Twentieth-Century Literary Criticism

Guide to Gale Literary Criticism Series

For criticism on	Consult these Gale series
Authors now living or who died after December 31, 1959	*CONTEMPORARY LITERARY CRITICISM (CLC)*
Authors who died between 1900 and 1959	*TWENTIETH-CENTURY LITERARY CRITICISM (TCLC)*
Authors who died between 1800 and 1899	*NINETEENTH-CENTURY LITERATURE CRITICISM (NCLC)*
Authors who died between 1400 and 1799	*LITERATURE CRITICISM FROM 1400 TO 1800 (LC)* *SHAKESPEAREAN CRITICISM (SC)*
Authors who died before 1400	*CLASSICAL AND MEDIEVAL LITERATURE CRITICISM (CMLC)*
Black writers of the past two hundred years	*BLACK LITERATURE CRITICISM (BLC)*
Authors of books for children and young adults	*CHILDREN'S LITERATURE REVIEW (CLR)*
Dramatists	*DRAMA CRITICISM (DC)*
Hispanic writers of the late nineteenth and twentieth centuries	*HISPANIC LITERATURE CRITICISM (HLC)*
Poets	*POETRY CRITICISM (PC)*
Short story writers	*SHORT STORY CRITICISM (SSC)*
Major authors from the Renaissance to the present	*WORLD LITERATURE CRITICISM, 1500 TO THE PRESENT (WLC)*

ISSN 0276-8178

R

Volume 55

Twentieth-Century Literary Criticism

**Excerpts from Criticism of the
Works of Novelists, Poets, Playwrights,
Short Story Writers, and Other Creative Writers
Who Lived between 1900 and 1960,
from the First Published Critical
Appraisals to Current Evaluations**

Marie Lazzari
Editor

**Joann Cerrito
Laurie Di Mauro
Nancy Dziedzic
Jennifer Gariepy
Margaret A. Haerens
Kelly Hill
Drew Kalasky
Thomas Ligotti
Lynn M. Spampinato**
Associate Editors

 *Gale Research Inc.*

An International Thomson Publishing Company

 I(T)P

NEW YORK • LONDON • BONN • BOSTON • DETROIT • MADRID
MELBOURNE • MEXICO CITY • PARIS • SINGAPORE • TOKYO
TORONTO • WASHINGTON • ALBANY NY • BELMONT CA • CINCINNATI OH

STAFF

Marie Lazzari, *Editor*

Joann Cerrito, Laurie Di Mauro, Nancy Dziedzic, Jennifer Gariepy, Margaret A. Haerens, Kelly Hill, Drew Kalasky,
Thomas Ligotti, Lynn M. Spampinato, *Associate Editors*

Pamela Willwerth Aue, Christine M. Bichler, Martha Bommarito, Ian A. Goodhall, Matthew McDonough, *Assistant Editors*

Linda M. Pugliese, *Production Supervisor*
Donna Craft, Paul Lewon, Maureen A. Puhl, Camille P. Robinson, Sheila Walencewicz, *Editorial Associates*

Sandra C. Davis, *Permissions Supervisor (Text)*
Maria L. Franklin, Josephine M. Keene, Michele Lonoconus, Shalice Shah, Kimberly F. Smilay, *Permissions Associates*
Jennifer A. Arnold, Brandy C. Merritt, *Permissions Assistants*

Margaret A. Chamberlain, *Permissions Supervisor (Pictures)*
Pamela A. Hayes, Arlene Johnson, Keith Reed, Barbara A. Wallace, *Permissions Associates*
Susan Brohman, *Permissions Assistant*

Victoria B. Cariappa, *Research Manager*
Mary Beth McElmeel, Tamara C. Nott, Tracie A. Richardson, Norma Sawaya, *Research Associates*
Maria E. Bryson, Eva M. Felts, Shirley Gates, Michele McRobert, Michele P. Pica, Amy T. Roy, Laurel D. Sprague,
Amy Beth Wieczorek, *Research Assistants*

Mary Beth Trimper, *Production Director*
Catherine Kemp, *Production Assistant*

Cynthia Baldwin, *Product Design Manager*
Barbara J. Yarrow, *Graphic Services Supervisor*
Sherrell Hobbs, *Macintosh Artist*
Willie F. Mathis, *Camera Operator*

Library of Congress Catalog Card Number 76-46132
ISBN 0-8103-2435-0 (set)
ISBN 0-8103-2436-9 (main volume)
ISBN 0-8103-2437-7 (index)
ISSN 0276-8178

Printed in the United States of America
Published simultaneously in the United Kingdom
by Gale Research International Limited
(An affiliated company of Gale Research Inc.)
10 9 8 7 6 5 4 3 2 1

I(T)P™   Gale Research Inc., an International Thomson Publishing Company.
ITP logo is a trademark under license.

Contents

Preface   vii

Acknowledgments   xi

Preface

Since its inception more than fifteen years ago, *Twentieth-Century Literary Criticism* has been purchased and used by nearly 10,000 school, public, and college or university libraries. *TCLC* has covered more than 500 authors, representing 58 nationalities, and over 25,000 titles. No other reference source has surveyed the critical response to twentieth-century authors and literature as thoroughly as *TCLC*. In the words of one reviewer, "there is nothing comparable available." *TCLC* "is a gold mine of information—dates, pseudonyms, biographical information, and criticism from books and periodicals—which many libraries would have difficulty assembling on their own."

Scope of the Series

TCLC is designed to serve as an introduction to authors who died between 1900 and 1960 and to the most significant interpretations of these author's works. The great poets, novelists, short story writers, playwrights, and philosophers of this period are frequently studied in high school and college literature courses. In organizing and excerpting the vast amount of critical material written on these authors, *TCLC* helps students develop valuable insight into literary history, promotes a better understanding of the texts, and sparks ideas for papers and assignments. Each entry in *TCLC* presents a comprehensive survey of an author's career or an individual work of literature and provides the user with a multiplicity of interpretations and assessments. Such variety allows students to pursue their own interests; furthermore, it fosters an awareness that literature is dynamic and responsive to many different opinions.

Every fourth volume of *TCLC* is devoted to literary topics that cannot be covered under the author approach used in the rest of the series. Such topics include literary movements, prominent themes in twentieth-century literature, literary reaction to political and historical events, significant eras in literary history, prominent literary anniversaries, and the literatures of cultures that are often overlooked by English-speaking readers.

TCLC is designed as a companion series to Gale's *Contemporary Literary Criticism,* which reprints commentary on authors now living or who have died since 1960. Because of the different periods under consideration, there is no duplication of material between *CLC* and *TCLC*. For additional information about *CLC* and Gale's other criticism titles, users should consult the Guide to Gale Literary Criticism Series preceding the title page in this volume.

Coverage

Each volume of *TCLC* is carefully compiled to present:

- criticism of authors, or literary topics, representing a variety of genres and nationalities

- both major and lesser-known writers and literary works of the period

- 10-15 authors or 4-6 topics per volume

- individual entries that survey critical response to each author's work or each topic in literary history, including early criticism to reflect initial reactions; later criticism to represent any rise or decline in reputation; and current retrospective analyses.

Organization of This Book

An author entry consists of the following elements: author heading, biographical and critical introduction, list of principal works, excerpts of criticism (each preceded by an annotation and followed by a bibliographic citation), and a bibliography of further reading.

- The **Author Heading** consists of the name under which the author most commonly wrote, followed by birth and death dates. If an author wrote consistently under a pseudonym, the pseudonym will be listed in the author heading and the real name given in parentheses on the first line of the biographical and critical introduction. Also located at the beginning of the introduction to the author entry are any name variations under which an author wrote, including transliterated forms for authors whose languages use nonroman alphabets.

- The **Biographical and Critical Introduction** outlines the author's life and career, as well as the critical issues surrounding his or her work. References to past volumes of *TCLC* are provided at the beginning of the introduction. Additional sources of information in other biographical and critical reference series published by Gale, including *Short Story Criticism, Children's Literature Review, Contemporary Authors, Dictionary of Literary Biography,* and *Something about the Author,* are listed in a box at the end of the entry.

- Most *TCLC* entries include **Portraits** of the author. Many entries also contain reproductions of materials pertinent to an author's career, including manuscript pages, title pages, dust jackets, letters, and drawings, as well as photographs of important people, places, and events in an author's life.

- The **List of Principal Works** is chronological by date of first book publication and identifies the genre of each work. In the case of foreign authors with both foreign-language publications and English translations, the title and date of the first English-language edition are given in brackets. Unless otherwise indicated, dramas are dated by first performance, not first publication.

- Critical excerpts are prefaced by **Annotations** providing the reader with information about both the critic and the criticism that follows. Included are the critic's reputation, individual approach to literary criticism, and particular expertise in an author's works. Also noted are the relative importance of a work of criticism, the scope of the excerpt, and the growth of critical controversy or changes in critical trends regarding an author. In some cases, these annotations cross-reference excerpts by critics who discuss each other's commentary.

- **Criticism** is arranged chronologically in each author entry to provide a perspective on changes in critical evaluation over the years. All titles of works by the author featured in the entry are printed in boldface type to enable the user to easily locate discussion of particular works. Also for purposes of easier identification, the critic's name and the publication date of the essay are given at the beginning of each piece of criticism. Unsigned criticism is preceded by the title of the journal in which it appeared. Some of the excerpts in *TCLC* also contain translated material. Unless otherwise noted, translations in brackets are by the editors; translations in parentheses or continuous with the text are by the critic. Publication information (such as footnotes or page and line references to specific editions of works) have been deleted at the editor's discretion to provide smoother reading of the text.

- A complete **Bibliographic Citation** designed to facilitate location of the original essay or book follows each piece of criticism.

- An annotated list of **Further Reading** appearing at the end of each author entry suggests secondary sources on the author. In some cases it includes essays for which the editors could not obtain reprint rights.

Cumulative Indexes

- Each volume of *TCLC* contains a cumulative **Author Index** listing all authors who have appeared in Gale's Literary Criticism Series, along with cross references to such biographical series as *Contemporary Authors* and *Dictionary of Literary Biography*. For readers' convenience, a complete list of Gale titles included appears on the first page of the author index. Useful for locating authors within the various series, this index is particularly valuable for those authors who are identified by a certain period but who, because of their death dates, are placed in another, or for those authors whose careers span two periods. For example, F. Scott Fitzgerald is found in *TCLC,* yet a writer often associated with him, Ernest Hemingway, is found in *CLC*.

- Each *TCLC* volume includes a cumulative **Nationality Index** which lists all authors who have appeared in *TCLC* volumes, arranged alphabetically under their respective nationalities, as well as Topics volume entries devoted to particular national literatures.

- Each new volume in Gale's Literary Criticism Series includes a cumulative **Topic Index,** which lists all literary topics treated in *NCLC, TCLC, LC 1400-1800,* and the *CLC* yearbook.

- Each new volume of *TCLC,* with the exception of the Topics volumes, includes a **Title Index** listing the titles of all literary works discussed in the volume. In response to numerous suggestions from librarians, Gale has also produced a **Special Paperbound Edition** of the *TCLC* title index. This annual cumulation lists all titles discussed in the series since its inception and is issued with the first volume of *TCLC* published each year. Additional copies of the index are available on request. Librarians and patrons will welcome this separate index; it saves shelf space, is easy to use, and is recyclable upon receipt of the following year's cumulation. Titles discussed in the Topics volume entries are not included *TCLC* cumulative index.

Citing *Twentieth-Century Literary Criticism*

When writing papers, students who quote directly from any volume in Gale's literary Criticism Series may use the following general forms to footnote reprinted criticism. The first example pertains to materials drawn from periodicals, the second to material reprinted from books.

[1]T. S. Eliot, "John Donne," *The Nation and the Athenaeum,* 33 (9 June 1923), 321-32; excerpted and reprinted in *Literature Criticism from 1400 to 1800,* Vol. 10, ed. James E. Person, Jr. (Detroit: Gale Research, 1989), pp. 28-9.

[2]Clara G. Stillman, *Samuel Butler: A Mid-Victorian Modern* (Viking Press, 1932); excerpted and reprinted in *Twentieth-Century Literary Criticism,* Vol. 33, ed. Paula Kepos (Detroit: Gale Research, 1989), pp. 43-5.

Suggestions Are Welcome

In response to suggestions, several features have been added to *TCLC* since the series began, including annotations to excerpted criticism, a cumulative index to authors in all Gale literary criticism series, entries devoted to criticism on a single work by a major author, more extensive illustrations, and a title index listing all literary works discussed in the series since its inception.

Readers who wish to suggest authors or topics to appear in future volumes, or who have other suggestions, are cordially invited to write the editors.

Acknowledgments

The editors wish to thank the copyright holders of the excerpted criticism included in this volume, the permissions managers of many book and magazine publishing companies for assisting us in securing reprint rights, and Anthony Bogucki for assistance with copyright research. We are also grateful to the staffs of the Detroit Public Library, the Library of Congress, the University of Detroit Mercy Library, Wayne State University Purdy/Kresge Library Complex, and the University of Michigan Libraries for making their resources available to us. Following is a list of the copyright holders who have granted us permission to reprint material in this volume of *TCLC*. Every effort has been made to trace copyright, but if omissions have been made, please let us know.

COPYRIGHTED EXCERPTS IN *TCLC*, VOLUME 55, WERE REPRINTED FROM THE FOLLOWING PERIODICALS:

American Indian Quarterly, v. 3, Autumn, 1977. Copyright © Society for American Indian Studies & Research 1977. Reprinted by permission of the publisher.—*American Journal of Sociology,* v. LXIII, May, 1958. © 1958, renewed 1986 by The University of Chicago. Reprinted by permission of The University of Chicago Press.—*American Notes and Queries,* v. XX, September-October, 1981. Reprinted by permission of the Department of English, University of Kentucky.—*AUMLA,* n. 69, May, 1988. Reprinted by permission of the publisher.—*Book Forum,* v. V, 1981 for "American Indian Intellectuals and the Continuity of Tribal Ideals" by Tom Holm. Copyright © 1981 by The Hudson River Press. Reprinted by permission of the author.—*The Connecticut Review,* v. IV, October, 1970. © Board of Trustees for the Connecticut State Colleges, 1970. Reprinted by permission of the publisher.—*The International Fiction Review,* v. 9, Winter, 1982 for "Literary Dimensions of 'Robert Elsmere': Idea, Character, and Form" by Mildred L. Culp. © copyright 1982 International Fiction Association. Reprinted by permission of the author.—*The Journal of General Education,* v. 11, April, 1958. Copyright 1958 by The Pennsylvania State University Press. Renewed 1986 by The University of Chicago. Reprinted by permission of the publisher.—*Kentucky Romance Quarterly,* v. 27, 1980. Copyright © 1980 Helen Dwight Reid Educational Foundation. Reprinted with permission of the Helen Dwight Reid Educational Foundation, published by Heldref Publications, 1319 18th Street, N.W., Washington, D.C. 20036-1802.—*Modern Drama,* v. XXXI, March, 1988; v. XXXIV, September, 1991. Copyright 1988, 1991 *Modern Drama,* University of Toronto. Both reprinted by permission of the publisher.—*New Literary History,* v. II, Spring, 1971 for "Dramatic Analysis and Literary Interpretation: 'The Cherry Orchard' as Exemplum" by Bernard Beckerman. Copyright © 1971 by *New Literary History.* Reprinted by permission of the publisher and the Literary Estate of Bernard Beckerman.—*The New York Times Book Review,* December 21, 1924; December 20, 1925; November 9, 1941; September 18, 1949. Copyright 1924, 1925, 1941, 1949 by The New York Times Company. All reprinted by permission of the publisher.—*Nineteenth-Century French Studies,* vs. 12 & 13, Summer & Fall, 1984; v. XV, Spring, 1987. © 1984, 1987 by T. H. Goetz. Both reprinted by permission of the publisher.—*The Saturday Review of Literature,* v. XXIV, December 6, 1941. Copyright 1941, renewed 1969 *Saturday Review* magazine.—*The Sewanee Review,* v. XCIII, Fall, 1985. © 1985 by The University of the South. Reprinted with the permission of the editor of *The Sewanee Review.*—*The South Carolina Review,* v. 14, Spring, 1982. Copyright © 1982 by Clemson University. Reprinted by permission of the publisher.—*Studies in American Humor,* n.s. v. 3, Spring, 1984. Copyright © 1984 by Southwest Texas State University. Reprinted by permission of the publisher.—*Studies in Short Fiction,* v. 26, Fall, 1989. Copyright 1989 by Newberry College. Reprinted by permission of the publisher.—*Western Illinois Regional Studies,* Spring, 1981. Reprinted by permission of the publisher.—*Women's Studies: An Interdisciplinary Journal,* v. 12, 1986. © Gordon and Breach Science Publishers. Reprinted by permission of the publisher.—*Zagadnienia Rodzajów Literackich,* v. XXV, 1982 for "Structure in Octave Mirbeau's 'Le jardin des supplices'" by Aleksandra Gruzińska. Reprinted by permission of the author.

COPYRIGHTED EXCERPTS IN *TCLC*, VOLUME 55, WERE REPRINTED FROM THE FOLLOWING BOOKS:

and Innovation in Native American Autobiography. Oxford University Press, Inc., 1992. Copyright © 1992 by Oxford University Press. All rights reserved. Reprinted by permission of the publisher.—Yates, Norris W. From *The American Humorist: Conscience of the Twentieth Century.* Iowa State University Press, 1964. © 1964, renewed 1992 by Iowa State University Press. All rights reserved. Reprinted by permission of the publisher.—Yates, Norris W. From *Robert Benchley.* Twayne, 1968. Copyright © 1968 by Twayne Publishers, Inc. All rights reserved. Reprinted with the permission of Twayne Publishers, Inc., an imprint of Macmillan Publishing Company.

PHOTOGRAPHS AND ILLUSTRATIONS APPEARING IN *TCLC*, VOLUME 55, WERE RECEIVED FROM THE FOLLOWING SOURCES:

Reproduced by permission of Gluyas Williams and HarperCollins Publishers, Inc.: **p. 7, 18;** Angus McBean Photograph, Harvard Theatre Collection: **p. 39;** Courtesy of Prints and Photographs Division, Library of Congress: **p. 190;** Jacket of *The Last Tycoon*, by F. Scott Fitzgerald. Scribner's, 1941. Reprinted with permission of Charles Scribner's Sons, an imprint of Macmillan Publishing Company: **p. 200;** Princeton University Library: **p. 227;** Fales Library, Elmer Holmes Bobst Library, New York University: **p. 265;** Cover of *Der Spiegel 35*, no. 24 (8 June 1981). Reprinted by permission of New York Times Syndicate, Paris: **p. 372.**

Robert Benchley

1889-1945

American humorist, essayist, critic, actor, and screenwriter.

INTRODUCTION

One of the most popular American humorists of the early twentieth century, Benchley is best remembered for his essays and film monologues depicting a slightly befuddled average man struggling to cope with the complexities of modern life. His self-described middle-class perspective shaped his commentary on such subjects as the peculiarities of business, nature, and human relationships. With Dorothy Parker, James Thurber, Robert Sherwood, George S. Kaufman, and others, Benchley was a member of the Algonquin Round Table, a group of highly influential American writers of the 1920s and early 1930s.

Biographical Information

Benchley was born and grew up in Worcester, Massachusetts. He attended Harvard University, where he quickly developed a reputation as a humorist. His drawings, satires, and parodies appeared regularly in the *Harvard Lampoon*, along with those of classmate Gluyas Williams, who would later illustrate Benchley's collections of humorous essays. During his college career, Benchley also enjoyed success as an actor, specializing in the amusing, rambling monologues which would later characterize his works as both an essayist and a screenwriter. Following two decades as a prolific writer, during which he worked as an editor for *Life* and a drama critic and essayist for the *New Yorker*, Benchley turned his attention to acting in short films based on his popular essays. An avid party-goer and a popular host, Benchley was also devoted to his family, from whom he drew both emotional support and inspiration for many of his essays. His son, Nathaniel, became a well-known journalist and novelist, and his grandson, Peter Benchley, is the author of the best-selling novel *Jaws*.

Major Works

During his prolific career Benchley produced more than six hundred essays for a variety of magazines, weekly drama reviews for the *New Yorker*, and scripts for numerous films—many of which he also acted in. Benchley's first book, *Of All Things!* (1921), is a collection of his popular essays originally published in *Vanity Fair*, the *New York Tribune*, *Collier's*, *Life*, and *Motor Print*. Subsequent volumes were patterned after this model, comprised of a cross-section of comic essays, literary parodies, and sharp commentaries on life according to Benchley. In 1928, Twentieth Century-Fox released the film version of "The Treasurer's Report," starring Benchley. During the next

decade, Benchley divided his time between writing and acting, winning an Academy Award in 1935 for the MGM short film "How to Sleep." Benchley wrote his final drama review for the *New Yorker* in 1940, and during the next five years his work centered on his film monologues. Several collections of essays appeared after he announced his official retirement as a writer, including the posthumously published *Benchley–Or Else!* (1947) and *Chips Off the Old Benchley* (1949), which some critics believe contains some of Benchley's finest essays.

Critical Reception

Throughout his career Benchley enjoyed the approval of his peers and the public for his humorous, self-effacing approach to life in the early twentieth century. He was also highly regarded as a genial and tolerant drama critic whose observations were always well-considered. Commentators generally applaud Benchley's unique brand of humor, echoing James Thurber's assessment that the critics who underrate Benchley have overlooked "his distinguished contribution to the fine art of comic brevity."

PRINCIPAL WORKS

Of All Things! (essays) 1921
Love Conquers All (essays) 1922
Pluck and Luck (essays) 1925
The Early Worm (essays) 1927
20,000 Leagues under the Sea; or, David Copperfield
  (essays) 1928
The Treasurer's Report (essays) 1930
No Poems; or, Around the World Backwards and Sideways
  (essays) 1932
From Bed to Worse (essays) 1934
My Ten Years in a Quandary, and How They Grew
  (essays) 1936
After 1903—What? (essays) 1938
Inside Benchley (essays) 1942
Benchley Beside Himself (essays) 1943
Chips off the Old Benchley (essays) 1949

CRITICISM

Edmund Wilson, Jr. (essay date 1922)

[*Wilson was an American poet, essayist, lecturer, editor, and social and literary critic. In the following review of* Of All Things! *he lauds Benchley's wit and suggests that his satire ought to be more sharply focused on issues of wider societal concern.*]

Mr. Benchley's collected burlesques are, of course, exceedingly funny: they are a little like Stephen Leacock, but more urbane than Leacock. Mr. Benchley, if he has not the force of Mr. Leacock's violent and barbarous imagination, has not developed Mr. Leacock's vice of making five bad gags to one good one. He nearly always makes you laugh and he never makes you ill—which is high praise for an American humorist.

But it is not of Mr. Benchley's farces that I propose to speak in this review. Indeed, if he were only an Irvin Cobb, there would be no reason to review him at all. But there is a phase of Mr. Benchley—(and of the humorists of whom he is the leader)—which has a certain intellectual importance and which might have a great deal more. They are perhaps unconscious of it but it is nevertheless true that Mr. Benchley and his companions amount to something like an antidote to the patent medicines administered by the popular magazines. The great function which they perform is making Business look ridiculous. It is not enough that people should laugh at Mr. Addison Sims of Seattle: they must also learn to laugh, as Mr. Benchley teaches them to, at Window Card Psychology and the Woonsocket Wrought Iron Pipe—nor must they forget Mr. Joseph L. Gonnick and his Cantilever Bridges. Mr. Benchley's burlesques of Business and of the Business magazines are surely the most inspired things in his book and, it seems to me, the funniest; there is almost a note of savagery about them which he all too seldom lets us hear.

But why does Mr. Benchley stop here? Why isn't he more savage? Why does he cling so long to the pleasant nonsense of *The Harvard Lampoon?* We know that he can write first-rate satire from his sketch **"The Making of a Red".** (Why has he omitted it from the book [*Of All Things!*], by the way? It is perhaps the best thing he ever did.) Why does he never let his private indignations get into his humorous work? Does he hesitate for the same reason that he hesitates (according to one of his sketches) about giving the number of his floor to the elevator boy? What self-consciousness, what timidity has divorced his convictions from his jokes?

The truth is, I suppose, that if Mr. Benchley and his friends do not set out to écraser l'infâme, it is because they are not sufficiently detached from it. In spite of the fact that they make fun of it, they still identify themselves with it. In order to attack it effectively they would have to tear themselves up by the roots. What might happen if they did, we have already seen in *Main Street.* Mr. Lewis burst bellowing from the advertising agencies and the popular magazines and gave vent to a bitter caricature of the life he was saturated with. —But what is to prevent Mr. Benchley, at least, from doing something of this kind? He has not the creative energy nor the violent reaction of Mr. Lewis, but he has at least a gift of burlesque, a nose for the silly and the cheap and a passion against intolerance. It is precisely such ridicule as his which can destroy the tyranny of our gods and he can surely not plead at this date that there is not an audience for it. Let him turn from an outworn genre which should have passed away with Bill Nye and devote himself to the deflation of the gas-bags that crowd our world: the journalism, the commercial booming and the barbarous public opinion.

Edmund Wilson, Jr. "Mr. Benchley's Message to His Age," in The New Republic, *Vol. XXIX, No. 382, March 29, 1922, p. 150.*

Edwin Clark (essay date 1925)

[*In the following excerpt from a review of* Pluck and Luck, *Clark praises Benchley's development as a satirist.*]

It is our duty to confess that Mr. Benchley is changing. No longer can the book seller honestly tell you that this is just good, clean, wholesome humor. It isn't so. His carefree spirit has been darkened by the presence of satire. Acid has risen in him and given expression to bitterness just when he seemed about to be nice and funny. The tendency to fancy has increased. He is always slipping away from this orderly and practical world into a world of incongruous fantasy. Really, it is rather irreverent, this neglect of this best of all possible worlds, particularly, as in the world of fancy, he seems to be making faces at this nice practical world he has slipped away from. So perhaps it should be said that Mr. Benchley has joined with Ring Lardner, Donald Stewart, Frank Sullivan and such exponents of our new crazy humor.

Being funny is quite often difficult and trying, isn't it? He isn't like the conventional essayists, improvising upon a theme until he gets a quaint aspect. His subjects are the headline events in a fellow's life and are treated precisely.

We are blessed with papers on **"The Church Supper,"** **"How to Watch Football,"** **"Christmas Pantomimes,"** **"The Musical Club Concert,"** **"Paul Revere,"** **"Editha's Christmas Burglar,"** **"The Big Bridegroom Revolt,"** **"The Romance of Digestion,"** **"French for Americans,"** **"Amateur Theatricals,"** **"The Last Day,"** and several probing pieces upon science and recent discoveries of great illumination.

"Kiddie-Kar Travel" has both luminosity and terrific human insight. It will bring joy and gladness to those who have children and those who have no children. This record of the high adventure of little Roger is unique in sustaining this two-way interest. His antics are a constant cynosure—no other word could possibly describe it—for all eyes.

> He doesn't act like this at home. In fact, he is noted for his tractability. There seems to be something about the train that brings out all the worst that is in him, all the hidden traits he has inherited from his mother's side of the family.

The brief note on Paul Revere is a historical document. We suspect that Mr. Benchley rather fancies this one with affection. Certainly, with us, it is prize winning. Revealed to Paul is a vista crammed with people:

> He saw fifty million of them trying to prevent the other sixty million from doing what they wanted to do and the sixty million trying to prevent the fifty million from what they wanted to do.. .. He saw ten million thin children working and ten thousand fat children playing in the warm sands. And now and again he saw five million youths, cheered by a hundred million elders with fallen arches, marching out to give their arms and legs and lives for Something to be Determined Later. . . .
>
> And so Paul changed his mind and did not ride forth to rouse the Middlesex farms.

Turning from history to literature, it once more becomes evident that murder will, like yeast, rise and be called to your attention. The several phases of literature, including biography, the novel and the theatre reappear in the dress of comic parody. Nor should one forget a most iconoclastic discussion of Shakespeare. Galsworthy, Arlen and May Sinclair have their styles taken off in hilarious burlesque. An intimate autobiography of the life and times of R. Benchley is written in the manner of Mark Twain. A series of new letters gives new insight into the love life of Goethe. The sea-searching of Beebe is guyed. A critical discussion examines the question of picking the best novels and play of the year, with two examples given in illustration. Finally we reach the subject of the modern drama. Here the critic of Life bares his soul.

There is in this fooling of Benchley's, as is obvious, some excellent criticism. While the parodies of Galsworthy and May Sinclair aren't quite so devastating they represent, as does the Arien burlesque, sound discernment of technique and style. Which suddenly brings us to Shakespeare and the modern fad of producing and acting his plays. In almost the best manner of the old Quarterly Reviews Benchley boldly remarks that

the only trouble with acting Shakespeare is the actors. It brings out the worst that is in them. With a company consisting of one or two stars and the rest hams (which is a good liberal estimate), what can you expect? But you can't blame the actor entirely. According to present standards of what constitutes dramatic action most of Will's little dramas have about as much punch as a reading of a treasurer's report. To be expected to thrill over the dramatic situations incident to a large lady's dressing up as a boy and fooling her own husband or to follow breathlessly a succession of scenes strung together like magic lantern slides and each ending with a perfectly corking rhymed couplet is more than ought to be asked of any one who has in the same season seen "Loyalties" or any one of the real plays now running on Broadway. I wouldn't be surprised if things keep on as they are if Shakespeare began to lose his hold on people. I give him ten centuries more at the outside.

The front-page appearances of the theatre, with the vexing-involved problems, are considered in a paper on **"Drama Cleansing and Pressing."**

> Something has got to be done about the sex-play market in New York. It is all shot to pieces owing to the fact that a manufacturer can't tell whether he has turned out an obscene play or a work of art. He doesn't know in advance whether his show is going to be found guilty of corrupting public morals or put on President Eliot's list of the Fourteen Most Ennobling Plays on the Atlantic Seaboard. Each opening night there is equal chance that the next week will find him having an audience with either a Judge or the Pope. A pretty good way to judge in advance about the intrinsic art of a sex play is to see whether the characters have a good time at it or not. If they have fun out of the thing then it's a harmful play; if they hate it it's a work of art.

Two samples are introduced as evidence into this perplexing discourse—or dilemma—or what have you; a farce in one act entitled **"Wrong Number, Please,"** and **"Sunk,"** a drama in one act. It is the reader's privilege to decide which is which—if any.

The readers of the jury have now had the evidence presented. Can or can't Robert Benchley make you laugh? The court suggests that he be encouraged and that Gluyas Williams be urged to continue his illustrations for Benchley.

Edwin Clark, "Mr. Benchley Takes an Acid Bath," in The New York Times Book Review, *December 20, 1925, p. 9.*

Walter Blair   (essay date 1942)

[*Blair was an educator, editor, and critic who is recognized as one of the first American scholars to appraise humor academically. In the following excerpt from his* Horse Sense in American Humor, *he distinguishes Benchley as one of the most popular humorists of his day, and suggests that the uniqueness of his sketches derives from the neurotic nature of his protagonists.*]

Mr. Robert Benchley tells of the trouble he had when, like

Ward, he became worried about grammar and the sound of words. It all started when he tried to figure out the present tense of the verb of which "wrought" is the past participle:

> I started out with a rush. "I wright," I fairly screamed. Then, a little lower: "I wrught." Then, very low: "I wrouft." Then silence.
>
> From that day until now I have been murmuring to myself: "I wrught—I wraft—I wronjst. You wruft—he wragst—we wrinjsen. . . ."
>
> People hear me murmuring and ask me what I am saying.
>
> "I wrujhst," is all that I can say in reply.
>
> "I know," they say, "but what were you *saying* just now?"
>
> "I wringst."
>
> This gets me nowhere.

It is easy to see why this writer claims that "One of the easiest methods of acquiring insanity is word-examining. Just examine a word you have written, and then call up Dr. Jessup and tell him to come and get you. Tell him to wear just what he has on."

Mr. Benchley—in his role as a humorist, at any rate—has the same sort of random associations Ward had when he was on the platform in the sixties. Riding on a train, he sights a dust storm, which calls to his mind the fact that "a dust-storm. . . . is a lot like life. It has its entrances and its exits, and it is the strongest team that wins. And by 'the strongest team' I do not mean the team with the most muscle, or sinew, or brawn. I mean the strongest team." Weirdly his mind maunders on, from the strongest team, to the lives of people in shacks, to mountain trout, to old miners and what they might have thought, to what trout have thought, then to Indians and what "they think when they see sand-storms and mountain trout."

Again . . . this fellow is faced with the job of getting up before an audience and making a speech. Hear him galumphing around:

> Now in connection with reading this report, there are one or two points which Dr. Murnie wanted brought up in connection with it, and he has asked me to bring them up in connec—to bring them up.
>
> In the first place, there is the question of the work which we are trying to do up at our little place at Silver Lake, a work which we feel not only fills a very definite need in the community but also fills a very definite need—er—in the community. I don't think that many of the members of the Society realize just how big the work is that we are trying to do up there. For instance, I don't think that it is generally known that most of our boys are between the age of fourteen. We feel that, by taking the boy at this age, we can get closer to his real nature—for a boy *has* a very real nature, you may be sure—and bring him into closer touch not only with the school, the parents, and with each other, but also with the

town in which they live, the country to whose flag they pay allegiance, and to the—ah— *(trailing off)* town in which they live.

Here there is both the snakelike fascination of rhythms and phrases that worried Ward and the jittery uncertainty that scrambled the phrases of Adeler. A humorist at work today, in other words, is nicely carrying on with one of the good old devices of American humor.

Mr. Robert Benchley is one of the most popular men in the business of being funny today [1942]. He has syndicated his skits, at various times, to a large number of newspapers; his books have sold well above 120,000 copies; he has done well on the stage, on the screen, and on the radio.

Son of a New England family and graduate of Phillips Exeter Academy, Mr. Benchley began to show a knack for humor when he was an undergraduate at Harvard. There he made college mates laugh by giving a burlesque lecture which had qualities closely akin to those of his later comic writings—one which, by the way, used many tricks like those which had been used by Artemus Ward, when that old-timer had given his burlesque lecture in London. Young Benchley's talk was on the woolen-mitten industry, and he used a napkin for a screen and an umbrella for a pointer. Part of it went like this:

> Our first slide shows that in 1904, it took 1487 man hours to produce 1905, which, in turn, required 3586 man hours to hold its own. This made 3,000,000 foot-pounds of energy, a foot-pound being the number of feet in a pound. This is, of course, all per capita. . . . Next slide, please!. . . . I'm afraid my assistant has it upside down. . . . There! that's better!

Inevitably, some years after graduation, the man who had made such an analysis of industry as this, having found that the world of business was not for him, turned to humor.

The pages of the books he wrote, as has been suggested, often remind one of the humor of his forerunners. Many times he shapes his paragraphs and sentences as they did: instinctively, probably, he hits on tried and true ways of making people laugh. But there is a difference between his writings and the older ones. . . .

This difference is suggested by a look at the kind of a character who woefully makes his way through the strange happenings set down in Mr. Benchley's writings. Any of the books shows the chief thing about this poor devil— that his whole life is a series of humiliations and frustrations. He is constantly bedeviled by all sorts of petty little things which a masterful man would easily be able to take in his stride. As a critic of this writer, Mr. Bryant, says,

> . . . . he sees himself. . . . not the master of high comedy, but the victim of low tragedy. King Lear loses a throne; Benchley loses a filling. Romeo breaks his heart; Benchley breaks his shoelace. They are annihilated; he is humiliated. And to his humiliations there is no end. His whole life has been spent as the dupe of "the total depravity of inanimate things." Today a knicknack leaps from his hand and shatters to

the floor. Tonight his slippers will crawl away
and wheel around backward . . . .

Happier men could laugh little troubles like these off—but
they happen so often to the fellow who appears in the
Benchley pieces that he develops a persecution complex
about them.

A book of his, aptly called *My Ten Years in a Quandary,*
shows this character sloshing around in a sea of troubles.
Furious, eager to take arms—as Shakespeare puts it—
against the waves, he finds himself unable to do anything.
All the time he is bothered by frustrations—in general and
in particular. He cannot leave a party at a decent time,
cure hiccoughs, wear a white suit, smoke a cigarette, or
read while eating—though he wants passionately to do all
these things. Pathetically, this victim of suppressions
looks forward to a total eclipse, when darkness will give
him "a chance," as he says, "to do a lot of things I have
planned to do, but have been held back from." And what
are these daring deeds to be? Simply these—he will put on
a white suit, pick some flowers, waltz, exercise on a rowing
machine, read some books, and make some faces. All these
innocent little diversions he has been afraid to enjoy in the
bright light of day.

Plainly, the difference between this victim of fate and
healthier men is that the healthier men would not want to
do such things or—if they did—would do them. But the
man in a Benchley sketch, paralyzed by these tremendous
frustrations, worries and worries about them. A chronic
worrier, he is tormented by other things besides those
which have been mentioned—fur-bearing trout, a bird
which breaks down his morale, a ghost which worries him
into spending a whole night in the Grand Central Station,
meteorites, a Scottie (to which he feels inferior), the Younger Generation (which he fears is hatching a sinister plot),
and dancing prairie chickens.

Read on in the book and you will find that even more serious troubles pester him. When this poor creature lies
down to sleep, his throat closes up and he stops breathing.
He has dementia praecox and a phobia for barber chairs,
and he goes crazy in a lonely shack on the seashore. All
these psychopathic woes are made known in one volume.
Read the rest of his volumes, and it will be clear that the
man—if his books are to be believed—is just a mess of
frustrations and phobias. As Mr. Bryant has said, "Madness so dominates the landscape of his humor that a second reading is necessary to recognize its other features."
When another humorist not long ago published a volume
called *A Bed of Neuroses,* he might well have used a picture of Mr. Benchley's four-poster for a frontispiece.

Walter Blair, "Crazy Men," in his Horse Sense in American Humor from Benjamin Franklin to Ogden Nash, *The
University of Chicago Press, 1942, pp. 274-94.*

James Thurber   (essay date 1949)

[*James Thurber was a celebrated American humorist best
known for his essays, stories, and cartoons published in the*
New Yorker *during the 1930s and 1940s. In the following
excerpt from his review of the posthumously published*

Chips Off the Old Benchley, *Thurber commends Benchley's skill as a humorist and suggests that other critics have
overlooked Benchley's gift for "comic brevity"*]

The heavier critics have under-rated Benchley because of
his "short flight," missing his distinguished contribution
to the fine art of comic brevity. He would thank me not
to call him an artist, but I think he was an artist who
wouldn't give up to it, like a busy housewife fighting the
onset of a migraine headache.

It was an artist, to cite outstanding proof, who wrote (in
another book) that brilliant and flawless parody of Galsworthy called **"The Blue Sleeve Garter."** He had all the
equipment for the "major flight," but he laid it aside to
lead one of the most crowded private lives of our century.
Even so, he somehow found time to work on an ambitious
enterprise, a book about the satirists of the Queen Anne
period, which he later turned into a history in play form.
For all its seriousness, it seems to have been a kind of monumental hobby, and a man is never done with a hobby.
Benchley didn't finish his.

Chips Off The Old Benchley contains eighty pieces never
put in a book before. I don't know why. All of it is highly
readable, and much of it is top-flight Benchley, gathered
from *The New Yorker, Vanity Fair* and a dozen other
sources. It goes back as far as 1915, but forty-eight of the
pieces are from the vintage years of 1930-34. As in all
Benchley, a fresh wind stirs in these pages. In this collection you find him everywhere, ducking swiftly, looking
closely, writing sharply.

I have space for a few gleams and swatches:

> This God-given talent which I have must be
> tossed aside like an old mistress (or is it mat-
> tress?).
>
> He is a little man who has difficulty in breathing
> (not enough, however).
>
> There was a big bull-pigeon walking about on
> the window ledge and giving me an occasional
> leer with its red eyes.
>
> Sun shining on closed eyelids (on my closed eye-
> lids) soon induces large purple azaleas whirling
> against a yellow background.
>
> At a hundred yards he could detect a purple
> wolf's cup (or Lehman's dropsy) and could tell
> you, simply by feeling a flower in the dark,
> which variety of bishop's ulster it was.
>
> Working on the piece-system as we do (so much
> per word or per piece—or perhaps) . . .
>
> The London illustrated weeklies are constantly
> making remarkable discoveries in the Etruscan-
> tomb belt.

I could go on till dusk.

Benchley has been placed in the Leacock "school," but
this is too facile a classification. For just one thing, Benchley did more funny things in, and to, banks than Stephen
ever dreamed of. Leacock was an "I" writer and Benchley,
even in the first person, a "You" writer. Leacock is Lea-

cock, but Benchley's Mr. Ferderber is practically every man.

Comparison is easy. A facet of the Benchley fancy resembles the comic approach of the late Max Adeler, but I never heard him mention the Comparable Max—or Leacock either. To most of us, he stands alone, in a great, good place all his own.

James Thurber, "The Incomparable Mr. Benchley," in The New York Times Book Review, *September 18, 1949, pp. 1, 31.*

On Benchley's career as an actor:

There came a time early in the 1940s when Benchley, after years of resisting identification as an actor, had to concede that he no longer considered himself a writer. Nathaniel Benchley tells of his father's announcement, in November 1943, "that he was through with writing and was resigned to being a radio and movie comedian," but he had already issued much the same statement two years earlier in a Columbia Studios press release. According to this source, he had wearied of trying to maintain several careers and had decided to narrow his activities: "Put me down as an actor. . . . From now on I am going to cut out everything but screen work, and limit that to acting." Between 1940 and his death in 1945, he played supporting roles in thirty feature-length pictures, starred in fifteen more short subjects, and continued his frequent guest appearances on radio broadcasts, though his own radio series ended in 1940.

Robert Redding, in his Starring Robert Benchley: "Those Magnificent Movie Shorts," *University of New Mexico Press, 1973.*

Norris W. Yates (essay date 1964)

[*Yates is an American educator and critic. In the following excerpt from his* The American Humorist: Conscience of the Twentieth Century, *he characterizes Benchley's comic narrator as an ordinary man beset by the forces of nature. In addition, Yates examines Benchley's work as a literary critic.*]

It is impossible to say just when the bemused householder and white-collar man became really prominent in American humor, but by 1910 Stephen Leacock, Simeon Strunsky, and Clarence Day, Jr. were writing pieces in which the disguise of each author was just that. As noted before, one of Benchley's direct models was Leacock, whose *Literary Lapses* appeared in that year. "Leacock [to quote Ralph L. Curry] found much of his fun in the little man beset by advertising, fads, convention, sex, science, cussedness, machinery—social and industrial—and many other impersonal tyrannies." Benchley's favorite piece of humor was "My Financial Career," in *Literary Lapses,* where a bedeviled Little Man of the lower middle class is overawed and confused by a bank and its officials. Robert once stated, "I have enjoyed Leacock's work so much that I have written everything he ever wrote—anywhere from one to five years after him." Leacock wrote of the Little Man in an urbane prose that owed much to the familiar essays of Addison and Lamb, to the English tradition of parody as found in *Punch* (one of whose columnists, A. A. Milne, was another favorite of Benchley), to nonsense humor as exemplified in the verse of Edward Lear and Lewis Carroll, and to the newspaper columnists on Leacock's own side of the Atlantic. In its liveliness, it resembled most perhaps the last-named kind of writing. Despite Benchley's statements of his indebtedness, he might conceivably have written much as he did had he never read Leacock, but his work included all of the elements that went into Leacock's humor. The nonsense element, expressed by such bits as the line from Leacock's *Nonsense Novels,* "Lord Ronald said nothing; he flung himself from the room, flung himself upon his horse and rode madly off in all directions," was to recur with special effectiveness in Benchley's writing. . . .

In stressing the irrational side of [such American humorists as] Benchley, Thurber, and Perelman, Walter Blair calls them "Crazy Men" and says that "Benchley constantly assumes the role of 'Perfect Neurotic.' " Blair cites *My Ten Years in a Quandary,* in which the main character "cannot leave a party at a decent time, cure hiccoughs, wear a white suit, smoke a cigarette, or read while eating . . ." A worrier over trifles, this man with his "persecution complex" and his fear of dementia praecox is "just a mess of frustrations and phobias." All of this is true, and one can add to Blair's examples indefinitely.

In *Of All Things!,* the Little Man as a suburbanite is stalled by the furnace, stumped by auction bridge, and strapped by household expenses; as a family man he is badgered by children and relatives. His middle-class status augments his frustration: " . . . when I am confronted, in the flesh, by the 'close up' of a workingman with any vestige of authority, however small, I immediately lose my perspective—and also my poise." Out-of-doors, he is thwarted by **"Old Step-Mother Nature"** as much as was Mr. Dooley or the *persona* of Day in *After All:* when he tries to garden he will allow that nature is wonderful only if something he has planted grows—and that is unlikely.

In recounting the collapse of his efforts to learn to drive a car, this Little Man says, "Frankly I am not much of a hand at machinery of any sort . . . the pencil sharpener in our office is about as far as I, personally, have ever got in the line of operating a complicated piece of mechanism with any degree of success." In *No Poems,* he admits that even such simple articles as bedroom slippers conspire against him, as do also "the hundred and one little bits of wood and metal that go to make up the impedimenta of our daily life—the shoes and pins, the picture books and door keys, the bits of fluff and sheets of newspaper." Nature, technology, people—all give him a hard time.

But he is not really licked, though he says he is. Nor is he "crazy," in the sense of having fostered an image of himself and a picture of the world that are out of touch with reality. He has moments of aberration—as who does not? Benchley's narrator is the normal man, with the ordinary degree of neurosis slightly exaggerated. Except during these brief moments, this character is acutely conscious that his images of self and of the world have lost contact with realities, and the loss worries him. He is usually quite aware that there *are* realities other than his images, and at moments his illusions vanish and he sees truth with painful clarity. Between these moments, his frequent if vague awareness that a difference exists between his actual self and the self-image that he wishes were valid (but knows is not) produces a continual flow of comic irony.

In an ethical sense, he is never seriously aberrant. Benchley's Little Man has an integrity that can be strained but never quite broken; it gleams sullenly through his foggiest notions. In *The Neurotic Personality of Our Time,* Karen Horney says that one refuge of the intellectual sort of neurotic is a detachment in which he refuses to take anything seriously, including himself. The self-mockery of Benchley's fictive double is never carried to the point where he loses his wholesome awareness that man's environment was made for man, not he for it, and if things don't seem that way (here the reformer speaks)—well, things had better be changed. Miss Horney also states that the neurotic feels a compulsion to be liked. Benchley's double is less concerned with being liked than with preserving his integrity and his ethical vision.

Applied to nature this statement is certainly fatuous, and the Little Man looks littlest—he is most consistently rebuffed and humiliated—in his conflicts with the nonhuman environment. Benchley's friend and fellow-humorist Frank Sullivan once said (in referring to Robert himself rather than to the Benchley *persona*), that nature "had him stopped cold." Benchley felt heckled by pigeons, and once he was attacked by terns on the beach at Nantucket. But his Little Man, though afraid of thunder, could at least take the stand that "Nature can go her way and I'll go mine." Thus, loosely speaking, Benchley is "naturalistic" in the same sense as Stephen Crane, Theodore Dreiser, and Ernest Hemingway. To these writers, man was all but helpless in the grip of vast nonhuman forces and was lucky if these forces seemed merely indifferent, as in Crane's "The Open Boat," rather than malignant. But far from yielding to nature more than he had to, man still must live as man. This unsentimental view of man's relation to nature is the source of the irony in Benchley's numerous parodies of the "Hail, vernal equinox!" school of nature writing.

In a sense, Benchley's view of man's relationship to nature was more pessimistic than the Darwinian attitude that nature is a ruthless struggle for the survival of the fittest. Such a view implies order and purpose in nature, however irrelevant to man's desires, a view that Benchley did not hold. He is more like Will Cuppy in distrusting both the "hearts-and-flowers" and the "tooth-and-claw" approach. To both humorists, nature is purposeless and chaotic as is much of man's "civilization."

Behind some of Benchley's parodies of nature writing lies an attack on both the sentimental and the scientific, or at least the Darwinian, approaches to nature. Examples of this attack may be seen in the futility of **"The Social Life of the Newt"** and in the remarks on eggs in *The Early*

Worm, where the utter purposelessness of the shape of the egg is pointed out:

> If you will look at these eggs, you will see that each one is *Almost* round, but not *Quite.* They are more of an "egg-shape." This may strike you as odd at first, until you learn that this is Nature's way of distinguishing eggs from large golf balls. You see, Mother Nature takes no chances. She used to, but she learned her lesson. And that is a lesson that all of you must learn as well.

It was not that Benchley actively disbelieved in evolution but that he had not (like fellow-Yankee Robert Frost) himself worked up "that metaphor" and was not much interested in it—except as material for parody. His narrator cannot defeat nature but can at least laugh at it even as he laughs at his own losing struggle with natural phenomena.

If Benchley's man can do little about nature he can occasionally make headway against certain man-made phenomena—for instance, letters. One of Benchley's more revealing pieces is **"Mind's Eye Trouble,"** in *No Poems.* Here Benchley (wearing his mask) confesses with ostentatious humility that, "I seem to have been endowed at birth

A Gluyas Williams sketch from The Benchley Roundup: *"One day I look like Wimpy."*

by a Bad, Bad Fairy with a paucity of visual imagination which amounts practically to a squint." This limitation causes him to picture the events in any book he reads as taking place in the home town of his youth. Victor Hugo may not have had Yankee-land in mind when he wrote *Les Miserables;* "However, regardless of what Hugo had in mind, *I* have Front Street, Worcester in mind when I read it." All scenes from classical Roman life are vivified for this reader only in the driveway of the House at May and Woodland Streets where lived the girl he courted, and the mob of Romans listening to Antony's famous speech "extended 'way over across the street to the front lawn of the Congregational Church parsonage." Similarly, the characters of Charles Dickens "all made their exits and their entrances by the door at the left of the stairway and delivered all their speeches in front of the fireplace in the 'sitting-room' of this house at No. 3 Shepard Street." The yard on one side is fixed in this Little Man's mind as the Solid South and as the place where "Werther wrestled with his sorrows." In "this stunted imagination of mine," the yard of his Aunt Mary Elizabeth is the West, "and the West had better accommodate itself to my whim." Scenes from the works of Byron, Samuel Richardson, Mark Twain, Katherine Mansfield, Frank Swinnerton, and Hugh Walpole are inevitably re-created in the playground of the Woodland Street School or its vicinity. The narrator even finds himself "sending Proust walking up and down Woodland Street with Albertine."

The "confession" of this well-read wise fool is the literary equivalent of Mr. Dooley's testing the validity of political ideas by showing how they would operate in Archey Road. Benchley is implying that if certain overrated works of literature do not retain their reality and power when their characters and events are imagined within the frame of the normal, modern man's everyday experience, it is these works that are at fault, not the man. Uncritical readers may worship this stuff without putting it to the test, but not Benchley's narrator.

According to Nathaniel Benchley, his father had burrowed through Dr. Eliot's "Harvard Classics" and "concluded that it hadn't been worth the effort." Robert's own comment was, "If one adopts the Missourian attitude in reading the masters, and, laying aside their reputation, puts the burden of proof on them, many times they are not so impressive." The views of Robert are similar to those reflected by his narrator in **"Mind's Eye Trouble"**; Benchley's mask in that piece distorts his true self only by exaggeration. The confession is no *mea culpa* but an affirmation of Benchley's faith in his own tastes as an educated but not academic reader.

Benchley's attitude toward Shakespeare too is that of the cultivated fellow who reads or goes to a play for pleasure and not to worship the highbrowed god of scholarship. Benchley scoffs at Shakespeare revivals and insists that on the stage Shakespeare brings out the worst in actors (he excepts certain specific productions from this criticism, including most of the efforts of Maurice Evans and Orson Welles). He is particularly severe with Shakespeare's humor, condemning his low comedy as "horsy and crass" and claiming that, "It is impossible for a good actor, as we know good actors today, to handle a Shakespearean low comedy part, for it demands mugging and tricks which no good actor would permit himself to do." If alive today, the Bard would write slapstick movie scripts for Mack Sennett. In **"Shakespeare Explained,"** Benchley parodies the dissection of Shakespeare by pedants in editions overburdened with footnotes. The way to enjoy Shakespeare, he suggests elsewhere, is to read snatches from his plays now and then when you want to, and *stop* reading when you want to. This attitude will at least be one's own, not borrowed from some teacher.

Benchley spoke for a more literate type of man than did Ade, Dooley, or Lardner, but his point of view toward letters was scarcely less middlebrow, especially when he dealt with contemporary authors. Like Marquis and Lardner, he parodied many of them, although in Benchley's case parody did not necessarily imply a dislike of the writer thus treated. For instance, he satirized Sinclair Lewis' "flair for minutiae" but elsewhere praised "the remarkable accuracy with which he reports details in his 'Main Street.'" Other moderns whom he parodied included Robert Louis Stevenson, H. G. Wells, Mencken and Nathan, James Branch Cabell, and Marcel Proust. Benchley had no patience with flamboyant, arty, or grotesque styles. He said of William Faulkner, "A writer who doesn't make his book understandable to a moderately intelligent reader is not writing that way because he is consciously adapting a diffuse style, but because he simply doesn't know how to write." Not caring whether he was accused of lack of imagination or not, Benchley insisted on testing all literature, both classic and modern, by trying to fit it into his familiar frame of reference, and by setting it against the standards of his *persona*. In spite of the Little Man's absurdities, Benchley felt that this man was the only possible measure of things. The "great" writers did not "live" in the notes of a few scholars but must overcome a perfectly natural resistance to the new, archaic, or unfamiliar by a substantial body of practiced but nonprofessional readers-for-pleasure.

At various times, Benchley ran the theater department in three publications: the *Bookman, Life,* and the *New Yorker*. As a drama critic, he let others speak for show business or the intellectuals while he consciously tried to represent the man who goes to plays for pleasure (not necessarily amusement). Benchley's comments on Bernard Shaw's *The Apple Cart* and on some Chinese pantomimes amount to a theater-goer's credo. To the argument that we shouldn't be bored by traditions of theater not our own but should make allowances for them, Benchley replied, "Why *need* we be bored? Why should we have to make allowances for *anything* when we go for entertainment? Why is it incumbent on the audience which has paid its money for an evening in the theatre to adjust itself to Shaw or to Mei Lanfang? Other playwrights and other actors have to adjust themselves to their audiences if they want to hold their attention. . . . My suggestion would be that *nobody* be allowed to bore us."

The limitations of this view were surely those of most audiences. One might argue that every tradition was new to its public once and that Benchley's attitude would stultify the attempts of any experimental playwright to reach an audience beyond the narrow circle of professional theater folk and arty bohemians. One might further protest that the sort of playgoer who takes the trouble to read drama reviews usually does not just pay his money for an evening at any play; he at least knows that G. B. Shaw and George M. Cohan purvey different kinds of fare, whatever he may think of either, and he is at liberty to neglect whichever kind he fears will bore him. However, in his practice as reviewer, Benchley was less strict than in his general pronouncements. He praised many specimens of every kind of play, from musicals by Cohan and comedies by Noel Coward to *Murder in the Cathedral* by T. S. Eliot, though his chief criterion was always whether the piece in question stimulated and held the interest of the audience. Through this criterion, Benchley as drama critic kept Benchley the moralist sternly in check, and when he praised the sociological dramas of the nineteen-thirties, including the "message" plays by Paul Green, Maxwell Anderson, Elmer Rice, and Clifford Odets, and the documentary offerings by the Federal Theater Project, he praised them as effective plays, not as trumpet-calls to reformers. To bad plays he was merciless, whether they were musical fluff, or documentaries about the plight of sharecroppers in the South or Jews under Hitler. He sympathized warmly with the liberal purposes of such documentaries, but they were not necessarily *theater.*

Besides demanding entertainment, Benchley often applied the frame-of-reference test as a dramatic standard. He did much to boost the reputation of Eugene O'Neill, but he criticized the exaggerated picture of misery and crabbedness in *Desire Under the Elms,* and parodied—though he frankly enjoyed—the melodramatic aspects of *Mourning Becomes Electra.* In reviewing *Marco Millions* for the *Bookman,* he criticized the author on the ground that

> during his poetic passages designed to set off the idealism and aesthetic superiority of the East over the fierce commercialism and blindness of the West there still runs the debatable thesis that money and numbers and luxury are in themselves ignoble things and that, if a man prefers the sensuous charms of good food, a buxom wife and bags of gold to speculating on Truth and the Idea and consorting with a lyric and love-sick princess, he is in a way a bounder and fit only to be crushed on the wheel.

Here the Little Man as Broadway playgoer was resisting values that did not meet the test of his experience. In view of Benchley's refusal to meet the artier arts halfway, it is not surprising that he cared almost as little for grand opera as did Ade and Lardner and followed their example by largely ignoring it except in parody.

Norris W. Yates, "Robert Benchley's Normal Bumbler," in his The American Humorist: Conscience of the Twentieth Century, *Iowa State University Press, 1964, pp. 241-61.*

Norris W. Yates   (essay date 1968)

[*In the following excerpt from his* Robert Benchley, *Yates analyzes Benchley's approach to, and definition of, humor.*]

The closest Benchley came to defining humor was a hint that it depended much upon conventions shared by the humorist and his public: A joke is funny only if the jokester and his audience think it is. This view was not exactly original, nor was his feeling that analyzing a quip kills it and that "The chances are that the person to whom you have been explaining it won't think that it is funny anyway." Benchley implied that if the audience is larger than one, the likelihood of humorous conventions being entirely shared decreases proportionately. Naturally he took a dim view of Max Eastman's analytical, not to say psychoanalytical, approach in *Enjoyment of Laughter;* and in a parody of that book he suggested that laughter is really caused by a small tropical fly carried from Central America to Spain by Columbus's men, "returning to America, on a visit, in 1667, on a man named George Altschuh."

Conceivably, Benchley was also irked by Eastman's just criticisms that his own humor was sometimes wordy and labored; in addition, he certainly shared the instinctive repulsion felt by many humorists at being picked apart by scholars, regardless of the slant or "school" of approach. Humor was supposed to be fun. It should also involve a laugh *with* rather than *at* its object; here Benchley agreed wholeheartedly with Leacock, an agreement natural in a humorist who likewise poked a great deal of fun at himself. Yet Benchley resembled Mark Twain in disliking the role of a mere funnyman whom no one would take seriously. He worried about writing something "Really Good" that would contribute to Progress, rated humor, including his own, outside the category of good writing, and thought of it mainly as a vehicle of entertainment rather than of enlightenment. The contradiction between his low rating of his calling and his gusto in the pursuit of it was never resolved. Yet this conflict may have had something to do with his occasional spurts of biting social satire and his uncharacteristic outburst at a party against Robert E. Sherwood just after the latter had won the second of his three Pulitzer prizes.

In his "funning," Benchley, on the whole, preferred metropolitan subtlety to crossroads crudity. Of Frank Crowninshield he wrote: "As a boy he conceived a bitter dislike for the joke in which a fat man is shown sitting down on a bench marked 'Fresh Paint.' . . . Humor which needs gesticulation and powerful wrinklings of the visage for its best effect leaves him mirthless." Benchley too voiced his scorn for those who laugh when someone slips on a banana peel. He also disliked the crude misuse of words and the inverted anti-intellectual snobbery of the cracker-box oracles. Leo Marx has said that the uncombed American vernacular, shaped into a great literary medium by Whitman and Mark Twain, was more than a literary technique; it was "a view of experience"—a view narrowed by anti-intellectualism. Benchley and the contemporary humorists whom he respected—for example, Stephen Leacock and Franklin P. Adams—were trying to intellectualize the vernacular (one might say) and thus to broaden the American experience.

To Benchley, however, intellectualized, or "high-brow," humor involved much more than use or non-use of the vernacular. In *The Seven Lively Arts* (1924) Gilbert Seldes had praised Lardner, Irving Berlin, the stage comic Joe Cook, and the creator of "Krazy Kat," George Herriman. Benchley commented on Seldes' views thus:

> To us it is quite understandable that Mr. Seldes, a highbrow, should revel genuinely and without affectation in the work of Lardner, Cook, Berlin and Herriman, because these gentlemen are Grade-A highbrows themselves. Each has a universal quality which renders him popular, but at his best he is so far over the heads of the average reader and audience that he might as well be working in a foreign medium.
>
> Lardner's entire structure is built on an unsparing and sophisticated exposure of the lowbrow mind, so subtle and delicate that thousands of readers of the *Saturday Evening Post* unquestionably found nothing amusing in it except the quite adventitious misspelling and slang. Messrs. Cook and Herriman are entirely mad at heart, and sheer madness is, of course, the highest possible brow in humor. They have, just as Ring Lardner has, certain fundamental comic elements which make everybody laugh, regardless of brow-elevation, but in the upper reaches of their imagination they are for only the sophisticates.

On the other hand, Benchley classed Mencken's humor, Shakespearian comedy and the Russian ballet as lowbrow:

> Mr. Mencken, while sophisticated enough for all practical purposes in his mental processes and serious criticism, is, when he wants to be funny, dependent on the extremely lowbrow medium of comic-sounding words like "pish-posh" and "*sitz-platz,*" and figures of speech reminiscent of Public School 165 when sitting down heavily and kicking in the seat of the pants were considered good enough fun for anyone. When Mr. Mencken has said something funny to you it is all over your face like a pail of whitewash, and he has nothing left for himself.
>
> The comedy of the Russians and Shakespeare, with its concomitant cheek-blowing and grunting, is comparable with the Mencken method in tonnage, but is without Mr. Mencken's mature intent. It all is derived from the whitewash pail and all is particularly delightful to auditors under eight years of age or their equivalent.

Benchley's distinction between sophistication and mere erudition was as sound as his differentiation between "pratfall" humor and more sophisticated funmaking. However, for the sake of those "certain fundamental comic elements," Benchley sometimes combined the "pratfall" and the thoughtfully knitted highbrow. Just as Ignatz Mouse repeatedly beans Krazy Kat with a brick, Benchley's Uncle George stumbles over a child's electric train, Papa Benchley lunges at son Bobby and falls off his bicycle, and football fans find themselves frozen to their seats. All of these episodes illustrate a fundamental comic element that Benchley recognized but seldom bothered to summarize explicitly: the incongruity between what man is and what he ought to be. Thus, in context, his bits of low comedy also offer something to the thinking minority—to the custodians of George Meredith's "Comic Spir-

it" and to the sort of readers Harold Ross hoped for. The first two of the examples just cited from Benchley's work are taken from parodies of Dickens and of "scientific" journalists, respectively; the third is from a critique of the mob-man as football fan. In all three, and elsewhere, Benchley simply ignores his own theoretical distinctions.

One type of humor for the thoughtful was, Benchley felt, "a broad burlesquing of modern entertainment formulae and clichés, with a strain of pleasant insanity running through the whole." In 1926 he found this kind of humor in "certain New York supperclubs" that were sponsoring "a crazy and highly amusing form of comedy, miles and miles in advance of the conventional revue stuff." Jimmy Durante, for instance, "mystifies some, irritates others, and provides incomparable entertainment for those whose minds swing free and loose and who are sick unto death of the old forms." In other words, this "greatest of all madmen" appealed mainly to connoisseurs, as did Joe Cook, whose praises Benchley also sang. Unfortunately, Benchley seldom quoted or described their material, but, in 1924, Edmund Wilson too had noticed "the revolution in humor that seems to be taking place in New York." Wilson stressed the "nonsense of Joe Cook and Robert Benchley" as part of this revolution, and recounted, "Joe Cook asks 'the Senator,' his stooge, 'How's your uncle?' —and the Senator answers, 'I haven't got an uncle.' 'Fine,' says Cook, 'How is he?'"

Like this rather flat bit, Cook's nonsense was presented mostly for laughs and was devoid of satire, as was much of the earlier buffoonery of the Marx brothers. Benchley, whose mind swung free and loose before he discovered Cook, went beyond the stage comedians in controlling his "insanity" for purposes of parody. Thus, he put a deaf elk and a woman weaving tapestry together into a greenhouse in order to parody amateur analysts of dreams. To parody art songs, as represented by their vapid synopses in program notes, Benchley mixed personification and nonsequitur:

> It is the day of the bull fight in Madrid. Everyone is cockeyed. The bull has slipped out by the back entrance to the arena and has gone home, disgusted. Nobody notices that the bull has gone except Nina, a peasant girl who has come to town that day to sell her father. She looks with horror at the place in the Royal Box where the bull ought to be sitting, and sees there instead her algebra teacher, whom she had told that she was staying at home on account of a sick headache. You can imagine her feelings!

Bullfighting and the sentimentalizing over quaint peasant mores also get hit here. Thus Benchley combined nonsense, topical satire, and parody.

Much of the supper-club humor was in the form of parody, and most of Benchley's pieces were, or included, parody (or burlesque, to use the term he preferred). For example, seven of the first ten pieces in *The Benchley Roundup* are parodies of "modern entertainment formulae and clichés," and two of the remaining three may be so considered (**"Take the Witness!"** and **"The Tortures of Week-End Visiting"**). Five of the pieces are almost exclusively parody. In print, parody undiluted by author comment is the equivalent of oral delivery with a poker face, and Benchley delivered most of his oral monologues with a face like a graven image. Of a man who died laughing at his own joke, Benchley said, "If he had given it with a dead pan he would have been alive today and would have been visiting me in New York at my expense."

But to enjoy fully this form of humor—parody—the receiver must share a common body of knowledge and feelings with the parodist, perhaps more fully than is required with other forms of humor. To get the most out of Benchley's parodies, one should have absorbed nature-study lectures, Shakespearean scholarship, Dickensian sentimentality, the drab realism of certain twentieth-century novels, and some specialized papers like those published by the American Psychiatric Association. Benchley's part in the "revolution," as summarized by Edmund Wilson, included much parody of the more complex and intellectual forms of communication and "entertainment," and relatively little lunacy for its own sake.

Not caring whether he was a "revolutionary" in humor or not, Benchley insisted on a commonplace: humor must convey the effect of spontaneity. This humorist, who sweated over his own writing, felt that such an effect required presentation in one's own language, "freshness" (up-to-dateness), and, preferably, understatement. As a result, he was cold to humor in translation or in the English of previous periods, such as the ages of Shakespeare, Queen Anne, and Mark Twain. (His collection of notes for a study of humor of the Queen Anne period was begun partly as proof that he could do some "serious" writing and was abandoned when he finally decided that no humorist of this period was funny.) His already mentioned preference for the cultivated Franklin P. Adams instead of Mark Twain's dialect humor was part of his demand that humor be up-to-date. Freshness was also needed in the handling of character types, situations, and jokes; but on this topic Benchley found it easier to say what he didn't like than what he liked.

His theater reviews are seasoned with sarcasms about trite material, and in **"Visitors' Day at the Joke Farm"** certain character types associated with stock situations reminisce at the "Home for Aged Jokes"—the grandiloquent old actor, the comic tramp, and the Broadway dandy—exchange memories with the missionary who was always being cooked by cannibals and with the man who was always kicking a hat on the sidewalk that had a brick in it. In the background hover Alkali Ike the cowboy, Willie Tenderfoot; the Irate Father who calls "Lydia, hasn't that young man gone yet?"; and the little girl who asks "Muvver, what did Daddy mean when he said—." In **"Old Wives' Tale,"** the author scoffs at early versions of the henpecked husband theme that included the throwing of dishes and the use of the rolling-pin. In both essays, much of the humor of *Life, Puck,* and *Judge* at about the time of "Grover Cleveland and the Full Dinner-pail" is explicitly rejected.

By "freshness" Benchley did not mean mere topicality. He did respect originality of situation; he thought Max Beerbohm's "Enoch Soames" was "an original idea, remarkably well told" and "the best short story I have ever read." (The story concerns a bad poet who is granted a vision of the future; instead of experiencing the fame that he has confidently expected would be his, he stares into oblivion.) However, Benchley wrote best about the confused American who, during the early years of Robert's career, was already becoming a stock figure on the stage (in 1920 and 1921 Benchley praised Ed Wynn and W. C. Fields for their portrayals of the bumbler), and he wrote some of his most effective humor about this type-figure long after his earlier pieces had helped to make the Little Man a stock character in the humorous essay as well. To Benchley, freshness meant, in part, up-to-dateness in language, so that one of his objections to Shakespeare's comedy was that Elizabethan English was archaic and therefore dead. Accordingly, as a drama critic he was hard on Restoration and eighteenth-century comedy largely because, as he admitted, dialogue in a play simply had to be "in my own set" to be effective.

Besides freshness of language, another attribute that Benchley associated with up-to-dateness was understatement. Here, too, his practice deviated from his theory. He felt, however, that modern comedy was better than Shakespeare's because it had less noise, less mugging, and less cruelty. He therefore praised Charlie Chaplin for his frozen face, and he awarded palms to the cast of George M. Cohan's *The Tavern* for underplaying this "burlesque of romantic drama." Although Benchley's attitude toward Chaplin vacillated—Nathaniel Benchley says that "He hated Chaplin. Called his humor 'rectal kicking' "—he could hardly avoid taking an interest in Chaplin's playing of bumbler roles.

Again denying his own practice in part, Benchley felt that the subject matter of humor was severely limited. Although current social and political events like the Eighteenth Amendment, the Palmer raids, the Five-Year Plan, and the New Deal—along with the latest developments in science, technology, books, and drama—supplied most of the pegs for his humor, Benchley felt that only a rare specialist should try to be topical: "Our idea would be to leave all timely matters and quips on the news to Mr. Will Rogers, and have everyone else confine himself to being funny with the eternal verities and all that sort of deathless thing." Despite his admiration for Rogers, Benchley preferred the wackiness of Fanny Brice and the clumsiness of W. C. Fields as he "fretted over the Ford."

On topicality, Benchley stood in controversial territory. His position was close to that of Max Eastman; but Gilbert Highet, one of the more recent and readable commentators about humor and satire, feels that satire must be topical, although it should also be more than that. But from "the eternal verities" with which humor was fit to deal, Benchley tended to subtract, as has been noted, not only the currently topical but the sexual and the obscene; as might be expected, his zest for up-to-date humor did not, therefore, include the bawdy, modern, or otherwise. He could be raffish in private and before restricted audiences—solemnly he informed a group of naval officers that prophylaxis after shore leave was to be made compulsory for officers as well as for enlisted men—but to defenders of Rabelaisean humor in plays, he replied: " 'Rabelaisean humor' is dirty talk that Daddy can laugh at and not lose cast. 'Dirty talk' is what Junior gets spanked for." The idea that children's conversation and Broadway plays might be different and not comparable media either did not occur or was not acceptable to him at the time.

True, he said of a show by Fred Stone, "There is such a thing as clean fun reaching a point of cleanliness where it is practically sterile," and he praised *Lysistrata* as a sex comedy that was both open and clean. Besides a categorical distaste for the hypocritical snigger, Benchley disliked triteness in the presentation of sex as of other themes: "Sex, as a theatrical property, is as tiresome as the Old Mortgage," he announced in 1930, three years before *Tobacco Road* began its record-breaking run. Nonetheless, he offered no real defense for his theoretical exclusion of sex from humor; his queasiness seems entirely visceral, especially if viewed with Highet's observation in mind that much first-rate satire is redolent with sex and obscenity.

One should note that Benchley's severities about the subject-matter of humor were typical of American columnists and essayists during the 1920's and 1930's. Public affairs was a major theme of only two outstanding humorists in these media, Will Rogers and E. B. White. Sex got somewhat more attention. White and Thurber asked, *Is Sex Necessary?* (1929) and decided that it was if other human problems received due weight; but the exploitation of sex by humorists in the shorter forms was slight compared to the slavering over this material by playwrights, by "serious" novelists, and by such writers of comic romances as James Branch Cabell, John Erskine, and Thorne Smith.

Perhaps the greater freedom enjoyed by playwrights and novelists stimulated their literary sexuality. Writers in the shorter forms labored under the restrictions of the newspapers and magazines for which they wrote on salary, on assignment, or as "free" lancers. *Vanity Fair* was too well-bred to get very daring; *Life* had allowed some naughtiness to creep into its illustrations around 1910 but thenceforth seldom sinned. Harold Ross was no prude and rejected only incest and major blasphemy as themes for humor; but when Lardner, Benchley, Day, and Marquis wrote for *The New Yorker,* they gave the editor little trouble on the score of sexual liberality. On this subject they were their own severest monitors. Either because they remained prisoners of their Victorian childhoods or because they had been too well trained during long careers under more timid editorial chiefs than Ross, they easily sacrificed up-to-dateness for old-fashioned reticence.

"I laugh," said Beaumarchais' Figaro, "that I need not weep." Benchley, too, belonged to the impressive band who have felt that humor was very close to its opposite. Thurber said of humorists that "The little wheels of their invention are set in motion by the damp hand of melancholy," and Groucho Marx retells the story of Grock, the clown, who went to a doctor about his melancholia and was advised to go see Grock. Benchley admired "that approach to tragedy which marks great comedy," and he respected Ed Wynn in part because "He has that same aura of pathos which sublimates Charlie Chaplin and makes him by turns a great comedian and a great tragedian."

Yet Benchley made little use of pathos, a restraint that was both good and bad. He never dragged tear-jerking situations out of stock, as did Finley Peter Dunne in describing how a fireman, killed in the collapse of a rickety building, was brought home, or as Lardner did in "There Are Smiles," where a flapper with a heart of gold and a weakness for reckless driving was killed by the snap of an O. Henry ending. On the other hand, apart from the pieces in which he sprayed acid on social injustices, Benchley's work suffers from excessive blandness. His muse was not cankered enough; one misses the controlled pathos and brooding melancholy that lend variety and tension to the best writing of Lardner and Thurber.

Such darkness as there is in Benchley will receive its due in our discussion of his imagery. Meanwhile, as one ponders Highet's statements that excellent satire must be big, coarse, and hearty and that polite and sophisticated satires are "untypical, almost paradoxical, one wonders whether the *New Yorker* humorists were too thoroughly Benchleyized and even whether the entire trend of metropolitan humor and satire in the twentieth century has not veered from the main path marked by Chaucer, Boccaccio, Rabelais, Cervantes, Swift, and Fielding. Perhaps the suave, sophisticated moderns have laid out a new track; perhaps the "black humorists" of the angry, bawdy comic novel are the true "main-liners."

Whatever Benchley's limitations in theory and in practice, his comments on brow-elevation, spontaneity, the deadpan, social content, and sex not only link him with the older humorists of his generation but show his relationship to such younger, jumpier contemporaries as James Thurber, E. B. White, Wolcott Gibbs, and S. J. Perelman who further intellectualized the vernacular and made *The New Yorker* a magazine of distinction.

Norris W. Yates, in his Robert Benchley, *Twayne Publishers, Inc., 1968, 175 p.*

Louis Hasley   (essay date 1970)

[*Hasley is an American writer, educator, and critic. In the following excerpt, he provides a thematic and stylistic analysis of Benchley's personal essays.*]

[Robert Benchley] wrote humor, satire, reportage and criticism; but all of his writing that found its way into books may be broadly categorized as personal essays. These essays assumed various shapes, of course, including some narration and a substantial amount of dialog; they were always Benchley on, or off, some subject. And *he* was always more important than his subject. His writing career extended roughly from 1915 to 1945, during which time many hundreds of such pieces, originally published in magazines, were reprinted in periodic collections. An additional source of Benchley's fame arose from his work in Hollywood, where he made forty-eight shorts and appeared in, or collaborated on, forty-seven feature pictures. Many of these contributed to making his name synonymous with comedy of a quietly distinctive sort.

More than with any other humorist, it is hard to distinguish his literary reputation from his personal reputation as perpetuated by his many acquaintances who sought his friendship and paid lavish tribute to his warm personality and his charm. To James Thurber he was "the humorist's humorist . . . and . . . a wonderful guy." Howard Dietz called him "the most entertaining personality that ever decked the tables of New York and Hollywood. . . . Among other sacred things," continued Dietz, "I consider him the wisest man I have ever known." Not having known Robert Benchley personally, nor having known how many wise men Mr. Dietz has known, and possessing no idea of Mr. Dietz's conception of wisdom, I cannot deal with this last testimony. What one does learn, however, is that such fondness is the rule, not the exception, among those who were Benchley's close associates. . . .

[Benchley] is one of the most subjective of writers and one of the most personal of personal essayists. Almost all his subjects seem trivia, but they become stamped with the unique genius of his highly subjective reactions. Overtly, however, he declares for subject matter. "Being simply a person who writes little articles sporadically, and with no distinction," he wrote in **On Saying Little at Great Length,** "I am always forced to have something in mind about which to write. . . . Even if I could sell an article about nothing in particular, I wouldn't feel quite right in doing it." (Here he has begun slipping into a lightly mocking irony and goes on.) "When I write a thing, I do it because I have something fairly vital burning with me which I feel it is only my simple obligation to the State to express. . . ." Among American writers of Benchley's stature, probably only S. J. Perelman has less formal content in his essays.

Benchley does, of course, use 'subjects' as springboards for expressing his prejudices, preferences, and reactions. Travel, sleep, birds (he had a thing against birds, especially pigeons), language, games, finance, theatre, and science—these are but a few of the dozens of everyday topics that he teed off from. Since his formal content was so slight, the onus of literary enjoyment to be had from his work must rest, to a very great extent, on the satisfactions of style. Like his contemporaries, James Thurber and E. B. White, Benchley was master of a style remarkably pure. He animadverted on writers who were not understandable to moderately intelligent readers. His own writing was a model of lucidity. Respect for language shows in the ceremonious completeness of his sentences, a patient grace that reflects the gentleman. He indulges few figures. The lines move flawless and unruffled, breathing a disciplined restraint and understatement. The rhythms carry us along in sinuous psychological progressions that eventuate often in surprising *non sequiturs,* or a quick descent to a contrastingly lower level of language, or a quiet collapse into cockeyed nonsense. Delicacy of touch is nowhere better realized than in this bit from **"More Songs for Meller,"** which Benchley purports to be a program synopsis for a song sung in Spanish by Señorita Raquel Meller:

> A coquette, pretending to be very angry, bites off the hand of her lover up to the wrist. Ah, naughty Cirinda! Such antics! However does she think she can do her lessons if she gives up all her time to love-making? But Cirinda does not care. Heedless, heedless Cirinda!

In person and in print the kindliness of Benchley is widely evident, but it must not be inferred that his writing is without grain. Satire of a quiet but unmistakable sort appears versus—among other topics—women, children, college football, sentimentality, scientists, and heroes like Paul Revere. Women, especially, challenge his charity. In **"Ladies Wild"** he ridicules women poker players. In **"Cocktail Hour"** he complains of women's tearooms that advertise 2:30 p.m. as a cocktail hour when men at that time are just returning to work from lunch. In **"Matinees— Wednesday and Saturdays"** he does not spare the afternoon theatre audiences, made up primarily of women, who giggle over chocolates at a seduction scene that would be taken seriously at an evening performance. In **" 'Ask That Man' "** he focuses on the wife who believes that any other man knows more than her husband. In **"The Wreck of the Sunday Paper"** a man wonders how his wife could have got the paper in such a mess—was she trying to dress herself in it?

It seems more than likely that Benchley's confessed "New England streak" manifested itself in a preference for masculine company, specifically for his literary and theatrical friends and *bon vivants.* They hobnobbed (I mean nothing sinister) with him in his uptown hotel suite, which Thurber characterized as "The combination men's club, museum, and art gallery," his wife meanwhile remaining in their home in Scarsdale not only when he stayed over in New York but also, so far as can be learned from Nathaniel's biography, while he was working in Hollywood. In that biography the role assigned to Mrs. Benchley seems hardly more than a statistic, though it is true that Robert's late-at-night theatrical reviewing or his acting on Broadway often made staying in town a practical necessity.

But there are complementary attitudes toward children as unrelieved encumbrances (an attitude widely shared in this country and much exploited by comics). **"Kiddie-Kar Travel"** begins:

> In America there are two classes of travel—first class, and with children. Traveling with children corresponds roughly to traveling third class in Bulgaria. They tell me there is nothing lower in the world than third-class Bulgarian travel.

In **"The Children's Hour,"** he is apprehensive of the mysterious rushing into and out of the house by clusters of children, who he speculates may be plotting a revolution. "All I hope is that they start something—anything— before I am too old to run." **"Museum Feet"** is practically a case study of what happens when you take two small boys to a museum. This is the way he describes bringing the nightmarish visit to an end: "It is but the work of a minute to hit Herbert over the head till he is quiet and to yank Arthur into the cab along with you." Perhaps the attitudes here toward spouses and children relate to the larger one of the humorist in general. He must take his material where he finds it, and it must have wide, if not universal appeal. And what has wider or more universal appeal, especially in our time, than the follies, shortcomings, and annoyances experienced within the family circle? Of a list of eight leading American humorists of this century (say Ade, Marquis, Lardner, Thurber, Benchley, White, Nash, and McGinley) only one had more than two children (Lardner had four), one never married, two had only one child, one was divorced and remarried. Is it simply a sober fact that, for one pursuing a career, a spouse is a 'necessary luxury' and children an encumbrance? It would often seem so, and it would also seem that the same facts and attitudes exist, with rare exceptions, among the entire intellectual and artist class. End of *obiter dictum.*

Among other favorite Benchley topics was that of the spectator—bridge kibitzer, chess watcher, football fan, or sidewalk superintendent. The ceremony of the old grad returning for the Big Game, as well as the game itself, comes in for pricking by Benchley's needle. Because of the impossibility of understanding the game by reason of the frequent rules changes, "All that the spectator gets out of the game now is the fresh air, the comical articles in his program, the sight of twenty-two young men rushing about in mysterious formations, and whatever he brought along in his flask." As to watching a chess match, he said:

> At first you may think that they are both dead. . . . I once heard of a murderer who propped his two victims up against a chess board in sporting attitudes and was able to get as far as Seattle before his crime was discovered.

For the purpose of illustrating his peculiar humorous quality, it is ordinarily difficult to quote from Benchley because his effects are likeliest to come as an emanation rather than as epigrammatism. His style in itself—often so elaborately, brightly dim-witted, alternately so bravado and so fumbling—is seen to be a continuing satire of obvious and superficial minds, as in the following unflappable paragraph, with its artificial naivete turning into an embarrassment:

> The best part about a meteorite (I always try to look on the bright side) is that you can hear it coming. The sound has been variously described as 'the bellowing of oxen,' 'the roaring of a fire in a chimney' and 'the tearing of calico.' I certainly hope that mine doesn't sound like the tearing of calico, as that is a sound that drives me crazy. I would almost rather be hit by the meteorite without any warning. (Cross that out, Miss Schwab, please.) ("Duck, Brothers!")

Like every other humorist, Benchley employs a number of devices. One of these is literalism, used to enforce the reader's image of the author, or his persona, as something of a nitwit. ("Most people today do not look in the best of health owing to not being in the best of health." Or: "Tell us your phobias and we will tell you what you are afraid of.") The literalism easily is transformed to a vapid repetition or circularism:

> If you are planning to go abroad, it is easy to see that you must have a passport. They won't let you abroad without a passport or something to show to the man. If you haven't got a passport, you can show him some of the snapshots you took at the beach last summer, but he would rather look at a passport.

> A worker, whom we will call Cassidy, because his name was Cassidy. . . .

Another device by which Benchley gets some of his best effects is reversalism. It usually takes the form of his first making an assertion and then abruptly denying, diminishing, or recanting it.

> My grandfather Corporal Benchley (later Private Benchley). . . .

> He is a little man, who has difficulty in breathing (not enough, however). . . .

> We find ourselves confronted by a pretty serious situation. The cow has been called 'Man's best friend.' No, that is the dog. . . . Sorry.

> My hundreds, nay dozens, of friends. . . .

Use of outright nonsense puts Benchley, along with Lardner and Perelman, among the forerunners of post-World War II surrealism. Easily his most obvious use of nonsense is found in some of the titles of his books, e. g., ***20,000 Leagues Under the Sea, or David Copperfield; The Treasurer's Report and Other Aspects of Community Singing; My Ten Years in a Quandry, and How They Grew.*** But, with him, nonsense is likely to crop up anywhere. Here's what happened with a safety device on a "beater" in a Massachusetts paper mill.

> Cassidy got flustered and dropped one leg of his trousers in the safety device with the result that he was caught up in the machine and swished around until all they had to do was to dry him out and they could have printed the Sunday *Times* on him. In fact, that is just what they did do, and it was one of the best editions of the Sunday *Times* that was ever run off the presses. It had human interest. (**"Safety Second"**)

> Europe has often claimed that Las Los was not a part of it, and in 1356, Spain began a long and costly war with France, the loser to take Las Los and two out-fielders.

Terminology applicable to humorous devices is often overlapping. Possibly this next example should be called confusionism.

> Look at the time-table for a train which leaves about 2:45 (Eastern Standard Time). Write down '2:45' on a piece of paper. Add 150. Subtract the number of stations that Valhalla is above White Plains. Sharpen your pencil and bind up your cut finger and subtract the number you first thought of, and the result will show the number of Presidents of the United States who have been assassinated while in office. Then go over to the Grand Central Terminal and ask one of the information clerks what you want to know.

Among other prominent humorous devices, Benchley derives a great deal of entertaining mileage from his brash, fumbling, or nonsensical translations of foreign words and phrases, particularly French and German.

The intelligent reader need not be told that assessing the character and quality of a literary humorist is more than describing his general style and specifying a number of his devices by which to categorize examples. There are, indubitably, numerous such devices; but many of them are used resourcefully perhaps only once or a few times, and provide much of the reader's ongoing enjoyment from page to page. These scattered, less frequently used devices, varied in nature as they are, can obviously be only hinted at through samples, which I will refrain from labeling.

> To these simple, childish people . . . cleanliness is next to a broken hip.

> Someone has just estimated that the velocity of wind on some of the stars is 140,000 miles an hour. That's too fast for wind to blow.

> . . . The life of one American dollar has been estimated at one-third that of a sugar lozenge under a faucet.

> I have no liking for migraine headaches, but I would rather have them than a responsible job.

A great amount of Robert Benchley's popular fame came from one piece, **"The Treasurer's Report,"** first launched as a speech in 1922. Son Nathaniel observed that it marked "a new and completely different kind of comedy." It was a comedy without gags but depending for its humor on an alternately brisk and fumbling delivery, with stops and starts, and irrelevant phrases that just seem to creep in unbidden. "I guess that no one," Benchley wrote,

> ever got so sick of a thing as I and all my friends have grown of this Treasurer's Report. I did it every night and two matinees a week for nine months in the Third Music Box Revue. Following that, I did it for ten weeks in vaudeville around the country. I did it at banquets and teas, at friends' houses and in my own house, and finally went to Hollywood and made a talking movie of it. In fact, I have inflicted it on the public in every conceivable way except over the radio and dropping it from airplanes.

From such exposure by audio-visual media of his Hollywood shorts and his roles in full-length features, he became more famous than he had ever been as an essayist, drama critic, and Broadway actor. He also found that performing in and producing motion pictures was vastly easier and more lucrative than his literary work, and so his writing for the printed page fell off to almost nothing.

In attempting to evaluate an author's writings as literature, a critic cannot ignore the view of life which such writings embody. People were surprised to find, says Nathaniel Benchley,

> that Robert was deeply religious. . . . he was such a determined antiformalist as to appear practically agnostic. But . . . his belief in God and the hereafter was so strong as to communicate itself to others, and if not actually to convert them, at least to reaffirm their own faith.

He added that his father and mother had a strong feeling for Christmas and that Robert wrote "two biting satires on how the spirit of Christmas gets lost through the dogged determination of the celebrants to preserve it. . . ."

Not to scamp the issue, this critic found little religious spirit, express or implied, in the two satires; and the judg-

ment that Robert Benchley was deeply religious must be left to those who knew him, for this trait does not show in his work. Perhaps humanistic, rather than religious, is the accurate term. There is, in fact, a clear strain of disillusion about life in many of his essays. In recounting his experiences as a reporter covering some two hundred banquets, he speaks of having been "seared and calloused with a premature cynicism [and] bitter distrust of mankind" from listening to "the great minds of the nation giving expression to palpable bologna." In another piece he mentions that a certain civilization was probably superior to ours, and adds, "and what civilization wouldn't be?" In a third he deprecates "our wonderful Human Machine (wonderful except for about three hundred flaws which can be named on the fingers of one hand). . . ." In **"A Little Sermon on Success,"** he asserts that "taking Life as it comes along isn't a very satisfactory way, but it is the *only* way. (I should be very glad to try any other way that anyone can suggest. I certainly am sick of this one.)"

He goes still further metaphysically and theologically in **"The World of Grandpa Benchley,"** where he speculates on the future thoughts of himself when he will be an old man.

> I sometimes wonder what it is all about—this world I mean. I am not so sure about the next world. Sometimes I think there is one and sometimes I think there isn't. I'll be darned if I can make it out. . . .

> I don't think there is any doubt about there being some Motive Power which governs the world. But I can't seem to get much beyond that.

What we do see in Robert Benchley's writings are a fine humanity, urbanity and decorum—as well as an impeccable taste, as Howard Dietz declares, that passed up numerous opportunities for obvious jokes. He stays well within the bounds of conventional ethics and morality. There is no traffic with sordidness or vice or the realism that flirts with pornography. In this he is in the main-stream of twentieth century American literary humor. He had, said Frank Sullivan, "humility, honesty, and integrity." We are told by Nathaniel that he read much, though we have scarcely any detail on his favorites except that he almost worshipped George Ade. There are traces of an influence on him by nineteenth century humorist Bill Nye; and there is considerable kinship to, if not influence by, the Canadian humorist Stephen Leacock, who was twenty years his senior, and who paid tribute to Benchley as # "perhaps the most finished master of the technique of literary fun in America." Writers like Thurber, E. B. White and others on the *New Yorker* sometimes feared that what they were writing had already been done, and done better, by Benchley.

He composed slowly, painstakingly. His biographer pictures him as sometimes poised over his typewriter for fifteen minutes before pecking in a comma. But against him duty had a hard line to type, for, as he declared, he found no greater pleasure in the world than being dilatory. Once he left a poker game and, in an effort to start writing, sat down in his hotel room and typed "The." But nothing followed, so he went down and met some acquaintances for an hour or so, went back to write, found "The" still staring blankly at him, typed after it "hell with it," and went happily out for the evening. In this incident, one feels, we glimpse the real Benchley that his friends so highly cherished.

"The heavier critics have underrated Benchley because of his 'short flight,' " wrote James Thurber in a commemorative tribute. Very likely. For the form of his pieces is light, airy, personal, and fragile. Many of his short flights, however—most of them in fact—today lack the sense of nervous urgency that our turbulent time seems to demand. A few of them have a synthetic quality, while a sizeable number have a too-low pulse that does not hold today's harried reader. *The Benchley Roundup* (1954) presents a selection of eighty-eight pieces which the editor, son and biographer Nathaniel Benchley, says are "those which seem to stand up best over the years." I am constrained, however, to file a dissenting judgment. Not more than half of these are the ones that I would nominate for any healthy longevity. I can only suspect that quite a number were included, or excluded, not on their literary merits, but on other considerations. To a reader of the whole Benchley canon who comes to a similar conclusion, I confess that I have a list of several dozen that do not appear in *The Benchley Roundup,* among them **"The Treasurer's Report"**—pieces that, if given a favorable chance for survival in the next century, might go on delighting discriminating readers for many decades to come.

Louis Hasley, "Robert Benchley: Humorist's Humorist," in The Connecticut Review, *Vol. IV, No. 1, October, 1970, pp. 65-72.*

Nathaniel Benchley on his father's purported laziness:

He wasn't lazy. He liked to put things off as long as he could. He was a procrastinator. He got his copy done just in the nick of time for the *New Yorker.* They often had to send runners out to get it. Benchley's law is "Any man can do any amount of work, provided it's not the work he's supposed to be doing." So he would find all manner of things to do rather than start a piece.

At one point he was doing three pieces a week for the King Features Syndicate and a radio show and in the winter, covering the theatre openings for the *New Yorker.* It was a hell of a pile up. Writing got harder and harder until he finally gave it up altogether. He "quit while he was ahead." I think that could have been a little rationalizing . . . to salve his conscience.

Nathaniel Benchley, cited by Robert Luhn, in "In Good Spirits: Robert Benchley Remembered," Book Forum *VI, No. 2, 1982.*

Walter Blair and Hamlin Hill (essay date 1978)

[*In the following excerpt from their book* America's Humor: From Poor Richard to Doonesbury, *the critics* *distinguish* Inside Benchley *as the volume they consider to be most representative of Benchley's flair as a comic writer.*]

The collection which we think displays Benchley at his most brilliant is the 1942 volume of reprints, *Inside Benchley.* The title page shows the Gluyas Williams caricature of Benchley peering into his bedroom mirror and seeing the image of Wimpy from *Popeye* reflected there. In the back of the book, we come upon an utterly worthless Glossary of Kin, Native and Technical Terms, a list of Abbreviations from the Old and New Testaments and the Apocrypha, a Bibliography of books in sexual psychology, and an Index which is a page of the New York City telephone directory. Preceding this bufoonery are some of the best examples of vintage Benchley.

The mock-lecture, **"The Social Life of the Newt,"** points out that newt courtship occurs "with a minimum distance of fifty paces (newt measure) between the male and the female. Some of the bolder males may now and then attempt to overstep the bounds of good sportsmanship and crowd in up to forty-five paces, but such tactics are frowned upon by the Rules Committee." In **"Cell-formations and Their Work,"** we are told that

> in about 1 / 150000 of a cubic inch of blood there are some five million cells afloat. This is, as you will see, about the population of the City of London, except that the cells don't wear any hats. Thus, in our whole body, there are perhaps (six times seven is forty-two, five times eight is forty, put down naught and carry your four, eight times nine is seventy-two and four is seventy-six, put down six and carry your seven and then, adding, six, four, three, one, six, naught, naught, naught), oh, about a billion or so of these red corpuscles alone, not counting overhead and breakage.

Perhaps even less information comes across in **"The Romance of Digestion."** This essay reveals a lecturer trying to get cute: The teeth and the tongue ("which we may call the escalator of the mouth or Nature's nobleman for short") "toss the food back and forth between them until there is nothing left of it, except the little bones which you have to take out between your thumb and forefinger and lay on your butter-plate":

> And now comes the really wonderful part of the romance which is being enacted right there under your very eyes. A chemical reaction on the tongue presses a little button which telegraphs down, down, down,' way down to the cross old stomach and says: "Please, sir, do you want this food or don't you?" And the Stomach, whom we shall call "Prince Charming" from now on, telegraphs (or more likely writes) back: "Yes, dear!" or "You can do what you like with it for all of me. . . ."

The food is then placed on a conveyor, by means of which it is taken to the Drying Room, situated on the third floor, where it is taken apart and washed and dried, preparatory to going through the pressing machines. These pressing machines are operated by one man, who stands by the conveyor as it brings the food along and tosses it into the vats. Here all rocks and moss are drawn off by mechanical pickers. . . . From here the food is taken to the Playroom where it plays around awhile with the other children until it is time for it to be folded by the girls in the bindery, packed into neat stacks, and wrapped for shipment in bundles of fifty. . . . The by-products are made into milk-bottle caps, emery wheels, and insurance calendars, and are sold at cost.

The utterly inappropriate names ("Nature's nobleman" and "Prince Charming"), the unexpected and irrational non sequiturs, the anti-climaxes, incongruous catalogues, associational leaps, and childlike but confusing "explanations" of the lecturer produce an effect close to hallucination.

Inside Benchley also includes one of the author's finest parodies, **"Family Life in America,"** a take-off on the Naturalistic novel and others in the modes of Dickens and H. G. Wells. **"More Songs for Meller"** recalls George H. Derby in summaries of Spanish songs that Senorita Meller sings; for instance:

> (3) La Guia
> (The Time-Table)
> It is the day of the bull fight in Madrid. Everyone is cock-eyed. The bull has slipped out by the back entrance to the arena and has gone home, disgusted. Nobody notices that the bull has gone except Nina, a peasant girl who has come to town to sell her father. She looks with horror at the place in the Royal Box where the bull ought to be sitting and sees there instead her algebra teacher whom she had told that she was staying at home on account of a sick headache. . . .

All of Senorita Meller's songs are equally surreal.

Most important, there is a whole series of minor dilemmas before which the Little Man quails. Pushed by uneasiness into a spoonerism in **"Coffee, Megg and Ilk, Please,"** the "I" tells about his abject terror before any workingman. "I become servile, almost cringing. . . . When, for instance, I give an order at a soda fountain, if the clerk overawes me at all, my voice breaks into a yodel." **"The Tooth, the Whole Tooth, and Nothing but the Tooth"** records the terror of a dentist appointment: "Of course, there is always the chance that the elevator will fall and that you will all be terribly hurt. . . . Things don't work as happily as that in real life." **"Kiddie-Kar Travel," "The Last Day," "Traveling in Peace"** ("I myself solved the problem of shipboard conversation by traveling alone and pretending to be a deaf-mute"), and **"Howdy, Neighbor!"** record the anguish of train travel, packing up at the end of vacation, ship travel, and visiting with friends. **" 'Ask that Man' "** confronts the awesome trauma of getting directions from strangers. Ordered by his wife to ask which train went to Boston, the Little Man approaches the stationmaster and "simulating conversation with him, I really asked him nothing":

> Eight months later we returned home. . . .

> From Arkansas, we went into Mexico, and once, guided by what I told her had been the directions given me by the man at the news-stand in Vera Cruz, we made a sally into the swamps of

Central America in whatever that first republic is on the way south.

Whether he blusters, bumbles, or lies deliberately, the Little Man is trapped. Neither the common sense of his crossroads antecedents nor the logic and erudition of the urban wits gets him out of his predicaments.

It's noteworthy, too, that Benchley managed to transfer many of the qualities of the Little Man from the rarefied atmosphere of *The New Yorker* and other highbrow periodicals to the mass media. Robert Redding, looking at Benchley's movie career in *Starring Robert Benchley,* argues convincingly that when Benchley played the role of lecturer, "his monologue . . . invariably took some unexpected and inexplicable turns; then the speaker's words or manner might betray an awareness that all was not going well, but as often as he would briskly proceed, apparently satisfied that his outlandish discourse was altogether lucid and instructive." Redding sees Benchley in other movies becoming "Joe Doakes," "a fumbling, ineffectual, supposedly average citizen, reenacting trivial, everyday humiliations of the sort that, again, most of his viewers could recognize. They watched him being intimidated, or defeated outright, by supercilious clothing salesmen, uniformed attendants, precocious children, malevolent ironing boards and furnaces and window shades." In the film of his most famous lecture, **"The Treasurer's Report,"** a substitute completely messes up the annual financial statement before the members of his organization.

That Benchley was able, almost singlehandedly, to define the character of the Little Man is possibly less important than that he managed to find a sympathetic audience among the middle-class moviegoers of the late thirties and forties. His popular success suggests that his "sheer madness" was in fact recognizable to brows of all levels in America. Something of the futility, the hopeless bravado, the glorious confusion, and the lurking terror that Benchley embodied in his invention struck universal chords.

Part of the explanation may be that his subjects were everyday annoyances. His language, while it was formal rather than colloquial, imitated the hesitancy and informality of spoken English. His allusions—though they frequently required special knowledge on his reader's part—never soared over the common man's head into the stratosphere. Though Benchley did a beautifully faithful rendition of "The Secret Life of Walter Mitty" for radio in 1940, his own zaniness never quite reached the clinical level that Thurber's Mitty did. Benchley managed to walk a razor edge between in-group faddishness and universal appeal. He came closest to clinical schizophrenia in one story, **"My Subconscious,"** when he wrote, "One of the many reasons for my suspecting that I am headed for the last break-up . . . is my Subconscious is getting to be a better man than I am." But, he had to confess, "on the whole, my Subconscious makes a much better job of things than I do."

Walter Blair and Hamlin Hill, "Benchley and Perelman," in their America's Humor: From Poor Richard to Doonesbury, *Oxford University Press, Inc., 1978, pp. 427-37.*

Gluyas Williams drawings always appeared in Benchley's books, illustrating Benchley himself (above) and his "Little Man" persona.

Eric Solomon   (essay date 1984)

[*In the following essay, Solomon focuses on the scope and significance of the "Wayward Press" and "Theatre" columns Benchley wrote for the* New Yorker *during the 1930s.*]

During the Depression decade, Robert Benchley wrote nearly seventy-five casual essays for the *New Yorker,* most of which have been collected in the five books he published in the 1930s—*The Treasurer's Report* (1930), *No Poems* (1932), *From Bed to Worse* (1934), *My Ten Years in a Quandary* (1936), *After 1903—What?* (1938). Some of these pieces are brief humorous asides—similar to his contributions of the late 1920s, when he provided many fillers for an issue—some rank among his finest parodies (**"How Seamus Commara Met the Banshee"**—1932), mock scientific essays (**"A Brief Study of Dendrophilia"**—1933), false nostalgia (**"New Plays for Old"**—1930), and the little man's dreams (**"Take the Witness"**—1935). Benchley scholarship has taken appropriate notice of these contributions.

Less noted, and certainly uncollected in book form, are

some of the best, the funniest, the most intelligent, and the most politically concerned pieces Benchley wrote. During the Thirties, over the pseudonym "Guy Fawkes," forty of his seventy Wayward Press columns appeared. Benchley not only prepared the way for his successor, A. J. Liebling, but also wrote some of the magazine's strongest political commentary as he questioned newspapers' coverage of such matters as the Lindbergh kidnapping, peace conferences, red scares, the Roosevelt elections, and the Supreme Court packing struggle.

Even more forgotten are Robert Benchley's rich exercises in comic appreciation and, sometimes, wry rejection: his Theatre Reviews. After coming over from *Vanity Fair* in late 1929 and before leaving permanently for Hollywood in early 1940, Benchley wrote close to three hundred and fifty drama reviews for the *New Yorker,* sometimes treating as many as four plays or musicals per column. He wrote admiringly of actors and actresses and positively of most of the dramatists whose reputations have held up: Ibsen, Coward, O'Casey, O'Neill, Anderson, Kaufman, Howard, Rice, Hellman, Kingsley, Sherwood, Behrman, Green; as a critic he supported strongly the leftist plays of Odets, Blitzstein, Maltz, Wexley, Lawson, and the Federal Theatre. (One exception to Benchley's praise was anything by A. A. Milne; "The Milne Menace," is the head of one of Benchley's columns.) He reviewed plays each week during the early 1930s except for brief periods when other staffers such as E. B. White, Charles Brackett, or Dorothy Parker would cover for him. Later, he shared the column with the man who would inherit it, Wolcott Gibbs. Benchley reviews are at once trenchant and comic, and many of the greatest humorous effects he ever created appear in these old *New Yorker* pages. He was superb at this kind of critico-comic writing under pressure, as Parker realized when she tried to fill his slot and ended each column with a plea—"Robert Benchley please come home. Nothing is forgiven"; or "Baby is taking terrible beating." Dorothy Parker is quite explicit: "Not I nor anyone else . . . can do what he does to the drama."

Although most of Robert Benchley's Wayward Press commentaries are essentially tough-minded and disillusioned criticisms of both contemporary journalistic practices and the contradictions of the American scene, Benchley employs many of the humorous approaches that make his memoirs and parodies some of the finest humorous prose of his time. While he often attacks papers like the New York *Times* for awkward, overdone, and cliché-ridden coverage of the young Charles Lindbergh or for reportorial venality in writing straight-forwardly respectful stories about, say, Calvin Coolidge in Wild West garb; and despite his fiercely liberal stance when he mocks the *Herald Tribune* for trying to document a Soviet attempt to stir up a revolt by American blacks or to deny the realities of Roosevelt's victory over Landon—Benchley can still be warmly funny.

His openings are brisk and absurd. He treats Memorial Day newspapers with affectionate acceptance of the holiday jinx of dullness: "Except for those who are going to march and want to know the course of the parade, the papers on Memorial Day can be used for wrapping without a glance." Benchley's skill in expanding comic metaphor is often on display. "The *Times* has, for several years now, maintained its own private hatchery for news-heroes. Selecting the bird when it is very young, the editors have nailed its feet to the ground and stuffed it with selected bits of prepared publicity until it is ready with a large and succulent *foie gras* featuring a New York *Times* copyright stamp right on the middle of it. Practically all the polar explorers, planet-detectors, and long-distance fliers . . ." are thus nurtured. And Robert Benchley's particular brand of comic diminution is always in evidence. Since there were no newsworthy items in a Naval Conference, "This left the gigantic press organizations in London with just a little less to do than they previously had. They could either play badminton, go and look at the Italian art exhibition at Burlington House, or choose up sides among themselves and have a hare-and-hounds race. Many of them settled down to writing little themes for their home school papers entitled 'My Vacation in England'." His own self-mockery tempers his criticisms. Dealing with sports pages' emotional over-reaction to Knute Rockne's death, Benchley uses a familiar self-denigrating ploy to ease in comic fashion his criticism. "The question is whether or not sporting writers are ever to be trusted with matters of a sentimental nature. We are clutching in our chubby fist one black ball, signifying 'No-no-no!'" The "chubby" is pure Benchley.

Benchley's basic tone is ironic, satirizing the press's generally conservative attitude. The irony always shows a genuine wit, which is often heavier than the whimsical approach that distinguishes his comic articles. In a 1930 issue—and he seems to have written nearly the entire magazine—Benchley turns to what he calls the newspapers' celebration of "Russian Godless Week." Here, he remarks, " . . . it is not too much to say that when the day has arrived on which the New York *Times* is taken to task for publishing pro-Soviet news we may confidently expect the entire Appalachian range to get up and walk over to the ocean for a dip." There is a feeling of weary sarcasm in his remarks, as in his glance at the 1932 Democratic convention—**"The Reportorial Dance Marathon"**—which intensely bores this critic of reportage. "But they keep right on doing it, every four years, perspiring and giggling at themselves, until the last peal of the organ has sounded and they sink exhausted to the floor, poorer by sheaves of expense accounts and richer only by several million words which nobody but the copy desk have read." One conjectures that this mordant critical outlet released Benchley to be the jolly comic in his more typical essays. Certainly, his anger shows clearly in **"The Third-and-a-Half Estate,"** where he excoriates the press for its mendacious and insensitive handling of the Lindbergh kidnaping (May 7, 1932—the flier continued to draw Benchley's attention throughout the decade).

Benchley employs his most savage indignation when discussing matters connected with World War I or any future conflict. A deeply sincere pacifist, he gives his humor a nervous edge as he mentions either reporters' blandness or nations' blindness in matters of war and peace. He fiercely attacks, for example, the efforts of a particular journalist who Benchley says "will be pleasantly remembered as the man who got America into the World War by his stirring editorials in the *Tribune*. He does not feel quite so strongly about this next war, but there is no telling when the old fighting spirit will flare up again, and, having made such a success of his last war, he may be tempted to get the boys into khaki again just for a final fling before the law is passed making editorial and special writers the first ones to be taken up in the draft." Ambrose Bierce could not have put the case more bitterly.

Many press failures peeve Benchley, most often when they involve some lack of humane response. Even what the papers omit can fall under Benchley's scorn. Sports: "The football season . . . is over, and we have received our daily news from the various stadia detailing what the scrubs did against the Varsity in Wednesday practice and what the Varsity did against the coaches on Thursday. What we *don't* get was that a young man was killed playing football at Brown University on November 1. That probably wouldn't be considered news." Advertising influence: he hails the fact in **"Real News"** that advertising or editorial pressures seem not to affect weather reports—but "Possibly, in a few days, the anti-administration papers may set out to prove that the Street Cleaning Department is shot through with graft and inefficiency, but in that glorious day after no reporter need fear getting all the news. . . . Nature doesn't advertise, though the *News* may eventually swing her into line." He finds reporters deliberately misleading in **"Expert Dope"** as far as Roosevelt's re-election is concerned; in **"The Sound and the Fury,"** Benchley terms reportage on the conflict between FDR and the Supreme Court "propaganda by saturation"; and—remarkably, from a historicist standpoint—discovers that the coverage of fads takes up all the space in newspapers so that stories of the Nazi persecutions of the Jews are buried. **"Vanishing News"** is his title for this Wayward Press column, and Benchley goes so far as to hint at a cover-up plot.

Irony is Robert Benchley's special technique in these press analyses. He is devastating on newspapers' uses of red plot scares to shift the public's minds from bank failures: "So, thank God, we're safe from that quarter!" He is mightily amused by writers he calls Christopher Robins creating roguish picture captions of "*Snow Flake, Esq.* and Family" on a visit to Washington. "We can hardly wait for the first visit of *Little Christine Crocus* and her family when spring comes to the *World* offices." What he most laughs at are the lengths to which journalists go to provide copy when there are no newsworthy events. Benchley himself compensates for boredom with typical whimsy—as he does in his Theatre columns—"(Probably between the closing date of this magazine and its appearance on the stands . . . the Reds will have taken the city as far north as Fourteenth Street, and a new mountain range will have sprung up overnight along the Jersey Shore)." Benchley is always alert to one of humor's staples, the contradictions between genuine beliefs and stated positions. The quick shift of newspapers from support of government action to attacks on government action when NRA regulations threaten the publishers' positions fascinates the Wayward Press observer. "Guy Fawkes," indeed. The column releases Robert Benchley's iconoclastic, radical inclinations, and he directly attacks in the same context not editorial matter but slanted news columns that move seamlessly from attacks on Roosevelt's National Recovery Act to praise for Mussolini's statism.

While always eschewing theoretical formulations, as drama or journalism critic, Robert Benchley does indicate to the readers the basis for his comical/critical stance. Speaking of the New York *Times,* Benchley points out that it "on occasion goes out of its way to invite a genial leer from outsiders, and it is on such leers that this department is founded!" Elsewhere, he watches newspapers start to kid one another, "and now, perhaps, our particular *mission of vilification* will be taken over by the papers themselves" (my italics). Benchley's critical self-awareness is one of the hallmarks of his humor, whether mocking himself as the inadequate little man caught in Gluyas Williams' illustrations to the books—the Robert Benchley of the genial leer—or revealing himself as the angry satirist of social hypocrisy discovered in his direct statements of rueful dismay—the "Guy Fawkes" on a mission of vilification.

As a play reviewer, Robert Benchley is at once the clear, acute critic and the warm, discursive humorist. His basic tone is genial and tolerant. He enjoyed evenings at the theatre (but not restive or tardy audiences), and he is inclined in his reviews to reflect his pleasure by leniency towards actors and playwrights. No abstract conceptualist, he knows what he likes and draws on his practical sense of both good acting and good writing; after all, he was himself both writer and actor.

The persona developed by Benchley in his humorous essays carries over to his theatre work. Benchley the drama critic is always Robert the amiable blunderer. As his essays focus on this silly self, so in a review he can state, "And now, having checked up on the actors, I will check up on myself." He goes on to admit a mistake in a previous column: "My error was nothing but gross, palpitating stupidity. *I* should go around spying on actors." And he develops this play-going characterization, in the manner, perhaps, of a latter-day Samuel Pepys (Benchley was fascinated by the Queen Anne period, always planning a scholarly book on the subject; he makes no attempt, however, to imitate Pepys in form as was Franklin P. Adams' wont). After viewing *Uncle Vanya,* Benchley gets inside his own comic figure. "I love to be depressed by these Russians. As I go out into the street after an evening in one of their high-civilized, mid-Romanoff houses where a lot of people are stuck for the rest of their lives, I feel somehow that I have myself become an object of pity and that people ought to be a little nicer to me from now on. I walk along the street with what seems to me to be a rather sadly beautiful detachment, smiling wanly at the quips of my pleasure-mad companions, waiting for some sensitive Stranger to come up and press my hand and murmur: 'I understand, I understand.' This is a swell feeling." The humor may tell us more about Benchley than about Chekhov, but maybe not. Surely Benchley's foolishness enlivens what is customarily a rather rigid form. What other drama critic would spin such a rhetorical web as this? "Things picked up a little in the theatre last week. They lay right back

down again, it is true, but they *did* pick up at first, which is a comfort. A little picking up here and there each week, be it ever so slight, and we shall soon have our little girl downstairs again, sitting out in the sun in the garden for a few minutes every day. And then perhaps will come solid food, and something nice from Uncle Bob." The Robert Benchley a generation of readers loved and identified with wanders through a decade of *New Yorker* theatre reviews. He adores the drama. "It was a very exciting task to set myself, and my little face flushed with pleasurable anticipation as I dressed in my best bib (my best tucker was in the laundry) to make the rounds."

Benchley's great strengths as a comic essayist are his unexpected openings and his brilliant one-liners. One example of an opening will suffice: "As far as this week's drama page is concerned, you are over into the advertising right now. There need be nothing to detain you here, unless you like the monotonous hissing of plays on the pan—and not very much of that. For Spring, the Great Reaper, is here, and the pall of vernal death is slowly settling down on Broadway." And the number and skill of his witty throwaway lines are unmeasurable. "It was one of those plays in which all the characters, unfortunately, as it turned out, enunciated very clearly." After viewing a great acting performance in Marc Connelly's *The Green Pastures,* Benchley conjectures, "If the Lord is really anything like Mr. Harrison, maybe I have been wrong all these years." One phrase is sufficient to dismiss a play forever: "I must have seen a play called 'Dora Mobridge' because I have the program for it right here on my desk. All right. So I saw 'Dora Mobridge'." He can be orotund—"But it does seem as if at our age, we might have been spared a thing like 'Made in France.' Our civilization can't have incurred sufficient divine wrath to deserve that. Not only was it old, old stuff, but it was bad, bad, old, old stuff. . . ." At times, wit alone is enough; a play seems adequate on its own merits, "nothing much, but all right as such shows go. Considered as the Golden Calf brought in on the Ark of the Covenant, it was a complete bust." He can encapsulate his credo in one short line: "Never give an actor a cape to wear," or "It is too bad that people who feel strongly about good causes do not know more about writing good plays." And Benchley is a master at reducing a weak play by quick ridicule. "But it must also be said that it contains volley after volley of some of the most immature gags ever conceived by an adult mind. [Then comes the unmistakable Benchley twist.] I take it for granted that they are the product of an adult mind. No child could have had the stamina to stay up as late at rehearsals as must have been necessary in the fight to keep them in." Knowing that he is writing in a cliché-ridden genre, Benchley depends on his knack of creating quaint comic phrases to enliven the prose. "The rest of the cast took their parts well as my grandmother once said of Julia Marlowe. . . ."

If Benchley can swiftly make a humorous point, he can also break the conventional mold of drama criticism to find room for more extended flights of comic invention. He is at his best, I think, either when the week's plays are not worthy of discussion, when there are no new plays, or in his yearly summaries—in which he always avoids summarizing. Here is part of his 1930 **"In Conclusion,"** where he approaches sheer nonsense in a mini-comic essay.

> There is always a certain sadness incident to writing a summary of a dramatic season which is just closing. In the first place, it involves a lot of work. One has to look up the summaries which the newspaper reviewers have compiled in the preceding Sunday papers and then try to re-write them, using different verbs and adjectives. [Awk! ES] This, in itself is cause enough for depression.
>
> In the second place, when it comes time to make a digest of a waning season, it means that summer, with its unpleasant and depressing contacts with Nature, is at hand. And summer is, at best, the death's head at the feast of the season, poets and travel bureaus to the contrary notwithstanding. Everything worth while, with the possible exception of the pores, is closed during the summer. People disappear. Lights go out. All work, aside from the renting of rowboats, ceases. And, with no work to evade, play loses its charm. *There,* now I've said it!

Certainly these paragraphs—which are a humorous version of a similar passage in "Rich Boy," one of the finest stories written by Benchley's good friend F. Scott Fitzgerald—represent as fine a contribution to an anthology of American humor as any work collected in Robert Benchley's canon of books.

Again, see his marvelous philippic against daylight saving, "that newfangled legal monster created by the Communistic Brain Trust." Benchley detests entering a theatre in sunlight, for, "No system of entertainment can flourish under the blighting influence of such Left Wing Farmer-Labor party legislation as Daylight Saving. No government can hope long to endure." And this piece appears in the Theatre column! This political travesty of conservative paranoia closes on a wonderful riff as "the Communists get an extra hour of daylight in which to overthrow the established order." Benchley promises to question "a certain Mr. Tugwell" and brings down the curtain on a superb piece of humorous writing.

Benchley also develops more traditional comic sections, which closely parallel his humor in the *New Yorker* and elsewhere during the 1930s. Because a week in 1931 turns up only two flawed foreign plays and some pretentious experimental theatre, Benchley falls back on sheer silliness of style to report the drama news. The result is hilarious.

"Last week was Prom Week for us play reviewers—just one round of good times and gaiety. Saturday night we saw a Greek actress doing a French play in Greek. Monday night there was Rajah Raboid with his Knights of the Orient in a mystifying program of unfortunate accidents and maladjustments. And on Tuesday night the graduating class of Miss Lea Gallienne's School of Acting put on a show in the Gym, to which all the parents were invited." Benchley cannot miss the chance for a typical conclusion: "On Wednesday night we tried to find a Punch and Judy show to go to, but they were all closed, which was probably just as well as we were all worn out with our fun-making and ready to burst into tears if anyone pointed a

finger at us." He retains a clear sense of what works best in this humor and often turns to a familiar mixture of nostalgia and whimsy. "In a book, probably to be called 'Footlight Memories,' you will be able to read of the good old days along Broadway in the early thirties, and you will lay the book aside with those old eyes dimmed with tears and, cracking one of your grandchildren over the head, will murmur: 'Tsk-tsk [some day I am going into a room by myself and try making that noise] those were the times when Titans strode the earth'."

Benchley retains the stance of literary iconoclast that qualifies his excellent critical essays and parodies. His negative remarks show a special drive, a rhythm: "Whipping myself along with a youthful prejudice against the sisters of Haworth Parsonage, I have succeeded in maintaining a dogged and sullen indifference to their many biographers, in the face of what has turned out to be a world movement to Know More About the Brontes. . . . I happen to have been more interested in Emily Dickinson's family life, that's all. (I do suppose that I might possibly have been able to swing both during my half-century of research. . . .)." His attack on autograph hounds is an inspired venture into absurd invective. "Nobody knows where they spring from, or what they do in the daytime, for they look and behave like no one you have ever seen before. They are small, and dark, and fairly loathsome, like mature pygmies." Tolerance for the absurd assists Benchley in surviving illogical structure and stupid plotting in the plays he must watch. Deploring a wretched Civil War melodrama, Benchley strikes out on his own comic path. "Would a man in his position actually let himself be arrested as a Confederate spy when he had such important documents [and here Benchley departs] pertaining to the Suez Canal?" Why the Suez Canal? Because Robert Benchley wants it. "An interesting story," he continues in this review of a play treating America in 1864, in, really, his own comic attempt to provide interest, "is told of the Suez Canal. It seems that this fellow Disraeli (George Arless) was on the inside of the whole Canal project—in a nice way, you know. Sidney Smith said some funny things, too, in his day. . . ." Pity the unfortunate dramatist who wondered when his play would actually be discussed by American humor's master of the irrelevant, digressive ramble.

Benchley's special form of mild paranoia directs him to create tiny comic fictions within his reviews. When he is negative about a show based on the life of the gambler Arnold Rothstein, the reviewer imagines dark strangers following him, which "sent me ambling back into the theatre, remarking, in a tone loud enough for them to hear, that it certainly was a great show. I am now using all my influence with the editors of the *New Yorker* to print a limited edition of this particular issue. . . ."

From such playing with fictional devices, it is only a short step to Robert Benchley's favorite form of fiction—parody. From Sherwood Anderson to Marcel Proust, from Charles Dickens to Henry Adams, from H. G. Wells and Theodore Dreiser to John Galsworthy and Thornton Wilder, the excesses of novelists provided Benchley with some of the best material to be exploited for his particular parodic gifts. Equally, the plays he must review are often best discussed through the medium of parodic take-offs. On one occasion, interestingly, the *New Yorker* opens with Benchley's **"New Plays for Old,"** a first-rate parody of Chinese drama, "out of the Golden Age of Chinese Drama (80,000—76,000 B. C.)," which serves as a reference point a few pages later in his Theatre column that questions if audiences deserve to be bored by the lengthy plays of George Bernard Shaw or Mei-Lan-fang. Benchley makes no distinction between the genuine offering on the New York stage and the one invented by the humorist in the magazine's columns. On a dull week, Benchley writes a parody of the theatre critic's dream, to be in Europe, "writing back trenchant criticism of the foreign drama and studying types. It is *Doppel-Bräu* Week in Munich and people are flocking from all over the land to get a load of fresh, newly made headaches. In Paris (*dear* Paris) the potato chips are just beginning to poke their little heads up in the Rue Caubon and all the world is young again. What drama criticism I could be sending back from Europe." "Could be" sets a challenge that this writer cannot resist; there follows a report on Edgar Wallace's *Auf den Flesch,* which treats gangster life in Chicago's "Underwelt." And if the British drama critic St. John Irvine can use his Theatre column in the *Observer* to describe a trip to Scandinavia, Robert Benchley is up to parodying even a drama review—he describes carefully *his* trip to New Bedford, by boat.

Although kindliness is Benchley's trademark, even the genial lover of acting and playwriting succumbs to the temptations of irony, sometimes heavy irony. (Yet not as heavy as Dorothy Parker's, who when filling-in for the Hollywood-bound Benchley, keeps the faith by describing A. A. Milne's drama *The House Beautiful* as "The Play Lousy"). When Robert Benchley feels that the public is being diddled—to say nothing of the weary reviewer—he can employ strong satire. In an Ed Wynn vehicle, "You will discover," Benchley warns, "without much searching, a Mother Goose story of such banality as to affront even the children for whom it was written, and a series of the highest-pensioned gags in the G. A. R. Just the manual labor of chopping them from old funny papers must have been stupendous." He can be direct yet retain his penchant for whimsicality. "There's a lineup for you! There's a line-up for a firing squad. If spring is determined, year after year, to push these little things through the ground along with her shoots of grass and crocuses, then by all means let us do without the grass and crocuses and leap right from winter into mid-summer. At least then the new shows will have music in them."

Most often, Benchley develops little side-references to make his ironic message clear. Here he condemns amateurish acting by referring to one of his favorite themes, the not-so-cute child, thus joining two forms of immaturity. "The one-act plays which I was able to sit through last week seemed to be a little better done than those of last year, but this is like saying 'Little Roger is coming along better in this schoolwork. He holds his book right side up now.' That wouldn't mean that I would recommend going to hear Roger give a reading in the Town Hall." The audience doesn't escape Benchley's ironic notice, especially

those he calls unsophisticated mothers who have led sheltered lives and who laugh too hard at simplistic comedy. "It must have been a big night for them," he muses, "what with seeing the trolley cars and electric signs, and all the automobiles in the streets, to say nothing of the play itself. In fact to say nothing of the play itself would be much the easiest way out." It is manifest that he reserves his most severe ironic anger for weaknesses in comedy, as if Benchley feels most pain at flaws in the basic craft of humor that he practices well himself. His irony then is clear and cutting. To a wretched comedy he gives no mercy; the play "might have been translated from the French, or the Hungarian, or from both at once. I could detect not one item in its composition that even savored of originality." When American dramatic humor is threatened, Benchley springs to the defense of what he cares deeply about by attacking those who misuse the form. His attacks show little restraint—and, after all, he knows what he is doing: "I use the word 'stupendously' after careful conference with our Restraint Editor. . . ."

As that line makes clear, Robert Benchley is intensely self-conscious throughout his humorous writing, and his Theatre work shows this reflexiveness. Like many humorists whose gambit is to laugh at themselves, Benchley is a constant critic of his own work. When he grants faint praise, he watches himself doing it. Thus, on *A Month in the Country,* "It was a long evening, and not a very exciting one, but it certainly was not boring—at least not to this section of the theatregoing public, whose boring-point is 96F." After a disquisition on matters of some substance—Helen Hayes's demand for fifty-word-only reviews, difficulties in purchasing theatre tickets—Benchley self-consciously undercuts his editorializing: "Next week we will take up the subject of Stage Censorship about which we know nothing also." Of course, he often falls into the word-play temptation, a technique that calls attention to the humorist who seemingly apologizes for his verbal tricks while in the act of playing them: "It is on us play-reviewers that the brunt of such a retrenchment policy falls. We are black and blue from falling brunts."

Reflexiveness can lead to theorizing. And despite the myth, one certainly promulgated strongly by Benchley himself, that he holds no critical credos, that he is merely a funny man, that he is but the public's surrogate, he holds, like any genuine humorist, well-defined standards of professionalism in acting and craftmanship in playwriting. While he may not articulate them directly, he does so obliquely, though his humorous throw-away lines, which, if brought together in one essay, would provide Robert Benchley's Poetics of the Theatre.

Early on, Benchley denies that his close relationships with Parker, George Kaufman, Adams, Edna Ferber *et al.* can define his approach to drama reviewing. He responds to a writer who is prejudiced against "that mythical group of demons known as 'the critics at the Algonquin.' In the first place, he cannot keep up with the menace market or he would know that the Algonquin coterie has been practically eliminated as a sinister influence on the arts, thanks chiefly to the fact that it never existed." Thus, he belongs to no critical school. That Benchley refused to state critical rules largely stems from his belief in the (undefinable) magic of the theatre. In a wistful reminiscence largely undiluted by comic effects, he recalls himself as a little boy putting on a play in his attic and being disappointed that the audience didn't grasp his transformation from beggar to prince since he had *thought* hard about the change. "It was my first big disillusion on the matter of magic, and I have never dared write another play since." If he can't create the magic himself, he can certainly recognize the gift in others—a gift that excessive analysis would make stale. Playwriting's loss is reviewing's gain, and Robert Benchley is always more an admirer of magic than a carper at flaws.

To discover Benchley's standards for plays and actors, one only has to read carefully through the humor and seek the firm bases. For example, after mocking Ibsen's *The Vikings* as a "punk play," Benchley disingenuously pretends to laugh off his obvious respect for the dramatist: "I am one of the best friends that Ibsen ever had and the Ibsen estate recognizes this and sends me a hundred cigarettes each year on my birthday." For all the familiar self-mockery that surrounds his assessment of George M. Cohan as comic actor now and ten years earlier, the admiration shines through. "(I must stop using that phrase 'ten years ago.' It depresses me.) I was a novitiate then, and easily excited. Would I be moved to jump up and down as I did in 1920 and hail Mr. Cohan as the greatest man in the world since Martin Luther?"

Pretentious theatre journals attract Benchley's contempt as "those magazines with uncut pages and dull-finish halftones showing four parallelograms in various stages of disarray with captions such as: 'Act VIII, Scene 4, of the Kalpfleisch production of "Charlie's Aunt," Luftspielhaus.' " Faintly humorous but fiercely direct, Robert Benchley's most forthright critical statement denies the usefulness for himself of any abstract rules: "I have never been able to analyze whatever it is that makes some plays sound like manuscripts and others like life. It isn't in the words or dialogue itself, but I have thought of that point and checked up." He is straightforwardly pragmatic in the great American humorist tradition of Huck Finn and Simon Suggs: if it works, leave it alone. Robert Benchley could play the critic's game, but his own sense of humor keeps him in the reviewer's camp. "Every once in a while this department wakes up in a cold sweat thinking of how little it really gives its readers in the matter of cultural dialectics. No stimulating discussions on the Theory of Acting ever seem to come from the opinions printed on this page, and Sir Henry Irving or the team of Beaumont and Fletcher might as well have been civil engineers for all the attention they ever get under our all-too-parochial heading, 'The Theatre.' " Well, perhaps. But Benchley then mocks himself a bit too harshly, and the reader knows that the reviewer doesn't mean to put himself *too* far down on the scale of criticism. Benchley remarks that in London papers "the words 'subjective' and 'objective' are as common in their pages as 'swell' and 'punko' are in these." He has his standards, all right, but he can be humorous and indirect in setting them forth. Benchley admires good, thoughtful left-wing drama, as he makes clear in many positive reviews. That he dislikes propaganda in its cruder

forms, he also makes clear—to the readers who have the humor to draw the idea from the wisecrack. "Why," Benchley asks as if grimacing in pain, "can't someone write a propaganda play about the St. Lawrence Waterways Project, just for once?" Funny, sure. A critically valid attack on political oversimplifications, too, sure.

Since D. H. Lawrence wisely warns us to trust the tale, not the teller, we should not take to heart Benchley's typically overmodest advice about his *New Yorker* work. "This, then, concludes our analysis of the middle week of May, 1930. You may destroy your notes, as you will have no need for them again." I very much doubt it. We should preserve some of the very best American humorous writing of our century that Robert Benchley has left buried in the Wayward Press and Theatre columns to be found now only in dusty library stacks or sticky microfilm drawers. He was a humorist for all seasons, theatrical and journalistic, and his critical writing is as valuable as his creative achievement.

Eric Solomon, "Notes towards a Definition of Robert Benchley's 1930s 'New Yorker' Humor," in Studies in American Humor, *n. s. Vol. 3, No. 1, Spring, 1984, pp. 34-46.*

Gerald Weales   (essay date 1985)

[*Weales is an American writer, educator, and critic. In the following excerpt, he focuses on the "Wayward Press" columns Benchley wrote for the* New Yorker *from 1922-1939 under the pseudonym "Guy Fawkes."*]

A. J. Liebling's name is so firmly identified with the *New Yorker's* Wayward Press column—even now, more than twenty years after his death—that the work of his illustrious predecessor in that department is almost forgotten. Yet Robert Benchley wrote press criticism for the magazine from 1927 to 1939, and to read through his seventy-four columns, as I have just done, is not only to taste the pleasures of Benchley's prose but to recognize that he was a man with firm opinions about what a newspaper should be and do and a sharp if occasionally idiosyncratic sense of the metropolitan press's failure at being and doing.

Benchley was not the first of the *New Yorker's* press critics. The seeds of the Wayward Press can be found in a column that appeared in just two issues, the second (February 28, 1925) and the third (March 7) in the magazine's first year. It consisted of short pieces by various writers, but the emphasis was not so much on press coverage as on the manipulations that its title—"Behind the News"—suggests. The first column devoted to the reporting of the news was "The Current Press," which first appeared on August 15, 1925.

Guy Fawkes (Benchley) took over "The Press in Review" on July 23 and, at the end of the year (December 24), the column was happily rechristened "The Wayward Press." At the time Benchley, already an occasional contributor to the *New Yorker,* was an editor at *Life,* a position that he held until 1929, when he joined the *New Yorker* staff as drama reviewer. In a foreword to Stanley Walker's *City Editor* Alexander Woollcott said that the "fitfully recurrent feature in *The New Yorker*" was a "toddle" if not "a step in the right direction" toward serious press criticism. Woollcott was right about the fitfulness at least. In his first five years as Guy Fawkes, Benchley produced a regular column almost once a month, but by 1933 he had begun to act regularly in the movies, which meant that he spent much time in Hollywood, a continent away from Guy Fawkes's raw material. The column appeared less and less frequently during the second half of the 1930s and ended with a whimper on January 14, 1939, with a weak one-page piece about the lack of news between Christmas and New Year's Day. By that time, as Nathaniel Benchley indicates in his biography of his father—*Robert Benchley*—Benchley was increasingly unhappy with his writing and finding it more and more difficult to put words to paper. Although there is much fine commentary during his last five years as Guy Fawkes, Benchley's own doubt about the column surfaces as early as January 7, 1933, when he wonders if newspapers are improving or if he is reading less well because he is having difficulty finding "material for sneering," and he contemplates the possibility of the department's closing down or being forced to burlesque itself, "stressing those features that have come to be staples in our monthly philippic." Even *sneering* is a sign of distress, for *sneer* is an unlikely word to describe Benchley's prose even at his most critical.

The unhappy note on which that paragraph ends is misleading. The columns as a whole display Benchley's quiet vigor as a writer and his continued fascination with (or love of) newspapers. "He read every New York paper every day," says Nathaniel Benchley, "scanning the columns for items of minor interest that he considered funny, or about which some humorous comment could be made." His first contribution to the *New Yorker* (December 26, 1925), for instance, grew out of a news story about a doctor who insisted that there was "no such thing as absolute sex." His regular reading, as a humorist in search of material and as a newspaper addict, had only to be shaped to Guy Fawkes's purposes as newspaper critic. "Benchley wrote purely as a newspaper reader," Liebling says in *The Wayward Pressman.* "He had little of what Max Fischel called the newspaper 'taint' on him." What he had—his brief stint (1916-1917) on the New York *Tribune*—he plays self-deprecatingly whenever autobiographical material invades the column. In a parenthetic remark on April 20, 1929, he writes: "Incidentally, any doubt as to his qualifications to comment in this space on reporting or reporters can be dissipated—and his mysterious identity established—by asking any city editor of a decade ago who was known far and wide as the Worst Reporter in the City of New York." It is a label he liked so well that he repeats it on November 19, 1932. He gives the impression that he belongs properly in that long line of ineffectual reporters that he played in the movies from the theater columnist who can never find a pencil in *Dancing Lady* to the bibulous space-filler in *Foreign Correspondent.* Yet he has "taint" enough to know how newspapers and reporters operate. He simply chooses to work "from the point of view of a human being rather than from what is known as a 'news hawk's' angle," as he once said in praising Alva Johnston.

The form of Benchley's column is that devised by Morris Markey for "The Current Press." Having seined a month's papers for usable ore, he usually devotes a long opening section to a single subject and then allows the column to trickle off into small items that do not need or deserve much space. Only very rarely—pieces on the Lindbergh kidnapping and the Hauptmann trial, for instance—does he devote a whole column to a single subject. One difficulty with his catch-all organization is that very sharp comments on journalistic derelictions are sometimes followed by frivolous remarks on newspaper foolishness. The latter often resemble the kind of bottom-of-the-page filler that became characteristic of the *New Yorker.* Even when Benchley is funny in these items they tend to undermine the seriousness of the longer entries in part because the same wit and the same cast of mind are being used for two different purposes.

Benchley is stylistically at his best when he allows a throw-away phrase to make a point, as in his insistence that Hoover's appointing Coolidge and Al Smith to a committee "rocked the country from Maine to northern New Hampshire." He dwells lovingly on the extensive coverage of the wedding of Coolidge's son to John H. Trumbull's daughter, but it is not until the last line ("Oh, and while we are felicitating the young couple, may we offer to Governor Trumbull our best wishes for his coming Senatorial campaign") that we realize that his point is not newspaper preoccupation with celebrity but the reporter's dependence on the self-interest of participants even in social events. The column is the more effective for following so closely on the one in which he indicates the frustration of the press at the care with which Lindbergh and the Morrows protected the privacy of the colonel's marriage to Anne. Benchley is capable of grandly inventive metaphor, as in a piece clocking the degree of hysterical response to Roosevelt's plan to pack the Supreme Court in which he says, "the *Sun* just took off all its clothes and stood screaming in the middle of the market place." For the most part, however, he sticks to direct statement or mildly deceptive undercutting.

For the most part Benchley sticks to the journalistic hierarchy that he had established from the beginning. His primary target is the New York *Times,* with the *Herald Tribune* and the *World* as its closest competitors for Guy-Fawkesian space. The evening papers come in for less comment, partly because he likes to begin the day reading the papers and partly because of "the array of junk issued by the evening papers in lieu of news." He explains his position in his March 8, 1930, column. "In case this department seems unduly attentive to the little foibles of the New York *Times,* we may say it is because the New York *Times* is the only newspaper we really give a hang about." The *Times* gives him something to talk about, he says, and then adds: "The little excursions of the evening papers into sociology and pet-culture do not count, because they are really comments in themselves. The tabloids and the Hearst papers are too easy."

Although there is a great deal of cheerful kidding in Benchley's Wayward Press, he is seriously interested in good reporting. Like Markey and Harold Ross, Benchley believed that a good news story presents the facts with a minimum—ideally, an absence—of overwriting, invention, and editorializing. "There is somebody on the *Times* rewrite staff who is doing his best to bring that impersonal journal into the lists of romantic fiction," Benchley writes on August 18, 1928, quoting one example at length, "and if style-with-a-tear-in-it can perform this feat the writer is going to do it, too." In his next column he wonders if "the special dialogue rewrite man of the *Times* . . . has gone over to the *Herald Tribune*." He regularly deplores the "Rover Boys Afloat" tone of the stories filed to the *Times* from the Byrd expedition to the South Pole. He likes to invent little scenes in which he imagines the overhearing of obviously faked conversation passed off as factual reporting; he puts the reporter under the table in his column on the abdication of Edward VIII, and imagines, since the dialogue stops abruptly, that the king and Stanley Baldwin wandered out of earshot.

Part of this reaction grows out of a fastidiousness in Benchley that reveals itself in other ways in the columns. In one odd instance he chides Will Rogers for "one of the most distasteful stories ever run in the *Times*," but the questionable item is a characteristic Rogers joke using the heat in Houston to mock the rituals of the Democratic convention: "Have perspired for Jefferson, sweated for Jackson, fainted for Tilden and am dying slowly for Smith" (*Times*, June 27). Benchley's delicacy is more often used efficaciously, as in his asking "what the hell right the Public has to insist on knowing anything that a perfectly law-abiding citizen doesn't want to tell." In this column he differentiates between Lindbergh's desire for privacy and a secret ballot in a senate committee: "Here is a matter in which the Public is legally (if not actually) interested, and the newspapers are the only means of public information." Elsewhere he writes: "Never noted for their consideration of privacy, or even decency, the tabloid cameramen seem lately to have gone in for a specialty of closeups showing bereaved mothers in the throes of grief."

Benchley constantly complained about the way newspapers fill column after column, page after page, with non-news passing itself off as a big story. Election coverage is his King Charles's head. In the column of June 30, 1928, contemplating the legion of journalists that descended on Kansas City to file pointless copy about the Republican convention, Benchley imagines the lowly underlings who were forced to stay at home "dreaming of the day when they, too, will be big reporters and can tell a lethargic nation things it doesn't give a damn about reading." This is a recurrent theme of the Wayward Press columns, as persistent, if not quite as funny, as Benchley's response to endless stories in the *Times* ("the Great Mother of all Aviation, Discovery, Scientific Research, and Germ Culture," July 12, 1930) on science and exploration. He mocks the paper's eagerness to sign up the participants for exclusive by-line stories, but his special scorn is aimed at the *Times* editors' apparent need to run daily stories from whatever the current expedition. "You can't write a story a day about a lot of men in a snow hut and make every story important," he says of the Byrd expedition, "even with Frank Merriwell as the leader." He praises a story from an earlier Arctic expedition in which real news—the finding of some lost flyers—is reported, but in the same column he criticizes the paper again for its more characteristic coverage: "they are seeing oodles and oodles of jellyfish." He has a long list of false news—repetitive comments on the celebrated dead, Monday morning printing of sermons, detailed reports on football practice scrimmages.

If Benchley manages to be amused by all that print that he thinks no one wants to read, his impatience has a sharper edge when he is faced with stories obviously manufactured to fit the editorial policy of a newspaper. "Probably the least important news story during the month," he says in his first Guy Fawkes column, "was the *Herald Tribune's* spectacular two-day exposure of the Big Soviet Plot to stir up American Negroes to revolt." He reports that the story, carried for two days and picked up by no other papers, was dismissed in an editorial by the paper itself: "Thus, entirely within the four walls of the *Herald Tribune* building was the tocsin sounded and the 'false alarm' bell rung, the entire fright lasting only forty-eight hours, and America is safe again." Commenting on public indifference to a scare story, he says: "If what Mr. Hearst wants is a war with Mexico he had better use some other paper than the *American*. He would create more of a stir if he advertised for it." His was a long-standing quarrel with Hearst. The attempts of the Hearst papers to make jingoistic capital out of an incident in Mukden remind him of "the old days back in '98 when the *Journal* had goateed Spaniards disrobing ladies on board American ships and the question was 'HOW LONG WILL AMERICA STAND FOR THIS?'" Benchley, at nine, probably did not read Hearst's campaign for a war with Spain; but Benchley, at forty-two, presumably remembered that his beloved older brother died in Cuba in what Guy Fawkes thought of as Hearst's war. Related to such inhouse inventions and decorations is the use of *parti pris* reporters or those whose coverage of a story depends on where they are situated. Benchley regularly identifies Arnaldo Cortesi as the *Times*'s "special Fascist representative in Rome" and assumes, as he says on June 8, 1929: "If one read only the *Times* . . . one would have the impression that Italians did nothing but cheer Mussolini from morning until night." At the beginning of "the Japanese-Chinese ruction in Manchuria" the *Times* got stories from both Japan and China, he says on October 10, 1931; but "we gather that the *Times* personally is more or less for Japan, however, as Mr. Abend was suddenly sent to Nanking with the result that Japan has two boosters instead of one."

The most persistent criticism of the press in the Benchley columns is with the way newspapers allow themselves to be used for publicity and propaganda purposes. At the silly end of the continuum of collusion and cooption are the successful endeavors of publicity men and press agents. Benchley, who says that one of his newspaper chores was rewriting circus handouts, is almost affectionate about the flurry of feature stories that greet the yearly arrival of the circus. He is less amiable about a story of a pair of Siamese twins and the proposed operation to separate them, a publicity invention that got them press space shortly before they were to open at the Hippodrome: "It must be wonderful to be a newspaper man. You get sucked in by so many interesting people." He is almost venomous about the Roumanian royal family's romance with head-lines, suggesting that the AP man in Bucharest may also be "First Lord of the Publicity Chamber." In the same column he says of Queen Marie, "we have heard it ru-mored that she is coming over shortly incognito with Miss Elsa Maxwell. Incognito like the Graf Zeppelin." Queen Marie falls somewhere between show business and busi-ness for real. Newspaper kindness to the latter—space given to the birthdays, professional anniversaries, and other PR-engineered nonevents in the lives of tycoons—sprinkle the columns in which Benchley correctly identi-fies the non-news stories as free advertising; he has a funny account of the sentimental mileage that Owen D. Young and General Electric got out of a story about two little boys who wanted to trade their birds'-egg collection for a refrigerator for their mother. He is considerably blunter about the Automobile Show "with its attendant padding of the newspapers with trade articles written by local auto-mobile agents" and downright harsh about the commit-ment of newspapers, particularly the *Times,* to the bur-geoning aviation industry. "Once in a while something rather underhanded is pulled to convince the public that flying is really the safest method of travel," he says in a piece about how the papers tried to write around "three fatal crashes in one week" by blaming the pilot of one of them for being "drunk," a word that he says is almost never used in news stories: "But the aviation authorities said that Stultz was drunk, and Stultz was dead, so why not?"

More dangerous to the concept of a free press is the way in which newspapers allow themselves to be used, even in good causes. The Liberty Loan campaign is a historical in-stance that he occasionally recalls, and the annual Red Cross drive is his favorite example of propaganda as news. The cooperation between the press and the government at the expense of real reporting he finds particularly alarm-ing. In a column in which the press "had to take the rap" for printing stories that were handouts from the Treasury Department, he explains the press's acquiescence by pointing out that "governmental publicity" is "run on the dole system." An early example of press cooperation is "a barrage of quite credible publicity" which the strategic presence of Colonel Lindbergh and Will Rogers gave to the government's gestures of good feeling toward Mexico. "Of course, it is churlish to complain of any propaganda which has as its aim international good will," he says of the same operation in his March 3 column, "but even be-neficent propaganda, when it is so obvious, defeats its own end if it makes newspaper readers suspect that they are being fed prepared pap." Beginning with the crash of the stockmarket and continuing as the depression deepened came a welter of reassurance stories which Benchley re-sented because they treated newspaper readers as children who had to be protected and set the morale boosters ("the Head Masters' Association," he calls them on January 10, 1931) as a group apart. In **"After the Deluge"** he writes about the initial practice of burying news of bank failures in the business section while printing uplift stories in the front pages:

This system of giving the Public what Someone

thinks the Public should have in its news col-umns met its first gigantic failure during the first four days of March. It was a policy good enough to get us into a war, to keep us fighting a war, and to get us out of a war when the time came, but it couldn't save a banking system that was due for a crash even if it had to crash all by itself.

In **"A Free Press"** he celebrates "the end of the benevolent alliance between the Press and Pro Bono Publico" brought on by the NRA, which the newspapers saw as imposing restrictions on them ("Say, what *is* this? We're not the Public, you know"): "In fighting a bugaboo, the newspa-pers of the country have freed themselves from the tyran-ny of the good fairies." Fifty years later that seems a pre-mature conclusion.

Throughout his work as a press critic Benchley identifies with other readers, assuming that he and they are bored by the same kind of newspaper stories and that the editors use the readers' presumed rights and demands to further their own ends. Commenting on an attempt to justify inva-sion of privacy, he suggests that "the Public insists on knowing" is more correctly "the *editors* insist on the Pub-lic's insisting on knowing." Yet this image of the reader as the innocent victim of news manipulators, in and out of editorial offices, is exploded in an angry piece in which he talks about Roosevelt's landslide reelection in the face of constant chirpy predictions of a Landon victory from the *Herald Tribune,* the *Sun,* the *Mirror,* the *American.* Readers will shrug and go back to their favorite papers, he says; and he calls up World War I propaganda once again: "All this Spartan grinning over being played for suckers may be very fine for character-building, but until we learn to read our papers without moving our lips as we read, the hell with us. . . . The fact remains that the pub-lic likes to have its leg pulled, even if the leg comes out by the roots, as it did in the war."

Nathaniel Benchley tells us that his father dismissed his early work because it was not "the Really Good writing he was working toward"—which is to say that in his own eyes he never got there. "Really Good writing," we pre-sume, was Literature to Benchley, but to any reader who is concerned with the follies and triumphs of journalism and who appreciates the kind of mind that can recognize them and the clear and witty prose by which he praises or pillories them, Robert Benchley's Guy Fawkes columns are Really Good enough.

Gerald Weales, "Robert Benchley as Guy Fawkes," in The Sewanee Review, *Vol. XCIII, No. 4, Fall, 1985, pp. 601-09.*

FURTHER READING

Biography

Benchley, Nathaniel. *Robert Benchley.* New York: McGraw-Hill Book Company, 1955, 258 p.
    Study of Robert Benchley's life and work written by his

son. Includes a chronological list of Benchley's movies and eight pages of photographs.

Masson, Thomas L. "Robert C. Benchley," in his *Our American Humorists*, pp. 47-52. Freeport, N. Y.: Books for Libraries Press, Inc., 1931.
>Brief biographical sketch plus text of Benchley's essay "The Social Life of the Newt."

Rosmond, Babette. *Robert Benchley: His Life and Good Times*. New York: Doubleday & Company, 1970, 239 p.
>Biography of Benchley featuring numerous drawings by Gluyas Williams.

Criticism

Pinsker, Sanford. "Comedy and Cultural Timing: The Les-
sons of Robert Benchley and Woody Allen." *The Georgia Review* XLII, No. 4 (Winter 1988): pp. 822-37.
>Comparative analysis of the two American humorists.

Redding, Robert. *Starring Robert Benchley: "Those Magnificent Movie Shorts."* Albuquerque: University of New Mexico Press, 1973, 209 p.
>Overview of Benchley's work as a writer and actor in Hollywood short films and features.

Yates, Norris W. *Robert Benchley*. New York: Twayne Publishers, 1968, 175 p.
>Critical study of Benchley's work as a writer. Yates includes a chronology of Benchley's life and career and a selected bibliography of obscure essays.

Additional coverage of Benchley's life and career is contained in the following sources published by Gale Research: *Contemporary Authors*, Vol. 105; *Dictionary of Literary Biography*, Vol. 11; and *Twentieth-Century Literary Criticism*, Vol. 1.

The Cherry Orchard

Anton Chekhov

The following entry presents criticism on Chekhov's drama *Vishnevy sad* (1904; *The Cherry Orchard*). For information on Chekhov's complete career, see *TCLC,* Volumes 3 and 10. For criticism focusing on Chekhov's dramas, see *TCLC,* Volume 31.

INTRODUCTION

Considered by many critics to be Chekhov's greatest play, *The Cherry Orchard* is a portrayal of a family of aristocrats who lose their ancestral estate as a result of their failure to face the realities of the changing social, political, and economic order of late nineteenth-century Russia. Commentators praise the realism and artistry with which Chekhov illuminates the human condition through the plight of the Ranevskaya family. As Virginia Woolf stated in a review of the play: "Chekhov has contrived to shed over us a luminous vapour in which life appears as it is, without veils, transparent and visible to the depths."

Plot and Major Characters

The drama revolves around the impoverished Ranevskayas, their servants, and family friends as they discuss the approaching sale of their house and cherry orchard. Lopakhin, the son of a former serf of the family, urges them to chop down the cherry orchard and build cottages in order to make their property profitable. Chekhov's characters, however, are unable to act decisively in the face of a new socio-economic order. Eventually, Lopakhin purchases the estate. At the conclusion of the play, the characters disperse to continue their lives independently.

Major Themes

The Cherry Orchard blends elements of the tragic and the comic. Although the subject of the play—the Ranevskaya's loss of their ancestral home—is ostensibly a tragic one, Chekhov subtitled the play "A Comedy," presenting his characters in a comic light; their speech and actions are often absurd and most are ineffectual. Nevertheless, this work displays one of Chekhov's most important themes: the triumph of ignorance and vulgarity over the fragile traditions of elegance and nobility. Critics maintain that his depiction of the "ordinary drabness" of life, brings to the stage a realism that eschewed the epic scale of traditional drama. As Francis Fergusson has observed: "If Chekhov drastically reduced the dramatic art, he did so in full consciousness, and in obedience both to artistic scruples and to a strict sense of reality. He reduced the dramatic art to its ancient root, from which new growths are possible."

Critical Reception

Stagings of *The Cherry Orchard*, first performed by the Moscow Art Theater under the co-direction of Constantin Stanislavsky and Vladimir Nemirovich-Danchenko, reflect the pathos of the characters' situation. Initial critical reaction was mixed but Stanislavsky's treatment of the play as tragedy received unanimous praise and has thus become the predominant interpretation. Nevertheless, commenting on the humor of the work, Dorothy Sayers wrote that "the whole tragedy of futility is that it never succeeds in achieving tragedy. In its blackest moments it is inevitably doomed to the comic gesture." Most critics agree that the subtlety of *The Cherry Orchard,* which has neither a dominant protagonist nor traditional plot development, is a tribute to Chekhov's skill as a dramatist. Noting the ethereal quality of Chekhov's work, Joseph Wood Krutch has commented: "Others build upon a solid foundation. They are architectural and they attain solidity by placing stone upon stone; but he merely throws out one thread after another. Each is so fragile that a wind would blow it away, but we are soon enmeshed in a thousand of them. Out of delicacy laid ceaselessly upon delicacy comes strength."

CRITICISM

Virginia Woolf   (essay date 1920)

[*One of the most prominent figures in twentieth-century literature, Woolf rebelled as a novelist against traditional narrative techniques, developing a highly individualized style employing the stream-of-consciousness mode. She was also esteemed for her critical essays, which cover a broad range of topics and contain some of her finest prose. In the following review of a performance of* The Cherry Orchard, *Woolf asserts that the play is foreign to English sensibilities yet is emotionally moving regardless.*]

Although every member of the audience at the Art Theatre last week had probably read Tchekhov's *The Cherry Orchard* several times, a large number of them had, perhaps, never seen it acted before. It was no doubt on this account that as the first act proceeded the readers, now transformed into seers, felt themselves shocked and outraged. The beautiful, mad drama which I had staged often enough in the dim recesses of my mind was now hung within a few feet of me, hard, crude, and over-emphatic, like a cheap coloured print of the real thing. But what right had I to call it the real thing? What did I mean by that? Perhaps something like this.

There is nothing in English literature in the least like *The Cherry Orchard.* It may be that we are more advanced, less advanced, or have advanced in an entirely different direction. At any rate, the English person who finds himself at dawn in the nursery of Madame Ranevskaia feels out of place, like a foreigner brought up with entirely different traditions. But the traditions are not (this, of course, is a transcript of individual experience) so ingrained in one as to prevent one from shedding them not only without pain but with actual relief and abandonment. True, at the end of a long railway journey one is accustomed to say goodnight and go to bed. Yet on this occasion, since everything is so strange, the dawn rising and the birds beginning to sing in the cherry-trees, let us gather round the coffee-cups; let us talk about everything in the whole world. We are all in that queer emotional state when thought seems to bubble into words without being spoken. The journey is over and we have reached the end of everything where space seems illimitable and time everlasting. Quite wrongly (since in the production approved by Tchekhov the birds actually sing and the cherries are visible on the trees) I had, on my imaginary stage, tried to give effect to my sense that the human soul is free from all trappings and crossed incessantly by thoughts and emotions which wing their way from here, from there, from the furthest horizons—I had tried to express this by imagining an airy view from the window with ethereal pink cherries and perhaps snow mountains and blue mist behind them. In the room the characters spoke suddenly whatever came into their heads, and yet always vaguely, as if thinking aloud. There was no "comedy of manners"; one thought scarcely grazed, let alone struck sparks from, another; there was no conflict of individual wills. At the same time the characters were entirely concrete and without sentimentality.

Not for an instant did one suppose that Madame Ranevskaia was wrapping up a mystic allusion to something else when she spoke. Her own emotions were quite enough for her. If what was said seemed symbolical, that was because it was profound enough to illumine much more than an incident in the life of one individual. And, finally, though the leap from one thought to another was so wide as to produce a sense of dangerous dislocation, all the separate speeches and characters combined to create a single impression of an overwhelming kind.

The actors at the Art Theatre destroyed this conception, first, by the unnatural emphasis with which they spoke; next by their determination to make points which brought them into touch with the audience but destroyed their harmony with each other; and, finally, by the consciousness which hung about them of being well-trained English men and women ill at ease in an absurd situation, but determined to make the best of a bad business. One instance of irrepressible British humour struck me with considerable force. It occurred in the middle of Charlotte's strange speech in the beginning of the second act. "I have no proper passport. I don't know how old I am; I always feel I am still young," she begins. She goes on, "When I grew up I became a governess. But where I come from and who I am, I haven't a notion. Who my parents were—*very likely they weren't married*—I don't know." At the words I have italicised, Dunyasha bounced away from her to the other end of the bench, with an arch humour which drew the laugh it deserved. Miss Helena Millais seemed to be delighted to have this chance of assuring us that she did not believe a word of this morbid nonsense, and that the old jokes still held good in the world of sanity round the corner. But it was Miss Ethel Irving who showed the steadiest sense of what decency requires of a British matron in extremity. How she did it, since she spoke her part accurately, it is difficult to say, but her mere presence upon the stage was enough to suggest that all the comforts and all the decencies of English upper-class life were at hand, so that at any moment her vigil upon the bench might have been appropriately interrupted by a man-servant bearing a silver tray. "The Bishop is in the drawing-room, m'lady." "Thank you, Parker. Tell his Lordship I will come at once." In that sort of play, by which I mean a play by Sheridan or Oscar Wilde, both Miss Irving and Miss Millais would charm by their wit, spirit and competent intellectual outfit. Nor, though the quotation I have made scarcely proves it, have we any cause to sneer at English comedy or at the tradition of acting which prevails upon our stage. The only question is whether the same methods are as applicable to *The Cherry Orchard* as they are to *The School for Scandal.*

But there are four acts in *The Cherry Orchard.* How it may have been with the other readers I do not know, but before the second act was over some sort of compromise had been reached between my reader's version and the actor's one. Perhaps in reading one had got the whole too vague, too mad, too mystical. Perhaps as they went on the actors forgot how absurd such behavior would be thought in England. Or perhaps the play itself triumphed over the deficiencies of both parties. At any rate, I felt less and less desire to cavil at the acting in general and more and more appreciation of the acting of Mr. Cancellor, Mr. Dodd, Mr. Pearson and Miss Edith Evans in particular. With every word that Mr. Felix Aylmer spoke as Pishchick, one's own conception of that part plumped itself out like a shrivelled skin miraculously revived. But the play itself—that was what overwhelmed all obstacles, so that though the walls rocked from floor to ceiling when the door was shut, though the sun sank and rose with the energetic decision of the stage carpenter's fist, though the scenery suggested an advertisement of the Surrey Hills rather than Russia in her wildness, the atmosphere of the play wrapped us round and shut out everything alien to itself. It is, as a rule, when a critic does not wish to commit himself or to trouble himself that he refers to atmosphere. And, given time, something might be said in greater detail of the causes which produced this atmosphere—the strange dislocated sentences, each so erratic and yet cutting out the shape so firmly, of the realism, of the humour, of the artistic unity. But let the word atmosphere be taken literally to mean that Tchekhov has contrived to shed over us a luminous vapour in which life appears as it is, without veils, transparent and visible to the depths. Long before the play was over we seemed to have sunk below the surface of things and to be feeling our way among submerged but recognisable emotions. "I have no proper passport. I don't know how old I am; I always feel I am still young"— how the words go sounding on in one's mind—how the whole play resounds with such sentences, which reverberate, melt into each other, and pass far away out beyond everything! In short, if it is permissible to use such vague language, I do not know how better to describe the sensation at the end of *The Cherry Orchard,* than by saying that it sends one into the street feeling like a piano played upon at last, not in the middle only but all over the keyboard and with the lid left open so that the sound goes on.

This being so, and having felt nothing comparable to it from reading the play, one feels inclined to strike out every word of criticism and to implore Madame Donnet to give us the chance of seeing play after play, until to sit at home and read plays is an occupation for the afflicted only, and one to be viewed with pity, as we pity blind men spelling out their Shakespeare with their fingers upon sheets of cardboard.

Virginia Woolf, A review of "The Cherry Orchard," in New Statesman, *Vol. XV, No. 380, July 24, 1920, pp. 446-47.*

Joseph Wood Krutch   (essay date 1928)

[*Krutch was one of America's most respected literary critics. Noteworthy among his works are* The American Drama since 1918 *(1939), in which he analyzed the most important dramas of the 1920s and 1930s, and* "Modernism" in Modern Drama *(1953), in which he stressed the need for twentieth-century playwrights to infuse their works with traditional humanistic values. In the following review of a performance of* The Cherry Orchard, *Krutch offers the play as evidence of Chekhov's genius and singularity as a dramatist.*]

For the third new production of its season the Civic Repertory Theater has chosen *The Cherry Orchard* of Che-

khov and has made of the play, familiar as it is, by far the most interesting of the three. It is true that here, as usual, Miss Le Gallienne's production leaves something to be desired—that the limitations, financial and other, of her enterprise preclude the possibility of perfect finish, and that her sorely tried company is called upon by the exigencies of the repertory to perform feats of versatility beyond their capacity. It is true, furthermore, that neither her own good performance in the role of the self-effacing Varya nor that of Alla Nazimova (guest for the occasion) as the charmingly incompetent mistress of the orchard is enough to dispel that somewhat impromptu air which often marks the production at this theater. And yet the intelligence of the direction, coupled with the intelligence of the play, is sufficient to make *The Cherry Orchard* delightful to all those capable of seeing below a surface not quite so smooth as that to which Broadway is accustomed, and of relishing the delicately humorous genius of the author.

Important novelists have often been seduced by promises of fame and money to try their hands at the stage, but they have very rarely enriched either themselves or the drama. Chekhov stands almost alone among the great writers of fiction who have, with results other than regrettable, allowed themselves to be persuaded by importunate managers; and his unusual success is probably due in a very considerable measure to the fact that instead of going to the theater he made the theater come to him—a highly unusual proceeding, since nothing is more pathetic than the respect generally paid by the layman to the infantile "mysteries" of conventional stagecraft. Grave professors are reduced to a state of awed wonder by the pronunciamentos of any fourth-rate hack who talks about the "laws of the theater," and first-rate novelists who would show the door to any one who told them how to write in any other form accept complacently the imbecile suggestions of the "practical man of the theater," producing, as a result, plays which have none of the virtues of the professional litterateur and all the defects of the amateur dramatist. Chekhov, on the other hand, had the good sense to conclude that the public wanted him to be, in the theater as elsewhere, not a lumbering imitation of another, but Chekhov himself; accordingly he wrote two plays which are like no others ever seen upon any stage but which are, nevertheless, replete with all the virtues which made his stories unique.

The very soul of his method had always been the avoidance of anything artificially "dramatic," and he was wise enough not to alter it when he came to write drama. In *The Cherry Orchard* as in his stories the plot is insignificant; instead of clothing a narrative skeleton with thought and feeling he generates his moods and delivers his reflections in a manner which appears to be in the last degree casual. Strokes of characterization, flashes of humor, and unexpected touches of nature seem introduced almost at random; and yet somehow an unforgettable picture is evoked. Doubtless there is art in every line of this seeming artlessness, and Chekhov, indeed, complained at one time that he was writing it at the rate of four lines a day; but the art is not of any familiar sort. Others build upon a solid foundation. They are architectural and they attain solidity by placing stone upon stone; but he merely throws out one thread after another. Each is so fragile that a wind would blow it away, but we are soon enmeshed in a thousand of them. Out of delicacy laid ceaselessly upon delicacy comes strength.

If Chekhov meant to say, as in **The Cherry Orchard** he apparently did, that the touching absurdity of the society he pictures was destined to be gradually and peacefully replaced by the cruder, though sturdier, race of peasants turned capitalists, then he was a very bad prophet indeed so far as Russia was concerned, but it is not for prophecy that we turn to him.

What we get instead is as delightful pictures as any contained in the whole realm of Russian literature of the charming childishness of those gentle people whose incompetence precipitatcd onc of the bloodiest upheavals of history—pictures whose moods vary, as gracefully as the moods of the people who are their subjects, from bubbling gaiety to hopeless melancholy and back again. Never, moreover, was penetration more gentle than his. His insight spares no one and yet no one is really wounded. He is merciless in his exposure of every character and yet every one of them finds mercy. No one else ever stripped his characters barer than he, but no one else ever held helpless victims up to a kindlier ridicule. Good art is perpetually revealing how it can accomplish the impossible. Smiles and tears, satire and sentiment—what combination is generally more nauseous? But the combination is Chekhov's and Chekhov is great.

Joseph Wood Krutch, "The Greatness of Chekhov," in the Nation, *New York, Vol. CXXVII, No. 3304, October 31, 1928, p. 461.*

Irving Deer   (essay date 1958)

[*Deer is an American critic and educator. In the following essay, he perceives the dialogue in* The Cherry Orchard *both as a manifestation of the characters' inner turmoil and as a means of avoiding action.*]

Both directors and actors are confronted with many perplexing problems when they deal with Chekhov's full length plays. Perhaps the most perplexing are those which they meet in the attempt to discover and express the dramatic significance of Chekhov's dialogue. The difficulty is not that Chekhov's dialogue requires any unusual acting techniques, but rather that it has no obvious form. It seems to be rambling, disconnected, and irrelevant. Take for example a brief scene from the first act of **The Three Sisters.** Olga has been grading papers and thinking aloud about her father's funeral, the drudgery of her job, and her long held hope of going to Moscow. Irina picks up the Moscow refrain and then Olga again goes into one of her "catch-all" speeches:

> You look radiant today, lovelier than ever. And Masha is lovely, too. Andrey would be good looking if he hadn't got so heavy, it's not becoming to him. And I've grown older, a lot thinner; it must be because I get cross with the girls. Now that I'm free today and am here at home and my head's not aching, I feel younger than yesterday. I'm only twenty-eight. . . . It's all good, all

God's will, but it seems to me if I had married and stayed at home all day long, it would have been better. (A pause) I'd have loved my husband.

When one realizes how much of this kind of associative talk goes on in Chekhov, it is not too difficult to understand why some critics (Walter Kerr and William Archer, for example) see in Chekhov's plays only a formless mass without conflict or progression.

The apparent formlessness of Chekhovs' dialogue is even more clear when we compare Olga's speech with a more conventional speech in modern drama, say a speech by Lady Utterword in Shaw's "Chekhovian" play, *Heartbreak House.* Lady Utterword is home after an absence of twenty-three years and shc finds everything as chaotic as ever. Her father and the nurse are disrespectful. She cannot even get a cup of tea. "Sitting down with a flounce on the sofa," she says to Ellie Dunn, who also has not been received properly:

> I know what you must feel. Oh, this house, this house! I come back to it after twenty-three years; and it is just the same: nobody at home to receive anybody, no regular meals, nobody ever hungry because they're always gnawing bread and butter or munching apples, and what is worse the same disorder in ideas, in talk, in feeling. When I was a child I was used to it: I had never known anything better, though I was unhappy, and longed all the time—Oh, how I longed! to be respectable, to be a lady, to live as others did, not to have to think of everything for myself. . . . And now the state of the house! the way I'm received! the casual impudence of that woman Guinness. . . . You must excuse my going on in this way; but I am really very much hurt and annoyed and disillusioned. . . .

Like Olga, Lady Utterword is also "thinking aloud" about her home, her past and her family. She also is distressed. But unlike Olga, her speech is obviously prompted by events around her. She feels herself horribly insulted and everything she says represents her reaction against those who affront her sense of conventional decency. She sticks to the point; her ideas are clearly connected. The speech is obviously dramatic.

Even when the ideas in a Chekhov speech are clearly and logically connected, the speech is often confusing for another reason. Conventionally, speech in drama is a device for simultaneous two way communication: the characters talk directly with each other and at the same time they talk indirectly to the audience. But in Chekhov, these two functions of dialogue seem often separated. The characters seem to be talking to themselves in a daze primarily for the purpose of giving the audience direct exposition. Chekhov appears to have done Scribe one better. Scribe had to have two servants dusting while they gave the audience background information. Chekhov can get by with only one character, who need not even be dusting.

Consider, for example, the opening conversation between Lopahin and Dunyasha in **The Cherry Orchard.** Lopahin, the merchant, and Dunyasha, the maid, have been anxiously awaiting the train which will bring Madame

Ranevskaya and her entourage. Dunyasha tells Lopahin that the train has arrived. He answers: ". . . thank God . . . But how late was the train? Two hours at least. (Yawning and stretching.) I'm a fine one, I am, look what a fool thing I did! —You could have waked me up." Dunyasha then replies: "I thought you had gone. (Listening) Listen, I think they are coming now." Lopahin listens and then says:

> No—no, there's the luggage and one thing and another. (A pause) Lyuboff Andreyevna has been living abroad five years. I don't know what she is like now—She is a good woman. An easy-going simple woman. I remember when I was a boy about fifteen, my father, who is at rest—in those days he ran a shop here in the village—hit me in the face with his fist, my nose was bleeding. —we'd come to the yard together for something or other, and he was a little drunk. Lyuboff Andreyevna, I can see her now, still so young, so slim, led me to the wash-basin here in this very room, in the nursery. "Don't cry," she says, "little peasant, it will be well in time for your wedding"—(a pause) Yes, little peasant—My father was a peasant truly, and here I am in a white waistcoat and yellow shoes. Like a pig rooting in a pastry shop—I've got this rich, lots of money, but if you really stop and think of it, I'm just a peasant—(turning the pages of a book) Here I was reading a book and didn't get a thing out of it. Reading and went to sleep. (A pause)

As if she had not heard a word, Dunyasha replies: "And all night long the dogs were not asleep, they know their masters are coming."

As we can see, Lopahin and Dunyasha communicate with each other only occasionally. Although they both share the stage, they seem to be talking more to themselves than to each other. Lopahin's long monologue seems to be there merely to get background information across to the audience. Dunyasha does not engage in any conflict with Lopahin which would force him to talk at such length. She either knows most of what he says or she is not interested in it at the moment. It does not affect her in any way. There seems to be no dramatic relationship between the characters or between them and the situation in which they find themselves.

When a Shakespearean character speaks to himself, he is obviously engaging in a struggle which is an expression of the central conflict of the play and which leads to new action. Take Macbeth's "If it were done when 't is done" speech for example. Everything Macbeth says there expresses his struggle to overcome his qualms of conscience or his fear of retribution. This speech is part of the process by which he whips himself up to the point of murdering Duncan. Like Shakespeare's soliloquies, most modern soliloquies are obviously relevant to the central conflict and plot of the play. When Peer Gynt, for example, expostulates to himself on the beauty of Anitra the slave girl [in Henrik Ibsen's *Peer Gynt*], we are not at a loss for one moment. We have seen his daydreaming tendencies before. The contrast between his idealized version of the girl and her dirty legs and selfish actions shows us immediately not

only what kind of a man Peer is, but also points ahead to his financial ruin at her hands.

Even if we suppose that Lopahin is in a semi-conscious state, and therefore cannot be expected to talk with as much point as Macbeth or Peer Gynt, the speech still seems mere verbiage. Arthur Miller's salesman, Willy Loman, is a dazed and broken character who often talks to himself. But although he may be dazed and prone to "lose himself in reminiscences," Miller always makes obvious the meaning of Willy's speeches to himself. As the flashbacks which usually attend Willy's "thinking aloud" sessions indicate, he is either trying to relive an idealized dream of the past, or he is punishing himself for having committed some wrong. On the other hand, nothing Lopahin says seems to express his feelings or desires. It is no wonder then that directors and actors have difficulty understanding how Chekhov's speech reveals character or expresses the conflicts within the play.

But a close examination of the dialogue reveals that Lopahin's rambling remarks are, in fact, actually expressive of internal conflict which is an integral part of the central conflict of the play. Lopahin has only partially accomplished his purpose of greeting the Ranevskayas by going to the Cherry Orchard. Once there, instead of going to the station to meet the returning party, he goes to sleep. Upon awakening, he chides himself for not completing his purpose. He both starts and ends his musings on this chiding note. He seems to be scolding some impulse or desire within himself which has prevented his conscious will from achieving its aim.

Lopahin is torn by guilt for deeper causes, however, than mere oversleeping. He questions his right even to be at the Cherry Orchard. "My father was a peasant truly, . . . I'm just a peasant [too]. . . ." As a peasant by birth and upbringing, he feels that he is subservient to the Ranevskayas. He still remembers the time when the honor of being in the nursery could compensate for his father's beatings. Yet, as a freed serf, he has the money and the desire to be an aristocrat. He scolds himself for desiring to rise above his class, "like a pig rooting in a pastry shop," and yet he wants to do just that. Thus, when he meditates upon the incongruity of the peasant in white waistcoat, he is struggling to reconcile the conflicting desires within himself.

He is so torn by conflicting desires that even his attempt to "talk himself awake" becomes a form of day dreaming. For at the very moment that he is trying to "wake up" so that he can greet the Ranevskayas, he goes into a kind of reverie about what the orchard has meant to him in the past: "I remember when I was a boy about fifteen. . . ." His reverie begins as an attempt to define his problem, but it becomes a means of escaping from it. By concentrating on what appears to him an insoluble conflict, he loses the will to act. Instead he ends by merely scolding himself because he really does not properly use his aristocratic skill of reading. He substitutes recognition of his problem for solution of the problem.

Lopahin's apparently non-functional speech is really functional in several ways. In the first place, it is a means by which he chides himself for shirking his responsibilities toward the Ranevskayas. Second, it helps to build up in his own mind the importance of those responsibilities and to define them more clearly so that he will try harder to accomplish them. And third, it allows him to talk and thus escape the reality of his problems by letting him concentrate on merely recognizing the problem instead of on trying to solve it. Since the third of these functions is opposed to the other two, Lopahin's speech works like his dream-seeking action: it sets up a tension which keeps him acting in the attempt to reconcile the contradictions within himself.

All of the major characters in the play face problems similar to Lopahin's: like him, they are torn by contradictory impulses and desires. Madame Ranevskaya and Gayeff can passionately desire to save the Orchard at any cost, and yet refrain completely from doing anything to save it because they desire to keep the Orchard intact as a symbol of past bliss. Anna and Trofimoff can love each other deeply and yet refrain from marriage because of their dedication to abstract ideals.

Since the characters' attempts to achieve any of their important aims are thwarted by their opposing desires, like Lopahin they indulge in daydreams. But again like Lopahin, they do even this for two opposing reasons: one, to reaffirm their aims, and two, to escape from the difficulties they have in achieving those aims. Madame Ranevskaya and Gayeff grow angry when faced with the reality of their problems, and like Lopahin, they escape into the past. Madame Ranevskaya rhapsodizes about what the nursery has meant to her; Gayeff makes a speech to the desk about how it has served the family. But rhapsodizing about the nursery and eulogizing the desk serve finally to again remind Madame Ranevskaya and Gayeff of their present problems. Like Lopahin, they become more determined to solve the problems; and also like Lopahin, they use recognition of a problem as a comfortable escape from attempting any real solution to it.

Like the daydreams of Lopahin, Madame Ranevskaya, and Gayeff, those of the other important characters usually take the form of sentimental talk about the Cherry Orchard. Nearly everyone envisages it as a Utopia where he can achieve the purposeful, unified life he so desperately wants. It becomes for everyone a symbol of the ideal for which he is striving. By thinking and talking about the ideal world they envision, Chekhov's characters gain a feeling of purpose. They delude themselves into believing that they are actually bringing unity and purpose into their lives.

But occasionally they discover that their escape into sentimental daydreams is actually preventing them from solving any of the problems. As Trofimoff says, "Apparently, with us, all the fine talk is only to divert the attention of ourselves and of others." Varya, too, realizes that talk will not make Lopahin propose. As she says, "It's two years now; everyone has been talking to me about him, everyone talks, and he either remains silent or jokes." It is this partial awareness of the discrepancy between their aims and their achievements which keeps them struggling to achieve their aims. Lopahin tries again and again to persuade Madame Ranevskaya that she must divide the Orchard into commercial lots if she is to save it. Gayeff tries to face his problems despite his tendency to lapse into daydreams or sentimental talk. Madame Ranevskaya struggles to keep her mind on her present problems, and not on her past bliss. But always the characters allow the dream of unity and purpose to substitute for actions which will achieve their purpose. And since they allow their thoughts and words to take the place of any direct action which might help them achieve what they want, they must fall. As Lopahin says to Madame Ranevskaya after he has bought the orchard, "Why, then, didn't you listen to me? My poor dear, it can't be undone now. Oh, if this could all be over soon, if somehow our awkward, unhappy life would be changed!"

Chekhov's dialogue then is functional because of its rambling, formless quality, not in spite of it. With such dialogue Chekhov has hit upon a perfect means of making objective the constant struggle his characters have between their desire to act realistically in order to solve their problems and their desire to daydream in one form or another in order to avoid their problems. But because talk gives them both a way of struggling and a way of avoiding strug-

---

***The Cherry Orchard* as a comedy:**

[The first production of] ***The Cherry Orchard*** was not a success. The press was, on the whole, favorable, but the reviewers were not enthusiastic, and both the production and the acting were criticized. As to the play, the consensus appeared to be that it was no great thing; the theme was dated; the vein had been worked to death. The play was taken to be a portrayal of the passing of the old order. Nobody suggested that there was anything in the least funny about this. Nevertheless Chekhov persisted in his notion that Stanislavsky had ruined his comedy by playing it tragically. On April 10, he wrote [to his wife] Olga: "Why is it that my play is persistently called a *drame* in the posters and newspaper advertisements? Nemirovich-Danchenko and Stanislavsky see in my play something absolutely different from what I have written, and I am willing to stake my word that neither of them has read it through attentively even once. Forgive me, but I assure you that this is so."

It is strangely ironical that Chekhov never saw his play produced as a comedy, as he intended, nor has anyone, apparently, ever ventured to produce it in this manner. ***The Cherry Orchard*** has many comic passages, some of them so broad as to approximate farce but, generally speaking, directors have been unable to fathom the author's comedic intention. The reason is not far to seek. The play, on the whole, is not funny. The characters have their comic side, but the situation is sad. No rationalization has ever succeeded in giving it a comic bias.

Maurice Valency, in his The Breaking String: The Plays of Anton Chekhov, *Oxford University Press, 1966.*

gle, they allow it to divert them from saving the Orchard. Thus, far from being irrelevant, Chekhov's dialogue is actually the essential expression of the central conflict in *The Cherry Orchard.*

Irving Deer, "Speech as Action in Chekhov's 'The Cherry Orchard'," in Educational Theatre Journal, *Vol. X, No. 1, March, 1958, pp. 30-4.*

Daniel Charles Gerould   (essay date 1958)

[*Gerould is an American playwright, critic, and educator who has written and edited several works about drama. In the following essay, he argues that* The Cherry Orchard *is a true comedy rather than a tragedy, social drama, or problem play.*]

Chekhov's *The Cherry Orchard* often occupies a peculiar position in the general education curriculum. Since it is included in many anthologies of world drama, *The Cherry Orchard* is readily available for use in those humanities courses which would consider such works as Sophocles' *Oedipus Rex* and Jonson's *Volpone,* along with two or three plays by Shakespeare, as the appropriate texts for a study of the drama. The critical reputation of Chekhov's play, coupled with this accident of availability, leads those who feel that modern drama should somehow be represented in a humanities course to select *The Cherry Orchard* for this purpose. Thus *The Cherry Orchard* is most often chosen by teachers of the humanities with a sense of reluctance, for lack of a better alternative rather than for any intrinsic qualities of the play as a work specially suited to the purposes of general education.

It is for this reason that I believe the position of *The Cherry Orchard* in most humanities courses is insecure and uneasy. Such a contention is borne out by the widespread perplexity about how to teach the play in the classroom. This uncertainty about the play may even produce in some teachers a feeling of distaste for the work as something questionable, strange, and abnormal in both form and content. "Morbid" and "decadent" are words frequently used to characterize Chekhov's subject, if not by implicit extension his method and point of view. As far as structure is concerned, the play is admitted to be "formless," and it is only in terms of lyricism, symbolism, and atmosphere that Chekhov's dramatic technique seems susceptible of treatment.

In these terms, *The Cherry Orchard* would appear to be a literary anomaly, indeterminate in its artistic shape and in its moral dimensions. The case against its inclusion in a humanities course seems very strong, for what could serve as a poorer introduction to the drama than a formless play which utilizes non-dramatic means to create a mood of pathos? Therefore, once a humanities course has adopted *The Cherry Orchard,* the problem of justifying its inclusion in the curriculum becomes an acute one. What type of play do we intend *The Cherry Orchard* to represent in a general education course? Since this question is usually asked only after the problem has arisen, the customary answer resembles a rationalization or apology rather than an enthusiastic argument on behalf of the play.

The usual reply to the question is that *The Cherry Orchard* is a representative of the type of play that deals with social problems. The term "problem play" is often heard. The editors of anthologies in their introductions tell us that *The Cherry Orchard* deals with "the passing of the old regime in Russia," with "changing Russian society," and with "the tragedy of pre-revolutionary Russian life." It is felt that the social theme gives *The Cherry Orchard* dignity and seriousness and prevents the play from being merely morbid and depressing.

I should like to challenge the value of this approach. No one questions that *The Cherry Orchard* has value as a social document, just as almost any great play or novel does. However, to make *The Cherry Orchard* "an augury of a new order in Russia" (as Beaumarchais's *The Marriage of Figaro* has been made a prophecy of the French Revolution) is to distort the meaning of the play in order to make it serve the ulterior purposes of the historian and the social scientist. If we are to justify the use of *The Cherry Orchard* in general education, it will not be by reducing Chekhov to the role of providing data on social conditions. Rather, it must be by the qualities of the drama as a drama. If it is really anomalous, it is inappropriate for a general humanities course, whatever its social preoccupations. Should we seriously maintain that its failings as representative drama are compensated for by its being an accurate picture of Russian society in transition?

Unfortunately, *The Cherry Orchard* continues to be regarded as social drama, and this is the aspect of the play which receives public attention and conditions our thinking about it. For example, not very many years ago an adaptation of the play appeared on Broadway. In this version the plot and characters were transferred to an American setting because the adapter thought he saw a parallel between the social picture given by Chekhov and the conditions in the South toward the end of the last century. In this play, called *The Wisteria Trees,* Madame Ranévskaya is transformed into a slightly faded southern belle who owns a plantation overrun with wisteria, and the characters drink mint juleps and eat corn bread instead of vodka and cucumbers. The social theme—which has become the relation between the races—even gains in emphasis by the transposition. The only quality lost is, I should maintain, the entire sense of the play as Chekhov wrote it.

Once we are willing to abandon the idea of *The Cherry Orchard* as a problem play or social drama, I believe it is possible to find the real justification for its inclusion in a humanities course. It will even be possible to assert that *The Cherry Orchard* can be a crucial work in such a course because of the important literary questions that it raises. If it comes at the end of discussion of certain tragedies and comedies, it can appropriately serve as a vantage point from which to survey all that has been learned from such a study of the drama. At this point the students should profit from being confronted with a play that does not seem to fit into any recognizable pattern and that at first puzzles them as to how to react to what they read.

For these reasons, *The Cherry Orchard* represents a challenge to the students' newly acquired skills in reading and interpreting a complex and difficult work of art. That this is not merely a matter of labels, not an imaginary or an academic problem, can be indicated by the different and contradictory interpretations that have been given to Chekhov's play by actors, directors, and critics.

I should like to suggest in this [essay] how I believe such an investigation of *The Cherry Orchard* as a literary type can be carried out along lines relevant to a general course in the humanities. By the examination of a difficult play like *The Cherry Orchard* in terms of a genre with which the students are already acquainted, not only will the play itself receive a thorough exploration, but also the concept of the genre will be tested and enlarged. If we assume that the students in a humanities course first read several English comedies such as *Volpone* and *Twelfth Night,* then a discussion of *The Cherry Orchard* as another representative type of comedy will serve a special function as a conclusion to the study of this genre. Therefore, from the following analysis of *The Cherry Orchard,* I shall attempt to show ways in which we may deduce some general principles about comedy which, I hope, will illuminate some of the differences between comedy and tragedy.

As I have already suggested, this investigation starts with a problem and should be especially suitable to treatment by the discussion method. I shall therefore present my analysis in the terms of such a discussion and first raise objections in the form of typical questions and then attempt to answer them.

The first reaction to any proposal to consider *The Cherry Orchard* as a comedy will probably be one of disbelief. This must be our starting point. How could anyone possibly call a comedy a play in which the heroine's husband dies of drink, her son drowns, her lover deserts her, and she returns to the one thing in the world she loves—her home and cherry orchard—only to have them taken from her and destroyed, only to be turned out into the unfriendly world again, all alone? Furthermore, the other characters, who also love the orchard, are scattered at the end of the play, and the faithful old servant Firce is left behind, locked up in the deserted house—perhaps to die. Wouldn't a person have to have a warped sense of humor to find this story comic? Here is the first objection to calling *The Cherry Orchard* a comedy. It is an objection in terms of the plot, which seems to be composed of unhappy events and to have an unhappy outcome.

A further objection might be made in terms of the characters and their emotions. Practically every character in the play from Madame Ranévskaya to Dunyasha the maid is deeply sensitive. Hardly a page passes that someone doesn't weep or give voice to strong feelings. At the end of the play Madame Ranévskaya and her brother Gaieff fall into each other's arms and sob. Aren't these the reactions we expect from serious, not comic, characters? How could we possibly reconcile the strength of feeling all the characters display toward the orchard with a comic point of view?

A final objection might then be formulated on the basis of our reaction as audience to what we see on the stage or to what we read. Don't we pity the central characters and feel sorry for them in their misfortunes? Then doesn't a play of this sort have a depressing effect rather than a comic one? Don't we close the book or leave the theater feeling sad?

It would seem, then, that neither the plot of the play, nor the characters, nor the effect of these two upon the audience is in any way comic. This is the problem and these are the questions that *The Cherry Orchard* raises. If we imagine for a moment that we are producing and directing a production of the play, it becomes of the greatest importance to answer these questions satisfactorily before attempting to tell the actors how to speak their lines. By making the problem as real and as difficult as possible through the use of these three objections, we can insure that our answers and explanations will involve us in a thoughtful examination of each of the elements of the play and be the result of a thorough reading. It will be appropriate to take up each of the objections in order.

The first objection is that the plot is made of unhappy events, has an unhappy outcome, and is thus not at all comic. However, in such a summary of the action of the play, we are telling the story as it might appear in a novel, starting with Madame Ranévskaya's unhappy marriage, following her through the death of her son Grisha, her unhappy love affair in Paris, and her desertion by the man who had lived off her money, and finally ending with her return home and the loss of her estate. Now the play itself presents only the last stages of this long story, and we learn what happened in the past, not by seeing it presented directly, but by having it narrated by various characters in the course of the play.

Thus we can say that *The Cherry Orchard* begins toward the end of a sequence of events which goes back over many years, instead of showing us directly that whole sequence. In this respect, *The Cherry Orchard* is unlike a play such as *Macbeth* which traces through the major events of the plot over a period of many years; and it resembles to some degree a Greek play like *Oedipus* which begins at the very end of a long story with the final moment of crisis. However, *The Cherry Orchard* does cover a period from May to October of one year and therefore presents not only the final moment in a long progression but also several selected stages leading up to the final moment. We shall return a little later to this question of time, and then we shall have to ask why Chekhov, concentrating as he does on the moment of crisis, wishes to present the elapsing of several months.

The important point for our present discussion is to fix the limits of the action in order to determine what sort of plot the play has. We notice now that the action of the play is inclosed within the arrivals of the first act and the departures of the last act. In Act I we see the various characters assemble about the cherry orchard—some coming from far off, some from nearby. In the last act we see all these characters dispersed and scattered, with the exception of old Firce, who is forgotten. The action of the play in some way brings about the change from arrival to departure, from gathering to dispersal.

What is it that brings about this change? Obviously, it is the selling of the estate and orchard. Most plays contain some basic problem or conflict which the characters must face; and the resolution of this problem or conflict, either successfully or unsuccessfully, will affect the lives of these characters. Clearly, the problem in *The Cherry Orchard* is the approaching sale of the property. Can the sale of the estate be avoided and the orchard saved? This is the central question for all the characters; the fact that they are unsuccessful in dealing with this problem brings about the end of the play, the departures in Act IV.

That people are unsuccessful in solving a problem involving the loss of what they love most may not yet strike us as comic, but at least we have a new and accurate formulation of the action of *The Cherry Orchard,* which we can now describe as the unsuccessful efforts of the owners of the orchard to save their property in the face of its approaching sale.

Then the plot of the play will be concerned with these efforts to save the orchard. What are these efforts? Gaieff has four different ideas: the first is that he might inherit a fortune from somebody; the second that his niece Varya might marry a rich man; the third that his rich aunt might give him enough money; the fourth that he might get a job in a bank. How sensible or practical are any of these hopes? When we consider that to pay their debts they need several hundred thousand rubles, we see that Gaieff's schemes are ridiculous and absurdly unrealistic daydreams. For example, in Act II, Gaieff says: "I have the promise of an introduction to a General who may lend me money on a note." His sister comments: "He's out of his head. There's no General at all."

And what does Madame Ranévskaya do herself to prevent the loss of her homestead? She lends money to Pishchik, a needy neighbor; she gives money to a tramp; she holds a ball and hires an orchestra the day of the auction. Here is plenty of action, but it is all of a sort not to save the orchard but rather to make its loss absolutely certain. Therefore, we can say that the characters act in such a way as to insure that what they are trying to prevent *will* take place. Their actions, supposedly designed to save the orchard, are so futile and ludicrous that either they are utterly useless or they even tend to impoverish the family still more.

In other words, the actions of the characters are inappropriate, inadequate, and irrelevant to the situation in which they find themselves and to the problem they face. It is for this reason that we can say the action of the play is purely a comic one and one of the most perfect comic plots ever created.

Very early in Act I Varya tells Anya, "The place will be sold in August," and a little later Lopákhin announces to all: "If we can't think of anything and don't make up our minds, then on August 22 both the cherry orchard and the whole estate will be sold at auction. Make up your mind! I swear there's no other way out."

As Dryden points out in his *Essay of Dramatic Poesy,* it is a highly effective dramatic device to set a long-awaited day when something decisive will take place, on which the action of the whole play hinges. Chekhov uses the ever present threat of the sale of the orchard to contrast with the ludicrous preoccupations of the characters and their ridiculous responses to the threat. They reveal themselves to be totally incapable of the necessary, practical activity.

Let us look a little more closely at Chekhov's technique. In Act II Lopákhin continues to plead with Madame Ranévskaya to make a decision. He says: "We must decide once and for all: time won't wait. After all, my question's quite a simple one. Do you consent to lease your land for villas, or don't you? You can answer in one word: yes or no? Just one word!" "Who's been smoking such abominable cigars here?" replies Madame Ranévskaya.

Those two speeches contain in miniature the essence of the whole play, its plot and its humor. Most of Chekhov's comedy comes from this kind of incongruity—the trivial response to a serious situation. Thus there are many references to petty, undignified objects which seem to obtrude upon the important problem of how to save the orchard. Trofimov can't find his galoshes, Gaieff continues to eat candy and play his imaginary billiard game, and all kinds of food keep popping up at what should be solemn moments—frogs legs and herring and nuts and pickled cherries. While Charlotta Ivanovna, the lonely German governess, delivers her soliloquy at the beginning of Act II, "I haven't anybody to talk to . . . I haven't anybody at all," she is munching on a cucumber. Likewise, when Gaieff returns from the auction, where he could do nothing to prevent the loss of his estate, he comes back not entirely empty-handed; he says, weeping, to old Firce: "Here, take this. Here are anchovies, herrings from Kertch. . . . I've had no food today." His heart is broken, but he remembered the anchovies.

I should like to suggest as a general axiom that such an incongruity between situation and response, between the serious and the trivial, is one of the fundamental sources of comedy. Nothing more quickly deflates the tragic dignity of a character and brings him down to the level of common humanity than a sudden annoyance at cigar smoke or a craving for a cucumber. Imagine Macbeth during his soliloquy: "I have lived long enough. My way of life / Is fall'n into the sear, the yellow leaf," all at once overcome with an urge to have a bowl of home-made Scotch broth with barley.

We are now in a position to look a little more closely at this type of comic plot and see whether we can describe precisely the kind of comic incongruity with which we are dealing. For example, in a comedy such as *Volpone* there is an incongruity between the wit, intelligence, and eloquence of Volpone and Mosca and the unworthy and degraded ends for which all their talent is expended.

In *The Cherry Orchard* the reverse is true. The end of saving the orchard is worthy, but the characters are unable to engage in even the simplest plans or schemes to raise money; they are incapable of managing any business affairs. Although both plays center around money problems, in *The Cherry Orchard* squandering, not greed, is the comic failing of Madame Ranévskaya and her brother. In Act II, Madame Ranévskaya tells her friends: "I've always scattered money about without being able to control myself, like a madwoman." *The Cherry Orchard* is the comedy of the spendthrift or the wastrel. With the exception of Lopákhin, the principal characters are too foolish and footless to hold on to their dearly beloved possessions.

A brief examination of the structure of *The Cherry Orchard* should confirm these observations about the nature of the plot and the incongruities which it presents. We might begin this discussion of the organization of the play with a simple question: Why does the action of the play begin with the return of Madame Ranévskaya from Paris? In order to answer this question, we must first ask about her motive for coming home.

Here the gradual unfolding of the past gives us the explanation. We learn that after running off to Paris with her lover, Madame Ranévskaya continued to spend money recklessly, even buying a villa at Mentone on the Riviera by mortgaging her Russian estate and getting head over heels in debt. Finally, the French villa was sold to pay her debts, her lover ran off with another woman after robbing her of everything she had, and Madame Ranévskaya was left penniless and unable to pay her debts on her Russian estate. At this point she comes home, and the action of the play begins.

We can now see that the reason why she returns is that she has no more money left; she must attempt to save the estate and solve her financial problem. Thus the action of the play begins with her coming home, since it is her return which poses this central financial problem.

The turning point in the play occurs in Act III, when we learn that the merchant Lopákhin has purchased the estate. What is the nature of this turning point? It is a complete reversal, a total upset, since the estate now passes into the hands of the man who seemed least likely ever to own it—Lopákhin, son of a former serf on that very property! Here is another aspect of the comic incongruity of *The Cherry Orchard*: Not only have the owners lost their estate through their own folly, but it now belongs to the man that no one could have imagined as the new owner. The incongruity is made doubly ludicrous by the fact that Lopákhin is the one character in the play who had sincerely made repeated efforts to save the estate for its rightful owners. Chekhov has made this reversal quite probable, yet at the same time comically surprising, by his careful development of the relationship between Madame Ranévskaya and Lopákhin.

In Lopákhin there is a constant alternation between his old self, the son of a serf, and his new self, the rich businessman. At the turning point in Act III, when Lopákhin arrives flushed with his purchase to announce that he is now owner of the estate, Chekhov reminds us of the incongruity of his new position by the fact that Varya, who has threatened to hit the pompous, insolent clerk Yepikhodov, actually strikes Lopákhin by chance as he enters. The new master of the estate is hit over the head with a stick as he arrives to proclaim his new power, and this incident recalls to us the other Lopákhin—the small peasant boy beaten by his drunken father.

If the announcement of the sale of the orchard represents the turning point in the play and the resolution of the central problem, what is the function of the final act? The last act presents the consequences of this solution; we must see how the failure to save the orchard will affect all the characters. Thus if the arrival of Madame Ranévskaya initiates the action and poses the basic problem, it is not until her departure that the action ends, that her failure to solve the problem is presented to us in its entirety. Thus the setting of Act IV parallels that of Act I, except that the room is now empty and dismantled. As before, the characters were waiting for the train to arrive, now they are waiting for it to depart.

These remarks will have to suffice as an examination of the plot, the structure, and the revelation of the past. Our observations about the inability of the characters to change and meet new circumstances bring us to our second point. We raised the objection that the emotions of the characters are of too great depth and seriousness to be comic. For example, there are the passionate outbursts of Trofimov, Madame Ranévskaya, and Gaieff. Perhaps these characters are incapable of *acting* effectively in a given situation, but they can at least *feel* profoundly, and this makes them pathetic and moving rather than comic. After all, King Lear is incapable of acting effectively, yet he is deeply tragic. Couldn't a similar case be made for Madame Ranévskaya and the others?

In order to answer this question, we must return to an earlier problem we left unresolved: the elapsing of time in *The Cherry Orchard.* Why does the play cover a period of six months? We can see now that this period from May to October is necessary to show the characters' repeated and continuous failure to act intelligently in a situation that demands practical action. A more limited time-span would not have shown effectively the change in the circumstances of the family, and, at the same time, their complete inability to change themselves and to grasp the reality of what is happening to them. To estimate rightly their flagrant wasting of opportunity, we must feel the passing of time and experience the difference between the household bustling with activity in May and the deserted room in October, without curtains, furniture and with suitcases piled in the corner.

Here we touch on the central fact about the characters in *The Cherry Orchard.* Their responses are always the same. To Dunyasha's announcement about Yepikhodov's proposal, Anya says, "Always the same . . ."; Madame Ranévskaya tells Gaieff, "You're just the same as ever"; and Varya says of Madame Ranévskaya herself: "Mother hasn't altered a bit, she's just as she always was." Trofimov will always go on being a student—like all the others, he is growing old without growing up. The characters age but remain unchanged, learning nothing from life.

They share a common past which they love to talk about; they would really like to go back to those good old days. They wish to return to their childhood and be children again; they can't seem to realize that things aren't as they used to be, that they have to face certain responsibilities. Instead, they refuse to face reality. By living in the past, in a world of dreams, they hope to avoid having to live in the present and make hard decisions. Although the orchard will be sold in a few months, all they do is talk about the wonderful old days.

Naturally enough, the old servant Firce is an extreme of this type; he lives entirely in the past. He even regrets the emancipation of the serfs. He remembers in the happy old days of slavery, fifty years ago, they dried the cherries from the orchard and made them into a most wonderful jam—when he is asked how it was done, he mutters that the recipe is lost and no one remembers how. Old Firce lives his life in this foggy, imaginary past when everyone was happy and didn't know why. And so it is with all their past happiness: the recipe is lost, and no one remembers how.

Madame Ranévskaya and her brother are like Firce in that they recall without cease the nursery and their ecstatically happy childhood. But by the end of the play they seem to have learned nothing at all from their experiences and to have matured in no way as a result of all their emotions. We can well imagine that Madame Ranévskaya will feel the loss of the estate chiefly when she talks about it to others, that she will weep and gush sentimentally about the orchard and the nursery, about her girlhood and days of innocence, as she sits in that small smoke-filled room on the fifth floor in Paris. Likewise, her brother Gaieff will embarrass and bore the people at the bank with his repetitious effusions about the "dear and honored" hundred-year-old cupboard, instead of doing the least bit of work.

It is this fixity, this lack of adaptability of the characters' emotional responses that makes them comic. We soon come to assess the emotions of Madame Ranévskaya and Gaieff as sentimental and excessive rather than tragic. That we are to laugh at Gaieff's foolish sentimentality is clear because the other characters try to shut him up and make gentle fun of his outbursts. His continual stock response: "Red into the corner!" as though he were playing billiards, is an example of such comic fixity on a simple, mechanical level. The self-pitying, self-dramatized outbursts of Madame Ranévskaya represent the same source of comedy on a psychological level.

On the basis of the foregoing analysis, I should like to suggest another axiom: In comedy the characters do not change profoundly because of the experiences they undergo, but they continue making the same responses, repeating the same errors, committing the same follies. The more we learn about Madame Ranévskaya's past, the more we see that her present difficulties are a result of an incorrigible nature which has not changed. She is consistent in her behavior; having created the unpleasant situation in which she finds herself, she is unable to extricate herself from it for just the same reasons. Furthermore, we can easily picture a comic figure such as Madame Ranévskaya continuing to act in the same way even after we have left the theater or closed the book. This is just the opposite of the shattering experience of tragedy which either ends the hero's life or utterly transforms it.

On the other hand, Madame Ranévskaya has never come to grips with reality and never will; she will go on living in the world of illusion, talking about herself and weeping over herself. It is this contrast between illusion and reality which makes all the characters in **The Cherry Orchard** part of the same comic vision. Let us now look at the other characters and see the particular illusions in which they live.

The servants are caricatures of their masters, with whom they mingle in a ridiculous and incongruous fashion. Dunyasha is just a maid, but she dresses and acts like a lady, her hands are white and delicate, and she has become so sensitive that she almost faints from nerves. Yasha is only a footman, but he has turned into such a Frenchified fop in Paris that he feels quite superior to his masters and turns up his nose at Lopákhin's bottle of domestic champagne (although he manages to finish it single-handed).

Yepikhodov is a lazy clerk who has great intellectual pretensions because he has read Henry Thomas Buckle's *The History of English Civilization,* but his shoes squeak. He also accidentally tips over chairs, breaks dishes, and puts trunks on hatboxes, and these calamities lead him to proclaim grandiloquently: "Fate, so to speak, treats me absolutely without mercy, just as a small ship, as it were." He finds cockroaches in his wine glass and becomes a fatalist, threatening to commit suicide if Dunyasha throws him over for Yasha. As he strums his guitar lugubriously, he says: "Now I know what to do with my revolver." In other words, Yepikhodov is a pompous fool who imagines he is as poetic and mysterious as Hamlet.

Lopákhin is all dressed up "in a white vest and brown shoes," seemingly successful and cultured, but the reality is that he's a peasant in origin and in spirit, and his past keeps showing through the veneer. In Act II he confesses that he's really a fool and an idiot and that his handwriting is just like a pig's!

The one character who understands and explains this kind of contrast between illusion and reality is the student Trofimov. He points out to the others: "It's obvious that all our nice talk is only carried on to delude ourselves and others." Trofimov sees clearly the contrast between ideals and facts, wishful thinking and actual practice. Because of this, we might suspect that Trofimov is a spokesman for the author and not a comic figure, and we might think that we are to take quite seriously his talk about the future.

Let us look at Trofimov a little more closely. His creed is expressed in the phrase: "We must work"—which is what none of the characters do, Trofimov included. In fact, he has been wasting his time for years with some vague and endless course of study at the university. Trofimov penetrates the delusions of everyone but himself. He is perceptive enough to recognize that by clinging to the orchard the others are refusing to face reality, but he doesn't see that he likewise is escaping from the present with his beautiful dreams of the future. His talk of the future is as much sentimental rhapsodizing as Madame Ranévskaya's gushing about the orchard and poor little Grisha her dead son.

Trofimov informs all the others: "Mankind goes on to the highest possible truths and happiness on earth, and I march in the front ranks!" But he's marching without his galoshes, which he still can't find. He is the perfect type of the seedy, balding bohemian with elaborate theories and very little common sense. His contemporary counterpart is well known to all of us.

A scene from the Royal Shakespeare Company's 1961 production of The Cherry Orchard *with Peggy Ashcroft and John Gielgud.*

From these observations about character, it would be possible to indicate as another axiom that one of the basic incongruities in comedy lies in the inability of the characters to tell illusion from reality. Here we can make a distinction between *The Cherry Orchard,* on the one hand, and earlier English comedies such as *Volpone* and *Twelfth Night,* on the other. In the two Elizabethan plays, one group of characters deliberately dupes or tricks another and helps to produce the delusion, whereas in *The Cherry Orchard* the characters are self-deluded. In fact, they wilfully resist any efforts made to enlighten them on their true characters and state of affairs; they prefer to remain oblivious to the real world.

Such self-delusion manifests itself in a variety of ways. One of the principal forms it takes is egotism or self-centeredness. Each character is so wrapped up in himself that he is hardly aware of those about him. Although all the characters are intimately connected to the family group through deep ties in the past and through their love of the estate and the orchard, preoccupation with self produces an isolation of each character from all the others. The comic separateness of characters who should be close to one another is emphasized by their disregard for and deafness to what others are saying and by their persistence in thinking their own thoughts aloud.

On the simplest level, this deafness is quite literal, as in the case of old Firce, who once again represents the extreme

toward which all the other characters tend in varying degrees. Firce lives in a world of illusion all his own because he is hard of hearing. His comments are nearly always irrelevant because he does not know what the others are talking about, quite literally as well as figuratively. When Madame Ranévskaya first sees him after her return, she goes up to him and says emotionally, "Thank you, dear old man. I'm so glad you're still with us." Firce replies, "The day before yesterday." A little later on, a propos of nothing at all, he mumbles, "They were here in Easter week and ate half a pailful of cucumbers."

On a less obvious plane, all the characters are deaf and go on muttering irrelevant things to themselves, unheeded by the others. When Dunyasha tells Anya that Yepikhodov has proposed to her, Anya says, "I've lost all my hair pins . . ." and later Anya falls asleep while Varya is talking to her. Pishchik even falls asleep in the middle of his own conversation when he is talking! Just at the moment that Varya first announces to Anya that the estate will be sold in August, Lopákhin sticks his head in the door and, for a joke, moos like a cow. There is a special comic irony here in that this is the future owner of the estate commenting on the central problem of the play, the chances of saving the orchard. No one pays any real attention to anyone else. Gaieff even talks to waiters in restaurants about the decadents!

Thus the self-centered isolation of the characters produces

a lack of communication, a failure in expression. This lack of communication is one of the principal sources of comedy in *The Cherry Orchard* and appropriately brings us to a discussion of the comic use of language. If, in tragedy, language is used for maximum eloquence and expressiveness, in comedy language is abused for maximum nonsense and confusion. I should like to propose as another axiom that in comedy the resources of language are deliberately misused. This misuse takes the form of excess in many English comedies of the Shakespearean period. For example, in *Volpone* we see eloquence and rhetoric pushed to ludicrous extremes and put to unworthy uses in Volpone's mountebank speeches and in his pleas and arguments to Celia.

In *The Cherry Orchard* there is also an abuse and misuse of language, but it is in the opposite direction. Rather than an excessive glibness, there is a deficiency in articulateness. Old Firce's disconnected mutterings give us the essence of the comic use of language in *The Cherry Orchard.* Each character talks to himself about something irrelevant to the present situation, usually about something in the past either trivial or personal to the speaker, the significance of which cannot be grasped by the other characters.

Characteristically, the non sequitur or meaningless remark which doesn't logically follow what has gone before is the primary source of humor in Chekhov's use of language. The non sequitur not only expresses a momentary illogicality but, in the comic world that Chekhov creates, expresses the characters' reaction to their situation. Their response to the approaching sale of the estate is a non sequitur indicating the world of illusion in which each lives.

Even if these answers to the first two objections to calling *The Cherry Orchard* a comedy are found to be satisfactory, won't it still be possible to assert that the spectacle of this group of foolish, bungling, impractical characters being dispossessed and cast out into a world with which they are not fit to cope is not a comic one? A perceptive reader may be willing to grant that the characters are as incompetent as we have described them and that their actions are futile and inappropriate, but he will insist that the effect of seeing lonely, irresponsible people come to an unhappy end is one of sadness, not comedy. He might well argue that we feel sympathy and even pity for Madame Ranévskaya, Gaieff, Varya, old Firce, and all the rest, and ask whether these emotions are compatible with the conception of comedy which we have been developing. It will then be necessary to investigate the problem of the unhappy ending and the matter of comic sympathy if we are to convince this perceptive reader that he is actually experiencing comic, not tragic, emotions.

As concerns the unhappy ending and its supposedly sad effect, there are two answers. The first is that the denouement of the play is not quite so unhappy as it may at first appear. Although Madame Ranévskaya and her brother dread the loss of the estate before it takes place, after it has happened they seem to be surprisingly indifferent to the reality. Gaieff comments gaily: "Yes, really, everything's all right now. Before the cherry orchard was sold we were all excited and worried, and then when the question was solved once and for all, we all calmed down, and even became cheerful. I'm a bank official now, and a financier . . . red in the center; and you, Liuba, look better for some reason or other, there's no doubt about it." Madame Ranévskaya replies: "Yes. My nerves are better, it's true. I sleep well. . . . I'm off to Paris. I'll live on the money your grandmother from Yaroslavl sent to buy the estate—bless her! —though it won't last long."

A fine use for grandmother's money—to go back to Paris and live with her lover! Here is the crowning irony and incongruity: the money that was to be used to save the beloved estate will actually be used so that Madame Ranévskaya can continue a little longer in her loose, shiftless life!

If we remember Madame Ranévskaya's resolve in the first act when she said, "I'm through with Paris" and tore up the telegrams from her lover, we see the comical nature of the denouement in which, after all her noble intentions to save the orchard and reform her life, she continues true to her unregenerate nature, throwing away her own and other people's money in a completely unworthy cause.

In the second place, it is a mistake to suppose that comedies always have happy endings for the comic or ridiculous figures. In fact, the reverse is usually true: the ridiculous figures do *not* achieve their ends, but they are in some way frustrated, chastised, or held up to laughter or scorn. Thus it is that the denouement of *The Cherry Orchard* is in some way frustrating for all the characters. It is this very frustration which unifies all the different lines of action in the play; everything goes wrong, no one accomplishes any of the things he sets out to. All the minor mishaps and failures are related to the loss of the estate as lesser frustrations around one central failure. For example, Lopákhin in Act I comes to meet the party at the train station, but he falls asleep and misses the train; Varya would like to marry Lopákhin and he her, but neither can ever get around to talking about it. Such misfortunes are even personified in one almost farcical figure, the clerk Yepikhodov, nicknamed "Two-and-Twenty Troubles." This frustration of the purposes of ridiculous figures is of the very essence of comedy. Just a moment ago we saw that the unhappiness produced thereby is not so great or so deeply felt as to be tragic and bring about any radical change in the lives of the characters. Therefore, we can conclude that the so-called unhappy end of *The Cherry Orchard* produces a true comic effect.

As for the objection that we feel sympathy for the characters, I should say that there is no reason why a comic figure should not be sympathetic. If we think of Don Quixote or Falstaff or Charlie Chaplin, we see that many of the greatest comic creations are very sympathetic. If we take sympathy to mean an "affinity between persons," a "liking or understanding arising from sameness of feelings," and the "ability to enter into another person's mental state" (*Webster's New World Dictionary of the American Language*), then in one important aspect comic characters are much more sympathetic than tragic ones. We are more like comic figures. We admire and respect a man like Oedipus from a distance, and we are awed by Lear's sufferings; but we feel we share the same weaknesses and the same fallible human nature as comic characters like Madame

Ranévskaya. We are close to them and do the same foolish things they do: we procrastinate, waste time, choose poor companions, spend money foolishly, and then feel sorry for ourselves and invent excuses. And many of us are like Trofimov: we've spent far too many years at the university over imaginary studies, until our hair has grown thin and we wear spectacles.

It is in this sense that comedy is just as profound as tragedy and perhaps more universal. Tragedy presents only the exceptional cases, individuals whose experiences are unique; comedy deals with types, with those traits all men have in common: their pettiness, egotism, foolishness, weakness, and hypocrisy.

From this point of view, tragedy and comedy are not to be distinguished one from the other by an unhappy or a happy ending. Rather, they are two fundamentally different ways of looking at the world. In the tragic view we see nobility and relentless self-honesty even in the cornered murderer Macbeth; in the comic view we see an unkempt philosopher looking about on the floor for his galoshes and a middle-aged woman, ignobly in love, deceiving herself with sentimental lies. In this way, comedy sees the contrast between what man should be and what he is, between what he claims to be and what he actually does; and it exposes all imposture.

In these terms, comedy is a criticism of life and a critical view of human nature, and not merely a form. All the great comic writers from Aristophanes and Molière to Chekhov and Shaw have been interested not only in creating works of art but, first and foremost, in criticizing the foibles and extravagances and the faults and vices of men and women. Jonson wrote: "The office of a comic poet is to imitate justice and instruct to life . . . to inform in the best reason of living." Chekhov says almost exactly the same thing: "All I wanted was to say honestly to people: 'Have a look at yourselves and see how bad and dreary your lives are!' The important thing is that people should realise that, for when they do, they will most certainly create another and better life for themselves."

Despite their similarity of purpose, Chekhov, unlike Jonson in *Volpone,* is not concerned with vices like greed, jealousy, and lust which lead to violence and crime. Rather Chekhov is submitting to comic scrutiny the lesser follies of the bunglers in life—the half-baked sentimentalities, the fatuous emotionalism, and the wasteful absurdities of Madame Ranévskaya and her family and servants. Because they are kind, gentle fools with generous hearts and good intentions, we can sympathize with them and even pity them at the same time that we laugh at their utter lack of sense.

Such is the main line of argument which I believe can be profitably followed in a presentation of *The Cherry Orchard* as a comedy. However, the enunciation of these general principles and theories will be chiefly useful insofar as they enable us to understand and to enjoy more fully the play itself. Therefore, as a conclusion to this analysis, it will be of the utmost importance to present a detailed examination of certain portions of the text as concrete illustration of all that we have been saying about *The Cherry Orchard.* I should like to offer the following explications of two short scenes as examples of what can be done to show exactly how Chekhov's comic view operates in practice.

The first scene is the quarrel between Madame Ranévskaya and Trofimov which occurs during the ball in Act III.

In the course of this quarrel, each tells the other painful truths. Trofimov tells Madame Ranévskaya that she is deceiving herself both about the orchard which must be sold and also about her lover in Paris, who is no better than a thief. In anger, Madame Ranévskaya answers that Trofimov is nothing but a schoolboy who has never grown up. She says: "You're not above love, you're just what our Firce calls a bungler. Not to have a mistress at your age!" Trofimov leaves in horror at the things that have been said, vowing, "All is over between us." It seems for a moment that there may have been a tragic realization of the truth of their accusations and hence a discovery leading to a final rupture between the two, which would be grave, since we know how much they care for each other.

But what actually happens? We hear a loud crash and learn that Trofimov has fallen downstairs in his haste to make an effective exit. A moment later he is back in the room dancing with Madame Ranévskaya, and the whole episode is forgotten. There could be no better illustration of the way in which comic characters bounce back and go on in their old unthinking manner, quite unchanged by what has happened. The fall downstairs ludicrously deflates Trofimov's solemn, "All is over between us," and his speedy return to dance with Madame Ranévskaya contradicts his words.

In this scene we see how Chekhov transforms what might have been a tragic quarrel into a ridiculous scene with an unmistakable comic effect by the use of the surprising anticlimax that terminates the scene. At just the most serious moment, the rug is almost literally yanked out from underneath Trofimov, and he falls flat on his face. The next moment he's back on his feet again—dancing!

The second scene I should like to examine comes at the very end of the play, the short scene in which we see old Firce locked up in the deserted house. I have mentioned this scene several times because I feel that it is of central importance to an understanding of the play. What is the effect of this scene which gives us our final impression of **The Cherry Orchard**?

Before Firce appears, we have the departure of Madame Ranévskaya presented in the grand manner. She and her brother fall in each other's arms and sob. This seems to be the great emotional climax of the play. Madame Ranévskaya exclaims: "My dear, my gentle, my beautiful orchard! My life, my youth, my happiness, good-bye! Good-bye!" This is where the ordinary dramatist would end his play, with the exit of the leading actress, as beautiful, as tearful, as emotional as possible. In fact, this is where the author of *The Wisteria Trees* did end his play, and, in the terms of the trade, this is called "good theater."

But a great dramatist like Chekhov does something much

more than that. What Chekhov has done in ending the play, not with the farewell of Madame Ranévskaya to her orchard, but with the appearance of old Firce is exactly the same kind of comic anticlimax which we saw in the quarrel scene. Nothing shows better the shallow sentimentality of Gaieff and his sister about the orchard than the fact that they've entirely forgotten to insure that Firce will be taken care of, Firce the one person who has been blindly faithful to his masters.

Madame Ranévskaya has just said, "We go away, and not a soul remains behind." As if to contradict her, to show her persistence in error, old Firce then comes shuffling in, wearing slippers and white vest and dress jacket, and we have the final comic surprise and incongruity of the play. Failure and frustration of purpose prevail to the very end. The contrast of the sound of the axes, practical and efficient in their destruction of the orchard, with the picture of the feeble old servant still in livery lying down and falling asleep in the empty house expresses the central contrast between reality and illusion which has run through the whole play.

Firce reacts as he always has, thinking that Gaieff has forgotten his overcoat. "Oh, these young people!" he exclaims. It is appropriate that Firce end the play and have the last words, since he represents the extreme obliviousness to reality; his falling asleep is the final lack of response to the external world.

His last words enforce the whole comic meaning of the play. He says: "Life's gone on as if I'd never lived. . . . Oh, you . . . bungler!" This word *bungler,* which is a favorite with Firce, is used to describe practically every character in the play. It is the key word in **The Cherry Orchard** because it portrays the bumbling, muddled, sentimental failures that all the characters are. Thus **The Cherry Orchard** ends with delusion triumphant: Madame Ranévskaya leaves, intoxicated with her own words but failing to realize that her one loyal follower has been abandoned, and Firce himself remains bunglingly devoted to his bungling masters. The comedy is complete.

Lest this reading of **The Cherry Orchard** be thought too personal and unconventional to be sound for the purposes of general education, I should like to point out that we have Chekhov's own words about the play to serve as a guide. The following remarks which appear in different letters Chekhov wrote concerning **The Cherry Orchard** support not only the contention that the play should be regarded as a comedy but also the view that failure to approach the work in terms of its proper genre will result in serious misinterpretation.

Chekhov writes: "I shall call the play a comedy. . . . It has turned out not a drama, but a comedy, in parts a farce . . . the last act is gay, the whole play is gay, light . . . why on the posters and in the advertisements is my play so persistently called a *drama?* Nemirovich and Stanislavsky see in it a meaning different from what I intended. They never read it attentively, I am sure."

Therefore, what I am urging is that we restore **The Cherry Orchard** to the proper tradition, the humanistic tradition; only by treating it as a comedy, along with other comedies,

shall we be able to understand the play as Chekhov wrote it. We must read the play attentively, as the author suggests we should, and restore to the title the part most editors of **The Cherry Orchard** omit: *A Comedy in Four Acts.* In this way, I believe **The Cherry Orchard** can occupy an important position in any humanities course.

Daniel Charles Gerould, " 'The Cherry Orchard' as a Comedy," in The Journal of General Education, *published by The Pennsylvania State University Press, University Park, PA, Vol. 11, No. 2, April, 1958, pp. 109-22.*

John Kelson   (essay date 1959)

[*In the following essay, Kelson argues that the superficially formless plot of* The Cherry Orchard *is undergirded by extensive patterns of historical allegory, structural symmetry, and myth.*]

The Cherry Orchard, which dramatizes the lives of a group of "job-lots," people whose sense of isolation and futility is perhaps most forcefully expressed in the ambivalent, Villonesque "Je ris en pleurs" feelings of Madame Ranevsky, is widely admired for the psychological realism of its characterizations and for the theatrical effects it achieves by subtle employment of mood and atmosphere. To use another line from Villon, who, like the characters in **The Cherry Orchard,** lived in an agonizingly transitional age, the play as a whole seems to be saying: "Ou sont les neiges d'antan?"

It is my intention to show that, while this impression is certainly a part of the total effect that the play has upon the reader, beneath this surface of seemingly aimless existence there is a patterning so rigorous as to give every impulsive speech and despairing gesture an almost predetermined significance. Thinking of the play as a person, one can say that beneath the quivering, oh so sensitive flesh there is a very firm bone structure and a strongly beating heart.

The structure of the play allows for at least three levels of meaning: literal, historical, and mythical. On the literal level of psychological realism, the play gives a picture of humanity in which loneliness, futility, and frustration are the dominant emotions. It is on the literal level, of course, that the play makes its most immediate appeal to the reader. In addition to this emotional content, however, there is historical allegory which, like the allegory in Orwell's *Animal Farm,* depends for its appeal on the knowledge of Russian history that the reader can correlate with the naturalistic events and characters of the literary work. Some of the characters, as a matter of fact, are motivated in ways difficult to explain satisfactorily except on the level of historical allegory; I am thinking particularly of Charlotte and Barbara, the governess and adopted daughter, respectively, of Madame Ranevsky.

Following is a brief schematization of the allegorical correspondences of the various characters, with occasionally a suggestion as to the way particular characters are motivated in response to other characters in terms of the historical allegory. Madame Ranevsky, Gayef, Anya and Pishtchik correspond, in that order, to the pleasure-seeking, dilettantish, idealistic and opportunistic elements of Russian aristocracy at the turn of the century. Barbara, the *adopted* daughter, the one in charge of the estate during the mistress' absences, the one who feeds the servants on peas while dreaming of the day she can cast off her responsibilities for the life of a pilgrim, represents the Russian Orthodox Church. Her ambivalent relationship with Lopakhin, who stands for the Bourgeois class, is understandable in terms of Russian history, just as is her fear of the Tramp, a symbol of atheistic Marxism. The Bolsheviks had declared themselves as a separate identity in 1903, just a year before ***The Cherry Orchard*** was produced. Trophimof, as the Intellectual class, and Firs, Yasha, and Dunyasha as representing aspects of the Servant class, can be easily identified. Of the two remaining characters, Ephikhodof fits readily into his role as the type of the Bureaucrat, as he is left in charge of the estate during the absence of Lopakhin. His delusions, seeing a spider straddled over him upon awakening, and his misfortunes, clumsily breaking things as he moves about, remind one of other fictional clerks in recent European literature, among whom are the hero of Gogol's *The Overcoat,* the Underground Man and the Double of Dostoevsky, and, most famous of all, the man-turned-insect of Kafka's *Metamorphosis.* Finally, there is Charlotte. She embodies the spirit of the modern Russian artist, as composer painter and writer. Her cries of loneliness, of not being understood, reflect the attitude of the modern artist, whether Russian or otherwise. At the beginning of Act II, when she reminisces about her earlier days, mentioning the *salto Mortale* and the old German lady, what we have on the allegorical level is a brief resume of the development of Russian musical culture in particular, and in general a statement of the progress of the Fine Arts through imitation of foreign models to the establishment of a native, national art. She has become, that is, a governess. Her theatrical background, her ventriloquism and her conjuring tricks make her a suitable representative of the Artist, the dealer in entertaining illusions.

To turn to a reading of the play as the representation of myth is to penetrate deeper than surface emotion (the raw nerves of psychological realism) or intellectual amusement (the jigsaw of allegory). It is on this level, I believe, that the play gives us a meaning which will account for the most enduring appeal that the play has.

To begin with, although the cherry orchard is certainly the central image of the play, it is the seasonal cycle of Nature that provides the basic structure for the action of the drama. The four acts correspond to the four seasons: spring, summer, fall, and winter. The first act, for example, is so constructed that everything in it tends to reinforce the atmosphere associated with springtime, with birth and planting. The act opens with the reveries of Lopakhin, representative of the forces in Russian society that are going to displace the aristocracy, and it closes with the reveries of Anya, who represents the youthful, idealistic element of the established aristocracy, that element which, by joining hands with the intellectuals, can contribute to the growth of the new order. The time of year is May, the setting is the nursery, and the atmosphere is one of hopefulness; enthusiastic plans for the future are in the air. Lo-

pakhin has a plan to save the orchard for his beloved benefactress; Dunyasha has fallen in love again; and Gayef is full of schemes that reassure Anya, causing her to doze off contentedly as the curtain falls, just as Lopakhin had been dozing contentedly when it rose. The ecstatic remark of Trophimof as he gazes on Anya provides an appropriate curtain line: "My sunshine! My spring!"

In Act II the time is late June, the setting is the open fields. Being summer, there are evidences of growth and development, of active cultivation of planted things. Telegraph poles are in sight, the outline of a big town may be discerned off in the distance. Here, as in Act I, there is parallelism between the first and last scenes. Charlotte, at first, and Trophimof, at the end, express feelings of "mysterious anticipation." Just as Trophimof represents the Russian intellectual, cultivating dissatisfaction with things as they have been, so Charlotte represents the Russian artist, conscious of a profound unrest after having been educated by Italians and Germans and having become now a governess, one who is trying to train and discipline the native Russian capabilities in art. All the characters talk about the way they have spent their lives, the things they have done in their youthful enthusiasms. For just as the theme of Act I is Infancy, so the second Act centers upon Youth. As in Act I, Anya and Trophimof are center stage as the curtain falls, now having definitely committed themselves to the stirrings of the new society. The Tramp, in his mysterious passage across the stage, has proffered an invitation—"Brother, my suffering brother . . . Come forth to the Volga. Who moans?" . . . —and Anya and Trophimof seem to have accepted it, for Anya says, "Let us go down to the river. It's lovely there."

As the curtain rises on Act III, the time is autumn, the orchard, now ripe for harvest, is being sold, and a celebration is in progress. Now is the time at which the plantings made in the spring will be gathered in, if they have thrived, or cast aside, like the chaff from the wheat, if they have not prospered. The parallelism between first and last scenes continues. This time Pishtchik, with his talk of the horse of Caligula that became senator, and a representative of the aristocracy which can no longer harvest anything but tares, is paralleled with Lopakhin, the founder of a new dynasty, another breed of work horse that has been transformed into a senator. Everything has now come to maturity. That which must die can look forward only to death, while the "young wood, green wood" that has been growing through the spring and summer will continue on into the next cycle of life.

The wintry mood of late October dominates the last act; the hopefulness of Lopakhin, Anya and Trophimof, among the representatives of the new life, is subdued by their sympathy for those who have only a short span left. The parallelism of opening and closing scenes in this act involves, on the one hand, the delegation of servants who have come to pay their last respects to the dispossessed landlord, and, on the other, old Firs, who sinks down to die in silence and loneliness in the abandoned nursery. Just as the delegation at the beginning is characterized by the distant murmur of their voices, dying away into silence, so does Firs mumble inaudibly as he resigns himself to his fate.

The most important element in this framework of the seasons, however, has not yet been mentioned. The beginnings and endings of the four acts enclose centrally placed scenes in which Madame Ranevsky is the dominating figure. Her musings in each act are appropriate to the season: in the first she recollects her childhood, in the second she speaks of more recent years, in the third she disputes with Trophimof about her present lover whose appeals for her sympathy and protection she will not reject, and in the fourth act all of her concern is with finding secure places for all those who have been in her service, particularly Barbara and Firs. Since, on the mythic level, the play is mimesis of the cycle of Nature, it is appropriate that one character should represent the continuing, sustaining and life-giving power of Nature. Thus Madame Ranevsky is in the first act the Sorrowing Mother for, in grieving over her lost son Grisha, she is another Demeter mourning the Persephone snatched from her. Her Grisha is taken from her, but what Lopakhin says of her at the beginning of the play, mentioning the way she wiped the blood from his face and took him in her arms, suggests that on the mythic level Lopakhin is the son returned to her, and in his return there is the renewal of life, the beginning of a new cycle. She is, in the second act, a Goddess of Fertility, eternally procreant, carelessly spilling gold coins from her lap as she sits in the midst of a burgeoning field. In the third act she is represented as a Love Goddess, a Venus lamenting over her Adonis ill and alone in Paris. (Note that Trophimof says he does not want to be an Adonis, after saying which he succeeds in making a complete fool of himself.) As she was a Demeter in the first act, she becomes a Persephone in the last. She reigns as Queen of the Dead, tenderly concerned for Barbara and Firs; but also, like Persephone, she will return to the world of the living, and when she does she will bring life back to the earth again. As she says to Anya, "I'll come back, my angel."

Thus the play has at its center a character who, seen only in her human and finite appearance, is the very picture of helplessness and ineffectuality, but who, in her mythic character, is actually that which sustains and renews the life around her. It is she, not Lopakhin, who triumphs, for Lopakhin, like all the others in the play, is only another one of the unhappy children on earth whom she gathers into her arms to comfort and console.

John Kelson, "Allegory and Myth in 'The Cherry Orchard'," in Western Humanities Review, *Vol. XIII, No. 3, Summer, 1959, pp. 321-24.*

J. L. Styan   (essay date 1962)

[*Styan is an English critic and educator who has written numerous studies of the theater, including the three-volume* Modern Drama in Theory and Practice *(1981). In the following excerpt, he undertakes a detailed explication of the fourth act of* The Cherry Orchard *in order to reveal the development toward the climax and subsequent denouement of the play.*]

The Cherry Orchard is a play which represents an attitude

to life under stress and a way of life in transition. The orchard itself summarizes the hopes and regrets, the desires and ideals of this way of life. Just as the orchard with the town on the horizon epitomizes all Russia, so the play in its structure at once encompasses the range of social class from landowner to domestic serf, and brings the past hard against the future in its three or four generations. It achieves in its design as wide a statement as a naturalistic play could hope to do.

In the last act of the play, this structure of change and decay is welded into a firm whole, both because its parts are here drawn together and because the sympathies of the audience are under careful restraint and precise control. In this act the crescendo of finely chosen discords is heard and felt with inimitable impact. The following account is written, not to repeat what is well known, but to discover how the impact is caused.

The mood of the act is conjured immediately with the rise of the curtain. It is late autumn and the cherry trees stand bare outside the window. The nursery is in a pitiful state of nudity, with fade-marks on the walls where the pictures were, furniture stacked or covered with dust-sheets, luggage waiting for removal. 'There is an oppressive sense of emptiness'. It was a brilliant stroke to have this final scene played in the nursery of Act I rather than in the drawing-room of Act III, not only to balance the arrival of the family with their departure, but also because a setting of birth and childhood challenges the affections of *all* the generations, young and old.

In the desert spaces of this room stands waiting the new master of the cherry orchard, now an embarrassed and rather lonely man, Lopakhin. Embarrassed because the family has always been unable to forget his peasant origins; lonely because he now realizes how he has hurt those he loved by taking from them what they loved. He waves his arms a little in nervousness; beside him stands Yasha with a tray of champagne, Lopakhin's offering of farewell, according to Russian custom. He has done what is expected, but coming from him this same champagne needles them all, except Yasha.

We in the audience take in the situation at a glance: this is a situation we can recognize and know from experience. We can fully understand, and thus sympathize with, this man in this position, but if we see him only at the level of one who has to speed the parting guest, the irony of his situation keeps us from a complete identity. We now see him as the merchant away from his merchandise, the shopkeeper out of his shop, fish out of water, for all that, as Chekhov told Stanislavsky, 'he must behave with the utmost courtesy and decorum, without any vulgarity or silly jokes . . . it must be borne in mind that such a serious and religious girl as Varya was in love with Lopakhin; she would never have fallen in love with some cheap moneymaker'. We see him in his 'white waist-coat and brown shoes' (this is Chekhov to Nemirovich-Danchenko now), taking long strides when he is lost in thought, stroking his beard back and forth. At this moment the comedy of his characterization half rises to the surface.

The irony of his situation is accentuated, too, because

Chekhov so carefully contrasts this scene with the last. Act III bustled visually to an emotional climax; Act IV is toned so much lower as to be almost an anticlimax. It offers a pause in its first few minutes for us to soak up its bitterness. We left Lopakhin in a drunken hysteria, proclaiming half in joy, half in self-reproach, 'Here comes the new landowner, here comes the owner of the cherry orchard!' He is now involved in the complexities of sentiment which surround the departing family, unable fully to grasp what we in our Olympian seats assimilate in a flash.

His helplessness is enacted when Mme Ranevsky, with her brother Gaev, enter feverishly, cross the stage quickly, and go off, leaving him standing there perplexed, offering them the champagne they have ignored: 'Have some champagne, please do, please!' We balance this gesture against the depth of feeling in Mme Ranevsky; yet, in its own way, it too commands our sympathy.

The exchanges which follow with Yasha and Trofimov are all to explore the nature of Lopakhin's embarrassment with that clinical eye which is to keep us alert to the meaning of his suffering. The same Lopakhin is there displaying his classical comic obsession: business-like in his appreciation of the cash value of the wine—'eight roubles a bottle', he tells Yasha; business-like in his time-keeping—'there are only forty-six minutes before the train's due to leave'. Though Chekhov uses him to supply one of his illuminating moments of the mood and atmosphere in the house with his 'It's devilishly cold in here', the practical man with his feet on the ground must add, 'Good building weather'.

Thus by suggestion we are told that Lopakhin is floundering, and the more he turns for reassurance to matters of money, of time and of business, measurable, accessible, firm and concrete things, the more we smile. Should we have wept to see him unable to cope with the huge and complex agony of a lost cause? So he puppets it back and forth across the bare stage, obeying the little laws of his own habits, while we weigh his inadequacy with mixed amusement against tender impressions sustained over three acts.

The image grows denser when Trofimov, with an incongruous air of efficiency and youthful egotism, enters echoing Lopakhin: 'I think it's time to start. The horses are at the door'. We begin to notice now how Chekhov applies pressure to our sense of time in this last act, squeezing out our sympathy for the general distress on the stage, while at the same time neatly indicating how little the 'eternal student's' assumption of command for the operation of departure is justified. Against Lopakhin's 'We must start in twenty minutes. Hurry up' is set the dubious 'I think . . .' of Trofimov. Especially since he is chiefly bothered because he cannot find his galoshes; and in a personal flutter he calls to the one least likely at this time to be able to help him—Anya (it is Varya who throws a pair of galoshes at him a few minutes later). The humble detail derides the total appearance.

However, Lopakhin is grateful to have someone, even someone he in his soul despises, to talk to at the moment.

Without being asked, he pours out his heart with an abrupt, 'And I must be off to Kharkov . . .'. Then follows a long speech during which he is talking only to himself. Meanwhile Trofimov continues to hunt among the luggage and ignore him, until a breathless pause from Lopakhin brings Trofimov to a halt. With a bitter look and a curt reply, Trofimov puts him in his place: 'We'll soon be gone, then you can start your useful labour again'. Trofimov can be cruel in a way that the family itself would never dare to be.

Lopakhin now begins to draw on our sympathy more warmly, and it is Trofimov who comes more under scrutiny. Lopakhin in a sudden gesture of friendship, prompted perhaps by guilt, offers some of the champagne which Yasha is busily quaffing alone upstage. He is curtly refused. A little quarrel flashes out, and the sparks of their slight differences in social class and their greater differences in wealth catch fire, reminding us dramatically that behind the emotionality of the farewell unquenched antagonisms still burn:

> LOPAKHIN. Well, well . . . I expect the professors are holding up their lectures, waiting for your arrival!
>
> TROFIMOV. That's none of your business.
>
> LOPAKHIN. How many years have you been studying at the university?
>
> TROFIMOV. I wish you'd think up something new, that's old and stale.
>
> Incidentally, as we're not likely to meet again, I'd like to give you a bit of advice. . . .

He goes on to criticize the 'wide, sweeping gestures' of Lopakhin's talk about building villas. We know that his criticism is really a criticism of himself, since he is the one who speaks in wide, sweeping gestures. We know, furthermore, that a Lopakhin who can buy the cherry orchard can also calculate precisely the profits from its summer residents. This is a farcical quarrel of tit-for-tat, but one with an ugly gist.

As if he suddenly realizes that he is dealing with a man of different calibre from himself, indeed that he may be saying things he will regret, Trofimov lets his anger die quickly. He sees that his comments on Lopakhin's personal behaviour have hurt far more than any criticism of his business methods: this attack on Lopakhin's social graces is of course a direct thrust at his class background. So Trofimov retracts and intuitively says the right thing, incidentally illuminating a little the mystery of the most complex character in the play: 'When all's said and done, I like you, despite everything. You've slender, delicate fingers, like an artist's, you've a fine, sensitive soul . . .'. We are reminded of Lopakhin's dreams in Act II, that men should be 'giants' to live in consonance with a country of 'vast forests, immense fields, wide horizons'.

They would then have parted friends, and the moral would have suggested itself, we may suppose, that there is a basis for progress and co-operation between opposing classes on grounds of human tolerance, and so on, and so forth. Chekhov indeed hints at the need to link industry with culture and culture with industry, as he does less obliquely in the mouth of Vershinin in *The Three Sisters.* But here Chekhov doesn't allow us any such immediate response. Lopakhin, in a final mistaken gesture of friendship, offers the younger man money for his journey—the sort of offer he might have valued himself in earlier days perhaps, an offer that makes sense to the practical man he is. Trofimov is of course touched on another raw spot. He sees Lopakhin's generosity as a further sign of the vulgarity that distinguishes them, and the quarrel again flares up. He tells a lie about having had a translation accepted in order to refuse with dignity. They are, we recognize, two of a kind in matters of personal pride.

So Trofimov the idealist speaks. He is a free man, money can mean nothing to him, and, with the grand, abstract sweep of the arm of one who has nothing to lose and everything to gain, he drops into cliché:

> Humanity is advancing towards the highest truth, the greatest happiness that is possible to achieve on earth, and I am in the van!
>
> LOPAKHIN. Will you get there?
>
> TROFIMOV. Yes. (*A pause.*) I'll get there myself, or show others the way to get there.

In that pause Chekhov allows just time enough to let the insidious irony seep back. During that moment of hesitation, Chekhov permits us to pin down all youthful revolutionary leaders with their own doubts: pathetic Trofimov becomes comic again, and Lopakhin makes his point. The vision of a glorious future clouds slightly, but it does not disappear, for we hear of it again with Anya. As if to mark the impression, the first sound of an axe cutting into a cherry tree is heard distantly off-stage. 'Life is slipping by', says Lopakhin in a real gesture of shared sympathy, and irreverently identifies Trofimov's grand rhetoric, as we have already done, with infinite numbers of us, and not merely in Russia: 'how many people there are in Russia, my friend, who exist to no purpose whatever! Well, never mind, perhaps it's no matter'. He at least feels happier for working hard—he slips into the pragmatic view of the practical man again.

These two in their characteristic duologue embrace the conflict in our own minds. They offer not merely a restatement of a class difference in society, or of youthful idealism corrected by a maturer wisdom, though this symbolism is there. For it is a mark of the darkness of the comedy that both of these characters are specimens of broken-hearted clown: neither can therefore teach us a complete truth or give us a final answer. In the acumen of the one and the optimism of the other, Chekhov points to a rooted error of judgment. Behind them both lies the fading nostalgic beauty of all the cherry orchard stood for when circumstances were different. Chekhov is not indicting the Russian merchant or the Russian intellectual, any more than he is telling us what fools Lopakhin and Trofimov are: Chekhov is more subtle than this. There is some truth in Lopakhin's view and some in Trofimov's. We are to imagine a blend of Lopakhin and Trofimov, perhaps together with a little of Anya's lack of affection and a good deal of Mme Ranevsky's heart. He is pressing us, in other words, to take a more balanced view. We are to discover that these two confused men are, like us, groping in a dark room while an unknown hand moves the furniture. Their differences of pragmatism and ideality are those that struggle within ourselves with each new experience that comes. If Chekhov leaves us in uneasy doubt about the righteousness of either, it is to encourage us towards impartiality; it is to induce a greater awareness of serious comic meaning in the extraordinary series of little episodes, particularities and attitudes that make up the *dénouement* of the play.

As if suddenly to reduce the scale of our view, Chekhov now places the manservant Yasha centre-stage and completes the little story of the triangle Epihodov—Dunyasha—Yasha.

Yasha would be the one unsympathetic character in the play were he not also a little comic, and one must ask the reasons for this. As Lopakhin represents the new aristocracy of business-men, so Yasha represents a new breed of underlings, the smart servants who cheat their masters and lord it over their equals. They astutely take advantage of the social changes that only bewilder their superiors. They grease their hair, Chekhov is saying, and, when they can, they smoke cigars and ape their betters. They can mesmerize silly girls like Dunyasha, and, for what they are worth, break their hearts. They despise the genuine affection towards the family of a domestic serf like old Firs. For Chekhov they sum up all that is *poshlost,* vulgar.

Somewhat indirectly, Yasha is to suggest what might happen to the minds of the other young people of the same generation, like Anya and Trofimov, had they too to fend for themselves in a commercial world. In this he is the complement of Lopakhin, illuminating a side of this character we would not otherwise see, the Smerdyakov facet of Dostoevsky's Ivan Karamazov, the Svidrigailev of his Raskolnikov. He is denied any of Lopakhin's sensitivity and generosity of spirit. Now a little drunk from champagne, he speaks with casual disrespect to Anya when she inquires whether Firs, his foil, has been taken to hospital: 'I told them to take him this morning. He's gone, I think'. But Anya knows Yasha too well, and calls to Epihodov, 'Semyon Panteleyevich, will you please find out whether Firs has been taken to hospital?' Yasha is not concerned. With the gentlest of touches, we are told incisively that the man is wholly egocentric and contemptuous of all about him.

This is confirmed when Varya calls that his mother has come to say goodbye to him before he returns to Paris. This reminder of his former life is unwelcome, and he shrugs off her old-fashioned sentiment with a superior air: 'She just makes me lose patience with her'. We may criticize this as altogether too strongly contradicting psychological truth: a rejection of a mother by her son shocks. It condemns him, and illuminates the impression that was dim before, that there is an amoral and destructive aspect of progress. Like Lopakhin's unwitting negation of what is personally delicate and living in the cherry orchard home, like the eliminating of the Mme Ranevskys who have their own contribution to make to the harmony of existence, subtle changes in the social order can tear up what is deep-rooted and valuable in human life.

Unlike some farcical intrusions into modern domestic comedy, Yasha's presence in the play is relevant to the whole. His part faintly echoes that of Lopakhin, for it shows us how silly ignorance may injure silly innocence. This is done lightly: the regrets and distress of Dunyasha, the pert maidservant, are her just deserts; there is no real suggestion that Epihodov's love for her has been mortally wounded—no melodrama here. In their miniature comedy, played very much in the remoter background, Epihodov is the sort who can say how much he envies Firs because he is 'beyond repair' and must soon 'join his ancestors', and this part, written for brittle comedy, written for the Russian comedian Moskvin, must exclude bitterness. In the same way, Dunyasha is quite an accomplished actress: she shams 'delicacy', falls too easily in and out of love, powders her nose, faints at appropriate moments, and so on. Her story must exclude tragedy, although it allows for pathos.

Nevertheless, all that Yasha stands for is thereby effectively diminished. He drinks his champagne in spite of the fact that 'it isn't the real thing', dreams of the journey in the express train, and longs for Paris where something is always 'going on', where there is less 'ignorance'. In view of the character who purveys these ideas, they are received by us only with scepticism. This is given open expression in laughter when Gaev enters, fixes one look on Yasha's hair, and says, 'Who's smelling of herring here?'

The late owners of the cherry orchard, Lyubov (Mme Ranevsky) and Gaev, are two lovable fools, held in affection by all around them. They now re-enter. 'In ten minutes we ought to be getting into the carriage . . .', and again we are reminded of time. Time was dogging us through the scene of the party in Act III, and now we realize that its pressure is not only of dramatic hours and minutes, but a poetic urgency fixing a paralysed attention on the treasure that is escaping. The loss of the orchard, prefigured from the outset, has grown in the imagery of the play to mean the loss of a whole way of life, with all the particularity of its hopes and frustrations, all the living experience of its memories and its expectations. There are ten minutes left for us, as it were, breathlessly to savour its sadness.

In the grip of a genuine nostalgia and a deep regret, Mme Ranevsky takes a last look round her nursery: 'Goodbye, dear house, old grandfather house'. With the simplest of epithets, Chekhov paints a picture of generations, while directly expressing the character's emotions. It would seem we are to expect an emotive sequel, flushed with sentiment. Yet there is an ironic edge to every gesture and statement which is to follow. Our view of the play remains carefully under control.

Lyubov's ardent kissing of Anya, with all her desire for her future happiness, hardly conceals the dilemma of a woman caught between her uncertain regret for the past and her uncertain hope for the future. She is not happy, but perhaps her daughter is:

MME RANEVSKY. Are you glad? Very glad?

ANYA. Yes, very. Our new life is just beginning, Mama!

GAEV (*brightly*). So it is indeed, everything's all right now.

Anya unaffectedly sees no past standing over her like a judgment as her mother does: she unknowingly clouds the nostalgic image of the dear past, and looks fearlessly forward to a bright future. But we sense that Anya is her mother as she was, and Lyubov is as her daughter will be.

Gaev's effort of gaiety confirms the ambiguities beneath the surface of their mood. Our impression of the inadequacy of Mme Ranevsky, for all her unselfishness, is here as elsewhere reinforced by the greater weakness of her brother. This man who has no money-sense at all, who let the orchard slip between his fingers also, is simulating happiness as obviously as she: we immediately recognize his instinct to console himself. He tells us that he is to become a bank-clerk, of all things, 'a financier'.

Passionately embraced and passionately embracing, Anya, the innocent who has yet to face the world of hard experience, dreams of Mama's return, of passing examinations and working hard . . . 'We'll read during the long autumn evenings, we'll read lots of books, and a new, wonderful world will open up before us . . .'. For a perceptible moment seventeen-year-old Anya reverses their roles; she is the little mother comforting Lyubov, till she relaxes into golden fancies. Almost symbolically the child curls up on the dust-sheet over the sofa, seeing with the bright eyes of youth, reassured by the caresses of the mother who tells her she will come back. We have the authority of the play's cumulative ironies to doubt what we see and hear.

In case we too grow sentimental over this imaginary prospect, too reassured by the archetype of mother and child, Chekhov plays an ace. He had brought in Charlotta, the German-bred governess, and has had her downstage, looking with our eyes at the scene. Now, half to cheer the company, it would seem, half to express her and our scepticism, she plays one of her tricks:

> (*Picking up a bundle that looks like a baby in swaddling clothes.*) Bye-bye, little baby. (*A sound like a baby crying is heard.*) Be quiet, my sweet, be a good little boy. (*The 'crying' continues.*) My heart goes out to you, baby!

This must strike us as a naughty burlesque of the pathetic exchange we have just seen, belittling and colouring the impression the other three have created. The burlesque is offered with less of the gentle, shaded touch so familiar in Chekhov, and more with that callous juxtaposition to be found later in works like Anouilh's *Point of Departure*. Chekhov feels it necessary to give a more severe shock to dispel the more subversive sentiment. It is Chekhov's command to us to return to earth, and it is enacted when Charlotta almost viciously throws the bundle down and says, 'Are you going to find me another job, please? I can't do without one'. She is practical, for we remember what she told us on the garden seat in Act II, that she does not know who her mother was, that she has no past, that she is alone—as Anya may well be.

By the matter-of-fact tone of her last remark, a moment of farce is turned to wormwood. 'You should only sit down to write', Chekhov told Bunin, 'when you feel as cold as ice'.

Pishchik, 'strong as a horse', eternally penniless, high with blood-pressure, puffing and sweating, is most part clown. He is an ineffectual landowner from another cherry orchard, and we are really unable to take his financial distresses seriously. His constant borrowing of money is his comic 'gimmick', and Gaev by his scuttling exit reminds us of Pishchik's apparent role in the play. He will enter now to provide us with some crazy horse-play perhaps, a little knock-about relief, 'what a phenomenon!' But he too has a calculated place in the pattern.

He blusters in, out of breath as usual, greeting Mme Ranevsky and Lopakhin, pouring a glass of water, fumbling in his pocket, swallowing a mouthful. Between his gasps for air and comic business with the tiresome glass, he drags from his pocket—a handful of notes! Too late he repays money that might have paid the mortgage interest on the unhappy estate. For in bewilderment he has found that science and progress have overtaken him unawares, to his advantage and amazement. In joy and confusion he explains what has happened: 'Wait a moment . . . I'm so hot . . . A most extraordinary thing happened. Some English people came to see me and discovered a sort of white clay on my land . . .'.

His perpetual simple astonishment at the phenomena of life around him is now given real cause for expression. Foreign capital was in fact being invested in Russia in the 1890's. Now indeed he can ridicule his naïve search for a philosophical justification for the forgery of banknotes—or taking one's own life. 'Just now a young fellow in the train was telling me that some great philosopher or other . . . advises people to jump off roofs. You just jump off, he says, and that settles the whole problem. . . . Fancy that!' Thus subtly, farcically, does the author drop a thought among the audience, brushing it off as soon as it has settled. The sequence of the dialogue suggests that Pishchik had thought for a gossamer moment of a resort to suicide: now providence has relieved him of the need, just as it had left her token, ignored, with Mme Ranevsky. Could this same thought have occurred to her? —oh, but no—we dismiss the idea: Chekhov is teasing.

As if to strengthen our feelings, Pishchik has dashed about the room, sat down, stood up, drunk his water and gone—at such a pace that we have hardly had time to assimilate the impression he leaves us with. He has gone without noticing that the family is on the eve of departure. Lyubov calls after him, and the pace abruptly halts as he turns back and looks unhappily about him. He sees the bare room at last. Something did not 'turn up' for them this time. His tone changes: 'Well, never mind. (*Tearfully.*) Never mind. . . . These Englishmen, you know, they're men of the greatest intelligence. . . . Never mind. . . . I wish you every happiness, God be with you. Never mind, everything comes to an end eventually'. Jumping off the roof was not so outrageous a notion after all—'everything comes to an end eventually'. What was stated in jest is now

echoed with deep embarrassment; the puppet becomes a man.

Pishchik's little scene, brief and funny and pathetic as it is, fits into the design. The comedy misleads us momentarily, but the contrast in the tempo of playing between the time of Pishchik's entrance and that of his exit again reorients by a fine degree the play's whole meaning. Pishchik's primary function is to introduce that recognizable element of fatalism into the structure of the life being demonstrated, though we remain free to dismiss it. The chance purchase of Pishchik's clay by the astonishing Englishmen is the counterpart of the sale of the cherry orchard: the positive and the negative of the same picture. Are we equally subject to chance? Only death is inevitable. Comic Pishchik epitomizes mankind faced with insoluble problems: in bewilderment he blusters with joy, and in the same bewilderment he frets in misery. It is all very droll.

Characteristically, Chekhov allows his good-hearted Pishchik a tender moment before he takes his departure from the play. This is quoted in all its subtlety, and without comment:

> And when you hear that my end has come, just think of—a horse, and say: 'There used to be a fellow like that once. . . . Simeonov-Pishchik his name was—God be with him!' Wonderful weather we're having. Yes. . . . (*Goes out, overcome with embarrassment, but returns at once and stands in the doorway.*) Dashenka sent greetings to you. (*Goes out.*)

The tiny tragedy of Charlotta is followed by the tiny comedy of Pishchik, and this in turn is followed by the tiny tragedy of Varya. But just as Charlotta could never of course have risen to any real stature, neither can Varya. Chekhov wrote to Nemirovich-Danchenko that she was to be 'a little nun-like creature, somewhat simple-minded, plaintive'. Plaintive, but still a comedienne: 'she is a crybaby by nature and her tears ought not to arouse any feelings of gloom in the audience' [David Magarshack, *Chekhov the Dramatist,* 1952].

Yet the sequence which follows that of Pishchik's exit moves into the friendly territory of common experience far enough to colour the action with a sufficient tincture of pathos.

First Mme Ranevsky gives us another reminder of time: there are but five minutes remaining. However, as she insists, there is still time enough to settle a final problem, that of Varya's future. It is firmly in the mother's mind, in spite of many protestations from the parties concerned, that Lopakhin must propose to her. 'We have another five minutes or so . . .'. A moment later: 'You'll hardly need more than a minute, that's all'.

Much of the comedy, and much of the pathos, of this episode rests upon counterpointing two senses of time: on the one hand, that which presses from without, the waiting carriage and the approaching train; and, on the other, the inner reluctance of Lopakhin, whose emotional indigestion makes it so impossible to hasten the passing of this most embarrassing moment. His scene with Varya is to be played so slowly as to make an audience conscious of an intentional dramatic meaning through tempo. The contrast with the quicker pace of Pishchik's speech and movement is to make us feel Lopakhin's own confusion of mind about time. When he looks at his watch and when he finally leaves the room in unseemly haste, we must be made to ask ourselves, were these actions the result of his anxiety for the family's prompt departure, or for his own? If this scene is to illuminate one more facet of the agony of the relentless advance of tomorrow, we must feel the state of Lopakhin's shuttlecock mind in wanting the moment to fly, and yet wanting it to stop. He asks only that human relationships may resolve themselves in natural harmony, for they will not obey the clock.

Chekhov's dialogue for this episode is masterly. With brevity, and yet with an adroit mustering of points in favour of a marriage, Mme Ranevsky is made to use all her feminine wit to accomplish a mother's last duty to a daughter. She excuses her for looking thin and pale. But this is only because she has no work to do—an appeal to a Lopakhin who would be expected to want an industrious wife. She tells him that her Varya cries a lot—an appeal to his protective sympathies. Finally she tells him that Varya loves him—an appeal to his masculine pride. '. . . And I just don't know, I just don't know why you seem to keep away from each other. I don't understand it'. She implies a question: what reason can you give for your delay?

Anton Chekhov and his wife Olga Knipper in Yalta, 1902.

What reason *can* Lopakhin give? We guess: although Varya is only adopted into the household to earn her keep as a housekeeper, perhaps an illegitimate daughter of Lyubov's husband, nevertheless, like Lopakhin's purchase of the cherry orchard, his marriage to Varya would perhaps be a glancing blow against social tradition, which he has always instinctively accepted. Lopakhin could never aspire to the manners and graces Varya has acquired in her years with Lyubov. A social barrier, however, is hardly used by Chekhov as a dramatic crux: there is to be no melodramatic gesture of defiance. The mother wants the marriage, as does the foster-daughter; but how strong are the ties that bind Lopakhin to the older respect for class? There is no defiance in his proposal, and Lopakhin remains human, humble, and no puppet. But he is equally reluctant to make a proposal of marriage because he is as shy as any man might be. Thus with sure control, Chekhov presents a socially symbolic situation under a wholly naturalistic guise, as he had done with Trofimov's poverty, Yasha's pertness, Pishchik's unexpected wealth. Neither Mme Ranevsky nor Lopakhin are aware of the forces present on the stage with them at this moment of decision.

> MME RANEVSKY. . . . I don't understand it.
>
> LOPAKHIN. Neither do I myself, I must confess. It's all so strange somehow. . . .

We feel Lopakhin's emotional immaturity and awkwardness compared with Mme Ranevsky's experience and grace. But the practical man will at last face the situation, and other members of the family are ushered out of the room, and Varya is called, while Lopakhin waits alone on the stage.

We are prepared for comic relief by the interminable pause that holds us in suspense after the exit of the mother. It is a pause redolent of the agony of making an irrevocable personal decision. We are held until we are ourselves self-conscious and Lopakhin's discomfiture is ours. So we are ready to laugh when we hear the 'suppressed laughter and whispering' of the others behind the door, and when in even greater embarrassment Varya enters pretending to hunt among the luggage: 'It's strange, I just can't find . . .'. It is with this new pause that the character of the scene begins to change, and a warmth of feeling begins to spread over it.

In a series of false starts, Lopakhin tepidly endeavours to make the bright opening gambit which might lead to the happy embrace of a potential bride and groom. But each time his leading questions only stress the misery of Varya's present position, and because she is the 'simple-minded, plaintive' little creature presented in the play, they lead her quickly to tears. He asks where she will go now that the family is leaving—she will go to the Rogulins to be a housekeeper. What is worse, her post will be seventy miles away—it might as well be in the antipodes. Husband and home will be left far behind, and for both Varya and Lopakhin a marriage must be contracted now or never. 'So this is the end of life in this house . . .'. Upon Lopakhin's saying this, Varya, in the anguish of nostalgia and longing, buries her tears furiously among the luggage. She has not dared to look at him.

Lopakhin has said the wrong thing, and he must start again. But the same nostalgia grips him too. As he looks out of the window, he sees the cold sun of autumn and feels the frost descending. With another of his fine imaginative strokes, Chekhov invokes the weather to epitomize the mood of the scene and at the same time extend and make articulate the feelings that surround the characters. The irony of Lopakhin's estimating the degrees of frost with the accuracy of a farmer, and of Varya's exasperated retort that their thermometer is broken, echoes painfully through a further long pause. Time rushes onwards.

Suddenly a voice, perhaps Epihodov's, calls his name, and Lopakhin is gone, his dilemma resolved for him. Varya is left to weep uninhibitedly with her face in a bundle of clothes. The precious moment is destroyed. How? By fickle accident, by the pressure of extraneous situation, certainly by a human inadequacy, perhaps by a deeper power of birth and blood, by all these things, by Chekhov's seeing life like this in such moments of time.

The idea of the mutation of things emerges through a succession of innumerable minute insights that are discovered to us. It will depend on what we contribute to the interpretation of this episode, however, and what these characters have grown to represent to us, if we are to see the scene as something more than an unhappy little fragment in two small lives that do not matter so very much; the rather pathetic surface of the action on this level will fail to affect us or the play. However, we are so well prepared for the anticlimax when it comes, that we must pay another kind of attention to its meaning.

The false starts and proprieties of the man, the gentility and discretion of the woman, our sense of the limitations of a conventional behaviour in such a situation as this, must vividly illuminate human weakness. Varya and Lopakhin, if indeed the busy man ever really wanted marriage, cannot make a sufficient adjustment to the requirements of change. Two small people who cannot see their position except subjectively, are shown buffeted by forces they cannot recognize, even less control. With an appalling irony, Varya, virtual mistress of the house, who had thrown her keys at Lopakhin's feet in Act III, must now go to the Rogulins 'to be their housekeeper, or something'. While she becomes a servant, he will be master. Against such a reversal, Lopakhin's well-meaning decorums are wholly misplaced, almost laughable. A pathetic loneliness, half-conscious maybe, is balanced by a comic awkwardness.

Chekhov is saying to us in as positive a way as he can without breaking his naturalistic convention, that the smashing of one order need not necessarily comprehend the end of an existing harmony of relationships, certainly not of individual happiness. He is inviting us to see the position with an objectivity denied to his characters. He does it by enlarging and emphasizing their feelings, and presenting these in the white light of their comic littleness.

Chekhov now crowds his stage in order to empty it at the curtain. This is his last opportunity to bring together his small host of characters with the cumulative impact of all their petty, but overwhelming, little troubles. Before he finally dismisses the world of the cherry orchard, its fragmentary impressions are to be blended into a total image.

The room fills with people, as it did in Act I when it was a springtime, happier time of homecoming: Varya, Mme Ranevsky, Anya, Gaev, Charlotta with her dog, Yasha, Epihodov, Dunyasha, with other servants and coachmen. Trofimov and Lopakhin will enter in a moment. The house bustles with life and urgency once more, but it is the urgency of departure. The attitudes characteristic of this or that generation, each with a contrasting outlook fixed upon the future or the past, are by simple strokes compressed into a tone of voice, a gesture, a familiar form of words, which seem to echo and re-echo from the far walls of the play till they merge into its sombre reverberations.

The mother who resigned herself so quickly to the failure of her plan that we suspect that she had hardly anticipated its success, says flatly, 'Now we can start on our journey'. But her heart is in the past. Anya, representative of a younger generation, happy at new prospects and widening experience, echoes her joyfully: 'Yes, our journey!' Equally unrealistic, she is living in the future. Gaev, overwhelmed with personal memories, is least in command of his feelings, and after his habit slips from sentiment into rhetoric: 'My friends, my dear, kind friends! Now as I leave this house for ever . . .'. Here it is dear old Gaev whom Chekhov permits to strike the seemingly false note of comedy, and it is emphasized by the girls who implore him to stop.

Amid all the activity of preparation and dressing and gathering of personal luggage, Mme Ranevsky sits centre-stage, silent and alone in a pool of quietness. By her stillness she catches our eye: 'I'll just sit down for one little minute more. I feel as if I'd never seen the walls and ceilings of this house before, and now I look at them with such longing and affection . . .'. She is sincere and articulate about her emotions, and suddenly this apparently featherweight heroine becomes solid for us: Chekhov uses her as his spokesman for the suffering, conscious and unconscious, of all. But only for that moment: she will be once more fussing about the luggage as soon as she hears her brother's voice take on the oratorical tone again. She tears herself out of her mood: 'Have they taken out all the luggage?' For us, the serious mood remains and continues under the surface of trivialities.

Now with inspired cunning, forcing us to enter into his peculiar war of nerves, the author has the most obvious comedian in the play, Epihodov, register his one truly fetching moment of pathos. As a result of Lopakhin's 'See that everything's all right, Epihodov', we digest the following exchange:

> EPIHODOV (*in a husky voice*). Don't worry, Yermolai Alexeyevich!
>
> LOPAKHIN. What are you talking like that for?
>
> EPIHODOV. I've just had a drink of water. I must have swallowed something.
>
> YASHA (*with contempt*). What ignorance!

Like Pishchik, Epihodov is allowed his feelings, however limited, before the end. But precisely because he has never before done other than make us mock at his emotion, his present frog in the throat startles us, just as it surprises Lopakhin and challenges Yasha. Yasha asserts his difference from the peasant by a characteristic remark of derision. This mild friction between the two servants adds nearly the last of the pieces to the jigsaw of class rivalries, here well thrust home by pressure of exceptional circumstances.

The limelight shines on Lopakhin too, for a last time. Again, Chekhov cleverly serves a double dramatic purpose by a single expedient.

> MME RANEVSKY. When we leave here there won't be a soul in the place. . . .
>
> LOPAKHIN. Until the spring.

Hearing the despondency in Lyubov's voice, he tries to respond with a brightly engaging comment. Like the realist he is, he is concerned with the present. But again he has said the wrong thing. In his odd effort to make amends, he has intensified her distress. Spring is when strangers will live where they live; spring is when the orchard would have been in blossom; spring was when they came home, only to leave again.

At this moment, Varya pulls an umbrella from a bundle. It flies up, and she seems to be about to strike him. In a gesture that catches our eye immediately, an echo of the incident with the billiards cue in Act III, Lopakhin's reaction summarizes in a flash his place in the pattern: he raises his arm to ward off the blow, and we are reminded of his peasant relationship with the family. Yet it also reflects his essential lack of confidence and the guilt he feels surging up as soon as he has spoken, that of his outrageous presumption in buying the estate. With a laugh, he promptly turns his instinctive fear into a little pantomime that relaxes the tension between himself and Varya and makes them friends again. Like the whole play, it is a token of confused emotions.

As a gesture, it is also a signal for renewed activity by everyone. Trofimov takes charge and orders the party into the carriage. Varya finds his galoshes at last—Chekhov leaves no detail unfinished. Trofimov has to put them on while still giving his orders—Chekhov deflates even his last assumption of dignity. Lopakhin efficiently counts the heads. Anya and Trofimov, the younger ones, leave first, hailing the future:

> ANYA. Goodbye, old house! Goodbye, old life!
>
> TROFIMOV. Greetings to the new life!

The older ones leave their lives behind them; youth has the world before it. The rest follow, Varya unwillingly, Yasha willingly, Charlotta coldly, Lopakhin warmly. Lyubov and Gaev are left alone, two small figures clasping each other in grief in the centre of the bare, blank stage.

With unparalleled simplicity of effect, Chekhov has his two forlorn puppets stand motionless in the deserted nursery. The cherry orchard is already forsaken, and they are the life that used to be. The lightness in Mme Ranevsky is now heavy, her feelings squeezed dry: and she says what the orchard and the house mean to her in explicit terms.

They express the salt and bitter taste, the uneasy ache of the experience of the whole play: 'Oh my darling, my precious, my beautiful orchard! My life, my youth, my happiness . . . goodbye! . . . Goodbye!' The orchard is the symbol for just those things: life, youth, happiness, and their passing. The symbolism is not a loose sentimentality: it is recognized in the astringency of our criticism.

They listen, as we do, to the excited cries from Anya and Trofimov impatient outside the house in the carriage, impatient to plant another cherry orchard. A world outside is calling, and another beyond that. Inside, the sobs of regret are counterpointed with the shrill calls outside, until Lyubov and her brother leave: 'We're coming . . . (*Both go out*).' The play is over; the point is made.

But is it? The curtain refuses to fall, and Chekhov tries his most daring stroke. For an age we sit looking at empty, half-lit space, while the master of pauses employs the longest pause of his career. We are to assimilate the implications of the drama by the tempo he ordains: '*The stage is empty. The sound of doors being locked is heard, then of carriages driving off. It grows quiet. The stillness is broken by the dull thuds of an axe on a tree. . . .*' The spirit of the cherry orchard is allowed time to seep into us, and by sheer radiogenic dramatics, we learn what it is to be left in a house when all have departed; we learn what it is to *be* that house and to feel the axe in our soul. There is no comedy here now: it is all twilight.

We wait again for the curtain to fall, but again it does not. We hear instead the shuffle, the slow shuffle of old feet, and we dimly discern Firs as he creeps in. The old servant has been left behind in the general confusion. He moves with difficulty to the door that has just been bolted, tries it unsuccessfully, and stumbles to the sofa covered with its dust-sheet. He sits. 'They forgot about me. Never mind . . .'. He is content, for the world outside no longer has any call upon him. Those of his generation cannot lose their cherry orchard now. At his age, neither past, present nor future have much meaning. With a final prick of comedy, almost a lifetime is compressed in his speech: 'I don't suppose Leonid Andreyevich put on his fur coat, I expect he's gone in his light one. . . . These youngsters!' He lies still, while once more we await the fall of the curtain.

Yet even now there is a last bold trump to play: '*A distant sound is heard, coming as if out of the sky, like the sound of a string snapping, slowly and sadly dying away.*' Just as Chekhov had gathered together his players for their last *ensemble,* visually gathering together the joy and the sadness, hope for the future and regret for the past, so he attempts to epitomize the mixture of all our feelings in one unearthly and inexplicable sound, the sound we heard, unexplained, in Act II. To interpret it is to interpret the whole play. The curtain falls slowly with this in our ears, this and the sound of an axe striking a tree in the orchard far away.

The teasing structure of **The Cherry Orchard** easily accounts for its misinterpretation by producers from Konstantin Stanislavsky onwards. Where Chekhov's effect rests on a knife-edge balance of comedy and pathos in so many details, it is only too easy to tip the play towards one or the other. By inclination the sentimental majority of us leans towards the emotionality of the passing of an order. The substitution of one world for another is an excuse for melodramatics. Yet Chekhov was constantly making a plea to redress the balance: 'I am writing about life . . . this is a grey everyday life indeed . . . but not an eternal whimpering'. He believed that a full, objective statement of what he saw of the behaviour of people would be sufficient to paint the unbiased picture he wanted. Although some may feel he should have made more direct statements, relying less on the vagaries of arbitrary mood of the audience, less on the caprices which abound in the theatre, to the end he preferred, as he said, to *show* us horse-thieves rather than condemn them.

Chekhov put on the stage a group of people. He made this the centre of attention; not events, unless they affected the characters; not characters, unless they were to disturb or cast a reflection on the group. His group lives by the commonplaces of life they display, and these carry the weight of the play. Thus he found a form for drama suited to the stage. He is accused of having no plot, but it is not the absence of plot, rather the presence of many little plots, suggestive phases of many little lives woven intricately together, that gives his play its careful, taut pattern in which every detail is intensely relevant. Every detail is relevant, that is, to the creation of that particular balance of sympathies which can recreate for an audience the fluid feel of life. It is not a gallows humour he offers, nor mere exuberance, but it embraces each of us in its restless appeal to truth.

On language in *The Cherry Orchard:*

In *The Cherry Orchard,* language is hardly shared by the characters. The merchant Lopakhin explains what the family must do in order to save their estate, but they cannot understand him. As the catastrophe nears, they expend themselves in useless dialogue calculated to distract them from reality. Even the student Trofimov, who expresses . . . Chekhov's own hopes for an ideal future, is an "eternal student" who knows nothing of life and whose high-sounding words are perhaps ludicrous. He says of his relationship with Anya:

> "We are above love. To avoid the petty and the illusory, which prevent our being free and happy—that is the aim and meaning of life. Forward! We are moving irresistibly toward the bright star that burns in the distance! Forward! Do not fall behind, friends!"

Anya, delighted, exclaims: "How well you talk!" And the emphasis surely is on the word "talk," an ironic emphasis since it implies the young man's own illusory condition. The same sort of substitution of talk for action is found everywhere in the absurdist theater. . . .

Joyce Carol Oates, in The Edge of Impossibility: Tragic Forms in Literature, *Victor Gollancz Ltd., 1976.*

J. L. Styan, "Naturalistic Shading," in his The Dark Comedy: The Development of Modern Comic Tragedy, *Cambridge at the University Press, 1962, pp. 59-126.*

Walter Kerr   (essay date 1969)

[*Kerr is an American dramatist, director, and critic who won a Pulitzer Prize for drama criticism in 1978. A longtime drama critic for the New York* Times, *as well as the author of several book-length studies of modern drama, he has been one of the most important and influential figures in the American theater since the 1950s. In the following excerpt, Kerr discusses the merits of Chekhov's and Stanislavsky's respective conceptions of* The Cherry Orchard.]

Now, here's a curious thing. **The Cherry Orchard,** perhaps all of Chekhov, cannot be truly sad *unless* it is funny.

I had never seen a Moscow Art Theater performance of **The Cherry Orchard** until the company paid a courteous visit to City Center, and I went with a half-dozen contending questions in my head. Chekhov had never liked what Stanislavski did with the play: the author insisted he had written a comedy and that the director had made tragedy of it. But the quarrel had ended in a terrible irony. Chekhov's comedy had apparently been scuttled, but Chekhov's reputation had been enormously enhanced. The production had been successful *against* its author. Why?

What comedy was missing? And what had Stanislavski put into its place with such authority that forever after the play would be seen as he saw it, would be duplicated and imitated time and time again until the entire world would think of Chekhov in terms that Chekhov himself detested?

I couldn't hope that a performance in 1965 would answer questions first raised in 1904. Though the physical staging might still be Stanislavski's—people might dance behind archways or nestle against haystacks as he had directed them to so long ago—at least two things were bound to have changed. New actors may try hard to echo a tradition of performance; but they cannot help bringing *themselves* into the tradition, which means they cannot help altering it in subtle ways. And the political and social changes in Russia since 1904 must, willy-nilly, have done something to the atmosphere. An institution may be revered and told to go on doing its work as before, no matter what aesthetic is being imposed upon newer playwrights and their playhouses. But what is happening on the street, or in an auditorium five blocks away, is bound to drift in through the stage doors, if only as an awareness. A change in the climate is noticed, and felt, even by an actor who is bundled protectively to his ears. Was there any chance at all now of estimating Stanislavski's original tone—and hence Chekhov's dismay with it?

In point of fact no one can be certain how much the interior intellectual life of **The Cherry Orchard** has changed color with regimes. One can suspect—but not prove—that the student Trofimov has gained earnestness with the years. Trofimov looks to a nobler future and makes impassioned speeches about it. He sees stupidity and corruption about him; he will have none of the old way of life; he expects that one day mankind will march boldly into a much purer dawn. Possibly the first actor who played the part saw some humor in it, as I now feel certain Chekhov did. Trofimov is, after all, as much a prattling dreamer as the sentimental, irresponsible, wool-gathering Gayev is. By the end of the third act he is going to look a good bit of a fool as he falls all over himself and tumbles downstairs in one of his temperamental fevers. But after a revolution any character who seems to have prophesied a revolution must inevitably acquire a small halo. The part is presently played as though Trofimov had spent time in the wilderness with John the Baptist and had come back clear-eyed, an accredited visionary. Has his stature as a seer grown week after week since 1917, without orders from above or without anyone's quite noticing it? The question is probably unanswerable, and must be passed.

But there was illumination aplenty, on other scores, in the production brought us. To begin with, the Moscow Art Theater feels its way toward rather more comedy in *The Cherry Orchard* than we who have heard Stanislavski's edict but seen little of his work are inclined to give it in our own performances. Indeed some of the comedy is surprisingly broad: the clerk Epikhodov is not merely accident-prone, breaking a billiard cue a moment after he has picked it up; he is a Dromio, unable to leave the stage without backing successively into three pieces of furniture which are by no means in his way.

There is comedy in the complacent money-grubbing of a corpulent neighbor, comedy in the way in which a servant who has risen above himself elegantly spits out his cigar ends, playful comedy in the determination of lovers not to be spied upon at sunset. The outer edges of the play are conceived lightly; not everyone anticipates doom.

But—and here no doubt is where Chekhov's blood pressure rose—there is no fatuity, no giddiness, no transparent thoughtlessness of a gently amusing sort at the center of the piece. When we come to the brother and sister who own the estate that is to be lost, and above all when the sister, Ranevskaya, lets her temper flare at the idealist Trofimov, we come to something that is as hard and inflexible as Medea's mighty will. In the Moscow Art production, Ranevskaya does not let a world slip through her fingers out of flightiness, or charming presumption, or a womanly affectation of being unable to cope with figures. She stands sturdy as a rock, surveying her diminishing world with alarmed but far-seeing eyes, an intelligently tragic figure who knows that she is about to be bent by the wind but is ready for it. When she lashes out at Trofimov for his endless prating of things to come, the scene is not a delightfully exasperated tussle of cross-purposes, an explosion of misunderstandings. It is a showdown. Willed death confronts willed hope, with countenances of granite.

Actually, there is nothing in the earlier portions of the play, nothing in the texture of the play, to justify so rigid and inexorable a duel. Ranevskaya is simply not a tragic figure. She has no purpose, no intention, no passion to make her one. It is the very purposelessness of her life, her ingratiating ability to circumvent decisions, that defines her. The business of turning her into Brünnhilde, or into a kind of dowager Prometheus, does not work. We look at her displaying so much keenness of mind and force of character and decide that she would not only have accepted the peasant Lopakhin's offer for the estate; she would have sat at the table with him and bargained until she had forced the price higher. If the present interpretation of the role is in the Stanislavski tradition, then this is the point at which Stanislavski overreached himself and outraged his playwright.

But there is a further consequence that interests me more. As the lady of the orchard becomes increasingly hardheaded, strong-willed, tragic, we feel less and less for her. At the center of the Moscow Art's *Cherry Orchard* there is little pity. The axes are closing in and we feel no sorrow. Ranevskaya will be dispossessed; but her plight will not move us.

It may be one of the distinguishing marks of Chekhov's work that tears come only when they are not asked for, only, in fact, when there is a sustained—if unrealistic—surface gaiety. The Ranevskaya who touches us will most likely always be the woman who puts the brightest, most impossible face on things, who dances and mothers and cajoles when she should be taking stock, who flies into a tantrum with a talkative student because she is temperamentally incapable of listening to anyone. A charmer, an optimist, inadvertently a fool.

When we see that her silken, impulsive, endearing evasions are funny because they are hopelessly out of kilter with the facts, when we laugh because she is helplessly prisoner of a grace that is now irrelevant but still a grace, when we cannot help smiling that she should mismanage things so adroitly, then we will feel sorry for her, too. Pathos cannot be bought with long faces; it is a reflex from having noticed something absurd that cannot change itself. At least I think it is in Chekhov.

Why, then, was Stanislavski's *Cherry Orchard* so successful, so successful that its mood has been imposed upon most productions of Chekhov for sixty years? The Moscow Art Theater production seems to give us an answer to that, also. It is filled—even now—with a superb sense of continuing life, of dancers who go on dancing even after the ballroom doors are closed, of old servants who must surely be in the kitchen when they are not actually before our eyes, of restless footsteps going up and down stairs we never see and no doubt pacing the floor above us though we never hear a sound above. The people of the production are busy with themselves. They leave the scene with something in mind; when they return, their eyes have changed as eyes do when something that needed doing has been done. Nothing is ever forgotten. The probabilities of the day behind and the night ahead are constantly in mind; they fill the personalities we learn to recognize with a twenty-four-hour history. No actor seems to reflect on anything that is not in the play. The play fully occupies its residents. They are never going to be anywhere but in it.

The physical, visual, aural, tactile echoes are overwhelmingly dimensional. You could walk with Varya, in her black dress and with the keys at her belt, throughout the house and never see her work finished. The stage is composed of planes, receding infinitely. There is no corner you could look around and see only scenery. I don't think I have ever attended a production in which the naturalistic flow of event was so matter-of-fact that there was no event at all, only the indisputable comings and goings of the of-course people, the people who of course live there, always have. Where else should they be? How else should they dispose themselves?

Chekhov ought to have complained. And the production ought to have been as successful as it was.

The theater plays tricks like that.

Walter Kerr, "Chekhov and Others," in his Thirty Plays Hath November: Pain and Pleasure in the Contemporary Theater, *Simon and Schuster, 1969, pp. 146-83.*

Bernard Beckerman   (essay date 1971)

[*An American critic and educator specializing in the field of drama, Beckerman wrote* Dynamics of Drama: Theory and Method of Analysis *(1970) and served as the editor of the "Theater and Dramatic Studies" series published by UMI Research Press. In the following essay, he contrasts dramatic analysis and literary interpretations of* The Cherry Orchard, *maintaining that most critics fail to acknowledge the distinction.*]

Peter Trofimov is a contradictory fellow. He attacks the depressing habits of Russian life and prophesies happiness to come. Articulate and idealistic, he expresses what lies beyond the felling of the cherry orchard. But he also takes a condescending tone towards others, quite convinced of his superiority. Priggish and insensitive, he exhibits a ludicrous obliviousness to primary human concerns. The Soviet critic, Vladimir Yermilov, considers him "good for nothing." Admittedly Peter has a positive side, for he does help Anya to face the future, but he himself does not "belong to the progressive fighters for future happiness" [Yermilov, *Anton Pavlovich Chekhov*]. [In *The Breaking String*] Maurice Valency eschews such doctrinaire judgment. For him Trofimov is "lovable, believable, and a little ridiculous . . . [yet not] altogether healthy." "For all his earnestness, [he is] merely another passionate drifter in the universities, a member of that intelligentsia which he himself derides . . . for its laziness and lack of purpose."

Neither Yermilov nor Valency allude to two passages that I consider particularly significant for an understanding of Trofimov. Twice in the play Trofimov has an abrasive exchange with the merchant Lopakhin. Neither exchange is more than half a dozen speeches long. Yet their importance exceeds their duration. The first occurs in Act II. Trofimov, Anya and Varya have just joined the older people at an abandoned chapel near the cherry orchard. Lopakhin teases Trofimov for being a perennial student. Peter responds curtly, "Mind your own business." Lopakhin persists, and then asks "What's your opinion of me?" Peter responds by comparing him to a beast of prey. There is general laughter. The second exchange occurs in Act IV immediately after Trofimov joins Lopakhin in the old nursery. Again Lopakhin teases him for being a perennial student, again Trofimov tells the merchant to mind his own business, and when irritated further, again anato-

mizes Lopakhin, this time commenting on his behavior and his aspirations. In the middle of his remarks, however, Trofimov interrupts himself and then says, "Anyway, all the same, I like you. You have fine, delicate fingers, like an artist, you have a fine, delicate heart—" Lopakhin senses the change of tone, for he immediately interrupts Trofimov with an embrace.

The two exchanges are remarkably similar and yet different. Although the second is shorter than the first, their structures are parallel. Lopakhin teases, Trofimov rebuffs him, Lopakhin persists, Trofimov criticizes him. The major difference between the two passages occurs when Trofimov checks himself and expresses affection for Lopakhin. Chekhov prepares for this change in a subtle way, untranslatable into English. During the first exchange, when Trofimov tells Lopakhin: "Mind your own business," he employs the second person plural. In the second exchange he repeats the same line, but utilizing "thy," the intimate form of address. Both in the broader structure as well as in this small detail, Chekhov shows care in juxtaposing these two passages precisely. What did he wish them to express?

Robert Brustein is one of the few critics to refer to these exchanges between Trofimov and Lopakhin. [In *The Theatre of Revolt* (1962) he] treats the first, where Trofimov calls Lopakhin a beast of prey, as evidence that Trofimov is wrong in his assessment of Lopakhin and the second as evidence that despite his error Trofimov does "in a more generous moment" appreciate Lopakhin's finer side. In effect, he adopts an image of an unchanging Trofimov whose views on Lopakhin are hardly modified in the course of the play. Of the parallel structure of the two exchanges, nothing is said. In this Brustein exemplifies the practice we find fairly common among critics, a practice that can be seen even more clearly in David Magarshack's comments on Trofimov. [In *Chekhov the Dramatist,* 1960] Magarshack, who is a knowledgeable and sensitive interpreter of Chekhov, draws a full scale portrait of Peter. "The only idealist in the play, . . . [he is] essentially a comic character. His exterior itself is comic. . . . But his outward appearance is merely a pointer to the deepseated comic streak in his nature. He is 'an eternal student' . . . eternal adolescent . . . reason means everything to him and experience nothing. . . . [Although] a queer fellow . . . [that] does not prevent [him] from having a great aim in life." It is through his mouth that "the theme of hard work as the key to future happiness is expressed." What we see exemplified in Magarshack and what we found in the previous summations of Trofimov's character is the static quality of the descriptions. Here I am not concerned with the interpretations these critics offer so much as with the *way* they express their interpretations. They are interested in what Peter *is,* not what experience he *goes through*. Their descriptions stress *being,* not *doing,* a fixed nature not an evolving one. From the variety of circumstances in which Trofimov is involved, they select a mosaic of lines and incidents to illustrate a finished view of his character. I would like to offer another mode of description, one that defines a character by his encounters not his sentiments.

When Trofimov interrupts himself in Act IV and then addresses Lopakhin warmly, he reveals a sensitivity to someone else's nature for the first time in the play. He finally accepts Lopakhin for what he is, no longer judging him by austere and rather arrogant standards. How he arrives at this point can only be understood by tracing the events that lead from the one exchange in Act II to the other in Act IV.

The second act, from the entrance of Trofimov, Anya and Varya to the end, can be divided into two major segments. The first segment deals with the gathering of the Ranevsky household at the abandoned chapel. They talk, they fall silent, they hear a "breaking string" in the distance. A stranger intrudes upon them. Mme. Ranevsky refers to Varya and Lopakhin's marriage. They depart leaving Trofimov and Anya behind. All of this is arranged in a carefully modulated pattern of activity that has the appearance of rambling talk. Let us not consider, however, the subject of this talking, but the kind of event the talking produces and the sequence it follows.

As human activity, their talking can be classified as pleasurable indulgence in speech making or, in stage terms, that special Chekhovian activity of speechifying. First, at the urging of the women Trofimov delivers a lengthy oration on the state of human affairs. He compares a utopian future to the present shiftlessness of the Russian intelligentsia, concluding with a call for silence. Lopakhin carries on one of Trofimov's themes, the necessity for work, but he begins in a more personal vein only to slip into rhetorical bombast. He is deflated by Mme. Ranevsky. In the silence Epikhodov, the inept accountant of the estate, passes by. The old uncle Gaev addresses a third speech to astonishing nature, but in turn he too is interrupted by Anya and Varya. After a long silence two brief declamations follow. One is delivered by an intruding passer-by. The second, in the form of a slightly distorted quotation from *Hamlet,* is pronounced by Lopakhin. After Mme. Ranevsky tells Varya that her marriage to Lopakhin has been arranged, Lopakhin intones: "Akhmelia, get thee to a nunnery," and goes on to "Nymph, in thy orisons. . . ."

Together these five "speeches" provide the structural support for the scene. As the action proceeds, each becomes progressively shorter and more extravagant. A serious deeply felt passion pervades Trofimov's speech. Similarly, Lopakhin begins his observations in a straightforward, common sense manner, only to leap into high style with his address: "Lord, thou gav'st us the great forests. . . ." Gaev directly invokes Nature in his customary rhetorical manner. The passer-by, in effect, parodies their declamations with his call: "Brother, suffering brother. . . ." Lopakhin's quotations from *Hamlet* are the final reduction of speechifying to absurd and senseless mockery. All these speakers have the purpose, as Trofimov observes, of diverting attention from themselves. The talk is entertainment, nothing more, as we can readily deduce from the attitude of the listening women. They treat Trofimov's words as clever, fashionable diversion, Gaev's invocation as tiresome fustian.

Counterbalancing this urge to talk endlessly is an impulse to end talk. After his speech, Trofimov calls for silence.

Mme. Ranevsky's interruption of Lopakhin is followed by silence again during which Epikhodov strolls past, strumming his guitar. Finally, the interruption of Gaev's praise of nature is followed by a pervasive stillness.

> All sit absorbed in thought. Silence. The only sound is FIERS muttering to himself softly. Suddenly a distant sound is heard, as if from the sky, the sound of a breaking string, sadly, dying away.

Here is the crux of the segment. Once the characters give themselves to silence, they are vulnerable to the ominous, intangible foreboding that fills the atmosphere. They guess at the source of the sound. Mme. Ranevsky shudders. Fiers recalls having heard the same sound just before the troublesome days when the serfs were emancipated. There is silence again. All prepare to leave, but are stopped by a passer-by who uses declamation as a beggar's ploy and after begging successfully, laughs at them. Thus, the impelling forces of the segment can be described as consisting of two contrasting urges: one, to speechify, the other, to yield to silence. The speeches get shorter and shorter, the pauses lengthen until they overwhelm the characters. Paralleling this action-pattern is another contrasting shift. The speeches move from a serious to a comic, even grotesque, tonality while the silence moves from a comic irony (Trofimov calling for silence after his long speech) to a somber and ominous apprehension.

In the last major segment of Act II, Trofimov, now alone with Anya, returns to his speechifying. This time he addresses her directly so that his style is more personal than it has been. Nevertheless, the same interplay exists as before. Proclaiming that they are "above love," Trofimov elaborates on the contrast between past and future. He talks about living in the present but can only look behind or beyond. Anya is thrilled by "how well you speak!" To his appeal, "Be free, like the wind," she replies in rapture, "How well you say it!" It is obvious that she is in love with his eloquence and the idealism it arouses, and therefore, happy in the present. She finds the night wonderful, she is aware of the rising moon, later she wants to go down to the river where it is lovely. Although Trofimov and Anya talk to each other, it is clear that they are in touch with different planes of experience. He is wrapped in "inexplicable visions of the future," she imbibes the romance of high flown words ringing in the moon-filled night. Insensitive to her mood, he repeats "Happiness is coming. . . ." They are interrupted by Varya's call for Anya. He repeats his prophecy that happiness is on its way, approaching nearer and nearer. Again Chekhov introduces a comic touch, for it is Varya who comes nearer and nearer, calling "Anya, where are you," naming for him, if he were only aware, an immediate source of happiness. In this manner Chekhov recapitulates the movement from serious persuasion to heady bombast, revealing thereby the ironic divorce between words of men and the language of nature, and showing Trofimov to be a faintly ridiculous fellow who fails to see any connection between what he says and what exists before him.

In Act II then, Chekhov reveals the most compelling aspects of Trofimov's idealism: his articulateness, his ability to stir Anya's soul, and his priggish superiority to such tender feelings as love. But already Chekhov reveals the other side of his loquacity and idealism. The attack is oblique. Trofimov speaks about work. Lopakhin works. But he too is bitten by the rhetorical bug. The case is not simple. Trofimov is not a fool, yet he is not wholly to be taken seriously. By the progressive satirization of speechifying, Chekhov casts doubt on the value of Trofimov's words without undermining his ideals.

In the third act, Trofimov's superiority towards others is manifested once again. He teases Varya, mocks Pishtchik, and lectures Mme. Ranevsky. With Mme. Ranevsky, this superiority finally encounters a resistance strong enough to unnerve him. Mme. Ranevsky wants him to understand a heart aching with love. At first she asks him to be less unkind to Varya, unhappy because Lopakhin reveals no signs of an inclination towards her. Trofimov scorns Varya who has misinterpreted his attitude towards Anya: he is above love. Mme. Ranevsky interprets his reply as a criticism of herself, finally asking him for comfort as she waits for word about the sale of the estate. He insists she face the truth. What truth? She isn't as sure of the truth as he seems to be. What she pleads for is sympathy. "Pity me," she weeps. He utters words of sympathy, but in tones of disapproval, for she observes, "But it must be said in another way, another way. . . ." This is a turning point. She criticizes him gently, then confesses how deeply she adores her man in Paris who has made her suffer so much. Sensing Peter's disapproval, she once again pleads with him not to condemn her, but he attacks her lover. They quarrel. She mocks him for his ridiculous behavior. Above love? He's not above love. He's a fool. "At your age not to have a mistress!" Shocked, disconcerted, he mutters to himself, throws two or three sentences at her, "All is over between us," and goes out, promptly to fall down a flight of stairs. This is the last word Trofimov speaks in Act III. Thereafter, we see him dancing with Mme. Ranevsky and at the very end of the act we see him observe how Anya comforts Mme. Ranevsky with words he taught her.

The structure of this sequence is a product of Mme. Ranevsky's longing for humane sympathy coming into conflict with Trofimov's determination to judge others according to idealistic yet uncompromising standards of behavior. These standards, unfortunately, make him insensitive to the personal needs of others. Mme. Ranevsky thinks he merely lacks a sexual outlet, but Trofimov's real failure is his unwillingness to recognize the claims of affection, whether sexual or non-sexual. When Mme. Ranevsky punctures Trofimov's manner, the result, as so often in Chekhov, is a comic denouement to a serious clash. Trofimov's fall downstairs is only the external expression of an inner explosion. It quiets him so that he no longer speaks. Instead, he is content to receive a lesson in human tenderness. Not the word spoken but the tone used truly comforts.

The next time we meet Trofimov is at the beginning of Act IV. Now that Lopakhin has bought the cherry orchard, everyone is leaving the estate. Trofimov enters the partly vacated nursery looking for his galoshes. Lopakhin is there. Keeping the first exchange between Trofimov and

Lopakhin in mind, we see that in echoing its structural pattern, Chekhov is deliberately pointing up the change in Trofimov. At first Lopakhin's teasing and Trofimov's irritation seem to indicate that nothing has altered. This impression is further supported when Trofimov starts to criticize Lopakhin once again. But then Trofimov stops. An ellipsis in the text makes it quite clear that the actor must alter the tone of his voice, whether by a shift in timbre, inflection, rhythm, or all three. Just as in Act III Chekhov depends upon the actor's voice to convey the contrast between Trofimov's words of sympathy to Mme. Ranevsky and his tone of criticism, so in Act IV he depends upon the actor to reveal the change within Trofimov that has occurred since the end of Act III. For the first time in the play Trofimov speaks intimately to another person. The change is further reinforced by Trofimov's subsequent announcement to Lopakhin that he has earned money translating a book. He has stopped talking and started working.

Chekhov casts additional light on Trofimov in the curious and superb way he dramatizes Trofimov's relationship to Anya in Act IV. Oddly enough, they do not exchange a single word. Nevertheless, Chekhov creates the definite effect that they are in harmony with one another. The harmony is not necessarily physical. He is off to Moscow, she off to study. Will they be together in the future? Who knows? It is sufficient that at this point in their lives they are in accord. Chekhov achieves this impression of unity in an extremely oblique manner. First, they are both engaged in the same sort of activity, getting people out of the house. They display similar kinds of energy in checking on details and calling on others to leave. Secondly, they have four pairs of speeches. In each of the pairs Anya speaks first and Trofimov reinforces or extends what she says without speaking directly to her. Anya asks Lopakhin not to start cutting down the cherry trees before her mother leaves. Trofimov reinforces her remarks by admonishing Lopakhin: "You really might show more tact." The second pair expresses their farewell to the house:

> ANYA. Good-bye house. Good-bye, old life.
>
> TROFIMOV. Welcome, new life. (*Goes out with Anya*)

The third and fourth pairs are identical. From off stage Anya calls "Mama" and Trofimov echoes with a cry of joy. It is true that the details of their personal lives remain hazy, but their spiritual life is vigorous. They are free of the crippling effects of speechifying, and eager to work appropriately for the future.

From the close scrutiny of Trofimov's experiences in the play, we can readily see the fallacy of drawing a static character sketch of him. At first he is both idealistic and ridiculous, a talker not a doer. But in the course of the action he is purged of his vain pretensions. He becomes capable of personal affection and though not completely freed of grand speeches, he can assert modestly, as he does when Lopakhin asks if he will ever accomplish his utopian goals, "I'll get there or show others how to get there." No longer does he use words to entertain Anya. Indeed, in each of the four parallel passages cited, Anya is the first to speak. Without conversing they convey a common purpose and strength.

Although my reading of the foregoing events may appear to be interpretive, it is not so in actuality, as a close scrutiny of the text will show. I regard the reading as essentially descriptive. In the main it keeps to the work as written. It does not seek to create the effect of the play but to define the structural pattern of the action. This aim, however, runs contrary to widespread literary practice. American critics by and large tend to distrust "objective" structural analysis of the drama. Symptomatic of such distrust is Robert Jackson's introduction to a collection of critical essays on Chekhov [*Chekhov: A Collection of Critical Essays,* 1967, edited by Robert Jackson].

In the course of summarizing the various essays, Jackson compares the work of S. D. Balukhaty ("*The Cherry Orchard:* A Formalist Approach") with that of Francis Fergusson ("*The Cherry Orchard:* A Theater-Poem of the Suffering of Change"). Although Jackson feels that there is much to recommend Balukhaty's formal method, he acknowledges that many will find it unsympathetic, for Balukhaty "divorces analysis of structure and device from poetic ideas and meaning." By comparison, "Francis Fergusson's sensitive analysis of poetic structure and device . . . appears almost as a living thing beside Balukhaty's hard algebra of criticism." And indeed Fergusson does evoke a poetic vision of "suffering of change." In his interpretive scheme of *The Cherry Orchard,* the second act is the agon which embodies awareness of such suffering. His detailed discussion of the gathering at the chapel stresses the atmosphere of the scene, that is the longings and emotional contrasts in the characters. By doing so he supplies a sensitive sketch of the dramatic effect that this act *can* have upon a reader or a spectator. In effect, he offers a literary equivalent of a stage performance. But he does not provide a satisfactory description of what *is happening* among the characters. For instance, he treats the silences perceptively, but fails to give due consideration to the nature and purpose of the speeches. Nor does he adequately trace the modulations of tragedy and comedy. In fact, his stress upon mood tends to cast a pall of unrelieved somberness upon the action which obscures the shifts from tragic to comic tonalities. In preferring this "sensitive analysis of poetic structure" to Balukhaty's "hard algebra," Jackson reinforces the prevailing taste for sensibility and the prevailing distrust of schematic approaches. Unfortunately, such distrust stands in the way of refining the tools of dramatic analysis so that they will have sufficient flexibility to overcome the rigidity of formalism and yet adequate preciseness to enable critics to distinguish between structure and effect. Admittedly, Fergusson's essay is a superior example of literary interpretation. But I am less concerned with interpretation and more concerned with the primary processes of analysis out of which interpretation springs.

The basis for a sound dramatic analysis is significantly different from the practice of literary interpretation, at least as exemplified by Fergusson. After summarizing the second act of *The Cherry Orchard,* he compares it to Canto VIII of Dante's *Purgatorio.* "The action is the same; in both, a childish and uninstructed responsiveness, an unpremeditated obedience to what is actual, informs the suffering of change." He sees a similarity between the rhythms and pauses of the poem and the play, finding the mode of awareness in Dante the Pilgrim similar to that in Gaev when, just prior to invoking Nature, he announces that the sun has set. Again, let us examine the method rather than the conclusion of his comparison. Implicit in such a comparison is the assumption that artistic effect is independent of artistic form. A poem and a play, two quite distinct forms of expression, can produce identical effects, Fergusson indicates. A further assumption is that the unified context of a poem corresponds to the diffused context of a play such as *The Cherry Orchard.* Dante's mode of awareness, as part of a literary progression, is a central event in the poem; Gaev's "awareness," to the extent it is separable from that of the other characters, is only one aspect of a mosaic of responses, the impact of which depends upon the context of a larger action. But both of these assumptions can be summed up in one overriding assumption. In linking Chekhov to Dante, Fergusson is joining poet to poet. For him *The Cherry Orchard* is a poetic achievement.

In taking this position Fergusson is not unlike G. Wilson Knight who [in *The Wheel of Fire,* 1930] felt that the metaphoric reality of Shakespeare's plays existed above and somewhat independent of the dramatic form. Both critics, not unfamiliar with theatrical production themselves, abdicate their responsibility to illustrate the workings of dramatic art. When Fergusson states that Chekhov can create a "single action with the scope, the general significance or suggestiveness, of poetry," he does nothing more than bestow an accolade upon Chekhov's ability to express a complex action. In such a sentence the term poetry has a purely *evaluative* significance; it is a synonym for profound goodness. But Fergusson uses the term in a more technical sense, as evidenced by his reference to "the rhythms, the pauses, and the sound effects" of both writers. It is here that his comparison breaks down. It may be that quite different aesthetic forms or, for that matter, quite different life experiences can arouse similar responses in us. But this similarity is apparent only in *isolation,* as single analogous moments. Artistic events occur in context, however, and the context of *poetry-as-a-form* is significantly distinct from the context of *drama-as-a-form.* In the context of poetry Dante's awareness emerges as an acute sensitivity to the nuances of day and hour, a sensitivity that links together the far flung sailor and the departing pilgrim. In the context of drama, Chekhov, utilizing an analogous mood, depicts not the mood itself but the way various characters encounter it, setting against the sense of the dying day the impulse to resist and alter it. Conceived as *poetry,* Gaev's "awareness" is a moment of static sensibility. Conceived as *drama,* it is a spring board into embarrassing sentimentality. Its final effect depends on sequence (contrasting steps in Gaev's behavior) and relationship (his attitude in comparison to the reactions of others) as manifested through the thrust of the actor and the corresponding energies of the other performers. To achieve a comprehensive sense of such a context, a critic cannot base his conclusions upon the habits of literary interpretation, but upon sound analytic processes peculiar to the dramatic mode.

These analytic processes, I admit, are difficult to separate from interpretation because in most instances, analysis and interpretation mingle in a critic's mind. Nevertheless, there are distinctive methods of dramatic analysis that can be stated, transmitted, and employed in teaching, production and criticism. They are not nor need to be "hard" or "algebraic." In fact, they should be simultaneously "objective" and intuitive, systematic and flexible. In tracing Trofimov's development, I looked at what was happening, not merely at what was said. I kept to the exact sequence of events rather than ignored sequence to suit a particular theme. With Chekhov especially, it is not enough to examine the attitudes and views of the characters. Even more important, it is necessary to analyze the type and form of segments as well as the relative emphasis he places upon each segment. This principle is immediately evident when one attempts to answer the question: what is *The Cherry Orchard* about? Is it about the loss of the estate, and by extension, about the passing of an old order? Well, yes—and no.

The cherry orchard—its loss and the meaning for the family—is certainly prominent in the action. On one hand, the fate of this property is the crucial event of the play. On the other, Chekhov treats its sale as much background as foreground. If one were to calculate how much of the play is devoted to the imminent loss of the orchard, one would find that it occupies a relatively small portion of the action. In the first act there is one substantial segment and about five speeches that deal with the subject. In Act II there are two short segments and one speech. The fullest treatment of this motif occurs in Act III where there occur twelve short speeches and a climactic scene when Lopakhin reveals his purchase of the estate. During the last act there are a few references to the loss although, of course, the entire act is suffused with awareness of it.

By contrast, more time is devoted to the various love affairs, abortive and otherwise, that abound in the play. There are four relationships that reveal contrasting aspects of love between man and woman: Mme. Ranevsky and her lover in Paris, Trofimov and Anya, Varya and Lopakhin, and finally a triangle, Dunyasha the maid, Yasha the valet, and Epikhodov. There is a further hint that Lopakhin has an especially deep affection for Mme. Ranevsky although this liaison is implicit rather than operative. Act by act, Chekhov reveals periodic glimpses of the state of these relationships: in one, the promise of a fulfilment that seems likely but that never comes; in another, the shabby consummation and dissolution of a back stairs intrigue. These love affairs parallel the unfolding fortune of the estate. Sometimes they echo, sometimes they counterpoint the problems of saving the orchard. How ironic it is that Lopakhin's efforts to persuade Mme. Ranevsky to cut down the cherry trees is a reverse enactment of Mme. Ranevsky's futile attempt to get him to marry Varya. It is through the contrasts in the ways these people deal with love and business that Chekhov evokes the rich complexity of life. To grasp its full range, we need a far more subtle instrument of dramatic analysis than we now have.

Because dramatic presentation is a personal, aesthetic experience achieved through a social act, an adequate method of dramatic analysis requires the synthesis of a wide variety of disciplines. The influence of verbal analysis—imagery, meter, rhythm, linguistic conventions—is already strong. What is now being channeled into the new mode of analysis are techniques derived from the stage. The means by which a skillful actor or director dissects a script and discovers the flow of action are necessary tools in any competent dramatic study. Essentially, they identify the rhythmic units of action and the distinctive sources of energy that provide the interaction among characters.

A greater, and potentially more significant, synthesis is required, however. Half of our task is to achieve an adequate description of the interaction between performer and playgoer, for the art of the theater lies in that interaction. The other half is to enlarge the comparative study of dramatic forms in order to distinguish how recurrent patterns of action are developed and altered by successive dramatists.

To make progress in either half of this task, we shall have to turn to nonliterary disciplines for information and stimulation.

First, we need to learn more about perceptive processes. The pioneer studies of the Gestalt school have been absorbed and modified by successive psychologists, and in fact the philosophical implications of these perceptual studies have had a major influence upon contemporary structuralism. Since most of these studies have stressed visual perception, it is to be expected that their findings would be applied to the analysis of visual response in the fine arts. E. H. Gombrich and Rudolf Arnheim have shown how experimental results can illuminate our understanding of both the creative and appreciative processes. The stress on visual perception, however, limits the relevance of these studies for the theatre. Fortunately in the last few years, psychologists like J. J. Gibson and Jean Piaget have broadened their treatment of perception, and have shown how perceptual organs function as perceptual systems. Their efforts can be of immense importance to dramatic analysis if they succeed in describing how the visual, auditory, and haptic systems absorb presented objects and events.

Secondly, we need to examine theatrical response as an aspect of learning, which in turn depends upon our understanding the processes of knowing. Here the ideas of Michael Polanyi can be invaluable in discriminating modes of cognition. In his exploration of the tacit dimension, for example, Polanyi distinguishes between peripheral and focal awareness of an object, showing how learning mediates between the two levels of attention. This distinction is of first importance for our understanding of theatrical perception. Applied to *The Cherry Orchard,* for instance, it helps to explain the relative degrees of attention we give to the motifs of financial hardship and thwarted love. As we attend to the play, the impending loss of the orchard is brought into focus from time to time, but for much of the action it remains in the background. We are aware of the problem peripherally at the same time as we are focally concentrated on the various situations involving love or aspirations for the future. Exactly how these levels of awareness are related to each other and how together they produce the effect of complex reality remains to be investigated.

Thirdly, we need to examine the role of dramatic structure as both the embodiment of meaning and a mode of communication. The comparative method devised by other disciplines like anthropology and sociology and stressed by structuralist philosophy may help us here. Contemporary dramatic analysis proceeds from the scene unit to the entire play, not from the play as a whole to its subordinate parts. In future cross-cultural studies, the scene unit will serve as the element for comparison. As such, it is analogous to the story function that Vladimir Propp used as the basis for his monograph, *The Morphology of the Folk Tale.* This pioneer study, which has profoundly affected the course of folklore research, suggests one way in which a comprehensive method of dramatic analysis can be constructed.

As yet comparative study utilizing the scene unit is in its infancy. There are some promising preliminary results, nevertheless. Along with several doctoral students, I have conducted research into long dramatic speeches, and already we are finding two or three dominant patterns in works selected from the entire range of dramatic literature.

Ultimately, what distinguishes dramatic analysis from literary interpretation is not any single aspect of textual examination. Instead, the difference is a factor of the contexts of literary and dramatic works. If indeed the perceptive process is an essential part of aesthetic response, as all studies on perception indicate, then the distinction between reading a poem and witnessing a play will make it impossible to speak of a common response. For the critic the literary text is a finished work perceived through a single, highly concentrated perceptual system: vision. The dramatic text, by contrast, is a work perceived visually but intended to be perceived totally. Acknowledging the vast amount of work yet to be accomplished in refining an adequate mode of dramatic analysis, we can still list a series of principles that underly such analysis when applied to playscripts.

1. Presentation is the *primary* experience intended by the dramatist. This is more than stating that a play is written for presentation. It means that the core experience of drama is living through the events of the play, that before anything else, the enjoyment of these structured events in a theater is both its own reason for being as well as the precondition for any other response. By no means does this imply that reading a play, by Shakespeare for instance, is less valid than witnessing its performance. We must recognize, however, that reading a play by Shakespeare *as a poem* provides a different artistic experience from witnessing it as drama.

2. To allow for the presentational character of drama, dramatic analysis requires a vertical rather than a horizontal method. The horizontal method is the prevailing one. Through it a play is divided into temporal strands of plot, character, diction, spectacle, and thought. We do not experience plays in this fashion, however. Instead we experience them vertically, that is, all elements (character, story,

etc.) are perceived simultaneously as total segments of time, in effect, as scene or segmental units.

3. The structure of the segmental unit is a product of a limited number of variables. These are not composed of character and story but of interactions among agents who embody active and reactive thrusts of energy.

4. The impact of drama depends upon the sequential unfolding of the segments. Therefore, sound analytic procedure requires description of characters or events in terms of temporal context. The portraits of Trofimov drawn by Yermilov, Valency, Brustein, and Magarshack violate this principle.

5. Theatrical response is total. It is not purely emotional, not intellectual, but a complex affective-cognitive reaction that is not very well understood. The crucial factor in response is the dynamic element in the play to which the individual attends. This is embodied in the structure of the segment as well as in the structure of relationship between segments. Therefore, the appreciation of the structure of a segment is the key to a potential dramatic response.

6. The purpose of dramatic analysis is not to arrive at definitive interpretations of a work, but to discover and test dramatic possibilities. Beyond analysis, there is interpretation. In that respect, the description of the segmental structure leads not so much to an appreciation of meaning so much as to an appreciation of unresolved states in

Chekhov on the balcony of his house at Yalta.

which human action is captured. For example, Chekhov repeatedly arranges segments in such a way that one character exerts pressure upon another, seems to bring the other to a point of confrontation, but just at the moment the issue is to be faced, the character under duress either dismisses or avoids the issue. Lopakhin trying to get Mme. Ranevsky to face the imminent loss of the estate, she trying to get him to accept Varya, she castigating Trofimov, in each of these sequences the person under attack changes the subject or, in a characteristic manner, changes his behavior. Comic response highlights the inability of a person to deal with a significant problem. Thus, in terms of action, the characters do not suffer change in a rather metaphysical manner. Quite the contrary. They assert themselves, often with determination, but without the ability to bring matters to a head.

Ultimately, what distinguishes a major dramatist are not his ideas nor his psychological penetration of people nor, perhaps, even the beauty of his expression, so much as his instinct for shaping human relationships into provocative, unresolved actions. He created illusions of imminence, of energies about to burst, of impacts just made. Since he cannot show action itself, he shows the symptoms of internal action, and arranges them carefully in planes of contrast. His art lies in the engineering of precise relationships which have maximum evocative power. Chekhov's mastery lies in his capacity to initiate a number of motifs (loss of the cherry orchard, variants of male-female love relationships) and to utilize them as aspects of the antagonism between loving and doing. Mme. Ranevsky is keenly aware of human yearning and affection; she is incapable of utilizing that capacity to direct her or her family's life. She depends upon the past and the chance generosity of the present. Lopakhin is her opposite. He has a rudimentary capacity for human feeling, but cannot apply it in any systematic way. We never know how much genuine affection he has for Varya, but whatever its extent he cannot display it to her or act upon it. On the other hand, he can act resolutely in business. Trofimov lies between. Less sensitive than either of the two, filled with the desire to act but content to talk about acting, he finally gains the capacity to both feel and perform. The two capacities are connected, Chekhov seems to show. Yet even then one cannot be sure. Just as Chekhov contrasts loving and doing, he seems to contrast the social and the personal planes of existence. Is he showing that the loss of the orchard is irrelevant, that Lopakhin is pathetic because he cannot translate his money making capacity into human relationships and that Trofimov is strengthened by becoming aware of others?

These contradictory Chekhovian contrasts which offer us alternatives can be so clearly seen in the conclusions of his plays. In the last moments of *The Cherry Orchard* a number of off-stage noises succeed one another. The joyous cries of Anya and Trofimov call Mme. Ranevsky forth. Sounds of departure follow. Then "a dull sound is heard, the stroke of an axe on a tree." On stage Fiers appears, left behind. The sound of the breaking string dies away sadly. Finally, the sound of the axe is heard again. Each of the sounds has its own significance: the cries of youth heralding the future, the thud of the axe proclaiming a change

from one era to another, the echo of a breaking string mourning the passage of an ancient life. By arranging these in a sequence of future, present, past, and present again, Chekhov does not make a statement about either the past or the future; he merely juxtaposes stimuli. Their succession stimulates a complex movement in our imagination, a movement induced over and over again each time we contemplate the forms of his action.

Bernard Beckerman, "Dramatic Analysis and Literary Interpretation: 'The Cherry Orchard' as Exemplum," in New Literary History, *Vol. II, No. 3, Spring, 1971, pp. 391-406.*

Harvey Pitcher   (essay date 1973)

[*Pitcher is an English critic who has written extensively about Russian literature. In the following excerpt, he contrasts* The Cherry Orchard *with Chekhov's other plays.*]

What most clearly distinguishes the content of **The Cherry Orchard** from its predecessors is that it has by far the simplest of Chekhov's plots. The play's 'shape' is no more than a straight line, which passes through the threat to the estate, ineffectual attempts to save it, the sale, and the dispersal of the family. It is the simplest and also the least dramatic of Chekhov's plots, in which for the first time, as he himself noted, 'there isn't a single pistol shot'. A certain amount of suspense is generated in Act III, but whether or not the estate has been sold seems trivial when compared, for example, with the outcome of the duel in **Three Sisters.** The final act may be very poignant, but again it has none of that deep anguish which one associates with the finales of **Uncle Vanya** and **Three Sisters.**

Moreover, the complex interlocking love intrigues of **The Seagull** and **Uncle Vanya** are not repeated in **The Cherry Orchard,** except in the comic love triangle of the minor characters; nor can it be described as a 'polyphonic' play in the manner of **Three Sisters,** where four distinct stories are developed in parallel. What happens to individuals in **The Cherry Orchard** is seen largely within the context of what happens to the estate, and the 'individual fates hanging in the balance' quality of **Three Sisters** is never so keenly felt. In contrast to the young characters of the earlier play, Ranyevskaya and Gayev are both well into middle age; they are not standing at the crossroads, they have already made or marred their lives, whatever happens to them now. Ranyevskaya's inability to break finally with her lover in Paris is an emotional undercurrent that runs beneath the surface throughout the play, but the outcome of this story is obviously dependent on whether or not the estate is sold. Trofimov claims that he and Anya are 'above love', but even if one overrules him and sees their relationship as a 'love story', it is neither very dramatic nor of great interest in its own right: Anya changes, she grows up perceptibly during the few months of the play, but this is because Trofimov makes her see the orchard and the whole of her past in an entirely different light. Only the story of Varya and Lopakhin does have some dramatic interest of its own—will Lopakhin propose or won't he? Their story recalls Irina and Tuzenbach, and Sonya and Astrov. Varya, like Sonya, is twenty-four, at the crossroads; yet even here the parallel is not quite exact, for what Varya would really like to do with her life is not to marry Lopakhin, but to become a pilgrim and to wander from one holy place to another.

So what then is *The Cherry Orchard?* What has made it the best known of Chekhov's plays, and why does it exert such a continuing fascination?

When Stanislavsky recalls that by the autumn of 1903 Chekhov had still not decided on a title, his memory must certainly have been at fault, for Chekhov had referred to his new play as *The Cherry Orchard* as far back as December 1902, not only long before the time recalled by Stanislavsky, but before he himself had even put pen to paper. And indeed it does seem to me of considerable importance for the evolution of the Chekhov play that this particular title had been chosen at such an early stage of composition. In contrast to *The Seagull* (a symbol to be identified with one or more characters), *Uncle Vanya* (one individual) and *Three Sisters* (a group of individuals), the new title is both inanimate and 'supra-individual'. It immediately conjures up the whole *situation* of the play (the inevitable sale of the estate of which the orchard forms part), a situation that is bound to cause disruption in the lives of all the characters. The play's disruptive element, in other words, is contained within the situation itself and not, as before, within particular individuals. Previously Chekhov had used the technique of making his outsiders cause disruption in the lives of the residents. Emotional tension had been generated by making these characters bring with them into the play elements of friction and antagonism, so causing the emotional network to vibrate in painful and urgent ways.

Now it would not have been at all difficult for Chekhov to follow a similar procedure in *The Cherry Orchard,* since at first sight the merchant Lopakhin appears to be an obvious successor to Natasha in *Three Sisters*—if not more than a successor, for he wields much greater power. Strikingly, however, Lopakhin is not treated as an unsympathetic figure by Chekhov. Soviet critics may regard him as the villain of the play, but one need only quote Chekhov's remark that Lopakhin is 'a very decent man in every sense' to refute such a view. Moreover, with the possible exception of the minor character, Yasha, *The Cherry Orchard* alone of the four major plays has no unsympathetic characters whatsoever. At the end of the play, *all* the characters depart with the exception of Firs; and this avoids that sense of contrast and unresolved opposition between outsiders and residents, between sympathetic and unsympathetic characters, which is implicit in the endings of *Uncle Vanya* and *Three Sisters.*

Thus in *The Cherry Orchard* Chekhov is no longer relying on the contrast between sympathetic and unsympathetic characters as a means of activating the play's emotional network. This change would have come about because he was attracted in the first place to a situation rather than to particular characters (the sisters, for example). That situation—the plight of the aristocratic family forced to sell its beautiful estate—would have seemed to him rich in emotional and social implication, though, as in *Three Sisters,* I [suggest] that the social landscape interested Chekhov not so much for its own sake, but more as a back-

cloth for the emotional processes. In itself the situation was neither especially dramatic nor momentous: it would not be possible to activate the emotional network by introducing intense drama into the characters' personal lives—exposing them to extreme emotional situations so as to evoke an extreme response; nor would it have seemed appropriate to activate the network by making the characters fall in love with one another. On the other hand, many people might be involved in this situation, for a variety of reasons, and their lives would all pass through the situation as through an emotional focal point, each life being more or less deeply affected by the orchard's fate. Their common relationship to this situation would create the emotional network between them.

The new and final evolutionary departure in *The Cherry Orchard* is therefore to bring out the emotional interrelatedness of a group of people who are not 'linked' by emotional hostility, and who at the same time are not linked by special ties of family or background. It was by making the situation central that Chekhov found himself able to do this. In *Three Sisters* emotional responsiveness is largely associated with the harmonious family relations among the Prozorovs. In *The Cherry Orchard,* though family relations play a part, there is less harmony but more general responsiveness. It is not necessary for characters to be all that close to one another for emotional responsiveness to start to operate. Lopakhin and Ranyevskaya, for example, are divided by their background, yet Chekhov brings out the emotional interrelatedness between these two very different characters.

We have come a long way from *The Seagull,* where emotional interaction only occurred within the suffocatingly close relationship of mother and son.

Dramatic technique in *The Cherry Orchard:*

[Chekhov] uses farce as a satiric device, to alienate us from a character so that we will not become too sympathetically involved with his spurious self-pity or melancholy posturing.

More interesting, because more subtly hidden, is Chekhov's use of melodrama. And I refer not only to melodramatic devices. (Many observers have already commented on Chekhov's weakness for effective act curtains, often brought down after a pistol shot: a killing, a suicide, or an attempted murder occurs in every play except *The Cherry Orchard,* where a sound like a broken harp string and the noise of an axe replace the zing of bullets.) I refer, rather, to Chekhov's use of the melodramatic formula. For each of his mature plays, and especially *The Cherry Orchard,* is constructed on the same melodramatic pattern: the conflict between a despoiler and his victims—while the action of each follows the same melodramatic development: the gradual dispossession of the victims from their rightful inheritance.

Robert Brustein, in The Theatre of Revolt: An Approach to the Modern Drama, *Little, Brown and Co. 1964.*

Harvey Pitcher, in his The Chekhov Play: A New Interpretation, *Chatto & Windus, 1973, 224 p.*

John Tulloch   (essay date 1980)

[*In the following excerpt, Tulloch analyzes the thematic and symbolic structure of* The Cherry Orchard.]

The Cherry Orchard is unusual among Chekhov's dramas in that the central focus is not the problem of choice among the intelligentsia. Whereas **The Seagull, Uncle Vanya** and **The Three Sisters** are all related to fundamental questions of identity for their author as a professional doctor and writer—the problem of art, the problem of science, the problem of education and upbringing—**The Cherry Orchard** is a play about social mobility and change. In particular, the play examines a moment in time when large-scale industrialisation had made possible a proletarian solution in addition to the evolutionist-technological vision of his earlier literature. The estates on which the action of the earlier dramas takes place are of course historically typical, insofar that the specific problems and the conflicting responses are typical of the situation of intellectuals in a modernising autocracy. But they appear timeless, and the epic vision becomes a commitment of method, a matter of endurance, a programme for living in which a better future lies in the hands of each individual.

In **The Cherry Orchard** the estate is no longer timeless. It is threatened by a new order of modernisation which enables a peasant to become master of the estate which owned his family as serfs; and threatened, too, by other, more violent, aspects of industrial growth. The cherry orchard is confronted with the modern capitalist and the modern revolutionary. The question of choice, and with it the crisis of identity, while remaining individual is subsumed within broader social movements.

Each character typifies a social position in his response to the orchard. Trofimov sees in the trees dead souls; Lopakhin sees in them the opportunity for technology and growth; Madame Ranevskaya thinks only of style, elegance and the white figures of the past; Varya, a girl raised above her station by the kindly condescension of a status-conscious society, thinks only of saving that order through petty cheeseparing and recourse to religion, its official ideology. To say, however, that Chekhov poses the question of individual choice within the framework of social movements is not to interpret his play in the light of a straightforward class struggle. Chekhov is favouring neither an aristocratic, nor a bourgeois, nor a proletarian solution.

By choosing the decay of a landed estate (and the complete inability of the old landowners to come to terms with the problem of farming without serfs) for his theme, Chekhov was not only selecting a problem about which he had written more than once, and of which he had a close personal experience, but also a typical contradiction of a society which tried to modernise yet, in terms of social stratification, stay the same. The *situation* in **The Cherry Orchard** is the moment when the autonomous world of tradition has been breached by the serf reforms and the will to modernise; when in Firs' words, 'everything is muddled', and action must be rational and decisive, yet within mores and institutions which remain ascriptive. The reactions of each landowner to the problem of debt differ at the personal level—Ranevskaya escapes to Paris, Gayev into dreams of liberal gentry and superfluous men, Simeonov-Pishchik into money-grubbing and a hand-to-mouth existence from day to day while he waits for something to turn up. But *socially* their reactions are qualitatively the same. They are simply incapable of adapting to the demands of a new rationality; Pishchik is as incapable of entrepreneurial activity when profitable minerals are discovered on his land, as Madame Ranevskaya is of profiting from the spread of new urban wealth to the country. Essentially they are people preoccupied with the old style of life, servants in livery, large tips to the waiters, casual philanthropy and amateur medical treatment for the poor—people who act from day to day, move from place to place, but really stay the same.

Yet the *contradictions* of the modernising autocracy have deprived these people of sureness of response. There is in **The Cherry Orchard** none of the rhythmic Arcadian symbolism of the English conservative tradition when *it* was threatened by the 'mob' beneath; nor yet a negative perspective, of angst, as the hero fights against frightful odds and fails. Neither allegory nor angst are possible moods for an author who stands outside a social group in decline, and views that decline with intellectual approval mixed with personal sympathy for those he knew and respected. Rather, the mood is elegiac, compounded of an intensely human crisis of identity at the personal level and a distancing, comic inconsistency of interaction.

In their isolation the landowners are marginal and anomic figures. Ranevskaya, the aristocratic woman who married beneath her station, travels from place to place seeking purpose in locations and in a lover who cheats her. Faced with the sale of the orchard she retreats into her past when everything was elegant and certain. Gayev also retreats into the past, given an extra and pompous dignity by his references to learning and social service. But his relationship to reason and the Enlightenment is empty; it goes no further than justifying the continued existence of the unproductive orchard on the grounds that it was mentioned in the Encyclopaedia. For all his escape into a pathetic flow of words, his refrain, 'I'll be silent, I'll be silent', is that of a man lost. Anya is aroused by the revolutionary ideals of Trofimov, but the vision of a new life of this naive girl is strangely mixed with the intention of planting another orchard and living happily ever after with her mother as they read to each other in the long evenings. Varya is divided between a desperate attempt to save the old order, to which she would somehow or other attach Lopakhin, and a desire to escape into the nun-like existence of Ol'ga in **"Big Volodya and Little Volodya."** Increasing mobility within this crumbling, self-conscious structure simply intensifies social marginality which, in the absence of a confident and coherent symbolic system becomes spiritual anomie as each individual faces alone the meaninglessness of his existence.

But there is little tragedy. Spiritual isolation is signified by a comic failure of communication when characters are *collectively* faced with the reality of change. So when Lopakhin first suggests the need to cut down the cherry orchard and let the land for summer villas, the reaction among the landowners is a comic and trivial dialogue of escape. Firs speaks of an old recipe for drying cherries; Ranevskaya asks for the recipe, but it is lost. Pishchik then asks whether they ate frogs in Paris, and Ranevskaya says she ate crocodiles, which Pishchik greets with great wonder. Lopakhin tries again with his plan. Gayev replies 'what idiocy!' and after a brief exchange between Varya and Ranevskaya which reveals both the former's workaday ritual and the latter's asylum in Paris, Gayev launches into his famous oration to the old and venerable bookcase which has been the source of his family's devotion to the people for so long. Silenced by Lopakhin's irony, he retreats into his billiards talk, and almost immediately the remaining landowner, Pishchik, reveals his extraordinary unconcern for the realities of life (and medical science!) by swallowing all of Ranevskaya's pills. Each individual responds quite typically to Lopakhin's suggestion; and each response reveals inner isolation. Yet the interaction, revealed as a collective style of life, is comic and absurd. The private worlds of Ranevskaya, Gayev, Varya and Pishchik, sad and lyrical though they may be, are a focus of irrationality, and thus, situationally, of the absurd.

It is within this overtly comic and nostalgic mood (which is nevertheless serious and sometimes fearful) that Chekhov is able to portray the genuine human values which are *overcome* in his works. As in *The Seagull,* the typical time perspective associated with the ascriptive society is a tension between time that passes meaninglessly, often absurdly, and the desire to make time stand still. The tension is rendered in *mood* by the relationship between broad comedy and nostalgia in the play; and *scenically* by beginning and ending the play in the same location, yet a location grievously altered.

Act 1 introduces the problem of the cherry orchard in a location of compulsive nostalgia: the nursery of generations of cherry orchard owners, each one (as in *The Three Sisters,* but in a more genteel setting) growing in the image of his parents. For Lopakhin active decisions about the future of the orchard are urgent, 'time flies by'; but for the landowners, accustomed to a different time scale, there can be no meaning in its passing. It is better not to consider the matter; something will turn up—an act of God, or of rich grandmamma; Anya may marry a wealthy man, or money may be won on a lottery ticket. Meanwhile resort to nostalgia can convince that nothing has changed:

> Oh, my childhood—my dear, innocent childhood! I once used to sleep in this nursery. I looked out from here at the orchard. Each morning that I awoke happiness awoke with me, and then the orchard was exactly as it is now. White all over—it hasn't changed a bit.

Objects which relate them to their youth are plentiful in the nursery: toys, little tables, aged bookcases, faithful retainers. And when the thought arises, 'strange though it may appear', that action must be taken to save it all, they can look into the eternal orchard and see the ghost of their mother walking. Faced by the visible passage of time, the dying and ageing servants, the balding Trofimov, the compulsion to nostalgia is even greater. For Ranevskaya, who throughout the play is torn most acutely by the tension between time passing and time past, Trofimov can only bring to mind the memory of her dead son—which is, in itself, a sign of an uncertain future. Nostalgia is then incorporated within a wider but equally escapist mood—fatalistic guilt in which everything, the passing of time, the sale of the orchard, the death of her child, are the punishment for her past and an act of God. Varya takes up the theme of dependence on God's mercy, while Anya, whom Ranevskaya loves with all the resonances of nostalgia, lives anew the innocent naivety of her mother's early days. Thus the dialogue between the flower-like innocence of youth and a trust in God for its passing, which continually tears Madame Ranevskaya, is acted out by her 'daughters'. As the close-knit family prepares to sleep with its memories and pious hopes, these two girls, these two values, see the Act to its close. Everything is in decay, but the scene is tranquil. 'From far away' the sound of a shepherd's pipe is heard, an echo of Chekhov's story **"The Pipe"**, where an old shepherd plays nostalgically, complaining that Fate, God, the Emancipation, have destroyed the real gentry (when half were generals), and destroyed with them the fertility of Nature. The mournful sound responds to the nursery's proper tone, relating it to the orchard just outside—but to the cherry trees' timeless and beautiful past (when, as Firs too would say, the place was full of generals) and not to their present decay. It is a sound which evokes the enclosed nostalgia of the nursery, embalms the dialogue of fragile innocence and fatalistic experience, and speaks of man's inability to comprehend the world beyond the nursery walls.

Act 2 confronts us with a dramatic scene change. The nostalgic claustrophobia of the nursery is gone, and the world beyond assumes its contemporary form. In sharp contrast to the enclosed space of Act 1, the author insisted on a boundless view of Nature, 'a sense of distance unusual on the stage'. In this place beyond the nursery, time is clearly not without significance. Man has related with Nature, and technology has spread; for beyond the poplars there are telegraph poles, and a town is to be seen on the far horizon. The drama is purely visual, in the scene change itself. The vision of Nature and technology stands in quiet testimony to the meaningless enclosure of time and purpose in the previous Act. The sound of the shepherd's pipe belonged to the nostalgia of the nursery. The world of change, however, is no more than a *mute* backcloth to the antics of both masters and servants.

When the sound of change does come out of this vast environment, these people will not recognise it, because they do not understand its sequence or its laws. For Gayev the railways are useful merely to take him to town, where he can converse with the waiters about the Decadents, and then to bring him back in time for a game of billiards. For Ranevskaya the sequence of life's change, from innocent upbringing, through marriage to a drunken spendthrift, to the arms of the usual lover, and from the death of her son, through desertion in Paris, to attempted suicide, is explicable only in religious terms—sin, and appeal to the mercy of God. Meanwhile she squanders money just the same, pours her love and her hopes on Anya and Varya, and prefers to ignore the issue of the orchard for 'what we were talking about yesterday'. The lives of these 'improvident, unbusinesslike and strange people' has simply not been patterned to ordered change, and when something new occurs passive fatalism is the only available response.

Time for them has always been cyclical—the filtering of generations through the nursery—and when instead it manifestly destroys, their reactions are confused and fearful. Madame Ranevskaya clings helplessly to Lopakhin (the agent of change whose message she cannot heed or even understand) because 'I keep imagining that something awful is about to happen . . . like the house collapsing on us'. A tramp comes by, and, like the peasants on the steppes, they are filled with wonder and fear by the sounds and strange figures of the expanse beyond them. And also like the peasants who cling to their protective fire, they retreat to their own enclosed world where, in Act 3, we find them once more, amidst the brightly lit chandeliers and luxurious fittings, whirling to the dance and drowning the outside world with the brash sounds of the ball.

Act 2 has opposed a world of purposeful change to the encapsulated time of Act 1; and the response of the landowners is, typically, not so much to reject as to flee from it as something disturbingly incomprehensible. Pishchik's dance calls, which, like the lotto calls in *The Seagull,* assert a timeless repetition, are more familiar and more comforting. Yet time does move on; it is the day of the auction, and the social poverty of the ball itself is an insistent comment on change. Madame Ranevskaya waits helplessly for this final judgment on her past, Varya continues to call on God, and Anya dances, a butterfly heedless of time. Meanwhile Sharlotta, engaged as always in tricks, produces something from nothing, thus parodying by sleight of hand the full scope of the landowners' vision. For Ranevskaya it is a time of pitiful decline and, with the entry of the new owner, collapse. This woman, once brought up with the tenderness of a flower like Anya, has no knowledge or inner resources with which to face the crisis; and when to Trofimov's claim to be above love, she answers 'I suppose I am below love', there is an echo once again of the ascriptive division of the Russian woman between the idealist and the seducer. Her only recourse, in fact, has to be external, back to her seducer. Though she knows she will be 'going to the dregs', she cannot bear to hear Trofimov speak in spiteful categories about her lover—it is the kind of callous 'truth' with which the revolutionary, like Lvov in *Ivanov,* destroys.

In Act 4 the family location has shrunk back to its real temporal and spatial proportions, the enclosed nostalgia of the nursery. But the nursery is bare. All the objects of nostalgia in which Gayev and Ranevskaya could hide from their fate have been stripped away. Time has actually passed, and the absurdity of it all for these people is emphasised by Pishchik's unexpected and quite undeserved fortune, and his final 'Don't worry, all things finish in their time'. Gayev will take a job in a bank, which will certainly prove to be a fiasco. Ranevskaya will return to Paris, keep

her lover on the limited sum grandmamma sent for the estate, and then will be a pauper. Even her last wish comes to nothing: the sick Firs is not taken to a hospital but is left in the deserted house; and Varya will never be married to Lopakhin.

In a most moving scene, alone on a bare stage, illusions spent, Gayev and Ranevskaya weep quietly together, unheard by Trofimov and Anya whose illusions are just beginning; and whose naively hopeful calls begin the whole process of empty dreams again in a new form. Finally Firs, alone and near to death, speaks Chekhov's deep sympathy for those caught in this process of meaningless time:

> Life's over as though I'd never lived.

The summary of life by an abandoned servant is entirely appropriate, for in this play without the foregrounding of the usual love triangles, servants perform an important structural role. In plays which considered the mediating role of art, education etc. such as *The Seagull,* Chekhov was able to portray the relationship of authentic and false choices as relations of love, and so give them dramatic immediacy. *The Cherry Orchard* demanded a rather different thematic organisation since here he was dealing with a whole order in decline, in which he knew people as deserving of sympathy as Trigorin and Treplev, yet who collectively created the world of Arkadina. In a play which demonstrates the humanity of these people, yet also displays the harsh social network on which the humanity rests the close analysis of the world of the servants is not coincidental.

Each of the landowning group finds a reflection here. Thus Firs, like Gayev, is always looking into the historical past; Yasha, like Ranevskaya, seeks escape to Paris; Dunyasha, like Anya, escapes into dreams; Sharlotta, like Varya of doubtful birth, drowns her unhappiness in ritual too (Varya in keys and dried peas and Sharlotta in tricks); and Yepikhodov, as submissive to fate and to women as Pishchik, like him stumbles from one chance occurrence to another. Moreover, the servants' style of *interaction* reflects that of their masters. At the beginning of Act 2, their response to the natural and technological world beyond them is prologue and paradigm for the landowners' mixture of spiritual isolation and comic interaction. Thus Sharlotta, abandoning her tricks for a moment, says thoughtfully,

> . . . Where I'm from or who I am I don't know . . . I don't know anything . . . I'm longing for someone I could talk to, but there is no-one. I have no-one.

The desire for direct relations and the weariness with rank of a governess who performs tricks on command is identical with the loneliness of Chekhov's **"Bishop":** her words are his:

> I've got nobody to talk to. I'm alone, quite alone. I have no-one and . . . and who I am, or what I am alive for, no-one knows.

The theme is taken up by the clerk Yepikhodov:

> I don't really seem to know the direction I want

to go, or what I'm really after—that is to say,
should I live or should I shoot myself, as it were.

(In an earlier version of the play which, according to
Stanislavskii, Chekhov rather unwillingly altered, Firs too
was incorporated in the anomic theme).

These lonely cries are enmeshed in a trivial and comic interaction in which Yepikhodov courts Dunyasha while
she courts Yasha, who shows off to everybody, Sharlotta
munches a cucumber, and Yepikhodov waves a gun about,
explaining the fact that cockroaches get into his kvass by
fatalistic laws of history. However, the structural importance of the servants is not simply as a comic parody of
their masters (who, after all, do that for themselves). It is
not the pretension of the masters that is laid bare by the
servants, as, say, in a play by Molière, but their humanity—which is genuine, but at a cost. The servants have an
'alienating' function in the Brechtian sense, a 'making
strange' of familiar scenes (there was certainly nothing
new about dramatising the decline of a landed class)—
thereby, supposedly, channelling the audience's patterns
of response away from emotional identification with a
group which, *intellectually,* Chekhov disapproved.

Hence Firs' nostalgic aspiration for a time when the 'peasants knew their place and the gentry knew their place'—
when in fact peasants were flogged, generals danced at the
balls and there was no proper medical treatment for the
servants—puts into historical focus Gayev's effusive:

> you have promoted within us the ideals of public
> service and social consciousness.

Similarly, the social climbing Yasha, who is prepared to
dally with Dunyasha (but not publicly because of his status) and who is ashamed of his peasant mother, not only
reproduces at a lower social level the avarice and vulgarity
of Ranevskaya's lover, but comments on the whole framework of ascriptive love relations—on Ranevskaya, who
like Dunyasha, is 'below love', on her sin of marrying 'beneath her', and even on the attempted match of Varya and
Lopakhin which would have fitted social convention so
well. Dunyasha, 'like a flower', and with her preoccupation with makeup and mirrors, reflects not only the 'spring
blossom' Anya, but her mother's giddy and lost innocence
too, and beyond that all the other cherry orchard ladies,
dressed in white, educated to dazzle socially with the latest hair-style and Paris fashion. Sharlotta, whose spiritual
isolation is less protected by the layers of nostalgia of her
betters, parodies with her baby noises in the final Act
Ranevskaya's only remaining resource: personal and familial resurrection in Anya—so a moving and human moment is shown to be an empty response to the pressure of
choice. One can only pity Ranevskaya, but her actions
have deprived Sharlotta and Varya of meaning too. And
when in Act 2 Yepikhodov, with his back to the expansive
technology beyond him, assigns to unchangeable historical laws the trivial events of his life, he too goes beyond
comedy, lighting up not only Gayev's equally futile attitude to technology and his 'you'll still die in the end, whatever you do' response to Trofimov's ideals, but also the
whole immobile crowd of these cherry orchard people
who find change 'so vulgar'. Even the tramp, emerging as
if out of the sound of the breaking string, has an alienating

function: Varya is frightened of this man who speaks of
the suffering people she has been raised above;
Ranevskaya gives him money, and her kindly generosity
is given perspective as the typically static philanthropy
which, Chekhov once wrote to [A. F. Koni, 26 January
1891], 'in Russia has such an arbitrary quality'. A man
wanders ill, he is given money and wanders out again—
and behind him there is the growth of a rational technology.

A whole order is tied together with this immobile procedure; and the same reforms which created zemstvo medicine are here seen as the 'troubles'. Moreover, the order
in decline may itself 'leave its mark'. Everyone is involved
in ritualised actions:

(a) the class in decline—Ranevskaya always giving money
away, Gayev potting the red and eating sweets, Pishchik
borrowing money and saying 'extraordinary thing';

(b) the lower classes who aspire to rise—Dunyasha always
powdering her nose, Yasha always giving himself airs and
saying 'what stupidity';

(c) and even those who have risen—Varya always cheeseparing and spying on the lovers, and Lopakhin constantly
being deferent and waving his arms about. Thus the new
order of social mobility is threatened with inclusion as the
traditional world adapts and renews itself.

It is clear in the values of the younger servants, in the deference that Anya and Varya expect from them, and particularly in Lopakhin's consciousness of hierarchy, that the
real human crisis does not lie in the historical decline of
a particular group. It lies in the division of human personality by ascriptive values which existed in Firs' golden
past, continue in the present, and threaten to be incorporated in the merchant values of the future (as Chekhov
had shown in earlier works, such as **"The Mask"** and **"My
Life"**). The *social* crisis of the landowning class, and their
particular anomie, is thus not the central one of the play.
The social crisis rather clarifies the loss of wholeness by
tearing away the comfortable ideology which hid it hitherto. Just as in **"Dreary Story"** and **"Bishop"** Chekhov used
the impact of physical decline to reveal the meaningless
passage of time, so in ***The Cherry Orchard*** he uses the impact of social decline to reveal the same thing. The question of identity and the problem of meaning extends beyond this class to the process of modernisation itself. As
Lopakhin says, 'what hordes of people there are in Russia,
my friend, who have no aim in life at all!'

Against the passive and hierarchical world of the landowners, Chekhov sets two forms of modernisation, embodied in two major characters, the revolutionary Trofimov, and the merchant (and former peasant) Lopakhin.
It is their activist dialogue which carries Chekhov's vision.
Trofimov in fact articulates a number of Chekhov's cherished beliefs—in the importance of science and art, education, and an intelligentsia which works:

> Mankind is constantly marching forward, con-
> stantly perfecting itself. Everything which we
> can't understand at the moment will one day be
> comprehensible. But to reach this point we have
> to give everything to our work, and we have to

help those people who are seeking after truth. Here in Russia, hardly anyone has begun to work as yet. The great majority of intellectuals that I know don't search for anything, don't do anything and as yet are incapable of working. . . . They merely chatter on about science and don't know a lot about art either.

Yet for all his talk about love for the people, unremitting toil and science, Trofimov is conspicuously unable to love, work or be scientific. Despite the obvious tenderness of the inner man, Trofimov does his best to drive out sentiment. He claims that his relationship with Anya is above love:

> . . . we are above love. The whole object and meaning of our life is to rid ourselves of everything that is petty and illusory in life, everything that hinders our happiness and freedom.

Like Shamokhin in **"Ariadne"**, he abstracts love, denying feeling. Nor does he work; he is the 'eternal student' who not only is criticised by the other characters for doing nothing, but himself admits that he will probably be a student for the rest of his life. And . . . in his eagerness to generalise, he also denies the achievements of contemporary science. His famous speech about the frightful condition of workers draws too much on revolutionary abstraction to be accurate. In denying the great advances made in zemstvo medicine (of which Chekhov was so very proud) Trofimov is opposing the evolutionary vision.

Like all of Chekhov's revolutionaries Trofimov has become, despite his undeniably sympathetic qualities, a 'walking tendency', with a simplistic ideological vision that makes him prone to categorise quite brutally all those about him. Thus his attitude to the orchard is not scientific but revolutionary—the landowners must atone for the dead souls who cry from the trees about years of persecution. Significantly, he tries to categorise Lopakhin according to a determinist Marxian formula—the *necessary* evil of a bourgeois period in Russia:

> My opinion of you, my dear Lopakhin, is simply this: you're a rich man, and soon you'll be a millionaire. Now, as part of the natural process by which one kind of matter is converted into another, you are a necessary evil—just as Nature needs beasts of prey which devour everything in their path.

It is interesting that Trofimov speaks a language of fatalistic Darwinism reminiscent of Van Koren to disguise the Marxist content from the censor; but it is not untypical, since for Chekhov both these value systems were part of the same 'inauthentic' paradigm.

Trofimov's vision of the future is as boldly uncontradictory as his evaluation of the complex Lopakhin. Having told Anya that they are above love, he continues, 'Onwards! We must march irresistibly together to that brilliant star shining there in the distance! Onwards, my friends! Let us not lag!'; and again 'It's upon us! Happiness is drawing closer and closer. I can almost hear its footsteps!' The speeches are as rhetorical as the vision is simplistic, and the whole thing is put into perspective by Chekhov in making Anya translate this new life into planting a new orchard with her mother, and in making Trofimov

himself ludicrous and laughable. Like the revolutionary Dr Lvov in *Ivanov,* Trofimov is a prig, and Chekhov is eager to make him appear absurd, with a beard that won't grow and a premature impotence. He is, in Madame Ranevskaya's words, 'an absurd prude, a freak', and is so upset by her suggestion to take a lover that he falls downstairs. Also, like Chekhov's other revolutionary creation at this time, Sasha in **"The Betrothed"**, Trofimov is dirty and down-at-heel. In every way he lacks beauty and wholeness, and despite his statement that man should not be proud since physically very imperfect, he claims to take a pride in being a 'moth-eaten gent'. He claims too, like Gusev, to be strong, and above the need for other men— yet he trails along on the coat-tails of the landowners.

Between on the one hand the student who deeply loves his mistress and her daughter, and on the other the revolutionary who believes that landowners have to atone for their oppression, there is an ambivalence of identity which deprives Trofimov of action, and so immerses him in the familiar rhythm of comic trivia and personal crisis with all the other characters of immobility. He is as irresolute as the family he clings to—and like them (and like Sasha again) this revolutionary is strangely anachronistic. At the end of Act 2, Trofimov tells Anya:

> Your mother, you yourself, your uncle don't understand that you are living in debt, at the expense of others. You live off people whom you don't even allow into the house. We are at least two hundred years behind the times.

But at the end of Act 3, Lopakhin puts Trofimov out of date:

> Oh, if only my father and grandfather could rise up from their graves and see what's happened here. . . . I have bought the very estate on which my father and grandfather were serfs, where they weren't even allowed into the kitchen.

In Chekhov's view it is the rational and beauty-loving merchant that makes the revolutionary anachronistic, and not the other way around.

In a play of ritualised action and withdrawal, it is Lopakhin alone who is mobile—both socially and dramatically. Undoubtedly there are elements of the old-fashioned, subservient Russian merchant about him, as well as elements of the more independent new capitalist who had just begun to appear in Russia. He is acutely conscious of his peasant origins and of the eternal hierarchy of the old order. At the same time he shows an equally acute understanding of change, and the profits to be gained from it. But he is certainly not the ruthless capitalist that Trofimov describes, nor even the type of grasping merchant Chekhov portrayed in earlier works—which is what contemporaries seemed to expect him to be. In his letters Chekhov insists that Lopakhin is not this type of merchant:

> You have to remember that he is not a merchant in the crude sense of the word. [Chekhov to Ol'ga Knipper, 28 October 1903]

Quite unlike the shiftless Trofimov, it is around Lopakhin

that the action moves. Chekhov's letters suggest that he structured his whole play round his development:

> Yes, Lopakhin is a merchant. But he is a good man in the fullest sense; and his presence must suggest considerable dignity and intelligence. There should be no trickery or pettiness attached to him. I thought that you would make a great success of Lopakhin's role, which is the central one of the play. If you decide to play Gayev, get Vishnevskii to play the part of Lopakhin—he won't succeed in being an artistic Lopakhin, but he'll avoid being a petty one. Luzhskii would play the ruthless foreigner and Leonidov would make a kulak out of him. [Chekhov to K. S. Stanislavskii, 30 October 1903]

Chekhov's letter to Stanislavskii rejects the Western 'capitalist' *and* the Russian 'kulak' interpretation of the merchant, and calls for him to be artistic, intelligent, and thoroughly human, thereby countering those Soviet and Western interpretations which prefer to see Lopakhin as a brutal destroyer of beauty. (The Western 'aesthetic' analysis is as misconceived as the Soviet class one—typical of the former is Magarshack's [in *Chekhov the Dramatist*]: 'The cherry orchard indeed is a purely aesthetic symbol which its owners with the traditions of the old culture behind them fully understood . . . to Lopakhin it is only an excellent site for "development".' In fact it is Lopakhin and not the owners who understands this decaying orchard.)

Chekhov was equally adamant about the centrality of Lopakhin's part to Nemirovich-Danchenko:

> If [Stanislavskii] decides to play Lopakhin and succeeds in the part, the play will be a success. But if Lopakhin is made trivial, played by a trivial actor, both the role and the play are certain to fail. [2 November 1903]

To emphasise the artistic sensitivity and humanity of Lopakhin, Chekhov added some words to the final version of the play, in which he makes even Trofimov recognise his qualities:

> Your fingers are fine and gentle, like an artist's, and you are refined and sensitive at heart.

And to the actor Leonidov, Chekhov insisted that Lopakhin should 'look like a cross between a merchant and a professor of medicine at Moscow University'.

We are given in the letters the image of a man of intelligence, sensitivity and humanity, with features of both the artist and the scientist about him; and this is the image which Chekhov draws with great care in the play itself. Lopakhin loves beauty, but recognises the brutal reality of the world of serfdom which fashioned the values of the cherry orchard people; he regrets his poor education, but as a man of intelligence recognises the emptiness behind Trofimov's supposedly scientific conversation. Like Chekhov, Lopakhin was the grandson of a serf, and too near the people to romanticise them in an abstract or nostalgic manner. Like Chekhov, he was brutally beaten by his shopkeeper father as a child. And like Chekhov, the career of this man with artist's hands and the appearance of a professor of medicine is much concerned with squeezing

the serf out of his soul—in terms not just of social mobility, but spiritual mobility as well. His tipsy but joyous cry from the heart in Act 3 is one of liberation, but his search for identity does *not* end with a merchant's possession of real estate. Lopakhin has a creative vision, of a new life evolving as the unproductive orchard is replaced by gardens where people grow things. In place of the decayed old order and their orchard where beauty hides stagnation, 'our grandchildren and our great-grandchildren will one day see a new living world springing up here'—as always in Chekhov, the reference to the future children, and to the particular time-scale, is significant.

So it is Lopakhin, not Trofimov, who finds meaning in work, and who responds 'scientifically' to the problem of the cherry orchard. It is Lopakhin who has the evolutionary and epic vision of a world of limitless potential peopled by giants. It is Lopakhin alone who, awkward and out of place with his gauche gestures in the claustrophobia of the nursery, does not turn his back on the sweeping horizons and growing technology of Act 2. Yet, unlike Trofimov, his visions are never left as vast generalities. While Trofimov talks arrogantly and abstractly of his place in the vanguard of progress in Act 4, Lopakhin's practical policy of replacing the infertile orchard goes methodically ahead:

> TROFIMOV. Mankind is on the march to the ultimate truth, the most supreme happiness that can be achieved on earth—and I am in the vanguard!
>
> LOPAKHIN. Will you get there?
>
> TROFIMOV. I will . . . Either I'll get there or I'll light the way for others!
>
> (The sound of an axe striking a tree is to be heard in the distance)
>
> LOPAKHIN. Well, my friend, goodbye. It's time we went. We torment each other, and meanwhile life goes on just the same. When I work long hours without a break I think a bit more clearly, and then I seem to know the reason for living.

Trofimov's pause contrasts with the relentless sound of the axe, and his generalities with Lopakhin's enduring work. Thus in Act 2, in response to Trofimov's speech about the need of the intelligentsia to work on behalf of science and art, which concludes with the inaccurate generalisation about workers' conditions, Lopakhin answers pragmatically:

> Now, I want to tell you that I am always up by five every morning. I work from morning till night. I invariably have my own and other people's money around me, and I get plenty of opportunity to see what kind of people they are. You only have to begin work to find out how few honest, decent people there are around.

Trofimov's speech begins with the exhortation to work by a man who never does, and concludes with a false generalisation; Lopakhin responds with a speech about real work in the present and concludes with the vision of a land fit for giants. It is the pragmatist *as well as* the visionary we need to remember. Lopakhin does not oppose Trofimov's appeal to science—indeed he subsumes it in his following words and actions. But he does oppose the abstractions Trofimov is committed to.

Despite the inconsistencies and occasional naivety of a peasant who has become a landowner, Lopakhin has no simplistic solutions. He recognises the human suffering as well as the hope that accompanies progress, and at the moment of his triumph weeps genuinely for the woman he had desperately tried to help. His maturity is of a dialectical kind: he wants to save the old class by changing it; he wants to preserve its human values while removing their social basis. The values of the old order should not be killed, as Trofimov would have it, but subsumed, incorporated within a new, growing humanity—just as Trofimov's vision of science is incorporated. Ranevskaya and Trofimov, master and revolutionary, are given value—or more precisely, both synthesised and rejected—by Lopakhin. But the way is hard, and unlike the revolutionary, Lopakhin cannot hear the footsteps of the new life:

> How I wish we could get past this stage. If we could just change this unhappy and arbitrary life soon.

Lopakhin can *feel* Ranevskaya's tragedy, and knows, like Gurov at the end of **"Lady with a Little Dog,"** that the way ahead is not simple.

Against Ranevskaya's suffering there is hope, and against Trofimov's hope, suffering: it is in this context that the sound of the breaking string can be understood. A detailed reading of the text surrounding its first appearance reveals a typical pattern. Ranevskaya wants to avoid the question of the cherry orchard by reverting to the talk of the past. Trofimov talks of the future of man and science—punctuated by Gayev's fatalistic pessimism, by Ranevskaya's eagerness to find some meaning in him, and by Lopakhin's irony over his pseudo-science. There follows Trofimov's speech about Russian intellectuals and the condition of the workers, then Lopakhin's practical refutation of it and his vision of a land fit for giants. Ranevskaya immediately trivialises Lopakhin's vision with her own fears:

> Why on earth do you want giants? They're fine enough in fairy tales but they terrify me anywhere else.

The juxtaposition of her banality and Lopakhin's sense of potential induces a feeling of melancholy, emphasised by the guitar of 'twenty-two misfortunes', Ranevskaya's pensive 'There goes Yepikhodov' (repeated by Anya) and the going down of the sun. There follows Gayev's typically fatalistic acceptance of the separation of Nature and man:

> (quietly, as if reciting): Oh, Nature, glorious Nature! You shine with your eternal light, so beautiful and yet so impervious to our fate.

Anya and Varya as usual beg him not to talk so pompously, and Trofimov emphasises the escapism of Gayev's vision with 'You'd better double off the red back into the middle pocket'. Gayev relapses into his other refrain, 'I'll be silent. I'll be silent'. There follows a pensive silence, broken only by the subdued muttering of Firs. Suddenly, out of the dark vastness of Nature itself comes a cry of melancholy—as in **"The Steppe"**; there it was a bird calling for understanding, here it is the sound of a breaking string from the technological world these nursery people have ignored.

The reactions are typical and significant. Lopakhin explains the sound rationally and practically—it comes from the mine. Gayev continues his thoughts about Nature, and thinks it was some bird, perhaps a heron. Trofimov converts this into a bird presaging ominous and great events, the owl. Ranevskaya is frightened and almost immediately gives more money away, as though buying off something incomprehensible. Varya is also frightened, but worries about her mistress' improvidence. Firs dreams of the golden days before the great 'troubles'. Gayev shakes and wants to escape from implacable Nature to his billiard room, just as Trofimov had suggested. So the sound of the breaking string, like the cherry orchard which began this conversation of evasion, distinguishes the alternatives of action in a world where 'everything's muddled'. Afterwards the landowners, as always, escape, Lopakhin turns to the practical question of the cherry orchard, and Trofimov stays with Anya to talk of revolution.

The second sound of the breaking string also takes place in the silences around the muttering Firs; and is directly stimulated by the contradictions, the hope and suffering (of Anya/Trofimov against Ranevskaya/Gayev; more personally of Lopakhin against Varya), which dramatise the question of the cherry orchard. The sad sound of the axe punctuates Firs' statement of the tragedy of human potential:

> Life's over as though I'd never lived. . . . You've got no strength left, you old fool. Nothing's left, nothing.

As this last, decayed man falls motionless, the sound of the breaking string coming out of the wide sky again speaks the elegy of man separated from value. The betrayed potential of the cherry orchard people is evident in this isolated old servant in the abandoned nursery where he is the only object of nostalgia left. The shepherd's pipe calling to the youthful Anya and Varya in the enclosed nursery of Act 1, which is an ambivalent call of potential and stagnation, is not answered. But the ambivalence is clarified. The true value of the nursery is now clear; for nostalgia there is emptiness, for naive youth there is abandoned old age. And outside, in the final moment of the play, there is the sound of Lopakhin's axe. Real value, real time, like Lopakhin's more successful actions, lie beyond the nursery, and that is the dramatic point of the play. . . .

[At] the social level **The Cherry Orchard** clarifies the potential responses of stagnation, revolution and scientific evolution to the contradictions of the modernising autocracy; at the personal level, it dramatises the struggle of a man of artistic and scientific sensitivity to squeeze the serf mentality of Russia and of his childhood out of his soul. The struggle for development was both Russia's and Chekhov's own.

John Tulloch, in his Chekhov: A Structuralist Study, *The Macmillan Press, Ltd., 1980, 225 p.*

Clayton A. Hubbs and Joanna T. Hubbs   (essay date 1982)

[*In the following essay, the critics study mythic and folkloric motifs in* The Cherry Orchard.]

In the climactic scene of *The Cherry Orchard,* Gayev recites the following hymn to the Great Mother Goddess:

> Oh, glorious Nature, shining with eternal light, so beautiful and yet so indifferent to our fate . . . you whom we call Mother, uniting in yourself both Life and Death, you live and you destroy. . . .

Gayev's speech is followed by an embarrassed silence *"only broken by the subdued muttering of Feers. Suddenly a distant sound is heard, coming as if out of the sky, like the sound of a string snapping, slowly and sadly dying away."* In the stage directions for the scene, the trees of the cherry orchard are contrasted to man-made trees, telegraph poles:

> *A road leads to Gayev's estate. On one side and at some distance away there is a row of dark poplars, and it is there that the cherry orchard begins. Further away is seen a line of telegraph poles, and beyond them, on the horizon, the vague outlines of a large town, visible only in very good, clear weather.*

In the final scene of the play we hear the breaking string a second time, this time against the background of the cherry trees being cut down to make way for construction. Liubov, whose name means "love" and whose role in the play suggests her identification with the Mother Goddess, is cast out into the profane world as if she were Eve being cast out of Paradise: "Oh my darling, my precious, my beautiful orchard! My life, my youth, my happiness . . . good-bye! . . . Good-bye!"

Gayev's evocation of nature as an indifferent goddess juxtaposed with the sound of a breaking string produces a sense of sadness and dislocation, the prevailing tone of *The Cherry Orchard* and all of Chekhov's plays. "Out of the sky" suggests a break between man and the sustaining cosmos. The association of Liubov with the tree (the chopping down of the trees and the departure of the mother occur together against the sound of the breaking string) provides us with a clue to the complex symbolism and structure of the play: The role of the Great Goddess changes from that of the bringer of life to the agent of death, from an initial association with the Tree of Life to a final association with the Tree of Knowledge, from the central and totemic figure of the Goddess to the denigrated and sinful Eve.

The mother, in the double aspect that Gayev describes her, as the agent of life and of death, is clearly the central figure that informs *The Cherry Orchard.* The play's four acts follow the movement of the seasons, from spring and the promise of renewal of life with the return of the mother in act one to winter and the coming of death in act four. By isolating one aspect of the Great Mother Goddess, her totemic association with trees (in this case the cherry trees of the orchard) and noting the change that occurs as the nature of that association moves from one with the Tree

of Life (the cherry as the fruit-bearing tree which feeds both peasant and gentry) to the Tree of Knowledge (telegraph poles, man-made trees which indicate the dislocation and human isolation of industrial society), we will disclose the controlling symbolism of the play and outline its movement from the promise of renewal of comedy and to the suffering and death of tragedy.

The historian of religion Fedotov argues [in *The Russian Religious Mind,* 1960] that the cult of nature as mother is deeply embedded in Russian life and is the source of Russian religiosity. Christianization merely transformed the caring Russian Demeter into the all-encompassing *Bogoroditsa* (Mother of God). At the same time the evil aspects of the Mother Goddess—as death dealer—were identified in part with the temptress Eve, the sinful rebel, mother of mankind whose action condemned her children to exile and death. Eve became the prototype for the disobedient and hence evil wife against whose snares the Orthodox church warned its male members. But the cult of the pagan all-powerful Great Mother continued in Russia into the twentieth century. As Gayev's speech reminds us, the two aspects of the Great Goddess as bringer of life and death are clearly united. What is involved here is a gradual displacement of her functions. To appreciate fully Chekhov's use of the complex symbolism of the double aspect of the mother and of the feminine, we must consider the

Chekhov and Maxim Gorky, 1900.

disparity between her image in Russian folklore and in Christian mythology.

Russian folklore is suffused with the worship of "Mother Moist Earth" (*Mat' Syra Zemlia*) embodying the forces of nature and the family bond. She appears to bear her children parthenogenetically. Though she is without name, she is akin to Demeter, goddess of fertility and motherly love. The peasant is her child, tied to the earth umbilically as though to the body of the nurturing mother. Fedotov describes him as "the fatherless son of Mother Earth" and though she taught him fidelity, he continues, she did not instill in him the male virtues of freedom and valor. Since she represents the totality of being and nature, she is the good, nurturing mother; but she is also the evil *hetaera* and hag. Russian folklore presents us with these two distinct aspects of her being in the figures of the witch Baba Yaga and the nymphs called *rusalki*. It is through them that the linkage of earth and tree, of the Goddess with her Tree of Life, seems most apparent.

The cannibal witch Baba Yaga lives alone in the forest but is frequently represented as the mother of many daughters and surrounded by all forms of animal life. Through her fearsome hut on hen's feet youths must pass in their rites of passage into manhood and womanhood. They must escape her oven, her maw. But she is not merely a dangerous obstacle in the quest; she can also provide the key to success to the hero or heroine who knows how to win her favor or outwit her. This dual function, good and evil, is also shared by the *rusalki*. Here the sexual aspect suggested metaphorically in Baba Yaga's oven and her "heraldry," the mortar and pestle, is more pronounced, while the maternal aspects are diminished. The *rusalki* or Russian sirens are thought to live in all three elements of nature—water, earth, and sky—and their movement from one to the other suggests their role in the process of fertility as self-inseminatory. They are represented often as half-birds, half-fish. From their perches in the trees to which they migrate in the spring from their abodes in lakes, rivers, or springs, they lure men to their death. At the same time they bring fertility to the land.

Both the Yaga and the *rusalki* are linked with trees—the first as the mother living in the midst of her primeval forest; the latter as *hetaera*, who lure the unwary. The tree, which in the form of the birch is associated with the Greek Goddess in Russian lore, is often represented as her homologue. In folk art, particularly embroidery, one often finds the motif of a goddess (perhaps "Mother Moist Earth" herself) flanked by horsemen, animals, birds, and many forms of vegetation. Frequently, the figure of a woman is replaced by that of the universal symbol of the Tree of Life, suggestive of the Mother Goddess encompassing her male child-consort. In Russian folk tradition the tree has an especially significant function. It is closely associated with the natural cycle of fertility for which it is the totem. The "priestesses" of the Tree of Life are peasant women—both young and mature. In the rites of the agrarian calendar which regulate all social and personal life of the peasantry, women are the midwives of nature who help deliver her child in the form of the harvest. Their homology with the fertile earth is suggested in the following Christianized proverb: "Your first Mother is Mary, your second mother is the earth, and your third is your own mother." In the calenderic rites that fertility is linked with trees. The festival of "bringing in the spring" which began the pagan year rites was the most joyous of the Russian festivals. In some areas before the Revolution, girls brought a doll figure or a tree from the forest into the village and called it "our Blessed Mother Spring"; and as though to suggest the persistence of rites in Russia which recall those of Demeter and Kore, they sang: "My spring, where is your daughter?" This ritual initiated a series of festivals in which women appeared to transfer the power of the tree, its rising sap—represented mythologically as the migration of the *rusalki* from water to tree—into the village to stimulate seeds planted in the fields and, analogously, human fertility. Going into the forest during the spring festival of Rusalia, girls and women decorated and chopped down a tree called a "Rusalka." This tree was used to augur future marriages.

While the tree is perceived as the symbol of the mother as nature and has the significance of the Tree of Life in the folkloric context, in Christian symbolism the Edenic tree is no longer called the Tree of Life but the Tree of Knowledge and is presided over by an angry male god rather than a maternal goddess. The feminine, once analogous with the cosmos, is derogated to the function of the helpmate of Adam, created rather than creating, born through the masculine "womb"—Logos. (One might call her "manufactured.") As Eve, she is the source of man's fall, his willful seductress; and yet she is also the mother of mankind—a disobedient and hence evil mother who condemns her progeny to death. In her rebellion against the just Jehovah, she sinned by reassociating herself with the forbidden tree through the act of eating its fruit.

In *The Cherry Orchard* we see precisely the movement from the orchard presided over by the ancient form of the goddess as the Tree of Life, the fruit-producing tree, to the orchard which begins to lose its life-giving harvest, abandoned by its goddess and ceding to the Edenic Tree of Knowledge—of the bitter and divisive fruit. Chekhov's image of the orchard dissolving into the line of telegraph poles clearly suggests the displacement of one by the other: the domain of nature is to be dominated and subjected to man's design. Liubov, the mother, thus embodies both pagan and Christian mythologems: She is a mother goddess, giver of life and fertility, as her name implies; but she becomes increasingly impotent and thus evil, suggesting the unpredictable aspects of the *rusalki* and the Yaga who avenge themselves on those who disobey them. The once all-powerful goddess is displaced from her orchard—her own creation. As the fallen Eve, Liubov betrays the old Adam, her weak brother Gayev who is under her power, and abandons the orchard to the "New Adams," Trofimov and Lopahin. As the degraded Eve, her act is one of rebellion: She showers her last gold on the ground until she has none to give and leaves those who will no longer worship her former glory and her orchard. In so doing, she condemns the orchard to destruction and those who remain to the routine of meaningless work "by the sweat of their brow."

We now see the context for the complex symbolism of *The*

Cherry Orchard. The Tree of Life which produces fruit is now, if not useless, not used. It stands as the "totem" of agrarian Russia, the place in which gentry and peasants communed in the cycle of nature. As old Feers says, "The peasant belonged to the gentry and the gentry belonged to the peasant; and now everything is separate and you can't understand a thing." All this has resulted from the orchard's falling into neglect after the initial departure of Liubov. The final break comes with her sale of the orchard and its abandonment. Liubov thus appears as a last representative of the sustaining power of the pagan nature myth; her "fall" brings to an end the old comic cycle of death and rebirth and suggests the "linear" finality of modern tragedy.

Having outlined the thematic and structural bases of the play in myth and folklore, we will examine its dramatic movement from the hope of renewed life to the fact of death. Despite our emphasis on chronology to show the mythic analogues, we wish to emphasize that Liubov's transformation from the goddess of love to the fallen Eve does not come as straightforward progression. Like the literal and historical levels of meaning, the mythic one remains richly ambiguous and cuts across the other two.

Liubov's springtime arrival as the sun comes up brings with it the promise of renewal. She is escorted by her worshipful entourage. Her daughters, her former serf, and her brother Gayev bring her, like the Goddess of Spring, into the nursery where she appears both as the resurrected child ("I feel as if I were little again") and the mother of her drowned son and two unmarried daughters. She is both a Russian Demeter and a Kore. However, the goddess has already foresaken her land; her beautiful Adonis-like child has died—as a result of what she calls "her sins," her sexual transgressions—and the peasants go hungry. It is the death of the child which has driven her away. To pay the debts for her sins, the orchard must be sold and her trees sacrificed.

But for the moment there is hope of a paradise regained, of the old order renewed. Only her adopted peasant daughter Varia, who "lives like a nun," suspects that "in fact there's nothing in it, it's all a kind of dream." But the old serf Feers, embodiment of the old order, says: "The Mistress is home again! Home at last! I don't mind if I die now . . . (*Weeps with joy*)." Coming right after Ania's recapitulation of the past and announcement to the audience that little brother Grisha was drowned in the river, this reference to a "happy" death as though it were an old man's return to the maternal womb ironically unites the child-Adonis to the old man. Liubov leaves because of an unexpected death over which she appeared to have no control and returns not to life but to another death—that of the old man Feers, of the orchard, and of the "grandfather house" contained within it. Child, old man, house, and orchard—encompassing all in a maternal bond—will disappear at play's end as Liubov leaves. But for now she has returned, and she is happy: "God, how I love my own country! I love it so much, I could hardly see it from the train, I was crying all the time [*through tears*]. However, I must drink my coffee. Thank you, Feers, thank you, my dear old friend. I am so glad I found you still alive."

In her tears she evokes the Orthodox version of the God-bearer Madonna whose image co-exists among the peasantry with that of Mother Earth. In her iconic as well as ritual and folkloric representation—as the embodiment of the orchard and the symbol of the Goddess of Love—she will be destroyed for money. But as we have seen, she is not only the grieving Madonna who weeps for the death of humanity, she is also the pagan goddess of sexual and profane love. She is a *rusalka*, a *siren*, in the guise of the Christianized temptress Eve. In Paris—the image of the West through which industrialization reaches Russia and through which the cycle of the seasons is superseded by the dictates of society and machine, in which woman rules as "coquette" rather than in her maternal role as goddess of bonding love—the consort of the former goddess is a sickly lover. Maternal love is replaced by a shady "liaison" in a society where pairings are determined by man, not nature, and not for the reproduction of life but for profane pleasures.

Meanwhile the orchard languishes. The "debate" over its fate is the apparent action of the play. Lopahin, who loves Liubov and still worships her, insists that the cherry orchard be cut down to pay the family debts. Although Lopahin's spiritual attachment to Liubov remains, his dependence on the natural cycle has been replaced by a compulsion to work and to accumulate capital. In the past the orchard provided nourishment to the entire county. In the old days, Feers says, "they had a recipe." But the "recipe," the contract or bond with the natural order made by both peasant and gentry, cemented by the nurturing mother, is now forgotten. Lopahin, the embodiment of one form of the new Adam, sums it up:

> Up to just recently there were only gentry and peasants living in the country, but now there are all these summer residents. All the towns, even quite small ones, are surrounded with villas. And probably in the course of the next twenty years or so, these people will multiply tremendously. At present they merely drink tea on the verandah, but they might start cultivating their plots of land, and then your cherry orchard would be gay with life and wealth and luxury. . . .

Liubov's weak brother, Gayev, who remains more strongly under her spell, can only say, "What nonsense," anticipating the very words with which Liubov will chastise Lopahin for his sentimental belief in the future and work. Gayev—like the landowner Pishchik, Feers, and her children—are still in her sphere.

In act one it is Gayev who reminds Liubov of her identification with the orchard:

> GAYEV [*opens another window*]. The orchard is all white. You haven't forgotten, Liuba? . . . Do you remember? You haven't forgotten?
>
> LIUBOV ANDRYEEVNA [*looks through the window at the orchard*]. Oh my childhood, my innocent childhood! I used to sleep in this nursery; I used to look on to the orchard from here, and I woke up happy every morning. In those days the orchard was just as it is now, nothing has changed. [*Laughs happily.*] All white! Oh, my

orchard! After the dark, stormy autumn and the cold winter, you are young and joyous again. . . .

She sees her mother "walking through the orchard . . . in a white dress! [*Laughs happily.*] It is her!" The orchard is not only Liubov in youth, as Kore, it is also her Mother Demeter whose role she herself has now assumed in regard to her children. The cherry trees dressed in white appear as an embodiment of woman. Trofimov, who enters in his shabby clothes, links the orchard in its bloom with her drowned son Grisha: In a literal as well as symbolic sense he takes Grisha's place. While Lopahin will take the place of Liubov as the "owner" of the land which is organically attached to her, so Trofimov will take the place of the youth unattached to the mother and looking forward to history and man's actions outside the organic sphere of nature as mother. Trofimov, a prototype for the forward-looking intelligentsia which wishes to propel Russia into the industrialized and westernized future, replaces Grisha, the child-Adonis attached to the mother. Liubov at first fails to recognize him and then strongly dislikes him:

> LIUBOV ANDRYEEVNA [*quietly weeping*]. My little boy was lost . . . drowned . . . What for? What for, my friend? [*More quietly.*] How is it that you've lost your good looks? Why have you aged so?
>
> TROFIMOV. A peasant woman in the train called me "that motheaten gent."
>
> LIUBOV ANDRYEEVNA. In those days you were quite a boy, a nice young student, and now your hair is thin, you wear glasses. . . . Are you still a student? [*Walks to the door.*]
>
> TROFIMOV. I expect I shall be a student to the end of my days.

The image of the mother and her drowned child suggests the interruption of the nurturance and continuance of life through the body of the mother. One can see in Trofimov, the petrified *puer eternus,* the symbol of that interrupted cycle. He is implicated in the child's death—most clearly in the sense that Grisha had been passed into his hands by Liubov to be "educated." Trofimov, the child substitute, exists only through his continued attachment to the Tree of Knowledge—the symbol of alienation, sin, and exile.

In the second act the focus shifts from the past to the present, from spring to summer, and the dream of regeneration of the first act is dramatically shattered. All the ancient folkloric motifs linking nature to mother and family are present in the background against which the servants, aping their betters, complain of loneliness and isolation. Here Gayev delivers his hymn to the Great Goddess. The shrine in the open fields is by a well, sacred in the folk tradition to the water nymphs, the *rusalki*; the discarded gravestones in the disused shrine evoke the image of the disintegration of the family clan with the dissolution of the worship of the mother-centered natural cycle. The action will still take place in the field, but the outline of a town looms on the horizon. The trees cede to telegraph poles threading their way out of the orchard and into the city. The servants' "dumb show" anticipates the one at play's

end, the death of old Feers. Chekhov includes each character in the tragic action.

Lopahin attempts to persuade the lady to sell the estate for building plots. Liubov complains that her servants go hungry (the old servants get nothing but dried peas from her daughter Varia) while she spills coins on the open field. But she is not too distracted to admonish Lopahin, as she has Trofimov, for the drab and meaningless life he leads and to suggest, unsuccessfully, that he marry Varia. Liubov as matchmaker, as the goddess of the family who determines fates, finds herself unable to mate her own daughter to these "new men." Feers reminds them that in the old order "peasants belonged to the gentry and the gentry belonged to the peasants; but now everything is separate and you can't understand anything." As a counterpoint, Trofimov pompously lectures Liubov and Gayev on the "progressive" opinions of a segment of the intelligentsia. Man is not a child of Mother Nature; he is a self-created being: "Where's the sense of being proud when you consider that Man, as a species, is not very well constructed physiologically and in the vast majority of cases is coarse, stupid, and profoundly unhappy too? We ought to stop all this self-admiration. We ought to—just work." Trofimov and Lopahin thus come together in opposition to Liubov and her weakling brother as the new men whose recipe for salvation is to oppose the natural order, "to work." Trofimov works for a new humanity, an "advanced" mankind; Lopahin, more practically, works to enhance his financial worth. One is absorbed in ideas, the other in amassing wealth. Neither has time for love.

As an ironic counterpoint to the progressive visions of these "new men," Gayev, the Old Adam, sings his hymn to the Great Goddess, and we hear the sound of the breaking string. The break with nature and the past is complete; but the men of the future, Lopahin and Trofimov, are false prophets. As it was for the three sisters, Chekhov shows us that all this knowledge is useless without a sustaining myth, a reason for existing.

In the autumn of act three the future already belongs to Trofimov and Lopahin. Liubov is now the patriarchalized version of the Great Mother of the ancient world, Eve, whose sin makes mankind suffer. It is Liubov's regrettable inattentiveness which results in the sale of the orchard and the necessity to "toil in the sweat of one's brow." It is through her that man is expelled from sacred to profane time, from the mythic realm of Eden to the stage of history where his sins must be expiated through labor and torment. She is the scapegoat and will be expelled in act four. As the orchard goes, so goes Mother Russia, Old Russia—subdivided into plots, industrialized to the rhythm of the machine and the clock. Liubov has lost all power:

> LIUBOV ANDRYEEVNA. What truth? *You* can see where the truth is and where it isn't, but I seem to have lost my power of vision. I don't see anything. . . . You look ahead so boldly—but isn't that because life is still hidden from your young eyes. . . . I can't conceive life without the cherry orchard and if it really has to be sold then sell me with it. . . . [*Embraces* TROFIMOV, *kisses him on the forehead.*] You know, my son was drowned here. . . . [*Weeps.*] Have pity on me.

Trofimov has replaced Grisha, but he has not grown up; her daughter wishes to marry a "freak" who is "above love." When Lopahin enters to gloat over his purchase of the estate and order the trees cut, the sense of rape and despoliation of nature and her daemon Liubov is complete. Lopahin's "new life" will come at the expense of the destruction of an organic unity with nature. Chekhov's irony here is perhaps almost too apparent. The tyranny of nature—and of the old social order—is replaced by the tyranny of labor and of money:

> LOPAHIN. Everything must be just as *I* wish it now. [*Ironically.*] Here comes the new landowner, here comes the owner of the cherry orchard!

Only Ania and Varia, the daughter "priestesses" of the Great Mother, each one linked with one aspect of the New Men, Trofimov and Lopahin, still attempt to worship Liubov's now empty powers.

Act four, winter, is marked by *"an oppressive sense of emptiness."* Liubov, the Great Goddess as Demeter, promising fertility and renewal in the spring of the first act, has now become Kore and Eve, reigning over the house of the dead. Lopahin and Trofimov combine as the patriarchal figures of Pluto and Jehovah who have captured her forever perhaps. When spring comes again, the house and its remaining inhabitants will no longer exist, ceding to the new industrial, patriarchal order.

Lopahin and Trofimov see salvation only in continuous planning for the future and in work. No longer attached to the regular cycle of the seasons, work becomes neurotic repetition with no cosmic pivot. Lopahin says, "When I work for long hours on end without taking any time off, I feel happier in my mind and *I even imagine I know why I exist*" (emphasis added). Man is not expendable in nature: he rejoins his family and ancestors and forms a collective unit with them in the natural cycle. However, in society he is expendable, an often unnecessary cog—Trofimov's "coarse, stupid" humanity. With the departure of the mother goddess from whom the peasantry as well as their masters drew strength, meaningful life comes to an end.

> GAYEV [*with despair in his voice*]. Sister, my sister. . . .
>
> LIUBOV ANDRYEEVNA. Oh my darling, my precious, my beautiful orchard! My life, my youth, my happiness . . . good-bye! . . . Goodbye!

The world left in its new cycle of history and labor—the "new life" welcomed by Trofimov in his last line in the play—appears doomed to sterility and its children to a sense of orphanage, unable to communicate their sorrow or their love. The mother, as the totem holding the family together, leaves her children scattered. The extreme pathos of Chekhov's plays is thus focused in the breaking string—the break with nature as mother, the eternal ground of communion for humanity.

We must conclude that in Liubov's final relinquishment of the cherry orchard Chekhov presents us with the end of a myth, the displacement of the Tree of Life by the Tree of Knowledge and of the Great Mother Goddess by the sinful Eve. Man is driven from the paradise of comedy by a destiny which finally denies his cyclically based perceptions. In place of the reassuring continuum of the natural cycle, Chekhov's characters face discontinuity and death. In *Three Sisters,* Vershinin considers what it would be like to start life all over again: "If that happened, I think the thing you'd want most of all would be not to repeat yourself." In *The Cherry Orchard* we see that hope fulfilled, with a suggestion of its consequences. It may be argued that Chekhov's plays represent the end of the evolution of drama from the fertility rites of traditional man who lives in myth to the empty repetitions of modern man who lives in a condition of constant material and spiritual dislocation. In Chekhov's earlier plays the mother's absence is the major source of pathos. In *The Cherry Orchard,* the reasons for the absence and the consequences are fully presented: Liubov, who first abandons and then is betrayed by her children, loses her power; with her departure the cord which had attached them to the land and its cyclic laws is broken.

In re-examining Chekhov's plays from the perspective of the archetypes from myth and folklore which inform them, we may better understand not only the structure of individual works but the nature and significance of all of Chekhov's dramatic works. We see that they are not limited to what Francis Fergusson has called "the little scene of modern realism" or to the absurd drama of arbitrary issue. Like the tragic drama of the ancient Greeks, Chekhov's plays dramatize man's relation to natural forces over which he attempts—and fails—to gain control. Attempts to subdue the forces of nature lead to psychic dissolution, alienation, and abandonment. The central archetypes remain the same; the specific forms are drawn from the tradition of Russian folklore and Christian myth.

On the climax of *The Cherry Orchard:*

In Chekhov the actions that occur are irrelevant to the willed desires of the characters. What is scrupulously denied is a catharsis of any recognizable sort, even a true dramatic climax. When climaxes are provided they are always out of focus, for Chekhov's people cannot see clearly enough to do what might be expected of them by ordinary standards. . . . The climax of *The Cherry Orchard*—the merchant Lopakhin's revelation that it is he who has bought the estate on which his father was once a serf ("I bought it," he announces with pride and awe)—initiates wrong reactions from everyone, for Lopakhin is the central character and had wanted in some confused way recognition for what he had done; this leads into the strange fourth act, an act of abandonment and leave-taking conducted with the most banal of conversations. Technically, a climax occurs in each play, but thematically, it is somehow not the right climax. The true issues are always avoided.

Joyce Carol Oates, in her The Edge of Impossibility: Tragic Forms in Literature, *Victor Gollancz Ltd., 1976.*

Clayton A. Hubbs and Joanna T. Hubbs, "The Goddess of Love and the Tree of Knowledge: Some Elements of Myth and Folklore in Chekhov's 'The Cherry Orchard'," in The South Carolina Review, *Vol. 14, No. 2, Spring, 1982, pp. 66-77.*

Greta Anderson (essay date 1991)

[*In the following essay, Anderson proposes that linguistic and phonic patterns reinforce the structure and meaning of* The Cherry Orchard.]

Kay Unruh Des Roches has recently demonstrated how an analysis of the verbal repetitions in the original text of Ibsen's *The Lady from the Sea* contributes to a specific understanding of the play which a close study of its English translations would not be able to yield ["A Problem of Translation: Structural Patterns in the Language of Ibsen's *The Lady from the Sea,*" *Modern Drama,* 30 (1987)]. Her essay suggests that all plays in translation "need a criticism based on a detailed description of untranslatable elements in the original text," a criticism which would be as relevant to the theater as to the classroom. Chekhov's major plays certainly merit such an approach, not only because they are so popular in both settings, but because, even in translation, their verbal repetitions (and acoustic repetitions) are such a significant part of our experience of them. Here, a reading of the Russian text of *The Cherry Orchard* will reveal the original shape and sound of its repetitions and probe the meanings inhering in their arrangement. As in Ibsen's play, the repetitions in Chekhov create local patterns which telescope into the play's larger thematic structure. By understanding the play in terms of musical structures, we can appreciate in greater detail the measured grace and good humor with which the playwright has his characters conduct themselves together, in the face of an uncertain future. Attention to structural rhythms tends toward a reading of the play more in accord with Chekhov's designation of the play as a comedy than do most interpretations, particularly those which focus on its closing moments. Of the final snapped string, [J. L. Styan has written in *Chekhov in Performance,* 1971], "to interpret that sound is to interpret the play": this essay will explicate the rhythmic framework in which that note sounds.

Throughout this play in which "nothing happens," Chekhov creates a dramatic "action" based on community and place—ultimately, the severance of the two. Thus, the characters appear on stage just as they would appear on the family estate, engaged in casual conversation or hysteric outburst, as the case may be. What makes such a loose "ensemble" structure cohere is, at least in part, the interplay of different types of verbal and acoustic repetition, with intermittent repetitions establishing a base rhythm upon which are layered the lyrical swells and lulls of local repetition. Through the effects of these two techniques on the audience's experience of time and emotion, Chekhov creates the boundaries of scenes and acts, and structures the play's close. The most common form of intermittent repetition occurs in character-specific "motifs," from Gayev's "cue ball into the corner" to Yepikhodov's sad song on the guitar. Such repetitions function to count-

er the strange with the familiar, the tragic with the perpetually comic, and, recurring from beginning to end as they do, mark the play's progress through time, evoking the pulse of particular lives through fateful vicissitudes. Local repetitions, as when a word is sounded twice—"doubling"—or when characters repeat their own words or others' within the space of a speech or exchange, often serve to amplify the tenor of the moment, but may also "round off" scenes within acts and close the acts themselves, returning heightened emotions to a baseline level, bringing silence to the stage.

The first line we hear Pishchik utter is the phrase "Think of that now!" in response to Charlotta's out-of-the-blue assertion: "My dog even eats nuts." He repeats this phrase twelve times in the play. This repetition establishes him as a gaping, vacuous character, but his character type is less important here than Chekhov's use of his "Think of that now!"'s. The second delivery occurs later in Act One, following an equally bizarre exchange:

> PISHCHIK. How was it in Paris? What's it like there? Did you eat frogs?
>
> LYUBOV. I ate crocodiles.
>
> PISHCHIK. Think of that now!

Moments later, Pishchik interrupts Gayev's verbal tribute to an antique bookcase with the exclamation: "A hundred years! . . . Think of that now!"

Pishchik's repetitive exclamations form a pattern of response to the more eccentric, potentially discordant elements in the play. The absolute predictability of his reaction domesticates the wild unpredictability of speeches like those cited above, balancing out the outrageousness in which Chekhov, and Chekhov's audience, delights. Both *Uncle Vanya* and *The Three Sisters* are much about the social carrying capacities of their communities, and the strain on equilibrium caused by certain combinations of personalities. In this sense, the community of *The Cherry Orchard* could not tolerate another Charlotta, nor could it do without Pishchik's normalizing responses, "Think of that now!" But Pishchik is not a "blank" background character. We take interest in him, not only because he swallows a boxful of pills, but because his speech is so consistently vacant. Pishchik's repetitive domestications of eccentricity are in fact just another genre of eccentricity.

Like Pishchik's expressions, Gayev's billiards speeches, though strange or obsessive by the standards of the outside world, form a normalizing subtext within the play. In almost every scene in which he appears, we witness the soon familiar "Cut shot into the corner" or one of its variants, accompanied by an appropriate pantomime. Other characters encourage this behavior. Lyubov is the first to articulate the standard line, responding to her brother's gestural "cue" with "How does it go? Let's see if I can remember . . . cue ball into the corner! Double the rail to center table," a speech which, being her first upon entering the stage, reveals her desire to resume the patterned discourse of the community she left and now returns to. In a later scene, Trofimov suggests that Gayev "cue ball into the center," his attempts at grandiloquence having been unanimously shut down. Gayev's billiards habit is endorsed by his family as more tolerable than his tendency to apostrophize the closest object at hand. Other characters rave, but Gayev is silenced as soon as he launches into his fustian extemporizations, and it is precisely because the others are allowed to rave that Gayev must be limited to his billiards motif. Trofimov, Lyubov, and to a lesser extent, Lopakhin all express deeply held and contrasting points of view—about tradition and change, love, the peasants; Gayev's idiosyncratic lyricism clutters the arena of situated conflict, and participates in communal discourse only to be silenced.

"Cue ball into the corner" and its variants not only provide Gayev's community an alternative to his excessive speechifying, they also provide him a viable response to personal crisis. According to Chekhov's stage directions, he announces his imaginary billiards shots *"in deep thought," "forlornly,"* and finally, *"afraid of bursting into tears."* Gayev's habitual dislocation of emotion in the billiards game is not acutely demonstrated in Act Three, during the public disclosure of his financial ruin. Gayev enters the scene of the party weeping from the auction's outcome. When, from the adjacent room, the click of billiard balls is heard, his expression changes: he stops weeping, and returns to his everyday concerns, leaving with Firs to change out of his business clothes. The allusion to billiards in this scene is most poignant because the symbolic language of billiards and the emotion Gayev brings to it are so unequal in value. Billiards is just a game, but it is Gayev's stronghold against debilitating change.

The repeated instances of Gayev's verbal tic might be charted as "ticks" on the play's temporal axis. Since these utterances are distributed equally throughout the play and, as Lyubov's initial speech makes clear, existed before the play, they form a constant that we can imagine will continue into the next phase of Gayev's life. Pishchik's banal "Think of that now"'s produce a similar rhythmic effect. But while these intermittent repetitions might be said to "keep time" in the play, its local repetitions serve to amplify the dimensions of individual moments, as characters use them to express their joy or grief—their passions. Likewise, while the pre-existence and continuation of certain verbal patterns suggest the sensation of unbounded or existential time, those rhythms are counterbalanced by the containing power of local repetitions at the ends of scenes and acts.

Of the play's characters, Lyubov, Anya and Varya most frequently use local repetition for emotional emphasis:

> LYUBOV. Today my fate is decided . . . my fate. (Act III)

> ANYA. I'm at peace now! I'm at peace! (Act I)

Local repetition is often syntactically enhanced, as in these cases of anaphora and epistrophe:

> LYUBOV. You should be a man, at your age you should understand those who love. And you yourself should love . . . you should fall in love! [*Angrily*] Yes, yes! (Act III)

> CHARLOTTA. But where I come from and who I am—I don't know. . . . Who my parents were—perhaps they weren't even married—I don't know. . . . I don't know anything. (Act II)

Doubling, or the immediate repetition of a word, occurs frequently in the play; the words most often repeated thus are those of silencing or coming and going:

> VARYA. Don't talk about it, don't talk about it. (Act I)

> GAYEV. I'll be silent, silent. (Act II)

> LOPAKHIN. I'm going, I'm going. (Act I)

> GAYEV. I'm coming, I'm coming. (Act I)

In the following passage, Gayev and Trofimov attempt to silence Lyubov by doubled repetition. The scattered repetition in Lyubov's initial speech reflects her disrupted emotions: "son," the word best modified by "my," is separated from her two utterances of that pronoun. As Lyubov gains control, she uses repetition—"For what? For what, my friend?" —to intensify her expression of grief:

> GAYEV [*embarrassed*]. Now, now, Lyuba.

> VARYA [*crying*]. Didn't I tell you, Petya, to wait until tomorrow?

> LYUBOV ANDREYEVNA. My Grisha . . . my little boy . . . Grisha . . . son . . .

> VARYA. What can we do, Mama dear? It's God's will.

> TROFIMOV [*gently, through tears*]. There, there . . .

> LYUBOV ANDREYEVNA [*crying softly*]. My little boy is dead, drowned . . . For what? For what, my friend? . . . But Petya, why do you look so bad? Why have you grown so old?

Lyubov's repeated question paradoxically purges her emotion as it contains it; it aestheticizes, through rhythm, an emotion too strong for ordinary syntax. This frees her to move on to another gesture better suited to the social setting; she teases Trofimov about his "mangy" appearance. In other words, her verbal repetition ends the "scene" which her weeping began.

Chekhov broke from contemporary dramatic convention when he chose not to subdivide into "french scenes" his later one-acts and the acts of his full-length dramas from *The Seagull* onward. Still, though they are not demarcated, there are within the acts distinct units of action, usually initiated or closed off by characters' entrances and exits, or one of the forty-three pauses written into the stage directions. For example, in Act One, Dunyasha's exit as she goes to prepare coffee leaves Anya and Varya alone in a distinct scene. Her reappearance ends the scene. Verbal repetitions often directly precede or follow such breaks in the action, emphasizing the boundaries of what we identify as scenes. In this case, Varya begins and ends the tête-à-tête with the phrase: "My darling has arrived! My pretty one has arrived!" Afterwards, the coffee serving begins: a new scene. This perpetual ending and beginning conditions the audience's response to the ends of acts, and to the end of the play. The audience comes to expect the continuation of action after closure and silence.

The scene immediately preceding the first snapping of the string is initiated by a dramatic entrance, concluded by a pause, and bounded also by verbal doubling. Like so many scenes in Chekhov's plays, it does not further the action, but holds the characters in a static suspension. The logic that effects its dramatic coherence is based on musical structures, rather than the signifying processes of the serial increment—the "what happens" of the plot unit:

> [*Yepikhodov crosses at the rear of the stage, playing the guitar.*]
>
> LYUBOV ANDREYEVNA [*pensively*]. There goes Yepikhodov . . .
>
> ANYA [*pensively*]. There goes Yepikhodov . . .
>
> GAYEV. The sun has set, ladies and gentlemen.
>
> TROFIMOV. Yes.
>
> GAYEV [*in a low voice, as though reciting*]. Oh, Nature, wondrous Nature, you shine with eternal radiance, beautiful and indifferent, you whom we call mother, unite within yourself both life and death, you give life and take it away . . .
>
> VARYA [*beseechingly*]. Uncle dear!
>
> ANYA. Uncle, you're doing it again!
>
> TROFIMOV. You'd better cue ball into the center.
>
> GAYEV. I'll be quiet, I'll be quiet.
>
> [*All sit, lost in thought. Silence. All that's heard is the quiet muttering of* FIRS. *Suddenly a distant sound is heard, as if from the sky, like the sound of a snapped string mournfully dying away.*]

The snapping string is the structural close to a scene which opens with several musical elements. Yepikhodov enters playing a guitar. The repeated anapests of *Yepikhódov idyót, Yepikhódov idyót,* create a distinct rhythm, to which the trochees of the next line answer: *Sólntze syélo, gòspodá.* Finally, the last syllable of this line is repeated immediately in Trofimov's "*Da.*" In fact, the repeated *-da,* or the acoustic image *-oda,* seems, as much as the setting sun, to inspire Gayev's rhapsody addressed to Nature, or *priróda.* Gayev expands beyond the acoustic coincidence to deliver a lyric speech crammed full of literary language: nature is divine, indifferent; she lives and destroys. His phrase "whom we call mother" acknowledges this literariness, as does the stage direction: ". . . *as though reciting.*" Finally, the abstraction of phonic repetition which introduced or generated Gayev's bathetic verbalization is reinstated in the silence urged upon him by his nieces, and by the sound which follows.

The reasons for this specific suppression of verbality may be found in a long speech by Trofimov immediately preceding the passage cited above. In it he proclaims the hypocrisy of the intelligentsia, and states his distrust of "fine talk" and "serious conversations." But by its length and its polemical sophistication, the speech of the "eternal student" itself might well qualify as "fine talk." The others ignore his conclusion—"Better to remain silent"—and

continue their verbal seriousness until they are interrupted by the entrance of Yepikhodov. The music which Yepikhodov introduces to the stage provides a simple alternative to literary language and political debate, and the ensuing "conversation" utilizes musical principles. In it Gayev, like a player in an orchestral ensemble, is instructed to either play his part or be silent.

The above scene illustrates Chekhov's use of local repetition to create verbal borders for scenes within the larger dramatic framework. But the repetitive element which closes the action also connects the unified part to the continuous whole, and to a time line which extends beyond the drama's borders. The sisters' pleas for silence are a motif introduced in Act One when Gayev makes a stupid speech shortly after lamenting this tendency of his. Here, Anya's "Uncle, you're doing it again!" comes close to duplicating her earlier complaint, "You're doing it again, uncle!" But Varya, in this second instance, and in a similar instance in Act Four, does not restate the substantive imperative, "be quiet"; she simply cries out, "Uncle dear." The content of the sisters' verbal gesture is implicit because it is a repetition, yet part of that content has shifted to the very fact of its repetition: we smile at the "[not] again!" Formally, the expression begins to approach the enigmatic "Cue ball into the center" as a trope of rhythmic continuity in communal discourse, a seme that constitutes both a constant and a constraint in lives which are now changing course, dispersing.

Chekhov's use of local repetition to contain dramatic action is most evident in the endings of his acts. The first three acts of *The Cherry Orchard* conclude with the doubled utterance of the Russian verb *poidyóm* (variously rendered in translation as "let's go," "come," or "come along"). The repetition of this verb at the end of acts works like a refrain or chorus in a ballad, closing off each part, while linking those parts in a continuing series, simultaneously creating linguistic closure and prompting a renewal of linguistic activity. Interestingly, the element of narrative stasis in a ballad becomes the repeated action of the play. Something does happen: the characters come and go. Finally, they go. The doubled *poidyóms* which close the first three acts prepare us for the last enunciation of this verb in the final and decisive exit of the family from the estate; the patterns created in the first three instances help inform our experience of that exit, and of the play's final events as a whole.

Varya supplies the refrain to Act One as she ushers her sister to bed:

> VARYA. Come to your little bed . . . Come along. [*Leading her*] My little darling fell asleep. Come along. . . . [*They go*]
>
> [*In the distance, beyond the orchard, a shepherd is playing on a reed pipe.*
>
> TROFIMOV *crosses the stage and, seeing* VARYA *and* ANYA, *stops.*]
>
> VARYA. Sh! She's asleep . . . asleep . . . Come along, darling.
>
> ANYA [*softly, half-asleep*]. I'm so tired . . .

Those bells . . . Uncle.. . darling . . . Mama and Uncle . . .

VARYA. Come along, darling, come along. [*They go into* ANYA'S *room*]

TROFIMOV [*deeply moved*]. My sunshine! My spring!

In Act Two, the refrain is rendered by a shared repetition, heard over the familiar strum of Yepikhodov's guitar:

VARYA'S VOICE. Anya! Where are you?

TROFIMOV. That Varya again! [*Angrily*] It's revolting!

ANYA. Well? Let's go down to the river. It's lovely there.

TROFIMOV. Let's go. [*They go*]

VARYA'S VOICE. Anya! Anya!

Anya's speech comforting her mother concludes Act Three:

ANYA. Mama! . . . Mama, are you crying? My dear, kind, good mama, my pretty one, I love you . . . I bless you. The cherry orchard is sold, it's gone, that's true, true, but don't cry, Mama, you still have your life before you, you still have your good, pure soul . . . Let's go together, let's go, darling, away from here, let's go!.. . We'll plant a new orchard, more splendid than this one, you will see it and understand, and joy, deep, quiet joy will sink into your soul, like the evening sun, and you will smile, Mama! Come, let's go, darling! Let's go! . . .

Established in the endings of the first three acts is a pattern of alternating harmony and discord, from Trofimov's effusive infatuation to Varya's peskiness back to the shared dreams of mother and daughter. This pattern prepares us for the discord of the ending, and mollifies that discord with promise of a rhythmic renewal of joy and harmony. The invocation of the sun in the two upbeat passages is significant, presenting an image of that which is ever repeating. Like other motifs, this natural one both divides time and stresses its infinite extension; it also comforts the community with its rhythm. Paired with spring, as in Trofimov's speech, the sun suggests bright renewal; imagined at sunset, as in Anya's speech, it evokes suffusing warmth. The relative timing of these two images—sunshine and spring in the first act; the colored dusk in the third—might imply a dramatic progression in synch with the natural temporal structures of days and years. In fact, the play begins in spring and ends with the onset of winter. But Chekhov would remind us that nature's changes are cyclical and continuous; Lopakhin refers to the next spring twice in the final act. Likewise, the opening of Act One subverts temporal closure even as it establishes a structural correspondence to the unit of "day." In the play's first exchange, Dunyasha, responding to Lopakhin's query "What time is it?" replies, "Nearly two," snuffs the candle that she carries, and continues, "It's already light." The enacted drama begins at day's beginning, but alludes to the everpresent past, to the dark of the previous night.

Act One opens with Lopakhin's awakening and closes with Anya's retreat to her bedroom for sleep. Act Three also closes with the suggestion of bedtime, rendered by the lullaby qualities of the repetitions in Anya's speech to her mother. In inflected languages like Russian, the possibilities for acoustic repetition, especially through suffixal assonance, are greatly increased. In Russian, assonance through inflection is particularly pronounced in feminine nominative and accusative adjective endings, where the vowel sound is doubled, —"-aya, -yaya/ -ooyoo, -yooyoo"—and acoustically imitates the feminine noun endings—"-a, -ya/ -oo, -yoo." Chekhov utilizes this feature of his language in Anya's speech ending; the string of adjectives—*Mìlaya, dóbraya, khoróshaya, moyá . . . moyá, prekrásnaya*—modifying "mama," and also those modifying the feminine nouns "joy" and "soul," add to the verbal repetition and syntactic parallelism a distinct acoustic repetition. These repeated soft sounds effectively calm and silence Lyubov. And by silencing Lyubov, Anya silences the stage, bringing the act to a rounded close.

But while Act Three ends precisely with the by now familiar refrain, *Poidyóm . . . poidyóm!*, the previous acts end with a refrain and a coda, a focused conclusion followed by an expression from off-center, or even offstage. Act One ends, not with the repetitive final words of the two characters whose conversation is central to the drama, but with the exclamation of the observing Trofimov, "My sunshine! My spring!" Likewise, Varya's call, from offstage, tags behind the happy closure of the lovers' exit at the end of Act Two. The end of Act Four and of the play itself is structured on a similar model of closure and coda, amplified and expanded.

Toward the close of Act Four the audience hears the sequence—

GAYEV. My sister, my sister!

ANYA'S VOICE. Mama!

TROFIMOV'S VOICE. Aa-ooo!

—repeated twice, then completed by Lyubov's *"Poidyóm"* as she and Gayev exit. A silence then falls upon the empty stage. The audience which has been sensitive to the play's structures feels the resolution of this moment, yet nevertheless anticipates a further note. And indeed, the stillness is broken by the thud of an axe against a tree somewhere offstage. The ensuing appearance of Firs, presumably removed to a hospital, is as shocking as if he had risen from the dead—and we understand that he is to die. His ragged speech provides the coda to the closing departure of his previous masters:

FIRS [*goes to the door and tries the handle*]. Locked. They have gone . . . [*Sits down on the sofa.*] They've forgotten me . . . It's nothing . . . I'll sit here awhile . . . I expect Leonid Andreich hasn't put on his fur coat and has gone off in his overcoat. [*Sighs anxiously.*] And I didn't see to it . . . The greenhorn! [*Mumbles something which can't be understood.*] That life is gone, as if it never were lived . . . [*Lies down.*] I'll lie down awhile . . . There's no strength left in you, nothing's left, nothing . . . Ugh, you . . . addlepate! [*Lies motionless*]

Early in his speech, Firs acknowledges the fact that would tend to give the play's ending a pessimistic tone: "They've forgotten me." But Firs goes on, repeating the habitual concern for and affectionate criticism of Gayev he has voiced all along, asserting the endurance of their relationship beyond the dramatic, or material, relevance of that relationship: Leonid Andreich is gone for good. It is as if Firs says, "They've forgotten me; what's more, as usual, the greenhorn's forgotten his coat. He'll never change." Firs lives for his master and through his master; in expressing that fussbudgety love of the life that will go on without him, he, in a sense, transcends his own death. The moment is followed by a darker view of his fate, and of the play's action. The line, "That life is gone, as if it never were lived," might serve as a gloss on the play itself. Soon the audience will leave the theater and leave these other lives behind. "Nothing's left, nothing . . ." seems to be a definitive ending to the play, a doubled repetition to arrest the propulsive "Let's go . . . let's go" of previous endings. But this end too has a coda. Firs's last utterance subverts the closure of his death with a gritty assertion of continuity. "Addlepate" may be Firs's last word and the play's last word, but it is not the last time his word will be used. Lyubov has already adopted this epithet in her put-down of Trofimov in the third act, acknowledging Firs as her source: "You! You're not above love. As our Firs would say, you're just an addlepate!" Firs's cranky expression will continue to sound in the community of which he was once an integral part.

Non-verbal sound has the "last word" in the play. A distant sound is heard, that of a snapped string "mournfully dying away." While the same sound in Act Two invited the characters' interpretations, this time it invites the audience's interpretation. Finding no referent for that noise, the audience might interpret the sound based on what it knows about the play's ending, rather than the other way around. Firs is abandoned, left to die alone. Outside someone is chopping down the orchard. In this context, the distant sound might be heard as the end punctuation to a cruel tragedy.

Searching for Chekhov's "intentions" regarding the sound raises difficult questions about the difference between playgoing versus play-reading. It is crucial to keep in mind that the reading audience will experience this "sound" differently from an audience in the theater; it will note that the string has sounded "*(as if) from the sky*" (angels on high?), that it is "*(like) the sound of a snapped string*" (reminiscent of Atropos's snip), that it "*dies away*" (like Firs), and that it does so "*mournfully*." But it might well note that these figures do not constitute but describe the sound, and that they are, to the word, the same figures used to describe it in Act Two. Chekhov is thwarting the reader's expectation for variation in literary language; his linguistic repetition stresses the structural, phonic identity of the two sounds, the acoustic repetition that a live audience would hear.

"The sound of the snapped string," in other words, indicates more a recurring motif than the sound *of* a snapped string. Recall the description of the first issuance of the string's sound:

> *All sit, lost in thought. Silence. All that's heard is the quiet muttering of* FIRS. *Suddenly a distant sound is heard, as if from the sky, like the sound of a snapped string mournfully dying away.*

In Act Two, silence, and Firs's mumbling, preceded the sonic event. In the second issuance, the volume is turned up, as it were; we hear the fragments of Firs's disconnected speech. The significance of the ending note may likewise seem amplified, momentous, but the momentum generated by its repetition prepares us for another act, another sounding of the string. Because of the patterns established and developed throughout the play, we expect another coda.

So, finally, the snapped string is followed by the sound of an axe continuing its work on the orchard. This sound is rhythmic, repetitive, and does not cease. It epitomizes not so much the ending or beginning of an era, but the current of the ongoing present, the infinitely receding coda to joy and grief, day and night, arrivals and departures, life and death. It answers the play's opening speech not with an apocalyptic gong, but with the repeated ticking of tocks. And thus the action of the play merges with the "action" of our own lives—the changes we do not so much "suffer" as endure or experience, the music we make with others while we can. For the final coda, the members of the audience will say to their companions, "Let's go," and, as they emerge outside under a changed sky, they may check their watches and note, as Lopakhin does in Act One: "Time passes . . . Time passes, I say."

Greta Anderson, "The Music of 'The Cherry Orchard': Repetitions in the Russian Text," in Modern Drama, *Vol. XXXIV, No. 3, September, 1991, pp. 340-49.*

FURTHER READING

Bibliography

Lantz, K. A. *Anton Chekhov: A Reference Guide to Literature.* Boston: G. K. Hall & Co., 1985, 287 p.
    Annotated bibliography of Chekhov criticism arranged chronologically by publication date. Includes English, Russian, French, and German sources.

Meister, Charles W. *Chekhov Bibliography: Works in English by and about Anton Chekhov; American, British and Canadian Performances.* Jefferson, N.C.: McFarland & Co., 1985, 184 p.
    Lists editions of *The Cherry Orchard* in English, critical and biographical sources, and information on stage performances of the play.

Biography

Priestly, J. B. *Anton Chekhov.* London: International Profiles, 1970, 87 p.
    Overview of Chekhov's life and career.

Criticism

Balukhaty, S. D. "*The Cherry Orchard*: A Formalist Approach." In *Chekhov: A Collection of Critical Essays*, edited by Robert Louis Jackson, pp. 136-46. Englewood Cliffs, N.J.: Prentice-Hall, 1967.
>   Rigorous formalist analysis of thematic structure in *The Cherry Orchard*.

Brandon, James R. "Toward a Middle View of Chekhov." *Educational Theatre Journal* XII, No. 4 (December 1960): 270-75.
>   Apropos of viewing performances of *The Cherry Orchard* and *Three Sisters* by the Moscow Art Theatre, Brandon states: "We should set aside our natural inclination to think of Chekhov's plays as being either tragic *or* comic, and instead recognize that . . . they are both at the same time."

Brustein, Robert. "Anton Chekhov." In his *The Theatre of Revolt: An Approach to the Modern Drama*, pp. 135-79. Boston: Little, Brown and Co., 1964.
>   Examines the complex nature of Chekhov's plays, maintaining that *The Cherry Orchard* "functions . . . as a satire on conventional melodrama, achieved through the reversal of melodramatic conventions."

Cross, A. G. "The Breaking Strings of Chekhov and Turgenev." *The Slavonic and East European Review* 47 (January-July 1969): 510-13.
>   Asserts that Chekhov's theme of the passing of the old social order in *The Cherry Orchard*, symbolized by the sound of breaking string, has precedence in Ivan Turgenev's works. Cross states that "there is every likelihood that Chekhov had read" particular writings by Turgenev that would have provided inspiration.

Durkin, Andrew R. "*The Cherry Orchard* in English: An Overview." In *Yearbook of Comparative and General Literature* 33 (1984): 74-82.
>   Compares translations of *The Cherry Orchard* available in English, assessing their relative success in conveying the intent of the original Russian text.

Fergusson, Francis. "*The Cherry Orchard*: A Theater-Poem of the Suffering of Change." In *Chekhov: A Collection of Critical Essays*, edited by Robert Louis Jackson, pp. 147-60. Englewood Cliffs, N.J.: Prentice-Hall, 1967.
>   Analyzes Chekhov's artistry as a dramatist, focusing on the second act of *The Cherry Orchard*.

Hahn, Beverly. "*The Cherry Orchard*." In her *Chekhov: A Study of the Major Stories and Plays*, pp. 12-36. Cambridge: Cambridge University Press, 1977.
>   Maintains that the play "brilliantly assimilates comic and tragic possibilities to one another until practically every scene is both light in texture and pervaded by a subtle melancholy—a true merging of tragic and comic possibilities."

Latham, Jacqueline E. M. "*The Cherry Orchard* as Comedy." *Educational Theatre Journal* X, No. 1 (March 1958): 21-9.
>   Argues that *The Cherry Orchard* is a comedy, not a tragedy. Latham concludes: "In his revelation of the ludicrous in human nature Chekhov successfully achieves a very rare blend of sympathetic and judicial comedy; the audience is aware of the triviality and inadequacies of the comic characters yet they cannot completely dissociate themselves from them, to assume a superior position."

Lewis, Allan. "The Comedy of Frustration—Chekhov." In his *The Contemporary Theatre: The Significant Playwrights of Our Time*, pp. 59-80. New York: Crown Publishers, 1962.
>   Comments on the comic elements in *The Cherry Orchard*.

Orr, John. "The Everyday and the Transient in Chekhov's Tragedy." In his *Tragic Drama and Modern Society: A Sociology of Dramatic Form from 1880 to the Present*, pp. 57-83. London: Macmillan, 1989.
>   Thematic overview of *The Cherry Orchard*.

Pavis, Patrice. "Textual Mechanisms in *The Cherry Orchard*." *Assaph: Studies in the Theatre*, No. 4 (1988): 1-18.
>   Addresses stylistic and structural elements of the play, as well as thoroughly analyzing the symbolic function of the cherry orchard on the estate.

Reed, Walter L. "*The Cherry Orchard* and *Hedda Gabler*." In *Homer to Brecht: The European Epic and Dramatic Traditions*, edited by Michael Seidel and Edward Mendelson, pp. 317-35. New Haven: Yale University Press, 1977.
>   Asserts that Chekhov's use of "comic and tragic archetypes" signifies his "desire to get beyond the conventional resolutions that literature provides."

Silverstein, Norman. "Chekhov's Comic Spirit and *The Cherry Orchard*." *Modern Drama* 1, No. 2 (September 1958): 91-100.
>   Views *The Cherry Orchard* as a comedy, providing biographical anecdotes about Chekhov in order to support the claim.

Stanislavski, Constantin. "*The Cherry Orchard*." In his *My Life in Art*, translated by J. J. Robbins, pp. 420-24. New York: Robert M. MacGregor, 1948.
>   Recalls Chekhov's ill health in the last year of his life, during which *The Cherry Orchard* was first performed, and notes his sense of humor.

Styan, J. L. "Shifting Impressions: *The Cherry Orchard*." In his *The Elements of Drama*, pp. 64-85. Cambridge: The University Press, 1960.
>   Explicates a passage from the fourth act of *The Cherry Orchard* in order to show that the effect of Chekhov's drama arises from his focus on relationships between the characters rather than on actions, events, or the characters themselves.

———. "The Cherry Orchard." In his *Chekhov in Performance: A Commentary on the Major Plays*, pp. 239-337. Cambridge: Cambridge University Press, 1971.
>   Provides an act-by-act analysis of *The Cherry Orchard*.

Toumanova, Nina Andronikova. "Sunset in the Cherry Garden." In her *Anton Chekhov: The Voice of Twilight Russia*, pp. 204-21. New York: Columbia University Press, 1937.
>   Offers a plot summary of *The Cherry Orchard*, stressing the play's dimensions as a drama about social classes.

Valency, Maurice. "*The Cherry Orchard.*" In his *The Breaking String: The Plays of Anton Chekhov*, pp. 251-88. New York: Oxford University Press, 1966.

Recounts the circumstances of the composition of *The Cherry Orchard* and provides an overview of the play.

Additional coverage of Chekhov's life and career is contained in the following sources published by Gale Research: *Contemporary Authors*, Vols. 104, 124; *DISCovering Authors*; *Short Story Criticism*, Vol. 2; *Twentieth-Century Literary Criticism*, Vols. 3, 10, 31; and *World Literature Criticism*.

Freeman Wills Crofts

1879-1957

Irish-born English detective novelist, short story writer, and radio scriptwriter.

INTRODUCTION

Crofts is best known for novels that feature the character Inspector French, a meticulous police detective whose systematic examinations of crimes bring villains to justice despite their virtually unshakable alibis. Crofts's novels were among the first to emphasize the role of hard-working, unglamorous official investigators who laboriously pursue lead after lead until they bring the perpetrators of a crime to justice. Along with such writers as Dorothy Sayers and Agatha Christie, Crofts is credited with being one of the founders of the period known as the Golden Age of English detective fiction, which lasted from about 1918 to 1939.

Biographical Information

Crofts was born in Dublin, Ireland, to a British army doctor from a Protestant family. His father died when Crofts was a boy, and his mother later married an archdeacon of the Church of Ireland. Crofts attended the Methodist and Campbell Colleges in Belfast, and after graduation was offered a job as an apprentice civil engineer by his uncle, who was chief engineer of the Belfast & Northern Counties Railway. Crofts had a long, successful career, eventually attaining the rank of chief assistant engineer for the railway. He began writing detective fiction in 1919 as a means of passing time while he was recovering from a serious illness. Crofts published his first novel, *The Cask*, a year later. This novel and his subsequent works were well-received, and by 1929 Crofts was able to retire from his railway job to devote his time to writing. In the 1930s he and his wife moved to the south of England, where they lived until his death in 1957.

Major Works

The Cask remains Crofts's best-regarded work, though he produced several dozen novels, collections of short fiction, and scripts for BBC radio dramas. *The Cask* focuses on a police detective's effort to discover the murderer of a woman whose body has been packed in a large barrel and shipped from France to England. Crofts employs his typical scenario: an innocent man is arrested while the real killer goes free on the strength of his alibi; through the careful work of the police detective, the alibi is finally broken and the murderer caught. Other characteristics of Crofts's novels include thoroughly unsympathetic portrayals of crime and criminals and the use of such realistic details as actual train schedules and minutely accurate descriptions of real locales. The solution to a crime often de-

pends on some small inconsistency such as the difference between the time a suspect claimed to have taken a train and the time a train was scheduled to run on that day. Commentators familiar with Crofts's works and the English countryside have maintained that one could retrace the steps of a character in any of Crofts's novels and find the details of landscapes, especially railways, to be exactly as Crofts described them.

Critical Reception

In general, critics have praised Crofts's works for their careful construction and close attention to realistic detail, finding *The Cask* and *Inspector French's Greatest Case* to be particularly fine examples of the detective novel. Commentators agree that Crofts's characterizations are somewhat stereotyped, and many cite his later works for lagging plots and an overabundance of minutiae; however, critics also agree that these faults do not prevent Crofts's fiction from being thoroughly entertaining. As Howard Haycraft wrote, "In the opinion of a vast number of readers and critics he has never been equaled, much less surpassed, in his particular field."

PRINCIPAL WORKS

The Cask (novel) 1920
The Ponson Case (novel) 1921
The Pit Prop Syndicate (novel) 1922
Inspector French's Greatest Case (novel) 1925
Inspector French and the Cheyne Mystery (novel) 1926
Inspector French and the Starvel Tragedy (novel) 1927
The Sea Mystery: An Inspector French Detective Story
     (novel) 1928
Sir John Magill's Last Journey: An Inspector French Case
     (novel) 1930
Death of a Train (novel) 1946
Murderers Make Mistakes (short stories) 1947
Many a Slip (short stories) 1955
The Mystery of the Sleeping Car Express, and Other Stories
     (short stories) 1956
Anything to Declare? (novel) 1957

CRITICISM

The New York Times Book Review   (essay date 1924)

[*In the following review, the critic praises* The Cask *for its careful construction.*]

Innumerable detective stories are written and many are published, yet a really good one, ingeniously contrived, plausibly worked out, and so constructed as to be without quite evident flaws, is almost as rare as the proverbial black swan. There are a few, a very few, authors from whom we may confidently expect tales of this type, and to the list must now be added the name of Freeman Wills Crofts. This story [*The Cask*] with which he makes his bow to American readers is clever, interesting and well constructed.

Though much longer than the average tale of its kind, the narrative never drags for a moment; moreover, the manner in which the truth is finally discovered is entirely convincing, depending neither on mechanical devices, superhuman perspicacity, far-fetched coincidence nor extraordinary good luck. And from first to last Mr. Crofts plays fair with the reader. All that his detectives—and there are no less than three of them—know is imparted at once to the reader, who follows them step by step, from complete perplexity to knowledge of the truth. It is a knowledge won by hard work, the careful investigating of every clue, the careful checking up of every statement. There are plenty of clues and plenty of statements, but at first no one of them seems to throw any real light on the problem.

The tale opens in London; the freight steamer Bullfinch had just arrived at St. Katharine's Docks, bringing among other things a large consignment of casks of wine. When these were removed from the hold, another cask was brought out with them, one larger and considerably heavier. By accident, it fell from the sling to the dock, and was cracked. Through the crack a tiny stream of sawdust began to trickle. There was nothing peculiar or alarming about sawdust, especially when it came from a cask which was stenciled "Statuary only," and bore the label of a Paris firm. But when gold pieces were discovered in the sawdust, the curiosity of the clerk and of the foreman was naturally aroused. They widened the crack, peered into the cask, and caught sight of a human hand; it was a woman's hand, slight and delicate, with rings on the fingers.

It would be unfair to the reader to give more than this hint of the mystery surrounding the cask. Inspector Burnley of Scotland Yard was the first detective to take up the case. When the investigation shifted from London to Paris, M. Lefarge of the Sûreté joined Burnley, and they worked together. Then, at the last, Georges La Touche, a private detective, the son of a French father and an English mother, entered the case and found the weak spot in the criminal's dexterous arrangements, the thing Burnley and Lefarge had missed, clever and painstaking though they were. *The Cask* is a story no one should begin with the idea of putting it aside in a little while, for that reader will be strong-minded, indeed, who can lay the book down until the very last page is reached.

"Sawdust and Gold," in The New York Times Book Review, *December 21, 1924, p. 17.*

H. Douglas Thomson   (essay date 1931)

[*In the following excerpt, which was originally published in 1931, Thomson discusses the use of realistic detail in Crofts's crime fiction.*]

> "He will present you with a magnificent alibi, an alibi that cannot be gainsaid." GABORIAU: *L'Affaire Lerouge.*

The greatest apostle of the matter of fact is Mr. Freeman Wills Crofts. Mr. Crofts is an Irishman, born in Dublin of an old County Cork family. He is a keen musician; was organist at Coleraine Parish Church, and has trained many prize-winning choirs. By profession, however, he is a civil engineer, having worked for many years on the L.M.S. Railway as chief-assistant engineer to the Northern Counties Committee. This fact will at once account for the important part played by the railways in his novels and for his extraordinary knowledge of different localities.

Indeed, Mr. Crofts's writing derives much of its effectiveness from the introduction of local colour. His novels have their setting in some precise district. Thus, to those who already know that particular district, there is an added charm. Whether the scene is the Welsh coast, or the Yorkshire moors, or Southampton, or Castle Douglas, he retains throughout his uncanny accuracy. The dénouement of *The Starvel Tragedy* takes place in the Waverley Station at Edinburgh, and not in some imaginary Grand Central. If he describes a lane, a level-crossing, or a bridge in some district, you can take a train there and see these self-same objects for yourself. For Mr. Crofts goes over his ground before he pens a line. I have seen actual snapshots taken by Mr. Crofts of several key positions described in *Sir John Magill's Last Journey.* Not the least interesting point about them was the pencilling on their backs of the most intriguing stage directions—"Path taken by So-and-So."

Mr. Crofts prefers the unvarnished narrative, and it is only when he would adorn his tale with these geographical asides, or when he would plunge into the treacherous waters of sensationalism, that his style seems to lose its hundred per cent. efficiency. Even his crimes, cold and premeditated as they appear in the dispassionate telling of them, lack that gusto which would serve to make them more attractive and also more credible. There is no careless rapture about his criminals, no sense of humour, no emotion. His writing is for the most part succinct and business-like, and resembles a well-informed newspaper article.

This treatment has two prominent weaknesses. In the first place the more matter of fact Mr. Crofts becomes, the more liable is he to fly to clichés of expression. Thus Inspector French is persuaded to "have something to fortify his inner man"; L'Affaire Magill is "terribly baffling," and so forth. The besprinkling of his text with these paste-jewelled phrases is an unnecessary fault, and, therefore, hard to forgive. Secondly, Mr. Crofts is so carried away by his love for detail that he exalts the trivial to a false prominence. Where any other writer would simply have said, "He travelled by night to Stranraer," Mr. Crofts gives us pages of description made up of paragraphs like the following: —

> He began, therefore, by engaging a sleeping berth at Euston. On inquiry he was directed to a stationmaster's office on No. 6 platform. There a clerk made the reservations, handing him a voucher. This voucher he presented at the booking office when taking his tickets. . . . The train left at seven-forty from No. 12 platform. . . . His name was on the list on the window of the sleeping car.

Take again such a paragraph as the following: —

> But later the excellent dinner served while the train ran through the pleasant country between Abbeville and Amiens brought him to a more quiescent mood, and over a good cigar and a cup of such coffee as he had seldom before tasted, he complacently watched day fade into night. About half-past six o'clock next morning he followed the example of the countless British predecessors, and climbed down on the long platform at Bâle to drink his morning coffee.

One is at liberty to argue that by such devices the action is held up, that the rattle of coffee cups is out of place in the detective story. Yet (Mr. Crofts might reply) what better respite from concentration is there for the detective who scorns Trade Union hours? What more pleasant rest-and-be-thankful for the conscientious reader who takes a hand in the case?

Along with Dr. Austin Freeman, Mr. Crofts has acquired the unenviable reputation in certain quarters of being a "highbrow." This is a comic anomaly, for they both cultivate unashamedly a prosaic reality. The charge of high-browism—always snobbish or else it is a misnomer—

denotes a strong dissatisfaction with certain alleged poses. Mr. Crofts cannot be a highbrow *qua* realist. Let us dismiss this absurd charge; but let us also mention the imputed faults which have given birth to the libel.

The sensational element, it is true, is minimised in the typical Wills Crofts novel. There is plenty of action, but not apparently of that type of action in request by the fault finder. The reports of pistol shots are often in "indirect speech." The suspense is thus sometimes more the detective's than our own. But even so there are exceptions. Several of his novels, in particular the early ones, combine adventure with detection. Even when in more serious vein, Mr. Crofts does let himself go at the dénouement. A Mills bomb nearly wrecks the saloon bar in the penultimate chapter of *The Starvel Tragedy*. And Inspector French all but finds his quietus at the end of *The Sea Mystery*. In these close shaves, one must confess, Mr. Crofts seems rather off colour. He cannot keep his cake till it seemed a permanency, only to gobble it up for an effect so long despised.

Then again, the action being moulded to fit certain measurements, there is a similarity of situation, a clockwork movement. In reading the average Wills Crofts novel one is conscious each time of experiencing very much the same "thought-process." His plots run like his railway trains. This allows one's reason or intuition to take one a chapter ahead of Inspector French. The "leads," the "startling new lines" along which the detective plunges out of the blue at regular intervals beckon to one's intelligence and shout for premature recognition. To forecast the state of affairs twenty pages after is genuine solace to the reader; it is flattering. But there, as a rule, his self-sufficiency ends. If the solution of each step in the investigation actually coincides with his pretty prognostications, the dénouement will shatter his complacency.

In construction he is the supreme technician. It is this quality that has earned for him an international reputation in Europe and America, and made him an Oracle of Detective Fiction, for whose praise publishers would go far to bartering their souls—this quality, too, that all but drew enthusiasm from the *Saturday Review*. No writer of detective fiction has ever produced a neater plot. Every brick fits exactly into the edifice. The plots of Gaboriau are not more exquisitely complicated. In Mr. Crofts's technique there are two great merits. The first is the cunning creation of the central idea, and the other the round-about rediscovery of it. A lesser artist than Mr. Crofts would have been severely handicapped by the conscientious deference to realism just mentioned.

To set off the sombre background he has his fireworks. He is an admirable conjurer, and a prolific "ideas-man." And because he is prolific, his tricks are seldom expanded into themes. Here is a haphazard selection—the changing of the numbers on the lorries and the smuggling of the pit-props in *The Pit-Prop Syndicate*. The drugging, and the solution of the diagrammatic cipher in *The Cheyne Mystery*. The solution of the dictionary cipher in *Inspector French's Greatest Case*. The planting of the twenty-pound notes in *The Starvel Tragedy*. The adventures with the rope ladder in *Sir John Magill's Last Journey*.

The realist having made his bed has got to lie in it. Of a necessity it must ever be sagging, for all the time he must be in the know. A knowledge of medicine and chemistry was indispensable to him even in the days of Sherlock Holmes. He must besides be as familiar with police methods as Mr. Edgar Wallace. Like Miss Sayers he must have common law and legal procedure at his finger tips. All this knowledge emanates without any gushing from Mr. Crofts. He is a criminologist and a cryptologist. I imagine he is a close student of the technical press, and files of *Police Journals* and *Reviews* adorn his shelves. He can tell one all about banking and brokerage; customs and excise; distilling; motor engines; seacraft, and a hundred and one different subjects. He approximates to the old-fashioned sleuth on whose omniscience emphasis was so plaintively but so necessarily laid.

In short, there are few writers in whom one could find such a wealth of interesting detail. If one were to count up to a hundred technical details in a story of his, one would be hard put to it to find a single flaw. I have heard that legal and medical experts have sat in judgement on his novels, prior to their publication and have picked out at the most three or four possible, but by no means certain, errors.

The *pièce de résistance* of his realism is his characterisation of the detective, that is of Inspector French, for the Burnleys, the Tanners and the Willises are only other editions of this favourite. The Inspector French that frowns on one from the insets on the dust wrappers seems quite an ordinary young man, clean-shaven, sharp of feature, well groomed and neatly dressed—just such a young man, in fact, as might adorn an advertisement of Austin Reed's or Three Nuns Tobacco. In the Elysian Fields he will assuredly be prejudged a gate-crasher by Sherlock Holmes and the super-detectives. His private life can boast no quixotry, no aesthetic capers. Being an ordinary sort of chap, it did not surprise us to learn that he was married. His Emily—true to the associations that that name has acquired—sits at home in their suburban villa knitting his socks. Mr. Crofts, seldom obsequious to the conventionalities, throws an unnecessary bouquet to contemporary fashion.

> When Inspector French felt really up against it in the conduct of a case, it was his invariable habit to recount the circumstances in the fullest detail to his wife. Sometimes she interjected a remark, sometimes she didn't . . . but she listened to what he said, and occasionally expressed an opinion, or, as he called it, 'took a notion.' And more than once it happened that these notions had thrown quite a different light on the point at issue, a light which in at least two cases had indicated the line of research which had eventually cleared up the mystery.

In the circumstances it was natural that Mr. Crofts should have had no use for "the superior amateur." His detective is the professional expert, the C.I.D. man, caring more for the material guerdon of advancement and an increase of salary than the fulsome flattery of a neighbour. So far he remains in the force (although merely from the point of view of realism Mr. Crofts must have recently considered French's resignation). He is energetic, ambitious, but not infallible; deferential to his superiors, he recognises the guiding genius of Chief-Inspector Mitchell and the Big Four.

The Inspector's methods are a true reflection of the man. He worries things out and is always "up against it." He never jumps to a conclusion, and that is the great difference between him and the Father Browns and Hanauds. If one theory fails, he tries another. This point is of some importance; for it is tantamount to the laying of all cards on the table. The fairplay method inaugurated by the fragmentary *Mystery of Marie Roget,* and both tentatively and temporarily adopted by various hands, has at last found its complete expression. The data are given. The detective's inferences are assembled in detail and from time to time a résumé is presented demonstrating the point reached in the investigation, and the points remaining to be solved; the cruxes, as it were, underlined, and the "leads" tabulated. This is something to be going on with. This is business.

To the puzzle-worm the subjectivity of French's reasoning is reassuringly natural. Yet it would be strange if he did not from time to time realise that the other fellow was doing all the work; that the mystery was being taken entirely out of his hands; that all the clues with which his imagination might have dallied for brief intervals between the chapters, were exposed in detail one after the other.

French looks for his information in the likeliest quarters. He does not don fancy dress and slouch off to Soho or the docks. He does not readily impose upon people by facile impersonations of antiquarians desirous of seeing the reredos. One has usually not long to wait for the curt, formal introduction, so much more dignified after all than the Transatlantic seizure of the lapel. He spends many hours in hotels, chatting to their managers and studying the register. He is frequently to be seen in shops and banks. Somehow he reminds one of a commercial traveller, so ingratiating a way he has with tradesmen.

The alibi was Mr. Crofts's first love and he made it the pivot of his plots. In life the mere presentation of an alibi is three-quarters proof—thanks chiefly to politeness and a disinclination on the part of normal people to make a scene. The alibi has only to pass an elementary test of probability, and circumstantial evidence gains another victory. This was Mr. Crofts's chance and this his angle of approach. If the novelist never wearies of turning the handle of circumstantial evidence to incriminate the too innocent hero, why should the use of circumstantial evidence to shelter the villain be not equally legitimate? The comforting maxim that the prisoner is innocent until proved guilty—logically an impossible restriction to all juries as being prejudice ridden—was another string to Mr. Crofts's bow. Yet another fact exalted the alibi. To the public, press-fed and expecting sensation, the vital attraction is always the human interest of the trial. Public interest soon wanes if the criminal is not forthcoming. It is the pros and cons of the alibi, and failing that, as a bad second, the veracity of the statements of the accused, that lead from one pint to another at the Rose and Crown. And circumstantial evidence, by the way, although the object of the super-detective's contumely, will yet turn a one-reel Movie into an "attraction."

Circumstantial evidence's strongest foothold in fiction thus rested with the possibility of concocting a "cast iron" "honest to goodness," "unobjectionable" alibi—all these epithets meaning, of course, the very reverse, that the alibi was pre-arranged. In Gaboriau's *L'Affaire Lerouge,* Père Tabaret discourses on the theme: —

> He (the suspect) will present you with a magnificent alibi, an alibi that cannot be gainsaid. He will show that he passed the evening and the night of Tuesday with personages of the highest rank. He had dined with the Count de Machin, gamed with the Marquis of So-and-So, and supped with the Duke of What's-his-name. . . . In short, his little machine will be so cleverly constructed, so nicely arranged, all its little wheels will play so well, that there will be nothing left for you but to open the door and usher him out with the most humble apologies.

But Père Tabaret's method of putting a cog in the wheels of the little machine presupposes a most alarming knowledge of the circumstances, and besides, if adopted to-day, would immediately bring into being a commission to report on third degree methods, ending in the dismissal of the detective.

> I have my man arrested. . . . I go right to the mark. I overwhelm him at once by the weight of my certainty, prove to him so clearly that I know everything that he must surrender. I should say to him, "My good man, you bring me an alibi. It is very well, but we are acquainted with that system of defence. It will not do with me. Of course, I understand you have been elsewhere at the hour of the crime; a hundred persons have never lost sight of you. It is admitted. In the meantime, here is what you have done. . . ."

But the parallel is of value with reference to Mr. Crofts's alibis. He constructs his little machine so cleverly that the reader does feel that there is nothing left for him but to dismiss the alibi-mongers from the circle of suspects. This is because the work of pre-arrangement is so deft, and because again we are misled by a false law of probabilities. Then the Inspector proceeds to break the little machine to pieces, and we "knew all the time"—but not quite honestly—that there was a snag somewhere.

With this new element as the central *motif,* the construction was bound to be modified. The suspects, for example, might be marshalled with promptitude as in *The Ponson Case* and their alibis be tested one after the other, and the artistic values of these alibis be enhanced by the juxtaposition. Or suspicion might be postponed until the tardy testing of the star alibi as in *The Cask.* In the earlier novels the alibi was a new toy to Mr. Crofts. Systematically he ran through a number of variations. In time he saw the tinsel, for it his plots were to be built up from the testing of unobjectionable alibis, the secret would soon be out; so he gave his tale a twist with the introduction of bogus impersonations and dual rôles.

In the execution of the alibi theme Mr. Crofts exploited

to the full his professional knowledge of the railways and found in Bradshaw an indispensable *vade mecum.* The original composer cannot even in his fondest flights of fancy have imagined to what diverse uses his *magnum opus* would be turned—to the composition of Latin hexameters and the concoction of alibis for detective stories. The principal alibi in *The Ponson Case* was worked out from a careful examination of the L.N.E.R. main line to Scotland—the "Flying Scotsman's" track—and the local service from King's Cross to Grantham. Boirac's alibi in *The Cask* was also based on the railway time-table, and in *The Cheyne Mystery* a similar trick is played, although strictly speaking it is not an alibi. You see Mr. Crofts trades upon the reader's gullibility. The little machine is perfect. The reader never dreams of opening his Bradshaw. He is too lazy—or too polite. In passing, Mr. Crofts has not had the heart to keep his inspectors from the restaurant car whenever he has noticed in his time-table a capital "R" adjacent to the selected train. Realism achieved so easily has its points.

The Cask, Mr. Crofts's first book, is his most famous detective story. In fact *Trent's Last Case* and *The Cask* are judged by the critics to be the most scintillating stars in our crowded constellation. Mr. Crofts's own account of how *The Cask* came to be written is interesting: —

> In 1916 I had a long illness, and it was after this that I tried writing a novel as a relief from the tedium of convalescence. I wrote most of *The Cask,* but on recovery, put it away and thought of other things. Some time later I re-read it, and thinking it did not seem so bad as I had imagined, I set to work to finish it.
>
> I was delighted when Messrs. Collins accepted it, even though this acceptance was accompanied by an extremely kind note from no less a person than Mr. J. D. Beresford, suggesting that Part III was unsatisfactory, and would I re-write it?

The Cask, like all Gaul, is "quartered into three halves." In the first part we read of the arrival of the cask; the clerk's discovery of the gruesome contents and disappearance of the cask; Inspector Burnley's discovery of it at Felix Leon's house; the opening of the cask and Leon's "My God! It's Annette," as the final curtain. An exquisite sandwich of action and detection.

In the second part Inspector Burnley and his colleague, Lefarge of the Sûreté, carry out exhaustive researches. The information acquired, in particular the fact that the victim, a Mme. Boirac, had *prima facie* tried to elope with Leon, leads to the building up of a perfect case against him. Perfect but in one important detail—the question of motive. In the circumstances thus imagined, it would be Boirac who would have cause to hate his wife. But Boirac was found to have an unassailable alibi. So Leon is arrested. The reader naturally asks himself whether the unfortunate Leon has not had too large a share of suspicion or whether it is a "double bluff." Boirac is the only alternative, as there is no other character important enough to fill the rôle of the villain. Is the alibi really cast iron? Thus the problem consists in the choice of one of two characters. In this respect *The Cask* is unique.

In the third part we are introduced to Georges La Touche, a private detective engaged by Leon's legal adviser. La Touche's task is to prove Leon's innocence. To do this he had to assume that Boirac is the murderer, just as Burnley and Lefarge had come to assume that Leon was guilty. (Had there been more than two suspects it might have been necessary to call in a fresh supply of detectives, constituting a small crime circle like Roger Sheringham's in Mr. Anthony Berkeley's *The Poisoned Chocolates Case.* Mr. Crofts happily steers clear of an obvious pitfall. He makes all three detectives contribute to the solution.) The final section consists in the breaking down of Boirac's alibi. La Touche was lucky at the start, for there was no real reason why he should have noticed, *qua* detective, the dark typist. His interest in her led to his ascertaining that the typed message found inside the cask and a typed letter of Leon's had both been typed on one of Boirac's machines. La Touche's next step was to show that it was possible for Boirac to get to England, etc., and to check up the "times" of his alibi. Thereafter it was plain sailing.

The Cask is a splendid illustration of Mr. Crofts's unsurpassed exercises in detection. Maybe he relies now and again on catches (the faked telephone message, for example), but as a rule he relies more on the *minutiae* furnished by the evidence which the careless reader will not notice. "Careless" is used relatively, otherwise it would be gross hyperbole. Mr. Crofts believes in making it hard for the reader. In one particular he goes too far—his time schedules. He may be as optimistic as the B.B.C., but the average reader will not feel disposed to take out his pencil. Life is too short for that. In justice to Mr. Crofts one is obliged to emphasise the significance that arises out of this attention to detail. And that is the *raison d'étre* of the attraction that detection has for us. There is no fun in merely putting two and two together. I have in mind Burnley's inferences from the two footprints: —

> Well, I can only compare the heels (the sole of one of the footprints was missing) and there is not much difference between them. . . . "By Jove, Inspector," he went on, "I've got you at last." "They're the same marks. They were both made by the same foot . . . . The fourth nail on the left hand side is gone. That alone might be a coincidence, but if you compare the wear of the other nails and of the leather you will see they are the same beyond doubt. . . . How could Watty, if it was he, have produced them? Surely only in one of two ways. Firstly, he could have hopped on one foot. But there are three reasons why it is unlikely he did that. One is that he could hardly have done it without your noticing it. Another, that he could never have left so clear an impression in that way. The third, why should he hop? He simply wouldn't do it. . . . He walked up first with you to leave the cask. He walked up the second time with the empty dray to get it. . . ."

And this is only a detail; only one link in the long chain. Unfortunately it is impossible without a tortuous explanation to enlarge upon this topic.

Mr. Crofts's other works consist of pure detective stories—such as *The Ponson Case, Inspector French's Greatest Case, Inspector French and the Starvel Tragedy, The Sea Mystery, Sir John Magill's Last Journey,* and the hybrids—*The Pit-Prop Syndicate, The Cheyne Mystery* and possibly the *Box Office Murders.* The latter being a mixture of detection and adventure have several recurring features. The adventure portion is the excuse for the detection. The amateur, the conventional hero, has danger thrust upon him; for a time he struggles, quite effectively, with his antagonists. Suddenly he considers he is "up against it"—a conclusion prompted by the fact that he has fallen in love—and he rushes in a taxi to Scotland Yard. The professionals there magnificently smooth over the troubled waters; and detection is vindicated. (Really rather a pleasant allegory denoting the superiority of the intellectual detective story!) Whether it was necessary for the professionals to do it is another question. The amateurs were going great guns and the inspectors hadn't really very much to do.

The Ponson Case, The Starvel Tragedy and *Sir John Magill's Last Journey* are for many reasons the most interesting of the others. The success of the first is due to the brilliant central idea of accidental death upsetting a cartload of alibis. In the invention of the plot, it looks as if the alibi tricks preceded, and the original plot was suddenly modified by the afterthought. To be uncharitable, there is an outstanding weakness in the plot. The irritating love theme—reminiscent of Dr. Austin Freeman at his second best—is the only valid excuse for the continued silence of Austin and Cosgrove. As far as the latter is concerned, the thread is very slender. The love element does however, become pivotal when Lois Drew, the Wordsworthian heroine, steals a march on Inspector Tanner in the exposure of Cosgrove's alibi. Mr. Crofts makes great play with Cosgrove as a suspect. Observe the readiness with which one's suspicions immediately fasten on the business man whose finances are not too stable, and who has a liaison with an actress. The business man, as Van Dine discovered, is the perfect suspect.

Inspector French and the Starvel Tragedy is probably the most satisfactory of all double murder plots. In the historical method Mr. Crofts shows his superiority to Gaboriau. For although Dr. Philpot's first murder—the murder of his wife at Kirkintilloch—and the Ropers' discovery of it—are the hinges of the plot, the earlier event is never allowed to dwarf in interest the Starvel affair. The confusion and suspense in the reader's mind as to the real identity of the victims of the fire are splendid proof of Mr. W. Crofts's technique. The conduct of the coroner at the inquest is, however, extremely questionable; and I believe that it is possible nowadays to tell the sex and age from a small piece of charred bone, let alone a complete skeleton. I should have liked to hear Sir Bernard Spilsbury on the Starvel Case.

Sir John Magill's Last Journey is in many respects the most typical of all Mr. Crofts's novels. It is a railway murder and never has he demonstrated his professional knowledge to greater advantage. The atmosphere has never been so vividly conveyed, and the descriptions of Stranraer,

Castle-Douglas, Campbeltown, Larne and Whitehead help to intensify the realism. The problem is again paramountly a time-table one and involves the most intricate checking up of innumerable times. We have to contend with a quartet of alibis; and poor French has to follow up the itineraries of each member of the gang both on land and sea. The actual murder went off like clockwork—a particularly brilliant murder this. It is hardly necessary to add that all the details were worked out beforehand with the most extraordinary accuracy. The "Sillin" by-plot is one of the best red herrings ever dangled before a wary reader. One has only two minor grievances. When a villain is made to impersonate somebody, what obligation is there to mention that he had once been an actor? It gives the show away. Secondly, was it necessary for Mr. Crofts to borrow from *The Cask* the idea of the typewriter clue? But these are trifles, and the last journey of Sir John Magill is certainly French's greatest case to date.

H. Douglas Thomson, "The Realistic Detective Story," in his Masters of Mystery: A Study of the Detective Story, *1931. Reprint by Richard West, 1978, pp. 168-92.*

Howard Haycraft   (essay date 1939)

[*Haycraft is an American editor and critic specializing in mystery fiction. In the following excerpt, he provides an overview of Crofts's best novels.*]

The first of modern writers to find fictional possibilities in the step-by-step methods of actual police routine was Freeman Wills Crofts. In the opinion of a vast number of readers and critics he has never been equaled, much less surpassed, in his particular field. The son of a doctor in the British Army, Mr. Crofts was born in Dublin and lived a great part of his life in Northern Ireland. Educated at the Methodist and Campbell Colleges, Belfast, at seventeen he entered on his professional career as a civil and railway engineer, a vocation which contributed no little to his later almost mathematical detective plots. The first of these, however, had to await the author's fortieth year.

"In 1916," he writes, "I had a long illness, with a slow recovery, and to while away the time I got pencil and exercise book and began to amuse myself by writing a story. It proved a splendid pastime and I did a lot of it before getting about again. Then I put it away, never dreaming that it would see the light of day, but a little later I re-read it, thought that something might be made of it, and began to alter and revise. Eventually . . . to my immense delight it was published."

This story, as every devotee knows by now, was that masterpiece of practical crime detection, *The Cask* (1920). Mr. Crofts will presumably not object if one hazards the statement that not even he has succeeded in topping this well-nigh perfect example of its kind. In its quietly documented thoroughness, it is one of those timeless stories that improve rather than lose by the test of re-reading—preferably with pocket-atlases and maps of pre-Hitler London and Paris by the reader's side. Its central theme has become the trade-mark of Mr. Crofts' work in the field: the painstaking demolition of the "unbreakable" alibi. In fact, it has become almost a truism that the one

character in a Crofts' story who could not *possibly* have committed the crime will in the end be shown to have done just that!

If *The Cask* has a flaw, it is its failure to introduce Inspector French, the modest, believable police hero of most of the author's later works. This difficulty was remedied, however, with the appearance of *Inspector French's Greatest Case* (1924), a volume worthy in almost every way to find its place on the shelf beside *The Cask*. Unfortunately, not so much can be said of quite all the later Crofts books, for in recent years some impatient readers claim to have noticed evidences of weariness in the methodical Inspector's adventurings. Others feel that his narrator occasionally becomes too greatly preoccupied with time-tables and menus to serve the best interests of fiction. These complaints, one fears, are at one and the same time justified and inherent in the factual method when it gets out of hand. The detective story may not be an "art form," but in common with all fiction it partakes of the axiom that art can reproduce life only by being *selective*.

That Mr. Crofts carries his chosen method sometimes a little too far is regrettable but by no means fatal to the enjoyment of any of his numerous works, even the least of which are rewarding to the reader who is willing to meet the author half-way with time and attention. Certainly, fellow-practitioners and readers alike owe him a very considerable debt for his conscientious pioneering in the early 1920's, and for his contribution of several of the most enduring stories in the genre. It is a pleasure to record that this contribution has not gone unrewarded. *The Cask* has sold more than 100,000 copies in two decades, with *Inspector French's Greatest Case* only a little behind, and Mr. Crofts' more-than-a-score of works have been translated into at least ten languages. In 1929 he was able to retire from engineering and in 1939 he was made a Fellow of the Royal Society of Arts. At latest reports he and his wife were living quietly in the Guildford region of Surrey, which has served as the locale of several of his stories.

Whatever he may or may not produce in the future, Freeman Wills Crofts' permanent place in the history of detective fiction is already more than secure.

Howard Haycraft, "England: 1918-1930 (The Golden Age)," in his Murder for Pleasure: The Life and Times of the Detective Story, *D. Appleton-Century Company, Inc., 1941, pp. 112-58.*

Erik Routley   (essay date 1972)

[*Routley is an English clergyman, theologian, and nonfiction writer who has written numerous studies on ecclesiastical history and church music. In the following excerpt, he enumerates the major characteristics and themes of Crofts's tales.*]

Freeman Wills Crofts, perhaps the greatest puritan of them all, made his first appearance in 1920 with *The Cask,* a year after Agatha Christie had led off with *The Mysterious Affair at Styles*. Crofts (1879-1957) was an employee of the railways, brought up at a Methodist school, who wrote a great deal of his work after he had retired at fifty in order to do it. Among his other works was a translation of the New Testament—and that is about all he has in common with Ronald Knox.

He was as regular and industrious in his methods as Trollope, and scrupulously fair in his laying of clues. He was ruthless in disposing of his murderers, who were never in any circumstances attractive or deserving of the reader's sympathy. Their motives were sometimes passionate, but far more often associated with greed, a vice peculiarly hated by puritans. There is no levity in his work. It is all sober, systematic slogging. And that is why he is the creator of the first great policeman in the business.

Good policemen who take the centre of the stage are sufficiently familiar now (Ngaio Marsh and John Creasey show other ways of handling them) to make it necessary to remind the reader how relatively rare, taking the literature as a whole, the good policeman is. There are several possible ways of using the police in a detective story. They can be well-meaning perpetrators of injustice, corrected by the superior intelligence of an amateur (like Lestrade or Sidney Lomas); they can be a team of technicians who are grateful for the assistance of a brilliant amateur but do not look as if they would have ultimately gone wrong without him (like Stanley Hopkins and Charles Parker); they can be ruffians and incompetents—and this really didn't occur to any author as a possible line to take before the 1950s; or they can be simply the people that the story is all about.

Now if you are writing a police-novel about detection you have little room for romance. Give your policeman too much character and you'll soon get a protesting reaction from the reader's sense of credibility. Pack the story with too much incident, and you will get the same reaction from people who are persuaded that police work isn't like that. You are almost forced into writing straight documentary (like Creasey's 'Gideon' series). Your long suit must be the response you get from the readers to any writer who can make some well-known profession interesting by making use of the fruits of the most precise and sensitive observation. Given that, you can get away with a good deal. Novels about doctors have a long tradition of acceptability because they are bound to bring the reader into tense human situations, and they are always the better for precise observation of medical life. Court-room scenes are the best material for those who would present lawyers in novels because they can be dramatic, but again they are much better value if the author knows his law. (I was distressed and disillusioned to hear, in 1955, the comments of an eminent Q.C., now a Lord Justice of Appeal, on the court-room scene in Margery Allingham's *Flowers for the Judge.*) Novels about solicitors are rarer than those about barristers: the solicitor becomes easier material if he is something of a dissenter from established values, like Joshua Clunk or Arthur Crook. And of course it has been shown that it is possible to get insurance-men or business tycoons into sensational situations: but on the whole it is the inherent drama of the doctor's or the criminal barrister's life that the novelist welcomes most.

It is like that with the police, and either you must romanticise them (as Creasey does with Inspector West, or Ngaio Marsh, more winningly, with Alleyn) or you must hold the reader's attention by engaging his sympathy with the policeman as he is, taking the rough with the smooth. It was Crofts who showed how this might be done. His feet are firmly on the earth. He writes like an educated clerk. He gets his effect, like his famous Inspector French, by plain puritan hard work.

As a professional railwayman, Crofts was naturally the most eminent of railway-minded detective writers, and his timetables are one of the most conspicuous features of his stories. There is nothing sedentary about any of his policemen, who are never happier than when they are dashing about the country or the continent of Europe, always by train. Trains, symbol of the counterpoint between authority and adventure, appeal naturally to the puritan temperament of enterprise and moral rigour (I am told that in any railway society two of the best represented professions are likely to be low-church clergy and church organists).

The Great Train Robbery of 1963 was a pure Crofts situation, not least in that its motive was crude gain. That is his favourite motive, and murder, when we get it, is incidental to that: sex is usually secondary to it. And if anybody wants a two-page guide to the modern English puritan mind, he has only to study, or recall, the reactions of public opinion to the two major national scandals of that summer—the train robbery and the Profumo affair. The Profumo scandal generated a sense of helplessness (nicely expressed in the then Prime Minister's own words in Parliament)—a sense of being caught in a kind of epidemic: nothing to be done, and even a court case frustrated by a suicide. The train robbers, on the other hand, got considerable applause from the country and thirty years from the judge. You knew where you were with that: it was, in a sense, a 'good clean crime', almost a relief, so public comment seemed to imply, from the sinister implications of corrupt high life. All that is necessarily and designedly a trivial comment, but it was the comment of society. It exposes both the character and the limitations of the ethos which the Crofts detective tale assumes. There is no high life, apart from high business life, in Crofts. 'He was hanged on the 14th' is a perfectly possible final line in a Crofts short story. His accounts are unsensational enough to have pleased Holmes himself. And there, just as much as in Noël Coward, you see the spluttering bravura of the twenties. Coward is all style and champagne: Crofts is all no-nonsense moralism. It's all, to jaded eyes of the present, too good to be true, but in its way it's good all the same.

The Cask was a new kind of sober masterpiece, one of the finest first novels in detective history. Inspector French did not appear until 1925, in *Inspector French's Greatest Case,* which was quickly followed by *The Cheyne Mystery* (1927) and *The Starvel Tragedy* (1927). If you want the best example of the technique of arousing and holding a reader's interest in a specialised work-situation, worthy to stand alongside the best middle-period Sayers, it would be in *Death of a Train* (1946), one of his last books. Crofts found his length at once and held it. He knew just how to work within his limitations. He set many of his scenes in London or near the town where he lived (Guildford).

With him you get moral relaxation in an ethical armchair that will never let you down, and a celebration of ordinariness that supplies adventure without any reference to Puritania.

Erik Routley, "Coming of Age: E. C. Bentley, Freeman Wills Crofts, John Rhode," in his The Puritan Pleasures of the Detective Story: A Personal Monograph, *Victor Gollancz Ltd., 1972, pp. 119-28.*

Additional coverage of Crofts's life and career is contained in the following sources published by Gale Research: *Contemporary Authors*, **Vol. 115 (brief entry), and** *Dictionary of Literary Biography*, **Vol. 77.**

Emile Durkheim

1858-1917

French sociologist.

INTRODUCTION

A prominent figure in the French school of Sociology, Durkheim is best known for his establishment of a social theory which views sociology as a natural science subject to empirical study. Unlike his contemporaries, including English philosopher Herbert Spencer and anthropologist Edward Tylor, who emphasized the role of the individual in the development of cultural phenomena, Durkheim asserted the converse, maintaining that, although individuals comprise society, society is a separate and distinctive entity or reality, a causal result of the associations, reactions, and combinations of individuals' behaviors and psychic realities. His most influential contribution to social theory is his concept of the social fact, which he defines as "ways of acting, thinking, and feeling, exterior to the individual and endowed with a power of coercion."

Biographical Information

Durkheim was born in Epinal, France. The son of a rabbi, Durkheim also was intended for the rabbinate; his early religious education contributed to his scholarly command of Talmudic law and biblical history, which he synthesized into his later studies on religion. In 1879 he entered the École Normale Supérieure, where he studied philosophy under Emile Boutroux and two historians, Fustel de Couleanges and Gabriel Monod. After graduating he taught at various lycées near Paris. Taking a leave of absence in 1885, he visited Germany, where he became influenced by the work of renowned psychologist Wilhelm Wundt, from whose work on individual representations Durkheim derived his analogous theory to social phenomena, collective representations. Returning to France in 1886, he obtained a teaching position at the University of Bordeaux and established a reputation as a dynamic and inspiring instructor whose well-prepared lectures were widely attended. With the publication in 1893 of his doctoral dissertation for the University of Paris, *De la division du travail social: étude sur l'organisation des sociétés supérieurs* (*The Division of Labor in Society*), he established a reputation as one of the leaders of social theory in France. In 1896 he attained full professorship at Bordeaux and in 1898 founded the journal *L'année sociologique*, serving as editor for the next twelve years. Consisting of reviews aimed at scholars in the field of sociology, the journal featured articles in the fields of anthropology or sociology and Durkheim was a frequent contributor, publishing his ethnographic studies on incest, totemism, and the marriage practices of Australian aboriginal tribes. In 1902 he was summoned to teach philosophy at the prestigious University of Paris, gaining full professorship in 1906 as chair

of the department of Science of Education, which later became the department of Science of Education and Sociology specifically on behalf of Durkheim's teachings. Durkheim maintained his position in Paris until his death in 1917 following a protracted illness.

Major Works

Durkheim's works focus on a wide spectrum of societal institutions and social phenomena such as labor, religion, education, suicide, and morality. His seminal study on labor, *The Division of Labor in Society*, uses a comparative method and borrows from the Darwinian system of survival of the fittest and the Malthusian theory of population density to explain the morphological changes in labor in preindustrial and postindustrial societies. Noting that labor differentiation tended to increase in proportion to the social complexity and size of the population, Durkheim characterized labor in primitive societies as "mechanical solidarity" for its homogenous nature, and its industrial counterpart as "organic solidarity," signifying its heterogenous nature. In his next major work, *Les règles de la méthode sociologique* (*The Rules of the Sociological Method*), he explained his positivistic and statistical methodology, which was purely empirical, and established the fundamental basis of sociology as a discipline consisting of all the "beliefs, tendencies, [and] practices of the group taken collectively." In *Le suicide* (*Suicide*), Durkheim sought to explain, through a concise, statistical method, the phenomenon of suicide. He established his theories of altruism, anomie, fatalism, and egoism, explaining their contingencies upon social and cultural forces rather than individual psychological manifestations. Later, Durkheim turned his attention to the study of religion, and in 1912 he published *Les formes élementaires de la vie réligieuse* (*Elementary Forms of Religious Life*). Following a comparative method, he analyzed religious beliefs, practice, symbols, rituals, and the structural organization among Australian aboriginal tribes, as well as Indians of South America and the American Northwest coast. His conclusions, although deeply flawed according to many commentators, established the premise that religion and society are synonymous because the totem, a spiritual symbol, was also a symbol of the group or clan itself. Throughout his career, Durkheim was concerned with the French educational system and its significance in the socialization process. He published numerous articles on the topic, and his study *Education et sociologie* (*Education and Sociology*) was published posthumously in 1922.

PRINCIPAL WORKS

De la division du travail social: Etude sur l'organisation des sociétés supérieures [*The Division of Labor in Society*] (nonfiction) 1893

Les règles de la méthode sociologique [*The Rules of Sociological Method*] (nonfiction) 1895

Le suicide: étude de sociologie [*Suicide: A Study in Sociology*] (nonfiction) 1897

La prohibition de l'inceste et ses origines [*The Origins and the Development of the Incest Taboo*] (nonfiction) 1898

"Deux lois de l'évolution pénale" (essay) 1901; published in journal *L'annné sociologique*

"De quelques formes primitives de classification: contribution à l'étude des représentations collectives" (essay) 1903; published in journal *L'anné sociologique*

Les formes élémentaires de la vie religieuse: le système totémique en Australie [*The Elementary Forms of the Religious Life: A Study in Religious Sociology*] (nonfiction) 1912

"La famille conjugale: conclusion du cours sur la famille" (lecture) 1921; published in journal *L'anné sociologique*

Sociologie et philosophie [*Sociology and Philosophy*] (nonfiction) 1924

L'éducation morale [*Moral Education: A Study in the Theory and Application of the Sociology of Education*] (nonfiction) 1925

Le socialisme [*Socialism and Saint-Simon*] (nonfiction) 1928

CRITICISM

A. A. Goldenweiser (essay date 1915)

[*In the following review of* Les formes élémentaires de la vie religieuse, *originally published in* American Anthropologist *in 1915, Goldenweiser refutes all of Durkheim's "cardinal doctrines" discussed in the work.*]

A contribution by Émile Durkheim always commands attention. His *Les règles de la méthode sociologique, De la division du travail social,* and *Le Suicide* have exercised an appreciable influence on sociological theory and are still remembered and read. As editor of *L'Année sociologique,* Durkheim deserves credit for a methodical and extensive survey of anthropological and sociological literature. In this task he was ably assisted by his disciples and sympathizers, Hubert, Mauss and others. It is to be regretted that this excellent annual has now gone out of existence, its place having been taken by a triennial publication supplemented by occasional monographs constituting a series of *Travaux de L'Année sociologique,* of which *La vie religieuse* is the fourth volume.

As the title indicates, the work deals with Australian totemism, but is also meant as a general theoretical inquiry into the principles of religious experience. Durkheim is a veteran in Australian ethnology. It will be remembered that the first volume of *L'Année sociologique* (1896-1897) contained a study from his pen devoted to **"La prohibition de l'inceste et ses origines."** Volume V (1900-1901) of the Annual contains another study, **"Sur le totémisme";** and volume VIII (1903-1904) one on **"L'organisation matrimoniale australienne."** One need not therefore be surprised to find Durkheim's latest work replete with abundant and carefully analyzed data. In this respect the volume compares most favorably with much of the hazy theorizing called forth in such profusion by [Herbert] Spencer and [Francis James] Gillen's descriptive monographs. But Durkheim's work contains, of course, much more than a merely descriptive study. He had a vision and he brings a message. To these we must now turn.

While a comprehensive analysis of all of Durkheim's propositions is entirely beyond the scope of a review, his cardinal doctrines may be discussed under the headings of five theories: a theory of religion, a theory of totemism, a theory of social control, a theory of ritual, and a theory of thought.

Theory of Religion.—Durkheim vigorously objects to the theories of religion which identify it with belief in God or in the supernatural. A belief in the supernatural presupposes the conception of a natural order. The savage has no such conception nor does he know of the supernatural. He does not wonder nor inquire, but accepts the events of life as a matter of course. The attempts to derive religion from dreams, reflections, echoes, shadows, etc., find as little favor with Durkheim. Is it conceivable, he exclaims, that religion, so powerful in its appeal, so weighty in its social consequences, should in the last analysis prove to be nothing but an illusion, a naïve aberration of the primitive mind? Surely, that cannot be. At the root of religion there must lie some fact of nature or of experience, as powerful in its human appeal and as universal as religion itself. Durkheim sets out in search of that fact. Presently, the field of inquiry is limited by the reflection that the beings, objects, and events in nature cannot, by virtue of their intrinsic qualities, give rise to religion, for there is nothing in their make-up which could, in itself, explain the religious thrill. This, indeed, is quite obvious, for do not the least significant beings and things in nature often become the objects of profound religious regard? Thus the source of religion may not be sought in natural experience but must in some significant way be interwoven with the conditions of human existence. Now the most fundamental and patent fact in all religion is the classification of all things, beings, events in experience into sacred and profane. This dichotomy of the universe is coextensive with religion; what will explain the one will explain the other. The next important fact to be noted is that the content of religion is not exhausted by its emotional side. Emotional experience is but one aspect of religion, the other aspects being constituted by a system of concepts and a set of activities. There is no religion without a church.

The fundamental propositions thus advanced by Durkheim do not impress one as convincing. In claiming that primitive man knows no supernatural, the author fundamentally misunderstands savage mentality. Without in the least suspecting the savage of harboring the conception of a natural order, we nevertheless find him discriminating between that which falls within the circle of everyday occurrence and that which is strange, extraordinary, requiring explanation, full of power, mystery. To be sure, the line of demarcation between the two sets of phenomena is not drawn by the savage where we should draw it, but surely we should not thereby be prevented from becoming aware of the existence of the line and of the conceptual differentiation of phenomena which it denotes. If that is so, Durkheim commits his initial error, fatal in its consequences, in refusing to grant the savage the discriminating attitude towards nature and his own experience which he actually possesses. The error is fatal indeed, for the realm of the supernatural, of which Durkheim would deprive the savage, is precisely that domain of his experience which harbors infinite potentialities of emotional thrill and religious ecstasy.

Durkheim's objection to the derivation of the first religious impulses from what he calls illusions, strikes one as peculiar. For what, after all, is truth and what is illusion? Are not the highest religions, of undisputed significance and worldwide appeal, also based on illusions? Are not ideals, in more than one sense, illusions? Should one therefore be shocked if religion were shown to have its primal roots in an illusion? Thus Durkheim's search for a *reality* underlying religion does not seem to rest on a firm logical basis. The author's definition of religion, finally, represents a conceptual hybrid, the application of which could not but have the gravest consequences for his study. A religion, says Durkheim, is an integral system of beliefs and practices referring to sacred things, things that are separated, prohibited; of beliefs and practices which unite into a moral community called the church all those who partic-

ipate in them. This apparently innocent definition involves a series of hypotheses. While all will concede that religion has a subjective as well as an objective side, that belief is wedded to ritual, the equating of the two factors in one definition arouses the suspicion of an attempt to derive one from the other, a suspicion justified by a further perusal of the work. Closely related, moreover, as are belief and ritual, they belong to different domains of culture, their relations to tradition, for instance, and to individual experience, are quite different, and the methodology of research in the two domains must be radically different. Unless this standpoint is taken at the outset, inextricable situations are bound to arise. That the body of believers constitutes a moral community is another proposition which one may set out to prove but which should not be taken for granted in an initial definition. The proposition further prejudices the investigator in favor of the social elements in religion and at the expense of the individual elements. The introduction of the term "church," finally, as well as the designation of the religious complex as an "integral system," brings in an element of standardization and of unification, which should be a matter to be proved not assumed.

Theory of Totemism.—Durkheim takes pains to set forth his reasons for discarding the comparative method of inquiry. The pitfalls of this mode of approaching cultural problems being familiar to ethnologists, we may pass over the author's careful argumentation. As a substitute for the antiquated method Durkheim proposes the intensive study of a single area; for, he urges, the superficial comparison of half-authenticated facts separated from their cultural setting is pregnant with potentialities of error, while the thoroughgoing analysis of one instance may reveal a law. Australia is the author's choice; for from that continent come detailed and comprehensive descriptive monographs; moreover, there, if anywhere, are we likely to discover the prime sources of religion: the social organization of the Australians being based on the clan, the most primitive form of social grouping, their religions must needs be of the lowest type. The author thus takes as his starting-point the Australian clan, which he conceives as an undifferentiated primitive horde. Each horde takes its name from the animal or plant most common in the locality where the group habitually congregates. The assumption of the name is a natural process, a spontaneous expression of group solidarity which craves for an objective symbol. To the totemic design or carving must be ascribed an analogous origin. Of this type of symbolism tattooing is the earliest form; not finding much evidence on that point in Australia, the author borrows some American examples. The paintings and carvings of the Australian being very crude and almost entirely unrealistic, the author is again tempted to refer to the American Indian, while ascribing the character of Australian totemic art to the low degree of their technical advancement. The theory of social control will show us how the concept of power, *mana,* the totemic principle, originates in the clan. Here we take it for granted. Thus, on ceremonial occasions the individual is aware of the presence of a mysterious power; through the vertigo of his emotional ecstasy he sees himself surrounded by totemic symbols, churingas, nurtunjas, and to them he transfers his intuition of power; henceforth, they become for him the source from which that power flows.

Thus it comes that the totemic representations stand in the very center of the sacred totemic cycle of participation; the totemic animal or plant, and the human members of the totemic clan become sacred by reflection. When so much is granted, the other peculiarities of totemism follow as a matter of course. Totemism is not restricted to the clans, their members, animals, carvings, but spreads over the entire mental universe of the Australian. The whole of nature is divided and apportioned between the clans, and all the beings, objects, phenomena of nature partake, to a greater or less degree, of the sacredness of the totemic animal or plant or thing with which they are classified. This is the cosmogony of the totemic religion. Individual totemism, the worship of the guardian spirit, is a later derivative of clan totemism, for whereas clan totemism often appears alone, individual totemism occurs only in conjunction with clan totemism. Every religion has its individual as well as its social aspect. The guardian-spirit cult is the individual aspect of totemism. The subjective embodiment, finally, of the totemic principle is the individual soul. But whence the totemic principle? Before passing to the theory of social control which brings an answer to the query, we must pause to examine the theory of totemism as here outlined.

While the author's rejection of the comparative method deserves hearty endorsement, the motivation of his resolve to present an intensive study of one culture arouses misgivings. For thus, he says, he might discover a law. Applicable as this concept may be in the physical sciences, the hope itself of discovering a law in the study no matter how intensive of *one* historical complex, must be regarded as hazardous. And presently one finds that there is more to the story, for Australia is selected for the primitiveness of its social organization (it is based on the clan!) with which a primitive form of religion may be expected to occur. That at this stage of ethnological knowledge one as competent as Émile Durkheim should regard the mere presence of a clan organization as a sign of primitiveness is strange indeed. For, quite apart from the fact that no form of clan system may be regarded as primitive, in the true sense of the word, clan systems may represent relatively high and low stages of social development. Moreover, even were the social organization of the Australian to be regarded as primitive, that would not guarantee the primitiveness of his religion; just as his in reality complex and highly developed form of social organization appears side by side with a markedly low type of industrial achievement. Also from the point of view of the available data must the selection of Australia be regarded as unfortunate, for, in point of ethnography, Australia shares with South America the distinction of being our dark continent. A most instructive study in ethnographic method could be written based on the errors committed by Howitt, and Spencer and Gillen, as well as Strehlow, our only modern authorities on the tribes from which Durkheim derives all his data. The fact itself that the author felt justified in selecting the Australian area for his intensive analysis, shows plainly enough how far from realization still is the goal which his own life-work has at least made feasible, the *rapprochement* of ethnology and of sociology.

But let us pass to the concrete points. The conception of a clan name being assumed as an expression of clan solidarity is suggestive enough. On the other hand, one must not be forgetful of the fact that a name serves to differentiate group from group, and that at all times names must have been given by group to group rather than assumed by each group for itself. Not that names were never assumed by groups—such names as, "we, the people" or "men," etc., bespeak the contrary—but this process must be regarded as the exception rather than the rule. Moreover, groups of distinct solidarity such as phratries or the Iroquois maternal families, often appear without names (in the instance of the maternal family this is indeed always the case), so that the consciousness of solidarity in a group may not be regarded as inevitably leading to expression in the form of a name. As to the objective totemic symbol, the totemic carvings or drawings, it is discussed most loosely by our author. Not finding the totemic tattoo in Australia, he appeals to American examples, but this device, of course, does not strengthen his case except by showing that totemic tattoo occurs in America. Also, he completely neglects the cardinal differences between the totemic art of the Northwest Coast and that of the Aranda—to both of which he refers—in failing to note that whereas among the Tlingit or Haida the carved crests are positively associated with the totemic ideas, among the Aranda the churinga or ground and rock designs are at best but passive carriers of momentary (although recurrent) totemic associations. It is, in fact, quite obvious that the geometrical art of the area has neither originated in nor been differentiated through totemic ideas, but being of an extra-totemic origin, has been subsequently drawn into the totemic cycle of associations without, however, ever becoming actively representative of them. Similarly, with the so-called totemic cosmogony, the fact that social organization tends to be reflected in mythology cannot indeed be disputed; this fact, however, altogether transcends, in its bearing, the problem of totemism. Hence, when we find a sociological classification of the universe coexisting with a totemic complex, we are fully justified in regarding the two phenomena as genetically distinct and secondarily associated. The burden of proof, at any rate, falls upon those who would assert the contrary. Durkheim's treatment of these as of other aspects of the Australian totemic complex reflects his failure to consider that view of totemism which was designed to show, at the hand of relevant data, that totemic complexes must be regarded as aggregates of various cultural features of heterogeneous psychological and historical derivation. Needless to add, the adoption of that view would strike at the very core of Durkheim's argument necessitating a complete recasting of the fundamental principles of *La vie religieuse.* Nor does Durkheim's discussion of the relative priority of clan totemism carry conviction. Here his facts are strangely inaccurate, for far from it being the case that "individual totemism" never occurs unaccompanied by clan totemism, the facts in North America, the happy hunting-ground of the guardian spirit, bespeak the contrary. Whereas that belief must be regarded as an all but universal aspect of the religion of the American Indian, it has nowhere developed more prolifically than among the tribes of the Plateau area who worship not at the totemic shrine. To regard the belief in guardian spirits, "individual totemism," as an outgrowth of clan totemism is, therefore, an altogether gratuitous hypothesis! Having satisfied himself that all the elements which, according to his conception of religion, constitute a true religion, are present in totemism, Durkheim declares totemism to represent the earliest form of a religion which, while primitive, lacks none of those aspects which a true religion must have. Thus is reached the culminating point of a series of misconceptions of which the first is Durkheim's initial view and definition of religion. For had he given proper weight to the emotional and individual aspects in religion, the aspect which unites religious experiences of all times and places into one psychological continuum, he could never have committed the patent blunder of "discovering" the root of religion in an institution which is relatively limited in its distribution and is moreover, distinguished by the relatively slight intensity of the religious values comprised in it. In this latter respect totemism cannot compare with either animal worship, or ancestor worship, or idolatry, or fetichism, or any of the multifarious forms of worship of nature, spirit, ghost and god. Several of these forms of religious belief are also more widely diffused than totemism and must be regarded as more primitive, differing from totemism in their independence from any definite form of social organization. Resuming the author's argument, we now return to the "totemic principle," the origin of which must be accounted for.

The Theory of Social Control.—Analysis shows that society has the qualities necessary to arouse the sense of the divine. Social standards, ideals, moods, impose themselves upon the individual with such categorical force as to arouse the consciousness of external pressure emanating from a force transcending the powers of the individual. Through the action of this social force the individual on certain occasions behaves, feels, and thinks in a way which differs from the psychic activities of his daily experience. The psychic situation of the orator and his audience, on the one hand, and, on the other, the actions and psychic experiences of individuals in the crusades or during revolutions, may serve as examples. Now the social unit with which the Australian is most intimately allied is the clan. The life of the clan mates consists of periods of non-eventful daily activities alternating with periods of violent emotional disturbances accompanying ceremonial occasions. While "the secrets" hold sway, to speak with the Kwakiutl, the individual lives on an exalted plane, manifesting qualities which altogether transcend those he possesses under ordinary conditions. The periodic recurrence of these two sets of ideas, emotions, acts, cannot but evoke in the individual the tendency to classify the totality of his experience into profane and sacred. The former embraces all that is strictly individual, the latter all that is social. The sense of external power which acts through the individual on social occasions will tend to crystallize into a concept of an undifferentiated, powerful, mysterious force, which pervades nature and absorbs the individual who feels himself external to that power and yet part of it. This power, as it appears to the Australian clansman, may be called the *totemic principle.* It is not the clan emblem, the totemic design, which is worshiped, nor the totemic animal, nor the various beings and things which form part of the totemic cycle of participation; but the to-

temic principle, the mysterious substance which pervades them all and constitutes their holiness. It was shown in the preceding section how this sense of power, craving for objective expression, attaches itself to the totemic symbols which surround the individual on ceremonial occasions and thus gives the initial stimulus to the formation of a sacred totemic world. Comparison with American data shows that the totemic principle is a forerunner of the *wakan,* the *orenda* as well as of the Melanesian *mana.* The concept is the same, the only difference being that the totemic principle, originating as it does within the clan, reflects the clan differentiation of the tribe, whereas, the *wakan,* the *orenda,* etc., belonging to a higher stage of development, have freed themselves from the constraint of the clan limit, and transcending it, have acquired that character of generality and homogeneity which distinguishes these concepts.

Thus a solution is reached not alone of the totemic problem, but of the problem of religion. The reality which underlies religion is society itself. In the Australian situation society appears in its most primitive form—the clan. The totemic principle, the nucleus of the most primitive religion, is the clan itself reflected in the psyche of the individual. Not aware of the real source of his subjective sense of power, the Australian objectifies the latter in the form of religious symbolism, thus giving rise to the infinitely varied world of the concrete carriers of religious values. Thus, while here also there is illusion, it extends only to the content not to the existence of the ultimate reality, which is eternal.

We may first consider the minor issue raised in this section, namely the identification of the totemic principle with *mana.* On reading the pages devoted to this discussion the unprejudiced student soon perceives that the facts supporting Durkheim's contention are altogether wanting. There is no indication that the beliefs underlying totemic religion are generically the same as those designated by the terms *mana* or *orenda*; and that the *wakan* and *orenda* concepts should represent later stages of religious evolution, having superseded a stage in which the totemic principle reigned, is an imaginary construction which cannot be described otherwise than *aus der Luft gegriffen.* The main issue of the section, however, is the derivation of the totemic principle. This, in fact, is Durkheim's theory of religion, which is represented as a symbol of social control. Durkheim's theory has the charm of originality, for no one else before him has, to my knowledge, held such a view, nor has the author himself, in his former writings, ever gone so far in his social interpretations of psychic phenomena. Our first objection to the derivation of the sacred from an inner sense of social pressure is a psychological one. That a crowd-psychological situation should have aroused the religious thrill in the constituent individuals, who—*nota bene*—were hitherto unacquainted with religious emotion, does not seem in the least plausible. Neither in primitive nor in modern times do such experiences, *per se,* arouse religious emotions, even though the participating individuals are no longer novices in religion. And, if on occasion such sentiments do arise, they lack the intensity and permanence required to justify Durkheim's hypothesis. If a corroborree differs from an intichiuma, or the social dances of the North American Indians from their religious dances, the difference is not in the social composition but in the presence or absence of pre-existing religious associations. A series of corroborrees does not make an intichiuma; at least, we have no evidence to that effect, and human psychology, as we know it, speaks against it. Durkheim's main error, however, seems to our mind to lie in a misconception of the relation of the individual to the social, as implied in his theory of social control. The theory errs in making the scope of the social on the one hand, too wide, on the other, too narrow. Too wide in so far as the theory permits individual factors to become altogether obscured, too narrow in so far as the society which figures in the theory is identified with a crowd, and not with a cultural, historic group. The experience of all times and places teaches that the rapport of the individual, as such, with the religious object is of prime importance in religious situations. While, on the one hand, religious emotions are stimulated (not created) by the social setting, the leaders of religious thought, prophets, reformers, individuals whose lives must be conceived as protracted communions with the divine, do not require the social stimulant, they shun the crowd, the church, the world, their god is within them, and their emotional constitution is a guarantee of an interminable succession of religious thrills. The lives of saints are one great argument against Durkheim's theory. The psychic cast of many a savage medicine man, magician, shaman, is another. If the social pressure, the ceremonial whirl is so indispensable a factor in the religious thrill, how is it that the world over the novice, in anticipation of the most significant, if not initial religious experience of his life, withdraws from human companionship, spends days, nay months in isolation, fasts and purifies himself, dreams dreams and sees visions? If phenomena of this type are so important in religion at all times, can one with impunity brush them aside in his search for a plausible origin of religion? Or would Durkheim claim that the religious thrill, socially produced, did then in some way become part of the psychic constitution of man in the form of a hereditary predisposition? But our author has not advanced this theory, and it would perhaps be unfair to attribute it to him.

On the other hand, the scope of the social in the author's theory is too narrow. For, significant as are the functions ascribed to it, the content of the social setting, in Durkheim's religious laboratory, is curiously restricted. Religion, he says, is society, but society, we find, is but a sublimated crowd. The only aspect of the relation of the individual to the social drawn upon in Durkheim's theory is the crowd-psychological situation, the effect on the individual of the presence of other individuals who, for the time being, think, and above all, feel and act as he does. We hear nothing of the effect on the individual of the cultural type of the group of the tribal or national or class patterns of thought and action, and even emotion, patterns developed by history and fixed by tradition. Of all this we hear nothing. The only factor called upon to do such far-reaching service is that whimsical psycho-sociological phenomenon which equates a crowd of sages to a flock of sheep. Strange fact, indeed, that one who expects so much from the social should see in it so little!

Theory of Ritual.—It will be impossible to fully discuss in these pages Durkheim's suggestive analysis of rituals, negative and positive, mimetic, representative, and piacular. We shall restrict our remarks to the types of ritual which bear directly on the theories here discussed. Ritual is essential for belief. Nature goes through certain periodic changes; evidently, thinks the Australian, the divinities controlling nature must go through similar transformations. To this spectacle man may not remain indifferent; he must assist the divinities with all the powers at his command. The divinities, totems, etc., derive their sacred character from man, hence, the sacredness will decline unless revived. The group gathers intent on relieving the situation. But presently they feel comforted: "They find the remedy because they look for it together." On such occasions society becomes rejuvenated, and with it the soul of the individual, for is it not derived from society?

In the mimetic dances of the intichiuma the performers believe that they *are* the animals whose multiplication they crave, hence they imitate them in cries and actions. This identification of man and animal exists only to the extent to which it is believed, and the rite feeds the belief. The ceremony is beneficent for it constitutes a moral remaking of the participants. Hence the feeling that the ceremony has been successful. But it was intended to further the multiplication of the totemic animal, and now the belief that such multiplication has actually been achieved arises as a correlate of the feeling that the ceremony was successful. Such is ritualistic mentality.

In this case as in others the real justification of a religious rite is in the rite itself, that is, in the effect it produces on the social consciousness. The economic or other uses to which a rite is put are secondary, they vary and the same rite often does service for different purposes.

Another aspect of the ritualistic situation is what one might call an overproduction of thought, emotion, and activity. The elaboration of these processes is accompanied by pleasurable emotion, it becomes an end in itself. This is the threshold of Art.

A striking example of Durkheim's conception of ritual and of its effect on belief, is presented in his interpretation of mourning. When an individual dies, the social solidarity of his family is shaken. Driven by the shock of their loss, they unite. At first this leads to an intensification of sorrowful emotion: a "panic of grief" sets in, in the course of which the individuals sob, howl and lacerate themselves. But presently the effect of this exhibition of solidarity in sorrow begins to be felt. The individuals feel comforted, reassured. The mourning is brought to an end through the agency of the mourning itself.

But the individual remains perplexed. He must account for the strange exhibitions of mourning. Of social forces he knows nothing. All he is aware of is his suffering, and he seeks the cause for it in an external will. Now, the body of the deceased can surely not be held accountable, but his soul is there and it must be vitally concerned in the processes of the mourning rite; but these processes are highly disagreeable, hence the soul must be evil. When the mourning frenzy subsides, and a pleasurable calm ensues, the soul is again held responsible for the change, but now it appears as a benevolent agency. Not only the properties, but the survival itself of the soul, may, according to Durkheim, be an afterthought, introduced to account for the mourning rites.

Thus the ritual in this and similar cases appears as a spontaneous response of the group to an emotional situation. The beliefs, on the other hand, arise out of speculative attempts designed to interpret the phenomena of the ritualistic performance.

Durkheim's psychological interpretation of ritual, must, on the whole, be regarded as the most satisfactory part of his analysis. Nevertheless here, as elsewhere, he permits himself to lapse into a rationalistic and behavioristic attitude. While it is, of course, true that divinities exist only to the extent to which they are believed in and that belief is stimulated by ritual, this dependence of the gods on belief is certainly a fact which never enters the mind of the native. He, for one, is profoundly convinced of the externality and objectivity of his spiritual enemies or protectors, nor does he believe in the waning and waxing of their powers, to keep pace with the periodic changes in nature. Moreover, while the rite may properly be regarded as a battery by means of which the participants are periodically re-charged with belief, this function of ritual may easily be exaggerated, nor should other sources be disregarded which tend to preserve accepted belief, such as the forces of tradition, teaching and more strictly individual, as contrasted with social, experience. It must be remembered that ritualism on an extensive scale is, while a common, by no means a constant nor even a predominant characteristic of primitive society. An analysis, from this point of view, of the North American area, for instance, reveals the suggestive fact that ritual *en masse* occurs mainly in the Southwest, Southeast, Northwest, Plains area, and part of the Woodland area, whereas among the Eskimo, in the Mackenzie and Plateau areas and in California, ritual is, speaking generally, an individual or family function. In other words, ritual *en masse* is associated with tribes of a complex social type, where the group is differentiated into many definite social units some of which appear as the carriers of ceremonial functions; while the tribes with a relatively simple social structure, based on the individual family and the local community, are on the whole foreign to ritualism of the above type. This generalization cannot be accepted without certain reservations. The situation is really more complex, and other factors, such, for instance, as diffusion of rituals, would have to be taken into account; such tribes, moreover, as those of the Western Plains or the Nootka combine with a relatively simple type of social organization a relatively complex type of ritualism. Within certain limits, however, the generalization holds. Now, it becomes at once obvious that the intensity of religious belief is not correlated with complex ceremonialism. Among tribes devoid of complex ritualism, other factors must be operative to strengthen and perpetuate the existing belief; and, if that is so, we are also cautioned against the exclusive emphasis on ritual as a generator of belief even where it does occur on a large scale. The gods live not by ritual alone.

As a most glaring instance of an extreme behaviorist position we must regard Durkheim's attempt to account for the qualities nay, in part, even for the survival of the soul, by means of the "ritualistic mentality." Elaborate criticisms of hypotheses such as this are futile, for it obviously represents a deliberate effort to disregard the many emotional and conceptual factors which go to the making of the soul-belief in all its aspects, in favor of a simplicist behaviorist explanation. When Durkheim interprets the belief in the efficacy of the intichiuma as a reflection of the rise in social consciousness brought on by the ceremony, he commits a similar error. It seems unjustifiable for instance, to disregard as a contributing factor in furthering the belief, the observation often made by the natives that the totemic animals and plants actually do multiply soon after the performance of the ceremonies. Durkheim does, indeed, note the fact, but he fails to utilize it in his theory.

Theory of Thought.—Whereas the prime object of the author's work is to trace the origin of religious beliefs and notions, he turns repeatedly to the more general problem of thought, of intellectual categories. While the author's remarks on that subject are not extensive nor systematic, enough is said before the volume draws to a close, to make his position stand out in bold relief. No less than the categories of religion the categories of thought are of social origin. The importance of individual experience and of tentative generalizations derived therefrom should not be underestimated, but isolated individual experience lacks the elements necessary to give the notions which thus arise that character of generality and imperativeness which distinguishes the mental categories. *Mana,* the totemic principle, that objectified intuition of society, is the first religious force, but also the prototype of the notion of force in general; just as the concept of soul, the active element in man, is, as shown, of social derivation. Similarly with the category of causality. The "will to believe" aspect of ritualistic mentality, as manifested, for instance, in the intichiuma ceremonies, has been dwelt on at length. But the belief alone is not sufficient; it would, at best, result in a state of expectancy. The rites must be repeated whenever need is felt of them, and the emotional attitude must be supplemented by a concept, if the intichiuma as a method of constraining or assisting nature is to be counted on. The concept that like produces like becomes a fixed mental category, and behind it is a social mandate. "The imperatives of thought seem to constitute but another aspect of the imperatives of Will."

The notion that the qualities of objects can be communicated to their surroundings by a process of propagation, cannot be derived from daily experience, for the phenomenon in question does not occur within the domain of such experience, but constitutes a peculiarity of the religious world. Religious forces, qualities, being themselves but sublimated and transformed aspects of society, are not derived from objects but super-added upon them. The intrinsic virtues of the carriers of religious forces are thus indifferent, and the most insignificant things may become objects of greatest religious import. It is not strange that sacredness can be communicated by contagion from object to object for it is by contagion that sacredness becomes primarily fixed upon objects. Nor is this contagiousness of the religious irrational, for it creates bonds and relations between objects, beings, actions, otherwise disparate, and thus paves the way for future scientific explanations. What was heretofore called the cosmogony of totemism, the classificatory aspect of the most primitive religion, thus becomes the prototype of classification in general, the first source of the notions of genus, subordination, coördination.

The mental categories, concludes Durkheim, are not merely instituted by society, but they are, in their origin, but different aspects of society. The category of genus finds its beginning in the concept of the human group; the rhythm of social life is at the basis of the category of time; the space occupied by society is the source of the category of space; the first efficient force is the collective force of society, bringing in its wake the category of causality. The category of totality, finally, can only be of social origin. Society alone completely transcends the individual, rises above all particulars. "The concept of Totality is but the abstract form of the concept of society: Society is the whole which comprises all things, the ultimate class which embraces all other classes."

The author's attempt to derive all mental categories from specific phases of social life which have become conceptualized, is so obviously artificial and one-sided that one finds it hard to take his view seriously, but the self-consistency of the argument and, in part, its brilliancy compel one to do so. In criticism we must repeat the argument advanced in another connection in the preceding section: in so far as Durkheim's socially determined categories presuppose a complex and definite social system, his explanatory attempts will fail, wherever such a system is not available. The Eskimo, for example, have no clans nor phratries nor a totemic cosmogony (for they have no totems); how then did their mental categories originate, or is the concept of classification foreign to the Eskimo mind? Obviously, there must be other sources in experience or the psychological constitution of man which may engender mental categories; and, if that is so, we may no longer derive such categories from the social setting, even when the necessary complexity and definiteness are at hand.

In this connection it is well to remember that the origin of mental categories is an eternally recurring event; categories come into being within the mental world of every single individual. We may thus observe that the categories of space, time, force, causality, arise in the mind of the child far ahead of any possible influence from their adult surroundings by way of conscious or even deliberate suggestion. To be sure, these categories are, in the mind of the child, not strictly conceptualized nor even fully within the light of consciousness, but their presence is only too apparent: the individual experience of the child rapidly supplements the congenital predisposition of the mind. Instructive conclusions, bearing on these and other questions of epistemology, could be drawn from a systematic analysis of the grammars of primitive languages. Grammar is but a conceptual shorthand for experience and the means by which a relatively unlimited experience is squeezed into the frame of a strictly limited grammar is classification. Now, while the psychic processes underlying grammatical categories fall notoriously below the level of consciousness, they do nevertheless represent the deepest and most fundamental tendencies of the mind which, without doubt, provide the foundation for later, more conscious mental efforts, in similar directions. While no intensive study of primitive grammars, from the above point of view, has as yet been made, enough is known to foresee that but a fraction of the categories thus revealed will prove of specifically social derivation.

There remains another equally fundamental criticism to be made of Durkheim's doctrine. As we have seen, the author maintains that infectiousness is a specifically religious phenomenon. It does not seem that even the infectiousness of the sacred has been satisfactorily accounted for by the author. For, granting that sacredness is not inherent in objects but projected into them, that fact would not, *per se,* explain why sacredness should be so readily communicable from object to object. The Australian is not aware of the extraneous character of the sanctity of things, and surely it would be impossible for him to believe that his consciousness is if not the ultimate, yet the proximate source of that sanctity. Hence, the infectiousness of the sacred remains, from that standpoint, inexplicable. Another instance of the psychologist's fallacy! This, however, is but a minor point. But can we follow the author in his assertion that infectiousness is peculiar to the sacred and that the quality is foreign to experience outside of the religious realm? Assuredly not. Daily observation brings before the mind of the savage numerous instances of the communicability of qualities. Wet comes from wet, and cold from cold; red ochre makes things red and so does blood, while dirt makes them dirty; touching rough surfaces brings roughness of skin and soreness; intimate contact with strongly smelling substances communicates the smell; heat, finally, produces heat—and pain. If the sacred is infectious, so is profane nature, and the mind which learns from the one its first lesson in categorizing can learn it from the other as well. It will be seen that the above criticism is based on a special instance. It must now be generalized. The exclusive emphasis on the religious and ultimately on the social as the source of the fundamental categories of thought is unjustifiable in view of the rich variety of profane experience which is amenable to like conceptualization. While the point, when made in this general form, is fairly obvious, much interesting research work in this neglected field of primitive mentality remains to be done. The magico-religious aspect of primitive life and thought has for years monopolized our attention to such an extent that the less picturesque but no less real concrete experience of the savage has remained almost completely in the background. What does the savage know? should be the question. A vast store of data is available, on which to base our answer, and more can be procured.

The principal criticisms here passed on Durkheim's work may now be summarized as follows: The selection of Australia as the practically exclusive source of information must be regarded as unfortunate, in view of the imperfection of the data. The charge is aggravated through the circumstance that the author regards the case of Australia as typical and tends to generalize from it.

The Theory of Religion is deficient in so far as it involves the commingling in one definition of disparate aspects of the religious complex. Many of the special points made in the course of the work are thus prejudged; the individual and subjective aspect of religion, in particular, thus fails to receive proper attention.

The Theory of Totemism suffers from the disregard of the ethnological point of view which forces upon us the conviction that the institution must be regarded as highly complex historically and psychologically. The resulting interpretation of the totemic complex, while giving evidence of Durkheim's superior psychological insight and often brilliant argumentation, recalls by its one-sidedness and artificiality the contributions to the subject on the part of the classical anthropologists.

The Theory of Social Control must be rejected on account of its underestimation as well as overestimation of the social, involving a fundamental misconception of the relation of the individual to society. For, on the one hand, the individual becomes, in Durkheim's presentation, completely absorbed in the social; society itself, on the other hand, is not conceived as a historical complex but as a sublimated crowd.

The Theory of Ritual, while involving much true insight, is narrowly behavioristic and rationalistic and fails to do justice to the direct effect of experience upon the mind. The conception of the subjective side of religion as an after-thought, consequent upon and explanatory of action, must be vigorously rejected.

The Theory of Thought, finally, suffers from an exclusive emphasis on socio-religious experiences as the sources of mental categories, to the all but complete exclusion of the profane experience of the savage and the resulting knowledge of the concrete facts and processes in Nature.

Thus the central thesis of the book that the fundamental reality underlying religion is society, must be regarded as unproved.

A. A. Goldenweiser, in a review of Les formes élémentaires de la vie religieuse in Selected Papers from the American Anthropologist, 1888-1920, *edited by Frederica De Laguna, Row, Peterson and Company, 1960, pp. 717-35.*

The Nation, New York   (essay date 1916)

[*In the following mixed review of* The Elementary Forms of the Religious Life, *the critic, while praising Durkheim's methods for their brilliance and originality, questions the validity of his conclusion that all forms of religion have the same totemistic, rather than naturalistic or animistic, origins.*]

It was in 1912 that *Les Formes élémentaires de la vie religieuse [The Elementary Forms of the Religious Life]* appeared; and English readers are fortunate that not more than four years were allowed to elapse before the publication of an English edition. Mr. Swain's translation is hardly brilliant, and in a very few cases his understanding of the French and his choice of English words are not all that

could be desired. But his sentences are invariably clear and his version is faithful to the original.

The book is probably the most important contribution to the study of primitive religions that this century has as yet produced. After a careful analysis and critique of the animistic and naturalistic hypotheses, the author passes to an exposition of totemistic beliefs and rites in the light of his own sociology. The major part of the book is devoted to this elaborate exposition and analysis. For his facts Durkheim is dependent chiefly upon Spencer and Gillen and upon Strehlow—though he has practically exhausted the literature of his subject and draws liberally upon all the more important investigators. But the arrangement and interpretation of the facts are his own, and, whether one agrees with him or not, no one can deny that his methods and conclusions are both original and brilliant.

The essential thing about religion, according to Durkheim, is the distinction which it makes between the sacred and the profane.

> Sacred things are those which the interdictions (of society) protect and isolate; profane things, those to which these interdictions are applied and which must remain at a distance from the first. Religious beliefs are the representations which express the nature of the sacred things and the relations which they sustain, either with each other or with profane things. Finally, rites are the rules of conduct which prescribe how a man should comport himself in the presence of these sacred objects.

> A religion is a unified system of beliefs and practices relative to sacred things, that is to say, things set apart and forbidden—beliefs and practices which unite into one single moral community called a church all those who adhere to them.

If we would find the essential elements of religion in their most obvious form, the author argues, we must seek it in the most primitive religion discoverable; and this most primitive religion will be that belonging to the most primitive societies known. Now, the societies most simple in structure known to sociology are the tribes of central and northern Australia. For this and other reasons Durkheim concludes that the religion of these tribes is the most primitive of all religions; and he is the more convinced of this because he has been able, as he believes, to find in their religion the germs of all the higher forms. This primitive religion from which all other religions have developed is, of course, totemism. A possible attack upon his position from those who see the earliest form of religion in primitive man's concept of *mana*—the impersonal power—Durkheim avoids by incorporating *mana* into totemism as an essential part of it. Mana, in fact, is interpreted as the totemic force—the principle or "god" of which the totem is the symbol. But the totem is not only the symbol of this mysterious force; it is the symbol of the social group as well.

> It is its flag; it is the sign by which each clan distinguishes itself from the others, the visible mark of its personality, a mark borne by everything which is a part of the clan under any title what-

soever, men, beasts, or things. So, if it is at once the symbol of the god and of the society, is that not because the god and the society are only one? The god of the clan, the totemic principle, can therefore be nothing else than the clan itself, personified and represented to the imagination under the visible form of the animal or vegetable which serves as the totem.

Here we are at the very heart of Durkheim's thesis: society and the god of all historical religions are really identical.

> It is unquestionable that a society has all that is necessary to arouse the sensation of the divine in minds, merely by the power that it has over them; for to its members it is what a god is to his worshippers. In fact, a god is, first of all, a being whom men think of as superior to themselves, and upon whom they feel that they depend. . . . Now, society also gives us the sensation of a perpetual dependence.

And not only are we physically dependent upon it; it exerts upon us a moral constraint which no merely physical power could ever make us feel, and thus both morally and physically acts upon the individual as the god is always pictured as doing. Durkheim argues the point at length, and very brilliantly, with great force of illustration and originality of conception. The masses of facts that have been piled up by investigators in Australia and from our own West are worked over so as to yield results at which those who reported them would never have guessed, and in such fashion as to throw unexpected light on many a hitherto dark place in various higher stages of religion.

Yet brilliant as is Durkheim's argument concerning the original form and the essential nature of religion, it can hardly be called conclusive. A good deal may still be said for Animism, and particularly for Naturalism. In fact, most of Durkheim's facts might be taken out of the very clever arrangement he has devised for them, in which they point so clearly towards a totemistic origin of nearly everything, and be rearranged so as to lead to an animistic and naturalistic conclusion. As a fact, indeed, Spencer and Gillen, the great authorities on Australian matters, lean decidedly towards an animistic interpretation. Very much more evidence will have to be produced before it can be made even probable that totemism is the primitive form of all religions. Why, indeed, must all religions have had the same origin? The conditions in which men have lived in various parts of the world have been so varied that a plurality of origins for religion would, on the face of it, seem not at all improbable. To insist that all began in one way smacks a little of the dogmatic monism from which philosophy has suffered so long, and from which it is beginning to declare its independence.

Finally, it is very questionable whether we can ever get at all that is essential in religion by confining our study to its sociological expressions and to its most primitive forms. In early tribal societies we shall indeed find most easily its simplest elements; but it may well be that in its later developments there are truly essential elements which are far from simple. Or must we presuppose, without investigation, that nothing of fundamental importance has been added to religion in times subsequent to the simplest and

lowest? It may perhaps be shown—if further evidence be forthcoming—that for the Arunta and the Ojibway "the reality which religious thought expresses is society." But a good deal more must still be done to show that what is true for the Arunta must therefore also be true for the Buddhist and the Christian. The truth is, Durkheim's definition is too narrow except for the practical purposes of sociology. Religion as a psychical fact of modern life has significant aspects which can never be evolved out of any manipulation of the sacred and the profane.

"The Totem and Society," in The Nation *New York, Vol. CIII, No. 2663, July 13, 1916, pp. 39-40.*

Durkheim on individual behavior and society:

In the case of purely moral maxims, the public conscience exercises a check on every act which offends it by means of the surveillance it exercises over the conduct of citizens, and the appropriate penalties at its disposal. In many cases the constraint is less violent, but nevertheless it always exists. If I do not submit to the conventions of society, if in my dress I do not conform to the customs observed in my country and in my class, the ridicule I provoke, the social isolation in which I am kept, produce, although in an attenuated form, the same effects as a punishment in the strict sense of the word. The constraint is nonetheless efficacious for being indirect. I am not obliged to speak French with my fellow-countrymen nor to use the legal currency, but I cannot possibly do otherwise. If I tried to escape this necessity, my attempt would fail miserably. As an industrialist, I am free to apply the technical methods of former centuries; but by doing so, I should invite certain ruin. Even when I free myself from these rules and violate them successfully, I am always compelled to struggle with them. When finally overcome, they make their constraining power sufficiently felt by the resistance they offer. The enterprises of all innovators, including successful ones, come up against resistance of this kind.

Emile Durkheim, in his The Rules of Sociological Method, *translated by Sarah A. Solovay and John H. Mueller, 1938.*

George Simpson   (essay date 1933)

[*Simpson is an American professor, translator, and author who specializes in field work on religious cults in the Caribbean and religious sects in South America, the United States, Canada, and England. In the following essay, he analyzes Durkheim's social realism and the validity of his positivistic methodology in the study of society.*]

With good reason, Émile Durkheim has been called a social realist, and has so come to be known in the history of social thought. The description is accurate, however, only if one understands by realism what has generally been meant in philosophical thought. In epistemology, a realist [States R. B. Perry in *Philosophy of the Recent Past*], is one who believes that "some or all known objects owe their being to conditions different from those to which they owe their being known." Durkheim's realism is a study not of the relation of the known to the knower, but of the relation of the individual to society, and realism here means that society, its facts and products, exist outside of, and above, individuals. The existence of social facts, in short, is not dependent upon individuals. Accused by Tarde and Dunan of being a Platonic realist, of the most extreme type, Durkheim admitted a resemblance between his collective representations and the Platonic ideas. He says [in *Elementary Forms of the Religious Life*]:

> Face to face with this system of ideas, the individual mind is in the same situation as the *nous* of Plato before the world of ideas. The individual mind is compelled to absorb them, for it needs them in order to be able to have communion with its fellows. But the absorption is always imperfect.

But he says there is a difference.

> The ideas of Plato are self-sufficient. They have no need of matter in order to exist; they cannot mingle with matter without undergoing a kind of degradation. On the contrary, society has need of individuals in order to exist.

It may be thought that this last statement would redeem Durkheim and render much criticism directed against him nugatory. And so it might, if Durkheim had adhered to it. However, in his investigations,—those after *Le Suicide*—Durkheim became a thorough-going realist, and left little place for the individual. In practical affairs, during the late war, he was a leader of the extreme nationalistic school and spoke of the French soul and the collective conscience without much thought of the right of conscientious objectors and the growth of individuality which he so well demonstrated as an evolutionary law in his *De la division du travail social.* Before going further, let it here be said, that what has come to be known as Durkheim's system of sociology, his social realism, his making of social facts external and constraining, is a complete contradiction of his first and greatest study, that of the division of labor and the growth of organic solidarity. In that work, he was well on the way to solving in profound fashion the most vexing, and withal, the central problem of all social thought,—the relation of the individual to society.

This problem upon which all research and systematic constructions depend has been troublesome since the Greeks. It is ultimately the problem of the relation of a particular to its universal, of specificity to generality. The usual method of solving it, espousing individualism or collectivism, is only an apparent solution, for the problem is antinomial. True insight into social life is not to think of the two as antithetical, or as one being subservient to the other, but, as Croce has said, "There is no fact, however small it be, that can be otherwise conceived (realized and qualified) than as universal." The ultimate fact of all thought and understanding, in social science as elsewhere, is the universal particular conceived as the particular universal. We must start with society-as-individual, and with the individual-as-society or we shall get into arrant contradictions unresolvable because erroneously based on false

questions. This Durkheim seems to see in his *De la division du travail social,* but even there he is already on his way to social realism through a misunderstanding of what he is himself proving. He says there that he has proved that society lays the bases for individual behavior and thought, and continues by saying that this proof

> . . . is a sufficient reply to those who think that they prove that everything in social life is individual because society is made up of individuals. Of course, society has no other substratum, but because individuals form society, new phenomena which are formed by association are produced, and react upon individual consciences and in large part form them. That is why, although society may be nothing without individuals, each of them is much more a product of society than he is its maker.

This last seems to be a very reasonable and fruitful statement of the problem, and one that might serve as a good basis for study. Durkheim, in his later development, strayed from it, however. For an understanding of the development of Durkheim into a social realist, we must understand the forces that had shaped and were shaping his thought. Greatly influenced by the growth and acknowledged prestige of the new science of psychology, which was, in the closing years of the last century and the early years of this, looked upon as the key to open the Pandora's box where all the mysteries of human nature lay concealed, Durkheim reasoned that, if there is a psychology which studies individuals, there must be a psychology which studies the interaction of individuals, and this psychology must have categories similar to that of individual psychology. He therefore built up a theory of collective representations by analogizing from the theory of individual representations which was then the psychologist's clue for unlocking human nature. Consequently, we find this statement [in *Représentations individuelles et représentations collectives*]:

> The collective representations are exterior to the individual consciousnesses because they are not derived from the individuals taken in isolation but from their convergence and union. . . . Doubtless, in the elaboration of the common result, each individual bears his due share; but the private sentiments do not become social except by combining under the action of the forces *sui generis* which association develops. As a result of these combinations and of the mutual alterations which result therefrom, the private sentiments become something else. A chemical synthesis results which concentrates, unifies the elements synthetized, and by that very process transforms them . . . . The resultant derived therefrom extends beyond the individual mind, as a whole is greater than its parts. Really to know what it is one must take the aggregate in its totality. It is this that thinks, that feels, that wills, although it may not be able to will, feel, or act save by the intermediation of individual consciousnesses. This explains also why the social phenomenon does not depend on the personal nature of the individuals. It is because, in the fusion through which it evolves, all the individual characters, being divergent by definition, are

mutually neutralized and cancelled . . . . The group has a constitution different from that of the individual, and the things that affect it are of a different nature. Representations expressing neither the same objects nor the same subjects cannot depend on the same causes. To understand the way in which the society represents itself and the world surrounding it, one must consider the nature of the society and not that of the individual.

Thus, the first influence in making Durkheim a social realist is a theory of collective representations which are contained within what he calls the collective conscience. This theory is based on a misconstruing of the field of psychology, its methods and status as a science, and the erection of a hybrid, factitious subject called socio-psychology.

The second influence upon Durkheim which we must understand if we would estimate him aright is that of positivism and its view of science. Durkheim has often been spoken of as Comte's successor, and in this respect,—the nature of science,—that is correct. Comte had conceived of science as something that gave certainty and truth, that was devoid of values, religious and metaphysical. He had suggested that there is something constraining about science, something that forces us to acknowledge its truth. In *De la division du travail social,* therefore, Durkheim says that he is going to treat the facts of the moral life according to the method of the positive sciences. Now, the positive sciences, that is, the natural sciences, as well as sociology which in Comte's view crowned them, are value-free. Durkheim says:

> A certain manner of representing and explaining to ourselves the principal facts of the moral life has become habitual with us; a manner, however, having nothing scientific about it, for being formed by chance and without method, it results in summary superficial examinations made in passing, as it were. It we do not free ourselves from these ready-made judgments, we cannot grasp the considerations which follow; science, here as elsewhere, supposes a complete freedom of mind. We must rid ourselves of that habit of seeing and judging which long custom has fixed in us. We must submit ourselves rigorously to the discipline of the methodical doubt.

But how, in the study of moral and social facts, can we rid ourselves of all preconceived notions? How can we make a science that shall be positive as the other sciences are positive? Durkheim answers this by saying that we must find some external symbols, some aspect of the reality being studied which makes it what it is, which determines it accurately and which does not permit us to leave its province. Science is rigor; science is constraint. Therefore, to be scientific, sociology must find some symbols which are outside of the observer and constrain him within their precincts. Whereupon Durkheim does a strange thing. If scientific method demands that the scientist be objective and forces him to be so, then the phenomena studied by the scientist must themselves be objective and constraining for the phenomena themselves. He argues from the rigor of the method which the scientist must use to the rigor with which the data he is examining are existentially

determined. Hence, he arrives at a definition of a "social fact." He writes [in *Les règles de la méthode sociologique*]:

> Social facts consist in ways of acting, thinking, and feeling, exterior to the individual and endowed with a power of coercion, by reason of which they impose themselves upon him. Consequently they cannot be confused with biological phenomena, since they consist of representations and actions; nor with psychic phenomena which have existence only in the individual consciousness and through it. They constitute a new variety of phenomena and it is to them that ought to be given and reserved the epithet "social."

Hence, Durkheim has reduced himself to the position of making social only that which permits him to found a science of the social in the light of a certain theory of science which he holds. His definition of a social fact is not so much a definition of the social, as it is a disclosure of what he means by science. Thus he aligns himself with the determinists as against the proponents of free will, and the positivists as against the idealists. Unfortunately, his conception of science is totally erroneous and rests on a false epistemology. His desire for certainty, for positivism in social science, is a worthy desire. It is unfortunate that human problems do not lend themselves to certain solution.

The definition of a social fact shows us how Durkheim was led in the direction of realism and to the position that society was something outside of individuals and which had existential import without them and which molded them in its image. How Durkheim came to this position requires our understanding the third influence which shaped him in the direction of realism.

This was his study of primitive society, and his appropriation of concepts which he found helpful in anthropological work for the explanation of modern society. In *De la division du travail social* Durkheim splendidly shows how society has changed and evolved from the primitive type, the segmental type, and how the individual has become more and more an autonomous factor in social life. In his analysis of primitive society he speaks of the collective conscience which binds the individuals, of the constraining force of the mores. He then goes on to show how the collective conscience slowly grows weaker, how the power of tradition is undermined, and the force of heredity becomes very slight. In *Le Suicide,* he studies the possibility of constructing social groups to give individuals too unstable to be wholly autonomous in the new social world in which we live, a goal and an ideal. But from then on, 1895, his work is a wholesale misinterpretation of all that is fruitful in his thought up to that point. He proceeds to talk about the collective conscience as an explanatory key for contemporary society, as social facts being external, constraining, and coercive. This was so, as he well showed, in primitive society but is no longer so. Why, then, does he employ inappropriate concepts in the study of contemporary society? To answer this question we must go back to his conception of science as deterministic, objective, and coercive. Only if a body of knowledge is thus qualified is it a science for Durkheim. And these qualities must be exemplified in the data. Forthwith, Durkheim proceeds so to delimit and define the data that they will fit his conception of science.

In *Les formes elementaires de la vie religieuse,* Durkheim, following his realistic bent, attempts to explain the categories of logic and the concepts of thought in terms of society. He becomes the father of the whole "primitive mentality" school of which Levy-Bruhl is the best known expositor. And here again, he misinterprets the determinism in things as the determinism of thought, and draws a false analogy from primitive society. If religion has become a personal affair and thought free, as he shows in *De la division du travail social,* then surely modern religious life and modern science and philosophy have accordingly become free. There is nothing constraining in thought.

Despite all these objections and criticisms, there is something in Durkheim's assertion that we must study the individual through society. But that does not derive from Durkheim's method of so studying the individual. The problem which he posed for himself in *De la division du travail social* is a real problem, and one for which he offered a really sound solution. His later work, unfortunately, was a complete denial of the very valid conclusions he there reached. As he there says:

> This work had its origins in the question of the relation of the individual to social solidarity. Why does the individual, while becoming more autonomous, depend more upon society? How can he be at once more individual and more solidary? Certainly, these two movements, contradictory as they appear, develop in parallel fashion. This is the problem we are raising.

The conclusion which this work should have led him to was that modern society had reached such a state that the individual could no longer be studied as a type of a genus, but only as himself, and that he was no more, and no less, than the social activities of which he was partaking. Thus, to study the individual one should study the family, the economic milieu, the political situation, the religious life, the educational practice, of the society in which such an individual lives. Instead of that, Durkheim went off to belie his own doctrine, leveled all individuals, and set up what he thought was a science of society. And so it was, only the society he constructed a science around was a primitive society where social facts were exterior, constraining, and coercive, and where collective representations and the collective conscience did seem to have a reality.

The attempt here to delineate and criticize, in short compass, Durkheim's social realism has been made with a view to using Durkheim's system as a take-off for a discussion of how the individual and human nature should be studied by the sociologist. The exposure of the contradictions latent in Durkheim have been made with a view to showing the difficulty of the topic, and its surpassing importance. Must we become realists with Durkheim or some sort of collectivists, or must we say with Weber that the behavior that sociologists must study is the "behavior of one or more individuals," and that when we use collec-

tive concepts as sociologists we are using them only in order to understand how they affect the social behavior of individuals *qua* individuals? Whether we, as sociologists, must forsake the individual, or cling solely to him, as our field of study is the question that we have here tried to raise.

George Simpson, "Émile Durkheim's Social Realism," in Sociology and Social Research, *Vol. 18, September-October, 1933, pp. 3-11.*

Julius Stone   (essay date 1934)

[*An English-born educator and author, Stone was a leading scholar of international jurisprudence and wrote many works concerning the sociological aspects of law. Below, he assesses the development of Durkheim's theories on the role of law in society in his* On the Division of Labor in Society.]

For those who cannot read Durkheim in the French, Mr. Simpson has done a very real service. Emile Durkheim has long been recognized as the successor in France of Auguste Comte, and his later and perhaps most important work—*Les Règles de la Méthode Sociologique* (1895)—marks what Dean Pound calls the stage of unification of sociological thinking. For the student of jurisprudence the present work, first published in 1893, is itself rich in ideas of wide ramifications. . . . To read *De la Division du Travail Social* in 1934 is to see in procession before one's eyes the ghosts of the dead as well as the spirits of the then unborn.

Here is the battle-cry of positivist jurisprudence. "This book is pre-eminently an attempt to treat the facts of the moral life according to the method of the positive sciences." Moral facts being phenomena, it must "be possible to observe them, describe them, classify them, and look for the laws explaining them." Durkheim's theme is that social life rests upon a two-fold basis. In undeveloped societies men have similar needs, economic and cultural, and each member satisfies his own needs in a manner uniform over the entire society. Homogeneity of needs and function preserves and fosters homogeneity of mental and moral characteristics. The collective *conscience,* in Durkheim's phrase, is very powerful and all-pervading in such societies, and any variation from the uniform type is repressed, for it revolts the collective *conscience* binding men together. This bond Durkheim describes as "mechanical solidarity". The tendency of societies, however, through causes analogous to those in the organic world, is toward differentiation of functions for meeting the common needs. The total labor of a particular kind is concentrated in a few members of society instead of being distributed uniformly over all. Moreover, this process of division of labor tends, in itself, to create variations in the needs men have and to reduce even similarity of needs to a minimum. Thus, "mechanical solidarity" tends to weaken, whilst in its place there appears the bond of mutual interdependence due to specialization of functions. The whole society must rely for satisfaction of each particular need upon some small part of society. Here is the second basis of social life, which Durkheim calls "organic solidarity". Societies, therefore, as they advance, come to depend less on "mechanical solidarity" and more on "organic solidarity". To parody Spencer's barbarous phrase, the movement is from a simple undifferentiated homogeneity to a complex differentiated heterogeneity.

As this movement goes forward law becomes decreasingly a mere instrument for repressing variations which revolt the collective *conscience,* and increasingly an instrument for regulating the operation of a complicated but close-fitting system of specialized functions. Proceeding along this main highway of his theme Durkheim points out with all the wealth of his unrivalled store of facts many by-paths of intense interest to American law today. He sees administrative law as essentially a symptom of the shift from mechanical to organic solidarity. He diagnoses the pathology of the social division of labor in terms as apt for the present day as if they had been recently penned. His discussions of crime are not, perhaps, as up-to-date, but they are suggestive and hold the attention. He asserts in no unmistakable terms the necessary limits of psychology and the call for what, since McDougall, we know as social psychology. He has gone far beyond mechanical and biological sociology, but he still talks the language of his predecessors.

Among the ghosts in this procession, that of [Rudolf von] Ihering (who died in the preceding year) suffers most, though it walks unnamed. The imposing structure which he had reared on the basis of the ego seeking to fulfill its egoistic purposes [in *Der Zweck im Recht,* 1877] shakes before the Grotian assertion that "collective life is not born from individual life, but it is, on the contrary, the second which is born from the first." Indeed, it is startling to see so frank a reversion to the natural law proposition that the social nature of man is the basis of any sound criterion of law. But this is not alone the marriage of rationalism and positivism: Hegelian dialectic also plays its part. Durkheim conceives of the growth of organic solidarity as a process of liberation of the individual from the social repression of mechanical solidarity, and like the unfolding of "the idea" of Hegel, and the growth of the "acorn" of Campbell [in *Science of Law according to the American Theory of Government,* (1887)], this process is a continual one. "As all the other beliefs . . . take on a character less and less religious, the individual becomes the object of a sort of religion", or, as Dean Pound would put it, the social interest in the general security yields place to the social interest in the individual life. At the vision of such a transformation the ghost of Bentham contemplates wistfully its shattered "happiness" principle.

The procession through these pages of spirits still to be born in 1893 will already have been perceived. There is nothing significant in [Léon] Duguit which is not in this book. Social interdependence through similarity of needs and division of labor is the central idea of everything jurisprudential that Duguit ever wrote. But the paternal resemblances are perceivable in the detail as well as in the broad sweep. The vehement insistence on the enforcement of contracts only when they are of social value, on the identity [in *Les Transformations du Droit Public,* 1913] of public and private law—"all law is public, because all law is social"—these are traits as significant as any blood test.

Admirers of [Josef] Kohler will find here the Neo- as well as the Hegelian. The inevitable progress of organic solidarity through division of labor takes on at moments the loftiness of Kohler's "civilization", for though based in fact, it is also an ideal—"always definite . . . never definitive". Nor will Kantians and Neo-Kantians come away empty, for there is as exotic a variation of the metaphysical theory of property as the reviewer has ever seen. Alongside it will be found the profound observation, so emphasized by Dean Pound, that the sphere of contract, though expanding when Maine and Spencer taught, is now yielding to a relational regulation—a reversion to the medieval ideal of relationally organized society.

Only a few drops of the riches of Durkheim's mind have been tapped in this review. He who wishes to understand the "becoming" as well as the "being" of modern juristic thought will be amply rewarded for tapping the springs himself.

The distortion of Durkheim's own title—*De la Division du Travail Social*—typifies unfortunately the translation of this famous book. Our instinct of gratitude for Mr. Simpson's happy idea is constantly jarred by evidences of careless and sometimes even unintelligent transliteration. He renders *négotiant* as "negotiant", *plaideur* (meaning "party") as "pleader", *état des personnes* (meaning "status") as "state of the persons", *propriété immobilière* as "immobile property", *société* (meaning "partnership") as "society", *belles controverses* as "delicious controversies", *contractants* as "contractants", *penser bien* (meaning "to understand well") as "to think well of". One wonders whether Durkheim ever spoke of "the doing of a *legis actio*"; whether the translator does not know that *une* in French may mean either "a" or "one"; what kind of musical ear would begin a sentence: "It is not it, it is true. . . ." These examples among many indicate a rather slip-shod execution which, while not soothing, is not dangerous to a thoughtful reader. A final comment must be made, however, as to Mr. Simpson's deliberate departure from the usual translation of *conscience* as "consciousness". It is rendered by him as "conscience" on the ground that "a conscience for Durkheim (although never expressly defined) is pre-eminently the organ of sentiments and representations; it is not the rational organ that the term 'consciousness' would imply." It does seem to the reviewer, that when Durkheim identifies science with highly developed *conscience,* when he pronounces the progress of *conscience* to be "in inverse ratio to that of instinct", it is obviously not "conscience" in the English sense that he is talking about. Nevertheless, either rendition of the word is misleading, and had Mr. Simpson with due monitions chosen one way without calling the other "a gross misinterpretation", he would perhaps better invoke our sympathy in his difficulties.

Julius Stone, in a review of On the Division of Labor in Society, *in* Harvard Law Review, *Vol. XLVII, No. 8, June, 1934, pp. 1448-51.*

Robert K. Merton   (essay date 1934)

[*Merton is a leading American social theorist, educator,*

and author of the popular Social Theory and Social Structure *(1949). In the following review of* De la division du travail social, *he identifies some flaws in Durkheim's methods.*]

In a pedestrian, and somewhat infelicitous, fashion, Durkheim's *De la division du travail social* has been accorded a belated English translation, forty years after its initial [1893] publication. This testimony to the continued esteem with which Durkheim's work is regarded provides the impetus for a reconsideration of the first *magnum opus* of this hegemonic protagonist of the sociologistic school. The value of such an examination is twofold: it permits a re-estimation of the rôle played by Durkheim in the development of modern sociological thought, and it brings to a focus several conceptions fundamental to much of contemporary research.

An analysis of the theoretical context in which this work was written is of moment in appreciating its contributions. Deep in the current of the positivistic thought which stemmed from Comte, Durkheim's *Division* embodies many of its characteristic features. It seeks to adopt the methods and criteria of the physical sciences for the determination of those mechanically induced social laws, which, under given conditions, obtain with an ineluctable necessity. Explicit in this procedure is, of course, the assumption of the feasibility of so doing and of the susceptivity of social phenomena to such study. The fact that the concept of causation, more markedly perhaps in the social sciences than in the physical, is an epistemologic assumption, a matter of imputation and not of observation, is ignored. Within this positivistic tradition the *Division* is further classifiable as instancing the anti-individualistic, anti-intellectualistic approach. It is an avowed revolt from the individualistic-utilitarian positivism which, finding its prototypes in the systems of Hobbes and of Locke, characterized so much of English social thought. A radical sociologism seemed to Durkheim to be the one way of maintaining the autonomy of sociology as an independent discipline, and it is to this dominant preoccupation that many of his conceptions are due. Of especial significance is the fact that the *Division,* although it adumbrates many ideas which Durkheim subsequently developed in some detail, presents an objective approach, with implicit reservations, from which he later diverged sharply, notably in his *Formes élémentaires de la vie religieuse.*

The peregrinations of the ideas expressed in the *Division* have included this country, but a brief summary is none the less desirable to establish the basis of this discussion. The source of social life, maintains Durkheim, is twofold: the similitude of consciousnesses and the division of social labor. In one society-type, which he calls "primitive," solidarity is induced by a community of representations which gives birth to laws imposing uniform beliefs and practices upon individuals under threat of repressive measures. These repressive laws are external—that is, observable in the positivistic sense—indexes of this "mechanical solidarity." The division of social labor, on the other hand, while it enhances, nay compels, individuation, also occasions an "organic solidarity," based upon the interdependence of co-operatively functioning individuals and

groups. This type of solidarity is indexed by juridical rules defining the nature and relations of functions. These rules may properly be termed restitutive law, since their violation involves merely reparative, and not expiatory, consequences. Historically, the movement has been from mechanical to organic solidarity, though the former never disappears completely. The determining cause of this trend is found in the increased size and density of populations with the usual, if not invariable, concomitant, increased social interaction. This so intensifies the struggle for existence that only through progressive differentiation of functions is survival possible for many who otherwise would be doomed to extinction. This continuous trend occurs mechanically through a series of disturbed and re-established social dynamic equilibria.

Now, as previously suggested, Durkheim seeks to combat individualistic positivism which ignores the relevance of social ends as partial determinants of social action. He is hence faced with a perturbing dilemma: as a positivist, to admit the irrelevance of ends to a scientific study of society; as an anti-individualist, to indicate the effectiveness of social aims in conditioning social action, and thus in effect to abandon radical positivism. For, if, as positivism would have us believe, logic and science can deal only with empirical facts, with sensa, then a science of social phenomena, on that score alone, becomes impossible, since this attitude relegates to limbo all ends, i.e., subjective anticipations of *future* occurrences, without a consideration of which human behavior becomes inexplicable. Ends, goals, aims, are by definition not logico-experimental data but rather value judgments; and yet an understanding of social phenomena requires a study of their rôle. This does not involve a determinism-teleology embarrassment, but simply notes the fact that subjectively conceived ends—irrespective of their recognition of all the pertinent data in a given situation—as well as "external conditions," influence behavior. To ban ends as "improper" for scientific study is not to exempt sociology from metaphysics, but to vitiate its findings by a crude and uncriticized metaphysics.

At the time of writing the *Division,* Durkheim was too much the positivist to acknowledge explicitly the full force of this position, but his conscious methodologic doctrines notwithstanding, he surreptitiously slips between the horns of the dilemma and salves his anti-individualistic conscience by dealing with *social* ends. Thus, he indicates quite clearly that if society were simply a resultant of juxtaposed individuals brought into temporary contractual relationships for the satisfaction of their respective immediate interests, that if the typical social relation were the economic, then we should no longer have a society but Hobbes's "state of nature."

> For where interest is the only ruling force each individual finds himself in a state of war with every other since nothing comes to modify the egos, and any truce in this eternal antagonism would not be of long duration. [Durkheim, *On the Division of Labor in Society*]

This corresponds to Durkheim's description of *anomie.* But the fact is, he continues, that even in such highly contractual and "individualized" societies as our own, this brutish state of nature does not obtain. What, then, obviates this condition which, were the individualistic approach valid, one would expect to find characterizing a contractual society? It is the "consensus of parts," the integration of individual ends, the social value-complex. This is clearly seen in the legal regulation of contracts between individuals, for although it is true that these contracts are initially a voluntary matter, once begun, they are subject to society as the omnipresent and controlling "third party." Through a system of law, an organ of social control, the accord of individual wills is constrained for the consonance of diffuse social functions. Moreover, in this process, society plays an *active* rôle, for it determines which obligations are "just," i.e., accord with the dominant social values, and which need not be enforced. With this incisive analysis, Durkheim refutes one of the basic doctrines of an atomistic sociology, for he finds in the very relation which had been regarded as individualistic, *par excellence,* the significant interpenetration of social factors.

His conception is similar to Sumner's "strain toward consistency" and autonomy of the mores and to Goldenweiser's notion of the limit to the discrepancies between the various aspects of a culture. This view of society is linked to an acknowledgment of the previously mentioned rôle of social ends and to an acceptance of the doctrine of emergence. That social behavior cannot be explained through reference to the behavior of individuals in mere juxtaposition is maintained by both Durkheim and Pareto, and it is precisely this view which is held to justify sociology as a distinct discipline.

In Durkheim's discussion of social ends is a latent antimechanistic trend. For when instruments are fashioned for the attempted attainment of ends, by this very fact conditions are evolved which act not only in the direction of the goals, but react upon and frequently change the value-estimations. These new valuations may relieve man from the necessity of accepting the "conditions of existence"—Durkheim's *milieu*—and acting in the previously determined manner. His "definition of the situation" having changed, his behavior has a new orientation, and mechanistic determinism, based on a knowledge of the *objective* factors, no longer adequately accounts for this behavior. But as is frequently characteristic of mechanistic theorists, Durkheim does not properly distinguish his abstract conceptions, in this instance the external conditions of existence, from the concrete situation, which includes the usually suppressed elements of man's selection of objectives. The ineluctable conclusions derived from his abstract delineation of the situation he thinks to represent actual facts, in all their empirical variety. To put it in another way, Durkheim neglects to treat his conceptions as advisedly ideal constructions demanding appropriate alteration before they can adequately describe concrete social phenomena.

In his presentation of societal evolution, Durkheim professes to trace genetically a transition from mechanical to organic solidarity, and it is here that his defective ethnographic data lead him astray. With Maine and Steinmetz,

he affects to note the preponderance, even the exclusive existence, of *penal* law in primitive society. In point of fact, as recent field studies have demonstrated, primitive societies possess also a corpus of restitutive, civil law, involving rights and duties between individuals, and kept in force by social mechanisms. The existence of such essentially contractual relations among primitive peoples detracts from the plausibility of Durkheim's theory of unilinear development. Moreover, in affirming the preponderance of organic solidarity in modern societies, Durkheim tends to depreciate unduly the persistent factor of community of interests. This bias warps his analysis of the elements of social cohesion. Such group-integrative factors as conceptions of honor, *Ehre,* and the subsumption of individual under collective interests during periods of war and of conflict generally, which are significant elements in the cohesion of contemporary societies, are unwarrantably ignored by Durkheim in his endeavor to find in the division of labor the sole source of modern solidarity. The inviolate unity of a group becomes imperative during inter-societal conflicts, and this unity is largely achieved through appeals to common sentiments. Likewise, is the non-juridical notion of honor a powerful, if not always effective, regulatory device making for social cohesion. The fact that such forms of mechanical solidarity still subsist suggests additional grounds for rejecting Durkheim's argument of unilinear development.

Durkheim's conception of this unilinear evolution must, moreover, be reconsidered in the light of what has been appropriately termed the "principle of limits" of development. Development in a given direction may continue until it becomes self-defeating, whereupon reaction occurs in an opposite direction. Were it not that Durkheim attempts to extrapolate beyond the universe of his data, he might have found in the ever more frequently occurring states of *anomie* accompanying the increase of division of labor an index of this reaction. In the economic world, one need but note movements of reconsolidation after optima of differentiation have been passed, to realize that the process is not necessarily unidirectional.

To arrive at his conception of evolution, Durkheim does not, as has been alleged, abandon his sociologistic position. It is true that he finds the "determining cause" of increased division of labor in the growth and heightened density of populations, which is primarily a biological factor, but it is only in so far as this demographic change is associated with increased social interaction and its concomitant, enhanced competition, that the stipulated change will occur. It is thus this social factor—the "dynamic density," as he terms it—which Durkheim finds actually determinant. In a subsequent work [*Les règles de la méthode Sociologique*] he makes this point even more definitely by noting that population density and dynamic density are not always associated—in China, for example—and that in these instances the increase in division of labor is considerably inhibited. Hence the facile formula which attributes an increased differentiation of function solely to demographic changes must be revamped. To the extent that this differentiation is generalizable as a social process it may be said to be associated with competition between individuals and between groups, whatever the factors leading to such competition.

If we abandon Durkheim's unilinear theory we are left with an acute characterization of the two societies, mechanical and organic, taken as ideal-types, or as heuristic fictions. These may then be considered as limiting cases, never obtaining in empirical reality, which may be fruitfully employed as poles of reference toward which empirical data are theoretically oriented. Durkheim's work thus provides a conceptual scheme which may be used to advantage in the interpretation of processes of differentiation, integration, competition, and the like.

Another aspect of Durkheim's methodology, which characterizes not only the *Division,* but also his later works, is his use of "indices" which he considers the "external," measurable translation of the "internal," not directly observable social facts. Just as the physicist measures heat and electricity through certain objectively observable and easily measurable phenomena, such as the rise and fall of mercury in a glass tube and the oscillation of the needle of a galvanometer, so Durkheim hopes to use repressive and restitutive law as indexes of mechanical and organic solidarity, respectively.

At this point, a fundamental difficulty arises. If the observed facts (L) are to be significant and relatively accurate indexes of the types of solidarity (S), the following relationships must hold true. Let L ($x, y. \ . \ . \ $) be written for a function of measurable quantities ($x, y. \ . \ . \ $) (statistics of penal or restitutive law) and let it be so related to S ($x', y'. \ . \ . \ $) (the social fact—social cohesion) that these postulates are satisfied. When L varies in a determinate fashion, S varies correspondingly. When there are successive increases in L, the first changing L from $L1$ to $L2$ and the second from $L2$ to $L3$, so that the first increase is greater than the second, then the first increase in S (solidarity) is greater than the second. This postulate must still obtain when less is written for greater. This affords a concomitant variation between the social facts and their indexes, the variations of the former being directly unmeasurable and relative to the directly measurable variation of the latter.

It is precisely this sort of relationship which Durkheim fails to demonstrate. He does not establish with any precision the perfect associations which he assumes obtain between his types of solidarity and of law. For example, organic solidarity may be regulated by customary usages and mores without ever becoming definitely translated into civil law. This was notably the case during a great part of the Middle Ages. Furthermore, as has been suggested, much of mechanical solidarity in contemporary society—that evidenced by "honor," for example—finds no expression in repressive law. These necessarily brief indications must suffice to signify the debatable premises on which Durkheim bases his system of indexes.

In his generally brilliant chapter on the division of labor and happiness, Durkheim evidences another fundamental weakness of his method. He eliminates certain possible explanations of a particular set of social phenomena by demonstrating that the logical consequences of the rejected theories are not in accord with observed facts. He assumes that the possible number of explicative theories is determinable, x, and that having eliminated x-1 explanations he is left with the necessarily valid solution. Thus, he holds that "the desire to become happier is the only individual source which can take account of [the] progress [of the division of labor]. If that is set aside, no other remains." This method of projected experiment was brought into prominence by Descartes [in his "Discours de la méthod," *OEuvres,* 1902], to whom Durkheim was avowedly indebted, who maintained that in approaching reality one will find that many consequences result from initially adopted principles and that rational consideration will decide which of these consequences is realized. But the fallacy of this method lies in the initial assumption that one has exhausted the totality of possible explanations. The elimination of alternative theories in no wise increases the probabilities of the other alternatives.

Of Durkheim's *Division,* one may say in general that it presents an incisive and suggestive analysis of a determinate social process and its structural correlates. If its conclusions are too sweeping, if its method is at times faulty, one may yet acknowledge from the vantage point afforded by four decades of subsequent research that it remains one of the peak contributions of modern sociology.

Robert K. Merton, "Durkheim's Division of Labor in Society," in American Journal of Sociology, *Vol. XL, No. 3, November, 1934, pp. 319-28.*

Durkheim on religion and suicide:

If religion protects man against the desire for self-destruction, it is not that it preaches the respect for his own person to him with arguments *sui generis;* but because it is a society. What constitutes this society is the existence of a certain number of beliefs and practices common to all the faithful, traditional and thus obligatory. The more numerous and strong these collective states of mind are, the stronger the integration of the religious community, and also the greater its preservative value. The details of dogmas and rites are secondary. The essential thing is that they be capable of supporting a sufficiently intense collective life. And because the Protestant church has less consistency than the others it has less moderating effect upon suicide.

Émile Durkheim, in his Suicide, *translated by John A. Spaulding and George Simpson, 1951.*

Talcott Parsons   (essay date 1937)

[*Parsons was a prominent American figure in the social sciences whose theories on social systems were considered highly controversial. In the following excerpt from* The Structure of Social Action, *Parsons examines Durkheim's theory of suicide and compares it with the conceptual framework employed in* On the Division of Labor in Society.]

Le suicide seems at first glance to be concerned with an

entirely different range of problems from those of the division of labor. This is not so, however. In the respects which are of primary interest here it is to be regarded as a continuation of the same line of thinking, a new crucial experiment in a different factual field. As usually develops, in the course of the investigation the theory itself is not merely verified, but undergoes a change. It is this which is of primary interest here.

It will be remembered that Durkheim called attention to the possible significance of suicide rates in his critical discussion of the happiness hypothesis of the development of social differentiation. The monograph he published four years later is to be regarded as an intensive study following up the suggestive remarks made in that brief discussion.

After the statement of the problem and preliminary definitions the book starts with a systematic critique of previous attempts to explain variations in the rate of suicide. The various theories he criticizes fall into two main classes. One type, which he dismisses very briefly, is that which employs what are ordinarily called the motives of suicide, such as financial reverses, domestic [infidelity] and the like. The principal empirical argument he brings to bear is that, in so far as these motives are ascertainable at all, when they are classified the proportions of cases falling into the various classes remain approximately constant through wide variations in the general rate. Since it is the latter which he is attempting to explain, motives in this sense may be regarded as irrelevant. The "motive" type of explanation is important in the present context because it is the principal form taken, in relation to suicide, by the utilitarian type of theory. Suicide is regarded by it as a rational act in pursuit of a definite end, and it is not thought necessary to go beyond this end. The social rate would be a mere summation of such "cases."

The other theories discussed all invoke factors in explanation which can be classified for present purposes as belonging to the categories of heredity and environment. In the first place there are what Durkheim calls the "cosmic" explanations, in terms of climatic conditions and the like. He has little difficulty in demonstrating that the alleged relations between suicide rates and climate are at least open to other interpretations. Then there are race, alcohol, psychopathological states and imitation. In each case he succeeds in demonstrating, for the most part on purely empirical grounds, that previous theories embodying these factors, or any combination of them, are not capable of yielding a satisfactory general solution of the problem, though he has by no means succeeded in showing that they can have nothing to do with it. Except race, they are probably of greater significance as factors in incidence than in the rate, but Durkheim certainly has not eliminated them from the latter. He has however shown that previous explanations embodying them have not so completely explained the phenomenon that a new approach to it is ruled out from the start.

The only one of these which calls for special comment here is the case of psychopathological states. It should be remembered that Durkheim was writing in the 1890's and that psychopathology has advanced enormously since then. The psychopathological views he criticizes are primarily those which attribute suicide to a specific, hereditary psychopathological condition and he is able to show easily that this cannot account for the significant variations of suicide rates. His arguments do not, however, apply to the "environmental" and "functional" types of mental disturbance of which our understanding has been so greatly increased in the last generation, especially through psychoanalysis and related movements. But in so far as the ultimate causes of a mental disturbance which issues in suicide are "environmental," *e.g.,* not hereditary, there is every reason to believe that the social component of the environment plays a decisive part. In fact Durkheim's analysis, especially in connection with the concept of *anomie* which will be discussed below, throws a great deal of light on these causes. Psychopathology comes in to trace the mechanisms by which such social situations affect the individual and his behavior. Thus, as has been shown by Durkheim's principal follower in this field, Professor Halbwachs, the social and the psychopathological explanations of suicide are not antithetical but complementary. But at the time when Durkheim wrote neither psychopathology nor his own sociology had reached a point of development where it was possible to build the bridge between them.

One thing is to be noted particularly about Durkheim's critical work in this connection. In the **Division of Labor** his critique was directed primarily against the utilitarian type of theory. There was a more or less incidental critique of explanations of the division of labor in terms of heredity by which he there meant the hereditary component in differentiation of character and ability between individuals. At the same time he invoked, as has been seen, another hereditary factor, the principle of population, for his own purposes. Here is, on the other hand, a clear and self-conscious criticism of a group of hereditary and environmental theories. The results of his detailed empirical criticisms of particular theories are generalized into the position that no theory either in terms of motives in the above sense, or of these other factors, can be satisfactory. The latter are specifically characterized as individualistic and over against them is set, as his methodological program, the development of social factors. The social milieu is specifically distinguished from the nonsocial components of the environment of the acting individual. Correspondingly there is, in the **Suicide** no further use made of the population factor; indeed it drops out of his work altogether. The social milieu retains, however, one basic property in common with heredity and environment: as seen by the actor it is a matter of things beyond his power to control—this is the nub of Durkheim's rejection of the "motive" explanation of suicide. It remained for a long time the distinguishing feature of his sociological objectivism.

The factors in the suicide rate in which he is interested are, then, to be found in features of the social milieu. They are what he calls *courants suicidogènes*. His own positive analysis consists in the distinction between and working out of the empirical consequences of three such factors. In so far as one of the three factors is maximized in importance relative to the others there are three "ideal types" of suicide called, respectively, "altruistic," "egoistic" and "anomic" suicide. The principal task of the remainder of the present discussion of his treatment of suicide will be to analyze these three concepts, their relation to each other and to the conceptual framework of the *Division of Labor*. . . . The prototypes of all of them have, as will be seen, appeared in the earlier work. But the modifications from their use there are of the first importance.

The simplest case is that of *suicide altruiste*. It involves a group attachment of great strength such that in comparison with claims made upon the individual in fulfillment of the obligations laid upon him by the group his own interests, even in life itself, become secondary. This leads, on the one hand, to a generally small valuation of individual life, even by the individual himself, so that he will part with it on relatively small provocation; on the other hand in certain cases it leads to a direct social mandate to suicide. In modern Western societies the case which arrests Durkheim's attention is that of armies. It is a fact that the suicide rates of armies are in his data markedly higher than in the corresponding civilian populations. This is a matter of the peacetime situation, although when a soldier in obeying orders apart from coercion exposes himself to a risk of almost certain death in battle it would also be suicide according to Durkheim's definition. But the peacetime military suicide rate has generally been explained by the objective hardships of military life. This is not, however, satisfactory. For one thing, suicides are more common among officers than enlisted men, and surely the officer's lot is easier. Furthermore, the rate increases with length of service, while one would expect that there would be habituation to hardship so that its effect would be greatest in the first year or two. Finally, more generally there is no correlation between hardship as indicated by poverty, and suicide. Some of the poorest countries of Europe, such as Italy and Spain, have far lower general suicide rates than more prosperous countries like France, Germany and the Scandinavian countries. Moreover, within a country the upper classes, especially in the cities, have higher suicide rates than the lower. This cannot be due to hardship in the ordinary sense.

The explanation that Durkheim advances is quite different. What distinguishes the army in modern society is the stringency of its discipline. There the desires and interests of the individual count very little in comparison with the impersonal duties imposed upon him by his membership in the group. This situation generates an attitude which is careless of individual interests in general, of life in particular. This is manifested for instance by the ease with which the military man will commit suicide when his "honor" is impugned. Japan, a specifically militaristic society, furnishes a most striking example. The fact that in those countries where the general rate of suicide is high the army rate is relatively low and vice versa strikingly confirms the view that the army rate is due to causes different from those operative in the general population.

Altruistic suicide Durkheim also finds exemplified in primitive societies, and in certain religious groups. In some of these cases, such as the Indian custom of suttee, there is a direct social mandate to suicide.

It seems quite clear that the altruistic factor in suicide is, for Durkheim, on essentially the same theoretical plane as mechanical solidarity. It is a manifestation of the *conscience collective* in the sense of group pressure at the expense of the claims of individuality. But even here there is a slight shift of emphasis. It is no longer similarity which is the central point, but subordination of individuality to the group. It is not because the army is an undifferentiated group that it has a high suicide rate, not that there is no difference between officers and men or artillery and infantry, but because of the character of the discipline imposed. Already Durkheim is moving away from the identification of the problem of "solidarity" with that of social structure. Altruistic suicide is a manifestation of a *conscience collective* which is strong in the sense of subordinating individual to group interests, and which has the particular content of a low valuation of individual life relative to group values.

With "egoism" the explanation is more complicated, and there is a much more radical shift from the position of the *Division of Labor.* There are two main groups of empirical phenomena in connection with which Durkheim strongly emphasized this element. In the first place, he is much struck by the relation of suicide to family status. In general, married persons have distinctly lower suicide rates than unmarried, widowed and divorced. This difference is greatly increased by the presence of children and in proportion to the number in the family. The decisive factor with which Durkheim emerges after eliminating various others, especially selection, is the attachment to a certain type of group as a mitigating influence. People are, to a point, less liable to commit suicide in so far as their relation to a group of others is, in the sense noted above, one of emotional dependence. But so far as the formulation of the concept of egoism is concerned this leaves us with an essentially negative conclusion. Egoism seems to exist as a factor in suicide so far as people are freed from such group control, while altruism exists so far as the group control is excessively strong in certain respects. This leaves the relation of egoism to *anomie* distinctly unclear.

But in the discussion of the other body of data, those concerning the relation of suicide to religious affiliation, something much more definite emerges. The striking fact is that the rate for Protestants is very much higher than for Catholics. The relation holds when a number of other factors are eliminated, as for example, nationality. For instance, in both German and French Switzerland the Protestant rate is much the higher, and in Germany the rate is much lower in the largely Catholic sections of Bavaria, the Rhineland and Silesia than for the country as a whole. What is the explanation of this striking fact?

It lies, according to Durkheim, in the Protestant attitude toward individual freedom in religious matters. The Catholic, precisely in so far as he is faithful, has laid down for him a system of beliefs and practices which his membership in the church prescribes for him. He has no initiative in the matter; all responsibility belongs to the church as an organization. The very state of his soul and chances of salvation depend on his faithful adherence to these prescriptions. The case of the Protestant, on the other hand, is very different. He is himself the ultimate judge of religious truth and the rightness of conduct deduced from it.

The church is in a very different relation to him. It is an association of those holding common beliefs and carrying out common practices, but as an organized body it does not have the same authority over the individual in prescribing what these beliefs and practices shall be.

It is, then, in the relation of the individual to the organized religious group that Durkheim sees the decisive difference. In one sense the difference consists in the fact that the Catholic is subjected to a group authority from which the Protestant is exempt. But this negative aspect does not cover the full extent of the differences. For the essential point is that the Protestant's freedom from group control is not optional. It is not a freedom to take his own religious responsibility *or* to relinquish it to a church as he sees fit. In so far as he is a Protestant in good standing he *must* assume this responsibility and exercise his freedom. He cannot devolve it on a church. The obligation to exercise religious freedom in this sense is a fundamental feature of protestantism as a religious movement. It may be said that this exemplifies quite literally Rousseau's famous paradox [in *Du contrat social,* 1762], as a Protestant a man is, in certain respects, *forced* to be free.

This is surely not simply a matter of the effects of differentiation of function due to population pressure. Indeed it comes exceedingly close to being a manifestation of the *conscience collective.* For religious freedom in the above sense is a basic ethical value common to all Protestants. In so far as a man is a Protestant at all he is subjected to a social, a group pressure in that direction. But the result is a very different relation to the religious group as an organized entity from that of the Catholic. He is under pressure to be independent, to take his own religious responsibility, while the Catholic is under pressure to submit himself to the authority of the church. But this decisive difference is *not* a matter of the action of the Catholic being influenced by the values common to Catholics while the Protestant is emancipated from the influence of those common to Protestants; the freedom in question is freedom in a different sense. The difference lies in the different *content* of the different value systems. It may safely be inferred that in so far as the high Protestant suicide rate is due to egoism it is a result of the hold over the individual of a *conscience collective,* a system of beliefs and sentiments common to Protestants, which are not shared by Catholics.

This system of beliefs and sentiments does not operate by directly enjoining the Protestant to take his own life. On the contrary, for Protestants and Catholics alike suicide is a mortal sin. But by placing the Protestant in a particular relation to his religious group, by placing a particularly heavy load of religious responsibility upon him, strains are created of which, in a relatively high proportion of cases, the result is suicide. Durkheim throws little light on the actual mechanisms by which the result is produced in the individual suicide. But he has established the fact of the relationship beyond doubt.

Later in [*Suicide,* Book III] Durkheim generalizes this insight and puts forward the view that the leading common moral sentiment of our society is an ethical valuation of individual personality as such. This is the more general

phenomenon of which the Protestant version of religious freedom and responsibility is a special case. In so far as this "cult" is present men are under strong social pressure, on the one hand, to "develop their personalities"—to be independent, responsible and self-respecting. On the other hand, they are equally under pressure to respect others, to shape their own actions so as to be compatible with others attaining the same development of personality. There can be no doubt that on the empirical level Durkheim has here reached a solution of the problem of the "non-contractual element in contract." The fundamentals of the system of normative rules governing contract and exchange by virtue of which "organic solidarity" is possible, are, in certain respects at least, an expression of the cult of individual personality. This is not a matter simply of freeing the individual from ethical restraints imposed by society, it is a matter of the imposition of a different *kind* of ethical restraint. Individuality is a product of a certain social state, of the *conscience collective.* It is true that Durkheim leaves us there. He does not attempt to explain in turn what is the source of the cult of the individual; he is content with establishing its existence. But by contrast with the ***Division of Labor*** he has accomplished a great work of clarification. No longer is the common-value element tied to a state where there is similarity of individuals and lack of differentiation. Above all the freedom itself which is the basic prerequisite of a "contractual" society is seen to be capable of being related positively to a *conscience collective.* With that, all attempt to derive organic solidarity from differentiation as such drops out, and with it the "biologizing" tendency which appeared in the population thesis. . . .

This has been worked out by Durkheim with exemplary clarity in connection with one empirical phenomenon, the differential suicide rates of Protestants and Catholics. By implication it clarifies the confused thought regarding the family as a protection against suicide. For in so far as the individual responsibility and independence inherent in the cult of personality has tended to break down certain types of emotional dependence on the family group, to prevent people from marrying and to lead to divorce as well as to affect relations within the family, it is legitimate to speak of an egoistic component in the suicide rates of persons excluded from family ties. The whole matter is, however, much further clarified by the development, by contrast with egoism, of the concept of *anomie,* to which the discussion must now turn.

Anomie already had a part in the ***Division of Labor,*** but a relatively minor one descriptive of one of the "abnormal" forms of the division of labor, that is, one in which organic solidarity was imperfectly realized. In the ***Suicide*** it occupies a far more prominent place and the concept itself is much more completely worked out, hence its discussion has been deferred to this point. From a relatively minor position it has been elevated to a factor in suicide *pari passu* with egoism and altruism.

As in the other two cases there is a body of empirical fact which was particularly important to Durkheim in framing the concept. It is the fact that there are quite large variations in the rate of suicide concomitant with the business cycle. It would surprise nobody to learn that panic and depression were also accompanied by increases in the suicide rate; disappointment and suffering due to financial reverses and losses seems a plausible, common-sense explanation. The surprising thing is that the same is true of periods of unusual prosperity, and the fluctuation from the average rate over a long period, or its trend, is of about the same magnitude. Hence Durkheim questions that even the increase of suicides in depression is due to economic hardship as such, especially in view of the lack of general correlation between suicide and poverty already mentioned. The probability is that the increase, both in prosperity and in depression, is due to the same order of causes.

That cause Durkheim finds in the fact that in both cases large numbers of people are thrown with relative suddenness out of adjustment with certain important features of their social environment. In depression expectations relative to the standard of living, with all that implies, are frustrated on a large scale. In that of unusual prosperity, on the other hand, things which had seemed altogether outside the range of possibility become for many people realities. At both extremes the relation between means and ends, between effort and attainment is upset. The result is a sense of confusion, a loss of orientation. People no longer have the sense that they are "getting anywhere."

Durkheim's analysis goes yet deeper. The sense of confusion and frustration in depression seems not so difficult to understand, but why is the reaction to unusual prosperity not increased satisfaction all around, as any utilitarian point of view would take for granted as obvious? Because, Durkheim says, a sense of security, of progress toward ends depends not only on adequate command over means, but on clear definition of the ends themselves. When large numbers are the recipients of windfalls, having attained what had seemed impossible, they tend no longer to believe anything is impossible. This is, in turn, because human appetites and interests are inherently unlimited. For there to be satisfaction they must be limited, disciplined. It is as an agency of breakdown of this discipline that prosperity is a cause of suicide. It opens up the abyss of an endless search for the impossible.

This discipline which is indispensable to the personal sense of attainment, and thus to happiness, is not imposed by the individual himself. It is imposed by society. For it to serve this function, however, the discipline cannot be mere coercion. Men cannot be happy in the acceptance of limitations simply imposed by force; they must recognize them to be "just"; the discipline must carry *moral* authority. It takes the form, then, of socially given moral norms by which ends of action are defined. If anything happens to break down the discipline of these norms the result is personal disequilibrium, which results in various forms of personal breakdown, in extreme instances, suicide.

In the present context the relevant norms are those concerned with the standard of living. For each class in society there is always a socially approved standard, varying within limits to be sure, but relatively definite. To live on such a scale is a normal legitimate expectation. Both depression below it and elevation above it necessitate what

Durkheim calls a "moral re-education" which cannot be accomplished easily and quickly, if at all.

Durkheim also attributes to the same thing a part in the higher suicide rate of the widowed and divorced as against the married. The breaking of the marital tie, like the removal of limitations on the standard of living, puts men's standards in flux, creates a social and personal void in which orientation is disorganized. The result is the same sense of frustration, insecurity and, in extreme cases, suicide.

What are some of the theoretical implications of the concept of *anomie?* In the first place, in setting *anomie* explicitly over against egoism, Durkheim has completed the process discussed above. Instead of the *conscience collective* being contrasted with organic solidarity, there now are two types of influence of the *conscience collective,* and set over against *both* of them the state where its disciplining influence is weak, at the polar extreme altogether absent. In so far as this weakening of discipline is present, the state of *anomie* exists. The freedom from collective control, the "emancipation of the individual" in the cases of egoism and of *anomie* are on quite different levels. Above all the development of individual personality is not a mere matter of the removal of social discipline, but of a particular kind of such discipline.

In discussing the institution of contract, Durkheim was calling attention to an aspect of the normative regulation of action which is relatively "external" to the acting individual. It can to a point readily be treated as a set of given conditions of action. But the type of discipline formulated by contrast with *anomie* is of a much more subtle kind. It concerns not only the conditions under which men act in pursuit of their ends but enters into the formulation of the ends themselves. Moreover, it is only by virtue of such a discipline that an "integrated personality" exists at all.

This amounts to carrying the Hobbesian problem down to a deeper level. The level of social instability which Hobbes analyzed presupposes a plurality of individuals who are capable of rational action, who know what they want. But this is itself an unreal assumption. The man in the state of nature could not even be the rational being the utilitarians posit. Durkheim's sociological analysis is not merely relevant to the elements of order as between individuals, to the power problem, but has extended further into the elements of order in individual personality itself.

With this a fundamental methodological point is already foreshadowed, but it was long before Durkheim attained anything like methodological clarity on it, as on many other implications of this insight into the *anomie* problem. This is that the analytical distinction between "individual" and "social" cannot run parallel with that between the concrete entities "individual" and "society." Just as society cannot be said to exist in any concrete sense apart from the concrete individuals who make it up, so the concrete human individual whom we know cannot be accounted for in terms of "individual" elements alone, but there is a social component of his personality. . . .

To sum up, then, the change from the ***Division of Labor*** to the ***Suicide:*** The element of a system of moral beliefs and sentiments common to the members of a society, the *conscience collective,* has been freed of its confusion with lack of social differentiation, with similarity of social role. *Pari passu* with this has come the realization that the non-contractual element of contract is just such a system of common beliefs and sentiments, that this is an essential element in the basis of order in a differentiated individualistic society. Modern "individualism" including the egoistic component of suicide is not a matter of emancipation from social pressure, but of a particular kind of social pressure. In both cases it is primarily a matter of the discipline to which the individual is subjected by his participation in the common beliefs and sentiments of his society.

At the same time the concept of *anomie* emerges into a position of much greater prominence. With it the disciplining function of the *conscience collective* is extended from the relatively external action of rules governing action to the constitution of the ends of action themselves, and thus into the very center of individual personality. This brings Durkheim's empirical insight to a point far in advance of his general conceptual scheme.

Talcott Parsons, "Émile Durkheim, I: Early Empirical Work," in his The Structure of Social Action: A Study in Social Theory with Special Reference to a Group of Recent European Writers, *second edition, The Free Press, 1949, pp. 301-38.*

Harry Alpert   (essay date 1938)

[*In the following essay, originally published in 1938 in the journal* Sociology and Social Research, *Alpert explains Durkheim's theory of the function of ritual in Book III of his* Les formes élémentaires de la vie religieuse.]

Functionalism in sociology is seen at its best, perhaps, in Durkheim's analysis of ceremony and ritual. The French sociologist inquired into the nature and functions of ceremonial and ritualistic institutions in Book III of *Les Formes élémentaires de la vie religieuse.* His mode of analysis here follows his general theory of religion which he perceives as an expression, in symbolic form, of social realities. He first determines the religious functions of ceremonial and ritualistic behavior and then tries to get behind the symbolic beliefs and behavior to the social realities which they are purported to express. In thus "substituting reality for symbol," he brings religion down to earth, so to speak, and hence is able to ascertain the social functions of the religiously symbolic conduct.

A study of the proscribing rites—i.e., taboos and interdicts ("the negative cult")—and of the prescribing ones—such as sacrificial, imitative, commemorative, and piacular rites ("the positive cult")—reveals that ritualistic institutions have a number of vital social functions which vary, of course, with the nature of the particular ceremony being performed. The following are four social functions of ritual to which Durkheim pays special attention.

1. *A disciplinary and preparatory function.* Ritual prepares an individual for social living by imposing on him the self-discipline, the "disdain for suffering," the self-abnegation without which life in society would be impossible. Social existence is possible only as individuals are able to accept constraints and controls. Asceticism is an inherent element in all social life. Ritual, being formal and institutional and, hence, to some degree prohibitive and inhibitive, is necessarily ascetic. Durkheim observes:

> In fact, there is no interdict, the observance of which does not have an ascetic character to a certain degree. Abstaining from something may be useful or from a form of activity, which, since it is usual, should answer to some human need, is, of necessity, imposing constraints and renunciations.

But abstinences, he adds,

> . . . do not come without suffering. We hold to the profane world by all the fibers of our flesh; our senses attach us to it; our life depends upon it. It is not merely the natural theater of our activity; it penetrates us from every side; it is a part of ourselves. So we cannot detach ourselves from it without doing violence to our nature and without painfully wounding our instincts. In other words, the negative cult cannot develop without causing suffering. Pain is one of its necessary conditions.

Moreover, the positive cult is possible "only when a man is trained to renouncement, to abnegation, to detachment from self, and consequently to suffering. Ascetic practices, therefore, are "a necessary school where men form and temper themselves, and acquire the qualities of disinterestedness and endurance without which there would be no religion." Substitute, in the above quotations, *social rule* for *negative cult, social life* for *positive cult,* and *society* for *religion,* and one has a clear picture of the disciplinary function of social ritual.

2. *A cohesive function.* Ceremony brings people together and thus serves to reaffirm their common bonds and to enhance and reinforce social solidarity: "Rites are, above all, means by which the social group reaffirms itself periodically." Ceremonial occasions are occasions of social communion. They are necessitated by the inevitable intermittency of social life. The workaday, immediate, private, and personal interests of an individual occupy much of his everyday life. His social ties to his fellow men, their common pool of values, tend to become obscure, indistinct, and even to lapse from consciousness. But since society is a necessary condition of human civilized living, it is imperative that this condition be remedied, that periodically at least man be given the opportunity to commune with his fellow social beings and to express his solidarity with them. Ceremonial institutions afford just such opportunities. Whatever their stated purpose, "the essential thing is that men are assembled, that sentiments are felt in common, and that they are expressed in common acts." . . .

3. *[A] revitalizing function.* If society is to be kept alive, its members must be made keenly aware of their social heritage. Traditions must be perpetuated, faith must be renewed, values must be transmitted and deeply imbedded. In this task of vitalizing and reanimating the social heritage of a group, ceremony and ritual play an important part. Men celebrate certain rites in order to "remain faith-

ful to the past, to keep for the group its moral physiognomy." A large number of ceremonies include rites whose object it is "to recall the past and, in a way, to make it present by means of a veritable dramatic representation." These rites serve to sustain the vitality of the social heritage and to keep its essential parts from lapsing from memory and consciousness. In short, they "revivify the most essential elements of the collective consciousness." Through them, "the group periodically renews the sentiment which it has of itself and of its unity; at the same time individuals are strengthened in their social natures." Ceremony functions, then, "to awaken certain ideas and sentiments, to attach the present to the past, the individual to the group." Since it aids in transmitting the social heritage, it may also be said to have an educational function. . . .

4. *A euphoric function.* . . . [Ceremony and ritual also] serve to establish a condition of social euphoria, i.e., a pleasant feeling of social well-being. This function takes on special significance when a group is faced with an actual or a threatened condition of dysphoria. All societies are subject to crises, calamities, disappointments, losses of particular members, and other dysphoric experiences. In certain cases the very existence of the group may be in jeopardy. These socially adverse conditions tend to disrupt the smooth functioning of the group; they threaten its sense of well-being, its feeling that all's right with the world. The group attempts, therefore, to counterbalance the disturbing action of these dysphoric situations; and in smoothing its way through crises and adversities, ceremony and ritual are of invaluable service. They perform this function by requiring individuals to have and to express certain emotions and sentiments, and by making them express these sentiments and feelings together.

Consider, for example, the mourning ceremonies: "When a society is going through circumstances which sadden, perplex, or irritate it, it exercises a pressure over its members to make them bear witness, by significant actions to their sorrow, perplexity, or anger." Thus, in the face of a dysphoric experience such as the loss of a member through death, a group exerts moral pressure on its members to make their sentiments harmonize with the situation. They must show that they have been duly affected by the loss. In any case, the group cannot allow them to remain indifferent . . . :

> [T]o allow them to remain indifferent to the blow which has fallen upon it and diminished it would be equivalent to proclaiming that it does not hold the place in their hearts which is due it; it would be denying itself. A family which allows one of its members to die without being wept for shows by that very fact that it lacks moral unity and cohesion; it abdicates, it renounces its existence.

When someone dies, then,

> the family group to which he belongs feels itself lessened, and to react against this loss, it assembles. . . . Collective sentiments are renewed, individuals consequently tend to seek out one another and to assemble together.

This coming together of individuals, this entering into closer relations with one another, and this sharing of a like emotion give rise to "a sensation of comfort which compensates the original loss." Since the individuals weep together,

> they hold to one another, and the group is not weakened. . . . Of course they have only sad emotions in common; but communicating in sorrow is still communicating; and every communion of mind, in whatever form it may be made, raises the social vitality.

We see then that ritual and ceremony in general serve to remake individuals and groups morally. They are disciplinary, cohesive, vitalizing, and euphoric social forces.

The above summary sketch of Durkheim's analysis of the social functions of ceremony and ritual can do justice neither to its profundity nor to its wisdom. Durkheim may have been mistaken in his interpretation of certain Australian ceremonies and in his sharp differentiation between magic and religion, and no doubt he erred in considering only religious rites to the practical exclusion of secular ritual and in neglecting in general to give due attention to those phenomena that are social but nonreligious. His functional analysis of ceremonial and ritualistic institutions, nonetheless, remains, we believe, a major contribution to sociology.

Harry Alpert, in "Durkheim's Functional Theory of Ritual," in Makers of Modern Social Science: Émile Durkheim, *edited by Robert A. Nisbet, Prentice-Hall, 1965, pp. 137-41.*

Emile Benoit-Smullyan (essay date 1948)

[*Benoit-Smullyan was an American economist who specialized in the economics of disarmament and who served as a consultant to the United States Department of Defense in the 1960s. In the following essay, he discusses the origins and development of Durkheim's sociologism.*]

Sociologism, as we use the term here, is a synthesis of a positivistic methodology with a particular set of substantive theories, for which we have invented the name "agelecism" (from $\alpha\gamma\epsilon\lambda\eta$, meaning "group"). By "agelecism" we mean the general sociological doctrine which maintains the reality *sui generis* or the causal priority of the social group *qua* group. Agelecism in its modern form was introduced into the stream of French social thought by [Louis] De Bonald and [Joseph-Marie] De Maistre, who maintained that the social group precedes and constitutes the individual, that it is the source of culture and all the higher values, and that social states and changes are not produced by, and cannot be directly affected or modified by, the desires and volitions of individuals.

Positivism, the doctrine that the social sciences should adopt the methods or schemas of the physical sciences, was first given self-conscious development by Saint-Simon, who sketched a program for a "social physics" or "social physiology" which would search for the "necessary" laws of social development. He laid the basis for a sociologistic theory of morals by treating morals as relative to group structure and pointing out the analogy between an applied science of morals and medicine or hygiene. This synthesis of agelecism and positivism was further elaborated and systematized by Comte. By reviving Bonald's criticism of introspective psychology and by omitting psychology from his classification of the sciences, he introduced an important antipsychologistic bias into the methodology of sociologism. His strongly anti-individualistic program of social control, his theory of social consensus, his conception of society as a "Great Being," and his emphasis on the family as the true social unit all contributed elements to the development of a comprehensive theory of agelecism. De Roberty, who, although a Russian, has figured prominently in the evolution of French sociologistic thought, contributed the biosocial hypothesis which viewed psychology as a concrete and dependent science derived from biology and sociology and explained culture and the higher faculties of the human mind as the product of human interaction and the group situation. The latter doctrine was later echoed and elaborated by Izoulet and Draghicesco. Finally, the biologistic theorist, Espinas, working under the inspiration of Comtean positivism, proclaimed that the individual was only a society of cells and, conversely, that society might legitimately be considered a kind of superindividual possessing a collective consciousness.

The essential dependence of Durkheim on this particular stream of thought would be difficult to deny. Durkheim disagrees with Comte's law of the three stages and with his conception of humanity as composing a single society; and he disagrees with Espinas's biologistic assumptions. But he is profoundly in sympathy with the particular combination of methodological positivism and agelecism which constitutes the essence of the sociologistic tradition as here defined. Durkheim's achievement may be summed up under three heads: first, his brilliant synthesis of positivism and agelecism into a single theoretical structure; second, his investigation and analysis of a number of empirical problems in terms of this theoretical scheme; third, the founding and editing of the *Année sociologique* and, in connection with it, the guidance of an enthusiastic group of collaborators and disciples in a wide but unified program of empirical research. . . .

Some students of Durkheim have maintained that Durkheim's whole sociological system rests at bottom on a few methodological intuitions. There can be no doubt at least that methodological preconceptions played a very important role in shaping the Durkheimian sociology. Our first task, accordingly, is to analyze the essential elements in the Durkheim methodology and to trace their derivation from the positivistic faith with which Durkheim was inspired. Durkheim's continuity with the main Positivist tradition is immediately evidenced in his stand on the relation between sociology and philosophy. He begins by rejecting the assumption that sociology needs to rest on any philosophic presuppositions whatever. Sociology is to be completely independent of philosophy; yet this independence is not reciprocal, for an adequate philosophy will, of necessity, incorporate important elements contributed by sociology, especially an understanding of the basic processes of association. This is clear-

ly in line with the essential element in the positivistic philosophy, namely, the rejection of the main philosophic traditions as unscientific, together with the attempt to erect a new philosophy by generalizing scientific conclusions or by utilizing scientific methods to tackle such theoretical questions as still appear to be meaningful. Like Comte, Durkheim expects the renovation of philosophy to be based particularly on the results of the new science of society. His blueprints for methodological reform in this new science we now propose to examine.

According to his own statement, Durkheim's most basic methodological postulate [in the preface to his *Les règles de la méthode sociologique,* 1904] is that we should "treat social facts as things." The intended meaning of this formula has never been clear, because Durkheim used the term "thing" in four different and not closely related senses, viz., (1) an entity possessing certain definite characteristics which are independent of human observation; (2) an entity which can be known only a posteriori (as opposed, for example, to a mathematical relation); (3) an entity, the existence of which is independent of human volition; (4) an entity which can be known only through "external" observation (as, for example, the sensory observation of the behavior or physiological states of others, in psychology) and not by introspection.

The meaning of the prescription that we ought to treat social facts as things varies with the sense of the word "thing," taken as intended. In the first sense of the word, the prescription means little more than that the sociologist has a real subject matter. In the second sense it means that social facts can be known only through *some type* of experience, and not by an a priori insight. These two contentions would be admitted by virtually all sociologists. In the third and fourth meanings the prescription becomes more controversial. In the third sense it seems to require the assumption of determinism in interhuman relations. In the fourth sense it limits us to external observation of social facts and forbids the use of introspective evidence even if it is selected and checked with scientific caution.

The classical sociological systems of Comte and Spencer, as well as virtually the whole body of jurisprudence, economics, and the theory of morals, are all vitiated, Durkheim feels, by an excessive dependence upon deductive reasoning and by a normative or evaluative approach. Both these errors spring from the same source: a failure to treat social facts as things; for, if social facts are things, then they must be empirically observed at every stage and not merely deduced from certain initial assumptions; and, moreover, we must strive merely to know them and adapt ourselves to them. Valuation is irrelevant. To insure scientific objectivity, the sociologist must begin not with concepts but with sensory data. These will supply the elements of his definitions. The sociologist must find some "objective" set of sensory data, the variations of which will measure the variations in the internal life of society, just as the oscillations of the thermometer provide an objective index to replace the subjective sensory data of temperature. There are three such orders of facts which Durkheim accepts as possessing this objectivity and, at the same time, as being collective rather than individual. They are legal codes, social statistics, and religious dogmas.

Durkheim's basic rules of sociological explanation are, first, that the social fact should always be viewed as mechanically determined and, second, that it should be explained in terms of another social fact, never by a fact of a lower order (e.g., a biological or psychological cause). In his discussion of this topic [in *Les règles*] Durkheim attacks two opponents simultaneously: psychologism and individualism—as well as that particular mixture of the two which constitutes utilitarianism. The common procedure of explaining a social fact in terms of its utility or in terms of the satisfaction it yields to individuals is, Durkheim maintains, entirely fallacious, since our needs do not of themselves create conditions which satisfy those needs; and only an explanation in terms of efficient causation is scientifically acceptable. Furthermore, if we supposed the cause of the social fact to lie within the individual, we should be unable to explain the constraint which the social fact, by definition, exerts over the individual. Hence "the determining cause of a social fact must be sought for among the antecedent social facts. . . . The function of a social fact must always be sought in its relationship to some social end."

There still remains the question as to which particular order of social facts is to provide the ultimate explanatory principle. Durkheim reasons that, since social facts arise out of the act of association, they must vary in accordance with the forms of this association, "that is to say, according to the manner in which the constituent parts of the society are grouped." Thus "the ultimate origin of all social processes of any importance must be sought in the constitution of the internal social milieu."

This internal social milieu, to which Durkheim elsewhere refers [in the introduction to *L'Année Sociologique* II, 1899] as the social "substratum" is comprised of such morphological elements as: the number of people in the group, the degree of their proximity, the evenness with which they are diffused over a given area, the number and dispositions of the paths of communication and transport, etc. It is, therefore, essentially a matter of the spatial distribution of physical entities (even persons are here considered in their physical aspect). The asserted ultimacy of this factor has caused Durkheim to be taxed, by several writers, with sociological materialism. This criticism Durkheim attempts to avoid by maintaining that it is not simply the number of people in a given area (the "material density") which is important, but the number of people who have established effective *moral* relations ("dynamic density"). However, by introducing this nonmaterialistic element into the concept, Durkheim sacrifices much of its operational value, since the degree of its applicability can no longer be determined by wholly external observations.

An interesting phase of Durkheim's positivism is his program for an applied sociology to formulate rules for social guidance. This science not only would advise us as to the best way in which to achieve social objectives but also would select the ends which a given society ought to pursue, and would do so entirely on the basis of scientific observation of empirical data. This can be accomplished,

Durkheim claims, by finding an objective criterion of social health and social pathology. Once in possession of such a criterion, social science can apply the general laws of sociology to the preservation of social health, just as the science of medicine applies the laws of physiology to the preservation of the health of the individual organism.

Durkheim is quick to dismiss the criterion of utility, as requiring an appeal to the subjective states of individuals and, hence, as lacking in scientific objectivity. Instead, he defines health in terms of "normality" and adopts *generality* as the criterion of "normality." The socially healthful is that which is normal; and as "the normal type is identical with the average type. . . . every deviation from this standard is a pathological phenomenon." In the application of this criterion Durkheim is led to paradoxical conclusions. Since crime is prevalent in all or most societies, it must be considered normal and as an element in social health. On the other hand, certain phenomena which have been common in all the societies of Western civilization for the last century, such as a rising suicide rate, a weakening in the moral condemnation of suicide, and certain types of economic maladjustments, are all classified by Durkheim as pathological. Critics have pointed out also that this criterion of normality leads to an ultra-conservative morality of sheer social conformism, since every deviation from what is general in a society is classified as pathological. An implicit concession to this criticism is perhaps apparent in Durkheim's admission that, in periods of great social change (like the present), phenomena which are general may have only an "appearance of normality"; and some phenomena which are exceptional may be normal because they are closely bound up with the conditions of social existence.

Durkheim places great emphasis on his definition of the social fact in terms of constraint and exteriority. Unfortunately, the precise meaning of these criteria has never been clear. From his fundamental methodological postulate that we must treat social facts as things, Durkheim infers that the social fact must possess two important characteristics of a thing: it must be *exterior* to (in the sense of not identical with) the idea in the mind of the scientist, and it must impose a certain constraint on the scientist (in the sense of possessing independent characters not influenced by the scientist's volition, to which the scientific theory must conform, or which it must express, if it is to be true). By shifting the center of reference from the *scientist* who *studies* social facts to the acting *individual* who *lives* in an environment of social facts, Durkheim is able to endow the criteria of exteriority and constraint with a new and purely substantive set of meanings. To the acting individual the social fact is exterior in the sense that it is experienced as an independent reality which neither he nor any other individual created and which literally forms a part of his objective environment. In the same way the social fact possesses the characteristic of constraint in that it does not conform to the volitions of individuals but, on the contrary, imposes itself upon individuals, regulating their behavior and even their volitions.

The substantive doctrine of the exteriority of the social fact is thus identical with what we have called "agelic realism." It asserts that society is a reality *sui generis,* above and apart from the individuals. The evidence adduced by Durkheim in defense of this doctrine is of four main types. The first is the alleged heterogeneity of individual and collective states of mind. Thus it is asserted that in a time of national danger the intensity of the collective feeling of patriotism is much greater than that of any individual feeling and society's willingness to sacrifice individuals is greater than the willingness of individuals to sacrifice themselves. Similarly, the individual's hesitant and vague condemnation of dishonesty is said to stand in marked contrast [as stated in *Le suicide: étude de Sociologique,* 1930] to the "unreserved, explicit, and categorical disgrace with which society strikes at theft in all its forms." A second type of argument, which in one form or another is to be found in practically all Durkheim's writings, stresses the difference in individual attitudes and behavior which results from the group situation. When in a crowd the individual thinks, feels, and acts in a different fashion. It follows, thinks Durkheim, that a new reality must be created by the association of individuals and that this reality reacts upon the sentiments and behavior of the individuals and changes them. A third type of evidence is supplied by the uniformities of social statistics. Many types of social facts, like crimes, marriages, and suicides, show a surprising degree of numerical consistency from year to year, either remaining virtually unchanged or maintaining a uniform rate of change. Such uniformity, Durkheim argues, could not derive from the personal motives or characteristics of individuals, which are so variable as to comprise what is practically a random distribution. Nor can they be satisfactorily explained, Durkheim attempts to prove, by physical, biological, or psychological uniformities. The only remaining explanation is to be found in the influence of certain real social currents which form a (hitherto undetected) part of the individual's environment. A fourth line of argument is based on analogy and on the philosophical theory of emergence. Just as the phenomenon of life is not to be explained by the physicochemical properties of the molecules which form the cell, but by a particular association of molecules, and just as the phenomenon of consciousness resides not in the physiological nature of the cell but in a particular mode of molecular association, so we must assume that society is not reducible to the properties of individual minds but that it constitutes a reality *sui generis* which emerges out of the collocation and interaction of individual minds.

The other characteristic of the social fact, the "constraint" which it exercises over the individual, may be viewed as a simple corollary of its externality. Since the social fact is both real and external, it forms part of the individual's environment and, like the physical and biological parts of his environment, exerts upon him a certain constraint; for the hallmark of an independent reality is the resistance it opposes to our volitions and the counterpressure it exerts on our behavior. Moreover, the fact of social constraint enters into the direct experience of the individual. Legal and moral rules (which are the most typical orders of social facts) cannot be flouted by the individual without his experiencing the tangible evidences of social disapprobation. But if constraint is such an essential element in legal

and moral rules, it cannot be wholly absent in other types of social facts.

The principal problems treated by Durkheim in his book on the division of labor, *De la division du travail social,* concern the nature and the cause of social evolution. Durkheim agreed with Spencer and the Utilitarians that one important aspect of the change from primitive to civilized modes of social existence was to be found in the increase in the amount of division of labor, or specialization. But he felt that the Utilitarians in their description of social evolution unduly emphasized the economic changes and misunderstood or neglected the far more important moral and legal changes. As Durkheim sees it, the fundamental difference between primitive and civilized societies is in the type of morals or social solidarity, which is, in turn, reflected in the type of legal codes.

In primitive society, where division of labor is rudimentary, individuals are relatively homogeneous and bound together by a "mechanical" solidarity characterized by blind acquiescence to the dictates of public opinion and tradition. The legal system is designed primarily to punish those who violate the collective will and offend collective sentiments and to restore by this punishment a moral equilibrium. In such a society, moral and legal responsibility is collective, social status tends to be hereditarily fixed, and a relatively small part of social life is ordered by the contractual principle. In civilized societies, where division of labor is well developed, individuals have diverse personalities, experiences, and functions, and they are bound together by an "organic" solidarity rooted in their need for each other's services. The primary purpose of the legal system is to restore to the individual that which has been wrongfully taken away from him. In this sort of society individualism is the dominant morality, but individualism in a very special sense. Individualism, as a conscious moral attitude appropriate for our type of society, is not a claim for the unlimited right of the individual to pursue his immediate desires; it is, rather, an obligation laid upon him to individualize himself by intensive specialization in order to make his distinctive contribution to social welfare. It is a stern injunction to avoid the delights of dilettantism and to further the division of labor. Durkheim is intensely concerned to demonstrate that a purely egoistic and hedonistic individualism could never produce social solidarity or serve as a basis for social cohesion. He is at pains to point out that peaceful and beneficial contractual relations can exist only in the framework of a legal and moral order which limits the types of contracts that are valid, gives the definitive interpretation as to the obligations arising out of the contracts, and enforces their performance.

Still more sharply does Durkheim disagree with the Utilitarians as to the *causes* of social evolution. They had assumed that the division of labor and the resulting gains in economic productivity and material civilization derived, quite simply, from the desires of individuals for greater wealth and higher planes of living. Durkheim makes this a test case in his war against the explanation of social facts in terms of the motives of individuals and the tendencies of human nature. The general line of the argument is as follows. Human beings have only a limited and moderate capacity to enjoy economic goods, and therefore they would long ago have stopped increasing their wealth if happiness had been the motive for increased production. Happiness is connected with social health, which is imperiled by excesses of every sort, including a superabundance of material luxuries. Great social changes which disrupt settled habits create much suffering, and it could not be a desire for happiness which would lead a whole generation to make such sacrifices in order to produce luxuries which it did not consciously desire and from which only succeeding generations would profit. Finally, there is no evidence that material progress and civilization make men any happier. In fact, the apparent contentment in primitive society and the relative infrequency of suicides and neuroses reveal a far higher degree of average happiness than that in contemporary civilizations. Therefore, it is not the desire for happiness which created civilization.

Having disposed of the psychologistic and individualistic explanations of the division of labor, Durkheim now turns to his own morphological explanation, which accords very well with the requirement set forth in the ***Règles de la méthode sociologique.*** Division of labor is due to changes in social structure arising out of an increase in material and moral density. The increase in population intensifies competition and thus forces individuals to specialize, in order to survive. Thus Durkheim, rather reluctantly, comes to rest his entire explanation upon the factor of an assumed natural increase in population. This is obviously a biologistic rather than a sociologistic type of explanation and comes closer to an outright materialism than anything in Durkheim's later work.

Durkheim's intensive study of suicide is more than an interesting statistical analysis of an important empirical topic. As usual, Durkheim is vitally concerned to show how the empirical data support a theoretical doctrine, in this case the exteriority and constraining power of a given order of social facts.

He begins by refusing to define suicide as an intentional act of self-destruction, because intentions are not externally observable and are too variable to define a single order of phenomena. He then proceeds to an ingenious statistical refutation of theories which explain suicide in terms of various climatic, geographic, biological, or psychological factors. As an alternative he proposes a conception of suicide as a social fact, explicable in terms of social causes. The social, superindividual nature of suicide is supported by the observation that the rate of suicide (or its rate of change) in a given society is remarkably constant from year to year. Durkheim argues that such constancy would be inexplicable if the suicide rate depended on the highly variable and practically random traits of individual personality and volition. He infers that suicide must emanate from a single type of causal factor which preserves a uniform strength from year to year. Since climatic, geographic, biological, and psychological factors have been excluded by his statistical demonstrations, he concludes that only in the social realm can a comprehensive explanatory factor be found.

The social factors influencing the rate of suicide are re-vealed by the correlation of suicide rates with group affiliations and with important collective processes. Thus Durkheim uncovers evidence to prove that free thinkers have the highest suicide rates and Protestants the next highest; that Catholics have low rates, and Jews the lowest of all. The essential difference here, according to Durkheim, is not in the religious beliefs themselves but in the degree of integration of the religious group. Protestantism involves a higher degree of religious individualism than Catholicism, and the religious group is less integrated by uniformities of belief, while Judaism, because of its heritage of persecution, strongly binds its members together to face a hostile environment. Durkheim infers that one important type of suicide ("egoistic") is caused by an insufficient participation by the individual in the life of a group. The individual in himself is of little value; it is only what he derives from participation in a social group that can give his private existence purpose and significance. Hence the individual who remains aloof from strongly integrated social groups, who pursues his own personal ends exclusively, is more liable than others to be overcome with ennui and to find no reason for continuing his existence.

Another important type of suicide described by Durkheim is *"suicide anomique,"* or "normless" suicide. He observes that bachelors have much higher suicide rates than married men and that the general suicide rate decreases in time of war and increases in times both of sharp economic depression and of exceptional prosperity. Durkheim supposes that the individual's desires are in themselves boundless and insatiable and that mental health and contentment require that fixed limits be placed by society on the individual's expectation of personal gratification. During a period of exceptional prosperity, customary standards of living are easily surpassed, and no new norms or appropriate living standards are established. But unlimited expectations must sooner or later engender disappointments, which may easily prove fatal to the individual lacking a strong moral constitution. Similarly, the bachelor, who is less restricted in his sexual life than the married man, is easily disenchanted and disgusted with life. The degree of integration of the society is important, because upon it rests the capacity of the society to discipline the individual. Thus in wartime, when there is normally a strong unification of the society in response to an external threat, it imposes a firmer discipline on the individual and thereby preserves him against suicide. A serious depression, on the other hand, involves social disorganization, and the suffering which this disorganization produces in the social mind is reflected in the minds of individuals, a greater number of whom commit suicide.

The conclusion to which Durkheim comes is that there exist "suicidal currents" produced by the varying states of social organization, which act mechanically upon individuals and force a certain number of them to commit suicide. These suicidal currents are just as real and just as much external to the individual as are the physical and biological forces which produce death by disease. The suicidal current, like the biological epidemic, has a predetermined number of victims, selected from those who can offer the least resistance. There is an individual factor in suicide, just as there is in disease; but it determines who in particular will succumb and not the number of deaths. The individual may appear to himself and to others to be committing suicide from personal motives, but in reality he is being impelled to commit the act by impersonal forces, of which (unless he is a sociologist!) he is presumably unaware. Perhaps nowhere in the literature of sociologism has the doctrine of agelic fatalism been given a more dramatic application!

Around 1898, Durkheim entered on a new and distinct phase of his work. It is characterized, in the first place, by a more idealistic conception of the social group, with more emphasis on "collective representations" and less on the internal social milieu; and, in the second place, by adventurous speculation concerning the social origin of morals, values, religion, and knowledge. The social group is successively endowed by Durkheim with the characteristics of hyperspirituality, personality, creativity, and transcendence. The inception of this phase is marked by the publication of Durkheim's paper on individual and collective representations [entitled **"Représentations individuelles et représentations collectives,"** 1924].

The chief conclusion of this paper is that there exist collective mental states which are no more reducible to the mental states of individuals than the mental states of individuals are reducible to the physiological states of independent brain cells. The association of individuals gives rise to an emergent reality—society—which is relatively independent of the properties of the constituent individuals. Collective representations are undoubtedly influenced in their formation by the conditions of the material substratum; but, once formed, they are partially autonomous realities, which combine according to their own natural affinities and which are not closely determined by the character of the milieu in which they originated. This conception of social facts as constituting an independent reality is very far from materialism, says Durkheim. If the individual mind is a spiritual reality, social facts must be granted the attribute of "hyperspirituality."

The second major step in the development of a transcendental theory of the social group was taken by Durkheim in connection with the development of a sociologistic theory of morals. To begin with, he holds that the moral fact presents a peculiar duality. The moral rule inspires us with respect and with a feeling of obligation which is quite independent of its content; but, on the other hand, we must assume that this content is good and desirable (even if it does not at the moment correspond with our personal desires).

Now if we seek for the origin of the moral rule, we perceive immediately that it cannot emanate from the individual, since no act has ever been called "moral" which had as its exclusive end the conservation or self-development of the individual. If the agent in himself cannot be a source of moral obligation, neither can *other* individuals, for they are not essentially different from the agent. But disinterestedness and devotion are essential characters of the moral act, and these sentiments are meaningless or impossible unless we subordinate ourselves to another conscious being (preferably of higher moral value than ourselves). If, however, all human beings are excluded, there are only two further alternatives: there is God, and there is society.

At bottom these two alternatives are the same, for God is only society "transfigured and conceived symbolically." Thus, if the moral life is to have any meaning, we must assume that society itself is a true moral person, formed by a synthesis of individuals and qualitatively distinct from all the individuals taken distributively.

This solution accounts for the dual character of the moral fact. It is obligatory because it is the command of society, and society so infinitely surpasses the individual, both materially and morally, that its commands carry sufficient authority to produce unquestioning obedience. But, on the other hand, it seems good and desirable, because society is the source of all the higher values of civilization and the creator of that element in the individual which raises him above the animal level. Without society, language would not exist; and without language, the higher mental processes would be impossible. Without science, which is a social product, man would be helpless before the blind forces of nature. So it is to society that the individual owes his real liberty. "We cannot wish to leave society without wishing to cease to be men."

Durkheim ends by drawing certain important relativistic conclusions. Moral rules are always the product of particular social factors, and every moral system is closely dependent upon the social structure of the society in which it exists. There is no single moral system which would be moral for every society, and diversity of morals among different societies is not to be explained by ignorance or perversity. Each society has the moral system it needs, and any other morality would be injurious to it. The social scientist may sometimes help society by showing what moral judgments are truly consistent with the actual state of social organization, but this is as far as anyone can go. "To wish for a different moral system from the one which is implied in the nature of society is to deny society, and consequently to deny oneself."

The final stage in the completion of a doctrine of agelic transcendentalism was reached in 1911 with the elaboration of a general theory of value, which portrayed the social group as the transcendental creator of *all*, not merely of all moral, values. As his point of departure. Durkheim calls attention to the apparent objectivity of value-judgments. Assertions that Beethoven's music has aesthetic value, that honest behavior has moral value, that a diamond has economic value, are not intended as mere expressions of personal preference but as characterizations of an external reality.

They cannot, therefore, be supposed to refer to the personal likes and dislikes of myself or any other *individual*, or even of a majority of individuals. Since value-judgments do not refer to any individual's preference, they must express the hierarchy of preferences which society has established—and the fact that it is society which has established and imposed them gives them their objectivity.

The basic problem, however, concerns the source of the whole realm of values. How is it possible that man, who lives in a world of merely factual existence, should conceive and refer to an ideal world of values? How can we pass from what is to what ought to be?

According to Durkheim, the only natural forces which could suffice to account for the emergence of an ideal realm of values are those which are liberated by the association of individuals in the social group. When individuals come together and have vigorous mental interaction, "there emerges from their synthesis a psychic life of a new sort." It is in such periods of effervescence and collective enthusiasm, when gatherings and assemblages are more frequent and the exchange of ideas more intense, that the great ideals of civilization have been formed. Examples are offered by the student movement in Paris in the twelfth and thirteenth centuries, the Reformation, the Renaissance, the French Revolution, and the socialist upheavals in the nineteenth century. In such periods the individual lives a higher life, almost completely devoid of egoistic and vulgar considerations. Then, for a time, the ideal seems to coalesce with the real, and it almost seems as if the Kingdom of Heaven were about to be achieved on earth. However, this illusion cannot last, because the exaltation is too exhausting to be maintained indefinitely. "Once the critical moment has passed, the social network relaxes, the intellectual intercourse slows down, and the individuals fall back to their ordinary level." What is left behind is only a memory, a group of *ideas,* which would soon evaporate if they were not revivified from time to time by celebrations, public ceremonies, sermons, artistic and dramatic performances, and other forms of group concentration and social integration.

Society must be conceived as a mind composed of collective ideas, but these ideas are not simply cognitive representations. They are strongly imbued with sentiment and have important motor elements, i.e., they are stimulants to action. They are the expression of forces which are both natural and ideal at the same time. This is possible because society has a dual character: it comes out of nature, but it synthesizes natural forces to produce a result which is richer, more complex, and more powerful than these forces. "It is nature which has risen to the highest point in its development and which concentrates all its energies in order, in some fashion, to transcend itself."

It must be noted that Durkheim has arrived here at a definitely ambivalent conception of society. On the one hand, it is a transcendental reality, which can plausibly be considered the source of all the transcendent elements in human experience; and, on the other hand, it is still a natural phenomenon (a number of individuals in spatial proximity). An increase in the proximity of the members of the group provides a "naturalistic" explanation for the creation of the transcendental elements in experience, and a decrease in proximity provides an equally naturalistic explanation for the nontranscendent, secular, *alltäglich* element in experience. With the further assumption that the life of the group goes through a natural and necessary rhythm of concentration and dispersion, the doctrine of agelic fatalism becomes practically omnipotent as an explanatory hypothesis.

As is generally known, the fundamental idea of Durkheim's *Les Formes élémentaires de la vie religieuse* is that religion is entirely a "social thing." This involves two distinct theses: first, that religious ideas and practices refer to or symbolize the social group and, second, that association is the generating source, or efficient cause, of the religious experience. As usual, Durkheim begins with the careful framing of an *ad hoc* definition of the object of investigation.

The next step is the elimination of the chief individualistic and psychologistic theories of religion, especially the animistic theories of Sir Edward B. Tylor and Spencer and the naturistic theory of Müller. The chief objections brought against these theories are that they are unable to account for more than a part of the whole body of religious phenomena; that they fail to explain the radical heterogeneity between the sacred and the secular, which is the essential characteristic of religion; and, finally, that they "explain religion away" by interpreting it as an illusion without any basis in the real world.

Durkheim proceeds next to an examination of the totemic practices of the Aruntas in Australia. The assumption is that this society is about the most primitive society in existence and that its religious practices will therefore exhibit in its simplest form the original nature of religion. The fundamental characteristic of totemism is that the clan takes the name of, claims descent from, and exercises certain ritual restraints toward, some object in the environment, usually an animal or plant. According to Durkheim's analysis, the most fundamental belief implicit in totemism is the belief in a mysterious and sacred force or principle which animates the totem, provides a physical sanction for violation of the totemic taboo, and inculcates moral responsibilities. Now the strong emotions of awe and reverence for the totem can hardly have been derived from the physical properties of the totem itself, since this latter is usually some harmless and insignificant animal or plant. The totem must therefore be considered as a symbol. It symbolizes, first, the sacred totemic principle or god and, second, the clan itself, with which the totem is closely identified. Durkheim infers from this that the totemic divinity and the clan are really the same thing and, more generally, that God is only a symbolic expression of society.

The next problem concerns the origin of the religious experience; and Durkheim's explanation runs as follows: The life of the Arunta is divided into two phases. In the first, or secular, phase the clan is scattered in small groups of individuals pursuing their private economic objectives and living a life which is "uniform, languishing, and dull." In the second, or religious, phase the clan gathers together, and "the very fact of the concentration acts as an exceptionally powerful stimulant." A sort of electricity or collective euphoria is generated, which soon lifts the individuals to miraculous states of exaltation. The effervescence is so intense that delirious behavior and altogether exceptional actions (like violations of the most well-established taboos) are common. It is in these periods of intense agelic concentration and violent interaction that religious sentiments and ideas are born, and it is the sharp contrast between these periods and the dull and languishing periods of group dispersion which explains the radical heterogeneity between the sacred and the profane.

These general conclusions are reinforced by certain considerations concerning the similarity of our attitudes toward society and toward God. Society, it is asserted, is quite capable of inspiring the sensation of divinity in the minds of its members because of its power over them. The individual's feeling of perpetual dependence is alike in each case. Society, like God, possesses moral authority and can inspire disinterested devotion and self-sacrifice. It is also capable of endowing the individual with exceptional powers and is the source of all that is highest and best in human personality. Therefore, the religious man, who feels a dependence upon some external moral power, is not the victim of a hallucination. There is such a power: society. Of course, he may be mistaken in supposing that the religious forces emanate from some particular object (like a totem), but this is simply a mistake in the "letter of the symbol." Behind this symbol there is a reality which does have the ascribed properties.

In recent years one major development in sociology has been the elaboration of a "sociology of knowledge," an explanation of knowledge itself as a product of social conditions. In this field Durkheim must rank as one of the most important pioneers. Going beyond the generalities of his predecessors (to the effect that thought depends upon language, and language upon society), he tries to show in detail how both the forms of classification and the basic categories of cognition have been produced by society.

The problem of classification is treated in a monograph, ["De quelques formes primitives de classification," *Année Sociologique* VI (1901-2)], on primitive forms of classification (written in collaboration with M. Mauss). The present concept of a "class," we are told, does not go back beyond Aristotle; and our contemporary forms of classification (in terms of class and subclass, species and genus, etc.) are not innate but based upon "a hierarchical order for which neither the sensory world nor our own minds offer us a model." If we observe the classifications of primitive peoples, however, we discover that these classifications closely reflect the social organization of the tribe. The first "classes" were classes of men, and the classification of physical objects was simply an extension of previously established social classifications, since all the animals and objects in the environment were classified as belonging to this or that clan, phratry, or other kinship group. The hierarchy of type and subtype in logical classification reflects the hierarchical character of earlier forms of social structure. The imagery in which, even today, logical relations are expressed, reveals their social origin: things which are alike "belong to the same family"; an entity "possesses" certain characteristics; and one concept is "dependent upon or subordinate to" another.

Primitive classification is not primarily conceptual but is based largely on emotion and social sensibility. Scientific classification emerges when social sentiment becomes less important and when individual observation and speculation have more freedom. But the very framework of classification—the mental habits by which we organize facts in groups (themselves hierarchically related)—bears the indelible mark of a social genesis.

The last and most daring of Durkheim's speculative flights is a sociologistic explanation of the categories of thought and the forms of intuition. As usual, he begins with a criticism of existing theories. Empiricism, he holds, cannot account for the universality and necessity of the categories (i.e., why it is that the individual cannot "think away" or alter essentially his conceptions of space, time, substance, cause, etc.). The aprioristic point of view does not explain where these ideas originate and how it is that we can arrive at knowledge of objective relationships transcending our personal sensory experience. A theological explanation is not "experimental" and cannot account for the variation of the categories in different societies.

Durkheim's own explanation is that the categories are collective representations. As such, they are imposed upon the individual and create in him the impression of being universal and necessary. The uniformity of the categories within a given society is easily explained by the fact that agreement about such fundamental modes of thought as the categories is absolutely essential for social cooperation and thus for the very existence of society. In the interest of self-preservation, the society must impose a minimum of logical conformity. Our obligation to think in terms of space, time, cause and effect, etc., is "a special form of moral necessity which is to the intellect what moral obligation is to the will."

But the categories are not only imposed by society; they reflect its most general characters, and they are in this sense a social creation. The sense of time was derived from the rhythms of group life; "the territory occupied by the society furnished the material for the category of space"; and the power of the social group gave rise to the idea of an efficient force, upon which the category of causality depends. From his own limited temporal and spatial intuitions the individual could never derive the idea of space or time in general. It was necessary, first, to have the concept of totality, and only society, "which includes all things," could give rise to the concept of totality. With the world "inside of society," however, the space occupied by society becomes identified with space in general. Similarly, social rhythms, based on the concentration and dispersion of the social group, supply the generalized notion of time. The divisions of time into days, weeks, months, and years corresponds to the periodic recurrence of social functions; the calendar both expresses the rhythm of social life and assures its regularity.

The dependence of our conception of space on the regions occupied by the society is shown by the following [from *The Elementary Forms of Religious Life*]:

> There are societies in Australia and North America where space is conceived in the form of an immense circle, because the camp has a circular form; and this spatial circle is divided up exactly like the tribal circle, and is in its image. There are as many regions distinguished as there are clans in the tribe, and it is the place occupied by the clans inside the encampment which has determined the orientation of these regions. Each region is defined by the totem of the clan to which it is assigned.

Durkheim even hopes that evidence may yet be found to show conclusively that the principle of contradiction itself is a function of a given social system. He thinks that it has already been shown that the extent to which this principle has influenced human minds has varied historically from one society to another.

In the history of thought, agelecism has usually been accompanied by anti-individualism in ethics and conservatism in politics. This combination of elements is well exemplified in many phases of Durkheim's work. His sociology is primarily concerned with the problem of social control and is negatively disposed toward individual deviation from accepted social norms. Both the reality and the value of individual invention are systematically denied. It is a sociology of a static and monistic type, with no adequate explanation for social change. Moreover, it displays a remarkable lack of interest in those structures and processes of group life which are connected with internal division and conflict. There is little concern with social classes, with the clash of interest groups, or with processes of revolution and war.

It is not surprising, therefore, that Durkheim's diagnosis of our social ills and his therapeutic program of social reform should have assumed a pronounced anti-individualistic character. The prevalence of suicide, nervous disorders, and other pathological symptoms were due, he thought, to the fact that the individual was no longer sufficiently restrained by a social group. With the decline in the influence of the neighborhood, the religious group, and the extended kin group and with the increase in the size of the state and its impersonality and distance from the individual, there was no group left which could successfully impose a wholesome moral discipline on the individual. To remedy this deficiency, Durkheim proposed the creation of a type of corporatism which would endow the trade-union or professional association with sufficient authority to enter actively into the regulation and direction of the personal lives of its members. This program bears some resemblances (the importance of which should not, however, be exaggerated) to the corporatism established by Fascist regimes.

Yet, if we would do justice to Durkheim's thought, we must admit a complexity which baffles any simple interpretative pattern. Scattered throughout his work, but especially in the *Division of Labor* and in the *Suicide,* are numerous passages of praise for individualism. In his politics, moreover, he was regarded as a liberal. Certain biographical facts are of considerable relevance here. Durkheim was born in 1858 and came to intellectual maturity in a period when France was exerting enormous efforts to recover from the effects of the Franco-Prussian War. The unification and reintegration of the French nation was considered by most intellectuals of the period to be of the utmost urgency. An intense sentiment of nationalism provided the emotional background for Durkheim's belief in the transcendental reality of the social group (which, ordinarily, he implicitly identifies with the nation) and for his unvarying emphasis on the problems of social control. But the intellectuals were hopelessly divided in their opinions as to the proper *basis* of that social reintegration, the necessity of which they uniformly conceded. On the one hand, the conservatives urged a reversion to Catholicism, royalism, and traditionalism. On the other hand, the intellectuals who most staunchly supported the Third Republic hoped for a secular basis of integration, resulting from the growth and diffusion of scientific information. Durkheim's position was naturally with the latter group. As a social scientist of the positivistic persuasion, he could not fail to support the position that science could provide a new and quite adequate basis of social organization. As a scientific rationalist, he was necessarily distrustful of those *mystiques* which the traditionalists were offering as a substitute. Two other factors inclined him in the direction of liberal individualism: his own struggle against race prejudice, and the strong influence upon him of Renouvier's moral personalism.

What is truly distinctive, however, about Durkheim's individualism is that it is supported by entirely agelic arguments. The individual is sacred, it is claimed, because he bears within himself that culture which has been created by the group; and in doing violence to him we should be indirectly attacking the group. Moreover, the ideals of individualism and liberalism need no metaphysical justification: their rightness *for us* is guaranteed by the fact that they are implicit in our whole contemporary social organization (based on division of labor and specialization). We cannot restore this or that institution characteristic of an earlier civilization, because individualism and liberalism offer the only *possible* basis for integration in a society of our type.

The adequacy of this relativistic and pragmatic defense of individualism is highly questionable. It is not based on any appreciation of the intrinsic value and creative potentialities of the individual in himself but upon the assumed in-

---

Durkheim on analytical intelligence and primitive religion:

At the roots of all our judgments there are a certain number of essential ideas which dominate all our intellectual life; they are what philosophers since Aristotle have called the categories of the understanding: ideas of time, space, class, number, cause, substance, personality, etc. They correspond to the most universal properties of things. They are like the solid frame which encloses all thought; this does not seem to be able to liberate itself from them without destroying itself, for it seems that we cannot think of objects that are not in time and space, which have no number, etc. Other ideas are contingent and unsteady; we can conceive of their being unknown to a man, a society or an epoch; but these others appear to be nearly inseparable from the normal working of the intellect. They are like the framework of the intelligence. Now when primitive religious beliefs are systematically analysed, the principal categories are naturally found. They are born in religion and of religion; they are a product of religious thought.

Émile Durkheim, from the Introduction to his The Elementary Forms of Religious Life, *translated by Joseph Ward Swain, 1915.*

evitability of individualism at a given stage in the fixed evolutionary pattern of social change. In Durkheim's system, it appears as a paradoxical rationalization of an ideal which he found useful and which he wished to defend but which was, at bottom, incompatible with his fundamental sociological beliefs. The reversion, in recent years, of several civilized nations to a more barbaric principle of law and social organization dramatically illustrates the unsoundness of the doctrine of linear evolution. It may be true that individualism and liberalism are necessarily bound up with our present type of society, but Durkheim, who died too soon to see a Fascist revolution, apparently never realized that a society may actually change over—and quite rapidly—from a more to a less individualistic and liberal type. His relativistic defense of liberal individualism gives us no basis for deciding which of the two *types* is preferable.

Emile Benoit-Smullyan, "The Sociologism of Émile Durkheim and His School," in An Introduction to the History of Sociology, *edited by Harry Elmer Barnes, The University of Chicago Press, 1948, pp. 499-537.*

P. M. Worsley (essay date 1956)

[*In the excerpt below, Worsley draws from recent ethnographic evidence to reassess Durkheim's theory of knowledge, as exemplified by his study of totemism among aboriginal tribes in his* Elementary Forms of the Religious Life.]

As a theorist, Emile Durkheim is perhaps unique amongst recent writers in the extent of his influence upon both sociologists and anthropologists, though it is particularly the thinking of a whole generation of anthropologists which bears the impress of Durkheim's influence—either as a result of direct study of his works, or, indirectly, via the teachings of Radcliffe-Brown. In his comparative sociology, he never hesitated to utilize material from primitive society because such material shed light upon human institutions in their simpler forms.

But sociologists have also recognised Durkheim as a major theorist, even where he has taken his material from primitive society. What is conventionally an anthropological study, his *Elementary Forms of the Religious Life,* has been read as widely by sociologists as by anthropologists.

Many partial criticisms of this work have been made since its first appearance in 1912, but there appears to have been little attempt to revalue it more specifically in the light of the data on aboriginal society accumulated since Durkheim's day. Following the tradition of Durkheim himself in disregarding conventional barriers between anthropology and sociology, I propose to examine the basic notions of this work, particularly his theory of knowledge, and to draw the attention of sociologists to recent ethnographic material which makes such reassessment possible. I make no apologies, therefore for using anthropological material, since I use it because of its bearing on Durkheim's theory, not because of its intrinsic interest. Some of the material on Groote Eylandt is here presented for the first time, but this is incidental to my main purpose.

It is a tribute to Durkheim's logical powers, and to his precise and rigorous methodology, that his theories on the subjects of totemism and religion in general still command such attention. But let us look first at the purpose and scope of the work, and note the theoretical assumptions, explicit and implicit, upon which it is founded.

Durkheim was not interested in totemism merely as an exotic social phenomenon. He is quite explicit in his *Introduction* that he is concerned with the analysis of totemism, in the first place, as a critical illumination of his general theory of religion, this in its turn being merely one facet of his wider theory of knowledge. It is the theory of knowledge that is his principal, underlying concern throughout the study.

This concern is crystallized in his discussion of the categories of understanding. Durkheim is concerned to establish the derivation of these categories—concepts of space, time, class, force, substance, efficacy, personality, causality, etc.—concepts which are fundamental to all human thought. Examining existing theories, he first dismisses that type of idealism which depicts the ultimate reality behind the world as spiritual, or which depicts the categories as 'inherent in the nature of the human intellect.' This, he says, assumes that 'above the reason of individuals there is a superior and perfect reason from which the others emanate and from which they get this marvellous power of theirs, by a sort of mystic participation: this is the divine reason.' This apriorist position, he says, is refuted by the 'incessant variability' of the categories of human thought, in contradiction to the postulated immutability of divine reason. Again, it lacks experimental control, and thus 'does not satisfy the conditions demanded of a scientific hypothesis.'

Next, he sweeps aside certain varieties of subjectivism, in particular the theory that the individual creates the categories from the raw material of his own experience, from the ordering of his sensations. Though the categories vary greatly from society to society, he points out that within any one society they are characterised by universality and necessity, which therefore, he says, precludes any idea of their derivation from individual thought, and he criticises the theories of Tylor and Frazer from this point of view.

Nevertheless, Durkheim firmly dissociates himself from any materialist standpoint. His approach does not consist in 'a simple restatement of historical materialism: that would be mis-understanding our thought to an extreme degree.' In fact, he says, 'the world of representations . . . is superimposed upon its material substratum, far from arising from it.'

This 'plague on both your houses' theme is familiar today, when both materialism and idealism are dubbed 'metaphysics' by many writers. In adopting a standpoint which claimed to differ from either of these philosophies, Durkheim is, of course, developing the earlier ideas of Comte. In order to avoid deriving mind from matter, or calling on any super-experimental reality, it 'is no longer necessary to [go beyond] experience,' he says, and the specific experience to which he refers is the 'super-individual reality which we experience in society.' Men do not make the world in their own image, he states, any more than the converse: 'they have done both at the same time.' True, he makes occasional references to the 'nature of things,' the 'objective value' of concepts, etc., which might mislead one into thinking that he was speaking of a knowable material reality. He does, indeed, intend to refer to a super-individual reality, but this reality is not the material world; it is society.

For Durkheim, society is the fundamental reality; without it, there is no Man. But society can only become conscious of itself, can only make its influence felt, through the collective action of its members. Out of this action spring the collective ideas and sentiments of society, and further, the fundamental categories of thought.

Whereas positivist philosophers generally make the individual their point of departure, this does not satisfy such a sociologically-minded writer as Durkheim. For the sense-impressions of the individual as a *ne plus ultra* of thought, he substitutes the collective representations of society. In harmony with the findings of positivist philosophers he sets a limit to human understanding. The limit, however, is not merely the isolated individual's sense-impressions, but the sense-impressions of the individual as a member of a social group.

As far as the critical question of the existence and knowability of the external natural world is concerned, such a position, superficially agnostic, in fact denies that we can ever obtain such knowledge, since the categories are always interposed between the individual and the postulated reality. A person can know only society, can think only as a member of society. None, then, can assert that the material world exists. The categories themselves are limited by the limited development of society, and of science, which is 'fragmentary and incomplete' and slow to develop. Durkheim does note that ideas 'partially' persist because they are true, i.e. objective: 'we demand credentials of concepts before according [them] our confidence.' Objectivity, in the passage, is not merely impersonality; collective authority is not the criterion of truth. But he avoids the issue of distinguishing between truth as an accurate notion of an external material reality, and truth as collective endorsement, and merely remarks that 'scientifically elaborated and criticized concepts are always in the very slight minority.' This minority of concepts, however, raises problems that Durkheim does not develop. He goes on to emphasise the thinness of the dividing-line between this minority of ideas and those concepts which have only social authority. Science also depends upon opinion, he says, whilst collective representations receive verification in experience. Since the overwhelming weight of emphasis in the book is thrown upon the social nature of the categories, I do not think it is unfair to remark that this all too brief consideration of the distinction between objectivity in the sense of social authority or consensus, and objectivity as correspondence with nature counts for little in the total argument.

There is, indeed, ample confirmation of our analysis from Durkheim himself, for in other places he is more explicit:

> . . . there is one division of nature where the formula of idealism is applicable almost to the let-

ter; this is the social kingdom. Here, more than anywhere else, the idea is the reality, the part of matter is reduced to a minimum.

And there is a less abstract illustration of this viewpoint, when he remarks that totemism is:

> . . . inseparable from a social organisation on a clan basis. Not only is it impossible to define it except in connection with the clan, but it even seems as though the clan could not exist without the totem.'

It is clear that, for Durkheim, correspondences that may prevail between nature and collective representations are largely irrelevant to any consideration of the genesis, character and persistence of the representations.

To what extent does Durkheim's philosophy assist him in undertaking an analysis of totemism?

To answer this, we must examine his views on religion in general as well as his views on this particular religious phenomenon, totemism. If, for Durkheim, collective thought is super-individual, something eminently social, then religion must inevitably be so also. 'Religious representations are collective representations which express collective realities; the rites are a manner of acting which take rise in the midst of the assembled groups and which are destined to excite, maintain or recreate certain mental states in these groups.'

Now Durkheim, aware that totemism is found all over Australia, and having posited religion as a collective social product, needs must find some suitable group which can be linked with totemism throughout the continent. He finds it, of course, in the clan. 'The god of the clan, the totemic principle, can therefore be nothing else than the clan itself, personified and represented to the imagination under the visible form of the animal or vegetable which serves as a totem.' The totemic principle is not merely linked to the clan; it is nothing but the clan itself.

From here, with inexorable logic, he proceeds to derive all religious forces from society. These forces are only 'collective forces hypostatized . . . they are made up of the ideas and sentiments awakened in us by the spectacle of society, and not of sensations coming from the physical world.' The totemic principle itself; totemic objects and the totemic rites; the concept of the soul; of gods, taboos and sacrifice; imitative, representative and piacular rites, and even notions of causality—all are derived from society. There is much brilliant analysis in this part of the work, and Durkheim's control of abundant ethnographic material is masterly. One might draw particular attention to the brief passage in which he points out that the emphasis laid by Spencer and Gillen on 'increase' rites ('Intichiuma') as the mainspring of totemism overlooks the fact that in other social contexts, e.g. initiation, these Intichiuma rites do not have an 'increase' significance. This aspect entirely escaped Frazer's attention; he was preoccupied with the question of totemism as a form of magical control by Man over Nature.

Such a critical instance illustrates the merits and limitations of Durkheim's study of the social origin of totemism, for the rites, he suggests, cannot be derived from Man's attitude towards Nature, if, in the one context, they have an 'increase' function, and in another, are part of initiation *rites de passage*. The rites must therefore relate to some other reality, which is society.

After the spate of subjectivist theories about totemism which were thrown up around the turn of the century, Durkheim's stress on society has considerable value. To take one of the more bizarre notions of the origin of totemism, Wundt suggested [in his *Mythus and Religion*] that this special relationship between man and animal arose from the sight of a corpse in decomposition, since worms which crept out of the body were believed to embody the soul. He presumed that this belief was extended to snakes, and then to other animals.

But we cannot evaluate Durkheim's contribution by examining this part or that part of his work in isolation: we must look at his work as a whole. The stress he lays on society is placed on the morphological structure of society: the clan, phratry and tribe. He conceives of the social group as the key element. In this essentially mechanical picture, there is little attention paid to social *activity,* except where the group meets as a body and performs certain collective ritual actions. The whole field of social action is otherwise ignored. Durkheim's society exists in a virtual vacuum. The significance of a hunting-and-collecting way of life is ignored except to the extent that it brings groups together periodically for *ritual* activities.

Since the clan suits his theoretical scheme most effectively, he finds it necessary to dismiss (in footnotes) the existence of marriage-classes bearing totems as 'very rare,' 'badly established' and 'suspect,' although reported by fieldworkers such as Mathew, Howitt and Daisy Bates. The social importance of the marriage-classes was well-known long before he wrote. Similarly, phratry-totemism receives brief treatment. Radcliffe-Brown has since indicated the varied association of totems with sex, with moiety, phratry, clan, horde, marriage section or subsection, etc., etc., and has demonstrated that totems have more or less social importance from tribe to tribe. Such facts may scarcely be said to invalidate Durkheim's major assertion; they merely shift the social referent from the clan to *various* social groups, as Radcliffe-Brown does: to the section, moiety, and so on.

Yet since Durkheim stresses the coming-together and the collective ritual activity of the social group as the *fons et origo* of collective consciousness, and therefore of totemism, it must be observed that some of these totemic social categories have no corporate life at all, especially, and usually, the marriage-classes.

Applying Durkheim's own method, as illustrated above in the treatment of the Intichiuma rites, it may be observed that a social category of persons may possess a totem, and yet never act in a collective manner at all. The derivation of the totemic principle solely from the collective action of social groups is then inadmissible, though the affiliation of totem to social groups and associations is obviously correct.

But men's common interests as members of groups are not limited to their collective interest in group identity abstracted from the activities of the group. Firth has spoken of culture as the content of social relationships, and it is this content which Durkheim ignores. The ends of group existence, the activities and interests of the members of the groups, are missing from his scheme. The 'social' apart from this content of cultural activities is a label on an empty jar. It is because of this that Durkheim's limitation of the examination of group activities to the analysis of occasions of collective ritual appears so inadequate.

Radcliffe-Brown has raised the question 'Why are plants and animals the object of a ritual attitude?' Durkheim does, in fact, briefly touch upon this question when he remarks that the animal is 'an essential element of the economic environment,' the plant being secondary in a noncultivating society. This is too simple an interpretation of the stress upon animals in Australian society; many plants are totems, just as plants are vital in the economy. In fact, vegetable food provides the bulk of the diet. But meatfoods are the great luxuries, and, moreover, are produced by men, as Durkheim notes, without pointing to the dominant social status of men in aboriginal society.

He also notes the correlation of totemic centres with spots where certain natural species actually abound. Such a cursory treatment of the question—the equivalent of one page out of 447—can hardly be said to deal adequately with this aspect of the question. Elsewhere, his preconceived notion that religious forces 'do not translate the manner in which physical things affect our senses, but the way in which the collective consciousness acts upon individual consciousnesses' leads him to remark that the objective qualities of 'humble vegetables and animals . . . ducks, rabbits, kangaroos . . . surely were not the origin of the religious sentiments they inspired.' Again, the idea of a quasi-divine principle obviously does not arise, he says, 'out of the sensations which the things serving as totems are able to arouse in the mind; we have shown that these things are frequently insignificant.'

To Durkheim, these things were merely convenient symbols, material repositories for spiritual forces. Collective sentiments have to be expressed by 'fixing themselves upon external objects . . . they have acquired a sort of physical nature.' The implication is that almost any external object encountered by a society would serve adequately as a symbol for collective representations.

Durkheim must surely have known that Australian aborigines live by collecting wild plants and hunting wild animals. They have no knowledge of cultivation, keep no flocks, and have limited techniques of food preservation. The procurement of food is thus a primary necessity in their everyday life which keeps them on the move continually as they exhaust the food-supply of one area after another. They have, moreover, a detailed knowledge of the animal and plant resources of each ecological area, and of the seasonal variations of each relevant natural species.

Plants and animals are thus of major importance to every aborigine. For Durkheim, however, these are humble things unlikely to inspire religious sentiments. It appears to me that such a view, contrary to all that is known of the importance of these natural species in the life of the aborigines, must be the product, partly of 'armchair' isolation from the reality of aboriginal society, but also of a preconceived notion that the relationship of Man to the material world is unimportant, or something about which we can say nothing intelligible. In my opinion, it is still profitable to relate religious sentiments to society, but to society in a specific environment, with a particular economy, and not merely to its structural units abstracted from activity.

This general line of criticism was developed by Radcliffe-Brown, though he did not take the analysis to its logical conclusions. The implications become clearer when we turn to the question of classification.

Besides deriving religious representations from the morphological units of society, Durkheim finds that the logical category of class itself is similarly derived. Since aboriginal society is divided into phratries and clans, these serve as a framework for the classification of other things—animals, plants, the heavenly bodies, and so on. The systematic interrelations of these classes again stem from their association with social groups which are themselves associated; the separation of opposites arises from the opposition of social units. There could be no notion of class, nor any system of classification, without social groups integrated into such a system, he suggests.

This neat correlation is exemplified by taking Australian tribes which place markedly contrasting objects as phratry (actually moiety) totems, and which place markedly linked things together in the same clan within a particular phratry. In fact, the whole universe is said to be divided between the phratries and clans of a tribe.

Thus the Mount Gambier tribe (described by Fison and Howitt, and Curr) place the black cockatoo in one moiety, and the white in the other; the summer, sun, wind and autumn in one clan, and the stars, moon, rain, winter, etc. in two other clans of the opposite moiety.

[The] opposition of N.W. and S.E. winds, [totems on Groote Eylandt], seems to bear out the principles Durkheim expounded (though there is in addition, the less important north wind). As Durkheim suggests, there may be an 'obscure psychology which has caused many of these connections and distinctions,' i.e. there are often logical connections that we do not always know of between totems classified together in the aboriginal systems. Such connections are known and can be specifically stated for most of the Groote Eylandt totems.

If we examine the . . . totems, we find that they fall into three groups: those which are either natural species or topographical features of the environment; the wind-totems; and the Ship totem. Under the first heading fall the totemic complexes deriving from myths in which figure Central Hill (Jandarnga), the largest hill on Groote Eylandt, and Malirba Hill, on another island formerly inhabited by this tribe. In the first case, various totems such as Parrot, Stingray, Sawfish, the Jinuma River, the Shark-Ray, Neribuwa and Dumaringenduma are all derived from the main myth of Central Hill. The only connection between these totems is not any objective resemblance, but their occurrence in a myth. In the case of Malirba Hill, the totems

Water, Waterfalls, Water-creatures (such as Snake and Frog) are linked together. This is a connection which occurs not merely in mythology, but in Nature itself.

If we look at the other totems, we find differing reasons for their place in the totemic compendium. Ship is shared by four clans in neighbouring areas. This probably derives from the original route followed by the Indonesian voyagers and traders from whom this totem is derived. Ship has no connection with the various sub-totems in these four clans. The three wind-totems are associated with clans whose territories lie in the appropriate geographical quarters for these winds. Yet the multiplicity of links which may be utilized for allocating totems may be judged from the practice whereby a songman may create a new song about some historical event or innovation of social importance, and this song will thenceforward be assimilated to his clan. Again, if an event occurs in a particular clan-territory, this may well be the nexus that decides the allocation of a totem commemorating that event to a particular clan.

Other totems are borrowed from other tribes through intermarriage, etc., and are adopted by clans as a whole. Such are the totems Dove, Turtle, Goose and Crow—all of mainland origin. The methods of allocating these to different clans again vary.

It would be easy to exaggerate the systematization and orderly arrangement of these totemic compendia. Whilst the allocation of large numbers of natural phenomena to moiety or other divisions is commonly found, and in some tribes much more rigorous and rational divisions of types of trees, animals, etc., such a division is rarely thoroughgoing; it can naturally only embrace a part of the more obvious or important features of the environment, but rarely does one find this kind of attempt at rational classification within a totemic system.

In most systems (and even, outside the limited range of trees or certain kinds of animals, in the Queensland systems Kelly describes), the totemic compendium is often quite partial and fragmentary, and is certainly not constructed on any consistent principle derived from observation of objective natural resemblances of the totemic objects. Many important natural features may thus be missing from the totemic compendium: on Groote Eylandt, for example, the wallaby is only a recent importation as a totem; so also is the dingo, whilst vegetable-foods are almost entirely neglected as totems. Yet all these are important features of the environment. Nor are many modern innovations necessarily included, in spite of their importance, e.g. 'truck' and 'gun.' Each totemic system has its particular characteristics, and a varying range of classification, using various principles for associating the totems. Each is the product of specific historical and local conditions, and in most cases we cannot now discover how these links arose. We do not, then, find abstract and absolute principles used as a rational and consistent basis of classification in totemism, but rather many diverse principles for associating totem with social group applied haphazardly.

When we examine this great proliferation of totems in

some tribes, Durkheim's limitation of the totem to its function as the badge of a social group is plainly inadequate. He notes that writers such as Spencer and Gillen, Howitt and others recorded not merely one totem for each cclan, but large numbers for each clan, generally with one as the principal totem and the others as secondary or subtotems. Carl Strehlow noted 442 totems among the Aranda and Loritja alone. Indeed, it might be noted that far from serving as foci of group identity, some principal totems are shared by several clans on Groote Eylandt; it is the secondary totems which have a diacritical function. At one point, adhering to his standpoint that the totems derive from collective awareness of the morphological structure of society, Durkheim suggests that sub-division of the totemic groups is responsible for this proliferation of totems, elsewhere he suggests that the whole of the natural order is classified within the framework of phratry and clan. In fact, as we have seen for Groote Eylandt, the proliferation of totems may be derived from historical events and changes in social life (e.g. the coming of the Indonesians to Groote Eylandt, mirrored in the Ship totem, and the 1939-1945 War, mirrored in the Catalina-Army-Airbase totem). It may also occur as a result of the creation of myths and songs, from intermarriages with other tribes, and so on. Totemic changes do result from the formation and disappearance of groups, as I have described for Groote Eylandt, but they do not occur solely because of this. The totems always have some social referent, but this is not necessarily the social group; it may equally be some event of general concern to society, such as the opening of the Airbase, or an established institution, such as the custom of cicatrization (a stage in initiation).

The totemic compendium therefore omits some important natural species, as it includes some minor ones; it contains an arbitrary aggregation, and not a rational selection, of objects taken as totems; it is added to by processes of often fortuitous accretion, sometimes through the individual creation of songs. Though there is, of course, a stress in the compendium upon the plants and animals and other features of the environment which are of particular interest to the aborigines, and although only those individually-created songs which relate to phenomena which are of general social concern tend to persist and enter the totemic compendium, nevertheless the compendium is a somewhat wayward collection.

Social groups thus serve as a framework for the classification of totems, but, I would suggest, these groups are not the classification from which the categories of understanding emerge. In order to understand the true origin of the categories, let us look at some other aboriginal systems of classification.

The WaniNdiljaugwa divide food into animal and vegetable, though they have no generic term for 'food.' Vegetable food is *anunga* (or *enungwijegba*, or *amuraja* from *-muraja:* to be hungry). *Angwindjadja* describes the meat of land-animals, including flesh from fish caught in inland waters. *Augwalja* basically means fish, but so important is fish and marine flesh-food in the whole economy that *augwalja* is extended to cover any animal flesh, whether it be shark, goat, wallaby, goanna, or fish itself. The terms thus refer

primarily to rough-and-ready natural classifications; although social considerations govern the extension of the term *augwalja* to meat in general, there is no connection between this classification and the units of the social structure. This classification is a very limited one, however, when we compare it with that of the Wik-Monkan tribe of Cape York Peninsula.

Here plant and vegetable foods are *maiyi,* and all animal foods *minya.* Food in general is *maiyi* (the bulk of aboriginal diet is vegetable). The Wik-Monkan further 'prefix the specific name of every plant, or food derived from it, with the term *mai'*, and every animal, as well as flesh or animal food, with the term *min,* which is repeated in each case, before the actual name,' e.g. *mai' wu'umba:* arrowroot; *mai' erk:* water lily, etc. Similarly, *yukk* is the generic prefix for trees and wooden things; *koi* for strings; *wäkk* for grasses; *kek* for spears. These classifications are plainly independent of social units. But they are conditioned by social interests. Thus although 'bird' in general is *päntj,* and 'fish' in general is *nga'a,* since these are animal *foods* the names of specific birds and fish are prefixed by *min* (animal food), and not by *päntj* or *nga'a.* The social element here is not related in any way to the formal structure of society, but rather to the interests of society which arise from society's productive activity. The Wik-Monkan further classify the country, with precision, into ecological association-zones [according to Donald F. Thomson in his "Names and Naming in the Wik-Monkan Tribe," *Journal of the Royal Anthropological Institute* LXXVI, 1946].

It would be a work of supererogation to examine further aboriginal systems of classification. Enough has been said to reveal that the morphology of society is not the only model or framework for the categories of understanding.

The classifications I have just described are simple scientific classifications which are not completely objective in that they associate various phenomena in accordance with the use men make of them, whether as food, as materials for various productive activities, etc. But they are not entirely based on subjective interest: there is at least a partial approach to an objective classification based on careful observation of nature. Grasses are classed together, animals distinguished from vegetables, and so on. It has been well remarked that most of the basic research into the plant and animal species on which even our modern civilization depends was carried out by men in primitive societies. The experience of hundreds of years of study and field-research, observation and experiment which hunters and collectors have carried out in the course of their everyday task of getting a living has been the basis also of improved and more accurate modes of classification . . . As Thomson remarks, these classifications 'bear some resemblance to a simple Linnaean classification.' It is plainly from this sort of classification that our more precise systematization has arisen.

This is not true of totemic classification. Firstly, the aborigine does not attempt, in his totemic compendium, to follow any rational principle or principles consistently (though he may do so partially), on the basis of accurate observation of nature. It is true that the selection of totems is not arbitrary in so far as the animal and plant species which constitute the great majority of totems are not merely convenient receptacles for the totemic principle derived from society, but are of prime interest to the aborigine who cannot live without them. Food and the getting of food are constant themes of ordinary conversation.

The aborigine's interest in his environment is selective not only insofar as he adopts particular species as his totems; it is also selective in that he reveals a special interest in topography and locality, in the winds, and so on. I have shown elsewhere that major topographical features of Groote Eylandt, especially the well-watered regions, are themselves totems. The link between totem-centres and areas in which the totemic animal or plant abounds is well-known from the classifical literature, although it is not invariably found. But one should not overweigh the elements of rational systematization in any totemic compendium.

The universality and necessity of the categories, then, is not merely a projection of the social units of society. These features arise from common, but not necessarily collective, experience of the external natural order, and also from the selective social interest of men in certain aspects of the natural order. And, it may be noted, the productive activities of the aborigines are more often conducted individually or in small groups, not in collectivities.

There are thus two different kinds of classification. The first, which is proto-scientific, emerges from the common experience of men in social groups who formulate a primitive system of classification of nature on the basis of their interaction with the environment. The implications of this in relation to Durkheim's theory have already been indicated by other writers, notably Benoit-Smullyan, who writes:

> If primitive man could always classify his food-stuffs . . then the logical powers of classification were already his, anterior to, and independent of the classificatory powers derived from the structure of the group . . .

I hope that I have demonstrated this more abstract criticism in detailed specific analysis.

Whereas the proto-scientific type of classification relies on a rational, ordered, consistent and systematic approach, with objective analysis of natural phenomena, the type of classification which we find in totemism is of quite another kind. Though it does not exclude rational thought, it is marked by agglomerative, arbitrary and fortuitous accretions, which are often individual and subjective in their provenance. Far from assisting the development of the categories of human understanding, the totemic mode of classification would encourage free association and not logical thought. Scientific modes of thought, therefore, have not emerged as a result of the development of such primitive religious philosophies as totemism, *but in spite of them.* We cannot, then, accept the commonly-expressed view of religion as 'primitive science.'

Durkheim's work on religion was a great advance on the subjectivist writers precisely because of his focus upon the social nature of religion. But religion is also concerned with the specific content of social relations, with human culture, and not merely with generalized 'social existence.' If, then, Durkheim had not been impeded by his general philosophy from examining the question of the relationship of Man to Nature more objectively, he must needs have concluded that the categories are formed, not out of experience of the collective ritual activity, but out of the experience and wants of men living in groups and wresting their livelihood from nature.

P. M. Worsley, "Émile Durkheim's Theory of Knowledge," in Sociological Review, *n.s. Vol. 4, No. 1, July, 1956, pp. 47-62.*

Leo F. Schnore   (essay date 1958)

[*Schnore is an American sociologist and educator who specializes in the sociology of urban life. In the following essay, he identifies three dominant themes in Durkheim's work, explicates his theories, and faults earlier critics for misrepresenting his methods and conclusions.*]

Émile Durkheim, of course, was not himself a human ecologist. The ecological viewpoint did not develop within sociology until near the end of Durkheim's life, and then in America. There is no evidence that this new approach to social phenomena exerted any profound influence upon his thought, despite the fact that he regarded "social morphology" as one of the major branches of sociology. In Durkheim's scheme, this field was to be devoted to two major inquiries: (1) the study of the environmental basis of social organization and (2) the study of population phenomena, especially size, density, and spatial distribution. These areas of interest obviously converge with those of human ecology as it was originally formulated.

This paper consists of an exegesis and a critique of one of his major theoretical contributions and a consideration of the broad implications of his "morphological" analysis for contemporary human ecology. It is concerned, for the most part, with Durkheim's doctoral dissertation, *De la division du travail social: étude sur l'organisation des sociétés supérieures,* first published in 1893. More particularly, the discussion is largely limited to Book II, where he dealt with the "causes" of division of labor and where the morphological approach was most explicitly used. The brief exegesis is based on a selective restructuring of his main argument, which is unfortunately scattered through many pages. We trust that taking up the crucial elements in his thought in somewhat different order does no violence to the essential logic of his position. This procedure has been adopted in order to point up the contrasts between his morphological theory of differentiation and the alternative explanations that were available at the time that he wrote.

First, it must be emphasized that Durkheim's intention in Book II of *Division* was to account for differentiation and its obvious increase in Western societies. The very subtitle is the key: "A Study of the Organization of Advanced Societies." Second, it is necessary to preserve the historical context of his work. The division of labor had long interested social philosophers, especially in the West. As early as 1776, Adam Smith had pointed to division as the main source of "the wealth of nations," and the concept itself can be traced at least to the Greeks. Unfortunately, these earlier writers gave scant attention to the determinants of differentiation, contenting themselves with analyses of its nature and its implications for economic efficiency and productivity.

In the latter half of the nineteenth century, however, increasing effort was given to explaining the process, with special reference to the "advanced" societies of the time. By the time that Durkheim began his work, however, the dominant views in intellectual circles were still a peculiar admixture of utilitarian and evolutionary "explanations," both best represented in the works of Herbert Spencer. In large part, Durkheim's analysis must be seen as a reaction against the Spencerian view.

Durkheim's own analysis actually began in Book I, with a distinction between two forms of organization somewhat similar to the types sketched by Maine and Tönnies [in *Gemeinschaft und Gesellschaft,* 1887, translated in 1940 as *Fundamental concepts of Sociology* by Charles Loomis and *Über Soziale Differenzierung,* 1890, respectively]. The first type ("mechanical") was used by Durkheim to describe the relatively undifferentiated or "segmented" mode of organization characteristic of small and isolated aggregates, in which little control has been achieved over the local environment. The basis of social unity is likeness or similarity. There is minimal differentiation, chiefly along age and sex lines, and most members are engaged most of the time in the same activity—collecting, hunting, fishing, herding, or subsistence agriculture. The "social segments" of the community (families and kinship units) are held together by what they have in common, and they derive mutual support from their very likeness. Unity is that of simple "mechanical" cohesion, as in rock forms, and homogeneity prevails.

Durkheim was fully aware that structural differentiation is a variable characteristic of aggregates, for he recognized another and fundamentally different mode of organization. He saw that modern Western society was based increasingly upon differentiation, and his concept of the "organic" type of organization was designed to describe the complex and highly differentiated structural arrangements of his own time. According to Durkheim, a complex and heterogeneous society, like all but the most rudimentary organisms, is based on an intricate interdependence of specialized parts. Labor is divided; all men do not engage in the same activities, but they produce and exchange different goods and services. Moreover, not only are individuals and groups differentiated with respect to functions, but whole communities and nations also engage in specialized activities. In short, there has been a breakdown of internal "segmentation" *within* communities and societies and a reduction of isolation *between* them, although mechanical solidarity never completely disappears.

With this distinction between major types of organization in mind, Durkheim's task in Book II was to explain the conditions under which "mechanical" organization is superseded by the "organic" form. According to the mode of analysis that prevailed at the time that he wrote, Durkheim viewed this change in social organization as comprising a kind of "evolutionary" sequence, and much of his theory was cast in these terms. However, it would be extremely misleading to portray his work as that of an uncritical evolutionist, for Durkheim possessed a sensitive, critical mind and he considered and rejected a number of alternative hypotheses that had been widely accepted as explanations of increasing differentiation.

With respect to the popular utilitarian version, Durkheim vigorously attacked the idea that differentiation was somehow the product of man's rational desire to increase his own happiness. In fact, he rejected all individualistic interpretations. The notion that social structure is merely the product of the motivated actions of individuals was apparently almost repugnant to him. It ran directly counter to his conception of society as an entity *sui generis,* and it obviously violated his most famous principle [Stated in ***The Rules of Sociological Method,*** 1895]: that "the determining cause of a social fact should be sought among the social facts preceding it and not among the states of the individual consciousness."

Durkheim then turned his attention to the evolutionary portion of the Spencerian argument. The organismic analogy, of course, was in vogue at the time, and Spencer had used it brilliantly. As to the division of labor in society, Spencer had held [in *Principles of Sociology,* 1876] that

> along with increase of size in societies goes increase of structure. . . . It is also a characteristic of social bodies, as of living bodies, that while they increase in size they increase in structure. . . . The social aggregate, homogeneous when minute, habitually gains in heterogeneity along with each increment of growth; and to reach great size must acquire great complexity.

In other words, Spencer's theory of differentiation—despite its cosmic overtones and utilitarian underpinnings—reduced to an explanation based on sheer population size. At the very least he pointed to a universal association between size and differentiation.

Durkheim recognized the potential role of population increase in bringing about further differentiation. Along with Adam Smith, he was aware of the permissive effect of sheer size. Large aggregates allow greater differentiation to emerge, but Durkheim concluded that the population-size factor was a necessary, but not a sufficient, cause. His reasons for this conclusion are particularly instructive. In contrast to Spencer, who exemplified the deductive method of proceeding from first principles, Durkheim was very much the inductive analyst. In fact, he showed the underlying weakness of Spencer's theory by pointing to "deviant cases." Concretely, he called attention to large, densely settled areas in China and Russia clearly characterized, not by extreme differentiation (organic solidarity), but by homogeneity (mechanical solidarity).

Having thus rejected the Spencerian argument on empirical grounds, Durkheim tried to explain the absence of any marked differentiation in these places in the face of great size and density. It is at this point that Durkheim introduced a series of essentially sociological concepts, the first of which must be seen as an "intervening variable." First, he noted that social segmentation had not broken down (i.e., that there was minimal contact between the constituent parts of Chinese and Russian society). In the face of limited contact, these parts remained homogeneous, very much like each other with respect to structure and functions, representing a proliferation of essentially similar village units. Durkheim asserted that this "segmentation" disappears and that division increases only with an increase in "moral" or "dynamic density." In contrast to physical density—the number of people per unit of space—"dynamic density" refers to the density of social intercourse or contact or, more simply, to the rate of interaction—the number of interactions per unit of time. Until this rate of interaction reaches a high (although unspecified) level, the constituent social segments or parts remain essentially alike. According to Durkheim: "The division of labor develops . . . as there are more individuals sufficiently in contact to be able to act and react upon one another. If we agree to call this relation and the active commerce resulting from it dynamic or moral density, we can say that the progress of the division of labor is in direct ratio to the moral or dynamic density of society." In other words, differentiation tends to increase as the rate of social interaction increases.

Durkheim then asked the next logical question: Under what conditions does this rate of interaction increase? In answer, he first observed that dynamic density "can only produce its effect if the real distance between individuals has itself diminished in some way." He then pointed to two general ways in which this might come about: (1) by the concentration of population, especially in cities, i.e., via increases in *physical density;* (2) by the development of more rapid and numerous means of transportation and communication. These innovations, "by suppressing or diminishing the gaps separating social segments . . . increase the [dynamic] density of society."

Thus, to demographic factors (essentially the Spencerian explanation), Durkheim added a technological emphasis. An increase in population size and density *plus* more rapid transportation and communication bring about a higher rate of interaction. However, the crucial questions still remain: what brings about differentiation? Why should a simple increase in the rate of interaction produce greater division of labor? If social units (whether individuals or collectivities) are brought into more frequent contact, why should they be obliged to specialize and divide their labor? A simple identification of "factors" obviously was not enough; Durkheim was also compelled to indicate the mechanism that would produce further differentiation under the prescribed circumstances. As it turns out, he had in mind a particular type of interaction, viz., competition.

It is in his identification of competition as the vital mechanism that Durkheim borrowed most heavily upon Darwinian thought, and it is this part of his theory that has been most widely distorted. Durkheim's argument was based on Darwin's observation that, in a situation of scarcity, increased contact between like units sharing a common territory leads to increased competition. Being alike, they make similar demands on the environment. Inspired by the Malthusian account of population pressure on limited resources, Darwin had been led to stress the resultant "struggle for existence" as the essential condition underlying the differentiation of species. In the human realm, Durkheim reasoned in turn, individuals or aggregates offering the same array of goods or services are potential, if not active, competitors. Thus, according to Durkheim,

> If work becomes divided more as societies become more voluminous [i.e., larger in size] and denser, it is not because external circumstances are more varied, but because struggle for existence is more acute. Darwin justly observed that the struggle between two organisms is as active as they are analogous. . . . Men submit to the same law. In the same city, different occupations can co-exist without being mutually obliged to destroy each other, for they pursue different objects. . . . The division of labor is, then, a result of the struggle for existence, but it is a mellowed dénouement. Thanks to it, opponents are not obliged to fight to a finish, but can exist one beside the other. Also, in proportion to its development, it furnishes the means of maintenance and survival to a greater number of individuals who, in more homogeneous societies, would be condemned to extinction.

The division of labor is thus seen by Durkheim as essentially a mode of resolving competition and as an alternative both to Darwinian "natural selection" and to Malthusian "checks."

One might conclude from the foregoing that Durkheim merely substituted one variety of evolutionism for another, by pointing to a Darwinian struggle for existence between competitors as the mainspring of differentiation, rather than Spencerian cosmic forces leading inexorably to increased division. Indeed, the common interpretation of *Division* has been along these lines. Consider, for example, Benoit-Smullyan's remarks [from "The Sociologism of Emile Durkheim and His School," *An Introduction to the History of Sociology,* Harry Elmer Barnes (ed.), 1948]:

> Having disposed of the psychologistic and individualistic explanations of the division of labor, Durkheim now turns to his own morphological explanation. . . . Division of labor is due to changes in social structure arising out of an increase in material and moral density. The increase in population intensifies competition and thus forces individuals to specialize, in order to survive. Thus Durkheim, rather reluctantly, comes to rest his entire explanation upon the factor of an assumed natural increase in population. This is obviously a biologistic rather than a sociologistic type of explanation.

On the contrary, Durkheim tried to spell out the conditions under which one variety of "social evolution" would occur, by pointing to the factors underlying increased structural complexity. Far from assuming natural increase and then using population growth as the explanation (à la Spencer), Durkheim clearly asserted that differentiation will accompany growth only if interaction increases concomitantly; moreover, he suggested that this intensification of interaction ordinarily occurs as a result of technological changes that facilitate contact, exchange and communication. Thus Durkheim rejected a single-factor explanation—whether it be the individual's desire for happiness, cosmic evolutionary force, or population size—and proceeded to construct a multiple-factor theory.

But what of the charge that Durkheim disobeyed his own rules and thus became guilty of "biological reductionism"? This question can be answered best by recalling the explanatory concepts that he employed (i.e., dynamic density and competition). Both refer to interaction and can hardly be called intrinsically biological constructs without stretching the meaning of "biological" to the point where it loses all discriminatory value. If anything, these are clearly sociological concepts. Moreover, Durkheim's technological emphasis—his stress upon the role of improvements in transportation and communication—cannot properly be called "biological" reasoning.

As to the dependence of the theory upon an assumed natural increase, Durkheim's critics have again fallen into error. An increase in effective population size can obviously occur in several ways, of which natural increase is only one. Following out the implications of Durkheim's thought, it is readily apparent that improvements in transportation and communication can bring into sustained contact previously separate areas and populations. Historically, such "growth by merger" has frequently involved political merger, whether by violent subjugation or peaceful assimilation, and often has witnessed an extension of the area of regular economic exchange. These political and economic changes can be subsumed under the "biological" rubric only with difficulty, if at all.

Although Merton is also inclined to view parts of Durkheim's explanation as biological, he has pinpointed the truly sociological character of Durkheim's analysis in the following passage [from "Durkheim's Division of Labor in Society," *American Journal of Sociology* XL, 1934]:

> It is true that he finds the "determining cause" of increased division of labor in the growth and heightened density of populations, which is primarily a biological factor, but it is only in so far as this demographic change is associated with increased social interaction and its concomitant, enhanced competition, that the stipulated change will occur. *It is this social factor-the "dynamic density" as he terms it—which Durkheim finds actually determinant.* . . . To the extent that this differentiation is generalizable as a social process it may be said to be associated with competition between individuals and between groups, whatever the factors leading to such competition.

Even Durkheim's "evolutionism" is not really biological in orientation. Although he did use the language of evolutionary thought, he clearly rejected most of the prevailing evolutionist views on the nature of social change. There is no idea here of unilinear, irreversible development in a fixed sequence of stages, no suggestion of "progress" as a necessary consequence of greater complexity, no hint of blind cosmic forces animating the whole process, as in Spencer's thought. Durkheim simply attempted to specify the social conditions under which a particular change in

social organization tends to occur. In addition, he attempted to identify the general mechanism by which like units become unlike, through the resolution of competition. Unfortunately, the process is not described in any detail. Presumably the unsuccessful competitors (individuals, groups, or territorial aggregates) take up new functions and somehow become integrated in a more inclusive and complex system.

At any rate, it should be evident by this point that most criticisms of Durkheim's theory of differentiation have been misplaced. As they have been stated, they might better be aimed at Spencer—the theorist against whom Durkheim was contending throughout his entire analysis. The unfortunate effect of these errors of interpretation is plain: to the extent that these secondary sources are read in place of the original work, a whole generation of American sociologists has been given an essentially incorrect image of one of Durkheim's most important theoretical contributions. American sociology is probably the poorer for it. Durkheim clearly viewed "the origin of social species" as the product of social and not biological forces. If his analysis were not so clear on this issue, the apparent unanimity of his critics would be more compelling.

To say that most of the prevailing criticisms of Durkheim's theory are themselves unsound, however, is not to say that the theory is entirely satisfactory as it was originally stated. The major difficulty stems from his treatment of competition. In view of the great importance that he attached to it, his discussion is surprisingly brief. If differentiation is the resolution of competition that does occur and if a more complex organizational pattern does emerge to integrate the new specialties, it may be correct to view these developments as due to increases in effective size and improvements in the facilities for movement. However, a number of writers have suggested that differentiation is not the only resolution of competition.

"Competition" occurs whenever the number of individuals or units with similar demands exceeds the supply, whether it be food, raw materials, markets, or occupational positions. As Durkheim suggested, differentiation represents a less harsh resolution of competition than that stressed by Darwin and Malthus. But in the case of human populations, the competition resulting from an increase in demand (population) theoretically can be resolved in a number of ways. Among them are the following:

Demographic changes.—(1) As Durkheim recognized, following Darwin and Malthus, an increase in the death rate can bring population into line with resources. (2) Similarly, a decrease in the birth rate can have the same effect, although not so immediately. (3) Migration may remove excess numbers at least temporarily and thus reduce demand.

Technological changes.—A number of possible developments may redefine and expand the effective environment, thus altering the supply. (4) Previously unused local resources may be brought into use via technological innovation or diffusion; the result is a more intensive use of environmental elements already present but unexploited. (5) Technological changes in transportation and communication, whether indigenous or borrowed, can make new areas and new resources available; such changes may also improve the internal distribution of commodities. (6) The substitution of mechanical for human energy may increase production and release manpower for other pursuits, including new occupations; thus the shift in the energy base of modern societies can be viewed as a process of displacement of the affected sectors of the population.

Organizational changes.—As noted above, previously isolated areas, resources, and peoples can be absorbed by conquest or assimilation. However, internal reorganization of a given population can also result in supporting increased numbers. (7) "Revolutionary" changes may occur; the surplus formerly held by the few may be distributed among the many, and increased numbers can be supported, with perhaps an even higher average level of living. (8) The converse can also occur; for a variety of specific reasons, the average level of living may be lowered, permitting a given area and its resources to support even greater numbers. (9) Finally, as Durkheim suggested, occupational and territorial differentiation may occur.

This list of "alternatives" is probably not exhaustive, but it suggests that further differentiation is only one of a number of ways to resolve competition. It is also clear that these alternatives are not mutually exclusive, for a number of them have occurred simultaneously in the Western world. This observation suggests that the changes that have occurred are concomitants of differentiation itself. Indeed, closer analysis reveals that each of these "alternatives" involves either (1) elimination of excess numbers, (2) expansion of the resource base, or (3) functional differentiation, or some combination of these changes.

In view of the importance that Durkheim attached to competition, however, it is unfortunate that he did not present a more explicit and systematic treatment of its resolution. He was inclined to invoke competition and to let it go at that. In passing, he remarked that "Spencer ably explains in what manner evolution will be produced, if it does take place, but he does not tell us the source producing it." Durkheim, on the other hand, pointed to the sources of differentiation but offered little in the way of a detailed account of the manner in which it is produced. In fairness, of course, it must be said that such a statement has yet to appear.

A more serious weakness in Durkheim's theory is the inadequate attention accorded the physical environment. He apparently was reluctant to give such factors as climate and topography any major role in his analysis. In part, this probably is due to the restrictive character of his own rules, adherence to which obliged him to seek the explanation of social facts in other social facts. He tended to dismiss the physical environment as a relevant variable and to regard the "social environment" as the ultimate source of differentiation. But this procedure has its own blind alleys; for one thing, the analyst does not get "outside the system" in his search for relevant variables.

To accept Durkheim's view of the limited role of environmental variability is to ignore two key considerations, the first of which is implicit in his own thought. (1) As suggested above, the effective environment can be altered by technological and organizational changes. These changes redefine the environment by bringing new resources into use—local resources already "there" but unexploited or resources found at sites that were previously inaccessible because of limited transportation facilities and exchange mechanisms. Although the initial impetus may not be the environment itself, it may become an important condition with respect to further organizational change. (2) Environmental variability must be viewed in static as well as dynamic terms. The plain fact of the matter is that the physical environment confronting mankind is almost infinitely variable, in the sense that there are enormous geographical differences from place to place. Some of these differences may favor organizational change. Long before Durkheim's time, Adam Smith perceived the significance of this factor, pointing to the greater likelihood of differentiated units appearing at the water's edge. Since Durkheim wrote, the role of a favorable geographic position has been stressed frequently in discussions of the sites of early civilizations and of the deep-water orientation of most great cities throughout history. This emphasis also appears in [Charles Horton] Cooley's famous "break-in-transportation" theory [in his "Theory of Transportation," *Publications of the American Economic Association,* 1984], and it can be easily merged with Durkheim's own views on the crucial role of transportation and communication technology.

Nonetheless, Durkheim's own theory clearly minimizes the potential relevance for organization of variations in physical environment. The corrective probably lies in adopting the modern geographer's concept of the environment as a vital premissive factor with respect to human activities. This approach is best summed up in the view known as *possibilisme,* wherein the environment is viewed as a set of limiting conditions, which may be narrow or broad, depending upon the technological devices and modes of organization that prevail in a given population.

Despite these minor shortcomings, Durkheim provided a highly useful framework for the analysis of social structure and particularly for the examination of changes in structure. From the ecological standpoint, *Division*'s major contribution is its stress upon the significance of technological advances for the development of a more elaborate division of labor. As Durkheim correctly pointed out, the efficiency of transportation and communication affects the degree to which spatially separate and functionally dissimilar activities may be interrelated. This is especially evident in the case of territorial differentiation, in which whole areas are devoted to specialized functions. Such a development clearly depends upon the loss of isolation and the establishment and maintenance of sustained contact.

Division provides, though only in outline, a framework for studying one of the most salient aspects of social organization, viz., the degree of structural differentiation. It can be applied to static, cross-sectional analysis as well as to dynamic, longitudinal study. Although it stands in need of certain modifications, his morphological theory seems particularly useful in approaching the problem of structural differentiation within and between areally based aggregates, i.e., communities. It is to this contention that the following section is addressed.

The very first point to be made is that ecologists concern themselves with precisely the same problem as that attacked by Durkheim in Book II of *Division.* Just as he tried to explain one aspect of structure, contemporary ecologists attempt to identify the factors determining variations in structure. [Amos H.] Hawley, for example, defines human ecology as the study of the form and development of the community. At one point [in *Human Ecology: A Theory of Community Structure,* 1950], he adopts Durkheim's exact phraseology and describes the ecologist's objective as the elucidation of "the morphology of collective life in both its static and its dynamic aspects." Although he represents a more traditional ecological viewpoint, [James A. Quinn in his *Human Ecology,* 1950] also declares that the logic of ecological inquiry points to the study of "the occupational pyramid" as essential subject matter, despite the unfortunate preoccupation of some ecologists with spatial distributions. Thus modern human ecology deals with the Durkheimian problem of "morphology" and takes the same dependent variable (structure) as its *explanadum.* This is despite the fact that ecologists of Hawley's persuasion frequently limit themselves to discussing community structure, avoiding Durkheim's broader concern with society.

Second, once the environment is brought into the picture, modern ecology can be regarded as working with essentially the same array of *independent* variables—most broadly, population, technology, and the environment. Building on Hawley's theory, [Otis Dudley Duncan in his "Human Ecology and Population Studies," in *The Study of Population,* Duncan and M. Hauser, 1959] has labeled the resulting scheme "the ecological complex." Although it tends to be implicit rather than explicit, Hawley's own effort seems to consist of treating community structure as the product of the interaction of these broad factors. The structure of a given community is viewed as a collective adaptation on the part of a population to its total environment (including other organized populations, as well as physical features), an adaptation that is strongly modified by the technological equipment in use and by certain "purely" demographic attributes of the population itself, notably its size, rate of growth, and biological (age-sex) composition.

Thus the general relevance of Durkheim's thought to modern ecology is clear. He worked with essentially the same broad factors, taking one of them (structure) as his dependent variable. Moreover, his general mode of analysis is highly similar to that employed in current ecological theory. This becomes particularly apparent when one considers Hawley's treatment of differentiation [in *Human Ecology*], which clearly follows Durkheim in its major outlines. Moreover, there are obvious formal parallels between Durkheim's *mechanical-organic* typology and the concepts of *commensalism* and *symbiosis, categoric* and *corporate groups,* and *independent* and *dependent communities* in Hawley's work. Both writers point to (*a*) two modes of relationship, or forms of interaction, between like and unlike unit parts and to (*b*) two major forms of organization, depending upon which type of relationship is most prominent. Also deserving stress here is their common search for the factors that explain the progressive breakdown of isolation, the welding-together of larger and more inclusive functional units, and the emergence of a more complex structure.

An even more recent variety of ecological thought—Julian Steward's "cultural ecology"—is amenable to interpretation along the lines suggested here. In other words, the "ecological complex" appears to be in use throughout much of Steward's work, despite the fact that he does not consciously focus upon organization as the *explanandum,* preferring to work with "culture," a much broader dependent variable, and despite the fact that he gives a much larger role [in his *Theory of Culture Change,* 1955] to the physical environment than either Durkheim or Hawley. Durkheim's influence on Steward is apparently more indirect, via Durkheim's contribution to the development of "functional anthropology."

But we need not confine ourselves to the most recent statements of the ecological position to see the relevance of Durkheim's thought. A Durkheimian approach has informed human ecology since its inception. In one of his most influential essays—"The Urban Community as a Spatial Pattern and a Moral Order"—Robert E. Park ["The Concept of Position in Society," in *Human Communities: The City and Human Ecology,* 1952] identified the subject matter of human ecology as "what Durkheim and his school call the morphological aspect of society." It has probably also occurred to the reader that the use of the concept of competition in Durkheim's work is highly similar to Park's. To quote Park: "Competition determines the distribution of population territorially and vocationally. The division of labor and all the vast organized economic interdependence of individuals and groups of individuals characteristic of modern life are a product of competition." Thus both Durkheim and Park saw structure as ultimately emerging out of competition in a context of scarcity, although Park was no more helpful than Durkheim in providing a detailed account of the process as a whole.

In addition, it should be pointed out that Durkheim anticipated much of [R. D.] McKenzie's theoretical work, especially the latter's treatment of the rise of "metropolitan" communities. In Durkheim's analysis, we have seen that great stress is given to advances in transportation and communication technology, which lessen isolation and break down "social segmentation." McKenzie showed that this theory can be readily given an areal referent, since formerly isolated and territorially distinct populations are frequently brought into more intimate contact by virtue of improvements in transportation and communication. McKenzie saw the key feature of metropolitan development as the emergence of an intricate territorial division of labor between communities that were formerly almost self-sufficient, and he viewed the whole process as mainly due to technological improvements. In fact [in *The Metropolitan Community,* 1954], McKenzie went so far as to characterize the metropolitan community as "the child of modern facilities for transportation and communication."

Although Durkheim's analysis was largely at the societal level and dealt mainly with occupational differentiation, McKenzie used an essentially similar model in treating communities and regions, analyzing the problem of territorial differentiation. The process of differentiation is presumably the same in each case. Units that are brought into contact via technological improvements become competitors; such units necessarily compete to the extent that they offer the same goods and services to the same population. In the communal or regional context, the resolution of this competitive situation is frequently effected by territorial differentiation. Certain areal units, including whole communities, then give up certain functions and turn to new specialties. A case in point is the historical "flight" of certain specialties, particularly infrequently purchased goods and services, from nearby smaller cities to the metropolis, following the development of the automobile. In the process, formerly semi-independent centers, which once offered a rather full range of services, came to take up more narrowly specialized roles in a larger and more complex division of labor—the metropolitan community as a whole.

At any rate, whether we examine earlier or more recent versions of human ecology, Durkheim's stamp is clearly imprinted. In order to provide maximum utility in ecological analysis, Durkheim's theory needs certain modifications, particularly along the lines of bringing the environment into the schema as a factor worthy of recognition. As a result of its conceptual heritage from biology, human ecology has a rather full appreciation of the role of the physical environment as it affects social structure. This is not to say, however, that the ecologist is an environmental determinist; rather, he points to the relevance of the environment as it is modified and redefined by the organized use of technology. To paraphrase a recent compendium of valuable ecological data [entitled *Man's Role in Changing the Face of the Earth,* edited by William L. Thomas, 1956], man has a key role in changing the face of the earth. Although the human ecologist's initial concern may be with the interaction between "man and his total environment," as a sociologist he inevitably turns to a study of the organized relations between man and man in the environmental setting, i.e., to morphological considerations. As Park said [in *Human Communities*] for ecology, it is "not man's relation to the earth which he inhabits, but his relations to other men, that concerns us most." And in following out the interaction of a given aggregate with other organized populations, the ecologist necessarily concerns himself with what Durkheim called "the social environment."

The only American sociologists to make any intensive use of Durkheim's earliest and most ambitious work are those who have adopted the ecological perspective. Very little attention has been given to Durkheim's "social morphology," and his theory of differentiation has been widely misunderstood. Most American writers who have discussed *Division* have drawn upon Book I, where Durkheim treated the effects of division with his customary insight. His later works, especially those dealing with suicide and reli-

gion, have been much more influential in this country. In these later studies Durkheim was more frequently dealing with individual behavior, especially as it is "normatively defined" and modified by group ties.

This selective emphasis by American writers is probably related to the main drift of American sociology in this century (i.e., toward increasing concern with social-psychological considerations). Instead of taking social structure as the phenomenon to be explained—the dependent variable—most American sociologists habitually deal with social structure as an independent variable with respect to individual behavior. More particularly, structure is usually treated as it is perceived by the individual.

Now it must be made very clear that this procedure is an entirely legitimate enterprise; the variables with which one works and their analytical status depend upon the problem to be investigated. Moreover, this approach has vastly illuminated the human situation. Since the individual is somehow regarded as a less abstract unit than the organized aggregate and as a more interesting subject for study, social psychology has grown rapidly and has made giant strides toward acceptance in the scientific community. Witness the present status of "behavioral science." For all its past progress and future promise, however, the social-psychological sector of sociology still deals with some of the consequences of structural arrangements, leaving the determinants of structure to someone else.

In the light of these considerations, Durkheim's conception of *collective representations*—"shared norms and values" in the contemporary lexicon—provides an interesting sidelight on the position of social psychology within sociology. Durkheim regarded these social phenomena as mere "emanations" of underlying social morphology or structure. If one accepts this position, then he holds that the social psychologist be concerned with little more than the derivative manifestations or passive reflections of underlying structural arrangements. Such a view clearly poses the analysis of structure itself as a logically prior problem. However, if current sociological output is any measure, few of us are inclined to grant any kind of priority to a morphological approach.

It is true that Durkheim himself turned more and more to the analysis of individual behavior in his later years, but he rarely departed from his original position regarding the undesirability of attempting to explain "social facts" by reference to individual characteristics. This is in dramatic contrast to the direction taken in American sociology: toward the view that has been labeled "voluntaristic nominalism." As the most significant characteristic of American sociology, our fundamental postulates have recently been identified as follows:

> The feeling, knowing, and willing of individuals—though limited by cultural prescriptions and social controls—are taken to be the ultimate source of human interaction, social structure, and social change. . . . Social behavior is interpreted voluntaristically. Social structures are real only as they are products of individuals in interaction. [Roscoe C. Hinkle, Jr., and Gisela

J. Hinkle, *The Development of Modern Sociology,* 1954]

One must be impressed by the fact that so many American theorists now acknowledge a heavy indebtedness to Durkheim. If this voluntaristic position is actually dominant, however, we have only succeeded in turning Durkheim upside down.

Be that as it may, Durkheim's conception of "social morphology" suggests that one of the most promising areas of structural analysis lies in the development of a general taxonomy of aggregates and collectivities. Few sociologists seem to have addressed themselves to this task in recent years. To the extent that "types of society" are used today, they represent minor variants of the dichotomies presented long ago by Tönnies, Durkheim, and other writers of the nineteenth century. More important, most of the refinements and reformulations of these typologies in recent years have been left to writers like [Robert] Redfield and Steward. In other words, a genuinely sociological tradition is being kept alive by the efforts of anthropologists.

With respect to "types of community," the initiative has been taken by economists and geographers, despite the fact that many areas of current sociological interest absolutely require close attention to the community context. To choose only the most obvious example, community studies of stratification would probably be enormously improved if the over-all structure and functions of the selected research sites were indicated with some precision according to their taxonomic types. For one thing, the over-generalizations that seem to emerge from many such studies might be far less frequent. It is probably unfortunate that the few sociologists currently attempting to develop a systematic taxonomy of communities appear to be those who employ an ecological framework.

As for types of groups within communities and societies, we have not advanced very far beyond the rather rudimentary notions of "in-" and "out-groups" and "primary" versus "secondary" groups. Both of these dichotomies, of course, tend to be employed within a social-psychological context. The only notable recent addition to this limited array of group types is the notion of "membership" versus "reference" groups. However, the latter turn out not to be groups at all, for the distinction rests not upon structural or functional attributes of aggregates but upon the identifications and aspirations of individuals. It would be difficult to find a better index of just how far we have gone in bartering our sociological heritage for a mess of psychological pottage.

Morphological problems, including the development of fundamental structural taxonomies, deserve far greater attention than they have received in recent years. These are the tasks that have been largely ignored since Durkheim's day. Moreover, Durkheim's earliest work offers a challenge to those interested in the most neglected area of sociology—the analysis of the determinants of structure. As we have tried to suggest, Durkheim also provided a fascinating view of the problematics of social psychology. Given the current division of labor within American sociology, Durkheim's morphological theory of structural differentiation is probably of greatest value to ecologists, although not without relevance to other students of social organization. In this age of specialization, that he saw developing so rapidly, the sheer breadth and scope of Durkheim's achievement becomes all the more impressive with the years.

Leo F. Schnore, "Social Morphology and Human Ecology," in American Journal of Sociology, *Vol. LXIII, No. 6, May, 1958, pp. 620-34.*

Harry Alpert   (essay date 1959)

[*In the following essay, Alpert lauds Durkheim's establishment of and contribution to the social sciences.*]

Emile Durkheim was born on April 15, 1858, just seven months and ten days after the death of Auguste Comte. Comte had conceived the potentialities of a science of society and had provided sociology with its barbaric and controversial cognomen, but Durkheim was needed to provide the persistent efforts, by means of theoretical formulations and empirical demonstrations, which made possible the release of the new discipline from the near-pariah status it had acquired in France. Despite the warning of a Sorbonne professor of philosophy that sociological study leads to insanity, Durkheim dedicated himself to the establishment of sociology as a legitimate and respected science and as an instrument of rational social action.

The richness of Durkheim's sociological contributions serves as the dominant theme of this centennial celebration. One clear indication of the wealth of his permanent additions to sociological science is the variety of positions and movements with which he has been identified. That these positions are often contradictory suggests that textual exegesis is still a fine art and not a science.

To some, Durkheim is an arch nationalist and ideological father of Turkish despotic nationalism. To others, he is the philosopher of French secular republicanism and the spiritual god-father of more democratic human relations in industry. His Preface to the second edition of *De la Division du Travail Social,* with its emphasis on the need for developing occupational social units intermediary between the family and the state, has been cited to prove that he was a forerunner of technocracy, a precursor of corporative fascism, and an advocate of guild socialism and trade unionism. Human ecologists see his theories of social morphology as providing a systematic framework for research in their field, and students of symbolic behavior, for example, W. Lloyd Warner, note that Durkheim has been a major source of inspiration. Finally, as Dr. [Robert N.] Bellah points out in the paper published in [the August 1959] issue of the *Review,* Durkheim is widely thought of as an ahistorical functionalist, while, at the same time, he was a supreme advocate of the comparative historical method.

The history of sociology, to a large extent, is the graveyard of false dichotomies: nature *versus* nurture, society *versus* individual, theory *versus* research, ideas *versus* actions, case method *versus* statistics, and many others. A wise philosopher, Morris Raphael Cohen, some years ago warned against many of these false dichotomies [in *Reason and*

Nature, 1931], but few sociologists have given attention to his suggested application of the principle of polarity. Unfortunately, the functionalism *versus* historicism dichotomy seems still to have sufficient life in it. It apparently cannot be given a decent burial at this moment, but the funeral should not be far off.

With impressive scholarship, Bellah successfully defends his basic thesis that history was always of central importance in Durkheim's sociological work. The persuasiveness of his argument, however, is beguiling and may lead to erroneous impressions regarding Durkheim's views on history. For Durkheim, in the best sense of the term, was a sociological imperialist. He was anxious to establish the integrity, dignity, and independence of sociology as a science. He was prepared to enter into relations with geography, economics, history, linguistics, and related social disciplines—if they operated within sociologically relevant frameworks.

Thus, history, Durkheim would say, is fine and, indeed, essential, provided it is done sociologically, that is, provided it utilizes sociological constructs and theories; and above all, provided it uses a sound comparative method. In the [1898] Preface to Volume I of the *Année Sociologique,* Durkheim wrote: "History can be a science only to the extent that it explains and one can explain only by comparing." The comparative perspective, he added, is also essential for historical description. Durkheim alleged, for example, that Fustel de Coulanges misunderstood the nature of the *gens* because of his ignorance of its counterpart in primitive societies. In a second reference to his teacher at the *Ecole Normale Supérieure,* Durkheim later noted [in the preface to *L'Année*]: "Fustel de Coulanges was fond of repeating that the true sociology is history. Nothing is more incontestable provided that history be done sociologically." And in his posthumously published history of education in France [*L'Evolution Pédagogique en France,* 1938], Durkheim, discussing sources of ideas concerning human nature, observed that theories of human behavior should be developed in the psychological and sociological sciences. But he added, in view of the backward state of these sciences, that we must turn to history. History thus becomes a *pis aller,* a last resort in the absence of good social science and psychology.

In sum, then, Durkheim must indeed be viewed as a strong advocate of historical research, but his support of history rests on the proviso that it be reconstituted and revitalized by sociology.

With this understanding, we can grant the importance of Durkheim's historical emphases. It should be noted, however, that despite the international renown of *The Rules of Sociological Method,* methodological interests as such were not dominant in his thinking. Method, to him, was instrumental. He himself regarded *The Rules* as a sort of extended methodological footnote to the substantive studies he was pursuing on the family, ethical judgments, suicide, division of labor, and social morphology. He would certainly have agreed with Frank Knight who once remarked that "discussing methodology is like playing the slide trombone. It has to be done extraordinarily well if

it is not to be more interesting to the person who does it than to others who listen to it."

In the perspective of Durkheim's total sociological activities, as well as in the light of recent posthumous publications of his studies of Montesquieu and Rousseau and of his lectures on pragmatism and ethics, it is possible to identify three dominant themes which, in my judgment, were foremost in Durkheim's mind and deepest in his heart. They are, first, central preoccupation with ethics and theory of knowledge, second, establishment of sociology as a scientific discipline, and, third, demonstration of the fruitfulness of the sociological perspective or focus in studies relating to human social, psychological, and cultural behavior. These we shall refer to briefly as the philosophy theme, the science theme, and the social focus theme, respectively. They are interconnected threads of the fabric of Durkheimian sociology.

It has been noted, and even regretted [by A. Cuvillier in his *Où Va la Sociologie Française?,* 1953], that Durkheim, in developing his sociological studies, never shed his early interest in the possibility that the new science of society might provide solutions to the traditional philosophical problems of the foundations of knowledge and morality. The concern with ethics, especially, dominated much of Durkheim's activities and colored his sociological orientations. His own rabbinical background, the acknowledged influence of Renouvier and other French philosophers, and the desire to establish a secular and rational basis for ethical judgments all led to this concentrated preoccupation with a science of ethics. Durkheimism, it has been said, is Kantism revised and complemented by Comteism. Rejecting supernaturalism, mysticism, and traditional *a priori* metaphysical doctrines, Durkheim sought the foundations for a scientific, rational system of ethics in the realities of social living. Science, he believed, was a great invention of the human mind, and one of its crowning achievements would be the formulation of sound ethical principles based on systematic knowledge of human nature and society.

Similarly, Durkheim believed ardently in the possible contributions of sociology toward unraveling the difficulties inherent in understanding the nature of knowledge and the categories of thought. Here, too, his perspectives on the sociology of knowledge and thought may be seen as an attempt to exploit the positive science of society so as to solve the difficult epistemological problems posed by Kantian metaphysics. Cuvillier has effectively demonstrated the parallel nature of Durkheim's approach to the study of ethical judgments and his analysis of the problems of thought and truth. Both values and thoughts, in Durkheim's view, must be analyzed as living realities experienced as such by human beings in society.

But the study of human social behavior, insisted Durkheim, following Comte, can progress only through scientific inquiry. Durkheim would have vigorously applauded the recent observation by Ernest Nagel [in "The Place of Science in a Liberal Education," *Daedalus,* 88 (Winter, 1959)]:

> . . . competent familiarity with the knowledge
> acquired by scientific inquiry concerning the

structures of physical, biological, and social process is indispensable for a responsible assessment of moral ideals and for a rational ordering of human life. Ideals and values are not self-certifying; they are not established as valid by appeals to dogmatic authority, to intuitions of moral imperatives, or to undisciplined preference. Proposed moral ideals must be congruous with the needs and capacities of human beings, both as biological individuals and as historically conditioned members of cultural groups, if those ideals are to serve as satisfactory guides to a rich and satisfying human life. The adequacy of moral norms, and of proposed resolutions of moral conflicts, must therefore be evaluated on the basis of reliable knowledge acquired through controlled scientific inquiry.

Durkheim would also have agreed with Nagel's view that scientific method is a procedure of applying logical canons for *testing* claims to knowledge. For this reason, Durkheim placed greatest emphasis on the development of objective indexes. He saw the methodological problem of social science as fundamentally involving the objective study of subjective modes of behavior. Since these include feeling-states, relationships, ideals, values, ideas, and the like, which cannot be observed directly, a *science* of sociology must use its collective creative ingenuity in identifying the overt indexes by which these subjective phenomena can be observed and possibly measured. The theme of science, as Georges Davy has noted [in the Introduction to Durkheim's *Lecons de Sociologie: Physique des moeurs et du droit,* 1950] is one of the paramount features of the Durkheimian system of sociology.

Following a 19th century conception of science, Durkheim believed, however, that the firm establishment of a scientific sociology requires the clear identification of a distinctive subject matter and the staking out of a special domain. From this conviction stems his persistently forceful, but not wholly successful, polemics against psychology and his doctrines of disciplinary purity. The latter, as Alex Inkeles points out [in "Personality and Social Structure," in R. K. Merton, L. Broom, and L. S. Cottrell, editors, *Sociology Today,* 1959], sometimes created analytical blind spots. Nevertheless, the inspired dedication to the empirical demonstration of the *social* as a reality *sui generis* created a truly contagious enthusiasm which stimulated a whole generation of French philosophers and social scientists to develop a genuine sociological perspective. Durkheim taught, by example and by suggestion, how to identify the sociological elements of human social conduct. Considerations of institutional organization, social structure and function, social processes, social origins, and social interactions became significant conceptual tools for the development of sociologies of values, ethics, religion, law, economic life, art, thought and knowledge, mental states, language, and emotions. Durkheim himself became a master-surgeon of the *social;* he developed consummate skill in the sensitive utilization of a sociological scalpel to locate and lay bare the operation of social factors where none had been suspected or looked for before. Suicide, incest taboos, ethical judgments, magical and religious beliefs, division of labor, and social solidarity are but a few of the topics which were illumined by his sociologi-cal explorations. But equally important was his capacity to stimulate his colleagues and students, to fire their imaginations, and to interest them in pursuing the sociologically relevant aspects of their specialized research. To direct Durkheimian influence may be attributed not only the socio-historical studies of Marcel Granet and others to which Robert Bellah refers, but also the monumental studies of Lévy-Bruhl on primitive mentality, the linguistic and semantic research of A. Meillet, Robert Hertz's ingenious analysis of the role of religious and magical concepts in the preeminence of the use of the right hand, the Mauss and Beuchat investigation of seasonal variations in the social practices and religious and ethical beliefs of the Eskimo, Simiand's sensitivity to a social dimension in his studies of economic evolution, wages, and money, Halbwach's demonstration of the social frameworks involved in the memory processes, and numerous other investigations published, in large measure, as monographs and memoirs of the *Année Sociologique.*

A century after his birth, we can be grateful to Durkheim for reminding us that as students of the science of society we have much to do and for providing us with some of the conceptual tools, methodological precepts, and theoretical perspectives with which to do it. Without Durkheim, without his philosophical orientation, scientific emphasis, and identification of the social, social science would have made much slower progress in the systematic application of the methods of rational intelligence to an understanding of human social behavior.

Harry Alpert, "Émile Durkheim: A Perspective and Appreciation," in American Sociological Review, *Vol. 24, No. 4, August, 1959, pp. 462-65.*

Bruce P. Dohrenwend   (essay date 1959)

[*In the following essay, Dohrenwend provides a conceptual analysis of Durkheim's four types of suicide.*]

In recent years, there has been a growing number of empirical studies of relations between environmental factors and mental illness. Such work is confronted by large theoretical problems. Not the least of these is how to conceptualize social and cultural sources of psychological stress. Although existing theory in sociology offers no ready-made solution, it does contain some major guideposts. Perhaps the single most important source of these is Emile Durkheim's study of suicide. For in this study, Durkheim locates diverse social conditions or states as major sources of stress for individuals exposed to them.

The most dazzling of Durkheim's conceptions in his descriptions of these social conditions is that of anomie. It is so provocative, in fact, that there has been a tendency to overlook the conditions labeled by the companion-concepts of egoism and altruism; and the footnoted stepchild, fatalism, has been all but ignored. It may well be that failure to utilize the concepts Durkheim set forth in relation to anomie is in part responsible for the contradictory or divergent conceptions advanced in current approaches which acknowledge his work as their mainspring.

Yet it is not only preoccupation with anomie which has led to neglect of the other three concepts. There is a more general problem to be faced, one which inheres in Durkheim's descriptions of all four types. Recall some of his remarks about egoism, altruism, anomie, and fatalism:

Egoism is said by Durkheim [in **Suicide**] to be a state of society "in which the individual ego asserts itself to excess in the face of the social ego and at its expense. . . ." This state is one marked by "excessive individualism." It is characteristic, for example, of intellectuals and of Protestant societies.

Altruism, on the other hand, is a "state of impersonality in the social unit." Here "the individual has no interests of his own." He is rather "trained to renunciation and unquestioned abnegation. . . ." Duty and honor are of paramount importance. Ego is "blended with something not itself . . . the goal of conduct is exterior to itself, that is, in one of the groups in which it participates." Military societies and some "primitive" societies afford examples of this state.

Anomie, in contrast with both egoism and altruism, is a state of "de-regulation" and "declassification." "All the advantages of social influence are lost . . . moral education has to be recommended." Appetites increase, passions are unleashed, there is suffering, competition, "a race for an unattainable goal." This state is found in industrial sectors of modern society, but it is not restricted to them.

Fatalism, finally, is a state in which there is "excessive regulation" such that "futures [are] pitilessly blocked and passions violently choked by oppressive discipline." The case of slavery provides an example.

These are vivid descriptions which embody illustrations of original insights of first importance. They are often, however, ambiguous in themselves, sometimes indistinct, and infused with value judgments about what is "good" and "bad."

As [Paul F. Lazarsfeld and Allen H. Barton in "Qualitative Measurement in the Social Sciences: Classification, Typologies, and Indices," in Daniel Lerner and Harold D. Lasswell, editors, *The Policy Sciences,* 1951.] have pointed out, any typological system such as Durkheim's involves a reduction of various dimensions in the interest of summarizing what, to the conceptualizer, are the salient features of each type. Often the reader is left to reconstruct for himself the dimensions of the types from the summary descriptions of their salient features. To the extent that the impressions of these features are sharp and clear and devoid of moralizing value judgments, the process is not difficult. To the extent that some of their vividness is due less to objective description and more to the value terms in which they are phrased, the task is complicated. If the types are blurred and ambiguous, they have something of the quality of Rorschach's inkblots and hence serve, inevitably, as objects of the projections of the persons attempting the reconstruction.

The problem of this paper is to try to establish, conceptually, the systematic dimensions of the four types—egoism, altruism, anomie, and fatalism—as states of the most important norms in social aggregates of two or more individuals. Given the scope of Durkheim's work, which places his formulation of these states in the context of a number of assumptions about the nature of human personality and motivation, this is not an easy task to delimit. Given the ambiguities in Durkheim's descriptions, the analysis is confronted by serious obstacles. The paper is therefore an essay in conceptual analysis.

Society is viewed by Durkheim as controlling individuals primarily through the "moral power" of the social environment. Such moral power is invested in what Durkheim variously refers to as the "moral consciousness of societies," their "moral structure," their "moral constitution," or, more concretely, "the common ideas, beliefs, customs and tendencies" of societies. "Externalized" in part in legal codes embodying swift sanctions for his behavior, outnumbering him in the form of "public opinion," and preceding him as traditions in which he himself is socialized, this moral power bears down on the individual who is seen as a "spark" in the "collective current." Certain states of this "moral constitution" or "moral structure" approximate "pure types" which, in the extreme, constitute social conditions predisposing individuals to suicide. Durkheim singled out four such types: egoism, altruism, anomie, and fatalism.

Contemporary sociological terms have replaced such phrases as "moral consciousness of society" and provide a less cumbersome and loaded vocabulary for the analysis of Durkheim's work. [Robert K. Merton in *Social Theory and Social Structure,* 1957], for example, refers to anomie as "a property of the social and cultural structure." The term "social norm" has come to summarize many of the ideas conveyed by the "common ideas, beliefs, customs and tendencies" of society's "moral constitution." Thus, the types may be understood as describing certain "normative situations" [as explained by Robin M. Williams, Jr., in *American Society,* 1950] or, since one type has been characterized as "normlessness," certain "norm-states" of the cultural and social structure of social aggregates.

As Inkeles notes [in "Personality and Social Structure," in Robert K. Merton, Leonard Broom, and Leonard S. Cottrell, Jr., editors, *Sociology Today,* 1959] Durkheim makes a number of assumptions about the nature of personality, and these are invoked as intervening variables between the norm-states and suicide rates. The line between an assumption about a norm-state and an assumption about the nature of personality as related to such a state is not always easy to draw. For example, when Durkheim characterizes the norm-state of egoism as consisting of "excessive individualism," it is not readily apparent that the use of the adjective "excessive" is related to his assumption that it is human nature for the individual to *need* a goal larger than himself. Similarly, Durkheim's use of terms like "greed" and "the dreams of fevered imaginations" and "lost in an infinity of desires" to describe the "unleashed passions" of anomie are more understandable, though not more persuasive, in the light of his assumption that "the more one has, the more one wants" is a basic characteristic of human personality.

In contrast to "hypercivilization," which is said to breed

egoism and anomie and to produce a "refined" and "excessively delicate nervous system" which easily gives way to depression, the "crude, rough culture implicit in the excessive altruism of primitive man" is held to promote a "lack of sensitivity which favors renunciatior." This assumption and those cited above appear to consist more of moralistic interpretations or rationalizations about "human nature" than fruitful (and much needed) attempts to introduce psychological theory into the formulation. As this moralizing about "the nature of human nature" influences Durkheim's descriptions of the norm-states at many points, it serves for the most part as an obstacle to the analysis of these states.

Durkheim also speaks of "derivatives" of the norm-states which take the form of more prevalent responses to such states than that of suicide. Thus egoism is said to be accompanied by collective "currents of depression and disillusionment," and by "incurable weariness and sad depression." Altruism, in contrast, is described as being associated with "active renunciation," and "passionate exultation or courageous resolution." The companions of anomie, in turn, are "weariness," "disillusionment, disturbance, agitation and discontent," "anger," "irritated disgust with life," "exasperated infatuation," and "exasperated weariness." In these last examples we have, it seems, the rather primitive ancestors in Durkheim's work of what has come to be called [by Merton] "subjective anomie;" or better, individual "anomia"—when the focus is on the reactions of the individual *summed across his group memberships;* Srole's anomie scale is an example of such a focus. When the frame of reference is situational, centering upon the relation of the individual to the norm-state of a particular group, it is possible to see in these types of "derivatives" the forerunners of contemporary treatments of the problem of conformity and deviance; thus Durkheim's distinction between the responses to anomie and egoism resembles somewhat the active-passive dimension in the typology of deviance developed by Parsons and held to be essentially the same as that advanced by Merton. In the present context, these "derivatives" of the norm-states constitute another distinction which must be made if the states themselves are to prove susceptible to systematic analysis.

The focus of this paper, then, is on the norm-states themselves as distinct from their relation to ideas about basic human nature, situational reactions to them, or their personality correlates. The paper makes two debatable assumptions: that it is possible to develop a conception of norm from contemporary theory applicable to Durkheim's formulations; that the meaningful differentiations in the norm-states of egoism, altruism, anomie, and fatalism can profitably be discovered in the terms of this conception of social norms.

In an investigation of current work employing the term "social norm," [in Ragnar Rommetveit, *Social Norms and Roles,* 1955] finds three different usages: as "shared frame of reference," as "uniformity of behavior," and as "social pressure" or "role obligation." The three usages are not, of course, mutually exclusive. In the field of sociology, however, the "uniformity" and "social pressure" usages have been emphasized rather than the perceptual approach of the "frame of reference" usage, which has been more the concern of psychologists in what Rommetveit terms "the Sherif tradition."

When the term "social norm" is used in the "uniformity of behavior" sense, it is little more than a descriptive tool, another way of saying that sociology is concerned with regularities of social relationships. Any regularity (or structure) of social behavior, in this usage, is normative, and the emphasis is on end products of processes which are not analyzed in this variety of the concept.

Of considerably more power as an analytic concept, and closer to Durkheim's meaning, is social norm viewed as "social pressure." Attempts to systematize this usage, however, appear in several varieties of guises, designated here as, first, terminological guises, second, guises of operational definition, and, finally, guises of the connotations of the idea of stability—even "integration"—in group processes.

Consider the terminological guises. In the work of Parsons and Shils [editors of *Toward a General Theory of Action,* 1951] the social pressure emphasis is advanced in the term "value-orientation" which connotes the "normative ideas" or "regulatory symbols" of the culture. A similar conception is contained in Williams' formulation of "cultural norm" which "refers to a specific prescription of the course that action *should* (is supposed to) follow in a given situation." Merton's term is "normative values" which, as part of the "cultural structure," govern "behavior which is common to members of a designated society or group." Perhaps the most succinct formulation is that of Nadel who speaks of behavior [in his, *The Theory of Social Structure,* 1957] as being normative "in the sense that the shared attributes exhibited by individuals are understood to follow from the rules [in other guises, the value-orientations, cultural norms, or normative values] of the society or to involve them in some way."

The "social pressure" usage is also implicit in operational definitions of social norms. Nadel outlines three interconnected methods which, he holds, are used in any investigation of social norms. They involve, first, determining the frequency and regularity of behavior; second, eliciting assertions (or what Williams calls "testimony") concerning appropriate conduct; and third, investigating sanctions which [according to Nadel] "forestall or follow deviant behavior." The "social pressure" emphasis in the idea of social norm is unmistakable in this last reliance on sanctions that are called forth to maintain adherence to the cultural rule.

But the observation of sanctions employed to reward conforming and to punish deviant behavior provides only limited clues to the nature of the social pressures that function to maintain adherence to cultural rules. A less restricted lead is contained in discussions of the idea of "stability" of social systems. Parsons and Shils, for example, state: "A stable system of action requires above all the internalization of value-orientations to a degree which will sufficiently integrate the goals of the person with the goals of the collectivity." Thus, as Parsons had noted earlier in terms more similar to those used by Durkheim:

A weakening of control through moral authority tends to call forth . . . a substitution of unpleasant, external consequences to supply a motive of obedience in place of the internal moral sense of duty. . . . There can be no doubt that both [types of constraint' play their part in the actual functioning of social norms. [*The Structure of Social Action,* 1949]

These various ideas may be incorporated into a more complete definition of social norm than is usually found, as follows: *A social norm is a rule which, over a period of time, proves binding on the overt behavior of each individual in an aggregate of two or more individuals.* It is marked by the following characteristics: *(1) Being a rule, it has content known to at least one member of the social aggregate. (2) Being a binding rule, it regulates the behavior of any given individual in the social aggregate by virtue of (a) his having internalized the rule; (b) external sanctions in support of the rule applied to him by one or more other individuals in the social aggregate; (c) external sanctions in support of the rule applied to him by an authority outside the social aggregate; or any combination of these circumstances.*

This definition suggests the following questions about the dimensions of any types of norm-states: Do norms exist? What is their content? What is the source of their power to regulate—is it primarily through internalized or external sanctions? If external, are the sanctions administered primarily from a source of authority within or outside the social aggregate?

Durkheim describes the norm-states as "pure" types in the sense that, in most empirical situations, elements of them are combined to form composite varieties. The pervasiveness and relative importance of the elements of any one of the types in a given social aggregate is thus a matter of degree. In discussing the characteristics of the types in their pure or ideal form, Durkheim maintained that egoism and altruism are opposites, as are anomie and fatalism. The present examination considers these normstates as pure types, the elements of which are pervasive and all-important in the social aggregate. The assumption here is that each type can be differentiated from every other in terms of its polar oppositeness to *each* of the other types on at least one major dimension. What, then, are the dimensions of these polar classifications?

Parsons takes us part of the way, as he interprets Durkheim's major distinctions between altruism and egoism, on the one hand, and both of these and anomie, on the other. One of these distinctions refers to the content of the norms characterizing the states of altruism and egoism: in the case of altruism, the norms dictate a collectivistic orientation, which demands subordination of the little-valued individual to highly-valued group goals; in the case of egoism, the rules dictate an individualistic orientation, which stresses the initiative, responsibility, and dignity of the individual. Parsons' second major distinction refers to the absence of norms in the state of anomie: in contrast to both altruism and egoism, anomie is marked by the absence of common social rules which are binding on individuals in the social aggregate. In this sense, then, normative regulation characterizing the norm-states of both ego-

ism and altruism is opposed to "deregulation," or the "normlessness" of the state of anomie. Thus we have the first two dimensions of Durkheim's types: one is the presence *versus* the absence of social norms, distinguishing both altruism and egoism from anomie; the other is the collectivistic *versus* the individualistic content of norms, which distinguishes altruism from egoism, [following Parsons, Lazarsfeld and Barton have summarized these distinctions].

Anomie is characterized by Durkheim as a state of "deregulation" in the social aggregate. Fatalism, in contrast, is said to be a condition of the social aggregate in which there is "excessive regulation" and "oppressive discipline." The state of fatalism, then, provides common rules and these are binding on the overt behavior of the individuals in the social aggregate. Thus, by our definition, the norms of fatalism place this state as opposite (in this respect) to the normlessness of anomie. But how is fatalism differentiated from egoism and altruism, which are also characterized by the existence of norms?

To differentiate fatalism from either altruism or egoism on the basis of the *content* of norms is not useful. Content, in fact, appears quite irrelevant when we recall Durkheim's examples of social aggregates in which fatalism is most likely to prevail—the situations of prisoners and slaves. The conception of social norm developed here suggests inquiry into the *source* of regulatory power for norms in the state of fatalism, in contrast with egoism and altruism.

In the terms of this concept of norm, comparison of the slave society of fatalism, on the one hand, and Durkheim's egoistic-intellectual and altruistic-military societies, on the other, is instructive. In the case of fatalism, it would seem that the effective regulatory power of common rules is anchored in an authority external to the social aggregate as a whole and to each individual in it—vested, for example, in the "captor." In contrast (if differentiation is sought in terms of oppositeness), egoism and altruism, as pure types, must be norm-states in which the regulatory power of common rules is not only located within the social aggregate but internalized in each individual. Is there evidence in Durkheim's work to support this differentiation?

Durkheim speaks of the "moral consciousness" or "moral power" which distinguishes both egoistic and altruistic societies from anomic ones. Moral consciousness, he holds, is "external" to the component individuals of the society. If this statement is accepted at face value, there appears indeed to be no basis in his work for distinguishing internalized from external regulation. A closer reading indicates, however, that Durkheim is using the term "external" in a very special, even metaphysical, sense to present his view of the individual as but "a spark" in the "collective current." That Durkheim means something quite different from the "moral consciousness" of egoism and altruism by the "deregulation" or normlessness of anomie is clear enough. A hint that he also intends to distinguish the latter from the regulation involved in fatalism is contained in his discussion of the nature of moral obligation: "What actually matters in fact is not only that the regulation should exist, but that it should be accepted by the conscience. Otherwise, since this regulation no longer has moral authority and continues only through the force of inertia, it can no longer play any useful role. It chafes without accomplishing much." The interpretation of this passage depends to a considerable extent on whether the word *conscience* refers to a metaphysical "collective conscience" or to the conscience of each individual in the social aggregate. At the very least, it may be argued, the statement underlines a distinction between a coercive kind of regulation and one that has acceptance; at most, it implies internalization of the rule as a defining characteristic of whether or not it carries "moral obligation" for the individual.

Parsons, in analyzing this problem, sees Durkheim coming to distinguish between two varieties of normative control: "These two classes of normative control are distinguished [by] the mode of relation of the actor to them. By contrast with the morally neutral attitude associated with the sanction concept of constraint and with norms of 'efficiency' generally, emerges the attitude of moral obligation, of a specific respect toward the rule." Parsons, after noting that for Durkheim the basis of this "attitude of respect" toward a norm is simply a fact, adds the following interpretation: "insofar as the actor maintains an attitude of moral obligation toward it, the norm to which his action is oriented is no longer exterior. . . . It becomes, in the Freudian term, 'introjected'. . . . "

According to this interpretation, there is implicit in Durkheim's types a distinction (made explicit in the present conception of social norm) between two main sources of normative regulation: one stemming from rules which have been internalized by individuals in the social aggregate, the other from rules applied from a source of external authority. On the basis of this distinction, it seems reasonable to locate the third dimension of Durkheim's types—a dimension clearly revealed by examination of fatalism in contrast to the other three types—in the power of rules that regulate overt behavior of individuals in a social aggregate where norms exist.

Thus the four types can be differentiated, each from every other, in terms of oppositeness on at least one of three major dimensions: the existence of norms, their content, and their effective source of regulatory power. Both egoism and altruism are characterized by the existence of effective, internalized rules, but the content of the rules is individualistic in the first case and collectivistic in the second. Fatalism stands in strong contrast to egoism and altruism, for its effective source of normative power is an authority external to the social aggregate; nevertheless, all three types involve rules which are binding on the overt behavior of individuals. Anomie, however, appears to be a type apart, as it is marked by the absence of norms altogether.

But must the "absence of norms" be manifested in the "deregulation" that Durkheim associates with the state of anomie? What about the situation in which rules exist, to be sure, but call for inconsistent or contradictory behavior, without a superordinate rule to reconcile the conflict? As Williams has stated, this condition is evidenced "when two or more . . . standards enjoin actions that cannot,

both or all, be carried out by the same person in the same situation."

Other authors have been concerned about the possibility of more than one type of normlessness. Merton, for example, following a distinction made by Sebastian De Grazia, writes:

> *Simple anomie* refers to the state of confusion in a group or society which is subject to conflict between value systems . . . ; *acute anomie,* to the deterioration and, at the extreme, the disintegration of value systems. . . . This has the merit of ear-making the often stated but sometimes neglected fact that, like other conditions of society, anomie varies in degree and perhaps in kind.

Consider, however, that as a state in a social aggregate, the anarchistic clash of social rules is probably always a transitional phenomenon. For some individuals, perhaps in coalition or through access to outside authority, in the long run, can make rules which are binding on their own behavior, as well as the conduct of others. Only under certain conditions is it likely that the competing rules themselves will all "disintegrate."

Given these considerations, it may be argued that "normlessness," in the sense of unreconciled conflict among rules, is indeed a difference in degree and also, in a manner, in kind. But the difference is not necessarily between "simple" and "acute" anomie. Rather, it is a difference between a *transitional state* of anarchistic conflict in the rules and its resolution. The resolution itself assumes a form in which the characteristics of any one of the four ideal types—altruism, egoism, fatalism, or (acute) anomie—may be dominant.

In varying degrees of intermediacy between the transitional state and the four types are the empirical realities of norm-states in most existing social aggregates at any given point in time. The concept of social norm employed in this paper may be of use in the analysis of the wider environmental conditions affecting such aggregates, the processes of conformity and deviance which indicate tendencies toward one or another of the polar types, and the effects of the latter on individuals.

Little can be said here about the wider environmental conditions. Durkheim notes the effects of various crises on social aggregates—war, for example, leading to an increase in altruism, economic boom or disaster contributing to anomie. The precise relation of such crises to the norm-states is far from clear. It is suggested, however, that environmental changes of this order should be assessed in terms of their impact on the sources of regulatory power of the existing rules.

Moreover, understanding of the processes of conformity and deviance in social aggregates, requires analysis of the relations between internalized and external sources of regulatory power of the rules affecting the behavior of individuals. At present, there exists no theory of social motivation which attempts to predict modes of conformity and deviance on the basis of the relative strength of the individual's internalized rules, of the rules which he *and* other members of the group experience as external pressures, and of the rules external to him but stemming from other *in* the social aggregate. Yet such theory would seem essential if fruitful links are to be made with Freud's relevant concepts of id, superego, and objective anxiety. Similarly, theoretical development along these lines is needed in order to bring together the sociological study of normative behavior and the growing clinical and experimental investigation of stress and the direction of anger in relation to mental disorder.

Bruce P. Dohrenwend, "Egoism, Altruism, Anomie, and Fatalism: A Conceptual Analysis of Durkheim's Types," in American Sociological Review, *Vol. 24, No. 4, August, 1959, pp. 466-73.*

Robert N. Bellah   (essay date 1964)

[*The author of* Tokugawa Religion *(1957), Bellah is an American educator and writer with a special interest in Far Eastern and Middle Eastern societies. The following essay, first published in the August 1959 edition of* American Sociological Review, *discusses the importance of history to Durkheim's comparative method.*]

History was always of central importance in Durkheim's sociological work. Without understanding this, a full appreciation of his contribution to sociology is impossible. From his earliest to his latest work, Durkheim urges the closest rapprochement between sociology and history. In one of his earliest published papers, ["Introduction à la sociologie de la famille," in *Annales de la faculté des lettres de Bordeaux,* 10, 1888], he stresses the importance of history for sociology and of sociology for history. In the Prefaces of Volumes I (1898) and II (1899) of *L'Année Sociologique,* he lays down the policy of including a large proportion of historical works among the books reviewed, a policy from which *L'Année* never deviated, and addresses his colleagues: "It has appeared to us that it would be useful to call these researches to the attention of sociologists, to give them a glimpse of how rich the material is and of all the fruits which may be expected from it." In 1905 he calls to his students' attention the importance of history for the understanding of the sociology of education [translated in 1956 as *Education and Sociology*], and in 1912 he speaks of the crucial importance of history [in his *The Elementary Forms of Religious Life,* translated in 1947] for the sociology of religion. And in his last paper, "Introduction à la morale" of 1917, Durkheim once again notes the fundamental significance of history for the understanding of man.

At several points Durkheim went so far as to question whether or not sociology and history could in fact be considered two separate disciplines. In the Preface to Volume I of *L'Année* he quotes the great historian, Fustel de Coulanges—to the effect that "the true sociology is history." Durkheim approves of this on the condition that history be treated sociologically and, in a subsequent article ["Sociologie et Sciences Sociales," *Revue Philosophique,* 55, 1903], he traces the tendency of the writing of history during the last half of the nineteenth century to become in fact more and more sociological. His most extreme statement on the subject was made in the course of a discussion held by the French Society of Philosophy in 1908 where, in reply to the statement of a distinguished historian, he said: "In his exposition, M. Seignobos seemed to oppose history and sociology, as if they were two disciplines using different methods. In reality, there is nothing in my knowledge of sociology which merits the name, which doesn't have a historical character. . . . There are not two methods or two opposed conceptions. That which will be true of history will be true of sociology." When reviewing some articles by Salvemini, Croce, and Sorel [in *L'Année Sociologique* 6, 1903], however, he draws the distinction between the two fields that he maintained more or less constantly: history is concerned with the particular; sociology with types and laws, that is, with comparative structure and analytical theory, with the study of things not for themselves, but as examples of the general. But he adds that these are not two disciplines but two points of view which, far from excluding each other, support and are necessary for each other, although they should not be confused.

But Durkheim did not merely preach. Almost all of his own researches draw heavily from historical and ethnological sources and are in fact organized in a historical framework. This is true, for example, of his sociology of the family, his treatment of the division of labor, his theory of punishment, his discussion of property and contract, his sociology of education, his sociology of religion, his study of socialism. Even **Suicide,** which depends more on contemporary data than almost any other of his studies, derives its conceptual scheme in part at least from hypotheses about very long-term changes in the structure of solidarity in society.

If Durkheim was not an ahistorical theorist neither was he just another philosopher of history whose work stimulated little concrete historical research. Durkheim's profound influence on two generations of anthropologists and sociologists is well known, but what is perhaps less well known is his equally profound influence on cultural history—Hubert's work on the Celts, Granet on China, Harrison and Cornford on ancient Greece, Maunier on North Africa, and many others. Of course, Durkheim advocated comparative historical studies relevant to problems of analytic theory, not a narrow historicism.

What is the theoretical groundwork of Durkheim's lasting concern with history in his sociological thought? His Latin thesis contains an early formulation of his position:

> There are two types of conditions which move social life. One is found in present circumstances such as the nature of the soil, the number of social units, etc.; the other is found in the historical past (*in praeterita historia*). And in fact just as a child would be different if it had other parents, societies differ according to the form of the antecedent society. If it follows a lower society it cannot be the same as if it had issued from a very civilized nation. But Montesquieu, having not known this succession and this kinship of societies, entirely neglected causes of this type. He didn't take account of this force from behind (*vis a tergo*) which pushes peoples and only paid attention to the environing circumstances (*circum-*

fusa). ["The Contribution of Montesquieu to the Establishment of Social Science," in *Montesquieu et Rousseau: Précurseurs de la Sociologique* 6, 1903]

He then points out that Comte was equally mistaken in the opposite direction in thinking that placing a society in an historical series was in itself sufficient for sociological explanation.

The position maintained in the Latin thesis, however, was inherently unstable. In saying that both the historical past and the social milieu are causal factors in sociological explanation, Durkheim seems to be adopting an eclectic "both/and" position which leaves the fundamental antinomy unresolved. But in as early a work as the *Rules of Sociological Method* he adopted a stable position which he maintained with consistency thereafter. In the *Rules* he decisively rejects both causal finalism, which seeks to account for the emergence of sociological phenomena in terms of the use or advantage which will result from them, and historical determinism which explains sociological phenomena as the product of an inevitably operative sequence of stages. In opposition to both of these types of explanation, Durkheim holds to the position that only efficient causes are admissible in scientific explanation. Thus he maintains that only currently operative variables can account for the emergence of social phenomena and that neither a hypothetical sequence of past historical stages nor a hypothetical future utility can do so. Causes, then, are to be found only in the currently operative social milieu, or, as we might say, in the social system, a position which some have taken as Durkheim's renunciation of history.

Durkheim, however, had by no means renounced history. This is shown by his insistence, on the one hand, that currently operative variables cannot be understood without a knowledge of their history and his deepening understanding of those variables themselves, on the other. The Preface of Volume II of *L'Année* is instructive in this regard. Immediately after having commended historical researches to the attention of sociologists, he says:

> Perhaps, it is true, the busy sociologist will find this procedure uselessly complicated. In order to understand the social phenomena of today . . . , isn't it enough to observe them as they are given in our actual experience and isn't it a work of vain erudition to undertake research into their most distant origins? But this quick method is full of illusions. One doesn't know social reality if one only sees it from outside and if one ignores the substructure. In order to know how it is, it is necessary to know how it has come to be, that is, to have followed in history the manner in which it has been progressively formed. In order to be able to say with any chance of success what the society of tomorrow will be . . . , it is indispensable to have studied the social forms of the most distant past. In order to understand the present it is necessary to go outside of it.

Durkheim repeatedly warned that to study the present from the point of view of the present is to be enslaved by all the momentary needs and passions of the day. It is necessary to go into the past to uncover the deeper lying forces which, though often unconscious, are so largely determinative of the social process. Durkheim compares this stricture with the necessity of studying the past of an individual in order to understand the unconscious forces at work in him, thus urging a sociological analogue to the psychoanalytic method.

But history is not only essential to the understanding of the present. History is central to sociology by the very nature of the sociological method, namely, that it is *comparative*. This is precisely the point that Durkheim makes in Chapter VI of the *Rules*. There he argues that the comparative method is above all the appropriate method for sociology and, more specifically, within the general logic of comparative analysis, the method of concomitant variation—a position which the subsequent history of sociology has largely borne out. But Durkheim was always acutely aware of the problems of analysis and definition in sociological work. He therefore criticizes those sociologists and anthropologists who understand the comparative method to consist in the indiscriminate collection of facts and who believe that the sheer weight of documentation can prove anything. Durkheim, rather, insists that comparison can only be meaningful when the facts compared have been carefully classified in terms of a systematic and theoretically relevant typology. This means, for him, especially the typological classification of whole societies or what he calls "social species." Durkheim's work in this area, while far from definitive, did lay down some of the essential guidelines. His basic principle of classification, that of morphological complexity, as he plainly saw, has both analytical and genetic implications. The arrangement of social types or species shows a rough sequence, in that the more complex types emerge from the simpler. But there is no suggestion of "inevitable stages": the genetic concept was not tainted with unilinear evolutionism.

How, then, is the comparative method to be applied in sociology? It can, according to Durkheim, be used in a single society "when absolutely necessary" if certain conditions obtain, namely, when there are data for a considerable period of time and when the data themselves reveal extensive systematic variation, as in the case of suicide. Results obtained from several societies of the same species are desirable in confirming the generalizations reached on the basis of a single case. But by far the best use of the comparative method, from Durkheim's point of view, is its application to an extended series of social types, involving a wide range of historical and ethnographical material.

> To explain a social institution belonging to a given species, one will compare its different forms, not only among peoples of that species but in all preceding species as well. . . . This method, which may be called "genetic," would give at once the analysis and the synthesis of the phenomenon. For, on the one hand, it would show us the separate elements composing it, by the very fact that it would allow us to see the process of accretion or action. At the same time, thanks to this wide field of comparison, we should be in a much better position to determine the conditions on which depend their formation.

Consequently, one cannot explain a social fact of any complexity except by following its complete development through all social species. Comparative sociology is not a particular branch of sociology; it is sociology itself, in so far as it ceases to be purely descriptive and aspires to account for facts.

Here, as so often, Durkheim overstates his case. There are clearly some problems for which the historical and comparative method is less relevant than others. Still, it is important to remember that most of his empirical work was carried out in terms of just such a method of extended comparison, and that the great theoretical advances which have inspired so much valuable work in anthropology, history, and sociology directly emerged from the use of that method.

Thus, although Durkheim stresses that only currently operative variables can be accepted as causes of social phenomena, he insists with equal vehemence that such variables can only be understood by a comparative analysis involving a recourse to history. So in Durkheim's mature view there are not two alternative modes of explanation of social phenomena, one in terms of sociological function, the other in terms of the historic past. There is only one method of explanation, at once both sociological and historical.

We may now turn to an analysis of the chief types of social cause with which Durkheim worked, an analysis which will take us even more deeply into Durkheim's conception of the role of the historical in sociology. For here Durkheim went quite far in the direction of developing a theory of social change—which, presumably, static functionalists are not allowed to do.

In the early period, roughly from the **Division of Labor** through **Suicide,** Durkheim gives primary emphasis to morphological variables in the explanation of social causes. Schnore has recently published an excellent analysis of Durkheim's views on morphology and structural differentiation ["Social Morphology and Human Ecology," *American Journal of Sociology* 63, (May 1958)]; only the briefest summary is necessary here. Durkheim isolates two especially important morphological variables: the number of social units or the "size of a society"; and the degree of interaction taking place between the units of the system, which he calls "dynamic" or "moral" density. In general, as size and dynamic density increase, competition between unspecialized units engaged in the same activities also increases. Structural differentiation is then seen as an adaptive response to this increased competition: by specializing in different activities the units no longer come in conflict. Although his conception is schematic and oversimplified, Durkheim is unquestionably correct in seeing structural differentiation in response to adaptive exigencies as a major aspect of social change. This concern with structure, far from obscuring the problem of change, actually illuminates it.

Durkheim saw that the focus of structural differentiation is economic organization; but he also saw that structural differentiation had a profound effect on the total society and that it always involved important elements which were in no immediate sense economic. Examination of some of these noneconomic aspects of structural differentiation provides better understanding of Durkheim's conception.

In Durkheim's conception the starting point of the process of structural differentiation is the undifferentiated segment that he tends to identify with a "diffuse clan." This is the beginning of the development of the family as an institution. The diffuse clan has economic, political, religious, and other functions, as well as functions which, on the basis of our form of family (which Durkheim called "conjugal" and we sometimes call "nuclear"), are today often referred to as *familial.* Durkheim therefore believes that it is somewhat confusing to name the diffuse clan a "family" since by that term we mean something so different. He does recognize the existence of the nuclear family within such a unit but finds it weak in structural differentiation and institutional legitimacy compared with the family in our society. As the process of division of labor proceeds Durkheim sees the successive differentiation of religious, political, and economic functions away from the kinship unit itself. But together with these external changes there are also internal changes. As familial relations become disentangled from relations to property, political authority, and the like, they become more personalized. The external environment reaches into the family in the form of the state, which affords protection from abuse even within the family. Under these circumstances the conjugal family in modern society is enabled to carry out its indispensable function, namely the moral training of children or, as we would say, "socialization," and the provision of moral and emotional security for all family members. So brief a summary gives no idea of the richness of the comparative material which Durkheim presents in support of his argument. But the essential position is that in the process of structural differentiation the family does not merely lose functions but becomes a more specialized unit playing a vital role in more complex societies, although not the same role as in simpler societies. Not only does this analysis increase our understanding of the family, it adds an important principle to the theory of structural differentiation—namely, that when in the course of differentiation, a unit appears to lose important functions, it is not necessarily a weakened version of its former self; it may be a new, more specialized unit, fulfilling important functions at a new level of complexity in the larger system.

A similar conclusion may be drawn from the consideration of Durkheim's views on the changing position of the individual in society as the result of structural differentiation. This is a subject to which Durkheim devoted considerable attention, references to it being found in a great many of his books and articles. Taken as a whole, his work on this subject constitutes an important contribution to the "sociology of personality," or, as it may be put, a historical and comparative social psychology. Durkheim's great problem in this area is to explain the emergence of individualism on a sociological basis, avoiding both the abstract philosophical and purely psychological analyses of his predecessors.

The core of the problem is touched in **The Division of**

Labor. Individuality is at its minimum in the undifferentiated segment characterized by mechanical solidarity; here a single *conscience collective* guides all individuals alike. In a differentiated society where the division of labor and organic solidarity have become important, the sphere of the *conscience collective* has shrunk and individual differences are not only tolerated but encouraged. How does this occur? In the first instance, Durkheim cites a number of morphological factors. One aspect of the increase of dynamic density (the degree of interaction between units in a social system) is increased physical mobility. As individuals move away from their place of origin the hold of the older generation, defenders of tradition (itself the stronghold of the *conscience collective*), is weakened and consequently individual differences can occur more easily—especially in the process of urbanization. Another aspect of urbanization allowing greater individual variation is the anonymity afforded by large population aggregates, which renders the individual less subject to rigid traditional controls. In addition to these rather negative causes Durkheim adduces certain important positive factors. One of these is the emergence of the state, which he sees as an essential prerequisite for the emancipation of the individual from the control of the undifferentiated segment. The state, seeking to extend its own influence at the expense of the primary and secondary groups which immediately envelop the individual, operates to secure the rights of individuals against such groups. If the state destroys the secondary groups, however, it becomes even more oppressive than they were. Durkheim sees a dynamic balance between the state and secondary groups as maximizing individuality. As society becomes more voluminous it tends to become more universalistic—and here is another positive factor. Law, for instance, when it must apply to a vast empire must be more generalized than are the local customs of a petty hamlet. Religion, too, if spread over a wide area, must have a universal appeal and not be restricted by narrowly local and particularistic concerns. But a more generalized and abstract law and religion will bind the individual less closely than the minutely specific customs of the undifferentiated segment. Implicit throughout the *Division of Labor* is the notion that the performance of complex differentiated functions in a society with an advanced division of labor both requires and creates individual variation, initiative, and innovation, whereas undifferentiated segmental societies do not.

These more or less morphological hypotheses may serve as an introduction to Durkheim's sociology of the individual. His understanding of this problem was greatly deepened as he became aware of a second main type of causal variable, noted below. The foregoing discussion, however, is sufficient to indicate that Durkheim not only introduced a series of stimulating hypotheses about the role of the individual, but also added further important corollaries to the theory of structural differentiation. One of the most important of these is what Talcott Parsons calls [in his "Durkheim's Contribution to the Theory of Integration of Social Systems," in *Durkheim, 1858-1917,* edited by Kurt H. Wolff, 1960] "institutionalized individualism." This is the notion that the emergence of individuality involves the shift from one kind of social control to another, not the weakening of social control itself. Durkheim, then, stress-

ing the necessity of conformity in some sense for social order, turns our attention from the false issue of conformity *versus* nonconformity to a consideration of various types of conformity, including, of course, the pathological possibility of overconformity.

For our purposes, however, the point of special interest in Durkheim's views on the family and the role of the individual, for example, is that the basic analytic concepts of morphology and social differentiation, which supply the basis of so much of Durkheim's work, apply, as he uses them, both to current functioning and to long-term historical change. Here are concrete examples of that method of extended comparison which Durkheim advocated. If the concepts which have emerged from these comparisons—the types of solidarity, the types of suicide, and so on—have proven useful in the analysis of the functioning of social systems, these same concepts when organized around the master idea of structural differentiation have made very important contributions to our understanding of social change.

The second major type of social cause which Durkheim isolated, and which occupied him increasingly in his later years, is the *representation collective.* As is well known, Durkheim's interest turned increasingly to religion, especially primitive religion, and it was in relation to this interest that the idea of collective representation takes on prominence. It seems likely that Durkheim's concern with problems of structural differentiation turned his interest to religion. At any rate his work on religion is closely related to that earlier concern, as indicated in the preface of Volume II of *L'Année.* Durkheim is interested in discovering in religion, especially primitive religion, that undifferentiated whole from which the elements of social life gradually differentiated. (Durkheim twice speaks of this phenomenon in connection with the importance of the discovery of the unicellular organism in biology.) It is in this context, then, that we can understand why Durkheim came to devote so much attention to religion in the Australian clan, attention that led to the production of his greatest work, *The Elementary Forms of the Religious Life.* As early as the 1880s, Durkheim had seen what he called the "diffuse clan" as the simplest form of kinship structure. By 1898 he had come to view the clan as more fundamentally a religious group than a consanguineal one. With the example of the Australian clan and its religious life, he undertook to analyze the social analogue of the unicellular organism, the basic structural type from which all other social structures have differentiated.

For fifteen years Durkheim used Australian totemism as a "laboratory" in which to study with minute precision the relations between religion, social structure, and personality. During that time he mastered the concrete empirical data to such an extent that *Elementary Forms* anticipated discoveries made by Australian fieldworkers only several years later, and profoundly influenced subsequent work in this field. And it was during these long and painstaking experiments on Australian totemism that Durkheim made some of his most fundamental sociological discoveries—the symbolic nature of the sacred, the theory of ritual, the role of religion in the internalization of values, and so on. It is impossible here to give even a superficial summary of the *Elementary Forms.* We can only cite a single point of method and discuss the major contribution to the theory of social change—our theme—which emerged from Durkheim's study of primitive religion.

Durkheim clearly regarded the *Elementary Forms* as a vindication of his genetic method. He said on one occasion [in a discussion of "L'inconnu et l'inconscient en Histoire," published in *Bulletin de la Société Français de Philosophie,* 8 (1908)] that he understood the Australian primitives better than he did modern France. He found the fundamental facts simpler and the relations between them easier to grasp than in a more complex society. Unfortunately, he was unable to carry out his method extensively, that is, by a series of studies of religion in societies of successively more complex types. He did give some suggestions along these lines, however, some of which are noted below.

Turning to the main contribution to the theory of social change emerging from his work on religion we must consider the idea of *collective representations.* This idea appears in 1898—when Durkheim was deeply concerned with the sociology of religion. One of the earliest uses of the concept is in "La Prohibition de L'Inceste," an article which appeared in that year, and is the first paper drawing heavily on Australian sources. Both in this paper and in another publication in 1898, "Individual and Collective Representations," the fundamental point is made that while collective representations (which Durkheim later called "ideals" and which we might call "values"—although the original conception was broader than these terms suggest) arise from and reflect the "social substratum" (the morphological variables of the earlier period) they are, once in existence, "partially autonomous realities" which independently influence subsequent social development. Thus Durkheim, in the concept of collective representations, made the fundamental discovery of culture as an element analytically independent of social system, although the full significance of this insight remained somewhat obscured by his use of the word "social" to apply to both elements.

With the creation of the concept of collective representations Durkheim made a twofold contribution to the theory of social change. First and better known, he greatly increased our understanding of how collective representations arise by showing their relation to morphological features. (In this, incidentally, he anticipated [Karl] Mannheim by more than twenty years.) The greatest impact of the *Elementary Forms* on the study of primitive religion and on early societies in the ancient Mediterranean, the Far East, and elsewhere, was of this sort. But Durkheim, never a devotee of one-way determinism, also saw clearly that collective representations have a reciprocal influence on social structure and are independent variables in the process of social change. This is stated explicitly as early as 1898 [in "La prohibition de l'inceste et ses Origines," *L'Année Sociologique* 1] and receives something like a theoretical formulation in 1911 [in "Value Judgments and Judgments of Reality," *Sociology and Philosophy*]. But the

richest and most exciting elaboration of this view appears in that little known but extremely important book, published twenty years after Durkheim's death, *L'Évolution Pédagogique en France,* composed of lectures written in 1904 and 1905.

In this work Durkheim takes the history of French education as an index to the history of the French spirit and of the social and cultural framework out of which it arose: here is an intricate and sensitive analysis of the interplay of morphological and representational factors in the development of French culture from the early middle ages to the nineteenth century. In accordance with his penchant for origins, he begins by showing that French education first appeared in the church. He demonstrates how certain fundamental features of the Christian world-view colored the conception of the school as a place for the education of the total personality, a conception which still survives. Here a representational element is used as a fundamental point of reference without any attempt to explain it morphologically. There follows an interesting discussion of how the morphological factors involved in the political unification of Charlemagne and the religious unification of the high middle ages are related to the structure of the school system and to the predominance first of grammar and then of logic in the curriculum, although in this analysis he takes full account as well of cultural factors. Subsequently, the changes in social structure involved in the breakdown of the medieval system and the several cultural tendencies of the Renaissance are considered as alternative answers to the problems raised by the breakdown. The analysis of the factors involved in the French cultural synthesis of the seventeenth century is especially brilliant; and since the spirit of modern French culture derives from that period, this discussion is helpful in understanding the France of today as well as Durkheim's thought. A final example—there are many others—of Durkheim's historical sociology in this work is his analysis of the relation between Protestantism and the rise of "realistic education," especially the teaching of science. In linking the orientation of Protestantism to science Durkheim independently reached a conclusion better known from the studies of [Max] Weber and [Robert K.] Merton.

Two general conclusions may be drawn from Durkheim's treatment of such problems, which have reference to the theory of social change. One is his insistence that collective representations, once institutionalized, are capable of exerting an influence over an exceptionally long period of time and in the face of many social and cultural changes. He held, for example, that even modern secular ideas of duty, morality, and the like were derived from fundamentally Christian ideas, since Christianity was the chrysalis of Western culture itself, and that these ideas are quite different from the ethical views of the classical pagan world. Again, he maintained that the Cartesian spirit held a certain cultural dominance in France in spite of the tremendous political and economic revolutions which occurred after its formulation. The second general conclusion is that as long as the social system is running smoothly the accepted system of collective representations will not be questioned. Only when the old system is breaking down, when there is a great deal of turmoil and social ferment, new systems of ideals become formulated, and then contribute to the establishment of a newly stabilized social system. Durkheim's conclusions about the role of collective representations in social process together with his conception of structural differentiation, I believe, provide the outlines of a fruitful theory of social change and suggest the direction of future work in the development of such a theory.

Robert N. Bellah, "Durkheim and History," in Sociology and History: Theory and Research, *edited by Werner J. Cahnman and Alvin Boskoff, The Free Press of Glencoe, 1964, pp. 85-103.*

On Durkheim's Sociology:

By his ill-considered and scientifically pretentious psycho-mysticism Durkheim has contributed to give the color of justification to the new religion of the altar of *divus Augustus* and to the neopagan philosophy of Caesar-worship. This (scholastically speaking) "realistic" attitude toward society, although applied by Durkheim in sociology, as by Gierke in jurisprudence, for the benefit of the group, was philosophically indispensable for the new religion of the state. Political monism reappeared, out of the political pluralism in vogue in the first quarter of this century, in a form more formidable than even Hobbes ever dreamed.

George E. G. Catlin, in his "Introduction to the Translation" of The Rules of Sociological Method, *by Émile Durkheim, 1938.*

Anthony Giddens (essay date 1982)

[*In the following essay, Giddens discusses Durkheim's conception of socialism and its current value in his political writings.*]

My aim in what follows will not be to offer a textual examination of the various discussions and comments on socialism that are to be found scattered through Durkheim's writings. Rather, I want to pose the question: is there anything in Durkheim's account of socialism that remains of value today, when we inhabit a world which has changed profoundly since Durkheim's time? I do not write as a particular admirer of Durkheim's views about sociology. These views have had an enormous influence, in varying ways and contexts, upon the subsequent development of the social sciences, but in my opinion this influence has not always been a fruitful one. I do want to argue, however, that Durkheim's analysis of socialism—not an aspect of his work which has been debated as frequently as some others—contains some ideas that are a stimulus to reflection about contemporary political problems.

Let me first sketch in a few of the elements of Durkheim's discussion. Durkheim draws a distinction between 'communist' and 'socialist' doctrines. 'Communist' ideas, in Durkheim's use of the term, have existed at various different periods of history. Communist writings typically take the form of fictional utopias: examples are to be found in the diverse works of Plato, Thomas More and [Tommaso] Campanella. Such utopian writings tend to treat private property or wealth as the main origin of social evils; the private accumulation of wealth is regarded as a moral danger that must be kept strictly in check. In 'communist' utopias, political and economic life are kept separated, so that the latter should not be corrupted by the former. Thus in the ideal form of the republic as projected by Plato, the rulers have no right to intervene in the economic activities of the producers, and the latter are not permitted to participate in administration or legislation. This is because wealth and its temptations are a source of public corruption, a phenomenon 'stimulating individual egoisms'. The guardians of the state and the artisans or labourers even live in physical separation from one another: 'All communist theories formulated later,' according to Durkheim [in his *Socialism*, 1962], 'derive from Platonic communism, of which they are hardly more than variations.'

As such, they all stand in decisive opposition to socialism, which is much more recent, is related to social movements rather than being the isolated creation of individual authors, and has a different basic content in terms of the ideas which it involves. The word 'socialism' dates only from the turn of the eighteenth and nineteenth centuries, as do socialist movements themselves; socialism, says Durkheim, is a product of the social changes transforming the European societies from the late eighteenth century onwards. In complete contrast to communist theories, which presuppose that polity and economy must be separated, the main thesis of socialism, as Durkheim conceives of it, is that the two should be merged. That is to say, it is not wealth as such which is the source of social evils, but the fact that it is not socialised in the hands of a centralised directive agency. Here we come to a vital element of Durkheim's argument. In socialist doctrines, production is to be centralised in the hands of the state; but the state is conceived of in a purely economic way. The Saint-Simonian theme that, in the anticipated society of the future, the 'administration of human beings' will give way to the 'administration of things' is taken by Durkheim to be a specific and defining characteristic of socialist ideas as a whole. In this respect socialism, including its Marxist version, shares certain parameters of thought with one of its principal opponents, political economy. Each regards economic reorganisation as the essential basis for coping with the problems facing the contemporary societies; each considers it both possible and desirable to reduce the activities of the state to a minimum. The classical economists propose that the scope of government be limited to the enforcement of contracts, such that the market can be given free play; the socialists wish to replace market mechanisms by centralised economic control.

Communist theories usually have an ascetic character, but socialist ideas are founded upon the proposition that modern industrial production holds out the possibility of abundant wealth for all, if the economy is rationally organised. Communism and socialism, Durkheim claims, tend to be frequently confused or mingled with one another. This is partly because both seek to combat perceived sources of social disquiet, and partly because each proposes forms of regulation (*reglèmentation,* in Durkheim's term) to do with the relation between economic and political life. However, Durkheim adds, 'one aims to moralise industry by binding it to the State, the other, to moralise the State by excluding it from industry'. It seems evident, although Durkheim does not spell the idea out in detail, that the distinction between communism and socialism connects closely to the themes of *The Division of Labour in Society.* Communist ideals are those that appear sporadically in societies having a low division of labour, which are segmental in character, and where there is little co-operative dependence in production. Since there is little mutual dependence in production, the possibility of socialisation of economic life does not raise itself. Consumption, rather than production, is communal. Socialism, by contrast, could only arise in societies having a high degree of interdependence in the division of labour, i.e. in societies cohered by organic solidarity. It is a response to the pathological condition of the division of labour in societies undergoing the transition from mechanical to organic solidarity.

This explains Durkheim's guarded but undeniably positive attitude towards socialism (in his formulation of it). Parsons's comment, in his famous discussion of Durkheim in *The Structure of Social Action,* that Durkheim's sympathies were closer to communist than to socialist doctrines, seems entirely wide of the mark. Socialism, according to Durkheim, is in certain degree a symptom of the strains to which contemporary societies are subject; but socialists are correct in holding that these strains call for the regulation of economic activity in the interests of the whole of the community. I don't think it would be correct to call Durkheim a 'socialist' as such, either in terms of his personal involvement in politics—which was in any case fairly limited—or in terms of the overall themes of his social analyses. His political sympathies were close to liberal republicanism, and he saw socialist ideas as limited in respect of providing a programme of social reconstruction appropriate to the demands of the day. In the context of the Anglo-Saxon reception of Durkheim, it is important to accentuate these things, because one prominent line of thought has stressed a presumed association of Durkheim's thought with conservatism. The view that Durkheim's writings, if not his political attachments, are inherently conservative in character has been stressed by various commentators, most particularly by Nisbet and by Coser. It has contributed, in my opinion, to serious distortions in the interpretation of Durkheim's work—distortions that have had various ramifications for the development of social theory in recent times.

Of course, Durkheim was not a revolutionary, and one of the main features of his definition of socialism is his attempt to argue that the notion of class conflict is not fundamental to socialist thought. As he admits, this stance seems at odds with the importance that socialists, especially Marxists, attribute to class struggle in the constitution and transformation of society. But it is possible to demonstrate, he asserts, that the workers' movement is only of secondary concern in socialism. The improvement of the lot of the worker is merely one aspect of the more all-encompassing economic reorganisation that socialist doctrines point to; and 'class war is only one of the means by which this reorganisation could result, one aspect of the historic development producing it.' The main factor responsible for the degradation of the worker is that productive labour is not harnessed to the universal interests of the societal community, but instead to those of an exploitative class. The overthrow of this exploiting class is not an end in itself, but rather the mode whereby a rational and fair system of production can be set under way.

Durkheim's portrayal of the history of socialism unfortunately remained unfinished, and he did not continue through to an exhaustive discussion of Marx—although we can glean some idea of what his appraisal of Marx's writings might have involved via his review of Labriola's exposition of historical materialism [in *Revue philosophique,* 1897]. In lieu of such a discussion, we perhaps should be somewhat cautious in subjecting Durkheim's analysis of socialism to critique. None the less, it is not particularly difficult to point to basic difficulties in the contrast Durkheim wanted to draw between communism and socialism, and in the manner in which he sought to characterise socialist theories. The utopian writings Durkheim isolated were certainly not the only form of 'radical Leftism' to have existed prior to the origins of modern socialism in the late eighteenth century; one can think, for example, of the Levellers or of Winstanley in seventeenth-century England. Moreover, Durkheim seems not only to write as if socialist authors were unaware of differences between their ideas and those of 'communism', he also appears to attribute too much unity to 'socialism'. In criticising what he sometimes called 'utopian socialism', after all, Marx showed himself to be acutely aware of the importance of creating a socialist movement that would have a real part to play in furthering social change. A conception of what Habermas would call 'self-reflection' is built into Marx's writings. He was as aware as Durkheim was of the fact that socialist ideas both express circumstances of social transformation and simultaneously can be drawn upon critically to promote further social change.

Particularly dubious, I think, is Durkheim's effort to remove class conflict from occupying a central position in socialist thought. He accomplishes this rather remarkable feat only by virtue of a specious trick of definition. Having characterised socialism as 'in essence' concerned with the centralised control of economic activity, with the regulation of economic life, he is able to declare labour movements and class struggle as of secondary importance to socialist thought. But this conception only has any plausibility at all because Durkheim uses 'socialism' in a very broad sense, and because he suppresses any analysis of *capitalism* in Marx's usage of that term. In Marx's view, capitalism is a generic type of society, constituted upon an economic foundation of the capital/wage-labour relation. Class struggle is thus inherent in the capitalist mode of production; and the revolution due to be brought about by the rise of the workers' movement is the necessary medium of the realisation of a socialist society.

Durkheim's attempt to disconnect socialist thought from

class conflict by means of terminological juggling serves in some part to conceal some very profound divergences between Marx's conceptions and his own. Durkheim not only traces the origins of socialism primarily to Saint-Simon, his own thought is embedded in traditions that owe a considerable amount to Saint-Simon's specific doctrines. Saint-Simon helped to found what I have elsewhere called the theory of industrial society (besides coining the very term 'industrial society'). According to Saint-Simon, the emergent industrial order is already on the verge of becoming a 'classless' society, in the sense of a 'one-class' society of *industriels.* Durkheim developed the theory of industrial society well beyond the point at which Saint-Simon had left it, even if he only rarely used the term itself. For Durkheim, class conflict expresses the tensions involved in the maturation of an industrial order, in which organic solidarity in the division of labour has not yet fully matured. The conflicts deriving from the 'forced division of labour' will be overcome by the progressive removal of 'external inequalities'—barriers to equality of opportunity—and by the transcendence of anomie through the normative regulation of industrial relations. The *corporations,* or occupational associations, were to play a major role in each of these processes.

The revolution that Marx projected may not have occurred, but it seems to me quite plain that Marx's assessment of the endemic character of class conflict in capitalism is closer to contemporary industrial reality than the views which Durkheim offered. Labour unions have not ceded place to *corporations* such as Durkheim envisaged them. Class conflict appears inherent in the capitalist societies at two related 'sites'. One is class struggle at the level of day-to-day practices on the shop-floor. I have in mind here the attempts of workers to control or influence the nature of the labour process. The other is class struggle pitting the various sectors of organised labour movements against employers. These intersecting axes of class conflict, I think, can be readily explicated in terms of Marx's portrayal of the capitalist labour contract, but they are not particularly amenable to explanation within the frame of reference which Durkheim used. Marx emphasised that the capitalist labour contract contrasts radically with class relations in prior types of society. The worker sells his or her labour power in exchange for a monetary wage, but in so doing sacrifices all formal control over the labour process and over other aspects of the organisation of production. But wage-labour refuses to be treated as 'a commodity like any other'. Through modes of informal sanctioning, and through the substantive use of the threat of the collective withdrawal of labour, workers establish themselves as a force to be reckoned with at both sites of conflict.

While Marx's analysis of capitalism as a class society remains of great importance, nobody today can be content with an unreconstructed version of Marxism. For those who would situate themselves 'on the Left' today politically, whether or not they want to call themselves 'Marxists', it seems to me to be an increasingly pressing task to rethink the legacy of Marx. Has Durkheim's account of socialism, whatever its deficiencies, any contribution to make to such a process of reconstruction? I think perhaps

it has, although this does not entail accepting Durkheim's own formulations as they stand.

Durkheim criticised socialist ideas, as he understood them, by arguing that the solutions they propose remain upon a solely economic level. He allowed that various types of economic regulation envisaged by socialists are necessary as part of a programme of social reform. But they cannot be sufficient, because the difficulties facing contemporary societies are not wholly, not even primarily, economic. The contemporary *malaise* derives in an important sense from the very *predominance* of economic relationships over other aspects of social life. No amount of economic transformation will cope with the moral gap that has been left by the dissolution of traditional norms in the face of the expansion of industrial production. This leads Durkheim to an exposition of the nature of the state which contrasts considerably with that contained in Marx's writings. According to Durkheim, the state must play a moral as well as an economic role in a society dominated by organic solidarity. In conjunction with this argument, he rejects the thesis that the state can be 'abolished' in the emergent society of the future—or if the state were 'abolished', the results would be quite the opposite to those anticipated by socialists. Socialists, including Marxists, Durkheim argues, are only able plausibly to advocate the abolition of the state because they imagine that the state can be reduced to a purely economic agency. The state is supposed to restrict the scope of its operations to the 'administration of things'.

Durkheim's discussion of the state and democracy is worth taking seriously. It has to be read against the backdrop of the analysis of mechanical and organic solidarity established in *The Division of Labour.* The moral order of societies cohered by mechanical solidarity provided a binding framework of authority, in which problems of *anomie* did not arise. At the same time, however, they were repressive. The individual was subject to the 'tyranny of the group': the strength of the moral consensus involved in mechanical solidarity inhibited the development of freedom of expression or action. This emphasis is one reason why it is mistaken to see Durkheim as a conservative thinker, even in a broad sense of that term, because at no point in his writings did he evoke a nostalgia for this lost (or rapidly disappearing) moral community. On the contrary, the whole point of the arguments developed in *The Division of Labour* is to demonstrate that there can be no regression to mechanical solidarity, to traditional norms and values: for a new type of societal totality has emerged. The characteristic issue facing the modern world is that of reconciling the individual freedoms which have sprung from the dissolution of the traditional order with the sustaining of the moral authority upon which the very existence of society depends. The contemporary moral order, however, cannot be the same as that which used to exist, and it necessarily involves different institutional mechanisms.

Such mechanisms, in Durkheim's view, must both sustain the independence of the state from society, and at the same time not allow the state wholly to dominate the activities of individuals in the civil sphere. The expansion of the activities of the state, according to him, is an inevitable accompaniment of the maturation of societies having a complex division of labour. As a moral agency, the state takes the lead in fostering the sorts of changes involved in promoting the ideals of 'moral individualism'—ideals stressing the dignity of the individual, and justice and freedom among individuals. Where the state is not strong enough to assume a directive role in this way, the result is likely to be stagnation under the yoke of tradition. There has to be a two-way flow of information between the state and individuals in civil society; and there has also to be a balance of power between them, a balance of power in which the occupational associations are supposed to play an essential mediating role. In a developed 'industrial society', the state cannot be transcended as is presumed in socialist theory. If circumstances which approach this came about in fact, in a developed society, the result would precisely be a reappearance of the 'tyranny of the group' characteristic of mechanical solidarity.

By means of such an analysis, then, Durkheim sought to distinguish his political theory from those of both Right and Left. Thus in the former—in, for example, the works of Hegel and his followers—the state is the very incarnation of societal ideals, and envelops the individual. If put into practice, this type of political theory leads to despotism. The socialist conception of abolishing the state, of reabsorbing the state into civil society, on the other hand, if put into practice, produces tyranny. This is not, however, for Durkheim a tyranny of an individual ruler, rather a tyranny of blind habit or prejudice.

I have said that Durkheim's ideas on the state should be taken seriously, but this does not mean I am particularly persuaded by them. Some writers have tried to develop Durkheim's notion that there should be 'secondary groups' intervening between individuals and the state, into a theory of the origins of totalitarianism. But I do not think such attempts have proved to be illuminating. I do not believe any discussion of the state and democracy can be well founded unless it takes account of the class character of the capitalist societies; and, as I have previously pointed out, Durkheim's sociology is specifically opposed to such a view. Why Durkheim's political writings are worth taking seriously is because they focus upon themes which are at best confronted only in a rudimentary way in Marx. I shall single out only two such themes for discussion here: first, the problem of the importance of the range of individual rights which Durkheim labelled generically 'moral individualism' in the modern state; and second, the question of the relevance to Marxist thought of the Saint-Simonian notion of the state as concerned only with the 'administration of things'. Durkheim's writings on these matters are thought-provoking, and I believe they address issues of major importance. In discussing them here, however, I shall abandon Durkheimian terminology because, as I have said, I do not propose to try to salvage much of Durkheim's own mode of approach to these themes.

The rights involved in moral individualism are essentially those which Marx called 'bourgeois rights'. Marx quite often wrote in a dismissive fashion about them, on the basis that they form an ideological prop to the capitalist class system. The worker is 'free' to sell his or her labour-power to any employer; but this 'freedom' is actually closely bound up with the degradation of labour resulting from the nature of the capitalist labour contract. 'Political freedom', in the nineteenth century at least, was for the working class a sham in two senses. It was a sham in a quite manifest sense, in so far as property qualifications on the vote ensured that the mass of the work-force was not enfranchised. But Marx saw a more deep-lying limitation than this. For the participation of the 'citizen' as a periodic voter in the sphere of 'politics' leaves economic life untouched. On entering the factory gates, the worker leaves behind any rights of participation; democracy in the state permits the autocracy of capital over wage-labour.

I think this analysis to be broadly correct, but it has left something of an ambiguity for subsequent Marxist thought. Are 'bourgeois freedoms' wholly ideological, nothing more than a mode in which the dominant class supports its hegemony? Many Marxists have in fact taken such a view. But it is none the less quite a mistaken standpoint, in my opinion. 'Bourgeois freedoms' in Marx's terminology—rights attaching to 'moral individualism' in that of Durkheim, or, as T. H. Marshall says [in *Citizenship and Social Class*, 1949], 'citizenship rights'—have proved to be of great significance in explaining certain features in the development of the capitalist societies over the past century. Durkheim saw the state as the principal instrument of the furthering of citizenship rights, independently of class interests. Such a view will not do, for reasons I have mentioned. The state, in capitalism, is a state in a class society, in which political power is skewed by the nature of class domination. But the existence of citizenship rights, and the struggles of labour movements to actualise or expand them, have brought about major social changes. The nineteenth-century state was, as Macpherson has said [in his *The Real World of Democracy*, 1966] a 'liberal' state: one allowing the organised formation and competition of parties, but where such parties only represented certain dominant interests. The transformation of the liberal state into the 'liberal-democratic' state was in most countries in substantial degree the result of struggles of labour movements to form recognised parties and to achieve the universal franchise. As Marshall has pointed out, there has occurred in most Western countries a three-fold expansion of citizenship rights, leading from 'legal', to 'political', to 'social' (or welfare) rights.

I do not want to argue, as Marshall does, that the development and actualisation of citizenship rights have substantially dissolved pre-existing class divisions. But I do think it very important to resist the idea, which can no doubt be supported by various textual excerpts from Marx, that such rights are merely a means of 'ensuring the reproduction of labour-power'. This view radically undervalues the struggles of labour movements that have played their part in the formation of liberal democracy; and it therefore does not provide an accurate basis for analysing past transformations. But those of us who still have sympathy for socialist thought, however, have to give some considerable thought to the question of the normative significance of citizenship rights. Liberal democracy remains a sham in the second sense of Marx's critique mentioned above. However, rights which until quite recently many Marxists have accepted quite casually as of only marginal importance to a projected socialist society of the future turn out to be very important indeed. I shall rather arbitrarily mention here only two aspects of this, one from the West, and one from Eastern Europe. The resurgence of conservatism in various Western countries, including Britain and the USA, has made manifest the fact that the 'welfare state' is no mere comfortable functional mechanism cohering capitalism. Welfare rights and services are under severe attack, and in such a context it is surely not possible to see them as mere devices of capitalist domination. Rather, it seems that citizenship rights are important bases of freedoms that those in subordinate positions are able to sustain; and that, far from being able to take them for granted, we have to emphasise that in the context of liberal democracy they are continually subject to contestation.

The development of 'Euro-communism' has served to provide a focus for some of these issues. But there is no doubt in my mind that a good deal of re-thinking is required concerning the relation of socialism and democracy. Questions of the significance of various types of citizenship rights are of course only one angle on this; and at this point I can appropriately turn to the other aspect of Durkheim's writings on socialism which I have argued continues to have a certain relevance today. Durkheim's claim that, both in socialist theory in general and in Marxism in particular, the state is reduced to a purely economic agency is perhaps exaggerated and oversimplified. But in stressing certain common threads in political economy and Marx's views, he makes an important observation. Marx's writings were undeniably influenced by the form of social thought which he devoted most of his mature work to criticising. For both the political economists and for Marx, the expansion of industrial capitalism signalled the increasing pre-eminence of relationships of economic exchange over other types of social relation. Moreover, in the anticipation of the abolition of the state in socialism, there is more than an echo of the Saint-Simonian formula that 'the administration of human beings' will be replaced by 'the administration of things'.

Now we know that for Marx the term 'abolition', in the phrase 'abolition of the state', has to be understood as *Aufhebung*—transcendence. Marx was explicitly opposed to anarchism, and rather than doing away with the state altogether envisaged its radical reorganisation with the advent of socialist society. But he gave little indication of what form this would take, and how concretely it was to be achieved. The notion of the 'abolition of the state', I consider, is not simply an archaic idea to be forgotten about in the altered circumstances of the twentieth century. But, in the context of the history thus far of the 'actually existing' socialist societies, no one can afford to be in the least complacent about the thesis that there is some clear and direct tie between socialism and the transcendence of the state. Nor can we merely wish away the claims of right-wing political theorists that socialism is linked 'at source' with totalitarian elements which actually accentuate rather than diminish the power of the state over individuals in civil society.

But Durkheim's own conception of the state does not advance much beyond that of Marx. Durkheim's writings provide very little conceptual grasp of two features of the state that have proved to be of fundamental significance in our era. One of these refers to 'internal', the other to 'external', characteristics of the state. So far as the latter are concerned, we have at this point to stop talking of 'the state' in the abstract. For at least since the origins of industrial capitalism, 'the state' has been the *nation-state;* and nation-states have existed in interrelation with one another. Industrial capitalism, as a form of economic production, emerged in conjunction with a pre-existing European state-system. The recent writings of Tilly and Skocpol, among others, have done much to help explicate the nature of this relationship. The nation-state system today, of course, has become a world-wide one, a common denominator among political systems of otherwise widely variant complexions. Of the various elements of the modern nation-state by far the most important for us to seek to understand and analyse is its monopoly of the means of violence. Marxism specifically lacks a tradition that can provide the source for such an analysis. I have argued elsewhere that it *is* possible, however, to forge connections between Marx's discussion of capitalism and the concentration of the means of violence in the hands of the state. I have earlier drawn attention to the importance of the capitalist labour contract in Marx's explication of the nature of capitalist production. A singular feature of capitalistic enterprise, as involving formally 'free' wage-labour, is that the main form of constraint ensuring the compliance of the labour force is the need of workers to have paid employment in order to survive. The worker loses any rights of participation in the organisation of the labour process; but the employer also forgoes the capacity to achieve compliance through threat of the use of violence. In contrast to virtually all prior class systems, the dominant class does not have direct access to the means of violence in order to secure its appropriation of surplus production. Control of the means of violence becomes 'extruded' from the exploitative class relation itself, and monopolised in the hands of the state.

The historical conditions that gave rise to this 'extrusion' were complicated, and I have no space to offer an analysis of them here. But they involved concomitant processes of the 'internal pacification' of nation-states. The recent writings of Foucault and others, in my view, have helped considerably to illuminate the mechanisms contributing to these processes. For a distinctive trait of states from the late eighteenth century onwards has been a vast expansion in the range and intensity of their activities of *surveillance* over their subject populations. 'Surveillance' refers to two sets of related phenomena (although these are not distinguished as such by Foucault).

The first concerns the collation of information used to 'keep tabs' on those subject to the authority of the state. As archaeologists have frequently stressed, the close association between the formation of early agrarian states and the origins of writing is not accidental. Writing seems to have been invented first of all as a recording device whereby states could 'store' information used in their governance. Surveillance in this sense has always been closely bound up with states of all kinds. But there is no doubt that the eighteenth and nineteenth centuries in Western Europe witnessed a vast extension and intensification of the activities of the state in this respect. The mushrooming of 'official statistics' is perhaps the best single exemplification of this.

Surveillance in its second sense refers to the direct or indirect *supervision* of the conduct of subject populations on the part of the state. The development of internal police forces is a major element here. But 'policing', as Donzelot has recently argued [in *The Policing of Families*, 1979], has to be understood in a broader sense than it has come to assume in language today. When he talks of, and seeks to examine, the 'policing' of the family in the nineteenth century, he is concerned to study how the supervisory activities of states penetrate to the interior of family life. The very period at which the differentiation of 'state' from 'civil society' was most taken for granted in the political literature was the period at which states began to spread their tentacles into numerous spheres of everyday life. We should not ignore this when we acknowledge the importance of Marx's discussion of the severance of the 'economic' from the 'political'. One of the major errors of social theory from the eighteenth century to the present day has been to presume that the 'economic' can be equated with the sphere of 'civil society'.

The relation between citizenship rights and the nation-state is an interesting and in some part an asymmetrical one. Marx might have believed that 'the workers have no country', but this has hardly turned out to have been one of his most trenchant observations. Struggles to achieve citizenship rights have almost wholly been carried on within the bounds of nation-states, and the very notion of 'citizenship' (in contrast to its earlier association with towns in the context of post-feudal society) has come to be defined in nationalist terms. One consequence of this is that there is not necessarily a direct connection between the nature and prevalence of citizenship rights within particular states, and the external conduct of those states. In this sense, it could perhaps be argued, there is a basic asymmetry between the USA and the Soviet Union in the world today. One would be hard put to it to argue that the Soviet Union is a 'freer' society internally, as regards the rights of its citizenry *vis-à-vis* the state, than the USA. But the role of the Soviet Union in the world at large, Poland and Afghanistan notwithstanding, tends to be less reactionary than that of its capitalist adversary.

The relation between citizenship rights and the surveillance activities of states is also not an unambiguous one. Collation of information and the supervision of at least certain sectors of the behaviour of subject populations is part and parcel of, for instance, the operation of any universal franchise that is not corrupt. At the same time, surveillance activities of various kinds can be directly inimical to the freedoms of individuals in civil society. Brutal forms of police repression are probably not the most disturbing instance of such a phenomenon. More insidious and difficult to combat are the rapid development of centralised modes of information storage and processing made possible by modern computer technology. Surveil-

lance in the first sense of the term I distinguished threatens in the modern age to become a more potent threat to freedom than surveillance in its second sense. But in so far as Left political theory has tried to come to terms with surveillance at all as a mode of state domination, it is mainly in respect of its second aspect.

I cannot attempt in the compass of this discussion to work out the implications of all this for contemporary socialist thought. Anyone interested in, or sympathetic to, socialism today is quite clearly in a very different position from either Marx or Durkheim, writing in the nineteenth and early twentieth centuries. Socialism has to be theorised today on two intersecting levels, and it will not do to work on either without reference to the other. For both Marx and Durkheim, socialism was a project, a set of possible developments for the future. For us, however, socialism is an 'actually existing' reality, and yet at the same time remains a set of ideals capable of generating potentialities as yet unrealised anywhere. Herein reside some of the most urgent problems of political theory. The contemporary world is the world of the Gulag, of warlike confrontations between socialist nation-states, and of something close to genocide in Kampuchea. Socialism no longer walks innocently in this world. One possible response to this is to follow the direction taken by the 'new philosophers' in France. They are the protagonists of the 'May events' of 1968 who find themselves, not in a world of liberated humanity, but in an age of a 'barbarism with a human face'. In consequence, they have moved from Marx to Nietzsche, declaring power and the state to be intransigent barriers to the realisation of any sort of socialist ideals. In a certain respect they are correct: the state is an altogether more formidable and pervasive phenomenon than was ever conceived of in the dominant traditions of thought in the nineteenth century. We should not tread their path and acquiesce helplessly in the triumph of state power. But if we do not wish to follow them, if we do not wish to move from Marx to Nietzsche—if we want to keep socialist political thought alive—we may have to be prepared to place radically in question some of the most cherished concepts of classical Marxism.

Anthony Giddens, "Durkheim, Socialism and Marxism," in his Profiles and Critiques in Social Theory, *University of California Press, 1982, pp. 117-32.*

David Lockwood   (essay date 1982)

[*Lockwood is an English educator and author of works examining class consciousness and labor. In the following essay, he discusses Durkheim's concept of fatalism and why it "remains Durkheim's hidden theory of order."*]

The significance of Durkheim's concept of fatalism [in *Suicide*] is wholly unappreciated. The idea is seldom discussed and then only in relation to the study of suicide. Unlike anomie, it has had a most undistinguished sociological career. This is curious because if anomie can serve to illuminate in a quite general way the nature of social disorder, why should fatalism not be regarded as having the capacity to provide an explanation of order that is of equally wide scope? The aim of this essay is to show that hidden in the concept of fatalism there is indeed such a theory, though it bears little resemblance to what is taken to be Durkheim's major contribution to the analysis of social integration.

It is understandable that fatalism should have been neglected because Durkheim devotes no more than a few lines to the concept, and then only, it would seem, out of a logical instinct for symmetry. It appears as the opposite social state to anomie, which is a condition in which normative rules suddenly lose their power of regulating the wants of individuals. Consequently, fatalism is defined as 'excessive regulation', 'excessive physical or moral despotism', as a situation in which the future is 'pitilessly blocked and passions violently choked by oppressive discipline'. At one pole, then, there is an extraordinarily weak social regulation of wants, at the other an unusually stringent limitation of them. If anomie means that horizons become abruptly widened so that aspirations know no bounds, fatalism refers to hopes so narrowed and diminished that even life itself becomes a matter of indifference. As examples of the latter, Durkheim refers to suicides committed by slaves, and he concludes by saying that in order to 'bring out the ineluctable and inflexible nature of a rule against which there is no appeal, and in contrast with the expression "anomy" which has just been used, we might call it *fatalistic suicide*'.

As it stands, Durkheim's treatment of the concept hardly goes much beyond the dictionary definition of fatalism as 'submission to all that happens as inevitable', and the possibility of deriving a theory of social order from it would appear to be small. Nevertheless, a start can be made by considering the two main assumptions of his account. The first is that fatalism, like anomie, is a matter of degree. In characteristic fashion, he uses the term 'excessive' to describe both the fatalistic over-regulation of wants and their anomic de-regulation. It is reasonable then to suppose that fatalism is to be understood as varying according to the amount of 'oppressive discipline' involved. The second point is that there are two kinds of discipline; fatalism results from either 'physical or moral despotism'. In seeking the meanings that can be attached to these terms it is convenient to begin with physical despotism. The most obvious instance of this is coercion, and social organisations in which order is maintained by excessive and oppressive discipline of a direct and personal kind are all too familiar. These extreme cases, however, are of little relevance to an understanding of the more general problem of order because the degree of coercion required to ensure the compliance of inmates of organisations such as prisons and concentration camps is incapable of being reproduced as the sole or even as the major means of securing enduring social stability in a society of any size and complexity. The various arguments against a 'coercion theory' of social order have been well rehearsed and it is no part of the present argument to reiterate or to challenge them. Moreover, to identify fatalistic order with a coercive regimen of this kind would be completely out of keeping with Durkheim's view that the coerciveness of society lies in its supra-individual nature. It has been argued on good grounds that in the course of his work Durkheim's idea of social constraint changed from a view of social facts as things,

or conditions of social action, to a notion of social facts as moral forces which exert their influence by becoming internalised needs of the individual. This distinction between social conditions and moral beliefs is indispensable to a closer understanding of fatalistic order.

The first conclusion that can be drawn from it is that 'despotism' presents itself most effectively not as direct personal oppression but in the form of impersonal social constraint. What are called the 'unintended consequences' of 'latent functions' of purposive social action belong to this category. These terms refer to the systematic effects of social interactions which appear not to be the outcome of human volition and which thus acquire the property of objective conditions. In this way, massive unemployment or abject poverty have very often been experienced as unavoidable 'facts of life', privations that are due to anonymous forces over which no one has control. These conditions have the effects of narrowing people's horizons and inuring them to what seems to be part of the natural order of things. Students of the 'culture of poverty' have shown in some detail how such fatalistic attitudes are engendered and how they contribute to the maintenance of life styles which serve to accommodate people to conditions of adversity. In a similar fashion, the structure of social organisation itself may take on the property of unalterability or inescapability. When Weber speaks of 'the iron cage' of bureaucracy, or Marx of the 'fetishism of commodities', it is presumably to this kind of social fact that they refer. In all these instances, what is especially conducive to a fatalistic attitude is not so much the degree of 'oppressive discipline' involved, but rather the fact that social constraint is experienced as an external, inevitable and impersonal condition. For however oppressive direct personal coercion may be, it can never produce the same kind of acquiescence as that which is born of social conditions that appear to be unattributable to, and thereby inconvertible by, human agency.

This kind of 'conditional fatalism' probably comes closer to Durkheim's notion of 'moral despotism'. Indeed, it may be all that he means by the latter term. 'Moral' has such a wide and uncertain significance in Durkheim's vocabulary that any further discussion of its association with fatalism is bound to be fairly speculative. Nonetheless, it is worth pursuing the idea that the meaning of moral despotism is not exhausted by the concept of conditional fatalism. The clue to what might further be implied by it is to be found in Durkheim's distinction between 'the spirit of discipline' and 'attachment to social groups'. Throughout his writings, these two 'elements of morality', which are fundamental to his explanations of social order and disequilibrium, simply appear in different guises (egoism versus anomie, ritual versus belief, organic versus mechanical solidarity, and so on). Now fatalism, like anomie, has to do with the way in which wants are disciplined, and for Durkheim the principal source of this regulation is the system of values and beliefs which makes up the collective conscience. One entirely consistent interpretation of moral despotism, then, is that it refers to some aspect of the collective conscience which has the capacity to make individuals accept their life situation as unquestionable, because any alternative dispensation is, by virtue of the beliefs they hold, unthinkable. Here, by contrast with conditional fatalism, it is the constraint of a system of beliefs, rather than sheer force of circumstances, which is the key to social order. But if this interpretation is correct, it follows that moral despotism has its origin in precisely that aspect of the collective conscience which Durkheim deliberately excluded from his study of the religious life: namely, the 'confusing details' of the creeds and doctrines themselves. His silence on this subject is most remarkable. It is true that at one point in his writings, and in a manner not distinct from that of vulgar Marxism, he does appear to attribute to religious beliefs in general the capacity to induce a fatalistic ethos among believers. But this passing remark goes very much against the grain of his conception of sociology as a subject concerned with the co-variation of social facts; and the assumption that all religions and ideologies have the same social consequences affords no basis for the serious examination of moral despotism. If fatalism and anomie are the limiting cases of moral discipline, and if the chief source of the last is 'religious' (in the widest, that is to say Durkheimian, sense of the term), then moral despotism must vary according to differences in the *structure* of religious beliefs. In short, certain types of beliefs must be assumed to be more conducive than others to what Mannheim has called the 'ethics of fatalism'.

Before attempting to substantiate this point, two further general implications of the concept of fatalism need to be brought out. The first concerns its consequences for the Durkheimian, and therefore for the normative functionalist, solution of the problem of order. The second has to do with the connection between fatalism and ritual, which for Durkheim is the core of the 'religious life'.

There can be no more firmly established canon of sociological orthodoxy than the belief that Durkheim's major contribution to the understanding of social integration consists in his discovery and elaboration of the concept of the collective conscience. Renamed the 'common value system', this idea became the lynchpin of normative functionalism, which, as the most influential school of neo-Durkheimian thought, took it as axiomatic that widespread consensus on ultimate values is not only a normal feature of stable societies but the single most important precondition of social order. From these assumptions it follows that the basic point of reference in the analysis of social integration are the processes by which values become internalised in actors, and that the conformity of actors with institutional norms must be understood first and foremost as the outcome of this commitment to values legitimating specific role obligations. In this perspective, there is little room for explanations of order that emphasise the significance of either coerced compliance or the 'natural identity of interests'; explanations that are commonly believed to be the only possible alternatives to a 'consensus' theory of society. The last, as represented by normative functionalism, has been subject to much condign criticism, but attempts to displace it have resulted in little more than a regression towards some kind of equally unacceptable 'coercion' model of society. In this whole controversy, however, it has not been recognised that what is conventionally taken to be Durkheim's classical solution of the problem of order is not the only one that

can be derived from his conceptual scheme. In the idea of fatalism there are the makings of an alternative explanation that depends neither on the assumptions of consensus theory nor on those of the latter's two chief rivals. Most importantly in the present context, the concept of fatalistic order can dispense with the view that widespread agreement on the ultimate values legitimating institutions is a prerequisite of social stability. A sufficient condition of order is simply that the structure of power, wealth and status is believed to be inevitable, or, as Durkheim says, ineluctable. The general point has been well made by [S. M.] Tumin in his review of the evidence concerning the characteristic modes of response of lower strata to their position in the social hierarchy:

> The fact is that we have tended to infer, from the relative stability of caste positions and arrangements over time, that the denigrated and depreciated castes accept as legitimate and appropriate a status of denigration and depreciation. But this inference, taken from the absence of significant action designed to alter the situation, neglects the numerous other reasons for such inactivity by lower caste members or relatively deprived peoples all over the world. In the more general case, it is probably true that subordinate people's failure to improve their situation is as much due to their inability to conceive of a possible alternative, and/or when they do conceive and desire alternatives, to contrive ways to carry out these ideas. Only in a very restricted sense of the word can people under such circumstances be said to 'accept' their positions. And this degree of acceptance is a far cry from any acceptance of the legitimacy of the situation under which they live, if by legitimacy we mean more than nominal conformity to the dominant norms. [*Social Class and Social Change in Puerto Rico,* 1961]

This formulation, however, still leaves open the question of how the inability to conceive of an alternative state of affairs arises. For there is after all an important difference between fatalistic beliefs stemming from the individual's realisation that he is personally in the grip of circumstances over which he has no control and fatalistic beliefs resulting from his socialisation into an ideology that provides a comprehensive account of why circumstances are beyond his (or anyone else's) control. The distinction is important if only because equally adverse conditions do not always produce equally fatalistic beliefs or the same degree of acquiescence to adversity. This is another reason for thinking that it might be useful to view moral despotism as a system of 'oppressive' beliefs. But in this case, how does the explanation of order differ from that advanced by normative functionalism? Does it not also presuppose the existence of a common value system, of a moral consensus?

The difficulty here lies in a further ambiguity of the term 'moral', which Durkheim uses to refer not only to values or ethical standards but also to beliefs about the nature of the physical and social world. To speak of moral despotism is therefore to conflate two distinct elements that enter into any ideology and to treat as unproblematic the very connection between them which the idea of fatalism would seem to make questionable. The chief social fact that ideologies seek both to explain and to legitimate is human fortune and misfortune, and in particular inequalities of power, wealth and status. But they do so more or less successfully, depending on the extent to which the existential and moral beliefs of which they are composed are in harmony with one another; in this respect ideologies differ markedly in their 'closure' or 'exploitability'. They differ also in the degree to which it is the existential or the moral element which has the more extensive hold over the various groupings of society, and most importantly over its lowest strata.

These facts have not been sufficiently well recognised by normative functionalism, which has tended to treat values and beliefs as an integrated whole as far as the motivation of actors is concerned. The main advantage of the concept of fatalism would seem to be that it leaves open the question of whether, and to what extent, beliefs in the inevitability of social structures are associated with beliefs in their justness and legitimacy. Indeed, by making it possible to ask whether institutions would continue to be supported in the event of the collapse of beliefs about their inevitability, the concept helps to provide a closer definition of solidarity. For it could hardly be denied that a society in which people continue to support central values and institutions, even though they can conceive of realistic alternatives to them, is in a real sense more solidary than a society whose members cannot make this comparison. Finally, the concept of fatalism has the merit of being able to explain those fairly common cases of societies undergoing a sudden discontinuity from order to disorder as a result of their members' exposure to new beliefs: for example, so-called 'revolutions of rising expectations'. The only way in which the value consensus theory of order could attempt to explain this kind of discontinuity would be to assume that the pre-existing orderliness of such societies was really a condition of potential instability characterised by weak attachments to, or even alienation from, common values and beliefs. But since this type of theory rejects the argument that societies can be held together by expediency or coercion, it would still leave unexplained the sources of orderliness of a potentially unstable society. The concept of ideological fatalism involves no such dilemma.

The extent to which subordinate strata regard their positions as legitimate, as opposed to simply accepting them as unalterable, is a matter that is closely bound up with the question of whether social cohesion is based principally on beliefs or ritual. For while Durkheim defines a religious community by its adherents' shared beliefs and their participation in a common ritual, it is a frequently noted aspect of the variability of religious institutions that the strict observance of ritual practice is by no means always associated with a strong commitment to the beliefs the ritual symbolises; indeed, very often the beliefs in question are no more than superficially understood. Robertson Smith, to whom Durkheim owed a great deal in forming his theory of the elementary religious life, drew a firm distinction between the external constraints of ritual in ancient religions and the internal constraints of conviction in modern religions:

It is of the first importance to realise clearly from the outset that ritual and practical usage were, strictly speaking, the sum-total of ancient religions. Religion in primitive times was not a fixed system of belief with practical applications; it was a body of fixed traditional practices to which every member of the society conformed as a matter of course. To us moderns, religion is above all a matter of conviction and reasoned belief, but to the ancients it was part of the citizen's public life, reduced to fixed forms, which he was not bound to understand and was not at liberty to criticise or neglect. Religious nonconformity was an offence against the state; for if sacred tradition was tampered with the bases of society were undermined, and the favour of the gods was forfeited. But so long as the prescribed forms were duly observed, a man was recognised as truly pious, and no one asked how his religion was rooted in his heart or affected his reason. Like political duty, of which it was indeed a part, religion was entirely comprehended in the observance of certain fixed rules of outward conduct. [*The Religion of the Semites,* 1956]

Although the difference is certainly overdrawn, the point is an important one. It is exaggerated because the relative salience of ritual and belief varies with the rhythm of routinisation and renovation common to all sacerdotal institutions. Even so, societies can be graded according to the extent to which ritualisation is the predominant mode of religious integration, a tendency that is the more apparent the greater the intellectual gulf between the beliefs of dominant and subordinate strata. This is a line of analysis that Durkheim's theory excludes; or at least directs attention away from. It is true that he thought of ritual as the more fundamental aspect of the religious life, but it was also a mode of action that he considered to be inseparably connected with the reaffirmation and reinforcement of a common belief system. Ritualisation, which term may be used to refer to Robertson Smith's emphasis on the routinisation of religious conduct, thus differs markedly from the Durkheimian notion of ritual as an extraordinary moment of collective 'effervescence' in which a society undergoes a periodic act of moral communion and re-making. By concentrating on the 'elementary' case of a socially unstratified 'church', Durkheim was not led to consider the nature of religious integration in those far more numerous instances in which the refined soteriologies of the *Lehrstand* have at best only the most feeble and tenuous links with the substratum of folk magic. In such societies, the elementary fact of religious life is the chasm between elite and mass religiosity; and as a result the applicability of Durkheim's concept of the church as a morally unified community is severely limited. Under these conditions, ritualisation acquires its significance as the chief means by which the rudiments of the dominant belief system can be infused into the plebeian collective consciousness. But this superficial appropriation of popular beliefs is obtained only at the cost of the deformation and degeneration of elite ideology, through its embodiment in rituals whose symbolism has to accommodate religious needs that remain primarily oriented to magical solutions of everyday exigencies.

It is perhaps profitable, then, to think of ritual and belief as alternative and inversely related modes of religious, and hence, in Durkheim's understanding, of social integration. Ritual, or rather ritualisation, is likely to be the principal agency when the cultural stratification of society is profound. But it will be especially prominent if, in addition, widespread heterodoxy is freely tolerated or (and this might amount to the same thing) less easily manageable. Indian religion, for example, is characterised by just such an extensive ritualisation of conduct and by a correspondingly weak dogmatism. At the opposite extreme (the case from which normative functionalism seems to have generalised its peculiar ethnocentric idea of social solidarity), is the kind of society in which dominant values and beliefs, principally those of 'secular' religions, are much more accessible to the masses; and in which therefore the problem of consensus, the legitimation and delegitimation of the centre, becomes of much more crucial importance. In this case, the need to secure social integration through pervasive ritualisation is less imperative, and the resort to manufactured ritual of a quasi-Durkheimian kind is occasioned less by the lack of a 'common' value system than by the tension between an overly articulate ideological promise and the evident faultiness of the reality it enshrines.

The question of whether the mass of the population is integrated into a religious community through ritual rather than belief has a direct bearing on fatalism. The crux of the matter is that the concept of fatalism forces a distinction between a social order that is based on a commitment to ultimate values that legitimate it, and one that rests on the rather less secure foundation of beliefs in its unalterability. And ritualisation clearly approximates the latter case. For if the value and belief system communicated to the masses through ritual is remote from their understanding, then the question of its function in legitimating their life situation is otiose. Plamenatz makes this point well when he writes [in *Man and Society vol. II, 1969*]:

> In the Middle Ages, most people who were called or who called themselves Christians were ignorant and illiterate; and it is impossible that many of them understood what the religion they adhered to was all about. They were churchgoers and participants in ceremonies rather than persons having definite beliefs. We ought to say of them, as of the illiterate peasants in the Balkans and the southern parts of Italy as late as our own century, that they did not challenge the doctrines of the Church, and not that they accepted them. Where orthodoxy is unchallenged nothing more is required of most people than outward conformity, and orthodoxy is never less challenged than when the vast majority are illiterate, or almost so, and are incapable of either accepting or rejecting the doctrines which are orthodox.

Ritualisation has, then, a close affinity to fatalism; and there are several reasons why this should be so. When ritual symbolism provides the bridge between the disparate beliefs of higher and lower strata, it is in the nature of this syncretisation that the dominant belief system remains cognitively remote from the masses and is just as likely to be regarded as part of the same unalterable order of things as are the institutions it seeks to legitimate. Moreover, in having to meet the exigent, relatively crude, redemptory interests of the masses, this symbolism tends to reinforce fatalistic attitudes by parochialising the sense of injury, injustice and discontent, the more so when it is charged with magical significance. Fatalistic beliefs in chance and luck are very generally held by people who perceive their lives to be subject to supernatural forces that are only marginally within their control. And since magic operates within the interstices of the soteriology of the ruling stratum, far from weakening the ideological sanctioning of the existing social order, it buttresses it. Ritualisation is not, however, the cause of fatalism. Rather, they are respectively practices and beliefs whose mutually reinforcing and socially stabilising effects are most evident in those societies in which the lower strata stand at such a great distance from the ideological centre that its constraint over them consists chiefly in its inscrutability.

But while this is perhaps one sense in which Durkheim's notion of moral depotism may be understood, it is very much a conceptual point of reference, a limiting case. In one form or another, the rudiments of the dominant ideology are conveyed to the masses through ritual symbolism and stand in varying degrees of integration with popular beliefs. Because of this, it is important to return to the problem of what Mannheim has called the ethics of fatalism. For there is clearly a difference between the more general case of fatalism that is augmented by people's inability to question a remote and largely incomprehensible ideology, and fatalism that is grounded in their acceptance of a system of beliefs, which, however imperfectly it is understood, is, by virtue of its particular soteriology, an ideology *of* fatalism.

Probably the most thoroughgoing attempt to explain social order in terms of ideological fatalism is Weber's account of the Hindu doctrine of *karma,* which is part of his wider thesis that the theodicies of 'Asiatic religion' precluded the development of an ethical interest in radical social transformation. A major starting point of his work [*The Religion of India*] on Indian religions is the problem of why rebellion against the caste system had not been more frequent and widespread. In seeking to provide a solution of this problem primarily by reference to the basic presuppositions of Hindu soteriology, Weber was, it may be assumed, not oblivious of the political and economic conditions that would have placed obstacles in the path of any concerted 'class' action on the part of the most disadvantaged, and thus potentially revolutionary, castes. What he wished to prove was that the goal of social revolution was unthinkable in the first place. His most categorical statement of this view [in ***The Sociology of Religion,*** transl. E. Fischoff, 1963] is as follows: 'That these religions lack virtually any kind of social-revolutionary ethics can be explained by reference to their theodicy of "rebirth" according to which the caste system is eternal and absolutely just.' The logic of *karma-samsara-moksha* did not, however, prevent inter-caste hostility; and what Weber has to say about it brings out once again the highly questionable sense in which a social order based on a system of fatalistic beliefs may be said to be 'legitimate'.

Estranged castes might stand beside one another with bitter hatred—for the idea that everyone had 'deserved' his own fate did not make the good fortune of the privileged more enjoyable to the underprivileged. So long as *karma* doctrine was unshaken, revolutionary ideas or progressivism were inconceivable. The lowest castes, furthermore, had the most to win through ritual correctness and were least tempted to innovations. [*India*]

Furthermore, this doctrine, 'the most consistent theodicy ever produced by history' and shared by all Hindus, not only acted as an infallible prophylactic against lower-caste revolt, but decisively determined the other-worldly religious interests of the many sectarian movements that challenged Brahminical orthodoxy and found their adherents mainly among the middle and higher castes. As Weber puts it [in *India*], 'An absolute presupposition of Hindu philosophy after the full development of the *karma* and *samsara* doctrines, was that escape from the wheel of rebirth could be the one and only conceivable function of a "salvation".'

Since Brahmins awarded themselves the exclusive privilege of being able to seek release from the *karma* mechanism, it is understandable that there was a strong incentive to doctrinal innovation among those less fortunately placed. For example, heterodox sects, and in particular the Jains, appealed especially to relatively privileged groups whose positions in the secular and ritual hierarchies were incongruous, just as the *bhakti* movements, promising redemption through ecstatic devotion to a saviour deity, recruited extensively from lower castes who were, according to orthodoxy, condemned to the torment of a virtually endless cycle of reincarnations.

In general, the states and stages of salvation envisaged by Hindu philosophies were as myriad as the methods by which it was believed that they could be achieved. Weber's basic contention, however, is that although their specific goals and means might vary, all indigenous soteriologies were oriented to the same ultimate end, which Mrs Stevenson epitomises in the opening sentence of her book, [*The Heart of Jainism*], on Jainism: 'The desire of India is to be freed from the cycle of rebirths, and the dread of India is reincarnation.' Whatever the preferred salvation technology (meditation, asceticism, orgiasticism, *bhakti*), a radical denial of the purpose of worldly redemption was common to both orthodoxy and heterodoxy. There were many movements that rejected Brahminical authority, it was not unusual that caste was regarded as irrelevant to salvation, and some sects, most notably the Lingayats, even dispensed with the doctrine of transmigration. Yet, given the direction of the basic religious interest, the goal of protest could not be to reconstitute society in accordance with some external ethical commandment, to replace caste by another form of social organisation. It was constrained rather to assume some form of what Dumont [in his *Homo Hierarchicus: The Caste System and its Implications,* 1970] has called 'renunciation'. On this point, Weber is unequivocal. As regards 'open-door castes', namely 'Jainism, Buddhism, some of the revivals of Vishnu faith in a redeemer, and the Shiva sect of Lingayat, all

of which are considered absolutely heretical', [Weber's claim in *India*] is that 'there is no basic difference between their sacred paths and those of orthodox Hinduism' and that none of them undermined the prestige of mystic contemplation as the highest holy path. Finally, in Weber's estimation, these higher ethical currents scarcely touched the mass of the population who for the most part, as always, relied on what were essentially magical remedies against immediate distress.

Although Weber's thesis of *karma*-induced fatalism has not escaped criticism, much of which concerns issues that he himself considered problematic, it is not easily dismissed as a major element in the explanation of the stability of the traditional caste system. And while it is possible that the system was in certain respects more fluid than Weber thought, the results of recent anthropological and historical studies of social mobility have not removed the need to find an answer to his basic question of why the caste order remained so remarkably immune to rebellion. These studies show that, far from accepting their positions as unalterable, individuals and subcastes at most levels of the hierarchy consistently strove to elevate their ritual status, and that, where they achieved a dominant influence in terms of economic or other forms of power, such as numerical preponderance in a locality, they were generally successful in this endeavour. Although strict *karma* doctrine might have demanded undeviating conformity to the duties of immutable caste position, it is clear that aspirations for upward mobility were by no means limited to those that might legitimately be fulfilled in the next cycle of rebirth. Despite the spiritual penalty of demotion attaching to such conduct, it appears that status usurpation was endemic in the traditional caste order and, as in other systems of stratification, it was closely bound up with status incongruities stemming from shifts in the distribution of power. Nevertheless, the fact remains that this mobility involved positional rather than structural change; it left the caste system intact, and was indeed a means of stabilising it [according to M. N. Srinivas in his *Social Change in Modern India,* 1966; and Weber in *India* vol. III].

The same was true of radical sectarian protest movements that challenged orthodox beliefs and treated caste as irrelevant to salvation. Yet in this case, the way in which Weber seeks to explain how such movements were contained introduces an important qualification into his basic thesis that the stability of the social order was guaranteed by the fatalistic implications of *karma* doctrine alone. Virtually without exception, sects that sought to dissociate themselves from the caste system were, in one way or another, forced to accommodate to its boundary-maintaining ritual. Even movements that denied Brahminical authority, along with some of its most basic tenets, ended up by acquiring a quasi-caste status and undergoing internal differentiation that reproduced the main features of the wider ritual hierarchy. Of the Lingayat, which 'represented a type of particularly sharp and principled "protest" reaction to the Brahmans and the caste order', Weber notes tersely [in *India* vol. III] that it was 'pressed back into the caste order by the power of the environment. It did not escape again.' Here Weber refers to constraints of a very different kind than those imposed by fatalistic beliefs.

> When a principled anti-caste sect recruits former members of various Hindu castes and tears them away from the context of their former ritualistic duties, the caste responds by excommunicating all the sect's proselytes. Unless the sect is able to abolish the caste system altogether, instead of simply tearing away some of its members, it becomes, from the standpoint of the caste system, a quasi-guest folk, a kind of confessional guest community in an ambiguous position in the prevailing Hindu order. [*India* vol. III]

Generally speaking, this ambiguity was resolved, and the position of the sect determined, by the way in which its style of life accorded with orthodox ritual observances of the host society.

This line of argument raises certain doubts about the validity of Weber's basic thesis. First of all, inability 'to abolish the caste system altogether' is a very different matter from the inability to conceive of its rejection as a religiously meaningful objective. There are many reasons why the abolition of caste was not feasible, a major one being that the high degree of internal differentiation of the lower castes, together with their geographical dispersion and isolation in a myriad of what Bailey has called 'village microcosms', was a powerful obstacle to any concerted action.

In posing the problem of why lower-caste rebellion was ostensibly so limited, and in seeking to explain this mainly by reference to religious factors, Weber must have assumed that the social and economic conditions impeding rebellion were not essentially different from those obtaining in other comparable societies that did experience frequent and widespread peasant revolt. But he never attempts to substantiate this very large assumption; and this omission is a serious weakness in his argument.

Another difficulty arises in connection with his claim, which is undeniable, that anti-caste movements were generally neutralised by the 'power of the environment', that is to say, by the constraint of ritual, which was the core of the religious order. It is, however, essential to Weber's thesis that the observance of ritual duty was guaranteed principally through spiritual sanctions, by the beliefs in *karma* and *samsara*, 'the truly "dogmatic" doctrines of all Hinduism'.

But whether radical secular protest by lower castes was stifled mainly because of their indoctrination into these beliefs is a question that is highly debatable and unlikely ever to be settled by appeal to historical evidence. To begin with, while Weber was aware that caste discipline was enforced by a whole range of material sanctions, it is possible that he underestimated the extent of their deployment, especially against the untouchables, who were in fact, if not in theory, integral to the system, and who must have formed a substantial part of those whom he considered as potentially rebellious. He probably also underestimated the extent to which economic and other forms of power not only decided ritual ranking but helped to maintain the caste system as a whole. Quite apart from these considerations, it is quite impossible to know how far down the

caste system the ideology of fatalism reached and with what practical effects. What slight evidence there is does not always sit easily with Weber's thesis. For example, it is by no means clear that the stability and rigidity of caste was always regularly associated with widespread belief in *karma* doctrine. More importantly, the fact that anti-caste sects and movements recruited extensively from among lower castes shows that, even if *karma* doctrine was implanted in the minds of the masses, this did not make egalitarian ideas unattractive to them or prevent them from seeking to abandon their ritual duties.

This last point, however, leads back once again to the strand of Weber's argument that is at once most crucial and most difficult to disprove. For if, as many experts believe, the *bhakti* movements were the major expression of lower-caste 'rebellion' against the Brahminical order, what was it that prevented them from carrying their anti-caste ideology into practice outside their own religious communities? Weber's answer is clear. What impeded them was not mainly their inability to mount a frontal attack on the caste system as a whole, or the 'power of the environment' which ritually encapsulated them. What was decisive was that, especially insofar as these movements were anchored in, and constituted a reaction to, indigenous Hindu soteriology, the nature of their rejection of caste had to be passive and accommodative, rather than active and social-revolutionary. In the last analysis, these movements were directed to the same kinds of otherworldly goals as those of the multi-faceted orthodoxy they attacked.

This, then, is Weber's 'anti-critical final word' on the Hindu ethic. From a social scientific point of view it may be less than satisfactory. In the end his thesis is not open to empirical refutation and is hedged in by many refined qualifications. Nevertheless, in its range and power, it is at the very least a theory of ideological fatalism that has no rival. And that is why so much attention has been devoted to it here.

While Weber's attempt to explain the lack of revolutionary movements in traditional India must be regarded as inconclusive, it is necessary to recognise that his views on the fatalistic implications of 'Asiatic religion' relate also to China. And it is possible that the interpretations that have been put upon the significance of the Taiping rebellion provide much less unequivocal support of his thesis than any evidence that is likely to be forthcoming in the case of India. In Weber's estimation [in *The Religion of China,* transl. and ed. by Hans Gerth, 1951], the Taipings represented 'the most powerful and thoroughly hierocratic, politico-ethical rebellion against the Confucian administration and ethic which China had ever experienced'. His opinion is shared by many contemporary Sinologists, and most emphatically by [Joseph R. Levenson in his *Confucian China and Its Modern Fate* vol. II, 1964] who consider that the Taipings represented a decisive break with the previous pattern of inveterate, though intra-systemic, rebelliousness.

The significance of the Taiping rebellion for Weber's thesis [in *India*] can only be appreciated in the context of his theory of the general nature of 'Asiatic' soteriology, the distinctive feature of which was that 'knowledge, be it literary knowledge or mystical gnosis, is finally the single absolute path to the highest holiness here and in the world beyond'. The aim of this knowledge was the comprehension of an immanent and impersonal sacred order, and it generated a type of religious orientation that stood in fundamental contrast to the one that derived from the conception of a personal transcendental god whose ethical demands were in tension with the world and who had created man as his tool for fulfilling these demands. As Weber puts it [in *Religion*],

> None of these mass religions of Asia, however, provided the motives of orientations for a rationalized ethical patterning of the creaturely world in accordance with divine commandments. Rather, they all accepted the world as eternally given, and so the best of all possible worlds. The only choice open to the sages, who possessed the highest type of piety, was whether to accommodate themselves to the Tao, the impersonal order of the world and the only thing specifically divine, or to save themselves from the inexorable chain of causality by passing into the only eternal being, the dreamless sleep of Nirvana.

This distinction is not only vital to the way in which Weber seeks to discriminate between Occidental and Asiatic soteriologies, which find their respective limits in inner-worldly asceticism and other-worldly mysticism; it also has a direct bearing upon the difference between rebellion and revolution. The usual distinction between revolutionary and rebellious movements (irrespective of their success) is that, whereas the former seek to change the entire structure of authority, the latter seek only to replace particular occupants of positions of authority. If this distinction is accepted, then it is easy to see that there is a close relationship between fatalism, rebellion and the conception of the divine as an immanent principle of order. One way of defining an ideology of fatalism is to say that those who share it will be constrained to limit their social protest to rebellion. It is precisely this type of ideological constraint which Weber saw as inherent in the religions of India and China. There were differences, the most important one being that secular rebellion had a legitimate purpose within the Confucian world view, whereas in Hindu theodicy it was utterly meaningless and futile. But the revolutionary transformation of society was in both cases ruled out; it was, given the presuppositions of the belief systems, unthinkable.

The Chinese experience supports Weber's argument remarkably well. 'The Chinese have been called the most rebellious but the least revolutionary of peoples,' writes [Robert M. Marsh in *The Mandarins*, 1961], 'even the overthrow of a dynasty did not legitimise a basic, revolutionary change in the system of stratification. It signalled, rather, a return to a traditional, ideal *status quo*, which had been outraged in the downward swing of the dynastic cycle.' Moreover, what was crucial in legitimating, directing and limiting the traditional pattern of protest was the Confucian concept of 'Heaven', the impersonal and immanent cosmic order. According to Confucian orthodoxy, disturbances in this order were attributable to the rulers'

ritual impropriety, and their loss of the 'mandate' of Heaven was a legitimate ground for rebellion, through which the intrinsically harmonious order could be restored. It is against this background that the Taiping revolt stands out as distinctive in its aims, and the explanation of their novelty is one that adds considerably to the credibility of Weber's thesis.

There is fairly general agreement that, in contrast with previous movements, which had pursued restorationary goals, the Taiping uprising was revolutionary. And even though it failed to put its ideas into practice, it is considered to have had a lasting and shattering effect on the structure of Confucian authority. As Levenson puts it: 'Proto-revolutionary Taiping rebels took the Confucian-imperial order out of the path of rebellions, and set it up for the unmistakable revolutionaries who were still to come.' Whereas earlier rebellions had sought to replace emperors and ruling cliques through whose derelictions of ritual duty the natural social equilibrium had been disturbed, the Taipings envisaged a far-reaching transformation of social institutions, including the abolition of emperorship itself. In this way, it directly challenged the central Confucian doctrine of immanence, which had hitherto survived any challenge from Taoist and Buddhist ideas that had provided fuel for rebelliousness. The source of the new, utopian element in Taiping ideology was undoubtedly exogenous, deriving from Christianity, with its conception of a personal, transcendental god and its millenary promise. Taiping ideology was naturally a syncretisation of indigenous justifications of rebellion and 'imported' Christian beliefs; but it was the latter which appear to have been decisive in switching the movement from a rebellious to a revolutionary track.

This is all that Weber's thesis would require in the way of confirmation. It is therefore arguable that the nature of the entry of the Taipings into Chinese history provides much firmer evidence in support of his general theory of the religious determination of interests than any that is likely to emerge from the historical study of the caste system, or indeed from the protracted controversy over the 'protestant ethic' and the 'spirit of capitalism'. For what distinguished the Taiping uprising from previous ones was not so much a fundamental change in the social and economic setting of the movement as the extent of its ideological discontinuity. History is not a laboratory. It is, nevertheless, fairly safe to say that the social conditions that gave rise to the Taiping revolt were not basically different from those that were the occasion of previous rebellions. And the obstacles to revolutionary change remained largely the same. Among them, probably the most important was the well nigh invincible position of the Confucian ruling class, who, as landlords, officials and scholars linked by extensive kinship networks, virtually monopolised major power resources. In this respect, the fate of the Taipings was no different from that of any preceding rebellion. All of this, however, adds further support to Weber's thesis. He concluded that the Taiping revolt showed that 'it was not an insurmountable "natural disposition" that hindered the Chinese from producing religious structures comparable to those of the Occident'. In the light of subsequent work, he might have concluded that, until the Taipings, what hindered the Chinese from producing revolutionary movements was an insurmountable system of fatalistic beliefs.

Weber's studies of Indian and Chinese religions come nowhere near providing incontrovertible proof that beliefs in the immanent nature of the sacred are sufficient to account for the peculiar structural stability of these societies and the distinctive forms of social protest they experienced. Such a conclusion would anyway be completely out of keeping with his general observations on the determination and effects of religious interests. Nevertheless, his work still stands as the most thoroughgoing analysis of the 'ethics of fatalism'. It is ironic then that, although his studies of comparative religion are so highly esteemed by normative functionalists, their relevance to the Durkheimian theory of order has largely been ignored. For if the foregoing arguments have any substance, Weber's studies of 'Asiatic' religion provide grounds for thinking that the concept of fatalism, far from being an obscure afterthought deserving of no more than its relegation to a footnote of **Suicide,** is in fact the key to a completely different solution of the problem of order than the one Durkheim has been credited with. Most importantly, Weber's work shows that if any precise meaning is to be attached to the idea of moral despotism this can only be discovered through an analysis of the ideological constraints inherent in the structures of specific belief systems. This kind of enquiry has not been central in the theory of order and conflict propounded by Durkheim and elaborated by his successors. The neglect of it is one main reason why fatalism remains Durkheim's hidden theory of order.

David Lockwood, "Fatalism: Durkheim's Hidden Theory of Order," in Social Class and the Division of Labour: Essays in Honour of Ilya Neustadt, *edited by Anthony Giddens and Gavin MacKenzie, Cambridge University Press, 1982, pp. 101-18.*

FURTHER READING

Criticism

Alpert, Harry. *Émile Durkheim and His Sociology.* New York: Columbia University Press, 1939, 233 p.

Discusses Durkheim's conception of sociology as a "natural, objective, specific, yet synthetic, collective, independent and unitary science of social facts."

Beach, Walter Greenwood. "Attempts at Psychological Social Interpretation: Tarde and Durkheim." In his *The Growth of Social Thought,* pp. 175-81. 1939. Reprint. Port Washington, N. Y.: Kennikat Press, 1967.

Study of Durkheim's contribution to the development of social thought, comparing and contrasting his ideas about group behavior and social psychology with those of his contemporary, Gabriel Tarde.

Bierstedt, Robert. *Émile Durkheim.* London: Weindenfeld and Nicolson, 1966, 247 p.

Analysis of Durkheim's last four prominent works: *The Division of Labor in Society, The Rules of Sociological Method, Suicide,* and *The Elementary Forms of the Religious Life.*

Bogardus, Emory S. "Durkheim and Collective Representations." In *The Development of Social Thought,* pp. 418-35. New York: Longmans, Green and Co., 1940.

Explains the function of collective representations in Durkheim's theories of the division of labor, religion, and suicide.

Bowle, John. "Modern Sociologists: Durkheim on Environment: Graham Wallas and Social Psychology." In his *Politics and Opinion in the Nineteenth Century: An Historical Introduction,* pp. 445-64. New York: Oxford University Press, 1954.

Examines *Rules of the Sociological Method* and *Socialism* as prime examples of the environmental approach to the study of society.

Fenton, Steve; Reiner, Robert; and Hamnett, Ian. *Durkheim and Modern Sociology.* Cambridge: Cambridge University Press, 1984, 276 p.

Exegesis of Durkheim's writings in the context of recent critical interpretations of his work, "demonstrating the actual impact of Durkheim's thinking on important substantive areas of sociological inquiry—the state, the division of labour and class conflict, religion and ideology, race and society, education, and the problems of law and deviance."

Gehlke, Charles Elmer. *Émile Durkheim's Contributions to Sociological Theory.* New York: Columbia University, 1915, 188 p.

Explains Durkheim's major premises, theories, and methods, noting his development of a particular conception of sociology, including the study of psychic, moral, and political life as collective, social facts.

Giddens, Anthony. Introduction to *Émile Durkheim: Selected Writings,* pp. 1-50. Edited and Translated by Anthony Giddens. London: Cambridge University Press, 1972, 272 p.

Summary of Durkheim's major works and ideas.

Gisbert, Pascual. "Social Facts in Durkheim's System." In ANTHROPOS: *Revue internationale d'ethnologie et de linguistique* 54 (1959): 353-69.

Analyzes Durkheim's concept of social facts, distinguishing them from their psychological counterpart, collective representations. Gisbert acknowledges the primacy of social facts in Durkheim's sociology as "the pivotal point of his system."

Hammond, Phillip E. "Religious Pluralism and Durkheim's Integration Thesis." In *Changing Perspectives in the Scientific Study of Religion,* edited by Allan W. Eiste, pp. 115-42. New York: John Wiley & Sons, 1974.

Proposes a reinterpretation of what it means to speak of religion as being "integrative" in pluralistic societies. Hammond scrutinizes Durkheim's explanation for the function of religion as a unifying element of society, questioning the validity of his integrative thesis as applied to complex societies distinguished by religious pluralism.

Hatch, Elvin. "The Transcendence of Society." In his *Theories of Man and Culture*, pp. 162-213. New York: Columbia University Press, 1973.

> Explores Durkheim's theoretical basis for phenomena such as collective representations, consciousness, and group psychological behavior as transcendent of individual psychology.

Lukes, Steven. *Émile Durkheim: His Life and Work*. London: Allen Lane The Penguin Press, 1973, 676 p.

> A comprehensive study of Durkheim's life and works and their impact on sociological scholasticism. This volume also contains bibliographies of Durkheim's works and works about him, as well as his comments and inquiries to students during their oral examinations for doctoral theses at the University of Paris.

Nisbet, Robert A., ed. *Émile Durkheim*. Englewood Cliffs, N. J.: Prentice-Hall, 1965, 179 p.

> Divided into two parts: part one is a study by Nisbet, who uses Durkheim's own emphasis on milieu to examine his works and ideas in an historical context; part two is a collection of essays by various commentators on Durkheim's works.

———. *The Sociology of Emile Durkheim*. London: Heinemann, 1975, 293 p.

> Explains Durkheim's contribution to the areas of method, social structure, social psychology, political sociology, religion, morality, deviance, and social change.

Ottaway, A. K. C. "The Educational Sociology of Émile Durkheim." *The British Journal of Sociology* 6, No. 3 (September 1955): 213-27.

> Discusses Durkheim's theory of educational sociology.

Parsons, Talcott. "The Emergence of a Voluntaristic Theory of Action from the Positivistic Tradition," pp. 129-460. In his *The Structure of Social Action: A Study in Social Theory with Special Reference to a Group of Recent European Writers*. Glencoe, Ill.: The Free Press, 1937.

> Analyzes the development of sociology as "a theory of empirical science" and discusses Durkheim's contribution to this scheme.

Wallwork, Ernest. *Durkheim: Morality and Milieu*. Cambridge: Harvard University Press, 1972, 224 p.

> Examines Durkheim's moral philosophy on the premise that his sociology is a by-product of his background in classical moral philosophy stemming from Plato and Aristotle.

Wilson, Ethel M. "Émile Durkheim's Sociological Method." *Sociology and Social Research* 18, No. 6 (July-August 1934): 511-18.

> Analyzes Durkheim's concept of social facts and several of his scientific methods.

Wolff, Kurt H. *Émile Durkheim (1858-1917)*. Columbus: Ohio State University Press, 463 p.

> Collection of essays on Durkheim and his works; includes translations of some of his writings.

Charles Alexander Eastman

1858-1939

(Sioux name Ohiyesa) Santee Sioux autobiographer, lecturer, and essayist.

INTRODUCTION

Eastman is remembered as the author of numerous writings through which he sought to educate whites about Native American spirituality, morality, and mythology. His best-known works—among the first such Native American records to have been written rather than dictated by their subject—are the autobiographies *Indian Boyhood*, in which he recounts the events of his youth, and *From the Deep Woods to Civilization*, which chronicles his experiences as a Native American living in the United States.

Biographical Information

The son of a Santee Sioux father and a mixed-blood Sioux mother, Eastman lived the life of a traditional Santee Sioux until the age of fifteen. His mother died shortly after his birth, and his father disappeared and was believed to have been killed in the Minnesota Massacre of 1862. Eastman, who was raised in Ontario by his paternal grandmother and uncle, was beginning his quest to become a Sioux warrior when his father unexpectedly returned. After having been held prisoner in Minnesota, he had taken the name Jacob Eastman, converted to Christianity, and remarried. Eastman went with his father to a homestead in Flandreau, North Dakota, where he was baptized, renamed, and placed in a mission school. His education among whites took place in an era of "Indian reform," during which the U.S. government and many academic institutions were dedicated to "civilizing" Native Americans through schooling and Christian teachings. An accomplished student who attended Dartmouth College and earned his medical degree from Boston University, Eastman represented the ideal Sioux to many Indian reformers, including the woman he married, Elaine Goodale, who was a dedicated assimilationist. Eastman was one of the physicians who attended to the injured and dying after the massacre at Wounded Knee in 1890, and he was a well-known advocate for better treatment of Native Americans. He became a sought-after lecturer and public speaker and, with the help and encouragement of his wife, began publishing works in which he sought to bridge the chasm between white society and the Sioux way of life. Together they also opened wilderness camps to introduce Indian customs and culture to young white people. As Eastman found himself increasingly drawn back to the values of his boyhood, he reluctantly concluded that white society would never truly accept the wisdom of native ways and that traditional Sioux life as he had known it was over forever. His marriage—which has been called his wife's ultimate experiment in assimilation—eventually failed,

and his writing career, so dependent upon his wife's involvement, also ended. Weary of the strain of being "the model Indian," Eastman gradually withdrew from public life and lived alone until shortly before his death in 1939.

Major Works

Eastman began writing to provide his six children with a record of his Indian boyhood, and continued because he believed that white society could benefit from an understanding of the Sioux way of life. In *Indian Boyhood*, Eastman used traditional Sioux narrative forms, including legends, stories, and songs, to provide an account of the first fifteen years of his life. Later, in *From the Deep Woods to Civilization*, Eastman documented the difficulties associated with the assimilation process and attempted to overturn European and American stereotypes about Native Americans. His works also include several volumes of traditional tales, legends, and Native American lore, and numerous articles, many of which were published in such magazines as *Boy's Life*, *St. Nicholas*, and *The Craftsman*.

Critical Reception

While many of Eastman's works evidence ambivalent and sometimes contradictory feelings about his Native American heritage, critics note that Eastman never rejected his Sioux culture. Reviewers also acknowledge that critical interpretation of Eastman's works is difficult because he often blended history with Sioux legends—in Sioux culture the significance of events is considered more important than historical facts and chronology. Nonetheless, his works are praised for promoting respect for nature and the accomplishments of Native Americans, documenting Sioux history and culture, and revealing the pain and confusion associated with assimilation.

PRINCIPAL WORKS

Indian Boyhood (autobiography) 1902
Red Hunters and the Animal People (legends) 1904
Old Indian Days (legends) 1907
Wigwam Evenings: Sioux Folktales Retold [with Elaine Goodale Eastman] (legends) 1909
The Soul of the Indian (legends) 1911
Indian Scout Talks: A Guide for Boy Scouts and Campfire Girls (nonfiction) 1914; also published as *Indian Scout Craft and Lore*, 1974
The Indian Today: The Past and Future of the First American (nonfiction) 1915
From the Deep Woods to Civilization: Chapters in the Autobiography of an Indian (autobiography) 1916
Indian Heroes and Great Chieftains (nonfiction) 1918

CRITICISM

Henry Chester Tracy   (essay date 1930)

[*In the following excerpt, Tracy comments on Eastman's portrayal of Native American morality and spirituality in* Indian Boyhood *and* The Soul of the Indian.]

[When he was fifteen, Ohiyesa] was removed entirely from the loved wild life of the west and placed in school among white boys of his own age. With them he learned to express and to shape his thoughts in words that fitted a culture not his own. But with that achievement, and with such discipline as an American college can give, he remained a believer in the integrity of the Indian spirit and the poetry of the Indian mind. His own books are proof of it, and through them is diffused the convincing loyalty of his soul to its own upbringing, and a good forest life.

I do not feel that picture he has given us in *An Indian Boyhood* is idealized. A selection has been made, doubtless, of those episodes and experiences that served to shape him and which impressed him most, as well as of those tales and teachings which he was expected to remember. Perhaps there were things which he wisely forgot. Certainly there are included in the picture accounts of savage warfare and of beliefs and practices based on superstition. No

Indian is presented as a saint. Many, however, are seen as brave—not merely with an animal courage—and noble according to a consistent code. . . .

The Soul of the Indian is an important document. Written in grave, restrained English, without bitterness or unfairness, it strips away the veil of self-complacency that so often obscures a white man's view of his own culture in relation to the life he displaces. Necessarily a defense of the red man's code of morals, it is also an interpretation of forest man, of the spirit of man in nature. That spirit it finds ingenuous, yet profound in its intuitions, and therefore worthy. A fair reader concedes that worth because he feels it in the author. Cradled in the woods, familiar from birth with its sounds and lights and shadows, but no less with its struggle for life, its hungers and perils, Ohiyesa emerged in youth to take a white man's education. It schooled his mind but did not change his spirit. Indelibly impressed upon his inmost being was the red man's feeling for the communal good in nature and of responsibility toward the "Great Mystery" which controls all living creatures. What Ishi [the last surviving member of the Yahi tribe and the subject of Theodora Kroeber's *Ishi: Last of His Tribe* (1964)] could not have said, wanting words, Ohiyesa made clearly articulate, in a book of nature faith, any page of which is quotable. Two passages will suffice, and those who wish to know the fuller detail may go to the original.

> The worship of the "Great Mystery" was silent, solitary, free from all self-seeking. It was silent, because all speech is necessarily feeble and imperfect. . . . It was solitary, because they believed that He is nearer to us in solitude, and there were no priests authorized to come between a man and his Maker. None might exhort or confess or in any way meddle with the religious experience of another. Among us all men were created sons of God and stood erect, as conscious of their divinity. Our faith might not be formulated in creeds, nor forced on any who were unwilling to receive it; hence there was no preaching, proselytizing or persecution, neither were there any scoffers or atheists.

> Long before I ever heard of Christ, or saw a white man, I had learned from an untutored woman the essence of morality. With the help of dear Nature herself she taught me things simple but of mighty import. I knew God. I perceived what goodness is. I saw and loved what is really beautiful. Civilization has not taught me anything better.

Henry Chester Tracy, "Forest Man as Naturist," in his American Naturists, *E. P. Dutton & Co., Inc., 1930, pp. 264-82.*

David Reed Miller   (essay date 1976)

[*In the following excerpt, which was first presented as a paper at the 1976 Symposium of the American Ethnological Society, Miller explores Eastman's ambivalence toward his cultural identity as evidenced in his written works.*]

Since 1893, Eastman had been writing stories and remembrances of his childhood, primarily for his own children, which his wife polished and submitted to magazines like *St. Nicholas* and *Harpers.* Soon he began to gain a literary reputation, and to think of writing books. In 1900, he was appointed Agency Physician at Crow Creek Reservation, South Dakota, and in 1902 his first book, ***Indian Boyhood,*** was published. But due to political problems in 1902 he became the center of a controversial investigation, with his personal reputation at stake. He remained in government service only through the aid of Hamlin Garland, who was attempting to obtain standard surnames for Indians as a means of protecting their property rights. Garland, convinced Eastman was the man to rename the Sioux, obtained his transfer from Crow Creek to this special project. Although Eastman was occasionally lecturing and writing articles, which he assembled later as books, he worked as Renaming Clerk through 1909.

By 1910, at fifty-one years of age, Eastman remained in many ways a frustrated and disillusioned man, still not having found his "place" in life. In his restlessness, he sought some sort of renewal of identity:

> Early in the summer of 1910 the 'call of the wild' in me became very insistent, and I decided to seek once more in this region (northern Minnesota) the half obliterated and forgotten trails of my forefathers. I began to see the vision of real camp fires, the kind I knew in my boyhood days. So I hastily prepared for a dive into the wilderness, and on a morning in June found myself upon the pine-clad shores of Leech Lake, impatient to reach a remote camp of Indians on Bear Island, twenty five miles away.

Funded by the University of Pennsylvania Museum to conduct several months of fieldwork collecting folklore texts and museum artifacts, Eastman encountered the Ojibways of the lakes of Northern Minnesota, the hereditary enemies of his Sioux forefathers. Yet in visiting the north woods which he described as the "only one region left in which a few roving bands of North American Indians still hold civilization at bay," Eastman found the new sense of identity and spiritual renewal as an "Indian" that he was seeking. Eastman's writing upon his return from the wilderness became more philosophical, reflecting the depth of his experience in his reunion with nature. Although he wrote several articles about the events of the trip to the north country, the fall of 1910 was spent writing **The Soul of The Indian.** In this, his most expressive and articulate essay, Eastman created a text for understanding himself:

> Long before I ever heard of Christ, or saw a white man, I had learned from an untutored woman the essence of morality. With the help of dear Nature herself, she taught me things simple but of mighty import. I knew God. I perceived what goodness is. I saw and loved what is really beautiful. Civilization has not taught me anything better!
>
> As a child, I understood how to give; I have forgotten that grace since I became civilized. I lived the natural life, whereas I now live the artificial. Any pretty pebble was valuable to me then;

every growing tree an object of reverence. Now I worship with the white man before a painted landscape whose value is estimated in dollars! Thus the Indian is reconstructed, as the natural rocks are ground to powder and made into artificial blocks which may be built into the walls of modern society.

> The first American mingled with his pride a singular humility. Spiritual arrogance was foreign to his nature and teaching. He never claimed that the power of articulate speech was proof of superiority over the dumb creation; on the other hand, it is to him a perilous gift. He believes profoundly in silence—the sign of perfect equilibrium. Silence is the absolute poise of balance of body, mind, and spirit. The man who preserves his selfhood ever calm and unshaken by the storms of existence—not a leaf, as it were, astir on the tree; not a ripple upon the surface of shining pool—his, in the mind of the unlettered sage, is the ideal attitude and conduct of life.

In *The Soul of the Indian* Eastman created his own ideal of Indian-ness, very different from White American society. But Eastman was not unaware of "social evolutionism" as espoused by Spencer and Sumner. He examined the Indian in light of the inevitability of "civilization" over the "savage." In his writing Indians were referred to as "they," never "we." Eastman saw himself as set apart from his own people by education and life experiences. He subscribed to the notion that the "noble savage" with the "natural" virtue of close proximity to nature was on a low, simple, and pristine rung of the ladder of evolution to "civilization." In a sense he was scarred by western science and philosophy. As a marginal Indian and a marginal member of White society, Eastman felt uncomfortable with his status and sought in some way to resolve the ambiguity of his position. He believed that if his White readers could only understand the beauty and truth of the Indian way of life and learn to emulate the quality of truth found in it, a higher, more sensitive morality would eventually prevail in the larger American society.

However in all of Eastman's writings, many of them published repeatedly, first as articles and then as chapters in his books, he sought to teach and explain details about the native American way of life. In most of his early work he attempted to relate for young children the tales and stories of his childhood and the general folklore and woodlore of the Sioux. But were these stories or details intended to be ethnographic? For example, in the account from ***Indian Boyhood*** entitled "Hakadah's First Offering," Eastman was careful to avoid potential criticism by omitting the ethnographic detail that the dog which he had to give up to his grandmother was to be eaten. Eastman, in explaining the sacrifice of his playmate, implied that its only function was to deny the importance of material possessions and to appease the Great Mystery. He thus misled his reader by censoring an important ethnographic detail from his description. On the other hand, his 1893 address **"Sioux Mythology,"** delivered before the World Columbian Exposition in Chicago and reprinted in abbreviated form in *Popular Science Monthly* in 1894, was very important because it was Eastman's first scholarly presentation before a professional audience, in which he offered a succinct description of the key concepts of reasoning important to the Sioux in their view of the world. Included were the roles of death, religion, health, and medicine, and the behavior of animals as a model for proper human behavior. Among his first attempts to relate cultural values and concepts, this article remains his most ethnographically insightful.

Eastman conceived of himself as a "rememberer" much like his childhood teachers, his grandmother, and Smokey Days, the story teller. In this sense he saw himself to be a folk historian or recorder rather than an academic. In the foreword to *The Soul of the Indian,* he says:

> My little book does not pretend to be a scientific treatise. It is as true as I can make it to my childhood teaching and ancestral ideals, but from the human, not the ethnological standpoint. I have not cared to pile up more dry bones, but to clothe them with flesh and blood. So much as has been written by strangers of our ancient faith and worship treats it chiefly as matter of curiosity. I should like to emphasize its universal quality, its personal appeal!

During the twenty-five years of his literary career, an increasing tone of anti-intellectualism emerged. He rejected the intellectual and academic aspects of anthropology and history. He sought "human" and "personal" explanations. For example, in January of 1907 in St. Louis, Eastman contended that in all his childhood no word existed for an arrow-head made of flint. Because he had never heard the practice of flint knapping discussed and had never seen flint worked in his childhood, he rejected the idea that flint "arrowheads" were ever made by Indians. In the same address he denied that the Mound Builders had ever existed, maintaining that mounds were really battlefields, formed by the accumulation of dirt and sand over time. He also contended on the basis of his own knowledge of Sioux tradition that many theories of ethnology and archaeology could not be true. Although recognizing various ethnologists as contributors to knowledge, nowhere in print does he discuss adequately his opinion of the validity of anthropology or its study of the American Indian.

The most historically oriented article of Eastman's career appeared in *The Chatauquan* in July 1900, and was entitled **"The Story of the Little Big Horn (Told From the Indian Standpoint by one of Their Race)."** Writing the article while he was Outing Agent at Carlisle Indian School, Eastman contended that most accounts have exaggerated the number of Dakota and Cheyenne that were needed to engage and defeat Custer. Although the article was undocumented, his account appears to include the reminiscences of many of the warriors mentioned in the article.

> The battle of the Little Big Horn was a Waterloo for General Custer and the last effective defense of the Black Hills by the Sioux. It was a fair fight. Custer offered battle and was defeated. He was clearly out-generaled at his own stratagem. Had he gone down just half a mile farther and crossed the stream where Crazy Horse did a few minutes later, he might have carried out his plan

of surprising the Indian village and taking the Indian warriors at a disadvantage in the midst of their women and children.

> Was it a massacre? Were Custer and his men sitting by their camp-fires when attacked by the Sioux? Was he disarmed and then fired upon? No. Custer had followed the trail of these Indians for two days, and finally overtook them. He found and met just the Indians he was looking for. He had a fair chance to defeat the Sioux, had his support materialized, and brought their entire force to bear upon the enemy in the first instance.

> I reiterate that there were not twelve thousand to fifteen thousand Indians at that camp, as has been represented: nor were there over a thousand warriors in the fight. It is not necessary to exaggerate the number of the Indians engaged in the notable battle. The simple truth is that Custer met the combined forces of the hostiles, which were greater than his own, and that he had not so much underestimated their numbers as their ability.

In many of Eastman's writings, including *Red Hunters and the Animal People* (1904), *Old Indian Days* (1915), and *Indian Heroes and Great Chieftains* (1920), he gives much detail about the Sioux and their Algonquian neighbors and enemies. His sources must have included more than simple childhood memories. He apparently utilized interviews such as the ones conducted with the Ojibway in the summer of 1910. These interviews apparently were carried on with Indians of note whenever and wherever the opportunity arose. For the Little Big Horn article he undoubtedly had collected data for a number of years. While at Pine Ridge Agency in 1891-92, he and his wife had invited many Indians in for evening suppers and long sessions of story telling. Among those who visited from time to time were George Sword and American Horse, and possibly, Red Cloud. In 1896, Eastman visited the Oak Lake Reserve near Brandon, Manitoba, and saw many of the relatives he had left behind in 1873. He was able to see the elder of his two uncles again. Both these uncles had been at the Battle of the Little Big Horn. Joseph White Foot Print Eastman undoubtedly filled Charles in on the history of his people since 1873, and details of the battle were surely included. Later, during his period as Renaming Clerk (1903-1909), he talked with many old warriors including Rain-in-the-Face, whom he met and interviewed two months before the old man's death on Standing Rock Reservation. By such interviews he gained additional information that eventually was blended with the memories of his childhood. But his "fieldwork" methods were unsystematic and disorganized, as was his writing method itself.

One of Eastman's nieces related that while writing *Red Hunters and the Animal People* (1904), he would walk the woods alone in the mornings beside Bald Eagle Lake, Minnesota, where the family lived during the summer of 1903. Carrying a small note pad, he would jot notes of ideas as inspirations came to him. Returning around noon, he would explain his ideas to his wife, who then, under Charles' supervision, developed the ideas into prose, typing a draft for additional corrections and polishing. Elaine was indispensable to her husband's writing: after his separation from her in 1921, he published nothing new.

Because he was neither an intellectual nor an academic, Eastman blurred and distorted much of the data he presented. He contributed little new ethnographic information. The redeeming value of writings such as *The Soul of the Indian* (1911) and *Indian Scout Talks* (1914) was that an attempt was made in them to describe what it meant to be an Indian when the historical and environmental backdrop of the frontier wilderness was disappearing. Undoubtedly Eastman's relatives had been among the first to assimilate trade goods and new ideas such as literacy and settled life from the Euro-Americans. But Eastman saw the need to redefine the essence of Indian identity and, thus, a type of moral character. He joined the ranks of Americans who between 1900 and 1920 were turning to the out-of-doors for relaxation and inspiration. Many of the national parks were being established, summer camps for children and adults were appearing, and conservation measures were developing to maintain and cultivate "America the Beautiful." Groups such as the Camp Fire Girls, and the Boy and Girl Scouts, as well as increasing numbers of Indian hobbyists and enthusiasts, turned to the Heritage of the American Indian to learn moral and practical lessons about the out-of-doors.

Eastman heartily endorsed the outdoor movement. He wrote articles such as **"Education Without Books"** (1912) and **"What Can the Out-of-Doors Do for Children"** (1921). During the summer of 1914, he was employed as the camp director of a large Boy Scout camp near Chesapeake Bay in Maryland. Throughout the summer he compiled ideas for chapters to his book *Indian Scout Talks* (1914) which he dedicated as a guide for Boy Scouts and Camp Fire Girls. His essay, **"At Home with Nature,"** suggests the extent of his feeling for the natural life:

> To be in harmony with nature, one must be true in thought, free in action, and clean in body, mind, and spirit. This is the solid granite foundation of character.
>
> Have you ever wondered why most great men were born in humble homes and passed their early youth in the open country? There a boy is accustomed to see the sun rise and set every day; there rocks and trees are personal friends, and his geography is born within him, for he carries a map of the region in his head. In civilization there are many deaf ears and blind eyes. Because the average boy in the town has been deprived of close contact and intimacy with nature, what he learns from books he soon forgets, or is unable to apply. All learning is a dead language to him who gets it second hand.
>
> It is necessary that you should live with nature, my boy friend, if only that you may verify to your own satisfaction your school room lessons. Further than this you may be able to correct some error, or even to learn something that will be a real contribution to the sum of human knowledge. That is by no means impossible to a sincere observer. In the great laboratory of na-

ture there are endless secrets yet to be discovered.

> We will follow the Indian method, for the American Indian is the only man I know who accepts natural things as lessons in themselves, direct from the Great Giver of Life.

Neither an intellectual nor a great scholar, Charles Alexander Eastman tasted both success and failure. His readers, especially children, loved his stories and he was seen by many as an interpreter of one way of life to another. Whether he was an ethnographer is dubious. He sought a different level of meaning in terms of "personal appeal." He attempted to define ideals, moral codes, sex roles, mythology and cosmology; and finally, he attempted to influence White civilization by his version of the contribution of his Indian heritage. By teaching and even helping to invent a new conception of the American Indian, Eastman wanted American society to learn about itself using the mirror provided by the first Americans.

David Reed Miller, "Charles Alexander Eastman, Santee Sioux, 1858-1939," in American Indian Intellectuals, *edited by Margot Liberty, West Publishing Co., 1978, pp. 61-73.*

Ohiyesa remembers the past:

As a child I understood how to give; I have forgotten this grace since I became civilized. I lived the natural life, whereas I now live the artificial. Any pretty pebble was valuable to me then; every growing tree an object of reverence. Now I worship with the white man before a painted landscape whose value is estimated in dollars! Thus the Indian is reconstructed, as the natural rocks are ground to powder and made into artificial blocks which may be built into the walls of modern society.

The first American mingled with his pride a singular humility. Spiritual arrogance was foreign to his nature and teaching. He never claimed that the power of articulate speech was proof of superiority over the dumb creation; on the other hand, it is to him a perilous gift. He believes profoundly in silence—the sign of a perfect equilibrium. Silence is the absolute poise or balance of body, mind, and spirit. The man who preserves his selfhood is ever calm and unshaken by the storms of existence—not a leaf, as it were, astir on the tree; not a ripple upon the surface of the shining pool—his, in the mind of the unlettered sage, is the ideal attitude and conduct of life.

If you ask him: "What is silence?" he will answer: "It is the Great Mystery!" "The holy silence is His voice!" If you ask: "What are the fruits of silence?" he will say: "They are self-control, true courage or endurance, patience, dignity, and reverence. Silence is the cornerstone of character."

"Guard your tongue in youth," said the old chief, Wabashaw, "and in age you may mature a thought that will be of service to your people!"

Charles Alexander Eastman, in his The Soul of the Indian, *1911.*

Anna Lee Stensland   (essay date 1977)

[*Stensland is an American educator. In the following essay, she provides an overview of Eastman's works, focusing on the apparent blending of history and legend in his autobiographical works.*]

Charles Alexander Eastman, the Sioux, Ohiyesa, is unique among Indian writers. No other writer moved so far culturally in a lifetime, from the tribal life of the Santee Sioux, who were in exile following the Minnesota Uprising, to the white society of Dartmouth College and Boston University Medical School, a world in which he met Matthew Arnold, Theodore Roosevelt, Longfellow, Emerson and Francis Parkman. As a result, Eastman's autobiographies, biographies, and stories are told by him as he experienced and perceived them. His Indian contemporaries, on the other hand, have provided mainly "as told to" biographies, with all of the possible misunderstandings and misinterpretations which occur when there is a recorder or editor and often a translator as well. Consider, for example, Black Elk, who told his story in Sioux to his son Ben, who then translated it into English for John Neihardt, who then reworked it into his own style.

But because Eastman lived so successfully in two such diverse cultures, a number of problems appear in his recording of history and of the Santee Sioux tribal stories. The first problem arises because he was an Indian-thinking author writing for white readers. He is often quoted as an authority for historical fact. Yet it is not clear that in his own mind he separated historical fact from legend. A second and related problem is a failure at times to separate the historical incidents and stories told in the tribe from his own created short stories. A third problem is his conversion to a conservative Protestantism, which, as a result of strong influence upon him from the age of fifteen until his marriage at the age of thirty-three, probably led to certain interpretations of Sioux legends and customs.

George E. Hyde, American historian, in *Red Cloud's Folk* speaks of Eastman's *Indian Heroes and Great Chieftains* as "a spectacle of poor and distorted memory that is appalling, as nearly every date and statement of fact is incorrect." Eastman was not by nature nor by training an historian, his education having been that of a medical doctor. Hyde's own historical accuracy must be questioned when he expresses some disbelief that a full-blooded Sioux would belittle Chief Spotted Tail. Eastman was not a full-blooded Sioux, since his grandfather on his mother's side of the family was Captain Seth Eastman, white pioneer artist and professional soldier at Fort Snelling.

We know that to the tribal Sioux precise place and time were unimportant. What was important was where the buffalo herds were and in which river fish could be caught. Time was recorded mainly as seasons, the time of the summer rendezvous, or the first spring thaw, that period of the annual sugar-making. Most Indians of the nineteenth century did not know their exact time or place of birth.

If one expects to read *Indian Boyhood* as the chronological story of Eastman's early years, he will be disappointed. As an autobiographer, Eastman does start at the beginning, but he does not give his birth date nor a precise place of birth. What is far more important is who he is—the son of "the handsomest woman of all the Spirit Lake and Leaf Dweller Sioux," a child whose grandmother was descended from a haughty chieftain of the Dwellers among the Leaves and whose great grandfather was Chief Cloud Man. Far more important than precise time and place was the *story* of his birth, an event which he says his brothers recalled often with such mirth, "for it was the custom of the Sioux that when a boy was born his brother must plunge into the water, or roll in the snow naked if it was winter time; and if he was not big enough to do either of these himself water was thrown on him. . . . The idea was that a warrior had come to camp, and other children must display some act of hardihood." This first autobiography of Eastman's is more topical than it is chronological, containing such chapters as "My Indian Grandmother," "My Playmates," "Evening in the Lodge," and "A Winter Camp." He tells us about early hardships when the Santee Sioux were forced into exile by the Sioux Uprising in Minnesota. He does tell us that he was a little over four years old at the time. He describes the pursuit of part of the tribe by General Sibley across the Missouri River, the thrill of a blizzard which overtook them the following winter, during which the family lay for a day and a night under the snow, and the betrayal of his father and two older brothers at Winnipeg during the second winter after the Uprising. All of these events occurred between 1862 and 1864. But two chapters later he describes an Indian sugar camp in Minnesota, an event which had to take place before the Uprising. This is followed by yet another chapter, "A Midsummer Feast," an event at which the boy received his name, Ohiyesa, meaning winner. If the reader is thinking historically, he must realize that this chapter, too, took place in Minnesota, since Chief Mankato, who was chief of the village and played an important part in the selection of the name, was killed in the Battle of Wood Lake during the Uprising.

A good story is far more important to Eastman and to other tribal Indians than accurate history. A modern author, N. Scott Momaday, discusses the Indian relationship of art and reality in his consideration of myth and legend: "We are concerned here not so much with an accurate representation of actuality, but with the realization of the imaginative experience." As Momaday explains the process, when the imagination is superimposed upon the historical event, it becomes a story and is invested with meaning. Any suffering can be endured if it is given meaning through the tribal imagination.

Eastman's *Indian Heroes and Great Chieftains* cannot be considered history which records historical fact from native sources. By the time the Santee Sioux author recorded the stories of Red Cloud, Spotted Tail, Sitting Bull and others, their stories were already legendary in the tribe, given meaning through tribal imagination. Hyde says that the Oglala Sioux have almost no memory of the killing of Chief Bear Bull, the result of a feud which split their tribe into two hostile factions and influenced its later history.

As Eastman told the story, the cause of the trouble was the arrival of General Harney at Fort Laramie in order to make a treaty with the Sioux. Historically, there was no Fort Laramie at the time. General Harney first came into the vicinity fourteen years after Bear Bull's death and he did not come to make a treaty. But as Eastman tells it, General Harney bribed the wicked chief, Bear Bull, who attempted to bully the people into accepting the treaty. Red Cloud's father (who historically had been dead for many years) defied the chief. Bear Bull consequently killed both Red Cloud's father and brother. According to Indian tradition, young Red Cloud then had to kill Bear Bull, which he did, and was proclaimed a hero. According to Hyde, on the other hand, during a period of liquor peddling in Oglala camps, followers of Chief Smoke and followers of Bear Bull got into a quarrel while drinking. Bear Bull tried to stop the quarrel and was shot down, perhaps by Red Cloud.

In the historical version of the tale, Red Cloud's role in the incident is quite uncertain. In the version Eastman reports from his Indian sources, the heroic nature of young Red Cloud is established. He avenged both his father's death and his brother's. Every event in Eastman's version of Red Cloud's life, from his learning to discipline himself to ride a pony bareback to his resistance speeches, is told to develop the image of the brave and wise leader. The stories, coming from Eastman's Indian sources, members of the Oglala tribe, demonstrate Indian values—heroism, defense of family and tribe, and self reliance. Red Cloud's story was already legendary in the tribe, but it was not historically accurate. Eastman, the converted Christian, however, finds it necessary to add at the end of the selection that Red Cloud's private life was also exemplary: he was faithful to one wife, a devoted father to his children and a lover of his country, values not necessarily Indian.

Eastman's story of Chief Spotted Tail is a bit more confused. His Brulé sources in the early twentieth century probably did not agree completely on the heroic nature of the one chief who counselled submission to the superior forces of the white man. Even so, the story is legendary rather than historical. Hyde points out that Eastman's date for Spotted Tail's birth—1833—has to be wrong, since the chief would have been a warrior in 1839 at the age of six; he would have killed a man in a duel with knives in 1841 at the age of eight, have married in the same year and fathered a child the following year at the age of nine. In spite of the historical absurdity of such facts, many historians have accepted Eastman's date. Because Spotted Tail apparently had a certain vanity about his age, at forty he often told people that he was thirty, but later on in his life in a legal affidavit he said he was born in 1823 or 1824. To the Brulé Sioux who reported to Eastman, such confusion and lack of consistency was trivial. What was important was that the chief established himself as a warrior and attained the rank of shirt wearer at an early age: "It is personal qualities alone that tell among our people, and the youthful Spotted Tail gained at every turn. At the age of seventeen, he has become a sure shot and a clever hunter."

Hyde argues with Eastman about the tribe of Indians against which Spotted Tail made his reputation as a warrior. Eastman says it was against the Utes; Hyde argues that historical records indicate that it had to be against the Pawnees. By the time Eastman heard the story it did not make much difference which tribe the chief fought against. The important point was that the young man had distinguished himself against an enemy of the Brulés.

Spotted Tail has often been spoken of as a poor orphan, an idea which came originally from Eastman and has been continued by a number of historians. This may be further evidence of the legendary characteristics which had already penetrated the Brulé story of the chief. The poor, unpromising orphan boy who becomes the savior of his tribe or the recipient of the stories of the tribe is a common characteristic in the Indian myths of many tribes. The Sioux First Born, or Elder Brother, fathered by the Sun and mothered by the Earth, was an orphan on earth, who because of loneliness created Little Boy Man, who in turn had only the animals to play with. Little Boy Man was created innocent, trusting, and helpless, but with the guidance of Elder Brother, he learned to conquer the animal people and withstand the forces of the elements. The story of Stone Boy, told in several tribes, is also told by Eastman. In this story a young girl, who had lost all ten of her brothers through hunting, miraculously finds a baby boy, whom she names Stone Boy, an orphan, awkward and unpromising, who later rescues her brothers from the country of the Thunder Birds.

According to Eastman, Chief Spotted Tail was an orphan reared by his grandparents. Moreover, he was slow-moving as a boy, a child who because he had no parents to present him to the tribe and to give feasts in his honor, was greatly disadvantaged. This seems quite clearly the beginning of a legend. Hyde claims that history disputes this, pointing out that the diary of Lieutenant G. K. Warren for September, 1855, records that the chiefs Man-Afraid-of-His-Horse and Grand Partisan were at Fort Laramie with Spotted Tail's father. Hyde gives further evidence that Spotted Tail was not an orphan. But to the Brulés, Spotted Tail had already become a legend whose achievements were enhanced by his unpromising beginnings.

Eastman must also, however, report the less heroic side of Spotted Tail. Some Sioux felt that he had "copied the white politician too closely after he entered the reservation. He became a good manipulator, and was made conceited and overbearing by the attentions of the military and of the general public." The converted Christian author also condemns him for "high handed actions," including elopement with another man's wife.

In a chapter on storytelling in *Indian Scout Craft and Lore,* Eastman describes what happened to stories as they were told in the tribe: "True stories of warfare and the chase are related many times over by actors and eyewitnesses, that no detail may be forgotten. Handed down from generation to generation, these tales gradually take on the proportions of heroic myth and legend. They blossom into poetry and chivalry, and are alive with mystery and magic." The stories of the chiefs when Eastman heard them had already taken on some of that mystery and magic, since a good story was a higher value than historical accuracy.

A second problem as we study Eastman's writing is that of separating those stories which were tribal legends from Eastman's own storytelling. Perhaps it is simply the arrogance of our profession which makes us want to separate the two. The storyteller of the tribe was among the most respected of men: "He was not only an entertainer in demand at all social gatherings, but an honored schoolmaster to the village children. The great secret of his success was his ability to portray a character or a situation truthfully, yet with just a touch of humorous or dramatic exaggeration." No doubt, in Eastman's mind, the art of storytelling was a noble one. Why should he make a distinction between his own stories and those told in the tribe, simply because he was writing the stories rather than telling them orally? Indeed, he did tell his own stories orally during the year 1914, when he directed a Boy Scout camp in Maryland, and during the years 1914 to 1925 when his wife ran a girls' camp in Munsonville, New Hampshire.

In the earliest of the collections of stories, *Red Hunters and Animal People,* published first in 1904, he seems to be separating his own storytelling from the stories he heard in the tribe, either by having a member of the tribe tell an exciting story which happened to him, in the midst of Eastman's own story, or by having a tribal storyteller tell a legend about an animal in order to explain to children a phenomenon they had observed. An example of the first is **"The Sky Warrior,"** in which two Sioux hunters are tempted to shoot a pair of eagles, until one stops the other because he has seen that one of the eagles is a male who once saved him from starvation when he was injured. The eagle had killed a deer, off which both man and bird feasted. The result in Eastman's story is that the hunters do not shoot the two eagles. In another story, **"The Dance of the Little People,"** young boys around the age of ten assimilate a hunt by making small bows and arrows for a mouse hunt. But when they see a white mouse, which they presume to be the chief, one of the boys declares that they must cease the hunt because they will have good luck if the mice are spared after the chief's appearance. This is an excuse for the boys to ask Padanee, the old storyteller, to confirm this legend, as well as others about the Moon-Nibblers and their dances in the full moon. Thus Eastman in each case uses a native story teller to tell the legend, but he imposes his own super-structure on it in order to tell us about aspects of Indian life—the belief that certain humans had special relationships with particular animals or birds and the assimilation of the hunt by small boys, a custom the author also described in *Indian Boyhood.*

The problem of mixing history and legend with original stories becomes more complicated in *Old Indian Days.* In **"The Singing Spirit,"** what appears to be Eastman's story of some Yankton Sioux hunters who become lost in the late fall is attached to what seems like a partly historical and partly legendary account of a half-breed named Antoine Michaud, who plays a homemade violin in the wilderness. But before the hunters realize what the sound of Michaud's violin is, there is the opportunity to incorpo-

rate an old Santee legend of a strange little man named Chanotedah. An example of what seems to be mixing history and original short story is **"The Famine."** Since so little information exists about the Santee Sioux during the years of exile, it is tempting to assume that the story is historical. Near Fort Ellis in Manitoba, the tribe was starving, under the leadership of White Lodge, whose father was Little Crow, leader of the Sioux Uprising in 1862. A Scotch trader, Angus McLeod, who was in love with one of White Lodge's twin daughters, rescues the daughters and presumably the tribe. The beginning of the tale is quite factual but the ending becomes very romantic, so one must assume that at best only part of it is historical.

When he came to telling the mythological tales, yet another problem confronted Eastman and also confronts his readers. He was a converted Christian who was looking at the Sioux mythology out of changing values and assumptions. The fifteen year old boy, whose father appeared miraculously in southern Manitoba after having been thought hanged at Fort Snelling at the time that Chief Shakopee and other participants in the Uprising were, was still highly impressionable: "I could not doubt my father, so mysteriously come back to us, as it were, from the spirit land." Many Lightnings had been converted along with hundreds of other Santee Sioux while they were imprisoned in Davenport, Iowa. Later Dr. Alfred Riggs, second generation missionary among the Santee and the director of the Indian School at Santee, Nebraska, became his mentor: "Next to my own father, this man did more than perhaps any other to make it possible for me to grasp the principles of true civilization." Still later other influences—Beloit College; Knox College; Dartmouth College; Mr. and Mrs. Frank Woods of Boston, his white mother and father during his years at Boston University Medical School; and finally the woman he married, the white missionary and teacher at Pine Ridge, Elaine Goodale—led him to accept conservative Christian beliefs. The result is that certain truly Indian concepts had to be rejected and others made to conform to white values. His wife helped edit one collection of myths, *Smoky Day's Wigwam Evenings.* In the introduction to that volume, Elaine Eastman discusses some changes which had to be made for the white audience: Symbolism in some of the creation stories was too complicated for young readers, and stories which would take an entire evening to tell to Indian children because of the detailed descriptions had to be shortened.

In addition, there is no doubt that in spite of certain disappointments about the Great White Father in Washington, D. C., and "civilized man," in general following the Wounded Knee Massacre, Eastman still felt that the white man's civilization was superior to the Sioux way of life. In a *Popular Science* article of November, 1894, he wrote, "The human mind equipped with all its faculties is capable even in an uncultured state of logical process of reasoning." The result is an attempt to make many of the Sioux characters and concepts fit Christian Biblical characters and concepts. Mrs. Eastman speaks of Little Boy Man as the Adam of the Sioux, while Eastman himself equates Adam with Elder Brother, who became weary of living alone and so formed himself a companion, not from a rib but from a splinter he withdrew from his toe. The companion was not a wife but rather the Little Boy Man. Unk-to-mee, the spider, Eastman says is akin to the serpent which tempted Eve. The Battle of the Elements he compares to the Biblical story of the Flood.

The term *God* is often used by Eastman in place of the Great Spirit or the Great Mystery. Although different tribes have different concepts, many modern Indians have agreed that the Great Spirit is quite a different idea from the Christian God. Sanders and Peek, Indian editors, who use the term Wah'kon-tah for the Great Spirit, write: "The Native American religions encountered by the white man were . . . more subtle, more complex in that Wah'kon-tah is incapable of being anthropomorphized as is Elohim who created man in his own image. Wah'kontah lacks image, being all things." In his *Popular Science* article, however, Eastman writes, "There is a strong implication that the Great Mystery has made man after himself, and that he is in shape like man, but with a few modifications. For instance, he is supposed to have horns symbolic of command; and his eyes are like the sun—no one can gaze into them."

We must ask what changes in the myths Eastman made, consciously or unconsciously, because of his Christian conversion. Ethel Nurge, in a discussion of the diet of the Dakotas, points out that in describing the sacrifice of a dog to the Great Spirit, Eastman leaves out the fact that the eating of the dog was an integral part of the ceremony. This is probably, as Nurge says, a tailoring of his writing to white prejudices, or perhaps Eastman himself had adopted the white man's objection to the eating of dogs.

Eastman's writings are invaluable because he lived the experiences and wrote about them effectively. All of his historical information should not be written off as merely tribal "bad memory," as Hyde has done. Much that he has recorded is found no place else, both history and legend, but it must be examined in the light of tribal imagination. The Sioux did not have a George Bird Grinnell to collect their legends. The best-known collectors of myths—Stith Thompson, Tristram P. Coffin, Susan Feldman, and Alice Marriott and Carol Rachlin—include no Sioux legends. In the prolific writings of Charles Eastman there is probably more Sioux legend, myth and history than is recorded any place else.

Anna Lee Stensland, "Charles Alexander Eastman: Sioux Storyteller and Historian," in American Indian Quarterly, *Vol. 3, No. 3, Autumn, 1977, pp. 199-208.*

Marion W. Copeland   (essay date 1978)

[*In the following excerpt, Copeland asserts that Eastman's fictional works* Red Hunters and the Animal People, Old Indian Days, *and* Wigwam Evenings *together form a traditional Sioux "vision quest" autobiography.*]

Because Charles Eastman's best known book is his earliest, *Indian Boyhood* (1902), and because that autobiography and its sequel, *From the Deep Woods to Civilization* (1916), have been most often used as sources for studies of the cultural transition of the Sioux, the literary value

of those and of Eastman's later books has gone largely unexamined. Eastman subtitled the 1916 volume *The Autobiography of an Indian,* but one cannot therefore assume that the conventions of European-American autobiography control Eastman's work.

In *Plains Indian Autobiographies,* Lynne Woods O'Brien explains that Indian autobiography does not "limit itself to 'real' or historical events in the autobiographer's present or past life." In fact, the forms of Plains Indian autobiography suggest that the Indian's reality is quite distinct from the historical perspective of the European tradition. "Vision," for instance, "allows the autobiographer to explore his future life by spiritual means," while the war or *coup* story recounts what white culture would call a historical event. Chronological tracing of a life was not traditional among the Plains tribes because, in their days of solidarity, the life of one member of a tribe differed very little from that of any other member. Only great achievements and visions were recorded, and they were significant only in their effect upon the tribe.

Ohiyesa's (Eastman's) vision quest, he tells us in both *Indian Boyhood* and *From the Deep Woods,* began among his uncle's exiled band in the wilderness of Ontario's Turtle Mountains when he was fifteen.

> I had already begun to invoke the blessing of the Great Mystery. Scarcely a day passed that I did not offer up some of my game, so that he might not be displeased with me. My people saw very little of me during the day, for in solitude I found the strength I needed. I groped about in the wilderness, and determined to assume my position as a man. My boyish ways were departing, and a sullen dignity and composure was taking their place.

The youth's father, Many Lightnings, who was believed dead for over ten years, appeared at the apex of the boy's quest for vision. Determined to take his son back with him, Many Lightnings—whose story is a part of Eastman's autobiography rather than of his vision quest—seemed to the boy to be a ghost, a being from the Spirit Land, who snatched him away from a lifestyle appropriate for a Sioux warrior. In a state of shock, Ohiyesa, his grandmother, and young cousin left the band of Mysterious Medicine. "I felt," he would write later, "as if I were dead and travelling to the Spirit Land."

Eastman, feeling that he had been ripped untimely from the "womb of our mother, the Earth," came in time to understand the events recorded in *From the Deep Woods to Civilization* not as "real" but as a period of trial (*Seeing with a Native Eye: Essays on Native American Religion,* Walter Holden Capps, ed., is a helpful aid to the reader's vision). The intervening events, Eastman's autobiography, are a clear history up to the point where Eastman breaks off in *From the Deep Woods.* The vision quest takes place in the volumes not easily recognized as autobiography. . . .

The vision quest is recorded, as Sioux tradition demands, in the tales of the tribal story teller: *Red Hunters and the Animal People* (1904), *Old Indian Days* (1906), and *Wigwam Evenings* (1909). *The Soul of the Indian: An Inter-*

pretation (1911) and *The Indian Today: The Past and Future of the First American* (1915) serve as interpretive guides, making clear that Eastman saw himself and his audience—red and white alike—as late-comers, to whom the story-tellers' wisdom was alien. Nonetheless, Eastman strives to tell each story "as true as I can make it to my childhood teaching and ancestral ideals, but from the human, not the ethnological standpoint." It is an effort to share "flesh and blood," rather than "more dry bones."

Eastman himself tells us in *Soul of the Indian* that he knows that much of the "symbolism or inner meaning" of his journey will be "largely hidden from the observer." His audience must learn to look with a Sioux eye, to see that reality may be what the mind envisions rather than what the eye observes. To understand that the seven chapters of *Soul* imitate the sevenfold structure of nature and, in turn, the seven divisions of the Sioux nation, is a beginning. Even when historical vicissitudes and political convenience after 1850 created varying "actual" divisions among the Sioux, they saw themselves as comprised of the Seven Council Fires, meeting annually to reaffirm and reassert the "cohesiveness of the nation" through the ritual of the Sun Dance (Royal B. Hassrick, *The Sioux*). In other words, Eastman tries to point out that what the reader perceives largely as myth or theory—what is in the mind—defines the reality which the Sioux perceives.

The first of the seven chapters of *Soul* provides a glimpse of the reality, The Great Mystery, that possessed Eastman as Christianity never could. His grandmother's teaching had been that

> The worship of the "Great Mystery" was silent, solitary, free from all self-seeking. It was silent, because all speech is of necessity feeble and imperfect; therefore the souls of my ancestors ascended to God in wordless adoration. It was solitary, because they believed that He is nearer to us in solitude, and there were no priests authorized to come between a man and his Maker. . . . Our faith might not be formulated in creeds, nor forced upon any who were unwilling to receive it; hence there was no preaching, proselytizing, nor persecution, neither were there any scoffers or atheists.

In white culture, silence is thought of as a void to be filled and feared. In Sioux culture, silence is a positive expression of openness to the harmony of the natural order. Eastman tells us in *Soul of the Indian* that

> The religion of the Indian is the last thing about him that the man of another race will ever understand.
>
> First, the Indian does not speak of these deep matters so long as he believes in them, and when he has ceased to believe he speaks inaccurately and slightingly.
>
> Second, even if he can be induced to speak, the racial and religious prejudice of the other stands in the way of sympathetic comprehension.
>
> Third, practically all existing studies on this subject have been made during the transition period, when the original beliefs and philosophy of

the native American were already undergoing rapid disintegration.

He goes on to describe the problems inherent in white studies of native religions, but the relevant point is that he suggests his own incapacity at the time of the writing to discuss or to participate in the silence of the true believer.

In the foreword to *Four Indian Masterpieces of American Indian Literature,* John Bierhorst suggests that all American Indian narrative is revivalistic, "a focused progression away from the old and into the new, building to a climax in which the awaited transition is at last made possible through the mechanism of a sacred 'mystery'." Elaine Goodale Eastman and other Friends of the Indian, in all goodwill, understood the "new" to mean the transition into "civilization," into the ways of the white man; hence for them *Indian Boyhood* and *From the Deep Woods* represent progress. For the Sioux, progress is distinct from evolutionary progress. The looked-for transition is renewal of health and cleanliness, restoration of what was. The worshipper (or patient) reaches wholeness through a journey which returns him, renewed, to his point of departure.

The symbolic structure of *Soul of the Indian* prepares us for the symbolic progression of Eastman's volumes of Indian tales. Eastman assumed the role of the story-teller, and his narrative impetus was the shattering of the Sioux nation. Because he had been chosen as a "medicine man," his personal quest was for the sacred mystery that would return the Sioux to their original health and power. In *Red Hunters and the Animal People,* Eastman characterizes the narrator of these silent lives as a "biographer and interpreter." . . .

Ohiyesa [Eastman] had become a warrior when, at fifteen, he had been presented with his first gun, a flintlock. The "mysterious iron" filled him with echoes of the war songs he had heard as a child. The rite of passage, amply prepared for by his grandmother and uncles, was swift and silent: "It seemed as if I were an entirely new being—the boy had become a man!" and the man was eager and able "to avenge the blood of my father and my brothers!" To that end, as we have seen, he "had already begun to invoke the blessing of the Great Mystery" and had begun to seek the "sullen dignity and composure" necessary to his task. Then Jacob Eastman appeared. His son's comment is brief: "They were Indians but clad in the white man's garments. It was as well that I was absent with my gun."

The metaphor of Indians clad in white man's garments haunts *From the Deep Woods to Civilization* and *Soul of the Indian.* One has the sense that Eastman's view of himself is encompassed by this figure and that it is symbolic of his feeling that first his father and brothers and then he himself inhabited a foreign land, wore foreign garb, and participated in an alien mode of life Contrastingly, the figure is absent—or nearly so—in his books of tales: *Indian Boyhood, Old Indian Days, Red Hunters and the Animal People,* and *Wigwam Evenings.* It is in these recollections of Sioux myth and folklore that Ohiyesa best reveals the indelible education of his childhood, his true sense of self and of reality. . . .

In the eyes of his public, the years between the publication of *Red Hunters* (1903) and 1923 were successful ones. He was hailed by J. T. Faris in 1922 as one of the *Men Who Conquered.* Despite Eastman's efforts in his books and lectures, Faris still saw Eastman's story as an example of how a savage "Out of an Indian Tepee" could become a model of civilized living. It is no wonder that once Eastman had officially resigned as physician at the Crow Creek Agency (March 1903) his faith in finding a place in either white or red society dwindled. . . . He devoted himself to writing and lecturing, but the spirit of the storyteller/medicine-man was faint. Perhaps he created old Smokey Day in *Wigwam Evenings* (1909) to replace his own voice. *Old Indian Days* (1907), written only two years earlier, seemed to cast Eastman himself in the storyteller's rôle. It is a particularly interesting volume in that it outlines the education and role of both **"The Warrior"** (Part I) and **"The Woman"** (Part II).

The hero of Part I, Young Antelope, is first seen perched "spirit-like among the upper clouds" of Eagle Scout Butte, "fasting and seeking a sign from the 'Great Mystery'. . . ." His career opens where Eastman's autobiography ends in *Indian Boyhood,* and this narrative represents the spirit autobiography which Eastman needed. Chosen to protect the peace of his people, Antelope faces the encroachment of hostile tribes into the foothills of the Big Horn Mountains. The enemy is the Utes, traditional foe of the Sioux, and Antelope—like the wolf-hero, Manitoo, of *Red Hunters*—is capable of impeding their attack, proving himself a warrior and claiming a mate.

The tale shows that the traditional ways allow Antelope to deal even with the spirit-world. Returning from a raiding party, he finds that his band is gone and that only a single teepee—his own—remains. Taluta, his wife, lies in it, dead. Intense mourning, accompanied by ritual cleansing, allows him to "obtain a sign from her spirit," and rejoining the band, Antelope returns to his duties. In the course of a peace mission, he discovers Taluta's "twin" in Stasu, the daughter of a Ree chief. The allegory is thinly disguised. As long as the lovers remain isolated from relatives, their union is as Edenic as the first years of Eastman's had been: "man and wife, in their first home of living green." Quite literally arranged by a spirit, the marriage is kept holy in "a silent place."

It is fruitful, but in time their thoughts turn to their own people, and they envision their son taking his rightful place among them. Each "entertained the hope that he would some day be *waken,* a mysterious or spiritual man, for he was getting power from his wild companions and from the silent forces of nature." At length the wife proposes that they sacrifice pride and even life in order to return the child to one tribe or another. Being a typical Sioux warrior, Antelope prefers to sacrifice life to pride: "If I am to die at the hands of the ancient enemy of the Sioux, I shall die because of my love for you, and for our child. But I cannot go back to my own people to be ridiculed by unworthy young men for yielding to the love of a Ree maid." However, because the Rees admire Antelope's bravery, they accept the young family and receive Stasu as one returning from the dead. Such a return had been impossible for Eastman. But even here, the momentary peace is broken when, in the next tale, two young Yankton Sioux warriors shoot a Ree chief totally on impulse.

"The Madness of Bald Eagle" is a strange tale which questions the values of White Ghost, a Sioux patriarch who has not kept the old ways holy. Power passes from him to a young warrior who, like Antelope, reinforces the ritual ways. A strange wood spirit, Oglugechana (or Chanotedah), a hairy little man who lives in the hollow stump of a tree that has been downed by lightning, draws travellers to him, robs them of their senses, and makes of them great war-prophets or medicine men. To retain lucidity and to come upon the spright is to risk one's own death or that of a close relative. But Eastman's hero, Anookasan, is willing to take the risk, and he follows the Oglugechana's music. It leads him to a hairy white man in a log cabin playing what we recognize as a fiddle. Outraged, he attacks the musician—and the action of the tale freezes, to be held static until the end of Part II of the tales. The unusual narrative technique calls attention to itself.

In Part II, the mixed-blood Antoine Michaud—like Anookasan—finds himself alone in the woods. By winding the story back to the end of Part I, we slowly realize that Michaud is the bearded fiddler who was attacked by Anookasan and that the full-blood does not recognize the musician as being of his own kind. But the Yankton responds to Michaud's passivity, accepts him, and becomes destined to the fate of the Oglugechana's victims, for the Yankton Sioux will all die soon, as the fourth tale of Part I, **"Famine,"** suggests.

Alienation, loss, starvation, and death are clearly the themes of *Old Indian Days,* just as they are the themes of *Red Hunters.* But the time in this volume is closer to the time of the Sioux's real loss. The setting is in Manitoba on the Assiniboine sometime after the Minnesota Massacre of 1862. Little Crow, the last of the strong Sioux chiefs, is dead, and White Lodge, his son, controls only a small band of renegades. The medicine men prophesy famine and ascribe its cause to the people's desertion of the old ways. **"The Famine"** juxtaposes the spiritual battle of Face-the-Wind and Eyah, the god of famine, with the white man's interpretation of that battle. To McLeod, trader at Fort Ellis, where Face-the-Wind has come for help, the brave's dying request is simply "delirium," yet McLeod defeats Eyah by ringing the fort's bells as Face-the-Wind has requested. McLeod assumes that he has found the starving band because Magaskawee, one of White Lodge's twin daughters who had lived with missionaries for a time, had sent a written message with the runner to McLeod's son Angus. But the Sioux know that Eyah fears the jingling of metal and that the bell had saved them. It would be easy to miss the juxtaposition of realities at the end of the tale as Angus and Three Stars, the other twin's lover, arrive just in time—accompanied by "the jingle of dog-bells."

The fifth story, too, juxtaposes realities. It is the history of the 1862 massacre. Tawasuota, **"The Chief Warrior,"** having proved his bravery, has been made Little Crow's *ta akich-itah* (chief soldier). Details of treaties signed and broken are accurately recorded in the tale, but the Sioux code of honor is the real subject of the story. Obligated by his position, Tawasuota joins the attack on the agency and shoots a man who puts up no defense. At first he is so conscience-stricken by his act that he drops from the fight and rejoins his fellow warriors only when the United States cavalry appears. His uneasiness is accompanied by a strong sense of loss, and he finds his people possessed of a "strange stillness" that is distinct from silence. Some of them have retreated to the protection of the whites in Faribault, his wife and sons among them, and have thereby broken up the band irreparably.

In theme and tone, the tales of Part I of *Old Indian Days* move relentlessly away, from **"The Love of Antelope"** to **"The Grave of the Dog,"** from the days of Sioux glory to their days of agony. Although there are seven tales, no one remains who remembers that seven is a sacred number or what the number represents. The unity of the Sioux is forgotten. Passing wagons of fugitives, Tawasuota goes to Faribault and determines that his sons can survive only if they stay with his wife among "the lovers of the whites." Although she protests, "he disappeared in the shadows, and they never saw him again." Eastman's postscript to the tale summarizes: "The chief soldier lived and died a warrior and an enemy to the white man; but one of his two sons became in after years a minister of the Christian gospel, under the 'Long-Haired Praying Man,' Bishop Whipple, of Minnesota." There is no overlapping of the lives of the white lovers and haters, or of the agriculturalists and the hunters who are traditionalists. In historical terms, the agriculturalists had been led by Eastman's own maternal grandfather, Cloudman. To survive, they sold what was not theirs—the earth—and committed sacrilege by cutting into it with plows. The question which the story raises is whether survival is of itself worthwhile. Tawasuota becomes emblematic of the Sioux's dilemma.

The sixth story in *Old Indian Days* is also history. It opens by focusing upon the ritual arrangement of a Sioux camp: a circle or hoop with the council lodge at its center. In that center, "the minds of all were alike upon the days of their youth and freedom," days obviously past. The group recounts stories "of brave deeds and dangerous exploits . . . with as much spirit and zest as if they were still living in those days." The Sioux have slipped into the white man's historical time. Their stories have become history rather than reality. Zuyamani's tale of the winter that follows the Minnesota massacre is the autobiography of a man "upon the white man's errand" rather than a quest tale. Even as he wrote the words, Eastman knew himself to be upon the white man's errand.

The faithful dog, Shanka, becomes the narrator of the concluding tale, **"The Warrior."** While his master sleeps, the dog sets out "to discover the truth." The next day he leads the band to what remains of the buffalo, and when the hunters are overtaken by a blizzard, Shanka's barking leads rescuers to where his master lies beneath two frozen buffalo carcasses in a womb of hay and buffalo hair. His sense of loyalty, mission, and dedication to the truth serves as a contrast to the loss of loyalty, mission, and sense of truth in Tawasuota and Zuyamani, the heroes of Eastman's "historical fiction." It becomes clear, then, that

the real values which Eastman understands as Sioux values remain only in the silent peoples. **"The Grave of the Dog"** commemorates a way of life whose loss we have watched through the seven tales that would have marked a ritual way in *Old Indian Days.* One suspects that Shanka is the spiritual heir of the dog Ohitika, whose sacrificial death had marked the beginning of Eastman's initiation into the life of a Sioux warrior.

Part II of *Old Indian Days,* **"The Woman,"** develops "Winona" as the counterpart to Antelope. "Winona" is the name of Eastman's mother, who on her death-bed remained loyal to the Sioux. Her tale begins with a lullaby. The singer is her grandmother, who, like Eastman's own, takes her "among the father and mother trees" to learn their language. To be "nature-born" is to become a part of the Sioux reality. Essentially Part I of Winona's story is another tract on Sioux child-rearing. She learns much—as Eastman's reader must—from the four-footed peoples.

For Eastman a significant fact is that for

> the Sioux of the old days, the great natural crises of human life, marriage and birth, were considered sacred and hedged about with great privacy. Therefore the union is publicly celebrated after and not before its consummation.

Winona and her mate's silent time alone in the wilderness is a decided contrast to the highly public union of Charles Eastman and Elaine Goodale at the Church of the the Ascension in New York City and to the high society reception provided by the Frank Woods, in Dorchester. The reception and the honeymoon at "Sky-Farm in the Berkshires" received much attention from the press. In later years, headlines such as "She Will Wed a Sioux Indian" (*New York Times,* June 7, 1891) and "The Bride of An Indian" (*New York Times,* June 19, 1891) must have pained both of the Eastmans.

Winona concludes her tale with an example of "womanly nobility of nature." An orphan who was reared by her grandmother, Her-Singing-Heard used herself to form "a blood brotherhood" between the Sioux and the Sacs and Foxes, ending what she saw as "cruel and useless enmity." The fifth tale, **"The Peace Maker,"** shows how *Eyatonkawee* (She-Whose-Voice-is-Heard-Afar) brings together the disparate bands of Sioux into a nation. She herself, a member of Eastman's band, the Leaf Dweller Sioux, is a historical figure. The tale of her exploits served to retain peace among the bands of Sioux on several occasions. Her tale culminates with her chanting of how she countered the Sac and Fox attacks in which her young husband was killed. It ends with the young mother—"victorious over three!" —making her infant son "count with his tiny hands the first 'coup' on each dead hero." With the same ax that she used to kill the enemy, she puts a dramatic end to her chant by smashing the keg of whiskey from which her listeners drink—"So trickles under the ax of Eyatonkawee the blood of an enemy to the Sioux."

The seventh tale, which is symbolic of the harmony of nature and of the Sioux nation, recalls a more recent occasion, the celebration by the Uncpapa Sioux of their Sun Dance. Forty years before Eastman wrote *Old Indian*

Days, the way had been remembered, and man and animal had joined to keep the nation whole.

But Eastman's last tale shatters the harmony of the seventh. It introduces a new voice, that of Smokey Day, "for many years the best-known story-teller and historian of the tribe," but long dead at the time of the book's writing. The ghost voice continues as Eastman's narrator in *Wigwam Evenings,* suggesting that the living no longer remember the words of the traditional way. Smokey Day makes clear—as perhaps Eastman can not in his own "educated" voice—that the Sioux do not make the white man's distinction between fiction and history. In fact, he makes it clear that *Old Indian Days* and Smokey Day's own tales in *Wigwam Evenings* are perhaps a more accurate reflection of events than are Eastman's later herotales in *Indian Heroes and Great Chieftains* (1918).

In the eighth tale, Tamakoche's three sons are killed in battle; so he urges his daughter, Makatah, to think and act as a warrior. She rejects many suitors and instead of marriage chooses to accompany her three cousins on an attack upon the Crows.

When, in the retreat, her pony tires, the threat becomes a test of her suitors. The braggart, Red Horn, chooses to save his own life while the humble orphan, Little Eagle, sacrifices his life to save Makatah's. Returning to camp, she declares herself "the widow of the brave Little Eagle" and remains true to his spirit for the rest of her life. Although the Sioux woman's usual role was as "a link in the genealogy of her race," Eastman shows here that in the face of unworthy life, loyalty to the dead is preferable. Since no warrior was worthy, the woman must choose—as do so many of the silent people in *Red Hunters and the Animal People*—to break the genetic link. Thus subtly but undeniably, this eighth tale marks the conclusion of *Old Indian Days.*

In *Wigwam Evenings* Smokey Day is younger and less despairing than he is in the earlier books. But despite the efforts of Elaine Goodale, who co-authored the volume, Eastman's increasing despair surfaces. What should be parables for red children have become fables for white children, Ohiyesa's fable among them. The tales of *Wigwam Evenings* seem to use nature as Aesop might. Their morals are accented as though the teller has no faith in his audience's ability to respond to "every accent, every gesture" of the teller, as Smokey Day's original listeners had been trained to do. Despite this difference, the tales retain ritual emphasis and traditional values. We meet in them the balancers of nature which the whites hear only as voices of discord.

We learn that the Sioux emerged originally from a splinter in the toe of He-who-was-First-Created. This is a decidedly more modest vision of man's significance than the view which gives western man his sense of superiority over nature. We learn that originally all things spoke a single language and possessed a single spirit. Not until Man is destroyed by Unk-tay-keep does He-who-was-First-Created take on a Prometheus-like role, reviving man and giving him fire and weapons to help him survive in a world now unbalanced. When he uses fire and weapons instead of rit-ual, the animals and plants see Man as enemy. Reinforcing the lesson of *Red Hunters,* therefore, Eastman shows that man himself creates discord in nature. Only the coming of the Star Boy, son of Star and the Earth maiden, will return balance to the earth. The reality that the Star Boy represents is the interpenetration of the physical by the spiritual world which white logic has destroyed.

The two concluding tales of *Wigwam Evenings* are tales of magic and of the supernatural in which the Sioux spirit world penetrates white reality. But the penetration is possible only as long as the Sioux believe in and retain the conditions necessary to that coexistence. The old people in **"The Magic Arrows"** retain this belief, even though the young husband in **"The Ghost Wife"** forgets. His moment of carelessness loses him his family and his world. The loss is irretrievable, for the Sioux world is as dangerous and remorseless as the world of the animals in *Red Hunters.*

Ohiyesa (Eastman) is in the tales no longer an apologist or an apocalyptic prophet, but the revealer of an irreversible reality. Like the young warrior's, the Sioux's family and world are "gone from him forever." His people will produce no more heroes, chiefs, or warriors to replace those who are recalled in *Indian Heroes and Great Chieftains.* In *Soul of the Indian,* Eastman writes of the Sioux way as dead. Yet I think that each of the volumes is part of a ritual way that Eastman began later in life than was usual. In the narrative which is a substitute for the ritual he returns to that penultimate day when, at sixteen, he stepped into the Spirit Land. Considering his works as a ritual, one can see a strength in the developing character of Ohiyesa that he himself seems not to have seen until the late 1920's.

In a chapter called "Back to the Woods," in *From the Deep Woods to Civilization,* he details the first steps of his journey back from civilization to the deep woods. On Bear Island in Leech Lake, he came upon a group who "still sustained themselves after the old fashion by hunting, fishing, and gathering of wild rice and berries." Their hunting trails are "deeply grooved in the virgin soil," and they hold the Grand Medicine Dance annually. The voice of the narrator becomes poetic as it speaks of the "clear Black waters" which have "washed, ground, and polished these rocky islets into every imaginable fantastic shape." Leech Lake bestows a sense of the sacred, and from this point on, Eastman and his readers know that "the out-of-doors was the essential vehicle" for Eastman's spiritual quest.

Marion W. Copeland, in her Charles Alexander Eastman (Ohiyesa), *Boise State University, 1978, 43 p.*

Tom Holm   (essay date 1981)

[*In the following excerpt, Holm discusses Eastman's presentation of Sioux philosophy in his writings.*]

During the early part of this century there was a nationwide interest in American Indian life. As a result, Charles A. Eastman, a Sioux graduate of Boston Medical School, published a number of books about tribal life and culture. His style was genteel and not really upsetting to non-

Indians, yet he professed many tribal values and ideals that ran counter to Anglo-American economic, political and social thinking.

Eastman was initially concerned with providing proof to whites that American Indians were intellectually capable of American citizenship and should, therefore, be treated with equality. In his first book, an autobiography entitled *Indian Boyhood,* he emphasized the idea that Indian people learned and had the capacity to be taught even while in transition from "savagery" to "civilization." Indian cultures, however, were different and the Indian child was taught according to the dictates of his own society. In many ways Eastman anticipated the acceptance of cultural pluralism as a social ideal.

In terms of technological knowledge, Eastman most often gave the edge to Western European civilization. He lived in an era when people were convinced that industrialization held the answer to the problems of mankind. But when the conservation movement began to show a widespread popular base during the early years of the twentieth century, Eastman proudly wrote about, and to his mind demonstrated, the equality, if not the superiority of American Indian knowledge. In *Indian Boyhood* he attempted to prove that the tribal life he had lived as a boy was much healthier and more peaceful than life in the city. Indians, according to Eastman, lived in harmony with nature and because of the demands of the environment were physically as well as mentally capable of meeting any demand placed upon them.

It was easy for Eastman to move from being a philosopher on racial capabilities to becoming a teacher of "Indian lore." In addition to the widely read and admittedly instructional *Indian Boyhood,* Eastman continued his autobiography in *From the Deep Woods to Civilization.* His most popular tracts were youth books. *Red Hunters and the Animal People* (1904), *Indian Scout Talks* (1914) and *Indian Heroes and Great Chieftans* (1918) were among his best received monographs for young people. For a more mature audience, Eastman expounded on American Indian religious ideas in *The Soul of the Indian* (1911), and reported on conditions within American Indian groups and listed Indian contributions to American society in *The Indian Today.*

As a physician in touch with the trends in his own profession, Eastman was convinced that a back to nature movement was necessary to the life of the nation. He believed that his ancestors owed their strong physical characteristics to their "natural" life styles. In his mind, detriments to Indian health were measles, smallpox, tuberculosis and alcohol—all European introductions. He once expressed the opinion that these introductions would have annihilated the Indian race had it not been for the already strong physical conditioning acquired during a tribal upbringing.

He was consistent in reminding his readers of the tribal concept of balance. Eastman was against excess in all human endeavor, and if extremes had already been made he believed that measures should be taken to counterpose them. To him a back to nature movement would counter the deleterious effects of industrialization. Wise Americans, both Indian and non-Indian, should offset life in the cities with vacations in the wild. The wilderness was a healthful and spiritually stimulating environment designed to balance out human avarice. He fully supported every movement that advocated the preservation of nature, and was most active in promoting groups like the Camp Fire Girls and the Boy Scouts.

Although considered a romantic, Eastman was convinced that further destruction of the natural order would lead to chaos. Resources would be depleted as once game had been. Human survival actually depended on a rapid change of attitudes regarding the environment. He stressed that mankind should adopt Indian knowledge and admit that all forms of life were interdependent and akin to each other.

Far from being removed intellectually from tribal thought, Eastman was part of its continuous existence. He, like tribal spiritual leaders, adopted a holistic approach to knowledge and was acutely aware of the idea of universal order. His personal mission, he believed, was to extend this outlook so that all of mankind could learn and benefit from it. In that way the earth was to be saved from ultimate destruction. In the final analysis, despite his outward idealism, Eastman was not overly convinced that human beings were, on the whole, intelligent enough to learn the responsibilities of continued existence. This underlying pessimism was perhaps one of the reasons why he particularly aimed his books toward the young and why he decided to leave, in his later years, civilization for the peace of the wilderness. Perhaps, as his biographer Raymond Wilson once suggested, his return to nature symbolized a completion of the life cycle.

Tom Holm, "American Indian Intellectuals and the Continuity of Tribal Ideals," in Book Forum, *Vol. V, No. 3, 1981, pp. 349-56.*

Raymond Wilson   (essay date 1983)

[*Wilson is an American educator whose major area of research and writing is nineteenth- and twentieth-century Indian and white relations. In the following excerpt, he discusses Eastman's work as a writer and lecturer.*]

Charles Eastman made his greatest impact on society as a writer and lecturer. He originally intended to preserve a written record of his Indian childhood for his children. After moving his burgeoning family to St. Paul in 1893, Eastman began to record his thoughts and recollections. Elaine [Goodale Eastman] read what her husband had written and persuaded him to send these earliest sketches of his childhood to *St. Nicholas: An Illustrated Magazine for Young Folks* for possible publication. They were immediately accepted and were serialized in six installments. These articles would later be incorporated in his first book, *Indian Boyhood,* published in 1902. The six serialized articles were his first publications. In years to come he wrote many additional articles and eleven books (two of which were combinations of others and were published as special school editions).

Although all of these books except *Wigwam Evenings:*

Sioux Folk Tales Retold (1909) and *Smoky Day's Wigwam Evenings: Indian Stories Retold* (1910) bore only Eastman's name, he acknowledged his wife's collaboration. Indeed, she served as his principal editor. "Dr. Eastman's books left his hand," Elaine later wrote, "as a rough draft in pencil, on scratch paper." From these, she would then type copies, "revising, omitting, and re-writing as necessary," the same procedure undoubtedly employed in getting his articles ready for publication.

The subjects of Eastman's books and articles can be grouped into three general categories: autobiography; information concerning Indian life, customs, and religion; and information dealing with Indian and White relations. Two of his books which are specifically autobiographical in nature are integral to an understanding of the mental, spiritual, and attitudinal stages of development of Eastman's life. Although Eastman apparently planned to write a third book, concerned exclusively with the last years of his life, the book was never published.

His first book, *Indian Boyhood* (1902), dealt with his reminiscences of his first fifteen years of life as an Indian in the wilds of Minnesota and Canada. In *From the Deep Woods to Civilization: Chapters in the Autobiography of an Indian,* published in 1916, he continued the story of his life, emphasizing his schooling and subsequent work in white civilization up to about 1915. Both books contain material which Eastman had previously published in article form.

Written mainly for children, *Indian Boyhood* depicts the idyllic existence Indians once enjoyed. Eastman did not ignore the harsh realities associated with the type of life he led as a youth. He referred briefly to famine, disease, confrontations with other Indian bands, and intermittent conflicts with the white man, but he devoted greater attention to the more gratifying aspects of his childhood, idealizing and romanticizing his past and associating it with an atmosphere of childlike simplicity. In an informal and at times intimate tone, Eastman conveyed an unconscious longing to return to a world he viewed as naturally good. Even in the final chapter, in recounting what must have been a personal and emotional trauma at his father's request that he live in the white world, Eastman never revealed his true feelings about his displacement. Rather, he assumed an optimistic tone as he, his father, and his grandmother began their journey into white society.

The youthful optimism and idealism which Eastman possessed when he began his passage into an alien culture soon diminished with the sobering experiences of adulthood. As Eastman related in his second autobiographical work, *From the Deep Woods to Civilization,* his varied experiences in white society gave him a more realistic perspective of that society. Eastman presented a more candid and critical opinion of the white world, openly attacking the evils of white society and lamenting the sorrows Indians encountered as a result of cultural contact, yet never completely turning his back on the positive aspects of the dominant society but only exposing the wrongs which certain Whites perpetrated on Indians.

Certain omissions in *From the Deep Woods to Civilization* are noteworthy. Eastman's presentation of the facts regarding the Pine Ridge controversy is entirely one-sided. Although he did not present false information, he was guilty of neglecting all data which would cast doubt on his arguments. He also did not discuss the turmoil-filled years he spent as government physician at Crow Creek, possibly because of inherent fears that his readers would question his ability to get along with Indian agents and other government officials. He should have detailed thoroughly both incidents, letting his readers make the ultimate decision as to who was to blame.

Eastman's writings regarding Indian life, customs, and religion included many stories containing factual information about Indian culture, some of which were written especially for children. He heard many of these stories as a youth sitting around a campfire with other boys and listening to elders relate Indian tradition and history. In *Old Indian Days* (1907), Eastman presented fifteen stories—seven about Indian warriors and eight about Indian women. While all contained information about Indian customs, some stories were written far better than others. For example, one of the best stories on warriors, **"The Love of Antelope,"** concerned an Indian named Antelope and his love for Taluta. Besides presenting information on courtship, marriage, and the role of women in Sioux society, Eastman discussed the Indians' practice of counting coup—the way in which warriors received honor and eagle feathers for extraordinary feats, usually in battle. In turn, one of the most poorly written stories on warriors was **"The Madness of Bald Eagle,"** which contained information on the practice of accepting dares and explained the custom of redeeming peer approval through acts of bravery, but was sketchy and lacked character development.

His stories on women stressed their importance and function in Indian society. Two of his best were **"Winoa, The Woman-Child"** and **"Winoa, The Child-Woman,"** in which Eastman excellently portrayed the life and training of an Indian girl, from birth taught to accept her role in society: "to serve and to do for others." In **"The War Maiden"** Eastman wrote about the rather unusual practice of a woman going to war. She was not only accepted by the Indian men, but she also proved herself worthy in battle.

Other books containing accounts on Indian life included some written for children, in which Eastman explained the Indians' concept of creation and their close relationship to nature and animals. In several of these stories animals represented Indians as leading characters, and the tales ended with a moral similar to the Aesop Fables. For instance, in one story concerning a drake outwitting a falcon, the drake believed that the falcon was dead, and later, while he was boasting of this feat to others, he was overtaken and killed by the falcon. The moral was "Do not exult too soon; nor is it wise to tell of your brave deeds within the hearing of your enemy."

Another story concerned a turtle who had been captured by his enemies. In contemplating a manner of death, they suggested burning him, but the turtle replied that he would scatter the burning coals and kill them all. Next, they considered boiling him, to which the turtle said that he would dance in the boiling kettle and the steam would blind them forever. Finally, the turtle's captors suggested drowning. To this form of death the turtle remained silent, and his enemies suspected that this was the best way of disposing of him. After being thrown into the water, the turtle, of course, escaped. Eastman moralized that "patience and quick wit are better than speed."

One of his best books containing stories about Indian life was *Red Hunters and the Animal People* (1904), in which Eastman stressed the honor and closeness that Indians felt for animals. The twelve excellent pieces in this book ranged from how hunters learned from animals in hope of acquiring their resourceful ways, to the Indians' view that animals were placed on the earth as a means of a life line for them.

Eastman wrote many straightforward accounts about Indian customs and religion. To Eastman Indians lived the "freest life in the world," and their handicrafts, their rudimentary technology, and their medicine were indeed significant because many were adopted by or influenced white civilization. He described how Indians made bows and arrows, canoes, pottery, and pipes; discussed at length the work Indians did with leather and hides; and detailed information on such political and social subjects as Indian government, humor, and burial. From Indians, white men learned new agricultural methods for growing vegetables and fruits, and even borrowed the national emblem of the United States, the American eagle, from them.

Eastman also stressed the healthier aspects of Indian living over white living. He encouraged white parents to involve their children in more outdoor activities because fresh air and nature were God's gifts and should be utilized. In one book, written specifically for the Boys Scouts and the Campfire Girls, he used the Indian as the prototype of these organizations and presented useful information that these youths could employ in their activities, such as outdoor survival techniques. In addition, he suggested special and honored Indian names and secret signals that they could adopt.

Many of these books and articles brought out his belief in the compatibility between certain aspects of Indian worship and Christianity. Eastman syncretized his beliefs to a certain extent, yet spiritually he maintained an affinity with his past. His Indian religion seemed to be the source from which he maintained his identity, an aspect which he covered more thoroughly in *The Soul of the Indian,* published in 1911. The purpose, as he stated in the Foreword of the book, was "to paint the religious life of the typical American Indian as it was before he knew the white man." He presented his recollections knowing that "the religion of the Indian is the last thing about him that the man of another race will ever understand." His purpose for writing the book appears to have been his need to reaffirm his identity with the past rather than to explain that past to white society. Eastman let his readers know that he was proud to be an Indian and was proud of his ancestral religious beliefs, which seemed to give meaning and perspective to his life.

In the Foreword of this book, Eastman explained the sources of his religious knowledge. "It is as true as I can make it to my childhood teaching and ancestral ideals, but from the human, not the ethnological standpoint." He used the term the Great Mystery (Wakan Tanka) to explain the Indians' concept of God and His creation. They worshipped this all-powerful force in silence and solitude. The responsibility for religious instruction was given to the woman, who from the time the baby was conceived practiced a sort of spiritual training, praying and meditating "to instill into the receptive soul of the unborn child the love of the 'Great Mystery' and a sense of brotherhood with all creation." After birth, she began pointing out and explaining nature to her newborn baby. Eastman recalled his own surrogate mother, Uncheedah, through whose guidance he was taught to pray in silence, was told the history of his people, and was instructed in the art of storytelling.

An integral part of the ritual of passage in which a boy became a man was the first offering, which required that the Indian child sacrifice the thing most dear to him to the Great Mystery. Such a sacrifice instilled in the child an appreciation of others' needs. Eastman decided to sacrifice his beloved dog because it was the thing he most cherished. When detailing the procedure, he failed to mention to his readers, however, that he probably ate some of the dog's remains, most likely feeling that his white audience might be offended by this part of the ceremony.

In sum, Eastman described the Indians' concept of religion as recognizing "a power behind every natural force. He saw God, not only in the sky, but in every creation. All Nature sang his praises—birds, waterfalls, tree tops— everything whispered the name of the mysterious God." To Indians the supernatural was commonplace. "The virgin birth would appear," wrote Eastman, "scarcely more miraculous than is the birth of every child that comes into the world, or the miracle of the loaves and fishes excite more wonder than the harvest that springs from a single ear of corn."

He commented on white missionaries and their frequent attacks on Indian beliefs. He thought that their methods were unjust, characterizing them as "good men imbued with the narrowness of their age" and chastising their practice of classifying Indians as pagans because they followed a different religion. To substantiate this view, Eastman told about a group of Indians listening to a missionary tell about the creation and the fall of Adam and Eve. After he finished his account, the Indians, in turn, told him about their belief of how maize originated. When the missionary became outraged and discounted their story as false, the Indians calmly replied that they believed his stories, so why did he not believe theirs?

The most significant topics to Eastman were perhaps the ones concerning Indian and White relations, especially during the reservation period. In Eastman's opinion the coming of the white men destroyed forever the Indian's way of life. Labeling Indian and White contact as the Transition Period—a movement from the natural life to an artificial existence—Eastman declared that the two greatest white civilizers were whiskey and gunpowder. Contact with Whites forced Indian women into prostitution, altered or perverted Indian customs and manners, and caused divisions within tribes. He speculated that the mass killing of buffalo was a conspiracy by Whites to conquer the Plains Indians because it was less expensive to attack them economically than militarily.

Warfare between Indians and Whites was, according to Eastman, the usual and gravest result of contact. Originally, war among Indians was regarded as part of their life. "It was held to develop," wrote Eastman, "the quality of manliness, and its motive was chivalric or patriotic." He suggested incorrectly that these tribal wars were little more than tournaments and compared them to the white man's football games. "It was common, in early times, for a battle or skirmish to last all day, with great display of daring and horsemanship, but with scarcely more killed and wounded than may be carried from the field during a university game of football."

Eastman described how Indians revered a brave enemy in mourning by scalping him and holding a ceremony to honor his departed spirit. Warfare with Whites, however, was different. Eastman believed that all major Indian wars were caused by land-hungry Whites and broken treaties. He declared that "wanton cruelties and the more barbarous customs of war were greatly intensified with the coming of white men, who brought with them fiery liquor and deadly weapons, aroused the Indian's worst passions, provoking in him revenge and cupidity, and even offered bounties for the scalps of innocent men, women, and children."

Eastman had the opportunity to interview several famous Indian leaders and to write accounts of their lives and battles. Such prestigious individuals as Sitting Bull, Red Cloud, and Chief Joseph were included in a book entitled *Indian Heroes and Great Chieftains* (1918), which also contained excellent photographs of many famous Indians. His vivid portrayal of these Indians and other leading figures, as well as battles between Indians and Whites, appears, in the main, accurate in detail and sympathetic in tone.

He used the Battle of the Little Big Horn as an example of the consequence of broken treaties. In no uncertain terms he condemned historians and military personnel for inflating the number of Indians engaged in this encounter and for underestimating the Indians' military genius. In summing up the battle Eastman wrote, "The simple truth is that Custer met the combined forces of the hostiles, which were greater than his own, and that he had not so much underestimated their numbers as their ability." He stated, however, that this victory was short-lived, and the result of this war and most Indian wars with Whites was imprisonment on reservations.

Eastman sharply criticized the Indian bureau's responsibility for the wretched conditions on reservations, basing his observations on his own experiences as a government physician on reservations and as a visitor to several reserves. Commenting that many of the reservations were located in dry places and were unfit for agriculture except with proper irrigation, he complained that Indians were forced to eat unhealthful food. "In a word," wrote East-

man, "he lived a squalid life, unclean and apathetic physically, mentally, and spiritually."

Eastman held the Indian bureau and its system responsible, because though the bureau was set up to serve Indians, instead it became an autocracy over them. Furthermore, he believed that many Indian agents were "nothing more than a ward politician of the commonest stamp, whose main purpose is to get all that is coming to him. His salary is small, but there are endless opportunities for graft." Eastman recognized that there were good men in the Indian bureau, but their numbers were few and they were not in positions of authority to implement their views.

To rectify matters, he called for the abolition of the Indian bureau, whose political interests appalled him. He blamed it "for all the ills of our Indian civilization." He thought that the bureau had outlived its usefulness and was too paternalistic toward Indians, but he was not, however, in favor of complete termination of government services and aid. Indeed, he wanted the machinery updated possibly in the form of a commission that would serve as a guardian over Indians. He specifically stressed that at least half the members on the commission should be Indians, that it should be as free as possible from political pressures, and that it should have direct authority to handle Indian affairs without going through other departments for approval. Such a commission or program was never established.

Eastman also expressed his views about Indian policies and humanitarian organizations. He generally condemned Republican administration during the early 1860s for its extreme corruption in the handling of Indian affairs; but, in turn, he applauded President Abraham Lincoln's courage in pardoning hundreds of Indians held responsible for the 1862 Sioux Uprising in Minnesota. In addition, he praised Indian reform measures enacted under President Ulysses S. Grant, especially the upgrading of agency officials in order to curb graft and corruption on reservations. He expressed anger at the abandonment of the policy as partisan politics again dictated the selection of Indian agents.

Eastman, along with many other reform-minded individuals and organizations, supported the Dawes Severalty Act of 1887, which provided for allotments in severalty and the breakup of reservations. He called it the Emancipation Act of the Indian and praised such organizations as the Board of Indian Commissioners, the Indian Rights Association, and the Lake Mohonk Conference of Friends of the Indian, not only for their support of this act, but also for their work on behalf of Indians. Eastman supported the Dawes Act primarily because it granted citizenship to Indians who accepted allotments. By becoming citizens Indians could obtain rights of the dominant Americans, particularly the suffrage, which he hoped would give Indians a voice in decisions affecting their lives. His later publications, however, contain little praise and minimal mention of the Dawes Act but do contain criticism of the Burke Act of 1906, which dealt with Indian allotment fees, patents, and citizenship. Most reformers condemned the Burke Act, especially the provisions making it more difficult for Indians to acquire citizenship. Eastman chastised the framers of the act as interested only in graft and believed that such a law would confuse the status of Indians. Eastman can certainly be criticized for supporting the Dawes Act, especially by citing the devastating results of the act. The Dawes Act and related pieces of legislation operated for nearly fifty years, during which time Indians lost over 85 million acres. Yet, in his defense, most well-meaning reformers supported the Dawes Act, sincerely believing that it would bring the two races closer together. Perhaps Eastman was too naive and put too much faith in the Dawes Act as a means to achieve harmony between Indians and Whites.

Many of his later publications, written between 1910 and 1919, dealt with the contributions and needs of Indians. He wrote that Indians were no longer regarded as "bloody savages," and white civilization was finally recognizing their worth. He cited, for example, their native arts and crafts as much in demand, and he ridiculed the use of machine-made products in the place of handmade items. Furthermore, non-Indian painters, sculptors, authors, and other patrons were honoring and praising Indians for their achievements.

Even though Indians were at last being recognized, they still suffered from unhealthful living conditions and inadequate educational facilities. Eastman lamented that the annual death rate of Indians was alarming in comparison to the death rate of Whites, and he stated that tuberculosis and trachoma, an eye disease, were among the major diseases that attacked Indians. He believed that Indians were receiving better care and treatment than in previous years, but that there was still a need for more services. In addition, educational facilities for Indians were often overcrowded, unsanitary, and breeding grounds for disease. He called for the support of programs that directed more appropriations to improve Indian health and to teach Indians about proper hygiene.

Eastman continually stressed the need for Indians to obtain a proper education, believing that this was the best way for Indians to contribute to their people and to white society. He offered himself as an example of what an Indian could attain. Though he recognized that many schools were inadequate, he stated, "I would give up anything rather than the schools, unmoral [sic] as many of them are." He suggested that more qualified teachers and improved facilities were needed to eradicate the deficiencies, praising the Hampton Institute in Virginia and Carlisle School in Pennsylvania, two institutions attended by Indians, because they showed that Indians could be properly educated. He also remarked that more and more educated Indians were being accepted by their fellow tribesmen upon returning to the reservation.

The granting of citizenship to Indians continued to be, in Eastman's opinion, their most pressing need, particularly following World War I. He regarded Indian status in the United States as extremely confusing. "I do not believe," he wrote, "there is a learned judge in these United States who can tell an Indian's exact status without a great deal of study, and even then he may be in doubt." Eastman used Indian involvement in World War I and the goals of peace after the war as reasons for granting citizenship. Emphasizing the way they were actively involved in the

defense of liberty and their need to be adequately compensated, he used President Woodrow Wilson's goals of peace for European countries as a premise to what should be applied at home for Indians. He wrote, "We ask nothing unreasonable—only the freedom and privileges for which your boy and mine have fought." Indians had to wait for several more years, however, before receiving such a privilege.

Lucrative lecture engagements resulted from his writings. Addressing audiences was nothing new to Eastman, who during his college days had given speeches before groups and later spoke at the Lake Mohonk Conference of Friends of the Indian. After publication of ***Indian Boyhood*** he accepted a lecture invitation from the Twentieth Century Club in Brooklyn, New York, for which he received $100. While there, he met Major James B. Pond, a lyceum manager, who asked Eastman if he wanted "to go on the lecture platform under his management." Eastman found the arrangements satisfactory and accepted his offer. The two men developed a good rapport and worked together until Pond's untimely death. Because of the initial success of this first venture and a growing demand for more personal appearances. Eastman continued to give lectures. His wife took over the duties of handling all of his correspondence and publicity.

Eastman in Sioux regalia, ca. 1918.

Eastman wrote that he could lecture on any general or specific Indian topic. The subjects of his talks ranged from "The School of Savagery," "The Real Indian," "The Story of the Little Big Horn," to aesthetic topics such as, "Indian Wit, Music, Poetry and Eloquence." Frequently Eastman would be attired in full Sioux regalia while presenting these lectures. He must have cast a striking pose, wearing such items as an eagle-feathered war bonnet, a beautifully beaded tan costume made from animal skins, and carrying a tomahawk/peace-pipe. His stage presence and commanding voice must have been overwhelming.

Response to Eastman's writings and lectures was phenomenal. Almost every review of his books contained both laudatory remarks of their contents and high praise of the author. For example, *The Soul of the Indian* and *The Indian Today* (1915), two of his most profound books, received good reviews. In the case of the former, one reviewer wrote, "Not being influenced by the prejudices and legends which prevail in the mind of most white men concerning the Indian, Dr. Eastman is able to give us a clear idea of what the red man really thinks and feels" [*American Review of Reviews* 43 (Jan.- June 1911)]. Regarding the latter book, several reviewers believed that it was well written, forceful, and most enlightening.

In evaluating Eastman's expertise as a writer, several observations are in order. One of the major criticisms of his works is his neglect, at times, to make it clear to the reader whether he is discussing particular traits of all Indians or of just the Sioux, though most of what he wrote applied to his kinsmen. Because he seemed to draw little distinction between being an Indian and being a Sioux, his works tend to emphasize the similarities rather than the marked differences among Indian cultures. He helped to influence the contemporary stereotyped image of Native Americans. Today, non-Indians the world over have painted a mental picture of what an Indian is: a Plains Indian—more specifically, a Sioux.

In general, Eastman's depiction of Indian life and subsequent white contact is reinforced by several of his contemporaries, two of whom were Zitkala-Sa (Gertrude Bonnin), a writer, poet, and lecturer, and Luther Standing Bear, a noted Sioux author. In comparing Eastman to these writers, interesting and important distinctions emerge. Gertrude Bonnin, born in 1876 at Yankton Reservation, South Dakota, learned quickly from her mother to distrust and resent the white man. She sought a formal education despite her mother's wishes and later attended Earlham College in Indiana. A few years later, she studied at the Boston Conservatory of Music, when she began to write. Some of her articles were published in the *Atlantic Monthly* and in *Harper's Monthly.* Her most memorable book was *American Indian Stories,* published in 1921, in which she depicted her childhood, her initial rejection and eventual acceptance of Christianity, and her changing attitudes toward the white man. Like Eastman, her autobiography is romantic in scope and viewed the Indian way of life as a state of grace eventually corrupted by the coming of the white man. Bonnin's account, however, was less detailed on Sioux customs and more resentful toward the white man.

Luther Standing Bear, born in the 1860s, unlike Eastman, who was a Santee, or Eastern, Sioux, was a Teton, or Western, Sioux. Standing Bear attended Carlisle Indian School, where he acquired a trade, tinsmithing, which proved to be impractical on the reservation, and as a result, he undertook various jobs ranging from an assistant teacher at a reservation school to an agency clerk and storekeeper. He eventually became involved in show business. Later in his life he wrote four books, a noteworthy accomplishment for someone with only a rudimentary education as Carlisle provided. Two of his best works are *My People the Sioux* (1928) and *Land of the Spotted Eagle* (1933).

Standing Bear was not as prolific a writer as Eastman, but they wrote about many of the same topics. Although they expressed similar points of view regarding Indian and White relations, reservation life, and the role of women, Standing Bear tended to give a more elaborate account of certain events than did Eastman. Their descriptions of the Sun Dance, for example, reflect their different viewpoints. According to Eastman, the Sun Dance occurred when a Sioux warrior wanted to fulfill a vow made to the Sun for prolonging his life. Standing Bear, on the other hand, remembered the Sun Dance as a sacrificial rite which was fulfilled every year. Both writers had similar accounts of the elaborate selection and importance of the pole to the ceremony and also agreed on the symbolic importance of the figures which hung from the pole, but differed in their accounts of the final stage of the Sun Dance. Standing Bear recalled, in detail, the brutal aspects of the ceremony, from the piercing of the participant's breast, through which a wooden pin was inserted, to the ensuing results. Eastman, however, did not emphasize these points. The cut made, according to Eastman, was just deep enough to draw blood. The rawhide was then attached to the shoulders of the participant rather than the breast. In fairness to both writers, there are two rites of sacrifice of the Sun Dance—one which pierces the breast, and the other which pierces the shoulders. The lodge ceremony (breast) is the more spectacular. Unlike his conscious omission in *Indian Boyhood* regarding his consumption of his favorite dog, Eastman did not avoid the gruesome aspects of the Sun Dance to appease the sensibilities of the white audience. Rather, he paralleled the increase of cruelty in the event to the Indians' contact with white men. He declared, "The Sun Dance of the Plains Indians, the most important of their public ceremonies, was abused and perverted until it became a horrible exhibition of barbarism." The amount of brutality involved in the Sun Dance and aspects of the ceremony still remain matters of controversy.

The diversity in the writing styles and content of Standing Bear and Eastman can be attributed to many factors. Because they were from different bands, they probably had different versions of particular events. Standing Bear's tendency to write more detailed accounts than Eastman could be explained by having people like E. A. Brininstool, author of several books on western history, and Dr. Melvin R. Gilmore, an ethnologist, serve as collaborators on his books. Eastman, on the other hand, relied primarily on his own expertise and his wife's knowledge and editorial skills.

Eastman's books were so popular that some were translated into different languages. Even today, Eastman's works continue to be in vogue. Recently published anthologies contain selections from his works, and some of his books are still being reprinted. The *Wassaja/The Indian Historian,* a national Indian magazine, frequently cites and praises Eastman's works. As a source for Indian topics, Eastman's writings have been employed by several historians of the past and of the present. Indeed, Eastman's knowledge of historical data regarding Indian and White relations are quite accurate. For example, his views on the Custer debacle and on the Wounded Knee tragedy parallel most of the major accounts of these confrontations. In addition, the information he presented on Indian customs, the different ways in which Indians and Whites conducted warfare, the lack of respect most missionaries had toward Indian beliefs, and the deplorable conditions on reservations are valid and, in most cases, accurate observations. His interpretation that the mass slaughter of the buffalo—the Indians' lifeline—was a plot conceived by Whites to defeat economically the Plains Indians because it would be less costly to engage in economic warfare than major military operations is a view still held by many contemporary writers.

His statements on the corruption, graft, and inefficiency of the Bureau of Indian Affairs primarily surfaced after 1910. By that date, Eastman had had two bitter confrontations with white agents while serving under them as a government physician. Ironically, by criticizing the bureau, Eastman was demeaning the vehicle through which he pursued his original goal as a physician to his people. Failing in this role, he engaged in other pursuits, specifically writing and lecturing. Although certainly his criticism of the bureau was tempered by the unpleasant episodes he had encountered at Pine Ridge and at Crow Creek, he justifiably condemned the wretched conditions on reservations and called for desperately needed reforms.

Eastman received equal praise as a lecturer. The popularity of his books made him a sought after speaker in many cities throughout the United States and in England. People who heard his lectures found him to be a knowledgeable, dignified, and an attractive speaker.

Through his writing and lecturing, Eastman hoped to influence Whites, to make them aware of the "Indian problem" from an Indian point of view, and to spur them to the cause of reform. On some occasions he used powerful language to make a point, and at other times, his audience had to read between the lines to get his message. One of his nephews, Oliver Eastman, a Flandreau Sioux, believed that his uncle's books were popular because of their truthfulness. However, he thought that Eastman was forced to choose his words carefully in order not to offend his white readers. Although this may be true, he did, nevertheless, make some bold and valid statements regarding reform of Indian policy.

There is little doubt that Eastman believed Indians should adopt white ways; however, he did not favor total rejection of past customs and traditions. He supported many of the old customs but realized that Indians were doomed if they clung to the past and did not alter their ways. As a subjugated people, Indians had to acquire the more advanced aspects of white civilization to survive and then to compete in white society.

Eastman's writings are important to historians not only because he interviewed several famous Indians and recorded their views but also because he was writing about Indian history from his own perspective as an Indian—an uncommon perspective in the early twentieth century. Through his works he hoped to bring Indians and Whites closer together in an effort to break down the wall of prejudice which existed. That was his greatest contribution as author and lecturer. Indeed, commenting on the primary purpose of his lectures, which can also be applied to his writings as well, Eastman wrote:

> My chief object has been, not to entertain, but to present the American Indian in his true character before Americans. The barbarous and atrocious character commonly attributed to him has dated from the transition period, when the strong drink, powerful temptations, and commercialism of the white man led to deep demoralization. Really it was a campaign of education on the Indian and his true place in American history.

That his books are still widely read is testimony to his success.

Raymond Wilson, in his Ohiyesa: Charles Eastman, Santee Sioux, *University of Illinois Press, 1983, 219 p.*

The emergence of Pan-Indian leadership in the United States:

Often well educated in white schools and comfortable in white society, the first generation of Indian leaders to emerge on the national level included persons like Charles Eastman and Gertrude Bonnin. Yet despite their acceptance of assimilationist ideals, they also contributed a new ideal of their own: a Pan-Indian identity that emphasized the commonness of Indians of all tribes. They recognized things that Indians held in common, much more than previous tribal leaders had done. While they valued a "civilized" lifestyle, they also respected their native traditions enough to recognize the injustices of the federal colonial domination.

*Walter L. Williams, in his "Twentieth-Century Indian Leaders," *Journal of the West, *July 1984.*

H. David Brumble III (essay date 1986)

[*Brumble is an American educator, editor, and translator who has written numerous works about Native American autobiographies. In the following excerpt, he discusses late-nineteenth century Social Darwinism, evolutionary thinking, and their influence on Eastman and his writings.*]

Charles Alexander Eastman is the first Indian author who tried self-consciously to write autobiography after the modern, Western fashion (aside from the few Indians like

George Copway, Samson Occom, and William and Mary Apes who wrote pious accounts of their conversion to Christianity). His first volume of autobiography, *Indian Boyhood* (1916), begins in this way:

> The North American Indian was the highest type of pagan and uncivilized man. He possessed not only a superb physique but a remarkable mind. But the Indian no longer exists as a natural and free man. Those remnants which now dwell upon the reservations present only a sort of tableau—a fictional copy of the past.

This is a rather remarkable passage. For the first fifteen years of his life, Eastman lived according to the ancient tribal ways of the Santee Sioux. He was raised up to be a hunter and a warrior. He was taught never to spare a white enemy. Then, at the age of fifteen, he was abruptly taken out of this life and brought to Flandreau, South Dakota, to learn to live in the white man's way. Soon he outgrew the local school; he went on to Santee Normal School, in Nebraska, then to Beloit College, Knox College, Dartmouth College, and finally to the Boston University Medical School, where he took his degree in 1890. He had long since decided that he wanted to serve his people; and so, degree in hand, he went off to begin his work as Government Physician to the Sioux at Pine Ridge, South Dakota. He arrived one cold and windy day in November. Just one month later he was binding wounds and counting frozen corpses at Wounded Knee.

How could a Sioux Indian who had had such an experience, how could a man who came to know so many of the reservation Indians during his years as a reservation doctor, how could *Eastman* have written so dismissively of the Indians on the reservations? It is not surprising that those who write about Eastman either ignore this passage or agree with Arlene Hirschfelder that these sentiments are "unworthy of the rest of the book."

But the passage is not an aberration, really. The passage serves, in fact, as a perfectly apt introduction to some of the book's main concerns and themes. And it springs from Romantic Racialist and Social Darwinist assumptions fundamental to Eastman's thinking during these years—and fundamental as well to some other Indian autobiographies in the first decades of this century. *Indian Boyhood* can best be understood in the light of these assumptions and the feelings to which they gave rise.

Eastman was born in 1858, a year before the publication of *The Origin of Species.* But even in his mother's day, white-American attitudes toward race were undergoing a profound change. By the mid-nineteenth century, scientific and popular opinion had moved decisively away from the eighteenth-century ideas about the essential unity of the human race that had inspired the Jeffersonian declaration that "all men are created equal." The differences between savages and Americans, for Jefferson, could be explained in terms of environmental differences. Savages were deprived (or degenerate) humans. But by the time Eastman was fingering his first bow, environmental differences were no longer thought to be sufficient to explain human diversity. In 1847 the eminent craniologist S. G. Morton had proved to his own satisfaction that separate races were separate species. This was no mean feat, since scientists at this time assumed that the fertility of offspring was *the* test for species distinctions—and mulattos, after all, were obviously, indeed disturbingly, fertile. Morton argued that since hybrids—and he cited examples of hybrids among species of birds, fish, mammals, insects—are sometimes fertile, one can account for interracial fertility as a case of hybridity. Some species, Morton argued, are simply endowed with more capacity for hybridization than others, and none more than the several species of man.

And there were as well the separate creationists, those who believed, with Josiah Clark Nott, that all men could not have descended from Adam and Eve; not even God's mark on Cain could suffice to explain such great mental, moral, and physical differences. Racial variations could be scientifically explained only by positing separate acts of creation.

Obviously, such scientific theories often worked to justify deeply felt prejudices. But it is well to remember that even abolitionists could assume that blacks and Indians, because of their inherent inferiority or (more kindly) their inherent weakness, were unlikely long to survive. In 1863, for example, the Reverend J. M. Sturtevant wrote on "The Destiny of the African Race in the United States." He concluded that the direct competition with the white race, which would be the immediate result of emancipation, will have "inevitable" consequences for the Negro:

> He will either never marry, or he will, in the attempt to support a family, struggle in vain against the laws of nature, and his children, many of them at least, die in infancy. . . . Like his brother the Indian of the forest, he must melt away and disappear forever from the midst of us.

As George Fredrickson has written, Sturtevant's "racial Malthusianism" anticipates Darwin's idea of the struggle between the species—"as well as the 'social Darwinist' justification of a *laissez-faire* economy as the arena for a biological competition resulting in the 'survival of the fittest'."

Such ideas were at the peak of their influence when Eastman entered Dartmouth College in 1883. Just ten years earlier Whitelaw Reid, sometime influential Assistant Editor of the New York *Tribune* under Horace Greeley, had addressed the college, speaking about how quickly the new scientific ideas were winning acceptance:

> Ten or fifteen years ago the staple subject here for reading and talk, outside study hours, was English poetry and fiction. Now it is English science. Herbert Spencer, John Stuart Mill, Huxley, Darwin, Tyndall, have usurped the places of Tennyson and Browning, and Matthew Arnold and Dickens.

And in the year of Eastman's matriculation, for another example, *The New Englander,* an important periodical for Yankee clergymen, reversed itself and began to publish editorials to justify the ways of Darwin to man. Sizeable pockets of resistance remained, of course; but still it may be said that evolution had won the high ground in its battle with religion by the time Eastman began college. Much of the success of these ideas was due to Herbert Spencer. It was he who coined the phrase "survival of the fittest." It was Spencer who worked out most completely the social and racial implications of evolutionist ideas. Spencer managed, as well, much of the popularization of Social Darwinism. By the time Eastman published *Indian Boyhood*, Spencer's books had sold well over 300,000 copies—a figure probably unmatched by any other author dealing with subjects as difficult as sociology and philosophy.

It was largely to Spencer, then, that white Americans owed thanks for ideas that must have seemed divine compensation for the awkward religious choices forced upon them by Darwinian evolution. It was Spencer who did most to teach Americans that what was happening to the Indians was the inevitable—sad, of course, but certainly inevitable—working out of the laws of nature. And such ideas powerfully influenced those who concerned themselves with Indian affairs during these years. They provided the intellectual underpinnings of the Dawes Severalty Act of 1887—"the political expression of American thought about the Indian" throughout Eastman's adult years. This Act, which caused land to be taken from the tribes and allotted to individual Indians, assumed that the tribes were bound to die out. This was perfect Spencerism, perfect Social Darwinism. Societies, or races (it was so difficult, really, to distinguish between the two), were fundamentally like organisms. They had their span of life, and then they died, sooner if they were weaker than competing societies/races, later if they were strong of tooth and claw and intellect. The Indians, then, simply could not survive as *Indians*. Eastman was officially consulted about the provisions of the Dawes Act. And he was consulted precisely because he was rather famous proof that an individual Indian could compete with Americans. He approved of the Act and urged his Indian friends to embrace it. He and his fellow Indians could compete as *individuals*, each with his separate allotment; the tribes must, of course, inevitably vanish.

This kind of thinking produced a curious blend of fatalism and nostalgia. Indians are vanishing—and let us cherish our remembrances of real Indians. The Bureau of Indian Affairs even arranged an official farewell. With Joseph K. Dixon as prime mover, the Bureau arranged the Last Council, a meeting of chiefs and aging warriors from several of the Western tribes. This meeting took place in the Valley of the Little Bighorn in 1909. The record of that meeting was Dixon's *The Vanishing Race* (1913). In this book Dixon collected narratives (mostly autobiographical) from twenty-one Indians from fifteen tribes. The book was illustrated with Rodman Wanamaker's gorgeous sepia photographs. Dixon explained the Last Council and his book in this way:

> The preservation of this record in abiding form is all the more significant because all serious students of Indian life and lore are deeply convinced of the insistent fact that the Indian, as a race, is . . . soon destined to pass completely away. . . . These original Americans *Deserve a Monument*.

It is important to realize that Dixon is no champion of Anglo domination. He does not think of the Indians as morally inferior:

> The ruthless tread of cruel forces—we call them civilization . . . have in cruel fashion borne down upon the Indian until he had to give up all that was his and all that was dear to him—to make himself over or die. He would not yield. He died.

Dixon is certainly sympathetic; he feels a very personal sense of loss: "The door of the Indian's yesterdays opens to a new world—a world unpeopled with red men, but whose population fills the sky, the plains, with sad and spectre-like memories." He is thinking in social-Darwinist terms. "The white is the conquering race," he says; the Indians are "ancient forerunners." He is not as happy as Andrew Carnegie or Teddy Roosevelt was about the consequences of evolutionary forces, but he is every bit as certain that what has happened was inevitable. What he feels he can do now is to preserve as much of what is *really* Indian as he can. And so he gives us Red Whip's story of his fight with the Sioux—eleven against a hundred and thirty; he gives us Pretty Voice Eagle's remembrances of a time when there were no white men along the upper reaches of the Missouri; he gives us Mountain Chief's recollections of his boyhood sports. He also includes Wanamaker's photographs. And just as Dixon asked the questions that elicited the narratives, so Wanamaker posed the Indians for the photographs. The next-to-last photograph in the book shows the old warriors in their best buckskins and feathers riding in single file down a treeless hill toward the camera. This is captioned "Down the Western Slope." And in case we should miss the point, the last photograph in the book shows a huddle of riderless horses: "The Empty Saddle."

When all of this is taken into account, we may see that the opening epigraph in *Indian Boyhood* is not heartless. There is no failure of compassion here. The passage is a verbal equivalent of Wanamaker's "The Empty Saddle." The "real" Indians had been a glorious race; but it was a race that could not compete with the whites, and so it was dying out. Eastman saw upon the reservations the sad survivors of the Darwinian struggle. In his assessment of these people Eastman was agreeing with Spencer that contemporary primitive societies were sometimes retrograde. And he was agreeing with Dr. Carlos Montezuma, who was known as "the fiery Apache." Montezuma had been stolen from his family by raiding Pimas when he was four years old; he was then purchased and adopted by a Mexican-American reporter. Eventually, he worked his way through Chicago Medical College. He went on to serve as a physician on the reservations. And it was there, he said, that he "saw in full what deterioration is for the Indians." Montezuma bridled at the suggestion that he ought to live "among his people":

> Not that I do not revere my race, but I think if I had remained there on the reservation and not have been captured years and years ago, I would not be standing here defending my race. . . . I find that the only, the best thing for the good of the Indian is to be thrown on the world. . . . Better send every Indian away. Get hold and send them to Germany, France, China, Alaska,

Cuba, if you please, and then when they come back 15 or 20 years from now you will find them strong, a credit to the country, a help and an ornament to this race.

This was a view widely held by progressive Indians looking at the misery and poverty on the reservations. The pan-Indian and progressive Society of the American Indian argued that the BIA was very much mistaken to permit—let alone encourage—Indians to retain such vestiges of tribal life as the reservation system allowed. The Indians needed to be forced out of the tribes, off the reservation. The tribes must vanish as social institutions, for it was the tribe that kept individual Indians from achieving all that Eastman and Montezuma had achieved as individuals, away from their tribes.

Elaine Goodale, the woman who was to become Eastman's wife, provides another interesting case in point. She went to work in the Indian schools before she was twenty years old; she soon came to the attention of General Richard Henry Pratt, the founder of the Carlisle Indian School, and other prominent figures in the Indian reform movement. Her memoirs make fascinating reading for anyone interested in the enlightened attitude toward Indians in these years. Goodale steeped herself in the customs of the Dakota. She herself learned Sioux and thoroughly enjoyed her knowledge of the language. But utility and not sentiment, she was convinced, must rule in matters of education; and she saw no reason why teachers should know Sioux, since instruction was, quite rightly in her view, in English only. She was proud of her knowledge of Sioux customs, and observed them fairly punctiliously in her intercourse with her neighbors. The whole business, then, of Americanizing the Indians had for her and her progressive friends nothing to do with abhorrence of their ways. She had an explicitly romantic love of their ways. But the Americanizing was necessary, inevitable; consequently, sentiment had to be set aside.

The tribes must vanish, but they were important as memories. The glory of the tribe must be remembered. Goodale worked very hard and very ingeniously to turn Indians into civilized Americans. And yet she could write with real fondness of Indians as they were before their civilizing:

> Dear, lovable, intensely feminine Sioux women of days gone by! How affectionately I recall their devotion to their families, their innocent love of finery and gossip, eager curiosity and patient endurance.

It is in just this way, with the same limitations, that Montezuma can "revere" his race. And it is in this same way that Eastman hopes to convey a sense of the glory of his people. . . . All that Eastman can do now is try to record what he remembers of the old ways. What he can do is set down for his Anglo audience the nobility of the "real" Indians. Like Dixon and the Bureau, Eastman wants to set it all down before it vanishes.

There are other ways as well in which *Indian Boyhood* reflects evolutionist ideas. The book assumes, for example, that the races may be ordered, that some are higher, some lower. We should not be surprised, then, when we find

Eastman telling us that the Indians were a "primitive people." But for Eastman there were also distinctions—gradations—to be found among primitive peoples. As we have seen, Eastman began *Indian Boyhood* with the assertion that "The North American Indian was the highest type of pagan and uncivilized man." And if the North American Indians were "higher" than the South American Indians and the Africans, and the other primitive peoples, there are also gradations even among the Indians. Consider, for example, Eastman's comparison of the woodland Indians, like Eastman's Santee Sioux, and the Plains Indians:

> There was almost as much difference between the Indian boys who were brought up on the open prairies and those of the woods, as between city and country boys. The hunting of the prairie boys was limited and their knowledge of natural history imperfect. They were, as a rule, good riders, but in all-around physical development much inferior to the red men of the forest.

Environment alone could not account for such differences. Eastman believed that differing races have differing instincts. For example, Indians in general have an instinct for the hunt. So it is that when hunting, Eastman's Indian moves with an "inborn dignity" and "native caution." Eastman can even recall for his readers the moment when he first felt these native stirrings:

> I was scarcely three years old when I stood one morning . . . with my little bow and arrow in my hand, and gazed up among the trees. Suddenly the instinct to chase and kill seized me powerfully. Just then a bird flew over my head and then another caught my eye. . . . Everything else was forgotten and in that moment I had taken my first step as a hunter.

Eastman considered himself, then, to have inherited the blood of a superior tribe of the "highest" type of pagan people. And Eastman's family, it seems, was remarkable too—even among the Santee Sioux. His mother, Eastman wrote, was "sometimes called the 'Demi-Goddess' of the Sioux, who tradition says had every feature of a Caucasian descent with the exception of her luxuriant black hair and deep black eyes." His uncle "was known . . . as one of the best hunters and bravest warriors among the Sioux in British America." It was, however, his grandmother who was largely responsible for raising Eastman:

> It was not long before I began to realize her superiority to most of her contemporaries. This idea was not gained entirely from my own observation, but also from a knowledge of the high regard in which she was held by other women.

In some measure, of course, Eastman's sense of his tribe's and his family's superiority is quite traditional. It is well known that in some tribes the word for a member of the tribe was the same as the word for human being. And Eastman's pride in his family could have been matched by Achilles as readily as by other non-literate people whose sense of self-definition was shaped by ancient attitudes toward tribe and family. But ideas about the stages of human development are at work in Eastman's book as well, ideas that were central to much of social evolutionist thought. In 1877 Lewis Henry Morgan offered up a scientific rendering of Romantic conceptions of "national character" (such as we find, for example, in Carlyle and in Emerson's *English Traits*). He theorized that human history could be divided into three main "ethnical periods": Savagery, Barbarism, and Civilization. And these could further be broken down as follows:

> Lower Savagery: from "the infancy of the human race" up to the time of the discovery of fire; fruit and nut gathering; beginnings of language.

> Middle Savagery: fishing and use of fire; spread of mankind over the globe (examples: Australians and Polynesians).

> Upper Savagery: bow and arrow (examples: northern Atapascan tribes).

> Lower Barbarism: pottery making (examples: tribes east of the Missouri River).

> Middle Barbarism: in the Old World, the domestication of animals; in the New World, farming with irrigation and building with adobe and stone (examples: "Village Indians of New Mexico . . . and Peru").

> Upper Barbarism: commences with the smelting of iron (examples: Homeric Greeks)

> Civilization: from the time of the first use of phonetic alphabet up to present time.

Eastman did not see the history of the human race in quite the same way as Morgan did. For Eastman the North American Indian was "the highest type of pagan and uncivilized man," while Morgan would have graded Eastman's Santees no higher than the bow-and-arrow Upper Savagery stage. But it is quite clear that Eastman did assume, like Morgan and Spencer and others, that societies could be ranked in terms of their stage of evolution. And so, even though he considered his people, and especially his own family, to have been remarkably close to the Caucasian ideal, Eastman did realize that his family still was not fully evolved. His uncle, for example, was "a typical Indian—not handsome, but truthful and brave." The Santees in general were a "primitive people" and "superstitious."

Eastman saw himself as an embodiment of Social Darwinist notions about the evolution of the races. He had "evolved" from the woodland life of the Santee Sioux to the heights of white culture.

In *Indian Boyhood,* then, Eastman provides an explanation for just why it was that he was able to compete so successfully with the white man. . . . He could compete because he was a member of perhaps the best family of the best tribe of the "highest type of pagan and uncivilized man." This idea of competition is central to *Indian Boyhood*—just as it is central to Social Darwinism. Andrew Carnegie, for example, one of the best at the *practice* of Social Darwinism, was convinced by his reading of Darwin and Spencer that the "law" of competition was fundamentally biological. In an article for the *North American Re-*

view Carnegie argued that although we may object to what seems the harshness of this law,

> It is here; we cannot evade it; no substitutes for it have been found; and while the law may sometimes be hard for the individual, it is best for the race, because it assures the survival of the fittest in every department.

There is much in *Indian Boyhood* for Carnegie to applaud. "There was always keen competition among us," Eastman wrote. "We felt very much as our fathers did in hunting and war—each one strove to excel all the others." After hunting he and his mates would compare their kills: "We . . . kept strict account of our game, and thus learned who were the best shots among the boys." He remembers that the adult hunters "started before sunrise, and the brave who was announced throughout the camp as the first one to return with a deer on his back, was a man to be envied." There were even prizes for the young men who could hull rice the fastest. Because his mother died shortly after he was born, Eastman recalled, he "had to bear the humiliating name 'Hakadah,' meaning 'the pitiful last'." *Indian Boyhood* is, among other things, the story of how he earned—and how he continued through life to deserve—the name Ohiyesa, "winner."

This is certainly not to suggest that the Santee knew nothing of competition before Darwin, Spencer, and Carnegie whispered to them upon the wind. One has only to read *Two Leggings: The Autobiography of a Crow Warrior* to realize how intensely competitive a warrior society could be. But as he wrote about competition, as he thought about all the ways in which he had himself competed, Eastman must have been influenced by what he had learned about competition in the classroom and on the playing fields of Dartmouth. And Eastman was captain of athletic teams at Dartmouth.

Another striking feature of the book is its emphasis on childhood: the book is about an Indian boyhood, and the book was written for children. This, too, I think, is related to Eastman's Social Evolutionist assumptions. Notions about the childhood and the maturity of races were the common coin of Social Evolutionist explanations. The following passage from Spencer's *Principles of Sociology* is typical. I quote at length in order to demonstrate how rich the metaphor seemed to the Social Evolutionist:

> The intellectual traits of the uncivilized . . . are traits recurring in the children of the civilized.

> Infancy shows us an absorption in sensations and perceptions akin to that which characterizes the savage. In pulling to pieces its toys, in making mud-pies . . . the child exhibits great tendency to observe with little tendency to reflect. There is, again, an obvious parallelism in the mimetic propensity. Children are ever dramatizing the lives of adults; and savages, along with their other mimicries, similarly dramatize the actions of their civilized visitors. . . .

There was a time, then, when their enemies and friends could refer to Indians and blacks as "childlike" with the full authority of science. In her memoirs Elaine Goodale, for example, refers to the Sioux as being childlike, even though she could be infuriated by the official government statements that so often "were patronizing in tone, addressing the Indians as if they were children incapable of reason." There is no real inconsistency here, for Goodale wanted Indians to be treated like other Americans; she wanted them off the reservation, out of the reservation schools. Since she wanted them to become "adults," she wanted them to be treated like adults. And so in *Indian Boyhood* we find that the Santees were "children of the wilderness." When he was very young, Eastman conversed with squirrels and birds in "an unknown dialect"—he was, then, a child of Nature. As he was in years, so were his people in spirit:

> They are children of Nature, and occasionally she whips them with the lashes of experience, yet they are forgetful and careless. Much of their suffering could have been prevented by a little calculation.

But "calculation" is just what Spencer would not expect of savages, for "Lacking the ability to think, and the accompanying desire to know, the savage is without tendency to speculate." Eastman's formulation is a bit less brutal, but he is in fundamental agreement with Spencer. Eastman quite freely explains some of his people's behavior, for example, by speaking in terms of their "superstitions." And he devotes a whole chapter to making a distinction between the medicine men and women who worked upon the people's credulity and the herbal healers, whose remedies were real remedies. Eastman's grandmother was one of the latter, and so we see again that Eastman is descended from the best, most nearly rational, most fully evolved family of the best, most fully evolved tribe of the "highest type of pagan and uncivilized man."

There is, then, something quite consciously appropriate in Eastman's addressing *Indian Boyhood* to children. "I have put together these fragmentary recollections of my thrilling wild life," Eastman wrote in the dedication, "expressly for the little son who came too late to behold for himself the drama of savage existence." The hope would seem to be that his son, and his other youthful readers, might derive vicariously some of the benefits of a savage childhood:

> What boy would not be an Indian for a while when he thinks of the freest life in the world? This life was mine. Every day there was a real hunt. There was real game. Occasionally there was a medicine dance away off in the woods where no one could disturb us, in which the boys impersonated their elders, Brave Bull, Standing Elk, High Hawk, Medicine Bear, and the rest.

Much that Tom Sawyer urged his band to imagine, Eastman lived in fact. Eastman was very active in the Boy Scouts of America, and he wrote extensively for them. After he gave up doctoring, he ran for a time a woodsy camp for young women. He taught them archery and other Indian lore as being peculiarly appropriate to their formative years. In one book he described Indian life as the prototype for the Boy Scouts and the Campfire Girls. He considers his own remembrances of Indian ways, then, to be naturally well suited for children. It is no coinci-

dence that *Indian Boyhood* should end with Eastman's passage into the adult world *and* the white world. The passage into the white world *is* the passage into adulthood for the Indian.

Eastman was not alone in assuming that Indian life—the life of *real* Indians—provided good stories for children. Much of what was published about Indians during the first three decades of this century was intended for children. James Willard Schultz wrote many of his stories about his life among the Black-feet for *Youth's Companion* and *American Boy*. But among many examples, Luther Standing Bear provides probably the closest analogy. Standing Bear, like Eastman, was brought up in the old ways; he learned all that an Oglala boy ought to learn. He describes himself as having been precisely of an age to allow him the traditional Oglala education, but none of its application. This will say that he, too, conceives of himself as having been taken away from his people and brought to school just as he was entering upon the life of an adult. Soon after he killed his first and only buffalo he was whisked off to be a student in the first class at Carlisle Indian School. Standing Bear described his Indian life in *My Indian Boyhood*. He inscribed the book to children, "with the hope that the hearts of the white boys and girls . . . will be made kinder toward the little Indian boys and girls."

Standing Bear is like Eastman, too, in having written more than one volume of autobiography. Standing Bear went on to write *My People the Sioux* in 1928. And Eastman wrote *From the Deep Woods to Civilization* in 1916. Both were written for adults. But there are interesting differences between the adult books and Eastman's boyhood book that cannot be explained simply by the change of audience. For example, neither Standing Bear nor Eastman in their "adult" autobiographies is willing to dismiss Indian spiritualism as "superstition," the way Eastman had done in *Indian Boyhood.* Now, a good deal had happened since the publication of *Indian Boyhood* in 1902. By the time they wrote their adult autobiographies, both Standing Bear and Eastman had lived long enough in civilization to have felt some pangs of disillusionment. But it must also be remembered that the vogue for Social Darwinism had faded by this time. Boasian, particularist anthropology was in the ascendancy. The bright promise of the Dawes Act had faded, and Indian tribes were demonstrating a remarkable staying power. They were neither vanishing nor melting with quite the alacrity Social Darwinists had anticipated. The older he became, the more Eastman allowed himself to conceive of himself as a Santee, the more eager he was to return to the lakes and the woods and find there some of what he had left behind.

But *Indian Boyhood,* as we have seen, is driven by earlier, Social Darwinist assumptions. And so, at the end of the book, Eastman recalls his preparations for initiation into Santee manhood. When his Santee elders feel that he is ready to become a warrior, when they feel that he is ready to become an adult, they give him his first gun, the white man's "mysterious iron." This image of the first gun is full of meaning: it is symbolic of the rite of passage; it looks forward to the white world Eastman will soon enter; it implies white dominance; it suggests the imminent breakup of the old ways. It is "mysterious," and so it is suggestive, too, of the rationality of white civilization and the credulity of the Indians.

It is a powerfully ambivalent image. And it sums up a good deal of *Indian Boyhood*'s Social Darwinist thinking.

H. David Brumble III, "Charles Alexander Eastman's 'Indian Boyhood': Romance, Nostalgia, and Social Darwinism," in American Indian Autobiography, *University of California Press, 1988, pp. 147-64.*

Hertha Dawn Wong   (essay date 1992)

[*In the following excerpt, Wong examines the ways in which Eastman's personal bicultural tension is revealed through the tone, syntax, and content of his autobiographies,* Indian Boyhood *and* From the Deep Woods to Civilization.]

When his mother died shortly after his birth (1858) in the woodlands of southwest Minnesota, Hadakah (The Pitiful Last) was raised in the traditional Santee Sioux ways by his paternal grandmother (Uncheedah) and his uncle. A few years later, as an honor for his band's triumph in a lacrosse game, he was awarded the name Ohiyesa (The Winner). In 1862, when Ohiyesa was four years old, the first of three life-changing events occurred. Having been denied their rightful government annuities, factions of the starving Minnesota Sioux killed several hundred white settlers in what is now called the Minnesota Sioux Conflict. Believing Ohiyesa's father, Many Lightnings, had been arrested and executed by Euro-Americans, the rest of the family fled to Ontario, Canada. There Ohiyesa spent the next eleven years in the woods of the Turtle Mountains learning to be a hunter and a warrior in the pre-contact ways of his people.

At the age of fifteen, when Ohiyesa was just about ready to go on his vision quest, Many Lightnings appeared, as if returned from the dead, to take his son back to the United States to learn the ways of the whites. From this time on, Ohiyesa, soon to become Charles Eastman, had to contend with this second major disruption of his life. After attending Beloit College, Knox College, and Dartmouth College and graduating from Boston University Medical School in 1890, he arrived at Pine Ridge Reservation in time to care for the victims of the Wounded Knee Massacre, the third life-altering event of his life. Every idealistic notion he entertained about "the Christian love and lofty ideals of the white man" was strained severely as he tended to the wounded and dying members of Big Foot's band.

At Pine Ridge he met Elaine Goodale, a white New Englander teaching in Indian Territory. They were married in New England in 1891. To support his family of six children over the years, Eastman worked at a series of jobs in various locations: as a physician on and off reservations, as a YMCA representative to Indians, as a Bureau of Indian Affairs employee in numerous capacities, as an attorney for the Sioux in Washington, D.C., and as a writer and lecturer. In 1921, after thirty years of marriage, Elaine and Charles were separated. In the same year, his growing disillusionment with Euro-American Christian values led

him to leave New England for a quieter life in Minnesota. In the 1930s, he retreated to a cabin in the semiseclusion of the Ontario forest, retracing his steps back from "civilization" to the deep woods.

During the years of his marriage, Eastman, "always with the devoted cooperation" of his wife, wrote numerous books and articles about native life and Indian concerns. In the epilogue to her autobiography, *Sister to the Sioux*, Elaine Goodale Eastman, an author in her own right, wrote:

> In an hour of comparative leisure I had urged him to write down his recollections of the wild life, which I carefully edited and placed with *St. Nicholas.* From this small beginning grew *Indian Boyhood* and eight other books of Indian lore, upon all of which I collaborated more or less.

Goodale, then, provided the initiative and the editing for nine of Eastman's eleven books. After their separation in 1921, Eastman continued to write, but he never again published. Eastman's biographers tend to agree that Eastman was responsible for the ideas, while his wife was responsible for the editing. She seems to have been the force guiding his work into print as well. . . .

Filled with nineteenth-century "Friends of the Indian" notions of helping native people assimilate into the mainstream of American life (through education and Christianity), Elaine Goodale spent five and a half years teaching in small villages on what was then the Great Sioux Reservation. She was no idle curiosity seeker. She knew the Lakota language, went on at least one hunting trip with native friends, and was known as "Little Sister" to the Sioux. During this time, she wrote articles about the Lakota for newspapers and magazines in the East. In 1930, she admitted that her "songs of Indian life exhibit a pardonable coloring of romance." But, she added, she wrote "mainly in prose and with serious educational purpose." Some of this "coloring of romance" and "educational purpose" is evident in her husband's two autobiographies: *Indian Boyhood* (1902) and *From the Deep Woods to Civilization* (1916). This may not be due entirely to his wife's editing, however. Eastman himself believed in the Christian humanism he had been schooled in for eighteen years.

While most Native American autobiographers of this period *speak* their tribal stories to Euro-American editors, Eastman *writes* his personal history himself, relying on such Western autobiographical forms as education and conversion experiences. Although Eastman collaborated with his wife-editor, this may be less important than the extent to which he incorporated the collaborative process into himself, combining the functions of both white editor and Indian informant. In addition, Eastman was raised in the traditional ways of the Santee Sioux, but he received a Euro-American education. He worked closely with white Indian reformers who believed that assimilation was the answer to "the Indian problem," but at the same time, he was fiercely attached to traditional Sioux values. This uneasy alliance induced Eastman to attempt to consolidate Christian and Sioux values. Ohiyesa, as the young Eastman was called, whose childhood had been spent in the Ontario woods, became Charles Alexander Eastman, the transformed Sioux who was trained as a physician. One problem for him, then, was how to write about his Indian life for a white audience, how to reconcile truth and romance, how to balance his Sioux upbringing with his Anglo education.

. . . . .

Published in 1902, *Indian Boyhood* covers the first fifteen years of Ohiyesa's life. The narrative is not strictly chronological. Instead, it jumps ahead and back, moving from anecdote to dialogue to ethnological description. Eastman incorporates multiple voices into his life history. We hear dialogues with and stories from his grandmother Uncheedah, the "preserver of history and legend" Smoky Day, his uncle White Footprint, and the storyteller Weyuha. It is as though Eastman were re-creating for his children, for whom he wrote the book, the family and tribal storytellers of his youth.

Eastman relies on the oral and performance aspects of native personal narrative, but he does not include pictographs or drawings of any sort. Eastman includes stories from two of the three traditional Lakota narrative forms: *Ehani Woyakapi* (legend) and *Woyakapi* (true stories). Smoky Day tells the legend "The Stone Boy" and true accounts of the battle exploits of Jingling Thunder and Morning Star. Weyuah relates the legend of his people, while Uncheedah recites the true stories of an Ojibway raid and of the first battle of her son, Mysterious Medicine. After much coaxing by the young Ohiyesa, White Footprint tells him numerous hunting stories, including one about the beautiful female huntress, Manitoshaw. Humorous stories of real misadventures are told by the comic Matogee, and by his friends Chankpayuhah and Bobdoo.

In contrast to the numerous mythological and historical stories, songs are a minor part of the oral component of Eastman's autobiography. He includes three lyrics from three types of songs: a Strong Heart song to be sung in battle, a serenade from a wooer to a maiden, and a lullaby his grandmother sang to him. Together, these few songs give the reader a sense of the variety of songs and their importance to the Sioux; they provide ethnological details rather than insights into Ohiyesa's childhood.

Just as songs are scarce in *Indian Boyhood*, performance cues are few. Eastman does not elaborate on the storytelling styles of the speakers. Although he includes descriptions of the Bear Dance and the Maidens' Feast, he does so to explain them to a Euro-American readership rather than to dramatize the events or to illuminate their effect on his personal life. In so doing, he sounds more like an "objective" ethnographer than an autobiographer. In fact, like an outsider and one acutely cognizant of his Euro-American readers, he criticizes the belief in the Bear Dance as "one of the superstitions of the Santee Sioux."

Use of his Indian name, lack of rigid chronology, incorporation of multiple voices that emphasize tribal identity, and inclusion of Lakota narrative forms, all indicate a Native American perspective. There is much, however, that is distinctly Euro-American. *Indian Boyhood* is, in part, the "Indian Education of Charles Eastman" in which

Eastman attempts to rectify the Euro-American misconception that "there is no systematic education of their children among the aborigines of this country." "Nothing," he insists, "could be further from the truth." Certainly, he is trying to correct mistaken notions about indigenous people and life by describing the elaborate education every Indian child receives. Bo Schöler states that "by writing about his boyhood he wishes to illustrate the way things used to be in order to break down the stereotype of the Sioux. . . ." While this is true to a certain degree, Eastman's purpose and message are not that simple.

Brumble suggests Eastman's complexity when he notes that *Indian Boyhood* is based on "Romantic Racialist and Social Darwinist assumptions fundamental to Eastman's thinking during these years." Like other indigenous people trying to live biculturally, Eastman faced the difficult task of trying to translate Indian life for non-Indians. To counter the stereotypes of bloodthirsty savages killing wantonly, many Indian writers perpetuated the more positive stereotype of the noble savage. Eastman wished to illustrate how it was possible for a "child of the forest" to live with personal integrity and, through education and conversion to Christianity (believed to be a kind of evolutionary development), to live successfully among Euro-Americans. As a part of this impulse, Eastman describes his mother as "the Demi-Goddess of the Sioux," and to substantiate this claim he explains that tradition says she "had every feature of a Caucasian descent with the exception of her luxuriant black hair and deep black eyes." His mother's beauty, then, is due to her Caucasian physiognomy rather than to her Indian attributes. Perhaps Eastman intends to contradict demeaning popular images of Indians with oversized noses and ungainly bodies. One reviewer of this book aptly points out a parallel issue in African-American literature of the second half of the nineteenth century. At that time, African-American novelists created "tragic mulatto" heroines with white features in order to gain the sympathy of their Euro-American readers. In a similar fashion, Eastman describes his uncle who served as his adviser and teacher: "He is a typical Indian—not handsome, but truthful and brave." In this instance, Eastman may wish to emphasize the interior beauty of his uncle, again contradicting popular stereotypes of Indians as treacherous and untrustworthy. At the very least, his descriptions reflect a tenuous double vision. Eastman reconstructs native people who will gain the attention, sympathy, and respect of their oppressors/white readers.

As well as emphasizing Sioux internal and external beauty, Eastman presents romantic images of the Indian to counteract other predominantly negative stereotypes. He writes that "[t]he Indian boy was a prince of the wilderness," "a born hunter." Uncheedah, he says, helped her sons develop "to the height of savage nobility." Elsewhere he talks about "savage wealth" and "savage entertainments." When Ohiyesa has to offer his beloved dog to the Great Mystery, he describes himself from an outsider's perspective: "To a civilized eye he would have appeared at that moment like a little copper statue." Similarly, he talks of his "rude home" and his "untutored mind," and refers to himself as "the little redskin." In addition, he notes "the Indian's dusky bosom" and their "tawny bodies."

Even more evident than his Eurocentric descriptions of the Sioux is his ambivalence about which perspective is his. His double vision is part anthropological observer (he describes many Sioux customs and "superstitions") and part Santee Sioux participant:

> Such was the Indian's wild life! When game was to be had and the sun shone, *they* easily forgot the bitter experiences of the winter before. Little preparation was made for the future. *They* are children of Nature, and occasionally she whips *them* with the lashes of experience, yet *they* are forgetful and careless. Much of *their* suffering might have been prevented by a little calculation. (emphases mine)

Speaking of his people in the third person is, in part, a linguistic device to distance himself from them, to enhance his position as an "objective" observer and reporter of Sioux people. *He* describes *them* as though he were not one of them himself. At the same time, he perpetuates the stereotypes of Indians as innocent and incompetent "children of Nature" who do not know enough to plan for the future, and who consequently need the Great White Father to admonish and teach them.

Eastman, however, does not consistently use the third person to describe his people. A few pages later, for instance, he discusses "*our* native women" and "*our* food" (emphases mine). There seems to be no pattern to when Eastman talks about the Sioux in the first-person plural (we) and when he uses the third-person plural (they). What is striking are his abrupt shifts from a Santee Sioux to a Euro-American perspective and back again, a reflection, perhaps, of his own uncertain identity or perhaps his wife's editorial pen. Andrew Wiget comments on Eastman's "ambivalence toward both cultures": "His support of the Boy Scout Indian programs and his public appearance in tribal dress, though they did reinforce the 'noble savage' stereotype, were Eastman's attempts to assert the dignity of native culture in terms compatible with the best elements of Christianity in his emerging universalist perspective." The seeming contradictions and the evident tensions in Eastman's pronoun use, behavior, and dress reveal his struggle to reconcile two opposing cultures.

Part anthropological document, part personal narrative, *Indian Boyhood* [1902] is important background reading for understanding the more mature Eastman found in *From the Deep Woods to Civilization.* At the end of *Indian Boyhood,* Ohiyesa follows his father to Flandreau, South Dakota. "Here my wild life came to an end," he concludes, "and my schooldays began."

· · · · ·

From the Deep Woods to Civilization (1916) continues Eastman's education from the time he entered the white world. In the Foreword, Elaine Goodale Eastman explains:

> We are now to hear of a single-hearted quest throughout eighteen years of adolescence and early maturity, for the attainment of the modern

ideal of Christian culture: and again of a quarter of a century devoted to testing that hard-won standard in various fields of endeavor, partly by holding it up before his own race, and partly by interpreting their racial ideals to the white man, leading in the end to a partial reaction in favor of the earlier, the simpler, perhaps the more spiritual philosophy.

Eastman's 1916 autobiography, then, combines several Euro-American autobiographical forms. It is part secular conversion narrative (from "savagery" to "civilization"), part "the Anglo education of Charles A. Eastman," and part quest.

When his father, Many Lightnings (now Jacob Eastman), explains the importance of Euro-American education, he uses images of Eastman's former life. The ability "to think strongly and well," he tells his son, "will be a quiver full of arrows for you." He compares the whites' "way of knowledge" with the Indians' "old way in hunting." In both you start with a dim footprint, which, if pursued faithfully, "may lead you to a clearer trail." To encourage his reticent son, Many Lightnings says: "Remember, my boy, it is the same as if I sent you on your first war-path. I shall expect you to conquer." Prepared as he was to be a hunter and warrior, Ohiyesa sets out to hunt the white man's wisdom and to conquer his knowledge.

The young Santee Sioux is out of place in this new world, and in the beginning pages of *From the Deep Woods to Civilization,* he underscores this by referring to himself in metaphors of wild nature. He describes the dramatic change in his life "as if a little mountain brook should pause and turn upon itself to gather strength for the long journey toward an unknown ocean." Later, he compares himself to wild ponies roaming free on the prairie "who loved their freedom too well and would not come in." He is a "wild cub caught"; "a young blue heron just leaving the nest," balancing precariously on a flimsy branch; "a turtle" pulling himself into the safety of his shell; "a wild goose with its wings clipped"; and, to certain whites at Dartmouth, "a wild fox" in the midst of their chicken coop. Such metaphors emphasize his Sioux identity, and contrast his former free and natural life in the woods with his current restricted and uncertain life in "civilization."

Just as he did in *Indian Boyhood,* Eastman often describes his people using the positive stereotypes of Indians commonly used by those sympathetic to native people. He refers to Indians as the "children of nature"—the "sons of nature" and the "daughter[s] of the woods." When he seeks "rare curios and ethnological specimens" from the "wilder and more scattered bands" in Minnesota, he describes the area as "the true virgin wilderness, the final refuge . . . of American big game and primitive man." His collecting ethnological artifacts and considering "big game and primitive man" as dual aspects of the wilderness reveal his Euro-American education or at least his awareness of this Euro-American perspective. Similarly, he exults over his "wonderful opportunity to come into contact with the racial mind."

Eastman does not always write from such a seemingly Eurocentric point of view. He often vacillates between allegiance to the Indians and loyalty to the whites. Although he is critical of Euro-American society, aware of his audience, he is careful to temper his admonitions. Just after describing how he overheard a Beloit classmate call him "Sitting Bull's nephew," who might score a "scalplock before morning," he explains: "It must be remembered that this was September, 1876, less than three months after Custer's gallant command was annihilated by the hostile Sioux." Eastman's choice of adjectives reveals his awareness of his rhetorical predicament. Describing Custer's cavalry as "gallant" and the Sioux as "hostile" and using the highly charged verb "annihilated" echo newspaper accounts of the event and suggest that Eastman was sensitive to his classmates' perceptions of the battle and their consequent judgment of Indian people. Certainly, this is not the story that Eastman's two uncles who took part in the Custer battle would tell. Although this might be read ironically, in context this description seems to be a straightforward explanation. In addition, it reveals Eastman's and his wife-editor's clear awareness of his Euro-American readers.

Eastman tries to strike a balance between Native American and Euro-American concerns in order to mediate Indian perspectives to policymakers in the East. During the trouble at Pine Ridge in South Dakota in the winter of 1890, the moderate chief, American Horse, asks Eastman for advice about how to deal with his torn loyalties between the "ghost dancers, men of their own blood, and the Government to which they had pledged their loyalty." Eastman advises that they "reason with the wilder element" "for a peaceful settlement," but remember their "solemn duty to serve the United States Government." Certainly, such a precarious political position, part of Eastman's bicultural predicament, was difficult, and often dangerous, to sustain.

Nowhere is this bicultural tension more apparent than in his pronoun shifts. As in his earlier autobiography, he shifts his perspective between first-person plural (we) and third-person plural (they). As an attorney for the Sioux, Eastman learns about the treacherous history of treaties between the Sioux nation and the United States. In his description, he refers to himself as one of the Sioux. His pronouns are "we" and "us" until "the frightful 'Minnesota massacre' in 1862." After this episode, Eastman shifts to talking about the Sioux as "them." On the next page, he says he went to Washington with "great respect for *our* public men and institutions" (emphasis mine). Here "our" refers to the whites. Later in the same paragraph, "they" refers to the white "political henchmen on the reservations," who abuse the Sioux, and "our" alludes to the Sioux, who have been wronged. Eastman's transitions from first person to third person are rhetorical devices to remove himself from whichever group he is criticizing at the moment. He wishes to identify himself with only the best of both worlds. But later he describes Native Americans in the third person not to excoriate them as "hostiles," but to analyze them from an Anglo ethnological perspective:

> The philosophy of the original American was demonstrably on a high plane, *his* gift of eloquence, wit, humor and poetry is well estab-

lished; *his* democracy and community life was much nearer the ideal than ours today; *his* standard of honor and friendship unsurpassed, and all *his* faults are the faults of generous youth. (emphases mine)

The "original American," then, is a noble savage superior in many ways to the "civilized" white. But Eastman (perhaps with the influence of his wife) clearly aligns himself linguistically with white society. "Our" (i.e., Euro-American) philosophy is not so ideal, he insists. As well as the perspective of ethnographer, he adopts the typically Euro-American pose of generous and tolerant father when he excuses Indian faults as "the faults of generous youth."

At times Eastman *is* ironic. For instance, when he hears about the graft of Pine Ridge officials, he writes: "I held that a great government such as *ours* would never condone or permit any such practices" (emphasis mine). Similarly, he subverts the language usually limited to describing Native Americans and applies it to Euro-Americans. Disillusioned with the failure of white Christians to live their ideals, he describes the "savagery of civilization" and the "warfare of civilized life." Even Jesus, the embodiment of the Christian ideal, is described ironically. As a YMCA practitioner, Eastman travels among various tribes preaching about "the life and character of the Man Jesus." At one point, an elderly Indian man responds:

> I have come to the conclusion that this Jesus was an Indian. He was opposed to material acquirement and to great possessions. He was inclined to peace. He was as unpractical as any Indian and set no price upon his labor of love. These are not the principles upon which the white man has founded his civilization. It is strange that he could not rise to these simple principles which were commonly observed among our people.

With these words, spoken safely by an anonymous unreconstructed Indian elder, Eastman undercuts the fancied superiority of Euro-American ideals. His very next anecdote is about an Indian who converts a white man to Christianity, overturning expectations that it is the white man who "saves" the Indian. Still later, in another role reversal, he has a white guide lead him into the wilderness to seek Ojibway artifacts. By subverting Euro-American assumptions about the language, ideas, and activities of Indians, Eastman overturns Indian stereotypes (just as he seems to perpetuate them elsewhere). In the process, he educates whites and restores humanity to native peoples. Eastman's stance, though, is never absolute, as reflected in his linguistic ambivalence.

In *From the Deep Woods to Civilization,* Eastman includes few traditional Sioux modes of personal narrative. He mentions several *Woyakapi* and paraphrases a few stories, but elaborates on none. Through reconstructed speeches and dialogue, we hear numerous voices and gain a vague sense of performance. In part, the recurring dialogue between his father and grandmother serves to introduce and clarify his argument about the ideals of civilization versus the values of the deep woods. He continues this dialogic device throughout the autobiography, furthering his argument in the voices of others.

Instead of pictographs, Eastman includes sixteen photographs. Six are of individuals important in his life (a white influence: Reverend Alfred L. Riggs; his family: Many Lightnings, Mrs. Frank Wood [his "white mother"], Elaine, and his son Ohiyesa; and one historical figure: Kicking Bear). Five are of buildings (an Indian cabin, tipis, Santee Normal Training School, Chapel of the Holy Cross, and Pine Ridge Agency). He includes three pictures of himself, one of his Dartmouth class, and one of him and his wilderness guide. Like the written narrative, his photographs highlight education, religion, and the difference between Indian and white ways. Unlike narrative pictographs, these photographs do not tell his story themselves. Rather, they enhance his written account, illustrating personal and cultural details.

From the Deep Woods to Civilization as a whole can be seen as a reenactment of the tedious and painful process of Ohiyesa's assimilation into Euro-American culture, his transformation from Ohiyesa into Dr. Charles Alexander Eastman, whom Pine Ridge residents called "the 'white doctor' who was also an Indian." This is not the traditional, formalized enactment of tribal ceremony, but the new, undetermined drama of Native American acculturation.

Eastman ends his autobiography with a catalogue of his "civilized" pursuits. Just as if he were recounting brave battle deeds in a coup tale, he recalls his major accomplishments as an author, a public speaker, a representative of North American Indians at the First Universal Races Congress in England, an acquaintance of famous personages, a traveler, a correspondent and editor, and a Boy Scout proponent. Dropping the names of the famous as he proceeds through his list of achievements, Eastman means for the reader to marvel at his wondrous adaptation to the Euro-American world. Yet after this lengthy list, he criticizes the very basis of the culture he has adopted. He reflects on "the Christ ideal"—its potential good, but more important, the "modern divergence from that ideal." He condemns those who "are anxious to pass on their religion to all races of men, but keep very little of it for themselves." "Behind the material and intellectual splendor of our civilization," he declares, "primitive savagery and cruelty and lust hold sway, undiminished, and it seems, unheeded." It is Euro-American civilization, then, not Native American culture, that is primitive, that is savage, cruel, and lustful. Still, Eastman advocates "civilization" for two reasons: it is impossible to go back to the simpler life of pre-contact times, and Christianity is not to blame for the wrongdoings of whites.

In the carefully balanced final paragraph of his autobiography, Eastman's initial tension between Native American and Euro-American cultures remains unresolved:

> I am an Indian; and while I have learned much from civilization, for which I am grateful, I have never lost my Indian sense of right and justice. I am for development and progress along social and spiritual lines, rather than those of commerce, nationalism, or material efficiency. Nevertheless, so long as I live, I am an American.

With several qualifications, Eastman insists that he can be both Indian and American. It is important to keep in mind that this book was published in 1916, just one year before the United States entered World War I (in which many Indian men enlisted) and eight years before Indians were granted citizenship. This prismatic paragraph begins and ends with mirror images asserting his bicultural identity: "I am an Indian"; "I am an American." These are the two opposites he has tried to reconcile in himself, in the United States of the early twentieth century, and in his autobiography that deals with both.

Hertha Dawn Wong, "Oral and Written Collaborative Autobiography: Nicholas Black Elk and Charles Alexander Eastman," in her Sending My Heart Back across the Years: Tradition and Innovation in Native American Autobiography, *Oxford University Press, Inc., 1992, pp. 117-52.*

FURTHER READING

Biography

Faris, John T. "Out of an Indian Tepee: The Wonderful Story of Charles A. Eastman." In his *Men Who Conquered*, pp. 57-68. New York: Fleming H. Revell Company, 1922.

> Romanticized account of Eastman's Santee Sioux childhood significant for its representation of early twentieth-century popular cultural sentiment toward Native Americans.

Wilson, Raymond. *Ohiyesa: Charles Eastman, Santee Sioux.* Urbana: University of Illinois Press, 1983, 219 p.

> The most complete scholarly overview of Eastman's life and work.

Additional coverage of Eastman's life and career is contained in the following source published by Gale Research: *Yesterday's Authors of Books for Children.*

The Last Tycoon

F. Scott Fitzgerald

(Full name Francis Scott Key Fitzgerald) American novelist, short story writer, essayist, screenwriter, and dramatist.

The following entry presents criticism of Fitzgerald's novel *The Last Tycoon* (1941). For a discussion of Fitzgerald's complete career, see *TCLC*, Volumes 1 and 6; for a discussion of his novel *The Great Gatsby*, see Volume 14; for a discussion of his novel *Tender Is the Night*, see Volume 28.

INTRODUCTION

An unfinished novel, *The Last Tycoon* is concerned with the life of Monroe Stahr, a powerful Hollywood mogul. Published posthumously in an edition edited by Edmund Wilson, this work has been praised by critics for its realistic portrayal of Hollywood and its insight into the motion picture industry. Commentary on *The Last Tycoon* speculates on the ultimate form of the work as suggested by the six completed chapters and Fitzgerald's notes and outlines for the remaining sections of the novel.

Biographical Information

Despite his popular success as a novelist, Fitzgerald was plagued by money problems in the last years of his life, including the support of his daughter and his institutionalized wife, Zelda. To fulfill his mounting financial obligations, Fitzgerald moved to Hollywood in 1937 and secured a screenwriting contract with MGM studios. While working at the motion picture company he became interested in the life of film producer Irving Thalberg; in 1937 and 1938 Fitzgerald researched Thalberg's life and the history of MGM studios, and his copious notes became the basis for *The Last Tycoon*. When his contract with MGM expired in 1939, Fitzgerald began writing the novel. He continued work on the manuscript during the last year of his life, supplementing his income with freelance film scripts and short stories. He died of a heart attack in 1940.

Plot and Major Characters

The Last Tycoon is the story of the fall of a powerful Hollywood producer, Monroe Stahr, who rose from the streets of New York to head a major motion picture studio at the age of thirty-five. Following his wife's death, Stahr pursues a love affair with Kathleen Moore, an English actress who bears a strong resemblance to his late wife. His domination of the movie studio is threatened by the machinations of a scheming associate, Pat Brady, and labor disputes that culminate in a physical confrontation with a communist labor organizer. His power and influence waning, Stahr panics and arranges to have Brady murdered. Later, realizing the gravity of this action, Stahr attempts

to revoke the murder contract on Brady but is killed in a plane crash before the assassin can be contacted.

Critical Reception

Most critics view Monroe Stahr as representative of modern America, using his meteoric rise, fall, and resulting moral confusion as an allegory for the rapid change in American business and society in the early twentieth century. Initial reviews of *The Last Tycoon* were laudatory; several important critics asserted that the novel was destined to be considered Fitzgerald's best. Later critics have compared *The Last Tycoon* unfavorably with Fitzgerald's other work, denigrating the plot as melodramatic. Nevertheless, as Stephen Vincent Benét has remarked, *The Last Tycoon* demonstrates the "wit, observation, sure craftsmanship, the verbal felicity that Fitzgerald could always summon. . . . But with them there is a richness of texture, a maturity of point of view that shows us what we all lost in his early death."

CRITICISM

J. Donald Adams   (essay date 1941)

[*In the following review, Adams offers a positive assessment of* The Last Tycoon.]

It is a heavy loss to American literature that Scott Fitzgerald died in his forties. Of that fact this volume which Edmund Wilson has edited is convincing proof. When *Tender Is the Night* was published a few years ago there was reason to doubt whether the fine talent which had first fully realized itself in *The Great Gatsby* eight years before would develop sufficiently to arrive at the greater achievements of which it was capable. *Tender Is the Night* was an ambitious book, but it was also a brilliant failure. Coming after so long a lapse in Fitzgerald's serious writing, the disappointment it brought to those who had felt in *The Great Gatsby* the hand of a major novelist was keen.

So, too, is *The Last Tycoon* an ambitious book, but, uncompleted though it is, one would be blind indeed not to see that it would have been Fitzgerald's best novel and a very fine one. Even in this truncated form it not only makes absorbing reading; it is the best piece of creative writing that we have about one phase of American life—Hollywood and the movies. Both in the unfinished draft and in the sheaf of Fitzgerald's notes which Mr. Wilson has appended to the story it is plainly to be seen how firm was his grasp of his material, how much he had deepened and grown as an observer of life. His sudden death, we see now, was as tragic as that of Thomas Wolfe.

Of all our novelists, Fitzgerald was by reason of his temperament and his gifts the best fitted to explore and reveal the inner world of the movies and of the men who make them. The subject needs a romantic realist, which Fitzgerald was; it requires a lively sense of the fantastic, which he had; it demands the kind of intuitive perceptions which were his in abundance. He had lived and worked in Hollywood long enough before he died to write from the inside out; the material was clay in his hands to be shaped at will. One comes to the end of what he had written—something less than half the projected work—with profound regret that he did not live to complete the job.

As Mr. Wilson observes in his all too brief foreword, Monroe Stahr, the movie big shot about whom the story is centered, is Fitzgerald's most fully conceived character. "Amory Blaine and Antony Patch [*This Side of Paradise* and *The Beautiful and Damned*] were romantic projections of the author; Gatsby and Dick Diver were conceived more or less objectively, but not very profoundly explored. Monroe Stahr is really created from within at the same time that he is criticized by an intelligence that has now become sure of itself and knows how to assign him to his proper place in a larger scheme of things."

We have about 60,000 words of the novel in this uncompleted draft; it was originally planned to be of approximately that length, but, as the appended outline shows, the chapter on which he was working the day before his death brings the story little more than half way to its conclusion. Yet within these half dozen chapters, running to 128 pages, Fitzgerald had created a memorable figure in Stahr, Hollywood's "last tycoon"; he had marvelously conveyed the atmosphere in which a mammoth American industry is conducted; he would have ended, we can see, by bringing it clearly into focus as a world of its own within the larger pattern of American life as a whole.

As Mr. Wilson reminds us, the main activities of the people in Fitzgerald's early books "are big parties at which they go off like fireworks and which are likely to leave them in pieces." It is indicative of the broader scope of *The Last Tycoon* and of Fitzgerald's wider and deeper intentions that the parties in this book are "incidental and unimportant." Excellent as *The Great Gatsby* was, capturing as it did in greater degree than any other book of the period the feel of the fantastic Twenties, one closes it with the thought that Fitzgerald had not himself quite gotten outside the period. There is a detachment about his handling of *The Last Tycoon* that he could not fully achieve in *The Great Gatsby.* This is the more emphasized by the skillful technique employed in the telling of his story. The narrator is the daughter of a big producer, an intelligent girl, of the world of the movies, yet not in it as an active participant, who looks back on the events she describes after a lapse of several years.

The book as Mr. Wilson has edited it has a dual interest. There is the intrinsic interest of the story as we have it, written with all the brilliance of which Fitzgerald was capable; and there is besides, for those who give thought to literary craftsmanship, the pleasure of watching his mind at work on the difficult task he had set himself. In this respect the notes which follow the draft are fascinating reading.

Besides *The Last Tycoon,* the volume includes *The Great Gatsby* and several of Fitzgerald's best short stories. There is **"May Day,"** a kaleidoscopic picture of New York when the boys were coming back from the last war; that strange fantasy which out-Hollywoods Hollywood, **"The Diamond as Big as the Ritz"**; **"The Rich Boy,"** an early story, but good enough to stand with his mature work; **"Absolution"** and **"Crazy Sunday."**

In the chapter on "The James Branch Cabell Period" which he contributed to *After the Genteel Tradition,* Peter Monro Jack observed that Fitzgerald's titles were the best in fiction. No one, certainly, has more good ones to his credit: *This Side of Paradise, The Beautiful and Damned,* **"All the Sad Young Men"** in particular. Mr. Jack also remarked in that excellent essay that Fitzgerald was badly served by his contemporaries, maintaining that "Had his extraordinary gifts met with an early astringent criticism and a decisive set of values, he might very well have been the Proust of his generation instead of the desperate sort of Punch that he is." The lack of these no doubt delayed his development, but it is clear now that his feet were set on a forward path.

From the beginning Scott Fitzgerald wrote about the things and the people that he knew. His early material was trivial, and like the youngsters of whom he wrote, he was himself rudderless, borne swiftly along on a stream that emptied into nothingness. But from the outset his perceptions were keen, his feeling for words innate, his imagination quick and strong. There was vitality in every line he wrote. But he had to get his own values straight before he could properly do the work for which he was fitted, and the process took heavy toll of his vitality.

Fitzgerald's career is a tragic story, but the end is better than it might have been. And I think he will be remembered in his generation.

J. Donald Adams, "Scott Fitzgerald's Last Novel," in The New York Times Book Review, *November 9, 1941, p. 1.*

Stephen Vincent Benét   (essay date 1941)

[*Benét was an American literary figure whose poetry and fiction is often concerned with celebrating American history and culture. In the following review of* The Last Tycoon, *he praises Fitzgerald's realistic and complex portrayal of Hollywood.*]

When Scott Fitzgerald died, a good many of the obituaries showed a curious note of self-righteousness. They didn't review his work, they merely reviewed the Jazz Age and said that it was closed. Because he had made a spectacular youthful success at one kind of thing, they assumed that that one kind of thing was all he could ever do. In other words, they assumed that because he died in his forties, he had shot his bolt. And they were just one hundred percent wrong, as *The Last Tycoon* shows.

Fitzgerald was a writer, and a born writer, and a writer who strove against considerable odds to widen his range, to improve and sharpen his great technical gifts, and to write a kind of novel that no one else of his generation was able to write. How far he had come along the road to mastery may be seen in this unfinished draft of his last novel. We have had a good many books about Hollywood, including the interesting and staccato *What Makes Sammy Run?* But the difference between even the best of them and *The Last Tycoon* is not merely a difference of degree but a difference in kind. *The Last Tycoon* shows what a really first-class writer can do with material—how he gets under the skin. It doesn't depend for success on sets or atmosphere, local color or inside stuff; it doesn't even depend for effect on the necessary exaggerations of the life that it describes. All that is there—the Martian life of the studios, brilliantly shown. But it is character that dominates the book, the complex yet consistent character of Monroe Stahr, the producer, hitched to the wheels of his own preposterous chariot, at once dominating and dominated, as much a part of his business as the film that runs through the cameras, and yet a living man. Had Fitzgerald been permitted to finish the book, I think there is no doubt that it would have added a major character and a major novel to American fiction. As it is, *The Last Tycoon* is a great deal more than a fragment. It shows the full powers of its author, at their height and at their best.

The book begins with a brilliant description of a flight in a transcontinental plane. It breaks off after an equally brilliant drunken scene between Stahr, the producer, and Brimmer, the communist—breaks off with perhaps half its story told. In between, we get to know Stahr and we get to know Hollywood. But, chiefly, we get to know Stahr, the "last tycoon," the individualist, the man who has to make the decisions, who has to be right, or the whole machine will break down, yet the man who feels personally responsible to all the men who work for him. It is an extraordinary portrait, for you no more question Stahr's curious creative drive than you do his limitations. And the tragedy of the book is implicit in Stahr himself, in his strength as well as in his weaknesses. The machine and the life he had helped to create are bound to destroy him in the end. But—at least as Fitzgerald had planned it—he goes down whole.

Wit, observation, sure craftsmanship, the verbal felicity that Fitzgerald could always summon—all these are in *The Last Tycoon.* But with them, there is a richness of texture, a maturity of point of view that shows us what we all lost in his early death. You can take off your hats now, gentlemen, and I think perhaps you had better. This is not a legend, this is a reputation—and, seen in perspective, it may well be one of the most secure reputations of our time.

Stephen Vincent Benét, "Fitzgerald's Unfinished Symphony," in The Saturday Review of Literature, *Vol. XXIV, No. 33, December 6, 1941, p. 10.*

James Thurber   (essay date 1942)

[*Thurber was an American humorist, cartoonist, short story writer, and playwright. In the following review, he evaluates the significance of* The Last Tycoon *and speculates that if Fitzgerald had lived to complete the novel, it would have been his best work.*]

The novel F. Scott Fitzgerald was working on when he died in December, 1940, has been on the counters for three months now. His publishers tell me that it has sold only about 3,500 copies. This indicates, I think, that it has fallen, and will continue to fall, into the right hands. In its unfinished state, *The Last Tycoon* is for the writer, the critic, the sensitive appreciator of literature. The book, I have discovered, can be found in very few Womrath stores or other lending libraries. This, one feels sure, would have pleased Scott Fitzgerald. The book would have fared badly in the minds and discussions of readers who read books simply to finish them.

Fitzgerald's work in progress was to have told the life story of a big Hollywood producer. In the form in which the author left it, it runs to six chapters, the last one unfinished. There follows a synopsis of what was to have come, and then there are twenty-eight pages of notes, comments, descriptive sentences and paragraphs, jotted down by the author, and a complete letter he wrote outlining his story idea. All these were carefully selected and arranged by Edmund Wilson (who also contributes a preface) and anyone interested in the ideas and craftsmanship of one of America's foremost fiction writers will find them exciting reading.

No book published here in a long time has created more discussion and argument among writers and lovers of writing than *The Last Tycoon.* Had it been completed, would it have been Fitzgerald's best book? Should it, in a draft which surely represented only the middle stages of rewriting, have been published alongside the flawless final writing of *The Great Gatsby*? In the larger view, it is sentimental nonsense to argue against the book's publication. It was the last work of a first-rate novelist; it shows his development, it rounds out his all too brief career; it gives us what he had done and indicates what he was going to do on the largest canvas of his life; it is filled with a great many excellent things as it stands. It is good to be acquainted with all these things. In the smaller, the personal view, there is a valid argument, however. Writers who rewrite and rewrite until they reach the perfection they are after consider anything less than that perfection nothing at all. They would not, as a rule, show it to their wives or to their most valued friends. Fitzgerald's perfection of style and form, as in *The Great Gatsby,* has a way of making something that lies between your stomach and your heart quiver a little.

The Last Tycoon is the story of Monroe Stahr, one of the founders of Hollywood, the builder of a movie empire. We see him in his relation to the hundreds of human parts of the vast machine he has constructed, and in his relation to the woman he loves, and to a Communist Party organizer (their first contact is one of the best and most promising parts of the book). We were to have seen him on an even larger scale, ending in a tremendous upheaval and disintegration of his work and his world and a final tragedy. Fitzgerald would have brought it off brilliantly in the end. This would have been another book in the fine one-color mood of *The Great Gatsby,* with that book's sure form and sure direction. He had got away from what he calls the "deterioration novel" that he wrote in *Tender Is the Night.* He had a long way yet to go in *The Last Tycoon* and his notes show that he realized this.

In one of these notes he tells himself that his first chapter is "stilted from rewriting" and he instructs himself to rewrite it, not from the last draft, but from mood. It is good as it stands, but he knew it wasn't right. In the last of the notes, Fitzgerald had written, with all the letters in capitals: "ACTION IS CHARACTER." A brilliant perfectionist in the managing of his ultimate effects, Fitzgerald knew that Stahr had been too boldly blocked out in the draft which has come to us. There was too much direct description of the great man. He fails to live up to it all. Such a passage as this would surely have been done over: "He had flown up very high to see, on strong wings, when he was young. And while he was up there he had looked on all the kingdoms, with the kind of eyes that can stare straight into the sun. Beating his wings tenaciously—finally frantically—and keeping on beating them, he had stayed up there longer than most of us, and then, remembering all he had seen from his great height of how things were, he had settled gradually to earth." There are other large, unhewn lines which would have given place to something else, such as this speech by one of his worshipers: "So I came to you, Monroe. I never saw a situation where you didn't know a way out. I said to myself: even if he advises me to kill myself, I'll ask Monroe." The Monroe Stahr we see is not yet the man this speaker is talking about. I would like to see him as he would have emerged from one or two

more rewrites of what is here, excellent, sharp, witty and moving as a great deal of it is.

It must inevitably seem to some of us that Fitzgerald could not have set himself a harder task than that of whipping up a real and moving interest in Hollywood and its great and little men. Although the movie empire constitutes one of the hugest and therefore one of the most important industries in the world, it is a genuine feat, at least for me, to pull this appreciation of Bel-Air and Beverly Hills from the mind down into the emotions, where, for complete and satisfying surrender to a novel and its people, it properly belongs. It is a high tribute to Scott Fitzgerald to say that he would have accomplished this. I know of no one else who could.

James Thurber, "Taps at Assembly," in The New Republic, *Vol. CVI, No. 6, February 9, 1942, pp. 211-12.*

John Dos Passos   (essay date 1945)

[*Dos Passos was an American novelist, playwright, and social historian. In the following essay, he attempts to place* The Last Tycoon *within the context of American fiction in general and Fitzgerald's works in particular.*]

The notices in the press referring to Scott Fitzgerald's untimely death produced in the reader the same strange feeling that you have when, after talking about some topic for an hour with a man, it suddenly comes over you that neither you nor he has understood a word of what the other was saying. The gentlemen who wrote these pieces obviously knew something about writing the English language, and it should follow that they knew how to read it. But shouldn't the fact that they had set themselves up to make their livings as critics of the work of other men furnish some assurance that they recognized the existence of certain standards in the art of writing? If there are no permanent standards, there is no criticism possible.

It seems hardly necessary to point out that a well written book is a well written book whether it's written under Louis XIII or Joe Stalin or on the wall of a tomb of an Egyptian Pharaoh. It's the quality of detaching itself from its period while embodying its period that marks a piece of work as good. I would have no quarrel with any critic who examined Scott Fitzgerald's work and declared that in his opinion it did not detach itself from its period. My answer would be that my opinion was different. The strange thing about the articles that came out about Fitzgerald's death was that the writers seemed to feel that they didn't need to read his books; all they needed for a license to shovel them into the ashcan was to label them as having been written in such and such a period now past. This leads us to the inescapable conclusion that these gentlemen had no other standards than the styles of window-dressing on Fifth Avenue. It means that when they wrote about literature all they were thinking of was the present rating of a book on the exchange, a matter which has almost nothing to do with its eventual value. For a man who was making his living as a critic to write about Scott Fitzgerald without mentioning *The Great Gatsby* just meant that he didn't know his business. To write about the life of a man as important to American letters as the author of *The Great Gatsby* in terms of last summer's styles in ladies' hats, showed an incomprehension of what it was all about, that, to anyone who cared for the art of writing, was absolutely appalling. Fortunately there was enough of his last novel already written to still these silly yappings. The celebrity was dead. The novelist remained.

It is tragic that Scott Fitzgerald did not live to finish *The Last Tycoon.* Even as it stands I have an idea that it will turn out to be one of those literary fragments that from time to time appear in the stream of a culture and profoundly influence the course of future events. His unique achievement, in these beginnings of a great novel, is that here for the first time he has managed to establish that unshakable moral attitude towards the world we live in and towards its temporary standards that is the basic essential of any powerful work of the imagination. A firmly anchored ethical standard is something that American writing has been struggling towards for half a century.

During most of our history our writers have been distracted by various forms of the double standard of morals. Most of our great writers of the early nineteenth century were caught on the tarbaby of the decency complex of the period, so much more painful in provincial America than on Queen Grundy's own isle. Since the successful revolt of the realists under Dreiser, the dilemma has been different, but just as acute. A young American proposing to write a book is faced by the world, the flesh and the devil on the one hand and on the other by the cramped schoolroom of the highbrows with its flyblown busts of the European great and its priggish sectarian attitudes. There's popular fiction and fortune's bright roulette wheel, and there are the erratic aspirations of the longhaired men and shorthaired women who, according to the folklore of the time, live on isms and Russian tea, and absinthe and small magazines of verse. Everybody who has put pen to paper during the last twenty years has been daily plagued by the difficulty of deciding whether he's to do "good" writing that will satisfy his conscience or "cheap" writing that will satisfy his pocketbook. Since the standards of value have never been strongly established, it's often been hard to tell which was which. As a result all but the most fervid disciples of the cloistered muse have tended to try to ride both horses at once, or at least alternately. That effort and the subsequent failure to make good either aim, has produced hideous paroxysms of moral and intellectual obfuscation. A great deal of Fitzgerald's own life was made a hell by this sort of schizophrenia, that ends in paralysis of the will and of all the functions of body and mind. No durable piece of work, either addressed to the pulps or to the ages, has ever been accomplished by a double-minded man. To attain the invention of any sound thing, no matter how trivial, demands the integrated effort of somebody's whole heart and whole intelligence. The agonized efforts of split personalities to assert themselves in writing has resulted, on the money side, in a limp pandering to every conceivable low popular taste and prejudice, and, on the angels' side, in a sterile connoisseur viewpoint that has made "good" writing, like vintage wines and old colonial chairs, a coefficient of the leisure of the literate rich.

One reason for the persistence of this strange dualism and

the resulting inefficiency of the men and women who have tried to create literature in this country is that few of us have really faced the problem of who was going to read what we wrote. Most of us started out with a dim notion of a parliament of our peers and our betters through the ages that would eventually screen out the vital grain. To this the Marxists added the heady picture of the onmarching avenging armies of the proletariat who would read your books round their campfires. But as the years ground on both the aristocratic republic of letters of the eighteenth century and the dreams of a universal first of May have receded further and further from the realities we have had to live among. Only the simple requirements of the editors of mass circulation magazines with income based on advertising have remained fairly stable, as have the demands of the public brothels of Hollywood, where retired writers, after relieving their consciences by a few sanctimonious remarks expressing what is known in those haunts as "integrity," have earned huge incomes by setting their wits to work to play up to whatever tastes of the average man seemed easiest to cash in on at any given moment.

This state of things is based, not, as they try to make us believe, on the natural depravity of men with brains, but on the fact that for peace as well as for war industrial techniques have turned the old world upside down. Writers are up today against a new problem of illiteracy. Fifty years ago you either learned to read and write or you didn't learn. The constant reading of the bible in hundreds of thousands of humble families kept a basic floor of literacy under literature as a whole, and under the English language. The variety of styles of writing so admirably represented, the relative complexity of many of the ideas involved and the range of ethical levels to be found in that great compendium of ancient Hebrew culture demanded, in its reading and in its exposition to the children, a certain mental activity, and provided for the poorer classes the same sort of cultural groundwork that the study of Greek and Latin provided for the sons of the rich. A mind accustomed to the Old and New Testaments could easily admit Shakespeare and the entire range of Victorian writing: poetry, novels, historic and scientific essays, up to the saturation point of that particular intelligence. Today the English-speaking peoples have no such common basic classical education. The bottom level is the visual and aural culture of the movies, not a literary level at all. Above that appear all sorts of gradations of illiteracy, from those who, though they may have learned to read in school, are now barely able to spell out the captions in the pictures, to those who can take in, with the help of the photographs, a few simple sentences out of the daily tabloids, right through to the several millions of actively literate people who can read right through *The Saturday Evening Post* or *The Reader's Digest* and understand every word of it. This is the literal truth. Every statistical survey that has recently been made of literacy in this country has produced the most staggering results. We have to face the fact that the number of Americans capable of reading a page of anything not aimed at the mentality of a child of twelve is not only on the decrease but probably rapidly on the decrease. A confused intimation of this situation has, it seems to me, done a great deal to take the ground from under the feet of intelligent men who in the enthusiasm of youth decided to set themselves up to be writers. The old standards just don't ring true to the quicker minds of this unstable century. Literature, who for? they ask themselves. It is natural that they should turn to the easy demands of the popular market, and to that fame which if it is admittedly not deathless is at least ladled out publicly and with a trowel.

Scott Fitzgerald was one of the inventors of that kind of fame. As a man he was tragically destroyed by his own invention. As a writer his triumph was that he managed in *The Great Gatsby* and to a greater degree in *The Last Tycoon* to weld together again the two divergent halves, to fuse the conscientious worker that no creative man can ever really kill with the moneyed celebrity who aimed his stories at the twelve-year-olds. In *The Last Tycoon* he was even able to invest with some human dignity the pimp and pander aspects of Hollywood. There he was writing, not for highbrows or for lowbrows, but for whoever had enough elementary knowledge of the English language to read through a page of a novel.

Stahr, the prime mover of a Hollywood picture studio who is the central figure, is described with a combination of intimacy and detachment that constitutes a real advance over the treatment of such characters in all the stories that have followed Dreiser and Frank Norris. There is no trace of envy or adulation in the picture. Fitzgerald writes about Stahr, not as a poor man writing about someone rich and powerful, nor as the impotent last upthrust of some established American stock sneering at a parvenu Jew; but coolly, as a man writing about an equal he knows and understands. Immediately a frame of reference is established that takes into the warm reasonable light of all-around comprehension the Hollywood magnate and the workers on the lot and the people in the dusty sunscorched bungalows of Los Angeles. In that frame of reference acts and gestures can be described on a broad and to a certain degree passionlessly impersonal terrain of common humanity.

This establishment of a frame of reference for common humanity has been the main achievement and the main utility of writing which in other times and places has come to be called great. It requires, as well as the necessary skill with the tools of the trade, secure standards of judgment that can only be called ethical. Hollywood, the subject of *The Last Tycoon,* is probably the most important and the most difficult subject for our time to deal with. Whether we like it or not it is in that great bargain sale of five and ten cent lusts and dreams that the new bottom level of our culture is being created. The fact that at the end of a life of brilliant worldly successes and crushing disasters Scott Fitzgerald was engaged so ably in a work of such importance proves him to have been the first-rate novelist his friends believed him to be. In *The Last Tycoon* he was managing to invent a set of people seen really in the round instead of lit by an envious spotlight from above or below. *The Great Gatsby* remains a perfect example of this sort of treatment at an earlier, more anecdotic, more bas relief stage, but in the fragments of *The Last Tycoon,* you can see the beginning of a real grand style. Even in their unfinished state these fragments, I believe, are of sufficient di-

mensions to raise the level of American fiction to follow in some such way as Marlowe's blank verse line raised the whole level of Elizabethan verse.

John Dos Passos, "A Note on Fitzgerald," in The Crack-Up *by F. Scott Fitzgerald, edited by Edmund Wilson, A New Directions Book, 1945, pp. 338-43.*

It is too much to ask that F. Scott Fitzgerald cap the successes of his youth and compensate for the failure of his last years with his greatest work. It would be too much like a second-rate Fitzgerald story.

—*Kenneth Eble, in his* F. Scott Fitzgerald, *1963.*

Edmund Wilson   (essay date 1951)

[*Wilson was a prominent American literary figure who wrote widely on cultural, historical, and literary matters. He is often credited with bringing an international perspective to American letters through his widely read discussions of European literature. Perhaps Wilson's greatest contributions to American literature were his tireless promotion of writers of the 1920s, 1930s, and 1940s, and his essays introducing the best of modern literature to the general reader. In the following introduction to the 1951 edition of* The Last Tycoon, *Wilson discusses the development of Fitzgerald's work and commends the maturity of his last novel.*]

Scott Fitzgerald died suddenly of a heart attack (December 21, 1940) the day after he had written the first episode of Chapter 6 of his novel [*The Last Tycoon*]. The text which is given here is a draft made by the author after considerable rewriting; but it is by no means a finished version. In the margins of almost every one of the episodes, Fitzgerald had written comments—a few of them are included in the notes—which expressed his dissatisfaction with them or indicated his ideas about revising them. His intention was to produce a novel as concentrated and as carefully constructed as *The Great Gatsby* had been, and he would unquestionably have sharpened the effect of most of these scenes as we have them by cutting and by heightening of color. He had originally planned that the novel should be about 60,000 words long, but he had written at the time of his death about 70,000 words without, as will be seen from his outline, having told much more than half his story. He had calculated, when he began, on leaving himself a margin of 10,000 words for cutting; but it seems certain that the novel would have run longer than the proposed 60,000 words. The subject was here more complex than it had been in *The Great Gatsby*—the picture of the Hollywood studios required more space for its presentation than the background of the drinking life of Long Island; and the characters needed more room for their development.

This draft of *The Last Tycoon,* then, represents that point in the artist's work where he has assembled and organized his material and acquired a firm grasp of his theme, but has not yet brought it finally into focus. It is remarkable that, under these circumstances, the story should have already so much power and the character of Stahr emerge with so much intensity and reality. This Hollywood producer, in his misery and grandeur, is certainly the one of Fitzgerald's central figures which he had thought out most completely and which he had most deeply come to understand. His notes on the character show how he had lived with it over a period of three years or more, filling in Stahr's idiosyncrasies and tracing the web of his relationships with the various departments of his business. Amory Blaine and Antony Patch were romantic projections of the author; Gatsby and Dick Diver were conceived more or less objectively, but not very profoundly explored. Monroe Stahr is really created from within at the same time that he is criticized by an intelligence that has now become sure of itself and knows how to assign him to his proper place in a larger scheme of things.

The Last Tycoon is thus, even in its imperfect state, Fitzgerald's most mature piece of work. It is marked off also from his other novels by the fact that it is the first to deal seriously with any profession or business. The earlier books of Fitzgerald had been preoccupied with debutantes and college boys, with the fast lives of the wild spenders of the twenties. The main activities of the people in these stories, the occasions for which they live, are big parties at which they go off like fireworks and which are likely to leave them in pieces. But the parties in *The Last Tycoon* are incidental and unimportant; Monroe Stahr, unlike any other of Scott Fitzgerald's heroes, is inextricably involved with an industry of which he has been one of the creators, and its fate will be implied by his tragedy. The moving-picture business in America has here been observed at a close range, studied with a careful attention and dramatized with a sharp wit such as are not to be found in combination in any of the other novels on the subject. *The Last Tycoon* is far and away the best novel we have had about Hollywood, and it is the only one which takes us inside.

It has been possible to supplement this unfinished draft with an outline of the rest of the story as Fitzgerald intended to develop it, and with passages from the author's notes which deal, often vividly, with the characters and scenes.

It is worth while to read *The Great Gatsby* in connection with *The Last Tycoon* because it shows the kind of thing that Fitzgerald was aiming to do in the latter. If his conception of his subject in *Tender Is the Night* had shifted in the course of his writing it so that the parts of that fascinating novel do not always quite hang together, he had recovered here the singleness of purpose, the sureness of craftsmanship, which appear in the earlier story. In going through the immense pile of drafts and notes that the author had made for this novel, one is confirmed and reinforced in one's impression that Fitzgerald will be found to stand out as one of the first-rate figures in the American writing of his period. The last pages of *The Great Gatsby* are certainly, both from the dramatic point of view and from the point of view of prose, among the very best things

in the fiction of our generation. T. S. Eliot said of the book that Fitzgerald had taken the first important step that had been made in the American novel since Henry James. And certainly *The Last Tycoon,* even in its unfulfilled intention, takes its place among the books that set a standard.

Edmund Wilson, in a foreword to "The Last Tycoon," *an Unfinished Novel, Together with* "The Great Gatsby" *by F. Scott Fitzgerald, Charles Scribner's Sons, 1951, pp. ix-xi.*

Robert E. Maurer   (essay date 1952)

[*In the following essay, Maurer analyzes structural and stylistic aspects of* The Last Tycoon.]

In November of 1940 F. Scott Fitzgerald wrote to Edmund Wilson from Hollywood about the novel on which he was then working:

> I think my novel is good. It is completely upstream in mood and will get a certain amount of abuse but it is first hand and I am trying a little harder than I ever have to be exact and honest emotionally. I honestly hoped somebody else would write it, but nobody seems to be going to.

On December 21, 1940, the day after he had written the first episode of the sixth chapter of his book, Fitzgerald died. In 1941 Scribner's published all there was of *The Last Tycoon,* along with part of Fitzgerald's notes for its completion, as edited by Edmund Wilson. The uncompleted novel closely matches Fitzgerald's description of it: it shows signs of being good; it reveals the author's first-hand knowledge of his subject (Fitzgerald had been in Hollywood three years); its mood, like that of a drama or of Fitzgerald's most perfectly realized book, *The Great Gatsby,* is upstream throughout.

Perhaps we cannot take too literally Fitzgerald's statement that he "honestly hoped somebody else would write it"—the "it" referring to the particular story Fitzgerald had in mind, the story of one of the truly great men of the movies and of how he was defeated by the hugeness of the industry and the smallness of the men who superseded him in power. But at least we know, as Fitzgerald knew, that such a story had not yet been written.

Only one notable novel about Hollywood, Nathanael West's *The Day of the Locust,* appeared before the time of Fitzgerald's death. West's subject was Hollywood but not exclusively the movie industry. All Hollywood is affected by the movies, of course; West dealt with the inhabitants of Hollywood who live on the periphery of the industry—his narrator is a minor artist at one of the studios, the girl in the book sometimes works as an extra, and there is a movie cowboy. The main character, however, has nothing to do with the movies at all; he is one of the characteristic Hollywood immigrants, an Iowan, who, because his doctor had "an authoritative manner," moved to California for a "rest." West, then, chose for his characters people who might be called the more typical residents of Hollywood; certainly they outnumber movie magnates by several thousand to one. But West's people are never what we like to think of as normal. He refers to them as "the cream of American madmen"; their only solace is found in mob violence, cockfights, and bawdy houses. If West felt that the cream of American madmen were in Hollywood, he did not mean to imply that the rest of the American bottle is not liberally filled with milk. He had, several years earlier, indicated his predilection for madmen: his previous novel, *Miss Lonelyhearts,* though set in New York, is not one whit less grotesque, less downright horrible, than his book about Hollywood.

Fitzgerald made a comment about *The Day of the Locust*—a somewhat tongue-in-cheek comment, it seems to me. He said:

> The book, though it puts Gorki's "The Lower Depths" in the class with "The Tale of Benjamin Bunny," certainly has scenes of extraordinary power—if that phrase is still in use.

Fitzgerald went on to name the points in *The Day of the Locust* which particularly impressed him. He did not say, however, that he thought it was a fine book. Certainly it was not the book that he wanted to write. Fitzgerald, while he did not overlook unpleasantness, did not see America, humanity, or Hollywood with quite the jaundiced eye with which West saw it. Fitzgerald was interested, not in abnormality (however common it may have seemed to West), but in the problems of a conscientious artist, perhaps of himself, perhaps of a movie producer faced with an industry which had grown bigger than anyone in it. Fitzgerald placed himself within this industry and wrote exclusively about its members. The outer Hollywood, whose eccentricities quite likely derive as much from the presence of the movies as from the accident of climate, was only incidental to his story.

The Last Tycoon is primarily the story of Monroe Stahr, a producer who rules his studio "with a radiance that is almost moribund in its phosphorescence." But one could easily say that the book has two heroes: one, Monroe Stahr, a creation of the author; the other, Hollywood, the radiant Hollywood of an earlier decade (Fitzgerald set the time of the action as 1935—"to obtain detachment"), which existed as a piece of history, ripe for anyone's artistic purposes. The tragedy in the book is a dual one: the doom of the movie industry is sealed by the decline of its last individualist; when Monroe Stahr dies, it becomes certain that the lavish, romantic past of the early Hollywood will never return. If *The Great Gatsby* can be viewed in broad interpretation as the tragedy of a man who outlives his dreams, *The Last Tycoon* can be thought of as a tragedy of a man who, for a time, remains great while his surroundings, the old order of a creative Hollywood, deteriorate. In this novel the man and his surroundings are inextricably interwoven; in no previous work was Fitzgerald able to integrate two themes so successfully.

Three things hinder the making of a complete analysis of *The Last Tycoon* as it stands in the 1941 Scribner edition. The first is that the notes are cursed by the same kind of deficiency that Edmund Wilson later saw and roundly condemned in Matthiessen's edition of Henry James' notebooks—incompleteness. Only a few of the hundreds of notes that Fitzgerald made are included here. In the second place, some of the notes which are appended are meaningless: they indicate only that the author meant to change a certain passage, or that a new incident was to be included, the nature of which it is often impossible to determine. Finally, the book has the deficiencies of any uncompleted work: since the artist has not yet put his work into final focus, the completed portions are distorted. Fitzgerald had not yet decided how the novel was to end. As a result, we see him merely suggesting a character who in one version of the ending (Fitzgerald suggests at least three separate endings) might conceivably have played a part demanding much more than mere suggestion earlier in the book. In short, it becomes difficult to evaluate separate incidents as they stand; and even the significance of the major event of the finished portion—the romance between Stahr and Kathleen—cannot be fully determined from what we have been given here. However, we do have enough material to make an analysis of Fitzgerald's writing techniques and the form he intended for the novel, and to make such an analysis is the purpose of this paper.

One outline which Fitzgerald made tells us that the novel was to have been about 60,000 words long and to have been divided into nine chapters. As we now have it, the novel reaches a length of 70,000 words, an indication that, despite the cutting which would inevitably have come, Fitzgerald had underestimated the scope of his project. As Edmund Wilson points out in his Foreword, "the subject here was more complex than it had been in ***The Great Gatsby***," which was primarily the story of a man. ***The Last Tycoon,*** however, is both the story of a man and an examination of his surroundings, surroundings that were in many ways as important as the man himself. Yet, despite the generous proportions of the work, the reader does not get the impression that Fitzgerald is splashing paint on his canvas indiscriminately. His control of his brush is much firmer than it had been in the creation of his previous work, ***Tender Is the Night***; it is as if he approached ***The Last Tycoon*** with much more regard for structure, and, consequently, that he was able to handle the enlarged canvas which was essential for this work.

Fitzgerald's regard for the structure of the novel, and his fidelity to his original concept of it, cannot be stressed enough. The same outline that gives us an estimate of the word length also indicates the nine chapter divisions as well as the detailed division of chapters into specific episodes. Up to the first episode in the sixth chapter, which is as far as he wrote, Fitzgerald made no deviation from that outline. Unfortunately, not all his notes are dated, and it is therefore impossible to tell how far in advance of the actual period of writing this diagrammatic outline was prepared. But there is every indication that, despite the changes which took place between the first plotting given by Fitzgerald to his publisher in September, 1939, and this outline, Fitzgerald had laid in detail the foundation for the episode structure of the novel. Only the ending and the identity of the personality who was to bring about Stahr's death remained puzzling questions for Fitzgerald, and even in making these decisions the problem had become more that of selecting, from many possibilities, one solution that would produce the desired effect than it was of determining the effect desired. But more important than the planning of the plot (it might be supposed that any author would be aware of the important nature of a preplanned plot) is the fact that Fitzgerald set to work on these chapters and episodes with a larger purpose in mind.

Fitzgerald thought of the structure of this novel in terms of the drama. Any number of similarities between dramatic techniques of structure and handling and those employed in **The Last Tycoon** come to mind as one reads the novel and the notes. The question becomes: how much of this similarity did Fitzgerald intend? There is no doubt that he did think of the novel as a tragedy, and it is perhaps inevitable that the roots of tragedy in drama would come to his mind as a basis for structure. Such is the association that he seems to have made. In his outline he divides his nine chapters into five acts (he so labels them), and gives each act a title: Stahr, Stahr and Kathleen, The Struggle, Defeat, Epilogue. Fitzgerald evidently made this five-act division in direct imitation of the classic drama, and, having made the division, deliberately fitted his chapters into it. Throughout the novel there are many pieces of evidence to substantiate this reasoning.

For instance, the "completely upstream" mood is a fundamental characteristic of dramatic tragedy. **The Last Tycoon** is much like **The Great Gatsby** in this respect and unlike **Tender Is the Night,** which is much less tragic in its implication and hence much more uneven in its mood. Perhaps Fitzgerald realized that part of the weakness of **Tender Is the Night** was the diffusion of intensity. At any rate, in **The Last Tycoon** there is every indication that although each "act" reaches a peak of intensity in its concluding episodes—another characteristic of act-division in drama—the book as a whole would have followed a pattern of increasing tension. Fitzgerald even arranged his time (the novel starts in June and ends in early October) so that his reader would get, according to one of his notes, a sense of increasing heat, culminating in Stahr's final fling at romance and the plot to murder him.

The first "act" in the novel corresponds to the *exposition* in drama: Stahr is introduced, and the conflict between Hollywood's growing commercialism and Stahr's individuality is proposed. "Acts" two and three correspond to the *development* in drama: Stahr's failure to win the girl who might save him from destruction, and his struggle with the forces in Hollywood which are determined to extinguish tycoons of his type. The *climax* is reached when Stahr, himself plotted against, falls to the level of his opponent in attempting to bring about Brady's death, but boards a plane for the East before he makes his decision to stop the plot, and is therefore unable to do so. The plane crashes, and the *epilogue,* in which the funeral of Stahr takes place and a prophecy of Hollywood's future is given, corresponds to the last, tapering-off scenes in the classic drama, in which, after a resounding climax which usually included a few violent deaths, the stage was cleared, the moral driven home, and the audience given a few minutes to wipe their tear-stained faces and bring themselves back to reality before emerging into the flat world.

Although Fitzgerald, in writing a novel, was under no obligation to use the artificial arrangements of material which the more restricted form of a drama demands, a reader of **The Last Tycoon** is struck by the number of conventional dramatic techniques that he does use. In the first chapter, for instance, Schwartz, a down-and-out Hollywood underling heading for the West Coast on the same plane as Stahr, is attempting to get to talk to Stahr in order to secure footing for a new start. Stahr turns him down, and Schwartz sends a note to Stahr before committing suicide. The note is ominous and vague, but, like an omen in the first act of a classical drama, it announces the coming of Stahr's fall. It is interesting, also, looking at the novel from a dramatic point of view, that Stahr too meets his death while taking a transcontinental plane trip—this time in the opposite direction. Dramatically, one event in one part of the novel is balanced by a similar event in another part.

This arrangement of similar events at the beginning and at the end of the novel, in each case in an altered way or with an ironical twist (a common arrangement in drama), occurs again and again in **The Last Tycoon.** Following this pattern, in the first chapter Cecilia Brady, Schwartz, and Wiley White cannot enter The Hermitage, near which their plane is grounded. The event becomes a symbol of Hollywood's failure to understand and express the heart of America's tradition. Later in the novel Stahr himself, who earlier would have been able to connect Hollywood and America's past, now weakened by the opposition of commercial Hollywood to his high standards, becomes ill in Washington and is unable to make a tour of the city, the symbol of America's heritage, as he had planned. Similarly, Stahr is represented in studio conferences at the beginning of the novel as a leading constructive force in Hollywood. Fitzgerald had planned to show, later in the novel, Stahr's weakened position in a similar series of conferences in which he would be unable to make decisions such as his earlier one to produce a money-losing picture. Thus, too, Stahr's early and beautiful tryst with Kathleen was to have been contrasted with an abortive attempt to recapture their love in the stifling atmosphere of summer heat and lost hopes. These incidents are examples of the dramatically calculated balancing of events at various stages in the novel, and these events reflect the fall that has taken place in the protagonist. We see in such contrasts Fitzgerald's attempt to impose a kind of dramatic order on his novel.

After all, the subject matter itself, Hollywood, fits a dramatic presentation beautifully. There can be no doubt that Fitzgerald thought so, and that he even imitated Hollywood's dramatic technique as he portrayed the movie industry. That technique is explained early in the novel, during one of the conferences Stahr has with Boxley, a novelist turned script writer. Boxley, it seems, has fallen down on a writing assignment, and Stahr has put two hacks to work with Boxley to help speed up the job. Boxley is disgruntled about how the hacks spoil his ideas:

> "Why don't you write it yourself?" asked Stahr.
>
> "I have. I sent you some."
>
> "But it was just talk, back and forth," said Stahr mildly. "Interesting talk but nothing more."

Stahr then tells Boxley what he wants by setting up an imaginary story situation and arousing Boxley's interest in it. The point of Stahr's method of storytelling is that interest is action. Later we see Boxley taking over a script and applying the lesson he has learned from Stahr. But it is also a lesson which Fitzgerald evidently had learned from his work in Hollywood, the theory of which he applied in writing *The Last Tycoon.* Included in Fitzgerald's notes is one which he had written in capital letters: ACTION IS CHARACTER. In another note he speaks of a chapter in which he planned to give Stahr's background:

> Each statement that I make about him must contain at the end of every few hundred words some pointed anecdote or story to keep it alive. I do not want it to have the ring of an analysis. I want it to have as much drama throughout as the story of old Laemmle himself on the telephone.

Open *The Last Tycoon* at any point and it will be obvious that Stahr's dramatic method has been applied, and that there is a difference in technique from that of Fitzgerald's earlier works. Gone is the expansive and speculative rhetoric of his first four novels. Every page is packed with things happening. Rarely does Fitzgerald stop his physical action or mental action through conversation to go omnisciently into a character's mind. The pace is fast, kaleidoscopic. Chapters two and three and the first part of chapter four, dealing with Stahr at the studio and presenting Hollywood in action, are a panorama of quick-shifted scenes. The action is movie-like, eminently suited to the material. At one point Fitzgerald calls a group gathered for a conference "the cast" and gives a brief sketch of each "actor." When Fitzgerald wishes to slow down the pace, as in the romantic scenes between Stahr and Kathleen, he slows down the action and the scene-shifting. But even then the tale is not static; things happen to his lovers. When he wishes to remind his reader of the Hollywood theme permeating the romance, he inserts such bizarre Hollywood touches as an orangoutang introduced to Stahr by telephone, or a Negro fishing for grunion in front of Stahr's house because the motion-picture people have prohibited his fishing on Malibu Beach.

Fitzgerald's use of dramatic techniques results not only in a change in style from his earlier books but also in a change in his whole approach to the problem of writing. One of Fitzgerald's weaknesses had always been his inability to separate himself from his material. For instance, he confessed that as he wrote *The Great Gatsby* he identified himself more and more with his hero until, at the end of his writing, the two became one. However, the drama form requires an exercising of the imagination in such a way that the author speaks through his characters, who nevertheless retain their identity. Objectivity of craftsmanship is one of the chief characteristics of the drama. Like Yeats, Fitzgerald became more objective as he worked with a dramatic medium. In *The Last Tycoon* lyricism yields to classical hardness; obvious personal interference in his writing gives way to omniscient objectivity. The happy ability Fitzgerald has for seeing things sharply is evident in *The Last Tycoon,* but they are seen less obviously by the author than by the characters.

But for Fitzgerald to use the techniques of drama, whether of the classical drama or of Hollywood, was not enough to guarantee a unified structure in his book. There remained the problem of integrating his themes (one that had especially bothered him in *Tender Is the Night*) and of fixing his point of view. It is profitable in estimating Fitzgerald's final growth as an artist to view each of these problems separately and in detail.

Fitzgerald tells us (through his letters) that Hollywood had disappointed him. "My dreams about this place are shattered," he said in one letter; and in another, "Everywhere there is, after a moment, either corruption or indifference." He set out, then, in *The Last Tycoon,* to picture Hollywood as he saw it, exactly and honestly. He also tried to analyze what had happened to the Hollywood which, up to that point, had been leavened by a faith in the artistic possibilities of the movie medium. His conclusions, as one sees them in *The Last Tycoon,* were that the Hollywood of the past had been directed by individuals who had the movie qualities which he so much admired in his earlier novel-heroes—honesty, charm, creativity, consistency, and loyalty to an ideal—and that the power of these men had been undermined by the baser commercial brains of the industry, typified by Brady, and by the organization of labor by men like Brimmer, the Communist.

The solution of the problem of how to integrate the fall of a hero with the fall of Hollywood must have seemed obvious. He would present Hollywood through a study of the last of the individualists, the last great tycoon. He would picture Hollywood through the faithful representation of one of the men who saw it clearly. Cecilia Brady announces the plan on the first page of the book:

> It [Hollywood] can be understood too, but only dimly and in flashes. Not half a dozen men have ever been able to keep the whole equation of pictures in their heads. And perhaps the closest a woman can come to the set-up is to try and understand one of these men.

Thus the personal tragedy and the Hollywood tragedy are never allowed to be separated; while one has the stage the other insists on attention. That Fitzgerald saw the danger of letting either slip out of view is apparent from his notes and from the novel itself. In the chapter which pictures one of Stahr's typical days, for instance, the attention is on Hollywood. As already mentioned, the scenes shift rapidly. However, in order to avoid an overweighted interest in the Hollywood theme, Fitzgerald constantly brings in Stahr's personal story. Stahr had, the night before, found a love and lost her. During the day his efforts to locate the girl hold together the brief sketches of Hollywood routines. In his notes Fitzgerald indicates how intentional his method was:

> Chapters (C and D) are equal to guest list and Gatsby's party. Throw everything into this, with selection. They must have a plot, though, leading to 13.

The "13" he refers to is the point in the story at which Stahr and Kathleen get together. While Fitzgerald develops his picture of Hollywood, he keeps the reader conscious of Stahr's search for Kathleen. The seduction scene in the fifth chapter, which develops the theme of Stahr's personal tragedy, is kept from complete isolation from the

Dust jacket for The Last Tycoon.

Hollywood theme by the bizarre touches mentioned above.

The whole episode of Stahr's romance with Kathleen needed to have significance for either or both of the main themes of the book. In his original draft Fitzgerald called the love affair "the meat of the book." As first plotted, Stahr needs Kathleen (then called Thalia) to give him strength; he is physically sick as well as knee-deep in the struggle with his rival, Brady. Stahr lets Kathleen go, however, because she is "poor, unfortunate, and tagged with a middle-class exterior which doesn't fit in with the grandeur Stahr demands of life," as Fitzgerald says in his notes. Later Stahr realizes how much he needs Kathleen; they are going to be married, but on a trip East he is killed.

Such a romance *would* have been the meat of the book. Fitzgerald must have felt, however, that his book was not meant to be primarily a love story, and in later drafts he molded the Kathleen-Stahr affair more and more into his main themes. It seems likely that he would have realized, as he wrote on and reread, that the heavy emphasis on the sheer romance of the affair in the early chapters as we have them would have seemed out of place in view of the development of the Stahr-versus-Hollywood theme in the latter half of the book. Certainly the transition from romance to intrigue would have been awkward—and already begins to seem so.

In the published version of the book (which, when one tries to judge it, must always be carefully kept separate both from Fitzgerald's early plans and from what he might have done before the book reached the presses), Kathleen plays a fairly large part both in precipitating Stahr's crack-up and in the Stahr-Brady conflict. Stahr no longer hesitates because Kathleen is a middle-class figure. He does hesitate, but merely to be sure that his reason is ruling over his emotions; and in this brief interval Kathleen marries someone else. Her action becomes a factor which hastens his disintegration. The two attempt to get together again after her marriage, but are never successful in doing so. The girl "who promises to give life back to him" never is his, and thus she becomes part of his tragedy. Fitzgerald later decided to use Kathleen's husband, too. He was to be a tool for Brady, either by having him sue Stahr for alienation of affection at Brady's direction, or by some other yet undetermined means. We see now that romance-for-romance's-sake is subordinated, and that Fitzgerald made this decision to strengthen his book. **The Last Tycoon,** therefore, became more than a tragic romance.

Fitzgerald may have vacillated about the degrees of emphasis to be put on the Hollywood, tragic, and romantic themes, but his choice of a method of narration for the book never wavered. This choice is, obviously, among the first and most fundamental decisions which an author projecting a novel must make. He must decide from what *point of view* the story is to be told. Basically, he has two choices: he can have the story narrated by one individual, who may or may not be the central character; or he can, so to speak, tell the story himself, as an "omniscient author" writing in the third person rather than in the first. When an author decides to write a first-person narrative, so that the whole action will be seen through the eyes of one character, the author's problem is to manipulate his narrator so that he is constantly in a position from which he can view the principal actions of the other characters. *The Great Gatsby* is an almost textbook-perfect example of successful first-person narration. On the other hand, *Tender Is the Night,* in which Fitzgerald used the omniscient—author point of view, is a rather good example of what happens when the author loses control of his omniscience and allows it to encompass the minds and viewpoints of too many characters. As a result of this lack of control, a reader of *Tender Is the Night* finds himself, well into the story, still uncertain as to which character the book will eventually center upon. The fact is that Fitzgerald had great difficulty in writing *Tender Is the Night,* and as soon as it was published he realized that it was structurally faulty. He may have decided, as a result of this experience, that the first-person narrative form gives a book more unity and intensity. At any rate, he chose to return to this form, or point of view, for *The Last Tycoon.*

In the original outline of the book which he sent to his publishers, he set forth this plan:

> Cecilia [Brady] is the narrator because I think I know exactly how such a person would react to my story. She is of the movies but not *in* them. She probably was born the day *The Birth of a Nation* was previewed and Rudolf Valentino came to her fifth birthday party. She is, all at once, intelligent, cynical, but understanding and kindly toward the people, great and small, who are of Hollywood.

Cecilia remained the narrator of the book through all his subsequent outlinings and plot revisions, and there can be no doubt that his choice of Cecilia was a natural and a good one. And yet, despite his certainty in this matter, there are very vulnerable points, as far as point of view goes, in *The Last Tycoon.* Adequate handling of point of view is not dependent alone upon a good choice of narrative character.

Cecilia, at the time of the action of the book, is a junior at Bennington, and is home for the summer. Perhaps Fitzgerald felt that he had some insight into the workings of the undergraduate mind, for his daughter, Scotty, was corresponding with him from college at the time he was writing his last novel. Cecilia's Hollywood upbringing is another mark in her favor, as Fitzgerald pointed out. Besides, she has the dual advantage of two other involvements which make her a participant in the story, although she is not a major figure in it: she is the daughter of Stahr's antagonist, Brady, and she is in love with Stahr. Despite these close associations, she is a perfect mouthpiece for Fitzgerald because of her ability to detach herself from her surroundings: "I took it tranquilly," she tells us. "At the worst I accepted Hollywood with the resignation of a ghost assigned to a haunted house. I knew what you were supposed to think about it, but I was obstinately unhorri-

fied." She sees the best and the worst in Hollywood and reports them, honestly. Even when her disgust at what she sees should, by all rights, be overwhelming, she manages to stifle it somehow: seeing her father (whom she dislikes greatly) just after his mid-day encounter with his secretary, she is struck not so much by her father's action as by the degradation of the girl, "stuffed . . . naked into a hole in the wall in the middle of a business day."

In Cecilia, Fitzgerald not only selected a good character to view the action but also made her much more a part of the novel than he had made Nick Carraway in *The Great Gatsby.* His approach is different. The reader of the earlier book sees the character of Gatsby developing as it is revealed to the mind of Nick Carraway, and as Nick develops it for himself. Nick's own character remains rather static throughout. The character of Cecilia, on the other hand, develops, pathetically, along with that of Stahr, the hero of the book. His tragedy becomes hers. At the start of the novel she is a rather giddy young person, but as the novel grows she changes. She is struck by the pathos of Stahr's situation, until, at the end of the novel, stricken by the deaths of both her father and Stahr, she breaks down physically herself (as Fitzgerald planned it). He had even considered the idea of revealing at the end of the book that her story was being told by two fellow-tuberculosis patients to whom she had related it, thus making his novel a second-hand second-hand narrative. Exactly what the book would have gained by the use of such a tortured device is hard to say. This complicated machinery would not have altered Cecilia's story; and this story, though it is not essential to the novel (Fitzgerald omitted parts of it in his outline for a serial version), does add a great deal both to the pathos of the book and to its unity.

The partial failure of Fitzgerald's use of Cecilia is the result of the weaknesses inherent in the first-person narrative form, as well as of Fitzgerald's method of surmounting these weaknesses. The drawbacks of the strictly first-person narrative technique are obvious: the narrator ordinarily can report only what he actually witnesses or what he hears from someone who was a witness, and the latter plan cannot be used too often lest the verisimilitude of the narrative be destroyed. Nor can the narrator enter directly into the minds of the other characters. A first-person narration is comparatively easy to handle when the narrator is the hero of the story, but when, as is Cecilia or Nick, he is a secondary character, the task of the author becomes much more ticklish. Fitzgerald wanted to give himself more latitude than he was entitled to, and decided to grant himself "the privilege, as Conrad did, of letting her [Cecilia] imagine the actions of the characters." Fitzgerald hoped to get the impact of a first-person narrative and yet avail himself of the convenience of omniscience. As a full-grown author, Fitzgerald should have known that the answer to the Elizabethan proverb-maker's question, "Would yee both eat your cake and have your cake?" is no.

At the very beginning of the book the reader becomes aware of Cecilia's limitations as a narrator, and it is not long before Fitzgerald's awkward manipulation of her becomes as annoying as his disruptive interference with the established point of view in some of his earlier books. In the first chapter alone there are three incidents which are reported to Cecilia by other people: Wylie White tells her, after the plane ride, about Schwartz's note; the hostess tells her of a conversation between the pilot and Stahr; and the pilot tells her, years later, of his conversations with Stahr. Each of these incidents is important either to the development of Stahr's character or to the view of Hollywood which Fitzgerald wishes the reader to have. Yet the reader's acceptance of the narrative is not strengthened by the contrived coincidence necessary to develop these points.

Going further in utilizing Conrad's scheme of omnipotence, Fitzgerald has Cecilia report a typical studio day of Stahr, reconstructed, as she says, partly from a paper she wrote in college called "A Producer's Day" and partly from incidents she knew to be true. He has her justify this method by telling of Stahr's efforts to parry the spying of his competitors by working in secret, and the reason seems adequate enough to make her "reconstruction" acceptable. After all, it does not matter whether or not the reader has an exact description of a particular day in Stahr's life; actually, the description of a "typical" day is more representative and useful in coming to an understanding of the man. What becomes disturbing, however, is Cecilia's use of her imagination, which must have been extremely fertile, to describe in exact detail personal encounters such as Stahr's romantic afternoon with Kathleen. At such points the reader is likely to have one of two reactions: either he forgets that Cecilia is supposed to be telling the story and accepts the incident as if it were told by an omniscient author; or he realizes that Cecilia's imagination, vivid though it may have been, could not possibly have hit on the exact words and actions of two other characters at an intimate moment, and he has to accept this afternoon, too, as a "reconstruction." The question arises, then, whether such an atypical, even unique, afternoon in Stahr's life could have been reconstructed with enough accuracy to warrant its inclusion in its full detail. Most readers, it seems to me, will not give full credence to such an imaginative chronicle.

One cannot help comparing this unwarranted extension of the narrator's powers to the completely legitimate use of Nick Carraway in *The Great Gatsby.* In that book Fitzgerald never let himself forget that he was seeing the story through Nick Carraway's eyes. That simple consistency seems to be the answer to the debated question of whether or not Fitzgerald should have revealed what went on between Gatsby and Daisy after their reunion. Nick could not possibly have known, for, like Cecilia's his sources of information were limited. The author had to choose between changing his narrative approach in order to include descriptions of their meetings, or omitting those episodes entirely. The omissions in *The Great Gatsby* seem, in comparison with the attempts at inclusion in *The Last Tycoon,* by far the more graceful way out of the dilemma.

There are passages in *The Great Gatsby* in which Nick uses his imagination to reconstruct events, but they are always events which are plainly related to Nick in the course of the story; instead of using the words of his informant,

he uses his own. Usually he is reconstructing events which took place before the story opened. The passages are always short enough to prevent Nick's slipping out of the reader's mind. Again, *The Last Tycoon* provides an unfortunate contrast. Fitzgerald himself realized that, throughout many passages, Cecilia was likely to be forgotten; he has her bring herself back by saying "This is Cecilia taking up the story." Where, the reader may well ask, had she been during all the preceding narration, and who *had* been "taking up the story"?

Another subtle difference between Nick's narration and Cecilia's is that, when Fitzgerald has Nick reconstruct emotions, Nick's narration always conveys the surface degree of emotion which a spectator, or a hearer, would be able to reconstruct without violating truth, not the private details of such scenes as the Stahr-Kathleen love affair. And yet to sacrifice the Stahr-Kathleen episodes would have meant sacrificing the element of a love story in the novel. If Fitzgerald wanted to retain this element and still make his book a consistent, successful example of first-person narration, he would, I think, have had to handle differently the episodes which Cecilia does not witness herself. I cannot presume to solve Fitzgerald's problem and say what he should have done. But, giving him credit for the ability shown in a past performance, in *The Great Gatsby,* I like to think that, had he lived to finish the book, he would have found a satisfactory solution.

There is no doubt that he would have had to make some changes, for as the novel progresses the control of narration seems to become less and less firm. Sometimes the poor reader, if he ever was conscious that the events were being related to Cecilia, hears a completely new and unidentified voice—God's? —such as in the last part of chapter five, when this personage advises Stahr to take Kathleen while he can:

> . . . It is your chance, Stahr. Better take it now. This is your girl. She can save you, she can worry you back to life. She will take looking after and you will grow strong to do it. But take her now—tell her and take her away. Neither of you knows it, but far away over the night The American has changed his plans. . . . In the morning he will be here.

The most charitable thing that can be said about such passages is that they probably would never have seen print if Fitzgerald had lived to correct his proofs. An editor, not being able to remonstrate with a dead author, evidently feels morally bound not to edit him.

The Last Tycoon, had Fitzgerald lived to complete it, would have been the first step on his road back from physical and moral exhaustion. It was his last attempt to reassert himself, to find strength through the discipline of his craft. Despite the harrowing conditions under which he wrote the book, and with all its technical limitations, this fragment, with Fitzgerald's notes, reveals a maturity of conception which would very likely have made this book his finest work. Along with his new-found dramatic objectivity, Fitzgerald adopted a change of prose style for his book. It is not the style of *The Great Gatsby,* but both styles are identifiable as Fitzgerald at his best, which was very good indeed. I have mentioned sharpness and hardness. The sharpness of Fitzgerald's observation and the hardness of his narration are like the fine cruel point of a diamond cutting glass, and the results are just as true.

Robert E. Maurer, "F. Scott Fitzgerald's Unfinished Novel, 'The Last Tycoon'," in Bucknell University Studies, *Vol. 111, No. 3, May, 1952, pp. 139-56.*

John E. Hart   (essay date 1961)

[*Hart is an American educator and critic. Below, he examines autobiographical elements in* The Last Tycoon.]

In a sense all of F. Scott Fitzgerald's life had been a struggle with his "talent for self-delusion," a search for his "lost city." That search had led him from New York to Great Neck, to Paris, to the Riviera, and finally to Hollywood. When he died there in 1940, leaving the unfinished manuscript of **The Last Tycoon,** he was still trying to fit the pieces of his self-deluded past into a coherent and functioning whole. Edited by Edmund Wilson and published in 1941, the fragment and the notes which Fitzgerald had made for the novel indicate the care with which he was examining his theme and subject. Although **The Last Tycoon** describes the growing power of organized labor and Communist infiltration in Hollywood studios, it is more personal document than sociological tract; primarily, it is the story of a once-powerful and dominating personality, who, struggling with changing social patterns and with personal confusions and inner conflicts, falls into moral and spiritual bankruptcy. Conceived, as it was, after Fitzgerald's own psychological crack-up, the novel clearly represents not only the struggle with his own self-delusion, but also his final attempt to give shape and meaning to his own identity.

In this search for identity, a city like New York—and finally many cities—had a special meaning for Fitzgerald. Writing in 1932, he recalls that when he went there to become a writer, "New York had all the iridescence of the beginning of the world." It was both innocence and experience; it was the symbol of all those things that seemed important: money, success, romance, eternal youth. Its capture meant triumph, and with an early literary success, the conquest came easily. To the young outsider from the Midwest life seemed pretty much a romantic matter. Yet, however he had succeeded in the new jazz age—he was even becoming its spokesman—he actually knew very little about his relation to it. Speaking for both Zelda and himself, he wrote, "we scarcely knew any more who we were and we hadn't notion what we were." Then, as their "minds unwillingly matured" and the city changed, the triumph which had been so real seemed more like a glittering mirage: the "whole shining edifice that he had reared in his imagination came crashing to the ground." He discovered that New York was not a "universe" after all; *"it had limits."* The real values, the values to count on when the chips are down, lie not in the outside world of illusion, but in the limitless world of the inner "I." As he said, "I knew that triumph is in oneself."

But in analyzing his own psychological, moral, and spiritual breakdown, Fitzgerald discovered something

else:" . . . there was not an 'I' any more." Clearly, he must begin again. He had always believed that

> the test of a first-rate intelligence is the ability to hold two opposed ideas in the mind at the same time, and still retain the ability to function. . . . Life was something you dominated if you were any good. Life yielded easily to intelligence and effort. . . .

If a person could maintain a balance between such contradictions—e. g., the "dead hand of the past and the high intentions of the future," the "determination to 'succeed,'" the "inevitability of failure"—the "ego would continue as an arrow shot from nothingness to nothingness with such force that only gravity would bring it to earth at last." But now the "ego" was in pieces, and after the long silence, the "self-immolation," he found that, despite the man he "had persistently tried to be," he must "now at last become a writer only." With this new beginning, however, there was difficulty, the difficulty of contradiction. As the narrator says in **The Last Tycoon,** "Writers aren't people exactly. Or, if they're any good, they're a whole lot of people trying so hard to be one person."

In 1937 when Fitzgerald went to Hollywood, he was still trying to find that oneness, and just as New York and Paris and the Riviera had served as repeated beginnings, so Hollywood became the city of last resort, the self-deluding scene and symbol of success and failure. Hollywood was, of course, the logical choice for a new beginning. Here in this opulent world of gilt and glamour, the past as Fitzgerald had always known it still retained a certain validity. Here man had built a fabulous city on quick success and easy money, on innocence and love and romance, on hope for eternal youth. Using the only ingredients that were at hand—the shattered pieces of a personality given to self-delusion—he could show from personal experience how the "old dream of being an entire man in the Goethe-Byron-Shaw tradition" was not only obsolete, but suicidal.

As a writer Fitzgerald's problem was to find the right way of presenting man's loss of identity and moral disintegration artistically. In order to achieve "the verisimilitude of a first person narrative, combined with a Godlike knowledge of all events that happen to my characters," Fitzgerald borrowed a device from Conrad. The story of **The Last Tycoon** is told by an impersonal narrator, a kind of "center of revelation" through whom character and action are revealed. While recovering in a tuberculosis sanitarium, Cecilia, daughter of the Hollywood producer Brady, narrates the story of Stahr's rise and fall as she remembers it. She is of the movies, but not in them, a kind of outsider, as Fitzgerald himself had always been. Like the other characters, she is a fragment of the writer's own personality. A further problem in writing, as the notes indicate, was that of selecting the right name for the characters. Fitzgerald changed the name of the heroine from Thalia to Kathleen. The narrator's father becomes Brady instead of Bradoque. Although the problem of naming is perhaps trivial, it must have bothered Fitzgerald, for he even incorporates it as a major theme of the novel. As Wylie White says, "I didn't feel I had any rightful identity until I got back to the hotel and the clerk handed me a letter addressed to me in my name."

It is through the confusion of naming—is it not a search for identity? —that Fitzgerald introduces Monroe Stahr as the hero of the novel and reveals through action and symbol the pattern of behavior which has made Stahr's life one of disintegration and self-delusion. Stahr is actually made known through his friend Schwartz as they return to Hollywood on a transcontinental plane from New York. Although he has known Stahr for a long time, Schwartz cannot recall the name of the man who has taken the bridal suite on the plane. In conversation, he misnames him "Smith" and warns him to look out for enemies in Hollywood. Once a practical man of decision in the movies, but now a down-and-out producer, Schwartz clearly belongs to a past that Hollywood no longer represents. His face, as the narrator observes, has fallen into its "more disintegrated alignments." When the plane lands at Nashville, Tennessee, Schwartz leaves the airport alone and wanders to the statue of Andrew Jackson, and there commits suicide. Clearly, the self-destruction of a man who believes in the unity and importance of the individual signifies a loss of faith in such values, just as the sacrifice to the shrine of a man famous for his devotion to these ideals signifies continued belief in them. And just as the fall of Schwartz serves as a preview of Stahr's own life, so with Schwartz's death the fictitious "Smith" is annihilated, and the true identity of Stahr emerges as a normal, integrated, sane personality. As if having been reborn, Stahr can now be regarded in Hollywood as "the only sound nut in a hatful of cracked ones." Actually, however, he is struggling against inevitable failure in a changing world where his credo of life no longer has validity. If there are enemies at work in the movie studios, the real enemy lies in his own self-delusion.

The Last Tycoon is, then, the story of Monroe Stahr, a once "nameless" man, who, at the age of twenty-three, had first climbed his way to success. (Fitzgerald was also twenty-three when he published his first novel.) A small man, Stahr has always been a fighter. In his youth he headed a gang in the Bronx. Popular with men, he likes being with the boys; yet he is never one of them. Throughout his life he has always darted in and out of his various roles with dexterity. "If he could go from problem to problem, there was a certain rebirth of vitality with each change." Although success has come to him, he remains uncertain and indecisive. Direct and frank by nature, he has never quite known how he "got to be Mr. Stahr." As we shall see, Stahr's search for identity follows a kind of pattern of dying and rebirth, which Fitzgerald's use of flight and plane imagery peculiarly represents.

Introducing the plane trip in the first chapter, Fitzgerald makes the flight metaphor central throughout the novel. Stahr's whole life has been an "aerial adventure." It is flight that has given him vision and insight. Long ago he

> had flown up very high to see, on strong wings, when he was young. And while he was up there he had looked on all the kingdoms, with the kind of eyes that can stare straight into the sun. Beating his wings tenaciously—finally frantically—

and keeping on beating them, he had stayed up there longer than most of us, and then, remembering all he had seen from his great height of how things were, he had settled gradually to earth.

In Hollywood—this city of "mystery and promise"—Stahr achieves position and power. Here he has found a "new way of measuring our jerky hopes and graceful rogueries and awkward sorrows." But the flight metaphor has further meaning. In his note-book Fitzgerald observes that unlike the English

> Americans, restless and with shallow roots, needed fins and wings. There was even a recurrent idea in America about an education that would leave out history and the past, that should be a sort of equipment for aerial adventure, weighed down by none of the stowaways of inheritance or tradition.

Clearly, if up to now Stahr has been able to escape his past, that is, not be burdened by it, Schwartz has not, for is it not inheritance or tradition—Jackson, the monument—that kills him? Flight may save: it has always functioned as a new beginning for Stahr; he has even taken the "bridal suite" on the plane. But flight also destroys, as in the case of Schwartz. When Stahr returns to Hollywood, the "stowaways of inheritance or tradition" begin to weigh him down.

Stahr loses the city in which he has had his success by a series of blows that are struck from both without and within. Fitzgerald represents the disintegration through symbols. Stahr realizes that something has gone wrong when he discovers that the earthquake, which he has slept through, has burst not only the water mains in the studio lot, but also something inside himself. The back lot looks like the "torn picture books of childhood, like fragments of stories dancing in an open fire." As he watches the picture of his dead wife drift by on the surface of the water, he realizes with terrible fear that the past as he has known it has vanished. The personal loyalty of workers to an individual has been replaced by an organized union with its own spokesman and organizer. There are "clay feet everywhere." These outward signs of destruction and change aptly reflect the disintegration of Stahr's inner self. Confused, alone, he wonders who or what will nurse him back to "completeness"—what breast or shrine, what fragment of picture or illusion? The doctor tells him that he has a heart ailment. He decides that if he is going to die he wants "to stop being Stahr for awhile and hunt for love like men who had no gifts to give, like young nameless men who looked along the streets in the dark." Although Stahr seeks to obliterate a past that seems to have played him false, he also tries to use that past as a new beginning.

The earthquake that destroyed something in Stahr has also introduced him to love and romance, both of which give an illusion of security to his old identity. From the confusion that was the flooded lot, he remembers having seen two women. When he finally locates them he identifies the wrong one, a girl named Edna Smith, who introduces him, however, to the "right" one. Kathleen Moore is glamorous, yet "poor, unfortunate, and tagged with a middle-class exterior which doesn't fit in with the grandeur Stahr demands of life." He falls in love with her, and like the rest of his past with which she becomes identified, she becomes absolutely necessary to him. But clearly something has gone wrong. As the error in naming suggests, Stahr is no longer a man of authority and decision. Once he has been mistaken for Smith; now, as if occupying Schwartz's role, he has made the identical error in naming. Like Schwartz, Stahr is losing his grip on life.

If Stahr's new "aerial adventure" gives an illusion of unity to his life, his "aerial romance," burdened with obsolete values of a self-deluded past, ends with inevitable failure. Stahr invites Kathleen to his half-finished Malibu beach home; in metaphor that uses flight image, he confesses that he does not have sufficient material at hand to finish the "fuselage" of his new home. The luxury, the obsolete items of a past are there—built-in book cases, curtain rods, cushioned chairs, a ping-pong table, the trap in the floor for a movie projector—but the household necessities, the sides and roof, are missing. In this half-built "new world," Stahr is even now, as the narrator says of him later, playing a "losing battle with his instinct towards schizophrenia." Further realization comes when, in front of Kathleen, Stahr makes another error in naming. He believes the telephone call is from the President of the United States, but he has misunderstood. He has actually been speaking to an orang-outang. He knows someone has tricked him, but he tries to go along with the gag: "Hello, orang-outang—God, what a thing to be! —Do you know your name? . . . He doesn't seem to know his name." Twice mistaken over names, Stahr is helplessly confused, as if his error in identification reflects his own uncertainty of self. After the seduction Kathleen asks him: "Don't you always think—hope that you'll be one person, and then find you're still two?" Her question is ironic mockery. Stahr is two persons striving to be one, and Kathleen, to whom he has turned for even the illusion of unity and fulfillment, writes later that she intends to marry someone else.

The episode on the beach, which follows the seduction scene, underlines the growing incapacity of the last tycoon as a topflight Hollywood producer. When Stahr leaves the house, he meets an old Negro, who has "really come out to read some Emerson," but is busy picking up grunion. What bothers Stahr is that the Negro refuses to let his children attend movies. Since the man is a Rosicrucian, Stahr asks if the brotherhood is against pictures. "Seems as if they don't know what they are for," the Negro tells him. "One week they for one thing and next week for another." Stahr feels somehow personally responsible for such indecision, as if his own pictures were not "artistic" enough to merit the sanction of the brotherhood or the attention of a man who is self-reliant as Stahr is not. Has he not failed in the very exercise of talent that has always sustained him? Are there to be no new flights, except those burdened with a past of self-delusion? Returning to the studios, Stahr is confronted with a new problem: organized labor—the enemy of personal power and leadership—has struck a blow from the "outside."

If Fitzgerald had followed the outline which he had

worked out, part of the remaining action of the novel was to show the effect of this conflict on Stahr. The scenes are fragmentary and do not, of course, present a final statement, but Fitzgerald's meaning, his point of view, seems clear. Stahr's meeting with Brimmer, the Communist labor organizer, clarifies what Stahr has begun to realize—his loss of personal power and leadership in the movie industry. The only leadership that Stahr really understands is that of individual triumph, the personal loyalty between employer and employee. At the interview he is white and nervous. He accuses Brimmer of trying to breakup the "unity" in his "model plant." Since Stahr is—or has been—that unity, he feels that the Communists are trying to "get" him personally. Actually, of course, Stahr is right, and when he asks Brimmer, "You don't really think you're going to overthrow the government," and Brimmer replies, "No, Mr. Stahr. But we think perhaps you are," Stahr is clearly reminded of his loss of prestige, his waning power. The interview leaves him weak and confused. The once powerful tycoon seems to be on neither one side nor the other. "The Reds see him now as a conservative—Wall Street as a Red."

Whatever the weakness of Stahr's position, Fitzgerald does not side with the Communists. As he writes in 1940, "You can neither cut through, nor challenge nor beat the fact that there is an organized movement over the world before which you and I as individuals are less than the dust." He clearly sees the danger of this "intensely dogmatic and almost mystical religion" to the individual: "whatever you say," the Communists "have ways of twisting it into shapes which put you in some lower category of mankind . . . , and disparage you both intellectually and personally in the process." On Stahr the blow from without is also a blow from within. Clinging to beliefs that are, perhaps, obsolete equipment for "aerial adventure," he fails because he now lacks the authority of self-conviction. Like Schwartz at the beginning of the story, Stahr no longer belongs.

Surrounded by enemies from without and weakened by confusions from within, Stahr is doomed to failure. In order to gain control of the studio management, Brady, a rival producer and the narrator's father, sides with the union, and with the help of Kathleen's husband, W. Bronson Smith, plots to have Stahr murdered. Again the name of Smith appears at a moment when death—if not rebirth—of personality is imminent. Although these final episodes must be reconstructed from the notes, the inevitable outcome for Stahr is failure and death. In a final effort to retain power, Stahr hires a thug to kill Brady and then escapes by plane. If, as the notes indicate, Stahr does not survive the plane crash, his life as we know it has begun figuratively and ended literally with flight.

Stahr's "aerial adventure" has become, then, a life of contradiction between the dead hand of the past and the high intentions of the future. If flight has served as a way of beginning, it has been burdened with self-delusions, with the disintegration and loss of identity. Thus Stahr's actual death only spells out what has already happened to him on a moral and intellectual level; the realization is for him—as it was for Fitzgerald—a psychological crack-up.

The very beliefs which have once sustained Stahr in his way of life—the "old dream of being an entire man," as Fitzgerald said of himself—have also played him false; he has lost confidence and integrity, even the merited respect from others. In a sense, his death is, like that of Schwartz, suicidal. The only part of his past "left over from a world that glitters" is Kathleen, who is now really Mrs. Smith, a fragment of memory whose very name connotes loss of individuation. Having left her husband as a result of the plot against Stahr, she remains, as she has always been, "on the outside of things—a situation which also has its tragedy." Indeed, the tragedy here is that of identity, or rather loss of identity; it is, as Fitzgerald believed and as Stahr demonstrates, the tragedy of being deluded by the iridescence and glitter of a world that seems to be made of diamonds, but is only rhinestones. It is the mockery in discovering that, although the triumph lies within oneself, now there is no self. There are only struggle and determination and failure.

When read in terms of image and symbol, **The Last Tycoon** is the personal statement of a writer who has seen a way to reorganize the ingredients of his shattered life into an artistic whole. In a note to himself that suggests conscious intention, Fitzgerald wrote: "repeat my own fear when I landed in Los Angeles with the feeling of new worlds to conquer in 1937 transferred to Stahr." Here was a new city with all the freshness of a new beginning, and as it whispered of success—of money, of romance, of eternal youth—so it revived the old determination to dominate life, to make it yield to "intelligence and effort." During the last week Fitzgerald was working faithfully and well, as if he really believed that "the redeeming things are not 'happiness and pleasure' but the deeper satisfactions that come out of struggle." Once again he had found a "splendid mirage." And then the sudden ending. "Come back, come back, O glittering and white!"

John E. Hart, "Fitzgerald's 'The Last Tycoon': A Search for Identity," in Modern Fiction Studies, *Vol. 7, No. 1, Spring, 1961, pp. 63-70.*

James E. Miller, Jr.   (essay date 1964)

[*Miller is an American educator and critic who has written extensively on such American writers as Fitzgerald, Walt Whitman, and J. D. Salinger. In the following excerpt, he provides an overview of* The Last Tycoon.]

In spite of all his physical and spiritual difficulties near the end of his life, Fitzgerald ambitiously began **The Last Tycoon** in Hollywood, where he spent the greater part of his last years writing for the motion pictures. There is a kind of heroic determination in his letters to his daughter during this period: "Any how I am alive again—getting by that October did something—with all its strains and necessities and humiliations and struggles. I don't drink. I am not a great man but sometimes I think the impersonal and objective quality of my talent and the sacrifices of it, in pieces, to preserve its essential value has some sort of epic grandeur." On November 25, 1940, Fitzgerald wrote to Edmund Wilson: "I think my novel [**The Last Tycoon**] is good. I've written it with difficulty. It is completely up-

stream in mood and will get a certain amount of abuse but it is first hand and I am trying a little harder than I ever have to be exact and honest emotionally. . . . This sounds like a bitter letter—I'd rewrite it except for a horrible paucity of time. Not even time to be bitter." Fitzgerald's acute consciousness of the swift passage of time now seems like a prophetic awareness of approaching death. He died within the month, in December, 1940, without completing his novel, but it was published posthumously with his notes and plans in 1941.

In September, 1940, Fitzgerald wrote to a friend: "But it [**The Last Tycoon**] is as detached from me as **Gatsby** was, in intent anyhow." In another letter, in which he outlined the story for Scribner's Maxwell Perkins, Fitzgerald said, "If one book could ever be 'like' another, I should say it is more 'like' **The Great Gatsby** than any other of my books." Given only its rough, unfinished state, it is impossible to know whether **The Last Tycoon** would have achieved or surpassed the brilliance of **The Great Gatsby**. But Edmund Wilson, who edited the fragment, together with Fitzgerald's notes, has pointed out the chief value of Fitzgerald's last novel: "This draft of **The Last Tycoon** . . . represents that point in the artist's work where he has assembled and organized his material and acquired a firm grasp of his theme, but he has not yet brought it finally into focus." In other words, the creative act is "frozen" in all the complexity of its intricate movement; it is fixed in time for all the curious to see. The effect is not unlike a visit behind the stage, where all the machinery and costumes and stage furniture are available for inspection.

John Dos Passos wrote extraordinarily powerful praise for this last novel: "It is tragic that Scott Fitzgerald did not live to finish **The Last Tycoon**. Even as it stands I have an idea that it will turn out to be one of those literary fragments that from time to time appear in the stream of a culture and profoundly influence the course of future events" ["A Note on Fitzgerald," **The Crack-Up**]. What struck Dos Passos so forcibly—the book's "unshakable moral attitude"—has not (as yet, anyway) been widely remarked or unusually influential. Indeed, there has been a tendency in Fitzgerald criticism to regard the book as something less in achievement, realized or potential, than **The Great Gatsby**. Typical is an opinion from *The Times Literary Supplement*: "It is hard to agree with the many critics who have said that **The Last Tycoon** would have crowned Fitzgerald's achievement. . . . Although the novel has a kind of distinction that clung to Fitzgerald's writing, even in the depths of his least engaging journalism, there is nothing in this final book to compare with **The Great Gatsby**."

It is, of course, highly speculative and probably unprofitable to judge a work in terms of what it might have become had it been finished. It is perhaps better to accept the work for what it is, an unfinished novel of a highly gifted writer, valuable for revealing how a genuine craftsman goes about his craft. As with Dickens' *Edwin Drood*, each reader can finish the novel to his own taste, on the basis of all the clues he can find.

Fitzgerald had exploited his knowledge of Hollywood before, notably in his short stories **"Magnetism"** (1928) and

"Crazy Sunday" (1932). But never before had he attempted such an ambitious narrative, not just set in Hollywood but *about* Hollywood. He intended not only to tell a story but to describe a way of life. In its scope, then, **The Last Tycoon** resembles **Tender Is the Night** more than **The Great Gatsby.** The outline published with the unfinished novel permits us to reconstruct the action that Fitzgerald intended to portray. The protagonist is Monroe Stahr, a high-powered Hollywood producer who, at thirty-five, is at the peak of his influence and productivity. Since the death of his beloved wife, he has, as a kind of compensation, driven himself in his work to the point of emotional and physical exhaustion. Although he is pursued by Cecilia Brady, his associate's young daughter, his interest is aroused only by Kathleen Moore, an English woman who resembles his late wife. His encounter with Kathleen, although it is romantically consummated, comes too late to prevent her planned marriage with an American who had previously extricated her from an unhappy life with a displaced European king. Stahr's attention is absorbed by the labor problems of the studio and particularly by the Communist manipulation of the workers, and he finds himself deeply involved in a power-struggle with Cecilia's corrupt and scheming father, Pat Brady. In all the liaisons, double-dealing, and black-mailing, Stahr attempts to maintain his moral equilibrium, but gradually he becomes entangled in the malignant morass surrounding him. He plots Brady's murder, and just as he realizes the degradation of the act and decides to call it off, he is killed in a plane crash.

What has all the marks of a melodramatic plot turns out to be remarkably believable, if not commonplace, in Fitzgerald's skillful rendering, at least in the six finished chapters of the projected nine. His notes show him taking great care to work out the method for telling his story. The most notable technical device he has hit upon is to use the young, somewhat sophisticated, partly naive girl, Cecilia Brady, as narrator: "This love affair [between Stahr and Kathleen] is the meat of the book—though I am going to treat it . . . as it comes through to Cecilia. That is to say by making Cecilia, at the moment of her telling the story, an intelligent and observant woman, I shall grant myself the privilege, as Conrad did, of letting her imagine the actions of the characters. Thus, I hope to get the verisimilitude of a first person narrative, combined with a God-like knowledge of all events that happen to my characters." The clarity with which Fitzgerald saw his method is remarkable, and the return to the craft of **Gatsby**—and Conrad—is unmistakable.

In creating an appropriate narrator, Fitzgerald was no doubt discovering his own attitude toward his material. It would have been easy, in depicting a Hollywood tycoon, to perpetuate a stereotype, either Hollywood's romantic conception of its own, or an anti-Hollywood caricature. Distance, Fitzgerald saw, would be everything if he were to escape both cynicism and sentimentality. Cecilia would provide just the right tone for making Monroe Stahr breathe the breath of life: "Cecilia is the narrator because I think I know exactly how such a person would react to my story. She is *of* the movies but not in them. She probably was born the day *The Birth of a Nation* was previewed

and Rudolf Valentino came to her fifth birthday party. So she is, all at once, intelligent, cynical, but understanding and kindly toward the people, great or small, who are of Hollywood." Cecilia does provide the breathless quality that we have come to identify as that special evocation of Hollywood—but without compromising the serious note that Fitzgerald wanted to sound. Her freshness, not unlike Rosemary Hoyt's in **Tender Is the Night,** revitalizes what might be tired material. Her bright young passion for Stahr endows him with a glamour that does not cheapen or mock.

From the opening page Cecilia beckons us into the novel and onto the plane which is carrying her home to Hollywood. We feel the immediacy of the events taking place—but we sense a distance, too. Before very many pages, we learn that the events, though vivid, are filtering through time, when Cecilia says, "I wonder what I looked like in that dawn, five years ago." This casual remark, we discover, has more meaning than at first appears when we reach Fitzgerald's notes and come upon the fragments he had once written for the opening of the novel and then discarded. These passages are written from still another point of view—two men who have encountered a fascinating young woman in a hospital in the canyons of Colorado: "this girl's face in the sunset, and with the fever, seemed to share some of the primordial rose tints of that 'natural wonder.' " She is, of course, Cecilia, wasting away with tuberculosis, recalling for her visitors the events of five years ago—the events of **The Last Tycoon.** Fitzgerald decided, and it seems wisely, that the whole scene was too gloomy for an opening to his story, but he intended to place it at the end to add its depressing note to the tragedy which preceded. Upon discovering these plans for Cecilia, we come to understand why, though resembling Rosemary Hoyt, she transcends her greenness and naivete. We come to know the source of the cynicism that tinges her intelligence. In trying to capture the feelings and tone of a young girl, product of Hollywood, from the inside (after all, Rosemary Hoyt was viewed from outside), Fitzgerald was hazarding a great deal. In placing her, and thus her recollections, in a sanatorium five years after the events, perhaps he was narrowing the gap between her perspective and his own, beset as he was by the illnesses of his last years. However that may be, Cecilia seems to come off with immense skill, providing the precisely right angle of vision, physical and emotional, for the story of Monroe Stahr.

But, as Fitzgerald indicated in one of his notes, he did not leave the whole task to Cecilia. In letting her "imagine the actions of the characters," he freed himself from the absurdity of inventing excuses for her being present at or learning about everything that had to be represented in the action. A brief account of the six finished chapters will show the ease with which he moved into and out of Cecilia's orbit. Chapter I describes the return flight to Hollywood, all narrated by Cecilia and introducing Monroe Stahr as the mysterious Mr. Smith ironically occupying the "bridal suite." Chapter II describes in a few vivid strokes the flooding of the studio lots (as the result of the earthquake) and Monroe Stahr's glimpse of the woman who resembles his dead wife floating by on a studio prop, "a huge head of the Goddess Siva." The first part of the chapter is Cecilia's, and she explains how she reconstructed the latter part:" . . . it was Robby [Robinson, Stahr's trouble-shooter] who later told me how Stahr found his love that night."

Chapters III and IV omit Cecilia almost entirely, but she introduces them:" . . . I have determined to give you a glimpse of [Stahr] functioning, which is my excuse for what follows. It is drawn partly from a paper I wrote in college on 'A Producer's Day' and partly from my imagination. More often I have blocked in the ordinary events myself, while the stranger ones are true." After some of the most brilliantly finished passages of the novel, describing Stahr setting an inhuman pace at his job, Cecilia steps in to wind up Chapter IV:

> That was substantially a day of Stahr's. I don't know about the illness, when it started, etc., because he was secretive, but I know he fainted a couple of times that month because Father told me [the doctor predicts Stahr's death within months]. Prince Agge [a studio visitor] is my authority for the luncheon in the commissary where he told them he was going to make a picture that would lose money—which was something, considering the men he had to deal with and that he held a big block of stock and had a profit-sharing contract.
>
> And Wylie White [a writer] told me a lot, which I believed because he felt Stahr intensely with a mixture of jealousy and admiration. As for me, I was head over heels in love with him then, and you can take what I say for what it's worth.

Chapter V alternates the point of view between Cecilia and Stahr, first person and third, with scenes developing the affair between Stahr and Kathleen Moore (the woman on the Siva head) counterpointed with scenes portraying the frantic Cecilia trying to discover the facts of Stahr's secret love life. In this chapter, there are some awkward touches; for example, at one point we read: "This is Cecilia taking up the narrative in person." But in general the difficult technical feat is carried off with unobtrusive skill, not calling attention to itself. Chapter VI is again given over largely to Cecilia, as it is through her (and her connections in the East, at Bennington) that Stahr arranges to meet the Communist, Brimmer. Her presence at their friendly discussions and her attempt at intervention when the argument threatens to become a brawl (Stahr, disappointed in the loss of Kathleen, is drinking heavily) seem not like technical manipulation at all but like natural advances in the action of the novel. The chapter breaks off, incomplete—and indeed none of these chapters may be regarded as finished. Fitzgerald wrote on the last draft of his first chapter: "Rewrite from mood. Has become stilted with rewriting. Don't look [at previous draft]. Rewrite from mood." In all their unfinished state, these six chapters reveal a novelist in full command of his craft, wresting from his abundant material the full range of its rich possibilities.

The last note included with *The Last Tycoon* is written in capitals, as a kind of warning, "ACTION IS CHARACTER." Fitzgerald's novel seems to be something of a demonstration of this "rule." We are never told directly what kind of man Monroe Stahr is, but we are shown continuously through his varied activities—and, furthermore, we see him as many others see him, each through his own distorting lens. It is not easy, then, to assess the special quality of his being that arouses such a complex mixture of respect and distaste, irony and awe. But this complexity is not new with Fitzgerald's heroes—Jay Gatsby and Dick Diver both attracted and repelled. Though radically different in their motives and their careers, their lives and their milieus, all these heroes, in spite of their shortcomings, share a kind of moral awareness that ultimately wins our grudging admiration.

In his haunting search for the woman who resembles his dead wife, Stahr resembles Gatsby in his determined pursuit of Daisy. Both men try in some sense to repossess the past, and both are doomed to emotional disappointment. But although Stahr in the savage dedication to his profession and in the lordly manner in which he operates resembles Gatsby imperiously managing his far-flung enterprises—both are tycoons—there is a creative aspect to Stahr's endeavor that is missing from Gatsby's. Stahr is, after all, boldly willing to make a picture for its intrinsic value, even though it will lose money. Gatsby's shabby business ventures are certainly immoral and probably illegal. In a way, Stahr is an inside-out Dick Diver. While Diver cannot find in himself the will or the drive to stick to his serious profession, Stahr can find almost nothing else; while Diver squanders the rich emotional resources of his being, Stahr seems almost unable to reach the depths where his emotional life lies buried.

Stahr is a modern American type, consumed by ambition, deriving from his work the kind of emotional satisfaction an ordinary man expects from marriage. He has the traits of the mythical American pioneer, tremendous energy and drive, a variety of skills, immense resources of cunning and craft—and a fundamental sense of fair play. He is a pioneer of a new frontier, America's last—Hollywood, California. But he is also the *last* tycoon; his notions of running a large, complex business enterprise are primitive and old-fashioned. He holds every detail and decision to himself, and he cannot rise above the paternalistic view in labor relations. He is the American self-made man, with all his virtues and all his faults. Although unread, he is creative; although autocratic, he is fair. In short, he is a unique example of a specimen fast fading from the American scene, displaced by organization men and corporate images.

The Hollywood of Stahr's day has already passed, and nobody has captured its essence more vividly than Fitzgerald. By portraying in detail one of Stahr's days, Fitzgerald captures the essence of a fabulous industry and a bygone era. Whether in his office hounded by visitors and phone calls, in a story conference with directors and writers, at an executive luncheon with builders and owners, or in his private theater viewing rushes, Stahr remains cool-headed through a multitude of demands and decisions. Right or wrong, he must decide, and decide he does, ingeniously combining sound judgment, intuitive insight, and shrewd guesswork. In situations in which indecisiveness would be ruinous, Stahr cuts boldly through the uncertainties with his firm command—and cooly accepts the shattering responsibilities for being wrong as he takes for his own the considerable rewards for being right.

In the whirlwind that is Stahr's day, a multitude of characters emerge briefly, are vividly *there*, and then fade from view. Fitzgerald's genius for handling an immense cast of characters in confined space is here again put to the test, as it was in the accounts of Gatsby's parties or in the description of life on the Riviera beaches in *Tender Is the Night*—and again his achievement is brilliant. In a few fine strokes, a telling phrase, Fitzgerald brings a minor functionary or an important personage springing to life.

Jacques La Borwitz, the studio commissar, "had his points, no doubt, but so have the sub-microscopic protozoa, so has a dog prowling for a bitch and a bone." Mr. Roderiguez, famous and successful actor, has fallen out with his wife and pours out his problems to Stahr: "I think *Rainy Day* grossed twenty-five thousand in Des Moines and broke all records in St. Louis and did twenty-seven thousand in Kansas City. My fan mail's way up, and there I am afraid to go home at night, afraid to go to bed." Jane Meloney, "the best writer on construction in Hollywood, . . . had ulcers of the stomach, and her salary was over a hundred thousand a year." Reinmund, the supervisor, was a "handsome young opportunist" who had "an almost homosexual fixation on Stahr." Broaca, the director, had to be watched or he made the same scene over and over for his pictures: "A bunch of large dogs entered the room and jumped around the girl. Later the girl went to a stable and slapped a horse on the rump. The explanation was probably not Freudian. . . ." Old Marcus, top man in the company: "His grey face had attained such immobility that even those who were accustomed to watch the reflex of the inner corner of his eye could no longer see it. Nature had grown a little white whisker there to conceal it; his armor was complete." Red Ridingwood, the dismissed director: "It meant he would have slight, very slight loss of position—it probably meant that he could not have a third wife just now as he had planned." Birdy Peters, Brady's secretary, who, when Cecilia opens her father's office closet, "tumbled out stark naked—just like a corpse in the movies." These are only a few of the people who populate the novel, providing a backdrop of richly textured life for the story of Stahr.

If the existing chapters of *The Last Tycoon* reveal that the novel was to be about Stahr and about Hollywood, they suggest also that it was to be in some sense about modern life, about American life. No doubt the theme would have emerged with clarity from the finished novel, but there are enough signs to indicate Fitzgerald's direction. In the very opening chapter, the plane must land and stay over in Nashville, Tennessee, and the characters find their way out to Andrew Jackson's Hermitage. Accompanying Cecilia and Wylie White, the writer ("Cecilia, will you marry me, so I can share the Brady fortune?"), is Manny Schwartz, a tense ex-big-shot now rebuffed by the busy Stahr. When Cecilia and White return to the plane, Schwartz stays behind in the hopeless dawn: "He had come a long way from some Ghetto to present himself at that raw shrine. . . . At both ends of life man needed

nourishment: a breast—a shrine. Something to lay himself beside when no one wanted him further, and shoot a bullet into his head."

This grotesque juxtaposition is echoed in a comic scene in the studio, when the visiting Danish Prince Agge comes upon a familiar face, Abraham Lincoln. Startled, Prince Agge continues to stare at the figure, "his legs crossed, his kindly face fixed on a forty-cent dinner, including dessert, his shawl wrapped around him as if to protect himself from the erratic air-cooling." As Prince Agge gapes, like a tourist staring "at the mummy of Lenin in the Kremlin," "Lincoln suddenly raised a triangle of pie and jammed it in his mouth." The affinity with the opening Hermitage scene seems certain, as both episodes suggest some kind of debasement of the national heritage, some kind of degeneration of a heroic vision. Though modern America sits in the presence of its own past of transcendent achievement, the vital relationship has run out, become mechanical and meaningless.

In a later chapter Fitzgerald intended to return to this estrangement between past and present, between the serious and superficial aspects of life in America. Stahr was to make a trip to Washington, D. C., but he was to be suffering from a high fever and therefore unable to see anything in its true perspective or to apprehend the meaning of what he did see. Such a scene would, of course, modify our feelings about what we witness in the first six chapters of the book, and it would also subtly affect our relationship to Stahr. And if the scene had been done in Fitzgerald's finest suggestive style, the meanings would have radiated out into many dark corners of modern life and modern America. Like *The Great Gatsby, The Last Tycoon* might well have provided a commentary on the ultimate debasement of the American dream. As it is, we must accept the chapters that we have and the notes that survived with them for what they actually are—interesting evidence of Fitzgerald's involvement not only with plot but with technique as well. The outpourings of *This Side of Paradise*—the novel of saturation—have long since been replaced by a style that is the result of conscious and avowed concern for structure and selection.

James E. Miller, Jr., in his F. Scott Fitzgerald: His Art and His Technique, *New York University Press, 1964, 173 p.*

Sergio Perosa   (essay date 1965)

[*Perosa is an Italian educator and critic with a special interest in English and American literature. In the following excerpt from his critical study* The Art of F. Scott Fitzgerald, *he explores thematic, stylistic, and structural elements of* The Last Tycoon, *viewing the unfinished novel as a turning point in Fitzgerald's career.*]

> Once one is caught up into the material world, not one person in ten thousand finds the time to form . . . what, for lack of a better phrase, I might call the wise and tragic sense of life.

> *Letters*

The Last Tycoon has much in common with *The Great Gatsby* and with *Tender Is the Night,* and yet it represents a notable turning point in Fitzgerald's fiction. Like *Gatsby* it is a tightly knit and well-constructed novel—even in its unfinished state—based on the skillful juxtaposition of "dramatic scenes" filtered through the eyes of a narrator involved in the story. Its affinity with *Tender Is the Night* is in the informing idea, if it is true that the story concerns a "superman in possibilities," almost an artist and a creator, who finds his defeat in a psychological and emotional *épuisement* and at the same time is crushed by adverse circumstances. But in comparison with Gatsby the protagonist of *The Last Tycoon* is more extensively defined, both on the psychological and on the social and ethical level of his conflict, while in comparison with Dick in *Tender Is the Night* his predicament is more deeply rooted in a context of external circumstances and his struggle is less passive and more virile. Moreover, the adventure of Monroe Stahr is presented in a fairly realistic way, and Fitzgerald was availing himself of a quite different type of diction—a diction which came as close as possible to the ideal of immediacy and concreteness that is present in Hemingway's fiction. This is why *The Last Tycoon*, although basically in line with the motives and methods developed in his previous works, is an original achievement which shows the degree of renewal that Fitzgerald could reach without denying himself or his past. While remaining faithful to his inner convictions and "traditions," the writer was not prevented from asserting himself with a final *tour de force* that might have radically changed his line of development.

The incompleteness of the novel does not allow any excessive speculation on the entity and the eventual future bearing of such a change, and it is safer to consider the novel in its relationship with the preceding works. But it will be necessary, from time to time, to stress the differences, and even if we have to suspend final judgment because of its incompleteness, it would be amiss to neglect its unsuspected potentiality of new motives and new techniques.

Checked in the "game of life," Fitzgerald was also betrayed by his luck. He was betrayed by his weakened physical condition, which prevented him from gathering the reward of his assiduous effort under adverse conditions, and as in no other case death came at the wrong moment. Of this novel that should have marked his triumphant return among the leading authors of the Forties, Fitzgerald was able to complete only five chapters out of nine. We are left with little more than half a novel, even considering the scattered notes, outlines, and fragments that remain. It is probably too little for us to speak of a "novel," especially since Fitzgerald used to rework his novels even when he had completed them (*Tender Is the Night* is typical in this sense). Nevertheless, *The Last Tycoon* belongs to the canon of Fitzgerald's fiction, and it must be considered as an important part of it. For Dos Passos, who cannot be suspected of any tenderness toward Fitzgerald, it represents "one of those literary fragments that from time to time appear in the stream of a culture and profoundly influence the course of future events." If this is an exaggerated and questionable statement, the fact remains that this fragment has all the intensity, the effectiveness, and the significance of a final outburst of artistic vitality.

The first idea of a new novel was conceived by the writer

three or four years before his sudden death. "This has been in my mind for three years," he wrote in a note, and his first idea was to write a love story set in Hollywood. The protagonist was to be a brilliant producer, possessing many of the qualities and limitations of the producer Irving Thalberg whom Fitzgerald had met as far back as 1927. From the very start he committed himself to an objective rendering, since for this character he could not use his own traits and personal experiences as such, but had to embody them in a character seen from the outside, who would lead his own independent life. According to a first outline of the plot, the brilliant producer would have been ruined by his love for a woman whose resemblance to his wife would stir him to a longing for a new home, a new affection, and a new form of life. Realizing that in this way he would break the prospect of a happy marriage for the woman, the producer was to have left her, only to find himself alone in his daily struggle for survival and preeminence in the movie world. Physically worn out, emotionally disappointed and persecuted for his attempt to continue his relations with the woman after her marriage, he was to break down like Dick Diver. An accident in an airplane during his "flight" would have sealed his ruin. The theme had much in common with the theme in the first drafts of *Tender Is the Night*: Stahr's tragic flaw appears to be mainly his need for love, while it is his blind dedication to the woman that determines more than anything else his *épuisement* and his collapse.

There is no indication, at this point, of how Fitzgerald intended to handle the difficult problem of the point of view. In other notes, however, he faced the problem and ended by making the narrator a girl, Cecilia, daughter of Stahr's fellow-producer and rival; Cecilia's unrequited love for Stahr was to have colored the whole story with an intense participation, while at the same time objectifying it through the detachment of a limited point of view. In two detailed plans the story is then delineated and divided into eight chapters, subdivided into thirty-one episodes. In these plans the story was still described as a love story (the working title was quite revealing in this respect: The Love of the Last Tycoon), but it was already determined and conditioned by other, more realistic elements. The story of Stahr's love for Thalia made up the largest part of the episodes and was followed for a rather long span of time, although it was not marked by the breathless rapidity that characterizes it in the novel. There was also to be a conflict of interests between Stahr and Bradogue (Cecilia's father), which would push the former, after a hard struggle, to eventual defeat in a framework of conflicting social and economical forces. Stahr did not give in or fly as in the first outline, and even the plane crash was to happen when his defeat had been already determined. The two themes, however, were separately developed, and the inner and the outer conflicts remained independent of one another, without really coinciding or being structurally combined.

Fitzgerald's difficulty in freeing himself from the limitations of a pathetic love story and in dealing consistently with the theme of a more realistic conflict is evident in the second outline of the plot, which he sent to his publisher and to the editor of *Collier's*. Many of the definitions and statements of purpose in this outline clarify the purport or at least the intention of the story that he had in mind after the first attempts. Fitzgerald discussed at length the figure and the function of the narrator, the nature and the characteristics of Stahr and Thalia; he attempted a definition of the conflict that opposes Stahr to Bradogue and to the writers' union; he alluded to a struggle for the control of Stahr's company—but he insisted all the same that "the love affair *was* the meat of the book." Unexpectedly, the tragic end is here represented as an ironical twist of fate, since Stahr was to die when he had not only regained the love of Thalia, but was flying to New York to clinch his victory over his rival. In addition, a penultimate chapter would have represented a boy who would find in the wreckage of the airplane a "moral heritage" by simply reading Stahr's papers.

If the love story was to have been "the meat of the book" and was to end in reconciliation, it is difficult to see how the writer could have sustained it through a turbulent conflict of interests, which was also to work out favorably for Stahr, and then end it in an incongruous plane crash. There is no link of cause and effect among the various elements, between their development and their conclusion, especially if we consider that the love affair, far from precipitating the conflict of interests and deriving from it a dramatic tension as in the novel, has no apparent obstacle to overcome. It is compromised by Stahr's own indecision and particular form of mind, by his psychological and aesthetic requirements only. There is no other man in Thalia's life and nothing would prevent her from staying with Stahr. All the difficulties are in him: in his dream of an emotional as well as social superiority Stahr is unable to accept such a girl as Thalia, who has a poor background and humble appearance. It is he who alienates Thalia without realizing that she is much more important to him than he thinks, that she is in fact necessary to him. The motivation that Fitzgerald had envisaged is quite revealing. "Previously his [Stahr's] name had been associated with this or that well-known actress or society personality, and Thalia is poor, unfortunate, and tagged with a middle-class exterior which doesn't fit in with the grandeur Stahr demands of life." Everything seems to be the result of an excessive squeamishness on the part of Stahr; his hamartia is really a form of pathetic weakness—an incapacity to accept reality, a little like the early Dick, or Gatsby himself, not to speak of Anthony. If Fitzgerald had developed his story along these lines he would have run the risk of repeating himself, and it is significant that he defined the book as "an escape into a lavish, romantic past that perhaps will not come again into our time."

In the third diagram of the story, which seems to be connected with the previous outline, and which is divided into ten chapters and twenty-three episodes, the love affair is still the dominant theme of the book. A good four chapters (II, III, IV, and VII) are devoted to the meetings of Stahr and Thalia, while only two deal with the same material in the novel. The seduction is accomplished in Chapter VII (Chapter V in the novel) and the conflict of interests with Bradogue begins to take shape only in the eighth chapter, when the story is already turning to its logical conclusion. From this moment the story seems to be centered on this conflict, and the love affair seems to be almost forgotten.

The two motives, therefore, are not only separated in this diagram, but they seem actually to offer two separate possibilities, as if the second might at a certain point take the place of the first. It is Stahr again who seems to refuse the possibility of marrying Thalia, and Thalia herself, as is apparent in a first version of the second chapter based on this diagram, is represented without the elusive and slightly mysterious charm that she will have in the novel. Stahr saves her from the flood in the set, and in this immediate contact the girl not only loses every mysterious fascination, but in fact appears to him as " 'common' . . . ready for anything—a wench, a free-booter, an outsider." Cecilia, though with the irritation of a rival in love, later describes her as "that wretched trollop." If Thalia had been developed according to these premises, there is little doubt that the story would have never come to a logical formulation.

Fortunately, the story was reshaped in a fourth diagram, and when it was written down in an extended narrative the two main motives were blended and fused in a functional way. The story was developed in a tightened structure of episodes in which the elements found their proper place in the close relationship and interdependence of the two informing ideas. Stahr's love story preserves its necessary importance and its dramatic quality (the girl is about to marry another man and does so despite meeting the producer), but it is unfolded in close connection with the conflict that opposes Stahr to Bradogue for the control of the movie company and to the writers' union, over which he wants to maintain his paternalistic predominance. The *épuisement* of the impossible relation with Thalia undermines Stahr's chances of affirming himself in the double struggle and offers to both enemies the occasion for a frontal attack, while the straits of his material interests prevent him from finding in his love the evasion from or the solution to his problems.

In a fine example of *discordia concors*, **The Last Tycoon** has all the premises and many of the qualities of a highly dramatic story, complex in motivation, realistic in context and statement, rapid, immediate, and intense in diction. By following it step by step we can attain a clear idea of its nature and significance and establish both its relations to **Tender Is the Night** and **Gatsby,** and its intrinsic novelty in comparison with these two novels.

Like **The Great Gatsby, The Last Tycoon** opens with a careful characterization of the narrator and then introduces some of the secondary characters whose function is to bring us near the protagonist; Stahr is already caught sight of toward the end of the first chapter, but he is still detached. Like Nick Carraway, Cecilia is given all the qualities of a perfect narrator, including the ability to imagine certain episodes at which she was not present or which could not be related to her. "She is *of* the movies but not *in* them," as the writer warns us, and detached chronologically from the facts, which she reconstructs after five years have elapsed. Intelligent and observant, she is involved in the action and is a product of the social environment, but with a certain measure of disenchanted cynicism. Like Nick, she presents herself directly at the beginning, and if she declares that she accepts Hollywood "with the resignation of a ghost assigned to a haunted house," she proclaims nevertheless her capacity to be "obstinately unhorrified." Cecilia can be perturbed by the movie world (like the nun who wanted to study a script), but she does not question it. She takes it for granted, and to understand it she suggests that it is sufficient "to understand one of those men." She is flying back to this world from the East, but the haunting atmosphere of Hollywood is already present on the plane, and we are given a clear warning as to its possible destructive effects when the plane lands in Nashville during a thunderstorm. When she goes to the Hermitage of Andrew Jackson in the night, Cecilia can neither enter nor properly contemplate the sanctuary of the uncorrupted American faith in progress and democracy. And on its threshhold Schwartz, a Hollywood cast-off whom Cecilia has met on the plane, commits suicide.

He has killed himself because Stahr has turned against him, but he has warned Stahr of a mysterious danger that threatens him. Wylie, the script writer who is a friend of Cecilia and works for Stahr, also vaguely hints at a possible danger to the producer, even if he predicts his victory over his rival. When Stahr, traveling incognito on the plane, first chats with Cecilia and then holds a brief soliloquy in the pilot's cabin, his charm and his energy are still dominant. Cecilia discovers that she is childishly falling in love with him, and she sees only strength and amiable manhood in his personality; and as Stahr sits in the pilot's cabin to contemplate Los Angeles from the sky, all the writer's abilities are brought into play to give us a sense of enlightened grandeur. Fitzgerald attached an important symbolic significance to this episode, so much so that he prepared a longer version of it in which his intentions are made even more obvious. By sitting with the pilot, Stahr comes to identify himself with him: like the pilot he is a "leader" of men, aware of his responsibilities, quick and resolute in his decisions, somewhat isolated from the rest of the people and relying only on his intuition when it becomes a question of life or death. He too operates "on a high level"—far from the ground—master of his own destiny and of all who are with him. And when in the course of the story he is compelled to "come down to earth" and to measure himself with others on their own level, he will be bound to face his ruin; even the plane's landing acquires a symbolic meaning. It is significant that Stahr sees in the approaching lights of Los Angeles a sign of his passion for activity, and he returns to the city with the pleasure of an empire builder, of an artistic creator, almost, who is interested in it not because he possesses it, but because he has *created* it. Yet, his going down "into the warm darkness" will soon turn into a crash against a hostile ground. The lights go out, and his activity will languish, blighted by its own worm, wrecked by contrasting tensions; even his descent might be taken as a thematic forewarning of his fatal destiny, when he will crash in another plane into the snowy mountains.

In Hollywood the action moves on in a second, very brief chapter. Brady makes his first appearance on the scene, and during an earthquake, which is both functional and symbolic in the story, Stahr sees for the first time an unknown and mysterious woman who closely resembles his dead wife. The convulsive rhythm of the chapter, which was meant perhaps to convey an idea of the sudden illumination that was to strike Stahr, is smoothed and quieted in the two successive chapters, whose main purpose is to acquaint us with Stahr in an almost analytic way. Unable to forget Stahr, Cecilia tells us of his working day by reconstructing a broken series of episodes, a sequel of dramatic scenes which gives an idea of his character and his nature while also illustrating the Hollywood background. To believe that Stahr is "a marker in industry like Edison and Lumière and Griffith and Chaplin," we must see him at work to appreciate his qualities as a man and leader. He can show his humanity toward a cameraman who has attempted suicide, and thus restore him to his work and happiness; he can teach a presumptuous English writer what amount of imaginative power is needed to make a film; he can solve the personal crisis of an actor (even if he has to keep important people waiting); he is stubborn and dictatorial at the rushes, but always with competence and success. And when he joins the other producers at the commissary, he is willing to sustain the production of a quality picture even if it means losing money. Brady is already opposed to this idea, but Stahr turns a deaf ear to any opposition, without ceremony, and with almost too much precision gets rid of a director who is unequal to his job, and is not afraid to deal at cross purposes with the script writers. His only reward after a long, tiring day is his attempt to find the unknown girl he has seen on the set after the earthquake.

When the setting has been established and the nature of the various characters has been illustrated, the action begins to take shape. In the fifth chapter, which is described as the "dead middle" of the book, the various threads begin to be drawn together. A little like Rosemary—and using almost the same words ("Undertake me," she says to Stahr)—Cecilia tries to interest the tycoon, who is, however, deeply involved in his dream of repeating the past with Kathleen. Allusions at this point indicate that his health is not of the best, and Stahr attaches himself to Kathleen as a way out of his isolation and overwork. To meet her on a sad, long Sunday he neglects his work for the first time. This might be the beginning of a new life for him, but his affair with Kathleen worsens his inner conflict. If it is true that they meet "as strangers in an unfamiliar country," not even the closest intimacy will bring them really together and that country will never appear familiar to them. Kathleen recounts her past to Stahr, tells him of her impoverished childhood and of her humiliations, culminating in an impossible and weary relationship with a king. Her background is as artificial and incomplete as the house on the beach where the tycoon takes the girl on their first day together. The skeletal house, suggestive of a movie set and somehow constituting a symbol of the desolation of Stahr's unstable life, is where their bodies are united. It is a breathless union—almost in the open, without any shelter—that will never turn into a harmonious life.

Four times Stahr drives with Kathleen on the road that joins Hollywood with Malibu. Each time the tone and the atmosphere vary, in keeping with the state of mind of the two characters. The first trip is full of expectancy and uncertainty, the second (their first return to Hollywood) is sad and marked with dissatisfaction, the third is lively with expectancy and impatience—after a dreary dinner in a drugstore Stahr and Kathleen have decided to go back to the house, under the pressure of their emotions and the urgency of their senses. The act of love is accomplished in the unfinished house, and it is "immediate, dynamic, unusual, physical" as Fitzgerald had said in his letter, almost too quick in its urgency (there is only a broken piece of dialogue between them:" 'Wait,' she said."). For a time the atmosphere becomes idyllic, in the twilight on the beach, where they meet an old Negro awaiting the arrival of the grunion. During their fourth trip back to Hollywood the enchantment seems broken, and Stahr has a feeling that nothing has been achieved. The final blow comes when he learns that Kathleen is going to be married; only the pile of film scripts will be waiting for him at home.

Such a cruel disappointment needs silence, and in the meantime the other motive of the book is developed with the reappearance of Brady in the foreground—as he is surprised by his daughter with a nude secretary hidden in a closet. This is the vulgar and cheap counterpart of the previous love scene between Stahr and Kathleen, and it is easy to foresee that between these two opposing poles of behavior and sensitivity there will not be a lasting truce. Stahr, however, has still a chance of dissuading Kathleen from getting married, but his disappointment is too deep and he can no longer deal with her with his customary decision. Kathleen is attracted by him, and a word from him at this time would have been perhaps sufficient to win her back. But Stahr is unable to utter it, since his pride and his boundless egotism have been hurt. Like Gatsby, he is unable to accept a compromise or to bargain for the thing he wants, and being unable to accept Kathleen as she is, he is almost guilty himself of losing her. In this way his destiny is marked: "the dam breaks" in the sixth chapter, of which only the first part has been written. Disturbed to the point of getting drunk by the idea of Kathleen's marrying another, Stahr for the first time lets himself be taken "off guard" when he has the greatest need for all his strength. He is overcome in a discussion with the leftist union leader Brimmer, and even physically hurt, since in his impotence Stahr can think of nothing better than trying to strike the man. From then on we can assume that his decline was to be steady and inescapable, but the novel was cut off here by Fitzgerald's death.

The turning point, however, has been reached, and it is fairly clear from the scattered notes and the diagram that he left how he intended to end the story. Stahr's health was to decline rapidly, and he was to visit Washington in the summer, without being able in the empty city to make any contact with the traditional values of America. Crossed by Brady, who has imposed a wage cut during his absence, Stahr opposes the union also, with the result that "the Reds see him now as a conservative—Wall Street as a Red." Heedless of everything Stahr leaves Cecilia, whom he has accepted as a substitute for Kathleen, and Cecilia tells her father of Stahr's secret love for Kathleen, thus furnishing Brady with the possibility of blackmailing Stahr. Stahr blackmails Brady in his turn, argues with Wylie, and his affair with Kathleen becomes instrumental in his ruin. In the eighth chapter, Brady was to resort to

Kathleen's husband, an active union leader, who would seize the chance of suing Stahr. According to Fitzgerald's first conception, he was to murder the producer; in either case, Stahr was to be saved by Peter Zavras, the cameraman whom he himself had saved at the beginning of the story. Under the pressure of all these tensions, however, Stahr is on the verge of collapse. Suspecting that Brady wants to murder him he resorts to Brady's own means and hires gangsters to kill Brady. The murder is to be accomplished while Stahr is flying to New York. On the flight he is disgusted with himself for having stooped to Brady's methods and determines to stop the gangsters as soon as the plane lands. But the plane crashes and Brady is murdered. Stahr's funeral, an orgy of servility and hypocrisy, was to have ended the book with a bitter and ironic touch: a cast-off actor, invited by mistake to be one of the pallbearers, is immediately reinstated. The future of the movie industry was to be foreshadowed in the grim figure of Fleishacker, the unscrupulous and opportunistic company lawyer. Finally, having separated from her husband, Kathleen comes back to gaze from the outside on the studios in which she has never set foot, while Cecilia, overwhelmed by the events, has a nervous breakdown after she has given herself for spite to a man she does not love (Wylie or Fleishacker); she relates the story from the hospital where she has been confined.

It is clear enough that in the unfinished novel we are confronted with only part of this story. As Edmund Wilson has warned, "This draft of *The Last Tycoon* . . . represents that point in the artist's work where he has assembled and organized his material and acquired a firm grasp of the theme, but has not yet brought it finally into focus." This warning should be constantly borne in mind. Nevertheless, the part that was written, the many indications as to its conclusion, and the notes that Fitzgerald left allow us to define the nature and the significance of the unfinished book.

In a certain way *Tender Is the Night* could also be interpreted as a novel dealing with the tragedy of the creative artist. Dick Diver could be seen as an intellectual, whose main motivation has much in common with the creative motivations of a scientist or, by extension, of an artist. He creates or recreates an organism which is dependent on him (Nicole) and succeeds in giving life and consistency to what did not exist and was shapeless before his intervention. His problem and his tragedy would then become identified with those of any other creator who, when his work is completed, finds that he has exhausted all his energy for its benefit and is therefore depleted, defeated, and overcome by his own creation. James's fiction abounds in similar representations, not only in obvious examples such as "The Figure in the Carpet," "The Lesson of the Master," and "The Middle Years," but also in works less openly focused on the theme of the artist. In his "major" works, characters like Lambert Strether, Milly Theale, or Maggie Verver are represented as obsessed by the need of imposing an order on their emotions, experiences, and behaviors, while in *The Sacred Fount* the role of the artist is explored in his extreme commitment to the task of reordering the world. In most of James's works, as R. P. Blackmur has remarked, "The fate of the artist is somehow the test of society," and the same definition might apply to *Tender Is the Night,* if we bear in mind that Dick's defeat implied a more general surrender of the idealistic and creative impulse to the organized forces of a hostile society.

In *Tender Is the Night,* although implicit rather than explicit, there seems to be a clear thematic and stylistic derivation from James; in *The Last Tycoon* it would be difficult to find a precise link with James. Yet, in this novel, Fitzgerald offered a particular treatment of the theme of the artist which has a typically Jamesian flavor in its general outline. Stahr is, of course, a "limited" type of artist, but he also finds the test of society hostile to his attempts and is snared by the social context into an inglorious defeat. In *The Last Tycoon,* moreover, the protagonist meets his ruin both on the psychological and emotional level of his *épuisement,* and on the social level of a conflict of interests; and this is a clear link with *Tender Is the Night,* where the defeat of the "artist" had been dealt with precisely on those two levels.

Writing of *The Last Tycoon,* Fitzgerald had made a point of noting the differences between his new novel and the preceding one: "Unlike *Tender Is the Night,* this novel is not a story of deterioration—it is neither depressing nor morbid, in spite of the tragic ending." He was partly right, of course, because the new novel avoided the canons of the "philosophical novel" and aimed at a "compression" in many ways similar to the compression of *The Great Gatsby.* But art, like nature, does not take jumps, and Fitzgerald remained faithful to the "ideal line" of *Gatsby* without denying the experience of *Tender Is the Night,* even if he was bound to surpass both experiences in a new form of achievement. It is from the point of view of continuity of motives (if no longer of techniques) that we are best able to appreciate the purport of *The Last Tycoon.* The mechanics of the situation are quite familiar, although his new story was developed in a rather different way.

That Monroe Stahr is basically an artist is made clear in various places in the book and in the notes. He lives and works in Hollywood because it is an empire that he has created, not because he wants to make money, as Brady does. All his energies are directed to raising the movie industry to an artistic level, and the passion and competence with which he works qualify him for the role of leader. He gives unity to the movies that he produces, "he takes the gloom out of a picture and gives it style" (as we find written in a note). He is able to direct the energies of his script writers and to sustain them in the effort until he gets the best out of them. He has a gift of seeing "below the surface into reality"; after him, the movie industry will gradually decline. Lastly, as we have noted, he is not afraid of sustaining a quality production even if it will lose money—and all these details contribute to qualify the artistic role that Stahr is at least potentially supposed to play in the novel. As an artist he has the typical awareness of his limitations, and his character is made credible and mature since, like Gatsby, his greatness is only partial and he carries within himself the germ of destruction.

Like Gatsby, who did not cut the pages of the books in his library, Stahr has no time to read, and his culture is superficial. He reads synopses—whether of the Bible or of the *Communist Manifesto*—and he values literature from a utilitarian point of view. His potential artistic nature finds an outlet in his efficient organization, and bows to the slightly presumptuous ideal of the tycoon. The practical results, to be obtained at any price, make any means legitimate in the end, and in consequence the creative impulse becomes an exaggerated form of paternalistic individualism. Egotistical and self-centered, Stahr carries all his qualities to an excess. With his domineering character, he tends to become a despot; an enlightened tyrant, he mistakes himself for an oracle. An efficient leader, he ends by relying only on his own strength and ideas; he underrates his enemies and does not grasp the natural evolution of the times. He has good cause to stand up against Brady, but he shows as much hostility to the writers union. On the human level he can be generous and altruistic to Zavras, but he is so enraged with Brimmer that he has to resort to physical violence, and as we have seen, he stoops to Brady's methods when he feels threatened.

Great in a partial way, a character who cannot "give himself entirely" to others (not even to Kathleen) ends by compromising the greatness of his efforts. "Note also in the epilogue that I want to show that Stahr left certain harm behind him just as he left good behind him," Fitzgerald had remarked. And it is this undoubted negative touch that makes the defeat of Stahr less lamentable, though more "realistic" in the ordinary sense, almost more existential, than the defeat of Dick. Stahr's defeat is made more concrete in a specifically social frame of reference, and his struggle is more virile than Dick's. He is "more of a men's man than a ladies' man"; he likes combat ("he was Napoleonic and actually liked combat"), even if he is described by Zavras as the Aeschylus and the Euripides of the movie world. Stahr has enough in his life to struggle against; but his struggle is only partly legitimate or justifiable, and it is disproportionate to his forces. In this way, Stahr is a victim of Brady's ruthlessness, but also of the just opposition of the unions, and of his own weaknesses, disguised under an exaggeration of his own strength. He is above all victim of himself and of his own "artistic" creation. "Stahr didn't die of overwork—he died of a certain number of forces allied against him," Fitzgerald had stated. His overwork is a result, more than a cause, of his unbalance; yet, among Stahr's worst enemies, is the less noble aspect of his character, and the external forces allied against him find an easy access into his home front—the weakened home front of his inner contradictions, of his unhappy and irregular love affair, of his waning strength.

Brady is the natural opponent of Stahr—the typical, mean merchant, interested only in making money, whose motivations are dictated by "Wall Street" ethics. Stahr's friend as long as Stahr is "productive," Brady begins to turn against him when he realizes the artistic and idealistic sides of his character, and his opposition becomes greater when he discovers that Stahr is honest and considerate to his workers. Brady neither respects Stahr nor understands his enlightened motives. On the other hand, the union leaders do respect Stahr's efficiency and understand, perhaps, his fair play and his sense of responsibility to his men. But they are bound to oppose his methods and his despotic individualism, while Stahr opposes the union not so much out of personal interest as out of principle, fearing in a way that in a Hollywood where the social structure is changed his preeminence would no longer be possible. He cannot ally himself with Brady, nor compromise with the union, and as a result he is torn between these two forces when they join to attack him on his vulnerable home front.

Stahr has already been defeated in this respect, owing to his contradictions. As Rosemary was for Dick Diver, Kathleen might represent a way out for Stahr, or at least an anchor for him in his loneliness; she might still bring order and affection into his existence. It is for her that Stahr does not work on Sunday for the first time, that he breaks the iron rules of his long working hours. With Kathleen he might start a new life. But confronted with the possibility of a normal life, it is Stahr himself who withdraws: Kathleen is a modest woman, a bit too old perhaps for him, and she lacks "grandeur." To have her for himself, Stahr should ask her not to marry, take her from another, submit somehow to a compromise. And not knowing how to stoop to conquer, he lets her marry another, forfeiting all his chances of renewal. Kathleen attracts him because she does *not* belong to the movie world; yet for this very reason Stahr is unable to accept her completely. When he resumes the affair after she has married, everything is compromised, and he is bound to end up in *épuisement* and consequent ruin. When Brady learns of the affair and goes to the union leader, Stahr's home front, already weakened, collapses. The outer conflicts find the softened ground of an inner conflict to work on; as in *Tender Is the Night* the objective tensions break the resistance of a protagonist already weakened by his inner tensions.

Dick Diver had made his dangerous choice and had succumbed to it, betraying his real mission. There is no *trahison des clercs* in Stahr, who fights his battle to the bitter end in *his* world and with his own weapons, as long as he has any. When he has no more, he capitulates, but his spear has not been "blunted" and his capacities have not been "locked up" by a hostile social class as in Dick's case. He has been defeated in an open struggle which leaves him no escape. He has not moved from one milieu to another or from one profession to another: he has stayed in *his* world, and the poison has grown as it were in his hands, when the creature to which he has given life revolts against him. Dick was responsible for his initial choice; Stahr is guilty for the way in which he reacts to a situation and to a world where he is at home and which he should know better. There is actually no other choice for him, and therefore his end is less melancholy than Dick's, but perhaps more painful and inevitable. The whimper of Dick becomes here—not only in a metaphorical sense—the bang of a man who strikes against the reality of his own natural surroundings.

This realistic frame of reference is made more concrete and visible in *The Last Tycoon* than in *Tender Is the Night.* In the earlier novel, the psychological and social conflict was basically between two moral attitudes and two universal aspects of human nature—between the ide-alism of Dick and the corruption of the bourgeoisie. Here the social and moral conflict is rooted in a local framework of contrasting attitudes and activities which are typical of a precise and well-known social milieu. Hollywood is an equivocal milieu, where the artistic impulse is blighted and frustrated by an industrial organization. In that milieu the artist—any kind of artist—has to face a dilemma every day, and the tragic potentialities are inherent in its nature. Stahr sets them in motion, and his story, while perfectly in keeping with the milieu, is an illustration of its intrinsic nature. The novel, as Fitzgerald had warned, was not to be *about* Hollywood; and yet Hollywood is indispensable in the whole design, and it becomes an overwhelming presence, like the sea in *Moby Dick*. Hollywood is the *sine qua non* condition for the book to develop along its lines, and it is in the book not for documentary but for purely artistic purposes of consistency and effectiveness. Without that framework the novel would not be possible. Fitzgerald gave a picture of that world in all its minutest details, in its mechanics and in its essence, representing it, moreover, in a particular period of its development—the social crisis of 1935, when the writers' union was in fact constituted. It was a particular moment in which the consequences of the depression were still badly felt, and it is significant that Stahr's defeat was to have had all these social as well as economical connotations in its unfolding.

At this point the novel begins to draw away noticeably from *Tender Is the Night* and *The Great Gatsby.* Fitzgerald's use of Hollywood as a setting is proof of his mature seriousness and of his unsuspected capacity for a realistic rendering. For the first time Fitzgerald chose to represent a business world, which he then defined in all its functions and represented with a rigorous adherence to its secret motivations. The field of action is no longer that of the expatriates, of the college students, or of the outsiders like Gatsby, but rather of people who work for a living, who build and produce and create. Quite rightly, in the third and fourth chapters, Stahr is represented, in every sense of the word, at work. The characters are no longer romantic projections of the author, adolescents or flappers; they are people caught and revealed in the sphere of adult and responsible action. Parties, so important in *Gatsby* and in *Tender Is the Night,* are here only marginal and of small importance; there is only one, at the beginning of Chapter V, and it does not counterbalance the long hours that Stahr spends in his office, in the projection rooms, on the sets.

Thus, Fitzgerald seems really to have confronted an experience which imposed on him the task of a realistic and objective rendering. The love scenes themselves, which were at first surrounded by a dreamy halo of idyllic sentimentalism, are finally represented in a direct, immediate, and dynamic way. Fitzgerald responded to the exacting requirements of his subject matter by adopting a bare, unadorned style, perfectly in keeping with the crude reality it had to express. One might speak of dramatic realism, although not in the sense that the term realism is applied, let us say, to the works of W. D. Howells or J. T. Farrell. Its connotations are much more complex here. Like Melville, Fitzgerald seized upon a well-defined framework of reality and immediately distorted it with the urgency of his imagination, colored it with nightmarish hues and shades, violated its surface, and corrugated it to make it a vehicle for larger meanings. Melville built on his realism the myth of the chase of the white whale; on a lower level, Fitzgerald extracted from his glimpses of reality a more human legend, strengthening the sinews of his narrative with concretions and distortions of a clearly symbolic nature. One might even speak of expressionism, but it would be better to say that Fitzgerald followed the traditional pattern of American fiction, which finds in the balanced fusion of realism and symbolism the typical mark of its identity. Nothing that serves to characterize the Hollywood milieu and the figure of Stahr is neglected in *The Last Tycoon.* In this manner, we are given a representation of life and even a *tranche de vie.* The symbolic method, however, comes in to modify and distort the picture, enlarging and enhancing its representational significance. The initial flight from East to West is clearly symbolical—both of Stahr's leadership and of his final descent "into the warm darkness." The emergency landing shows that Stahr will have to face a more painful descent: like Alice in the rabbit hole, Stahr will sink into the ambiguities of his soul and see the Gorgon-like reflection of human experience. Isolated in the bridal suite or in the pilot's cabin, he will also be isolated in his life. Schwartz and Wylie—Cecilia herself—find that the gates of the Hermitage are closed, and Stahr will wander in a deserted Washington. The story is set in motion by the gushing forth of volcanic water: the earthquake and the flood, as the author says, set Stahr in front of his destiny and they "seem to release something in him." The unfinished seaside house recalls the movie set ("odd effect of the place like a set," we find in the notes), and it is clearly an indication of Stahr's unstable equilibrium. It is impossible for him to hear the President in that house—he can only hear the grotesque gibberish of a monkey. Against the idyllic background of the beach at night, the Negro who is waiting for the grunion and is in communion with nature refuses to give credit to the tycoon's activities. "The dam breaks" in the sixth chapter, and the beginning of the downfall is subtly represented by the symbolic battle with pingpong balls, among which Stahr ironically falls in the end. The detail seems ordinary and banal, but the turning point of the action revolves around this objective correlative of Stahr's final collapse.

The action was to end with the fatal return of the plane to New York, interrupted before its arrival there. The thematic correspondence with the beginning is evident, and it is just as clear that Fitzgerald wanted to convey the idea that Stahr was surrendering himself to the world of the East. In fact, if we bear in mind all these details, it becomes clear that in *The Last Tycoon,* as in *Gatsby,* the symbolic conflict is once more between the two moral and geographical poles of East and West. Brady, Stahr's antagonist, is basically linked with the world of the East, with the world of money and ruthless business, the world of Wall Street and competitive acquisition, of brutal and corrupt force. Stahr, on the other hand, tries to give life to his creation—which permits at times the flowering of art, humanity, and idealism—in the West. In this case, the West is not ruined by its contact with the East, but the East pushes its tentacles toward and into the West, crack-

ing and corrupting it from the inside. Stahr ends by accepting it as a component of his world and of his life. If he is thrilled by the lights of Los Angeles when he flies back to Hollywood at the beginning, he will find the Eastern corruption flourishing there, and he will have to surrender to its overwhelming pressure. Between East and West—in Nashville, Tennessee, or Washington, D.C.—are the traditional and genuine virtues of the country. But here the doors are closed; there is no communion with the men and women who have been tainted by the Eastern corruption.

Within this symbolical frame of reference, the "artist" finds that his own creation has turned against him and that the "test" of society has forced him to a moral compromise and eventually to defeat. It has brought to the surface the less noble aspects of his characters and has directed its attack against the tycoon in a subtle way—by making him instrumental in his own ruin. The "merchant" wins an easy battle, and Wall Street denies the potential flowering of a civilization that might have stood against its commercial predominance. And all this Fitzgerald recorded with an "unshakable moral attitude towards the world we live in and towards its temporary standards, that is the basic essential of any powerful work of the imagination," if we want to use again the words of John Dos Passos. There is perhaps some exaggeration in this statement, but it really seems that here Fitzgerald was attaining that "wise and tragic sense of life" which he proclaimed to be the ultimate achievement of the writer. Henry James had stressed "the perfect dependence of the 'moral' sense of a work of art on the amount of felt life concerned in producing it." In *The Last Tycoon* the amount of felt life concerned in producing the novel is such that its aesthetic significance coincides with the apprehension of a specific "moral" sense. It is an advance over *Tender Is the Night* and *The Great Gatsby* as well, and all the more so as the extensive analysis gives way here to a rapid and vivid foreshortening, and the elegiac tone of the "tragic pastoral" is substituted by an intense urgency of feeling and emotion. The style of this novel vibrates with immediate intensity, is compressed and, as it were, contracted, so that the magic suggestiveness of *Gatsby* and the analytic fullness of *Tender Is the Night* are left along the way. Although starting from the same thematic awareness of the two previous novels, *The Last Tycoon* aims at a typical form of modern essentiality both in its technique and in its diction.

In its structure, *The Last Tycoon* is basically in line with *The Great Gatsby,* but in its texture (if we want to adopt John Crowe Ransom's distinction) it is considerably different. Fitzgerald stated that "if one book could ever be 'like' another, I should say that it [*The Last Tycoon*] is more 'like' *The Great Gatsby* than any other of my books," and he had stressed the fact that his new novel was "as detached from *him* as *Gatsby* was, in intent, anyhow." But he also wrote to Edmund Wilson that he had written it with great difficulty and that it was "completely upstream in mood." These statements are a good starting point to determine to what extent *The Last Tycoon* is both similar to and different from the earlier novel.

> **While remaining true to himself, to his inner motives, and to his fictional "tradition," Fitzgerald was able to start (if not to accomplish, owing to his early death) a clear revolution in his narrative. He left us with a premature and unexpected gift of his rising artistic ability.**
>
> — *Sergio Perosa*

The detachment of vision is achieved through the use of a narrator. But Cecilia is more involved in the action than Nick Carraway, and she is even responsible for the turning point of the story—when she tells her father of Stahr's secret affair with Kathleen. Of course, Cecilia's main role is to give the story a center of interest, in the Jamesian sense, and a unity of structure. As in the case of *The Great Gatsby,* the "greatness" of the protagonist is emphasized here by the sympathy and the love of the narrator, and it is thanks to her emotional reactions that Stahr attains an almost fabulous dimension as a character. Cecilia writes down with impartiality (and therefore with some kind of objectivity) the main events of the story, but she also colors them with the warmth of her intense participation, going so far as to interpret the facts and to convey to the reader their moral significance. Moreover, with her gift of imagining the events at which she has not been present, she can register those details that are meaningful and symbolic in the story and emphasize in this way the symbolic aspect of her realistic tale. "By making . . . Cecilia an intelligent and observant woman"—Fitzgerald had written—"I shall grant myself the privilege, as Conrad did, of letting her imagine the actions of the characters. Thus, I hope to get the verisimilitude of the first person narrative, combined with a Godlike knowledge of all events that happen to my characters." This compromise, far from breaking the unity of the limited point of view, allows the "omniscient" narrator to give a personal and subjective twist to the story. Cecilia can record the events at which she has not been present with the objectivity of a reporter (especially in Chapters III, IV, and V), but when she takes part in the action (notably in Chapters I, II, and in some episodes of Chapters V and VI) her report becomes less documentary; it is full of passion and participation and vibrates with undisguised emotion. Thus, Cecilia introduces us to Stahr and reveals the baseness of her father, and it is quite natural that she should bring Brimmer and Stahr together in their confrontation. But when she is not in the foreground, she gives a chronicle of Stahr's working day with dramatic precision and absolute detachment, and this fictional device of her alternating absence and presence makes it possible for the book to shift from a purely realistic notation of the events to an intensely emotional presentation of the story.

With her good *ficelles* (a device clearly derived from James), Cecilia, like Nick in *Gatsby,* breaks down the action into dramatic scenes, and if she gathers information from Wylie, Robinson, and Prince Agge, she knows very well when and where to introduce it. But it is at this point that the method used in *Gatsby* becomes "upstream in mood," more and more distorted in order to emphasize the symbolic possibilities. Having learned a lesson from the negative example of a certain heaviness in *Tender Is the Night,* where the predominance of the analytic method had compromised the natural development of the action and excluded the necessary relief of the dialogues, in *The Last Tycoon* Fitzgerald had decided to resolve the characterization *exclusively* in the action and to stress the *essential* nucleus of each incident, to the extent of depending almost completely on the dramatic intensity of the dialogues. In his notes there are clear indications of the method that he proposed to follow, and this method is adopted in the parts of the novel that he was able to write. "This chapter must not develop into merely a piece of character analysis. Each statement that I make about him [Stahr] must contain at the end of every few hundred words some pointed anecdote or story to keep it alive . . . I want it to have . . . drama throughout." In characterizing Stahr he followed this method precisely, and to characterize Brady and Brimmer he used two highly dramatic incidents: Cecilia's discovery of her father with the nude secretary in the closet, and Brimmer's fight with Stahr. Kathleen is gradually developed as a character through her successive meetings with the tycoon, and only through their dialogues do we catch a glimpse of Wylie's and Robinson's characters. The action never slows down or stops to allow a reconsideration of the events, as in *Gatsby.* And if we want to resort once more to James's concept of the relationship between character and incident, we should say that here every possible consideration is given to the incident and that the character is subservient to it in the highest degree. In *The Great Gatsby* these two theoretical terms of reference had been balanced in the rendering; here the scales are weighed in favor of the dramatic incident, which, furthermore, is represented only in its intense *final* moment and is compressed by an extreme form of foreshortening.

The reader finds himself confronted with an incident when it is usually turning to its conclusion, and he must go back from that point to the antecedents of the situation, reconstruct its premises, imagine its slow preparation and its gradual development. The author gives the impression that he has no time or willingness to give us the facts in their unfolding, that he is too pressed by the urgency of the events, and that he can only give us the conclusion, the significant result of the facts. He seems to compress the full purport of any incident into the last few acts or words of the characters. In contrast to *The Great Gatsby,* it is not the connotative suggestion that indicates the meaning of each single moment of the story, but rather a violent illumination at the very end of each significant moment that sends us back to reconsider the possible purport of the episode. The narration moves in a rapid and impetuous way, with the bouncing momentum of a cataract, not with the full ease of an abundant stream or the precision of a narrow brook. At each bounce, one might say, the previous stretch is gathered in a single knot of meaningful suggestions, which must be unraveled backward at great speed so as to be prepared for the next. This is why the story is really upstream in mood and in movement. Each dramatic incident, at the very moment when it has given a new turn to the action, must be explained and as it were completed by a consideration of what has made it possible, of what has determined it, of what has in fact prepared it.

The ideal of essentiality, that is, is pursued in two ways. *The Last Tycoon* contains only those episodes which are strictly functional to a consequent development of the plot, have a definite thematic meaning, and give impulse to the action; in the compass of the single episodes only the culminating moment is represented in a dramatic way, to the exclusion of both the beginning and the outcome. For this double reason (and the role of Cecilia is of only secondary importance here) the story is really reduced to its essentials and moves with sudden leaps and daring elliptical transitions, without any continuity in the narrative pattern. The action proceeds from one intense nucleus to another, from one meaningful point to another, and these points are really flashes of intuition which throw light only on the essential part of each incident until the subject matter is reduced to its barest essence. The action develops at a speedy and breathless pace: the plane stops in Nashville and is soon off again, and there has already been a suicide; in Hollywood there is an earthquake. Stahr rushes from one activity to another without intermission. When he finally meets Kathleen "he remains breathless," and after four convulsive trips to and from the beach there is the sudden blow of Kathleen's marriage, and immediately after the fight with Brimmer. . . . The staccato (no longer the fading away) is almost compulsory here, and the same technical principle of an extreme form of staccato operates within the economy of the single scenes.

One single example should be sufficient to illustrate the point. When he put down some notes for the episode of the airplane crash, Fitzgerald made it clear that the episode should be as much as possible represented in a foreshortened and compressed way. "Consider carefully"—he had written—"whether if possible by some technical trick it might not be advisable to conceal from the reader that the plane fell until the moment when the children find it . . . the dramatic effect . . . might be more effective if he did not find at the beginning of the chapter that the plane fell." Far from "describing the fall of the plane," he wanted to hint at this crucial point only in a passing paragraph which was to be as "evasive" as possible, in order to move on immediately to the effect of the crash, to its consequences—that is to say to the situation of the three children who pick up the "moral heritage" of the people killed in the crash. If the whole passage is analyzed, it will become clear that we are confronted with the extreme development of a fictional technique which aims at the maximum degree of dramatic concision, even to the point of neglecting the gradual unfolding of the episodes. These episodes are not described or represented in the usual sense of the word—they are compressed in sudden and unexpected flashes which compel the reader to move backward in order to understand the "upstream mood" of the narration.

Most, if not all, of the episodes in the book are dealt with in the same manner, and the book as a whole is construct-

ed on the same principle, since Stahr is presented only at the crucial point of his long career. Kathleen makes up her story through a disconnected series of hints and suggestions, Brady is characterized in a single incident, and the other characters appear only to point out the significant changes of the story. Cecilia herself is present only at crucial points. A particular kind of foreshortening and a restricted angle of vision allow the writer to illuminate with flashes only a few dramatic scenes, which consequently acquire an unforgettable relief and cannot be dealt with in a descriptive way. There are no shades or hues of color in the canvas—only a heightened quality of chiaroscuro and a hallucinatory reflection of violent flashes of light. This is the exact contrary of a "rounded-off" narration, and the foreshortening is here much more drastic than it was in *Gatsby*. In that novel the dramatic scenes were suspended at times to allow for reconsiderations or elegiac intermissions. Here everything is dramatic—the general framework, the single scenes, and whatever portions of the single scenes Fitzgerald chose to represent in his urgency to get at the core of each significant moment. Such is the concision and the essentiality of the actions which *are* represented, that the diction itself is influenced by this urgency to the extent of being reduced to the bareness of an outline of a film script.

After all, we are in the world and in the atmosphere of the movies. Though the incompleteness of the novel might partly account for a certain rapidity of statement and the quick transitions from one episode to another, we must still recognize the mark of inner development in the use of this highly concise form of diction. The language is here constantly breaking into dialogue, and if we bear in mind that a similar phenomenon was recognizable in Fitzgerald's latest stories, it becomes clear that we are confronted with a real stylistic development. If the structure of the novel is reduced to essentials, so is the texture; and this is a new departure, unfortunately broken off at its inception, in Fitzgerald's fiction. If the single scenes or incidents are not represented in their gradual unfolding, but rather compressed into significant moments and sudden flashes, in the same way the sentences are compressed and reduced to simple statements. They follow one another in quick succession and find their natural measure in the broken rhythm of the dialogue. In *The Last Tycoon* the language seems to avoid any syntactical subordination and is entirely dependent for its effectiveness on the simplicity of the direct statement, which is immediately ended by a period. Adjectives and adverbs are seldom used in a context of isolated and barren enunciations, whose main purport is conveyed to the reader by the kinetic force of the verbs. "About *adjectives:* all fine prose is based on the verbs carrying the sentences. They make sentences move," Fitzgerald had written, taking his cue from a line of Keats. And in *The Last Tycoon* he adhered to this principle and to this ideal, because he wanted his sentences to move as quickly as possible and to be carried forward at a quickened pace by the urgency of the verbs. In this way, too, he developed a staccato form of diction, a clear-cut simplicity of sentences, avoiding the harmonious fullness of the paragraph or the soft musicality of the evocation.

Converging into the mainstream of twentieth-century literature, like Eliot and Pound, Sherwood Anderson and Hemingway, Montale and Valéry, to name only a few, Fitzgerald found and asserted in his desire for a bare language the sense of his modernity. Like Yeats and Juan Ramon Jiménez he came to realize that "there's more enterprise / In walking naked," in renouncing the ideal of an adorned style and accepting the bare facts of what Jiménez had called *"poesìa nuda."* In his own field and in his own way, he had eventually achieved this ideal: the language that he perfected in **The Last Tycoon** justifies a reconsideration of Fitzgerald on the level of twentieth-century adherence to the common yearning of poetry and fiction toward the concrete, the concise, and the essential. It is sufficient to give a single example, chosen from a number of passages that would equally bear out the point, because it deals with the subject—a love embrace—on which the author had previously exercised his skill in a different way. Stahr and Kathleen have gone back for the second time to the house on the beach:

> Immediately she spoke to him coarsely and provocatively, and pulled his face down to hers. Then, with her knees she struggled out of something, still standing up and holding him with one arm, and kicked it off beside the coat. He was not trembling now and he held her again, as they knelt down together and slid to the raincoat on the floor.

The urgency of their emotions transfers itself to the action and is reflected in the broken movement of the sentences. Everything in this passage seems to be in motion and the sense of movement is emphasized by Fitzgerald's insistence on the verbs (. . . *spoke . . . pulled . . . struggled . . . holding . . . kicked . . . trembling . . . held . . . knelt . . . slid . . .*). There are a few nouns in the context (five in all) and no adjectives to slow down or qualify the kinetic rhythm; there are three adverbs which define not the situation but the action (*immediately . . . coarsely . . . provocatively*) and the personal pronouns (which in English are actually *part* of the verb in the sense that they absorb the function of the lost terminations, but would not be necessary in some other languages). For the rest, the passage is completely dependent on the urge of the verbs, most of which are renderd still more effective and urgent by the prepositions or verbal adverbs that follow (*to him . . . down to hers . . . out of something . . . standing up . . . kicked it off. .. knelt down . . . to the floor*). In this case Fitzgerald was really able to express "the stress and passion at the core of each convincing moment" with the utmost bareness of language and diction. If there is poetry in this scene, in which Fitzgerald gave us for the first time a dramatic presentation of physical love, it is poetry achieved and expressed through the immediacy of the simple statement. The same is true of other episodes, and in particular of the episode in which Stahr is hit by Brimmer:

> Then Stahr came close, his hands going up. It seemed to me that Brimmer held him off with his left arm a minute, and then I looked away—I couldn't bear to watch.

When I looked back, Stahr was out of sight

below the level of the table, and Brimmer was looking down at him.

"Please go home," I said to Brimmer.

"All right." He stood looking down at Stahr as I came around the table.

"I always wanted to hit ten million dollars, but I didn't know it would be like this."

Stahr lay motionless.

"Please go," I said.

"I'm sorry. Can I help—"

"No. Please go. I understand."

The "stress and passion" of this episode are expressed in a series of brief notations of heightened intensity, with a bare and feverish language, elliptical in the extreme, that aims at conveying the effect of the action, not at describing it. The few notations are sufficient to give the sense of what has happened even if Cecilia "cannot bear to watch"; the effectiveness of this kind of language, to express it in linguistic terms, is dependent on the prevalence of the morphemes—the words that express relationships, the verbs of action, the dialogue reduced to stichomythia—over the other linguistic functions.

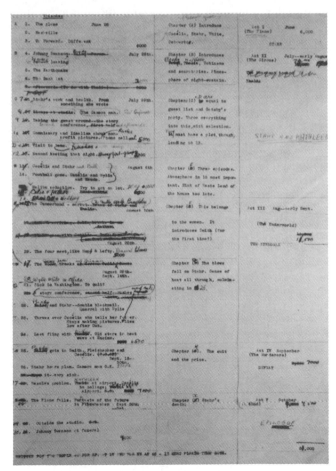

Fitzgerald's revised fourth outline-plan for The Last Tycoon.

One is tempted to see here a direct influence of Hemingway's style, and a certain similarity of manner is unquestionable. In an independent way, according to his own sensitivities, Fitzgerald recreated certain stylistic features typical of Hemingway's style: the hardness and precision of diction, the taste for the essential and the concrete, the predominance of the dialogue, the directness of statement, a refinement of language disguised as simplicity. One is reminded here of "Up in Michigan," among the *First Forty-Nine Stories,* or of the dialogue in *The Sun Also Rises* or, better still, of *To Have and Have Not* (1937), a novel that Fitzgerald seemed particularly to admire. In this novel Hemingway's imagination had been engaged in the realistic rendering of a situation that presupposed a definite framework of social and economic relationships. The story was concerned with the struggle of an individualist against the "organized worlds" of the leisure class and the gangsters, and his inevitable defeat had been represented in a rapid sequence of dramatic scenes, according to the principle of a violent compression (and even distortion) of foreshortened episodes. Even there the language, clear-cut and concise, elliptical and allusive, was based essentially on the verbs of action and reduced to the measure of the direct statement. Hemingway, of course, had something else in mind and was "tougher" than Fitzgerald would ever become in his general outlook on life and in his style, both of which if closely analyzed, reveal profound differences from Fitzgerald's. For our purposes it is sufficient to mention a momentary convergence, to indicate how Fitzgerald was nearing, if not actually meeting, a form of diction which might have had much in common with Hemingway's. It would be an idle speculation to carry the investigation too far, but even this assumption can give us an idea of the direction in which Fitzgerald seemed to be naturally evolving. The ultimate result might have been, quite logically, a kind of conscious expressionism: the potentialities are evident in *The Last Tycoon.*

While remaining true to himself, to his inner motives, and to his fictional "tradition," Fitzgerald was able to start (if not to accomplish, owing to his early death) a clear revolution in his narrative. He left us with a premature and unexpected gift of his rising artistic vitality. When it was published, *The Last Tycoon* was hailed as a little miracle. It was in fact an achievement and a personal conquest, linked with the past experiences of the author and yet open to new forms of artistic development. It finds its place next to *The Great Gatsby* and *Tender Is the Night* for the maturity of its conception and the intensity of its form. Together with *The Crack-up* and the last stories, these three novels must be seen as his lasting contribution to twentieth-century fiction. In the convulsed pages of *The Last Tycoon* there is a single, bizarre poetic quotation, taken from Gautier's *Emaux et camées.* We are no longer confronted with the "mysterious" (and in fact quite familiar) Thomas Parke D'Invilliers, or with the bitter irony of Anthony Patch, or with a recognizable allusion to Keats. We are confronted with a clear statement of the ideal that had inspired both Pound and Eliot—the ideal of a hard and "robust" type of artistic achievement:

> Tout passe. —L'art robuste
> Seul a l'éternité.

Fitzgerald's fiction seems in retrospect to be much more robust than we were (or still are) inclined to believe. Life is short—as James had complained with Chaucer and Horace—and Art is long; and it is always risky to speak of "eternity." In a world of relative values, however, only a lack of love or a deeply rooted prejudice can regard as of secondary value an artistic achievement that possesses all the marks of genuine identity and that can remain so fruitful for so long.

Sergio Perosa, in his The Art of F. Scott Fitzgerald, *translated by Charles Matz and Sergio Perosa, The University of Michigan Press, 1965, 239 p.*

Henry Dan Piper   (essay date 1965)

[*Piper is an American educator and critic. In the following excerpt, he discusses the development and characterization of Monroe Stahr, the protagonist of* The Last Tycoon.]

When, in the fall of 1936, Fitzgerald learned of [Irving] Thalberg's death, his first emotion had been one of relief. "Thalberg's final collapse," he wrote a friend, "is the death of an enemy for me, though I liked the guy enormously. . . . I think . . . that he killed the idea of either Hopkins or Frederick March doing *Tender Is the Night.*" But whatever resentment he had felt toward Thalberg living soon evaporated after he had spent eighteen months on the M-G-M lot that no longer had Thalberg to guide its destiny. For, as Crowther documents again and again in his history of Metro-Goldwyn-Mayer, neither M-G-M nor the industry at large was able to find a successor to fill his place. Thalberg's death marked the ultimate triumph of the commercialism that for so many years he had successfully held at bay. The battle between the idealists still loyal to Thalberg and the cohorts of the New York financiers was still raging on the M-G-M lot when Fitzgerald arrived a year later. But the end was already in sight. It was this epic conflict, symbolized by the heroic figure of the dead producer, that Fitzgerald intended to portray in the most ambitious of all his books, *The Last Tycoon.*

The earliest evidence that Fitzgerald had been thinking of writing a new novel occurs in a letter to [Maxwell Perkins of Charles Scribner's Sons] dated October 16, 1936, in which he said he had one "planned, or rather I should say conceived," that would make a book "certainly as long as *Tender Is the Night*" and would take at least two years to write. He was too broke at the moment even to think of starting work on it, however. "I certainly have this one more novel [in me]," he wrote, "but it may have to remain among the unwritten books of this world."

Since this letter was written soon after news reached him about Thalberg's death, one wonders if the book he mentions was to have been based on Thalberg's career. The first mention of *The Last Tycoon* does not occur until December, 1938, over two years later, again in a letter to Max Perkins. By then, according to Sheilah Graham, Fitzgerald had already accumulated a large collection of notes for his novel, though he had not yet begun to write it. Knowing what we do about Fitzgerald's methods of working, it seems quite possible that the idea for *The Last Tycoon* had been taking shape gradually in Fitzgerald's mind for several years.

As part of his preliminary planning during 1937 and 1938, he not only took copious notes about the more technical aspects of M-G-M's complex operations, but he read everything that he could lay his hands on relating to Thalberg, including an excellent article on the M-G-M organization that had been published in a 1933 issue of *Fortune,* as well as an article on movie making written by Thalberg himself and published in *The Saturday Evening Post* that same year. "Thalberg has always fascinated me," Fitzgerald wrote Kenneth Littauer in 1939, in a letter outlining his plans for *The Last Tycoon:*

> His peculiar charm, his extraordinary good looks, his bountiful success, the tragic end of his great adventure. The events I have built around him are fiction, but all of them are things which might very well have happened, and I am pretty sure that I saw deep enough into the character of the man so that his reactions are authentically what they would have been in life. So much so that he may be recognized—but it will be also recognized that *no single fact is actually true.* . . . This is a novel not even faintly of the propaganda type. Indeed Thalberg's opinions were entirely different from mine in many respects that I will not go into. I've long chosen him for a hero (this has been in my mind for three years) because he is one of the half-dozen men I have known who were built on the grand scale. . . . Certainly if Ziegfeld could be made into an epic figure, then what about Thalberg who was literally everything that Ziegfeld wasn't?

Among Fitzgerald's notes was the draft of a letter he intended to send his good friend Norma Shearer when *The Last Tycoon* was finished, asking her permission to make use of some of the incidents from her husband's life. Although he had not known Thalberg well, Fitzgerald wrote, the impression he had made had been "very dazzling." And Monroe Stahr, the hero of his novel, had been inspired primarily by that impression, "though I have put in some things drawn from other men, and, inevitably, much of myself. I invented a tragic story and Irving's life was, of course, not tragic except his struggle against ill-health because no one has ever written a tragedy about Hollywood. *A Star is Born* was a pathetic and often beautiful story, but not a tragedy and doomed and heroic things do happen here."

But, although Fitzgerald saw the heroic aspects of Thalberg's career, he did not intend to gloss over Monroe Stahr's very real limitations as a human being. Stahr shares Thalberg's hypochondria, his ruthlessness and his impatience with mediocrity, his inability to relax, and his rather middle-class artistic taste. "Stahr left certain harm behind him just as he left good behind him," Fitzgerald reminded himself in one of his many notes.

Primarily, it was Thalberg's superb managerial abilities that held Fitzgerald's fascinated attention: Thalberg—the head of a huge collaborative enterprise; the artful juggler of budgets, casting lists, shooting schedules; the skilled su-

pervisor of unit producers, directors, assistant directors, actors, cameramen, cutters, script writers, and craftsmen and technicians of every kind. Where was there a more striking illustration of the union of native managerial talent and modern mass-production techniques for the production of a unique work of art? From boyhood, Fitzgerald had always admired successful executives, from tycoons like James J. Hill and Grandfather McQuillan, and the politicos on the Princeton campus, to talented social impresarios and party-givers like Gerald Murphy.

It was not mere managerial talent alone that he admired, but the ability to use that talent in the creation of something of genuine aesthetic value—a magnanimous gesture, a heroic image, one of the Murphy's memorable Riviera parties, a colorful Broadway show, or a first-rate motion picture. Back in 1926, Fitzgerald had unsuccessfully tried to persuade Ring Lardner to write "the real history of an American [theatrical] manager—say Ziegfeld." But after he became acquainted with Thalberg, Ziegfeld's achievements paled by comparison.

Thus, it was important that Monroe Stahr's executive capabilities should be firmly established from the very beginning of the novel. In one of his notes for an episode in the first chapter, Fitzgerald said:

> This will be based on a conversation that I had with Thalberg the first time I was alone with him in 1927, the day that he said a thing about railroads. As near as I can remember what he said was this:
>
> We sat in the old commissary at Metro and he said, "Scottie, supposing here's got to be a road through a mountain and . . . there seem to be a half dozen possible roads . . . each one of which, so far as you can determine, is as good as the other. Now suppose you happen to be the top man, there's a point where you don't exercise the faculty of judgment in the ordinary way, but simply the faculty of arbitrary decision. You say, 'Well, I think we will put the road there,' and you trace it with your finger and you know in your secret heart, and no one else knows, that you have no reason for putting the road there rather than in several other different courses, but you're the only person that knows that you don't know why you're doing it and you've got to stick to that and you've got to pretend that you know and that you did it for specific reasons, even though you're utterly assailed by doubts at times as to the wisdom of your decision, because all these other possible decisions keep echoing in your ear. But when you're planning a new enterprise on a grand scale, the people under you mustn't ever know or guess that you're in doubt, because they've all got to have something to look up to and they mustn't ever dream that you're in doubt about any decision. These things keep occuring."
>
> At that point, some other people came into the commissary and sat down, and the first thing I knew there was a group of four and the intimacy of the conversation was broken, but I was very much impressed by the shrewdness of what he said—something more than shrewdness—by the

largeness of what he thought and how he reached it by the age of twenty-six, which he was then.

Gradually, as Monroe Stahr's image took shape in Fitzgerald's imagination, his resemblance to the historical Thalberg decreased, and he assumed a personality that was both more individualized and more representative. Fitzgerald began to think of him as embodying the virtues of the ideal executive, much as he had once conceived of Dick Diver as possessing heroic qualities of social leadership and charm. Turning from the facts of Thalberg's career, Fitzgerald investigated afresh the lives of several other well-known political and military leaders from the past. He read Philip Guedalla's biography of the Duke of Wellington, as well as A.H. Burne's study of three Civil War generals, *Lee, Grant and Sherman,* and J.A. Froude's *Julius Caesar.* In the last of these, the Victorian Froude portrayed the noblest Roman of them all as a nineteenth-century English liberal who fought in the name of the people against a corrupt, tyrannical, aristocratic senate that eventually betrayed and murdered him. Froude's Caesar was a skillful leader of men who possessed great executive abilities, and who, because of his insight into human nature, was able to direct the most diverse talents, welding them into a loyal, purposeful organization. Undoubtedly this interpretation of Caesar had a discernible influence on Fitzgerald's conception of Stahr. John O'Hara, visiting his old friend for the last time not long before Fitzgerald's death, was somewhat nonplused to find Fitzgerald constantly steering the conversation back to the exploits of Julius Caesar. He was further disconcerted when, at his departure, Fitzgerald insisted on lending him his old battered copy of Froude's book, so that O'Hara could read up on the subject.

Besides Stahr's affinities with Caesar, Fitzgerald also planned to emphasize certain parallels between his hero and two potent American political executives: Abraham Lincoln and Andrew Jackson. Jackson was intended to illustrate the ruthless, autocratic elements in Stahr's personality. Old Hickory was the first strong American president, and Stahr was a general waging war on a dozen fronts at once—against lazy subordinates, jealous associates, penny-pinching financiers, power-hungry labor unions. In his single-minded struggle to maintain independent authority over his organization, Stahr—like any other general—found it necessary at times to permit himself a minor moral infraction for the sake of a larger good. Stahr's ruthlessness in this respect is brought out at the beginning of the story by his attitude toward Manny Schwartz, the worn-out producer whom he brutally snubs because he has lost his usefulness. Significantly, Schwartz soon afterwards commits suicide on the steps of "The Hermitage," Andrew Jackson's homestead near Nashville. But even Manny Schwartz perceives Stahr's heroic qualities. Before he kills himself he takes the trouble to send Stahr a message warning him of his many enemies, and praising him as "the best of them all."

Further on in the novel, Fitzgerald planned to bring out Stahr's affinities with the somewhat different, and more compassionate, figure of Abraham Lincoln. Stahr was also to be an expert political strategist, an artist in human rela-tionships. Instead of removing his enemies, for instance, Stahr follows Lincoln's practice and keeps them where he can watch what they are doing. Like Lincoln, he knows how to use the element of play as a means of getting things done. At one stage in Fitzgerald's planning, he intended to have Stahr meet his death in front of the capitol in Washington. When Fitzgerald himself died, he was still not certain how he was going to work out the full implications of the Lincoln-Jackson association that he had so far indicated only in crude terms.

Fitzgerald also went out of his way to make Monroe Stahr's origins more lowly and impoverished than Thalberg's had been, in order to link his hero more firmly with the Lincolnesque myth of rags-to-riches success that he had already examined in *The Great Gatsby.* Here it is significant to recall that practically all of the manuscript of *The Last Tycoon* was written after the outbreak of the European War in September, 1939, and that Fitzgerald's beloved France and her allies were fighting for a cause Fitzgerald believed to be America's and his own. Back in 1928, in a newspaper interview foreseeing that crisis, he said that the nation's survival lay "in the birth of a hero who will be of age when America's testing comes." Such a leader, he believed, would probably emerge "out of the immigrant class in the guise of an East Side newsboy." Stahr, the poor tailor's son from the Bronx, derives from that Horatio Alger myth of success in which Fitzgerald still firmly believed.

But just as Monroe Stahr is a more complex and tragic symbol of that myth than the pathetic Gatsby had been, so Fitzgerald's view of his native country had changed drastically from that which he recorded in *The Great Gatsby* in the early 1920's. After the disillusioning expatriate years abroad, Fitzgerald no longer believed the United States to be that corrupted earthly paradise whose lost innocence he had hymned in the final sentences of *The Great Gatsby.* Instead, as the war clouds gathered, he saw both Stahr and the nation he represented as symbolizing the best values of the West. In one of the random notes lying between the pages of his *Last Tycoon* manuscript he said:

> I look out at it and I think it is the most beautiful history in the world. It is the history of me and my people. And if I came here yesterday like Sheilah I should still think so. It is the history of all aspiration—not just the American dream but the human dream and if I came at the end of it that too is a place in the line of pioneers.

Stahr was intended to exemplify the ideal qualities of the successful American business executive. His business is that of applying native production-line techniques to the mass production of unique works of art, at the rate of one each week. He is *par excellence* that most indigenous of all our achievements, the American business manager. The nature and extent of his managerial talents are best seen in Chapters II and III, in which we are shown one of Stahr's typical business days. Both chapters deserve thoughtful study by any aspiring junior executive. Here we see Stahr confronting and solving one major problem in human relations after another; tactfully but effectively removing a director who has failed to manage his movie crew; reviving the jaded spirits of a team of script writers; persuading a group of hard-nosed New York financiers that the artistic prestige to be gained from an unconventional film will more than make up for its probable financial losses; smoothing the jangled nerves of a spoiled, neurotic actress who, for better or worse, is still a valuable piece of studio property that must be kept in condition; restoring the shattered self-confidence of a cameraman whose services are irreplaceable; winning the confidence of a high-priced British novelist, who cannot get through his head just what picture making is all about.

Stahr's success in this role is due to two particular gifts—his articulateness, and the interest in people as individuals that allows him, despite his own aesthetic limitations, to work effectively with creative artists. Both are superbly brought out in one of the best scenes in the book in which Stahr explains to George Boxley, the British novelist, how movie making differs from other kinds of creative activity. Stahr does so merely by telling Boxley a story consisting of a series of dramatic actions. When Boxley's interest is inevitably aroused, Stahr suddenly stops, and reminds him that all he had been doing is "making pictures." Not only has Stahr made his point, but Fitzgerald has demonstrated his hero's genius for communicating with temperaments radically different from his own. The episode itself consists entirely of dialogue and images, and reads so smoothly that it seems to be nothing more than a literal transcription of something Fitzgerald had once observed. But it is more than this. Although some of the inspiration came from a conference that he had once witnessed at which Aldous Huxley was present, Fitzgerald also built the episode from his memories of many other such conferences, all of them carefully reported in his notebooks. As an author, Fitzgerald resented the script writer's menial position in the studio as vehemently as George Boxley did. But he did not let this resentment color his treatment of Monroe Stahr's very different view of the script writer's responsibilities. And, at the end, Boxley is brought around to a grudging admiration of Stahr's managerial genius. Stahr also is an artist, Boxley acknowledges, but he

> was an artist only, as Mr. Lincoln was a general, perforce and as a layman. . . . He had been reading Lord Charnwood and he recognized that Stahr like Lincoln was a leader carrying on a long war on many fronts; almost single-handed he had moved pictures sharply forward through a decade . . .

So far, the significance of Fitzgerald's portrait of Stahr as a heroic businessman has been overlooked by *The Last Tycoon*'s admirers. Yet Monroe Stahr is one of the best renderings we have had in our literature of that most typical of all American figures. Traditionally, the businessman in literature has been portrayed almost solely as the object of scorn and ridicule. From Trimalchio and Pantaloon, Volpone and Monsieur Jourdain, Bouvard and Pécuchet, to Père Grandet, and the Buddenbrooks and Forsytes, the business mentality has almost never been regarded as admirable. Even in the United States, that most businesslike of civilizations, the businessman has been portrayed more often as a Babbitt than a man of creative talent. Professor E. E. Cassady, after an exhaustive study of the dozens of American novels dealing with the subject, notes that the businessman has never been presented in our literature as "a large-minded, generous, disinterested, heroic character."

Henry James, with his characteristic insight, recognized the businessman as our civilization's most representative figure. But, lacking any practical contact with business itself, James was forced to admit (after several unsuccessful attempts to portray him in his fiction) that "before the American businessman I was absolutely and irremediably helpless." In more recent years, many other writers—Frank Norris, Theodore Dreiser, Edith Wharton, Sinclair Lewis, among them—have tried to come to terms with him in their work. But even they were content, for the most part, to describe him outside business hours. We see the businessman boring his wife, ruining his children's lives, stumbling on the social ladder. But we rarely see him in the office where whatever ability and imagination he possesses would be most tellingly demonstrated. What sets *The Last Tycoon* apart from other novels about the businessman (with the exception, perhaps, of Howells' *The Rise of Silas Lapham*) is that Fitzgerald conceived of Monroe Stahr as a doomed and heroic figure whose heroism and whose doom were both the consequences of his success as a man of business. Stahr, in short, is the self-made man whose destruction is brought about by the business organization that his talents and imagination have created. His studio has become so large and complex that he can no longer control its destiny. Instead, he is caught between the divisive forces that are fighting for domination. On the one hand there are the New York financiers and theater owners who provide the capital for Stahr's films. Interested only in profits, they see motion pictures solely as commodities to be made as cheaply and sold as dearly as possible. In the novel, forces representing these interests are scheming to replace Stahr by his more subservient and less competent rival, Pat Brady.

On the other hand, Stahr finds himself confronted by the ever growing threat of the labor unions. Here the danger is that his own artists will collectively force him to abandon the artistic standards he has hitherto defended against such odds. As a producer, Stahr knows that no picture can be better artistically than the director. Therefore the director must command absolute loyalty from his subordinates. This is the price for a first-rate product in any collaborative enterprise. Stahr insists on his sole right to dictate the artistic standards for the studio, but in exchange he shares his success generously with his artists.

But all this, he fears, is threatened by the growing power of the labor unions. They will insist on substituting watered-down, abstract, professional standards of competency for those that Stahr has created by himself. Moreover, the unions will divert his workers' attention from quality films to extraneous political, social, and economic considerations. This is implied by the figure of Brimmer, the Communist labor organizer who appears briefly in Chapter VI. The one thing both the unions and the New York moneymen share is their suspicion of Stahr's preoccupation with the artistic considerations of his job. This is a mystery neither is able to comprehend. Yet Stahr's battle is a hopeless one. In the past, he has been able to command his employees' loyalties by his personal friendship, but now the studio has become too large. Inevitably, his artists are beginning to look to one another for that respect and understanding they once received from Stahr. Ill, tired out by years of hard work, he no longer has the energy to resist the opposing forces closing in on him.

Although he is a doomed figure, it is wrong to say, as one commentator has, that Stahr therefore is "completely anomalous in the twentieth century." In a sense he is representative of the old-fashioned paternalistic employer. But as the head of a flourishing organization, Stahr surely has a more permanent significance. Every organization begins as the shadow of a man; but if it succeeds, it becomes an independent institution with an existence all its own. Then, like every other organism, it is responsible for its own survival. And in that struggle for survival no other organism, not even the individual who created it, becomes as important as itself. Stahr's predicament is thus a very familiar one. He is the individual locked in a struggle with the organization he has created, but which he no longer has the power to control. His plight is peculiarly relevant to our own super-organized society. Stahr, the tired businessman, grimly clinging to his job until he dies of a heart attack (or is carried away stubbornly sitting at his desk, like a recent president of Montgomery Ward)—is he really an outmoded hero? Fitzgerald's title, *The Last Tycoon,* was surely chosen for its ironic overtones. The *last?* How many other imaginative organizers—capitalistic, socialistic, communistic, or whatever their label—are destined to repeat Stahr's tragic destiny?

It is also ironic that Wylie White, the disillusioned screen writer who, of all the other characters in the book most resembles Fitzgerald, should be the person who understands Stahr best, and sees his tragic flaw. Stahr's strength, and his weakness, is that he cares too much. Herein lies his nobility and his pathos, his triumph and his doom. Instead of quitting while he is ahead, cutting his losses, and accepting the girl who loves him and wants to take care of him, Stahr insists on remaining at the helm of his sinking ship. Wylie White, like Fitzgerald, was "a free-lancer . . . [who] had failed from lack of caring." "But here," Wylie realizes, as he witnesses Stahr's tragedy, "here was Stahr to care for all of them."

Finally, quite apart from Stahr's role as the representative American business manager, Fitzgerald also thought of him as a moral symbol for the Hollywood film community itself—that glittering Babylon he had once described as "one of the most romantic cities in the world." Although Hollywood had defeated Fitzgerald as surely as it had destroyed Irving Thalberg, it continued nonetheless to fascinate him. Through the idea of Monroe Stahr, he hoped to be able to come to terms with his own ambiguous feelings about the screen colony.

He hoped to do this by telling Stahr's story from the point of view of someone as morally involved as Fitzgerald was with the problem of Hollywood. For this narrator he chose Cecilia Brady, the college-age daughter of Pat Brady, Stahr's bitterest enemy as well as his closest associate. Unlike both her father and Stahr, Cecilia has enjoyed the so-called "advantages." Born and bred a stone's throw from Sunset Boulevard, she is herself as much a Hollywood production as one of Stahr's "A" pictures. But she has also had the benefits of an exclusive Eastern girls' college. There, looking back on Hollywood from the greener perspective of a secluded New England campus, she has seen it in all its stark and pretentious ugliness. Although she can no longer accept the movie colony at its own inflated value, neither can she write it off as easily as her supercilious Eastern classmates. It is, after all, the most vital part of herself, and if Cecilia is ever to know herself, she must begin by understanding the culture that produced her.

In this sense, Cecilia Brady's desire to understand Monroe Stahr is the result of her need to comprehend Hollywood as a moral idea. How desperate that necessity was we can guess from the fact that in one version of *The Last Tycoon,* Fitzgerald planned to have Cecilia tell Stahr's tragedy while she herself was dying of tuberculosis. In this version Stahr was to have been murdered.

Was there actually any moral justification for Hollywood, anyway? Nathanael West, a talented Hollywood writer whose work Fitzgerald admired, had asked this question in *The Day of the Locust* in 1939, and replied with an unqualified negative. The Hollywood he described in that novel had been a nightmare so horrible that only the distortions of surrealism were able to do his hatred of it justice. West's Hollywood is a moral waste land not unlike the waste land of Dr. T. J. Eckelburg—but West's hatred burned more intensely than Fitzgerald's. At the end of *The Day of the Locust,* West destroyed Hollywood in a righteous, Old Testament holocaust of smoke and flame.

Much as Fitzgerald admired this novel, he could not accept West's over-simplified solution to the problem. *The Day of the Locust* was "literature," he said, but "the underworld of literature." It was concerned only with partial truths. To a novelist like West, or Wylie White, or George Boxley, or even Fitzgerald himself, Hollywood might indeed seem like a nightmare world. But what were good writers like these doing wasting their time in Hollywood? For those who were morally involved in the community, what help was the literary hatred of an acknowledged outsider? To someone like Cecilia Brady, the judgments of the Wests and Boxleys were, at best, irrelevant. Wasn't there some positive value to justify the movie community's existence and hence, her own? In the story of Monroe Stahr she found that vindication—Stahr, "who almost single-handed . . . had moved pictures sharply forward . . . to the point where an 'A' production was wider and richer than that of the stage."

"At certain points," Fitzgerald says in another note for the novel, "one man appropriates to himself the total significance of a time or place." For Cecilia, Stahr was such a man. "You can take Hollywood for granted," she tells the reader on the first page of her story, " . . . or you can dismiss it with the contempt we reserve for what we don't understand. It can be understood, too, but dimly and in flashes. Not half a dozen men have ever been able to keep the whole equation in their heads. Perhaps the closest a woman can come to the set-up is to try to understand one of these men."

Was there no *better* way to get at the meaning of Hollywood? By an odd coincidence, another investigation also got under way in January, 1939—the same month that Fitzgerald was fired from his Metro-Goldwyn-Mayer job and began to make serious plans for writing *The Last Tycoon.* This second project was nothing less than a full-dress sociological analysis of the movie community by a team of expert social scientists, backed by a quarter of a million dollars of Carnegie and Rockefeller foundation money. It was inaugurated with all the ballyhoo of one of the picture industry's own "A" productions. Among its distinguished sponsors were such well-known scholars as Margaret Mead and Gregory Bateson, with Walter Wanger himself serving as the representative of the industry's highest echelons.

For the next two years a team consisting of two sociologists, an economist, a statistician, and various foreign language translators, industrial engineers, personnel experts, management consultants, and their assistants, thumped and prodded the recumbent form of the ailing movie industry. They read everything that had been written about the subject, recorded hundreds of interviews, and prepared, distributed, tabulated, and analyzed some forty-two hundred questionnaires. The results were summarized in a book by Leo Rosten, *Hollywood: The Movie Makers, The Movie Colony,* which was published in 1941, the same year that Fitzgerald's unfinished *The Last Tycoon* posthumously appeared.

The Rosten volume was in every way the most comprehensive and authoritative study that had thus far been made of the movie industry. Yet its 368 pages of text, plus an additional 78 pages of charts and appendices, did little more than confirm the diagnosis of Hollywood's ills that Fitzgerald had reached in less than one hundred pages of memorable prose. Central to both works was the idea that the key figure in Hollywood was the director (or the producer, when he also exercised the responsibility for the direction of a film). The future of the movie industry depended on the creative ability and freedom that these men brought to the making of pictures. Once they had been provided with the money and other resources (human and mechanical) necessary for a film, they should be allowed to exercise total authority, just as they should be expected to take full responsibility for the results. This is the same conclusion Bosley Crowther arrives at in his history of M-G-M, *The Lion's Share.* It was also the conclusion Fitzgerald had reached back in 1924 in **"Why Only Ten Percent of the Movies Succeed,"** and it is the central theme of *The Last Tycoon.* Yet the film industry's failure to recognize this fact after Thalberg's death was the primary reason for its subsequent decline. World War II, when gas rationing temporarily provided the studios with a large captive audience, only postponed the inevitable day of reckoning. Television, instead of being responsible for Hollywood's downfall, merely administered the final *coup de grâce.*

Thus, *The Last Tycoon*—in spite of its fragmentary state—continues to be the most profound analysis we have had in fiction of the motion-picture industry. And writing this novel, under severe physical and emotional handicaps, constitutes Fitzgerald's most heroic act. Where the Carnegie and Rockefeller Foundation scholars were treated with every courtesy, Fitzgerald was obliged to pursue his writing secretly, convinced that if news of his novel got about, he would be blackballed by the major studios. When he found out that Max Perkins had innocently told Charles Scribner of his plans, he wrote Perkins desperately, denying everything:

> He [i. e., Mr. Scribner] seemed under the full conviction that the novel was about Hollywood and I am in terror that this misinformation may have been disseminated to the literary columns. If I ever gave such an impression it is entirely false: I said that the novel was about some things that had happened to me in the last two years. It is distinctly *not* about Hollywood (and if it were it is the last impression that I would want to get about).

So Fitzgerald struggled on alone in his doomed attempt to finish *The Last Tycoon.*

Henry Dan Piper, in his F. Scott Fitzgerald: A Critical Portrait, *Holt, Rinehart and Winston, 1965, 334 p.*

Richard D. Lehan   (essay date 1966)

[*Lehan is an American educator and critic who has written extensively on the twentieth-century American novel. In the following excerpt, he examines the diversity of influences on* The Last Tycoon.]

In October of 1931, Fitzgerald went to Hollywood where he made $6,000 for five weeks' work at M-G-M. There he met Irving Thalberg, who had come to Hollywood in 1919 to assist Carl Laemmle at Universal Pictures and who, in the meantime, had worked his way to the very top of the industry. In 1937, Harold Ober, Fitzgerald's agent, got him another contract at $1,000 a week with M-G-M. Thalberg had died, at the age of thirty-seven, the year before; and Fitzgerald saw his death was a turning point for the industry. Thalberg, Fitzgerald believed, was an idealist in a materialistic world. The feud at M-G-M between Thalberg and Louis B. Mayer was for Fitzgerald a matter of principle—whether the movies were an art form, as Thalberg maintained, or merely a profitable industry, as Mayer insisted; whether Hollywood should be more concerned with quality films or with profit.

Since Fitzgerald had depicted in Gatsby and Dick Diver [in *The Great Gatsby* and *Tender Is the Night*] the idealist in a materialistic world, he could warm to the struggle between Thalberg and Mayer. He was also excited by the personal qualities of Thalberg—a man of energy, power, and decision who lived a heightened and glamorous life—and Thalberg became the model for Fitzgerald's Monroe Stahr.

Monroe Stahr came to Hollywood when he was only twenty-two and became an important and powerful producer long before thirty-four, his age when we first meet him in the novel. Fitzgerald hoped to portray in Stahr a man who had helped build a dynasty—who had created the world of movies—and then to show that world come tumbling down around him. Fitzgerald says in his notes: "I want to give an all-fireworks illumination of the intense passion in Stahr's soul, his love of life, his love for the great thing that he's built out here, his, perhaps not exactly, satisfaction, but his feeling of coming home to an empire of his own—an empire he has made. I want to contrast this sharply with the feeling of those who have merely gypped another person's empire away from them like the four great railroad kings of the coast."

Fitzgerald made Monroe Stahr into the image of Thalberg and then fused this image with that of his own. Once again Fitzgerald created a heightened world and then invited himself in; once more he poured himself into the golden vessel of his imagination.

This method—starting with a heightened embodiment of self—had worked successfully in *The Great Gatsby* and in *Tender Is the Night,* but there is some doubt that it would have worked in *The Last Tycoon.* Monroe Stahr does not seem to be a consistent character. The man of integrity and character we meet at the beginning does not seem capable of the blackmail and murder he attempts, according to Fitzgerald's notes, at the end. He starts as Thalberg—with his energy, vitality, drive, and purpose—and ends as Fitzgerald—sick, frail, vacillating, and tired. At the beginning of the novel—as Stahr handles a board meeting, fires a director, criticizes the rushes—he is shrewd and decisive, makes accurate decisions, and is always in control. He is the source of unity, the emotional nucleus of the studio; he is the object of admiration, fear, and worship. At the end of the unfinished manuscript—as he talks with a Communist labor leader—he is loud and aggressive, boasts, misjudges his man, loses self-control, and makes a fool of himself. The transition from one man to the other is sudden and unjustified. Fitzgerald, in his notes, said that *The Last Tycoon* was not to be a novel about deterioration, but he seems to have made it one nevertheless—his own sense of reality affecting the way he depicted Stahr, although the tone of the novel never becomes as solemn as *Tender Is the Night.*

Fitzgerald once said that he "was a man divided." If he portrayed his divided nature by having Gatsby *seen* in double focus and by having Dick Diver *act* ambivalently, he did the same in *The Last Tycoon* by creating, in the person of Wylie White, an antimask of Monroe Stahr. If Stahr embodies some aspects of Fitzgerald's life and character, Wylie White embodies others—just as Nick Carraway is Fitzgerald the realist looking at Gatsby, Fitzgerald the romantic. Wylie White, however, is not a central observer; and where Nick is drawn toward Gatsby in the course of the novel, Stahr and White become enemies. Wylie White, like Fitzgerald, is separated (actually divorced) from his wife, is cynical about Hollywood, and is unable to write scripts that satisfy the producers. When Fitzgerald went to Hollywood in 1931, he was assigned to the movie *Red-Headed Woman,* based on a novel by Katherine Brush, which was eventually abandoned because the heroine was made too coarse and unappealing. Fitzgerald seems to have this in mind when Stahr, disappointed with one of

his scripts, tells his writers, " 'We've got an hour and twenty-five minutes on the screen—you show a woman being unfaithful to a man for one-third of that time and you've given the impression that she's one-third whore.' " Wylie White, like Fitzgerald, got the brunt of blame for the unacceptable script. Wylie is later also held responsible for a weak gangster scenario:

> "Who wrote the scene?" [Stahr] asked after a minute.
>
> "Wylie White."
>
> "Is he sober?"
>
> "Sure he is."
>
> Stahr considered.
>
> "Put about four writers on the scene tonight," he said. "See who we've got."

Fitzgerald hated the way the studios assigned writers to work "behind" him (writing the same material independently) and the way his scripts were mercilessly cut. One of the biggest disappointments in his life was when Joseph Manckiewicz, a producer at M-G-M, rewrote the script of *Three Comrades.* "I am utterly miserable," he wrote Manckiewicz, "at seeing months of work and thought negated in one hasty week."

Yet Wylie White, who seems to embody Fitzgerald's frustrations with Hollywood script writing, is not a wholly sympathetic character, and Fitzgerald's notes tell us that he betrays Stahr. Fitzgerald again seems to be putting his own experience in ironic context, writing against the grain of his own feeling by sympathizing with the Hollywood producer rather than the writer. Fitzgerald identified with both Stahr and Wylie White, and when he put them in opposition—seeing one as a kind of destructive complement to the other—he was again bifurcating his own dual nature, embodying both the mask and the antimask of that nature, seeing the writer in him destroyed and portraying the source of destruction. Wylie White sells out to the money grubbers. There is also a little of the writer *manqué* in Wylie. If the vital Monroe Stahr represents what Fitzgerald would have liked to become, Wylie White represents what Fitzgerald feared he would become. The final embodiment of this feeling is Pat Hobby—a pleasant drunkard, an inept cheat, a Hollywood failure; and Fitzgerald wrote against his own emotions—established an ironic distance between himself and his characters—when he made Wylie White unsympathetic and Pat Hobby pathetic.

The general structure of *The Last Tycoon* is similar to the business novels of Theodore Dreiser. We see Stahr, as we see Frank Algernon Cowperwood, as both financial genius and lover—we move from the board room to the bedroom.

Sheilah Graham, as she tells us in *Beloved Infidel,* is the model for Kathleen Moore, the object of Stahr's love. With Zelda in a North Carolina institution, Sheilah Graham took her place in Fitzgerald's life, as Kathleen Moore takes the place of Minna, Stahr's deceased wife. Stahr, who loved his wife dearly, is attracted to Kathleen because she looks like Minna, just as Fitzgerald was attracted to

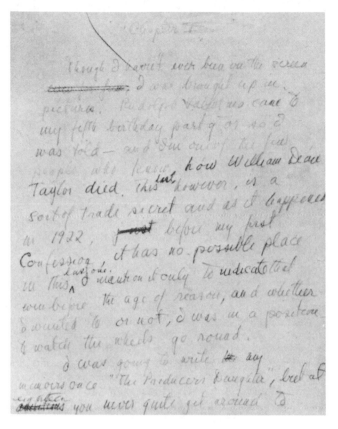

The discarded opening of The Last Tycoon.

Miss Graham who looked like Zelda—or so Miss Graham suggests. Fitzgerald first saw Miss Graham at Robert Benchley's party in the Garden of Allah; he left the party, and when he returned, he mistook her for Tala Birrell, in the same way that Stahr confuses Kathleen with her friend. Fitzgerald later met Miss Graham at a Writer's Guild dance, just as Stahr again meets Kathleen at a dance. Miss Graham ponders:

> . . . If I was Kathleen, Minna was Zelda. How much I must have reminded him of Zelda! Was this how I had appeared that night, when he stood at my door saying good-by, and I had not wanted to let him go and I had asked him in, and he had come in? Had he—has he—been reliving with me his life with Zelda?

There are other similarities between Kathleen and Sheilah Graham: Kathleen is Irish but she lived, as did Miss Graham, in London; like Miss Graham, she was divorced from an older man who had befriended her; at the time that Stahr met Kathleen, she was engaged to be married again, as Miss Graham was engaged to be married when Fitzgerald first met her.

Fitzgerald was again writing deeply out of his own sense of experience, just as he had in **The Great Gatsby** and in **Tender Is the Night,** novels which so richly represented two facets of his life and character. Although these novels are very different from each other, they both depict the idealist in a materialistic environment—one from Fitzger-

ald's point of view of the visionary, the other from his point of view of the *homme épuisé*. Monroe Stahr is also the idealist in the materialistic world, and in many ways he is an incongruous combination of Gatsby's vitality and Dick Diver's world weariness.

In a letter to Scribner's, Fitzgerald said: "If one book could ever be like another, I should say it is more like **The Great Gatsby** than any other of my books. But I hope it will be entirely different—I hope it will be something new, arouse new emotions, perhaps even a new way of looking at certain phenomena." Certainly **The Last Tycoon** reveals that as a novelist Fitzgerald had "a new way of looking at certain phenomena." Monroe Stahr has realized his dream, and he seems to have few regrets. Unlike Gatsby, Monroe Stahr is shrewd and experienced, and he makes very few mistakes. Yet, like Gatsby, the past has a tremendous appeal for Stahr, and he carries with him the memories of his wife Minna and his growing love for Kathleen is, in part, an attempt to recapture the dead past—it is, in fact, almost an attempt to recapture his lost sense of youthful excitement and romance. Fitzgerald makes it brilliantly clear what the death of Minna took from Stahr's life:

> As Stahr walked back from the commissary, a hand waved at him from an open roadster. From the heads showing over the back he recognized a young actor and his girl, and watched them disappear through the gate, already part of the summer twilight. Little by little he was losing the feel of such things, until it seemed that Minna had taken their poignancy with her; his apprehension of splendor was fading so that presently the luxury of eternal mourning would depart. A childish association of Minna with the material heavens made him, when he reached his office, order out his roadster for the first time this year. The big limousine seemed heavy with remembered or exhausted sleep.

Stahr realizes that Kathleen is his last hope—that his old and more vital point of view depends upon his marrying her. "This is your girl," he says of himself. "She can save you, she can worry you back to life." Like Dick Diver, Stahr needs to have people depend on him, and Kathleen "will take looking after and you will grow strong to do it." As Fitzgerald put all this in his notes, Kathleen "promises to give life back to [Stahr]."

But Stahr does not marry Kathleen. In the incompleted manuscript, Stahr and Kathleen seem to drift away because of each other's inertia, their failure to be decisive. In the letter to Scribner's, however, Fitzgerald said that Stahr did not marry Kathleen because she failed to come up to what his imagination demanded of a woman. She was "poor, unfortunate, and tagged with a middle-class exterior which [did not] fit in with the grandeur Stahr demand[ed] of life." When Fitzgerald wrote this letter, he had intended naming Kathleen "Thalia" and, in time, he may very well have decided to change Stahr's motives as well as Thalia's name.

Whether or not this is true, it does suggest that, at one point in his thinking, Fitzgerald conceived of Monroe Stahr as a kind of successful Jay Gatsby—as someone who made decisions on the basis of imaginative ideals. And these ideals seem to be the product of a youthful vision. Fitzgerald makes this clear in the Scribner's letter: "Success came to [Stahr] young, at twenty-three, and left certain idealisms of his youth unscarred." This idea finds its way into the novel itself, and it is said that Stahr "had flown up very high to see, on strong wings, when he was young. And while he was up there he had looked on all the kingdoms, with the eyes that can stare straight into the sun."

Yet, like Icarus, Monroe crashes rudely to earth, not on waxed wings but in a transcontinental plane, and his death is a metaphorical conclusion of his moral and physical decline. As Dick Diver is sometimes seen from the point of view of Rosemary, so Monroe Stahr is seen through the youthful eyes of Cecilia Brady, Fitzgerald's narrator, the nineteen-year-old daughter of William Brady, Stahr's rival. She has fallen in love with Stahr and admits that she had "the young illusion that most adventures are good." It comes as a shock for her to see Stahr humiliated by Brimmer, the Communist, who is trying to organize labor in the movie industry. Stahr considers himself a paternalistic employer, and it angers him to think that his workers would even want a union. This is the first defect that Cecilia has noticed in Stahr's armor and, in her embarrassment for Stahr, she wishes that he were ten years younger—not tired, worn-out, and the physically sick man she sees: "Suddenly I wished it had been about ten years ago—I would have been nine, Brimmer about eighteen and working his way through some mid-western college, and Stahr twenty-five, just having inherited the world and full of confidence and joy." Brimmer also looks at Stahr and speculates," 'Is *this* all? This frail half-sick person holding up the whole thing.' " One wonders how much Fitzgerald had himself in mind when Stahr's doctor thinks, "He was due to die very soon now. Within six months one could say definitely. What was the use of developing the cardiograms?"

The seeds of promise growing in time to ruin is as much the theme of *The Last Tycoon* as it is the theme of Fitzgerald's earlier novels. Fitzgerald suggests this through allusion and descriptive detail. When Stahr first sees Kathleen, she is floating on the head of the Goddess Siva in a current of water released by a broken water main in the earthquake of 1935. Siva, in Hinduism, is the Destroyer, the destructive principle in life, in contrast to Vishnu, the Preserver. Stahr's destruction is contained in the very moment of promise, in the very hope for a new life. Throughout the novel Fitzgerald plays upon this theme. He says of Monroe and Kathleen: "They existed nowhere. His world seemed far away—she had no world at all except the idol's head, the half open door." Later in the novel, Stahr and Kathleen watch from the beach in fascination as the grunion pile upon the shore intent on self-destruction.

Fitzgerald paralleled the destruction of Stahr with the destruction of Hollywood. He identified Stahr with the vital and romantic Hollywood of the past; and as Stahr declines there is the longing for the return of a golden age. In his letter to Scribner's, Fitzgerald said that he set *The Last Tycoon* "safely in a period of five years ago to obtain detachment, but now that Europe is tumbling about our ears this also seems to be for the best. It is an escape into a lavish, romantic past that perhaps will not come again into our time." "An escape into a lavish, romantic past": the theme here is the same as that of Fitzgerald's earlier fiction; only the perspective is different. Instead of putting the emphasis totally upon the loss of his hero's youth, the loss of illusion or of genius, Fitzgerald shifts the focus to a glamorous time and industry, an industry to which some of his most beautiful heroines aspired—Gloria Patch and Rosemary Hoyt, for example—and the decline takes place in the industry when it destroys its last tycoon.

In the synopsis of *The Last Tycoon,* put together from Fitzgerald's notes and from reports of persons with whom he discussed the novel, Edmund Wilson writes: "The split between the controllers of the movie industry, on the one hand, and the various groups of employers, on the other, is widening and leaving no place for real individualists of business like Stahr, whose successes are personal achievements and whose career has always been invested with a certain glamor. . . . In Hollywood he is 'the last tycoon.' " And Cecilia says that Hollywood can be understood "only dimly and in flashes," that fewer than half a dozen men have ever put the puzzle together, and that "perhaps the closest a woman can come to the set-up is to try and understand one of those men." In telling Stahr's story, Fitzgerald was telling the story of an industry. And Fitzgerald associated the Hollywood that Stahr knew with beauty—and with youth. When Gloria Patch turns thirty, she is too old for Hollywood. And when Monroe Stahr dies, Hollywood loses some of its appeal—its glamor, romance, and sense of promise. It is taken over, according to Fitzgerald, by an ugly and unimaginative group. In a very real way, at least for Fitzgerald, Hollywood loses all the attributes he had predicated of youth.

Fitzgerald moves from the story of Monroe Stahr to the story of Hollywood, and in *The Last Tycoon* he spirals out once more and relates the story of Hollywood to that of America. At the very beginning of the novel, the Hollywood people visit at dawn the Hermitage, the home of Andrew Jackson, in a scene that has so many of the grotesque qualities of *The Great Gatsby*. Andrew Jackson, who opposed the national bank, was also, as the novel points out, the inventor of the spoils system—the man, in other words, who cancelled out his ideals. The Hermitage becomes a historical extension of Monroe Stahr's contradictory nature and of Hollywood where artistic integrity is corrupted by materialism—and it is symbolically proper that Manny Schwartz, once a success now a failure in Hollywood, should commit suicide there, as if it were the proper shrine.

Throughout *The Last Tycoon,* Fitzgerald makes the same kind of use of Abraham Lincoln, the man who comes at the moment of colossal transition in American history, as he did of Ulysses Grant in *Tender Is the Night.* With both Lincoln and Grant, or so Fitzgerald suggests, their ideals came to naught in a crass material and commercial world. Fitzgerald rather uniquely conveys this feeling when a prince, visiting the studio, sees Abe Lincoln "his legs crossed, his kindly face fixed on a forty cent dinner, including desert, his shawl wrapped around him as if to protect himself from the erratic air cooling." If crass materialism was to profane the spirit of Lincoln, it was also to profane the spirit of Stahr because "Stahr like Lincoln was a leader carrying on a long war on many fronts; almost single-handed he had moved pictures sharply forward through a decade. . . . Stahr was an artist only, as Mr. Lincoln was a general."

As in *The Great Gatsby* and *Tender Is the Night, The Last Tycoon* spirals out from a story of an individual to a story of history, from the personal to the public. The story of Monroe Stahr is the story of Hollywood—and, by implication, the story of America as well. Kathleen tells us that Spengler was a name on her "reading list." The reference is significant because as Monroe Stahr loses his vitality and goes into decline so also does Hollywood and America itself.

Richard D. Lehan, in his F. Scott Fitzgerald and the Craft of Fiction, *Southern Illinois University Press, 1966, 206 p.*

Fitzgerald's death:

Like so much else in his life, his heroic effort to finish his last novel came too late; and the luck which might have kept him alive until he had finished was not with him. He had predicted to Perkins in the middle of December that he could complete a first draft by January 15, and at the rate he was going he might have done so; on December 20 he completed the first episode of Chapter VI. The next day he had a second, fatal heart attack.

He was buried with a flurry of ironies even thicker than he had himself dared to devise for Gatsby. His body was laid out in an undertaker's parlor on Washington Boulevard "which," as one observer remarked, "—to Beverly Hills—is on the other side of the tracks in downtown Los Angeles." He was not placed in the chapel but in a back room named the William Wordsworth room; no doubt it seemed to the undertaker the appropriate place for a literary man. Almost no one came to see him.

His old friend Dorothy Parker is said to have stood looking at his body for a long time and then, without taking her eyes off him, to have repeated quietly what "Owl-eyes" said at Gatsby's funeral: "The poor son of a bitch."

Arthur Mizener, in his The Far Side of Paradise: A Biography of F. Scott Fitzgerald, *Houghton Mifflin, 1940.*

Edward J. Piacentino   (essay date 1981)

[*Below, Piacentino offers a study of the moon imagery in* The Last Tycoon.]

Although regarded as a flawed fragment, a falling off from F. Scott Fitzgerald's earlier fictional achievements, *The Last Tycoon,* edited by Edmund Wilson and published posthumously along with the author's notes and plans in

1941, a year after Fitzgerald's death, is a work of conscientious craftsmanship. Rarely lavished with the same stupendous appraisal as some of Fitzgerald's earlier novels, particularly *The Great Gatsby* and *Tender Is the Night,* and some of his stories, *The Last Tycoon* has attracted considerable attention among some of Fitzgerald's most respected critics. Henry Dan Piper, for example, in commenting on the novel's technique and style [in *F. Scott Fitzgerald: A Critical Portrait*], viewed it as employing the "dramatic and more economical design of *The Great Gatsby.*" And James E. Miller, in his astute critical assessment [*F. Scott Fitzgerald: His Art and His Technique*], remarked that it is best to accept *The Last Tycoon* "for what it is, an unfinished novel of a highly gifted writer, valuable for revealing how a genuine craftsman goes about his craft." "The six chapters of *The Last Tycoon,* together with the sketches and notes," Miller continued, "provide valuable insight into the creative act. They tell us something of the art that, years before had gone into *The Great Gatsby,* and they tell us a good deal about the mastery of his craft that Fitzgerald had finally achieved . . ." Fitzgerald's fellow novelist, John Dos Passos, in what is perhaps the most complimentary and at the same time the most overrated acclaim accorded the novel, wrote in "A Note on Fitzgerald" that *The Last Tycoon* seems "of sufficient dimensions to raise the level of American fiction to follow in the same such way as Marlowe's blank verse raised the whole of Elizabethan verse." And Dos Passos indicated further that the book combined "two divergent halves, to fuse the conscientious worker that no creative man can ever really kill with the moneyed celebrity who aimed his stories at the twelve-year-olds."

While working on *The Last Tycoon* Fitzgerald himself had come to believe that he had rediscovered the same high standard of stylistic artistry he had employed so masterfully in *The Great Gatsby.* In a letter to his daughter Scottie, he tried to convey the sense of self-assuredness he had in his new novel: "Look! I've begun to write something that is maybe great, and I'm going to be absorbed in it four or six months. It may not *make* a cent but it will pay expenses and it is the first labor of love I've undertaken since the first part of *Infidelity* . . . Anyhow I'm alive again . . ." Also in a letter to Zelda, he partially explained the stylistic strategy he attempted to follow in the novel. "It is," he exclaimed, "a *constructed* novel like *Gatsby,* with passages of poetic prose when it fits the action, but no ruminations or side-shows like *Tender.* Everything must contribute to the dramatic movement."

In exploring the literary artistry of *The Last Tycoon,* it will not be my purpose to examine the entire range of the novel's stylistic achievement but only a single yet significant and previously uninvestigated aspect of the technical strategy, namely the recurring moon imagery—one of the novel's key and functional image patterns, and to attempt to justify the writer's probable rationale for employing this pattern. Most of the primary moon images serve to highlight the illusive quality of Hollywood and the motion picture industry generally and that of Monroe Stahr particularly, the latter a major influence on the Hollywood dream world. At the novel's outset Cecilia Brady, who serves as the retrospective narrator, has acquired at the time of recounting the events of the narrative a keen perception of Hollywood and the people associated with the movie industry. In part, Fitzgerald seems to use Cecilia as an agent for evoking the mood of mystery and illusion that informs the novel. As she discloses in the first chapter, Hollywood "can be understood . . . but only dimly and in flashes."

Cecilia further established this initial impression of the near make-believe, illusory feature of Hollywood in one of the first moon references when she relates in her own words Stahr's account of the flood at the motion picture lot in Chapter II. "Under the moon the back lot was thirty acres of fairyland—not because the locations really looked like African jungles and French chateaux and schooners at anchor and Broadway by night, but because they looked like the torn picture books of childhood, like fragments of stories dancing in an open fire. I now lived in a house with an attic, but a back lot must be something like that, and at night of course in an enchanted distorted way, it all comes true." Under the cover of faint and deceptive moonlight, the studio lot and its props take on a seemingly unrealistic, even ambiguous character, projecting an imaginative aura and creating concurrently a feeling of mystery and uncertainty for the observer.

Yet it is primarily through Stahr's special insight, what might be termed his uncanny perception into what really matters to him in life, that one can best comprehend the magic, the mystery, and the illusion that pervade his thoughts. According to Cecilia, Stahr, though not particularly tall, "always seemed high up [where] he watched the multitudinous practicalitities of his world like a proud young shepherd to whom night and day had never mattered." It was as if "he had flown high to see, on strong wings, when he was young. And while he was up there he had looked on all the kingdoms, with the kind of eyes that can stare straight into the sun. Beating his wings tenaciously—finally frantically—and keeping on beating them, he had stayed up there longer than most of us, and then, remembering all he had seen from his great height of how things were, he had settled gradually to earth." The metaphor of flight here becomes significant, for in Richard D. Lehan's cogent estimation [in *F. Scott Fitzgerald and the Craft of Fiction*] it aptly implies "the spirit of adventure, the sense of yearning, that characterizes the Romantic hero." "Flight," Lehan further observes, "suggests a desire for experience and a quest for meaning and the attainment of beauty . . . When this attitude of mind leads to desires that are impossible to achieve, it becomes destructive and self-defeating."

Viewed then within the intended mythical context, Stahr becomes an Icarus-like figure whose perceptions from above, from the moon, to speak figuratively, take on associations imaginary and perhaps even magical. According to Lehan's conception of Stahr's character (his very name is a homonym for star), he represents the mythical Icarus who "crashed rudely to earth, not on waxed wings but on a transcendental plane, and his death is a metaphorical conclusion of his moral decline." Thus Stahr's mythic stature established him as one whose perceptions may, or perhaps should, be interpreted as imaginary, as a departure from the confinement of visual reality.

Stahr's first wife, Minna Davis, dead at the time of the central narrative, had attracted Stahr, Fitzgerald makes clear, with her ethereal beauty and charm. On the night of the earthquake when Minna dies, as "the one-way French windows were open and a big moon, rosy-gold with a haze around, was wedged helpless in one of them," the moon, as Stahr perceives it, seems to foreshadow her doom. And later when Stahr sees the face of his dead wife in the moonlight, he is enchanted and at the same time frightened by her eyes, her "familiar forehead," her smile, and her lips— all of which significantly the soft light of the moon illuminates. To Stahr, Minna's beauty remains the same even in death as it had been in life, and the mystique of the "warm and glowing" night does not disappear until "the river passed him in a rush, [and] the great spotlights swooped and blinked."

After the earthquake Stahr frequently reminisces about Minna. In fact, "a childish association of Minna with the material heavens" prompts him to go for a ride in his roadster in the summer moonlight and causes him to feel a nearness to her when he leaves the other Hollywood lights—the "misty glare" of open markets, the winking "stop-signal of a car," and the ubiquitous floodlights shining in the evening sky. Yet still he must encounter the natural glow of the moon before recapturing the spiritual bond that he had felt with Minna.

In Kathleen Moore Stahr also seems to recognize this same magical illusion, this same mystical fascination, he had previously discovered in Minna. Furthermore, he tends to idealize Kathleen, seeing her, even though only temporarily, as a near double of Minna herself. When Stahr first sees Kathleen he immediately recognizes what seems to be a near replica of Minna's face—"the very skin with that peculiar radiance as if phosphorus had touched it." "He thought," Fitzgerald also discloses, "whether it might not be a trick to reach him from somewhere. Not Minna and yet Minna." Even Kathleen's eyes attract Stahr, enticing him "to a romantic commmunion of unbelievable intensity."

Soon afterwards, when she walks with Stahr to his car, "her glowing beauty and her unexplored novelty" are likewise recognizable; "but there was a foot of moonlight between them when they came out of the shadow." Like Minna, Kathleeen, at least as Stahr discerns her at this point, emits a radiance suggesting moon-like affinities. And in Chapter V, when Stahr and Kathleen meet again— but on this occasion in the afternoon—the upper section of her face, "luminous, with creamy temples, and opalescent brow," bears an uncanny resemblance to Minna's. Importantly, the parallels between Minna and Kathleen appear to be neither incidental nor coincidental. The apparent deliberate choice of such words as "luminous," "creamy," and "opalescent" implies a close assocation with the moon itself, particularly qualities relating to the impressions of enchantment and pleasing fantasy that occupy Stahr's mind.

Despite having been enthralled by Kathleen's beauty, Stahr seems to know very little about her. From his perspective, "a vague background spread behind her, something more tangible than the head of Siva in the moonlight." Her luminous and radiant beauty still nevertheless overwhelms him to the extent that he idealizes her. At the Screenwriter's Ball when he walks toward Kathleen, "the people shrunk back against the walls till they were only murals; the white table lengthened and became an altar where the priestess sat alone." And when she comes near him, "his several visions of her blurred; she was momentarily unreal." The effect of this spell continues even as they drive to Stahr's house: "The fog fell away . . . Out here a moon showed behind the clouds. There was still a shifting light over the sea." Moreover, this spell is kept alive as they enter his house, for as Fitzgerald emphatically relates, "they could just see each other's eyes in the half darkness." And again later on the night of Stahr's last meeting with Kathleen, when they return to her house—"a dark night with no moon"—Stahr experiences the same ecstatic feeling that had so enthralled him on previous occasions. "The hill they climb now," Fitzgerald states, "gave forth a sort of glow, a sustained sound that struck his soul alert with delight." This illusion proves deceptive and Stahr's vision destroyed, however, when on the following morning he receives a telegram from Kathleen announcing her marriage. The absence of moonlight on their final night together perhaps portends the termination not only of their short-lived romance but of Stahr's own uncontrollable infatuation as well. And this action decidedly transports Stahr back to earth, back to the uneventful reality of ordinary concerns. Therefore once outside the keen of the moon's influence, Stahr becomes compelled to confront directly terrifying, sometimes disillusioning actuality.

In *The Last Tycoon,* then, the skillful manipulation of moonlight may lead one to conjecture justifiably that recurring moon images function as part of a deliberate authorial design. The moon, in each of the scenes previously examined, is not a mere prop, some inconsequential backdrop to enhance or embellish visual scenic effects, but a viable and functional element, a recurring image that serves to emphasize the magic, the fantasy, and above all the mystique that invades Stahr's dreams, dreams that clearly go beyond the physical reality of commonplace existence, and that emanate from the highest and most irresistible lunar light. In sum, the moon imagery Fitzgerald uses in *The Last Tycoon* becomes almost a catalyst for evoking imaginative reverie in Stahr and perhaps in the reader as well. And significantly, this reverie proves ephemeral and permanently disillusioning.

Edward J. Piacentino, "The Illusory Effects of Cynthian Light: Monroe Stahr and the Moon in 'The Last Tycoon'," in American Notes and Queries, *Vol. XX, Nos. 1-2, September-October, 1981, pp. 12-16.*

FURTHER READING

Biography

Bruccoli, Matthew J. "Planning *The Last Tycoon* [Fall 1939]" and "Writing *The Last Tycoon* [1940]." In his *Some Sort of Epic Grandeur: The Life of F. Scott Fitzgerald,* pp. 461-68, pp. 470-80. New York: Harcourt Brace Jovanovich, 1981.

   Recounts the conception and drafting of *The Last Tycoon.*

Criticism

Eble, Kenneth. "The Last Tycoon." In his *F. Scott Fitzgerald,* pp. 148-51. New York: Twayne Publishers, 1963.

   Compares *The Last Tycoon* to other Fitzgerald novels.

Freeman, David. "The Great Hollywood Insider." *Los Angeles Times Book Review* (3 April 1994): 2.

   Mixed review of Matthew Bruccoli's 1994 edition of Fitzgerald's *The Last Tycoon.*

Giddings, Robert. "*The Last Tycoon*: Fitzgerald as Projectionist." In *Scott Fitzgerald: The Promises of Life,* edited by A. Robert Lee, pp. 74-93. London: Vision Press, 1989.

   Asserts that *The Last Tycoon* is "an impressive and moving fragment" because in this novel Fitzgerald explored "some of his driving interest in the creative processes and their relationship with industry and mass society."

Mizener, Arthur. "The Maturity of Scott Fitzgerald." In his *F. Scott Fitzgerald: A Collection of Critical Essays,* pp. 157-68. Englewood Cliffs, N.J.: Prentice-Hall, 1963.

   Traces the maturation of Fitzgerald's work, focusing on *The Last Tycoon.*

Seiters, Dan. "The Last Tycoon." In his *Image Patterns in the Novels of F. Scott Fitzgerald,* pp. 119-34. Ann Arbor: UMI, 1986.

   Analyzes various imagery in *The Last Tycoon.*

"Power without Glory." *The Times Literary Supplement* (20 January 1950): 40.

   Survey of Fitzgerald's works, maintaining that "it is hard to agree with the many critics who have said that *The Last Tycoon* would have crowned Fitzgerald's career."

Additional coverage of Fitzgerald's life and career is contained in the following sources published by Gale Research: *Authors in the News,* Vol. 1; *Concise Dictionary of American Literary Biography, 1917-1929; Contemporary Authors,* Vols. 110, 123; *Dictionary of Literary Biography,* Vols. 4, 9, 86; *Dictionary of Literary Biography Documentary Series,* Vol. 1; *Dictionary of Literary Biography Yearbook, 1981; DISCovering Authors; Major 20th-Century Writers; Short Story Criticism,* Vol. 6; *Twentieth-Century Literary Criticism,* Vols. 1, 6, 14, 28; and *World Literature Criticism.*

Susan Glaspell

1876-1948

(Full name Susan Keating Glaspell) American dramatist, novelist, short story writer, and biographer.

INTRODUCTION

Glaspell is known as an important figure in the development of modern American drama and as a cofounder of the influential Provincetown Players theater group. In many of her plays Glaspell used experimental techniques to convey her socialist and feminist ideals, portraying female characters—some of whom never appear onstage—who challenge the restrictions and stereotypes imposed on them by society.

Biographical Information

Glaspell was born in Davenport, Iowa. She graduated from Drake University in Des Moines in 1899 and accepted a position as a reporter at the *Des Moines News* the same year. After she published several short stories in such magazines as *Harper's Monthly* and the *American Magazine*, Glaspell left journalism to concentrate on publishing novels and short fiction. In 1913, Glaspell married George Cram Cook, a noted socialist. Dissatisfied with American popular theater, the couple moved to Provincetown, Massachusetts, and cofounded, with a group of writers, artists, and intellectuals, the Provincetown Players. Inspired by the independent theater movement in Europe, which had presented the works of Henrik Ibsen, Emile Zola, August Strindberg, and Maurice Maeterlinck, among others, the Provincetown Players were dedicated to developing an American theater movement alternative to the commercial theater of Broadway. The Provincetown "little theater" group included such writers as Djuna Barnes, Edna Ferber, Neith Boyce, Edna St. Vincent Millay, Paul Green, and Eugene O'Neill, most of whom wrote, directed, and acted for the group. The Provincetown Players began to disband with the personal successes of some of the members, including Glaspell. After the failure of his own work outside the company and what he considered the defection of other members, Glaspell's husband also resigned from the group. Glaspell and her husband moved to Greece and resided there until Cook's death in 1924. The following year, Glaspell married Norman Matson. In 1931, she received a Pulitzer Prize for *Alison's House*, the last of her plays to be produced. She served as midwestern director of the Federal Theater Project for a brief period before returning to Provincetown to write novels. Glaspell died of pneumonia in 1948.

Major Works

While Glaspell achieved some success with her novels—most notably her last two, *Ambrose Holt and Family* and

Judd Rankin's Daughter—she is best remembered as one of the first American experimental playwrights. For her first play, *Trifles*, Glaspell turned for inspiration to a murder case she had covered as a reporter. Glaspell's lead characters, Mrs. Hale and Mrs. Peters, accompany the sheriff and two other men to the isolated farmhouse of Minnie Wright—who dominates the play, yet never appears onstage—to collect some clothes for her while the men search for evidence to use in her trial for the murder of her husband. Surveying Minnie Wright's kitchen, the women piece together a motive from such evidence as untidy stitching on a quilt Minnie was constructing and a strangled canary in her sewing basket. The three male characters search the rest of the house fruitlessly, leaving the women to their "trifles." In her starkly realistic rendering of the characters and incidents, Glaspell disputed the notion that women's concerns and activities within the home are trivial, and exposed the harsh life frontierswomen endured in a male-dominated social and legal system. In *Bernice*, Glaspell again used the technique of keeping offstage the character who motivates the action of the play, which takes place following the death of the title character. Glaspell focuses on Bernice's friends and relatives, who attempt to understand her life and death, but can only articulate their thoughts in abstract, usually meaningless words and phrases. *The Verge*, which is generally acknowledged to be Glaspell's most ambitious work, is presented from the point of view of Claire Archer, a botanist who develops new species of plants. Claire rejects traditional gender and social roles and, with the exception of her friend Tom, is misunderstood by everyone because of her desire to transcend the limits of human reality. The play ends with Claire on the brink of madness, having failed to create a new form of life, speaking in a cryptic mix of poetry and prose.

Critical Reception

After receiving critical acclaim during her lifetime, Glaspell fell into obscurity after her death and has only lately been rediscovered due to an increase in feminist scholarship. Because of the experimental nature of many of her plays, she is considered with Eugene O'Neill to be a founder of modern American drama. Her one-act play *Trifles* and the short story into which she adapted it, "A Jury of Her Peers," are widely anthologized as exemplars of their respective forms. Additionally, critics note Glaspell's contribution to the canon of midwestern American literature, citing her use of frontier landscapes and elements of her Iowa upbringing in her work. While some commentators initially regarded her plays as overly intellectual and inaccessible to the average audience, she is now generally considered to be one of the most important figures in modern American drama and twentieth-century feminist literature.

PRINCIPAL WORKS

The Glory of the Conquered (novel) 1909
The Visioning (novel) 1911
Lifted Masks (short stories) 1912
Fidelity (novel) 1915
Suppressed Desires [with George Cram Cook] (drama) 1915
Trifles (drama) 1916
Close the Book (drama) 1917
The Outside (drama) 1917
The People (drama) 1917
Tickless Time [with George Cram Cook] (drama) 1918
Woman's Honor (drama) 1918
Bernice (drama) 1919
Inheritors (drama) 1921
The Verge (drama) 1921
Chains of Dew (drama) 1922
The Road to the Temple (biography) 1926
A Jury of Her Peers (short story) 1927
Brook Evans (novel) 1928
The Comic Artist [with Norman Matson] (drama) 1928
Fugitive's Return (novel) 1929
Alison's House (drama) 1930
Ambrose Holt and Family (novel) 1931

Cherished and Shared of Old (juvenilia) 1940
The Morning Is Near Us (novel) 1940
Norma Ashe (novel) 1942
Judd Rankin's Daughter (novel) 1945

CRITICISM

Ludwig Lewisohn (essay date 1922)

[*A German-born American novelist and critic, Lewisohn was an authority on German literature, and his translations of Gerhart Hauptmann, Rainer Maria Rilke, and Jakob Wassermann are widely respected. In 1919 he became the drama critic for the* Nation, *serving as its associate editor until 1924, when he joined a group of expatriates in Paris. In the essay below, originally published in the* Nation, *Lewisohn provides a mixed assessment of Glaspell's early plays.*]

In the rude little auditorium of the Provincetown Players on MacDougall Street there is an iron ring in the wall, and a legend informs you that the ring was designed for the tethering of Pegasus. But the winged horse has never been seen. An occasional play might have allured him; the acting of it would invariably have driven him to indignant flight. For, contrary to what one would expect, the acting of the Players has been not only crude and unequal; it has been without energy, without freshness, without the natural stir and eloquence that come from within. This is the circumstance which has tended to obscure the notable talent of Susan Glaspell. The Washington Square Players produced *Trifles* and thus gave a wide repute to what is by no means her best work. *Bernice,* not only her masterpiece but one of the indisputably important dramas of the modern English or American theatre, was again played by the Provincetown Players with more than their accustomed feebleness and lack of artistic lucidity. The publication of Miss Glaspell's collected plays at last lifts them out of the tawdriness of their original production and lets them live by their own inherent life.

That life is strong, though it is never rich. In truth, it is thin. Only it is thin not like a wisp of straw, but like a tongue of flame. Miss Glaspell is morbidly frugal in expression, but nakedly candid in substance. There are no terrors for her in the world of thought; she thinks her way clearly and hardily through a problem and always thinks in strictly dramatic terms. But her form and, more specifically, her dialogue, have something of the helplessness and the numb pathos of the "twisted things that grow in unfavoring places" which employ her imagination. She is a dramatist, but a dramatist who is a little afraid of speech. Her dialogue is so spare that it often becomes arid; at times, as in *The Outside,* her attempt to lend a stunted utterance to her silenced creatures makes for a hopeless obscurity. The bleak farmsteads of Iowa, the stagnant villages of New England, have touched her work with penury and chill. She wants to speak out and to let her people speak out. But neither she nor they can conquer a sense that free and intimate and vigorous expression is a little shameless. To uncover one's soul seems almost like uncovering one's body. Behind Miss Glaspell's hardihood of thought hover the fear and self-torment of the Puritan. She is a modern radical and a New England school teacher; she is a woman of intrepid thought and also the cramped and aproned wife on some Iowa farm. She is a composite, and that composite is intensely American. She is never quite spontaneous and unconscious and free, never the unquestioning servant of her art. She broods and tortures herself and weighs the issues of expression.

If this view of Miss Glaspell's literary character is correct, it may seem strange upon superficial consideration that four of her seven one-act plays are comedies. But two of them, the rather trivial *Suppressed Desires* and the quite brilliant *Tickless Time,* were written in collaboration with George Cram Cook, a far less scrupulous and more ungirdled mind. Her comedy, furthermore, is never hearty. It is not the comedy of character but of ideas, or, rather, of the confusion or falseness or absurdity of ideas. *Woman's Honor* is the best example of her art in this mood. By a sound and strictly dramatic if somewhat too geometrical device, Miss Glaspell dramatizes a very searching ironic idea: a man who refuses to establish an alibi in order to save a woman's honor dies to prove her possessed of what he himself has taken and risks everything to demonstrate the existence of what has ceased to be. The one-act tragedies are more characteristic of her; they cleave deep, but they also illustrate what one might almost call her taciturnity. That is the fault of her best-known piece, *Trifles.* The theme is magnificent; it is inherently and intensely dramatic, since its very nature is culmination and crisis. But the actual speech of the play is neither sufficient nor sufficiently direct. Somewhere in every drama words must ring out. They need not ring like trumpets. The ring need not be loud, but it must be clear. Suppose in *Trifles* you do not, on the stage, catch the precise significance of the glances which the neighbor women exchange. There need have been no set speech, no false eloquence, no heightening of what these very women might easily have said in their own persons. But one aches for a word to release the dumbness, complete the crisis, and drive the tragic situation home.

The same criticism may be made, though in a lesser degree, of Miss Glaspell's single full-length play, *Bernice.* No production would be just to the very high merits of that piece which did not add several speeches to the first and third acts and give these the spiritual and dramatic clearness which the second already has. Crude people will call the play "talky." But indeed there is not quite talk enough. Nor does Miss Glaspell deal here with simple and stifled souls. That objection is the only one to be made. The modern American drama has nothing better to show than Miss Glaspell's portrait of the "glib and empty" writer whose skill was "a mask for his lack of power" and whose wife sought, even as she died, to lend him that power through the sudden impact of a supremely tragic reality. The surface of the play is delicate and hushed. But beneath the surface is the intense struggle of rending forces. Bernice is dead. The soft radiance of her spirit is still upon the house. It is still reflected in her father's ways and words. Her husband and her friend hasten to that house. And now the drama sets in, the drama that grows from Bernice's last words to her old servant. It is a dra-

matic action that moves and stirs and transforms. There is hardly the waving of a curtain in those quiet rooms. Yet the dying woman's words are seen to have been a creative and dramatic act. Through a bright, hard window one watches people in a house of mourning. They stand or sit and talk haltingly as people do at such times. Nothing is done. Yet everything happens—death and life and a new birth. What more can drama give?

. . . . .

While managers are returning from early spring trips to London and Paris with the manuscripts of plays ranging from Shaw to Bataille, our native drama is gathering an ever more vigorous life. The process has few observers. But all great things have had their origin in obscurity and have often become stained and stunted by contact with the world and its success. It need matter very little to Susan Glaspell whether her play *Inheritors,* which the Provincetown Players are producing, ever reaches Broadway. Nor need it affect her greatly whether the criticism of the hour approves it or not. If the history of literature, dramatic or non-dramatic, teaches us anything, it is that Broadway and its reviewers will some day be judged by their attitude to this work.

Inheritors is not, in all likelihood, a great play, as it is certainly not a perfect one. Neither was Hauptmann's *Before Dawn.* Like the latter it has too pointed an intention; unlike the latter its first act drifts rather than culminates and needs both tightening and abbreviation. But it is the first play of the American theatre in which a strong intellect and a ripe artistic nature have grasped and set forth in human terms the central tradition and most burning problem of our national life quite justly and scrupulously, equally without acrimony or compromise.

In 1879 two men occupied adjoining farms in Iowa: Silas Morton, son of the earliest pioneers from Ohio who fought Black Hawk and his red men for the land, and Felix Fejevary, a Hungarian gentleman, who has left his country and sought freedom in America after the abortive revolution of 1848. The two men were lifelong friends, and Morton, who had had but two months of schooling, absorbed from his Hungarian friend a profound sense of the liberation of culture and left the hill which the white man had wrung by force from the red to be the seat of a college that was to perpetuate the united spirits of liberty and learning. In the second act we are taken to the library of this college. The time is October, 1920. Felix Fejevary, 2nd, now chairman of the board of trustees, is in consultation with Senator Lewis of the finance committee of the State legislature. Fejevary wants an appropriation and recalls to the senator that the college has been one hundred per cent. American during the war and that the students, led by his son, have even acted as strike-breakers in a recent labor dispute. The son, Horace Fejevary, is introduced, a youth who thinks Morton College is getting socially shabby—too many foreigners! —and who is just now enraged at certain Hindu students who have plead the cause of the Indian revolutionists and quoted Lincoln in defense of their position. Senator Lewis thinks the lad a fine specimen. But, talking of appropriations, there is a certain Professor Holden who does not think that the Hindus ought to be deported, who has said that America is the traditional asylum of revolutionaries, and who seems to be a Bolshevik in other ways. Fejevary promises to take care of Holden, and the ensuing scene between these two with its searching revelation of spiritual processes, its bitter suppressions, its implication of an evil barter in values not made with hands touches a point of both dramatic truth and force which no other American playwright has yet rivaled. The ironic and tragic catastrophe is brought about by another member of the third generation, Madeline Fejevary Morton. To her mind, natural and girlish though it is, the monstrous inner contradictions of the situation are not wholly dark. It is two years after the armistice. Yet a boy chum of hers, a conscientious objector, is still in a narrow and noisome cell; the Hindu students who are to be sent to certain destruction are but following the precepts of Lincoln's second inaugural. She interferes in their behalf and proclaims in public, crudely but with the passionate emphasis of youth, the principles for which her two grandfathers founded Morton College. Her offense, under the Espionage Act, is no laughing matter. People with foreign names have got twenty years for less. Her uncle and her aunt plead with her; Holden asks her to let herself ripen for greater uses; her father's state pleads for itself. Miss Glaspell has been careful to make her neither priggish nor tempestuous. Some inner purity of soul alone prompts her to resist. Suddenly an outcast, she goes forth to face her judges and suffer her martyrdom.

No competent critic, whatever his attitude to the play's tendency, will be able to deny the power and brilliancy of Miss Glaspell's characterization. The delineation of the three Fejevarys—father, son and grandson—is masterly. Through the figures of these men she has recorded the tragic disintegration of American idealism. The second Felix remembers his father and his inheritance. But he has faced the seeming facts so long and compromised so much that he is drained dry of all conviction and sincerity. His son is an empty young snob and ruffian. With equal delicacy and penetration we are shown the three Morton generations—the slow, magnificent old pioneer, his broken son, his granddaughter Madeline whose sane yet fiery heart symbolizes the hope and the reliance of the future. Alone and pathetic among them all stands Holden, the academic wage slave who knows the truth but who has an ailing wife; who yearns to speak but who has no money laid by; a quiet man and a terrible judgment on the civilization that has shaped him.

In the second and third acts Miss Glaspell's dialogue expresses with unfailing fitness her sensitive knowledge of her characters. It has entire verisimilitude. But it has constant ironic and symbolic suppressions and correspondences and overtones. This power of creating human speech which shall be at once concrete and significant, convincing in detail and spiritually cumulative in progression, is, of course, the essential gift of the authentic dramatist. That gift Miss Glaspell always possessed in a measure; she has now brought it to a rich and effective maturity.

Ludwig Lewisohn, "Susan Glaspell," in his The Drama and the Stage, *Harcourt Brace Jovanovich, 1922, pp. 102-110.*

Isaac Goldberg   (essay date 1922)

[*As a critic, Goldberg's principal interests were the theater and Latin-American literature. His* Studies in Spanish-American Literature *(1920) and* Brazilian Literature *(1922) are credited with introducing two neglected national groups of writers to English-language readers. In the following essay, Goldberg surveys Glaspell's plays, noting the emphasis on thought and self-conscious emotional expression evident in her characterizations of women.*]

Between Susan Glaspell and Eugene O'Neill there lies a fundamental artistic difference that may be rooted in the difference of sex as well as of temperament. Allowing for the fact that clear-cut contrasts are more or less illusory, we may yet assert that where O'Neill is at bottom the man of feeling, Glaspell is the woman of thought. From this distinction may be derived a list of antitheses. With O'Neill's overflow of feeling comes a straining toward violence and melodrama; he reveals little humor; he is fond of primitive persons, usually men bent upon achieving their purpose at whatever cost; he is voluble, as if his persons' thoughts were struggling to clarity through the mist of inchoate feelings. Glaspell's intensity of thought, on the other hand, induces a straining toward wit, an eminently intellectual process; her humor—leaving aside the question of its body or successfulness—presupposes persons of sophistication. As O'Neill inclines toward the masterful man, so she leans toward the rebellious woman. Where the author of *The Hairy Ape* spurts out words like the gushing of a geyser, Glaspell is reticent, laconic; O'Neill is expression, where Glaspell is repression. "Do you know, dearest", says Ian in her ***Tickless Time,*** "you are very sensitive in the way you feel feeling? Sometimes I think that to feel feeling is greater than to feel."

Now, Miss Glaspell is indeed very sensitive in the way she feels feeling, and by that very token is she the woman of thought, for the process implies an acute consciousness of one's emotions, a standing outside of them even as they are being experienced. And this is precisely what her most significant characters are forever doing, until their very language acquires a difference from ordinary expression that renders it exotic and mirrors the exotic difference of the characters. They speak of their "otherness", of the "outness", or "apartness", as no character in O'Neill has ever spoken. For language, too, is a matter of sophistication, and though O'Neill's people feel their "otherness", they do not feel the feeling, to use Ian's words; they have not achieved self-consciousness. It is thus something more than mere playing with words to affirm that where O'Neill feels his thoughts, Glaspell thinks her feelings. Contrast the descent of *The Emperor Jones* and his white brother *The Hairy Ape* with the ascent of Madeline in Glaspell's ***Inheritors*** or of the overwrought Claire in ***The Verge*** and the seeming trickery of words acquires validity. "Do you know why you're so sure of yourself?" cries Claire to her daughter, Elizabeth. "Because you can't *feel.* Can't feel—the limitless—out there—a sea just over the hill." Miss Glaspell's underscoring of the word feel reveals the difference in *thought* which she packs into that word.

But thought, too, has its misty zones, and more than once Glaspell flutters into them. "We're held by our relations to others—" says Fejevary in *Inheritors.* So far, so good. Few plays fill one with a realization of these necessary, yet numbing, ties, as deeply as does *Inheritors.* Then the speaker adds, "—by our obligations (*vaguely*) to the ultimate thing." Now that "ultimate thing" is what troubles one even in Miss Glaspell's best work, such as *Bernice.* The *vaguely* of her stage direction is something that bothers, not only Mr. Fejevary, but herself and her women protagonists as well. Now and again her women—whether in her lesser things or in her chief labors—feel "big things", but with that same vagueness which necessitates such words as "otherness", "apartness", and similar crepuscular formations. Not that the dramatist is wholly unjustified either in word or procedure; she is dealing with twilight persons, transitional souls, in the nobler meaning of transition; Claire herself is perhaps as puzzled as we; she is a Madeline of *Inheritors* grown up into motherhood and complex selfhood—a Madeline whose problems are no longer exclusively social, but whose individual problem is badly crushed beneath the weight of social pressure. Such a grip has this twilight "apartness" upon Miss Glaspell that she even hints abstractions in her stage-directions. *The Verge,* for that matter, is one long abstraction in three acts, not entirely untrammelled by a pervading symbolism. Glaspell, then, as a serious dramatist—one of the few Americans whose progress is worth watching with the same eyes that follow notable European effort—is largely the playwright of woman's selfhood. That acute consciousness of self which begins with a mere sense of sexual differentiation (exemplified in varied fashion in *Trifles, Woman's Honor, The Outside*) ranges through a heightening social sense (*The People, Close the Book, Inheritors*) to the highest aspirations of the complete personality, the individual (*Bernice, The Verge*). I would not be understood as implying that these plays exhibit solely the phases to which they are here related; all of Miss Glaspell's labors are an admixture of these phases, as is the life of the thinking and feeling woman of to-day. And there is more than rebellious womanhood in these dramas; there is consciousness of valid self, or of a passion for freedom, of dynamic personality; there is craving for life in its innermost meaning.

Miss Glaspell's one-act plays run the gamut from farce to drama. At times her more comic self is the caricature of her more serious. Even allowing for the influence of collaboration in *Suppressed Desires* and *Tickless Time,* are not these laughable creatures but replicas of her more sober protagonists reflected in a distorting mirror? She can poke fun at amateur Freudianism gone mad (*Suppressed Desires*) and then create serious characters that are almost clinical types for the psychoanalytical laboratory (*Bernice, The Verge*). Even her farce reveals her predominantly intellectual interests, as witness *Tickless Time.* Everywhere her ideas, as opposed to her feelings, will out. Thus *The People* is, in part, ostensibly a satire upon the cranks that infest the offices of radical publications, but the dramatist does not seem sure of her footing. Shall it be straight satire, burlesque, or what? As a result the humor becomes too heavily freighted with the suggestion of seriousness, the characters merge into caricature, and the spectator listens to the preachment of some beautiful thoughts that live as words, as ideas, but surely not as drama. So, too,

Woman's Honor, containing some acute criticism of the masculine mind, wavers between the farce and the serious play.

Out of the conversation in the sheriff's house, among the women who have assembled to save the life of a young man by offering as sacrifice their coveted honor, arises a protest against the lily-white ideal of virtue in which men have so long stifled woman's passional existence. They are sick of man's "noble" feeling toward womanhood and recognize, with feminine uncanniness, the source of that feeling in the emotional satisfaction which it breeds in man. "Did it ever strike you as funny," asks the Scornful One, "that woman's honor is only about one thing, and that man's honor is about everything but that thing?" And later in the same piece, from the same personage: "Why, woman's honor would have died out long ago if it hadn't been for men's talk about it." And the Shielded One:

> Oh, I hope you women can work out some way to free us from men's noble feelings about it! I speak for all the women of my—(*Hesitates*) under-world, all those others smothered under men's lofty sentiments toward them! I wish I could paint for you the horrors of the shielded life. (*Says "shielded" as if it were "shameful".*) . . . Our honor has been saved so many times. We are tired.

There are ideas enough in this little piece to float more than one long social satire, yet as Miss Glaspell has presented *Woman's Honor* it is, like *The People,* valuable for the detached ideas and for little else. For realism it is patently impossible; for satire it is too bald; for fantasy, too corporeal. The piece asks for different treatment and should receive it; the idea is too good to be wasted upon an indeterminate parlor entertainment.

The same predominance of idea over character and plausibility pervades *Close the Book,* in which the social status of Jhansi, the gypsy, provides the pivot upon which turns a very pithy critique of genealogical snobbery that proves a boomerang. O'Neill's weakness, particularly in his one-act plays, is the degeneration of feeling into a melodrama redeemed by gleams of originality in conception; Glaspell's weakness in her short pieces is the lapsing of intellectuality into brittle, discerning statement with little relation to organic artistry. And as O'Neill triumphs over these shortcomings in his later and longer work, so too, does Miss Glaspell in her longer subsequent pieces. "Life grows over buried life", says Allie Mayo in *The Outside.* And art grows over buried art. The real Glaspell is not in these one-act plays, however often they may be produced and read. It is in the oft-cited *Trifles,* with its tribute to woman's supposedly finer intuitions as opposed to the supposedly coarser fibre of man,—with its wise if overdone reticence—its foreshadowing of the longer dramas.

O'Neill's women do not understand their menfolk; recall the situation between Curtis and his wife in *The First Man,* between the wives and their men in *Ile,* in *Gold.* Glaspell's men do not understand their women. The Prisoner, in *Woman's Honor,* rather than be saved by the chorus of self-sacrificing females, cries out, *"Oh, hell. I'll plead guilty!"* Craig, in *Bernice,* has neither the profound intuitions that flow at the bottom of creative artistry (he is a writer who utterly misses the tragic plot that is his own married life), nor the appreciation of his wife which would have prevented her virtual suicide. Fejevary, in *Inheritors,* only half understands his niece, Madeline, while Professor Holden, who understands her attitude, cannot after all comprehend her radical action. As for *The Verge,* most of the men are entirely at sea as to Claire, and none more so than her eminently normal husband.

In *Bernice,* first of the full-length dramas, Miss Glaspell seems to carry her reticence to a fault, yet I believe her method is fully justified because it is a spiritual mirror of Bernice's own life tragedy. To add reticence to reticence, Bernice does not even appear, she is dead at the beginning, yet alive in every gesture, every utterance, made by her mourners. (Compare Glaspell's method in *Trifles.*) Her presence fills the intensity of a play that is as chary of deeds as of words; here, too, the idea gives life to the whole, but a genuine, dramatic life. The talk is all of her, and out of the stray phrases a vivid woman arises as if in the round before us. Miss Glaspell's irony is all the more difficult to appreciate in that she is as half-communicative as was Bernice herself; but it is an irony that cuts sharply and deeply into the quick of existence. A double irony, even as it is a double reticence; for her women, not understood of their men, but half understand themselves. That is the price they pay for their ever-groping superiority.

Inheritors, dealing with a social rather than an individualistic theme, is clearer in facture, even as Madeline is more direct in deed. Three generations pass before our eyes: the visionary pioneer who has been inspired by his Hungarian friend with an educational ideal, the son of that Hungarian friend who marries the pioneer's daughter and becomes the president of the college founded by his father-in-law, the motherless niece of that president. Again irony, for the vision of the pioneer degenerates into the corrupted and corrupting opportunism of the college president. But hope, too. For the brave niece refuses to profit by her uncle's social influence; she champions the cause of a handful of liberty-loving foreigners at a time when free speech has been forgotten in her own country, preferring the jail of the body to the jail of ideas. A heroine of the Glaspell tradition, then, who conquers her feelings in the glorious battle of the Idea.

Out of this play rises not only the irony of the succeeding generations, but that of life's inextricable tangle itself. These are no conventional heroes, heroines, and villains of a cause. The danger that besets the dramatist now and again in her one-act pieces is here conquered through a thorough immersion in her theme. "If you sell your own soul," explains Holden, the independently-minded professor who, for the sake of his sick wife, must recede from his noble stand, "it's to love you sell it". Whereupon Madeline: "That's strange. It's love that—brings life along, and then it's love—holds life back." This, to me, is fully as important in the play as are Madeline's social heroics or the shifting of values from one generation to the other. And I may be pardoned if I call attention to the punctuation of the sentence just quoted from Madeline—to the dashes. That is the way Miss Glaspell's women talk—with words

occasionally underscored and parted by dashes. This is no idiosyncrasy of orthography, I imagine. It is the intellectual groping of one who feels her feelings.

It is in the final act of *Inheritors* that Madeline's mentally unbalanced father, Ira, at last breaks his brooding silence and pours forth a flood of words that for all their apparent rambling are pregnant with farseeing sanity. Another irony, this. And it is in *The Verge* that insanity becomes almost the only sanity open to the shut-in personality of Claire. Her speech in the opening act may stand as epigraph to the play:

> (*With difficulty, drawing herself back from the fascination of the precipice.*) You think I can't smash anything? You think life can't break up and go outside what it was? Because you've gone dead in the form in which you found yourself, you think that's all there is to the whole adventure? And that is called sanity. And made a virtue—to lock one in. You never worked with things that grow! Things that take a sporting chance—go mad—that sanity mayn't lock them in—from life untouched—from life—that waits.

Now this, as Dick soon tries to explain, is merely "the excess of a particularly rich temperament", and certainly the playwright has succeeded in projecting a sense of the bewilderment that Claire works upon her husband, her daughter, and her friends. Among these is included the one whom she loves, who breaks through to her (to use her own style of expression) too late. "No, I'm not mad," cries Claire as the obsession grows upon her. "I'm too—sane!"

It would be easy to select strange-sounding passages from the progress of Claire to the murder of him she most loves, and to make easy mock of them. Her "outness", "otherness", "aliveness", provide jutting pegs upon which uncomprehending reviewers may hang the pearls of their journalistic wit. They are, as we have seen, merely verbal images of the woman's difference from her spiritual milieu. A more valid criticism would be directed against the unrelieved tension of its straining toward something which never becomes quite clear. That same criticism may be leveled against *Bernice,* as may the opposite against the too symmetrically patterned *Inheritors.* Yet *The Verge* is the brave protest of an artist-soul against the cramping patterns of existence. It is filled with the cry that ends one of Amy Lowell's best poems: "Christ! What are patterns for?" "Alles Ewige die Erfüllung fürchtet," declares someone in Franz Werfel's most recent drama, *Bocksgesang.* "All things eternal fear their fulfillment." True, a paradox lurks in the phrase, but few words could better describe the fear in which Claire lives amidst the plants which she is trying to nurture into new, inedited existences—the plants which are the symbol of her own little world. And something of of this same fear keeps Miss Glaspell at times half mute—chokes her personages with the fulness of unplumbed possibilities.

It is this refusal to be shut up into a shell, this everlasting aspiration toward newer and different life, that Miss Glaspell has significantly breathed into her long plays. All in all, here is a dramatist who oversteps mere national cataloguing. What she has already done pledges her to even higher things.

Isaac Goldberg, "Susan Glaspell," in his The Drama of Transition: Native and Exotic Playcraft, *Stewart Kidd Company, 1922, pp. 472-81.*

Andrew E. Malone   (essay date 1924)

[*In the following essay, Malone places Glaspell at the fore-front of early twentieth-century American dramatists and judges her plays to be "perfectly constructed."*]

The drama in America is gathering strength and individuality. Little more than a year ago Europe became aware of Eugene O'Neill; it must now recognise a very considerable dramatist in Susan Glaspell. Behind these two is a host of playwrights of more than average quality: Elmer Rice, Channing Pollock, Lula Vollmer, Gilbert Emery, and many others. While it remains perfectly true that one swallow does not make a summer, it remains equally true that a number of swallows certainly indicates that "Sumer is icumen in." The number of considerable dramatists in the United States at present is an indication that within a comparatively short time American drama may lead in quality as well as in quantity. In proportion to its population and its wealth America has yet done very little for drama. The plays of European writers provided the theatrical fare for American citizens, and upon American citizens depended, to a very large extent, the financial status of European authors. There is now a perceptible change; plays which have long run in America are now as often of American as of European authorship. *Sun Up,* by Lula Vollmer, and *Tarnish,* by Gilbert Emery, have shared their great successes in New York with *Saint Joan* and *Outward Bound.* This emergence of the distinctively American drama is one of the most significant things in our time. America is beginning to examine its conscience, having just lately discovered that it had a conscience of its own, and that interestingly significant examination is passing into literature as in *Main Street, Poor White, The Three Black Pennys, The Hairy Ape,* or *Inheritors.* This searching of conscience is certain to be very good for America—it will make Americans more tolerant and tolerable.

Because of this, one is glad to welcome Messrs. Ernest Benn's new series of plays, entitled *Contemporary American Dramatists,* of which the first three volumes have recently been published at four shillings each. All three are by Susan Glaspell, and it may be said at once that they are three of the most arresting plays yet published by this enterprising firm, to which the contemporary drama owes so much. Hitherto Susan Glaspell has been a name only on this side of the Atlantic; but as these plays become known her name will loom larger and larger, as that of a most original and accomplished dramatist. That she already holds a prominent place in American drama is evidenced by the notes on the covers of these volumes. On the cover of *The Verge* it is stated that Susan Glaspell is, "in the opinion of many American critics, the most important of contemporary American dramatists, while, in the opinion of almost all, she vies for the first place with Eugene

O'Neill." Of *Inheritors* the New York *Nation* has said: "The first play of the American Theatre in which a strong intellect and a ripe artistic nature have grasped and set forth in human terms the central tradition and most burning problem of our national life, quite justly and scrupulously, equally without acrimony or compromise." Of *Bernice* it is said: "This achievement is typical of Susan Glaspell's power as a dramatist, just as the slow building up, through the speech and actions of others, of a rare and vital personality, is characteristic of her extraordinary psychological insight." These claims may seem to be extravagant; they are certainly very high, and they make the reader expect much. It must be said that the expectation is more than realised. Susan Glaspell is certainly a remarkable and capable dramatist.

Dissatisfaction and aspiration are the driving forces in *The Verge.* It is a symbolist play, which seems to derive from *The Cherry Orchard* and *The Wild Duck.* Life is too awful, and it might be so different; so much better had humanity the courage, as it has the power. So far is Susan Glaspell from that satisfaction with things-as-they-are, which is so markedly American, that Bolshevism seems conservative beside the revolutionary ardour of her Claire in *The Verge.* A yearning which amounts to a faith keeps Claire on the verge of that Something which is always "beyond the horizon." Life, as lived by humanity, is not enough; to make life better and happier is not enough; only courageous adventuring and experimenting justify life, break through, even if the only result be disaster and chaos! That seems to be the philosophy of Claire. The curtain rises upon a greenhouse that is also a laboratory. Outside there is snow, and patterns have been made upon the glass "as if—as Plato would have it—the patterns inherent in abstract nature and behind all life had to come out, not only in the creative heat within, but in the creative cold on the other side of the glass." Claire is experimenting with a plant which she calls the Edge Vine. This plant is being given an opportunity of breaking out of the ordinary and being "different," but it fails to take advantage of its opportunity. "It's had its chance," Claire says; "it doesn't want to be—what hasn't been." There is the symbol and the reality; an exposition, in American terms, of the philosophy of *Penguin Island.* The vine rejects its opportunity—Claire does not have the opportunity. Another plant is tried, called Breath of Life. All the heat in the house, she insists, must go to Breath of Life, and her very pedestrian husband, Harry, with his friends, Tom and Dick, must eat in the greenhouse. Claire had married Harry because he was a flying man. Flying would liberate man! She would be free, free as air. She would "be where man has never been! Yes—wouldn't you think the spirit could get the idea?" Even the war was a failure. "The war didn't help. Oh, it was a stunning chance! But, fast as we could—scuttled right back to the trim, little things we'd been shocked out of." The chance was lost because "the spirit didn't take the tip." "Plants do it. The big leap—it's called. Explode their species—because something in them knows they've gone as far as they can go. Something in them knows they're shut in to just that. So—go mad—that life may not be prisoned. Break themselves up into crazy things—into lesser things, and from the pieces—may come one sliver of life with vitality to find the future. How beautiful. How brave." Claire's daughter, Elizabeth, thinks that "the object of it all is to make them better plants." Claire, enraged, uproots the Edge Vine to strike Elizabeth with it, but is prevented by one of the men as the curtain falls.

Claire is next seen in a ruined tower with her husband's friend, Tom. The tower is lit by a lantern which throws on the wall a pattern "like some masonry that hasn't been." Somewhere about the Barcarolle from *Hoffman* is being played on a gramophone. Claire says, "Don't listen. That's nothing. This isn't that. (*Fearing.*) I tell you—it isn't that. Yes, I know—that's amorous—enclosing. I know—a little place. This isn't that. (*Her arms going around him—all the lure of 'that' while she pleads against it as it comes up to them.*) We will come out—to radiance—in far places. (*Admitting, using.*) Oh, then let it be that! Go with it. Give up—the otherness, I will! And in the giving up—perhaps a door—we'd never find by searching. And if it's no more—than all have known, I only say it's worth the allness! (*Her arms wrapped round him.*) My love—my love—let go your pride in loneliness and let me give you joy." In the end she strangles Tom, for what reason it is very difficult to comprehend, and she passes from the scene singing hymns.

The Verge is a play of absorbing interest. It contains much that may be said to be nonsense, but it is shot through with passages of great beauty. Technically the play is perfect; every incident and every line of dialogue are fraught with direct and cumulative significance. On the stage it should be thrilling, but it will require acting of a very high order. Fresh from its triumphant performance of *Henry IV.,* perhaps the Dublin Drama League will give the public an opportunity of seeing *The Verge.*

Inheritors is objective and ironic. Yearnings there are, but they are yearnings that are realisable in this life and in this world. The curtain rises on the Morton sittingroom, in the Middle West, in 1879. The Mortons had been pioneers, taking the land from the Indians, and Felix Fejevary, a political refugee from Hungary, had settled close by. Silas Morton says to Fejevary: "I'm seeing something now. Something about you. I've been thinking a good deal about it lately—it's something to do with—with the hill. I've been thinkin' what it meant all these years to have a family like yours next place to. They did something pretty nice for the corn belt when they drove you out of Hungary. Funny, how things don't end the way they begin. I mean, what begins don't end. It's another thing ends." Silas Morton's dream is to see a college on the hill, which the red men loved, where "the best that has been thought and said in the world" would be studied and acted upon. "That's what the hill is for! (*Pointing.*) Don't you see it? End of our trail, we climb a hill and plant a college. Plant a college, so's after we are gone that college says for us, says in people learning has made more: This is why we took the land!"

The college is founded, and in the second act the fortieth anniversary of the opening of Morton College is being celebrated in the year 1920. Felix Fejevary, son of the Hungarian refugee, is discovered in conversation with Senator Lewis. "Morton College did her part in winning the war," he says, "and we're holding up our end right along. You'll see the boys drill this afternoon. It's a great place for them, here on the hill—shows up from so far around. They're a fine lot of fellows. You know, I presume, that they went in as strike-breakers during the trouble down here at the steel works. The plant would have had to close but for Morton College. That's one reason I venture to propose this thing of a state appropriation for enlargement. Why don't we sit down for a moment? There's no conflict with the State University—they have their territory; we have ours. Ours is an important one—industrially speaking. The State will lose nothing in having a good strong college here—a one-hundred-per-cent. American college." Silas Morton's gift has become the exact opposite of the old man's intention. It is a "hundred-per-cent-American" institution; snobbish, narrow, mean and vulgar, with no more relation to scholarship and fine thinking than the State Senator. American virtues are merely British vices transplanted and exaggerated. Silas Morton tried to prevent it being so, but he failed. His college merely stifles thought, restricts liberty, salaams to wealth. Professor Holden, the college's only scholar, is threatened with dismissal because he is a Radical; Jordan, a brilliant student, is expelled because he is a conscientious objector; Hindu students are mauled for daring to quote Lincoln, and in the ensuing melee, Silas Morton's granddaughter, Madeline, is arrested for aiding the Hindus and assaulting the police. The third act introduces the plant motif of *The Verge.* Ira Morton, the son of Silas, takes no interest in the college, his only interest is the improvement of his corn. The corn improves with each generation, but despite the college, mankind does not improve. The corn which improves and spreads is contrasted with man, who grows mean and narrow. All this is emphasised, and the play ends with the compromise of Professor Holden and Madeline going to jail because she only realised Silas Morton's ideal.

Inheritors is deep and bitter satire. It is a strong, definite attack upon that jingoism which masquerades as nationalism, and which makes nationalism itself a menace to civilisation. The gradual perversion of the spirit of freedom is a grave problem for America—it is no less grave for the people of other nations. Here is the Ibsen of *An Enemy of the People;* the satire is more obvious, more crude, more American. But *Inheritors* is a very fine play, technically as perfect as *The Verge,* more definite in its meaning, and, therefore, likely to be more popular in its appeal.

The third play, *Bernice,* somewhat resembles *The Verge.* It is in three very short acts which develop a personality that never appears. By the speech, action, and suggestion of five people a sixth person is made not only definite but dominant. Bernice is dead, not long dead; her corpse is still in the house with her father and an old servant when the curtain rises. They await the arrival of Bernice's husband, Craig Norris, and her friend, Margaret Pierce. About these people is woven the most common and the least noticed of human tragedies—the tragedies of imperception and incomprehension. Eyes do not see, minds do not understand; and there is sorrow, misery, and waste. Remorselessly, every word striking, this tragedy of quiet works to its end. It is a wonderful play.

Upon meeting the statement that Susan Glaspell "vies for first place with Eugene O'Neill," the first impulse is to smile derisively. Having read these three plays the attitude must change. The two dramatists have little in common save their nationality. In technique Susan Glaspell is undoubtedly the superior of Eugene O'Neill. There is no trace of O'Neill's loose construction about these plays; they are as perfectly constructed as a first-class watch. There is little of O'Neill's humanity about them either. Except in *Inheritors* the characters are somewhat remote from life, they are the exceptions who feel deepest and perhaps see farthest. Yet the plays are essentially studies in personality. Behind the body, behind the mind, is the searching ground where Susan Glaspell finds her treasures. She is a dramatist of the Ego—not so flamboyant as Toller, and with the ironic pity of Galsworthy. The psychology is as scrupulously studied as is that of *The Emperor Jones,* without any of the wildness of setting to heighten the effect. These plays would be tremendously effective upon the stage, and it may be hoped that an opportunity will soon be afforded to playgoers to make acquaintance with the work of one of the most interesting dramatists of to-day. Of course, there are the echoes from others in her work, but the echoes are all arranged to produce not only harmony, but a powerfully vivid personality, which is a very welcome addition to contemporary dramatists.

Andrew E. Malone, "Susan Glaspell," in The Dublin Magazine, *Vol. II, August, 1924-January, 1925, pp. 107-11.*

The Spectator (essay date 1926)

[*In the following review, the critic faults Glaspell for being too strident in her plays, but ultimately praises her work for its experimental themes and characterizations.*]

We owe Mr. Norman Macdermott, and the company of the Liverpool Repertory Theatre, a great deal for an excellent performance of Miss Susan Glaspell's *Inheritors,* at the Everyman Theatre.

It is the most ambitious play of this very remarkable American dramatist, the one that obviously ranges farthest—traversing a long stretch of time, and including an extensive criticism of American mental limitations. This is not to say that *Inheritors* is Miss Glaspell's *best* play. If, in the theatre, you like a light thrown upon secret places—the theme working itself out from the individual soul—you will prefer *The Verge* or *Bernice:* the first given by Miss Thorndike not long ago; the other, for a few performances, at the Gate Theatre.

These two are curiously enclosed, hothouse dramas, in which a few characters turn within a narrow circle, or strive to be free of it. But whether Miss Glaspell narrows or broadens her argument, she is primarily the dramatist, under a new guise, and using a sturdy, if often strained, language, of the very old quarrel between love or habit and duty; of the opposition between what appears to be fixed, in convention, or in mere amiability of acquiescent character, and the possibilities of an expectant creative life. Never to rest in a sameness of what *is,* never to close a door upon oneself, ever to be ready for the otherness, the allness, the awareness waiting for the receptive soul; this appears to be her "message," and these are the striving terms of the new American metaphysic. Well, we knew them, or something like them, in Emerson. Spiritually, these Puritans, after so many generations, have become anarchists. Miss Glaspell is, I think, the first effectively to dramatize their creed.

In *Inheritors* the prologue (far too long) shows us a liberal America, welcoming, "way back" in 1879, the Hungarian refugee, whose way of putting things so nobly inspired the farmer, Silas Morton, that he determined to found the college on the hill, where the light thus vouchsafed might continue to shine before men. Idealists are like that. Suddenly illuminated themselves, they hope always that the *vitai lampada,* the torch of intellectual brilliance will be caught from hand to hand. And perhaps their belief in education will be the last of their illusions to be destroyed.

When the curtain rises again, we see the seed scattered by trusting Silas already in the mildewed ear. In a word, we see—a University. Its prudent head would still be a-scattering, if he could get money for that purpose from a "hundred-per-cent. American" Senator, who demands that the radical Professor Holden shall not preach too boldly, but confine himself within an "unimpeachable Americanism." Holden bows the head, for he has a delicate wife to keep. This great hospitable college will thereupon deport the Hindu students who love freedom for India as well as for America. So is the lesson of Silas misapplied. Who will now sow the golden grain in other men's fields? The duty, with Miss Glaspell, is always reserved for some gallant *woman*—in *Inheritors* for the girl, Madeline Morton, who will preach to her deaf elders the pure doctrine of eternal receptivity. In dramatic terms, Madeline will go to prison for defending the persecuted Hindus with her best tennis racket.

Inheritors, you see, is less the separate story of the rebel Madeline than a shrewd questioning of two stages in a growing civilization. But, although Madeline is perhaps a little conventionally painted—observe her fond fingering, at the end, of the new tennis racket that replaces the one smashed on a policeman's head—Miss Glaspell, even here, never becomes the mere thesis-dramatist. Her characters live; though they help, as living people do, to illustrate ideas.

Yet I feel that, in her other plays, we get more of her feverish grasp upon the inner life. With the extraordinary "Miss Claire"—she is really Mrs. Archer—of *The Verge,* the pursuit of the ideal, of otherness, takes the odd thwarted form of petting certain plants—symbols, to her, of her longing to make grow "what wasn't there before." Claire should have been content with her flowers. But there is always sex; and she compromised with that other craving—afraid of its diverting her purpose, yet resigning herself *en passant* to three slightly sketched men, actually named Tom, Dick and Harry, in mockery, I suppose, of their "sameness." Tom was presumably the only danger. He might have moulded her to the love that imprisons. So she strangles him. Claire reminds one of *Hedda Gabler.* Only, she is more dangerous; for Hedda was content to use General Gabler's pistols on herself.

The keen self-consciousness of Claire Archer strove for expression by grasping at something beyond itself. She was deceived—so it seems to me—in taking a projection of her innate egotism for a divine frenzy: "a leading from above, a something given." This cult of hers brought her to the "verge" of mania. In *Bernice,* the wonderful woman, who has died suddenly, mysteriously, before the play begins, has tried to influence her weaker husband by letting him be told a lie about her death. Bernice wished him to believe that she had killed herself—apparently in order to reanimate his flagging "awareness," to inspire him, from her death-bed, to a new conviction of his worth, proved by his power to prompt such devotion in a martyr. And this, like Pirandello's *The Life I Gave,* or Ibsen's *Little Eyolf,* is one of those retrospective plays that depend for their reactions upon the influence of an unseen agent—here, the dead wife who makes this perilous experiment; in Ibsen, the dead child; in Pirandello, the dead man whose body lies in the next room. It is an eerie dramatic device, which, however, compels too much hovering and brooding over the virtues or vices of a character not seen by the audience, and therefore undefined. It is the sort of situation that would have appealed to Henry James, and one supposes that he, together with Ibsen, is an important influence upon Miss Glaspell. One may fancy that *Bernice* is just the sort of play that the author of *Guy Domville* might have written, had he not been too soon discouraged from "theatricals." He too would have perhaps a little wearied us—remember *The Portrait of a Lady*—by too much insistence upon the personality of one woman around whom the others revolve. It is nothing but Bernice, Bernice all the time; as in *The Verge* poor Tom, Dick and Harry hardly matter, but as foils to the horticultural Claire; as in *Inheritors* Madeline Morton, once launched upon her crusade, easily dominates the rest.

A great sincerity (often incompatible with a sense of humour) prevents Miss Glaspell from realizing the importance of not being *too* earnest. She insists, hammers in her points, repeats herself. Her plays would be the better for condensation. And no doubt English audiences are puzzled by such flowers of American speech as the subtle Claire's "What inside dope have you on what I was meant to be?" But this unimpeachable Americanism of style fits in well enough with a tense Emersonian preoccupation with the spirit. One would not have it revised. All one would like would be to temper Miss Glaspell's restlessness, her Western obsession about progress—to convince her that the individual conscience can mislead, to make her laugh a little. But, indeed, in creating the strange tiresome heroine of *The Verge* she has already shown, perhaps, that she *can* turn round upon herself, contradict herself, and see the defects of her great qualities. If she can do that, she should go far. She has already gone a good way.

R. J., "An Anarchist of the Spirit," in The Spectator, *Vol. 136, No. 5090, January 16, 1926, pp. 80-1.*

Bartholow V. Crawford   (essay date 1930)

[*In the essay below, Crawford presents an overview of Glas-*

pell's works up to 1930 and discusses the influence of her Iowa upbringing on her writing.]

Unlike some of the literary great, who, in making themselves into cosmopolites, have travelled so far actually and figuratively from the place of their birth as to pass quite out of any connection with it, Susan Glaspell is still at heart a daughter of Iowa. The surroundings of her girlhood, it is evident, made an ineffaceable impression upon her memory. While some of the stories in *Lifted Masks,* her first volume, have a Chicago background, and at least one other, that of Paris, several have the settings that she knew so well while an undergraduate at Drake University, and a newspaper woman, covering the doings of the legislature. To her drama, *The Inheritors,* she has given a setting strongly suggestive of Davenport, with its references to Black Hawk, and to the steel works. The denominational college of the drama might well be a composite of several such Iowa institutions, while the radical professor, with his long-suppressed passion for Greece, must remind every reader of her late husband, George Cram Cook. Her general experience of rural life also served her in good stead in the composition of her powerful novel, *Brook Evans.*

The Iowa experiences of which these works are the record were those from birth to early maturity. Born in Davenport in 1882, she was educated at Drake University, where in 1899 she was an unsuccessful candidate for the editorship of the *Delphic.* She remained for some time in Des Moines as a practical newspaper woman on the *Daily News* and the *Capital.* Following this, she was for a time a postgraduate student at the University of Chicago. *The Glory of the Conquered* (1909), with its background inspired by Chicago, was sufficiently successful to finance a year in the Latin quarter of Paris.

The desire to live life at its fullest, and to experience all its varieties, took her thereafter to a ranch in Idaho, and then to Provincetown, Massachusetts, where some of her most memorable years were destined to be spent. A succession of works followed; some fiction, some drama. *The Visioning* (1911), *Lifted Masks* (1912), *Fidelity* (1915), *Brook Evans* (1928), and *Fugitive's Return* (1929) belong to the first named group.

Association at Provincetown with George Cram Cook, whom she married in 1913, made her a sharer, as actress and producer as well as author, in the project known then and now as the Provincetown Players, one of the most significant dramatic enterprises of our generation. Among the plays written by her for this group of intellectual amateurs were *Suppressed Desires* (1914) and *Trifles* (1917)—two of the best short plays in our language. Following the removal of Cook and Miss Glaspell to Greenwich Village, New York, in 1917, where he was manager and she was chief playwright, *Woman's Honor* (1918), *Bernice* (1919), *The Inheritors* (1921), and *The Verge* (1922) were produced.

Immediately afterward came the journey to Greece with her husband in 1922, which ended with his death and burial at Delphi. The incidents of this journey, and indeed of their entire married life, are contained in her volume, *The*

Road to the Temple (1926). To a volume printed the year previous, *Greek Coins,* some poems by George Cram Cook, with memorabilia by Floyd Dell, Edna Kenton, and Susan Glaspell, she had contributed an affectionate memoir. Shortly thereafter, she married Norman Matson, author and critic, and with him produced her latest works, *The Comic Artist* (1927), and *Fugitive's Return* (1929). They have moved to an old farm house at Truro, Cape Cod, where they plan to write in retirement.

The work of Susan Glaspell reveals considerable variety in form, setting, and style; but there is also a degree of continuity and coherence in ideals and point of view. In her early volume of stories, *Lifted Masks,* in her novel, *Brook Evans,* and in her play, *The Inheritors,* she exhibits a sensitiveness to human injustice, an insight into human nature, and a realization of the unceasing struggle between idealism and the animal which is not cynical but sympathetic. No one can follow her through the moving pages of *Brook Evans,* and her analyses of the feelings and motives of her chief characters, without feeling the complexity and contradictoriness of the natures of men and women; nor, it might be added, without realizing that the author of this novel of rural life is herself a daughter of the soil.

The Inheritors, more than most of her works, emphatically dates itself. There is the satire on babbittism (French authors assure us that no capital is now required) and one hundred per cent Americanism. There is, too, the specific reference to the injustice of keeping in federal prisons, two years after the end of the war, men who opposed our entrance into that war. No one can doubt, reading this play, where Miss Glaspell's sympathies were in such matters. Clearly, she was no jingo; no narrow nationalist. This play, curiously enough, has about it more than a passing suggestion of Ibsen's *The Friend of the People.* Though talky, and at times tiresome, it has power, as evidenced by its revival by Eva Le Gallienne at the Civic Repertory Theatre. It will not soon be forgotten.

The Comic Artist, one of her latest works, is a sophisticated drama of artist life. The local color, acquired through years of life in Bohemian circles, is utilized with skill, while the clash of characters ends in an inevitably tragic conclusion.

Some of her remaining works are too little known to warrant comment; others, such as *Suppressed Desires* and *Trifles,* are so familiar as to make discussion superfluous. Suffice it to say that in Susan Glaspell Iowa claims an author of wide experience, varied capabilities, and undoubted genius. The Middle Western scene was for her not something to be lived down or forgotten, but one of her richest resources; and, in every reference to the region of her birth, there is affectionate understanding and sympathy.

Bartholow V. Crawford, "Susan Glaspell," in The Palimpsest, *Vol. XI, No. 12, December, 1930, pp. 517-21.*

Arthur E. Waterman (essay date 1966)

[*Waterman is an American critic and educator. In the fol-*lowing excerpt from his book Susan Glaspell, *he examines Glaspell's early novels* The Glory of the Conquered, The Visioning, *and* Fidelity.]

During the years in which she was writing her short stories [Susan] Glaspell was also writing novels, and she published three between 1909 and 1915. In these longer works she moved beyond the restricted local-color tradition to the larger and more significant movement called "regionalism." The turn to the longer form of the novel meant that she would have to develop different techniques, more complicated plots, larger characters, and, most importantly, she would have to come to terms with her region, to move beyond the oversimplified attitude she held in most of her short stories. She had to see the Midwest as more than a locale, as more than a pleasant place where problems could be neatly resolved by a twist of fate and a happy ending. The novel demands that the writer create a world with all the attendant complexities, ambiguities, and elements of disorder that any region has. In other words, when she turned to the novel, Miss Glaspell had to enlarge her technique and her ideas.

A first novel, *The Glory of the Conquered* (1909) does not show Miss Glaspell's maturity as a writer at all. It has the same sentimentality, optimism, and idealism of the short fiction; and it is directed toward the feminine reader looking for a romantic story quite removed from the humdrum reality of ordinary life. The subtitle of the novel, "The Story of a Great Love," indicates the plot, for the story traces the love and marriage of Ernestine Stanley, girl painter, and Karl Hubers, boy scientist. Love is the agent which binds art and science together, uniting opposites, bringing happiness. When Karl goes blind, then dies, we see that love not only conquers all but also overcomes all. Ernestine learns to find glory in being conquered; her love gives meaning to her defeat. The novel closes as she resolves to carry on by painting the world she and Karl loved, by showing others the beauty that transfigured their lives.

In case the reader misses the significance of the power of love, Ernestine explains the meaning of Mercie's statue *Gloria Victus,* stating clearly the idealistic moral: "The keynote of it is that stubborn grip on the broken sword. I should think every fighter would love it for that. And it is more than the glory of the good fight. It is the glory of the unconquerable will. . . . What we call victory and defeat are incidents—things individual and temporal. The thing universal and eternal is this immortality of the spirit of victory."

I quote this passage to illustrate not only the theme but also the extremely vague style of the novel and to show the kind of trite idealism Miss Glaspell had to overcome as a writer before her art could achieve any structure.

In addition to Karl and Ernestine there are three other characters who figure prominently in the novel. Karl's cousin Georgia, a newspaper woman who sees things with a journalist's eye, adds a note of realism and comedy to the romantic tale. Usually after an emotional scene between Ernestine and Karl (and there are more than enough of these) the reader laughs at Georgia, and her romance with a paper bag manufacturer called Joe Tank, before returning to the heavier melodrama in the main plot. Georgia disappears in the middle of the book where the tragedy deepens, and the reader has to take the emotion "straight." Dr. Parkman, Karl's closest friend, remains throughout the novel. He has been wounded by life, has slackened his grip on the sword, we might say, and has become a misanthrope with a gruff and fundamentally honest approach to matters. He serves as a kind of counterpoint to Ernestine's lyrical faith, but even he is moved to tears several times in the story. Finally there is Beason, Karl's student assistant, who gets involved in a trivial plot from which Karl helps him escape; this incident shows the nobility of our hero and his kind patronage of the lesser people surrounding him. These minor characters illustrate how neat and well-made the whole story is—how artificial and unreal.

The major defect of *The Glory of the Conquered,* then, is its lack of credibility. Not only is the writing consistently as bad as in the quoted passage, but the characters are shallow and unconvincing. We never have any concrete evidence that these are real people living real lives. We never see Ernestine actually painting or doing housework; we see Karl in the laboratory only when he is making great discoveries. Usually the two recline in front of a fire while the coterie of hired help hover in the background. The main characters remain cardboard figures whose symbolic purpose conceals their living identities. The Chicago background of the novel is likewise unrealistic. Although Miss Glaspell mentions a few streets, she does not make her locale an integral part of her story. Finally, the theme itself is too easy, too naïve to support our credence. As the reviewer of *The Nation* complained, "Now, if this is a great love, every Hamlet knows greater ones. Ernestine had sacrificed only her art work, a mean thing beside the good names, well being, and honor which many a woman has given for another's sake." At first glance we might suppose the novel ends unhappily—after all, Karl is dead—but we are supposed to accept the idea that Ernestine has triumphed; her defeat has become victory.

The Glory of the Conquered indicates how much Miss Glaspell needed to learn not only about artistic control but about her world before she could create more than the trivial stuff of romantic sentimentality. She needed to grow up. Between 1909 and 1911, the date of her next novel, she matured considerably, both as a woman and as an artist. She traveled to Europe in 1910, spent a winter in Colorado, and returned to Davenport a much traveled, cosmopolitan woman. About 1907, too late to affect her first novel, she met George Cram Cook, the radical son of a leading Davenport family, and his friend Floyd Dell, an ardent young Socialist. These two had started in Davenport the Monist Society, a club for the radicals, freethinkers, and eccentrics of the town. In her biography of Cook [*The Road to the Temple*], Miss Glaspell writes that attending the society's meetings was for her a kind of rebirth: "Some of us were children of pioneers; some of us still drove Grandmother to the Old Settlers' Picnic the middle of August. Now—pioneers indeed, that pure, frightened, exhilarating feeling of having stepped out of your own place and here, with these strange people, far

from your loved ones and already a little lonely, beginning to form a new background."

Dell implies that Cook and he helped shape Miss Glaspell's literary education when he says in his autobiography that "Susan was a slight, gentle, sweet, whimsically humorous girl, a little ethereal in appearance, but evidently a person of great energy, and brimful of talent; but, we agreed, too medieval-romantic in her views of life." Cook's political novel *The Chasm* and Dell's enthusiasm for the new directions in art which were just beginning the Chicago little-renaissance introduced Miss Glaspell to a new kind of writing, one with fresh concepts about the nature of art that were quite different from popular magazine stories and Romantic novels like *The Glory of the Conquered.* Cook had written: "Our fiction is juvenile—written for people who are no longer children but who have never grown up. . . . There is no hope for American writers until they can forget the existence of immature adults. Literature is, to be sure, a social product, created not only by the artist but by his audience; but it is for the artist to intensify his audience." Under the tutelage of Cook and Dell, Miss Glaspell began to view life in other than "medieval-romantic" terms and to read in a literary tradition concerned with an immediate, realistic sense of the present, often with a political basis.

All these factors help explain why *The Visioning* (1911) marks such an advance in her fictional approach. It has what *The Glory of the Conquered* so critically lacked: a realistic background, believable characters, and a conscious sense of its relevance for the contemporary reader. In this novel, Katherine Wayneworth Jones, the daughter of an old army family, lives on a military post in Iowa. In a quick opening scene, Kate saves a girl from drowning herself. Protected by her family's position and her own sense of class, Katie cannot understand why anyone would want to die on a sunny day. The girl, Ann Forrest, answers: "It would be foolish to try to make a girl like you understand that nothing can be so bad as sunshine." The rest of the novel concerns Katie's initiation into a world that could drive a person to suicide, which in turn leads her to a clear understanding about the nature of army life, the class struggle, love, and her own destiny.

As Ann grows to an emotional maturity, Katie grows to an intellectual one; she changes from a sublimely innocent, blindly assured girl to a socially responsible, politically aware woman. The two girls hold opposing but equally illusive ideas about life. Ann is the daughter of a stern Midwestern preacher who taught her that all pleasure is sin. Working in Chicago, she was exploited because she was poor and she was driven into an affair which left her guilt-ridden and suicidal. Katie, on the other hand, sees life as all pleasure. She winks at life and tampers with Ann's future in a frivolous game which ignores Ann's desperate need for love and security.

The climax of the novel occurs when Ann meets her Chicago seducer, coincidentally an army friend of Katie's, and runs away. Searching for Ann, Katie encounters a world completely different from her sheltered, special position: a world which shatters her illusions. Chicago is so different from the misty setting of *The Glory of the Conquered* that she says it is "too loathsome for the civilized man and woman of today to set foot in." When Katie visits Ann's family, she meets the intolerance and cruelty of so-called religion; she regards Ann's father "as product of something which had begun way back across the centuries, seeing far back of Reverend Saunders that spirit of intolerance which had shaped him—wrung him dry." She discovers woman's suffrage, evolution, and Socialism. She meets Alan Mann, an ex-enlisted man and a Socialist, who makes her realize the basic inequality of military life. Her marriage to Mann at the end of the novel indicates how far in development she has come, for he represents a new political-social involvement that she could not have accepted before her initiation. Ann, too, finds peace. In a rather far-fetched arrangement, she marries Katie's brother.

Miss Glaspell clearly reflects her own awakening to the reality of her environment through Katie's initiation. Underlying Katie's story is a symbolic meaning suggested by the title of the novel: a vision of a better world, with better people in it who have undergone the same growth she has. "A Vision," Mann says, "of what the world might be—world with the army left out, with all the army represented to me vanished from the earth. With men not ruling and cursing other men; but working together—the world for all and all for the world."

Thus *The Visioning* represents a combination of protest and hope. It attacks the shallow views of the ruling class and the cruelty of a society that exploits the poor; but the novel also predicts that social conscience, liberal thought, and true love can lead to a better America. Miss Glaspell's portrayal of army life is remarkably incisive, touching both the officer with his arrogance of privilege and the enlisted man who escapes responsibility for three "squares" and a dollar a day. Her condemnation of the different aspects of her society is not so slanted as the attacks in the muckraking novels of the time, but the details show those sharp touches of realism that were a part of her local-color training.

The hope of the novel is not nearly so clear. Katie's political progress gets all mixed up with her romantic attachment for Mann, and his Socialistic ideals degenerate into a more conventional desire to live happily ever after. Instead of allowing Ann to work out her future within a political-economic context suitable to her background, Miss Glaspell marries her to the wealthy brother of Katie. Apparently Miss Glaspell was sufficiently influenced by her travels and acquaintance with Cook and Dell to begin to question quite severely her previously easy acceptance of the world around her; but, as yet, she was not ready, nor able, to relinquish her middle-class attitudes. Marriage is still the goal for her heroines; the city a place of slums; and liberal thought a kind of hazy abstraction. In other words, the novel merges two schools of writing: the middle-class novel of Romance and the Naturalistic novel of revolt. The result is not so chaotic as we might expect. It is a smooth, readable story, which for its day makes a definite and noteworthy point; and, in light of the war about to break out in three years, it contains a prophetic warning.

As is customary in novels of initiation, the growth of the main character symbolizes a larger issue. Katie represents the rich, privileged class of prewar America who must accept the responsibility of their wealth, revise their attitude toward labor, and join in the struggle for a new democratic society where the poor can keep their dignity and not be driven to suicide as Ann was. Katie's brother renounces his experiments with new weapons in order to become a forest ranger who reclaims land instead of furthering destruction. The crucial test for such novels is whether the characters can shoulder their symbolic meaning without losing their validity as people. Katie comes through as a delightful girl, a fine example of the idle rich. But her initiation is not quite so convincing, nor is her marriage to Mann. Ann is believable as a study in neurosis and as an example of the typical working-class girl; but Mann, no better than a mouthpiece for the author's beliefs, lacks any real substance as a true person. All in all, *The Visioning* makes a remarkable advance over Miss Glaspell's first novel, and it indicates that she was beginning to realize that her art had to speak first to the present about the political and social ideas of the immediate scene.

Fidelity (1915), also a novel of protest and hope, realistically pictures the small Midwestern town with its narrow morality that limits the individual's freedom; to do so, it depicts the life of one woman who dares to challenge provincialism. Perhaps Miss Glaspell realized that the vague political ideals in *The Visioning* had been overwhelmed by the love story, so she turned in *Fidelity* to a more feminine theme that she knew something about. She had been in love with a married man, Cook, who had to wait for his divorce before he could marry her; therefore, she could treat this problem with firsthand knowledge.

Whatever the reason, *Fidelity* is about a woman who has run away with a married man, breaking the strongest tenet of the Midwestern moral code. The novel revolves around the woman's concept of fidelity: to marriage, to her lover, to her society, family, above all, to herself. Ruth Holland has to account for the consequences of her act, has to judge herself as either immoral and unfaithful to society's laws or as right and faithful to herself. Obviously, Miss Glaspell means us to see that fidelity is ambiguous: one has to choose—at least Ruth does—between conformity and individualism, although each exacts a price, and offers a reward. At the end of the novel Ruth chooses individualism, for she rejects a chance to marry her lover and legalize her long affair with him. She decides instead to go to New York where she can join the "new" women engaged in the feminist revolt. Ruth takes a new future rather than a dead past. "Don't you think, Stuart," she asks her lover, "that the future is rather too important a thing to be given up to ratifying the past?"

Fidelity, however, is not a feminist novel; Miss Glaspell wasn't ready to present the "new woman" until her play *The Verge.* Ruth's actions and decisions take place within the confines of the Midwestern town of Freeport where there are moral attitudes she must consider before she can reject them and leave. When she meets a young girl in love with a married man, Ruth is forced to relive emotions she once felt and, with her own experience in mind, to answer the question Mildred asks her: "Was it worth it?" Knowing that her love for Stuart has died, that habit has replaced passion, that her family, friends, and Stuart's wife have suffered because of what she has done, Ruth tries to make Mildred see the price she will have to pay for illicit love; and in answering her, Ruth judges herself:

> "But what are you going to put in the place of that social world, Mildred?" she gently asked. "There must be something to fill its place. What is that going to be?"
>
> "Love will fill its place!" came youth's proud, sure answer.
>
> Ruth was looking straight ahead; the girl's tone had thrilled her—that faith in love, that courage for it. It was so youthful!—so youthfully sure, so triumphant in blindness. Youth would dare so much—youth knew so little. She did not say anything; she could not bear to.
>
> "Love can fill its place!" Mildred said again, as if challenging that silence. And as still Ruth did not speak she demanded sharply, "Can't it?"
>
> Ruth turned to her a tender, compassionate face, too full of feeling, of conflict, to speak. Slowly, as if she could not bear to do it, she shook her head.

The ambiguity of Ruth's sin is suggested by the use of the Jamesian technique of shifting points of view. Miss Glaspell lights her subject with various "lamps," each of whom has his own attitude to fidelity. Dr. Deane Franklin is one of the few people in Freeport who has any sympathy for Ruth; his wife, Amy, expresses the conventional view of Freeport society—the female scorning the outcast: " 'Ruth Holland,' she began very quietly, 'is a human being who selfishly—basely—took her own happiness, leaving misery for others. She outraged society as completely as a woman could outrage it. She was a thief, really, —stealing from the thing that was protecting her, taking all the privileges of a thing she was a traitor to. She was not only what we call a bad woman, she was a hypocrite.' "

Ted, Ruth's younger brother, articulates the family's resentment and suffering from her crime; and Stuart's wife, Marion Williams, vehemently states the feelings of the wronged woman. Thus fidelity is put into a total perspective: we have the inner circle of Freeport society codifying and enforcing the moral standards; the outer circle of the offenders; the understanding doctor who communicates with both circles; and the ones who have suffered because of Ruth's act.

Whether Miss Glaspell was consciously imitating James or not, I cannot say, but the effect of her use of multiple points of view in this novel was to render in all its complexity one of James's most consistent themes: the ambiguity of moral issues. *Fidelity* has two concerns: an attack on the moral narrowness of the small town, which condemns any violation of its stringent code; and an expression of the individual's search for the meaning and direction of her life, regardless of social mores. Like the short story " 'Finality' in Freeport," this novel shows Miss Glaspell's sharp awareness of the defects in the Mid-

west of her day. Since she was living in Greenwich Village when *Fidelity* was written, she could view her birthplace with some detachment and its limitations, especially in terms of moral conventionality, from the perspective of the Village's extreme unconventionality. The novel indicates what this narrowness can do to the sensitive individual who refuses to play the game according to the rules, who wants more than clubroom gossip and provincial pursuits.

Like George Cram Cook, who had suffered a certain amount of ostracism because of his odd behavior, Miss Glaspell was disturbed by the failure of the Midwest to sustain its pioneer heritage of individuality, integrity, and simple virtue. Implicit in *Fidelity* is a comparison between the pioneer, agrarian past and the new, superficial, prudish present; between the land and the town; or, in different terms, between Ruth's open passion for her beliefs and those people like Amy who use convention to cloak their incapacity for genuine feelings.

Unfortunately, Miss Glaspell could not present Ruth's aspirations for the future with the same careful details she used to attack the town. The dream of individual freedom, vague by its very nature, is difficult to define and to render in narrative terms. Ruth doesn't seem to know what she expects to find in New York. She looks for life as if it were something that might fall from the skies at her feet. She says, "I want more life—more things from life. And I'm going to New York just because it will be so completely new—and because it's the center of so many living things. . . . It's as if a lot of old things, old ideas, had been melted, and were fluid now, and were to be shaped anew." We can guess at what the "old things" are— outmoded conventionality for one—but we have no indication as to how they are "to be shaped anew."

Like *The Visioning, Fidelity* shows that Miss Glaspell wanted her novels to express ideas, to be more than a reflection of Midwestern life. But she had yet to find the narrative strategies that could make these ideas meaningful within the details of her story. After her plays, in which her ideas could be given dramatic focus, she conveyed in the later novels, using more successful techniques than in *Fidelity,* Ruth's search for a meaningful life.

By 1915, with the exception of a few short stories, the first part of Miss Glaspell's writing career was over. With her marriage to Cook in 1913 and with her new interest in the drama, her life and literary concerns changed radically. In her beginnings as a writer, she used the local-color tradition, accepting its established form and appeal as easily as she accepted her Midwestern home. Gradually she worked out her own formulas and themes, but in general she was neither markedly better than nor different from other local colorists of the time. Her eventual shift away from excessive sentimentality to more realistic and contemporary concerns followed the general trend toward Realism which occurred in American writing at the turn of the century. By and large she sensed the changes in literary taste and was able to write accordingly. Although none of the early work would warrant for her any more than a minor place in our literary history, a few of the stories and two of the novels show her increasing capacity for serious and successful fiction.

In fact, the two historians of American fiction who have paid the most attention to her fiction place her in the tradition of the feminine writers who followed the manner of Henry James. George Snell compares Miss Glaspell to Edith Wharton, Willa Cather, and other women writers in his Chapter "The James Influence" in *The Shapers of American Fiction* (1947). Arthur Hobson Quinn, in *American Fiction* (1936), also groups her with such women as Mary Austin, Zona Gale, and Dorothy Canfield Fisher, who wrote novels concerned with the individual's search for independence. Snell and Quinn are correct only in regard to her early novels. To those causes that influenced her choice of tradition—namely, family background, environment, literary influences, and the demands of her audience—we should add the obvious fact that she was a woman. She shares with many other female authors certain feminine traits: an insistence on romance, an inability to create successful male characters, a tendency to sentimentality, and a vague desire on the part of the heroine, such as Ruth Holland, for independence. Neither Snell nor Quinn, however, adequately defines Miss Glaspell's importance in respect to the later novels and plays in which her feminine qualities, her Jamesian emphasis on manners, and her "defense of the village" are less significant than her dramatic achievement and her concern with the meaning of the Midwestern heritage for our time.

What we have been following as we have traced Susan Glaspell's development from a short-story writer to a novelist is her growth from local-color writing to regionalism. Her second and third novels comprise her first attempts to define her region, both for herself and for her readers. She had to broaden her appeal to reach the heterogeneous readers of novels who would not accept the oversimplified concerns of the short tales. In these novels she was no longer exploiting the unique aspects of a Midwestern town, as in her Freeport stories; instead, she was beginning to show that the Midwest was faced with the same problems other regions had. Consequently, her heroines moved in larger, more ambiguous and complex circles than the restricted environment of Freeport. She was changing from a writer who idealized the specialness of her world to one who expanded its qualities in order to make it important anywhere.

This latter intention can still be idealistic, for the regional setting becomes a microcosm of contemporary life. In her local-color tales, Freeport is carefully depicted as a unique place where a fight over a dangerous book happens because of the town's peculiar origins and beliefs. Freeport in *Fidelity,* on the other hand, is any small town that has failed to maintain its respect for the individual by succumbing to an insistence on social conformity; and Ruth's search for independence is allied to the larger issue of the feminist revolt. The difference is between a locale we are interested in because of its separateness from the contemporary situation, and a region we are concerned with because it is a part of our world.

In defining her region, Miss Glaspell was forced to see it more clearly and to qualify her commitment to its charms while she was gaining insights into its failures. As the Midwest came to mean more to her in terms of its importance to modern life, its defects became clearer, like the spots on a balloon which grow more apparent as the balloon gets bigger. Conversely, seeing its limitations from the vantage points of experience and travel, she was in an odd way moved to defend it more strongly. Attacking its superficial defects, she saw its underlying worth; she removed one level, so to speak, to reveal another. Thus the realism and the idealism of these two novels are part of the same intention: both help to define her region.

This desire to place the Midwest in a significant relationship with the modern world affected her style. She could point out its limitations in detail, using local-color techniques. But to convey the universal qualities of her region she had to create symbols. For a writer like Susan Glaspell—one concerned with such abstractions as fidelity, love, and the meaning of life—the need to fashion a credible, detailed locale which also suggested a universal meaning was especially important. In her first novel, symbols—like the statue *Gloria Victus*—were too crude; they were merely pegs on which she draped her moral. In the next two novels, the symbols were more effective, emerging smoothly from the particular scenes. She was still liable to forget the immediate context, however, and to let abstract words and gestures take over the story, as in Ruth's decision to go to New York. She still needed to learn how to unify realism and idealism in her work—to make the symbolic intent an integral part of the plot, so the meaning was there under the surface, covered by the skin of the details, but in truth the novel's core. This major artistic problem was one she had to solve in all of her fiction.

We can see an increasing concern with the novel form in these three novels. The first continues to use the techniques of her short stories and conveys its simple romantic plot through the point of view of the heroine. *The Visioning* counterpoints two narrators, Katie and Ann; and they develop the plot by the contrasts between their opposing perspectives. This novel has a few pages of compressed details and tight writing, but it is for the most part a loose novel that covers a large area and eventually loses its focus on the two heroines in order to state its message. It is a much better novel than *The Glory of the Conquered,* but it lacks compression and unity. *Fidelity* adopts a more difficult form by using several points of view to enrich the story and the theme. It avoids the excesses of the first novel and the sprawling effect of the second, for it centers on a single issue and treats it more dramatically.

As she matured, Miss Glaspell was able to use her own life and experiences with more imagination, to create heroines who were not puppet Susan Glaspells, and to change the facts of her own experience to suit the needs of her fiction. As a result of this technical growth, her third novel received more than the perfunctory reviews given her first novel. Both in quality and quantity the reviews showed that she was gaining her rightful recognition as a novelist.

When she stopped writing novels in order to concentrate on the drama, therefore, Miss Glaspell was just beginning to consider the question of the meaning of the Midwestern heritage. Her plays and later novels continue her search for the forms of expression and the symbolic motifs that could render this theme.

Arthur E. Waterman, in his Susan Glaspell, *Twayne Publishers, Inc., 1966, 144 p.*

Marcia Noe   (essay date 1980)

[*In the following essay, which was originally presented as a paper in 1980 at the annual convention of the Modern Language Association of America, Noe analyzes the metaphorical significance of Glaspell's dramatic settings, asserting that they represent her characters' psychological isolation and need for human contact.*]

Susan Glaspell is best known today, if she is known at all, as one of the Provincetown Players, the little theater group active during the second decade of this century whose eagerness to stage original American dramas brought to light the talents of Eugene O'Neill. What is generally unknown today is that during this period, Glaspell shared the spotlight with O'Neill as one of the two most prolific and imaginative playwrights of the group. "In technique Susan Glaspell is undoubtedly the superior of Eugene O'Neill," wrote Andrew Malone in *Dublin Magazine.* Isaac Goldberg called her "one of the few Americans whose progress is worth watching with the same eyes that follow notable European effort . . ."[*The Drama of Transition,* 1922]. "If the Provincetown Players had done nothing more than to give us the delicately humorous and sensitive plays of Susan Glaspell they would have amply justified their existence," was critic John Corbin's verdict in his New York Times review of *Bernice.*

The special talents cited by these and other observers of the American stage were recognized in 1931 when Glaspell won the Pulitzer Prize for *Alison's House.* They are evident in her skillful handling of a variety of dramatic modes, ranging from the social satire of *Suppressed Desires* and *Chains of Dew* to the dramatic realism of *Trifles* and *Inheritors* and the expressionism of *The Verge.* Her ability to focus audience attention on a character who never appears onstage was applauded by many who saw *Alison's House, Bernice,* and *Trifles;* those qualities of her plays most often remarked upon were indirection, idealism, and experimentalism.

Another notable quality of many of Glaspell's plays is their regional emphasis. "I live by the sea, but the body of water I have the most feeling about is the Mississippi River. . . ." she wrote near the end of her life, alluding to the two areas of the country that had most influenced her writing. Born in Davenport, Iowa, Glaspell was raised and educated in the Mississippi Valley and began her writing career as a reporter in Davenport and Des Moines. Iowa's cornfields, pioneer homesteads, and Indian heritage are prominent in five of her plays, most notably in *Trifles* and *Inheritors.* Three other plays are set in Provincetown, where Glaspell spent most of her adult life, living, working and socializing with a circle of artists and writers that included Floyd Dell, Sinclair Lewis, Mary Heaton Vorse, and Edna St. Vincent Millay during the time of the Provincetown Players and, later, Edmund Wilson, Mary McCarthy and John Dos Passos. In *The Out-side* and *The Comic Artist,* especially, the windswept outreaches of Cape Cod and the Truro woods are settings that bring alive the Provincetown area. These four plays—*Trifles, Inheritors, The Outside,* and *The Comic Artist*—have a uniquely regional flavor in that nature images from the Midwest and the Cape Cod region are used to reveal various characters' mental states.

Throughout her career as a novelist and short story writer, Glaspell used this technique frequently, creating a storm to suggest a character's troubled spirit or a great wind to represent the passion of two lovers. Her use of these not very original metaphors was a result of her studies at Drake University, where, as a philosophy major, she became familiar with Emerson's theory that human emotions have correspondences in nature. The idealistic vision that informs her novels and plays—her faith in intuition and insight as superior modes of knowing, her belief in the primacy of the spirit and in the unity of all experience—is most appropriately expressed through metaphors from nature.

Just as Glaspell used nature metaphors in her fiction to express these ideas and reflect her characters' mental states, so in her plays, setting is used metaphorically for the same purpose. In *Trifles, Inheritors, The Outside,* and *The Comic Artist,* the Iowa heartland and the Cape Cod seacoast serve as metaphors for isolation, illustrating various characters' attitudes about their relationship with others. Setting these plays in an Iowa farmhouse, at a Midwestern college in a cornfield, in an abandoned lifesaving station near Provincetown harbor, and at a sequestered Cape Cod artist's retreat respectively, Glaspell shows the effect of isolation upon the human spirit and affirms the importance of the human community for the individual.

A regional play has been defined as one in which "Characters must be rooted and branched like the natural flora of the region" [Felix Sper, *From Native Roots: A Panorama of Our Regional Drama,* 1948]. By this definition, the plays discussed here are truly regional, for the characters who inhabit them bear the mark of their regions on their speech, manners, and attitudes. "Last night wasn't the *best* night for a dory," comments one of the lifesavers in *The Outside,* betraying his Cape Cod origin through his use of understatement. "You ain't seen no *wrecks,*" he later boasts. "Don't ever think you have. I was here the night the *Jennie Snow* was out there. There was a *wreck.*" The farm women of *Trifles* also reveal their regional background through their speech, as does Silas Morton of *Inheritors.* "My father used to talk about Blackhawk—they were friends," he tells his neighbor. "I saw Blackhawk once—when I was a boy. Guess I told you. You know what he looked like? He looked like the great of the earth. Noble, Noble like the forests—and the Mississippi—and the stars." Some characters have been warped by the severity of the demands of their regions. Allie Mayo of *The Outside* epitomizes the taciturn New England seaman's widow who has responded to a life-time of fear and uncertainty by withdrawing from society. Ira Morton of *Inheritors* is also withdrawn and resentful of the sacrifices his family has made for their Iowa community.

Another definition of regional drama has been provided

by John Wertz, in his article "American Regional Drama—1920-40: Frustration and Failure." He describes a regional play as "a dramatic composition in which essential elements of plot, theme, tone, characterization, motivation, or conflict are at least partially determined by strongly emphasized local peculiarities of a specific non-urban geographic setting." By this definition, too, the plays discussed here are truly regional. The studio setting of *The Comic Artist* has an unmistakably Cape Cod flavor, for it is filled with things from the sea. Stage directions read, "The prow of an old boat protrudes from right. An anchor leans forgotten in a corner . . . a sea chest under the window serves as a bench." The characters' two-hundred-year-old home makes the Cape Cod past constantly present, from the driftwood bookshelves in the living room to the beach plum jelly and wine they savor and the sound of the surf that accompanies them as they go about their daily chores. Likewise, the Iowa farmhouse where the first and third acts of *Inheritors* take place is filled with artifacts of the Morton family's Iowa past, as Glaspell shows how the spirit of that pioneer heritage has survived through four generations of Mortons.

Glaspell drew upon her experiences as a reporter covering a downstate Iowa murder trial for *Trifles,* her best known and most widely anthologized play. The murder that is the center of interest in *Trifles* raises not the question whodunit? but why?, and setting plays the key role in suggesting the motive for the murder. The perpetrator of the crime, Minnie Wright, has been taken into custody and is never on stage during the play, which unfolds the story of the murder investigation. The sheriff and state's attorney can discover no clues that would indicate why Minnie would strangle her husband, but the farm wives who have accompanied the men to the Wrights' farmhouse find several clues in Minnie's kitchen. The dirty towels, unbaked bread, and unfinished quilting are evidence of a disturbed mind; the canary with its neck wrung found in Minnie's sewing basket is the tip-off clue.

Trying to decide whether to tell the men of their discoveries, Minnie's neighbors blame themselves for abandoning her to a grim life with a taciturn Iowa farmer who refused her a telephone, or even a canary for company. "I could've come," says Mrs. Hale. "I stayed away because it weren't cheerful—and that's why I ought to have come. I—I've never liked this place. Maybe because it's down in a hollow and you don't see the road. I dunno what it is, but it's a lonesome place and always was." Mrs. Peters, although married to the sheriff, eventually condones Minnie's crime. "I know what stillness is. When we homesteaded in Dakota, and my first baby died—after he was two years old, and me with no other then." The farm women allude to the desolate environment of the Wright homestead to show that Minnie strangled her husband out of the desperation people feel when they are isolated from human contact; their feeling of sisterhood with Minnie motivates them to conceal the evidence of her crime. Hence, in *Trifles* Glaspell uses the lonely Iowa farmhouse metaphorically to illustrate the psychological isolation that drove Minnie Wright to murder the man who denied her the relationships with others she needed to function as a fully human person.

Glaspell with her husband George Cram Cook in Greece, 1924.

The Mississippi Valley represents not only psychological isolation, but political isolation as well in *Inheritors.* This play shows how three generations of Iowans deal with the conflict between individual rights and the obligation to the larger human community. The pioneer settlers of the region espouse to the view that people's concerns should go beyond themselves and their families, an attitude vital to their survival in a harsh wilderness environment. Some go beyond a neighborly concern to include other generations, races, and nationalities. Count Felix Fejevary fought for freedom in Hungary in 1848, then emigrated to Iowa and lost an arm fighting in the Civil War. His neighbor, Silas Morton, is determined, over the objections of his mother, to found a college on family land so that future generations can benefit. He sees this act as a means of making restitution to the Indians for the land his people took from them, and he tells Count Fejevary, "I see that college rising from the soil itself. . . ." But the next generation of Mortons and Fejevarys fails to carry out Silas's dream. By the end of World War I, under the management of Count Fejevary's son, Felix, the college has become conservative and isolationist, sending students into the steel mills as strikebreakers, arresting and expelling Hindu students protesting Britain's colonial policy.

Just as Morton College has withdrawn from world concerns in order to curry favor with Iowa legislators, Silas's son, Ira, has withdrawn from life into a less emotionally draining world of silence and self. Ira's bitterness began when his wife died of diphtheria after nursing a neighboring immigrant family, and it became stronger after his son died fighting in France. As his retreat from life approaches madness, Ira, hostile to anyone not of his immediate family, becomes obsessed with his drive to breed corn that will be superior to his neighbors'. The same Iowa farmland that represents Silas's dream of engendering learning and a richer life on the prairie also illustrates Ira's isolation from that richer life. As the latter says, "What good has ever come to this house through carin' about the world? What good's that college? Better we had that hill. . . . "

Although the middle generation has withdrawn from all causes except their own, Silas Morton's spirit is alive in his granddaughter, Madeline, who understands the interconnectedness of all people throughout time and space. To her father's insistence, "I want my field to myself," she replies, "The world is all a—moving field. Nothing is to itself." Whereas Ira resents the wind which carries the pollen of his near-perfect corn to a neighbor's field, Madeline welcomes the wind. To her it represents the spirit of giving to others in the tradition of Silas Morton. As she explains, "Father has been telling me about the corn. It gives itself away all the time—the best corn a gift to other corn."

Madeline is not only an idealist, but an activist as well. She is thrown into jail after defending the right of the Hindu students to demonstrate against Great Britain, and only her repudiation of this effort will move Fejevary to arrange her release. She stands firm, choosing community and brotherhood—her grandfather's dream—rather than her own self-interest, an expression of Susan Glaspell's conviction that people must resist the impulse toward psychological and political isolation that the Midwestern environment encourages and choose instead a commitment to all human persons. In this play, the Iowa rural setting is used as a metaphor for both isolation and growth, suggesting the barrenness of Ira Morton's and Felix Fejevary's outlooks as well as the vision of brotherhood that Silas and Madeline Morton share.

Just as the Iowa of Susan Glaspell's youth functions as a metaphor for isolation in *Trifles* and *Inheritors,* the Cape Cod of her adult years plays a similar role in *The Comic Artist* and *The Outside.* The latter play takes place on the outside shore of Cape Cod, a lonely area where the struggle of the trees to grow against the countervailing force of the sand dunes suggests the struggle of the forces of life to prevail against the forces of annihilation. The setting of *The Outside* also represents the struggle that takes place between the play's main characters. Mrs. Patrick, who has taken up residence in an abandoned life-saving station there, wants to desert life as her husband has deserted her; Allie Mayo has lost a husband to the sea and finds the en-

vironment of the outside shore congenial for similar reasons. The efforts of a pair of sailors to revive a drowned man make Allie Mayo realize the folly of rejecting the human community, and she tries to make Mrs. Patrick realize this, too. To bolster her argument, she uses the outside region as a metaphor to describe the struggle of the human spirit to live and prevail in a world of conflict, frustration, and heartbreak. "I know where you're going! What you'll try to do. Over there. Bury it. The life in you. Bury it—watching the sand bury the woods. But I'll tell you something! *They* fight too. The woods! They fight for life the way that Captain fought for life in there!" Although the lifesavers are unable to revive the drowning victim, Allie Mayo is able to make Mrs. Patrick see that there is value in the struggle to live, grow, and develop as a person among others, however difficult and painful that struggle may be.

In *The Comic Artist,* one of Susan Glaspell's most complex and ambiguous plays, her attitude toward isolation is ambivalent. The play concerns two brothers, Karl Rolf, a successful and gifted cartoonist, and his older brother, Stephen, a painter who is only slightly talented. The irony inherent in the mismatch of talents and crafts is compounded by the irony of their respective situations. Karl's social-climbing wife, Nina, encouraged by her mother, Louella, demands a fancy car, a fur coat, and a country club lifestyle. Strangely enough, her materialistic impulses don't impede Karl's work. By contrast, Stephen's wife, Eleanor, has carefully created a serene environment in the secluded Cape Cod home of her ancestors that has somehow failed to inspire her husband to paint a great picture.

In the plays previously discussed, the regional setting has worked for the most part as a metaphor for an isolation depicted as life-denying and dehumanizing, but in *The Comic Artist* self-sufficiency rather than isolation is suggested by the setting of the play. From the home where her great-grandfather set off on whaling voyages, Eleanor has gathered about her the artifacts of her past and the bounty of Cape Cod to give herself a sense of identity and to give Stephen the sense of security and self-sufficiency they both believe to be necessary for his development as an artist. "We've been so deep in it here—painting, gathering things, making wine, we forget about the post office," Stephen explains to Louella. Just as the outside coast of Cape Cod was used as a metaphor for Mrs. Patrick's withdrawal from life, the harmonious seclusion Eleanor has created suggests her belief that it is important to be self-reliant and to refrain from imposing one's beliefs and values upon others.

But the arrival of Karl, Nina, and Louella for a weekend visit and the events that their stay precipitates show Eleanor's quest for a life of harmony apart from others to be as futile as Ira Morton's desire that the wind cease to blow pollen from his perfect corn into his neighbor's field. Nina's attempt to seduce Stephen, her former lover, shatters the peace of Eleanor and Stephen's refuge. When Stephen suggests they make Karl aware of Nina's unworthiness, Eleanor reiterates her belief that it is wrong to interfere in others' lives, yet when she finds Stephen and Nina in an embrace, she shares her discovery with Karl and later tells Nina that Stephen's response was merely a ploy to trap her into betraying Karl so that he will leave her for his own good. Nina fights back by rushing out and threatening to throw herself into the sea, hoping that Stephen will leave Eleanor to comfort her. Louella then tells Karl of what she has done, representing what is obviously a play for attention as an act of desperation in the hope that Karl will pursue her and they will reconcile. Ironically, it is Karl whom the sea destroys when he goes out to rescue Nina. His death completes a chain of events that proves Eleanor's insistence that it is wrong to meddle in other's lives.

But the play also suggests that just as manipulation and interference can have tragic consequences, our lives are so bound up with others within the human community that our actions have an ineluctable impact upon other lives as well as upon our own. *The Comic Artist* raises many questions and conveys many ironies. Is Stephen's response to Nina's advances sincere or contrived? Can the artist who isolates himself from others better practice his craft than the artist who participates fully in life? Is it more selfish to draw back and refuse to intrude upon the lives of others, or to force upon others our own values and insights? All of the ambiguities in *The Comic Artist* are heightened by the Cape Cod seacoast setting, used as a metaphor for an isolation which can be both a nurturing and a destructive force for the artist.

In the regional dramas of Susan Glaspell, the Mississippi Valley and the Massachusetts coastal region function as metaphors for isolation: the isolation sought by the artist from a society that threatens his talent, the psychological isolation that is a refuge for the individual from whom life has exacted too much emotional tribute, the isolated environment that can precipitate madness and violence if some contact with others is not provided, the political isolationist spirit of the post-World War I era. In *Trifles, Inheritors, The Outside,* and *The Comic Artist,* Glaspell shows through her regional settings that isolation can be a powerful force in crushing the human spirit, and that our connections with others in the human community are crucial to our development as individuals and are inextricably bound up with our individual destinies.

Marcia Noe, "Region as Metaphor in the Plays of Susan Glaspell," in Western Illinois Regional Studies, *Spring, 1981, pp. 77-85.*

Elaine Hedges   (essay date 1986)

[*An American critic and educator, Hedges is the author of* Land and Imagination: The Rural Dream in America *(1980; with William L. Hedges) and* In Her Own Image: Women Working in the Arts *(1980; with Ingrid Wendt). In the essay below, she argues that a full understanding of the symbolism in Glaspell's story "A Jury of Her Peers" requires an academic reconstruction of women's social history in the nineteenth-century American West.*]

Susan Glaspell's **"A Jury of her Peers"** is by now a small feminist classic. Published in 1917, rediscovered in the early 1970s and increasingly reprinted since then in anthologies and textbooks, it has become for both readers and critics a familiar and frequently revisited landmark on our "map of rereading." For Lee Edwards and Arlyn Diamond in 1973 it introduced us to the work of one of the important but forgotten women writers who were then being rediscovered; and its characters, "prairie matrons, bound by poverty and limited experience [who] fight heroic battles on tiny battlefields," provided examples of those ordinary or anonymous women whose voices were also being sought and reclaimed. For Mary Anne Ferguson, also in 1973, Glaspell's story was significant for its challenge to prevailing images or sterotypes of women—women as "fuzzy minded" and concerned only with "trifles," for example—and for its celebration of female sorority, of the power of sisterhood. More recently, in 1980, Annette Kolodny has read the story as exemplary of a female realm of meaning and symbolic signification, a realm ignored by mainstream critics and one, as she urges, that feminist critics must interpret and make available. Rediscovering lost women writers, reclaiming the experience of anonymous women, reexamining the image of women in literature, and rereading texts in order to discern and appreciate female symbol systems—many of the major approaches that have characterized feminist literary criticism in the past decade have thus found generous validation in the text of **"A Jury of her Peers."** The story has become a paradigmatic one for feminist criticism.

Whatever their different emphases, all of these approaches, when applied to Glaspell's story, have in common their central reliance, for argument and evidence, on that set of small details describing women's daily, domestic lives, which constitutes the story's core. These details—the "clues" through which in the story the two farm women, Mrs. Hale and Mrs. Peters, solve the mystery of the murder of John Wright—include such minutiae as a soiled roller towel, a broken stove, a cracked jar of preserves, and an erratically stitched quilt block. So central are these details not only to the story's plot but to its larger symbolic meanings, that Glaspell gave them precedence in the title of the dramatic version she originally wrote, the one act play, *Trifles,* that she produced for the Provincetown Players in 1916. It is by decoding these "trifles," which the men ignore, that the two women not only solve the murder mystery, but develop their sense of identity as women with Minnie Wright, and demonstrate their sisterhood with her by acting to protect her from male law and judgment. It is, therefore, essentially through these trifles that Glaspell creates in her story that female world of meaning and symbol which, as Kolodny says, feminist critics must recover, and make accessible.

My interest here is in extending the story's accessibility, making it more possible for contemporary readers to enter into and respond to the symbolic meanings of the details on which it is so crucially based. Any symbol system, as Jean Kennard for one has shown in her discussion of literary conventions, is a shorthand, a script to which the reader must bring a great deal of knowledge not contained in the text ["Convention Coverage; or, How to Read Your Own Life," *New Literary History,* 1981]. Critical exegeses of the symbolic worlds of male writers—the forest, the river, the whaling ship—may by now have enabled us imaginatively to enter those worlds. But the same is not yet true for women writers. What is needed, as Kolodny says, is an understanding of the "unique and informing contexts" that underlie the symbol systems of women's writing. Only after these contexts are made accessible are we likely to be able to enjoy that "fund of shared recognitions" upon which, as Kolodny also notes, any viable symbol system depends ["A Map for Rereading; or, Gender and the Interpretation of Literary Texts," *New Literary History,* 1980].

In Glaspell's story, Mrs. Hale and Mrs. Peters comprise an ideal (if small) community of readers precisely because they are able to bring to the "trivia" of Minnie Wright's life just such a "unique and informing context." That context is their own experience as midwestern rural women. As a result they can read Minnie's kitchen trifles with full "recognition and acceptance of . . . their significance." For contemporary readers, however, who are historically removed from the way of life on which Glaspell's story depends, such a reading is not so readily available. Superficially we can of course comprehend the story's details, since women's work of cooking, cleaning, and sewing is scarcely strange, or unfamiliar, either to female or to male readers. But to appreciate the full resonance of those details requires by now an act of historical reconstruction. Glaspell's details work so effectively as a symbol system because they are carefully chosen reflectors of crucial realities in the lives of 19th and early 20th century midwestern and western women. The themes, the broader meanings of **"A Jury of her Peers,"** which are what encourage us to rediscover and reread it today, of course extend beyond its regional and historical origins. Women's role or "place" in society, their confinement and isolation, the psychic violence wrought against them, their power or powerlessness vis-à-vis men, are not concerns restricted to Glaspell's time and place. But these concerns achieve their imaginative force and conviction in her story by being firmly rooted in, and organically emerging from, the carefully observed, small details of a localized way of life.

I would therefore like to reenter Glaspell's text by returning it to that localized, past way of life. Such reentry is possible by now, given the recent work of social historians in western women's history. The past six to seven years, especially, have seen the publication of works on the lives of western women by such historians as John Faragher, Julie Jeffrey, Norton Juster, Sandra Myres, Glenda Riley, and Christine Stansell. And the same years have seen a resurgence of interest in women's writings in non-traditional forms—the diaries, letters, journals, and autobiographies of 19th and early 20th century pioneer and farm women, women less silenced than Minnie Wright in Glaspell's story—on which, indeed, much of the published social history depends. It is this body of material, as well as my own researches into the autobiographical writings of 19th century women, on which I shall draw in order to recreate, however imperfectly, some of the historical reality that informs the responses of Mrs. Hale and Mrs. Peters to Minnie Wright's life. Again and again in **"A Jury of her Peers"** Mrs. Hale and Mrs. Peters perform acts of perception in which a literal object opens out for them into a larger world of meaning. At one point in the story Glaspell describes these acts as a way of "seeing into things, of seeing

through a thing to something else." To uncover that "something else"—the dense, hidden background reality of rural women's lives—may enable us to participate more fully in those acts of perception and thus to appreciate Glaspell's achievement—the way in which, by concentrating on a small, carefully selected set of literal details, she communicates, in one very brief short story, an extraordinarily rich, multilayered sense of women's sociocultural "place" in late 19th and early 20th century American society.

By the time she published **"A Jury of her Peers"** in 1917, Susan Glaspell had been living in the east for several years, both in Greenwich Village and in Provincetown, Massachusetts. But she had been born and raised in Iowa, and her earliest fiction had dealt with the people of her native midwest, and especially with the confined lives, whether on the isolated farm or in the midwestern small town or village, of women. In writing her play, *Trifles,* and then her story, therefore, she was returning to her midwestern origins, and to the lives of women of her mother's and grandmother's generations.

"A Jury of her Peers" is set in the prairie and plains region of the United States. The story itself contains a reference to the county attorney's having just returned from Omaha, which would literally locate the action in Nebraska. And a further reference to "Dickson County," as the place where the characters live, might suggest Dixon County, an actual county in the northeastern corner of Nebraska where it borders on Iowa. In the narrowest sense, then, given Glaspell's own Iowa origins, the story can be said to refer to the prairie and plains country that stretches across Iowa into Nebraska—a country of open, level or rolling land, and few trees, which generations of pioneers encountered during successive waves of settlement throughout the nineteenth century. More broadly, the story reflects the lives of women across the entire span of prairie and plains country, and some of the circumstances of Minnie Wright's life were shared by women further west as well. While emphasizing Iowa and Nebraska, therefore, this paper will draw for evidence on the autobiographical writings by women from various western states.

Glaspell's references to the outdoor setting are few. As the story opens she emphasizes the cold wintry day, and the emptiness of the terrain through which the characters travel on their way to the Wright homestead, where they are going to investigate the murder. But the very sparseness of her detail serves to suggest the spare, empty lives of her characters, and especially of Minnie Wright's. What Mrs. Hale notes as the group approaches the Wright farm is the "loneliness" both of the farmhouse and its surroundings. Three times in as many sentences she uses the words "lonely" or "lonesome" to describe the locale. (The road is lonely, and the farm, "down in a hollow," is surrounded by "lonesome looking poplar trees.") Kolodny has suggested that this sensitivity to place distinguishes the women in the story from the men, who confine their talk to the crime that was committed the day before. Whether or not one can generalize from this difference (as Kolodny does) to conclusions about gender-linked perceptions, it does seem to be the case that 19th century pioneer women were more strongly affected than men by a sense of the loneliness of the landscape they encountered in the west.

In spring, when the wild flowers were in bloom, the western prairie might seem "a perfect garden of Eden," as it did to an Iowa woman in 1851. But frequently the women's voices that we hear from that pioneer past express dismay at what they saw when they arrived. A prairie burned by the autumn fires that regularly ravaged the land might understandably seem "black and dismal," as the Illinois prairie did to Christiana Tillson in 1822. Other women, however, even when viewing a less seared and searing landscape, found the prairie unsettling especially as they moved farther west. "What solitude!," exclaimed the Swedish visitor, Fredrika Bremer, arriving in Wisconsin in the 1850s. "I saw no habitation, except the little house at which I was staying; no human beings, no animals; nothing except heaven and the flower-strewn earth." And Mrs. Cecil Hall, visiting northern territories in 1882 wrote, "O the prairie! I cannot describe to you our first impression. Its vastness, dreariness, and loneliness is [sic] appalling."

When a male pioneer registered his sense of the land's emptiness, it was often to recognize that the emptiness bore more heavily upon women. Seth K. Humphrey wrote of his father's and his own experiences, in Minnesota territory in the 1850s and in the middle northwest in the 1870s, and he remembered that "the prairie has a solitude way beyond the mere absence of human beings." With no trees, no objects to engage or interrupt the glance, the eyes "stare, stare—and sometimes the prairie gets to staring back." Women, he observed, especially suffered. They "fled in terror," or "stayed until the prairie broke them." Women themselves reported that it was not unusual to spend five months in a log cabin without seeing another woman, as did a Marshall County, Iowa woman in 1842; or to spend one and a half years after arriving before being able to take a trip to town, as did Luna Kellie in Nebraska in the 1870s. The absence both of human contact and of any ameliorating features in the landscape exacerbated the loneliness felt by women who had often only reluctantly uprooted themselves from eastern homes and families in order to follow their husbands westward.

Minnie Wright is not of course living in circumstances of such extreme geographical isolation. By the time of Glaspell's story, established villages and towns have replaced the first scattered settlements, and networks of transportation and communication link people previously isolated from one another. But John Wright's farm, as we learn, is an isolated, outlying farm, separated from the town of which it is, formally, a part. Furthermore, he refuses to have a telephone; and, as we also learn, he has denied his wife access to even the minimal contacts that town life might afford women at that time, such as the church choir in which Minnie had sung before her marriage. Minnie Wright's emotional and spiritual loneliness, the result of her isolation, is, in the final analysis, the reason for her murder of her husband. Through her brief opening description of the landscape Glaspell establishes the physical context for the loneliness and isolation, an isolation Min-

nie inherited from and shared with generations of pioneer and farm women before her.

The full import of Minnie's isolation emerges only incrementally in Glaspell's story. Meanwhile, after the characters arrive at the Wright farm, the story confines itself to the narrow space of Minnie's kitchen—the limited and limiting space of her female sphere. Within that small space are revealed all the dimensions of the loneliness that is her mute message. And that message is of course conveyed through those "kitchen things," as the sheriff dismissingly calls them, to which Mrs. Hale and Mrs. Peters respond with increasing comprehension and sympathy.

One of the first "kitchen things" or "trifles" to which Glaspell introduces us is the roller towel, on which the attorney condescendingly comments. Not considering, as the women do, that his own assistant, called in earlier that morning to make up a fire in Minnie's absence, had probably dirtied the towel, he decides that the soiled towel shows that Minnie lacked "the homemaking instinct." The recent researches of historians into the lives of 19th century women allow us today to appreciate the full ironic force of Mrs. Hale's quietly understated reply: "There's a great deal of work to be done on a farm." One of the most important contributions of the new social history is its documentation of the amount of work that pioneer and farm women did. The work was, as one historian has said, "almost endless," and over the course of a lifetime usually consisted of tasks "more arduous and demanding than those performed by men." Indoors and out, the division of labour "favored men" and "exploited women." Sarah Brewer-Bonebright, recalling her life in Newcastle, Iowa in 1848, described the "routine" work of the "women-folk" as including "water carrying, cooking, churning, sausage making, berry picking, vegetable drying, sugar and soap boiling, hominy hulling, medicine brewing, washing, nursing, weaving, sewing, straw platting, wool picking, spinning, quilting, knitting, gardening and various other tasks. . . ." Workdays that began at 4.30 a. m., and didn't end until 11.30 p. m., were not unheard of. Jessamyn West's description of her Indiana grandmother— "She died saying, 'Hurry, hurry, hurry,' not to a nurse, not to anyone at her bedside, but to herself "—captures an essential reality of the lives of many 19th and early 20th century rural women.

The work involved for Minnie Wright in preparing the clean towel that the attorney takes for granted is a case in point. Of all the tasks that 19th and early 20th century women commented on in their diaries, laundry was consistently described as the most onerous.

> Friday May 27 This is the dreaded washing day
>
> Friday June 23 To day Oh! horrors how shall I express it; is the dreaded washing day.

This entry from an 1853 diary is typical of what are often litanies of pain, ritualistically repeated in the records that 19th century women have left us of their lives. In her recent study of housework, *Never Done*, Susan Strasser agrees that laundry was woman's "most hated task." Before the introduction of piped water it took staggering amounts of time and labor: "One wash, one boiling, and one rinse used about fifty gallons of water—or four hundred pounds—which had to be moved from pump or well or faucet to stove and tub, in buckets and wash boilers that might weigh as much as forty or fifty pounds." Then came rubbing, wringing, and lifting the wet clothing and linens, and carrying them in heavy tubs and baskets outside to hang. It is when Mrs. Peters looks from Minnie's inadequate stove, with its cracked lining, to the "pail of water carried in from outside" that she makes the crucial observation about "seeing into things . . . seeing through a thing to something else." What the women see, beyond the pail and the stove, are the hours of work it took Minnie to produce that one clean towel. To call Minnie's work "instinctual," as the attorney does (using a rationalization prevalent today as in the past) is to evade a whole world of domestic reality, a world of which Mrs. Hale and Mrs. Peters are acutely aware.

So too with the jars of preserves that the women find cracked and spoiled from the cold that has penetrated the house during the night. It is the preserves, about which Minnie has been worrying in jail, that lead Mr. Hale to make the comment Glaspell used for the title of the dramatic version of her work. "Held for murder, and worrying over her preserves. . . worrying over trifles." But here again, as they express their sympathy with Minnie's concern, the women are seeing through a thing to something else: in this case, to "all [Minnie's] work in the hot weather," as Mrs. Peters exclaims. Mrs. Hale and Mrs. Peters understand the physical labor involved in boiling fruit in Iowa heat that one historian has described as "oppressive and inescapable." By the same token, they can appreciate the seriousness of the loss when that work is destroyed by the winter cold.

The winter cold is, as has been said, one of the few references to outdoor setting that Glaspell includes in her story. When at the beginning of the story Mrs. Hale closes her storm door behind her to accompany the others to the Wright farm, it is a "cold March morning," with a north wind blowing. Later we are told that the temperature had fallen below zero the night before. Historians have described the prairie and plains winters, their interminable length, the ceaseless winds that whipped across the treeless spaces, the "infamous" blizzards peculiar to the region—storms not of snow but of ice particles that penetrated clothes and froze the eyes shut. Eliza Farnham, travelling through the prairie in 1846, described the cold in the uninsulated log cabins and frame houses: "the cups freeze to the saucers while [the family] are at table." And Mary Abell, living in Kansas in 1875, related how "my eyelids froze together so I picked off the ice, the tops of the sheets and quilts and all our beds were frozen stiff with the breath. The cold was so intense we could not breathe the air without pain." Such weather demanded heroic maintenance efforts to keep a family warm, and fed. Engaged as they were in just such maintenance efforts (at the beginning of the story Mrs. Hale is reluctant to leave her kitchen because her own work is unfinished) the women can appreciate the meaning of the loss of Minnie's laboriously prepared food.

Hard as the work was, that it went unacknowledged was often harder for women to bear. The first annual report of the Department of Agriculture in 1862 included a study of the situation of farm women which concluded that they worked harder than men but were neither treated with respect as a result nor given full authority within their domestic sphere. And Norton Juster's study of farm women between 1865 and 1895 [*So Sweet to Labor: Rural Women in America 1865-1895,* 1979] leads him to assert that women's work was seen merely as "the anonymous background for someone else's meaningful activity," never attaining "a recognition or dignity of its own." Indeed, he concludes, women's work was not only ignored; it was ridiculed, "often the object of derision." Mr. Hale's remark about the preserves, that "women are used to worrying over trifles," is a mild example of this ridicule, as is the attorney's comment, intended to deflect that ridicule but itself patronizing—"yet what would we do without the ladies." It is this ridicule to which Mrs. Hale and Mrs. Peters especially react. When Mr. Hale belittles women's work we are told that "the two women moved a little closer together"; and when the attorney makes his seemingly conciliatory remark the women, we are further told, "did not speak, did not unbend." Mrs. Hale and Mrs. Peters, who at the beginning of the story are comparative strangers to each other, here begin to establish their common bonds with each other and with Minnie. Their slight physical movement towards each other visually embodies that psychological and emotional separation from men that was encouraged by the nineteenth century doctrine of separate spheres, a separation underscored throughout the story by the women's confinement to the kitchen, while the men range freely, upstairs and outside, bedroom to barn, in search of the "real" clues to the crime.

Women's confinement to the kitchen or to the private space of the home was a major source of their isolation. Men didn't appreciate how "their own toil is sweetened to them by the fact that it is out of doors," said one farm woman; and Juster has concluded that the lives of farm women in the second half of the 19th century were lives "tied to house and children, lacking opportunity for outside contacts, stimulation, or variety of experience." In Glaspell's story, Mrs. Hale moves only from one kitchen to another. That she hasn't visited Minnie, whom she has known since girlhood, in over a year she guiltily attributes to her antipathy to the cheerlessness of the Wright farm. But there is truth in Mrs. Peters' attempt to assuage that guilt: "But of course you were awful busy . . . your house—and your children."

"A walking visit to neighbors was not a casual affair but could take an entire morning or afternoon," says [John Mack Faragher] in describing the settlement on separate farmsteads, often far distant from each other, and like Juster he concludes that "the single most important distinction between the social and cultural worlds of men and women was the isolation and immobility of wives compared to husbands" [*Women and Men on the Overland Trail,* 1979]. "Grandma Brown," whose one hundred year life span from 1827 to 1927 is recorded in her autobiography, lived on an Iowa farm for fourteen years, from 1856 to 1870. They were, she said, "the hardest years of my life. The drudgery was unending. The isolation was worse."

Both during the frontier stage and in later periods of village settlement men routinely enjoyed more opportunities for social life than women. They travelled to town with their farm produce, to have their grain and corn milled, to trade surpluses, to have wool carded or skins tanned. In **"A Jury of her Peers"** John Wright's murder is discovered because Mr. Hale and his son stop at the Wright farm while travelling to town with their potato crop. Once in town, men had places to congregate—the market, the country store, the blacksmith shop, the saloon. That "women really did little more than pass through the masculine haunts of the village," as Faragher concludes, was a reality to which at least one 19th century male writer was sensitive. "The saloon-keepers, the politicians, and the grocers make it pleasant for the man," Hamlin Garland has a character comment in his story of midwestern rural life, "A Day's Pleasure"; "But the wife is left without a word." Garland wrote "A Day's Pleasure" to dramatize the plight of the farm wife, isolated at home, and desperate for diversion. Mrs. Markham has been six months without leaving the family farm. But when, over her husband's objections and by dint of sacrificed sleep and extra work to provide for her children while she is gone, she manages to get into town, she finds scant welcome, and little to do. After overstaying her leave at the country store, she walks the streets for hours, in the "forlorn, aimless, pathetic wandering" that, Garland has the town grocer observe, is "a daily occurrence for the farm women he sees and one which had never possessed any special meaning to him."

John Wright's insensitivity to his wife's needs parallels that of the men of Garland's story. Lacking decent clothes, Minnie doesn't travel into town. What she turns to in her isolation is a bird, a canary bought from a travelling peddler. It is after her husband strangles that surrogate voice that, in one of those "intermittent flare-ups of bizarre behavior," as one historian has described them, which afflicted rural women, she strangles him [Jeannie McKnight, "American Dream, Nightmare Underside: Diaries, Letters, and Fiction of Women on the American Frontier," in *Women, Women Writers, and the West,* edited by L. L. Lee and Merrill Lewis].

Here again Glaspell's story reflects a larger truth about the lives of rural women. Their isolation induced madness in many. The rate of insanity in rural areas, especially for women, was a much-discussed subject in the second half of the 19th century. As early as 1868 Sarah Josepha Hale, editor of the influential *Godey's Lady's Book,* expressed her concern that the farm population supplied the largest proportion of inmates for the nation's insane asylums. By the 1880s and 1890s this concern was widespread. An article in 1882 noted that farmer's wives comprised the largest percentage of those in lunatic asylums. And a decade later *The Atlantic Monthly* was reporting "the alarming rate of insanity . . . in the new prairie States among farmers and their wives." Abigail McCarthy recalled in her autobiography stories she had heard as a girl in the 1930s about the first homesteaders in North Dakota, two generations earlier. Women could be heard, she wrote

> screaming all night long in the jail after the first spring thaw. Their husbands had brought them into town in wagons from the sod huts where

they had spent the terrible Dakota winter; they were on their way to the insane asylum in Jamestown.

That the loss of her music, in the shape of a bird, should have triggered murderous behavior in Minnie Wright is therefore neither gratuitous nor melodramatic, as is sometimes charged against Glaspell's story. In the monotonous expanses of the prairie and the plains, the presence of one small spot of color, or a bit of music, might spell the difference between sanity and madness. Mari Sandoz, chronicler of the lives of Nebraska pioneers, describes in her short story "The Vine" a woman so desperate for some color in the brown, treeless expanse of the prairie that she uses precious water—scarce during a drought—to keep alive a trumpet vine outside the door of her sod house. When her husband, enraged at her wastefulness, uproots and kills the vine, she goes mad. In *Old Jules,* her account of the life of her homesteading father, Sandoz relates the true story of a farm wife who suddenly one afternoon killed herself and her three children. At her funeral a woman neighbor comments, "If she would a had even a geranium—but in that cold shell of a shack—." Again and again in their recollections of their lives on the prairie and plains, women described the importance of a bit of color, or music. The music might come, as it did for Minnie Wright, from a canary in a cage. Late 19th century photographs of families outside their Dakota and Nebraska sod huts routinely show the bird cage hung to one side of the front door. Indoors, it was likely to be one of the deep windows carved into the thick sod walls that provided the "spot of beauty" so necessary to psychological survival. As late as 1957 the *Nebraska Farmer* published interviews it had secured with women who had experienced the conditions of pioneer settlement. The comment of Mrs. Orval Lookhart is typical of many the journal received. She remembered the special window in the prairie sod house that was invariably reserved for "flowers and plants . . . a place where the wife and mother could have one spot of beauty that the wind the cold or the dry weather couldnet (sic) touch." There is no spot of beauty in Glaspell's description of Minnie's kitchen, which is presented as a drab and dreary space, dominated by the broken stove, and a rocking chair of "a dingy red, with wooden rungs up the back, and the middle rung was gone, and the chair sagged to one side." When the women collect some of Minnie's clothes to take to her in prison, the sight of "a shabby black skirt" painfully reminds Mrs. Hale by contrast of the "pretty clothes" that Minnie wore as a young girl before her marriage.

Unable to sing in the church choir, deprived of her surrogate voice in the bird, denied access to other people, and with no visible beauty in her surroundings, Minnie, almost inevitably one can say, turned in her loneliness to that final resource available to 19th and early 20th century women—quilting. Minnie's quilt blocks are the penultimate trifle in Glaspell's story. The discovery later of the strangled bird and broken bird cage explain the immediate provocation for Minnie's crime. But it is with the discovery of the quilt blocks, to which the women react more strongly than they have to any of the previously introduced "kitchen things," that a pivotal point in the story is reached.

The meaning of quilts in the lives of American women is complex, and Glaspell's story is a valuable contribution to the full account that remains to be written. Quilts were utilitarian in origin, three-layered bed coverings intended to protect against the cold weather. But they became in the course of the 19th century probably the major creative outlet for women—one patriarchically tolerated, and even "approved," for their use, but which women were able to transform to their own ends. Through quilting—through their stitches as well as through pattern and color—and through the institutions, such as the "bee," that grew up around it, women who were otherwise without expressive outlet were able to communicate their thoughts and feelings.

In *Trifles* Glaspell included a reference she omitted from **"A Jury of her Peers,"** but which is worth retrieving. In the play Mrs. Hale laments that, given her husband's parsimony, Minnie could never join the Ladies Aid. The Ladies Aid would have been a female society associated with the local church, where women would have spent their time sewing, braiding carpets, and quilting, in order to raise money for foreign missionaries, for new flooring or carpets, chairs or curtains for the church or parish house, or to add to the minister's salary. Such societies, as Glenda Riley has observed [in *Frontiers Women: The Iowa Experience,* 1981], provided women with "a relief from the routine and monotony" of farm life. They also provided women with a public role, or place. And through the female friendships they fostered they helped women, as Julie Jeffrey has noted [in *Frontier Women: The Trans-Mississippi West 1840-1880,* 1979], to develop "feelings of control over their environment," mitigating that sense of powerlessness which domestic isolation could induce.

Denied such associations, Minnie Wright worked on her quilt blocks alone, and it is the effect of that solitude which the women read in her blocks and which so profoundly moves them. It is, specifically, the stitches in Minnie's blocks that speak to them, and particularly the "queer" stitches in one block, so unlike the "fine, even sewing," "dainty [and] accurate," that they observe in the others. Nineteenth century women learned in childhood to take stitches so small that in the words of one woman, it "required a microscope to detect them" [Clarissa Packard, *Recollections of a Housekeeper,* 1834]. Mothers were advised to teach their daughters to make small, exact stitches, not only for durability but as a way of instilling habits of patience, neatness, and diligence. But such stitches also became a badge of one's needlework skill, a source of self-esteem, and of status, through the recognition and admiration of other women. Minnie's "crazy" or crooked stitches are a clear signal to the two women that something, for her, was very seriously wrong.

Mrs. Hale's reaction is immediate. Tampering with what is in fact evidence—for the badly stitched block is just such a clue as the men are seeking: "Something to show anger—or sudden feeling"—she replaces Minnie's crooked stitches with her own straight ones. The almost automatic act, so protective of Minnie, is both concealing and

healing. To "replace bad sewing with good" is Mrs. Hale's symbolic gesture of affiliation with the damaged woman. It is also the story's first intimation of the more radical tampering with the evidence that the two women will later undertake.

In so quickly grasping the significance of Minnie's quilt stitches, Mrs. Hale is performing yet another of those acts of perception—of seeing through a detail or trifle to its larger meaning—on which Glaspell's dramatic effects depend throughout her story. As she holds the badly stitched block in her hand, Mrs. Hale, we are told, "feels queer, as if the distracted thoughts of the woman who had perhaps turned to it to try and quiet herself were communicating themselves to her." Resorting to needlework in order to "quiet oneself," to relieve distress, or alleviate loneliness, was openly recognized and even encouraged throughout the 19th century, especially in the advice books that proliferated for women. One of the earliest and most popular of these was John Gregory's *A Father's Advice to his Daughters,* published in 1774 in England and widely read both there and in the United States well into the 19th century. Gregory recommended needlework to his female readers "to enable you to fill up, in a tolerably agreeable way, some of the many solitary hours you must necessarily pass at home." By 1831, as advice manuals began to be produced in this country, Lydia Child in *The Mother's Book* urged mothers to teach their daughters needlework, such as knitting, as a way of dealing with the "depression of spirits" they would inevitably experience in later life. "Women," Child wrote, "in all situations in life, have so many lonely hours, that they cannot provide themselves with too many resources. . . ." And as late as 1885 popular writer Jane Croly introduced a book of needlework instructions with a parable, in which an angel, foreseeing the "abuse" that woman would suffer from men, urged God not to create her. God refused. However, out of pity woman was given "two compensating gifts." These were "tears, and the love of needlework." Although one woman who read Croly's book tartly rejoined, in a letter to *The Housekeeper,* a magazine for women, that she would prefer to keep the tears and give men the needlework, for numbers of others needlework served, in Croly's words, as "that solace in sorrow—that helper in misfortune." That it might have so served Minnie Wright Mrs. Hale can immediately appreciate.

Minnie's stitches speak with equal directness to Mrs. Peters. It is she who first discovers the badly stitched block, and as she holds it out to Mrs. Hale we are told that "the women's eyes met—something flashed to life, passed between them." In contrast to the often outspoken Mrs. Hale, Mrs. Peters has been timid, self-effacing, and "indecisive," torn between sympathy for Minnie and resigned submission to the authority of the law, which her husband, the sheriff, represents. She has evaded Mrs. Hale's efforts to get her more openly to choose sides. The flash of recognition between the two women, a moment of communication the more intense for being wordless, is, as one critic has said, "the metamorphizing spark of the story" [Kathy Newman, "Susan Glaspell and 'Trifles': 'Nothing Here but Kitchen Things,'" *Trivia: A Journal of Ideas,* Fall 1983]. It presages Mrs. Peter's eventual revolt against male authority. That revolt occurs when she snatches the box containing the dead bird—the evidence that could condemn Minnie—in order to conceal it from the men. Her defiant act is of course the result of the effect on her of the accumulated weight of meaning of all of the "trifles" she has perceived and interpreted throughout the story. But it is here, when she reads Minnie's stitches, that she is first released from her hesitancy into what will later become full conspiratorial complicity with Mrs. Hale.

In examining Minnie's quilt blocks Mrs. Hale observes that she was making them in the "log cabin pattern." The log cabin pattern was one of the most popular in the second half of the 19th century, frequently chosen for its capacity to utilize in its construction small scraps of left-over fabric. For Minnie in her poverty it would have been a practical pattern choice. But there accrued to the pattern a rich symbolism, which would not have escaped a farm woman like Mrs. Hale and which adds yet another rich layer of meaning to Glaspell's exploration of women's place. The log cabin quilt is constructed of repetitions of a basic block, which is built up of narrow overlapping strips of fabric, all emanating from a central square. That square, traditionally done in red cloth, came to represent the hearth fire within the cabin, with the strips surrounding it becoming the "logs" of which the cabin was built. As a replication of that most emotionally evocative of American dwelling types, the log cabin quilt came to symbolize both the hardships and the heroisms of pioneer life. More specifically it became a celebration of women's civilizing role in the pioneering process: in the words of one researcher, "women's dogged determination to build a home, to replace a wilderness with a community" [Suellen Jackson-Meyer, "The Great American Quilt Classics: Log Cabin," *Quilters' Newsletter,* October 1979].

The 19th century ideology of domesticity defined woman's sphere as that of the home, but within that home it gave her, in theory, a queenly role, as guardian and purveyor of the essential moral and cultural values of the society. That role was frequently symbolized, especially in the popular domestic fiction of the 19th century, by the hearth fire, over which the woman presided, ministering, in the light of its warm glow, to the physical and emotional needs of her family. Julie Jeffrey has demonstrated the willingness and even determination with which women resumed this domestic role upon their arrival in the trans-Mississippi west after the dislocations induced by the overland journey, their sense of themselves as the culture bearers and civilizers. And in her recent *The Lay of the Land: Fantasy and Experience of the American Frontiers, 1630-1860* Annette Kolodny shows that on the earlier Mississippi Valley frontier (and in Texas as well) women's dreams were above all domestic—to create a home as a paradise.

That Minnie is making a log cabin quilt—and the women find a roll of red cloth in her sewing basket—is, both in this historical context and in the context of her own life, both poignant and bitterly ironic. The center of her kitchen is not a hearth with an inviting open fire but that stove with its broken lining, the sight of which, earlier in the story, had "swept [Mrs. Hale] into her own thoughts,

thinking of what it would mean, year after year, to have that stove to wrestle with." In Glaspell's story the cult of domesticity has become a trap, Minnie's home has become her prison. Minnie has asked Mrs. Peters to bring her an apron to wear in jail, a request the sheriff's wife at first finds "strange." But when Mrs. Peters decides that wearing the apron will perhaps make Minnie feel "more natural," we can only agree, since in moving from house to jail she has but exchanged one form of imprisonment for another.

In 1917 when Glaspell rewrote and retitled *Trifles,* feminists were engaged in their final years of effort to free women from at least one of the "imprisonments" to which they had been historically subject—the lack of the vote. Her change of title emphasized the story's contemporaneity, by calling attention to its references to the issue of woman's legal place in American society. The denouement depends on that issue. It is immediately after the county attorney, patronizing as always, expresses his confidence that in carrying things to Minnie in jail Mrs. Peters will take nothing suspicious because she is "married to the law," that she proceeds to divorce herself from that law by abetting Mrs. Hale in concealing the dead bird. With that act the two women radically subvert the male legal system within which they have no viable place. Throughout much of the 19th century married women were defined under the law as "civilly dead," their legal existence subsumed within their husbands, their rights to their own property, wages, and children either non-existent or severely circumscribed. Nor did they participate in the making and administering of the law. In 1873 Susan B. Anthony had challenged that legal situation, in a defense that was widely reprinted and that would have been available to Glaspell at the time of the final agitation for the vote. Arrested for having herself tried to vote, and judged guilty of having thereby committed a crime, Anthony had argued that the all-male jury which judged her did not comprise, as the Constitution guaranteed to each citizen, a "jury of her peers." So long, she argued, as women lacked the vote and other legal rights, men were not their peers but their superiors. So, in Glaspell's story, Mrs. Hale and Mrs. Peters decide that they, and not the men, are Minnie's true peers. They take the law into their own hands, appoint themselves prosecuting and defense attorneys, judge and jury, and pass their merciful sentence.

In committing her "crime," Mrs. Peters resorts not to any constitutional justification but to a bit of sophistry cunningly based on the trivia which are the heart of Glaspell's story. Why reveal the dead bird to the men, she reasons, when they consider all of women's concerns insignificant? If the men could hear us, she suggests to Mrs. Hale, "getting all stirred up over a little thing like a—dead canary . . . My, wouldn't they *laugh?*" But it is the women who have the last laugh (in a story in which potential tragedy has been transformed into comedy), and that laugh hinges upon a very "little thing" indeed. Glaspell gives literally the last word to one of the story's seemingly least significant details. As the characters prepare to leave the Wright farm, the county attorney facetiously asks the women whether Minnie was going to "quilt" or "knot" her blocks. In having Mrs. Hale suggest that she was probably going to knot them (that is, join the quilt layers via short lengths of yarn drawn through from the back and tied or knotted at wide intervals across the top surface, rather than stitch through the layers at closer intervals with needle and thread) Glaspell is using a technical term from the world of women's work in a way that provides a final triumphant vindication of her method throughout the story. If, like Mrs. Hale and Mrs. Peters, the reader can by now engage in those acts of perception whereby one sees "into things, [and] through a thing to something else," the humble task of knotting a quilt becomes resonant with meaning. Minnie has knotted a rope around her husband's neck, and Mrs. Hale and Mrs. Peters have "tied the men in knots." All three women have thus said "not," or "no" to male authority, and in so doing they have knotted or bonded themselves together. Knots can entangle and they can unite, and at the end of Glaspell's story both men and women are knotted, in separate and different ways, with the women having discovered through their interpretation of the trifles that comprise Minnie's world their ties to one another. One 19th century woman described quilts as women's "hieroglyphics"—textile documents on which, with needle, thread, and bits of colored cloth, women inscribed a record of their lives. All of the trifles in Glaspell's story together create such a set of hieroglyphics, but it is a language we should by now begin to be able to read.

Elaine Hedges, "Small Things Reconsidered: Susan Glaspell's 'A Jury of Her Peers'," in Women's Studies: An Interdisciplinary Journal, *Vol. 12, No. 1, 1986, pp. 89-110.*

Christine Dymkowski (essay date 1988)

[*In the following essay, Dymkowski discusses Glaspell's portrayal in her plays of the paradoxical nature of women's social roles as outsiders still capable of influencing society.*]

Until recently, Susan Glaspell has been little more than "a footnote in the history of drama," remembered chiefly for her association with Eugene O'Neill and the Provincetown Players; her contemporary reputation as one of the two most accomplished playwrights of twentieth-century America may come as a legitimate surprise even to serious students of dramatic history. Her plays have rarely been performed by professional companies and, apart from the often-anthologized **Trifles,** have been unavailable in print; such marginalization of Glaspell's work is the most obvious way in which her drama can be said to be "on the edge." Its own preoccupation with the limits of experience is another.

Central to Glaspell's plays is a concern with fulfilling life's potential, going beyond the confines of convention, safety, and ease to new and uncharted possibilities, both social and personal. This need to take life to its limits and push beyond them implies a paradoxical view of life's margins as central to human experience—as the cutting edge that marks the difference between mere existence and real living. This edge is imbued with both possibility and danger, the one concomitant with the other; Glaspell makes this clear not only in the plays but in her account of her response to the Provincetown dunes:

> I have a picture of Jig [her husband] at the edge of the dunes, standing against the woods, that line he and I loved where the woods send out the life that can meet the sand, and the sand in turn tries to cover the woods—a fighting-line, the front line.

It is, in the widest sense, the front line between life and death.

This focal point is at once evident in the titles of some of Glaspell's plays: **The Outside** and **The Verge** speak for themselves, while **Trifles** ironically alludes to the discrepancy between the vitality of women's experience and the male view of it as petty. Indeed, inherent in almost all of Glaspell's work is a consciousness that identifies women as outside the mainstream of life and thus capable of shaping it anew.

The paradoxically central nature of the edge informs Glaspell's theatrical methods and themes. Her first play, **Trifles** (1916), illustrates its use in several ways, the irony of the title already having been noted. The plot revolves around the visit to a farmhouse by County Attorney Henderson and Sheriff Peters to investigate the murder of John Wright; they are accompanied by the farmer who discovered the murder and, almost incidentally, by the farmer's and sheriff's wives. The men's assumption is that Minnie Wright, already in custody for the crime, has killed her husband, and they are there to search the house for clues to a motive. The audience undoubtedly sees them as protagonists at the start of the play.

The stage directions immediately call attention to the women's marginality: the men, *"much bundled up"* against the freezing cold, *"go at once to the stove"* in the Wrights' kitchen, while the women who follow them in do so *"slowly, and stand close together near the door."* The separateness of the female and male worlds is thus immediately established visually and then reinforced by the dialogue:

> MRS. PETERS. (*To the other woman*) Oh, her fruit; it did freeze. (*to the* LAWYER) She worried about that when it turned so cold. . . .
>
> SHERIFF. Well, can you beat the women [*sic*]! Held for murder and worryin' about her preserves.
>
> COUNTY ATTORNEY. I guess before we're through she may have something more serious than preserves to worry about.
>
> HALE. Well, women are used to worrying over trifles.
>
> (*The two women move a little closer together.*)

Not surprisingly, the women are relegated to the kitchen, while the men's attention turns to the rest of the house, particularly the bedroom where the crime was committed: "You're convinced that there was nothing important here—nothing that would point to any motive," Henderson asks Peters, and is assured that there is "Nothing here but kitchen things." However, while the men view the kitchen as marginal to their purpose, the drama stays centered there where the women are: contrary to expectation, it becomes the central focus of the play.

Ironically, it is the kitchen that holds the clues to the desperation and loneliness of Minnie's life and yields the women the answers for which the men search in vain; moreover, the understanding that they do reach goes beyond the mere solving of the crime to a redefinition of what the crime was. Mrs. Hale blames herself for a failure of imagination: "Oh, I *wish* I'd come over here once in a while! That was a crime! That was a crime! Who's going to punish that? . . . I might have known she needed help! I know how things can be—for women. I tell you, it's queer, Mrs. Peters. We live close together and we live far apart. We all go through the same things—it's all just a different kind of the same thing." The empathy both women feel for Minnie leads them to suppress the evidence they have found, patiently enduring the men's condescension instead of competing with them on their own ground. Conventional moral values are overturned, just as the expected form of the murder mystery is ignored: the play differentiates between justice and law and shows that the traditional "solution" is no such thing.

Just as Glaspell sets the play in the seemingly marginal kitchen, she makes the absent Minnie Wright its focus, a tactic she was to use again in *Bernice* and *Alison's House;* although noted by critics, this use of an absent central character has not received much comment. It is yet another way in which Glaspell makes central the apparently marginal—indeed, in stage terms, the non-existent. It is a point I will return to in discussing the later plays.

Woman's Honor (1918), like *Trifles,* is concerned with the gulf between female and male experience, centering on the ways men define and limit the world in which both sexes live and the ways in which women challenge those definitions and limitations. At its start, it appears to focus on Gordon Wallace, a man accused of murder who refuses to give an alibi because his "silence shields a woman's honor"; without his knowledge, his lawyer Foster has leaked the fact to the press in the hope that "Wives—including . . . jurors' wives—will cry, 'Don't let that chivalrous young man die!' Women just love to have their honor shielded."

Foster is quickly proved wrong as a succession of women enter the sheriff's conference room, all ready to provide Wallace with the alibi he so desperately needs, despite the loss of "honor" this will entail. Unlike the men, none of the women have names but are described somewhat expressionistically in the stage directions as the Shielded One, Motherly One, Scornful One, Silly One, Mercenary One, and Cheated One. As these seemingly anonymous figures discuss their motives and attitudes towards "woman's honor," they acquire far more reality than the men, who become ciphers pushed from center stage. What has seemed the play's central human situation—a young man "ready to die to shield a woman's honor"—becomes totally unimportant, indeed farcical, as the action progresses. The women have gathered not so much to save Gordon Wallace as to destroy an empty idea.

The reasons behind the women's action are as varied as

their names and, except for the Silly One who finds Wallace's attitude "noble beyond words," belie male attitudes towards them; however, the behavior of the Silly One undermines her position—she is a "*fussily dressed hysterical woman [who] throws her arms around the* LAWYER'S *neck,*" exclaiming "I cannot let you die for me!" The only other dubious motive comes from the Mercenary One, who makes it quite clear she has financial reasons for her presence; it eventually emerges that the women have been talking at cross-purposes, and she has come to apply for a stenographer's job.

The discussion among the rest of the women identifies "woman's honor" as a male concept, beneficial only to men; the Scornful One indicates its hypocrisy on several levels:

> So you were thinking of dying for a woman's honor. (*He says nothing.*) Now do you think that's a very nice way to treat the lady? (*He turns away petulantly.*) Seems to me you should think of *her* feelings. Have you a right to ruin her life? . . . A life that somebody has died for is practically a ruined life. For how are you going to think of it as anything but—a life that somebody has died for? . . . Did it ever strike you as funny that woman's honor is only about one thing, and that man's honor is about everything but that thing? . . . Now woman's honor means woman's virtue. But this lady for whom you propose to die has no virtue. . . . You aren't dying to keep her virtuous. I fancy few lives have been laid upon that altar. But you're dying to keep us from knowing what she is. Dear me, it seems rather sad.

The Motherly One agrees that the notion is an empty one not worth dying for, but wonders if it should perhaps "be kept up, as . . . it gives men such noble feelings." The Scornful One replies: "That man—the one [who seduced me] when I was seventeen—he's that sort. He would be of course. Why this instant his eyes would become 'pools of feeling' if any one were to talk about saving a woman's honor."

Eventually the discussion focuses on which of the women should stay to provide the alibi. It is agreed that the Motherly One has "too many other things to do" and that the Scornful One is not appropriate because "Woman's honor never hurt" her; since the Silly One subscribes to male ideals, the choice is between the Shielded and Cheated Ones. The decision involves choosing between personal and political objectives: the Cheated One insists on providing the alibi as a means of self-determination and personal fulfillment ("It's the first thing I ever wanted to do that I've done"), while the Shielded One wishes to claim she spent the night with Wallace as a means of freeing "all [women] smothered under men's lofty sentiments towards them." A vagueness about the way in which the Shielded One will liberate all others of her type weakens the play somewhat: the women are inconsistently treated as types or as individuals according to thematic needs. Nevertheless, the women aim at a resolution that will involve both the Shielded and the Cheated Ones, thus encompassing both personal and general salvation. Although we do not hear what this solution might be, it is clear that it is reached: "Here! Yes! On the night of October 25—(*Their heads together in low-voiced conference with* LAWYER . . .)." At this point, however, the prisoner, who is now both marginal and powerless, attempts to regain control; he "*slips around the* CHEATED ONE . . . *and makes for the door. It opens in his face, and the doorway is blocked by a large and determined woman.* PRISONER *staggers back to* LAWYER'S *arms*" and says, "*Oh, hell. I'll plead guilty,*" as the play ends.

The comedy of the conclusion entails one of Glaspell's serious concerns; her preoccupation with "the battle between the life force and the death force" has already been admirably discussed elsewhere. Wallace's life-denying attitude, however, gains added meaning when placed within the context of being on the edge. The imbalance of power between the sexes acts as an advantage to women, a disadvantage to men, when they reach the "front line" of struggle and change. It is precisely *because* "men . . . determine the world in which . . . women are . . . required to live" that women may have a perspective on it of which men are incapable; they have always been on the outside looking in. Their position on the edge gives them an alternative power—the power to move beyond what is, just as the women in *Trifles* and *Woman's Honor* move beyond male definitions of crime and justice and honor. Men placed on the edge, however, are excluded from a power to which they subscribe—Wallace, put in this position, cannot reshape his world from a new perspective; he can only affirm the old one. He prefers to die rather than redefine his notion of woman's honor. The perspective of gender can go some way to explain the inherent optimism of Glaspell's plays, even though they center on women who have died or go mad or face long spells in prison, as well as the unwitting pessimism and defeatism of so much of O'Neill's work.

By recreating the Provincetown coastline that Glaspell describes in *The Road to the Temple,* the setting of *The Outside* (1917) embodies the life/death struggle inherent in the edge:

> . . . *through [an] open door are seen the sand dunes, and beyond them the woods. At one point the line where woods and dunes meet stands out clearly and there are indicated the rude things, vines, bushes, which form the outer uneven rim of the woods—the only things that grow in the sand. At another point a sand-hill is menacing the woods. . . . The dunes are hills and strange forms of sand on which, in places, grows the stiff beach grass—struggle; dogged growing against odds. At right . . . is a drift of sand and the top of buried beach grass is seen on this.*

The set's significance is not left to the audience's inference but is underlined by the dialogue: Allie Mayo, embracing "The edge of life," speaks *"tenderly"* of the "Strange little things that reach out farthest," while Mrs. Patrick gloats that they "will be buried soonest"; Allie recognizes that they will nevertheless "hold the sand for things behind them" and so contribute to life. Mrs. Patrick, who throughout the play has denied life and struggle, finally starts to *"feel . . . her way into the wonder of life,"* understanding what it is to "Meet . . . the Outside."

Both women had originally retreated from life as a result of losing their husbands, and in dramatizing their re-embracing of it, the play affirms women's autonomy. The relationship between women and men in the play is, however, more complex than this statement suggests, and, not surprisingly, the perspective of gender also informs critical interpretation of it: Bigsby regards the male life-savers, who at the beginning of the play struggle unsuccessfully to revive a drowned man, as catalysts of the change ("paradoxically, [with Allie they] succeed in their efforts 'to put life in the dead,' " while Ben-Zvi sees Glaspell's focus "on the failure of men to accomplish what women can do. . . . [The men's] physical activity has proven a failure. The passive, mute Allie, however, is victorious in her own personal resuscitation of Mrs. Patrick." While a persuasive interpretation of the play can encompass both viewpoints, Glaspell's focus is unquestionably on the women and on the triumph of Allie's vision, which goes beyond the men's mere recognition of the life/death struggle to an understanding of the way in which that struggle itself shapes life.

While the line between woods and dunes in *The Outside* locates its focus in a symbolic struggle between life and death, the edge in *Bernice* (1919), Glaspell's first full-length play, is the interaction between literal life and death. The play focuses on the recently-deceased title character, whose body lies in a room just off-stage. Despite her physical absence from the action, the play creates and reinforces Bernice's presence in several ways. First, the setting is *"The living-room of Bernice's house in the country,"* and it is clear that Glaspell expected the stage set to create a powerful sense of her character: *"You feel yourself in the house of a woman you would like to know . . .";* furthermore, the house's evocation of its dead owner begins the action of the play:

> FATHER. Bernice made this house. (*Looking around.*) Everything is Bernice. (*A pause.*) Change something, Abbie! (*With growing excitement.*) Put something in a different place. [He moves some of the furnishings.] (. . . *helplessly.*) Well, I don't know. You can't get Bernice out of this room.

In addition, the other characters all focus on their relationships to Bernice, and indeed, relate to each other *through* that relationship. Their focus on the dead woman is theatrically realized by their constant approaches to the closed door behind which her body lies, the door itself acting as this play's concrete symbol of the edge. In fact, these approaches dramatize the continuing development of their relationship to her—for example, Bernice's faithless husband cannot bring himself to enter the room when he first arrives at the house, but eventually finds a solace there unavailable from any of his fellow-mourners. Through the characters' discussions and the action on stage, Glaspell makes her dead hero the vital mover of the drama.

That drama focuses, as implied, on the way the other characters—father, friend, husband, sister-in-law, and maid/companion—understand Bernice, and on the way that understanding shapes and transforms their lives. Craig, horrified to learn from Abbie, the maid, that Bernice killed herself, blames his infidelities for her action and berates himself for underestimating her passion for him: Margaret, her friend, cannot believe that Bernice took her own life, and when she forces the truth from Abbie—that Bernice, ill on her deathbed, made her promise to deceive Craig—she is devastated by the thought that Bernice's "life was *hate*." By the end of the play, Margaret understands that the deception was Bernice's final gift to Craig, one that breaks the mould of his life up till then and so gives him the opportunity to reach beyond his limits.

As always, this need to "break through" the "bounded circle" of life is Glaspell's central concern, and again, it is the character on the edge who is most successful in doing so; the dead Bernice has far more effect on the other characters than anyone else in the play. However, this influence is not simply due to the way death can alter relationships; despite Bernice's isolated country life, Margaret, who has devoted herself to active work for political and social causes, can say:

> I do things that to me seem important, and yet I just do *them*—I don't get to the thing I'm doing them for—to life itself. I don't simply and profoundly get to *life*. Bernice did.

The audience need not take Margaret's assessment on trust, but recognition of Bernice's achievement does depend on an understanding of power, an understanding determined in the play by gender. Craig's unfaithfulness to Bernice arose from his failure to dominate her, to "have" her completely; as Margaret explains, he "turned to women whom [he] could have" and " 'had' all of them simply because there was less to have." He could not appreciate Bernice because he had not "the power to reshape" her, and as Margaret astutely remarks, he wanted "no baffling sense of something beyond" him. Thus, Glaspell depicts male occupation of the central position in a woman's life as limiting for both, keeping them within the "bounded circle" of life. This is not "the power to reshape" that Craig thinks it is, but merely the power to circumscribe.

By using her death to convince Craig that he had the power over her he yearned for, Bernice, from her remote position, exercises a liberating power of her own. Craig now rejects his old life as "make-believe": "Pretending. Fumbling. Always trying to seem something—to feel myself something." Bernice's father recognizes that her spirit was generous enough to give as much as possible, but that paradoxically its very greatness meant she could not give "all she was." Even more paradoxically, the play shows how that magnanimity could clothe itself as something venal, and in so doing, manage "to give—what couldn't be given." Glaspell makes clear that Bernice's power over Craig is not one imposed on him, like man's power over woman, but one which allows him free scope. As Bernice's father remarks, "she wanted me to do what—came naturally to me. . . . She was never trying to make us some—outside thing."

Inheritors (1921), Glaspell's next play, emphasizes that growth into new ways of being *is* organic rather than imposed: just as the pollen from Ira's corn blows across neighboring fields, making other corn richer, so humankind develops from a desire to extend oneself; in discussing the evolution of the hand, for example, one character explains that "from aspiration has come doing, and doing has shaped the thing with which to do." True life is process, not product: "we aren't *finished* yet." Thus, the edge in this play is "the impulse to do what had never been done," which develops human potential. Importantly, this potential is both individual and social; the two are inextricable in this play.

The structure of ***Inheritors*** allows Glaspell to explore the development from impulse to achievement. Act I takes place in 1879, when the pioneer Silas Morton and his Hungarian refugee friend Felix Fejevary discuss Silas's intention to found a college for the girls and boys of the cornfields; the next three acts, set in 1920, show what has happened to the ideals of forty years before. Right from the beginning of the play, Glaspell takes every opportunity to highlight ironically the betrayal of earlier ideals through present self-interest. The action is set on the fourth of July, 1879—Independence Day, but the celebrations mentioned commemorate the Civil War of a decade earlier. Grandmother Morton, the first settler in the area with her husband and son Silas, "never went to bed without leaving something on the stove for the new ones that might be coming," but now balks at Silas's plan to give away some of their vast land holdings to start a college. The portrait of Lincoln which hangs in the Morton farmhouse during Act I is ironically recalled by the audience in the next act when his inaugural address, affirming the right to revolution, is subverted by a state senator and a bigoted student, the latter, the grandson of the "revolutionist" Fejevary, is hounding Indian students who call for an end to British imperialism in their country. He can say without any conscious irony: "This foreign element gets my goat." The dangers of moving from the edge to the center are made very apparent.

It is entirely appropriate and theatrically effective that the portrait of Silas Morton hanging in the college library should overhear the giddiness and snobbery of students in whom he had hoped to nurture sensitivity and love of learning: they dissolve into hysterical giggles because another student is "trying to run a farm and go to college at the same time." It also overhears the discussion between Fejevary's son, now president of the Board of Trustees, and State Senator Lewis about the "radical" views of Professor Holden, who has championed the cause of his former student Fred Jordan, a conscientious objector still held in solitary confinement two years after the war's end; so that the college can receive money from the state, Fejevary agrees to silence the professor. As he later explains to Holden, "we [the college] have to enlarge before we can grow. . . . Yes, it is ironic, but that's the way of it."

Everything in the play goes to show that that is *not* "the way of it"; while Holden is eventually compromised by the need to pay his wife's medical bills, Madeline Fejevary Morton, granddaughter of the pioneer and the revolutionary, is able to "go . . . against the spirit of this country," standing up for the rights of the persecuted Indian students and refusing to use her privileged position as a way of escaping the consequences of her assault on the police. In discussing her decision with Holden, Madeline articulates the dangers and potential of being on the edge: "I'd like to have been a pioneer! Some ways they had it fierce, but think of the fun they had! A whole big land to open up! A big new life to begin! . . . Why did so much get shut out? Just a little way back—anything might have been. What happened?" Holden answers that "It got—set too soon," and Madeline concludes that prosperity was the cause: "That seems to set things—set them in fear." She understands the importance of "Moving" and regrets that "We seem here, now, in America, to have forgotten we're moving. Think it's just *us*—just now." The town itself epitomizes her analysis: once a settlement at the very edges of civilization, nurturing people of vision and courage and generosity, it is now a city in the heart of the nation, full of unthinking conformists. Its college students are happy to act as strike-breakers, and the only courage that is recognized is in fact a fear of being different: those who went to war "had the whole spirit of [their] age with [them]," unlike the truly courageous Fred Jordan.

In the last three acts of the play, those characters with the greatest integrity are the most marginal ones. Seen by society as both extremists and outsiders, in stage terms Fred Jordan and the Indian students do not exist: they never appear. However, near the beginning of the last act, Glaspell provides this stage direction, which occupies several minutes of performance time:

> *Rises, goes to [the] corner closet. . . . She gets a yard stick, looks in a box and finds a piece of chalk. On the floor she marks off* FRED JORDAN'S *cell.* [It is "two and a half feet at one end, three feet at the other, and six feet long."] *Slowly, at the end left unchalked, as for a door, she goes in. Her hand goes up as against a wall; looks at her other hand, sees it is out too far, brings it in, giving herself the width of the cell. Walks its length, halts, looks up.*

In this way, Glaspell makes the absent Fred Jordan the center of our attention, without having him appear on stage. The audience is forced to imagine the experience of this political prisoner through Madeline's imagining of it; indeed, because the focus is on Madeline's *attempt* to experience Fred Jordan's confinement, the audience's mental and emotional engagement is greater than it would have been if Jordan were actually shown on stage in his cell.

Madeline, as hero, is of course central in terms of plot and stage presence, but she chooses to marginalize herself in the society which the play depicts. When Holden tries to dissuade her from "do[ing] a thing that [will put her] apart," fearing she will thereby lose the "fullness of life," Madeline pinpoints the self-interest that leads him to this view: "You don't think that—having to stay within—or deciding to, rather, makes you think these things of the— blight of being without?" She dismisses his argument, neatly summarizing Glaspell's own view: "I don't see it— this fullness of life business. . . . I think that in buying it you're losing it."

While *Inheritors* deals with the social and political significance of being on the edge, *The Verge* (1921) is concerned solely with the individual. Its hero, Claire, experiments with plants, hoping to shock them "out of what they

were—into something they were not." Her goal is to break "the old pattern," a prison that substitutes form for life. For Claire, the edge is a jumping-off-point for "otherness," for liberation from old and dead ways of being: "anything may be—if only you know how to reach it." Her experiments have led to two potentially new plants: the Edge Vine, which eventually runs "back to what it broke out of," and Breath of Life, "alive in its otherness."

Claire's attempt to create new plant forms is, of course, analogous to human potential: "We need not be held in forms moulded for us. There is outness—and otherness." The way to such creation is through destruction of the old order: "If it were all in pieces, we'd be . . . shocked to aliveness. . . . Smash it." Claire's understanding informs her otherwise incomprehensibly urgent plea to her conventional husband to "Please—please try [your egg] without salt" and validates a response to her daughter which others condemn as unnatural: Elizabeth, in her own words, studies "the things one studies" and does "the things one does" and "Of course . . . is glad one is an American"; it is not surprising that Claire is repulsed by the idea that such a daughter "ever moved [her] belly and sucked [her] breast."

Although another critic has found Claire's name ironic, her vision is essentially the same as Madeline Morton's, and as clear. Indeed, her clarity seems to be underlined by the amorphousness of the names of the men who surround her—Tom, Dick, and Harry, respectively her friend, lover, and husband. However, Tom's surname, Edgeworthy, distinguishes him somewhat from the others; it links him with the idea of the edge and, more particularly, with Claire's Edge Vine, which had the chance to be other, but "Didn't carry life with it from the life it left." Tom shares Claire's aspirations and values, but to a limited extent: whereas she is terrified that she will "die on the edge," without achieving "otherness," he is content with merely being "outside life." When Claire suggests to him that their friendship and shared sympathy should lead to a fulfilling sexual relationship, one that may help to achieve the otherness she desires, Tom refuses on the grounds that it would instead be a going-back. His concern for her, however, is suspect: while in sympathy with Claire's aims and ideas, he has also shown himself afraid of them. Tom realizes that the "door [to otherness is] on the far side of destruction," but he cannot face the risks, even vicariously. He warns Harry not to try to stop Claire's botanical experiments: "If she can do it with plants, perhaps she won't have to do it with herself." Again, Glaspell shows woman as the risk-taker and seer.

Tom's position as an avoider is not redeemed by his ultimate desire for sexual union with Claire. Instead of meeting her on the basis she had earlier proposed, he claims her according to the old pattern of female and male relationships: "I'm here to hold you from where I know you cannot go." Claire, who like Breath of Life wants to create herself anew, recognizes that Tom "fill[s] the place— should be a gate" and strangles him, ultimately achieving her freedom in madness.

That Claire's madness *is* liberating in the way she desires is determined by her own attitude to madness and sanity.

She repeatedly refers to the latter as a prison: "sanity. . . . [is] made a virtue—to lock one in. . . . Things that [grow] take a sporting chance—go mad—that sanity mayn't lock them in— . . . from life—that waits." She has always supposed that "If one ever does get out . . . it is—quite unexpectedly, and perhaps—a bit terribly." In this way, Claire's madness at the end of the play is a personal triumph, but one to be understood symbolically rather than realistically.

Glaspell's choice of settings gives her further opportunity to emphasize her theme. Acts I and III take place in Claire's greenhouse laboratory, Act II in her private tower. Both places are extremities of the house she lives in, and yet all the action of the play occurs there. Moreover, these edges force awareness of their centrality—all the characters are drawn into them, *must* enter them, in order to engage with Claire. Indeed, the comedy of the first act revolves around the retreat of Tom, Dick, and Harry to the greenhouse in order to eat breakfast comfortably; Claire has diverted to it all heat from the house so that the plants' temperature may be consistently maintained in the freezing weather.

Glaspell's decision to depict Claire's tower complete on stage actively involves the audience in the tension between the edge and the center; her stage directions at the beginning of Act II explain that the tower's "*back is curved, then jagged lines break from that, and the front is a queer bulging window. . . .* CLAIRE *is seen through the huge ominous window as if shut into the tower.*" It is most unusual for a playwright to separate characters from the audience with an actual physical barrier rather than a merely imagined fourth wall; seen through and enclosed by the glass, Claire is both the focus of the audience's attention and an outsider in its world. The tower, at once isolating Claire and making her its center, resembles Breath of Life, an "outer shell" with "something alive" and glowing within it; we hardly need Tom's reference to the plant as a "womb [Claire] breathes to life" to recognize the metaphor's aptness both for Claire's experiment and Glaspell's stage-picture. By identifying Claire in her tower with an embryo in the womb, Glaspell underlines several ideas: the organic nature of growth and development, the naturalness of the violence of creation, and the uniquely female capacity to give birth to new life; it is not only Tom's personal failings which prevent his journeying as far as Claire.

The Verge, which itself moves across different dramatic genres, is in many ways Glaspell's most complete expression of the complexities of being on the edge, and forms a fitting conclusion to this discussion. Throughout her career as a playwright, Glaspell was preoccupied with the central importance of people and ideas outside the mainstream of life, and the sterility of the status quo. Her consistent point-of-view, however, did not lead to a depressing staleness but to wide experimentation with different dramatic genres and theatrical devices which would embody her ideas. Her present appeal should in fact be wide: her relative critical neglect offers scholars and theatre historians varied research opportunities; her perspective on women and her creation of a variety of strong female protagonists should attract feminist critics, actors, and audiences; her insistence on the dangers of complacency should find a ready response in those who despair of the social and political myopia not just of Reagan's America but also of most other western democracies.

Glaspell clearly deserves a more central place in the history of twentieth-century American drama than she has so far been given. That she has not is in large part due to her sex. To those who will retort that Glaspell gave up the theatre, writing only one play between the end of her association with the Provincetown Players in 1922 and her death in 1948, while O'Neill went on from strength to strength, the answer is simply that gender contributed to those developments as well. Theatre, like the critical scholarship that determines "major figures," is still male-dominated, its edges inhabited by women. It is time those edges were seen as the challenging and important areas Glaspell recognized them to be.

Christine Dymkowski, "On the Edge: The Plays of Susan Glaspell," in Modern Drama, *Vol. XXXI, No. 1, March, 1988, pp. 91-105.*

Leonard Mustazza   (essay date 1989)

[*In the essay below, Mustazza argues that in adapting* Trifles *to the short story form in* "A Jury of Her Peers," *Glaspell changed the focus from the elements of women's lives judged as trivial by men to women's lack of power in the American legal system.*]

Commentators on Susan Glaspell's classic feminist short story, **"A Jury of Her Peers"** (1917), and the one-act play from which it derives, *Trifles* (1916), have tended to regard the two works as essentially alike. And even those few who have noticed the changes that Glaspell made in the process of generic translation have done so only in passing. In his monograph on Glaspell, Arthur Waterman, who seems to have a higher regard for the story than for the play, suggests that the story is a "moving fictional experience" because of the progressive honing of the author's skills, the story's vivid realism owing to her work as a local-color writer for the *Des Moines Daily News,* and its unified plot due to its dramatic origin. More specifically, Elaine Hedges appropriately notes the significance of Glaspell's change in titles from *Trifles,* which emphasizes the supposedly trivial household items with which the women "acquit" their accused peer, to **"A Jury of Her Peers,"** which emphasizes the question of legality. In 1917, Hedges observes, women were engaged in the final years of their fight for the vote, and Glaspell's change in titles thus "emphasizes the story's contemporaneity, by calling attention to its references to the issue of women's legal place in American society" ["Small Things Reconsidered: Susan Glaspell's 'A Jury of Her Peers,'" *Women's Studies,* 12, No. 1 (1986)]. Apart from these and a few other passing remarks, however, critics have chosen to focus on one work or the other. Indeed, thematic criticisms of the respective pieces are virtually indistinguishable, most of these commentaries focusing on the question of assumed "roles" in the works.

On one level, there is good reason for this lack of differentiation. Not only is the overall narrative movement of the works similar, but Glaspell incorporated in the short story virtually every single line of the dialogue from *Trifles.* By the same token, though, she also added much to the short story, which is about twice as long as the play. The nature of these additions is twofold, the first and most obvious being her descriptions of locales, modes of utterance, characters, props, and so on—the kinds of descriptions that the prose writer's form will allow but the dramatist's will not. The other type of alteration is more subtle, and it involves the revisions, embellishments, and redirections that occur when an existent story is retold. When, for instance, a novel is turned into a film or a play, the best that can be said about the generic translation is that it is "faithful," but never is it identical. So it is with **"Jury."** It is certainly faithful to the play, but it is also different in a variety of ways, and it is these differences, which took place in the act of generic translation, that I would like to consider here.

In her article on *Trifles,* Beverly Smith makes an interesting observation. Noting that the women in the play, Mrs. Hale and Mrs. Peters, function as defense counsel for and jury of their accused peer, Minnie Foster-Wright, she goes on to suggest that the men's role, their official capacities notwithstanding, are comparable to that of a Greek Chorus, "the voice of the community's conscience," entering at various points to reiterate their major themes—Minnie's guilt and the triviality of the women's occupations, avocations, and preoccupations ["Women's Work—Trifles? The Skill and Insight of Playwright Susan Glaspell," *International Journal of Women's Studies,* 5 (March-April 1982)]. This equation is, I think, quite useful, for the periodic entries, commentaries, and exits of the male characters in both Glaspell works do in fact mark the progressive stages of the narrative, which primarily concerns the women, including the absent Minnie Foster. Though not on stage for the entire drama, as is the Greek Chorus, the men nevertheless function in much the same way, providing commentary and separating the major movements of the narrative. What is more, if we regard the men's exits from the stage as marking these movements, we will recognize the first principal difference between the play and the story—namely, that the latter contains twice as many movements as the former and is therefore necessarily a more developed and complex work.

Trifles opens with Mr. Hale's account of what he found when he arrived at the Wright farm the day before. Of the women themselves, we know almost nothing beyond their general appearances as described in the opening stage directions—that Mrs. Peters, the sheriff's wife, is "a slight wiry woman [with] a thin nervous face"; and that Mrs. Hale, the witness's wife, is larger than Mrs. Peters and "comfortable looking," though now appearing fearful and disturbed as she enters the scene of the crime. Standing close together as they enter the Wrights' home, the women remain almost completely undifferentiated until, some time later, they begin to speak. Thus, Glaspell underscores here the male/female polarities that she will explore in the course of the play.

Her entire narrative technique is different in the prose version. That story begins in Mrs. Hale's disordered kitchen, which will later serve as a point of comparison with the major scene of the story, Mrs. Wright's kitchen. Annoyed at being called away from her housework, she nevertheless agrees to Sheriff Peters' request that she come along to accompany Mrs. Peters, who is there to fetch some personal effects for the jailed woman. Quite unlike the play's opening, which emphasizes the physical closeness of and the attitudinal similarities between the women, **"Jury,"** taking us as it does into Mrs. Hale's thoughts, emphasizes the women's apartness:

> She had met Mrs. Peters the year before at the county fair, and the thing she remembered about her was that *she didn't seem to like the sheriff's wife.* She was small and thin and didn't have a strong voice. Mrs. Gorman, the sheriff's wife before Gorman went out and Peters came in, had a voice that somehow seemed to be backing up the law with every word. But if Mrs. Peters didn't look like a sheriff's wife, Peters made up for it in looking like a sheriff. . . . a heavy man with a big voice, who was particularly genial with the law-abiding, as if to make it plain that he knew the difference between criminals and non-criminals. (emphasis added)

Interestingly, for all the added material here, Glaspell omits mention of what the women look like. In fact, we will get no explicit statements on their appearance.

On the other hand, what we do get in this revised opening is much that sharply differentiates the story from the play. In the latter, we are provided with no indication of Mrs. Hale's bad feelings about the sheriff's wife, and, if anything, their close physical proximity leads is to conclude the opposite. Although the women in the story will later assume this same protective stance when they enter the accused's kitchen and then again when the county attorney criticizes Mrs. Wright's kitchen, the movement together there is little more than reflexive. Elaine Hedges has argued that the latter movement together begins the process of establishing "their common bonds with each other and with Minnie." This may be so because of their physical proximity in the play, where no distance is established between the women at the outset, but the story presents a different situation altogether, for any emotional closeness we might infer from their act is undercut by our knowledge of Mrs. Hale's lack of respect for Mrs. Peters, particularly by comparison with her predecessor, Mrs. Gorman.

Ironically, however, despite her seeming mismatch with her husband, her lack of corporal "presence," Mrs. Peters turns out to be more suited to her assumed public role than Mrs. Hale had suspected—all too suited, in fact, since she perfectly assumes her male-approved role. "Of course Mrs. Peters is one of us," the county attorney asserts prior to getting on with his investigation of the house, and that statement turns out to be laden with meaning in the story. In *Trifles,* when the men leave to go about their investigative business, the women, we are told, "listen to the men's steps, then look about the kitchen." In **"Jury,"** however, we get much more. Again here, the women stand motionless, listening to the men's footsteps, but this momentary stasis is followed by a significant gesture: "Then, *as if releasing herself from something strange,* Mrs. Hale began to arrange the dirty pans under the sink, which the county attorney's disdainful push of the foot had deranged" (emphasis added). One is prompted here to ask: what is this "something strange" from which she releases herself? Though the actions described in the play and the story are the same, why does Glaspell not include in the stage directions to the play an indication of Mrs. Hale's facial expression?

The answer, I think, lies again in the expanded and altered context of **"Jury,"** where the author continually stresses the distance between the women. If Mrs. Peters is, as the county attorney has suggested, one of "them," Mrs. Hale certainly is not, and she distances herself from her male-approved peer in word and deed. The something strange from which she releases herself is, in this context, her reflexive movement towards Mrs. Peters. Mrs. Hale is, in fact, both extricating herself from the male strictures placed upon all of the women and asserting her intellectual independence. Karen Alkalay-Gut has correctly observed that, to the men, the disorder of Mrs. Wright's kitchen implies her "potential homicidal tendencies, inconceivable in a good wife" ["Jury of Her Peers: The Importance of Trifles," *Studies in Short Fiction* 21 (Winter 1984)]. For her part, Mrs. Hale is rejecting the men's specious reasoning, complaining about the lawyer's disdainful treatment of the kitchen things and asserting, "I'd hate to have men comin' into my kitchen, snoopin' round and criticizin'," obviously recalling the disorder in her kitchen and resenting the conclusions about her that could be drawn. Lacking that opening scene, the play simply does not resonate so profoundly.

Even more telling is a subtle but important change that Glaspell made following Mrs. Hale's testy assertion. In both the play and the story, Mrs. Peters offers the meek defense, "Of course it's no more than their duty," and then the two works diverge. In *Trifles,* Mrs. Peters manages to change the subject. Noticing some dough that Mrs. Wright had been preparing the day before, she says flatly, "she had set bread," and that statement directs Mrs. Hale's attention to the half-done and ruined kitchen chores. In effect, the flow of conversation is mutually directed in the play, and the distance between the women is thus minimized. When she wrote the story, however, Glaspell omitted mention of the bread and instead took us into Mrs. Hale's thoughts, as she does at the beginning of the story:

> She thought of the flour in her kitchen at home—half sifted, half not sifted. She had been interrupted, and had left things half done. What had interrupted Minnie Foster? Why had that work been left half done? She made a move as if to finish it, —unfinished things always bothered her, —and then she glanced around and saw that Mrs. Peters was watching her—and she didn't want Mrs. Peters to get that feeling she got of work begun and then—for some reason—not finished.
>
> "It's a shame about her fruit," she said. . . .

Although mention of the ruined fruit preserves is included

in the play as well, two significant additions are made in the above passage. First, there is the continual comparison between Mrs. Hale's life and Mrs. Wright's. Second, and more important, we get the clear sense here of Mrs. Hale's suspicion of Mrs. Peters, her not wanting to call attention to the unfinished job for fear that the sheriff's wife will get the wrong idea—or, in this case, the right idea, for the evidence of disturbance, however circumstantial, is something the men may be able to use against Mrs. Wright. In other words, unlike the play, the story posits a different set of polarities, with Mrs. Peters presumably occupying a place within the official party and Mrs. Hale taking the side of the accused against all of them.

We come at this point to a crossroads in the story. Mrs. Hale can leave things as they are and keep information to herself, or she can recruit Mrs. Peters as a fellow "juror" in the case, moving the sheriff's wife away from her sympathy for her husband's position and towards identification with the accused woman. Mrs. Hale chooses the latter course and sets about persuading Mrs. Peters to emerge, in Alkalay-Gut's words, "as an individual distinct from her role as sheriff's wife." Once that happens, "her identification with Minnie is rapid and becomes complete."

The persuasive process begins easily but effectively, with Mrs. Hale reflecting upon the change in Minnie Foster Wright over the thirty or so years she has known her—the change, to use the metaphor that Glaspell will develop, from singing bird to muted caged bird. She follows this reminiscence with a direct question to Mrs. Peters about whether the latter thinks that Minnie killed her husband. "Oh, I don't know," is the frightened response in both works, but, as always, the story provides more insight and tension than does the drama. Still emphasizing in her revision the distance between the women, Glaspell has Mrs. Hale believe that her talk of the youthful Minnie has fallen on deaf ears: "Much difference it makes to her whether Minnie Foster had pretty clothes when she was a girl." This sense of the other woman's indifference to such irrelevant trivialities is occassioned not only by Mrs. Hale's persistent belief in the other woman's official role but also by an odd look that crosses Mrs. Peters' face. At second glance, however, Mrs. Hale notices something else that melts her annoyance and undercuts her suspicions about the sheriff's wife: "Then she looked again, and she wasn't so sure; in fact, she hadn't at any time been perfectly sure about Mrs. Peters. She had that shrinking manner, and yet her eyes looked as if they could see a long way into things." Whereas the play shows the women meandering towards concurrence, the short story is here seen to evolve—and part of that evolution, we must conclude, is due to Mrs. Hale's ability to persuade her peer to regard the case from her perspective. The look that she sees in Mrs. Peters' eyes suggests to her that she might be able to persuade her, that the potential for identification is there. Hence, when she asks whether Mrs. Peters thinks Minnie is guilty, the question resonates here in ways the play does not.

Accordingly, Mrs. Hale will become much more aggressive in her arguments hereafter, taking on something of the persuader's hopeful hostility, which, in the case of the

Ida Rauh and Glaspell in the Provincetown Players' production of Bernice.

story, stands in marked contrast to the hostility she felt for Mrs. Peters' official role earlier. Thus, when Mrs. Peters tries to retreat into a male argument, weakly asserting that "the law is the law," the Mrs. Hale of the short story does not let the remark pass, as the one in *Trifles* does: "the law is the law—and a bad stove is a bad stove. How'd you like to cook on this?" Even she, however, is startled by Mrs. Peters' immediate response to her homey analogy and *ad hominem* attack: "A person gets discouraged—and loses heart," Mrs. Peters says—"That look of seeing . . . through a thing to something else" back on her face.

As far as I am concerned, the addition of this passage is the most important change that Glaspell made in her generic translation. Having used this direct personal attack and having noted the ambivalence that Mrs. Peters feels for her role as sheriff's wife, Mrs. Hale will now proceed to effect closure of the gap between them—again, a gap that is never this widely opened in *Trifles.* Now Mrs. Hale will change her entire mode of attack, pushing the limits, doing things she hesitated doing earlier, assailing Mrs. Peters whenever she lapses into her easy conventional attitudes. For instance, when Mrs. Peters objects to Mrs. Hale's repair of a badly knitted quilt block—in effect, tampering with circumstantial evidence of Minnie's mental disturbance the day before—Mrs. Hale proceeds to do it anyway. As a measure of how much she has changed, we have only to compare this act with her earlier hesitation to finish another chore for fear of what Mrs. Peters might

think. She has no reason to be distrustful of Mrs. Peters any longer, for the process of identification is now well underway.

That identification becomes quite evident by the time the women find the most compelling piece of circumstantial evidence against Mrs. Wright—the broken bird cage and the dead bird, its neck wrung and its body placed in a pretty box in Mrs. Wright's sewing basket. When the men notice the cage and Mrs. Hale misleadingly speculates that a cat may have been at it, it is Mrs. Peters who confirms the matter. Asked by the county attorney whether a cat was on the premises, Mrs. Peters—fully aware that there is no cat and never has been—quickly and evasively replies, "Well, not *now.* . . . They're superstitious, you know; they leave." Not only is Mrs. Peters deliberately lying here, but, more important, she is assuming quite another role from the one she played earlier. Uttering a banality, she plays at being the shallow woman who believes in superstitions, thus consciously playing one of the roles the men expect her to assume and concealing her keen intellect from them, her ability to extrapolate facts from small details.

From this point forward, the play and the short story are essentially the same. Mrs. Hale will continue her persuasive assault, and Mrs. Peters will continue to struggle inwardly. The culmination of this struggle occurs when, late in the story, the county attorney says that "a sheriff's wife is married to the law," and she responds, "Not—just that way." In **"Jury,"** however, this protest carries much greater force than it does in *Trifles* for the simple reason that it is a measure of how far Mrs. Peters has come in the course of the short story.

Appropriately enough, too, Mrs. Hale has the final word in both narratives. Asked derisively by the county attorney what stitch Mrs. Wright had been using to make her quilt, Mrs. Hale responds with false sincerity, "We call it—knot it, Mr. Henderson." Most critics have read this line as an ironic reference to the women's solidarity at this point. That is quite true, but, as I have been suggesting here, the progress towards this solidarity varies subtly but unmistakably in the two narratives. Whereas *Trifles,* opening as it does with the women's close physical proximity, reveals the dichotomy between male and female concepts of justice and social roles, **"A Jury of Her Peers"** is much more concerned with the separateness of the women themselves and their self-injurious acquiescence in male-defined roles. Hence, in her reworking of the narrative, Glaspell did much more than translate the material from one genre to another. Rather, she subtly changed its theme, and, in so doing, she wrote a story that is much more interesting, resonant, and disturbing than the slighter drama from which it derives.

Leonard Mustazza, "Generic Translation and Thematic Shift in Susan Glaspell's 'Trifles' and 'A Jury of Her Peers'," in Studies in Short Fiction, *Vol. 26, No. 4, Fall, 1989, pp. 489-96.*

Linda Ben-Zvi (essay date 1989)

[*In the following essay, Ben-Zvi discusses Glaspell's influence on modern women playwrights.*]

The name Susan Glaspell is followed in her biographical sketches by some of the most illustrious credentials in all of American theater history: cofounder of the Provincetown Players, the seminal American theater company; prodigious playwright, who contributed eleven plays to the Provincetown theater in its seven years of existence, surpassed only by Eugene O'Neill, who wrote fourteen under the aegis of the group; talented actress, praised by the visiting French director Jacques Copeau for her moving depiction of character; director of her own plays, including *The Verge,* one of the first expressionist dramas seen on the American stage; winner of the Pulitzer Prize for drama in 1931 for her play *Alison's House,* only the second woman to be so honored; head of the Midwest bureau of the Federal Theatre Project in Chicago in the thirties, credited with reviewing over six hundred plays and instrumental in the production of several important works by black playwrights; significant influence on others, particularly Eugene O'Neill, who she brought to the Provincetown theater in the summer of 1916 and with whom she continued to have a close personal and professional relationship until her departure for Greece with her husband in 1923, thus ending the original Provincetown experiment.

Few have been so successful in so many areas of theater, yet, ironically, few have so completely disappeared from the dramatic canon as Susan Glaspell. Critics in her own

period such as Heywood Broun, Ludwig Lewisohn, Isaac Goldberg, and Barrett Clark praised her and O'Neill for creating an indigenous American dramatic idiom, experimenting with new forms and new subject matter, and leading the way for those who followed. Yet while O'Neill's reputation grew over the years, Glaspell was virtually ignored by subsequent critics. In the forty years following her death, only one book devoted to her dramas and novels and only one biographical essay on her life appeared. And with the exception of her first one-act play, *Suppressed Desires,* which has remained a standard work for amateur theater companies, her other writings—six one-act and six full length plays and eleven novels—were allowed to go out of print.

Interest in Glaspell and her work began to resurface only in the last ten years, when research devoted to women writers uncovered her masterpiece *Trifles,* and the play, along with the short story version, **"A Jury of Her Peers,"** began to appear in anthologies of women's writing, particularly Mary Anne Ferguson's popular *Images of Women in Literature* and Judith Barlow's drama collection *Plays by American Women: The Early Years.*

While feminist criticism has brought Glaspell's name back from the dead and uncanonized, it has not yet produced studies of Glaspell's contributions to dramatic writing. Most discussions of her plays concentrate on them as documents of female exploitation and survival. Certainly, they are important because they are among the first modern writings to focus exclusively on female personae, but they go even further. They offer a new structure, a new dramatic language appropriate to their angle of vision, and a new depiction of character which accommodates the experience of the central figure they delineate, a woman seeking her way in a hostile and often unfamiliar world.

Glaspell's relevance to women playwrights is particularly important because she illustrates in the body of her works the kinds of questions they must face, questions of form determined by the sensibility that the plays embody. Glaspell was among the first writers to realize that it was not enough to present women at the center of the stage. If there were to be a radical break with plays of the past, women would have to exist in a world tailored to their persons and speak a language not borrowed from men. She shared this awareness with her contemporary Virginia Woolf, who, in a 1920 essay, described the problems of female representation on the stage:

> It is true that women afford ground for much speculation and are frequently represented; but it is becoming daily more evident that lady Macbeth, Cordelia, Clarissa, Dora, Diana, Helen, and the rest are by no means what they pretend to be. Some are plainly men in disguise; others represent what men would like to be, or are conscious of not being; or again they embody the dissatisfaction and despair which afflict most people when they reflect upon the sorry condition of the human race.

Glaspell's women *are* what they seem to be: tentative and often halting, trying to find themselves and their voices. Her explorations on the stage are similar to those described by the critic Susan Rubin Suleiman in her 1986 essay entitled "(Re)Writing the Body: The Politics and Poetics of Female Eroticism":

> Women, who for centuries had been the *objects* of male theorizing, male desires, male fears and male representations, had to discover and reappropriate themselves as *subjects*. . . . The call went out to invent both a new poetics and a new politics, based on women's reclaiming what had always been theirs but had been usurped from them; control over their bodies and a voice with which to speak about it.

Glaspell, seventy years earlier, was aware of both responsibilities. She offered a form, a poetics, and a politics which Suleiman and others writing today describe as vital to female-centered art. Glaspell saw that if the world portrayed is the world of women—if the locus of perception is female—then her plays would have to strive for a shape which reinforces this new vantage point and a language which articulates it. And while her particular experiments may at first glance seem removed from those of women writing in modern and postmodern modes of the sixties, seventies, and eighties—who employ transformations, nonrepresentational situations and characters, fragmented temporal and spatial distinctions—they are in fact part of the same ongoing search for dramatic means to depict female experience. A study of Glaspell's works thus provides illustrations of how women can function as protagonists and how structures, language, and subject matter can act as extensions of such women-centered drama.

When Susan Glaspell first came to New York with her husband George Cram Cook in April 1913, she was disturbed by the theater she saw. In *The Road to the Temple,* her biography of Cook, she writes, "Plays, like magazine stories, were patterned. They might be pretty good within themselves, seldom did they open out to—where it surprised or thrilled your spirit to follow. They did not ask much of you, those plays." Like O'Neill and the other contributors to the Provincetown Players, she was conscious of the limitations of traditional dramatic form. The Dublin-based Abbey Theatre had toured America in 1911 and had shown the possibilities of dramas not limited to narrowly defined shapes. Yet Glaspell's desire to smash existing structures stems from more than the contemporary abhorrence of limitation, permeating the society in which she moved: Greenwich Village in the first decades of the century. To understand Glaspell's work with form and language, it is necessary to understand something of her biography. Her wish to see plays which "open out" and require the audience "to follow" springs most directly from her pioneer roots.

Susan Glaspell was born in Davenport, Iowa, in 1876, a grandchild of one of the early settlers of the territory. When asked to compile notes for a biographical sketch, she wrote, "Though my home has for some years been in the East, almost everything I write has its roots in the middle west; I suppose because my own are there." In an essay for *Twentieth Century Authors* she repeats this idea: "I have never lost the feeling that is my part of the country."

The impetus for pioneers such as her ancestors, that thing that made them leave comfortable homes for unknown places, continually puzzled Glaspell and became the central motif in all her writing. In *The Road to the Temple* she asks, "What makes a man who has an orchard or a mill in Massachusetts or New York where there is room enough for him . . . get into a covered wagon and go to Indians, rattlesnakes, to the back-breaking work of turning wilderness into productive land." "They go to loneliness and the fears born in loneliness," she says of these pioneers. Young enough herself to remember her grandmother's stories, Glaspell also recognized the difficulty facing the following generations. How do those who come after retain the pioneering spirit? In *Inheritors,* her historical drama, the protagonist Madeline Morton says to her college professor Dr. Holden, "Just a little way back—anything might have been. What happened?" He answers (speaking with difficulty), "It got—set too soon." Unlike O'Neill, who attributed America's failure to an inability of the country to "set down roots," Glaspell saw roots as dangers, marks of fixity and stagnation, usually leading to stultifying institutions against which her characters struggle, much as their pioneering forebears did, in order to move into a new sphere, if not of place then of spirit.

While Glaspell indicates that both men and women need constantly to question institutions and to change them and themselves if both become too rigid—a situation she describes in *Inheritors*—it is to her women characters that she usually attributes this desire for change. It is they who seem to suffer most from the fixity of society. Glaspell continually sunders the stereotype of women desiring stability and the comfort of place. Her works stand in juxtaposition to arguments such as the one set forth in Leslie Fiedler's *Love and Death in the American Novel,* where women are depicted as perpetuators of the status quo, those agents of society against whom male characters battle by going down the Mississippi, into the wilderness, on the road. Invariably in the world Glaspell describes, it is the women, not the men, who want to "lit out," for fixity impinges more directly on them than on the men. As figures of power—American versions of Ibsen's "pillars of society"—the male characters in Glaspell's works have most to lose by change, they hew most closely to routine, and allow virtually no freedom to the women with whom they live. Glaspell's women, for the most part, are required to uphold traditional patterns and remain in place—both physically and mentally.

Mrs. Peters in *Trifles* is typical of such personae. She is described as "married to the law," and expected as such to mouth the ideas of her husband, the sheriff, to trace his conservative path, reflecting his opinions and his decisions. Mr. Peters and the men in the play are untouched and unchanged by the events they witness at the scene of a murder; they are "the law," and the law, Glaspell indicates, is a fixed thing incapable of dealing with either nuances of a case or variations of human behavior. Mrs. Peters, however, assimilates the evidence she stumbles across; she "opens out" into new areas of self-awareness. It is her emancipation which becomes the central theme of the play, overshadowing the murder investigation, the ostensible subject of *Trifles.*

In *The Verge,* Glaspell's expressionist masterpiece, her protagonist Claire Archer experiments with plants in an attempt to move vicariously in new directions that have not been attempted before. Her "Edge Vine" timidly clings to the familiar patterns of the species, and she destroys it. It is to the plant she calls "Breath of Life" that she next turns, hoping that in its courageous "thrusting forward into new forms" it will enter worlds which she too wishes to know. When asked why she breeds new plant forms that do not seem "better" than the familiar varieties, she attempts to explain: "These plants (*beginning flounderingly.*) —perhaps they are less beautiful—less sound—than the plants from which they diverged. But they have found—otherness. (*Laughs a little shrilly.*) If you know what I mean?" When her husband tries to stop her words as he has tried to stop her experiments, she continues excitedly, "No; I'm going on. They have been shocked out of what they were—into something they were not; they've broken from the forms in which they found themselves." In Claire's own life, "form" takes the familiar configurations: wife, mother, friend, lover. She too would move outward, but she is kept back by a circle of men appropriately called Tom, Dick, Harry—friend, lover, husband—and by her sister and child. "Out there— lies all that's not been touched—lies life that waits. Back here—the old pattern, done again, again and again. So long done it doesn't even know itself for a pattern," Claire says to those who thwart her in her desires.

In *Inheritors,* again woman is shown as pioneer, this time not seeking emancipation from conventional gender roles or attempting exploration into unknown areas, but seeking the reinstatement of democratic values which have been subverted in succeeding generations. Madeline Morton, the protagonist, refuses to believe that the practices of America in 1920, with its Red-baiting, condemnation and imprisonment of conscientious objectors, and limitations on freedom of speech, are correct. An "inheritor" of the pioneering spirit of her grandfather, she alone questions the values of the "100 percent Americans" whose jingoism reflects the period in which the play is set and in which it was written.

The image of pioneering is a recurrent one in all of Glaspell's plays; it shapes all her writing. Yet what makes her significant as a model for modern women playwrights is less the paradigm itself than the fact that Glaspell creates a form which reinforces it. Like modern playwrights such as Beckett and Pinter, she recognizes that it is not enough to have subject matter discuss new ideas; a playwright must also offer a dramatic form appropriate to the ideas expressed. The impossibility of logic and linearity cannot be adequately shown in a conventional three-act play which abides by the laws of time and place; so, too, the desire of women characters to break the rules of their societies cannot be depicted in plays which follow conventional rules. The form of a Glaspell work becomes an extension of the theme: each play attempts to break with the formulaic conventions of dramaturgy so pervasive during her period and to offer possible new structures to shape the explorations of her female personae.

Nothing in a Glaspell play is linear. Plots do not have clearly defined beginnings, middles, and ends; they self-consciously move out from some familiar pattern, calling attention as they go to the fact that the expected convention will be violated, the anticipated order will be sundered. If the play seems to be a traditional detective story, as in *Trifles,* the emissaries of the law—the men—will not be the focus of attention. The center of interest, instead, will be the women, those peripheral, shadowy figures in the play who have come on the scene to accompany their husbands and each other.

The notion of linearity in Glaspell's plays is always connected with suppression and with social institutions which have become rigid and confining. For example, the men in *Trifles* walk and talk in straight lines, crisscrossing the scene of the murder as they crisscross the facts of the murder case. When Mr. Hale, a witness to the murder scene, relates his story, he is chided by the district attorney to recount just the facts. "Well Mr. Hale, tell just what happened when you came here yesterday morning." Whenever Mr. Hale veers in the slightest way from the straight narrative line, the county attorney returns him to the narrow parameters of the discourse. "Let's talk about that later, Mr. Hale. I do want to talk about that, but tell now just what happened when you got to the house." In his insistence on the limitations of discourse, the attorney makes clear that he is able to proceed only in prescribed ways. It is significant that Mr. Hale is not part of the legal system; he seems less confined by the narrowness of the lawmen and more in spirit with the freer, unstructured methods of the women, one of whom is his wife. Yet because of his sex, Mr. Hale is afforded the privileges of the men. He is not confined to the kitchen, but follows the attorney and the sheriff around the house seeking clues which will help convict Mrs. Wright, the woman accused of strangling her husband.

Unlike the men, Mrs. Hale and Mrs. Peters show flexibility in their actions and their words. They are limited by the patriarchal power structure clearly working within the scene Glaspell describes, but they are free in the limited confines of the kitchen where the play takes place. One of Glaspell's radical departures is to place the action in the kitchen, one of the few plays of the period to follow *Miss Julie* in doing so. But unlike in Strindberg's play, there are no men in this female province to control the action. Here the women freely retrace the steps of Mrs. Wright. Slowly, almost without volition, they piece together the motive for murder, quilting a pattern of awareness as they randomly move across the stage and speak about the events of the case.

The central image Glaspell chooses for this play is quilting, and, like quilters, her female characters carefully sew together disconnected pieces, making new patterns out of old materials, intuitively sifting through the details around them without any preconceived pattern limiting their actions. It is they who solve the case, not the lawmen who are committed to set ways of investigation.

The dichotomy Glaspell presents is between male fixity— the fixity of a society gone rigid—and female exploration at the outskirts of that society in the world of women, among "trifles." She underlines this dichotomy by offering a form which has the same randomness and openness as the quilting process itself, in apposition to the constrained, formalized actions of her male characters.

Even more innovative is Glaspell's manipulation of point of view. What she is able to do in this play and in her other works is to force the audience to share the world of her women, to become fellow travelers with her pioneering protagonists. While the men in *Trifles* are almost immediately shunted offstage and only appear as they traverse the playing area of the kitchen, the women remain stationary. It is with them that the audience—men and women—remain, not privy to the conversations of the men, not afforded their mobility. The audience is therefore forced to see the world through the eyes of Mrs. Hale and Mrs. Peters. As a bond is gradually forged between the women and the absent one for whom they act as surrogates and judges, a bond is gradually created between the women and the audience who has gained some insights into their female world and has—at least for the duration of the play—seen as they see. When, at the end of the work, Mrs. Hale places the box containing the strangled bird into her pocketbook in order to destroy the incriminating evidence which provides the only motive for murder, the audience generally applauds her gesture and by so doing becomes itself an accessory to the act.

By placing women at the center of the drama and the audience captive in the kitchen with them, Glaspell does more than merely upend the conventional detective format or offer an unusual locale for a play—at least in 1917. She actually overturns the very hierarchical values of the society she depicts. The men in the play chide "the ladies" for being concerned with the "trifles" of the farm kitchen: the unbaked bread, dirty towel rack, and sewing left undone. Yet Glaspell indicates during the course of the play that such "trifles" can reveal truths, that the concerns of women may have as much significance as the "facts" of men.

She overturns both conventional dramatic form and conventional gender demarcations and values in her other plays as well. In *The Outside* men again play the seemingly active agents. They are lifesavers who attempt to resuscitate a drowning victim. And again—as in *Trifles*—men are unsuccessful; their attempts to save life fail. But as they go through the motions of resuscitation, two women—a maid and her employer—watch silently and themselves perform another kind of "lifesaving." As in *Trifles,* once more Glaspell depicts the inarticulate power of women to understand the shared experiences of other women, unstructured by language but nevertheless communicated through mutually shared pain. Using single words, pauses, and broken sentences, the maid, Allie Mayo, reaches out to the other woman, Mrs. Patrick, drawing her back to the life she has rejected. Little outward action occurs, but once more Glaspell indicates that events of great moment may take place in near-silence among those not accustomed to heroic deeds; individuals may be saved by a few well-chosen words, by a gesture, by "trifles," as well as by physical valor.

In *The Verge* Glaspell's protagonist is less fortunate than the two women in *Trifles* and *The Outside;* she is afforded

no victory in her quest for freedom. Unable to move "outside," like the plant she has cultivated, Claire Archer reverts to one of the two traditional ends for women who would break with societal restrictions. She lapses into madness, a variation on the suicide that so often is the end of pioneering women, at least in literature in the early part of twentieth century. Glaspell's great accomplishment in this play is to provide a perfect dramatic structure to shape her hero's efforts. Antedating O'Neill's *Hairy Ape* by several months, she creates one of the first expressionist settings in American theater. The play has an odd, open-ended shape to it, depicted visually on the stage by the two playing areas: the narrow, low greenhouse in which Claire works and the tower—"*a tower which is thought to be round but does not complete the circle,*" the stage directions say. Claire calls it her "thwarted tower." Both areas are lit in special ways. In act 1, patterns are superimposed on the greenhouse "*as if—as Plato would have it—the patterns inherent in abstract nature and behind all life had come out.*" Periodically, light from a trapdoor illuminates the laboratory. The interior of the tower in act 2 is dark and brooding, lit by an old-fashioned watchman's lantern whose "innumerable pricks and slits in the metal create a marvelous pattern on the curved wall—like some masonry that hasn't been."

The form of the play is also experimental. Beginning like a conventional comedy of the twenties—weekend guests discomforted because the heat in the house has been diverted to the plants in the greenhouse—the play moves in act 2 to a psychological investigation of Claire that stands in odd juxtaposition to the levity and ambiance of act 1. Yet this discontinuity between acts seems to be Glaspell's way of once more having form reinforce theme. Repeatedly in act 1 Claire is chided by the men around her to be "cheerful," "witty," "fun." Enforced gaiety is what Claire wishes to escape as much as she wishes to escape the restrictive roles of traditional womanhood. By contrasting the style and mood of the laboratory scene with the introspective world of the tower, Glaspell indicates the forces working on her protagonist. Only in her tower home is Claire relatively free to pursue a course not dictated by others. However, there are still stairs which lead up to her haven, more often trod than the parallel stairs which lead from her laboratory down to a temporary, subterranean refuge. She may escape down the latter, but she cannot avoid the intrusions of those who will ascend the former.

In act 3, again in Claire's laboratory, as she waits for the unveiling of her new plant form, the tensions between the two styles of the preceding acts and the two venues explode in violence. Using the same ending that O'Neill will employ in *The Hairy Ape*—the hug of death—Glaspell has her protagonist strangle Tom, the man who presents the greatest obstacle to her freedom. She then concludes her play with Claire lapsing into insanity, what appears to be the only refuge from the world depicted in the play. Conflating the initial comedy of manners and the psychological investigation, Glaspell creates a play which fits no simple category, a fitting structure for a protagonist who wishes to escape easy classification.

Glaspell's plays foreground women and provide open, unrestricted, asymmetrical dramatic structures in which women operate. The same can be said for the language characters use. Repeatedly, Glaspell connects language to action. Since her women are exploring new areas of their lives, they find traditional language unsuited to their needs. They may be women unused to speech or women all too aware that the words they speak do not express their thoughts. In either case the results are the same. Her characters are virtually inarticulate, or are rendered so because of the situations in which they find themselves. The most common punctuation mark she uses is the dash. It is used when the character is unsure of the direction in which she is going, as yet unprepared to articulate consciously a new awareness or unwilling to put into words feelings and wishes which may collapse under the weight of words.

One of Glaspell's most important contributions to drama is to place these inarticulate characters in the center of her works, to allow them to struggle to say what they are not sure they even know. While O'Neill's personae usually end statements with exclamation points, Glaspell has the courage to allow her women to trail off their words in pauses, devices against the tyranny of language. And while those inarticulates O'Neill does present are unable to speak because of the limits of their class or education, Glaspell's women, despite their class, share the limitations of their gender and find speech difficult. It fails to describe the new areas into which they are attempting to move and is often perceived as the language of male experience.

In many ways Glaspell's recognition of the inherent connection between female independence and language makes her a forerunner of contemporary feminist critics who see language at the heart of any possible realignment of the sexes. While Glaspell did not write essays about the subject, her plays speak to the same concerns that occupy feminist critics such as Julia Kristeva, Hélène Cixous, and Luce Irigaray. And while Glaspell's struggles to create a female language do not go as far as those espousing *écriture féminine* would probably accept, they are predicated on some of the same beliefs: that women's subjugation in society is connected to the subjugation imposed by language.

Prefiguring psychoanalytic critics such as Irigaray, Glaspell actually offers on the stage the absent woman—woman as void—against whom male characters react, upon whom they impose a shape—much as Woolf described—making of the absent woman a kind of palimpsest upon which to inscribe their own identities, desires, and language. Bernice in the play of that name, Alison in *Alison's House,* and Mrs. Wright in *Trifles* are all hovering presences who never appear. Since they are not physically present, their voices are co-opted by males who speak for them. This dramatic depiction of woman as void is one of Glaspell's most innovative and modern techniques, employed by contemporary women playwrights as well as by feminist critics.

One of the most direct examples of male usurpation of female speech appears in *Trifles,* which begins with Mr. Hale acting as the spokesperson for the absent Mrs. Wright. Her words come through his mouth. The women present say nothing as the voice of man speaks the words of woman. Only when the women are alone does sound come, and it is—and remains—a halting sound. Yet as the awareness of their shared subjugation develops, the women begin to seek a verbal form for this knowledge. Appropriately, it is a language of stops and starts, with lacunae—dashes—covering the truths they still cannot admit or are unused to framing in words. What the audience sees and hears are people learning to speak, constructing a medium of expression as they go. The way is not easy, and the language they frame is awkward. But it is clearly their language, no longer the words of others which they have been taught to speak.

One of the most effective moments in the play, a point of anagnorisis, is when Mrs. Peters recalls the time when she too felt powerless, like Mrs. Wright, and she too had murder in her heart: "When I was a girl—my kitten—there was a boy took a hatchet, and before my eyes—and before I could get there—if they hadn't held me back I would have—hurt him." Unwilling or unable to say more, Mrs. Peters talks in half sentences, covering her growing awareness in pauses more telling than the words she actually employs. The sentence becomes a verbal concomitant to the patchwork investigation the two women have conducted in the kitchen.

In another section of *Trifles,* Glaspell points directly to the connections between quilting and growing awareness, doing so through seemingly flat, banal phrases. Three times during the course of the play, the women discuss the stitches Mrs. Wright has used for her work. The first time the men overhear them and laugh when Mrs. Hale asks, "I wonder if she was goin' to quilt it or just knot it." Several minutes later the question turns to a qualified statement when Mrs. Peters says, "We think she was going to—knot it." The last words of the play, after the women have hidden the evidence and silently rebelled against their husbands, are Mrs. Hale's: "We call it knot it." From interrogative to qualified statement to assertion—the sentences mark the changes in the women, changes the men overlook because they do not hear the import of the words the women use. To the men, the words refer to "trifles"; the language is foreign, the shape of the sentences irrelevant. That seems to be Glaspell's point. The women speak in a different voice, to use Carol Gilligan's apt phrase. There is the voice of law and fact and the voice of connection and caring. The two voices do not hear each other. What is important, however, is that the audience, who has begun to decipher the words of women, can understand the import of the lines as the men with whom these women live cannot. The audience has begun to listen to, if not to speak in, "a different voice."

Glaspell employs other alterations of language in *The Verge.* In that play Claire Archer suffers from too many words, other people's words. When she desires to express her own ideas, she finds herself unable to do so because the words she must use are already misshapen by the uses others make of them. "I'm tired of what you do," Claire tells her fatuous sister,

> you and all of you. Life—experience—values—
> calm—sensitive words which raise their heads as

indications. And you *pull them up*—to decorate your stagnant little minds—and think that makes you—And because you have pulled that word from the life that grew it you won't let one who's honest, and aware, and troubled, try to reach through to—what she doesn't know is there.

Unsure of what she seeks, Claire realizes the dilemma she faces: the language which is her only means of investigation is the language of those she would leave behind. It is against the fixed forms of the society which Claire inveighs, just as it is against the imposition of an alien language which she struggles.

To compound the problem, Claire also recognizes that when trying to give voice to ideas which are still inchoate, she forces upon them a pattern that limits the exploration itself. "Stop doing that!" she demands of language, "—words going into patterns; They do it sometimes when I let come what's there. Thoughts take pattern—then the pattern is the thing." Here Glaspell refers not to the limits women experience speaking the language of men but to the limits of language itself.

Claire Archer is one of the first female characters in drama whose main concern is to create a new language and whose failure illustrates the difficulties in doing so. Sixty years later, in his play *Not I,* Samuel Beckett would place a gaping mouth eight feet above the stage and reenact a similar struggle for articulation of self—and a similar failure. By making language the primary focus of the struggle for selfhood, Glaspell is radically expanding the possibilities of thematic material for theater and the uses of stage language.

Further, Glaspell was one of the first women playwrights to present female personae engaged in violent acts: killing a husband offstage in *Trifles,* strangling a lover onstage in *The Verge.* Glaspell's choice of subject matter in both plays may not seem shocking or innovative in the contemporary period, where a playwright depicts a woman taking the grotesque shape of a circus freak and having her genitals excised (Joan Shenkar's *Signs of Life*); or examines lesbianism, homosexuality, and masturbation as liberating alternatives to, or perhaps direct results of, colonial values and mores (Caryl Churchill's *Cloud Nine*); or describes the ritual slaughter of a random male (Maureen Duffy's *Rites*); or depicts lady mud wrestlers performing in a bar in New Jersey (Rosalyn Drexler's *Delicate Feelings*); or makes Joan of Arc and Susan B. Anthony fellow travelers (Lavonne Mueller's *Little Victories*). Yet, in her own period, Glaspell's material was culled from events and subjects considered sacrosanct, controversial, and—in the case of *Inheritors*—subversive. Her first play was *Suppressed Desires,* written in collaboration with her husband, George Cram Cook. It parodied a movement which her own circle of friends in Greenwich Village took most seriously: psychoanalysis. "You could not go out to buy a bun without hearing of someone's complex," Glaspell wrote about her first days in New York in 1913. Blind adherence to analysis becomes the comic subject of the play, subtitled *A Freudian Comedy.* It was one of the first plays written in America to employ, albeit sarcastically, the new

theories Freud introduced to the country only a few years before in his Clark University lectures.

Glaspell consistently wrote about controversial topics throughout her career, sometimes treating them to ridicule, sometimes offering them a platform for development. For example, her last play for the Provincetown theater, *Chains of Dew* (1922), has as its protagonist a young woman named Nora (the name probably borrowed from Ibsen) whose mission is to spread news about contraception and who in the process radicalizes the women with whom she comes into contact in the play and, by extension, those in the audience.

Glaspell's most challenging use of subject matter, however, comes in the play *Inheritors.* In order to appreciate the risks taken in this work, it is necessary to have some idea of the climate in which the play was written in 1920. In 1917, as a result of Woodrow Wilson's declaration of war—an act Glaspell and her friends vigorously opposed—Congress passed the Selective Service Act, which required general conscription for eligible males, exempting only those who on narrowly specified grounds opposed all wars. Others resisting the draft for moral or political reasons were tried as deserters, and when convicted often faced brutal treatment. Along with conscription, Congress also enacted laws intended to quell dissent about the war. The Espionage Act, on pain of a ten-thousand-dollar fine and twenty years in jail, made it illegal to refuse duty or impede recruitment in the military. The appended Sedition Act went further and prohibited uttering, printing, or writing any disloyal, profane, or scurrilous language about the form of government in the United States. Various alien laws made it a crime, punishable by deportation, to speak out against America or any of its allies.

During the postwar period the theater was generally silent about such abuses in society. Burns Mantle's *Best Plays of 1920-21* lists such hits as *Good Times* and *Irene.* Glaspell's *Inheritors* was the exception to this escapist fare. It directly condemns the treatment of conscientious objectors after the war, the deportation of aliens and strikebreakers, and the abridgment of personal freedom of speech. The play also makes direct references to the excessive patriotism which persisted after the end of the war. "That's the worst of a war—you have to go on hearing about it for so long," and "Seems nothing draws men together like killing other men," and "The war was a godsend to people who were in danger of getting on to themselves" were lines still liable to bring Glaspell—like her protagonist—a possible fine and jail sentence under the espionage and sedition laws. Glaspell's friends Big Bill Haywood, head of the Wobblies, Emma Goldman, and Jack Reed had already experienced the effects of the repression. Yet Glaspell went ahead with her play, which was well received and may have had some part in reversing the climate of the period. It is interesting to note that as a mark of the universality of the issues Glaspell raises, the Hedgerow Theatre of Moylan, Pennsylvania, headed by Jasper Deeter, an original member of the Provincetown Players, performed the play every year from 1923 to 1954, except during the war. When the play was revived by the Mirror Repertory Company in New York in 1983, the critics all mentioned one point: the picture of the past which it offers is as valid in the eighties as it was for Glaspell's audience in 1921.

Glaspell's focus on contemporary issues—either to mock them or to promulgate them—follows a tradition among women playwrights which goes back as far as Mercy Otis Warren and forward to Megan Terry and Maria Irene Fornes. Yet when Terry wrote *Viet Rock* in the sixties and Fornes wrote *The Danube* and *The Conduct of Life* in the eighties, they risked far less censure or danger than Glaspell faced in her own stand against a repressive society.

As important as her political positions were in keeping alive the tradition of outspoken women playwrights, Glaspell is probably most important to women writers as an example of someone who dared to give dramatic shape to the struggles of women. The two women in *Trifles* can be prototypes of Everywoman; Claire Archer can be a fictional surrogate for feminist ideologues who are presently engaged in altering language to fit their own needs and possibilities. Certainly, Glaspell is not the only woman playwright who provides a her/story from which others may draw sustenance. Those writers represented in Barlow's collection—Mowatt, Crothers, Gale, and Treadwell—as well as innovators such as Gerstenberg and those many, until recently anonymous black women playwrights of the twenties and thirties, offer a body of works that open up the range of experimentation for the present group of women playwrights.

I would argue that having read the work of Glaspell and other women writing at the beginning of the century, one has a better idea of the ongoing movement which is American women's drama. There is the shadow of Glaspell and the others behind such experiments as the Women's Project of the American Place Theatre, which one of its participants described as giving to women "a place to raise their voices without apology." While Helene Keyssar in *Feminist Theatre* is correct in saying that it was only in the late sixties that playwrights "*in significant numbers* became self-consciously concerned about the presence—or absence—of women as women on stage" (my italics), there were women much earlier in the century, and before, who shared these concerns and wrote plays which led the way. Susan Glaspell was one of the most important of these pioneering playwrights. Although she has been ignored by those who shape the canon, she should not be ignored by those who are attempting to reconstitute it.

Linda Ben-Zvi, "Susan Glaspell's Contributions to Contemporary Women Playwrights," in Feminine Focus: The New Women Playwrights, *edited by Enoch Brater, Oxford University Press, Inc., 1989, pp. 147-66.*

Barbara Ozieblo   (essay date 1990)

[*In the essay below, Ozieblo argues that Glaspell's female characters reveal her personal ambivalence about the role of women in society, oscillating between rebellion against and dependence on men.*]

Susan Glaspell (1876-1948) is a prime example of the "peculiar eclipsing" so frequently suffered by women writers. She devoted eight years to the Provincetown Players, and

her plays alone would have justified the claim that the sand dunes of Provincetown were the birthplace of modern American drama. But Glaspell's voice was silenced, and although feminist literary criticism has rediscovered some of her work, she is still largely unknown. Experimental in form and content, her plays brought expressionism and social criticism to the American stage, and her contribution on this count is so significant that it cannot be treated adequately in a short essay. Here I have set a less ambitious goal: by focusing on those facets of her work that threaten male authority, I hope to account for Glaspell's exclusion from the dramatic canon.

The American dream is undeniably a man's dream: "the green breast of the new world" flowered for Dutch sailors while Margaret Fuller's earlier cry in vindication of women's rights, "Let them be sea-captains," became the butt of sexist jokes. As Nina Baym points out in her work on American fiction, "the essence of American culture means that the matter of American experience is inherently male" and that it is conditioned by a deeply romantic promise, the myth that "a person will be able to achieve complete self-definition" ["Melodramas of Beset Manhood: How Theories of American Fiction Exclude Women Authors," in *The New Feminist Criticism: Essays on Women, Literature, and Theory*]. In American literature, this quest for identity has traditionally been the quest of men, with society, symbolically embodied in woman, identified as the obstacle. Glaspell's protagonists are women; they are superior to the male characters and have a disturbing habit of arrogating to themselves divine powers over life and death. Clearly, Glaspell's female characters threaten patriarchal authority. We should not be surprised, then, that many of Glaspell's reviewers dismissed her plays as nonsense and that the management of the Players deleted them from their repertoire after she had left.

Glaspell started her writing career in the Midwest as a newspaper-woman, short-story writer, and novelist; it was not until her marriage to George (Jig) Cram Cook catapulted her into the heart of Greenwich Village bohemia that she tried her hand at playwriting. In the summer of 1915, Cook's enthusiasm for the theater, which he saw as the life-giving force of ancient Greece, culminated in the first productions of the Provincetown Players—in a rickety old fishhouse on the end of an abandoned wharf. The following summer, Glaspell wrote *Trifles,* which was an immediate success and is still her best-known play. That autumn, Cook galvanized the Players into opening their first season in a converted warehouse on MacDougal Street, New York, where their principal playwrights were Eugene O'Neill and Susan Glaspell. O'Neill had joined the Players that summer with a "trunkful" of plays awaiting performance; Glaspell, not similarly equipped, conceived her plays specifically for the Provincetowners, experimenting with their "untramelled little stage" and working out "her ideas in freedom."

A stint on the *Des Moines Daily News* had early aroused Glaspell's interest in local and domestic politics; she was assigned to the statehouse and legislature, and this experience gave her material for many short stories and plays.

It also convinced her that the local socialist party was too conservative, and she readily abandoned it when Jig Cook founded the more liberal Monist Society. New York City widened Glaspell's horizons further; but whereas Cook plunged joyfully into the "New Bohemia"—an exotic amalgam of the old Parisian bohemia, the Industrial Workers of the World, and the New Feminist Movement—Glaspell's poor health, which included a weak heart and gynecological problems, forced her to remain on the sidelines. In an interview in 1921, she justified her position by saying, "I am interested in all progressive movements, whether feminist, social or economic, but I can take no very active part other than through my writing." And it was indeed through her work that she voiced her dissatisfaction with right-wing politics, forcefully expressing the "concern with wrongs to human beings in their times" that marks her as a feminist writer.

At a time when the established American theater refused to deal with social problems (excepting those of marriage), Glaspell dared to tackle controversial issues, among them political dissent and the ambitions of a female Zarathustra.

The 1917 and 1918 Espionage and Sedition Acts, for example, outraged her democratic spirit, and she responded with *Inheritors,* which the Provincetown Players produced in 1920. The setting is a midwestern college campus that had been founded by the idealist Silas Morton, one of the earliest settlers, and Felix Fejevary, an exiled Hungarian revolutionary whose son is now on the board of trustees. The play opens in 1879 with a discussion of the pioneer days and of the importance of learning, and Act 1 ends with Morton's decision to bequeath his best land to the building of a college. Act 2 shows how the expansion of the college brings about financial problems that must be solved. Felix Fejevary Junior does his best to convince Senator Lewis that the state should appropriate the college and so assure its future. Lewis agrees but imposes one condition: Professor Holden, a radical idealist and supporter of conscientious objectors, must go. By Act 4, Fejevary has persuaded Holden of the advantages of silence, but he then is defeated by his niece—the granddaughter of both Silas Morton and Felix Fejevary Sr. —who insists on supporting Hindu students in their fight for independence. As the play ends, Madeline Morton leaves for the court hearing; there is no doubt that she will be imprisoned for her ideals.

This play is a feeling riposte to a historical moment, and although it is the least overtly feminist of Glaspell's plays, the surface plot thinly disguises her disappointment with patriarchal society, with man's weakness and his readiness to forego his ideals under pressure. Discretely, Glaspell mocks several male myths: the frontier myth; the myths of progress, learning and civilization; and in particular, the myth of male superiority. Her "leading" men, although endowed with redeeming virtues, are far from being supermen and frequently frustrate the expectations of the female protagonists. In *Inheritors,* Glaspell intelligently refuses to condemn or praise the individual outright, and her sympathies waver between Holden and Madeline, finally settling on the side of the female charac-

ter. Holden's pusillanimous decision is excusable in the light of Mrs. Holden's costly illness, and Madeline's action, although it will bring sorrow to the family, is seen in the idealistic terms of the individual's self-sacrifice in the cause of freedom.

As a result of her first-hand experience, Glaspell was never tempted to sentimentalize pioneer life. She was a Midwesterner by birth and spent many years on Cape Cod, only a few miles from the Mayflower Pilgrims' reported first landing place and still a rough place to live in the 1910s. Thus, she could authoritatively expose the frontier myth of machismo, with the white man defending his women from savage Indians and wresting the land from barbarity, and she did so in a number of her novels and plays, but nowhere so incisively as in *Inheritors.* Silas Morton's grandmother used to give cookies to the Indians, who, in her words, were "mostly friendly when let be"; they did not attack or rape till the white man had "roiled them up" by taking their land. Grandmother Morton had observed in the white man a similar attachment to the land, and her sympathetic understanding of his weaknesses is mingled with disgust at his love of violence. She herself had always been prepared to feed and help strangers, and she finds it difficult to accept that "nothing draws men together like killing other men." She knew the hardships of pioneer life for a woman, and the news of the death of a Civil War veteran's wife provokes from her the heavily laden comment, "Well, I guess she's not sorry." Self-reliant and hardworking, Grandmother Morton is reminiscent of Willa Cather's Alexandra in her love of the land: "A country don't make itself. When the sun was up we were up, and when the sun went down we didn't."

The learning myth also is stripped of its romantic fallacies. Morton's generous spirit, love of the land, hard work, and initial friendship with the native Indians inspired him to build a college on a hill, visible for miles "for the boys of the cornfields—and the girls. . . . 'Twill make a difference—even to them that never go." In Silas Morton's "dreams for the race," the college offered a "vision of what life could be," and it atoned for the wrong the white man had done to the native: "That's what that hill is for! Don't you see it! End of our trail, we climb a hill and plant a college." Echo of the Puritan City on a hill and founded with the explicit purpose of redeeming the white man's bloody role in the Blackhawk War, the college ultimately generates the overwhelming desire for expansion and state appropriation—a "sivilization" that not all are free to reject. Holden's Whitmanesque vision of each man "being his purest and intensest self " is sourly compromised by financial interests—a consequence of patriarchal society Glaspell deplored.

Founder Morton's expansionist dream fails on another count. He had worked the fields to bring wealth to his family and community, but now his son Ira, who has experimented with corn and created an improved variety, curses the wind for carrying seeds to his neighbor's farm. The community tries to excuse Ira's obsession as a mental disorder and believes he is the price the white man pays for progress and growth, the "scar" left by the "lives back of him," that were too hard.

Ira's daughter Madeline compensates for his mean spirit when she takes up the cause of a group of Hindu students who have been inconsiderately preaching "the gospel of free India—non-British India" on the day when Senator Lewis visits the college. Madeline is depicted first as a carefree, fun-loving, tennis-playing college senior who has no time or respect for her ancestors or elders. By play's end, however, she has shed her egotism and consciously adopted ideals that will require her to sacrifice her freedom. Madeline's first act of rebellion is to hit a policeman with a tennis racket: this childish reaction to the police harassment of the Hindu students sends her to prison. Released almost immediately after her uncle intervenes, she is shocked to discover that Fejevary has done nothing for the Hindus and horrified at their imminent deportation. The ensuing argument with Fejevary transforms the naive and impetuous college girl into an articulate adult aware of her feelings for her grandfather, the college, freedom, and what she always, although only half-consciously, believed to be the ideal of American democracy:

> MADELINE. (*In a smoldering way.*) I thought America was a democracy.
>
> FEJEVARY. We have just fought a great war for democracy.
>
> MADELINE. Well, is that any reason for not having it?

Moments later, when the gang of students led by Fejevary's son provokes the Hindus and the police intervene again, Madeline has so far learned to control her impulses that she can respond without reverting to childish tantrums to express herself. Her impassioned speech proves her worthy of both of her grandfathers: "My grandfather gave this hill to Morton College—a place where anybody—from any land—can come and say what he believes to be true!"

Although she does not come anywhere near the "superwoman" stature achieved by the protagonists of the later plays, Madeline does prefigure them, particularly the heroine of *The Verge* (1921). Claire is an older Madeline, weighted down by social and moral pressures; whereas Madeline is ingenuously prepared to sacrifice her physical freedom for the ideal of democracy, Claire despairs of ever attaining real freedom for woman, artist, or humanity. She realizes that the older order—symbolized in the play by a plant that grows in the shape of a cross—has failed her, but she is still afraid of challenging it; she finds it difficult to believe in the existence of a new and better dispensation or to express her vision of it coherently.

The Verge is Glaspell's most provocative play. The Provincetown Players "kept alive a stage dedicated to the experimental production of plays by American playwrights," and by 1921 Glaspell was sufficiently self-confident to use the many innovations both in content and stagecraft that the Players had adopted from Europe. They took Strindberg, Ibsen, and Shaw for their models, although the Players' insistence on their own nationalistic aesthetics made them very reluctant to stage the Europeans; they assimilated the work of Stanislavski and Reinhardt, and they were ready to incorporate at least some of the tenets of expressionism then coming to the fore in Germany. Cook insisted on building a dome for O'Neill's *The Emperor Jones* to create an illusion of expanded space, for example, and he was impatient to try out the ideas of Adolphe Appia and Gordon Craig. *The Verge* is an example of the assimilation of European trends in using characteristically expressionistic settings to reveal the mind of the protagonist. Concerning content, the play criticizes the stifling doll's house a marriage can become; but by not insisting on the gender of the protagonist, it portrays successfully the lot of humankind, trapped by established norms and unable to overcome itself.

The play opens in a luscious and overheated greenhouse in which Claire experiments with plants. She believes she can exploit a technique of transplanting to create new organisms that are liberated from the previous forms and functions of plant life. Tom, Dick, and Harry (confidant, lover, and husband) violate this sanctum when they seek a warm spot for breakfast. Hoping to end the farcical bickering that follows, Claire attempts to express her Nietzschean desire to overcome established patterns and to break into whatever lies beyond; of the three men in her life, only Tom gropes toward an understanding of her disjointed sentences. In Act 2, Claire's sister Adelaide invades her study, a strangely twisted and uncannily lit tower that is an outward sign of Claire's disturbed mind. Adelaide's mission is to convince her sister to play the part of the dutiful mother and wife, but Claire is too close to transcendence to take heed. On the brink of uncovering her latest experiment, the plant she calls "Breath of Life," she is staggered by fear of the retaliation of the God whose life-giving powers she has appropriated. Claire seeks a haven in consummating her relationship with the sympathetic Tom, but, in deference to her superior spirit, he denies her that ordinary human refuge. The second act ends with Claire's hysterical plea for "Anything—everything—that will let me be nothing!" In Act 3, back in the greenhouse, we witness the unveiling of the new plant and Claire's success in creating a hitherto unknown life form. Yet the achievement is clearly ambivalent; any organism is condemned to repetition and stagnation unless it continually overcomes itself. Claire is fully aware of that baleful dilemma; when Tom finally offers his love, she is appalled at the prospect of being engulfed by mediocre patterns and relentlessly chokes him to death. The murder parallels the suffocating norms of society, that inevitably silence the creative urge in those who refuse to conform, but the family sees Claire's convulsive action as final proof of her insanity. The play ends on a savagely ironic note as Claire chants the hymn "Nearer, my God, to Thee," which Adelaide, intuiting blasphemy, had refused to sing previously in her presence. Claire, a female Faust, now is her own God and cannot be reached by societal structures and compunctions; she has broken out and is free existentially, alone in the transcendental beyond. Like the protagonist of *Inheritors,* Claire rejects the laws of the patriarchal world, but unlike her she refuses to deal with them on their own terms.

Glaspell is careful in *Inheritors* not to be too harsh on the male characters, but in *The Verge* she is not so generous; she allows each in turn to prove his inferiority to Claire. As their names suggest, Tom, Dick, and Harry are stereotypes; they are incapable of helping Claire define herself fully in a patriarchal society or of protecting her from the consequences of transcending it. Harry, the husband, does his utmost to understand her, but his down-to-earth character is an impossible barrier to comprehension or communication. Dick paternally dismisses Claire's strange behavior as "the excess of a particularly rich temperament"; Tom commits the unforgivable error of offering her a bourgeois relationship. In the earlier play, which is less fiercely feminist, Fejevary and Holden are neither dim-witted nor guilty of paternalism; they are motivated by less idealistic concerns than Madeline, and Fejevary duly convinces Holden that his wife's health is more important than his ideology: "You'd like, of course, to be just what you want to be—but isn't there something selfish in that satisfaction?" he asks.

Claire is selfish—a male prerogative in the 1920s—and it is precisely her determination to create a satisfactory life for herself that aroused the fervent admiration of the Greenwich Village feminists and brought "religious excitement" to their voices and eyes when talking of *The Verge.* This was Glaspell's most impiously feminist play, although she had touched on the same issues in *Inheritors;* in the earlier play, she had established Madeline's need for the freedom to define herself as an individual, contrasting physical with mental imprisonment and allowing her to choose the former. As a result of her death-dealing, Claire also will be confined to four walls, but she too will have the satisfaction of a mind free of the restrictions society imposes. Both women rebel against conventional roles in their determination to make themselves new; and although the author approves their defiance, she presents it as meriting social punishment.

The protagonist of an earlier play, **Bernice** (1919), escapes society by literally moving into another life: she dies, and in death wields absolute power over her husband. Neither the husband Craig nor the trusted friend Margaret who "sees everything" arrives in time to hear Bernice's last words. The cause of death is never revealed; a long illness and a sudden, unexpected death are all we know. Bernice's marriage had not been successful; she was too independent to need Craig, an inferior writer whom she could never admire, and he accordingly sought admiration from other women and was openly unfaithful to her. As in Claire's case, patriarchal society imposes a twofold denial of self-definition on Bernice: as a woman in her own right, she is trapped by marriage; as a woman bound to her husband's love and professional failure, she is trapped by his inadequacy. Craig is a more dangerous opponent to Bernice than any of Claire's to her; he wishes for the power to destroy and reshape the terms of existence, but that is a faculty only Glaspell's female protagonists are given to exercise. Craig had presumably battled with Bernice for this power and had always lost; "her life wasn't made by my life," he tells Margaret. In death, Bernice wins the battle once and for all. Before dying, she extracts from Abbie, her servant, the promise to tell Craig that she had taken her own life. Through this ruse, she hopes to confer on him the delusion of power over herself that he had always coveted, and Craig convinces himself that he was *"everything* to Bernice." On the other hand, Margaret cannot be-

lieve that her friend could have committed suicide and finally works out Bernice's Freudian logistics. Even from the grave, the female protagonist assumes power over the living; as in the later plays, the principal male character is shown to be undoubtedly weaker than his female counterpart.

Glaspell's men cannot understand their women; with the exception of Silas Morton, they are vastly inferior intellectual and moral beings. The logical corollary of this inequality would be that the women join forces against them, creating a higher caste. But Glaspell has no preconceived notions of women's superiority. In **The Verge,** Claire cannot bond with her daughter, that creditable young American who goes with all the girls, or with her sister, the prototypical self-sacrificing Mother. Bernice and Margaret, whose bonding ensures the latter's final comprehension of her friend's action, must contend with Craig's sister, who is prepared to defend him come what may, while in **Inheritors** Mrs. Fejevary, in spite of her maternal feelings toward Madeline, can only echo her husband's arguments. Nonetheless, the possibility of real understanding between women attracted Glaspell, and her first play was a study of female bonding.

Trifles (1916) opens with the sheriff and his men looking hopelessly for clues to the murder of Minnie Wright's husband, who has been strangled with a rope. Although they cannot bring themselves to believe that a woman—Minnie herself—could have done the deed, their wives, who visit the house to collect some clothes for Minnie to wear in prison, spot and interpret certain clues: a dirty kitchen, bread not made, crooked sewing, a broken canary cage, a dead canary. The women had been prepared to condemn Minnie, but as they talk of her they learn to give credit to old Grandmother Morton's knowledge of pioneer life and realize how they could have helped: "Oh, I *wish* I'd come over here once in a while! That was a crime! That was a crime! . . . We live close together and we live far apart. We all go through the same things—it's all just a different kind of the same thing." They begin to perceive that Minnie Wright has "effectively triumphed over a cruel male jailer" and to understand that the annihilation of male authority, which oppresses them too, depends on their bond.

Although Glaspell never again used female bonding as the main theme of a play, it surfaces in **Bernice** and is significant in the later **Alison's House** (1930). This thinly disguised life of Emily Dickinson begins after the protagonist's death, when we learn that Alison, the poet, had long ago sacrificed her forbidden love to avoid bringing scandal on the family. Elsa, her niece, has run off with a married man, and although that is precisely what Alison had not done, Elsa feels a special understanding between them. When a cache of unpublished poems by Alison is discovered, Elsa claims them for herself because she alone can "know their value." Alison, the seer, the one who always "knew" and understood and had the courage to sacrifice love and find "victory in defeat," has left a legacy for all women in the form of her poetry.

Glaspell's attitude to society and to women's duty toward it is ambivalent. Rejection of responsibility to a society that "exerts an unmitigatedly destructive pressure on individuality" is the inescapable consequence of the American myth. In men's writings, society is assumed to be the adversary, the obstacle to self-definition, and is depicted as female. In Glaspell's plays, society is not simply the enemy that must be defeated but an integral part of her protagonists' lives, to be examined and, if possible, understood. Glaspell's women seek self-definition as women at home and beyond; that is, they enter the male sphere, thus being both inside and outside society. Glaspell is caught between the patriarchal myth she had been taught to respect and her realization that it is false. Although women must choose between their individuality and their role in society, Glaspell never presents this choice clearly—in terms of right and wrong. Madeline must satisfy either herself or her family; Claire's impulse to create new forms of life is commendable, and yet it brings anguish to her and to those who love her; Bernice's lie, viewed from the outside, is wicked, but it gives Craig confidence in himself. Alison rejected love, gave her life to her family and poetry, and achieved self-definition, which love alone, as Elsa learns, cannot offer. Glaspell cannot condemn her women for opposing society, but she is painfully conscious of the consequences of their rebellions.

Glaspell's protagonists do rebel: they insist on appropriating to themselves the traditionally male quest for self-definition. They are aware that they transgress the laws of society and that retribution will follow. This is abundantly clear in *Trifles* and in *Inheritors,* in which the law steps in bodily. Retribution in *The Verge* is more subtle and ironic; Claire is conscious that she has gone too far and that the law of man no longer applies to her. Yet she has put herself under the supposedly higher law of a man-made God and realizes that her only salvation lies in insanity.

In her plays, Susan Glaspell challenges the prevailing patriarchal myth and pays the consequences. While she enjoyed the "protection" of her husband and the circle of friends that had originally formed the Provincetown Players, her plays were produced, published, and praised. In 1922, however, just before the first night of *Chains of Dew,* she left for Greece with Cook; when she returned after his death two years later, the Provincetown Players had already forgotten their founder and his wife. Lacking support, Glaspell retired to her clapboard cottage in Provincetown and returned to writing fiction, the only medium in which she could examine her discontent with society in relative independence.

Barbara Ozieblo, "Rebellion and Rejection: The Plays of Susan Glaspell," in Modern American Drama: The Female Canon, *edited by June Schlueter, Fairleigh Dickinson University Press, 1990, pp. 66-76.*

FURTHER READING

Bibliography

Bach, Gerhard. "Susan Glaspell (1876-1948): A Bibliography of Dramatic Criticism." *Great Lakes Review* 3, No. 2 (Winter 1977): 1-34.

Annotated bibliography of secondary sources on Glaspell's plays.

Papke, Mary E. *Susan Glaspell: A Research and Production Sourcebook.* Westport, Conn.: Greenwood Press, 1993, 299 p.

Contains a complete bibliography of Glaspell's works, including archival material; plot summaries, production histories, and review summaries of the plays; and an annotated bibliography of secondary sources.

Waterman, Arthur E. "Susan Glaspell (1882?-1948)." *American Literary Realism* 4, No. 2 (Spring 1971): 183-91.

Bibliographic essay on Glaspell, including a reception study, a primary bibliography, and a selected bibliography of recent critical works about Glaspell.

Biography

Dell, Floyd. *Homecoming: An Autobiography.* New York: Farrar and Rinehart, 1933, 368 p.

Includes biographical information on Glaspell and George Cram Cook, and describes the formation of the Provincetown Players.

Larabee, Ann. "Death in Delphi: Susan Glaspell and the Companionate Marriage." *Mid-American Review* VII, No. II: 93-106.

Studies Glaspell's marriage to and collaboration with George Cram Cook, arguing that "Many women found themselves in collaborative arrangements with their husbands as the second half of a writing couple, a hierarchical organization which asserted a rhetoric of equality."

Criticism

Alkalay-Gut, Karen. "Jury of Her Peers: The Importance of Trifles." *Studies in Short Fiction* 21, No. 1 (Winter 1984): 1-9.

Suggests that readers may best understand "A Jury of Her Peers" and *Trifles* by analyzing and connecting small, telling details, just as the women in the story analyze the murder scene.

Andrews, Clarence A. *A Literary History of Iowa.* Iowa City: University of Iowa Press, 1972, 287 p.

Discusses Glaspell and other writers strongly influenced by their Iowa background.

Bach, Gerhard. "Susan Glaspell—Provincetown Playwright." *Great Lakes Review* 4, No. 2 (Winter 1978): 31-43.

Questions whether Glaspell was a representative member of the Provincetown Players. Bach faults critics who assume the association was a "happy marriage."

Ben-Zvi, Linda. " 'Murder, She Wrote': The Genesis of Susan Glaspell's *Trifles.*" *Theatre Journal* 44, No. 2 (May 1992): 141-62.

Discusses the murder case on which Glaspell based *Trifles* and "A Jury of Her Peers."

Bigsby, C. W. E. Introduction to *Plays by Susan Glaspell*, pp. 1-31. Cambridge: Cambridge University Press, 1987.

Provides a history of Glaspell's life and her involvement with the Provincetown Players, as well as a brief overview of *Trifles, The Outside, The Verge,* and *Inheritors.*

Carpentier, Martha C. "Susan Glaspell's Fiction: *Fidelity* as

American Romance." *Twentieth Century Literature* 40, No. 1 (Spring 1994): pp. 92-113.

> Disputes the popular critical notion that Glaspell's drama eclipses her fiction in quality, noting that in the novel *Fidelity,* "Glaspell shows how hollow the American romantic ideal of self-definition at the expense of community is, especially for women."

Deutsch, Helen, and Hanau, Stella. *The Provincetown: A Story of the Theatre.* New York: Farrar and Rinehart, 1931, 313 p.

> Provides a history of the Provincetown Players.

Gould, Jean. *Modern American Playwrights.* New York: Dodd, Mead and Company, 1966, 302 p.

> Somewhat romanticized account of Glaspell's involvement with the Provincetown Players.

Makowsky, Veronica. *Susan Glaspell's Century of American Women: A Critical Interpretation of Her Work.* New York: Oxford University Press, 1993, 169 p.

> Traces Glaspell's writing career and treatment of female characters in light of the changing cultural image of the American woman.

Smith, Beverly A. "Women's Work—*Trifles*?: The Skill and Insights of Playwright Susan Glaspell." *International Journal of Women's Studies* 5, No. 2 (March-April 1982): 172-84.

> Discusses the symbolism and depiction of female relationships in *Trifles,* as well as the theme of spousal abuse and murder in light of present-day criminal justice.

Stein, Karen F. "The Women's World of Glaspell's *Trifles.*" In *Women in American Theatre,* pp. 253-56. Edited by Helen Krich Chinoy and Linda Walsh Jenkins. N. p.: Crown Publishers, 1981. Reprint. Rev. ed. New York, Theatre Communications Group, 1987.

> Describes the ways in which *Trifles* is "an anomaly in the murder mystery genre, which is predominantly a masculine tour de force."

Waterman, Arthur. "Susan Glaspell's *The Verge*: An Experiment in Feminism." *Great Lakes Review* 6, No. 1 (Summer 1979): 17-23.

> Contrasts *Inheritors* and *The Verge* and argues that *The Verge* addresses questions not only of feminism, but also of the place of geniuses and eccentrics in society.

Additional coverage of Glaspell's life and career is contained in the following sources published by Gale Research: *Contemporary Authors,* Vol. 110; *Dictionary of Literary Biography,* Vols. 7, 9, 78; and *Yesterday's Authors of Books for Children,* Vol. 2.

Octave Mirbeau

1848-1917

(Full name Octave-Marie-Henri Mirbeau) French novelist, playwright, journalist, critic, and short story writer.

INTRODUCTION

Mirbeau is best known for writing intensely polemical and satirical works in which he attacked many of the institutions and individuals representing the established social and political order of his time. The targets of Mirbeau's wrath included the Catholic Church, the bourgeoisie, the government of the French Third Republic, politicians, foreigners, and his numerous personal enemies. Critics have noted that although his political views changed during the course of his life from monarchist to Bonapartist to republican, and finally to anarchist, throughout his career Mirbeau consistently championed the causes of individual liberty and intellectual honesty.

Biographical Information

The son of a physician, Mirbeau was born and raised in Normandy. In 1859 he began attending a Jesuit school in Vannes, Brittany, but was dismissed four years later for unknown reasons. Mirbeau continued his studies at various boarding schools, earned a baccalaureate diploma in 1866, and spent the next three years studying law. When the Franco-Prussian War began in 1870, Mirbeau joined the military and eventually rose to the rank of lieutenant before being wounded in December of that year. He was granted a leave to seek medical attention, but when he returned he found that he had been falsely accused of desertion. Although Mirbeau was cleared of all charges after an eight-month-long investigation, the incident left him with a profound mistrust of authority. In 1872 he went to Paris and began a career as a journalist and editor, focusing primarily on art, theater, and politics for Bonapartist and monarchist papers. His opinions were often controversial: he was dismissed from the staff of several journals and at least four of the twelve duels Mirbeau is known to have fought during his life were provoked by his articles. He began publishing short stories and novels during the late 1880s, achieving his first notable literary success with the novel *Le Calvaire* (1887; *Calvary*). During the 1890s Mirbeau began to sympathize with anarchist causes, and although many of his early articles had been anti-Semitic in tone, he also wrote in support of Alfred Dreyfus, a Jewish military officer whose unjust conviction on charges of treason had caused a major political crisis for the French government. Mirbeau remained active as a playwright and novelist until 1913, but wrote little thereafter as his health declined. He died in 1917.

Major Works

Often noted for their autobiographical elements, Mirbeau's first three novels are sometimes referred to as his "novels of revenge" because they contained fictional portrayals of persons who had offended Mirbeau and expressions of outrage at the social institutions he believed responsible for the suppression of individual liberty. In *Calvary*, the narrator Jean-François-Marie Mintié relates his experiences as a soldier in the Franco-Prussian War, concluding that the cause of patriotism hardly justifies the horrors of war. When the war ends he returns to Paris to start a literary career, but, after becoming disgusted with the corruption of Parisian society and the infidelities of his mistress, Mintié flees to the countryside to begin his life anew. *L'Abbé Jules* concerns the effects of sexual repression on a defrocked Catholic priest who is given responsibility for supervising the education of his nephew, whom he advises to follow his natural instincts. The eponymous hero of *Sébastien Roch*, Mirbeau's last novel of revenge, is a young boy who is sent to a Jesuit school where he is raped by a priest and later dismissed from the school when the same priest accuses him of having a homosexual relationship with another student. Sébastien later serves in the

Franco-Prussian War, where he is killed in action. Mirbeau's other novels include *Le jardin des supplices* (1899; *Torture Garden*), which allegorically equates the corrupt political atmosphere of the French Third Republic with the sadistic diversions of a Chinese torture garden, and *Le journal d'une femme de chambre* (1900; *Celestine: Being the Diary of a Chambermaid*), which examines the hypocrisy of the French bourgeoisie from the perspective of a servant girl. *La 628-E-8* is recognized as one of the earliest novels to use the automobile as subject matter. Mirbeau's most famous play, *Les affaires sont les affaires*, focuses on a wealthy entrepreneur whose obsession with making a profit leads him to ignore the elopement of his daughter and the death of his son.

Critical Reception

Commentators have observed that while Mirbeau's works were usually popular and financially successful, his novels were generally valued more for their social and political ideas than their literary style. Controversy over the pacifist theme of *Calvary* significantly contributed to the work's popular success. As an art critic he is credited with championing the work of such unknown but soon-to-be-famous artists as Auguste Rodin and Claude Monet, and his articles on political issues, particularly anarchism and pacifism, were widely read during his lifetime. Summarizing Mirbeau's literary career, Edmund Wilson observed that he was "not only outspoken and tactless: he did not even value the classical *'bon sens français'*—behaved habitually, from the French point of view, intemperately, quixotically, absurdly. A Normand, he was in some ways quite close to the English . . . , that is, he was blunt, self-willed, and not particularly intelligent at the same time that he was subject to moral passion and capable of profound insights and had the courage to give voice to both at the risk of being thought eccentric."

PRINCIPAL WORKS

Maîtres modernes. Le Salon de 1885 (criticism) 1885
Lettres de ma chaumière (short stories) 1885; also published as *Contes de la chaumière* [revised edition], 1894
Le Calvaire [*Calvary*] (novel) 1887
L'Abbé Jules (novel) 1888
Sébastien Roch (novel) 1890
Les mauvais bergers (drama) 1897
L'epidémie (drama) 1898
Le jardin des supplices [*Torture Garden*] (novel) 1899
Le journal d'une femme de chambre [*Celestine: Being the Diary of a Chambermaid*] (novel) 1900
Les amants (drama) 1901
Vieux ménages (drama) 1901
Interview (drama) 1902
Le portefeuille (drama) 1902
Scrupules (drama) 1902
Les vingt et un jours d'un neurasthénique (novel) 1902
Les affaires sont les affaires (drama) 1903
La 628-E-8 (novel) 1907

Le foyer [with Thadée Natanson] (drama) 1908
Dingo (novel) 1913
Un gentilhomme (novel) 1920
Théâtre I (dramas) 1921
Théâtre II (dramas) 1922
Théâtre III (dramas) 1922
Œuvres illustrées. 10 vols. (novels, short stories, dramas, criticism, and essays) 1934-36

CRITICISM

James Huneker   (essay date 1920)

[*Huneker was a prominent American literary critic. In the following essay, he discusses Mirbeau's writings on literature, art, theater, and politics, as well as his fiction.*]

Octave Mirbeau was a prodigious penman. When Remy de Gourmont called Paul Adam "a magnificent spectacle" he might have said with equal propriety the same of Mirbeau. A spectacle and a stirring one it is to watch the workings of a powerful, tumultuous brain such as Mirbeau's. He was a tempestuous force. His energy electric. He could have repeated the exclamation of Anacharsis Clootz: "I belong to the party of indignation!" His whole life Mirbeau was in a ferment of indignation over the injustice of life, of literature, of art. His friends say that he was not a revolutionist born; nevertheless, he ever seemed in a pugnacious mood, whether attacking society, the Government, the Institutes, the theatre, the army or religion. There is no doubt that certain temperaments are uneasy if not in opposition to existing institutions, and while his sincerity was indisputable—an imperious sincerity, a sincerity that was perilously nigh an obsession—Mirbeau seemed possessed by the mania of contradiction. After his affiliations with Jules Vallès and the anarchistic group he was nicknamed "Mirabeau," and, indeed, there was in him much of the fiery and disputatious, though he never in oratory recalled the mighty revolutionist. Nevertheless, he was a prodigious penman.

He was born in Normandy, 1850 (Ernest Gaubert says 1848), the country of those two giants, Gustave Flaubert and Barbey d'Aurevilly. He died early in 1917. His Odyssey, apart from his writings, was not an exciting one. Well born and well educated, he took a violent dislike to his clerical instructors, and as may be noted in **Sébastien Roch** (1890), he suffered from the result of a shock to his sensibilities because of an outrageous occurrence in the course of his school years. He early went to Paris, like many another ambitious young man, and began as an art-critic, but his first article on Monet, Manet, and Cézanne was also his last in the journal *l'Ordre;* it created so much scandal by its attack on those mud-gods of art, Meissonier, Cabanel, Lefebvre and Bouguereau, that he was drafted into the dramatic department. There he did not last long. After a violent diatribe against the House of Molière he found himself with several duels on his hands and enjoyed the distinction of a personal reply from Coquelin. He wrote for a little review *Les Grimaces,* and in 1891 defended Jean Grave's *La Société Mourante* and composed a preface for that literary firebrand. He had dipped into the equivocal swamp of politics and had been a sous-préfet (at St. Girons, 1877), but the experience did not lend enchantment to his patriotism. He saw the inner machinery of a democracy greasy with corruption and it served him as material for his political polemics.

His first decade in Paris he wrote for such publications as *Chroniques Parisiennes, La France, Gaulois,* and *Figaro.* The entire gamut of criticism was achieved by him. He was fearless. His pen was vitriolic and also a sledgehammer. Like old Dr. Johnson, if his weapon missed fire he brained his adversary with its butt-end. A formidable antagonist, yet the obverse of his medal shows us a poet of abnormal sensibilities, a loather of all injustice, a Quixote tilting at genuine giants, not missing windmills; also a man of great literary endowment and achievement. His critics speak of a period of discouragement during which he smoked opium, though without ill consequences. His was not a passive temperament to endure inaction. Like others, he had perversely imitated Baudelaire and De Quincey, but soon gave up the attempt. A nature trembling on the verge of lytic pantheism and truculent satire, Mirbeau had a hard row to hoe, and it is gratifying to learn that as he conquered in his art so he conquered himself. He waged war against Octave Mirbeau to the last. And no wonder. He has written stories that would bring a crimson blush to the brow of Satan.

Turning the pages of the principal Paris reviews to which he copiously contributed we find him calling the financial press blackmailers; the law reporters "vermine judiciaire"; French journalism decidedly decadent: "The press kills literature, art, patriotism; it aggrandizes the shop and develops the shopkeeping spirit. It exalts the mediocre painters, sculptors, writers. Its criticism is venal." As for the theatre—from the frying-pan into the fire! The theatre is the prey of mediocrity, wherein *Le Maître de Forges* is pronounced a masterpiece!

The comedians ("les tripots revenus; cabotinisme") of La Comédie Française come in for their share. Emile Zola, naturally enough, has his allegiance, but he dealt hard raps on the skulls of his followers, the Zolaettes, who hung on the fringe of the novelist's dressing-gown. He admired Barbey d'Aurevilly and Elémir Bourges, as well he might; he attacked Daudet, Paul Bourget, Ohnet, Legouvé, Feuillet, Sarcey—dear old Uncle Sarcey, how Huysmans and Mirbeau did pound him! —and, last and worst, the art-critic of the *Figaro,* Albert Wolff. But he deserved the flaying.

In *La Presse* Mirbeau saluted the genius of Rodin, Maupassant, and praised Paul Hervieu. He adored Victor Hugo, not only as supreme poet but as humanitarian—the very quality that to-day so many find monotonous in his lyrics. But there was more than a strain of humanitarianism in Mirbeau. He was truly a Brother to Man, but he never exploited it as do sentimental socialists. It was the spectacle of poverty, of the cruelty of man to man, of the cruelty to animals—he wrote a novel about a dog—that set the blood boiling in his veins and forced him to utter terrible, regrettable phrases. His friends grieved, yet the spectacle was not unlike a volcano in action. That all this

was prejudicial to the serenity of his art is not to be doubted. Mirbeau cared little. Let art perish if he accomplished a reform! Yet he has written some almost perfect pages, and in the presence of nature his angry soul was soothed, ennobled. A poet was slain in him before his vision became voice. He loved the figure of Christ and he drifted into the mystic and lovable theories of Kropotkin, Elisée Reclus, and Tolstoy. Their influence is manifested in his *Lettres de ma Chaumière* (1886). These tales overflow with sympathy and indignation. The French peasant as he is, neither idealized by Millet nor caricatured by Zola, is painted here with an intimate brush—it is painted miasma, one is tempted to add. That he was an unyielding Dreyfusard is a matter of history.

It may be said in passing that Mirbeau had not the stuff in him to make a sound or satisfactory critic of the Fine Arts. He was too one-sided in his Salons, his enthusiasms were often ill-placed, and he resembled Zola in his vocabulary of abuse if any one disagreed with him. M. Durand-Ruel, where he was liked for his sterling qualities, has a pamphlet of Mirbeau's on the Impressionists. Published here it would have resulted either in a libel suit or a prosecution for obscenity. His definition of a certain art-critic is unprintable. When he hated he stopped short of nothing. A true Celt. But how he could tune down the peg of the false heroic to make sound the mean music of mean souls! There are a dozen men in Paris who were riddled by his shot and shell. He did not spare the Government and told some wholesome truths about the Tonkin affair. But he was not all fire and fury. He had intellectual charity, and the artist in him often prevailed. He was destructive, and he could be constructive. He could be charming and tender, too, and his style ranged from thunder-words to supple-sweet magic.

The constructive in him was artistic, but when the propagandist reins were between his teeth his judgments were muddied by his turbulence. And how clearly he could judge was proved by his clairvoyant article in *Le Figaro* on an unknown Belgian, by name Maurice Maeterlinck (1890). Mirbeau literally discovered Maeterlinck; and while we now smile over the title of "Belgian Shakespeare," there is no denying the flair of the Parisian critic. Certainly he made a better guess than the amusing Max Nordau, who once described the author of *The Treasures of the Humble* as "a pitiable mental cripple." In 1888 *L'Abbé Jules* appeared. It was Mirbeau's first novel. For the chief character he went to his uncle, a priest of rather singular traits. The book became a burning scandal.

Le Calvaire (1887) confirmed the reputation of the young writer. He certainly had a predilection "pour la poésie de la pourriture," as one critic puts it. But *Calvary* is a masterpiece and his least offensive fiction. The story of the little soldier who shoots an Uhlan in the war of 1870 and then tries to revive the dead man, finally kissing him on the forehead as a testimony of his fraternal feeling, is touching. *Sébastien Roch,* the third novel, is full of verity and power only marred by a page, one of the most hideous in French fiction (irrespective of avowedly crapulous stories). But Mirbeau has testified to its truth elsewhere. The hero becomes a victim to aboulia, or the malady of doubt.

Happiness is not for him and he dies in the Franco-Prussian conflict. *Le Jardin des Supplices* (1899) set Paris cynically shivering with a new sensation. This garden of tortures is the most damnably cruel book in contemporary fiction. It was conceived by a Torquemada of sadism. Yet Mirbeau disclaimed any notion of writing for mere notoriety. These sombre pages of blood and obscenity were printed to show the cruelty and injustice of all Governments. The Chinese were selected as masters of the most exquisite tortures. A vile nightmare is the result. It demands strong nerves to read it once through; a rereading would seem incredible. Swift is in comparison an ironical comedian.

Les Mémoires d'une Femme de Chambre (1901) is backstairs gossip, though the purpose is not missing; again satire of the better classes, so-called. *Les vingt-et-un jours d'un Neurasthénique* (1902) need not detain us, nor such one-act pieces as *Vieux Ménage* (1901), *Amanto* (1901), *Scrupules* (1902), or *Le Foyer,* with Natanson (1908). He also wrote a preface to Margaret Andoux's story, *Marie Claire.* The first important dramatic work of Mirbeau was *Les Mauvais Bergers,* in five acts, produced at the Théâtre de la Renaissance (December 14, 1897). We can still evoke the image of Sarah Bernhardt in the last act, an act charged with pity and irony. The play, because of its political and social currents, created a dolorous and profound impression. The work has in it something of both *The Conquest of Bread* and *The Weavers.* In *Les Affaires sont les Affaires,* produced at the Théâtre Français (April 20, 1903), Mirbeau is at his satirical best. The play has been shown here, but in a colorless, unconvincing style. In De Feraudy's hands the character of Isidore Lechat, both a type and an individual—one of our modern captains of industry (in the old days, a chevalier of industry?)—was perfectly exhibited. After witnessing in June of the same year a performance of this bitterly satirical comedy I met the author, who appeared as mild-mannered a pirate as ever cut a poet or scuttled a ship of State.

Paul Hervieu told me at the time that the bark of this old growling mastiff was worse than his bite; but his victims did not believe this. He was, in his dynamic prime, the best-hated publicist in all Paris—and that is saying a lot, for there were also Barbey d'Aurevilly, Ernst Hello, Louis Veuillot, J. K. Huysmans and several other virtuosi in the noble art of making foes. Decidedly, Mirbeau was not a lagger behind those pamphleteers and dealers in corrosive verbal values.

That he could be human was shown in his vertiginous automobile story *La 628-E8,* where, after retelling what Victor Hugo had hinted at in his *Choses vues,* Mirbeau made an apology to the daughter—or was it granddaughter?—of Mme. Hanska Balzac for a certain chapter which relates the Russian lady's doings on the heels of her great husband's death. Mirbeau was not legally compelled to withdraw this chapter, as it was a thrice-told tale in Paris, but a friend explained to him the lady's distress and he promptly made the only amend he could. This man had also a prodigious heart.

James Huneker, "The Passing of Octave Mirbeau," in his Bedouins, *Charles Scribner's Sons, 1920, pp. 64-72.*

René Lalou   (essay date 1924)

[*Lalou was a prominent French essayist and critic and the author of a comprehensive history of modern French literature entitled* La littérature française contemporaine (Contemporary French Literature, *1922; revised editions 1924, 1941). In the following excerpt from that work, he provides a brief assessment of Mirbeau's major fiction and dramas.*]

There are few writers as tiresome and as diverting as Octave Mirbeau—tiresome to read, but so diverting on reflection! Mirbeau's work accomplishes as a matter of fact, the miracle of clothing with the most outworn Romantic ornaments a naturalistic philosophy the meditations of which invariably end in platitude. Beginning with *Sébastien Roch,* dedicated to Edmond de Goncourt, he extolled "the sublime beauty of the ugly." *Le Jardin des supplices,* inspired by this thought, that "Love and Death are identical," pretends to imitate, in a garden borrowed from the Paradon, the art of the Chinese executioner who "extracts from the human flesh all its prodigies of suffering." *Le Journal d'une femme de chambre* expresses "the sadness and the comedy of being a man—a sadness which makes noble souls laugh, comedy which makes them weep." *Les 21 Jours d'un neurasthénique* proves that "men are everywhere the same" and *Dingo* sings the praises of a dog which, in spite of some vices borrowed from man, has kept its precious canine superiority. Everything in Mirbeau is enormous, and first of all the puerility. Generous, ever ready to write the article or the preface which would launch some unknown genius, which would denounce some social injustice, his enthusiasm was often mistaken. In his books, monotonous examples of the novel of odds and ends, he relieves himself of a scorn for modern society which would be scathing could it be taken quite seriously. They are receptacles into which he casts pell-mell his rancours as an anti-clerical, as a Dreyfusist and as a pamphleteer. His love of opposition carries him, in *La 628-E8,* to the point of a eulogy of Germany which the Prussian "squirearchy" must have relished. The results he obtains have always this paradoxical character. If he gives well-known names to his heroes, no one accepts these caricatures. If he portrays a Père Roch or an Abbé Jules, the author's truculence alone is appreciated. If he talks about himself, the reader yawns. He dreams of writing "pages of murder and blood," pages which will exhale "a strong stench of rottenness," and succeeds in attracting only the amateurs of pure pornography. He goes lion-hunting and brings back merely a little vermin. Excellent when he narrates, in his natural voice, some rough Breton buffoonery, he usually wearies by the outbursts of a uniform violence. Huysmans had embalmed dead Naturalism in his decadent style. Mirbeau rejects this artifice and gives back the corpse its odour.

Yet this man has composed the one play of our epoch which stands comparison with Becque's. Perhaps he sought in the theatrical form an opportunity to discipline his impetuosity. *Les Mauvais Bergers* reveals a schematic Mirbeau who imagines a revolutionary workman, a wavering employer and a young idealistic bourgeois to pit them against each other in a brutal, mystic strike. *Le Foyer,* on the contrary, in spite of Thadée Natanson's collaboration, is written in the same ink as his novels. This virulent, painful caricature which in vain caused a sensation, shows above all his inability to confine his fierce and infantile misanthropy in a living action. To compare Armand Biron with Isidore Lechat is useful only to emphasize the extraordinary relief of *Les Affaires sont les affaires.*

This comedy offers a fine artistic situation. Its exposition is admirable. Two scenes suffice to evoke the setting in which the action is to take place and to paint soberly two characters one of whom, by his revolt, will provoke the crisis. Isidore Lechat enters. Mirbeau's habitual excess threatens to compromise this beginning. In his protagonist he has accumulated everything he detests in contemporary society: bourgeois cruelty, garrulous egotism, belief in material facts, scorn for artistic truth, opportunist socialism; but the necessity for rendering this symbolical character convincing on the stage has compelled Mirbeau to depict the business man in full strife. There he is great. The interview with the engineers reveals his power and, in the principal scene with the Marquis, he achieves quite naturally a lyric breadth which would not be unworthy of Toussaint Tourelure. The author conducts his drama with implacable determination towards the double catastrophe. His impenitent romanticism unleashes the fatalities of modern life. Of all the images of fright he so frantically sought none surpasses the tragic final scene in which Isidore Lechat, whose daughter has just run away and his son been killed, foils the two partners who wanted to take advantage of a father's grief to outdo the business man of whom Mirbeau has drawn this grandiose and enduring portrait.

René Lalou, "The Contemporary Drama," in his Contemporary French Literature, *translated by William Aspenwall Bradley, Alfred A. Knopf, 1924, pp. 271-86.*

Edmund Wilson (essay date 1949)

[*Wilson is generally considered twentieth-century America's foremost man of letters. A prolific reviewer, creative writer, and social and literary critic endowed with formidable intellectual powers, he exercised his greatest literary influence as the author of* Axel's Castle *(1931), a seminal study of literary symbolism, and as the author of widely read reviews and essays in which he introduced the best works of modern literature to the reading public. In the following essay, which originally appeared in the* New Yorker *in 1949, he reflects on Mirbeau's career and literary reputation.*]

> Dear me, how far from infinite the world is! Talking to my cousin today, I mentioned Octave Mirbeau's name. "Why, Mirbeau," she said, "let me see—that's the son of the doctor at Remalard, the place where we have our estate. I remember that two or three times I lashed him over the head with my whip. He was an impudent little thing as a child—his great idea was to show his bravado by throwing himself under the feet of our horses when we or the Andlaus were out driving."
>
> Edmond de Goncourt: *Diary,*
> August 26, 1889

I should like to take the occasion of the reprint of a very respectable translation by Alvah C. Bessie of Octave Mirbeau's novel *Le Jardin des Supplices* to look back at a remarkable French writer whose reputation, after his death in 1917, almost immediately evaporated both abroad and in his own country. Mirbeau belonged so much to his period that I may perhaps be pardoned for explaining that I first read him, and almost completely through, at the time of the first World War, and that he will always remain for me an old companion of my experiences of those years. As such a companion, he had perhaps more value than he might have had in other conditions. In the first place, he is at his best when he is describing those wretched French villages, with their doll-bedecked rundown churches, their diseased and deformed inhabitants and their pervasive smell of manure, among which I was then living on more intimate terms than those of the tourist who stares at them from the train and is thrilled by their look of antiquity. It is enough for me to open certain books of Mirbeau to see again their gray walls embedded in mud. In the second place, his favorite theme, the persistence in modern society of predatory and destructive appetites at variance with civilized pretentions, was particularly acceptable then, at a time when it was actually reassuring to read someone who was not trying to convince you that only the Germans had ever been bloodthirsty, who had never even fooled himself with the assumption that our exploiting competitive world was a respectable and reliable affair. And though I saw Mirbeau's faults even then, my opinion of him will always be colored by a certain special affection.

His compatriots, as we trace him through their criticism and journals, seem to have become toward him colder and colder. For Edmond de Goncourt, in the eighties, Mirbeau was a young colleague in the naturalistic movement, who was beginning to show distinguished abilities and who dedicated a novel to him. On André Gide, in the first years of this century, when Gide was an ally of the symbolists by no means enamored of naturalism, Mirbeau made a mixed impression. He responded to Mirbeau's warm indignations and admired some of his work, but complained that "the satirical spirit prevents his having any critical sense." By this time, it had become apparent that Mirbeau repudiated defiantly those versions of the French tradition that were in vogue at the turn of the century. He was not elegant and detached, like the Parnassians, not exquisite like the followers of Mallarmé, and he sometimes made heavy fun of the professional Parisian aesthetes. Nor would he attempt to adjust himself to the demands of a bourgeois audience. He scored against Paul Bourget, in his *Journal d'une Femme de Chambre,* by attributing to his servant-girl heroine a passion for the works of that fashionable novelist but making her conclude, after meeting him once, that, in the eyes of M. Bourget "people didn't begin to have souls below an income of a hundred thousand francs"; and he had none of the quiet discretion in running counter to accepted ideas that caused Anatole France to say of himself that the principal business of his life had been doing up dynamite in bonbon wrappers. He had not even the detachment of the naturalists. He was not only outspoken and tactless: he did not even value the classical *"bon sens français"*—behaved habitually, from the French point of view, intemperately, quixotically, absurdly. A Normand, he was in some ways quite close to the English, who figure in his books in a way that shows a special interest in them—that is, he was blunt, self-willed and not particularly intelligent at the same time that he was subject to moral passion and capable of profound insights and had the courage to give voice to both at the risk of being thought eccentric. In his character as publicist and journalist, in which he played for years a conspicuous role, he was vigorous and audacious. At the time of the Dreyfus case, he went on the stump in the provinces, rousing opinion in Dreyfus' defense; he forfeited by his very first article, in 1889, a job as a newspaper art critic by running down the academic painters and praising Manet and Cézanne; he loved to champion unrecognized writers like Maeterlinck and the seamstress Marguerite Audoux whose work had a lily-like innocence at the opposite pole from his own productions. In politics, he passed at an early stage from fire-breathing royalism to fire-breathing anarchism—the two attitudes having in common a violent hatred of politicians; and remained thereafter consistently pro-worker, anti-bourgeois and anticlerical. He wrote a labor play, **Les Mauvais Bergers,** produced in 1897, with Sarah Bernhardt and Lucien Guitry, the long heroic speeches of which make very dull reading today, but which differs from most such dramas by its pessimism in regard to the workers' cause; and he created a scandal in 1908 by a play (written with Thadée Natanson), **Le Foyer,** that attacked the philanthropical workshops subsidized by the rich for the relief of the poor.

Nor did the literary cuisine of Mirbeau quite come up to the current French standards. He was always a conscientious workman: his books are never botched or sloppy; he has trained himself with earnest discipline to make the very best of his powers, and he can sometimes write with trenchant lucidity, if rarely with felicitous brilliance. But the seasoning is a little coarse; the ingredients are not well mixed. The flavor is sometimes flat; and there is even a kind of false taste that is calculated to horripilate the French. For example, Mirbeau had a passion for flowers, which he raised and of which he was a connoisseur, but his writing about them—of which there is a good deal in **Le Jardin des Supplices**—combines the botanical and the gaudy in a way that does not conduce to good literature. And his writing about love—exemplified, also, in this book—has similar characteristics. He thus scandalized the bourgeois public and often bored the men of letters, and when he died, his countrymen dropped him. I once talked about him with Jean Cocteau just after the last war. Cocteau expressed surprise that anybody at that late date should be reading Mirbeau at all. "That's a whole generation," he said, "that my generation has skipped." But he approved of **Sébastien Roch,** one of Mirbeau's early books, which had made an impression on me, and suggested that a serious and chronic illness had caused a deterioration in his later work. If you consult the *Histoire de la Littérature Française Contemporaine* by René Lalou, published in 1922, you will find a discussion of Mirbeau, which is almost completely contemptuous and which takes it for granted that his novels are no longer of any interest. Though there are two or three brochures on Mir-

beau in various journalistic series dealing with the writers of his period, there is, so far as I know, no reliable biography of him, and it is curiously difficult at the present time even to find out the main facts about his life.

Octave Mirbeau's fiction falls into two groups, quite distinct from one another and with a gap of a decade between them. His first three novels—**Le Calvaire, L'Abbé Jules** and **Sébastien Roch**—were written during the late eighties. All deal more or less with provincial life, and especially with personalities which have become distorted or stunted by not finding their true vocations or appropriate milieux. There is a good deal of original insight—contemporary with Freud's first researches—into the infantile causes of neurosis and the consequences of sexual repression. The first of these books is a study of an unstable young man from the country demoralized by a Parisian cocotte; the second, a strange and repellent tale, is a kind of imaginary memoir which a nephew has written of his uncle: a man of superior abilities, from a bourgeois village background, whose personality has been deformed by his mistake of entering the priesthood—a profession in which his intellectual arrogance, his intractable sensual appetites and his very gift of moral vision make him tragically out of place. **L'Abbé Jules** has vivid flashes when the subject is brought to life dramatically—as when the abbé, returning to his family, frustrated, embittered, forbidding, and hardly condescending to talk to them, examines as if astonished the quilt that they have handed him for a carriage-robe; and both books have a clinical interest: Mirbeau, like Flaubert, was a doctor's son. But the third novel, **Sébastien Roch,** is much better and was to remain probably Mirbeau's best book. This is the story of a gifted boy who is sent away from home to a Jesuit school, where one of the priests seduces him, and who then comes back to his little town, with his emotions in agonized disorder and with no field for the exercise of his talents. He tries to give himself an outlet by writing in a diary and has an awkward love affair with a girl whom he has known since childhood, and, finally, conscripted for the Franco-Prussian War, is unheroically, ridiculously killed. Everyone who has read this book knowing James Joyce's *A Portrait of the Artist as a Young Man* has been struck by parallels between them, in form as well as in content. One would like to know whether Joyce had read **Sébastien Roch.** It is not quite up to the *Portrait*. It has elements of the romantic sentimentality and of the dead mechanical caricature that impair the soundness of all Mirbeau's work. But Mirbeau did his most successful writing in his description of the Breton countryside, and the anguish of adolescence has never been more truthfully treated. If one compares these early stories of Mirbeau with the fiction of his friend Guy de Maupassant, who worked also in the naturalistic tradition, the advantage is not all with the latter. Maupassant has more skill and more style. But such a figure as the conventional wife and mother of Maupassant's *Une Vie* is simply the victim of a melodrama in which the villain is the masculine sex. In **Le Calvaire,** the mother of the hero is a somewhat similar case, but Mirbeau's psychological insight makes it impossible for him to deal in this one-sided pathos, and he shows us that the woman, from a "trauma" of her childhood, has a special predisposition to succumb to such a situation as that later created by her marriage. To the brilliant raconteur of *Boule de Suif,* the war of 1870, again, presents itself mainly in terms of the hatred between Germans and French, whereas with Mirbeau, when he touches on it, the patriotic antagonisms are undercut by a sense of what all men have in common.

Between *Sébastien Roch* of 1889 and *Le Jardin des Supplices* of 1899, Mirbeau published no more fiction; but the first two of his plays were performed, and in the years that immediately followed he wrote half a dozen others. These plays are less interesting than his fiction, but they occupy, in the history of the French theater, an almost unique place. When Bernard Shaw bestowed his accolade on the second-rate Eugène Brieux, accepting him as the great French practitioner of his own peculiar kind of drama, the comedy of social analysis, he might better have selected Mirbeau. Mirbeau's plays are, so far as I know, the only French work of merit that has anything in common with this English school. One of them, *Les Affaires sont les Affaires* (1903), enjoyed an immense success. It was admitted into the repertoire of the Comédie Française at a time when the Comédie produced almost no modern plays, and it continued to be done there for years, thus becoming the only work of Mirbeau's that has been endorsed as a classic, so that it is always well spoken of by such writers as M. Lalou. It is certainly Mirbeau's best play, though not so good as the best of his novels. It suffers from his characteristic fault of introducing incredible monstrosities, against a familiar realistic background, into a story that is meant to be plausible; but such a scene as the conversation between the business man and the ruined marquis is admirable in its confrontation, very similar to such scenes in Shaw, of the spokesmen of two social classes, who expound their opposing roles. And Mirbeau's one-acter *L'Epidémie,* in which a provincial town council declines to do anything about a typhoid epidemic that is killing off the local garrison, till they hear that a bourgeois has died of it, is closer to English satire than to the irony of Anatole France. "Typhoid fever," declares in a quavering voice the oldest member of the council, "is a national institution. Let us not lay impious hands upon our old French institutions"; and, "Let us not," seconds the doctor, "present foreign countries with the deplorable spectacle of a French army beating an ignoble retreat before a few problematical microbes."

Sébastien Roch, the Abbé Jules and the hero of *Le Calvaire* are all subject to a waking delirium—day-dreams in which sexual images are mixed nightmarishly with images of horror—of which Mirbeau sometimes gives descriptions almost as elaborate and solid as his accounts of actual events. The key to most of these fantasies is to be found in Mirbeau's perception that inescapable sexual repression or neurotic emotional impotence may result in sadistic impulses. Now, in the fiction of his second period, he ceases to try to present us with difficult cases of real human beings: it is as if he had allowed these fantasies to take possession of his imagination and to impose themselves upon him as generalized pictures of life. At their soundest, these later novels arrive through distortion at satire; at their worst, they are artistically meaningless, a mere procession of obsessive grotesques.

The first of these books, *Le Jardin des Supplices,* is an epitome of Mirbeau's whole vision after his shift to phantasmagoric mythology from naturalistic observation, and it states the Grand Guignol philosophy which he tries to derive from this vision. The story opens in the noxious atmosphere of corrupt Parisian politics under the Third Republic. A scoundrelly Cabinet Minister, whose future is a toss-up between jail and advancement, is blackmailed by one of his jackals and buys him off by sending him away to Ceylon on a scientific expedition financed by government funds. The object of this expedition is to study marine biology in the Indian Ocean—"to discover the primordial cell," as his chief rather vaguely explains to him, "the protoplasmic initium of organized life, or something of the kind." The lesser scoundrel (who tells the story), pretending to be a great biologist, embarks for the East and meets on the ship a beautiful young English lady named Clara, the daughter of an opium-dealer, who is returning to her home in Canton. She gives the impression of great virtue and dignity, and the impostor falls deeply in love with her. He has retained, unlike his chief, some remnants of moral feeling, and all the idealism of which he is capable comes to life under the influence of his passion. He grows ashamed of his bogus role, of his debauched and dishonest past—cannot bear that he should be deceiving a being whom he so much respects, and one day makes a clean breast to Clara of all the disgraceful truth. To his astonishment, she shows at once, and for the first time in their acquaintance, a vivid interest in him. She had paid no attention to him when she had thought he was a serious scientist, but the idea of his vileness pleases her. She is, it turns out, more corrupt than he: more positively perverse and more formidable. She goes to bed with him immediately in her cabin, and he becomes her abject slave. Instead of getting off at Ceylon, he goes on with Clara to China.

The second half of the novel is devoted to a detailed account of their visit to a Chinese prison. This prison has a magnificent garden, in which the convicts are tortured. The Frenchman is shocked and revolted, but he recognizes in what he sees simply a franker and more elegant version of the kind of thing that is going on, in a disguised and hypocritical way, in the Europe he has left behind. It is in vain that, trying to shut out the garden, he summons his familiar Paris. In a moment of revelation, he identifies these executioners with "all the men and all the women whom I have loved or imagined I loved, little indifferent frivolous souls, on whom is spreading now the ineffacable red stain," with "the judges, the soldiers, the priests, who everywhere in the churches, the barracks and the temples of justice, are busy at the work of death," and with "the man as individual and the man as mob," and with "the animal, the plant, the element, all nature, in fact, which, urged by the cosmic forces of love, rushes toward murder, in the hope of thus finding beyond life a satisfaction of life's furious desires, which devour it and which gush from it in spurts of dirty froth." Clara, however, is enjoying herself. Among the gorgeous flowers which are a feature of the garden and which seem to grow out of its putrescence and blood, she becomes hysterically excited and later, when they leave the garden, collapses in a fit of convulsions. When she comes to, she seems calmed and purged, and declares that she will never return there, but her Chinese maid assures her lover that she will be back on the next visitor's day. The traveller, though he has given up his mission, has, after all, from one point of view, discovered the secret of life.

It will be seen that *Le Jardin des Supplices* has, in conception, its Swiftian strength. The trouble is that, though the scenes in the garden sometimes verge on a true tragic irony, Mirbeau, where a Swift or a Dante would have kept them under severe control, indulges himself, like his Clara, a little too much in horror. The same kind of wrong exploitation of a promising satirical idea—which Swift, again, would have handled better—appears in the second of these later books, *Le Journal d'une Femme de Chambre.* Here Mirbeau set out to expose the meanness and sordidness of the French bourgeoisie by showing how they look to a servant who goes from one of their households to another. But the book is full of scandalous episodes that are not merely repulsive but also completely unreal. The whole effect is turbid and boring. Almost the only memorable thing in the book is the chapter that describes the humiliations to which women looking for jobs are subjected in employment agencies, and this suffers, like so much else in the later Mirbeau, from systematic exaggeration. The moral of *Le Jardin des Supplices* is repeated by the unlikely conclusion, in which Mirbeau has the victimized *femme de chambre* marry a brutal coachman whose attraction for her is partly due to her believing him to have committed an atrocious murder.

If one has read the contemporary accounts of Mirbeau during the years when he was writing these books, it is quite easy to diagnose the reason—aside from his overindulgence in the salacious aspects of his subjects—that they do not succeed as satires or as what he called some of his plays, *"moralités."* There is much testimony on the part of those who knew Mirbeau at this period that, however one might like him, his conversation made one uncomfortable, because it consisted so largely of the hair-raisingly implausible stories he would tell about every kind of public figure and about all the people he knew. He was not merely trying to be funny; nor were his stories merely exercises in the expected professional malice of the Parisian literary man. What made his talk disconcerting was that he had evidently fabricated these scandals yet believed them to be actual happenings. (He was, also, it seems, untruthful in his ordinary relations with people.) And his books produce the same effect. In Swift, one feels almost to the end, no matter to what lengths he goes, a sound basis in common sense: he is perfectly well aware that human beings are not really Yahoos and that the poor cannot eat their babies. But Octave Mirbeau does not seem to know when or how much he is deforming reality. The truth is that these stories are a little mad. For all their careful planning and deliberate execution, they represent psychological hypertrophies that are destroying a true sense of the world and preventing the development of the artist. Even the texture of the writing is coarser than that of the early novels. If Mirbeau began by anticipating Freud in the case histories of his early fiction, he took later, in a retrogression, to concocting the kind of nightmare that Freud found it profitable to analyze.

Much the best of Mirbeau's later books is the last thing he published, *Dingo,* which appeared in 1913, four years before his death; but, containing no scandalous material, it has never been translated into English and has attained less celebrity than *Le Jardin des Supplices* and *Le Journal d'une Femme de Chambre. Dingo,* which is told by the author as if in his own character and which sounds as if it were based on a real experience, is the story of an Australian wild dog that has been sent as a puppy to France and grows up in a small French town: perhaps the most debased and revolting of all Mirbeau's dreadful towns. The animal, more wolf than dog, is handsome, remarkably intelligent and devoted to his master and the family; but as soon as he grows out of puppyhood, he begins killing sheep, fowl and game at a rate that makes him a menace. In all this, however, we are made to see, with a subtlety rare in the later Mirbeau, how the master, without at first quite admitting it even to himself, is deriving a certain satisfaction from these crimes against his neighbors, whom he has gradually come to loathe for their self-righteous pusillanimity and cruelty. On one occasion, when he has gone to visit a family of old friends, whom he supposes himself to like, he vicariously betrays his real scorn of them by doing nothing to prevent the dog from slaughtering their pet sheep, which he associates with their feeble personalities. This dog, at least, is frankly a hunter and loyal to those who have cared for him as well as to a family cat with which he has been brought up. But he becomes more and more of a problem. The master is forced to leave the village; he goes to live in Paris, but here Dingo one day leaps at the throat of a man who is trying to steal him and gives rise to disquieting doubts. Then they travel abroad, but wherever they go, they get into some kind of trouble, and the owner is finally obliged to settle down in the country, at the edge of a large forest, in which the dog is free to roam and where he sometimes disappears for days. While they are living there, the master's wife breaks her ribs in a runaway, and the dog, understanding what has happened, keeps watch day and night in her room, resisting attempts to turn him out and refusing to take any food. He wastes away and dies.

This makes a much better book than my summary may suggest. *Dingo* and *Sébastien Roch* are Mirbeau's most successful novels. He loved animals, and in his later phase sometimes wrote about them more satisfactorily than he did about human beings. André Gide is quite correct in singling out the episode of the fight between the hedgehog and the viper as one of the only interesting things in *Les Vingt et un Jours d'un Neurasthénique,* another of Mirbeau's books of this period, the Arabian Nights of a nerve sanitarium, which in general represents an even less appetizing combination of dreariness with abnormality than *Le Journal d'une Femme de Chambre.* In *Dingo,* the dog and the cat are splendidly depicted and analyzed, and the humans are more human than usual. The book has an emotional effect, creates a disturbing suspense. Animal stories were rather fashionable in the early nineteen hundreds, but this is one of the most unconventional and one of the most remarkable, and almost achieves the plane of Tolstoy's wonderful horse story, *Kholstomer.* (Mirbeau, who greatly admired Tolstoy, is said to have had the dubious reciprocal honor of being regarded by the latter, in his later years, as the most important living French novelist.) Yet, like everything else of Mirbeau's, it misses the highest level. Dingo's depredations are on too enormous a scale. His virtues—he loves the poor and makes a point of cheering up the unhappy—a little too sentimental (the Ernest Seton Thompson touch); for Mirbeau has his great sentimentalities to compensate for his chronic ferocities. And the master's inexhaustible complacence, and the immunity that both he and the dog enjoy in connection with Dingo's killings, become rather improbable, too. The element of fantasy gets in again, and it impairs the interest of the record of what was evidently a real animal.

And now what about Mirbeau today, when the ferocity of modern man has demonstrated itself on a scale that even he had not imagined? Already at the time of the first World War, a book like *Le Jardin des Supplices* seemed definitely out of date. Mirbeau did have hold of a terrible truth; and yet, reading the book, as I did, in a military hospital behind the lines, one realized that the impression made by human pain as a part of one's daily routine was different from anything felt by a prosperous pre-war civilian writing at his ease about it (I have not been able to learn whether Mirbeau actually served in the war of 1870). There was too much Parisian upholstery, too much conventional literature, about *Le Jardin des Supplices.* The characters of Ernest Hemingway, with their bad nerves and their ugly conduct, reflected the cruelty of the time more effectively than Mirbeau's enormities and his rhetorical paroxysms. Brett of *The Sun Also Rises* is the Clara of the later generation, and a more convincing creation. Since then, the indiscriminate bombings of London and Berlin, the death-houses of Dachau and Belsen, the annihilation of Hiroshima, have made Mirbeau and Hemingway both seem somewhat obsolete. Is anyone troubled at present by the idea that human beings are torturing or murdering each other? Don't the bugaboo books of the later Mirbeau, with their mélange of human sympathy and sadism, look today like the slightly cracked fairy-tales of a not ungenial old romantic who was still naïve enough not to take such things for granted?

Edmund Wilson, "In Memory of Octave Mirbeau," in his Classics and Commercials: A Literary Chronicle of the Forties, *Farrar, Straus and Company, 1950, pp. 471-85.*

Reg Carr   (essay date 1977)

[*In the following excerpt Carr discusses the anarchist themes of Mirbeau's three novels of revenge—*Le Calvaire, L'Abbé Jules, *and* Sébastien Roch.]

Political campaigner, administrator, financial speculator, journalist, editor, critic and short-story writer—Mirbeau had tried his hand at all of these, and still he had not found his niche; no area of activity had satisfied him for long, and nothing that he had so far written was of any lasting literary worth. His old friend Maupassant had often expressed his regret, as he did in a letter written early in 1886, that Mirbeau had not yet put his 'talent très ardent et très réel' to more worthwhile use. Mirbeau's mistress, whom he was soon to marry, had literary pretensions of her own and was very keen that Mirbeau should make a success of writ-

ing as a career. The *Lettres de ma chaumière* had passed unnoticed by critics and public alike, and Mirbeau was faced with the hard fact that if he did not attempt some new form of expression he would pass into middle age as a competent journalist and nothing more.

The advice of his friends, the promptings of his mistress, and his own awareness of the need to branch out into something new, were not however sufficient in themselves to transform Mirbeau into the hotly-discussed, best-selling novelist he became with the publication of *Le Calvaire* in December 1886. The all-important stimulus was provided by his contact with the radical ideas of the political, artistic and social Left, which had enabled him at last to throw off the shackles of his origins. At once Mirbeau felt free to express the feelings he had been obliged to conceal, or of which he had only vaguely sensed the existence, and *Le Calvaire* was to be the first of many books into which Mirbeau emptied the rancour of his liberated soul. In his short stories Mirbeau had observed the life of society and had described it with a satirist's pen; in his articles he had defended or attacked those with whom he came into daily contact. But now, in his novels, he was to turn to his own very personal experiences, choosing to lay bare his own existence, and with such intensity that it is difficult to disentangle the purely fictional from the strictly autobiographical.

Le Calvaire, if it is remembered at all, is now remembered as a love-story in the tradition of *Manon Lescaut;* and there is no doubt that Mirbeau used his first novel to ease the painful memory of his ill-treatment at the hands of an unfaithful mistress. The echoes of Mirbeau's unfortunate experience still reach us through the pages of Goncourt's diary, where we read in the entry of 20 January 1886:

> Le seul amoureux sincère, le seul amoureux vrai de ce temps serait le nommé Mirbeau, —une sorte de réduction d'Othello! Un soir qu'il était venu passer la nuit avec la femme pour l'amour de laquelle il s'était fait coulissier et qu'il la surprenait découchée, il entrait dans son cabinet de toilette et déchirait et mettait en lambeaux, de ses mains homicides, le charmant petit chien de sa maîtresse, le seul être qu'elle aimât sur la terre.

This incident from Mirbeau's life figured prominently in *Le Calvaire* when it was written later in 1886, and it illustrates not only the depths of Mirbeau's emotions but also the extent to which his novels are a reflection of his private life and a guide to his intimate thoughts.

The letters of Paul Bourget, with whom Mirbeau was friendly at this time, also make reference to Mirbeau's unhappy love-affair. Mirbeau had known Bourget for some time prior to 1886; they had sat together at the *Boeuf Nature* dinners organised by Zola in the 1870s, and they had met again at Barbey d'Aurevilly's, and shared the favour of the 'Connétable des lettres'. Mirbeau had praised Bourget's *Essais de psychologie contemporaine* in *Les Grimaces* (November 1883), and Bourget in his turn gave Mirbeau's first novel an enthusiastic write-up in January 1887 [in *La Nouvelle Revue*]. In 1886, at the time *Le Calvaire* was written, Bourget and Mirbeau met on common ground:

their literary aspirations were sufficient to make them companions. But Bourget, who had fraternised in his youth with the revolutionaries of the Paris Commune, was now beginning to adopt right-wing ideals, and was already frequenting the opulent circles of the upper middle class. Mirbeau was plainly heading in the opposite direction, as this later reminiscence by him illustrates:

> J'ai connu Bourget autrefois . . . Je l'ai beau-coup connu . . . Nous étions fort amis. Cela me gêne un peu, pour en parler . . . Et puis, il a pris par un chemin . . . moi, par un autre . . . Etant plus jeune que moi, il me protégeait, m'éduquait, me tenait en garde contre ce qu'il appelait les emballements un peu trop naïfs, un peu trop grossiers aussi de ma nature . . . Un jour que nous remontions les Champs-Elysées, il me dit: "Laissez donc les pauvres . . . ils sont inesthétiques . . . ils ne mènent à rien." Et, me montrant les beaux hôtels qui, de chaque côté, bordent l'avenue: "Voilà, cher ami . . . c'est là! . . ."

Mirbeau's increasing social awareness and Bourget's growing social ambition finally drove the friends apart, and the Dreyfus Affair only confirmed the wedge which had been driven between them. Bourget in fact became one of Mirbeau's favourite whipping boys during the Affair, and later novels like *Le Journal d'une femme de chambre* and *La 628-E8* are full of satirical references to Mirbeau's former friend whom he repudiated out of social conscience.

Yet in 1886 it was Bourget who was indirectly responsible for the publication of *Le Calvaire.* It was he who introduced Mirbeau to the milieu of *La Nouvelle Revue,* presided over by the celebrated Juliette Adam. It was in this periodical that Mirbeau's first novel was published, in serial form, from September to November 1886. Mirbeau enjoyed the intellectual stimulation this new milieu afforded him, yet even here he was unable to secure the complete expression of his views, even within the compass of a work of art, for the second chapter of *Le Calvaire* was politely 'withheld' from publication because of its antipatriotic sentiment. Mirbeau nevertheless succeeded in having this important chapter reintegrated when the novel was published by Ollendorff in December 1886, and once again he found himself the centre of a scandal.

This second chapter of *Le Calvaire* contains a detailed description of the narrator Jean Mintié's experience in the French army during the disastrous campaign of 1870-1. The selfishness, the brutality and the stupidity of men at war are depicted in minute detail; and as Mintié's regiment prepares to meet the Prussians, the iniquity of it all dawns on him in a way which clearly mirrors Mirbeau's own spiritual awakening. There are two or three pages here redolent of the influence of Tolstoy's Christian anarchism, with which Mirbeau had so recently been in contact. And not only the philosophy, but also the style and even the situations of this section of *Le Calvaire* reveal the debt which Mirbeau owed to the author of *War and Peace.* The chapter reaches its climax with the involuntary killing of a Prussian cavalryman, and Mirbeau takes the opportunity, through the mouth of Mintié, to express his antipathy to war, and, like Tolstoy, to appeal to the feelings of humanity and universal brotherhood which lie dormant in the human soul.

The similarities to Tolstoy were so marked that even the editors of *La Nouvelle Revue* found space to comment on them in the same breath as their refusal to print this chapter:

> A notre grand regret, il nous est impossible d'insérer, dans la *Revue,* le deuxième chapitre du roman de M. Mirbeau . . . Les tableaux, traités à la manière de Léon Tolstoï, sont si cruels, que nous n'avons pu les lire sans être pris d'un véritable désespoir patriotique.

Mirbeau replied in unusually restrained terms, insisting that as an artist he had the right to see things in his own way, and that he had the obligation to describe truthfully what he had seen:

> Je m'efforce d'exprimer les chose telles que je les vois et comme je les vois et comme je les sens. J'ai la passion de la vérité, si douloureuse soit-elle, et je n'entends rien aux précautions oratoires, aux réticences académiques, qui me semblent inutiles chez un écrivain sincère.

The incriminated chapter was evidently good publicity, and it dominated the rest of the book, ensuring that Mirbeau's first novel became a best-seller. There were twenty editions of the novel in 1887 alone, and for the ninth edition Mirbeau saw fit to write a preface in which he answered the criticisms which had arisen as a result of his reflections on the Franco-Prussian war. It is a measure of the sensitivity of the French about the 1870 defeat that a single chapter of what was to all intents and purposes a love-story could excite such passions and provoke such anger as it did. The extremist patriots took great exception to Mirbeau's view of the French defeat, and were particularly angered by Mintié's symbolic gesture of embracing the dead Prussian soldier. In his preface to the ninth edition, Mirbeau lightly mocked those who had called him sacrilegious, iconoclastic and refractory, and who had even accused him of being a German spy; and insisting that he himself was patriotic, he penned some words which contain the key to many of his subsequent attitudes, revealing as they do a significant point of contact with the kind of patriotism which Reclus and the anarchists preached—in strict contradistinction to the noisy and sensation-seeking chauvinism of the post-1870 germanophobes who had taken such exception to *Le Calvaire:*

> Le patriotisme tel que je le comprends, ne s'affuble point de costumes ridicules, ne va point hurler aux enterrements, ne compromet point, par des manifestations inopportunes et des excitations coupables, la sécurité des passants et l'honneur même d'un pays . . .
>
> Le patriotisme, tel que je l'aime, travaille dans le recueillement. Il s'efforce de faire la patrie grande avec ses poètes, ses artistes, ses savants honorés, ses travailleurs, ses ouvriers et ses paysans protégés. S'il pique un peu moins de panaches au chapeau des généraux, il met un peu plus de laine sur le dos des pauvres gens.

Le Calvaire was based almost entirely upon Mirbeau's own experiences. In the chapter about Mintié's part in the war, Mirbeau was drawing upon his bitter memories of the disasters he had witnessed himself. Though his experiences were perhaps distorted by the suffering involved, Mirbeau's picture of the horrors of war was nevertheless far more authentic than that which could be read in the history books or that which was being taught in the history classes. Yet many critics denied the truthfulness of Mirbeau's portrayal of war, while others accused him of treason—as Jules Huret wrote several years later:

> L'hypocrisie de la critique a fait naturellement un crime à l'auteur de la sincérité de sa lamentable peinture. Combien de siècles d'éducation faudra-t-il encore à l'esprit français pour l'amener à l'amour de la vérité pour elle-même?

Le Calvaire, at the time it was written, was treated as much as a political and social touchstone as it was discussed as a realist novel. Its readers were either for or against Mirbeau's attitudes; not for the last time did one of his works divide his readers sharply into two classes in this way. *Le Calvaire,* and indeed all of Mirbeau's works, were never wholeheartedly accepted by the established critics, not because his works were necessarily inferior as works of art, but because few critics could safely or willingly endorse the radical ideas which permeated Mirbeau's writings, reflecting the change of 1885.

The story of *Le Calvaire,* written entirely in the first person, begins with the childhood of the narrator Jean Mintié at Saint-Michel-les-Hêtres in l'Orne. Mintié's father, the village notary, whom Mintié despised for his hypocrisy, and his mother, whom he admired for her sensitivity, both contain elements borrowed from Mirbeau's own parents. Mintié's childhood, like Mirbeau's, is not a particularly happy one. After recounting his mother's strange illness and premature death, Mintié tells of his boredom under a pedantic and incompetent private tutor, and here Mirbeau avails himself of the opportunity to avenge himself of the things he suffered at the hands of those who in his childhood were given charge over him, but who made no attempt to adapt their approach to his sensitive nature.

Mirbeau's criticism of his own upbringing and education is not however confined in *Le Calvaire* to remarks put directly into the mouth of the narrator: it is part of the very fabric of the story. The tragic figure of Mintié, his unhappy fate, and even the insufficiencies of his character, with which the reader becomes impatient, are clearly shown to be engendered by his inimical background, by his indifferent parents, and by his unsettling contact with war and with the corruptness of parisian society. Mirbeau, who was thirty-eight when he wrote *Le Calvaire,* had reached an age when he could look back at his life and see more clearly the motivating forces which had been operating in it; and the fact that he made the hero of his first novel the victim of so many hostile forces betrays to the reader the grudge which Mirbeau bore against the world in which he had grown up, or at least against that section of it with which he had been forced to keep in contact against his will.

From a Freudian point of view, Mirbeau's misfortunes with an untrustworthy mistress were responsible not only for the creation in *Le Calvaire* of the painful relationship between the fictional Jean Mintié and Juliette Roux but also for the evolution in Mirbeau himself of an enduring and deep-seated misogyny. In a man who prided himself in later years on having rid himself of all his former prejudices, this misogyny represented a flaw which was, however, too subconscious to mar the overall sincerity of Mirbeau's claim. From his suffering at the hands of a Parisian flirt, Mirbeau developed a philosophy of the female species which was to colour much of his creative work with an erotic sadism which often borders on the obscene. In its literary expression this philosophy drew much inspiration from the literature of the *femme fatale,* but it owed most to the satirical obscenities of the Belgian artist Félicien Rops, with whom Mirbeau was friendly at this time, and whom he greatly admired. For Mirbeau, Rops' portrayal of woman as the incarnation of evil tallied too closely with his own experiences for it not to impress him deeply, and Rops remained one of the most important of the formative influences on Mirbeau's literary style, as the savage eroticism of *Le Jardin des supplices* and certain parts of *Le Journal d'une femme de chambre* demonstrate. In *Le Calvaire,* Juliette Roux becomes a nightmarish figure, haunting Mintié like a demon of evil, corrupting and degrading him until he can sink no lower, and finally abandoning him when he has nothing left to offer. Only then, when he has suffered such systematic torture—whence the grim title of the novel—does Mintié turn his back on Juliette and on the kind of society she represents; and only then does he cease to be an aimless and spineless parasite, and staggers off, clad in the outfit of an honest workman, away to where his wounds can heal and to where he can start anew.

Le Calvaire is the meeting-place of the many themes of Mirbeau's chequered career. It is essentially a novel of revolt against the malevolent influences which had sought to bind his independent and generous nature. It was intentionally a novel of revenge against authority and despotism in their various forms, throwing the spotlight on them, revealing their nefarious influence on the individual, and accusing them of responsibility for the human weakness upon which the forces of evil could feed at will.

The painter Lirat in *Le Calvaire*—the friend who replaces Mintié in Juliette's arms—and the evident influence of Félicien Rops, bear witness to the personal interest which Mirbeau had begun to take in the visual arts. Mirbeau had long admired the Impressionist *avant-garde,* as the perspicacious art-critic Félix Fénéon noted in 1886 [in *Le Petit Bottin des lettres et des arts*], and he had written many articles in demonstration of his progressive artistic taste. But now he had begun to frequent more systematically milieux in which he became acquainted with most of the leading artists of his day. By the time *Le Calvaire* was written Mirbeau had formed lasting friendships with such men as Monet, Rodin and Gustave Geffroy, the truest friend of all—'le bon Gef', the one Barbey d'Aurevilly nicknamed 'le juste de *La Justice*'. There is little doubt that Mirbeau's friendship with Geffroy, journalist, art-critic, biographer of the revolutionary Auguste Blanqui, and himself a novelist of communard sympathies, cemented Mirbeau's allegiance to the Left and caused him to associate more clearly in his mind the revolutionary ideals of *avant-garde* art and of political agitation for social reform.

Mirbeau, who had almost lost his job on *L'Ordre* for his admiration for Monet, was delighted to receive a visit from the artist on Noirmoutier island in Brittany, where he had gone with Alice Regnault to prepare *Le Calvaire* for publication in 1886. This visit was the real beginning of a lifelong friendship, as the sustained correspondence between Mirbeau and Monet illustrates. Mirbeau was clearly referring to Monet and to the artists to whom Monet later introduced him, like Bonnard, Vuillard and Vallotton, when he wrote:

> C'était une joie que leur amitié, et, en même temps qu'une joie, un profit. Pour moi, j'y ai beaucoup appris, même dans les choses de mon métier. Ils m'ont ouvert un monde spirituel qui, jusqu'à eux, m'était en quelque sorte fermé, ou obscur . . . Je ne le dis pas sans émotion, ils ont donné à ma conscience, qui, trop longtemps, avait erré dans les terres desséchées du journalisme, une autre conscience.

The artists' debt to Mirbeau was no less considerable than the debt he owed to them—Monet, Rodin and Gauguin were not alone in benefiting from the enthusiasm which Mirbeau put at their disposal. It is for the historian of art to assess the importance of Mirbeau's role as the champion of the artistic *avant-garde* of his time; but it is clear that from an intellectual point of view, Mirbeau's contact with the world of art was of capital importance to him. Mirbeau's growing appreciation of the freedom expressed in the works of the rising generation of artists was part and parcel of the same spiritual awakening that revitalised his whole outlook on life, giving him a new awareness, and inspiring him to creative activity of his own.

By the summer of 1887 Mirbeau was a successful novelist; and this fact was no doubt a contributory factor to his marriage in May of that year to his mistress Alice Regnault. His union with this ex-*Variétés* actress set the seal on his break with his family and his right-wing origins. The rural bourgeoisie from which he stemmed and the right-wing circles in which he had moved for so long had tolerated his occasional outbursts of criticism and had pardoned them as youthful peccadilloes. But with *Le Calvaire,* and with his marriage to an actress, Mirbeau had openly declared his hostility to his caste, and he was now at the point of no return. After the personal revenge which he exacted by means of his first novel, Mirbeau's attitude towards his background began to harden out of intellectual conviction. Not only his new friends but also the books he read caused him to recognise the need for radical changes in the political, economic and artistic life of French society. Spencer, Büchner, Darwin and Guyau were among the scientific philosophers Mirbeau was reading at this time, and their ideas coloured Mirbeau's own philosophy with the atheistic and evolutionary rationalism which was calling into question the authority of ancient institutions and undermining the very fabric of society. These writers, along with Tolstoy, Kropotkin and Reclus, provided Mirbeau with the ammunition he needed to intensify his opposition to the kind of social organisation

he saw around him and to the intellectual tyranny under which he had suffered for so long himself.

The vehemence of Mirbeau's criticisms increased in proportion to his awareness of the cause of the ills besetting society. In *L'Abbé Jules* and *Sébastien Roch* he was to show what harm could result from the repression of an individual's natural self-expression, while in *Le Jardin des supplices* his field of criticism was to widen to take in the whole of society. *L'Abbé Jules* and *Sébastien Roch* were based, like *Le Calvaire,* on Mirbeau's own life, and it was by applying his new ideas to his personal experiences, in the writing of these novels, that Mirbeau prepared himself to face the larger issue of a society in need of correction.

L'Abbé Jules was conceived as a novel of the revolt of an individual against the middle class values which had been forced upon him. The eponymous hero of the book was intended to be a sympathetic villain whose misdeeds were the direct result of the repression to which society had subjected him. Under the hyperbolic pen of Mirbeau, however, the Abbé Jules degenerated into a monster, terrorising all with whom he came into contact. Based on a character taken from real life, he transcends reality, and causes the reader to doubt the validity of Mirbeau's criticisms of the society of which he is meant to be the victim. The monumental monstrosity of Jules' character would undoubtedly undermine the moral thesis of the novel were it not for the stratagem employed by Mirbeau to reduce this effect—that of narrating the story through the eyes of a child, the young nephew of Jules, Albert Dervelle. This ploy certainly rescues *L'Abbé Jules* from the tendency which Mirbeau had to overexaggeration and which reached its crescendo with *Le Jardin des supplices.* There were those who still accused Mirbeau of creating a meaningless and vulgar monster, an exception which proved nothing, but the perspicacious reader missed none of Mirbeau's sympathy for the Abbé Jules' sufferings due to the repression of his natural instinct. Mallarmé, for example, with whom Mirbeau was becoming friendly at this time, wrote him a letter which compensated Mirbeau for all the adverse criticism which his novel had received, for Mallarmé had clearly understood Mirbeau's intention in creating the Abbé Jules, as Mirbeau's reply to Mallarmé's kind letter reveals:

> Il y a, dans votre lettre, une phrase qui m'a vivement ému, car elle résume parfaitement ce que j'ai tenté dans l'*Abbé Jules*, et ce qu'on ne veut pas y voir: "Or vous avez créé là un douloureux camarade." Cette phrase me paie de tous mes doutes et de toutes mes angoisses.

Flushed with the success of *Le Calvaire,* Mirbeau had begun working on *L'Abbé Jules* immediately on his return from England after his marriage. The Mirbeaus set up house in Kérisper, near Sainte-Anne-d'Auray in Brittany, not far from Vannes, where Mirbeau had gone to Jesuit college over twenty years before. It was there, in July 1887, that he began writing his new novel, keeping his friend Monet informed of his painful progress. Surrounded by some of the loveliest countryside in France, Mirbeau saturated the character of the Abbé Jules with his own love of nature, and wove into his strange novel an impassioned appeal to humanity to learn the lessons of freedom and harmony which nature teaches to those who will stop to listen. The pantheistic philosophy which Jules tries to inculcate into his young nephew Albert is clearly a *reductio ad absurdum* of Mirbeau's own rousseauistic attitude to nature; and when Jules insists that he would not have been the degenerate rogue he was if he had been allowed to pursue his naturistic ideals, we feel that Mirbeau himself is speaking directly to us through the mouth of this fictional priest:

> . . . si j'avais connu autrefois ces vérités, je n'en serais jamais où j'en suis aujourd'hui. Car je suis une canaille, un être malfaisant, l'abject esclave de sales passions . . . Et sais-tu pourquoi? Parce que, dès que j'ai pu articuler un son, on m'a bourré le cerveau d'idées absurdes . . . On a déformé les fonctions de mon intelligence, comme celle de mon corps, et, à la place de l'homme naturel, instinctif, gonflé de vie, on a substitué l'artificiel fantoche, la mécanique poupée de civilisation, soufflée d'idéal . . . l'idéal d'où sont nés les banquiers, les prêtres, les escrocs, les débauchés, les assassins et les malheureux . . . [*L'Abbé Jules*]

This vague and sentimental anarchism is the motivating force behind the revolt of the Abbé Jules who, like Mirbeau himself, takes vengeance on society by mystifying and terrifying those who have contributed to its nefarious influence.

The story of *L'Abbé Jules* begins, like *Le Calvaire*, with the narrator's childhood reminiscences; and here we are allowed to catch another glimpse of the boredom of Mirbeau's early years. Mirbeau again takes the opportunity to satirise the life of the provincial bourgeoisie, particularly in the relations between the Dervelle family and their neighbours the Robins. Mirbeau's enduring antipathy towards legal administrators is given full rein in his characterisation of Monsieur Robin, the local J.P. who makes the grand boast that he knows the Code by rote, but who is as venal and as corrupt as those on whom he is allowed to pass sentence:

> A la veille des audiences, on voyait entrer chez lui des paysans avec des paniers bondés de volaille et de gibier, qu'ils remportaient vides, à la suite de quelque discussion juridique, sans doute. [*L'Abbé Jules*]

The picture of the superstitious, money-grubbing villagers of Viantais is broken off by the narrator's account of the life and doings of the dreaded Abbé Jules. It had been a surprise to everyone when Jules Dervelle became a priest, but the narrator makes it quite clear that Jules did this to exact his revenge on the society which had stunted his natural development. Jules exploits his position for his own ends, and experiences an almost satanic joy in doing so; the catalogue of his crimes makes one wonder why his removal from office did not come sooner. His return to Viantais after six years' debauchery in Paris is the beginning of a closer association between the narrator and his uncle, and from this time on we begin to see more clearly that Jules has been the victim of society, and not the tormentor of it as he first appeared. Ironically, this contact

between Jules and his young nephew was permitted by Albert's parents, who overcame their antipathy towards Jules in the hope of inheriting the fortune which he had somehow managed to accumulate. Jules is even entrusted with Albert's education; and in a chapter which is reminiscent of Rousseau's *Emile,* the renegade priest sets about disabusing the young narrator of all the false notions which his family had taught him and the values he had learned to respect:

> Ecoute-moi donc . . . Tu réduiras tes connaissances du fonctionnement de l'humanité au strict nécessaire: lo L'homme est une bête méchante et stupide; 20 La justice est une infamie; 30 L'amour est une cochonnerie; 40 Dieu est une chimère . . . Tu aimeras la nature; tu l'adoreras même . . . [*L'Abbé Jules*]

It is not difficult to see why the critics and the public did not appreciate such lessons as this, of which *L'Abbé Jules* is full. Mirbeau himself was, as usual, mildly displeased with his novel; though in later years he said it was perhaps 'le moins mauvais', and he was heartened by its reception amongst his literary and artistic friends. Mallarmé in particular was unusually lavish with his praise, and the novel cemented the ties of friendship between him and Mirbeau, and led to a regular correspondence which ended only with Mallarmé's sudden death in 1898.

Mirbeau's friendship with Mallarmé brought him into contact with the rising generation of symbolists who frequented the Mardis of the rue de Rome; and though Mirbeau did not subscribe to the symbolist aesthetic—he was never a lover of poetry in any case—he learned to appreciate the originality of much symbolist talent, and found himself in agreement at least with the attitude of opposition to the bourgeois republic which prevailed in symbolist circles. It was through Mallarmé too that Mirbeau came into contact again with the leading symbolist critic Félix Fénéon, who was soon to begin expressing his opposition to society by writing anonymous articles in underground anarchist journals like *La Revue Libertaire* and *Le Père Peinard.* In 1888 Fénéon was co-editor with Jean Ajalbert of Dujardin's *La Revue Indépendante,* in which Mirbeau had published an article the previous year; and Fénéon was to be another friend who cemented Mirbeau's allegiance to the extreme Left.

L'Abbé Jules, then, was even more important in Mirbeau's personal life than it was in his career as a successful novelist. It gave him an entrance to a wider range of intellectual circles, and convinced any who still doubted that Mirbeau was now wholly committed to revolutionary ideals. It even brought Mirbeau's writings to the notice of the anarchists, with whom he had so far had no direct contact, but who immediately recognised in him a kindred spirit. *L'Abbé Jules* was published at a time when Jean Grave was busy publishing a literary supplement to his anarchist journal *La Révolte* and was casting about for suitable material to republish there. Grave could not fail to be struck by the revolutionary tone which Mirbeau adopted in *L'Abbé Jules.* The anarchism of the abbé is, as his young nephew says, 'un anarchisme vague et sentimental'; it does not progress far beyond the negative, and it is not based on any positive ideological formula other than that nature is good and can show humanity the way to beauty and truth. Yet this was undoubtedly true of much nineteenth-century anarchist thought. Though most anarchists, and Mirbeau as well, went on to build upon the ruins which their nihilistic theories left behind, the critical negation of society and its values was an essential first step, and *L'Abbé Jules* was very much in this tradition. Jules was a character dear to the hearts of all those who, like Mirbeau, objected to the repression of the individual, and sought to replace such repression with freedom from constraint. The abbé's final act, of leaving his fortune to the first priest to defrock himself, is the ultimate, ironical gesture of defiance against the society which had made him what he was, and against the cupidity of those who thought his fortune would be theirs. The anarchists especially appreciated the literary form which Mirbeau was able to give to ideas which they were trying, in their own way, to spread. Jules' lessons about naturism, free love and the non-existence of God were ready-made propaganda for those who preached these principles in a more doctrinal and less palatable form.

Owing to the copyright difficulties which Grave was likely to experience—and which he later experienced to his cost—he left republication of the relevant sections of *L'Abbé Jules* for a future occasion, and turned to Mirbeau's newspaper articles and to his earlier works of fiction for possible material to include in his literary supplement. And Grave did not have far to look, for the approaching elections inspired Mirbeau to write a stinging attack on the French electoral system, in an article which was so virulent, in fact, that he was very fortunate to squeeze it past the editorial censorship of *Le Figaro*, where it first appeared on 28 November 1888. The article, **'La Grève des électeurs'**, was deemed by Grave to be of such importance that he republished it almost immediately, and not in his literary supplement, but on the front page of *La Révolte* itself (19 December 1888). It seems to have been Grave's practice to request permission from any author he wished to republish in this way; and as he later noted, only a few writers refused him such requests. In view of this, and in view of the fact that Grave was 'en correspondance déjà' with Mirbeau when he wrote his first surviving letter to Mirbeau in 1890, it seems probable that he also wrote asking Mirbeau's permission to reprint his article, so that Mirbeau's first direct contact with the anarchist movement would come in the form of a letter which he received at the beginning of December 1888 requesting permission to republish **'La Grève des électeurs'**. Though Mirbeau's reply to Grave has not survived, it was evidently favourable to the anarchist's request, and thus began an epistolary acquaintance which was to bring Mirbeau still closer to the mainstream of nineteenth-century French anarchism.

Electoral abstention had long been a basic part of anarchist doctrine and practice. In 1885, Mirbeau himself had read these words in the *Paroles d'un révolté* [by Peter Kropotkin] concerning universal suffrage:

> . . . le suffrage universel, la liberté de la presse, etc. . . . ne sont qu'un instrument entre les mains des classes dominantes pour maintenir leur pouvoir sur le peuple.

This was a view shared by all the anarchists, and it was a view to which Mirbeau had come round through his own experience of the inadequacies of the electoral system. Mirbeau's article, though not intended as a means of anarchist propaganda, was nevertheless so close to the anarchist tradition, and it put the case against electoral participation in such a forceful and amusing way, that the anarchist readers of *La Révolte* clamoured for offprints of the article to be made, and not even 20,000 copies were able to silence the demand. **'La Grève des électeurs'** was so popular in anarchist circles that years later it was still being printed as the standard anarchist abstentionist pamphlet, and Jean Grave wrote of it: 'Nous n'en connaissons pas de meilleur que l'article de Mirbeau: **"La Grève des Electeurs,"** paru il y a sept ou huit ans, mais toujours d'actualité.' The French police naturally obtained their own copy of the article, and it went into the file which they had opened on Mirbeau, and which was soon to swell as his contacts with the extreme Left multiplied.

Jean Grave's idea of reproducing extracts of sociological interest from literary authors as a means of anarchist propaganda was originally the brainchild of his friend Baillet, who had published two numbers of the ephemeral *Glaneur Anarchiste* in January 1885, containing extracts from Diderot, Blanqui and Boucher de Perthes. The first number of Grave's literary supplement to *La Révolte* (19 November 1887), reiterated the same intentions as Baillet's *Glaneur:*

> . . . démontrer aux travailleurs que les idées dont nous nous faisons les défenseurs ne sont point nées d'hier . . . rappeler aux heureux du jour, —peut-être leur apprendre—qu'ils sont les bénéficiaires des révolutions précédents et qu'ils auraient mauvaise grâce à renier aujourd'hui ceux dont le seul crime consiste à vouloir mettre en pratique les théories de leurs devanciers eux-mêmes.

Though both Kropotkin and Reclus were initially cool about the efficacy of a literary supplement as a means of propaganda, Grave's persistence and his success made them and the anarchists as a whole admit that even such extracts from predominantly bourgeois literature could serve the anarchist cause.

Of all the writers who were co-opted into this kind of involuntary propaganda, Mirbeau was to be the one on whom Grave relied most heavily. In January 1889, the Boulanger affair caused Mirbeau to write a satirical article about the sad state of society, an article in which the key phrase—'le mécontentement général'—is lifted straight out of the *Paroles d'un révolté;* for Kropotkin, this 'general discontent' was a sign of the near decomposition of the ancient forms and traditions of society, and this was a subject on which Mirbeau loved to expatiate. In this article ('**Le Mécontentement**'), Mirbeau took hold of Kropotkin's ideas and elaborated on them; and thinking no doubt of the anarchists, Mirbeau argued that plebeian revolutionaries were fully justified in their conflict with society, for 'dans leur oeuvre farouche [ils] se montrent plus logiques, sinon plus rassurantes que les pleurardes bourgeoises'; Mirbeau's condemnation of all governments, 'qui ont toujours joué dans l'Humanité un rôle d'obstruction et de destruction', and of the legal system, was tailor-made for use as anarchist propaganda, and shortly after it had appeared, surprisingly, in *Le Figaro* (9 January 1889), it was reprinted in the literary supplement of *La Révolte* (4 February).

Le Calvaire, and indeed all of Mirbeau's works, were never wholeheartedly accepted by the established critics, not because his works were necessarily inferior as works of art, but because few critics could safely or willingly endorse the radical ideas which permeated Mirbeau's writings.

—Reg Carr

During the winter of 1888-9, which he spent mostly in Menton in an attempt to overcome the neurasthenia and fever which was plaguing him, Mirbeau began work on his third novel, **Sébastien Roch**. If **Le Calvaire** and **L'Abbé Jules** had contained elements of the anarchism which was now becoming Mirbeau's hallmark, **Sébastien Roch** was to be the novel most directly inspired by his extreme left-wing preoccupations and by his individualistic revolt against the pressures of a middle-class society. The most consciously anarchistic of his early novels, **Sébastien Roch** was also the one which gave him most trouble to write, for he wrestled with it for almost a year, and seemed ill-pleased with it at every stage of its composition.

Mirbeau returned to Paris from Menton in May 1889 with only a hundred pages of his novel written. He and his wife set up house at 26 rue Rivay, in the noisy district of Levallois-Perret, where Mme Mirbeau owned some property. By a strange coincidence, Levallois-Perret was also the part of Paris in which the anarchists were most numerous and most active; it was the home of many of the anarchist militants, including Louise Michel; there were two anarchist groups there at the very time when Mirbeau arrived, and the larger of the two groups bore the name La Révolte, and met in the Salle Isselée of the rue de Courcelles, only a short distance from Mirbeau's home. It seems impossible that Mirbeau could have had no contact with these *compagnons* on his very doorstep, especially as another of his friends, Jean Ajalbert, who also lived in Levallois-Perret, is known to have frequented the anarchist-inspired Club de l'Art social.

It was while Mirbeau was in Levallois-Perret in July 1889 that Grave began to republish the second chapter of *Le Calvaire*—the chapter which had caused the scandal three years earlier. It appeared in the literary supplement of *La Révolte* in six parts, between July and September, and the anarchist readers must have found it to their taste, for *Le Calvaire* became a firm favourite in the anarchist library. Six years later, an anarchist wrote of *Le Calvaire:* 'Ce livre, où s'affirment déjà les tendances socialistes de

l'auteur, mérite d'être lu surtout pour les pages admirables sur la guerre qui forment une partie du volume.' It was Mirbeau's concentration on war in that remarkable chapter which gave Jean Grave the idea, some years later, of grouping together by subject the pick of the extracts from the literary supplements of *La Révolte* and its successor *Les Temps Nouveaux*. Mirbeau's chapter was the first of these special volumes to be published, and it appeared, as it had done when Grave first reprinted it in *La Révolte*, under the title 'La Guerre'.

Mirbeau was still living in Levallois-Perret—he removed to Les Damps by Pont-de-l'Arche in August 1889—when the local elections came round again in Paris. Once more Mirbeau stepped into the fray with another article in the vein of **'La Grève des électeurs'**; this new article was called **'Prélude',** and it appeared in *Le Figaro* of 14 July. Mirbeau's cutting analysis of the electoral farce, of 'l'infinie sottise, l'infinie malpropreté de la politique', reveals him at his satirical best. His imaginative portrait of Boulanger, handing out promises of prosperity before the elections, and uniforms, knapsacks and rifles afterwards, is something which deserves a better fate than the one which seems reserved for such journalistic ephemera. The last paragraph in particular, in which Mirbeau expands his irony into direct address, deserves quoting, and it was for this no doubt that Jean Grave reprinted the whole article in *La Révolte* for, apostrophising the typical voter, Mirbeau wrote:

> Eh bien! mon brave électeur, normand ou gascon, picard ou cévenol, basque ou breton, si tu avais une lueur de raison dans ta cervelle, si tu n'étais pas l'immortel abruti que tu es, le jour où les mendiants, les estropiés, les monstres électoraux viendront sur ton passage coutumier étaler leurs plaies et tendre leurs sébiles, au bout de leurs moignons dartreux, si tu n'étais pas l'indécrottable Souverain, sans sceptre, sans couronne, sans royaume, que tu as toujours été, ce jour-là, tu t'en irais tranquillement pêcher à la ligne, ou dormir sous les saules, ou trouver les filles derrière les meules, ou jouer aux boules, dans une sente lointaine, et tu les laisserais, tes hideux sujets, se battre entre eux, se dévorer, se tuer. Ce jour-là, vois-tu, tu pourrais te vanter d'avoir accompli le seul acte politique et la première bonne action de ta vie.

Not only the electoral campaigning, and all the noise and show that went with it, but also the disruption caused throughout Paris by the Universal Exhibition being held there that year, made Mirbeau irritated by city life, and he became anxious to leave the capital and find a place in the country. And it was not simply the upset caused by the Universal Exhibition which annoyed Mirbeau; he saw it also as a further sign of the decadence of capitalist society, 'le dernier élan d'une société moribonde . . . le suprême cri d'une civilisation qui agonise'. In an article which the anarchists found to their liking, he even drew an implied comparison between the Paris of 1889 and ancient Babylon just before its overthrow by the Medo-Persians:

> Ce qu'il y a de plus incroyable, c'est que les classes dirigeantes se réjouissent. Elles sont fières de cette oeuvre, qui est la leur, et où je vois le *Mané-*

Thécel-Pharès de leur règne! Elles ne compren-
nent donc pas que les anarchistes, seuls, ont le
droit de se réjouir, car où donc trouveraient-ils,
autre part qu'ici, un meilleur recrutement de
révolte! . . . ['**La Granda Kermesse'**]

It was with articles like this, in which Mirbeau made common cause with anarchist theoreticians like Reclus and
Kropotkin, that he made his debut in the anarchist press.
He began by expressing ideas similar to those advocated
by the anarchists, and they were only too glad to give these
ideas an airing in their leading journal. Increasingly, however, their own ideas were to have an effect on Mirbeau,
and in his own individual way he became the leading literary interpreter of anarchist ideology. From July to December 1889 articles by Mirbeau appeared regularly, at
least once a month and sometimes more, in the literary
supplement of *La Révolte.* Almost every article which
Mirbeau wrote, whether in *Le Figaro* or in *L'Echo de
Paris,* on which he had begun to collaborate in January
1889, contained something which the anarchists could
turn to their advantage; and while Mirbeau settled himself
in his new country home in Normandy and occupied himself with the completion of *Sébastien Roch,* Jean Grave
continued to select material from Mirbeau's regular newspaper columns for republication in his anarchist literary
supplement.

Sébastien Roch, as Mirbeau had written to Mallarmé earlier in the year, was 'le roman d'un adolescent violé par
un jésuite, la conséquence de ce viol, sur la formation de
son esprit et la direction de ses idées'. It was like his two
previous novels in that it was basically autobiographical,
that it was the story of an individual's failure, and that its
thesis was that society was to blame. Yet *Sébastien Roch*
turned out to be an altogether tidier and crisper novel; its
characters are more well-defined, its plot is more feasible,
its thesis is more successful, and its criticisms more pointed and meaningful. In choosing to make a Jesuit responsible for the victimisation of his main character, Mirbeau
was able to centralise both the action and the social criticism of his novel. In *Le Calvaire* and in *L'Abbé Jules* a
diversity of influences had been responsible for the failure
of Jean and Jules, and none of these influences had stood
out sufficiently for Mirbeau to use as a focal point of his
social criticism. In *Sébastien Roch* however, Mirbeau was
able to focus the spotlight on one institution, the Jesuit
college of Vannes, on one group of people, the Jesuits who
ran it, and on one man, Father de Kern, the one who put
the finishing touches to the systematic destruction of an
innocent child. From this central theme proceeds all of
Mirbeau's condemnation of the social organism as a
whole; from Monsieur Roch's parental egotism in sending
his son to the famous Jesuit college to the perpetuation of
class-consciousness by the boarders there; and from the
strictness of Jesuit teaching-methods to their reliance on
fear and superstition in the maintenance of their religious
authority—each of these had wider implications, but all
are bound together by Sébastien's unfortunate experiences
in Vannes. The disastrous effect which these things have
on the life of this young adolescent—Sébastien dies at the
age of twenty—is Mirbeau's deliberate illustration of the

dangers of alienating the individual from his natural
course.

We meet Sébastien first as a healthy, fun-loving eleven-
year-old. His pompous father, who keeps the ironmongery
in the village of Pervenchères, is a pleasant enough character, described by Mirbeau with the kind of comic irony he
was to employ later throughout *Les Vingt et un jours d'un
neurasthénique.* Monsieur Roch has perhaps been guilty
of neglecting his son, but at least he has allowed Sébastien
a measure of freedom, and Sébastien's upbringing has been
far less repressive than that of either Jean Mintié in *Le
Calvaire* or Jules Dervelle in *L'Abbé Jules.* It is left to the
Jesuits to perform this work of deformation and repression, and the greatest mistake Monsieur Roch makes is to
confide his son to their tender care for the sake of his own
vanity.

Throughout his life Mirbeau reproached the Jesuits for the
kind of education they had tried to force upon him, and
for the adverse effect their efforts had had upon his character. In making the Jesuits responsible for the serious damage done to Sébastien, however, Mirbeau was expressing
far more than merely personal animosity towards a particular religious sect; by illustrating the dangerous menace
of education in the hands of the priesthood, Mirbeau was
undermining the validity of religion itself, and was giving
voice to the anticlerical feeling which was daily growing
stronger in France, and which the extreme Left—and the
anarchists in particular—were fomenting at that very
time.

In the very opening paragraphs of the novel, in a passage
which, through over exaggeration, almost loses the significance of the truth it contains, Mirbeau accuses the Jesuits,
with their religious superstition, of exploiting the abjec-
tion and poverty of their area of Brittany:

> Aucun décor de paysage et d'humanité ne leur
> convenait mieux pour pétrir les cerveaux et ma-
> nier les âmes . . . De tous les pays bretons, le ta-
> citurne Morbihan est demeuré le plus obstiné-
> ment breton, par son fatalisme religieux, sa résis-
> tance sauvage au progrés moderne, et la poésie,
> âpre, indiciblement triste de son sol qui livre
> l'homme, abruti de misères, de superstitions et
> de fièvres, à l'omnipotente et vorace consolation
> du prêtre. [*Sébastien Roch*]

The novel is riddled with such outbursts of anticlerical-
ism, of the 'haine de la prêtrise' which Mirbeau shared
with so many of his contemporaries—many of whom
knew what Jesuit college was like, having passed through
it themselves—and it is hardly suprising that Mirbeau
should invest Sébastien with this same hatred, as he noted
in his diary:

> Enfin, j'ai l'horreur du prêtre, je sens le men-
> songe de ses consolations, le mensonge du Dieu
> implacable et fou qu'il sert; je sens que le prêtre
> n'est là, dans la société, que pour maintenir
> l'homme dans sa crasse intellectuelle, que pour
> faire, des multitudes servilisées, un troupeau de
> brutes imbéciles et couardes . . . [*Sébastien
> Roch*]

Sébastien, endowed with an abnormal sensitivity, is made

to suffer horribly by the Jesuits. His only friend, the taciturn and thick-skinned Bolorec, suffers similar hardships but accepts them with quiet indignation. When Sébastien has been corrupted by the sensual Father de Kern, and has proved a disappointment to the Jesuit, he and Bolorec find themselves expelled from college on the grounds that a homosexual relationship has developed between them; and when Sébastien returns home in disgrace, we are able to measure the damage that has been done in the three years he has spent at Vannes. The diary which he keeps gives us a clear insight into the confused moral and mental state of this unfortunate victim of man's inhumanity. Sébastien shows himself to be incapable of forming normal relationships with people, especially with members of the opposite sex, like his childhood sweetheart Marguerite Lecautel. He is no longer the carefree self-confident child he once was; he is unstable, easily bored, misunderstood and disliked by his neighbours, and he is pursued by erotic nightmares which bring back all the horror of his days in Jesuit college. All this is a direct result of his three years in Vannes.

Beneath this marred existence however, we catch the occasional glimpse of what might have been if Sébastien had not been intellectually stunted by his education in Jesuit college. In his diary he struggles painfully to see clearly through the veils of prejudice and through the complexes the Jesuits have integrated into his personality; his generosity and his concern for the underprivileged make him feel the iniquity of the morality and the hollowness of the religion of his Jesuit teachers, and yet he is unable to formulate his own opinion—he cannot carry though his revolt to a true expression of himself:

> Révolte vaine, hélas! et stérile. Il arrive souvent que les préjugés sont les plus forts et prévalent sur des idées que je sens généreuses, que je sais justes. Je ne puis, si confuse qu'elle soit encore, me faire une conception morale de l'univers, affranchie de toutes les barbaries, religieuse, politique, légale et sociale, sans être aussitôt repris par ces mêmes terreurs religieuses et sociales, inculquées au collège. [*Sébastien Roch*]

The parallel between Sébastien and the young Mirbeau is obvious, and there can be little doubt that the character of Sébastien became a means whereby Mirbeau could explain, to his own satisfaction at least, his paradoxical conduct earlier in his life. Had he lived, Sébastien might ultimately have found himself, as Mirbeau did. As it was, his humanitarian impulses and his potentially anarchistic temperament proceeded little further than this grandiloquent apostrophe, inspired by the resigned submissiveness of the population of Pervenchères:

> Y a-t-il quelque part une jeunesse ardente et réfléchie, une jeunesse qui pense, qui travaille, qui s'affranchisse de la lourde, de la criminelle, de l'homicide main du prêtre, si fatale au cerveau humain? Une jeunesse qui, en face de la morale établie par le prêtre et des lois appliquées par le gendarme, ce complément du prêtre, dise résolument: 'Je serai immorale, et je serai révoltée.' Je voudrais le savoir. [*Sébastien Roch*]

When one day he receives a letter from his schoolfriend

Bolorec, who is plotting to bring about a proletarian revolution, Sébastien thinks again of his own concern for the poor and the underprivileged, and he regrets his inability to communicate with the common people. He remembers, for example, how he tried in vain to explain to the poor population of Pervenchères that public charity was simply a means used by the rich to perpetuate poverty and justify their wealth:

> . . . la charité, voilà le secret de l'avilissement des hommes! Par elle, le gouvernant et le prêtre perpétuent la misère au lieu de la soulager, démoralisent le coeur du misérable au lieu de l'élever. Les imbéciles, ils se croient liés à leurs souffrances par ce bienfait menteur, qui de tous les crimes sociaux est le plus grand et le plus monstrueux, le plus indéracinable aussi. Je leur ai dit: 'N'acceptez pas l'aumône, repoussez la charité, et prenez, prenez, car tout vous appartient.' Mais ils ne m'ont pas compris. [*Sébastien Roch*]

Sébastien is not able, as Bolorec is, to commit himself totally to the popular cause, and he is obliged to lead a tortured life of indecision. His mind is clear however, on one important point: the stupidity of militarism and its corollary, war between nations. This novel more than any other—*Le Calvaire* included—expresses Mirbeau's horror of war and his opposition to nationalistic patriotism. The ultimate fate which Mirbeau reserves for Sébastien is a meaningless death in a war he does not understand for a cause he knows nothing about. And before he goes off to war to die—supreme irony this—Sébastien is allowed to speak his mind in a passage which sums up not only Mirbeau's feelings, but also those of all those who were campaigning for the abolition of war:

> Je comprends que l'on se batte, que l'on se tue, entre gens d'un même pays, pour conquérir une liberté et un droit: le droit à manger, à penser; je ne comprends pas que l'on se battle entre gens qui n'ont aucun rapport entre eux, aucun intérêt commun, et que ne peuvent se haïr puisqu'ils ne se connaissent point. [*Sébastien Roch*]

The futility of Sébastien's death, in the arms of Bolorec, with whom he has met up again on the battle-front, fills the taciturn revolutionary with cold anger; and as he stumbles away into the smoke, bearing his friend's shattered body, he mutters dark threats of revenge on the world which has done this to an innocent youth.

It is tempting to agree with the critic Maxime Revon, who interprets the two friends as different aspects of Mirbeau's own personality: Sébastien the idealist, warm and generous, and Bolorec the revenge-seeking revolutionary, intent on making society pay for the death of the idealism personified by Sébastien. It is difficult not to see Sébastien as the younger Mirbeau, generous in impulse, but holding back through the reticence of prejudice, and Bolorec as the older Mirbeau, the revolutionary, the anarchist intent on making up for all the time that his indecisive self had lost. Whether this be the case or not, *Sébastien Roch* was certainly the novel into which Mirbeau put most of himself, a novel where he invites the reader to discern his philosophy of life, that amoral but humanitarian anarchism which was becoming more and more pronounced.

Such then was the novel which Mirbeau dedicated to the 'Maître vénérable et fastueux du Livre Moderne', Edmond de Goncourt; and though Goncourt did not exactly share Mirbeau's extremist views, least of all when the anarchists began to throw bombs about, he greatly admired the fine prose style of his younger friend, and *Sébastien Roch* remained his favourite of Mirbeau's works. Their friendship clearly transcended political considerations, and Mirbeau remained a regular visitor to Goncourt's Grenier.

The anarchists however, and Jean Grave in particular, were more interested in the sociological content of *Sébastien Roch* than in its literary merits, and they were quick to reprint the various sections of the novel which expressed ideas akin to their own. It had not long been published in book-form—it first appeared serially in *L'Echo de Paris* from January to April 1890—when the literary supplement of *La Révolte* published a section of it under the title 'La Guerre', closely followed by another under the title 'La Patrie', and then a third, 'Psychologie sociale'. These extracts, and the very fact of their republication in an anarchist journal, illustrate the gulf that separated Mirbeau from his former reactionary self. His three 'novels of revenge' not only enabled him to unburden himself of the painful memories of his youth, but by their defence of individualism and by the suppressed anger of their condemnation of the forces which repress man's natural instincts, these books brought him to the forefront of the anarchists' propaganda. . . .

Reg Carr, in his Anarchism in France: The Case of Octave Mirbeau, *McGill-Queens University Press, 1977, 190 p.*

Joseph Halpern   (essay date 1980)

[*In the following essay, Halpern discusses the themes of desire and the masking of reality in* Le journal d'une femme de chambre.]

Two liminal texts place Octave Mirbeau's *Journal d'une femme de chambre* under the sign of a particular kind of realism. One is a traditional "editor's" notice claiming authority for the book: "Ce livre a été véritablement écrit par Mlle Célestine R. . . . femme de chambre. Une première fois, je fus prié de revoir le manuscrit, de le corriger, d'en récrire quelques parties. Je refusai d'abord. . . . Mais Mlle Célestine R . . . était fort jolie . . . Elle insista. Je finis par céder, car je suis homme, après tout . . . j'ai bien peur . . . d'avoir remplacé par de la simple littérature ce qu'ily avait dans ces pages d'émotion et de vie." The other is Mirbeau's dedicatory letter to the journalist Jules Huret: "C'est un livre sans hypocrisie, parce que c'est de la vie, et de la vie comme nous la comprenons, vous et moi."

Both texts insist on the authentic life of the diary to follow. The editor's humble concerns "bring to life" a time-honored convention; in this instance, not only is the author real, but also desirable (*fort jolie*). She brings her charms with her into the literary marketplace and what follows should seem all the more real for it. Mirbeau in-

herited the subject of lower-class sexuality and its economics, treated as a slice of life, from the Goncourts, Huysmans and Zola, and the idea of "life as we understand it," in the dedication to Huret, is but a rephrasing of Zola's concession that literature necessarily filters reality through "temperament." By the publication of *Le Journal d'une femme de chambre* in 1900, however, the doctrines of naturalism were no longer law. Mirbeau's prefatory remarks locate his book in a subjectivist and decadent corner of late naturalism. The letter to Huret points to a postromantic aesthetics of the grotesque, of tragicomedy and the *rire en pleurs:* "c'est que nul mieux que vous, et plus profondément que vous, n'a senti, devant les masques humains, cette tristesse et ce comique d'être un homme . . . tristesse qui fait rire, comique qui fait pleurer les âmes hautes." Despite the novel's satirical references to Bourgetian elitism, Mirbeau's realism is understood to be of the standardly "artistic" sort, fully accessible only to superior souls who can perceive genuine emotion behind literary smoothness and the truths of human existence behind social postures.

These rhetorical principles take Maupassant's definition of realists as "illusionists" one step further toward expressionism, toward Cocteau's "mentir pour dire vrai." Mirbeau himself says elsewhere: "En l'art l'exactitude est la déformation et la vérité est le mensonge." As they are generally understood, Mirbeau's novels testify to the manipulation of outmoded naturalist conventions by a late romantic, decadent sensibility. The artist accentuates, exaggerates nature to express what he sees there and creates a romantic grotesque. In other words, the text holds the mask of realism up to its face: *Larvatus prodeo.* Paul Ricoeur glosses the Latin phrase as "comme homme de désir je m'avance masqué," and *Le Journal d'une femme de chambre* can be discussed in view of the three terms of that gloss: desire, mask and progression.

The thematically decadent, "black" realism of *Le Journal d'une femme de chambre* corresponds to the representation of a world of desire and the masking of desire. Mirbeau gives over a good half of the novel to an episodic collection of spicy tales and satirical portraits that tend toward the morbid: the writer's snobbish wife who sells her body for good reviews; the *bien pensant* fund raiser who delights in obscene magazines; the saintly spinster who finds and adores as a holy relic the phallus chipped off a statue; the well-kept old gentleman who dies with his teeth clenched on his maid's leather shoes; the honest gardener brought almost to murder because he is denied the right to have children; the consumptive youth exhausted and driven to death by love. Célestine's "petites histoires," as she calls them, are less exotic, less specific and milder than the horrors—the Wildean "wounds . . . like red roses"—detailed in Mirbeau's other, contemporaneous novel, *Le Jardin des supplices,* but the aesthetics of horror, the association of desire with death and corruption, is equally in evidence in both cases. Célestine's anecdotes, which are told in flashback, center on moments of violence, death, sexual obsession, degradation, humiliation, guilt and revenge. And so does the story of her own life, which serves to link together her rogue's gallery of funny and sad stories. Her own tale, which becomes a Cinderella romance in an ironic mode, a romantic quest perverted by neo-*Bovarysme,* is first of all predicated on a fall.

At the beginning of the narrative, Célestine, a young, blond, svelte and attractive *femme de chambre,* declares herself fallen upon hard days. "Ah oui, je suis bien tombée." Previously, she had been employed in fashionable Parisian homes where countesses and barons, poets and musicians were received, where she knew Paul Bourget and Jules Lemaître, where she was given splendid dresses and chic, tight uniforms to wear, where she read Baudelaire and Verlaine with romantic young lovers. Now her health is bad and she has left Paris to work in the squalid provinces. She has had a dozen places in two years, and in each of them she has been subjected to some "saleté," some ignominious humiliation indicative of the "débraillement moral" of contemporary society. She has now been washed away in a flood, "un flot ignoble et fétide," to a world of primeval chaos and decay. In her new job, the smart elegance and sharpness of her Parisian milieu has been replaced by the grotesque bestiality of Marianne, the cook, and "la grosse Rose," the neighbor's servant. The one is "grosse, molle, flasque, étalée, le cou sortant en triple bourrelet d'un fichu sale avec quoi l'on dirait qu'elle essuie ses chaudrons, les deux seins énormes et difformes roulant sous une sorte de camisole en cotonnade bleue plaquée de graisse, sa robe trop courte découvrant d'épaisses chevilles et de larges pieds chaussés de laine grise"; the other, "courte, grosse, rougeaude, asthmatique et qui semble porter péniblement un immense ventre sur des jambes écartées en tréteau . . . un sourire épais, visqueux, sur des lèvres de vieille licheuse . . . son corps tangue et roule, comme un vieux bateau sur une forte mer." This must be, Célestine muses, "le pays des grosses femmes."

She goes with Rose to meet the town's *épicière,* whose body, too, rolls like a liquid in a bottle, and there listens to the talk of the local domestic servants in a scene marked by its demonic imagery and its Sartrian/Hugolian evocation of primordial ooze:

> C'est un flot ininterrompu d'ordures vomies par ces tristes bouches, comme d'un égout. . . . Il semble que l'arrière-boutique en est empestée. . . . Je ressens une impression d'autant plus pénible que la pièce où nous sommes est sombre et que les figures y prennent des déformations fantastiques. . . . Elle n'est éclairée, cette pièce, que par une étroite fenêtre qui s'ouvre sur une cour crasseuse, humide, une sorte de puits formé par des murs que ronge la lèpre des mousses. . . . Une odeur de saumure, de légumes fermentés, de harengs saurs . . . Alors, chacune de ces créatures, tassées sur leur chaise comme des paquets de linge sale, s'acharne á raconter une vilenie, un scandale, un crime . . . j'éprouve quelque chose d'insurmontable, quelque chose comme un affreux dégoût. . . . Une nausée me retourne le coeur . . . ces voix aigres me font l'effet d'eaux de vaisselle, glougloutant et s'égouttant par les éviers et par les plombs.

Célestine may tell herself that she has nothing in common with these women, but nonetheless their stories are nothing but unshaped versions of her own anecdotes.

The *épicière*'s importance in this circle stems from the fact that she is the local abortionist. The implicit theme of abortion, which leads nowhere in terms of dramatic development, ties into the principal event that interests the town gossips: the rape, mutilation, and murder of a child in the neighborhood, which follows upon previous incidents of the kind. "Tiens! . . . encore une femme coupée en morceaux," says M. Lanlaire, Célestine's employer, while reading the newspaper. We can associate this image with a distinct constellation of themes in the text. First, there is Célestine's definition of a servant as "quelqu'un de disparate, fabriqué de pièces et de morceaux . . . un monstrueux hybride humain." The servant is a *déraciné,* uprooted from his class to live in bourgeois homes and breathe "l'odeur mortelle qui monte de ces cloaques." Secondly, the remorse, guilt and regret that Célestine feels is actualized in an interior pain, in "une douleur si aigüe que c'était à croire qu'une bête (lui) déchirait, avec ses dents, avec ses griffes, l'intérieur du corps."

Célestine thinks of herself as a child destroyed, and the source of that feeling is sexual: her mother and sister were sailors' sluts; she herself was already a "woman" and no longer a virgin at 12. She also pictures herself as a deep, open wound, and the violence of her history finds its correlate in the rape of the child: "Elle était un peu innocente, mais douce et gentille . . . et elle n'avait pas douze ans! . . . D'après Rose, toujours mieux informée que les autres, la petite Claire avait son petit ventre ouvert d'un coup de couteau, et les intestins coulaient par la blessure. . . . La nuque et la gorge gardaient, visibles, les marques des doigts étrangleurs . . . Ses parties, ses pauvres petites parties, n'étaient qu'une plaie affreusement tuméfiée, comme si elles eussent été forcées—une comparaison de Rose—par le manche trop gros d'une cognée de bûcheron."

The association of violence, death and sexual desire extends throughout the novel. The other servant in the Lanlaire household is Joseph, the gardener and coachman. Joseph exerts a sexual fascination on Célestine that grows in the measure that she considers him dangerous. He is a violent antisemite and patriot, bloodthirsty, cruel, ugly, sensual and menacing. To the moment of the murder of little Claire, he has represented only danger, but the rape triggers a new response in Célestine. The attack on Claire acts as a rape of the feminine consciousness of the community; it excites even the admiration of the police. So, too, does Joseph begin to fascinate Célestine. She assumes that he is the rapist. As he evokes more and more for her the devil, a wolf or wild beast, so he becomes increasingly endowed with mystery, with a "grande beauté horrible et meurtrière" and "une sorte d'atmosphère sexuelle, âcre, terrible ou grisante, dont certaines femmes subissent, même malgré elles, la forte hantise." Célestine imagines herself the plaything of his ferocious passions, the instrument of his crimes, and becomes obsessed by him: "Outre cet attrait de l'inconnu et du mystère, il exerce sur moi ce charme âpre, puissant, dominateur, de la force. Et ce charme . . . conquiert ma chair passive et soumise . . . C'est en moi un désir plus violent, plus sombre, plus terrible même que le désir qui, pourtant, m'emporta jusqu'au meurtre, dans mes baiser avec M. Georges."

Célestine's relation to Joseph develops coherently from the role she has been given in society. Her stories of her career cast her quite lucidly as the passive object of sexual degradation. As a servant, she defines herself as the slave of democratic society, the legalized prostitute characterized by her thing-like, alienated status. Her loss of identity is captured by her employers' mania for calling all their chambermaids "Marie"; she embodies what Sartre would call "matière oeuvrée," the essential passivity of the feminine condition in an unliberated society. Joseph, then, begins to possess her as she is possessed by the demon of revenge. Célestine, the Persecuted Maiden, that poor innocent from Richardson and the Gothic novels, thinks she feels the teeth of the decadent Fatal Woman growing within her. After almost every one of her humiliations, Célestine takes a verbal revenge, in a *réquisitoire* that humiliates the master, that ravages the icons of her society: politics, religion, art, etc. But Joseph's frightening, bulging muscles represent for Célestine the possibility of real, criminal revenge: the "rape" of the masters' goods, as Célestine calls it. When the Lanlaire's valuable silver service finally is stolen—by Joseph, it would seem—the "caisses éventrées," the "silence de mort" and the "visages morts" all bear witness to a nexus of crime, death and violation that constitutes the climax of this aspect of the novel:

> Le crime a quelque chose de violent, de solennel, de justicier, de religieux, qui m'épouvante certes, mais qui me laisse aussi—je ne sais comment exprimer cela—de l'admiration. Non, pas de l'admiration, puisque l'admiration est un sentiment moral, une exaltation spirituelle, et ce que je ressens n'influence, n'exalte que ma chair. . . . C'est comme une brutale secousse, dans tout mon être physique, à la fois pénible et délicieuse, un viol douloureux et pâmé de mon sexe. . . . C'est curieux . . . mais chez moi, tout crime—le meurtre principalement,—a des correspondances secrètes avec l'amour . . . un beau crime m'empoigne comme un beau mâle. . . .
>
> . . . Mais la gaieté, je l'éprouvai plus directe et plus intense et plus haineuse, à considérer Madame, affalée près de ses caisses vides. . . . Cette douleur honteuse, ce crapuleux abattement, c'était aussi la revanche des humiliations, des duretés que j'avais subies. . . . J'en goûtai, pleinement, la jouissance délicieusement farouche.

Célestine will never really know, however, if it was Joseph who organized the theft, if it was Joseph who murdered little Claire. The danger in Joseph will never become tangible. After the theft, Joseph and Célestine leave the Lanlaires; they marry and invest Joseph's mysterious fortune in a banal seaport café in Cherbourg. There Joseph, in his new role as *patron,* seems to become a new man. His once dangerous and violent patriotism turns into a tamed, commercial posture, a rightist enthusiasm that brings in a rowdy anti-Dreyfusard crowd. As for Célestine, the move to Cherbourg, in the spring, is a return to her origins:

"Née de la mer, je suis revenue à la mer." In her bourgeois triumph, we can see the basic closural devices of comic form—marriage and reintegration into society—as well as a parody of Disney's Cinderella after her marriage to the Prince: "Voilà enfin une partie de mon rêve qui se réalise. . . . Moi, je tiens la caisse, trônant au comptoir."

This pseudo-heroic story of upward social mobility, of ritual purification and rebirth, strikes a distinct false note. Célestine is still a passive object, there to flirt with the customers, a decoration at the bar in Alsatian costume, an instrument in Joseph's financial schemes. The honest social outrage that burned within her had opened up for her transcendent possibilities and given her life as an independent subject. But in her submission to Joseph it is revealed that her hopes were fed on the illusory fires of "des histoires romanesques," "des jolies romances qu'on chante au café-concert," as she says. Like Emma Bovary, she has read too much, and there seems to be little actual correlation between her sanguinary imagination and dull reality. "Chaque fois que je vois (Joseph) songeur, mes idées s'allument tout de suite. J'imagine des tragédies, des gens qui râlent sur la bruyère des forêts . . . Et voilà qu'il ne s'agissait que d'une réclame, petite et vulgaire."

The last line of the novel continues to assert passive aggressivity, potential revolution and an ascensional force toward an open future: "Je sens que je ferai tout ce qu'il voudra que je fasse, et que j'irai toujours où il me dira d'aller . . . jusqu'au crime!. . . ." The contractual syntagm and the three dots of ellipsis that end the text point in themselves to a "Pourrait être continué" that would build on the episodic and therefore additive aspect of the narrative. But at the same time Célestine is planning to add a *café-concert* to their establishment: formal openness is countered by ideological closure and narrative irony. The force forward toward crime and anarchy has already been undermined by Joseph's trivialization and by the specific admission of Célestine's romanticizing. Even more, Célestine's exchange of roles in life marks the completion of her sentimental education and underscores an aspect of narrative development that is not progressive and synthetic, but circular and chiastic. Throughout the novel Célestine's view of her employers as exploiters has been convincingly consistent—from the first page: "A la façon, vraiment extraordinaire, vertigineuse, dont j'ai roulé, ici et là, successivement . . . sans pouvoir me fixer nulle part, faut-il que les maîtres soient difficiles à servir maintenant! . . . C'est à ne pas croire." But in the closing pages of the text she has become an employer herself and her attack on them is devastatingly unmasked as mere rhetoric by a conventional "good help is hard to find" that reverses her earlier position: "Il est vrai qu'en trois mois nous avons changé quatre fois de bonne . . . Ce qu'elles sont exigeantes, les bonnes à Cherbourg, et chapardeuses, et dèvergondèes! . . . Non, c'est incroyable, et c'est dégoûtant." She is only repeating, of course, what has been said of her often enough; this is not revenge, but blindness.

Célestine has deserted her class. Without a viable social base, she no longer has an authentic claim to revolutionary fervor, and her criminal imagination is reduced to a case of right-wing feminine hysteria, from which the author takes his distance. Joseph and Célestine (or Joseph and Marie, if we accept the masters' name for her and define the pair as emblems of the servant class) can be taken for heralds of the new age only by a large stretch of the imagination; to a much larger degree, they form a society at the end that is only a parody of the old one.

The possibility of verbal revenge develops in the first place from Célestine's consistent role as revealer. The Balzacian observer was a lawyer, artist or author who perceived hidden beauty and horror, poems and dramas beneath banal appearances. Célestine inherits both this role and Zola's nose for dirty linen. As much as she has the recording eye of the journalist, she also has the roving satirical eye of the picaro. The picaresque model plays its traditional part here as the mirror image and deconstruction of the forms of romance; *Don Quixote, Moll Flanders,* and *Le Paysan parvenu* all form part of the background of this novel. We are invited to understand Célestine as the product of specific social forces in 19th century France, but she is nonetheless a typical literary picaro: a rogue or orphan, cut off from his roots and native city, originally naturally innocent but now determined to be as cruel to others as they have been to him, who drifts from place to place and from one level of society to another as he rises in it toward respectability. The picaro reveals the corruption of society in a series of disconnected portraits; he also reveals himself for what he is.

As she moves from one home to another, Célestine functions as the perfect revealer of society because she has access to its inner truths. The chambermaid sees things in their nudity and squalor, from the inside, and smells out corruption everywhere. "Ah! dans les cabinets de toilette, comme les masques tombent! . . . Comme s'effritent et se lézardent les façades les plus orgueilleuses!" The principal metaphorical system of the novel is thus that of *extérieur* and *intérieur, visage* and *âme, voile* or *masque* and concealed *pourriture:*

> Je connais ces types de femmes et je ne me trompe point à l'éclat de leur teint. C'est rose dessus, oui, et dedans c'est pourri . . . quand on va au fond des choses, quand on retourne leurs jupes et qu'on fouille dans leur linge . . . ce qu'elles sont sales!. . . .
>
> Je ne suis pas vieille, pourtant, mais j'en ai vu des choses, de près . . . j'en ai vu des gens tout nus. . . . Et j'ai reniflé l'odeur de leur linge, de leur peau, de leur âme. . . . Malgré les parfums, ça ne sent pas bon. . . . Tout ce qu'un intérieur respecté, tout ce qu'une famille honnête peuvent cacher de saletés, de vices honteux, de crimes bas, sous les apparences de la vertu . . . ah! je connais ça . . . ils ont beau se laver dans des machins d'argent et faire de la piaffe . . . je les connais! . . . Ca n'est pas propre . . . Et leur coeur est plus dégoûtant que n'était le lit de ma mère.

Célestine is an eye that sees, a surgical "regard" that penetrates through external facade into real corruption. But the masters are also eyes that watch and wound. Madame Lanlaire is a pure, objectified "regard" that seems to bore into Célestine's flesh and soul, a Medusean gaze that dehu-

manizes the servant. Thus Célestine also acts as a focal point for the eyes of others. She further exposes the souls of the Lanlaires because each of them reacts to her in a way that defines them: "Ils m'observaient, chacun, selon les idées qui les mènent, conduits, chacun, par une curiosité différente." In some cases, her employers project self-images through the manipulation of Célestine as a prop or fetish in their particular fantasy. Célestine reveals desire because she is its object. The masters see only what they want to see, and nothing below the surface but reflections of their own desire. The dialectical relationship of master and slave shapes itself here in the interplay of masking and unveiling, projecting and interpreting. To look within, in Mirbeau's novel, is to dominate and to violate.

Joseph's mystery, then, is one with his impenetrability. His relation to Célestine is always that of subject to object, master to slave, force to instrument, because Célestine can never see past his mask. Concomitant to the murder and theft, there exists a substantial tendency in *Le Journal* toward a detective form, that in the end will be entirely frustrated. The interpreting eye is first an inquiring eye. In order to discover Joseph's secrets, Célestine steals into his room. But where all the other household objects have spoken to her of their owners, Joseph's possessions reveal nothing. "Rien n'est mystérieux dans cette chambre, rien ne s'y cache. C'est la chambre nue d'un homme qui n'a pas de secrets. . . . Les objets qu'il possède sont muets, comme sa bouche, intraversables comme ses yeux et comme son front." Joseph is nothing but mask and surface, nothing but a power that reduces Célestine to passivity. It is his eyes, not hers, that dominate: "ses yeux parlent, à défaut de sa bouche. . . . Et ils rôdent autour de moi, et ils m'enveloppent, et ils descendent en moi, au plus profond de moi, afin de me retourner l'âme, et de voir ce qu'il y a dessous."

What Joseph claims to see in her is Evil: "Vous êtes comme moi, Célestine. . . . Ah! pas de visage, bien sûr . . . mais nos deux âmes sont pareilles . . . nos deux âmes se ressemblent." All this is pure Genet, of course, as read by Sartre—*Les Bonnes* and *Le Balcon* in period dress. Joseph claims to reveal to her her essential and unchangeable character—what Sartre speaks of in *Saint Genet* as an essentialism rooted in negation and passivity. On this premise, the circular aspect of the novel would be built into Célestine's static nature. Her return is to her true self, to the world of sailors and sailors' bars to which she belongs through her mother. Her new-found appreciation of authority and the rights of property, at the end, is neither a conversion nor a betrayal but a self-recognition as a negative, passive, "relative" being, who cannot exist outside a system of social hierarchy. And it is true that Célestine does seem to recognize herself—or what she has been made into—best in moments of degradation and futile rage. From the deathbed of poor M. Georges, her beautiful, consumptive lover, she throws herself into the arms of a brutal and vulgar companion: "Pour tout dire, je me reconnus, je reconnus ma vie et mon âme en ces paupières fripées, en ce visage glabre, en ces lèvres rasées qui accusent le même rictus servile, le même pli de mensonge, le même goût de l'ordure passionnelle, chez le comédien, le juge et le valet. . . ." If what she is is mirrored in Joseph's eyes, then we are to understand her in terms of the desires she imagines in him and a masochistic identification with evil. The affirmation of dissonance between the protagonist and his world that Lukàcs speaks of in his *Theory of the Novel* would thus be dissolved at the close of this novel. In her final role, exterior Célestine and interior Célestine are one; her soul is no bigger than her society.

Joseph's reading of Célestine is not the only possible one, however. Célestine's impulse toward self-punishment does hold her back from realizing her modest dreams of happiness here and there in the text: she turns down the rich old man who would have left her everything in a few months; she insults the only mistress to offer her love. But aside from these moments and her intermittent identification with evil, Célestine portrays herself as engaged in an affirmative existential quest. She pursues the positive image of what she could have been, an innocent girl open to Nature and poetic inspiration, kind of heart despite the corruption of her world. Her frequent moves from one job to another are explained as a search for an identity and an ideal: "j'ai toujours eu la hâte d'être 'ailleurs,' une folie d'espérance dans chimériques ailleurs, que je parais de la poésie vaine, du mirage illusoire des lointains . . . ce que je cherche, je l'ignore . . . et j'ignore aussi qui je suis." In this light, she casts herself as romantic heroine to the very end of the book. Admittedly, she accepts herself as a passive symbol of romantic disillusionment and nostalgia, in sorrow over a decomposing world, who looks forward to the barbarian rape of her society—"Avec quelle hâte j'attends Joseph!" —but still, in her romance, she remains to the last an unintegrated element of society, greater in spirit than the role she plays, and it is through her that a new society will be formed.

One can easily exaggerate the tone here, but clearly Mirbeau's satire plays off a similar model. Mirbeau is not Flaubert, and his novel does not dissolve into infinitesimal ironies of meaning. He is much more a journalist, and his text realizes, instead, two complete interpretative schemes, both of which are accessible to the reader. In fact, the novel has to be read in two ways. On the one hand, the text can be seen as dominated by structural closure, by a satirical and parodic tone, by a static main character, by its ideological inspiration as a *roman à antithèse*. In this light, the satirist's smile lies close to the surface of Célestine's prose; neither she nor her society are capable of redemption.

To reverse this reading is as simple as reading the fable of *The Grasshopper and the Ant* with sympathy for the grasshopper. A standard and not incorrect interpretation of the novel portrays it as a "cri d'angoisse et de douleur pour les victimes de la société," in which Célestine plays a heroic role as the author's *porte-parole*. *Le Journal d'une femme de chambre* would seem to recount, then, the desperate and foredoomed struggles of a working-class heroine toward self-realization; despite the oppressive nature of her society, she passes through a world of darkness to emerge partially in the light. The text marries a formal openness to a prophetic tone, latent social optimism, and mythical resonance.

In either of these versions, there is no doubt that Célestine is a victim; the question remains whether she transcends her condition, even in part, and if not, whether she shares society's guilt. Recourse to information about Mirbeau's Dreyfusard and anarchist position in the nineties would serve to separate the author from his main character to some degree, since Célestine half-heartedly shares Joseph's political prejudices, and thus to confirm a belittling view of her as a revolutionary *manqué*, but it would not eliminate the presence of an alternative and prior system of interpretation within the body of the text. To understand both that Célestine's posture and rhetoric comport elements of excess and inappropriateness that devalorize them and that they are markedly conventional to begin with, the reader must be aware at some level of the models and sub-texts inscribed within *Le Journal.* Mirbeau's novel elaborates elements of the quest romance, the epic, the picaresque tale, the detective story, the *Bildungsroman,* the naturalist novel, and the decadent *conte cruel* (all of which might be said to share common factors, to be sure). On the most basic level, Célestine's diary recreates the myth of a sun hero, who returns to life after a sojourn in the land of death: "Ce ne sont plus les paysages désolés d'Audierne, la tristesse infinie de ses côtes, la magnifique horreur de ses grèves qui hurlent à la mort. Ici, rien n'est triste; au contraire, tout porte à la gaieté. . . . C'est le bruit joyeux d'une ville militaire, le mouvement pittoresque, l'activité bigarée d'un port de guerre. L'amour y roule sa bosse. . . ." But that myth has been recast in an decadent mold: at Cherbourg Célestine is as much a prisoner as ever and as blind as ever. Or, at the least, these are the possible frameworks within which one can read the text, and to be aware of the full depth of an ironic, negative reading one has first to realize the text on a naively uncritical and sentimental level.

Parody, like irony, is a game of absence and presence. To create a parody of a specific text, I am obliged to recreate the elements that marked it as a recognizable sense-producing system. To make that parody accessible as parody, I have to negate the system of the original text and reverse its individual elements. In my parody, the reconstituted text functions as affirmation and negation; in its own repetition, it speaks against itself. It functions both as container and contained, figure and ground, and it produces meaning in the fullfillment of expectations and the reversal of expectations.

Models of interpretation and master-slave power relations are intimately bound together in Mirbeau's novel, as we have seen above. If the epic and romance forms behind *Le Journal d'une femme de chambre* may be heuristically subsumed under the heading of the quest for meaning and identity, then Célestine's story can be seen as the parodic revision of that quest, as an epic form in a fallen world, in which no self-creation or coherence is possible. The detective form, itself a derivation from romance, may be used as an example as it functions in the text. In a number of Célestine's anecdotes, she confronts enigmatic behavior on the part of her employers. In her first story, the entire household shows a peculiar interest in her footwear; in another, the mistress seems strangely concerned with Célestine's figure, her personal hygiene and the condition of her underclothes. In both cases, Célestine is puzzled and intrigued, and only gradually does she fit the clues together. "Je ne saisissais pas le lien qu'il y avait entre mon service et la forme de mon corps . . . je me demandais si Madame n'était point un peu loufoque, ou si elle n'avait point des passions contre nature." The reader makes much more rapid progress in discovering what particular humiliation awaits Célestine; he or she experiences a mildly delicious thrill of sadistic anticipation or masochism, depending on the nature of his or her investment in the character. On occasion, the reader may be surprised, but the clues hold together nonetheless; the picture is all of a piece. On a larger scale, however, the model breaks down. We are given a sufficiency of clues in regard to the murder of little Claire—M. Lanlaire serves as a possible suspect as well as Joseph—and the theft of the silver service, but there will be no ultimate revelation, no unmasking of secrets and no resolution of enigma. Célestine simply cannot put the pieces together. She accepts a basic identity as an adjunct to Joseph, but neither she nor the reader will ever know what Joseph really is.

If Célestine cedes political and sexual power to Joseph, there is still one aspect in which she attempts to retain control. Desire, the will to domination, channels itself into her role as author. It is as author that she can be most powerful and take her revenge the most thoroughly:

> Je me souviens de cette aventure comme si elle était d'hier. . . . Bien que les détails en soient un peu lestes et même horribles, je veux la conter . . . mon intention, en écrivant ce journal, est de n'employer aucune réticence, pas plus vis-à-vis de moi-même que vis-à-vis des autres. . . . J'entends y mettre au contraire toute la franchise qui est en moi et toute la brutalité qui est dans la vie. . . .
>
> J'adore servir à table. C'est là qu'on surprend ses maîtres dans toute la saleté, dans toute la bassesse de leur nature intime. Prudents, d'abord, et se surveillant l'un l'autre, ils en arrivent, peu à peu, á se révéler, à s'étaler tels qu'ils sont, sans fard et sans voiles oubliant qu'il y a autour d'eux quelqu'un qui rôde et qui écoute et qui note leurs tares, leurs bosses morales, les plaies secrètes de leur existence, tout ce que peut contenir d'infamies et de rêves ignobles le cerveau respectable des honnêtes gens. Ramasser ces aveux, les classer, les étiqueter dans notre mémoire, en attendant de s'en faire une arme terrible, au jour des comptes à rendre, c'est une des grandes et fortes joies de métier, et c'est la revanche la plus précieuse de nos humiliations.

The prevalent experience of Célestine's life in the Lanlaire household is boredom, which both acts as a setting for her naughty tales and concentrates her desire to talk and to write. Because all the days, all the tasks and all the faces have the same shapeless aspect, the stories she writes down serve to emphasize difference and to give form to her existence. In writing she attains the grammatical status of subject. To the degree that recounting her past gives it shape, Célestine's life begins to have a sense for her. To the degree that she can cast Joseph as a robber-hero of romance, she can deal with his mystery.

Each of Célestine's stories is coherent, complete and closed. Each is told in a tightly controlled and self-conscious style, which may vary with the nature of the anecdote: the simple, poignant story of the gardener is told "sous forme de récit impersonnel"; the lilial and neurasthenic mode of a decadent dinner party is reproduced in Célestine's own discourse: "un frémissement courut autour de la table, et les fleurs elle-mêmes, et les bijoux sur les chairs, et les cristaux sur la nappe, prirent des attitudes en harmonie avec l'état des âmes." However, this demonstration of authorial control, with the fact that Célestine usually has the last word, is all there is to her stories that constitutes a victory. Célestine's eventual rise in society is otherwise not foretold in her stories; in general, they recount moments of defeat and relapse. Her exercises in literary control, in subject status and in revenge are exercises in masochism as well. Within the story of her present progress, the episodic flashback of anecdotes outlines a series of symbolic falls, symbolic deaths. Prospectively, from the moment her desire transforms Joseph into a hero and she accepts a subordinate role as object, she begins to rise, and when she is finally enthroned at Cherbourg, her good health is no longer in question.

In the measure that Célestine imitates the gestures of the romantic hero she meets defeat. She gives way to the *fatalité* she feels hanging over her and to the sweep of greater forces: "ce qui devait arriver, arriva . . . et la vie me reprit." As a whole, the text gives evidence of a basic psychological conservatism. It effects a symmetrical return to equilibrium and to established hierarchical power patterns; it submerges anarchism under paternalistic power. It undercuts Célestine's role as formgiver and delegates authority to the Other. Célestine's individual stories created sense in the manipulation of symmetrical patterns, too, but they opened onto a psychological anarchism oriented toward defeat, masochism and death. They were keyed to the terms of sexuality and desire, which function in this text as disruption of given power patterns. The characters in her stories, Célestine says, only have life for her in their vices: "Enlevez-leur les vices qui les soutiennent comme les bandelettes soutiennent les momies . . . et ce ne sont même plus des fantômes, ce n'est plus que de la poussière, de la cendre . . . de la mort." Like the "bandages hypogastriques" that hold together Madame's corrupt flesh, vice—as a form of desire—is but a mask for interior rot and death, and life is synonymous with stagnation. Desire, seen as progression and intentional structure, is a movement toward death; life, as the distortion of desire, is the degradation of progression. The desire to control, in Célestine, to speak and to follow a sentence through to its end, masks an underlying impulse toward the explosion of form and control, but life, as she experiences it, means submission to an exterior force that diverts desire and denies ending.

Joseph Halpern, "Desire and Mask in 'Le journal d'une femme de chambre'," in Kentucky Romance Quarterly, *Vol. 27, No. 3, 1980, pp. 313-26.*

Aleksandra Gruzińska   (essay date 1982)

[*In the following essay, Gruzińska discusses the relationship between structure and subject matter in* Le jardin des supplices.]

Representative in style and in subject matter of the Literature of Decadence of the French *fin-de-siècle, Le Jardin des supplices* (1898) remains among Mirbeau's enduring novels. In spite of the suggestive title, its history appears less stormy and free of the notoriety that surrounded the publication of such works as *Le Calvaire* (1887), *La 628-E-8* (1907), or *Le Foyer* (1909). The book leaves the reader with a lasting impression. For many however, this impression may be negative, because the novel's subject and structure, and its seeming lack of unity raise many questions. Our attempt is to answer these questions by pointing out the complex relationship between structure and subject matter and by showing how the Frontispiece affects this relationship.

Among the first to point to the novel's loose construction was Marcel Revon, according to whom the book announces other novels by the author, "faits de pièces et de morceaux." His remark suggests indirectly that with *Le Jardin des supplices,* Mirbeau departs from a solidly constructed novel in order to adopt a different format. Yet, Revon fails to see that the "bits" and "pieces" which enter into its composition, in spite of their heteroclitic nature, ultimately mold the novel into a homogenous work of art.

The division of the novel into three extremely uneven parts, the various settings and historical background, the presence of two narrators (one of whom is probably the author and who is totally eclipsed by two major parts of the novel) and the variety of color and tone—all these factors create the impression of a loosely-constructed novel. Other elements, however, give support to the contrary. For instance, the universal presence of crime dominates the entire book: intellectual crime in the Frontispiece, social and political crime in Part I, the art of physical torture in Part II. The presence of the anonymous narrator also contributes to the unity of the novel, as does the metaphor announced by the title which is amply illustrated from cover to cover. The Frontispiece, on the other hand, in spite of its frontal position, serves not only as an introduction but, what is more important and often forgotten, it serves as the novel's conclusion as well. In this two-fold role, the Frontispiece plays an essential part in the structure and unity of the book.

The association of the garden with torture which is implied by the title and so vividly developed in Part II of the book, echoes throughout Mirbeau's private life, his novel and also his fictional universe. In his *Journal,* Edmond de Goncourt devoted an admirable page to the novelist's beautiful garden at Triel sur Seine. In letters to his friends, Mirbeau reveals himself an expert gardener who loved exotic flowers. He makes no reference to a garden in his first novel, *Le Calvaire,* however, the title brings to mind the garden setting of the Mount of Olives where Christ knew moments of profound anguish, and was soon followed by his crucifixion. Although the novelist never executed the project, he apparently had considered writing a sequel symbolically entitled "Resurrection", suggestive of an optimism seldom found in his works. In **"Le Concombre fugitif"**, first published in a newspaper, was later included

in the posthumous edition of **La Vache tachetée** (Paris: Flammarion, 1918), "Le père Hortus" speaks of difficulties he experiences in raising a rather common and popular vegetable. His rebellious cucumbers, endowed with human-like curiosity, play tricks on him by disappearing from the garden, in spite of the tall hedge that surrounds it. The cucumbers escape, according to the gardener, because they long for independence and freedom.

In *Sébastien Roch* (1890), we meet a gardener of a different kind, the priest-educator. The "Lycées" and "collèges" are "des univers en miniature", sample gardens of torture, where sensitive young boys (such as Sébastien, student at the Jesuit school of Saint-François Xavier in the Morbihan) receive their painful initiation into adulthood. This relationship between garden and torture culminates in the metaphorical vision of the world and is seen as "un immense [. . .] un inexorable jardin des supplices." "Inexorable," because there is nowhere to escape from it.

Mirbeau's translators sometimes introduce an element of nationality into the Mirbelian garden, situating it in China. Under the influence of the brothers Goncourt, the late nineteenth century had experienced a renewed interest in the Orient. Therefore, **A Chinese Torture Garden** would have only enjoyed a greater popularity as a book, had the author taken advantage of such a title. Aside from geographical precision, the translated title evokes exotic qualities; it brings to mind an ancient civilization; it awakens our curiosity to the mysteries associated with it. The French title, on the other hand, in its utmost simplicity draws attention to an image, a garden, and an experience of torture. Without making allusion to national boundaries, it maintains a geographical spaciousness and freedom, which probably was intentional. The French title is in harmony with the entire book, not only with Part II of the novel where the action takes place in China. Indeed, the metaphor, suggested by the title, applies to the universe and to the book as a whole. What is more, the desire to transpose the experience of one individual into a universal experience is not only in harmony with a tradition common in French letters, it is also characteristic of pointing to the book's homogeneity. The geographical spaciousness is closely related to the "anonymity" which surrounds the characters and which allows every reader to assume, in his turn, the characters' roles.

No doubt a novel divided into three such extremely uneven parts invites criticism. The first and the shortest of the three, the Frontispiece, raises many questions. Does it contribute an important dimension to the book or is it nothing more than a mere introduction by the author which we may discard if we so choose without altering the essence of the book? Or to the contrary, if for inexplicable reasons, the author had omitted it, would the meaning and the structure of the novel have become distorted? If the latter is true, of what artistic value would the reader be deprived?

The Frontispiece contains information which is not available anywhere else in the book and is closely related to what follows. Here the author describes a Parisian literary salon where outstanding scientists and men of letters discuss various aspects of crime. When their interest turns to women, we are not surprised to see this predominantly elitist group attribute crime to them: "Mais les crimes les plus atroces sont presque toujours l'oeuvre de la femme . . . On y retrouve, à leur caractère de férocité, d'implacabilité, sa présence morale, sa pensée, son sexe." To illustrate that "La femme a en elle une force cosmique d'élément, une force invincible de destruction, comme la nature," one of the participants proposes to share with those assembled in the "salon" a personal adventure of his own. Part I and II represent an account of this experience. However, before the Frontispiece comes to an end, the author relinquishes his role as narrator, assumes the pose of cynical listener, and seems to disappear from sight.

The setting, the tone and the mood of the novel change as we leave the *fin-de-siècle* atmosphere to enter the more naturalistic setting of Part I. Here the new narrator recalls his childhood and early adult life and provides us with his family background. His recollections go back to the French Revolution when his ancestors practiced the art of "doing others in," ("l'art de mettre les gens dedans.") Years later, the narrator himself enters the political arena of the Third Republic, shares in its corruption until it becomes expedient to vanish from public view. A former fellow student who has become an important minister in the government, rescues him from a difficult situation by suggesting a brief exile by means of a diplomatic mission to the East—an offer the narrator accepts. On a ship bound for Ceylon, he meets Clara, an eccentric English woman to whom he feels strongly attracted and who persuades him to abandon his mission:

> In Canton I own a palace amid marvelous gardens, where everything is conducive to a free life, and to love. What are you afraid of? What are you leaving behind? Who cares about you! When you don't love me any more, or when you are too unhappy [. . .] you'll go away!

Love and freedom so temptingly offered prove not only irresistible but illusory, as the protagonist later discovers. At first, the peaceful and happy ocean trip gives the voyagers a feeling of rebirth. In this small group of travelers isolated in mid-ocean, the passengers begin to seek greater pleasure in images of violence, cannibalism, exotic firearms. They dream of perfecting the latter and of increasing their power to kill; their sophistication consists ultimately in being able not only to annihilate men but also to eliminate even the traces of their victims:

> I have invented a bullet, [boasts one of the passengers]. I call it the Dum-Dum [. . .] You'd say it was the name of a fairy in one of Shakespeare's comedies. The fairy Dum-Dum! It enchants me. A laughing, light and quite blond fairy, hopping, dancing and bounding about amid the heather and the sunbeams [. . .] I sometimes wonder if it's not a tale out of Edgar Allan Poe or a dream of our Thomas de Quincey. But no, since I myself tested that admirable little Dum-Dum [. . .] The bullet had gone through [. . .] twelve bodies which, after the shot, were only twelve heaps of mangled flesh [. . .].

The superb seascape of blue skies and shimmering waters provides only a passing escape from the torture perpetrated here in the cannibalistic fantasies of the voyagers. The protagonist occasionally utters a weak protest of indignation but he remains, on the whole, a passive spectator and witness. This is not surprising. In fact, in the Frontispiece he had chosen to read from a prepared manuscript rather than to narrate his story, which indicates the hero's passivity. Furthermore, the act of reading betrays a greater complicity between narrator and reader and reminds us of Baudelaire's "hypocrite lecteur, mon semblable, mon frère." Moreover, because the narrator has chosen to remain anonymous, every reader, in his turn, assumes the role of protagonist and also remains anonymous. Everyone who opens the book participates in the personal adventure of the anonymous hero whose experience becomes a universal one.

Mini-flashes fill a two-year gap that separates Part II from Part I. During these two years, the narrator has discovered love, yet another instrument of torture, from which he has vainly tried to extricate himself. Although Clara had said, "when you don't love me any more, or when you are unhappy [. . .] you'll go away," to allow her lover to be free, the offer proves unworkable. The hero is never free of his love from Clara. Yet, loving Clara as he does, he is nonetheless very unhappy in her company, and infinitely more so away from her. This explains why, after a short separation, he returns and, unsuspectingly, submits to the ultimate torture. In Part II, the final and by far the longest segment of the novel, the anonymous narrator and Clara go to see a magnificent museum known for its artistic means of torture.

The action in the Frontispiece and Part I encompasses a series of events which move at a relatively brisk pace between 1789 and 1890. In Part II we suddenly come to a standstill as we live through what seems an endless visit to the torture garden. We are in China, yet the geographical location of the garden remains rather vague, perhaps intentionally so. In this garden maintained by the government, we find tortures lavishly displayed amid the most exotic and brilliant flora. Clara pays little attention to the natural beauty of the exotic vegetation while the narrator finds in it moments of relaxation and sometimes sheer delight. Once more we are immersed in a Baudelairian atmosphere of *Les fleurs du mal* with its two-fold meaning of evil and suffering, "ou les parfums, les couleurs et les sons se répondent." This brilliant floral spectacle serves to disguise and to increase simultaneously bodily torture and mental distress.

The endless spectacle which takes place every Wednesday lasts only a few hours. At its conclusion, Clara and her companion leave the garden. Except for the fact that Clara frequently returns to the museum, the novel offers no other information. However, since the events of Part II precede those of the Frontispiece, a re-reading of the latter becomes essential. The introduction, where we encounter the anonymous narrator for the first time, must now be examined in the role as the conclusion of the novel.

A writer who chooses to call "frontispiece" that which appears to be his prefatory remarks and prefers the word to more common headings such as "preface" or "introduction," betrays premeditation, intent and purpose. The italicized text and the pages numbered with Roman numerals used in the Frontispiece represent the standard practice in introductions. They separate typographically, so to speak, the introduction from the main body of the novel. Mirbeau goes one step further by dividing the book into two major time segments; the past (Part I and II) and the present. Indeed, the relatively recent events described in the Frontispiece unfold in a few hours time; what follows it represents a long flashback. At the end of the novel, when the reader re-reads the opening pages of the Frontispiece, the latter acquires a new dimension.

On the other hand, we may choose not to consider the Frontispiece an introduction but a part of an architectural construction, a "façade principale d'un grand édifice" (*Le Petit Robert*). Literature offers well-known works where an author uses architecture to introduce the reader to the emotional world of his novel. In Zola's *L'Assommoir* (1877) Gervaise's first contact with the house in the "rue de la Goutte d'Or," where she will eventually die, foreshadows her death. In describing the external structure of the "Pension Vauquer," Balzac introduces moral elements which he later amplifies in *Le Père Goriot*. As for Mirbeau, the reader who, unsuspectingly, opens his book, symbolically opens the door to the garden of tortures long before Clara and the anonymous narrator take him there. And what a garden the Chinese museum is in Part II, when the reader finally enters it, women rush in, fascinated, eager to share in the spectacle of torture. In the Frontispiece the exclusively male public is no less fascinated by crime. The Parisian "salon" and the Chinese museum differ in atmosphere, as well as in the practice of torture depending upon the participants. The exotic vegetation of the garden in China conceals and intensifies the agony inflicted upon body and mind. Nature and the instruments of torture remain conspicuously absent in the Parisian "salon", where the art of inflicting pain has reached the sophistication and refinement of a more decadent society, foreseen by the Chinese artists-tormentors: "We have been conquered by mediocrity," said one of them, "and the bourgeois spirit is triumphing everywhere. . . ."

Since the novel is "open-ended", it provides no further information about the protagonists once they leave the garden. However, in *Les Perles mortes* (*Le Journal*, Août 5, 1899), we see Clara Terpe returning to her native England, stricken with elephantiasis and her beautiful body distorted by swelling and pain. The disease which afflicts her body knows no geographical boundaries; no garden walls can immunize one against the intense suffering it brings. Clara Terpe's fate is identical to that of her beautiful friend Annie, who in *Le Jardin des supplices* frequently visited the garden of tortures. Stricken with elephantiasis, Annie developed a passion for pearls, then took her life. Clara Terpe experiences the same symptoms. Her physical pain turns into moral anguish as she watches the pearls decompose mysteriously on contact with her own decaying flesh.

In withholding from the readers of *Le Jardin des supplices* the information which he later included in the short story, Mirbeau endowed Clara with mysterious and mythical qualities. As beautiful as Eve, as evil as Lilith, this modern Ariadne guides her lover (and the reader) through an earthly maze of tortures. She is "La Femme" in whom the potential for good exists, though Clara herself finds pleasure in seeing others suffer:

> Et puisqu'il y a des supplices partout où il y a des hommes [. . .] je tâche de m'en accommoder et de m'en rejouir [. . .]

explained Clara at the time she initiated her lover into the art of torture.

As for the narrator, after the memorable visit to the garden we meet him in the Parisian literary "salon" described earlier by the author in the Frontispiece. Like Hortus' cucumbers, which sought freedom in the world outside the garden and discovered pitfalls everywhere, the narrator escaped from the unbearable atmosphere of the Chinese torture garden and from Clara's embrace only to find another impasse in Paris. Free from Clara and from physical pain, he seems, nevertheless, an anguished man. In observing the distinguished Europeans who surround him, we notice their resemblance to the Chinese tormentors. In the safety of the literary "salon" protected by walls like those of a garden, the prominent Europeans let their imagination freely explore crime. Indeed, the narrator cannot run away from torment or from anguish, because the entire universe is seen by Mirbeau as an "immense, inexorable torture garden," timeless and spaceless, yet always situated in time and space (China, Europe), always "en situation", as in Sartre's *No Exit*. Still, the splendorous nature of the Chinese torture garden afforded some consolation for the absence of natural beauty and color in Paris. The narrator soon finds a way to escape from Paris by taking his listeners and readers to a world of tortures, describing its natural beauty with such vividness that we have the illusion of being there.

The Frontispiece leads us to conclude that the practice of "decapitation, strangulation, flaying and tearing of flesh . . . ," witnessed in the archetypal Chinese museum, still goes on in the West. While the skillful Chinese tormentors mutilated the human body with primitive instruments, the distinguished Europeans practice the art of "doing others in." Their crimes remain undetected, and the criminal free from punishment. One guest, in describing his own father, the "docteur Trépan," says:

> Vous savez qu'il n'y a pas d'homme plus sociable, plus charmant que lui. Il n'y en a pas, non plus, dont la profession ait fait un assassin plus délibéré.

Someone else boasts of killing a man "d'une congestion cérébrale." No violence, no instruments of torture, nothing but a threat to strangle, followed by extreme shock, is needed to kill the victim. In short, Mirbeau's novel is a sampling of torture gardens: A Chinese museum, the French Revolution, the Third Republic with its corruption, an ocean voyage, a Parisian literary gathering. The contributions of the 20th century reaffirm the latter's solidarity with the past, giving the Mirbelian metaphor—the world seen as a vast garden of torture—its universal and timeless dimension. Like a frame around its picture, the

Frontispiece encloses the novel and reminds us at the end that Mirbeau's world affords no salvation nor resurrection.

Dedicated to men at large, the novel offers fleeting sadistic pleasures, murder and blood, coated with irony, artifact and art. In a world where torture is perpetrated by means such as education, justice, government, politics, business and love, the anonymous narrator remains the tormentor and the victim.

> My name matters little; it is the name of a man who has caused great suffering to others as well as to himself—even more to himself than to others. . . .

We enter into and we exit from the world of *Le Jardin des supplices* through the Frontispiece. Like a revolving door, it always leads us back to the museum where the art of gardening and the art of inflicting pain and moral anguish find a "harmonious" co-existence in the most exotic, paradise-like setting "où la torture se multiplie [. . .] de tout le resplendissemont qui l'environne." The Frontispiece occupies a privileged position; it is the essential key to Mirbeau's novel as art form; it serves to open and provisionally to close the open-ended novel; it gives the book a circular structure and the action a cyclic quality. Every time a reader opens the book, he re-enacts the ritual of the visit to the garden of tortures. Furthermore, every part of the novel contributes to illustrate the metaphor announced in the title. Without the Frontispiece all of these elements— the circular structure, the cyclic aspect of the action, the metaphorical dimension of the novel—are lost.

Aleksandra Gruzińska, "Structure in Octave Mirbeau's 'Le jardin des supplices'," in Zagadnienia Rodzajów Literackich, *Vol. XXV, No. 2, 1982, pp. 65-73.*

Robert E. Ziegler (essay date 1984)

[*In the following essay on* Le jardin des supplices, *Ziegler discusses the theme of the pursuit of non-reflective experience, or experience that is "not contaminated by thought or processed by interpretation."*]

Like an indictment containing a list of counts against an accused, Mirbeau's *Le Jardin des supplices* opens with a prosecutorial cataloging of every fault of the "fin-de-siècle" era in France. Targeted for criticism is each institution, each activity, which has the effect of stunting the blossoming of art and of thwarting the expression of intellectual energy. Commerce, having degenerated to the level of the corrupt trafficking of Huysmans' hated green grocers, becomes a kind of legal, doubly profitable theft, involving the misappropriation of goods from one party and their resale to another at inflated prices. Education is reduced to being a system which rewards young people for their sententiousness and fatuity, promoting the advancement of those bureaucrats most gifted at organizing others for the purpose of exploiting them. Those who rise the furthest in this system are like the peacocks described later in the novel: the ornamental parasites whose showiness enables them to live off social institutions already verging on collapse. Unscrupulous and glib, these men and women

articulate the ideology that both justifies the way they abuse others and condemns society to decay. Their language is the language of oppressors: "plenière, . . . gestuelle, théâtrale: c'est le Mythe," Barthes says [in *Mythologies*].

Foremost among this group is Eugène Mortain. Colleague and protector of the unnamed narrator, Mortain embodies the cynicism and opportunism which the Decadents saw as contributing to the decline of the West. Through his appeal to the interests of big business and the banks, and by his intimidation and extortion of support from figures of influence, Mortain is able to cling to his office. But the position he holds is dependent on the vagaries of public mood and political expediency, and without any moral or ideological underpinnings, the power he wields intends nothing more than its own continued exercise. Mortain knows that only a combination of ruthlessness and luck determines what position he will occupy next: the presidency of the Council or a cell in Mazas prison.

Science is similarly discredited, as the government-sponsored exile the narrator is sent away on takes the form of a fraudulent expedition to Ceylon in search of the "pelagic ooze," a fantastic research project providing an unworthy man with a sinecure of the kind the state habitually underwrites. Not surprisingly, the narrator is all too happy to accede to Mortain's suggestion that he leave the country: "Qu'est-ce que je risque? . . . La science n'en mourra pas . . . elle en a vu d'autres, la science!. . . ."

An examination of the first part of the novel shows the narrator leaving Europe to escape a civilization steeped in death and decay, a civilization originally founded on the principle of the repression of instincts and now devoted to their covert gratification. Further, his departure reflects a wish to reject a set of mythical, consensual values clearly shown to be invalid by the corruptness of its spokesmen. The France the narrator abandons is a country presided over by the likes of Mortain and the aging "entremetteuse" Madame G, in whose salon lesbian princesses flirt behind drawing room doors with Roumanian countesses, and sordid political and personal intrigues are discussed by all in the hope of some small self-advancement. The picture Mirbeau gives is one of a nation in a state of opulent morbidity, a society whose obsolete institutions were undergoing a final phase of vitiation before ending in extinction. As Jean Pierrot maintains, the belief in the imminent ruination of society was a conviction common to many of the Decadents, who associated it with the idea of "la dégénérescence de la race":

> Avant même que le journaliste allemand Max Nordau ne publie son énorme livre sur ce thème . . . , l'idée d'une dégradation générale des races européennes est largement répandue. . . . Les peuples européens, héritiers d'une longue évolution, seraient menacés par une décrépitude inévitable, et leur civilisation serait vouée à une mort prochaine, sous l'assaut de peuples demeurés dans un état plus proche de la nature. . . . [Jean Pierrot in *L'Imaginaire décadent (1880-1990)*]

Beginning with the voyage on the "Saghalien," the narrator's itinerary from Europe to the Orient traces his movement from the threat of decay to the promise of renewed vitality. Thus his journey reflects the Decadents' attraction to an experience of nature redeemed by the artifice they both depended on and realized to be the cause of the downfall of the culture they so despised. From this point on the story's structure follows a series of passages and crossings, over bridges, in steamers and sampans, as the narrator, together with his mistress Clara, realizes that to escape the corruption of the West, they must never stop moving, never pause too long lest they glimpse the germ of that corruption they carry within themselves: "[N]os deux âmes confondues ne songeaient . . . qu'à l'éternité du voyage, comme si le navire qui nous emportait dût nous emporter ainsi, toujours . . . et jamais . . . n'arriver quelque part. . . . Car arriver quelque part, c'est mourir!. . . ."

In a sense, the journey to the East betokened for the Decadents a wish to return to a primordial beginning, to step out of time—time which marked off the trajectory of the life of men and societies. For the Decadents this trajectory began and progressed through a stage of youthful vigor and then declined into one of ugliness and atrophy. Coupled with their fascination with and fear of the vitality of the barbarian races which threatened to overrun Europe, the Decadents saw in the Orient a place that was not so much filled with a crude, unchanneled energy as it was characterized by an ancientness that situated it outside of history altogether. It is appropriate in a psychoanalytic sense that Clara's garden be located in such a place, where all instinctive impulses could be expressed with impunity, in a place where, as "repression generates historical time . . . , unrepressed life would be timeless or in eternity" [Norman O. Brown, *Life Against Death: The Psychoanalytic Meaning of History*].

Yet in fleeing history, Clara and the narrator are also rejecting a society that thrusts upon them unquestioned assumptions, that perpetuates a particular and conventionalized world view. Members of a civilization that Barthes would say "fait passer le réel à l'état de parole," and that replaces experience with meaning, they seek to destroy its myths. Clara particularly claims to want to live in nature, rather than accept an ideology that is naturalized. Aware of the tendentiousness and superficiality of society's words and concepts, she no longer is satisfied being told the significance of things, but seeks instead to know the things themselves.

Most clearly, the flight from Europe represents a repudiation of a way of life based on institutionalized hypocrisy. There the superficial respect for honesty is belied by the business success of the narrator's father, whose ethic is to cheat his customers, to "mettre les gens dedans," as well as by the narrator's defeat in a legislative election by an opponent whose way of endearing himself to the electorate was to appear in the streets and public squares, proclaiming: "J'ai volé . . . j'ai volé. . . ." When a man who proudly admits his criminality is welcomed into the people's hearts, having provided them with a legitimation of their own immorality, when a transmutation of values takes place such that defects are turned into qualities and

wrongs into rights, it is easy to understand the accession to power of a man like Eugène Mortain. Yet even in his case the outward image remains important, since civilization's mechanism of repression continues to operate in the society of the Decadents too. First, the duality of their public and private selves is internalized in the respective functions of the actor and censor. Then, as the judgmental role of conscience becomes less pronounced in an age of widespread selfishness and cynicism, the self is divided simply into actor and observer. "Acteur et spectateur de lui-même et des autres, il n'est jamais acteur seulement," writes Maupassant of the Decadent figure. "Tout, autour de lui, devient de verre, les coeurs, les actes, les intentions secrètes, et il souffre d'un mal étrange, d'une sorte de dédoublement de l'esprit, qui fait de lui un être effroyablement vibrant, machiné, compliqué et fatigant pour lui-même."

What Clara in effect proposes to the narrator is that he pursue experience that is non-reflective, not contaminated by thought or processed by interpretation. She recommends that he throw off the repressive, inhibiting vestiges of his European upbringing, which evaluate experiences and refuse those judged to be too dangerous or abnormal. In so doing, she encourages him to cease being a spectator in order to free in him the actor that is hungry for new sensations.

> C'est cette contradiction permanente entre vos idées, vos désirs et toutes les formes mortes, tous les vains simulacres de votre civilisation, qui vous rend tristes, troublés, déséquilibrés . . . Dans ce conflit intolérable, vous perdez toute joie de vivre, toute sensation de personnalité . . . parce que, à chaque minute, on comprime, on empêche, on arrête le libre jeu de vos forces . . . Voilà la plaie empoisonnée, mortelle, du monde civilisé. . . .

Yet what Clara seems to set as her own goal is something more: the murder of the spectator or the consciousness of self, which would allow the automatic satisfaction of all instincts and the return to a perfect equilibrium between tension and release, hunger and satiation. More than the lifting of repression, Clara's philosophy proposes reverting to a state, in the garden of torture or of love, in which repression had never taken place at all. But rather than allowing her to achieve this balance, Clara's arrival at this state merely brings about an externalization of aggression, based on a desire to witness the pain and death of others, and not a deliverance from self-awareness and a fulfillment of her own desires.

The exploration of the issue of sadism and violence at its most extreme is clearly what gave Mirbeau's novel its notoriety and earned it the reputation as a kind of lurid and grisly "fin-de-siècle" masterpiece. In the "Frontispiece," during an after-dinner philosophic discussion among an all-male group of participants, the question of murder is broached by various parties, each of whom offers a theory on the psychology of aggression. A Darwinian scientist professes to see in murder the pretext for the founding of civilization, whose primary function is to check the spread of anarchy and bloodshed. According to him, the benefit of the socialization of the would-be assassin is that his homicidal tendencies can be redirected toward more positive or constructive ends: "l'industrie, le commerce colonial, l'antisémitisme." Next, a professor at the Sorbonne, pointing out how man's innate bloodthirstiness can be observed in the behavior of peasants at country fair shooting galleries, accuses the hypocrisy and inconsistency of a society that, in the name of patriotism, schools its citizens in an impersonal form of murderousness and hate, and then punishes them when they exterminate another individual for reasons of jealousy, resentment or personal pleasure. It is only later that the man to be revealed as the narrator injects himself into the discussion, insisting on the parallel between the sexual impulse and the impulse toward aggression: "C'est que les grands assassins ont toujours été des amoureux terribles . . . Leur puissance génésique correspond à leur puissance criminelle . . . Ils aiment comme ils tuent! . . . Le meurtre naît de l'amour et l'amour atteint son maximum d'intensité par le meurtre. . . ." Clearly, the fact that the narrator imputes the blame for all of mankind's crimes to "Woman," whom he describes as "une force invincible de la destruction comme la nature," reveals less about his theories on the general nature of violence than it does about his own personal susceptibility to Clara's charms and perverse teachings.

To follow the narrator, then, in interpreting his relationship with Clara abstractly, as a clash between the intellect of the male and the life of the instincts embodied by the female, would be to ignore the weaknesses of his character that eventually lead him to his downfall. If, as Praz says [in his *The Romantic Agony*], Clara is an embodiment of "the hysterical woman of exasperated desire, in whose hands man becomes a submissive instrument," the narrator is made to seem passive because not only Clara, but seemingly everyone, both man and woman alike, succeeds in dominating him. Without the ambition of Eugène Mortain or the raw instinctual energy of Clara, the narrator can enjoy, in his words, only the crumbs which others leave him. The traces of his civilizing conscience, rather than enabling him to discriminate between right and wrong, simply frighten him away from experiences that might prove too threatening or intense. The psychic life of the narrator is therefore characterized by a series of attractions and repulsions. Unable to generate by himself the experiences which might provide him with the physical or emotional shocks he desires, he alternately approaches and then withdraws from those people whose unrepressed behavior both seduces and alarms him. Thus he oscillates between hatred and admiration for Eugène Mortain; he departs from Paris for the East and returns to Paris at the end; he refuses and then accedes to Clara's appeal to accompany her to China, and flees his horrible captivation with Clara's garden for the wilds of Annam before going back to visit the prison-charnel house at her side.

In the division and apportionment of the self between actor and spectator, the narrator is able to function only in the latter capacity. "[P]ersonage-conscience, à la fois intelligent et inhibé, indépendant et impuissant," he is paralysed and helpless to initiate experience. Thus Clara assumes the dominant role in their relationship and then derides him for his weakness, calling him "mon bébé" and

"petite femme de rien du tout": "Non . . . non . . . insista Clara. . . . Tu n'es pas un homme. . . . Tu nous gâtais tout notre plaisir avec tes évanouissements de petite pensionnaire et de femme enceinte. . . ." Torn between his need for stimulation and a fear of the consequences of his actions, the narrator carries on an existence devoid of dynamism. A prisoner of his own timidity and ambivalence, he does not develop or grow, but simply moves back and forth between the two poles of his appetite for experience and his limited tolerance for newness, violence and change. His journey to the Orient does not have the effect of liberating his instincts and releasing him in eternity, but shows him still incapable of going beyond the conflicting pull of his morbid curiosity and fear.

Unlike the narrator, Clara longs totally to escape the repressive strictures of Western culture, to live where life is not a denial, but an affirmation of even the most destructive impulses. The Orient for her is a place where there is no more crippling sense of guilt, "[p]as d'autres limites à la liberté que soi-même . . . à l'amour que la variété triomphante de son désir." Clara's wish to reenter an earthly paradise means withdrawing to her garden, in which the free play of animal instincts is no longer inhibited by a knowledge of good and evil. And the method by which she hopes this knowledge can be erased and conscience silenced is to immerse herself in a flow of experiences that is so fast that it induces a kind of permanent "dépaysement moral." Thus Clara is forever hurrying her lover along, through the fetid, cavernous corridors of cells housing the starving inmates of the bagnio, up into the sunlight of the garden and onward toward the sound of the bell dying in the distance: "Clara, d'une voix douce, m'encourageait: 'Ce n'est rien encore, mon chéri . . . Avançons!. . . .'"

Clara, too, avoids stopping and giving her mind the time to catch up with her in her dizzying pursuit of new horrors. She recognizes that arresting her passage would mean another sort of death for her, would destroy the unity of the self as actor and kill the immediacy of the experience by forcing her to become conscious of it. As she hastens forward, she is not so much hungering for the new as fleeing the experience she has just left behind, fleeing it before the life of the sensation can turn into the deadness of a meaning.

The most explicitly developed theme of Mirbeau's novel, the fecundative power of death, is not in itself a new one, but is dealt with in a new way. As each organism perishes, undergoing decomposition and corruption, it returns to the undifferentiated. Individual living things, in losing their particular form or separateness in death, enrich the totality of life and ensure its immortality. Clara, too, affirms the regenerative property of death, but in a way that perverts the purpose and direction of the natural process. Rather than affirming her individuality first and then acquiescing to her own death as a means of adding to the life of everything else, she insists on subsuming the death of everything else to the expansion of the range of her bizarre experiences. From the singleness of the phenomenon of death which engenders a multiplicity of living forms,

> *Le Jardin des supplices* concludes on a note of pessimistic irony. The narrator, under the pretext of carrying out an important scientific expedition and bearing false credentials as an eminent "embryologist," sets out to find the "Urschleim," to discover in the warm waters off the island of Ceylon the secrets of the origins of life. Yet at the end of the journey which takes him to China and the torture garden, the secret of life is revealed to him in a puddle of blood, as maggots and flies.
>
> *—Robert E. Ziegler*

Clara seeks a multiplicity of deaths to bring about an enlargement of her individual sense of self.

At first, the flow of life by way of death in the prison garden seems to be from the human to the vegetal, from the grotesque and shrunken corpses of the executioner's victims to the strong shoots and buds and flowers of the plants which burst with life and flourish in such abundance there. A kind of agriculture in reverse is at work in the garden so that, instead of the cultivation of plants and cereals to be used for the raising of the livestock needed for the food of men, men are confined and left to wither in sunless cells, are slowly starved or fed with sanious meats so that plants may live and grow to no ostensible human purpose. But to Clara's mind, the end point of this process of organic degradation, from the complex to the simple, from man to flower, is not the creation of some useless floral spectacle. It is a new chance for self-discovery. That is why she experiences the plants not as mere ornamental bouquets, but as organisms to be joined with on a most intimate level, like the thalictrum with its phosphatic odor of semen or the spathaceous plant-carnivores which reek of carrion and thrive on death. Similarly, after one of the garden's executioners has shown the narrator and Clara a ranunculus flower, and has described it as an organ of passion in which twenty males are sometimes needed for the satisfaction of a single female, Clara asks the narrator about this account: "Tout à l'heure, le gros patapouf racontait que, chez les fleurs, ils se mettent quelquefois à vingt mâles pour le spasme d'une seule femelle?. . . C'est vrai, ça?" And when he answers "yes," she muses dreamily, then adds: "Je voudrais être fleur . . . je voudrais être . . . tout!" For Clara, then, death is not the means whereby living things are reproduced; instead, men die to fertilize the flowers in which she can behold a reflection, can experience a reproduction of herself.

However extraordinary are Clara's efforts to live on a purely biological level and thereby realize what she calls the fullness of personality, she remains unable to escape the process of "dédoublement," the resolution of the self into actor and spectator which she is so quick to criticize in the narrator. Not that the sight of men being crucified, disemboweled or flayed alive inspires in her a horror which causes her to dissociate herself from the spectacle; it is simply that the pursuit of these morbid pleasures leads her to objectify herself as a means of enabling her to better measure her own enjoyment. Clara herself never kills or tortures: she enjoys the commission of atrocities by others. And not only is she made a spectator in this sense; she further distances herself from the field of action by appreciating only the effects of the stimulation she receives from watching. Men are not killed to give Clara life, but to enable her to feel herself living more intensely.

Perhaps the figure in Mirbeau's novel that is most emblematic of the problem of consciousness and the duality it is based on is the peacock, a creature that is itself both an object and a reference, a simple organism and something more complex that transcends it. The peacock is an example of man's tendency to take what Barthes has called an empty signifier and fill it with a mythic signification. If, as a mythical object, the peacock exceeds or overruns its status as a signifier, it is because its signification is always one of excess: it is too vain, too gorgeous. In Mirbeau, too, the peacock signifies pure transcendence. It means more than what it is. So one might interpret Clara's adventures in the torture garden as an attempt to return to an instinctual, pre-signifying state, where objects are emptied of their historical, consensus-approved significations, where the peacock is a bird like any other and not a symbol of fatuousness or beauty. What Clara is seeking, beyond the enjoyment of men's deaths, is the destruction of all overlying meanings.

From a somewhat different standpoint [Gaston Bachelard in his *L'Eau et les rêves*] comments on the unusual markings on the peacock's plumage: "L'iris de la plume du paon, cet 'oeil' sans paupière, cet 'oeil permanent' prend soudain une dureté . . . il observe. . . . Le spectateur a alors le sentiment d'être en présence d'une 'volonté directe de beauté." Viewed in this light, the characters fail to show initiative even in their capacity as spectators: instead of seeing, they are seen. As the ornamental eye-pattern on the peacock's feathers commands their reciprocal and admiring regard, beauty is not so much a quality they attribute to the bird, as one imposed on them by way of a fascination over which they have no control. It is possible that their rebellion against the tyranny of meaning is directed secondarily at a situation in which beauty, rather than being in the eye of the beholder, derives from a "will to beauty" residing in the object itself.

This central image first appears when, at one point, on the steamer traveling to Ceylon, the narrator meets a fellow passenger, an empassioned hunter whose favorite game is the peacock. The hunter describes how a peacock will follow a tiger, how when the tiger has finished eating its prey, it relieves itself and the peacock descends to eat the tiger's dung. "C'est à ce moment . . . qu'on doit le surprendre," he says, exclaiming: "les paons . . . monsieur, comment vous dire. . . . c'est magnifique à tuer!" Both the hunter and another man on board, an explorer, regale Clara and the narrator with such tales, discussions of cannibalism and the like, all the while complaining of feeling imprisoned within the stultifying conventions of repressive European culture: "Je me trouve aveuli et prisonnier dans l'Europe, comme une bête dans une cage," says the explorer. "Impossible de faire jouer ses coudes, d'étendre les bras, d'ouvrir la bouche, sans se heurter à des préjugés stupides, à des lois imbéciles . . . à des moeurs iniques. . . ." As the peacock scavenger feeds on what the true predator has left behind, so do meanings fasten themselves to things and spectators gravitate to actions. For man to become himself a predator again, he must release his animal instincts from the cage of repression, must stop sublimating reality into spectacle and concealing objects behind what they signify. In this sense, hunting the peacock becomes an act of demythification; it constitutes an attack on a culture that generates transcendences, locks men inside ready-made meanings and away from things themselves.

Madame G, another embodiment of the superficiality, excess, gaudiness and parasitism of "fin-de-siècle" society which the hunter stalks in hopes of killing, is herself portrayed as a sort of peacock, her wizened person concealed by the resplendence of "fleurs, plumes et dentelles . . . soulevées . . . en vagues multicolores et parfumées. . . ." Like Clara, Madame G reigns over a garden, but too old and "ne pouvant plus cultiver la fleur du vice en son propre jardin," she too is obliged to satisfy herself with the droppings of a once vibrant and vital society, to survive on the lifeless pleasure of inducing vices in others and enjoying them vicariously, as a spectator.

Yet as the novel progresses, it becomes apparent that the move from the salon of Madame G to the gardens of the Orient has, if anything, brought about a lessening, not an increase of freedom. What the explorer on the steamer had referred to as the figurative entrapment of Western man in a cage of senseless laws and social prejudices has become the literal emprisonment in the bagnio of the Poet, a man stripped of his humanity and forced to bark like a dog for scraps of meat from visitors. Through the character of the Poet, who had earlier written of "la pourriture en qui réside la chaleur éternelle de la vie," Mirbeau suggests that an awareness of the fertility of death is not enough to put a man in closer harmony with his animal nature. A celebration in poetry of the death of repression does not have the effect of setting him free, but instead subjects him to systematic brutalization and degradation by his keepers which leaves him fit only to be kept behind bars.

Another ironic reversal seen later in the novel is that the peacock becomes the hunter, not the hunted, that rather than being the target of the sportsman's bullet, it lies in wait itself to seize the kill. As the hunter who stalks its prey sees the peacock non-symbolically, as just another game fowl to be brought down, so the peacock, moving in to glean the shards of human flesh from the instruments of torture, sees men as objects, too, as a meal, not as creators of myths or givers of meanings.

The ultimate impossibility of integrating or unifying the personality is shown in another scene in which the peacocks reappear, as Clara projects onto them the same inevitable tendency to divide into actor and spectator as a means of self-experience. As she is proceeding through the garden, and pausing to marvel at the horror and the beauty she is seeing there, she calls the narrator's attention to the spectacle: "Vois, mon chéri, . . . comme tout cela est curieux et unique. . . . Une salle de torture parée comme pour un bal . . . et cette foule éblouissante de paons, servant d'assistance, de figuration, de populaire, de décor à la fête!. . . ." How better could Clara describe herself than as play, setting and audience, than as the action, its locus and an onlooker all at once? Clara's attraction to promiscuity and death does not intend a breaking of the walls of ego, an obliteration of the self so that she can flow out and become one with other living things. Instead, Clara seeks out the experience of violation so that she can feel people's otherness enter into her, so she can absorb it and make it hers. Thus in the swell of the crowd surging forward toward the prison, the narrator observes: "Clara . . . se jetait au plus fort de la mêlée. Elle subissait le brutal contact et, pour ainsi dire, le viol de cette foule, avec un plaisir passionné. . . . Un moment, elle s'écria, glorieusement: 'Vois, chéri . . . ma robe est toute déchirée. . . . C'est délicieux!' " Even in death, Clara cannot imagine the eclipsing of the consciousness of her body as the medium of pleasure; even then she envisions herself standing apart from her corpse, which continues to register the piquancy of new sensations. "[Q]uand je serai morte," she declares to the narrator, "je voudrais que l'on mît dans mon cercueil des parfums très forts . . . des fleurs de thalictre . . . et des images de péché . . . de belles images, ardentes et nues. . . . Ah! mon chéri . . . je voudrais être morte, déjà!"

So at the end there is no final death for Clara, no definitive loss of self-awareness, only the intimation of an alternation between satiation and new appetites, between remorse and the subsequent rededication to the pleasures of debauchery. At the close of her day in the torture garden, Clara falls into a state of delirium and prostration and has the narrator conduct her to a brothel where, the owner of the sampan tells him, she is in the habit of going to recover from the excesses she subjects herself to on her visits to the prison. There, in her convalescence, she can enjoy the opposite spectacle of her feminine weakness, dependence and contrition, can represent herself, not as the strong and gorgeous and multicolored peacock feasting on the bodies of the dead, but as a little bird symbolizing fragility, purity and helplessness, "toute petite . . . et toute blanche comme ces petites hirondelles des contes chinois. . . ."

In a number of ways Mirbeau's novel concludes on a note of pessimistic irony. The narrator, under the pretext of carrying out an important scientific expedition and bearing false credentials as an eminent "embryologist," sets out to find the "Urschleim," to discover in the warm waters off the island of Ceylon the secrets of the origins of life. Yet at the end of the journey which takes him to China and the torture garden, the secret of life is revealed to him in a puddle of blood, as maggots and flies, "un pullulement de vie vermiculaire": the vermin and parasites which, like he and Clara, live and feed off death. By contrast, Clara's failure seems even more complete. In her flight from a culture founded on the tyranny of meaning, from a course of history which plunges civilization into corruption and decay, Clara seeks shelter in a way of life devoted to the immediacy of the instincts and in the time-lessness of China. Yet there too she runs up against men subjected to the "torture of the bell," put to death, not by time itself, but by the marking of its passage. Unable to exist on the level of tension and release, she offers herself her life as spectacle. She lives in her body to feed her imperious appetite for sensations, becoming both predator and prey. Depending thus for her experiential sustenance on a kind of cannibalism of the mind, she can do nothing but continue as she has before: always stalking, never satisfied, always hungry.

Robert E. Ziegler, "Hunting the Peacock: The Pursuit of Non-Reflective Experience in Mirbeau's 'Le jardin des supplices'," in Nineteenth-Century French Studies, *Vols. 12 & 13, Nos. 4 & 1, Summer & Fall, 1984, pp. 162-74.*

Aleksandra Gruzińska (essay date 1987)

[*In the following essay, Gruzińska discusses Mirbeau's portrayal of Honoré de Balzac's wife in* La 628-E-8 *and compares her portrayal with those of other women in* Le Calvaire, Le jardin des supplices, *and* Le journal d'une femme de chambre.]

The bizarre title of *La 628-E-8* suggests a mystery novel for which the work itself was once mistaken. Actually it is probably the first book ever written on the automobile, and it describes Mirbeau's tour through France, the Rhineland and, as he puts it in Montaigne-like fashion, "à travers un peu de moi-même."

The various episodes of *La 628-E-8* are a blend of fiction, reality and literary criticism, and seem to have nothing else to bind them together other than the author and his car. An occasional cameo-appearance by Mirbeau's friends and acquaintances may be intended to give the impression that the stories are true. What is more, the testimonies of such artists as Jean Gigoux and Auguste Rodin make it more difficult to distinguish fact from fiction. The situation becomes particularly sensitive when Mme Hanska, who is a historical figure, also becomes a protagonist in **"La Mort de Balzac."** In this episode of *La 628-E-8*, Mirbeau attributes to Rodin certain statements concerning Mme Hanska, which may receive today great attention because of his glory. They may not have seemed as impressive during Rodin's own life when he was less appreciated. The opposite may be true of Gigoux. He was deemed "un des plus célèbres portraitistes de l'époque," and had once enjoyed a great popularity, yet is today forgotten by many. Gigoux has left two portraits of Mme Hanska: first, a handsome painting exhibited at the Salon of 1852, and much later, he orally entrusted to Mirbeau his recollections about her. Even though he had once known Mme Hanska intimately, some critics consider Gigoux's testimony unreliable, owing to the artist's advanced age at the time he confided in Mirbeau. The latter, himself, calls the testimony "véridique" rather than "vrai," and this helps make it ambiguous.

On the surface, Mirbeau's travel in *La 628-E-8* unfolds in a chronological order, from day to day, from country to country. The trip affords Mirbeau an opportunity to observe the changing scenery and to record new sensations, for instance seeing a landscape in motion from a moving car. At times, when the auto stops, the passenger is under the deceptive impression that the landscape continues to flow. This illusion is a common distortion of reality which many drivers experience today as part of their daily life, but in Mirbeau's time, the car was a novelty and these were new sensations which gave rise to many questions on illusion and reality. What is more, within a relatively short time, the traveler of *La 628-E-8* sees his surroundings change, and this contributes to a strange feeling of being "dépaysé," or disoriented. The excitement of traveling and the movement of the car result in mental and physical fatigue, which adds another dimension to the travel experience and helps explain Mirbeau's moodiness, for instance his need to read a rare edition of Balzac, alone, in a hotel room.

The speed of the car, the changing scenery and the passenger's feelings are not the only factors which inspire the writer to reflect on new perceptions of reality. In fact, the emotional and intellectual meandering through space and time, now in the present, now in the past, does not prevent the traveler from clearly recording his observations from within and without. He no doubt introduces complexities of his own as he recalls his impressions of the journey, embellishing, exaggerating, and attenuating as he puts them in writing. Mirbeau believed that a writer should not copy reality, but rather he should deform it. According to him, deformation allows the artist to endow reality with new life. It helps him, perhaps, avoid creating a lifeless copy. These considerations lead us to re-examine Mirbeau's portrayal of Mme Hanska, and to study the metamorphosis she undergoes as a historical character when Mirbeau endows her with new life.

Our objective is, first of all, to clarify any ambiguities by studying in *La 628-E-8* the circumstances which led Mirbeau to become interested in Mme Hanska, and second, to explore "recurrent characteristics" in his portrayal of her. In transposing his vision of the world into one of art, Mirbeau reinforces certain images and patterns which suggest to us the dominant traits of his poetic landscape, and they prove helpful in identifying and isolating elements of fiction in his story. Our ultimate goal is to appraise the portrait in **"La Mort de Balzac,"** without determining what is historically true or false in the author's portrayal of Mme Hanska. This has already been attempted by others, i. e., Marcel Bouteron.

Mirbeau's obsession to shed light on Balzac's marriage revived an old controversy of which the public first became aware when the posthumous volume of *Choses vues* appeared in 1887. Here, Victor Hugo describes his last visit to the dying Balzac, and, in passing, refers to Balzac's wife, emphasizing Mme Hanska's absence from her husband's side at that crucial moment when a loving wife should be there. Hugo's contemporaries noticed this indifference, and following in Hugo's footsteps, other critics searched for evidence of a possible misunderstanding between Balzac and his wife. In 1907, some twenty years later, Mirbeau proposed his own version of the subject.

Having acquired a rare edition of Balzac's correspondence in Belgium, Mirbeau was inspired to study certain obsessions of Balzac, e. g., his infatuation with titles of nobility and with money. These infatuations helped Mirbeau clarify Balzac's marriage to a wealthy aristocrat, and he suggested that: "c'est par ses péchés qu'un grand homme nous passionne le plus."

Mirbeau's admiration for and interest in Balzac do not alone explain why he chose to speak of Balzac's wife. The presence in *La 628-E-8* of Paul Bourget helps shed some new light on the matter. Paul Bourget was a friend and a contemporary of Mirbeau, as well as a critic whose essay on Balzac Mirbeau had once admired. Later in his career, however, Mirbeau became very critical of Bourget. The criticism is felt in works like *Le Jardin des supplices* (1898), where Bourget appears satirized as "l'illustre écrivain," and again in *Le Journal d'une femme de chambre* (1900), where he plays the role of a writer who prefers women of high society and scorns chambermaids. Bourget explains to Célestine his lack of interest in her because chambermaids have no depth, no "âme."

Mirbeau, on the other hand, did not share this view. In a pointed reference to Paul Bourget he wrote: "[Balzac], cet esprit si averti, si aigu, si profondément humain, croyait, avec une ferveur théologale, aux grandes dames. Comme M. Paul Bourget. . . ." Mirbeau approaches Mme Hanska from a different point of view. In his portrayal of Eveline Hanska de Balzac, he focuses on the moral character of this "grande dame," who enjoys a unique social position, thanks to her title, her wealth as well as her marriage to a renowned novelist. Yet, in spite of these advantages, she does not fit into the mold of "grandes âmes"; for that matter few, if any, Mirbelian heroines do.

"La Mort de Balzac" represents the last episode in a three-part essay. We owe the account to Jean Gigoux's testimony who tells what happened on the eve of Balzac's death, thus providing Mirbeau with the most shocking and controversial passage of *La 628-E-8.* Mirbeau eventually withdrew the story and never allowed it to be published during his lifetime. In this episode, Gigoux claims to have been with Mme Hanska when her husband died, and he speaks of the event with a freshness of precision as if it had taken place only yesterday, and not on August 18, 1850. Gigoux vividly recalls hearing a knock at Mme Hanska's door "on the dot" of ten-thirty in the evening. To be able to recall with such an unusual sharpness a moment of forty years previous, the event must have either left a lasting impression on Gigoux, or Mirbeau is embellishing his story. The latter hastens to reassure us of his complete impartiality, denying in four categorical statements (why so many?) any intention to slant the testimony: "Je n'y change rien . . . Je ne le brode, ni ne le charge, ne ne l'atténue." Although he claims to be an impartial listener, we know that Mirbeau thought of deformation as a desirable literary technique. He further refers to Gigoux's account as "un fait . . . de la plus grande horreur tragique . . . ," "un fait" transformed by subjective elements, imagination and feelings, as is suggested by the use of the superlative. Moreover, as if he were using a microscope, Mirbeau singles out and magnifies the event, inevitably distorting it.

"La Mort de Balzac" brings to mind the many variations on the eternal triangle of the betrayed husband (Balzac), the unfaithful wife (Mme Hanska) and her lover (Jean Gigoux). The great Balzac plays a minor role and dies "off stage," so to speak, attended by an old woman, not even a member of the family, who watches over the dying man: "La vérité vraie est que Balzac est mort abandonné de tous et de tout, comme un chien!" Gigoux's exclamation and his use of the redundant epithet "vraie" (true) betray his emotions. On the other hand, the very common and trite comparison, "left to die like a dog," takes a new meaning because, in his works, Balzac constantly drew comparisons between the animal and human worlds.

Mirbeau proceeds to investigate the "dessous," or secrets, unknown to the public. He no doubt intends to expose them, in order to shed new light on the characters. While Balzac lies dying alone, his wife remains in the same house and spends the evening with Gigoux, "dans cette maison, en plein Paris, où, plus délaissé qu'une bête malade au fond d'un trou, dans les bois, mourait le plus grand génie du siècle. . . ." To abandon so completely Balzac no doubt illustrates, in Mirbeau's mind, the depth of indifference to which a woman can stoop in her scorn toward a great writer. By adroitly punctuating each of Jean Gigoux's utterances, Mirbeau makes certain that the reader fully understands the incongruity of the situation: "J'oubliais réellement que j'étais, à l'instant même où il mourait . . . dans la maison, dans le lit, avec la femme de Balzac! . . . Comprenez-vous ça?" While the rhetorical question needs no answer, we can almost visualize Mirbeau's disbelief and indignation.

According to a critic, Balzac, who was not inclined to tenderness, could not have imagined a scene more melodramatically cruel: "Balzac lui-même n'eût osé concevoir un semblable dénouement pour le plus tragiquement humain de ses romans." His own death becomes more poignant when we compare it to similar situations in his novels. Indeed, the characters of the *Comédie humaine* almost always receive some consolation which is denied to Balzac. The miser Grandet dies dreaming of the gold he so loved, while his tender daughter Eugénie watches over him. Although Goriot is abandoned by his daughters, he is attended by a young medical intern, the future Horace Bianchon, whom Balzac charitably places at the bedside of many characters. Legend has it that Balzac himself called for Bianchon during his last days of illness. Even the terrifying "cousine Bette," who repeatedly attempted to destroy the Hulot family, even she dies surrounded and mourned by the members of this family. As for the great seductress, Valerie Crevel, whose list of victims includes Baron Hulot, she receives the consolation of the last rites. Like his notorious protagonist, Balzac suffers from unpleasant odors and pus which emanate from his decaying body, and yet Mirbeau does not even grant him the comfort of religion and love.

In his portrait of Mme Hanska, Mirbeau only gradually introduces distortions. She who is blamed for cruelly abandoning Balzac first appears as the ideal woman: beautiful, exquisitely sensitive, compassionate, enticing and sensuous. She is the ideal woman of *Les Lettres à l'étrangère,* distant, mysterious and inaccessible, "une femme extraordinaire," "supérieure par l'intelligence et par le coeur. . . ." Mirbeau's ultimate goal, however, is to dispel the mystery surrounding "l'étrangère." He accomplishes this by enlisting the cooperation of two friends, Barbey d'Aurevilly and Jean Gigoux. According to the former, "[Mme Hanska] valait la peine de toutes les folies." But the latter's "confidences parlées" strike a fatal blow, destroying the traditional image of Mme Hanska, great lady and loving wife. By resorting to a variety of sources, i. e., Spoelberch de Lovenjoul and Mme Surville (Balzac's sister), and in particular to the oral testimony of Barbey d'Aurevilly and Jean Gigoux, Mirbeau injects new life into his subject. But in the process, the ideal woman of *Les Lettres à l'étrangère* loses her mystery and, what is more serious, acquires some mannerisms pertaining to other Mirbelian female protagonists. These recurrent mannerisms suggest that the author may have injected into his portrayal of Mme Hanska a vision of women yet to be defined.

Mirbeau recalls that in 1850, after eighteen years of correspondence, the aristocratic widow left her estate in Wierszchownia and married Balzac. When, finally, the couple arrived late at night in Paris, bizarre events forced them to resort to a locksmith before being able to enter their new home. The weary Balzac, whose poor health had made the journey more tedious, immediately retired, leaving Mme Hanska alone to weep in despair. According to Mirbeau, from this moment on Balzac and his wife avoided each other; they were mutually disappointed, he who dreamed of wealth and she of glory. Balzac soon discovered that Mme Hanska was not as "colossalement riche" as he had anticipated; she in turn found herself married to a very sick man, so different from the renowned novelist she had admired.

On the very eve of her husband's death, we penetrate into Mme Hanska's room. Gigoux, through whose eyes we see the room, speaks of stale odors which permeate it: "Avec cela m'arrivaient aux narines, des odeurs d'amour, d'écoeurantes odeurs de nourriture aussi, et de boisson, que la chaleur aigrissait." Soon after, an old woman comes to inform Mme Hanska of Balzac's precarious condition. The wife reacts strangely, to say the least: "[Mme Hanska] se bouchait les oreilles, ne voulant rien entendre. Elle la pria même [la vieille femme] de ne revenir que 'quand tout serait fini'." She wears very little clothing and frantically paces back and forth, bumping into furniture like a trapped animal. She appears quite unlike the mysterious and distant woman of *Les Lettres à l'étrangère*. In fact, Gigoux reduces her to nothingness, not even a "bête," beast or fool: "Elle, elle n'était plus rien . . . plus rien . . . Ce n'était plus un être de raison, ce n'était pas même une folle . . . pas même une bête . . . ce n'était rien." She shows neither sorrow nor sadness when Balzac finally dies. Instead she resents the inconvenience and the formalities which death entails. The disorder of her room, her skimpy clothing and her indifference, all make Mme Hanska appear as a sensuous but unfeeling courtesan in a bordello: "Mes vêtements, des jupons, traînaient sur les fauteuils, pendaient des meubles, jonchaient le tapis, en un désordre tel et si ignoble, que, n'eût été la splendeur royale du lit, n'eussent été les cuivres étincelants de la psyché, je me serais cru échoué, après boire, au hasard d'une rencon-

tre nocturne, chez une racoleuse d'amour." Gigoux's harsh portrayal brings to mind the "femme fatale" and the "belle dame sans merci" of the "fin de siècle" Decadents with whom Mirbeau shares certain affinities.

Balzac's contemporaries did not enter Mme Hanska's room, nor did they benefit from Gigoux's revelations and Mirbeau's elucidations ("éclaircissements"), which only became available after 1913. For her contemporaries, Mme Hanska remained dignified: "Andromaque elle-même quand elle perdit Hector . . . Elle émerveilla . . . tout le monde par la correction tragique." Mirbeau's readers, however, have a chance to notice various changes in the personality of the protagonist. Mme Hanska is seen, now as a mysterious woman or "l'étrangère," now as a courtesan or "racoleuse d'amour," and finally she becomes the ideal widow who recaptures the respect and admiration of the reader of *La 628-E-8.* Yet, when Gigoux compares Mme Hanska to the mythological Andromaque, his tribute seems only half-sincere: "Le plus comique, c'est, je crois, qu'elle fut sincère dans sa comédie." He seems to suggest that Mme Hanska only acts the part of Andromaque without actually possessing the attributes of the worthy widow. The final word "comédie" puts the emphasis on "play-acting" rather than sincerity, even though sincerity seems more desirable in this instance.

In Mirbeau's poetic landscape, the women aristocrats and the courtesans behave identically. Such a simplification affords the modern reader little comfort. Yet, each woman is observed by Mirbeau through a prism of ever-changing reflections and nuances of light, and becomes endowed with life, individuality and elusiveness, which compensate to some degree for the moral simplification: they are beautiful, self-centered creatures who repel and attract.

—Aleksandra Gruzińska

Since the episode of Balzac's death appears in a literary work, we may wonder if it is not embellished. The degree of embellishment may be determined by comparing the protagonist of **"La Mort de Balzac"** with other Mirbelian women. A comparison of this nature leads us to discuss recurring traits which give Mirbeau's fiction its characteristic relief.

In Mirbeau's earliest novel, *Le Calvaire* (1887), Jean Mintié falls in love with an innocent-looking Juliette Roux. As soon as their relationship reaches the breaking point, Juliette seeks new excitement, indulges in nightly orgies, loses her freshness, and begins to look tired, disheveled and unkempt. Jean Mintié admires Juliette, even after their final separation, and when he again meets her in the streets, he finds her most attractive and desirable: "Elle avait un chapteau rose, était fraîche, souriante, semblait heureuse. . . ." From a distance, Juliette resembles the ideal woman once more. Jean sees her younger-looking and idol-like: "L'idole impure, éternellement souillée, vers laquelle couraient des foules haletantes . . ." (*Le Calvaire*). Mme Hanska undergoes a similar transformation. First seen as the "ideal woman," she is later compared to a "racoleuse d'amour," and then again, to the ideal widow Andromaque.

In *Le Jardin des supplices* (1898), the anonymous narrator, who falls in love with Clara, is attracted by her beauty and mystery, and by the sadistic desires he later senses in her. Clara takes pleasure in human suffering, in feeling her dress torn by a blood-thirsty crowd, and in the atrocious scenes of the garden of tortures. Her sadism often reaches such an intensity that it results in pain and causes her to lose consciousness. During these moments of crisis, the helpless narrator sees Clara reach total exhaustion. Only then does she briefly recapture fleeting moments of innocence: "Et elle s'endormait . . . d'un sommeil calme, lumineux et lointain, et profond, comme un grand et doux lac, sous la lune d'une nuit d'été."

In *Le Journal d'une femme de chambre* (1990), by confronting her tyrannical masters, Célestine repeatedly loses her temper, and this results in her eventual dismissal. She later marries Joseph, a former servant, turned café owner in the provinces. Their rather uneventful provincial existence frees Célestine from servitude, but not from dreams of adventure and crime: "j'irai toujours où il [Joseph] me dira d'aller . . . jusqu'au crime . . . !" In spite of Célestine's attraction to crime, her behavior appears relatively innocent when we compare it with the bizarre and eccentric practices of her decadent and tyrannical masters.

Although Mirbeau endows all his heroines with the kind of uniqueness a reader hardly forgets, each woman conforms to a certain pattern of behavior. At first sight, she gives the impression of relative innocence. In the long run, certain signs contradict this: the forehead hardens, unpleasant furrows mold the corners of the mouth, and the voice takes on harsh vibrations. These are symptoms of anger and annoyance. The elegant dress becomes torn or dirty. The outward deterioration suggests a corresponding moral degeneration. The facial expressions suggest a change in the heroine's attitude as well. The gradual transformations convey a dynamic quality to the female protagonist and endow her with life. She retains a certain vitality in spite of Mirbeau's pessimistic portrayal of humanity in general, and of women in particular.

The same mixture of innocence and corruption which characterizes the courtesan Juliette, the sadist Clara, or the servant girl Célestine, also describes the aristocratic Mme Hanska. In fact, **"La Mort de Balzac"** reveals some shocking aspects about the woman whom we traditionally think of as a grandedame and a loving wife. Gigoux soon destroys these illusions as well as the elements of mystery and distance which Balzac had included in his *Lettres à l'étrangère*. His tale of unfaithfulness, eroticism and indifference erases the distance that separates the reader from Balzac's "ideal woman." The destruction is accomplished by scrutinizing Mme Hanska's face and searching for microscopic flaws: "Elle avait un pli amer, presque méchant, au coin de la bouche." Gigoux quickly adds a moral touch: "Et la bouche, d'un dessin si joliment sensuel, prenait alors une expression vulgaire, basse, qui avait quelque chose de répugnant . . . Sa voix, toute changée, sans cet accent chantant . . . devenait agressive." When in a moment of impatience Mme Hanska asks Gigoux to leave, her tone is "sec" and her voice is "dure."

After describing the expression on the face and the tone of the voice, Gigoux proceeds to criticize Mme Hanska's dress: "Je vis qu'elle allait sortir dans cet état de presque complète nudité. . . Je criai: 'Où allez-vous? . . . Habillez-vous un peu, au moins. Et puis, calmez-vous!' Je me levai, l'obligeai à revêtir une sorte de peignor blanc, très sale. . . ." The strategic position of the word "sale" at the end of the sentence, reinforced by an adverb of intensity, creates an effective contrast with the word "blanc" which immediately precedes. Mme Hanska's half-nakedness and the sad condition of her "peignoir" suggest the downfall of the ideal woman and accentuate further the traits which bring her closer to the courtesan to whom Gigoux has already compared her.

Perhaps the most trite, and yet the most expressive and fetishistic detail concerns hand gestures. Gigoux describes Mme Hanska's nervous pacing, back and forth, before the reader-spectator; like an actress on the stage, she sighs and files her nails: "Elle allait de son fauteuil à la fenêtre, revenait de la fenêtre à son fauteuil, tantôt limant ses ongles avec rage, tantôt poussant des soupirs." At the thought that Victor Hugo might visit Balzac and that she may have to face him, Mme Hanska frantically resumes filing her nails with increased vigor: "Et elle limait ses ongles avec plus de frénésie." The precision with which Gigoux remembers the trite gesture, forty years after Balzac's death, is like an obsession. He by no means is the first one to be so obsessed. **"La Mort de Balzac"** is neither the first nor the only story in which a Mirebelian female protagonist files her nails while being intently watched by an admirer. In fact, the gesture acquires greater significance because of its recurrence in other works. Indeed, already in *Le Calvaire* (1887), Juliette filed, polished and buffed her nails until they became hard as agate. She filed her nails with a persistence and a passion so great that Jean Mintié gave in to her, abandoning his literary ambitions in order to please her.

In a short story entitled **"Clotilde et moi,"** the narrator dreams of a sentimental encounter with Clotilde, in a romantic setting near the English seashore. Clotilde on the other hand only seems interested in inflicting torment on her male companion and postponing the moment of gratification: "La figure grave, le front serré d'un pli que je n'aimais pas . . . elle poussait un soupir, se remettait à polir ses ongles et ne répondit pas," or yet, "après avoir limé et poli consciencieusement ses ongles . . . elle s'ennuya." To make the situation typically uncomfortable, whenever Clotilde speaks, she does so in an imperious and irritating tone of voice.

This recurrent emphasis on facial expressions, the annoying vividness of hand gestures, the elegance or disrepair of clothing that was sometimes torn or dirty, even more, the impression of innocence which is inevitably followed by the discovery of cruel behavior in the loved woman, these devices seem common to Mirbelian heroines and lend them elusiveness and mobility, and ultimately create impressionistic portraits. Mirbeau was a friend, an ardent admirer and supporter of many impressionists, and in particular of Claude Monet, of whom he speaks in *La 628-E-8.* Monet's studies of nature, his pond of lilies, or his cathedral of Rouen, represent on canvas a succession of instants in the life of a landscape or a monument. Monet created his paintings of the cathedral of Rouen at varying moments of daylight, and each time his paintings underwent many changes. To what degree Mirbeau felt inspired to adapt Monet's ideas to literature is not certain. There is no doubt, however, that Mirbeau's female protagonists come to life through a succession of images, now of innocence and idealism, now of cruelty. The image changes depending on the angle, or the distance, or the circumstances from which the women are seen. Each change sheds new light on the protagonist, accentuating different aspects of her personality. What is more, the observer, through whose eyes we see Mme Hanska, be it Mirbeau, Gigoux, or the narrator (a male point of view), injects personal feelings into the portrait, inevitably distorting its psychological dimension. Mirbeau was always searching for new ideas and techniques of expression. He has even shown interest in representing reality "cinématographiquement." The cinema, like the car, was just emerging.

Whatever the technology, impressionistic or cinematic, the final creation contains subjective elements. This was evident to Mirbeau in the numerous accounts he had read or heard about Balzac: "Il y avait un peu de vrai, dans toutes ces histoires malsonnantes, mais du vrai mal compris, du vrai déformé, comme toujours." Ironically, he himself does not avoid "le vrai mal compris" or "le vrai déformé" he so well points out in the writings of others. Indeed, in **"La Mort de Balzac,"** he goes beyond describing Balzac's foibles, e. g., his fondness for titles of nobility and for money. He goes on to imply that Balzac and his wife avoided each other from the moment they arrived in Paris, and finally he uses an emotionally colored eyewitness account to support this idea. On the other hand, the impressionistic portrayal with its subtle but progressive deformation, and the use of recurring characteristics, suggest that the historical Mme Hanska is transformed when she becomes a Mirbelian protagonist. He endows her with the traits of a femme fatale, transforms her into a "belle dame sans merci," whose behavior strongly resembles that of his other heroines, Juliette and Clara, Clotilde and Célestine. "Eveline's" melodious and quasi-heavenly name, like the tender name of Juliette, or Clara or Célestine, barely disguises an egoistic, voluptuous and cruel nature, confirming what Mirbeau believed to be true: "Plus les noms sont charmants, plus méchantes sont les maladies."

On the other hand, Mme Hanska's attitude and behavior illustrate what Mirbeau has already suggested in *Le Jardin des supplices,* namely, that women, regardless of the social background from which they come, behave in the same manner: "les grandes dames et les bourgeoises . . . C'est la même chose... . Chez les femmes, il n'y a pas de catégories morales, il n'y a que des catégo-

ries sociales." In Mirbeau's poetic landscape, the women aristocrats and the courtesans behave identically. Such a simplification affords the modern reader little comfort. Yet, like Monet's cathedral of Rouen, or his pond of lilies, each woman is observed by Mirbeau through a prism of ever-changing reflections and nuances of light, and becomes endowed with life, individuality and elusiveness, which compensate to some degree for the moral simplification: they are beautiful, self-centered creatures who repel and attract.

Mirbeau's transposition of Gigoux's story does not flatter Mme Hanska. On the contrary, it aroused protests from her daughter. In a letter to *Le Temps,* she explained that her mother had met Gigoux two years after Balzac's death, therefore the events could not have taken place as they appear in *La 628-E-8.* Since the publication of her letter, critics have searched for documents to support Mirbeau's story, while others persist in discrediting it. In the heat of the debate, it was forgotten that *La 628-E-8* is a literary work which no doubt contains elements of truth, though not necessarily elements true to fact as in a biography.

There is a strong temptation to suggest that Mirbeau's own marriage may have influenced his vision of women in general, and his portrait of Mme Hanska in particular. Although he had the good fortune of marrying a talented and beautiful widow whose wealth, loving devotion and encouragement freed him from material worries and allowed him to devote his life to creative writing, his marriage was not free from disappointments. The future Mme Mirbeau, whom Robert de Montesquiou calls a "célèbre courtisane du Second Empire," was a wealthy widow before she remarried, though not an aristocrat like Mme Hanska.

One cannot help noticing interesting parallels between the marriage of Balzac and that of Mirbeau. Both married wealthy widows, who are compared to courtesans (by Montesquiou and Gigoux). Both were writers and married for love. This similarity notwithstanding, Mirbeau's letters to various friends suggest that, in his relations with women, he had met with disappointments long before he got married. On the other hand, his friendship with Claude Monet and his admiration for the artist lend support for Mirbeau's impressionistic art in portraying women. Furthermore, the recurring characteristics allow us to view Mme Hanska as part of Mirbeau's poetic landscape, as one of his "belles dames sans merci." Movie versions of *Le Jardin des supplices* and of *Le Journal d'une femme de chambre* and recent editions of the two novels have given Clara and Célestine a renewed lease on life. On the contrary, the protagonist of **"La Mort de Balzac"** died with the birth of *La 628-E-8,* for the book appeared without the Balzac episode. The latter remains nonetheless a testimony of Mirbeau's attempt to mold reality into a characteristic relief of his own poetic landscape.

Aleksandra Gruzińska, "Octave Mirbeau's Madam Hanska in 'La Mort de Balzac'," in Nineteenth-Century French Studies, *Vol. XV, No. 3, Spring, 1987, pp. 302-14.*

FURTHER READING

Criticism

Apter, Emily. "The Garden of Scopic Perversion from Monet to Mirbeau." *October* (Winter 1988): 91-115.
    Examines the theme of "the perverse curiosity of the gaze" in Mirbeau's *Le jardin des supplices.*

Carr, Reg. *Anarchism in France: The Case of Octave Mirbeau.* Montreal: McGill-Queen's University Press, 1977, 190 p.
    Studies the relationship between the anarchist movement in France and the works of Mirbeau. An appendix includes reprints in French of Mirbeau's major essays on anarchism.

Newton, Joy. "Emile Zola and Octave Mirbeau, with Extracts from Their Unpublished Letters." *Nottingham French Studies* 25, No. 2 (October 1986): 42-59.
    Scrutinizes the often stormy personal and professional relationship between Mirbeau and Zola.

Redfern, W. D. "The Pyromaniac Fireman." *The Times Literary Supplement* No. 3942 (14 October 1977): 1197.
    Review of Reg Carr's *Anarchism in France: The Case of Octave Mirbeau* and four reprint editions of works by Mirbeau.

Friedrich Nietzsche

1844-1900

(Full name Friedrich Wilhelm Nietzsche) German philosopher, philologist, poet, and autobiographer. The following entry presents an overview of Nietzsche's career. For further information see *TCLC*, Volumes 10 and 18.

INTRODUCTION

Nietzsche is considered one of the greatest philosophers of the modern era. Largely ignored and misunderstood during his lifetime, Nietzsche's revolutionary style of thinking and writing influenced a wide variety of twentieth-century disciplines, including psychoanalysis, existentialism, phenomenology, and hermeneutics. Trained as a classical philologist, Nietzsche's insight into the origins of ancient Greek culture provided the foundation for his critique of traditional philosophy. While he never achieved a systematic formulation of his ideas, Nietzsche's insights into the veiled motives of philosophy and morality inaugurated a wellspring of discoveries about the psychological, existential, and linguistic bases of human existence.

Biographical Information

Nietzsche was born in Röcken, Prussia, to a devout Lutheran couple. After considering and rejecting the study of theology, in 1865 he entered the University of Leipzig, where he concentrated on classical philology. Nietzsche acquired a reputation as a prodigy in his field, and though he had not yet finished his doctoral thesis, he was appointed as an associate professor at the University of Basel at the age of twenty-four. During this period, Nietzsche discovered the works of Arthur Schopenhauer, made the acquaintance of Richard Wagner, and published his first book, *Die Geburt der Tragödie aus dem Geiste der Musik* (*The Birth of Tragedy*). Nietzsche suffered chronically from numerous physical ailments, including severe headaches, gastrointestinal problems and partial blindness, and in 1879 he resigned his post at the university. With his retirement from teaching, Nietzsche devoted himself exclusively to the development of his philosophy. In 1889 he suffered a mental breakdown and partial paralysis. His condition gradually worsened over the ensuing decade. Nietzsche died in 1900.

Major Works

Many critics maintain that Nietzsche's works reflect three periods of development. The first, from 1872 to 1876, is exemplified by *The Birth of Tragedy,* in which Nietzsche contends that tragic drama and early Greek philosophy resulted from the interplay of Dionysian and Apollonian forces. *Unzeitgemässe Betrachtungen* (*Untimely Meditations*) advances Nietzsche's thesis that metaphysical reasoning is a symptom of decadence, though with respect to

German culture in the 1870s. In the second period, from 1878 to 1882, Nietzsche began to use an aphoristic style of writing to accommodate his radically skeptical and experimental mode of thinking. In such works as *Die Morgenröte* (*The Dawn*) and *Die Fröhliche Wissenschaft* (*The Gay Science*), Nietzsche began to probe psychological phenomena and to describe the functions of the unconscious. His analysis of Christian virtue as a sublimated drive for power and a symptom of "slave morality" foreshadowed the more rigorous formulation of the will to power in his later works. In *The Gay Science* Nietzsche also unveiled his dictum "God is dead," which metaphorically expresses the meaning of nihilism. The final period was initiated by Nietzsche's masterwork, *Also Sprach Zarathustra* (*Thus Spake Zarathustra*), a stylistic tour de force which embodies the central themes of Nietzsche's philosophy, particularly the eternal recurrence of the same. After the publication of *Thus Spake Zarathustra*, Nietzsche sought to disseminate his doctrines in a more accessible form in *Jenseits von Gut und Böse* (*Beyond Good and Evil*) and *Zur Genealogie der Moral* (*On The Genealogy of Morals*). While he drafted plans for a magnum opus, variously titled *The Will to Power* or *The Revaluation of All Values*, he was either unwilling or unable to systematize his philosophy, and he abandoned the project. Nietzsche did, however, produce three important works in the year before his breakdown. In *Die Götzendämmerung* (*The Twilight of the Idols*) Nietzsche formulated in his most succinct and penetrating style his opposition to metaphysical thinking, demonstrating that Platonic doctrines constitute the source of European nihilism. *Der Antichrist* (*The Antichrist*) is vitriolic and uneven, but also a profoundly insightful polemic against Christianity as a nihilistic religion. *Ecce Homo* is Nietzsche's unorthodox attempt at autobiography. Boastful to the point of megalomania, it nevertheless exhibits profound psychological insight and stylistic brilliance.

Critical Reception

While Nietzsche is now considered one of the greatest philosophers in history, his works were frequently denigrated by early commentators who objected to his "unphilosophical" use of aphorisms and irony. His professional isolation began with the bold but poorly documented insights of *The Birth of Tragedy*, which was scorned by a majority of classical scholars. By the turn of the century, however, Nietzsche's works began to generate considerable enthusiasm in literary circles, well in advance of his philosophical reception. Such authors as Thomas Mann, Hermann Hesse, and George Bernard Shaw embraced Nietzsche as a prophet of anti-humanist modernism. Serious consideration of the strictly philosophical aspects of his work did not appear until the advent of psychoanalysis and existentialism, though the taint of its association with Nazi ideology prevented a more widespread acceptance. This situation was radically altered in 1961, with the publication of Heidegger's four-volume study of Nietzsche, which outlined the central themes of his philosophy and asserted that Nietzsche's critique of traditional thought and value was at once the end point and culmination of Western metaphysics. During the 1960s Nietzsche became a central touchstone for such thinkers as Jacques Derrida and Michel Foucault, who detected in his revolutionary experiments with style a proto-deconstructionist understanding of language and conceptual reason. Since then, the rehabilitation of Nietzsche's reputation has continued unabated, with a torrent of studies from such diverse perspectives as feminism, Marxism, hermeneutics, and poststructuralism, and Nietzsche is commonly linked with Karl Marx and Sigmund Freud as a principal architect of the modern intellectual landscape.

PRINCIPAL WORKS

Die Geburt der Tragödie aus dem Geiste der Musik [*The Birth of Tragedy*] (essay) 1872
Unzeitgemässe Betrachtungen [*Untimely Meditations*] (essays) 1873-76
Menschliches, Allzumenschliches [*Human, All Too Human*] (essays and aphorisms) 1878-80
Die Morgenröte [*The Dawn*] (essays and aphorisms) 1881

Die Fröhliche Wissenschaft [*The Gay Science*] (essays, poetry, and aphorisms) 1882
Also Sprach Zarathustra [*Thus Spake Zarathustra*] (prose) 1883-85
Jenseits von Gut und Böse [*Beyond Good and Evil*] (essays and aphorisms) 1886
Zur Genealogie der Moral [*On the Genealogy of Morals*] (essays and aphorisms) 1887
Der Fall Wagner [*The Case of Wagner*] (essay) 1888
Die Götzen-dämmerung [*The Twilight of the Idols*] (essays) 1889
Der Antichrist [*The Antichrist*] (essay) 1895
Nietzsche contra Wagner [*Nietzsche contra Wagner*] (essay) 1895
Ecce Homo [*Ecce Homo*] (autobiography) 1908
Der Wille zur Macht [*The Will to Power*] (notebooks) 1909-10

CRITICISM

Martin Heidegger　(essay date 1954)

[*Heidegger was a German philosopher, critic, and educator. His magnum opus,* Sein und Zeit (*1927;* Being and Time), *exerted a profound influence on the development of existentialism, phenomenology, hermeneutics, and other contemporary philosophical disciplines. Heidegger's four-volume study of Nietzsche's philosophy was a major impetus for the renewed interest in Nietzsche among scholars in the mid-twentieth century. In the following excerpt from the second volume of that work, subtitled* The Eternal Recurrence of the Same, *Heidegger examines the meaning of the figure of Zarathustra in Nietzsche's philosophical thought.*]

Our question ["Who is Nietzsche's Zarathustra?"], it would seem, can be easily answered. For we find the response in one of Nietzsche's own works, in sentences that are clearly formulated and even set in italic type. The sentences occur in that work by Nietzsche which expressly delineates the figure of Zarathustra. The book, composed of four parts, was written during the years 1883 to 1885, and bears the title **Thus Spoke Zarathustra.**

Nietzsche provided the book with a subtitle to set it on its way. The subtitle reads: *A Book for Everyone and No One.* "For Everyone," of course, does not mean for anybody at all, anyone you please. "For Everyone" means for every human being as a human being, for every given individual insofar as he becomes for himself in his essence a matter worthy of thought. "And No One" means for none of those curiosity mongers who wash in with the tide and imbibe freely of particular passages and striking aphorisms in the book, and who then stagger blindly about, quoting its language—partly lyrical, partly shrill, sometimes tranquil, other times stormy, often elevated, occasionally trite. They do this instead of setting out on the way of thinking that is here searching for its word.

Thus Spoke Zarathustra: A Book for Everyone and No One. How uncannily true the work's subtitle has proven to be in the seventy years that have passed since the book first appeared—but true precisely in the reverse sense! It became a book for everybody, and to this hour no thinker has arisen who is equal to the book's fundamental thought and who can take the measure of the book's provenance in its full scope. Who is Zarathustra? If we read the work's title attentively we may find a clue: **Thus Spoke Zarathustra.** Zarathustra speaks. He is a speaker. Of what sort? Is he an orator, or maybe a preacher? No. Zarathustra the speaker is an advocate [*ein Fürsprecher*]. In this name we encounter a very old word in the German language, one that has multiple meanings. *For* actually means *before.* In the Alemannic dialect, the word *Fürtuch* is still the common word for "apron." The *Fürsprech* speaks "forth" and is the spokesman. Yet at the same time für means "on behalf of" and "by way of justification." Finally, an advocate is one who interprets and explains what he is talking about and what he is advocating.

Zarathustra is an advocate in this threefold sense. But what does he speak forth? On whose behalf does he speak? What does he try to interpret? Is Zarathustra merely some sort of advocate for some arbitrary cause, or is he *the* advocate for the one thing that always and above all else speaks to human beings?

Toward the end of the third part of **Thus Spoke Zarathustra** appears a section with the heading "The Convalescent." That is Zarathustra. But what does "convalescent," *der Genesende,* mean? *Genesen* is the same word as the Greek *neomai, nostos,* meaning to head for home. "Nostalgia" is the yearning to go home, homesickness. "The Convalescent" is one who is getting ready to turn homeward, that is, to turn toward what defines him. The convalescent is under way to himself, so that he can say of himself who he is. In the episode mentioned the convalescent says, "I, Zarathustra, the advocate of life, the advocate of suffering, the advocate of the circle. . . ."

Zarathustra speaks on behalf of life, suffering, and the circle, and that is what he speaks forth. These three, "life, suffering, circle," belong together and are the selfsame. If we were able to think this three-fold matter correctly as one and the same, we would be in a position to surmise whose advocate Zarathustra is and who it is that Zarathustra himself, as this advocate, would like to be. To be sure, we could now intervene in a heavy-handed way and explain, with indisputable correctness, that in Nietzsche's language "life" means will to power as the fundamental trait of all beings, and not merely human beings. Nietzsche himself says what "suffering" means in the following words: "Everything that suffers wills to live. . . ." "Everything" here means all things that are by way of will to power, a way that is described in the following words: "The configurative forces collide." "Circle" is the sign of the ring that wrings its way back to itself and in that way always achieves recurrence of the same.

Accordingly, Zarathustra introduces himself as an advocate of the proposition that all being is will to power, a will that suffers in its creating and colliding, and that wills itself precisely in this way in eternal recurrence of the same.

With the above assertion we have brought the essence of Zarathustra to definition—as we say at school. We can write the definition down, commit it to memory, and bring it forward whenever the occasion calls for it. We can even corroborate what we bring forward by referring specifically to those sentences in Nietzsche's works which, set in italic type, tell us who Zarathustra is.

In the above-mentioned episode, "The Convalescent," we read: "You [Zarathustra] *are the teacher of eternal return. . . !*" And in the Prologue to the entire work (section 3) stands the following: "I [Zarathustra] *teach you the overman.*"

According to these statements, Zarathustra the advocate is a "teacher." To all appearances, he teaches two things: the eternal return of the same and the overman. However, it is not immediately apparent whether and in what way the things he teaches belong together. Yet even if the connection were to be clarified it would remain questionable whether we are hearing the advocate, whether we are learning from this teacher. Without such hearing and learning we shall never rightly come to know who Zarathustra is. Thus it is not enough to string together sentences from which we can gather what the advocate and teacher says about himself. We must pay attention to the way he says it, on what occasions, and with what intent. Zarathustra does not utter the decisive phrase "You are the teacher of eternal return!" by himself to himself. His animals tell him this. They are mentioned at the very beginning of the work's Prologue and more explicitly at its conclusion. In section 10 we read:

> When the sun stood at midday he [Zarathustra] looked inquiringly into the sky—for above him he heard the piercing cry of a bird. And behold! An eagle soared through the air in vast circles, and a serpent hung suspended from him, not as his prey, but as though she were his friend: for she had coiled about his neck.

In this mysterious embrace about the throat—in the eagle's circling and the serpent's coiling—we can already sense the way circle and ring tacitly wind about one another. Thus the ring scintillates, the ring that is called *anulus aeternitatis:* the signet ring and year of eternity. When we gaze on the two animals we see where they themselves, circling and coiling about one another, belong. For of themselves they never concoct circle and ring; rather, they enter into circle and ring, there to find their essence. When we gaze on the two animals we perceive the things that matter to Zarathustra, who looks inquiringly into the sky. Thus the text continues:

> "These are my animals!" said Zarathustra, and his heart was filled with joy. "The proudest animal under the sun and the most discerning animal under the sun—they have gone out on a search.
>
> "They want to learn whether Zarathustra is still alive. Verily, am I still alive?"

Zarathustra's question receives its proper weight only if we understand the undefined word *life* in the sense of *will to power.* Zarathustra asks whether his will corresponds to the will which, as will to power, pervades the whole of being.

The animals seek to learn Zarathustra's essence. He asks

himself whether he is still—that is, whether he is already—the one who he properly is. In a note to ***Thus Spoke Zarathustra*** from Nietzsche's literary remains the following appears: " 'Do I have time to wait for my animals? If they are *my* animals they will know how to find me.' Zarathustra's silence."

Thus at the place cited, "The Convalescent," Zarathustra's animals say the following to him—and although not all the words are italicized, we dare not overlook any of them. The animals say: "For your animals know well, O Zarathustra, who you are and must become: behold, *you are the teacher of eternal return*—that is now *your* destiny!" Thus it comes to light: Zarathustra must first *become* who he is. Zarathustra shrinks back in dismay before such becoming. Dismay permeates the entire work that portrays him. Dismay determines the style, the hesitant and constantly arrested course of the work as a whole. Dismay extinguishes all of Zarathustra's self-assurance and presumptuousness at the very outset of his way. Whoever has failed and continues to fail to apprehend from the start the dismay that haunts all of Zarathustra's speeches—which often sound presumptuous, often seem little more than frenzied extravaganzas—will never be able to discover who Zarathustra is.

Sculpture of Nietzsche in a sick-chair (1898) by Arnold Kramer, with an anonymous work in the background depicting Nietzsche with Zarathustrian symbols of the snake and the eagle.

If Zarathustra must first of all become the teacher of eternal return, then he cannot commence with this doctrine straightaway. For this reason another phrase stands at the beginning of his way: *"I teach you the overman."*

To be sure, we must try to extirpate right here and now all the false and confusing overtones of the word *Übermensch* that arise in our customary view of things. With the name *overman* Nietzsche is by no means designating a merely superdimensional human being of the kind that has prevailed hitherto. Nor is he referring to a species of man that will cast off all that is humane, making naked willfulness its law and titanic rage its rule. Rather, the overman—taking the word quite literally—is that human being who goes beyond prior humanity solely in order to conduct such humanity for the first time to its essence, an essence that is still unattained, and to place humanity firmly within that essence. A note from the posthumously published writings surrounding ***Zarathustra*** says: "Zarathustra does not want to *lose* anything of mankind's past; he wants to pour everything into the mold."

Yet whence arises the urgent cry for the overman? Why does prior humanity no longer suffice? Because Nietzsche recognizes the historic moment in which man takes it on himself to assume dominion over the earth as a whole. Nietzsche is the first thinker to pose the decisive question concerning the phase of world history that is emerging only now, the first to think the question through in its metaphysical implications. The question asks: Is man, in his essence as man heretofore, prepared to assume dominion over the earth? If not, what must happen with prior humanity in order that it may "subjugate" the earth and thus fulfill the prophecy of an old testament? Must not prior man be conducted beyond himself, *over* his prior self, in order to meet this challenge? If so, then the "overman," correctly thought, cannot be the product of an unbridled and degenerate fantasy that is plunging headlong into the void. We can just as little uncover the nature of overman historically by virtue of an analysis of the modern age. We dare not seek the essential figure of overman in those personalities who, as major functionaries of a shallow, misguided will to power, are swept to the pinnacles of that will's sundry organizational forms. Of course, one thing ought to be clear to us immediately: this thinking that pursues the figure of a teacher who teaches the overman involves us, involves Europe, involves the earth as a whole—not merely today, but especially tomorrow. That is so, no matter whether we affirm or reject this thinking, whether we neglect it or ape it in false tones. Every essential thinking cuts across all discipleship and opposition alike without being touched.

Hence it behooves us first of all to learn how to learn from the teacher, even if that only means to ask out beyond him. In that way alone will we one day experience who Zarathustra is. Or else we will never experience it.

To be sure, we must still ponder whether this asking out beyond Nietzsche's thinking can be a continuation of his thought, or whether it must become a step back.

And before that, we must ponder whether this "step back" merely refers to a historically ascertainable past which one might choose to revive (for example, the world of Goethe), or whether the word *back* indicates something that *has been.* For the commencement of what has been still awaits a commemorative thinking, in order that it might become a beginning, a beginning to which the dawn grants upsurgence.

Yet we shall now restrict ourselves to the effort to learn a few provisional things about Zarathustra. The appropriate way to proceed would be to follow the first steps taken by this teacher—the teacher that Zarathustra is. He teaches by showing. He previews the essence of overman and brings that essence to visible configuration. Zarathustra is merely the teacher, not the overman himself. In turn, Nietzsche is not Zarathustra, but the questioner who seeks to create in thought Zarathustra's essence.

The overman proceeds beyond prior and contemporary humanity; thus he is a transition, a bridge. In order for us learners to be able to follow the teacher who teaches the overman, we must—keeping now to the imagery—get onto the bridge. We are thinking the crucial aspects of the transition when we heed these three things:

First, that from which the one who is in transition departs.

Second, the transition itself.

Third, that toward which the one in transition is heading.

Especially the last-mentioned aspect we must have in view; above all, the one who is in transition must have it in view; and before him, the teacher who is to show it to him must have it in view. If a preview of the "whither" is missing, the one in transition remains rudderless, and the place from which he must release himself remains undetermined. And yet the place to which the one in transition is called first shows itself in the full light of day only when he has gone over to it. For the one in transition— and particularly for the one who, as the teacher, is to point the way of transition, particularly for Zarathustra himself—the "whither" remains always at a far remove. The remoteness persists. Inasmuch as it persists, it remains in a kind of proximity, a proximity that preserves what is remote as remote by commemorating it and turning its thoughts toward it. Commemorative nearness to the remote is what our language calls "longing," *die Sehnsucht.* We wrongly associate the word *Sucht* with *suchen,* "to seek" and "to be driven." But the old word *Sucht* (as in *Gelbsucht,* "jaundice," and *Schwindsucht,* "consumption") means illness, suffering, pain.

Longing is the agony of the nearness of what lies afar.

Whither the one in transition goes, there his longing is at home. The one in transition, and even the one who points out the way to him, the teacher, is (as we have already heard) on the way home to the essence that is most proper to him. He is the convalescent. Immediately following the episode called "The Convalescent," in the third part of *Thus Spoke Zarathustra,* is the episode entitled "On the Great Longing." With this episode, the third-to-last of Part III, the work *Thus Spoke Zarathustra* as a whole attains its summit. In a note from the posthumously published materials Nietzsche observes, "A divine suffering is the content of Zarathustra III."

In the section "On the Great Longing" Zarathustra speaks to his soul. According to Plato's teaching—a teaching that became definitive for Western metaphysics—the essence of thinking resides in the soul's solitary conversation with itself. The essence of thinking is *logos, hon autē pros hautēn hē psychē diexerchetai peri hōn an skopēi,* the telling self-gathering which the soul itself undergoes on its way to itself, within the scope of whatever it is looking at.

In converse with his soul Zarathustra thinks his "most abysmal thought." Zarathustra begins the episode "On the Great Longing" with the words: "O my soul, I taught you to say 'Today' like 'One day' and 'Formerly,' I taught you to dance your round-dance beyond every Here and There and Yonder." The three words "Today," "One day," and "Formerly" are capitalized and placed in quotation marks. They designate the fundamental features of time. The way Zarathustra expresses them points toward the matter Zarathustra himself must henceforth tell himself in the very ground of his essence. And what is that? That "One day" and "Formerly," future and past, are like "Today." And also that today is like what is past and what is to come. All three phases of time merge in a single identity, as the same in one single present, a perpetual "now." Metaphysics calls the constant now "eternity." Nietzsche too thinks the three phases of time in terms of eternity as the constant now. Yet for him the constancy consists not in stasis but in a recurrence of the same. When Zarathustra teaches his soul to say those words he is the teacher of eternal return of the same. Such return is the inexhaustible abundance of a life that is both joyous and agonizing. Such a life is the destination toward which "the great longing" leads the teacher of eternal return of the same. Thus in the same episode "the great longing" is also called "the longing of superabundance."

The "great longing" thrives for the most part on that from which it draws its only consolation, that is to say, its confidence in the future. In place of the older word "consolation," *Trost* (related to *trauen,* "to trust," "to betroth," and to *zutrauen,* "to believe oneself capable"), the word "hope" has entered our language. "The great longing" attunes and defines Zarathustra, who in his "greatest hope" is inspired by such longing.

Yet what induces Zarathustra to such hope, and what entitles him to it?

What bridge must he take in order to go over to the overman? What bridge enables him to depart from humanity hitherto, so that he can be released from it?

It derives from the peculiar structure of the work *Thus Spoke Zarathustra,* a work that is to make manifest the transition of the one who goes over, that the answer to the question we have just posed appears in the second part of the work, the preparatory part. Here, in the episode "On the Tarantulas," Nietzsche has Zarathustra say: "For *that man be redeemed from revenge*—that is for me the bridge to the highest hope and a rainbow after long storms."

How strange, how alien these words must seem to the customary view of Nietzsche's philosophy that we have furnished for ourselves. Is not Nietzsche supposed to be the one who goads our will to power, incites us to a politics of violence and war, and sets the "blond beast" on his rampage?

The words "that man be redeemed from revenge" are even italicized in the text. Nietzsche's thought thinks in the direction of redemption from the spirit of revenge. His thinking would minister to a spirit which, as freedom from vengefulness, goes before all mere fraternizing—but also before all vestiges of the sheer will to punish. It would minister to a spirit that abides before all efforts to secure peace and before all conduct of war, a spirit quite apart from that which wills to establish and secure *pax,* peace, by pacts. The space in which such freedom from revenge moves is equidistant from pacifism, political violence, and calculating neutrality. In the same way, it lies outside feeble neglect of things and avoidance of sacrifice, outside blind intervention and the will to action at any price.

Nietzsche's reputation as a "free spirit" arises from the spirit of freedom from revenge.

"That man be redeemed from revenge." If we pay heed even in the slightest way to this spirit of freedom in Nietzsche's thinking, as its principal trait, then the prior image of Nietzsche—which is still in circulation—will surely disintegrate.

"For *that man be redeemed from revenge*—that is for me the bridge to the highest hope," says Nietzsche. He thereby says at the same time, in a language that prepares yet conceals the way, whither his "great longing" aims.

Yet what does Nietzsche understand here by "revenge"? In what, according to Nietzsche, does redemption from revenge consist?

We shall be content if we can shed some light on these two questions. Such light would perhaps enable us to descry the bridge that is to lead such thinking from prior humanity to the overman. The destination toward which the one in transition is heading will only come to the fore in the transition itself. Perhaps then it will dawn on us why Zarathustra, the advocate of life, suffering, and the circle, is the teacher who simultaneously teaches the eternal return of the same and the overman.

But then why is it that something so decisive depends on redemption from revenge? Where is the spirit of revenge at home? Nietzsche replies to our question in the third-to-last episode of the second part of *Thus Spoke Zarathustra,* which bears the heading "On Redemption." Here the following words appear: "*The spirit of revenge:* my friends, up to now that was man's best reflection; and wherever there was suffering, there also had to be punishment."

This statement without reservation attributes revenge to the whole of humanity's reflection hitherto. The reflection spoken of here is not some fortuitous kind of thinking; it is rather that thinking in which man's relation to what is, to being, is fastened and hangs suspended. Insofar as man comports himself toward beings, he represents them with regard to the fact that they are, with regard to what they are and how they are, how they might be and how they ought to be—in short, he represents beings with regard to their Being. Such representing is thinking.

According to Nietzsche's statement, such representation has heretofore been determined by the spirit of revenge. Meanwhile human beings take their relationship with what is, a relationship that is determined in this fashion, to be the best possible sort of relationship.

In whatever way man may represent beings as such, he does so with a view to Being. By means of this view he advances always beyond beings—out beyond them and over to Being. The Greeks said this in the word *meta.* Thus man's every relation to beings as such is inherently metaphysical. If Nietzsche understands revenge as the spirit that defines and sets the tone for man's relationship with Being, then he is from the outset thinking revenge metaphysically.

Here revenge is not merely a theme for morality, and redemption from revenge is not a task for moral education. Just as little are revenge and vengefulness objects of psychology. Nietzsche sees the essence and scope of revenge metaphysically. Yet what does revenge in general mean?

If at first we keep to the meaning of the word, although at the same time trying not to be myopic, we may be able to find a clue in it. Revenge, taking revenge, wreaking, *urgere:* these words mean to push, drive, herd, pursue, and persecute. In what sense is revenge persecution? Revenge does not merely try to hunt something down, seize, and take possession of it. Nor does it only seek to slay what it persecutes. Vengeful persecution defies in advance that on which it avenges itself. It defies its object by degrading it, in order to feel superior to what has been thus degraded; in this way it restores its own self-esteem, the only estimation that seems to count for it. For one who seeks vengeance is galled by the feeling that he has been thwarted and injured. During the years Nietzsche was composing his work *Thus Spoke Zarathustra* he jotted down the following observation: "I advise all martyrs to consider whether it wasn't vengeance that drove them to such extremes."

What is revenge? We can now provisionally say that revenge is persecution that defies and degrades. And such persecution is supposed to have sustained and permeated all prior reflection, all representation of beings? If the designated metaphysical scope may in fact be attributed to the spirit of revenge, that scope must somehow become visible in terms of the very constitution of metaphysics. In order to discern it, if only in rough outline, let us now turn to the essential coinage of the Being of beings in modern metaphysics. The essential coinage of Being comes to language in classic form in several sentences formulated by Schelling in his *Philosophical Investigations into the Essence of Human Freedom and the Objects Pertaining Thereto* (1809). The three sentences read:

> —In the final and highest instance there is no other Being than willing. Willing is primal Being, and to it [willing] alone all the predicates of the same [primal Being] apply: absence of conditions; eternity; independence from time; self-affirmation. All philosophy strives solely in order to find this supreme expression.

Schelling asserts that the predicates which metaphysical

thought since antiquity has attributed to Being find their ultimate, supreme, and thus consummate configuration in willing. However, the will of the willing meant here is not a faculty of the human soul. Here the word *willing* names the Being of beings as a whole. Such Being is will. That sounds foreign to us—and so it is, as long as the sustaining thoughts of Western metaphysics remain alien to us. They will remain alien as long as we do not think these thoughts, but merely go on reporting them. For example, one may ascertain Leibniz's utterances concerning the Being of beings with absolute historical precision—without in the least thinking about what he was thinking when he defined the Being of beings in terms of the monad, as the unity of *perceptio* and *appetitus,* representation and striving, that is, will. What Leibniz was thinking comes to language in Kant and Fichte as "the rational will"; Hegel and Schelling, each in his own way, reflect on this *Vernunftwille.* Schopenhauer is referring to the selfsame thing when he gives his major work the title *The World* [not man] *as Will and Representation.* Nietzsche is thinking the selfsame thing when he acknowledges the primal Being of beings as will to power.

That everywhere on all sides the Being of beings appears consistently as will does not derive from views on being which a few philosophers furnished for themselves. No amount of erudition will ever uncover what it means that Being appears as will. What it means can only be asked in thinking; as what is to be thought, it can only be celebrated as worth asking about; as something we are mindful of, it can only be kept in mind.

In modern metaphysics, there for the first time expressly and explicitly, the Being of beings appears as will. Man is man insofar as he comports himself to beings by way of thought. In this way he is held in Being. Man's thinking must also correspond in its essence to that toward which it comports itself, to wit, the Being of beings as will.

Now, Nietzsche tells us that prior thinking has been determined by the spirit of revenge. Precisely how is Nietzsche thinking the essence of revenge, assuming that he is thinking it metaphysically?

In the second part of ***Thus Spoke Zarathustra,*** in the episode we have already mentioned, "On Redemption," Nietzsche has Zarathustra say: "This, yes, this alone is revenge itself: the will's ill will toward time and its 'It was.'"

That an essential definition of revenge emphasizes revulsion and defiance, and thus points to revenge as ill will, corresponds to our characterization of it as a peculiar sort of persecution. Yet Nietzsche does not merely say that revenge is revulsion. The same could be said of hatred. Nietzsche says that revenge is the will's ill will. But *will* signifies the Being of beings as a whole, and not simply human willing. By virtue of the characterization of revenge as "the will's ill will," the defiant persecution of revenge persists primarily in relationship to the Being of beings. It becomes apparent that this is the case when we heed what it is on which revenge's ill will turns: revenge is "the will's ill will against time and its 'It was.'"

When we read this essential definition of revenge for the first time—and also for a second and a third time—the

emphatic application of revenge to *time* seems to us surprising, incomprehensible, ultimately gratuitous. It has to strike us this way, as long as we think no further about what the word *time* here means.

Nietzsche says that revenge is "the will's ill will toward time. . . ." This does not say, toward something temporal. Nor does it say, toward a particular characteristic of time. It simply says, "Ill will toward time. . . ."

To be sure, these words now follow: ". . . toward time and its 'It was.'" But this suggests that revenge is ill will toward the "It was" of time. We may insist, quite rightly, that not only the "it was" but also the "it will be" and the "it is now" also pertain just as essentially to time. For time is defined not only by the past but also by future and present. If therefore Nietzsche stresses the "It was" of time, his characterization of the essence of revenge obviously refers, not to time *as such,* but to time in one particular respect. Yet how do matters stand with time "as such"? They stand in this way: time goes. And it goes by passing. Whatever of time is to come never comes to stay, but only to go. Where to? Into passing. When a man dies we say he has passed away. The temporal is held to be that which passes away.

Nietzsche defines revenge as "the will's ill will toward time and its 'It was.'" The supplement to the definition does not mean to put into relief one isolated characteristic of time while stubbornly ignoring the other two; rather, it designates the fundamental trait of time in its proper and entire unfolding as time. With the conjunction and in the phrase "time and its 'It was,'" Nietzsche is not proceeding to append one special characteristic of time. Here the *and* means as much as "and that means." Revenge is the will's ill will toward time and that means toward passing away, transiency. Transiency is that against which the will can take no further steps, that against which its willing constantly collides. Time and its "It was" is the obstacle that the will cannot budge. Time, as passing away, is repulsive; the will suffers on account of it. Suffering in this way, the will itself becomes chronically ill over such passing away; the illness then wills its own passing, and in so doing wills that everything in the world be worthy of passing away. Ill will toward time degrades all that passes away. The earthly—Earth and all that pertains to her—is that which properly ought not to be and which ultimately does not really possess true Being. Plato himself called it *mē on,* nonbeing.

According to Schelling's statements, which simply express the guiding representations of all metaphysics, the prime predicates of Being are "independence from time," "eternity."

Yet the most profound ill will toward time does not consist in the mere disparagement of the earthly. For Nietzsche the most deepseated revenge consists in that reflection which posits supratemporal ideality as absolute. Measured against it, the temporal must perforce degrade itself to nonbeing proper.

Yet how should humanity assume dominion over the earth, how can it take the earth as earth into its protection, so long as it degrades the earthly, so long as the spirit of revenge determines its reflection? If it is a matter of rescuing the earth as earth, then the spirit of revenge will have to vanish beforehand. Thus for Zarathustra redemption from revenge is the bridge to the highest hope.

But in what does redemption from ill will toward transiency consist? Does it consist in a liberation from the will in general—perhaps in the senses suggested by Schopenhauer and in Buddhism? Inasmuch as the Being of beings is will, according to the doctrine of modern metaphysics, redemption from the will would amount to redemption from Being, hence to a collapse into vacuous nothingness. For Nietzsche redemption from revenge is redemption from the repulsive, from defiance and degradation in the will, but by no means the dissolution of all willing. Redemption releases the ill will from its "no" and frees it for a "yes." What does the "yes" affirm? Precisely what the ill will of a vengeful spirit renounced: time, transiency.

The "yes" to time is the will that transiency perdure, that it not be disparaged as nothing worth. Yet how can passing away perdure? Only in this way: as passing away it must not only continuously go, but must also always come. Only in this way: passing away and transiency must recur in their coming as the same. And such recurrence itself is perdurant only if it is eternal. According to the doctrine of metaphysics, the predicate "eternity" belongs to the Being of beings.

Redemption from revenge is transition from ill will toward time to the will that represents being in the eternal recurrence of the same. Here the will becomes the advocate of the circle.

To put it another way: Only when the Being of beings represents itself to man as eternal recurrence of the same can man cross over the bridge and, redeemed from the spirit of revenge, be the one in transition, the overman.

Zarathustra is the teacher who teaches the overman. But he teaches this doctrine only because he is the teacher of eternal recurrence of the same. This thought, eternal recurrence of the same, is first in rank. It is the "most abysmal" thought. For that reason the teacher comes out with it last, and always hesitantly.

Who is Nietzsche's Zarathustra? He is the teacher whose doctrine would liberate prior reflection from the spirit of revenge to the "yes" spoken to eternal recurrence of the same.

As the teacher of eternal recurrence, Zarathustra teaches the overman. According to an unpublished note, a refrain accompanies the latter doctrine: "Refrain: *'Love alone will make it right'*—(the creative love that *forgets* itself in its works)."

As the teacher of eternal recurrence and overman, Zarathustra does not teach two different things. What he teaches coheres in itself, since one demands the other as its response. Such correspondence—in the way it essentially unfolds and the way it withdraws—is precisely what the figure of Zarathustra conceals in itself, conceals yet at the same time displays, thus allowing the correspondence to provoke our thought.

Yet the teacher knows that what he is teaching remains a vision and a riddle. He perseveres in such reflective knowledge.

We today, because of the peculiar ascendancy of the modern sciences, are caught up in the strange misconception that knowledge can be attained from science and that thinking is subject to the jurisdiction of science. Yet whatever unique thing a thinker is able to say can be neither proved nor refuted logically or empirically. Nor is it a matter of faith. We can only envisage it questioningly, thoughtfully. What we envisage thereby always appears as *worthy* of question.

To catch a glimpse of the vision and the riddle which the figure Zarathustra manifests, and to retain that glimpse, let us once again cast our eyes on the spectacle of Zarathustra's animals. They appear to him at the outset of his journeyings:

> . . . He looked inquiringly into the sky—for above him he heard the piercing cry of a bird. And behold! An eagle soared through the air in vast circles, and a serpent hung suspended from him, not as his prey, but as though she were his friend: for she had coiled about his neck.
>
> "These are my animals!" said Zarathustra, and his heart was filled with joy.

A passage we cited earlier—yet purposely only in part—from the first section of "The Convalescent" reads: "I, Zarathustra, the advocate of life, the advocate of suffering, the advocate of the circle—I summon you, my most abysmal thought!" In the second section of the episode "On the Vision and the Riddle," in Part III, Zarathustra describes the thought of eternal recurrence of the same in identical words. There, in his confrontation with the dwarf, Zarathustra tries for the first time to think that riddlesome thing which he sees as meriting his longing. The eternal recurrence of the same does remain a vision for Zarathustra; but it is also a riddle. It can be neither proved nor refuted logically or empirically. At bottom, this holds for every essential thought of every thinker: something envisaged, but a riddle—worthy of question.

Who is Nietzsche's Zarathustra? We can now reply in the following formula: Zarathustra is the teacher of eternal return of the same and the teacher of overman. But now we can see more clearly—perhaps also beyond our own formula—that Zarathustra is not a teacher who instructs us concerning two sundry items. Zarathustra teaches the overman because he is the teacher of eternal return of the same. Yet the reverse is also true: Zarathustra teaches eternal return of the same because he is the teacher of overman. These doctrines are conjoined in a circle. In its circling, the teaching corresponds to that which is—to the circle which as eternal recurrence of the same makes out the Being of beings, that is, what is permanent in Becoming.

The teaching, and our thinking of it, will achieve such circling whenever they cross over the bridge called "Redemption from the Spirit of Revenge." In this way prior thinking is to be overcome.

From the period immediately following the completion of the work *Thus Spoke Zarathustra,* the year 1885, comes a note that has been taken up as number 617 in the book that was pieced together from Nietzsche's literary remains and published under the title *The Will to Power.* The note bears the underscored title "Recapitulation." Here Nietzsche with extraordinary perspicuity condenses the principal matter of his thinking into just a few sentences. A parenthetical remark appended to the text makes explicit mention of Zarathustra. Nietzsche's "Recapitulation" begins with the statement: "To *stamp* Becoming with the character of Being—that is the supreme *will to power*."

The supreme will to power, that is, what is most vital in all life, comes to pass when transiency is represented as perpetual Becoming in the eternal recurrence of the same, in this way being made stable and permanent. Such representing is a thinking which, as Nietzsche emphatically notes, *stamps* the character of Being on beings. Such thinking takes Becoming, to which perpetual collision and suffering belong, into its protection and custody.

Does such thinking overcome prior reflection, overcome the spirit of revenge? Or does there not lie concealed in this very *stamping*—which takes all Becoming into the protection of eternal recurrence of the same—a form of ill will *against* sheer transiency and thereby a highly spiritualized spirit of revenge?

We no sooner pose this question than the illusion arises that we are trying to discredit Nietzsche, to impute something as most proper to him which is precisely what he wants to overcome. It is as though we cherished the view that by such imputation we were refuting the thought of this thinker.

The officious will to refute never even approaches a thinker's path. Refutation belongs among those petty intellectual entertainments which the public needs for its amusement. Moreover, Nietzsche himself long ago anticipated the answer to our question. The text that immediately precedes *Thus Spoke Zarathustra* in Nietzsche's corpus appeared in 1882 under the title *The Gay Science.* In its penultimate section, under the heading "The Greatest Burden," Nietzsche first delineated his "most abysmal thought." Following it is the final section, which was adopted verbatim as the opening of the Prologue to *Thus Spoke Zarathustra.* In the posthumously published materials we find sketches for a foreword to *The Gay Science.* There we read the following:

> A spirit fortified by wars and victories, which has developed a need for conquest, adventure, hazard, pain; become accustomed to the crispness of the upper air, to long wintry walks, to ice and mountain crags in every sense; a kind of sublime malice and extreme exuberance of revenge—for there is *revenge* in it, revenge on life itself, when one who suffers greatly *takes life under his protection.*

What is left for us to say, if not this: Zarathustra's doctrine does not bring redemption from revenge? We do say it. Yet we say it by no means as a misconceived refutation of Nietzsche's philosophy. We do not even utter it as an objection against Nietzsche's thinking. But we say it in order to turn our attention to the fact that—and the extent to which—Nietzsche's thought too is animated by the spirit of prior reflection. Whether the spirit of prior thinking is at all captured in its definitive essence when it is interpreted as the spirit of revenge—this question we leave open. At all events, prior thinking is metaphysics, and Nietzsche's thinking presumably brings it to fulfillment.

Thus something in Nietzsche's thinking comes to the fore which this thinking itself was no longer able to think. Such remaining behind what it has thought designates the creativity of a thinking. And where a thinking brings metaphysics to completion it points in an exceptional way to things unthought, cogently and confusedly at once. Yet where are the eyes to see this?

Metaphysical thinking rests on the distinction between what truly is and what, measured against this, constitutes all that is not truly in being. However, what is decisive for the essence of metaphysics is by no means the fact that the designated distinction is formulated as the opposition of the suprasensuous to the sensuous realm, but the fact that this distinction—in the sense of a yawning gulf between the realms—remains primary and all-sustaining. The distinction persists even when the Platonic hierarchy of suprasensuous and sensuous is inverted and the sensuous realm is experienced more essentially and more thoroughly—in the direction Nietzsche indicates with the name *Dionysos.* For the superabundance for which Zarathustra's "great longing" yearns is the inexhaustible permanence of Becoming, which the will to power in the eternal recurrence of the same wills itself to be.

Nietzsche brought what is essentially metaphysical in his thinking to the extremity of ill will in the final lines of his final book, *Ecce Homo: How One Becomes What One Is.* Nietzsche composed the text in October of 1888. It was first published in a limited edition twenty years later; in 1911 it was taken up into the fifteenth volume of the *Grossoktav* edition. The final lines of **Ecce Homo** read: "Have I been understood? —*Dionysos versus the Crucified. . . .*"

Who is Nietzsche's Zarathustra? He is the advocate of Dionysos. That means that Zarathustra is the teacher who in and for his doctrine of overman teaches the eternal return of the same.

Does the preceding statement provide the answer to our query? No. Nor does it provide the answer after we have pursued all the references that might elucidate the statement, hoping in that way to follow Zarathustra—if only in that first step across the bridge. The statement, which looks like an answer, nonetheless wants us to take note, wants to make us more alert, as it conducts us back to the question that serves as our title.

Who is Nietzsche's Zarathustra? The question now asks who this teacher is. Who is this figure which, at the stage of metaphysics' completion, appears within metaphysics? Nowhere else in the history of Western metaphysics has the essential figure been expressly created in this way for its respective thinker—or, to put it more appropriately and literally, nowhere else has that figure been so tellingly *thought.* Nowhere else—unless at the beginning of Western thought, in Parmenides, though there only in veiled outlines.

Essential to the figure of Zarathustra remains the fact that the teacher teaches something twofold which coheres in itself: eternal return and overman. Zarathustra is himself in a certain way this coherence. That said, he too remains a riddle, one we have scarcely envisaged.

"Eternal return of the same" is the name for the Being of beings. "Overman" is the name for the human essence that corresponds to such Being.

On what basis do Being and the essence of human being belong together? How do they cohere, if Being is no fabrication of human beings and humanity no mere special case among beings?

Can the coherence of Being and the essence of human being be discussed at all, as long as our thinking remains mired in the previous conception of man? According to it, man is *animal rationale,* the rational animal. Is it a coincidence, or a bit of lyrical ornamentation, that the two animals, eagle and serpent, accompany Zarathustra; that *they* tell him who he must become, in order to be the one he is? In the figure of the two animals the union of pride and discernment is to come to the fore for those who think. Yet we have to know what Nietzsche thinks concerning these two traits. Among the notes sketched during the period when **Thus Spoke Zarathustra** was composed we read: "It seems to me that *modesty* and *pride* belong to one another quite closely. . . . What they have in common is the cool, unflinching look of appraisal." And elsewhere in these notes:

> People talk so stupidly about *pride*—and Christianity even tried to make us feel *sinful* about it! The point is that whoever *demands great things of himself, and achieves those things,* must feel quite remote from those who do not. Such *distance* will be interpreted by these others as a "putting on airs"; but he knows it [distance] only as continuous toil, war, victory, by day and by night. The others have no inkling of all this!

The eagle: the proudest animal; the serpent: the most discerning animal. And both conjoined in the circle in which they hover, in the ring that embraces their essence; and circle and ring once again interfused.

The riddle of who Zarathustra is, as teacher of eternal return and overman, is envisaged by us in the spectacle of the two animals. In this spectacle we can grasp more directly and more readily what our presentation tried to exhibit as the matter most worthy of question, namely, the relation of Being to that living being, man.

> And behold! An eagle soared through the air in vast circles, and a serpent hung suspended from him, not as his prey, but as though she were his friend: for she had coiled about his neck.
>
> "These are my animals!" said Zarathustra, and his heart was filled with joy.

Nietzsche himself knew that his "most abysmal thought" remains a riddle. All the less reason for us to imagine that we can solve the riddle. The obscurity of this last thought

of Western metaphysics dare not tempt us to circumvent it by some sort of subterfuge.

At bottom there are only two such routes of escape.

Either one avers that this thought of Nietzsche's is a kind of "mysticism" that our thinking should not bother to confront.

Or one avers that this thought is as old as the hills, that it boils down to the long-familiar cyclical notion of cosmic occurrence. Which notion can be found for the first time in Western philosophy in Heraclitus.

This second piece of information, like all information of that sort, tells us absolutely nothing. What good is it if someone determines with respect to a particular thought that it can be found, for example, "already" in Leibniz or even "already" in Plato? What good are such references when they leave what Leibniz and Plato were thinking in the same obscurity as the thought they claim to be clarifying with the help of these historical allusions?

As for the first subterfuge, according to which Nietzsche's thought of eternal recurrence of the same is a mystic phantasmagoria, a look at the present age might well teach us a different lesson—presupposing of course that thinking is called upon to bring to light the essence of modern technology.

What else is the essence of the modern power-driven machine than *one* offshoot of the eternal recurrence of the same? But the essence of such machines is neither something machine-like nor anything mechanical. Just as little can Nietzsche's thought of eternal recurrence of the same be interpreted in a mechanical sense.

That Nietzsche interpreted and experienced his most abysmal thought in terms of the Dionysian only speaks for the fact that he still thought it metaphysically, and had to think it solely in this way. Yet it says nothing against the fact that this most abysmal thought conceals something unthought, something which at the same time remains a sealed door to metaphysical thinking.

Martin Heidegger, in his Nietzsche: The Eternal Recurrence of the Same, Vol. II, *translated by David Farrell Krell, Harper & Row, Publishers, 1984, 290 p.*

William Barrett　(essay date 1958)

[*Barrett was an American critic, educator, and editor who was associated with the influential leftist journal* Partisan Review, *whose editors, including Lionel Trilling, Hannah Arendt, and Mary McCarthy, espoused Marxist and modernist ideas in politics and literature. Barrett reacted against the utopian strain in these ideologies and distinguished himself in translating and explicating the work of European existentialists. In the following excerpt from his much-praised study of existentialism,* Irrational Man: A Study in Existential Philosophy, *Barrett elucidates Nietzsche's contributions to existentialist thought.*]

By the middle of the nineteenth century . . . , the problem of man had begun to dawn on certain minds in a new and more radical form: Man, it was seen, is a stranger to himself and must discover, or rediscover, who he is and

An excerpt from *Beyond Good and Evil*

The will to truth which will still tempt us to many a venture, that famous truthfulness of which all philosophers so far have spoken with respect—what questions has this will to truth not laid before us! What strange, wicked, questionable questions! That is a long story even now—and yet it seems as if it had scarcely begun. Is it any wonder that we should finally become suspicious, lose patience, and turn away impatiently? that we should finally learn from this Sphinx to ask questions, too? *Who* is it really that puts questions to us here? *What* in us really wants "truth"?

Indeed we came to a long halt at the question about the cause of this will—until we finally came to a complete stop before a still more basic question. We asked about the *value* of this will. Suppose we want truth: *why not rather* untruth? and uncertainty? even ignorance?

The problem of the value of truth came before us—or was it we who came before the problem? Who of us is Oedipus here? Who is the Sphinx? It is a rendezvous, it seems, of questions and question marks.

And though it scarcely seems credible, it finally almost seems to us as if the problem had never even been put so far—as if we were the first to see it, fix it with our eyes, and *risk* it. For it does involve a risk, and perhaps there is none that is greater.

"How *could* anything originate out of its opposite? for example, truth out of error? or the will to truth out of the will to deception? or selfless deeds out of selfishness? or the pure and sunlike gaze of the sage out of lust? Such origins are impossible; whoever dreams of them is a fool, indeed worse; the things of highest value must have another, *peculiar* origin—they cannot be derived from this transitory, seductive, deceptive, paltry world, from this turmoil of delusion and lust. Rather from the lap of Being, the intransitory, the hidden god, the 'thing-in-itself'—there must be their basis, and nowhere else."

This way of judging constitutes the typical prejudgment and prejudice which give away the metaphysicians of all ages; this kind of valuation looms in the background of all their logical procedures; it is on account of this "faith" that they trouble themselves about "knowledge," about something that is finally baptized solemnly as "the truth." The fundamental faith of the metaphysicians is *the faith in opposite values*. It has not even occurred to the most cautious among them that one might have a doubt right here at the threshold where it was surely most necessary—even as they vowed to themselves, *"de omnibus dubitandum [all is to be doubted]."*

Friedrich Nietzsche, in his Beyond Good and Evil, *translated by Walter Kaufmann, Random House, 1966.*

what his meaning is. Kierkegaard had recommended a rediscovery of the religious center of the Self, which for European man had to mean a return to Christianity, but what he had in mind was a radical return that went back beyond organized Christendom and its churches to a state of contemporaneity with the first disciples of Christ. Nietzsche's solution harked back to an even more remote and archaic past: to the early Greeks, before either Christianity or science had put its blight upon the healthiness of man's instincts.

It was Nietzsche's fate to experience the problem of man in a peculiarly personal and virulent form. At twenty-four, an unheard-of age in the German academic world, he became Professor of Classical Philology at the University of Basel. The letter of recommendation written for him on this occasion by his teacher, Ritschl, is almost one continuous exclamation of awe at the prodigy of culture being sent to Basel. Besides being immensely learned in the classical languages, Nietzsche showed extraordinary literary promise and was also a gifted musician. But this prodigy was also a very delicate and sickly youth, with weak eyesight and a nervous stomach. Nietzsche had undoubtedly inherited this fragile constitution, but in later years he tended to think resentfully that it had been brought about by the excessive labors of scholarship. At any rate, intensive study had not helped his health. He thus knew at first hand the war between culture and vitality: he was himself, in fact, the field of battle between the two. He had to resign his professorship after ten years because of his poor health. Thereafter he became the wanderer and his shadow—to use the title of one of his books, which accurately describes his own life—traveling all over southern Europe in search of a health that he never could regain. In those disconsolate and lonely years all his glittering cultural attributes did not help him in the least; culture, in fact, was a screen between the wanderer and the natural man that he strove to resurrect. As a scholarly bookworm he had not even known that he was unknown to himself, but when his eyesight became too poor to read books he began at last to read himself: a text that culture up to that time had obscured.

Nietzsche had originally encountered the god Dionysus in his studies of Greek tragedy. Dionysus was the patron deity of the Greek tragic festivals, and so the cult of this god had received all the blessing of high culture, since it was associated with the most sublime and formally beautiful products of human art. On the other hand, the Dionysian cult reached back into the most primitive and archaic eras of the Greek race. For Dionysus was the god of the vine, the god of drunken ecstasy and frenzy, who made the vine come to life in spring and brought all men together in the joy of intoxication. This god thus united miraculously in himself the height of culture with the depth of instinct, bringing together the warring opposites that divided Nietzsche himself. The problem of reconciling these opposites was the central theme later of D. H. Lawrence, of Gide in his *Immoralist* (a fiction based upon Nietzsche's life), and of Freud in one of his last and most significant works, *Civilization and Its Discontents.* It is still the most formidable problem of man in our twentieth, the psychoanalytic, century. Dionysus reborn, Nietzsche thought, might become a savior-god for the whole race, which seemed everywhere to show symptoms of fatigue and decline. The symbol of the god became so potent for Nietzsche that it ended—as only symbols can do—by taking possession of his life. He consecrated himself to the service of the god Dionysus.

But Dionysus is a dangerous as well as an ambiguous god. Those in antiquity who meddled with him ended by being torn to pieces. When he took possession of his own followers he drove them to frenzies of destruction. He was called, among other names, "the horned one" and "the bull" by the Greeks, and in one of his cults was worshiped in the form of a bull who was ritually slaughtered and torn to pieces. So Dionysus himself, according to the myth, had been torn to pieces by the Titans, those formless powers of the subterranean world who were always at war with the enlightened gods of Olympus. The fate of his god overtook Nietzsche: he too was torn apart by the dark forces of the underworld, succumbing, at the age of forty-five, to psychosis. It may be a metaphor, but it is certainly not an exaggeration, to say that he perished as a ritual victim slaughtered for the sake of his god.

It is equally true, and perhaps just another way of saying the same thing, that Nietzsche perished for the sake of the problems of life that he set out to solve. The sacrifice of a victim, in the ancient and primitive world, was supposed to bring blessings upon the rest of the tribe, but Nietzsche was one of those who bring not peace but a sword. His works have divided, shocked, and perplexed readers ever since his death, and at the low point of his posthumous fortune his name was polluted by a Nietzschean cult among the Nazis. Nevertheless, the victim did not perish in vain; his sacrifice can be an immense lesson to the rest of the tribe if it is willing to learn from him. Nietzsche's fate is one of the great episodes in man's historic effort to know himself. After him, the problem of man could never quite return to its pre-Nietzschean level. Nietzsche it was who showed in its fullest sense how thoroughly problematical is the nature of man: he can never be understood as an animal species within the zoological order of nature, because he has broken free of nature and has thereby posed the question of his own meaning—and with it the meaning of nature as well—as his destiny. Nietzsche's works are an immense mine of observations on the condition of man, one that we are still in the process of quarrying.

Moreover, Nietzsche's life stands in a double sense as a great warning to mankind, to be heeded lest we too suffer the fate of being torn apart like Dionysus Zagreus. He who would make the descent into the lower regions runs the risk of succumbing to what the primitives call "the perils of the soul"—the unknown Titans that lie within, below the surface of our selves. To ascend again from the darkness of Avernus is, as the Latin poet tells us, the difficult thing, and he who would make the descent had better secure his lines of communication with the surface. Communication means community, and the adventurer into the depths would do well to have roots in a human community and perhaps even the ballast, somewhere in his nature, of a little bit of Philistinism. Nietzsche lacked such lines of communication, for he had cut himself off from the human community; he was one of the loneliest men that ever existed. By comparison, Kierkegaard looks almost

like a worldly soul, for he was at least solidly planted in his native Copenhagen, and though he may have been at odds with his fellow citizens, he loved the town, and it was his home. Nietzsche, however, was altogether and utterly homeless. He who descends must keep in touch with the surface, but on the other hand—and this is the other sense of Nietzsche's warning—modern man may also be torn apart by the titanic forces within himself if he does not attempt the descent into Avernus. It is no mere matter of psychological curiosity but a question of life and death for man in our time to place himself again in contact with the archaic life of his unconscious. Without such contact he may become the Titan who slays himself. Man, this most dangerous of the animals, as Nietzsche called him, now holds in his hands the dangerous power of blowing himself and his planet to bits; and it is not yet even clear that this problematic and complex being is really sane.

"In the end one experiences only oneself," Nietzsche observes in his *Zarathustra,* and elsewhere he remarks, in the same vein, that all the systems of the philosophers are just so many forms of personal confession, if we but had eyes to see it. Following this conviction, that the thinker cannot be separated from his thought, Nietzsche revealed himself in his work more fully than any philosopher before or since. Hence the best introduction to him may be the little autobiographical book *Ecce Homo,* which is his own attempt to take stock of himself and his life. Nietzsche is not the most prepossessing figure, as we are introduced to him here, for in this work he was clearly already in the grip of the psychological malady that three years later was to bring on his breakdown. But he is a great enough figure that he can stand being approached from his weakest side. And did not he himself say we must divest philosophers of their masks, learn to see the thinker's *shadow* in his thought? Paradoxical as it may sound, to praise Nietzsche properly we have also to say the worst possible things about him. This too is in line with his own principle, that good and bad in any individual are inextricably one, all the more so as the opposing qualities become more extreme. All of Nietzsche—in his extremes of good and bad—is summed up in *Ecce Homo,* and it is precisely the *all* that he himself could not see.

An unprejudiced psychological observer is at once fascinated and appalled by what he finds in *Ecce Homo.* The process of ego-inflation has already gone beyond the bounds of what we ordinarily call neurosis. And this inflation is already tinged with curious distortions of the facts: Nietzsche refers to himself swaggeringly as "an old artilleryman" as if he had had a robust military career, though we of course know that his service in the artillery was so brief as to be almost non-existent, and that it terminated with his illness after a fall from his horse. The relation with Lou Salome, which was in fact very slight, is described obliquely in such a fashion as to suggest that Nietzsche was a devil of a fellow with women. These are not the shallow lies of a calculating mind, but delusions in the systematic sense of psychopathology: that is, fantasies in which the man himself has begun to live. He rails against the Germans, yet he himself is German to the marrow. And while he proclaims himself above all resentments, we are aware throughout of a thin skin that is smarting with resentment at his lack of readers and of recognition in Germany. Nietzsche speaks of himself as the greatest psychologist who ever lived; and while there is some basis for so grandiose a boast—he was indeed a great psychologist—the overwhelming question his book raises is why this psychologist has so little insight into himself. The vision of his true self, we suspect, would have been too terrifying for him to face. The fantasies, the delusions, the grandiose inflation of the ego are only devices to shield him from the sight of *the other side of himself*—of Nietzsche, the sickly lonely man, emotionally starved, a ghost flitting from place to place, always without a home—the dwarf side, that is, of the giant about whom he boasts. Nietzsche's systematic shielding of himself from the other side is relevant to his explanation of the death of God: Man killed God, he says, because he could not bear to have anyone looking at his ugliest side. Man must cease to feel guilt, he goes on; and yet one senses an enormous hidden guilt and feeling of inferiority behind his own frantic boasts. Yet, though the wind of madness may already be blowing through *Ecce Homo,* at the same time the powers of Nietzsche's mind were never more formidable. The style is as brisk and incisive as anything he wrote, as he lays before us in bold and simple outline the guiding pattern of his ideas. It is this split between madness and coherence that makes the book so paradoxical. How could the mind of this man have so split off from the rest of himself—and this in a thinker who, above all other philosophers, seemed to have found access to the unconscious?

The title of the book itself *Ecce Homo*—"Behold the Man!", the words of Pontius Pilate spoken about Christ—supplies a very definite clue. The imitation of Christ, in however remote and unconscious a form, is something that almost nobody raised a Christian can avoid. ("All my life I have compared myself with Christ," exclaims the tramp in Samuel Beckett's *Waiting for Godot.*) Nietzsche had come from a line of Protestant pastors, had been raised in a very pious atmosphere, and was himself as a boy very devout. The religious influences of childhood are the hardest things to extirpate; the leopard can as easily change his spots. Had Nietzsche merely lost his Christian faith, or even simply attacked it intellectually, these acts would in themselves have been sufficient to create a conflict within him; but he went further by attempting to deny the Christian in himself, and thereby split himself in two. The symbol of Dionysus had possessed him intellectually; he identified with this pagan god (in one place in *Ecce Homo* he actually speaks of himself as Dionysus), and thenceforth, with all the energy of mind that he could summon, he devoted himself to elaborating the opposition between Dionysus and Christ. In the end, however, the symbol of Christ proved the more potent; and when his unconscious finally broke irremediably into the open, it was Christ who took possession of Nietzsche, as is shown by the letters written after his breakdown which he signed "The Crucified One."

In a life so filled with portents and omens it is remarkable that he should have recorded one–in a dream he had when a schoolboy of fifteen, at Pforta– that was prophetic of the central conflict out of which he was to write and live. In the dream he was wandering about in a gloomy wood at night, and after being terrified by "a piercing shriek from a neighboring lunatic asylum," he met with a hunter whose "features were wild and uncanny." In a valley "surrounded by dense undergrowth," the hunter raised his whistle to his lips and blew such "a shrill note" that Nietzsche woke out of his nightmare. Now it is interesting that in this dream he had been on his way to Eisleben, Luther's town; but on meeting the hunter it became a question of going instead to Teutschenthal (which means, German Valley). That is, the two roads diverge, one leading toward Lutheran Christianity, the other toward the primeval pagan German soil. Being a classical scholar, Nietzsche preferred to let his wandering German god assume the Greek guise of Dionysus. It would be farfetched to make much of this dream if it were merely an isolated revelation, but it is in fact of a piece with the other dreams and visions that Nietzsche poured into his writings. Even the frightening prophecy of madness that occurs in the dream is echoed among the images of *Zarathustra.* Nietzsche's life has all the characteristics of a psychological fatality.

Now all these self-revelations that we have been discussing, it might be said, reflect nothing but a pathological process, and therefore had best be left to one side while we discuss the philosophic ideas of this thinker. Unfortunately, nothing in life is *nothing but;* it is always something more. What we have been talking about is indeed a pathological process, but it is also a pathological process taking place in a thinker of genius, from whom the process thereby acquires an immense significance. It is just as much a mistake for interpreters of Nietzsche to cast aside this whole matter of Nietzsche's sickness, as it was for the Philistines, shocked by his ideas, to discount them simply as the ravings of a madman. It may be that genius and neurosis are inextricably linked, as some recent discussions of the subject have held; in any case Nietzsche would be one of the prime examples of the kind of truth neurosis, and even worse than neurosis, can be made to reveal for the rest of mankind. The pathological process in Nietzsche, which we have dealt with only briefly here, is in fact indispensable for an understanding of the philosophic meaning of atheism as he tried to live it. Nietzsche was engaged in a process of tearing himself loose from his psychological roots at the very moment in history that Western man was doing likewise—only the latter did not know it. Up to that time man had lived in the childhood shelter of his gods or of God; now that all the gods were dead he was taking his first step into maturity. This, for Nietzsche, was the most momentous event in modern history, one to which all the social, economic, and military upheavals of the nineteenth and indeed of the coming twentieth century would, as he prophesied, be secondary. Could mankind meet this awful challenge of becoming adult and godless? Yes, said Nietzsche, because man is the most courageous animal and will be able to survive even the death of his gods. The very process of tearing consciousness loose from its roots, which ends inevitably in *Ecce Homo* in the grandiose inflation of the ego, had for Nietzsche himself the significance of a supreme act of courage. Not a day goes by, he wrote in one of his letters, that I do not lop off some comforting belief. Man must live without any religious or metaphysical consolations. And if it was to be humanity's fate to become godless, he, Nietzsche, elected to be the prophet who

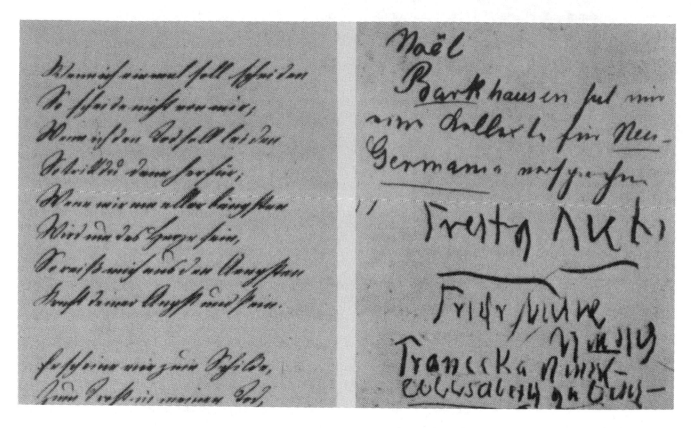

(Left) A page from the hand-written volume of poetry which the thirteen-year-old Nietzsche gave to his mother in 1857 for a Christmas present. (Right) A scrawled note (probably from 1892) including two attempts at signature and at writing the names of his mother and sister.

would give the necessary example of courage. It is in this light that we must look upon Nietzsche as a culture hero: he chose, that is, to suffer the conflict within his culture in its most acute form and was ultimately torn apart by it.

Now, there are atheists and atheists. The urbane atheism of Bertrand Russell, for example, presupposes the existence of believers against whom he can score points in an argument and get off some of his best quips. The atheism of Sartre is a more somber affair, and indeed borrows some of its color from Nietzsche: Sartre relentlessly works out the atheistic conclusion that in a universe without God man is absurd, unjustified, and without reason, as Being itself is. Still, this kind of atheism seems to carry with it the bravado of one who is ranging himself on the side of a less sanguine truth than the rest of mankind. Nietzsche's atheism, however, goes even deeper. He projects himself into the situation where God is really dead for the whole of mankind, and he shares in the common fate, not merely scoring points off the believers. Section 125 of **The Joyful Wisdom** [**The Gay Science**], the passage in which Nietzsche first speaks of the death of God, is one of the most heart-rending things he ever wrote. The man who has seen the death of God, significantly enough, is a madman, and he cries out his vision to the unheeding populace in the market place, asking the question: "Do we not now wander through an endless Nothingness?" Here we are no longer dealing with the abstractions of logical argument, but

with a fate that has overtaken mankind. Of course, Nietzsche himself tried elsewhere to assume the witty mask of the *libre penseur* of the Enlightenment and to make brilliant aphorisms about God's non-existence. And in his **Zarathustra** he speaks of "Zarathustra the godless" and even "the most godless." But godless is one thing Nietzsche certainly was not: he was in the truest sense possessed by a god, though he could not identify what god it was and mistakenly took him for Dionysus. In a very early poem, **"To the Unknown God,"** written when he was only twenty years old, he speaks about himself as a god-possessed man, more truthfully than he was later, as a philosopher, to be able to recognize:

> I must know thee, Unknown One,
> Thou who searchest out the depths of my soul,
> And blowest like a storm through my life.
> Thou art inconceivably and yet my kinsman!
> I must know thee and even serve thee.

Had God really died in the depths of Nietzsche's soul or was it merely that the intellect of the philosopher could not cope with His presence and His meaning?

If God is taken as a metaphysical object whose existence has to be proved, then the position held by scientifically-minded philosophers like Russell must inevitably be valid: the existence of such an object can never be empirically proved. Therefore, God must be a superstition held by primitive and childish minds. But both these alternative views are abstract, whereas the reality of God is concrete, a thoroughly autonomous presence that takes hold of men but of which, of course, some men are more conscious than others. Nietzsche's atheism reveals the true meaning of God—and does so, we might add, more effectively than a good many official forms of theism. He himself scoffs in one place at his being confused with the ordinary run of freethinkers, who have not the least understanding of his atheism. And despite the desperate struggle of the "godless Zarathustra," Nietzsche remained in the possession of this Unknown God to whom he had paid homage in his youth. This possession is shown in its most violent form in *Zarathustra,* even though Nietzsche puts the words into the mouth of the Magician, an aspect of himself that he wishes to exorcise:

> Thus do I lie,
> Bend myself, twist myself, convulsed
> With all eternal torture,
> And smitten
> By thee, cruelest huntsman,
> Thou unfamiliar—GOD

At this point we are ready to see what takes place behind the scenes in *Zarathustra,* where all the aforementioned themes become fully orchestrated.

No adequate psychological commentary on *Thus Spoke Zarathustra* has yet been written, perhaps because the materials in it are so inexhaustible. It is a unique work of self-revelation but not at all on the personal or autobiographical level, and Nietzsche himself ostensibly does not appear in it; it is self-revelation at a greater, more primordial depth, where the stream of the unconscious itself gushes forth from the rock. Perhaps no other book contains such a steady procession of images, symbols, and visions straight out of the unconscious. It was Nietzsche's poetic work and because of this he could allow the unconscious to take over in it, to break through the restraints imposed elsewhere by the philosophic intellect. For this reason it is important beyond any of his strictly philosophic books; its content is actually richer than Nietzsche's own conceptual thought, and its symbols of greater wisdom and significance than he himself was able to grasp.

Nietzsche himself has described the process of inspiration by which he wrote this book, and his description makes it clear beyond question that we are in the presence here of an extraordinary release of and invasion by the unconscious:

> Can any one at the end of this nineteenth century have any distinct notion of what poets of a more vigorous period meant by inspiration? If not, I should like to describe it. . . . The notion of revelation describes the condition quite simply; by which I mean that something profoundly convulsive and disturbing suddenly becomes visible and audible with indescribable definiteness and exactness. . . . There is an ecstasy whose terrific tension is sometimes released by a flood of tears, during which one's progress varies from involuntary impetuosity to involuntary slowness. There is the feeling that one is utterly out of hand. . . . Everything occurs quite without

volition, as if in an eruption of freedom, independence, power and divinity. The spontaneity of the images and similes is most remarkable; one loses all perception of what is imagery and simile; everything offers itself as the most immediate, exact, and simple means of expression.

"One loses all perception of what is imagery and simile"— that is to say, the symbol itself supersedes thought, because it is richer in meaning.

His most lyrical book, *Zarathustra* is also the expression of the loneliest Nietzsche. It has about it the icy and arid atmosphere not merely of the symbolic mountaintop on which Zarathustra dwells, but of a real one. Reading it, one sometimes feels almost as if one were watching a film of the ascent of Mount Everest, hearing the climber's sobbing gasp for breath as he struggles slowly to higher and still higher altitudes. Climbing a mountain is the aptest metaphor for getting above ordinary humanity, and this precisely is what Zarathustra-Nietzsche is struggling to do. One hears throughout the book, though, in the gasping breath of the climber, the lament of Nietzsche the man.

The book begins with the recognition of this human relevance as Zarathustra, about to leave his mountain solitude, declares he is going down among men "once again to be a man." The mountain is the solitude of the spirit, the lowlands represent the world of ordinary men. The same symbolic contrast appears in Zarathustra's pet animals, the eagle and the serpent: the one the creature of the upper air, the other the one that moves closest to the earth. Zarathustra, as the third element, symbolizes the union between the two animals, of high and low, heaven and earth. He is going down among men, he says, as the sun sets dipping into the darkness below the horizon. But the sun sets in order to be reborn the next morning as a young and glowing god. The book thus opens with the symbols of rebirth and resurrection, and this is in fact the real theme of *Zarathustra*: how is man to be reborn, like the phoenix, from his own ashes? How is he to become really healthy and whole? Behind this question we see the personal shadow of Nietzsche's own illness and his long struggle to regain health; Zarathustra is at once the idealized image of himself and the symbol of a victory, in the struggle for health and wholeness, that Nietzsche himself was not able to achieve in life.

Despite the intensely personal sources of his theme, Nietzsche was dealing in this work with a problem that had already become central in German culture. Schiller and Goethe had dealt with it—Schiller as early as 1795 in his remarkable *Letters on Aesthetic Education,* and Goethe in his *Faust.* Schiller has given an extraordinarily clear statement of the problem, which was for him identical in all its salient features with the problem later posed by Nietzsche. For man, says Schiller, the problem is one of forming *individuals.* Modern life has departmentalized, specialized, and thereby fragmented the being of man. We now face the problem of putting the fragments together into a whole. In the course of his exposition, Schiller even referred back, as did Nietzsche, to the example of the Greeks, who produced real individuals and not mere learned abstract men like those of the modern age. Goethe was even closer to Nietzsche; *Faust* and *Zarathustra* are in fact brothers among books. Both attempt to elaborate in symbols the process by which the superior individual—whole, intact, and healthy—is to be formed; and both are identically "immoral" in their content, if morality is measured in its usual conventional terms.

Placed within the German cultural context, indeed, Nietzsche's immoralism begins to look less extreme than the popular imagination has taken it to be; it is not even as extreme as he was led to make it appear in some of the bloody creations of his overheated imagination in his last work, *The Will to Power.* Goethe in *Faust* was every bit as much at odds with conventional morality as was Nietzsche, but the old diplomatic fox of Weimar was a more tactful and better-balanced man and knew how to get his point across quietly, without shrieking it from the housetops as Nietzsche did. The Faust of the second part of Goethe's poem is already, as we have seen, something of a Nietzschean Superman, beyond ordinary good and evil. The story of the other, moral Faust is told in the popular sentimental opera of Gounod, in which the character sells himself to the Devil and wrongs a young girl; the whole thing comes to an end with the girl's tragic death. But Goethe could not leave matters at this; the problem that had taken hold of him, through his creation of Faust, led him to look upon Gretchen's tragedy simply as a stage along Faust's way. A process of self-development such as his cannot come to a close because a young girl whom he has seduced goes crazy and dies. The strong man survives such disasters and becomes harder. The Devil, with whom Faust has made a pact, becomes in a real sense his servitor and subordinate, just as our devil, if joined to ourselves, may become a fruitful and positive force; like Blake before him Goethe knew full well the ambiguous power contained in the traditional symbol of the Devil. Nietzsche's immoralism, though stated much more violently, consisted in not much more than the elaboration of Goethe's point: Man must incorporate his devil or, as he put it, man must become better and more evil; the tree that would grow taller must send its roots down deeper.

If Nietzsche was not able to contain himself as tactfully as Goethe, on this point, he nevertheless had something to shriek about: The whole of traditional morality, he believed, had no grasp of psychological reality and was therefore dangerously one-sided and false. To be sure, this had always been known but mankind, spouting ideals, had looked at such realities and winked, or adopted casuistry. But if one is going to live one's life literally and totally by the Sermon on the Mount or Buddha's *Dhammapada,* and one cannot manage to be a saint, one will end by making a sorry mess of oneself. Nietzsche's point has already carried so far that today in our ordinary valuations we are actually living in a post-Nietzschean world, one in which the psychoanalyst sometimes finds it necessary to tell a patient that he *ought* to be more aggressive and more selfish. Besides, what does the whole history of ethics amount to for that half, and more than half, of the human race, women, who deal with moral issues in altogether different terms from men? It amounts to rather a silly man-made affair that has very little to do with the real business of life. On this point Nietzsche has a perfectly sober and straightfor-

ward case against all those idealists, from Plato onward, who have set universal ideas over and above the individual's psychological needs. Morality itself is blind to the tangle of its own psychological motives, as Nietzsche showed in one of his most powerful books, *The Genealogy of Morals,* which traces the source of morality back to the drives of power and resentment. There are other motives that Nietzsche did not see, or did not care to honor, but no one can deny that these two, power and resentment, have historically been part of the shadow behind the moralist's severity.

But it is precisely here, in the context of the Faust-Zarathustra parallel, that the chief problem arises for Nietzsche as man and moralist. Suppose the ethical problem becomes the problem of the individual; the ethical question then becomes: How is the individual to nourish himself in order to grow? Once we set ourselves to reclaim that portion of human nature that traditional morality rejected—man's devil, to put it symbolically—we face the immense problem of socializing and taming those impulses. Here the imagination of Faustian man tends to become much too high-falutin. For Western man Faust has become the great symbol of the titanically striving individual, so much so that the historian Spengler could use the term "Faustian culture" to denote the whole modern epoch of our dynamic conquest of nature. In Nietzsche's Superman the spiritual tension would be even greater, for such an individual would be living at a higher level than all of humanity in the past. But what about the individual devil within the Superman? What about Zarathustra's devil? So far as Nietzsche attempts to make the goal of this higher individual the goal of mankind, a fatal ambiguity appears within his ideal itself. Is the Superman to be the extraordinary man, or the complete and whole man? Psychological wholeness does not necessarily coincide with extraordinary powers, and the great genius may be a crippled and maimed figure, as was Nietzsche himself. In our own day, of course, when men tend more and more to be miserable human fragments, the complete man, if such existed, would probably stand out from the others like a sore thumb, but he might not at all be a creature of genius or extraordinary powers. Will the Superman, then, be the titanically striving individual, dwelling on the mountaintop of the spirit, or will he be the man who has realized within the world his own individual capacities for wholeness? The two ideals are in contradiction—a contradiction that is unresolved in Nietzsche and within modern culture itself.

The fact is that Zarathustra-Nietzsche did not come to terms with his own devil, and this is the crucial failure of Zarathustra in the book and of Nietzsche in his life. Consequently, it is also the failure of Nietzsche as a thinker. Not that Zarathustra-Nietzsche does not see his devil; time and again the latter pokes a warning finger at Zarathustra, and like a good devil he knows how to assume many shapes and disguises. He is the clown who leaps over the ropedancer's head at the beginning of the book, he is the Ugliest Man, who has killed God, and he is the Spirit of Gravity, whom Zarathustra himself names as his devil—the spirit of heaviness which would pull his too high-soaring spirit to earth. Each time Zarathustra thrusts aside the warning finger, finding it merely a reason for climbing a higher mountain to get away from it. The most crucial revelation, however, comes in the chapter "The Vision and the Enigma," in which the warning figure becomes a dwarf sitting on Zarathustra's back as the latter climbs a lonely mountain path. Zarathustra wants to climb upward, but the dwarf wants to pull him back to earth. "O Zarathustra," the dwarf whispers to him, "thou didst throw thyself high, but every stone that is thrown must fall." And then, in a prophecy the more menacing when applied to Nietzsche himself: "O Zarathustra, far indeed didst thou throw thy stone, but upon *thyself* will it recoil!" This is the ancient pattern of the Greek myths: the hero who soars too high crashes to earth; and Nietzsche, as a scholar of Greek tragedy, should have given more respectful ear to the dwarf's warning.

But why a dwarf? The egotism of Zarathustra-Nietzsche rates himself too high; therefore the figure in the vision, to right the balance, shows him to himself as a dwarf. The dwarf is the image of mediocrity that lurks within Zarathustra-Nietzsche, and that mediocrity was the most frightening and distasteful thing that Nietzsche was willing to see in himself. Nietzsche had discovered the shadow, the underside, of human nature, and he had correctly seen it as a side that is present inescapably in every human individual. But he converted this perception into a kind of romantic diabolism; it amused him to play at being wicked and daring. He would have been prepared to meet his own devil if this devil had appeared in some grandiose form. Precisely what is hardest for us to take is the devil as the personification of the pettiest, paltriest, meanest part of our personality. Dostoevski understood this better than Nietzsche, and in that tremendous chapter of *The Brothers Karamazov* where the Devil appears to Ivan, the brilliant literary intellectual nourished on the Romanticism of Schiller, it is not in the guise of a dazzling Miltonic Lucifer or a swaggering operatic Mephistopheles, but rather of a faded, shabby-genteel person, a little out of fashion and ridiculous in his aestheticism—the perfect caricature of Ivan's own aesthetic mind. This figure is *the* Devil for Ivan Karamazov, the one that most cruelly deflates his egotism; and Dostoevski's genius as a psychologist perhaps never hit the nail on the head more accurately than in this passage. Nietzsche himself said of Dostoevski that he was the only psychologist from whom he had had anything to learn; the remark is terribly true, and in a profounder sense than Nietzsche realized.

Zarathustra—to return to him—is too touchy to acknowledge himself as this dwarf. He feels his courage challenged and believes it will be the supreme act of courage, the highest virtue, to get rid of the dwarf. "Courage at last bade me stand still and say: Dwarf! Either thou or I!" It would have been wiser, and even more courageous, to admit who the dwarf really was and to say, not "Either thou or I" but rather, "Thou and I (*ego*) are one self."

The vision shifts and pauses for a moment, and Nietzsche now presents us with the idea of the Eternal Return. This idea has an ambiguous status in Nietzsche. He tried to base it rationally and scientifically on the premise that if time were infinite and the particles in the universe finite,

then by the laws of probability all combinations must repeat themselves over and over again eternally; and that therefore everything, we ourselves included, must recur again and again down to the last detail. But to take this as a purely intellectual hypothesis does not explain why the idea of the Eternal Return had such a powerful hold upon Nietzsche's emotions, and why, particularly, the idea is revealed at this most charged and visionary moment in *Zarathustra.* The circle is a pure archetypal form for the eternal: "I saw Eternity the other night," says the English poet Vaughan, "Like a great ring of pure and endless light." The idea of the Eternal Return thus expresses, as Unamuno has pointed out, Nietzsche's own aspirations toward eternal and immortal life. On the other hand, the notion is a frightening one for a thinker who sees the whole meaning of mankind to lie in the future, in the Superman that man is to become; for if all things repeat themselves in an endless cycle, and if man must come again in the paltry and botched form in which he now exists—then what meaning can man have? For Nietzsche the idea of the Eternal Return becomes the supreme test of courage: If Nietzsche the man must return to life again and again, with the same burden of ill health and suffering, would it not require the greatest affirmation and love of life to say Yes to this absolutely hopeless prospect?

Zarathustra glimpses some of the fearful implications in this vision, for he remarks after expounding the Eternal Return, "So I spoke, and always more softly: for I was afraid of my own thoughts, and afterthoughts." Thereupon, in the dream, he hears a dog howl and sees a shepherd writhing on the ground, with a heavy black reptile hanging from his mouth. "Bite!" cries Zarathustra, and the shepherd bites the serpent's head off and spits it far away. The uncanny vision poses its enigma to Zarathustra:

> Ye daring ones! Ye venturers and adventurers, and whoever of you have embarked with cunning sails on unexplored seas! Ye enjoyers of enigmas!
>
> Solve unto me the enigma that I then beheld, interpret for me the vision of the loneliest one.
>
> For it was a vision and a foresight. *What* did I then behold in parable? And *who* is it that must come some day?
>
> *Who* is the shepherd into whose throat the serpent thus crawled? *Who* is the man into whose throat all the heaviest and blackest will crawl?
>
> —The shepherd bit as my cry had admonished him; he took a good bite, and spit the head of the serpent far away: —and sprang up—
>
> No longer shepherd, no longer man—a transfigured being, a light-surrounded being, that *laughed.* Never on earth laughed a man as *he* laughed!
>
> O my brethren, I heard a laughter which was no human laughter.

"Who is the shepherd into whose throat the serpent thus crawled?" He is Nietzsche himself, and both the serpent and the dwarf set for him the same task: to acknowledge "the heaviest and the blackest in himself." We commonly speak of the truth as a bitter pill that we have to swallow, but the truth about ourselves may take even the more repulsive form of a reptile. Nietzsche does not swallow the serpent's head; he denies his own shadow, and out of it he sees a transfigured being spring up. This being laughs with a laughter that is no longer human. We know this laughter all too well: it is the laughter of insanity. A few years ago André Breton, the surrealist, published an *Anthologie de l'humour noir,* in which was included one of Nietzsche's letters written after his psychosis. If one did not know who the author was and what his condition was when he wrote it, one could indeed take the letter as a dazzling piece of surrealistic laughter, a high empty mad laughter. This is the laughter Nietzsche hears in his vision, and he speaks like a tragic character ironically ignorant of his own prophecy when he says, "It was a vision and a prevision." This laughter already began to sound eerily in the pages of *Ecce Homo.*

There is an inner coherence in the vision of Zarathustra, in that each of its three parts—the dwarf, the Eternal Return, and the shepherd spitting out the serpent—presents an obstacle and objection to Nietzsche's utopian conception of the Superman. They prefigure his own personal catastrophe; but since he was a thinker who really lived his thought, they indicate the fatal flaw in all such utopian thought. He who would launch the Superman into interstellar space had better recognize that the dwarf goes with him. "Human, all too human!" Nietzsche exclaimed in disgust at mankind as it had hitherto existed. But he who would try to improve man might do well not to make him inhuman but, rather, a little more human. To be a whole man—a round man, as the Chinese say—Western man may have to learn to be less Faustian. A touch of the average, the mediocre, may be necessary ballast for human nature. The antidote to the hysterical, mad laughter of Zarathustra's vision may be a sense of humor, which is something Nietzsche, despite his brilliant intellectual wit, conspicuously lacked.

The conclusions we have reached here on a psychological level become confirmed when we turn to Nietzsche's systematic philosophy of power.

Nietzsche is considered by many philosophers to be an unsystematic thinker. This view, a mistaken one, is based largely on the external form of his writings. He loved to write aphoristically, to attack his subjects indirectly and dramatically rather than in the straightforward solemn form of a pedantic treatise; he was one of the great prose stylists of the German language, and in his writing he could not, or would not, deny the artist in himself. He even went so far as to say that he was viewing science and philosophy through the eyes of art. But beneath and throughout all these belletristic forays a single consuming idea was moving in him toward a systematized development. As thinking gradually took over the whole person, and everything else in his life being starved out, it was inevitable that this thought should tend to close itself off in a system. At the end of his life he was making notes for a great systematic work which would be the complete expression of his philosophy. This work we now have in unfinished form in *The Will to Power.* The increase in sys-

tematization in Nietzsche's work is in many ways a psychological loss, since in pursuing his thematic idea he lost sight of the ambiguity in matters of the human psyche. However, there is a gain as well, for by carrying his ideas to the end he lets us see what they finally amount to. Heidegger has, in a recent memorable essay, called attention to the hitherto unrecognized fact that Nietzsche is a thoroughly systematic thinker. Indeed, according to Heidegger, Nietzsche is the last metaphysician in the metaphysical tradition of the West, the thinker who at once completes and destroys that tradition.

We do not know when the idea of the Will to Power first dawned upon Nietzsche, but there is a striking and picturesque incident, which he later told to his sister, that is relevant to it: During the Franco-Prussian War, when Nietzsche was a hospital orderly, he saw one evening his old regiment ride by, going into battle and perhaps to death, and it came to him then that "the strongest and highest will to life does not lie in the puny struggle to exist, but in the Will to war, the Will to Power." But it is a mistake to locate the birth of this idea in any single experience; it was, in fact, fed by a number of tributary streams, by Nietzsche's struggle against ill health and also by his studies in classical antiquity. Nietzsche's greatness as a classical scholar lay in his ability to see plain and simple facts that the genteel tradition among scholars had passed over. The distinguished British classicist F. M. Cornford has said of Nietzsche that he was fifty years ahead of the classical scholarship of his day; the tribute was meant to be generous, but I am not sure that the classical scholarship of our own day has yet caught up with Nietzsche. It requires much more imagination to grasp the obvious than the recondite, and a kind of imagination that Nietzsche had much more of than the classical scholars of his time. Take, for example, the obvious fact that the noble Greeks and Romans owned slaves and thought this quite natural; and that because of this they had a different orientation toward existence than did the Christian civilization that followed them. The humanistic tradition among classical scholars had idealized the ancients, and thereby, as in all idealistic views, falsified the reality. One does not need to be much of a classical specialist to note, on the first page of Julius Caesar's *Gallic Wars,* that the word *virtus,* virtue, means courage and martial valor—just the kind of thing that a military commander would most fear in the enemy and most desire in his own soldiers. (It is one of the odd developments of history—as one philosophical wag put it, making thereby a perfectly Nietzschean joke—that the word "virtue," which originally meant virility in a man, came in Victorian times to mean chastity in a woman.) Nor does it require any greater classical scholarship to recognize in the Greek word that we translate as virtue, *arete,* the clanging tone of Ares, god of battle. Classical civilizations rested on the recognition of power, and the relations of power, as a natural and basic part of life.

Nietzsche's idea also reflected the modern influence of Stendhal and Dostoevski, the two nineteenth-century novelists whom he most admired. Stendhal had shown the components of ego and power mingled in all the exploits of Eros: in the arts of seduction and conquest, in the battle of the sexes. Dostoevski had revealed how the most self-abasing acts of humility could be brutally aggressive. Nietzsche's own psychological acuity, however, once started on this path, did not need much prompting. He was able to see the Will to Power secretly at work everywhere in the history of morals: in the asceticism of the saint and the resentment of the condemning moralist, as well as in the brutality of the primitive legislator. All his separate insights on the theme accumulated finally in a single monolithic idea of all-comprehending universality: the Will to Power was in fact the innermost essence of all beings; the essence of Being itself.

Now, it is one thing to perceive that all the psychological impulses of man are mingled in some way with the impulse to power; it is quite another thing to say that this impulse toward power is *the* basic impulse to which all the others may be reduced. We are faced at once with that problem of reduction which haunts particularly the battle among the modern schools of psychology. As is well known, the individual psychology of Alfred Adler split off from Freudian psychoanalysis over just this point—Adler, who had read Nietzsche, declaring that the Will to Power was basic, Freud maintaining that sexuality and Eros were. But what—to confound matters by speaking paradoxically—if both are right and both wrong? What if the human psyche cannot be carved up into compartments and one compartment wedged in under another as being more basic? What if such dichotomizing really overlooks the organic unity of the human psyche, which is such that a single impulse can be just as much an impulse toward love on the one hand as it is toward power on the other? Dostoevski, at least as a novelist, preserves this sense of duality and ambivalence; and Nietzsche too, where his intuition was functioning as concretely as a novelist's, saw this interplay between power and the other drives. (In *Beyond Good and Evil* he remarked, rather as a good Freudian than an Adlerian, "The degree and nature of a man's sensuality extends to the highest altitudes of his spirit.") But later he had Zarathustra the loveless declare that "Love is the danger of the loneliest one," and suppress love and compassion; and so Nietzsche gave the last word to the Will to Power, making it the basis of every other psychological motive; he became one of the reductive psychologists.

What is most remarkable is that this Will to Power should have been made by him into the essence of Being. Remarkable because Nietzsche had ridiculed the very notion of Being as one of the most deceptive ghosts spawned by the brains of philosophers, the most general and therefore the emptiest of concepts, a thin and impalpable ectoplasm distilled from the concrete realities of the senses. He had perceived correctly that the principal conflict within Western philosophy lay at its very beginning, in Plato's condemnation of the poets and artists as inhabiting the world of the senses rather than the supersensible world of the abstractions, the Ideas, which represent true Being as opposed to the constant flux of Becoming in the world of the senses. Nietzsche took the side of the artist: The real world, he said, than which there is no other, is the world of the senses and of Becoming. Nevertheless, to become a systematic thinker Nietzsche had to become a metaphysician, and the metaphysician is driven to have recourse to the idea of Being. To be sure, Nietzsche's thought preserves his dynamism, for Being is turned into Becoming— becomes, in fact, essentially the Will to Power.

But what is power? It is not, according to Nietzsche, a state of rest or stasis toward which all things tend. On the contrary, power itself is dynamic through and through: power consists in the discharge of power, and this means the exercise of the will to power on ever-ascending levels of power. Power itself is the will to power. And the will to power is the will to will.

It is at this point that Nietzsche's doctrine begins to look rather terrifying to most people, and to seem merely an expression of his own frenetic and unbalanced temperament. Frenetic he had certainly become, in many passages of *The Will to Power,* where indeed he resembles nothing so much as "the pale Criminal" of his own description (in *Zarathustra*), the loveless one who thirsts for blood. But here, as elsewhere, the personal frenzy of Nietzsche had a much more than personal meaning; and precisely in this idea of power he was the philosopher of this present age in history, for he revealed to it its own hidden and fateful being. No wonder, then, that the age should have branded him as a wicked and malevolent spirit.

The fact is that the modern age has prided itself everywhere on its dynamism. In history textbooks we represent the emergence of the modern period out of the Middle Ages as the birth of an energetic and dynamic will to conquer nature and transform the conditions of life, instead of submitting passively to them while waiting to be sent to the next world as medieval man had done. We congratulate ourselves over and over again on all this. But when a thinker comes along who seeks to explore what lies hidden behind all this dynamism, we cry out that we do not recognize ourselves in the image he draws and seek refuge from it by pointing an accusing finger at his derangement. Technology in the twentieth century has taken such enormous strides beyond that of the nineteenth that it now bulks larger as an instrument of naked power than as an instrument for human well-being. Now that we have airplanes that fly faster than the sun, intercontinental missiles, space satellites, and above all atomic explosives, we are aware that technology itself has assumed a power to which politics in any traditional sense is subordinate. If the Russians were to outstrip us decisively in technology, then all ordinary political calculations would have to go by the boards. The classical art of politics, conceived since the Greeks as a thoroughly human art addressed to humans, becomes an outmoded and fragile thing beside the massive accumulation of technological power. The fate of the world, it now appears, turns upon sheer mastery over things. All the refinements of politics as a human art— diplomatic tact and finesse, compromise, an enlightened and liberal policy, good will—are as little able to avail against technological supremacy as the refinement of a man's dress and person are able to ward off the blow of a pile driver. The human becomes subordinated to the machine, even in the traditionally human business of politics.

Here Nietzsche, more acutely than Marx, expresses the real historical meaning of Communism and especially of the peculiar attraction Communism holds for the so-called backward or under-developed countries: it is a will to power on the part of these peoples, a will to take their fate in their own hands and make their own history. This powerful and secret appeal of Communism is something that our own statesmen do not seem in the least to understand. And America itself? Yes, we bear with us still the old liberal ideals of the individual's right to life, liberty, and the pursuit of happiness; but the actual day-to-day march of our collective life involves us in a frantic dynamism whose ultimate goals are undefined. Everywhere in the world, men and nations are behaving precisely in accordance with the Nietzschean metaphysics: The goal of power need not be defined, because it is its own goal, and to halt or slacken speed even for a moment would be to fall behind in achieving it. Power does not stand still; as we say nowadays in America, you are either going up or coming down.

But on what, philosophically speaking, does this celebrated dynamism of the modern age rest? The modern era in philosophy is usually taken to begin with Descartes. The fundamental feature of Descartes' thought is a dualism between the ego and the external world of nature. The ego is the subject, essentially a thinking substance; nature is the world of objects, extended substances. Modern philosophy thus begins with a radical subjectivism, the subject facing the object in a kind of hidden antagonism. (This subjectivism has nothing to do with Kierkegaard's idea of "subjective truth"; Kierkegaard simply chose his term unfortunately, for his intention is the very opposite of Cartesianism.) Nature thus appears as a realm to be conquered, and man as the creature who is to be conqueror of it. This is strikingly shown in the remark of Francis Bacon, prophet of the new science, who said that in scientific investigation man must put nature to the rack in order to wring from it an answer to his questions; the metaphor is one of coercion and violent antagonism. A crucial step beyond Descartes was taken when Leibnitz declared that material substances are not inert, as Descartes thought, but endowed with a fundamental dynamism: all things have a certain drive (*appetitio*) by which they move forward in time. Here the Cartesian antagonism between man and nature is stepped up by having added to it an intrinsic dynamism on both sides. Nietzsche is the culmination of this whole line of thought: the thinker who brings the seed to its violent fruition. The very extremity of his idea points to a fundamental error at the source of the modern epoch. Whether or not it points beyond that to a fundamental error at the root of the whole Western tradition, as Heidegger holds, is another matter, and one that we shall examine in the context of Heidegger's own philosophy.

Power as the pursuit of more power inevitably founders in the void that lies beyond itself. The Will to Power begets the problem of nihilism. Here again Nietzsche stands as the philosopher of the period, for he prophesied remarkably that nihilism would be the shadow, in many guises and forms, that would haunt the twentieth century. Supposing man does not blow himself and his earth to bits, and that he really becomes the master of this planet. What then? He pushes off into interstellar space. And then? Power for power's sake, no matter how far the power is extended, leaves always the dread of the void beyond. The attempt to stand face to face with that void is the problem of nihilism.

For Nietzsche, the problem of nihilism arose out of the discovery that "God is dead." "God" here means the historical God of the Christian faith. But in a wider philosophical sense it means also the whole realm of supersensible reality—Platonic Ideas, the Absolute, or what not—that philosophy has traditionally posited beyond the sensible realm, and in which it has located man's highest values. Now that this other, higher, eternal realm is gone, Nietzsche declared, man's highest values lose their value. If man has lost this anchor to which he has hitherto been moored, Nietzsche asks, will he not drift in an infinite void? The only value Nietzsche can set up to take the place of these highest values that have lost their value for contemporary man is: Power.

But do we today really have any better answer? An answer, I mean, that we live and not just pay lip service to? Nietzsche is more truly the philosopher for our age than we are willing to admit. To the degree that modern life has become secularized those highest values, anchored in the eternal, have already lost their value. So long as people are blissfully unaware of this, they of course do not sink into any despondency and nihilism; they may even be steady churchgoers. Nihilism, in fact, is the one subject on which we speak today with the self-complacency of commencement-day orators. We are always ready to invoke the term against a new book or new play that has anything "negative" to say, as if nihilism were always to be found in the other person but never in ourselves. And yet despite all its apparently cheerful and self-satisfied immersion in gadgets and refrigerators American life, one suspects, is nihilistic to its core. Its final "What for?" is not even asked, let alone answered.

Man, Nietzsche held, is a contradictory and complex being, and he himself is as complex and contradictory an example as one could find. One has the feeling in reading him that those ultimate problems with which he dealt would have been enough almost to drive any man mad. Was it necessary that he be deranged in order to reveal the secret derangement that lies coiled like a dragon at the bottom of our epoch? He does not bring us any solutions that satisfy us to the great questions he raises, but he has stated the central and crucial problems for man in this period, as no one else has, and therein lies at once his greatness and his challenge.

And Nietzsche's fate might very well prefigure our own, for unless our Faustian civilization can relax its frantic dynamism at some point, it might very well go psychotic. To primitives and Orientals, we Western men already seem half crazy. But it will not do merely to assert blandly that the tension of this dynamism has to be relaxed somehow and somewhere; we need to know what in our fundamental way of thinking needs to be changed so that the frantic will to power will not appear as the only meaning we can give to human life. If this moment in Western history is but the fateful outcome of the fundamental ways of thought that lie at the very basis of our civilization—and particularly of that way of thought that sunders man from nature, sees nature as a realm of objects to be mastered and conquered, and can therefore end only with the exaltation of the will to power—then we have to find out how this one-sided and ultimately nihilistic emphasis upon the power over things may be corrected.

This means that philosophers must take up the task of re-thinking Nietzsche's problems back to their sources, which happen also to be the sources of our whole Western tradition. The most thoroughgoing attempt at this, among philosophers in the twentieth century, has been made by Heidegger, who is . . . engaged in nothing less than the Herculean task of digging his way patiently and laboriously out of the Nietzschean ruins, like a survivor out of a bombed city.

William Barrett, "Nietzsche," in his Irrational Man: A Study in Existential Philosophy, *Doubleday & Company, Inc., 1958, pp. 158-83.*

Erich Heller   (essay date 1965)

[*A German-born American critic and educator, Heller has written extensively on modern German literature and culture in such books as* The Disinherited Mind *(1952),* Franz Kafka *(1969), and* Thomas Mann: The Ironic German *(1979). In the following essay from his* The Importance of Nietzsche, *Heller asserts that the central idea in Nietzsche's philosophy is the death of God, from which stemmed his prophetic insight that the nihilistic drive of modern science and politics would unleash technological warfare and destruction on an unprecedented scale.*]

In 1873, two years after Bismarck's Prussia had defeated France, a young German who happened to live in Switzerland and taught classical philology in the University of Basle wrote a treatise concerned with "the German mind." It was an inspired diatribe against, above all, the German notion of *Kultur* and against the philistine readiness to believe that military victory proved cultural superiority. This was, he said, a disastrous superstition, symptomatic in itself of the absence of any true culture. According to him, the opposite was true: the civilization of the vanquished French was bound more and more to dominate the victorious German people that had wasted its spirit upon the chimera of political power.

This national heretic's name, rather obscure at the time, was Friedrich Nietzsche. What he wrote almost a century ago about the perverse relationship between military success and intellectual dominance proved true: not then, perhaps, but half-a-century later. Defeated in two wars, Germany appeared to have invaded vast territories of the world's mind, with Nietzsche himself as no mean conqueror. For his was the vision of things to come. Among all the thinkers of the nineteenth century he is, with the possible exceptions of Dostoevsky and Kierkegaard, the only one who would not be too amazed by the amazing scene upon which we now move in sad, pathetic, heroic, stoic, or ludicrous bewilderment. Much, too much, would strike him as *déjà vu:* yes, he had foreseen it; and he would understand: for the "Modern Mind" speaks German, not always good German, but fluent German nonetheless. It was, alas, forced to learn the idiom of Karl Marx, and was delighted to be introduced to itself in the language of Sig-

mund Freud; taught by Ranke and, later, Max Weber, it acquired its historical and sociological self-consciousness, moved out of its tidy Newtonian universe on the instruction of Einstein, and followed a design of Oswald Spengler's in sending, from the depth of its spiritual depression, most ingeniously engineered objects higher than the moon. Whether it discovers, with Heidegger, the true habitation of its *Existenz* on the frontiers of Nothing, or meditates, with Sartre and Camus, *le Néant* or the Absurd; whether—to pass to its less serious moods—it is nihilistically young and profitably angry in London or rebelliously debauched and buddhistic in San Francisco—*man spricht deutsch.* It is all part of a story told by Nietzsche.

As for modern German literature and thought, it is hardly an exaggeration to say that they would not be what they are if Nietzsche had never lived. Name almost any poet, man of letters, philosopher, who wrote in German during the twentieth century and attained to stature and influence—Rilke, George, Kafka, Thomas Mann, Ernst Jünger, Musil, Benn, Heidegger, or Jaspers—and you name at the same time Friedrich Nietzsche. He is to them all—whether or not they know and acknowledge it (and most of them do)—what St. Thomas Aquinas was to Dante: the categorical interpreter of a world which they contemplate poetically or philosophically without ever radically upsetting its Nietzschean structure.

Nietzsche died in 1900, after twelve years of a total eclipse of his intellect, insane—and on the threshold of this century. Thinking and writing to the very edge of insanity, and with some of his last pages even going over it, he read and interpreted the temperatures of his own mind; but by doing so, he has drawn the fever-chart of an epoch. Indeed, much of his work reads like the self-diagnosis of a desperate physician who, suffering the disease on our behalf, comes to prescribe as a cure that we should form a new idea of health and live by it.

He was convinced that it would take at least fifty years before a few men would understand what he had accomplished; and he feared that even then his teaching would be misinterpreted and misapplied. "I am terrified," he wrote, "by the thought of the sort of people who may one day invoke my authority." But is this not, he added, the anguish of every great teacher? He knows that he may prove a disaster as much as a blessing. What he did not add was that on some of the pages of his writings he unmistakably enabled that "sort of people" to quote him verbatim in justifying their abominable designs. Still, the conviction that he was a great teacher never left him after he had passed through that period of sustained inspiration in which he wrote the first part of *Zarathustra*. After this, all his utterances convey the disquieting self-confidence and the terror of a man who has reached the culmination of that paradox which he embodies, a paradox which we shall try to name and which ever since has cast its dangerous spell over some of the finest and some of the coarsest minds.

Are we then, at the remove of two generations, in a better position to probe Nietzsche's mind and to avoid, as he hoped some might, the misunderstanding that he was merely concerned with the religious, philosophical, or political controversies fashionable in his day? And if this be a misinterpretation, can we put anything more valid in its place? What is the knowledge which he claims to have, raising him in his own opinion far above the contemporary level of thought? What the discovery which serves him as a lever to unhinge the whole fabric of traditional values?

It is the knowledge that God is dead.

The death of God he calls the greatest event in modern history and the cause of extreme danger. Note well the paradox contained in these words. He never said that there was no God, but that the Eternal had been vanquished by Time and that the Immortal suffered death at the hands of mortals: God is dead. It is like a cry mingled of despair and triumph, reducing, by comparison, the whole story of atheism and agnosticism before and after him to the level of respectable mediocrity and making it sound like a collection of announcements by bankers who regret they are unable to invest in an unsafe proposition. Nietzsche, for the nineteenth century, brings to its *perverse* conclusion a line of religious thought and experience linked with the names of St. Paul, St. Augustine, Pascal, Kierkegaard, and Dostoevsky, minds for whom God was not simply the creator of an order of nature within which man has his clearly defined place, but to whom He came rather in order to challenge their natural being, making demands which appeared absurd in the light of natural reason. These men are of the family of Jacob: having wrestled with God for His blessing, they ever after limp through life with the framework of Nature incurably out of joint. Nietzsche is just such a wrestler; except that in him the shadow of Jacob merges with the shadow of Prometheus. Like Jacob, Nietzsche too believed that he prevailed against God in that struggle, and won a new name for himself, the name of Zarathustra. But the words *he* spoke on his mountain to the angel of the Lord were: "I will not let thee go, except thou curse me." Or, in words which Nietzsche did in fact speak: "I have on purpose devoted my life to exploring the whole contrast to a truly religious nature. I know the Devil and all his visions of God."

"God is dead"—this is the very core of Nietzsche's spiritual existence, and what follows is despair *and* hope in a new greatness of man, visions of catastrophe *and* glory, the icy brilliance of analytical reason, fathoming with affected irreverence those depths hitherto hidden by awe and fear, and, side-by-side with it, the ecstatic invocations of a ritual healer. Probably inspired by Hölderlin's dramatic poem *Empedocles,* the young Nietzsche, who loved what he knew of Hölderlin's poetry, at the age of twenty planned to write a drama with Empedocles as its hero. His notes show that he saw the Greek philosopher as the tragic personification of his age, as a man in whom the latent conflicts of his epoch attained to consciousness, as one who suffered and died as the victim of an unresolvable tension: born with the soul of a *homo religiosus,* a seer, a prophet, and poet, he yet had the mind of a radical skeptic; and defending his soul against his mind and, in turn, his mind against his soul, he made his soul lose its spontaneity, and finally his mind its rationality. Had Nietzsche ever

written the drama *Empedocles,* it might have become, in uncanny anticipation, his *own* tragedy.

It is a passage from Nietzsche's *Gaya Scienza,* his *Joyous Science* [**The Gay Science**], which conveys best the substance and quality of the mind, indeed the whole spiritual situation, from which the pronouncement of the death of God sprang. The passage is prophetically entitled "The Madman" and might have been called "The New Diogenes." Here is a brief extract from it:

> Have you not heard of that madman who, in the broad light of the forenoon, lit a lantern and ran into the market-place, crying incessantly: "I am looking for God!" . . . As it happened, many were standing there who did not believe in God, and so he aroused great laughter . . . The madman leapt right among them . . . "Where is God?" he cried. "Well, I will tell you. *We have murdered him*—you and . . . But how did we do this deed? . . . Who gave us the sponge with which to wipe out the whole horizon? How did we set about unchaining our earth from her sun? Whither is it moving now? Whither are we moving? . . . Are we not falling incessantly? . . . Is night not approaching, and more and more night? Must we not light lanterns in the forenoon? Behold the noise of the gravediggers, busy to bury God . . . And we have killed him! What possible comfort is there for us? . . . Is not the greatness of this deed too great for us? To appear worthy of it, must not we ourselves become gods?" —At this point the madman fell silent and looked once more at those around him: "Oh," he said, "I am too early. My time has not yet come. The news of this tremendous event is still on its way . . . Lightning and thunder take time, the light of the stars takes time to get to us, deeds take time to be seen and heard . . . and *this* deed is still farther from them than the farthest stars—*and yet it was they themselves who did it!*'

And elsewhere, in a more prosaic mood, Nietzsche says: "People have no notion yet that from now onwards they exist on the mere pittance of inherited and decaying values"—soon to be overtaken by an enormous bankruptcy.

The story of the Madman, written two years before **Zarathustra** and containing *in nuce* the whole message of the *Übermensch,* shows the distance that divides Nietzsche from the conventional attitudes of atheism. He is the madman, breaking with his sinister news into the marketplace complacency of the pharisees of unbelief. They have done away with God, and yet the report of their own deed has not yet reached them. They know not what they have done, but He who could forgive them is no more. Much of Nietzsche's work ever after is the prophecy of their fate: "The story I have to tell is the history of the next two centuries . . . For a long time now our whole civilization has been driving, with a tortured intensity growing from decade to decade, as if towards a catastrophe: restlessly, violently, tempestuously, like a mighty river desiring the end of its journey, without pausing to reflect, indeed fearful of reflection . . . Where we live, soon nobody will be able to exist." For men become enemies, and each his own enemy. From now onward they will *hate,* Nietzsche believes, however many *comforts* they will lavish upon themselves, and hate *themselves* with a new hatred, unconsciously at work in the depths of their souls. True, there will be ever better reformers of society, ever better socialists, and ever better hospitals, and an ever increasing intolerance of pain and poverty and suffering and death, and an ever more fanatical craving for the greatest happiness of the greatest numbers. Yet the deepest impulse informing their striving will not be love and will not be compassion. Its true source will be the panic-struck determination not to have to ask the question "What is the meaning of our lives?" —the question which will remind them of the death of God, the uncomfortable question inscribed on the features of those who are uncomfortable, and asked above all by pain and poverty and suffering and death. Rather than allowing that question to be asked, they will do everything to smooth it away from the face of humanity. For they cannot endure it. And yet they will despise themselves for not enduring it, and for their guilt-ridden inability to answer it; and their self-hatred will betray them behind the back of their apparent charity and humanitarian concern. For *there* they will assiduously construct the tools for the annihilation of human kind. "There will be wars," Nietzsche writes, "such as have never been waged on earth." And he says: "I foresee something terrible, Chaos everywhere. Nothing left which is of any value; nothing which commands: Thou shalt!" This would have been the inspiration of the final work which Nietzsche often said he would write and never wrote: *The Transvaluation of All Values,* as he sometimes wanted to call it, or **The Will to Power,** the title chosen by his editors for their assemblage of a great many notes from his late years. Fragmentary though these are, they yet give a surprisingly full diagnosis of what he termed nihilism, the state of human beings and societies faced with a total eclipse of all values.

It is in defining and examining the (for him *historical*) phenomenon of nihilism that Nietzsche's attack on Christianity sets in, and it has remained the only truly subtle point which, within the whole range of his more and more unrestrained argumentativeness, this Antichrist makes against Christianity. For it is at this point that Nietzsche asks (and asks the same question in countless variations throughout his works): What are the *specific* qualities which the Christian tradition has instilled and cultivated in the minds of men? They are, he thinks, two-fold; on the one hand, a more refined sense of truth than any other civilization has known, an almost uncontrollable desire for absolute spiritual and intellectual certainties; and, on the other hand, the ever-present suspicion that life on this earth is not in itself a supreme value, but in need of a higher, a transcendental justification. This, Nietzsche believes, is a destructive, and even self-destructive alliance, which is bound finally to corrode the very Christian beliefs on which it rests. For the mind, exercised and guided in its search for knowledge by the most sophisticated and comprehensive theology the world has ever known—a theology which through St. Thomas Aquinas has assimilated into its grand system the genius of Aristotle—was at the same time fashioned and directed by the indelible Christian distrust of the ways of the world. Thus it had to follow, with the utmost logical precision and determination, a course of systematically "devaluing" the knowably real.

This mind, Nietzsche predicts, will eventually, in a frenzy of intellectual honesty, unmask as humbug what it began by regarding as the finer things in life. The boundless faith in truth, the joint legacy of Christ and Greek, will in the end dislodge every possible belief in the truth of any faith. Souls, long disciplined in a school of unworldliness and humility, will insist upon knowing the worst about themselves, indeed will only be able to grasp what is humiliating. Psychology will denigrate the creations of beauty, laying bare the tangle of unworthy desires of which they are "mere" sublimations. History will undermine the accumulated reputation of the human race by exhuming from beneath the splendid monuments the dead body of the past, revealing everywhere the spuriousness of motives, the human, all too human. And science itself will rejoice in exposing this long-suspected world as a mechanical contraption of calculable pulls and pushes, as a self-sufficient agglomeration of senseless energy, until finally, in a surfeit of knowledge, the scientific mind will perform the somersault of self-annihilation.

"The nihilistic consequences of our natural sciences"—this is one of Nietzsche's fragmentary jottings—"from its pursuits there follows ultimately a self-decomposition, a turning against itself," which—and this is one of his most amazingly precise predictions—would first show itself in the impossibility, within science itself, of comprehending the very object of its inquiry within one logically coherent system, and would lead to extreme scientific pessimism, to an inclination to embrace a kind of analytical, abstract mysticism by which man would shift himself and his world to where, Nietzsche thinks, they have been driving "ever since Copernicus: from the center towards an unknown X."

It is the tremendous paradox of Nietzsche that he himself follows, and indeed consciously wishes to hasten, this course of "devaluation"—particularly as a psychologist: and at the onset of megalomania he called himself the first psychologist in the world—"there was no psychology before me," a self-compliment which Sigmund Freud all but endorsed when incredibly, or at least not quite believably, late in his life, as he claimed, he came to know Nietzsche's writings. He had good reason to be impressed. Consider for instance, the following passage from Nietzsche's **Beyond Good and Evil:**

> The world of historical values is dominated by forgery. These great poets, like Byron, Musset, Poe, Leopardi, Kleist, Gogol (I dare not mention greater names, but I mean them)—all endowed with souls wishing to conceal a break; often avenging themselves with their works upon some inner desecration, often seeking oblivion in their lofty flights from their all-too-faithful memories, often lost in mud and almost in love with it until they become like will-o'-the-wisps of the morasses and simulate the stars . . . oh what a torture are all these great artists and altogether these higher beings, what a torture to him who has guessed their true nature.

This does indeed anticipate many a Freudian speculation

on traumata and compensations, on lusts and sublimations, on wounds and bows. Yet the extraordinary Nietzsche—incomprehensible in his contradictions except as the common strategist of two opposing armies who plans for the victory of a mysterious third—a few pages later takes back the guessing, not without insulting himself in the process: "From which it follows that it is the sign of a finer humanity to respect 'the mask' and not, in the wrong places, indulge in psychology and psychological curiosity." And furthermore: "He who does not wish to see what is great in a man, has the sharpest eye for that which is low and superficial in him, and so gives away—himself."

If Nietzsche is not the first psychologist of Europe, he is certainly a great psychologist—and perhaps really the first who comprehended what his more methodical successors, "strictly scientific" in their approach, did not see: *the psychology and the ethics of knowledge itself;* and both the psychology and the ethics of knowledge are of particular relevance when the knowledge in question purports to be knowledge of the human psyche. It was, strangely enough, Nietzsche's amoral metaphysics, his doubtful but immensely fruitful intuition of the Will to Power as being the ultimate reality of the world, that made him into the first *moralist of knowledge* in his century and long after. While all his scientific and scholarly contemporaries throve on the comfortable assumptions that, firstly, there was such a thing as "objective," and therefore morally neutral, scientific knowledge, and that, secondly, everything that *can* be known "objectively" is therefore also *worth knowing,* he realized that knowledge, or at least the mode of knowledge predominant at his time and ours, is the subtlest guise of the Will to Power; and that *as a manifestation of the will it is liable to be judged morally.* For him, there can be no knowledge without a compelling urge to acquire it; and he knew that the knowledge thus acquired invariably reflects the nature of the impulse by which the mind was prompted. It is this impulse which *creatively* partakes in the making of the knowledge, and its share in it is truly immeasurable when the knowledge is about the very source of the impulse: the soul. This is why all interpretations of the soul must to a high degree be self-interpretations: the sick interpret the sick, and the dreamers interpret dreams. Or, as the Viennese satirist Karl Kraus—with that calculated injustice which is the prerogative of satire—once said of a certain psychological theory: "Psychoanalysis is the disease of which it pretends to be the cure."

Psychology is bad psychology if it disregards its own psychology. Nietzsche knew this. He was, as we have seen from his passage about "those great men," a most suspicious psychologist, but he was at the same time suspicious of the suspicion which was the father of his thought. Homer, to be sure, did not "psychologically" suspect his heroes, but Stendhal did. Does this mean that Homer knew less about the heroic than Stendhal? Does it make sense to say that Flaubert's Emma Bovary is the product of an imagination more profoundly initiated into the psychology of women than that which created Dante's Beatrice? Is Benjamin Constant, who created the dubious lover Adolphe, on more intimate terms with the nature of a young man's erotic passion than is Shakespeare, the begetter of Romeo? Certainly, Homer's Achilles and Stendhal's Julien Sorel are different heroes, Dante's Beatrice and Flaubert's Emma Bovary are different women, Shakespeare's Romeo and Constant's Adolphe are different lovers, but it would be naïve to believe that they simply differ "in actual fact." Actual facts hardly exist in either art or psychology: both interpret and both claim universality for the meticulously presented particular. Those creatures made by creative imaginations can indeed not be compared; yet if they differ as, in life, one person differs from another, at the same time, because they have their existence not "in life" but in art, they are incommensurable above all by virtue of their authors' incommensurable *wills* to know the human person, to know the hero, the woman, the lover. It is not better and more knowing minds that have created the suspect hero, the unlovable woman, the disingenuous lover, but minds possessed by different desires for a different knowledge, a knowledge devoid of the wonder and pride that know Achilles, the love that knows Beatrice, the passion and compassion that know Romeo. When Hamlet has come to know the frailty of woman, he knows Ophelia not better than when he was "unknowingly" in love with her; now he knows her differently and he knows her worse.

All *new* knowledge about the soul is knowledge about a *different* soul. For can it ever happen that the freely discovering mind says to the soul: "This is what you are!"? Is it not rather as if the mind said to the soul: "This is how I *wish* you to see yourself! This is the image after which I create you! This is my secret about you: I shock you with it and, shockingly, at once wrest it from you"? And worse: having thus received and revealed its secret, the soul is no longer what it was when it lived in secrecy. For there are secrets which are *created* in the process of their revelation. And worse still: having been told its secrets, the soul may cease to be a soul. The step from modern psychology to soullessness is as imperceptible as that from modern physics to the dissolution of the concept "matter."

It is this disturbing state of affairs which made Nietzsche deplore "the torture" of psychologically "guessing the true nature of those higher beings" and, at the same time, recommend "respect for the mask" as a condition of "finer humanity." (A great pity he never wrote what, if we are to trust his notes, he planned to say in the abortive *Will to Power* about the literature of the nineteenth century. For no literary critic of the age has had a more penetrating insight into the "nihilistic" character of that "absolute aestheticism" that, from Baudelaire onward, has been the dominant inspiration of European poetry. Respectfully, and sometimes not so respectfully, Nietzsche recognized that behind the aesthetic "mask" there was a face distorted by the loathing of "reality." And it was the realistic and psychological novel that revealed to him that epoch's utterly pessimistic idea of its world. How intimately he knew those aesthetic Furies, or furious Muses, that haunted the mind of Flaubert, inspiring him to produce an oeuvre in which absolute pessimism, radical psychology, and extreme aestheticism are so intriguingly fused.)

For Nietzsche, however, *all* the activities of human consciousness share the predicament of psychology. There can be, for him, no "pure" knowledge, only satisfaction,

The eighty-eight-year-old Elisabeth Förster-Nietzsche greeting Hitler at the entrance of the Nietzsche archives in Weimar.

however sophisticated, of the ever-varying intellectual needs of the *will* to know. He therefore demands that man should accept *moral responsibility* for the kind of questions he asks, and that he should realize what *values* are implied in the answers he seeks—and in this he was more Christian than all our post-Faustian Fausts of truth and scholarship. "The desire for truth," he says, "is itself in need of critique. Let this be the definition of my philosophical task. By way of experiment, I shall question for once the value of truth." And does he not! And he protests that, in an age which is as uncertain of its values as is his and ours, the search for truth will issue in either trivialities or—catastrophe. We may well wonder how he would react to the pious hope of our day that the intelligence and moral conscience of politicians will save the world from the disastrous products of our scientific explorations and engineering skills. It is perhaps not too difficult to guess; for he knew that there was a fatal link between the moral resolution of scientists to follow the scientific search *wherever,* by its own momentum, it will take us, and the moral debility of societies not altogether disinclined to "apply" the results, however catastrophic. Believing that there was a hidden identity between *all* the expressions of the Will to Power, he saw the element of moral nihilism in the ethics of our science: its determination not to let "higher values"

interfere with its highest value—Truth (as it conceives it). Thus he said that the goal of knowledge pursued by the natural sciences means perdition.

"God is dead"—and man, in his heart of hearts, is incapable of forgiving himself for having done away with Him: he is bent upon punishing himself for this, his "greatest deed." For the time being, however, he will take refuge in many an evasive action. With the instinct of a born hunter, Nietzsche pursues him into all his hiding places, cornering him in each of them. Morality without religion? Indeed not: "All purely moral demands without their religious basis," he says, "must needs end in nihilism." What is left? Intoxication. "Intoxication with music, with cruelty, with hero-worship, or with hatred . . . Some sort of mysticism . . . Art for Art's sake, Truth for Truth's sake, as a narcotic against self-disgust; some kind of routine, *any* silly little fanaticism . . ." But none of these drugs can have any lasting effect. The time, Nietzsche predicts, is fast approaching when secular crusaders, tools of man's collective suicide, will devastate the world with their rival claims to compensate for the lost Kingdom of Heaven by setting up on earth the ideological rules of Love and Justice which, by the very force of the spiritual derangement involved, will lead to the rules of cruelty and slavery; and he prophesies that the war for global domination will be fought on behalf of philosophical doctrines.

In one of his notes written at the time of *Zarathustra* Nietzsche says: "He who no longer finds what is great in God, will find it nowhere. He must either deny or create it." These words take us to the heart of that paradox that enwraps Nietzsche's whole existence. He is, by the very texture of his soul and mind, one of the most radically religious natures that the nineteenth century brought forth, but is endowed with an intellect which guards, with the aggressive jealousy of a watchdog, all the approaches to the temple. For such a man, what, after the *denial* of God, is there left to *create*? Souls, not only strong enough to endure Hell, but to transmute its agonies into superhuman delight—in fact: the *Übermensch*. Nothing short of the transvaluation of all values can save us. Man has to be made immune to the effects of his second Fall and final separation from God: he must learn to see in his second expulsion the promise of a new paradise. For "the Devil may become envious of him who suffers so deeply, and throw him out—into Heaven."

Is there, then, any cure? Yes, says Nietzsche: a new kind of psychic health. And what is Nietzsche's conception of it? How is it to be brought about? By perfect self-knowledge *and* perfect self-transcendence. But to explain this, we should have to adopt an idiom disturbingly compounded of the language of Freudian psychology and tragic heroism. For the self-knowledge which Nietzsche expects all but requires a course in depth analysis; but the self-transcendence he means lies not in the practice of virtue as a sublimation of natural meanness; it can only be found in a kind of unconditional and almost supranatural sublimity. If there were a Christian virtue, be it goodness, innocence, chastity, saintliness, or self-sacrifice, that could not, however much he tried, be interpreted as a compensatory maneuver of the mind to "transvalue" weakness and frustration, Nietzsche might affirm it (as he is constantly tempted to praise Pascal). The trouble is that there cannot be such a virtue. For virtues are reflected upon by minds; and even the purest virtue will be suspect to a mind filled with suspicion. To think thoughts so immaculate that they must command the trust of even the most untrusting imagination, and to act from motives so pure that they are out of reach of even the most cunning psychology, this is the unattainable ideal, it would seem, of this "first psychologist of Europe." "Caesar—with the heart of Christ!" he once exclaimed in the secrecy of his notebook. Was this perhaps a definition of the *Übermensch,* this darling child of his imagination? It may well be; but this lofty idea meant, alas, that he had to think the meanest thought: he saw in the real Christ an illegitimate son of the Will to Power, a frustrated rabbi who set out to save himself and the underdog humanity from the intolerable strain of impotently resenting the Caesars: not to be Caesar was now proclaimed a spiritual distinction—a newly invented form of power, the power of the powerless.

Nietzsche had to fail, and fail tragically, in his determination to create a new man from the clay of negation. Almost with the same breath with which he gave the life of his imagination to the *Übermensch,* he blew the flame out again. For Zarathustra who preaches the *Übermensch* also teaches the doctrine of the Eternal Recurrence of All Things; and according to this doctrine nothing can ever come into being that had not existed at some time before— and, Zarathustra says, "never yet has there been an *Übermensch.*" Thus the expectation of this majestic new departure of life, indeed the possibility of any novel development, seems frustrated from the outset, and the world, caught forever in a cycle of gloomily repeated constellations of energy, stands condemned to a most dismal eternity.

Yet the metaphysical nonsense of these contradictory doctrines is not entirely lacking in poetic and didactic method. The Eternal Recurrence of All Things is Nietzsche's mythic formula of a meaningless world, the universe of nihilism, and the *Übermensch* stands for its transcendence, for the miraculous resurrection of meaning from its total negation. All Nietzsche's miracles are paradoxes designed to jerk man out of his false beliefs in time, before they bring about his spiritual destruction in an ecstasy of disillusionment and frustration. The Eternal Recurrence is the high school meant to teach strength through despair. The *Übermensch* graduates from it *summa cum laude et gloria.* He is the prototype of health, the man who has learned to live without belief and without truth, and, superhumanly delighting in life "as such," actually wills the Eternal Recurrence: Live in such a way that you desire nothing more than to live this very same life again and again! The *Übermensch* having attained to this manner of existence which is exemplary and alluring into all eternity, despises his former self for craving moral sanctions, for satisfying his will to power in neurotic sublimation, for deceiving himself about the "meaning" of life. What will he be then, this man who at last knows what life *really* is? Recalling Nietzsche's own accounts of all-too-human nature, and his analysis of the threadbare fabric of traditional values and truths, may he not be the very monster of nihilism, a barbarian, not necessarily blond, but perhaps a conqueror of the world, shrieking bad German from under his dark mustache? Yes, Nietzsche feared his approach in history: the vulgar caricature of the *Übermensch.* And because he also feared that the liberally tolerant, skeptically acquiescent and agnostically disbelieving heirs to Christian morality who had enfeebled the idea of civilized existence and rendered powerless the good would be unable to meet the challenges, Nietzsche sent forth from his imagination the *Übermensch* to defeat the defeat of man.

Did Nietzsche himself *believe* in the truth of his doctrines of the *Übermensch* and the Eternal Recurrence? In one of his posthumously published notes he says of the Eternal Recurrence: "We have produced the hardest possible thought—the Eternal Recurrence of All Things—now let us create the creature who will accept it lightheartedly and blissfully!" Clearly, there must have been times when he thought of the Eternal Recurrence not as a "Truth" but as a kind of spiritual Darwinian test to select for survival the spiritually fittest. There is a note of his which suggests precisely this: "I perform the great experiment: Who can bear the idea of the Eternal Recurrence?" This is a measure of Nietzsche's own unhappiness: the nightmare of nightmares was to him the idea that he might have to live his identical life again and again and again; and an ever deeper insight into the anatomy of despair we gain from this note: "Let us consider this idea in its most terrifying form: existence, as it is, without meaning or goal, but inescapably recurrent, without a finale into nothingness. . . . Those who cannot bear the sentence, There is no salvation, *ought* to perish!" Indeed, Nietzsche's *Übermensch* is the creature strong enough to live forever a cursed existence and even to transmute it into the Dionysian rapture of tragic acceptance. Schopenhauer called man the *animal metaphysicum.* It is certainly true of Nietzsche, the renegade *homo religiosus.* Therefore, if God was dead, then for Nietzsche man was an eternally cheated misfit, the diseased animal, as he called him, plagued by a metaphysical hunger which it was now impossible to feed even if all the Heavens were to be ransacked. Such a creature was doomed: he had to die out, giving way to the *Übermensch* who would miraculously feed on barren fields and finally conquer the metaphysical hunger itself without any detriment to the glory of life.

Did Nietzsche himself *believe* in the *Übermensch?* In the manner in which a poet believes in the truth of his creations. Did Nietzsche believe in the truth of poetic creations? Once upon a time when, as a young man, he wrote *The Birth of Tragedy,* Nietzsche did believe in the power of art to transfigure life by creating lasting images of true beauty out of the meaningless chaos. It had seemed credible enough as long as his gaze was enraptured by the distant prospect of classical Greece and the enthusiastic vicinity of Richard Wagner's Tribschen. Soon, however, his deeply Romantic belief in art turned to skepticism and scorn; and his unphilosophical anger was provoked by those "metaphysical counterfeiters," as he called them, who enthroned the trinity of beauty, goodness, and truth. "One should beat them," he said. Poetic beauty *and* truth? No, "we have *Art* in order not to perish of Truth" and, says Zarathustra, "poets lie too much"—and adds dejectedly: "But Zarathustra too is a poet . . . *We* lie too much." And he did: while Zarathustra preached the Eternal Recurrence, his author confided to his diary: "I do not wish to live *again.* How have I borne life? By creating. What has made me endure? The vision of the *Übermensch* who affirms life. I have tried to affirm life *myself*—but ah!" (There is, I believe, only one example of a confessed happy nihilist: the German poet Gottfried Benn. "*Nilismus ist ein Glücksgefühl,*" he said. He would be the perfect Nietzschean if his great mentor had died after *The Birth of Tragedy* and not essentially modified or even revoked the central thesis of that early book: that art is the only true "metaphysical activity." And Benn did claim that his "transcendent" appetites found satisfaction in the making of aesthetically successful things: poems, for instance. But in 1933, when Hitler came to power, he wrote not so much poetry, as he did, often brilliantly, in later years, but the most abject mumbo jumbo in praise of the crooked cross, symbol of a very different substitute religion.)

Was he, having lost God, capable of truly believing in *anything?* "He who no longer finds what is great in God will find it nowhere—he must either deny it or create it." Only the "either-or" does not apply. All his life Nietzsche tried to do both. He had the passion for truth and no belief in it. He had the love of life and despaired of it. This is the stuff from which demons are made—perhaps the most powerful secret demon eating the heart out of the modern mind. To have written and enacted the extremest story of this mind is Nietzsche's true claim to greatness. "The Don Juan of the Mind" he once called, in a "fable" he wrote, a figure whose identity is hardly in doubt:

> The Don Juan of the Mind: no philosopher or poet has yet discovered him. What he lacks is the love of the things he knows, what he possesses is esprit, the itch and delight in the chase and intrigue of knowledge—knowledge as far and high as the most distant stars. Until in the end there is nothing left for him to chase except the knowledge which hurts most, just as a drunkard in the end drinks absinthe and methylated spirits. And in the very end he craves for Hell—it is the only knowledge which can still seduce him. Perhaps it too will disappoint, as everything that he knows. And if so, he will have to stand transfixed through all eternity, nailed to disillusion, having himself become the Guest of Stone, longing for a last supper of knowledge which he will never receive. For in the whole world of things there is nothing left to feed his hunger.

It is a German Don Juan, this Don Juan of the Mind; and it is amazing that Nietzsche should not have recognized his features: the features of Goethe's Faust at the point at which he has succeeded at last in defeating the plan of salvation.

And yet Nietzsche's work, wrapped in paradox after paradox, taking us to the limits of what is still comprehensible and often beyond, carries elements which issue from a center of sanity. No doubt, this core is in perpetual danger of being crushed, and was in fact destroyed in the end. But it is there, and is made of the stuff of which goodness is made. A few years before he went mad, he wrote: "My life is now comprised in the wish that the truth about all things be different from my way of seeing it: if only someone would convince me of the improbability of my truths!" And he said: "Lonely and deeply suspicious of myself as I was, I took, not without secret spite, sides *against* myself and *for* anything that happened to hurt me and was hard for me." Why? Because he was terrified by the prospect that all the better things in life, all honesty of mind, integrity of character, generosity of heart, fineness of aesthetic perception, would be corrupted and finally cast away by the new barbarians, unless the mildest and gentlest hardened themselves for the war which was about to be waged against them: "Caesar—with the heart of Christ!"

Time and again we come to a point in Nietzsche's writings where the shrill tones of the rebel are hushed by the still voice of the autumn of a world waiting in calm serenity for the storms to break. Then this tormented mind relaxes in what he once called the *Rosengeruch des Unwiederbringlichen*—an untranslatably beautiful lyricism of which the closest equivalent in English is perhaps Yeats's lines:

> Man is in love and loves what vanishes.
> What more is there to say?

In such moments the music of Bach brings tears to his eyes

and he brushes aside the noise and turmoil of Wagner; or he his, having deserted Zarathustra's cave in the mountains, enchanted by the gentle grace of a Mediterranean coastline. Rejoicing in the quiet lucidity of Claude Lorrain, or seeking the company of Goethe in conversation with Eckermann, or comforted by the composure of Stifter's *Nachsommer,* a Nietzsche emerges, very different from the one who used to inhabit the fancies of Teutonic schoolboys and, alas, schoolmasters, a Nietzsche who is a traditionalist at heart, a desperate lover who castigates what he loves because he knows it will abandon him and the world. It is the Nietzsche who can with one sentence cross out all the dissonances of his apocalyptic voices: "I once saw a storm raging over the sea, and a clear blue sky above it; it was then that I came to dislike all sunless, cloudy passions which know no light, except the lightning." And this was written by the same man who said that his tool for philosophizing was the hammer, and of himself that he was not human but dynamite.

In these regions of his mind dwells the terror that he may have helped to bring about the very opposite of what he desired. When this terror comes to the fore, he is much afraid of the consequences of his teaching. Perhaps the best will be driven to despair by it, the very worst accept it? And once he put into the mouth of some imaginary titanic genius what is his most terrible prophetic utterance: "Oh grant madness, you heavenly powers! Madness that at last I may believe in myself . . . I am consumed by doubts, for I have killed the Law. . . . If I am not more than the Law, then I am the most abject of all men."

What, then, is the final importance of Nietzsche? For one of his readers it lies in his example which is so strange, profound, confounded, alluring, and forbidding that it can hardly be looked upon as exemplary. But it cannot be ignored either. For it has something to do with living lucidly in the dark age of which he so creatively despaired.

Erich Heller, "The Importance of Nietzsche," in his The Importance of Nietzsche: Ten Essays, *The University of Chicago Press, 1988, pp. 1-17.*

Henri Birault   (essay date 1966)

[*Birault is a French critic and educator in philosophy. In the following essay he explores Nietzsche's use of the concept of beatitude.*]

There is something paradoxical in choosing the idea of beatitude as an introduction to Nietzsche's thought. On the one hand, beatitude never presents itself as an introduction, but as a conclusion; it is not initial or initiating, but terminal or concluding. It is always at the end of a certain itinerary of the soul that we find it—as the recompense, the fine flower or beautiful mirage of a great labor achieved, a slow maturation, an old nostalgia. Logically, then, we should not begin with it; at most we might end with it.

But on the other hand, and especially because we are now concerned with the very legitimacy of the notion, we may justifiably ask what beatitude really has to do with Nietzsche's thought.

What are the fundamental concepts of his philosophy? Tradition distinguishes three: the Overman, the Eternal Return, and the Will to Power. The proper meaning and the logical (and even simply chronological) order of these three notions remain, even today, rather obscure. But at least one thing is clear: none of these three essential themes seems to have a direct relationship with beatitude. In connection with his thought, then, the idea that all the philosophies and religions of the world bring us of beatitude cannot fail to arouse immediate and perhaps invincible resistances in the informed Nietzschean.

The relatively well-informed Nietzschean easily forgets the Eternal Return and immediately wonders how one could ever reconcile the inevitable peace of beatitude with the idea of unlimited overcoming evoked by the theme of the Overman ("a bridge and not a goal," an arrow and not a target) and by that of the Will to Power—which, likewise, is always a will to *more* power.

The well-informed Nietzschean, however, remembers the religious or "evangelical" character of the doctrine of the Eternal Return. And he distrusts beatitude, for he recalls

---

Edgar Steiger on the possible origin of Nietzsche's idea of the eternal return:

The first time I read the words "eternal return" in Nietzsche I immediately had to recall Origen's *pochaastasix*. . . . For the Greek church father smuggled the genuinely Hellenistic idea of the eternal recurrence of things and the eternal repetition of the origin and end of the world without further ado into Christian theology and then built on it the magnificent doctrine of the bringing of men back to God. . . . But this divinization of the world was, for Origen, not just an end, but also a beginning. When the cycle of things had reached its beginning again, it began all over. The terrible spectacle of the fall, sin, punishment, redemption, and return to God is repeated over and over again—from eternity to eternity or, as one could better translate the word *aion* from one world-cycle to the next.

This adoration of iron necessity from the rostrum sounded like a Greek hymn. The old man up there [Karl Steffensen] had completely forgotten where he was and to whom he was speaking. And at his feet sat, in total rapture, the pale man [Nietzsche] whose book *The Birth of Tragedy from the Spirit of Music* was a single eulogy to the world-redeeming Dionysus, listening in amazement to Greek mystery-wisdom from the mouth of a church father. Despite myself I cannot escape the grotesque idea that "the seminal idea of the eternal recurrence, the idea in which every other way of thinking now perishes," first flashed through the Dionysus-disciple's brain like a sudden illumination at this moment, on this school bench, in old Steffensen's philosophy class.

Edgar Steiger, in Conversations with Nietzsche: A Life in the Words of his Contemporaries, *edited by Sander L. Gilman, 1987.*

---

that Nietzsche does not want to pour new wine into old vessels; he knows that the religion in this religion is formally different from that in all other religions—as essentially, substantially different as the joyous knowledge of tragic wisdom in its form and content is different from all the other kinds of wisdom, as different as the fifth gospel, that of Zarathustra, is from the other four. He knows that the Will to Power does not open upon, does not sink into the *amor fati* or the thought of the Eternal Return, finding in it something like the rest of the Seventh Day. For the Eternal Return is as much the *terminus a quo* as the *terminus ad quem* of the Will to Power—the Eternal Return is the "heaviest burden" that only the strongest of men can endure. In this sense, the Will to Power is the condition for the Eternal Return. But on the other hand, with this thought is produced "the greatest elevation of the consciousness of strength in man, as he creates the Overman." In this sense it is the thought of the Eternal Return that is now the condition for the Will to Power, conferring upon it that increase of force through which it can create the Overman. In the end, Heidegger is right when he writes [in his *Nietzsche,* Vol. I]: "The Will to Power is, in its essence and according to its internal possibility, the eternal return of the same."

Thus, the commentator who endeavors to think not *like* Nietzsche (foolish project, impossible imitation!) but to think *with* Nietzsche what Nietzsche wished to conceive—this commentator comes to disengage little by little the underlying, still enigmatic unity of the three themes. But everything that brings him closer to this unity seems to take him further from beatitude, for is it not true that at the very moment and in the very place that Nietzsche announces this sublime religion, he also asks us to have "tested all the degrees of skepticism" and to have "bathed with pleasure in icy torrents"? Otherwise, he says, "you will have no right to this thought. . . . I will be *on my guard,*" Nietzsche continues, "against credulous and exalted minds." And where is there more credulousness and greater exaltation, or at least greater *risk* of credulousness and exaltation, than in beatitude? If, as Nietzsche repeats several times, the doctrine of the Eternal Return is to be considered "as a hammer in the hands of the most powerful man"—how can there be contained in this most hammering and hammered-out doctrine anything that is still in any way close to what we call beatitude? How can the philosopher who philosophizes with a hammer ever be blissful, *agapé,* or *beatus?*

"I am bitterly opposed," Nietzsche writes, "to all teachings that look to an end, a peace, a 'Sabbath of Sabbaths.' Such modes of thought indicate fermenting, suffering, often even morbid breeds. . . ."

Why this animosity toward beatitude? Perhaps because Nietzsche perceives the abyss that separates true happiness from beatitude. Happiness (but not the happiness of the "last man," that bastard form of beatitude) arises out of chance, hazard, accident, events, fortune, the fortuitous. Beatitude is not the height of, but the opposite of, this free and gratuitous happiness. The concern for beatitude expresses the will to conjure away that part of contingency that is the very essence of happiness. The man of be-

atitude no longer wishes to be exposed to the thousand blows of fortune, to the stupor and the rending that happiness as well as unhappiness provoke, both of them always unwonted and rather monstrous. He wishes to have his feet on the ground once and for all. It is not enough for him to be happy; he wishes to be blissful, he wishes to rest in the certainty of the *unum necessarium.* He wishes to die, to sleep, and this eternal rest and sleep he calls eternal life and eternal bliss! Thus beatitude saves us—it works our salvation, we save ourselves, we flee from ourselves, we are no longer here below. A phenomenon of withdrawal, flight, and resentment, beatitude always wants the unconditioned, the absolute, the eternal; it refuses, it impugns the tender, innocent, puerile cruelty of chance; it casts an evil eye on all the favors and disfavors of existence. It says *no* to life.

The man who seeks beatitude is the man with an *idée fixe,* a solid block with one sole love, one sole god, one sole faith—a barbarian, in fact. "Love of one is a barbarism: for it is exercised at the expense of all else. The love of God, too." To this monoideism, this monotheism, this "monotonotheism" (Nietzsche's expression), incapable for two thousand years of inventing a single new god, Nietzsche constantly opposed a spirit of aristocratic tolerance, the virile and military (but not "militant") skepticism of those in whom the creative instinct for new gods awakens. The man seeking beatitude has finally entered the temple (*fanum*), the unique temple of virtue, truth, and felicity—curiously enough identified. How can such a man not be a fanatic? But fanaticism, always the symptom of a weak and servile will, is precisely what prevents us from becoming creators; he alone, Nietzsche says, is capable of creating who no longer believes in anything. "I no longer believe in anything—such is the right way of thinking of the creative man."

Thus, against "sabbatical" beatitude, and in the shadow of perfect nihilism, Nietzsche inaugurates a new alliance: that of heroic sentiments and warlike skepticism, of military discipline and scientific discipline, of the true creator and the noble traitor to knowledge. To everything that gapes in beatitude Nietzsche opposes the openness of an ever openended creation: to the Buddha's smile, Dionysus' demented laughter; to the man in search of beatitude, priest of his ideal, the Overman who is its master; to priesthood, mastery; to the spirit of faith, which is the subsiding or downward inclination of creation, the strange conjunction of love and scorn; to intuitive, infused, diffused, confused science, the perception, the sentiment, the "pathos of distance," and the clear gaze of him who no longer wishes to know other abysses than the "abysses of light;" to the ancient will to find the true, the young will to create it. At the same time the form, the very essence of this will is modified. It no longer has any moorings, any anchorage, anything more to lose, anything more to ask; it is finally left only for this will to be generous, imperial, legislating, ordaining, sense-giving. Precisely because there is no longer any being, any truth in things, everything must be given to this will; it does not give itself or lose itself in its gifts. It gives meaning because essences are dead; it creates values because there are no longer any existing values: it gives birth to new gods because there is no longer any

God. And thus, Nietzsche writes, Nihilism as the negation of a true world, of a being, might indeed be a divine way of thinking. It *might* be, Nietzsche says—but it is not yet so. . . .

For the image of solid earth Nietzsche substitutes that of the sea, a sea that he says was never full enough; to homesickness—a sickness that is indeed philosophy itself (philosophy is a true homesickness, Novalis said)—he opposes "the longing for a land without homeland." Since, in the end, the instinct for beatitude is only a death instinct, how can we still speak of beatitude in Nietzsche?

Now, then, we will attempt the impossible: we will try to find a certain idea of beatitude in Nietzsche. What path shall we take? The narrowest path. We will not compile all the passages in which Nietzsche speaks in positive terms of beatitude and, for example, of the happiness of forgetfulness, of the "blessed isles," of involuntary beatitude, etc. No, we will choose but three lines from the posthumous writings to try to acquire a necessarily narrow, not necessarily superficial, view of Nietzschean beatitude. These few lines are: "What must I do to be happy? That I know not, but I say to you: Be happy, and then do what you please."

According to the chronology set up by Nietzsche's editors, this fragment dates from 1882-84. Let us accept this hypothesis and consider the text in itself—first the aphoristic form of the text.

There is a question and an answer. The question is presumably that of a disciple, who presumably questions a master; the answer is that of a man who does not know given to a man who is presumed to know. The answer itself is composed essentially of two propositions: an admission of ignorance, this time a very explicit admission on the part of the master, and the declaration of a new maxim. Between the two, there is the transitional formula, "But I say to you."

The interplay of question and answer, and, in the answer, the mixture of ignorance and knowledge, modesty and prophecy, cannot fail to evoke in a rather troubling way the two hitherto most venerable forms of dialogue: the Socratic and the evangelical.

What is Socratic is, of course, first the apparent ignorance of the master, and then the apparent irony of an answer that does not answer the question raised, and finally the stupor and silence of the disciple before this paradoxical way to answer, which cannot satisfy him and to which he can still find nothing to say.

What is more evangelical than Socratic is that the initiative of the question comes from the disciple and not from the master; the question is put to a master who is not interrogating, but is first taciturn and then dogmatic enough. And what is frankly evangelical is the "But I say to you," which obviously echoes the distinctive *"sed dico vobis."*

The form of this passage is already instructive, for it has the twofold character, both metaphysical and evangelical, of Nietzsche's teaching. We must therefore consider it a little more closely before examining the content or the basis of the text.

Nietzsche presents himself often, on the one hand, as a philosopher of a new kind ("misosopher" as much as philosopher) and even as a metaphysician (a metaphysician, however, who is an enemy of all the worlds behind the scenes), and, on the other hand, as the messenger, the spokesman, the evangelist of news that could at last be the *good* news. His thought is thus, for example, said to be a *"Künstler Metaphysik"* and an *"Artisten Evangelium"* (an artist-metaphysics and an artist-gospel). This metaphysico-evangelical ambiguity of Nietzschean thought raises problems, for what is metaphysics? It is the ontological science of immutable being, of the eternal essence of all that is; it is the onto-theological science of the first principles and the first causes; it is the catholic and radical science of the *omnitudo realitatis.* And what is a gospel? It is the announcement of a blessed event, of good news, of something fundamentally historical—deeds and gestures of the man or the man-God that concern the destiny of men. But this announcement, the news of this deed, this knowledge by hearsay—all this does not have much to do with metaphysical speculation. Will we then have to choose between a "metaphysical" interpretation and an "evangelical" interpretation of Nietzsche's doctrine? Will we have to try to elaborate some patchwork compromise between these two possible readings? No; we should rather remember that Nietzsche wishes to rework both the form of metaphysics and the form of religion, and that this reworking is to be so profound that it will end by destroying even the possibility of such a compromise.

Nietzsche can say, for example, that the Will to Power is the essence of the world and present at the same time, and infinitely more modestly, this same Will to Power as a new fixation—a holding down, an arresting—of the concept of life. It is "the last fact back to which we can come." Here the word "fact" represents nothing else than the last instance, the final jurisdiction to which we can address ourselves to judge what life is about—or, rather, what it *could* be about.

No essence, as we see, is then lodged in the heart of things; "essence" is not something eidetic or ontological. On the contrary, it is the result of a certain subsumption, a certain schematization, a certain imposition—the imposition of a meaning, the assessment of a price; in the end, a fundamentally human appreciation, an estimation. This is why, far from being the in-itself or the true, "essence" is a view, a perspective, a position taken with regard to the thing on the basis of something other than itself: "The question 'what is that?' is an imposition of meaning from some other viewpoint. 'Essence,' the 'essential nature,' is something perspective."

This is also true for a *fact,* which at bottom is nothing else than the little in-itself with which the positivist physicists are ready to content themselves. It too is not simply self-made; it too is not: on the contrary, it is always the result of a certain setting up, the montage of a certain experience. A fact is never a mere fact, "stupid like a calf," Nietzsche says. It can only interest us; more, it only begins to be "produced" when it speaks. But in fact the facts never speak all by themselves, they always have to be made to speak a language that can only be our language; in short, we have to intervene to interpret them.

To conceive an essence as a meaning, a substance as an instance, and a fact as always "made" is to move toward bringing about a certain *rapprochement* between metaphysics and the gospel. What the essence has lost, the word—a certain word that at bottom is a will—will recuperate. The gospel is the announcement of a deed or exploit: this news, this announcement of itself, gives configuration to a certain history, a certain truth, always without foundation, but not necessarily always without value. Here the most "prosaic" saying is essentially "poetic," because it is fundamentally action and creation: it gives form to what is formless, meaning to what is meaningless, and being to what has no being; it is a veritable creation *ex nihilo*—that is, here, out of nihilism. In Nietzsche, to name things is always the privilege of the dominant classes, the creators, the legislators—in short, the masters, who teach and command by virtue of their word alone. The true master is both lord and teacher, despot and pedagogue: he states the elementary things and institutes them by stating them, and asks us to repeat them in order to instruct ourselves.

Zarathustra says: "I teach you the Overman! The Overman is the meaning of the earth. Your will says: the Overman is the meaning of the earth." The Overman is the meaning of the earth, and yet it is necessary that the will *state* this meaning in order that the being of meaning become the meaning of being.

What is meaning? It is the last residue of essences in a nihilistic philosophy. What is meaning? Meaning is a certain "wishing to say" that we ascribe to things—a desire to say that is, and yet must be stated in order that it be. What is meaning? It is also the direction, the goal, the end, that which things are on their way to, where they wish to come to, the last word of their history, this becoming that is their being, this being that is their becoming.

The saying that Zarathustra gives and commends to his disciples is always the saying of a will that orders, the saying of those genuine philosophers who, Nietzsche assures us, command and legislate: "They say, 'thus it *shall* be!'" Here what must be is what will be in any case, and yet what nonetheless can be only through the force of this will that states: a strange situation, in which meaning is and nonetheless is *only* if it is uttered. Thus, the word that states the meaning is here clearly ascribed to the will, and not to the understanding or to reason. This word is still *logos,* but in this imperious and ordaining *logos* there is now something that is akin to the *deka logoi* of the Decalogue. In Nietzsche, as in the Bible, the word is the scepter of power. And meaning, in turn, is a function of power.

But on the other hand, this will that states and dictates the form and the truth is in no way arbitrary. It is fully a will and a Will to Power only when it wills what is, when it loves the necessary: then it conceives itself as a destiny or a fatality, a storm or lightning bolt of truth. *Ego fatum,* Nietzsche often says, always conscious of the profound identity of the will (here the *ego*) and of necessity (here the *fatum*). The perfect will is delivered from the caprices of

desire, and destiny, for its part, is no longer (as Leibniz put it) a "Turkish fate" (*fatum mahumetanum*). Meaning is only for the will, and the will is only for meaning. Thus the authentic master of the philosopher is indeed the evangelical metaphysician, Nietzsche says: Caesar with the soul of Christ. It is such a master who speaks in the aphorism we have chosen. It is time to hear his words.

What does the master say—or rather, what does the disciple ask? He asks: "What must I do in order to become happy or blissful?" If the master does not answer this question, he nevertheless understands it. His silence is not that of distraction, but that of meditation and voluntary abstention. The proof of this is that in time he admits that he does not know what to answer, and this admission itself shows, on the one hand, the attention given the question, and, on the other hand, the distance that Nietzsche means to put between this demand and his own teaching.

Let us then first try to perceive the stress of the question, and, through the stress, the type of man who speaks. Nietzsche is and wishes to be a psychologist; let us then work out the psychology of the questioner, a psychology or psychoanalysis that in his eyes constitutes the sole genuine analysis of the question. There is no mistaking it: the stress of this question is the stress of distress, and the man who speaks here is an unhappy man who asks what he must do in order to be unhappy no longer. What, then, is the question? It is at bottom the oldest question in the world, the question that has fed all the religions and all the philosophies we know—all of them daughters of a poverty that seeks to evade its situation, to save itself from its poverty—daughters of a suffering that can no longer suffer its suffering. Philosophies of poverty, poverty of philosophy! Religions *of* suffering—they are always anxious to relieve the suffering from which they proceed, and that at the highest cost, the cost of death and sacrifice, the cost of a sublime and subtle cruelty, and hence at the price of an excess of suffering, a suffering "more profound, more inward, more poisonous, more deadly—but calming, reassuring, redemptive in spite of everything, because through it the primal pain of life is finally interpreted, justified, systematized, ordered, put into perspective: into the perspective of fault. Man suffered still and could suffer even more: he suffered because of . . . , through the fault of. . . . The pain henceforth had a cause, a reason, an end, a why, and this *meaning* allowed the *essential* to be saved—that is, the will, at least a certain will, that which wills the meaning of suffering because first it considers suffering an accident, a stumbling block, something that is but should not be and that elsewhere, in another world, another life, another nature, would *not* be. This will, avid for meaning, we see, is at bottom a will for annihilation, a will that begins by saying "no" to existence, to our meaningless, immoral, unreasonable existence. Revolt or resignation—what difference? —it is always first resentment, and also always first aversion to suffering. And yet this will to annihilation, this will to nothingness that generates the ascetic ideal, is something quite different from a nothingness of will: "It is and remains a *will,*" and, as Nietzsche says, in conclusion "man would rather will *nothingness* than *not* will.

Given this, why does the master not answer the question? Why does he remain deaf to the disciple's anxiety—not the anxiety of suffering (for man is the animal who calls for the most suffering, and in the end the animal that suffers most because he is the most courageous, and not the most courageous because he suffers the most), but, much more prosaically, the anxiety of this man *tired* of suffering, this candidate for beatitude, a rather insipid beatitude? "What must I do to become happy? That I know not!" Why this nonknowing, and this assurance and placidity in not knowing? Perhaps first, quite simply, because there is in the end never anything to say to the man who, being unhappy, asks what he has to do to become happy. Perhaps no action can ever make us pass imperceptibly from unhappiness to happiness, from the present reality of this unhappiness that *is* to the becoming of happiness that *is not yet*. Vanity of all those discourses! Vanity of all those practices, of all those becomings! Perhaps there is, strictly speaking, nothing to do to become happy when one is not already happy; perhaps there is no transition possible, but rather indeed an abrupt mutation, a qualitative leap, an instantaneous conversion—or, again, and to speak a more precisely Nietzschean language (one more in accord with that "intellectuality of suffering" Nietzsche continually insists on), a sudden change of outlook, of evaluation, of interpretation, of perspective?

Yet there is something else in this admission of ignorance on the part of the master. There is the will to establish distance from all the traditional philosophies, and, at the same time, the still unspoken elaboration of a new philosophy, or rather of a new manner of philosophizing: the joyous knowing—no longer the ascending knowing, but the declining knowing; no longer the knowing that rises from unhappiness toward happiness, but the knowing that descends, that overflows, that pours out of the over-full cup, the over-ripe cluster, the over-rich star: a primal abundance and superabundance, joyous and painful, of a Dionysian wisdom and beatitude! This joyous knowing, this tragic wisdom, has no connection with the question that has been put. The absence of a "response" is here the absence of a "correspondence." To respond to a question is always in the end to answer *for* the question—that is, to assume it, to take charge of it, to take "responsibility" for it. Nietzsche refuses this community of thought, its poverty and hope. That is why he keeps silence; that is also why he declares (and this time not without some pride) his resolute ignorance, his *will* to not know.

The beatitude that the unhappy man wishes to attain is that vesperal beatitude that Nietzsche calls an ideal state of laziness. To those sabbatical, hedonist, or Buddhist philosophers, those philosophers of the setting sun, those essentially reclining philosophers, Nietzsche opposes the philosophy of the morning and the midday, the standing philosophers, the men of the great north, "We Hyperboreans."

The Hyperboreans mock happiness and virtue, all the promised lands, the paths and the threads capable of taking us to this beatitude that has lost its first "terrorist" breath and today is nothing but the happiness of the last man.

But I ask you, gentlemen, what have we to do with happiness? What matters to us your virtue (the new way to happiness)? Why do we hold ourselves back? To become philosophers, rhinoceroses, cave bears, phantoms? Is it not to *rid ourselves* of virtue and happiness? We are by nature much too happy, much too virtuous not to experience a little temptation, to become immoralists and adventurers. We are especially curious to explore the labyrinth, we try to make acquaintance with Mr. Minotaur, about whom they tell such terrible things; but what matters to us your way that *ascends,* your thread that leads out, that leads to happiness and to virtue, that leads *to you,* I fear . . . You wish to save us with the aid of this thread? And we—we pray you earnestly, lose this thread!

There is always, in the same sense of this solar and glacial, divine and infernal wisdom,

> . . . preoccupation with itself and with its "eternal salvation" [that] is not the expression of a rich and self-confident type; for that type does not give a damn about its salvation—it has no such interest in happiness of any kind; it is force, deed, desire—it imposes itself on things, it lays violent hands on things. Christianity is romantic hypochondria of those whose legs are shaky. Wherever the hedonist perspective comes into the foreground one may infer suffering and a type that represents a failure.

The man who persists in saying, "*But I say to you . . .*" is a philosopher of a new kind. His doctrine is hyperborean: it is no longer a question of knowing what one must do to avoid unhappiness; it is now a question of letting everything that can issue forth from happiness do so. The "but" is the sign of this conversion.

What does the master say? He says: "Be happy or blissful and do what you please." The response is cavalier; it supposes the problem solved: in fact, the terms have been reversed. In the old perspective—that of Plato and of Hegel—desire, will, love, action, labor all proceeded from unhappiness, indigence, lack, need, hunger, appetite—in short, from negativity. Correlatively, happiness presented itself as the fulfillment, the contentment of this void, the release of this tension, the solution or the dissolution of what first presented itself as insoluble. In short, to will was fundamentally to will to will no more. Happiness was always at the end of the road—for tomorrow, for the day after tomorrow, for our children, our grandchildren, in another world, in another life. . . . Of course, this happiness could begin even now, but it never made anything but a timid beginning. Of course, we might find a certain happiness in preparing our happiness, but this transitional happiness was not yet the true happiness, beatitude.

In saying "be happy," Nietzsche shows himself a thousand times more impatient: what he wants is the whole of happiness and not only its premises, and this whole he wants at once. All happiness and at once—or else never! "Midday of life, second youth! Summer garden." Impatient happiness, under arrest, on the alert, looking forward.

We can now measure the abyss that separates these two apparently similar maxims: to make one's happiness, and to be happy. (But does not Nietzsche himself say that the narrowest abysses are the most difficult to cross?) Nietzsche implicitly opposes the baseness of the man who wishes to make his happiness, to prepare his beatitude, and to operate his salvation to the nobility of the man who has understood the grandeur of this new commandment: Be happy, blissful, eternally happy at the very heart of happiness, of one sole instant of happiness; at the very heart of unhappiness, of an abyss of unhappiness.

Happiness of adventure, happiness of the adventurer, to be sure—chance remains king, the contingency of happiness is intact. But it is also happiness in rest, perfect happiness, accomplished happiness—though still and always open—dazzling affirmation that no desire will ever more tarnish, and yet chaotic and creative affirmation. The identification of happiness and beatitude with that height, that depth of thought can be well understood only on the basis of another identification, that which this simple sentence of Nietzsche expresses: "Supreme fatalism, nonetheless identical with chance and creative activity (no repetition in things, but one has to first create it)."

The master goes on: "Be happy, and then do what you please." This means that, on the basis of beatitude, all desires are sanctified. He who would interpret in terms of facility this last proposition would be very mistaken. The precept is as strict as, even more strict than, those of all the old moralities; it does not open the way to all our desires—on the contrary, it closes the door to almost everything that up to now has been called love, desire, or will. All desires that proceed from unhappiness, from lack, indigence, envy, hatred are condemned. If Nietzsche's philosophy is not a new philosophy but a new way to philosophize, it is just because of this revolution worked in the very form or essence of desire. While the *sophia* changes its content, the *philein* changes its form. It is not a question of desiring other things or of desiring the same things by other means; it is a question of desiring all things in another way—the material and the spiritual, the good and the bad, for ourselves and for others.

What will this new desire be? And what will this new doing be? What can we will to desire and to do when we are blissful? Nothing. Such is the response that the disciple might make in his turn to the master's answer. And this response would be a new misunderstanding. The master's command is neither hedonist nor quietist. The master does not say to the disciple, "Do anything whatever," and he also does not tell him, "Do nothing." He rather tells him that it is only out of the over-fullness of his beatitude that all the desires and all the actions that please him can flow. Thus desire now has as its father (or rather its mother) wealth, and no longer poverty; action is the child of happiness and no longer of unhappiness; beatitude is initial and no longer terminal.

What will this desire be? Nietzsche tells us in **Zarathustra** that it will be the "great desire," that which wishes to give and no longer to take, to thank and no longer ask, to bless and no longer supplicate. Of this desire Nietzsche says, "All desire wills eternity—wills deep, deep eternity."

This desire wills eternity, but *what* eternity? Not an eternity that is beyond or above becoming, an eternity that casts an evil eye on the instant that passes, but, on the contrary, the eternity, the eternalization of what is and what is *at this very instant*. The blissful man has made his peace with reality. He is happy from what is and with what is, with the very brevity of the instant that passes. He does not demand the prolongation or the nonlimitation of this instant in time. To tell the truth, he does not demand anything at all; he orders, he wills that this instant return as it is, in its very fleetingness, an eternity of times. It is then not a mere coincidence that the fragment upon which we are commenting is contemporary with the time when Nietzsche conceived the doctrine of the Eternal Return of the same.

We can also understand that the "doing" issuing out of this beatitude is, in turn, totally foreign to the most traditionally admitted forms of action and praxis. The blissful man is more concerned with creating than with acting; or, rather, the sole action that seems to him to be at the height of his beatitude is precisely creation, that labor of creation which is that of child-bearing. A surprising word, one that seems to contradict what we have just said, affirming that the happy man rejoices over being, and, finally, over the becoming of things. This surprise rests, however, in the failure to recognize an essential difference between action and creation—or, more precisely, between action conceived in terms of Platonic, Hegelian, Marxist, or Sartrean (as one prefers) negativity, and creation as Nietzsche conceives it—that is, in essentially affirmative and playful terms, and this at the very moment when he associates it with destruction (but always under the aegis of love, of love that rejoices over what is).

Let us observe first, in general, that a philosophy of action is not necessarily a philosophy of creation, just as, conversely, a philosophy of creation (such as that of Bergson, for example) is not necessarily a philosophy of action. In reality, action is something quite different from a nascent creation, and creation for its part is something quite different from a fully developed action. It would perhaps not force Nietzsche's thought too much if we said that, for him, the principal source of all that we call action today is hatred for or discontent with what is, while every veritable creation proceeds from love and love only, from an immense gratitude for what is, a gratitude that seeks to impress the seal of eternity on what is and what, for Nietzsche, is always only in becoming. This is why the desire that wills eternity is an essentially creative desire, the extreme, playful, and artistic form of the Will to Power. It is then that the will becomes love, without ceasing to be will and Will to Power. It is then that this love becomes the love of the necessary, *"amor fati,"* without ceasing to be love and will for the contingency of the most contingent things. It is then that beatitude is beatitude in the heaven of chance, innocence and a fully positive indetermination. In this Dionysian beatitude, necessity is reconciled with chance, eternity with the instant, being with becoming—but all that outside of time, its lengths, its progress, its moments, its mediations. Speaking of this "recapitulation," in which the world of becoming comes extremely close to that of being—a "recapitulation that the doctrine of the

Eternal Return alone can accomplish—we see that it is not for nothing that Nietzsche calls it the "high point of the meditation."

Henri Birault, "Beatitude in Nietzsche," translated by Alphonso Lingis, in The New Nietzsche: Contemporary Styles of Interpretation, *edited by David B. Allison, 1977. Reprint by The MIT Press, 1985, pp. 219-31.*

Nietzsche's psychological collapse, in Turin, Italy, 1889:

On the morning of 3 January Nietzsche had just left his lodgings when he saw a cab-driver beating his horse in the Piazza Carlo Alberto. Tearfully, the philosopher flung his arms around the animal's neck, and then collapsed. The small crowd that gathered around him attracted Davide Fino, who had his lodger carried back to his room. After lying unconscious or at least motionless for a while on a sofa, Nietzsche became boisterous, singing, shouting, thumping at the piano. He probably thought he was clowning deliberately. . . . But the 'inspired clowning' which had already been hard to control by the end of November was now in unchallengeable possession of his mind. He wrote notes to the King of Italy ('My beloved Umberto'), the royal house of Baden ('My children'), and the Vatican Secretary of State. He would go to Rome on Tuesday, he said, to meet the pope and the princes of Europe, except for the Hohenzollerns. He advised the other German princes to ostracize them, for the *Reich* was still the enemy of German culture. Writing to Gast, Brandes and Meta von Salis, Nietzsche signed himself 'The Crucified', and writing to Burckhardt, Overbeck and Cosima Wagner, signed himself 'Dionysus'. The note to Meta runs: 'The world is transfigured, for God is on the earth. Do you not see how all the heavens are rejoicing? I have just seized possession of my kingdom, am throwing the pope into prison, and having Wilhelm, Bismarck and Stöcker shot.' The note to Burckhardt starts: 'That was the little joke for which I condone my boredom at having created a world.'

Ronald Hayman, in his Nietzsche: A Critical Life, *Penguin Books, 1980.*

Jean Granier   (essay date 1977)

[*A French critic and educator, Granier is the author of* Le Problème de la vérité dans la philosophie de Nietzsche *(1966). In the following essay he investigates Nietzsche's philosophy of the nature of truth.*]

One of the principal themes in Nietzschean thought is "the *interpretive* character of all that happens. No event exists in itself. Everything that happens consists of a group of phenomena that are gathered and *selected* by an interpretive being." For Nietzsche, these phenomena are not masks attached to a thing in itself, some lesser beings, or nothingness, or facts; their being belongs to an interpretive process, which consists only in the difference between an interpreting activity and a text. Being is text. It appears and makes sense; and the sense is multiple, manifested not in the way that an object is for a subject, but as an interpretation that is itself construed in terms of a multiplicity of perspectives. Interpretation, here, comprises the act of interpretation and the text interpreted, the reading and the book, the deciphering and the enigma. "One may not ask: 'Who then interprets?' for it is the interpretation, a form of the Will to Power, that exists." We are, Nietzsche claims, "ingenious interpreters and fortune-tellers whom destiny has placed as spectators on the European stage, faced with an enigmatic and *undeciphered* text whose meaning is gradually revealed."

Being is manifest, and this manifestation is a great rumbling and agitation of sense. But the sense is not directly decipherable. It receives nothing from beyond, and one would look in vain for an intelligible ground beneath the shimmer of appearance. No intuition or mental inspection can grasp it, still less synthesize it into a logical system. The very concept of totality—a logical system—is itself the product of an interpretation, and would not serve as immediate evidence. Because the phenomenon of being is a "text" and not a painting (which would display its contents to naïve perception or to the philosopher's intelligence), it is essentially ambiguous: it withholds as much as it shows, it is an opaque revelation, a blurred sense—in short, *an enigma*. Because of this quality of ambiguity, Nietzsche will call the phenomenon a *mask* or veil.

Once again, this mask conceals no transcendent reality. Perplexed by this peculiar state of affairs, the philosopher gives in to the temptation to break up the continuity of phenomena (a continuity whose dissonances agree and whose contraries blend) by separating out the clear and the obscure, being and its appearance. Thinking he can be clever in dealing with phenomena, the metaphysician becomes entrapped by them—*because phenomena cheat:* they *seem* to be masks that we can easily penetrate or remove as soon as we perform an intelligent critique upon them, guided by contradictions in the real world. But this is precisely not the case! The phenomenon masks what it manifests, *without enabling us to dissociate dissimulation from manifestation*. The phenomenon is a mask; it turns its own appearing into an appearance—i. e., it appears as pretense. Beyond it, one would find *nothing*—a nothing, moreover, that would still be qualified as a metaphysical negative of phenomenal being: the *nihil* of nihilism.

We must admit that there is something deceptive and frustrating to the human mind in this ambiguity of phenomena. But, instead of becoming indignant with this "travesty" of the sensible order, Nietzsche advises that we ask instead: what is it in man that becomes indignant and protests? The answer is that reason desires to recognize its own logical categories within phenomena. But, after all, why should the real world be compelled to please reason and logic? And what if the phenomena themselves directed this poem of the world to our aesthetic taste, to our will to art?

To try to imitate Parmenides by rejecting perceptible appearances for an absolute being (which would wholly conform to the principle of identity) would mean exchanging a convenient appearance—an authentic yet irrational

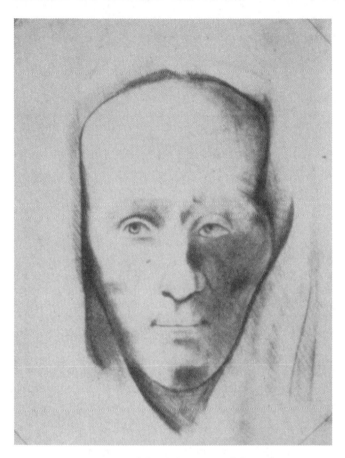

Undated pencil sketch from Nietzsche's youth.

manifestation of reality—for a fiction, for an inadequate appearance, an imaginary appearance:

> *Appearance,* as I understand it, is the true and unique reality of things; it is what all existing predicates belong to, and what to some extent could best be designated by the sum of these predicates, and this would even include contrary predicates. But this word plainly signifies a reality that is *inaccessible* to the operations and distinctions of logic, an "appearance," therefore, in relation to "logical truth," which—it must be added—is only possible in an *imaginary* world. I am not claiming that appearance is opposed to "reality"; on the contrary, I maintain that appearance is reality, that it is opposed to whatever transforms the actual into an imaginary "real world." If one were to give a precise name to this reality, it could be called "will to power." Such a designation, then, would be in accordance with its internal reality and not with its proteiform, ungraspable, and fluid nature.

If the wish to circumvent phenomena is idle, it is nonetheless legitimate *to describe them as they are,* in order to understand their organization and to disengage their subtle articulations. By describing them, we should be able to discern the texture of the text.

This texture corresponds to what Nietzsche calls a "scrawl." The phenomenon masks because it manifests a

sense that is not only multiple but subjected to a multitude of shiftings, transfers, superimpositions, overlappings, and sedimentations that produce the disconcerting impression of a rebus. The lines are broken, the contours blurred, the language anomalous, and the syntax incoherent. To all of this we must add the principal characteristic: the text is not static; it is not a monument, a museum; it is not really even a book, because everything in it changes, is transformed, *becomes.* The text itself is a becoming, and the interpreter, too, is a becoming. Interpretation, therefore, is the peculiar state of affairs that occurs, so to speak, at the intersection of these two sequences of becoming, where the one is determined as "sense" and the other as "the activity of deciphering."

Through concern for method, philosophers usually invoke a limiting principle that presupposes a primitive text, a base of sense that would serve as the real ground of the phenomenon—not, indeed, a substantial ground, but one that would prevent the phenomenon from dissolving into nothingness, one to guarantee precisely that it *exists.* What serves as this base, and is given within the phenomenon, is *nature.*

> To translate man back into nature; to become master over the many vain and overly enthusiastic interpretations and connotations that have so far been scrawled and painted over that eternal basic text of *homo natura;* to see to it that man henceforth stands before man as even today, hardened in the discipline of science, he stands before the *rest* of nature.

But be careful! The danger is to fall back into metaphysical illusion by turning the hypothesis of "nature" into an abstraction that would surreptitiously lead back to an intelligible *substratum* of being in itself. Let us resist the seduction of such a reading and say: if the phenomenon clearly warrants our distinguishing several levels within its interpretation and allows us to decipher the more or less archaic strata of sense by going back to a text that is said to be primitive—then this primitive text of nature has absolutely nothing in common with a "thing in itself," with an intelligible "being," or with a "cosmos." It is not a book written by a superior intelligence, it is what Nietzsche calls *chaos.*

The primitive text of nature is thus the *chaotic being that manifests itself as a significant process.* Its figures delineate not a system or a cosmos, but, precisely, a *mask. Nature and mask determine phenomenal being, the phenomenon in its being, as chaos.* In their very being, therefore, nature and mask are the same, and the worst possible mistake would be to oppose these two terms. In reality, they are strictly bound up with one another, and it is this interdependence that the sameness of their being expresses: the Same, and not a logical or ontological identity. *The Same*—the being that comes back in eternal recurrence, that renders nature and mask copresent in the equivocal unity of the *text.*

The Same—which denotes the being of the phenomenon—joins nature and the scrawl of interpretations together in such a way that the text is enigmatic for every interpreter. Performed and preserved by the Same, this conjunction is also a differentiation between terms. Thus, Nietzsche himself can distinguish a text from its interpretations, nature (the primitive text) from the inscriptions that cover it up. This difference has two dimensions, then: one, *epistemological* (the difference between an interpreted text and an interpretive operation); the other, *temporal* (the difference between the archaic and the recent, between the primitive and the modern). Since—as we have just pointed out—the sameness of chaos joins nature and mask, engendering the unique phenomenon of the text, and this sameness is the work of Eternal Recurrence, Nietzsche's thought here reveals its radicality: we see, in effect, that the theory of interpreted being, the theory of the text, involves an essential relation among *being, appearance,* and *time.* Because nature is subject to time, chaotic being constitutes itself as a text out of the confusion of appearance—i. e., across the perpetual "scrawl" of interpretations. Nonetheless, it is always the Same that is manifested; whether or not one attempts to restore its primordial truth, its "natural" truth, it is the Same that reappears across the flow of interpretations. There *really are* a text and its interpretations; moreover, the two are united (because the sameness is real) as Will to Power.

One essential element is still missing in our reconstruction of this Nietzschean problem of the mask: the *antagonism* that is played out between nature (chaotic being) and phenomena, whereby nature manifests itself while concealing itself. According to Nietzsche, this antagonism is what accounts for the difference, within the Same, between nature and interpretation: thus, nature is necessarily a mask, and the text is an enigma.

In an early fragment that prefigures the rest of his philosophical work, Nietzsche discusses the solution of the enigma: "For the Greek Gods, the world was an ever changing veil that hid the most terrible reality." For the Greeks, phenomena dissimulated what they showed, because what they showed was the most terrible. The name of this most terrible is chaos. In no other way can chaos appear than as masked: to look at it is intolerable—mortal. Every interpretation is thus in principle a concealment, since it cannot permit chaos to appear without masking it in a veil of appearance. "It would be possible that the true constitution of things was so hostile to the presuppositions of life, so opposed to them, that we needed appearance in order to be able to live."

Nietzsche calls this masking *art.* Art is the veil of beautiful appearance thrown over the horrors of chaos: "Greek art has taught us that there is no beautiful surface without a terrible depth." Beauty is the illusion that makes us forget that appearing is the manifestation of an unfathomable depth; it is the interpretation of its antagonist, the real.

To hold resolutely to appearances, to better accept an illusory mask, to interpret the text in such a way that its absurdity is concealed under the play of aesthetic significations and becomes a spectacle of beauty—this is the naïveté of the Greeks, those masters of interpretation. Naïveté characterizes the intentional superficiality of the profound man, the wisdom of the philosopher radical enough to become the poet of appearance.

In the Greek sense, the text phenomenon (or interpreted being) would stand as "the terrible in the mask of beauty."

What is most terrible, then, is also *the truth.* The truth designates the chaotic being of a groundless depth. If the mask is beauty, then truth is the ugliness of chaos: "because the truth is ugly." The phenomenon conceals its being in the appearance of beauty; thus, the beauty of the world hides the horror of nature. No more could one oppose being and phenomenon, nature and interpretation, text and "scrawl," revealed and concealed, than one could apprehend truth itself without its masks:

> We no longer believe that truth remains truth when the veils are withdrawn; we have lived too much to believe this. Today we consider it a matter of decency not to wish to see everything naked, or to be present at everything, or to understand and "know" everything.

As for the "grounds" of truth, we only imagine them. Chaotic being has no grounds, no reasons; it is *groundless*—an abyss. Mask, therefore, becomes one with life. "We should," Nietzsche emphasizes, "understand the fundamentally *aesthetic* phenomenon called 'life.' " Life is a beautiful appearance, then, one with no regard for truth, one that allows us to continue to exist despite the truth: "Is it to avoid chance that we take refuge in life? In its brilliance, its *falseness,* its *superficiality,* its shimmering falsehood? If we seem joyous, is it because we are profoundly sad? We are grave, we know the abyss." The most alive love what is most superficial—out of depth!

This conception of life, of course, is not the principal concern of the biological sciences. Rather, for Nietzsche, life determines the essence of interpreted being insofar as the latter involves a protective mask of lies. Lies, then, designate precisely the order of appearance—i. e., the texture of the text, the chaotic conglomeration of meanings. Lies indeed, since this phenomenon *masks* its own nature: it makes the illusion of truth surface from the terrible abyss—and because this is an illusion, truth is not so much divulged as denied, even when it seems to occur.

If the mask (life) characterizes interpreted being, then being in its interpretive aspect is an authoritarian insertion of sense, a sense-giving: Thus, when compared with the text, interpretation is a "creation." Life and art are two words that characterize a single creative act: namely, the act of ordering chaos, stabilizing becoming, and inventing categories by which the abyss of truth can be organized into various forms and constellations.

> Identity of nature between the conqueror, the legislator, and the artist—the same way of material expression. . . . Metaphysics, religion, morality, science—all of them only products of his will to art, to lie, to flight from "truth," to *negation* of "truth." This ability itself, thanks to which he violates reality by means of lies, this artistic ability of man *par excellence*—he has it in common with everything that is.

At this level of reflection, for Nietzsche, interpretation constantly takes the value of a creative imposition of form upon matter; here, the image of the relation between the artist and his material, the sculptor and his block of stone, replaces the textual metaphor and, thereby, enriches our understanding of phenomena. For Nietzsche, interpretation is synonymous with imposing sense, with molding chaos, with drawing a world of luminous figures out of what is hidden by the night of ignorance, impotence, and death. "The highest relation remains that between the creator and his material: that is the ultimate form of jubilation and mastery." To this, Nietzsche adds:

> This has given me the greatest trouble and still does: to realize that what things *are called* is incomparably more important than what they are. The reputation, name, and appearance, the usual measure and weight of a thing, what it counts for—originally almost always wrong and arbitrary, thrown over things like a dress and altogether foreign to their nature and even to their skin—all this grows from generation unto generation, merely because people believe in it, until it gradually grows to be part of the thing and turns into its very body. What at first was appearance becomes in the end, almost invariably, the essence, and is effective as such. How foolish it would be to suppose that one only needs to point out this origin and this misty shroud of delusion in order to *destroy* the world that counts for real, so-called "reality." We can destroy only as creators. —But let us not forget this either: it is enough to create new names and estimations and probabilities in order to create in the long run new "things."

Each individual, then, as an interpreter, is still creative.

Interpreted being, consequently, is itself the masking of chaos. The difference is still maintained here, since the mask both conceals the abyss and appears "alien" to the nature of things. Alien not because it would transcend, or be dialectically opposed, or be arbitrarily added on to this nature, but alien in that it would be the self-interpretation of chaos, its own self-informing, its cosmological structuring, its very life—something that could only be thought of as a proximity within the separation of its "difference," as simultaneously being *and* interpretation, as sense *and* nonsense, truth *and* lie. "It should be explained that the 'falsity' of things results from our own creative force." In other words, it is the act of interpretation and the interpreter that hide nature! And since the interpreter and the act of interpretation are already the life of being, it is being that interprets itself within its own self-dissimulation. We conclude the great cycle of being by returning to our starting point: being is mask, it is phenomenon.

Jean Granier, "Nietzsche's Conception of Chaos," translated by David B. Allison, in The New Nietzsche: Contemporary Styles of Interpretation, *edited by David B. Allison, 1977. Reprint by The MIT Press, 1985, pp. 135-41.*

Thomas J. J. Altizer   (essay date 1977)

[*An American critic and educator, Altizer has described himself as an atheistic Christian theologian. Altizer was deeply influenced by Nietzsche's critique of Christianity, and has authored such books as* Radical Theology and the Death of God *(1966),* Toward a New Christianity *(1967), and* Total Presence: The Language of Jesus and the Language of Today *(1980). In the following essay Altizer argues that Nietzsche's doctrine of the eternal recurrence of the same expands on a teaching of Jesus Christ that was subsequently obscured by orthodox Christianity.*]

Nietzsche's Zarathustra is a product of the Second Innocence of atheism, the new historical destiny created by the death of God. Man has been surpassed in Zarathustra, for Zarathustra has negated all previous history, and this negation is but the obverse of the deepest affirmation. As Nietzsche declares in **Ecce Homo:**

> The psychological problem in the type of Zarathustra is how he that says No and *does* No to an unheard-of degree, to everything to which one has so far said Yes, can nevertheless be the opposite of a No-saying spirit; how the spirit who bears the heaviest fate, a fatality of a task, can nevertheless be the lightest and most transcendent—Zarathustra is a dancer—how he that has the hardest, most terrible insight into reality, that has thought the "most abysmal idea," nevertheless does not consider it an objection to existence, not even to its eternal recurrence—but rather one reason more for being himself the eternal Yes to all things, "the tremendous, unbounded . . . Yes and Amen"—"Into all abysses I still carry the blessings of . . . saying Yes"—*But this is the concept of Dionysus once again.*

Zarathustra calls his hearers to a new Dionysian existence, an existence of total yes-saying to the sheer horror of a naked reality that is first revealed by Zarathustra and that can only be understood by a reversal of no-saying: Nietzsche's most profound symbol of the meaning of history. If as Nietzsche taught, bad conscience came into existence with the advent of history and originated with the interiorization or internalization (*Verinnerlichung*) of the instincts, with the birth of a "soul" opposed to the "body," then Dionysian existence demands a baptism of the instincts, a new innocence created by the sanctification of the forbidden. In short, Zarathustra calls for the resurrection of the body.

Nietzsche confessed that he chose the name of Zarathustra for his prophet of Eternal Recurrence because he believed that the Persian prophet Zarathustra created the first moral vision of the world: "the transposition of morality into the metaphysical realm, as a force, cause, and end in itself, is *his* work." Now Nietzsche, the first "immoralist," has created the exact opposite of the historical Zarathustra: "The self-overcoming of morality, out of truthfulness; the self-overcoming of the moralist into his opposite—into me—that is what the name of Zarathustra means in my mouth." Eternal Recurrence as the self-overcoming of morality? The self-overcoming not of self-righteousness or goodness itself? Through Zarathustra's self-overcoming, morality undergoes a metamorphosis and appears as the spirit of revenge: "the will's ill will against time and its 'it was.'" The life that Zarathustra promises is a life that will bring "it was" to an end:

> To redeem those who lived in the past and to re-create all "it was" into a "thus I willed it"—that alone should I call redemption. Will—that is the

name of the liberator and joy-bringer; thus I taught you, my friends. But now learn this too: the will itself is still a prisoner. Willing liberates; but what is it that puts even the liberator himself in fetters? "It was"—that is the name of the will's gnashing of teeth and most secret melancholy. Powerless against what has been done, he is an angry spectator of all that is past. The will cannot will backwards; and that he cannot break time and time's covetousness, that is the will's loneliest melancholy.

Can there be any doubt as to the Biblical identity of this "it was"? We have only to listen once again to the opening words of the Bible to be assured of this.

In the beginning God created the heaven and the earth. And the earth was without form, and void; and darkness was upon the face of the deep. And the Spirit of God moved upon the face of the waters. And God said, Let there be light: and there was light. And God saw the light, that it was good: and God divided the light from the darkness. And God called the light Day, and the darkness he called Night. And the evening and the morning were the first day.

The "first day" of creation was the day when God divided the light from the darkness, a division following His perception of the goodness of the light that He had created. But darkness existed before the creation; hence, it was not created by God, and the reader can only conclude that in some sense it is an "other" of God. In the primeval chaos or void, darkness was upon the face of the deep, and it was upon that face that God moved when He created light. God saw that the light was good, and clearly this light is the opposite of darkness. Even though for two millennia Christian theologians have declared that these words deny all ultimate forms of dualism, it would be idle to pretend that a dichotomy does not lie at the center of this myth. Can it be that it is "Zarathustra" and not "Moses" who is the first of our prophets?

Again and again in *The Antichrist*, Nietzsche portrays Jesus as a kind of innocent forerunner of Zarathustra; he is incapable of *ressentiment*, is free of history, and is himself exactly opposed to Christianity. The very word "Christianity" is a misunderstanding; there was only one Christian, and he and his gospel died on the cross.

—*Thomas J. J. Altizer*

Of course, *Isaiah II* and *Job* and not *Genesis* are the real ground and source of the Biblical understanding of God the Creator. *Isaiah II* comforts his people by speaking of the glory of the Lord:

Have ye not known? have ye not heard? Have ye not understood from the foundations of the earth? It is he that sitteth upon the circle of the earth, And the inhabitants thereof are as grasshoppers; That stretcheth out the heavens as a curtain, And spreadeth them out as a tent to dwell in: That bringeth the princes to nothing; He maketh the judges of the earth as vanity . . . He calleth them all by names By the greatness of his might, For that *he is* strong in power; Not one faileth.

To speak of God the Creator is to speak of the absolute sovereignty of God that can appear only as an infinitely distant transcendence, which reduces the earth to insignificance. Moreover, to know that God is the Creator is to know the ultimate impotence of man, as *Job* makes clear.

Then the Lord answered Job out of the whirlwind, and said . . . Where was thou when I laid the foundations of the earth? Declare, if thou hast understanding. Who hath laid the measures thereof, if thou knowest? Or who hath stretched the line upon it? Whereupon are the foundations thereof fastened? Or who laid the corner stone thereof; When the morning stars sang together, And all the sons of God shouted for Job?

Christianity knows God as the Creator, as the absolutely sovereign and transcendent Lord—what Nietzsche called the maximum god attained so far. But this maximum god, for Nietzsche, was accompanied by a maximum feeling of guilt, and was, indeed, the product of a madness of the will, the will of man to find himself totally and finally guilty. Of man's ultimate act of projection, Nietzsche says,

. . . he ejects from himself all his denial of himself, of his nature, naturalness, and actuality, in the form of an affirmation, as something existent, corporeal, real, as God, as the holiness of God, as God the Judge, as God the Hangman, as the beyond, as eternity, as torment without end, as hell, as the immeasurability of punishment and guilt.

While beyond any doubt Nietzsche judged this projection to be sickness, it is not an illusory sickness, as an earlier passage in *The Genealogy of Morals* makes manifest:

At this point I can no longer avoid giving a first, provisional statement of my own hypothesis concerning the origin of the "bad conscience": it may sound rather strange and needs to be pondered, lived with, and slept on for a long time. I regard the bad conscience as the serious illness that man was bound to contract under the stress of the most fundamental change he ever experienced—that change which occurred when he found himself finally enclosed within the walls of society and of peace. The situation that faced sea animals when they were compelled to become land animals or perish was the same as that which faced these semi-animals, well adapted to the wilderness, to war, to prowling, to adventure: suddenly all their instincts were disvalued and "suspended." From now on they had to walk on their feet and "bear themselves" whereas hitherto they had been borne by the water: a dreadful heaviness lay upon them. They felt unable to cope with the simplest undertakings; in this new world they no longer possessed their former guides, their regulating, unconscious, and infallible drives: they were reduced to thinking, inferring, reckoning, coordinating cause and effect, these unfortunate creatures; they were reduced to their "consciousness," their weakest and most fallible organ! I believe there has never been such a feeling of misery on earth, such a leaden discomfort.

Now, these words may well be as close as Nietzsche ever came to rewriting the opening page of the Bible. Certainly they give a new and decisive meaning to the "first day" of creation, and likewise they give an "innocent" meaning to the primordial division between light and darkness.

But is this meaning truly innocent? If the advent of man—of pure consciousness—is identical with the *internalization* of man, of the birth of a "soul" that is other than the body—then, in Nietzschean language, one may truly speak of creation as "fall." Here, the original fall would mean a primordial division between light and darkness, between "soul" and body that establishes a dichotomy at the center of life and existence. With the birth of consciousness, what Nietzsche calls our unconscious and infallible drives become reduced to thought or consciousness, and hence are no longer describable in terms of their original identity. Or, rather, they are describable only in the negative language of "bad conscience":

> The entire inner world, originally as thin as if it were stretched between two membranes, expanded and extended itself, acquired depth, breadth, and height, in the same measure as outward discharge was *inhibited.* Those fearful bulwarks with which the political organization protected itself against the old instincts of freedom—punishments belong among these bulwarks—brought it about that all those instincts of wild, free, prowling man turned backward *against man himself.* Hostility, cruelty, joy in persecuting, in attacking, in change, in destruction—all this turned against the possessors of such instincts: *that* is the origin of the "bad conscience."

Nor did bad conscience come into existence by way of a gradual and organic adaption to new conditions. On the contrary, it was the consequence of a fall, a sudden fall. Thus Nietzsche declares that the origin of the bad conscience was "a break, a leap, a compulsion, an ineluctable disaster which precluded all struggle and even all *ressentiment.*"

Consciousness as light? And our unconscious and infallible drives as darkness? Then the division of light from darkness becomes manifestly the primal originating event, and bad conscience appears as the origin of "man." If bad conscience is the serious illness that man was *bound* to contract under the stress of the most fundamental change he ever experienced, then it can neither be a simple illusion nor an accidental stumbling. It must rather be a necessary fate, an inescapable destiny, and hence a tragic fall. Furthermore, if the Christian God is identified as the projection of bad conscience, then that god is neither illusory nor accidental. The Christian God, the almighty and transcendent Creator, is the source and the ground of our tragic destiny, of the evolutionary movement of man. The utter holiness of the Christian God may well be a reverse image of the utter guilt of man. But that guilt is real, as real as the terror and cruelty of history; consequently, the Christian God is real, at least within the horizon of history, of "man." Or should we rather say that the Christian God is real so long as He is unnameable, is mysterious and beyond? And He must perish and disappear to the extent that His mystery is humanly spoken. Yet His mystery must remain mystery so long as it is apprehended in guilt, for it is guilt that evokes the mystery, just as it is the advent of bad conscience that establishes the infinite distance between the creature and the Creator.

Of course, morality is also a consequence of the advent of bad conscience. Morality is bound to that primal dichotomy between light and darkness or "soul" and body. Thereby it is sealed in a dual form, its every "yes" being inseparable from a parallel "no," and its every "no" a compulsive "no" that continually evokes an echoing "yes." This is the moral universe that Nietzsche called a madhouse, but it is identical with history itself and thereby inseparable from "man." The madness has an origin, a beginning, and thus it has a mythical meaning. *Genesis* is one expression of such a meaning, and *The Genealogy of Morals* is another. Both agree that morality is a consequence of an original and catastrophic fall. Paul anticipated Nietzsche in understanding morality, or the law, as a no-saying that makes guilt inescapable and final. Within this framework of understanding, Paul created a new dichotomy between "old" and "new," bringing a new and eschatological meaning to "it was." "It was" lies within the domain of "old aeon" or "old creation," and is therefore inextricably bound up with morality and law. This is precisely the domain that will come to an end with the Resurrection, for the realm of "it was" is the opposite of resurrection, if only because it is entirely subject to the judgment of guilt and death. From the standpoint of "new aeon" or "new creation," morality is the law of judgment and death, and as such it is not only the spirit but also the embodiment of revenge.

Paul, who may justly be regarded as the creator of Christian theology—indeed, of theology itself—offers us a means of understanding guilt and judgment as the contrary or reverse images of life and resurrection. Guilt only appears as total and irrevocable in the presence of its negation and transcendence. Here, guilt and death assume their full meaning only in an eschatological form, only when they are seen as even now coming to an end. Zarathustra, too, can realize the meaning of no-saying and *ressentiment* only by undergoing a self-overcoming of morality. Death and guilt become truly manifest only when they no longer sting, only when they no longer bind and enslave. Only then do they become all-comprehending images, for only the negation of their power can make their meaning manifest, can make it speakable. Just as hell, damnation, and final judgment are not found in the Old Testament, so the full meaning of guilt did not dawn until the modern age (beginning with Luther and culminating in Nietzsche). Even Augustine was unaware of the full meaning of guilt; his pagan roots protected him, for he was not aware of a guilt so complete that it ravages and inverts all expressions of consciousness and experience. The meaning of guilt can occur only when it comes to an end, only when its dark and negative ground becomes fully speakable.

Zarathustra is a prophet, that much is clear, at least to those who can hear his voice. Is not a prophet one who speaks what is unsayable to others, but which, once spoken, immediately carries its own authority? Prophetic speech is unmediated, unargued, and unadorned, but it nevertheless commands a hearing that cannot be denied so long as its voice is heard. The simple test of prophecy is whether or not its voice can be stilled or denied by those who hear it, and by that test Zarathustra is manifestly a prophet. One does not ask of prophecy whether or not it is true, for it lies far deeper than "truth," far deeper than logic, science, or knowledge. Even to inquire whether a prophecy is "good" is to evade its prophetic voice. Genuine prophecy invariably challenges what is established as goodness or truth—to the extent that one can even measure the degree to which prophecy is present by the shock that its utterance evokes. What is most shocking to us? Is it not quite simply the proclamation of the death of God? Nietzsche's madman, an earlier voice of Zarathustra, not only declares that God is dead, but that we have killed him—you and I. "How could we drink up the sea?" This is perhaps the most overwhelming question that Zarathustra asks us. Like all prophetic questions, it answers itself to the extent that we can speak it. To say that God is dead, and actually to say it, is to will the death of God. The prophet is the speaker, and his word is not his alone, it demands to be spoken by all who hear it. Here, listening is speaking. To hear the voice of prophecy is to speak it. Hence, to hear the prophetic announcement that God is dead is to proclaim the death of God oneself. How is such speech possible? How is such hearing possible? Is it not possible because we have finally been given the power both to hear and to speak the name of God? Zarathustra is the one who goes under, because he realizes the meaning of no-saying and *ressentiment*, that total guilt that is our "other," both our history and ourselves. That is the "other" that Zarathustra addresses when he pronounces the death of God. For to see that ultimate "other" and to name it is to proclaim the death of God.

Nietzsche concludes *Ecce Homo* by asking: "Have I been understood? —*Dionysus versus the Crucified.*" The new Dionysus, who is not simply to be identified with the Greek Dionysus, is the symbol of Eternal Recurrence. Nietzsche's Dionysus is fully born through the death of God, the most important event in history: "There has never been a greater deed; and whoever will be born after us—for the sake of this deed he will be part of a higher history than all history hitherto." Yet Nietzsche's opposition

to Christ is directed against religion itself, rather than against the actual figure of Jesus. In the same year that he wrote *Ecce Homo* (1888), he said in *The Antichrist:*

> Using the expression somewhat tolerantly, one could call Jesus a "free spirit"—he does not care for anything solid: the word kills, all that is solid kills. The concept, the *experience* of "life" in the only way he knows it, resists any kind of word, formula, law, faith, dogma. He speaks only of the innermost—all the rest, the whole of reality, the whole of nature, language itself, has for him only the value of a sign, a simile.

Viewed in this light, Jesus stands outside of Christianity, and Nietzsche's portrait of him bears a strong resemblance to the new Zarathustra:

> Make no mistake at this point, however seductive the Christian, in other words, the *ecclesiastical,* prejudice may be: such a symbolist *par excellence* stands outside all religion, all cult concepts, all history, all natural science, all experience of the world, all knowledge, all politics, all psychology, all books, all art—his "knowledge" is pure *foolishness* precisely concerning the fact that such things exist. *Culture* is not known to him even by hearsay, he does not need to fight it—he does not negate it. The same applies to the state, to the whole civic order and society, to work, to war—he never had any reason to negate "the world"; the ecclesiastical concept of "world" never occurred to him. To negate is the very thing that is impossible for him.

Again and again in *The Antichrist,* Nietzsche portrays Jesus as a kind of innocent forerunner of Zarathustra; he is incapable of *ressentiment,* is free of history, and is himself exactly opposed to Christianity.

> If one were to look for signs that an ironical divinity has its fingers in the great play of the world, one would find no small support in the *tremendous question mark* called Christianity. Mankind lies on its knees before the opposite of that which was the origin, the meaning, the *right* of the evangel; in the concept of "church" it has pronounced holy precisely what the "bringer of the glad tidings" felt to be *beneath* and *behind* himself—one would look in vain for a greater example of *world-historical irony.*

The very word "Christianity" is a misunderstanding; there was only one Christian, and he and his gospel died on the cross. "What has been called 'evangel' from that moment was actually the opposite of that which *he* lived: '*ill* tidings,' a dysangel." True Christianity is not "faith" in redemption through Christ, nor is it repentance or prayer; only Christian *praxis* is Christian: "True life, eternal life, has been found—it is not promised, it is here, it is *in you:* as a living in love, in love without subtraction and exclusion, without regard for station."

In the whole psychology of the "evangel" the concept of guilt and punishment is absent—as is also the concept of reward. "Sin"—any distance separating God and man—is abolished: *this is precisely the "glad tidings."* Blessedness is not promised, it is not tied to conditions: it is the only reality—the rest is a sign with which to speak of it. Only the practice, the immediate living, of the "glad tidings" leads to God. Indeed, Nietzsche proclaims that "it *is* God."

What god? Surely not the Christian God, the absolutely sovereign and transcendent God, the God of eternity. The God of Jesus? The God of the crucified? Less than a year after writing *The Antichrist,* when insanity was bursting upon him, Nietzsche alternately signed his notes "Dionysus" and "The Crucified." Of course, Dionysus *is* the crucified. At least, the Greek Dionysus is a god who dies and is resurrected. Zarathustra, too, is Dionysus, and Zarathustra suffers as a god. Again, what god? Is this the god or God who becomes manifest in the death of God? Could we say that the "glad tidings," both of Jesus and of Zarathustra, are the announcement of the death of God? Surely the death of God abolishes any distance separating God and man, and with that abolition, sin and guilt disappear. Does blessedness then become the only reality? All promise, all future hope and expectation, come to an end in the death of God. If the "glad tidings" are the announcement of the death of God, then living the "glad tidings" does lead to God. But it leads to that God who appears when all distance separating God and man disappears and is no more. True life is then found not in the life of God but in the death of God. Thereby life is not promised, it is here, it is *in you,* in you and me. For you and I have killed God, and we kill God when we pronounce His name, when we say life, and eternal life, and say it here and now. That life, that yes-saying, is not promised, it is found; and it is found in Christian *praxis,* in the immediate and total living of the "glad tidings" of the death of God.

The symbol of eternal life predominant in the New Testament is the Kingdom of God, but it eroded and virtually disappeared even before the completion of the New Testament itself. Yet it did not simply disappear—it reversed itself, becoming its own "other" in the Christian doctrine of God. This is the most fundamental insight of modern theology, and we owe it to Nietzsche. True, Hegel had fully realized it conceptually, but only conceptually, not humanly and immediately. The theme is also imaginatively worked out in Blake's apocalyptic epics, but, like the whole body of modern literature and art, they remain a theological cipher. *The Antichrist* is not a cipher, or not wholly so; in large measure it is luminously clear, and it is clearest in its portrait of the Christian God:

> The Christian conception of God—God as god of the sick, God as a spider, God as spirit—is one of the most corrupt conceptions of the divine ever held. It may even represent the low-water mark in the descending development of divine types. God degenerated into the *contradiction* of life, instead of being its transfiguration and eternal "yes!" God became a declaration of war against life, against nature, against the will to live; the formula for every slander against "this world," for every lie about the "beyond"; the deification of nothingness, the will to nothingness pronounced holy.

The Christian, at least, can recognize this as a true portrait of the God whom he knows in faith—albeit in bad faith, which is both a refusal of and a flight from the "glad tid-ings." Again and again the modern Christian has learned that his faith in God is a flight from the Gospel. But if it is a flight from the Gospel, a full and total flight, then the Christian God is opposed to the Kingdom of God.

Like Jesus, Zarathustra is a prophet of glad tidings, and his are of the "great noon" of Eternal Recurrence. Nietzsche regarded his discovery of Eternal Recurrence as his greatest creation, his triumphant hymn in praise of the earth, of life and immediate existence. Yet it was created out of the deepest pain, for Nietzsche himself looked upon the idea of Eternal Recurrence as the nightmare of nightmares. As early as *The Gay Science,* he expressed his conception in its most terrible form.

> *The greatest weight.*—What if some day or night a demon were to steal after you into your loneliest loneliness and say to you: "This life as you now live it and have lived it, you will have to live once more and innumerable times more; and there will be nothing new in it, but every pain and every joy and every thought and sigh and everything unutterably small or great in your life will have to return to you, all in the same succession and sequence—even this spider and this moonlight between the trees, and even this moment and I myself. The eternal hourglass of existence is turned upside down again and again, and you with it, speck of dust!" Would you not throw yourself down and gnash your teeth and curse the demon who spoke thus? Or have you once experienced a tremendous moment when you would have answered him: "You are a god and never have I heard anything more divine." If this thought gained possession of you, it would change you as you are or perhaps crush you. The question in each and everything, "Do you desire this once more and innumerable times more?" would lie upon your actions as the greatest weight. Or how well disposed would you have to become to yourself and to life *to crave nothing more fervently* than this ultimate eternal confirmation and seal?

The idea of Eternal Recurrence is the supreme challenge we can face, the ultimate test of courage, of life, for it poses the question whether we can affirm life, *our* life, here and now. Here is Nietzsche's categorical imperative—the most awful and awesome that man has ever faced, for it calls for an act of total affirmation.

Nietzsche knew that this conception was not new; found in ancient Stoicism, it parallels, if it does not exactly coincide with, the archaic myths of Eternal Return. What is new, radically new, is that Eternal Recurrence is here freed from the image of eternity. Eternity becomes identical with time itself. Zarathustra says:

> "Behold," I continued, "this moment! From this gateway, Moment, a long, eternal lane leads *backward:* behind us lies an eternity. Must not whatever *can* walk have walked on this lane before? Must not whatever *can* happen have happened, have been done, have passed by before? And if everything has been there before—what do you think, dwarf, of this moment? Must not this gateway too have been there before? And are not all things knotted together so firmly that this

moment draws after it *all* that is to come? Therefore—itself too? For whatever *can* walk—in this
long lane out *there* too, it *must* walk once more.

Eternity lies both behind and ahead of every actual and
present moment; it is a circle that cannot admit any eternal "other" beyond the present moment. Consequently,
the Eternal Recurrence proclaimed by Zarathustra is an
eternity, an actual and present eternity, embodying the
death of God.

The "great noon" of Eternal Recurrence is created by the
death of God, with which the beyond is abolished and disappears: eternal life is this life, the earth, the present moment.

> "O Zarathustra," the animals said, "to those
> who think as we do, all things themselves are
> dancing: they come and offer their hands and
> laugh and flee—and come back. Everything
> goes, everything comes back; eternally rolls the
> wheel of being. Everything dies, everything blos-
> soms again; eternally runs the year of being. Ev-
> erything breaks, everything is joined anew; eter-
> nally the same house is being built. Everything
> parts, everything greets every other thing again;
> eternally the ring of being remains faithful to it-
> self. In every Now, being begins; round every
> Here rolls the sphere There. The center is every-
> where. Bent is the path of eternity.

Nowhere did Nietzsche more triumphantly reach his goal
of speaking volumes in a few words than in this passage
of **Zarathustra**. The meaning of Eternal Recurrence shatters and reverses every sacred meaning of eternity. The
"wheel of being" is an archaic symbol in both East and
West of an eternal round of existence without meaning,
purpose, or direction, except insofar as mere existence in
such a "wheel" brings atonement from a primal guilt. At
a moment when Zarathustra himself cannot yet affirm the
Eternal Recurrence of all things, his animals celebrate the
wheel of being, not as a horrible cycle of perpetual pain,
but as an eternal dance. Now pain becomes joy, meaninglessness becomes order, guilt becomes grace. As opposed
to the Hindu symbol of the world as the divine but meaningless play (*lila*) of an ultimately inactive and unmoving
One, the Dionysian symbol of Eternal Recurrence reflects
the ultimate reality of things themselves as they here and
now become manifest as sheer delight. Only the Second
Innocence created by the death of God is wholly devoid
of guilt, and it is precisely through such innocence that the
most abysmal depths of a now naked reality become manifest as a cosmic dance.

Note the order of the images establishing this new meaning of reality or being: *Rad* ("wheel," "cycle"), *Jahr*
("year"). *Haus* ("house," "home," "family," "race"), and
Ring ("ring," "circle," "cycle"). The imagery itself is cyclical, moving to and from the image and idea of the circle,
and comprehending first a cyclical image of time (*Jahr*),
and then what can only have been intended as a cyclical
image of space (*gleich Haus*). Furthermore, all of these images are created by affirmation, by yes-saying, as is revealed by the first sentence of the passage ("to those who
think as we do, all things themselves are dancing"), and
then by the association of the word *treu* ("faithful,"

"loyal," "true") with the eternal cycle of being. When
manifest and known in total affirmation, the abyss of the
eternal round of suffering and pain is transformed into the
highest order of perfection, as symbolized by the circle.

The culmination of the passage is in the last three sentences, which are perhaps the most important lines that
Nietzsche ever wrote: "Being begins in every Now." When
Heidegger declared that Nietzsche's proclamation of the
death of God was the nihilistic fulfillment of our historical
destiny, he meant that with Nietzsche philosophy or primal thinking is completed; it has gone through the sphere
of its prefigured possibilities. Yet this ending is an eschatological ending, which is to say that it is a radical new beginning. The death of God, which brings to an end the
transcendence of being, the beyondness of eternity, makes
Being manifest in every Now. Being assumes a totally new
meaning and identity: no longer is it eternal; rather, it begins or dawns in every actual moment. Here, the verb *begins* is all-important, for it defines or establishes both the
subject and the predicate. We might even say that in this
affirmation the subject ceases to be, with the result that it
is no longer possible to say that being is, or that anything
whatsoever is, as everything *begins* in every Now. Thereby
it is revealed that the proposition "Being *is*" is a product
of the detachment of the speaker from the immediate moment: to be totally immersed in the Now is to be free of
a permanent existence of any kind.

When life or existence is most deeply affirmed, Being becomes identical with the Now: the actual moment of existence becomes *Being*. The act, the affirmation, the willing
of the moment is the eternal creation and re-creation of
everything. Totally to will the moment is to will that it
eternally recur, and eternally recur as the same, as this
moment, this life, this existence. It is the death of God or
the reversal of a transcendent eternity that makes possible
the resurrection of the Now, of time, of the body. This
transvaluation of the whole traditional identity of Being
is carried forward in the next phrase: "the world of There
revolves about every Here." If every moment is Being itself, then all moments of being are equivalent, because
every moment must coincide with every other. So, likewise, every point of space must be equivalent to every
other point, for there is no transcendent order to define either the meaning or the value of point or direction. Any
point in space—any fragment of world or self—can be said
to have neither direction nor meaning; therefore, the given
or established distinction between "here" and "there" collapses. To exist "here" is to exist "there," to will "here"
is to will "there." All things are firmly bound together; or,
rather, all things flow into one another, with the result that
it is no longer possible to say here or there, I or Thou, he
or it. The veil of Being crumbles and dissolves in the yes-
saying of Eternal Recurrence, a yes-saying negating and
bringing to an end those worlds and eternities created by
our primal flight or fall from the "body." "Man" has
thereby been surpassed, has been negated and transcended, and with him has been surpassed every meaning, every
order, every value created by our "soul." Yet what the
soul had known as chaos, the body now knows as bliss:
yes-saying delights in the resurrection of the brute reality
of things.

"The Center is everywhere." The new Dionysian life wants *all* things, wants all things now, and wants them eternally the same. Truly to accept, to know, the sameness of the same, is to know that the Center is everywhere. By dissolving the "here" and "there" of things, every unique and singular center disappears, and with that disappearance, all hierarchical judgment and comprehension become impossible. The traditional symbol of the Center is meaningful only when a chasm between it and the void is assumed. That chasm disappears when God is dead, and with it disappears every chasm or real or ultimate distance whatsoever. Now all transcendent centers pass into total immanence, and "center" as such ceases to be either singular or distinct. Therefore, real distinction becomes impossible; no longer is it possible to apprehend boundaries between things, to know a "this" which is "other" than a "that." When all things are firmly bound together, no lines or limits are possible, and all things spontaneously or immediately flow into each other. Now everything is a center, is *the* center, because the center is everywhere. God as the Center that is everywhere? Yes, but only when God is dead, only when the negation of his sovereignty and transcendence invests every point and moment with the totality of Being.

"The path of eternity is curved [*krumm:* also,'bent' or 'crooked']." Once again we find a circular image, although this time an ironic one, to symbolize eternity. The way of eternity is not only curved or bowed, it is also artfully crooked and circuitous. An image of a maze is evoked by this line—a circular maze, to be sure, and a maze that is never-ending, or eternal. What can Eternal Recurrence mean here? Being begins in every Now; the world of There revolves about every Here; and the Center is everywhere. Clearly, the very possibility of metaphysical or cosmological understanding has been denied by these affirmations: yes-saying can know no *logos* of things. There is no *logos* of eternity when its path is both curved and crooked, both circular and circuitous. Nietzsche's eternity is the very antithesis of the eternity of the philosophers and theologians, and he intends it to bring about a deep revulsion in the man of "faith." In his drunken midnight song, Zarathustra sings: "Woe says: Go! But all joy [*Lust*] wants Eternity—wants deep, deep Eternity." As Zarathustra himself interprets these words: "Joy, however, does not want heirs, or children—joy wants itself, wants eternity, wants recurrence, wants everything eternally the same."

> Have you ever said Yes to a single joy? O my friends, then you said Yes too to *all* woe. All things are entangled, ensnared, enamored; if you ever wanted one thing twice, if you said, "You please me, happiness! Abide, moment!" then you wanted *all* back. All anew, all eternally, all entangled, ensnared, enamored—oh, then you *loved* the world. Eternal ones, love it eternally and evermore; and to woe too, you say: go, but return! *For all joy wants*—eternity.

Finally, yes-saying and Eternal Recurrence are identical: the deepest affirmation of existence can only mean the willing of the Eternal Recurrence of all things, the willing of *this* life, of *this* moment, of this pain, and in such a manner as to will that it recur eternally, and recur eternally

the same. No metaphysical cosmology lies here at hand, nor even an "idea" of Eternal Recurrence, but rather a total existence in the present Now, a now that is here and there, a center that is everywhere.

At bottom, Eternal Recurrence is a way of totally loving the world, and not only a way of loving the world but also a way of speaking of love itself in a time and world in which God is dead. Zarathustra's symbol of Eternal Recurrence is radically distinguished from its classical and archaic counterparts, but so, likewise, is it distinguished from the historical language of Christianity. A decisive consequence of Christianity's loss of its original eschatological symbol of the Kingdom of God was that it was thereby led into an apprehension of a gulf or chasm between God and the world and a consequent apprehension of pure or total love as being "other" than the world. With the significant exceptions of its great mystics and its radical apocalyptic seers and groups, historical Christianity was more distantly removed from the proclamation of Jesus, for his "glad tidings" were a proclamation of the advent here and now of the Kingdom of God. Nietzsche knew this better than any theologian of his time or ours. Did he know it because of his very knowledge that God is dead? Does the death of the Christian God make manifest the Kingdom of God that Jesus proclaimed? Is the language of Eternal Recurrence a new eschatological language reflecting the presence of the Kingdom of God? A Kingdom of God that is totally present must necessarily empty the heavens of the absolutely sovereign and transcendent God, and consequently the ancient and sacred heavens are no more. With the disappearance of the Creator, creation ceases to be creation; or, rather, "old creation" becomes "new creation"; "it was" becomes affirmation and grace. Now, "old aeon" becomes identical with guilt and revenge, and "new aeon" becomes manifest as a radically new and total innocence. Is the new Zarathustra a new or renewed Jesus?

Thomas J. J. Altizer, "Eternal Recurrence and Kingdom of God," in The New Nietzsche: Contemporary Styles of Interpretation, *edited by David B. Allison, 1977. Reprint by The MIT Press, 1985, pp. 232-46.*

Karsten Harries   (essay date 1988)

[*Harries is a German-born American critic and educator in philosophy. In the following essay he examines Nietzsche's frequent metaphors likening philosophy to sea exploration.*]

In his preface to *Nietzsche as Philosopher,* Arthur Danto writes, appropriately enough given Nietzsche's understanding of himself as a seafaring discoverer, a new Columbus setting sail for uncharted seas: "His language would have been less colorful had he known what he was trying to say, but then he would not have been the original thinker he was, working through a set of problems which had hardly been charted before. Small wonder his maps are illustrated, so to speak, with all sorts of monsters and fearful indications and boastful cartographic embellishments!" This suggests that the special color of Nietzsche's discourse is inseparable from his failure to know what he was trying to say, a failure Danto links to Nietzsche's originality as a thinker.

Writing from the perspective of contemporary analytical philosophy, Danto insists that "we know a great deal more philosophy today." The seas Nietzsche first explored and sought to chart have apparently become much more familiar. Danto also suggests that we have a better understanding of what a philosophical sea chart should look like: such charts have no room for "monsters and fearful indications and boastful cartographic embellishments." The color of Nietzsche's prose is here tied to what makes it nonphilosophical.

But do we in fact know our way by now in the seas Nietzsche was trying to chart? And do we know what makes a discourse philosophical? Danto admits that his way of reading Nietzsche from a contemporary perspective "may precipitate some anachronisms" but claims that the progress of philosophy places us in a position to understand what is philosophically important in Nietzsche better than he himself was able to do; that to read Nietzsche as a philosopher, we may have to do violence to his texts, where such violence would be the price we have to pay if we are to grasp what in Nietzsche's work remains philosophically alive. But what sort of life is this?

Nietzsche himself insisted on the untimeliness of his writings. "The time for me hasn't come yet: some are born posthumously. . . . It would contradict my character entirely if I expected ears and hands for my truths today: that today one doesn't accept my ideas is not only understandable, it even seems right to me."

Do we now have ears and hands for Nietzsche's truths? Nietzsche remarks on the innocence of some professor in Berlin who "suggested very amiably that I ought to try another form: nobody read such things." Since then, taking up this professor's amiable challenge, countless interpreters have tried to recast what Nietzsche wrote into a more readily understood idiom, to make what he was trying to express more accessible. But, before we engage in such exercise in translation, we would do well to consider Nietzsche's insistence on the gap that separates the kind of reader he demanded from the readers available to him. Having understood six sentences of Zarathustra, Nietzsche claims, "would raise one to a higher level of existence than 'modern' man could attain." Nietzsche demands "postmodern" readers. Can we claim to be those readers? Should we even want to be such readers?

It is easy to reply that, when Nietzsche speaks of the untimeliness of his books, he is speaking in boastful hyperbole, especially in **Ecce Homo,** written on the edge of madness. And does he not go on to insist that he was speaking only of Germany? "Everywhere else I have readers—nothing but first-rate intellects and proven characters, trained in high positions and duties." He even mentions New York as one of the places where he has been discovered. Pain and irony are difficult to overhear.

But what kind of readers was Nietzsche looking for? His answer deserves our careful attention:

> When I imagine a perfect reader, he always

turns into a monster of courage and curiosity; moreover, supple, cunning, cautious; a born adventurer and discoverer. In the end, I could say no better to whom alone I am speaking at bottom than Zarathustra said it: to *whom* alone will he relate his riddle?

> "To you, the bold searchers, researchers, and whoever embarks with cunning sails on terrible seas—to you, drunk with riddles, glad of the twilight, whose soul flutes lure astray to every whirlpool, because you do not want to grope along a thread with cowardly hand; and where you can *guess,* you hate to *deduce.* . . ."

Such reading is difficult to reconcile with the kind of exploration and cartography Danto has in mind. This seafarer's monstrous texts demand monstrous readers, fearless sailors.

It is of course possible and instructive to read Nietzsche very differently, for example, from the perspective of contemporary analytical philosophy. But its style cannot do justice to Nietzsche's style, which must call the analytical approach into question. Not that other approaches, say a neo-Kantian approach or one indebted to Heidegger's fundamental ontology, are more likely to prove adequate. The difficulty is bound up rather with the very attempt to domesticate Nietzsche's monstrous texts by translating them into a philosophical idiom with which we are more at home and therefore more comfortable. Such translation may well help us to appropriate what Nietzsche has written, but we should ask ourselves whether such appropriation is not also a defense against a style and a thinking that puts the philosophy guarded by professional philosophers into question.

Just this, I want to suggest, makes Nietzsche a philosopher. In the *Philosophical Investigations,* Wittgenstein remarks that philosophical problems have the form "I don't know my way about." To be sure, not all problems having this form are therefore philosophical—to have lost one's way in some unfamiliar city hardly suffices to make one a philosopher. But in such cases our disorientation is only superficial. To reorient ourselves, we can fall back on a deeper and unchallenged understanding of where we are and what is to be done. Philosophy cannot fall back on such an understanding. The fundamental question of philosophy is, Where is man's place? Philosophy is born of a sense of homelessness that is inseparable from the insistence that man act and think for himself. At the center of philosophy thus lies an ethical concern born of the demand that we assume responsibility for our actions and the consequent refusal to rest content with what has come to be established, accepted, and taken for granted. Man's claim to autonomy forces him to put into question the authority of history and the place it has assigned to him. Philosophy is thus a critical enterprise. Not that this critique can rely on firmly established criteria. Quite the contrary—philosophy remains alive only as long as the question, What is man's place, his *ethos?* continues to be asked, because that place remains questionable, because man's vocation remains ambiguous. Once this ground of philosophy in radical questioning is recognized, the "monsters" and "cartographic embellishments" that are so much part of Nietzsche's maps will no longer seem eliminable ornaments that, born of fear and narcissistic boasting, only obscure what is philosophically significant. They challenge not only all philosophers who feel confident of their place and way, but also, and more important, our common sense. Measured by that common sense, what Nietzsche has to tell us may often seem nonsense. But this is a risk someone who would challenge common sense has to run. We serve Nietzsche ill when, refusing his challenge, we try to show that there is a quite acceptable sense behind such apparent nonsense. His teaching of the eternal recurrence, whose first statement in *Zarathustra* the lines cited in *Ecce Homo* serve to introduce, provides a key example. Citing these lines as he does to describe his perfect reader, Nietzsche suggests that, like that questionable doctrine, in some sense all he has written is a riddle demanding to be read by sailors.

The following remarks examine only that brief introduction in the hope that such an examination will shed some light on the profoundly questionable and, just because of this, philosophical character of Nietzsche's texts and of the demands this places on his readers.

Hermeneutics has taught us that we cannot really understand the meaning of a part until we have grasped its place in the whole to which it belongs. As Heidegger insists, interpretation (*Erläuterung*) cannot be separated from consideration of the place of what is being interpreted (*Erörterung*). Such consideration is especially important when we are seeking to understand a writer as preoccupied with the importance of setting and point of view, as fond of masks and self-dramatization, as aware of the importance of style and mood as Nietzsche. What then is the place of these introductory words?

The narrative of *Zarathustra* gives a first answer: the words are spoken by Zarathustra on a ship that is carrying him from the blessed isles back to the land of his mountain and his cave.

The words are spoken by Zarathustra. But who is Zarathustra? In *Ecce Homo,* Nietzsche tells his readers that to understand the Zarathustra type "one must first become clear about his physiological presupposition: this is what I call the *great health.*" This suggests that the place from which these introductory words are spoken is defined by "the great health."

There is an obvious objection: the words are spoken, after all, not just by Zarathustra, but by Zarathustra at a particular stage of his development, a Zarathustra who is coming home, still sick, still struggling to cure himself of the spirit of revenge, of "the will's ill will against time and its 'it was,' " still troubled by the soothsayer's "all is empty, all is the same, all has been," still resisting the thought of the eternal recurrence that, while still unspoken, yet haunts him, not yet "The Convalescent" ready to affirm himself as its teacher—a Zarathustra, in short, who is not only literally but spiritually at sea, bearing "riddles and bitternesses in his heart," a voyager in search of himself.

How then are we to understand the suggestion that the place from which these words are spoken is "the great health"? In just what sense is this great health the presup-

position of the Zarathustra type? Was that type born of such health? It would seem not, for, as Nietzsche tells us in the immediately preceding section, the Zarathustra type overtook him when he felt not at all well, in that cold and rainy winter of 1882-83 he spent in Rapallo, on walks he took whenever his frail health permitted. Like the words Zarathustra addresses to his sailors, all *Zarathustra,* and perhaps all Nietzsche's writings, are the work of a sick man. And yet, does this mean that their place may not also be that state of being Nietzsche calls "the great health"? "Health and sickliness: one should be careful! The standard remains the efflorescence of the body, the agility, courage, and cheerfulness of spirit—but also, of course, *how much of the sickly it can take upon itself and overcome*—how much it can *make* healthy. That of which more delicate men would perish belongs to the stimulants of the *great* health."

To explain this "great health," *Ecce Homo* quotes in its entirety the penultimate section of *The Gay Science,* which carries that phrase as its title. This section, too, is spoken by someone who needs and desires rather than possesses health: "Being new, nameless, difficult to understand, we premature births of an as yet unproven future, we need for a new goal also a new means—namely, a new health, stronger, more seasoned, tougher, more audacious, and gayer than any previous health." "Premature births of an as yet unproven future" once more suggests not health but a precarious state of being, precarious because that world in which it could thrive has yet to arrive, and may indeed never arrive. Presupposed is a dissatisfaction with the present age that is inseparable from a still worldless call to a different way of being issuing from beyond that age. He who heeds that call becomes "new, nameless, difficult to understand." Once again Nietzsche invokes the image of the sailor:

> And now, after we have long been on our way in this manner, we argonauts of the ideal, with more daring perhaps than is prudent, and have suffered shipwreck and damage often enough, but are, to repeat it, healthier than one likes to permit us, dangerously healthy, ever again healthy—it will seem to us as if, as a reward, we now confronted an as yet undiscovered country, whose boundaries nobody has surveyed yet, something beyond all the lands and nooks of the ideal so far, a world overrich in what is beautiful, strange, questionable, terrible, and divine that our curiosity as well as our craving to possess it has got beside itself—alas, now nothing will sate us any more!

Nietzsche's great health is the health required of a Jason, an Odysseus, or a Columbus, of a seafarer who, for the sake of the promise of some not yet discovered country is eager to surrender the comfort and the security of the familiar, ready to risk pain and even death, and who will not be sated. This refusal of satisfaction, of the old ideal of being at one with oneself, whole, entire, helps to define the great health.

The above discussion of the great health ends with the words "the tragedy *begins,*" referring the reader back to section 342 of *The Gay Science,* which is virtually identi-

Portrait of Nietzsche in 1868, when he was a lance-corporal in the Prussian Army.

cal with the opening paragraphs of "Zarathustra's Prologue." The beginning of *Zarathustra* is the beginning of tragedy, where we should keep in mind the hopes associated with tragedy in *The Birth of Tragedy,* the place of this book, which sought to locate the roots of the ills of our age in Socrates' optimistic embrace of both reason and the ideal of satisfaction and looked both backward and forward to tragedy as to a cure. Nietzsche's great health does not exclude suffering, disease, and death. Just the opposite, it affirms and appropriates them.

We learn more about the state of being Nietzsche calls the great health in *The Genealogy of Morals,* where he opposes it to the "evil eye" man has had all too long for his natural inclinations, for life, for the world, aspiring instead "to the beyond, to that which runs counter to sense, instinct, nature, animal." If this evil eye has supported "all ideals hitherto, which are one and all hostile to life and ideals that slander the world," Nietzsche would have us reverse this millennia-old tradition of self-torture in the name of "higher" values.

> The attainment of this goal would require a *different* kind of spirit from that likely to appear in the present age: spirits strengthened by war and

victory, for whom conquest, adventure, danger, and even pain have become needs; it would require habituation to the keen air of the heights, to winter journeys, to ice and mountains in every sense [the image of the mountain climber replaces here that of the seafaring discoverer]; it would require even a kind of sublime wickedness, an ultimate, supremely confident mischievousness in knowledge that goes with great health; it would require, in brief and alas, precisely this *great health!*

Nietzsche goes on to call for the person with great health as a redeemer not only from the reigning ethics of satisfaction but also from what was bound to grow out of it, the great nausea, the will to nothingness, nihilism, and identifies him with Zarathustra. Redemption here should be understood in the light of Zarathustra's understanding of redemption as an overcoming of the spirit of revenge. The great health is understood in opposition to the spirit of revenge, to "the will's ill will against time and its 'it was,' " in opposition to the evil eye that has determined the shape of our culture and alienated us from ourselves.

The dominant postwar critics have either condemned Nietzsche as centrally complicit in the Nazi evil or lauded him for being unblemished and opposed to all nazism's intentions and actions. Both these approaches were less interested in tracing actual historical paths than pursuing their own value-laden interpretations.

—*Steven E. Aschheim, in his* The Nietzsche Legacy in Germany 1890-1990, 1992.

The power that the spirit of revenge has over us is rooted in the temporality that constitutes our being, shadowing it with sad thoughts of losing all that we can call our own, even ourselves. Cast into a world that we have not chosen, vulnerable, mortal, too weak to secure even our own being, we find it difficult to accept ourselves as we are, especially difficult to accept what most insistently reminds us of our temporality, our corporality, and what is most intimately tied to it, such as sexual desire, hunger, disease, death. Willing power, lacking power, we find it hard to forgive ourselves that lack. So we turn against the reality that denies us power and that means also against ourselves. Seeking to escape the tyranny of time, which denies us what we so deeply desire, the spirit of revenge gives birth to another reality, a reality over which time has no power. Here, if Nietzsche is right, we must locate the origin of most religion and most philosophy.

Consider how Schopenhauer, represented by the soothsayer, whose gloomy pronouncements cast Zarathustra into such profound despondency, speaks of time [in *The World as Will and Representation*]:

> In time each moment is, only in so far as it has effaced its father, the preceding moment, to be again effaced just as quickly itself. Past and future (apart from the consequences of their content) are as empty and unreal as any dream; but present is only the boundary between the two, having neither extension nor duration. In just the same way, we shall also recognize the same emptiness in all the other forms of the principle of sufficient reason, and shall see that, like time, space also, and like this, everything that exists simultaneously in space and time, and hence everything that proceeds from causes and motives, has only a relative existence, is only through and for another like itself, i. e., only just as enduring.

Lack is constitutive of what we call reality. Reality knows no genuine plentitude. There is no presence we can really possess, no satisfaction that is not eroded and overtaken by time. What we so deeply want, to be at one with ourselves, is denied to us by what we are:

> Essentially, it is all the same whether we pursue or flee, fear harm or aspire to enjoyment; care for the constantly demanding will, no matter in what form, continually fills and moves consciousness; but without peace and calm, true well-being is absolutely impossible. Thus the subject of willing is constantly lying on the revolving wheel of Ixion, is always drawing water in the sieve of the Danaids, and is the eternally thirsting Tantalus.

To slake this thirst, the spirit of revenge gives birth to another reality that invites dreams of superhuman happiness, constructs "afterworlds," realms of being beyond becoming that promise the plenitude and presence that this world denies, a security not subject to the terror of time, that allow for genuine satisfaction, be it only the satisfaction of really knowing something. But the ideal of a satisfaction that stills care and desire has to turn against the very condition of our being. On reflection, all such ideals turn out to be metaphors of death, directed against life. Here, we have the source of that sickness which the great health would overcome. The great health names a mode of existing that has renounced the ideal of satisfaction, a mode in which it is important to keep in mind the way this ideal has shaped not only religion but philosophy, and not only moral philosophy but metaphysics and the theory of knowledge, to the extent that these have thought being and truth to be against time.

The very language of philosophy is governed by the spirit of revenge. Consider once more Danto's suggestion that Nietzsche's language would have been less colorful had he known what he was trying to say. What do we mean when we say that someone knows what he is trying to say? Presupposed is a distinction between thought and its linguistic expression. To know something is to have grasped the truth of some thought. Inseparable from such knowledge is the knowledge that what I know does not need to be expressed in just this way. The special color of a discourse comes to be understood as an at best dispensable, more often distracting, ornament. Knowledge is best served by

a discourse not so tied to the particular perspective of an individual or a group that, without it, it loses its meaning. So understood, knowledge demands objectivity, and objectivity demands translatability. Ideally, the medium of words should become totally transparent; language should be like clear glass so that it offers no resistance to the understanding as it appropriates what is to be understood. The "whiteness" of scientific discourse answers to this ideal.

Nietzsche could have replied that this ideal of a transparent language that does not contaminate the purity of our thoughts is just as much a chimera as the ideal of a transparent body that would not contaminate the chaste purity of our spirit. Both ideals prevent us from doing justice, to language in one case, to human being in the other. And in both cases the desire for purity presupposes that evil eye of which the great health is to cure us.

To say that the place from which Zarathustra tells his riddle is the great health is not to deny that the speaker is still fighting the poison left in him by the tarantula's bite, still struggling with the spirit of revenge, still trying to shake off the soothsayer's gloomy teaching; but it is to say that this struggle is illuminated by the possibility of a yes to time and all that is temporal, of a yes to the body, to hunger and disease, even to death. By choosing just this passage to describe his relationship to his perfect reader, Nietzsche invites us to understand him as someone still sick with revenge, still trying to renounce the ideal of satisfaction and the nihilism which is the unmasking of that ideal, but also haunted by another, still unnamed ideal as by a riddle, in love with life and full of hope.

As he likens himself to a seafaring explorer, Nietzsche likens his perfect reader to a sailor. Like his Zarathustra, he addresses his words to "bold searchers, researchers, and whoever embarks with cunning sails on terrible seas," who "drunk with riddles, glad of the twilight," are lured astray by flutes "to every whirlpool."

[Nietzsche translator Walter] Kaufmann's "searchers, researchers" fails to capture the challenge of the word play *Sucher, Versucher,* which calls attention to the prefix *ver* and helps to interpret the nature of the search Nietzsche would have his reader be engaged in. *Versuchen* means first of all "to attempt." To make a *Versuch* is to try something, uncertain of whether such trial will prove a success. A scientific experiment is a *Versuch* in this sense. We engage in experiments to test our conjectures; such testing presupposes a readiness to retract one's presuppositions and to rethink one's assumptions. Nietzsche's texts invite such hermeneutic experimentation.

But *Versucher* means first of all not a scientific researcher but a tempter. The devil, who tempted Adam and Eve with the promise that their eyes would be opened and they would be like God, knowing good and evil, is *the Versucher.* Nietzsche's sailors, it would seem, are of the devil's party, tempted by and tempting with the promise of truth. But the devil is only the mask in which Dionysus presents himself to Christians subject to the spirit of revenge, this "tempter god and born pied piper of consciences whose voice knows how to descend into the netherworld of every soul," this god of explorers and philosophers to whom Nietzsche offered his firstborn as "a *sacrifice.*"

Called by Dionysus, Nietzsche's sailors, too, are possessed of "that sublime inclination of the seeker after knowledge who insists on profundity, multiplicity, and thoroughness, with a *will* which is a kind of cruelty of the intellectual conscience and taste" and which counters the "will to mere appearance, to simplification, to masks, to cloaks, in short to the surface." Better than perhaps any other philosopher, Nietzsche knows about the importance of being superficial: "Anyone who has looked deeply into the world may guess how much wisdom lies in the superficiality of men. The instinct that preserves them teaches them to be flighty, light, and false." But if there is a superficiality in the service of life, and our ordinary concern for truth is superficial in this sense, there is also a superficiality born of a fear of life, a pursuit of truth born of fear of a deeper truth.

Already in *The Birth of Tragedy* Nietzsche had located in just such a fear the origin of our culture, a culture shaped by the "sublime metaphysical illusion" that "thought, using the thread of logic, can penetrate the deepest abysses of being, and that thought is capable not only of knowing being but even of *correcting* it." Man's will to power here blinds him to the lack of power constitutive of his being and thus alienates him from his own reality, from his life. Such a Socratic-Cartesian culture needs "to translate man back into nature; to become master over the many vain and overly enthusiastic interpretations and connotations that have so far been scrawled and painted over the eternal basic text of *Homo natura;* to see to it that man henceforth stands before man as even today, hardened in the discipline of science, he stands before the *rest* of nature, with intrepid Oedipus eyes and sealed Odysseus ears, deaf to the siren songs of old metaphysical bird catchers who have been piping at him all too long, 'you are more, you are higher, you are of different origin!' "

The basic text Nietzsche would have us interpret is *Homo natura.* His own texts serve such interpretation first of all as a restorer's solvents would, which help to "translate" a painting disfigured by what later generations have painted and scrawled over it back into its original state. Such "translation" is fraught with danger. Instead of allowing us to recover the original, it may only destroy it. And can we even be sure that there is an original to be recovered?

How are we to understand Nietzsche's expression "the eternal basic text of *Homo natura"*? This suggests that in principle it is possible to read human nature as one reads a text, even if countless translations have so obscured the original that our interpretation has to be at the same time an archeological excavation. But will such excavation yield a *Grundtext* [original text]? Has not Nietzsche himself taught us to be wary of any philosopher who would base his teaching on such a *Grund* [ground]?

Nietzsche knows that there is something profoundly unnatural about the refusal to remain with superficial appearance, about the insistence to descend to the *Grund,* the claim to a wisdom deeper than common sense. In *The Birth of Tragedy,* Nietzsche thus says of Oedipus that,

precisely because he possessed such wisdom, because he was able to solve the riddle of the Sphinx, he had to fall into a whirlpool of unnatural deeds. Nietzsche knows that to want to solve the riddle of the Sphinx is already to have fallen out of the natural order. But just Oedipus's refusal to remain on the surface, a refusal that subverts the natural order and the moral world and lets Oedipus blind himself, issues in a more profound vision that prepares the foundation of a new world on the ruins of the old.

Nietzsche demands such courage of his readers. This courage requires us to be deaf to the siren song that places man's essence beyond nature and time. Nietzsche's reference to the seafaring Odysseus in this place would appear to involve a misreading, for Odysseus did not seal his own ears with wax but those of his fellow sailors. Lashed to the mast, he listened to the siren's songs, as Nietzsche himself listened all too eagerly to the siren song of eternity, as his teaching of the eternal recurrence demonstrates; and it is tempting to link the disaster that overtook him to the absence of those who would tie him to some mast. But, like Odysseus, Nietzsche would seal the ears of his fellow sailors to this siren song, as he would seal his own ears were he only able to do so. We should not forget that, when Nietzsche speaks of standing before the riddle that is man with intrepid Oedipus eyes and sealed Odysseus ears, he is stating a task. Thus, he would also want his readers open to what lies beneath the surface of his texts, its ambiguities, its multivalence, open to the absence of a single unspoken meaning that could gather this text into a whole, to a chaos of affects only superficially gathered into a whole.

Sich versuchen can also mean to lose one's way while searching, as the wise Oedipus, searching, loses his place in the natural and moral order—and Nietzsche liked to think of the genuine philosopher in the image of Oedipus. Wittgenstein, as we saw, understands the philosopher as someone who has lost his way; he is, we can say, *einer, der sich versucht hat.* The existence of a method that would provide us with a way of solving all philosophical problems would mean the end of philosophy. Nietzsche's sailors are philosophers precisely because they demand the questionable for their horizon. To open our eyes to this horizon, and this also means to recall us to life, is one goal of Nietzsche's reflections. This goal is quite the opposite of that of Wittgenstein, who tried to show that the philosopher is someone who has allowed himself to become bewitched by language: as the unity "of language and the activities into which it is woven" that organizes ordinary language is destroyed, language begins to "idle" or "go on a holiday." Wittgenstein, too, rejects the metaphysician's promise of a terra firma. The would be terra firma of philosophers is unmasked as no more than a castle in the clouds. But the point of such unmasking is to return us to the language games of the everyday as the only ground given to us: *Wir legen den Grund der Sprache frei* (we are clearing up the ground of language).

If Wittgenstein would recall philosophers from their airy heights back to the earth, Nietzsche would set them afloat by shaking their confidence, not only in metaphysical construction but also in those language games to which Wittgenstein would have us turn as to a ground, not, however, to replace it with some other terra firma but to render the very idea of such a ground questionable. Nietzsche, too, calls words "the seducers of philosophers," who are likened to fish struggling in the nets of language. But instead of giving up this struggle. Nietzsche tears at this net to open us to what more immediately claims and moves us than all words, to open us to the sea, to life. Nietzsche's style is a tearing of language in the service of life. If Nietzsche's sailors are impatient with what is generally accepted and taken for granted, this is because they are haunted by the promise of a life richer than all common sense, richer also than philosophy, and haunted also by the possibility of a philosophy that, unlike all philosophy born of the spirit of revenge, would interpret and justify that life. Such a philosophy would not claim to have discovered a new terra firma. It would not be a philosophy for all times, nor would it be for everyone. It would be a necessarily precarious *Versuch* to answer the riddle of life with a discourse that would allow us to interpret it as a meaningful whole while yet aware that all such understanding must do violence to what it seeks to understand and that it therefore should not be dogmatic. Life overflows every interpretation. All the moral philosopher can furnish are precarious perspectives: "The moral earth, too, is round! The moral earth, too, has its antipodes! The antipodes, too, have their right to exist! There still is another world to be discovered—and more than one! Board the ships, you philosophers!"

Nietzsche knows that his call challenges the way philosophers have understood their task as one of securing human existence and more especially the project of knowledge by placing them on firm ground. Think of Hegel's famous suggestion that it is only with Descartes's establishment of the *cogito* as an unshakable foundation that "the education, the thinking of our age begins." "Here, we can say, we are at home and like the sailor, after long journeying about the raging sea, call 'land.'" Hegel describes Descartes as the thinker who marks the beginning of the end of philosophy's age of discovery, which, if philosophy requires the horizon of the questionable, heralds the end of philosophy. And, as a lover of truth, must the philosopher not welcome that end? Must he not be impatient with riddles and insist on clearly framed problems that leave no doubt as to what constitutes a satisfactory solution? Must he not be glad of a light that allows us to see things as they are, distrustful of a twilight that renders ambiguous, inviting us to mistake one thing for another, distrustful of that adventurism Nietzsche practices as a writer and demands of his readers? To Nietzsche, we can oppose Kant, who, in the *Critique of Pure Reason,* presents himself not as an adventurous seafarer but as a sober explorer on firm land:

> We have now not merely explored the territory of pure understanding, and carefully surveyed every part of it, but have also measured its extent, and assigned to everything in it its rightful place. This domain is an island, enclosed by nature itself within unalterable limits. It is the land of truth—enchanting name! —surrounded by a wide and stormy ocean, the native home of illusion, where many a fog bank and many a swiftly melting iceberg give the deceptive appearance of

> farther shores, deluding the adventurous seafarer ever anew with empty hopes, and engaging him in enterprises which he can never abandon and yet is unable to carry to completion.

The *Critique of Pure Reason* is written against such philosophical adventurism, and Kant was confident that his transcendental recasting of metaphysics heralded its imminent completion, which he expected to have been accomplished before the end of his century. Kant knows about the lure of the sea, about our dissatisfaction with the land given us to survey and cultivate, about a proud freedom that would have us seize what our finitude denies us; there is something in us that resists the completion he promises and insists on the sublimity of the questionable, even on the terrible. Kant, however, would have us resist the siren songs of the questionable.

But does this island to which Kant gives the "enchanting name" "the land of truth" deserve that title? Nietzsche might have asked whether Kant does not allow himself here to be enchanted by our natural tendency to transform that place where we happen to be, the way we happen to think, into a terra firma. Does Kant's "land of truth" even deserve to be called an island? Is it not rather a ship, perhaps even one whose timbers are beginning to rot and give way? And who is to say that such a shipwreck would be a disaster?

> That immense framework and planking of concepts to which the needy man clings his whole life long in order to preserve himself is nothing but a scaffolding and toy for the most audacious feats of the liberated intellect. And when it smashes this framework to pieces, throws it into confusion, and puts it back together again in an ironic fashion, pairing the most alien things and separating the closest, it is demonstrating that it has no need of these makeshifts of indigence and that it will now be guided by intuitions rather than by concepts.

What Kant considers firm land is to Nietzsche a floating prison. To open philosophy to life, to the sea, Nietzsche's discourse challenges ossified and taken-for-granted ways of speaking; semantic oppositions and collisions deny us the security of what is expected and accepted, opening up the horizon of the questionable.

But is Kant not right to warn us against trying to journey beyond the land of truth? Truth demands the liberation from the rule of perspective and the all-too-subjective; it demands objectivity. Objectivity, again, demands a discourse as free as possible from the colors added to what is thought by care and desire. Forsaking so readily the part of the suitor of truth, does Nietzsche not become "only fool, only poet"? Nietzsche could reply that it is just because he remains a suitor of truth that he has to challenge Kant's claim to have put an end to speculative metaphysics with his Copernican revolution and to have charted the boundaries of the land of truth once and for all. Are Kant's transcendental subject and the correlative idea of a knowledge of objects, which is free from perspectival distortion, not fantastic constructions? Can human thinking free itself from its subjective point of view and inherited prejudice? Herder already had protested both the elision of the concrete person and of language in *The Critique of Pure Reason,* insisting that we are always bound by what happens to be our nature, that we think with words, not concepts, and that we cannot think in a language other than our own. Thought will never become pure or innocent. There is no language unburdened by past prejudice, no intuition free from the distortion of perspective, no presence not hopelessly entangled in what remains concealed, absent, mysterious. Does the pursuit of truth not demand that we open ourselves to this mystery which our understanding vainly seeks to master? Kant's revolution can be charged with having been insufficiently Copernican. The progress of transcendental reflection since Kant, which has sought to bring Kant's transcendental structures down to earth, can be understood as a response to Nietzsche's call: "Board the ships, you philosophers!"

In this connection, it is interesting to note that Copernicus himself, citing Virgil, relies on the metaphor of the seafarer who is oblivious to his ship's movement to explain and thereby disarm his reader's reluctance to acknowledge that it is the earth that moves and revolves around its axis, and not the firmament: "The relation is similar to that of which Virgil's Aeneas says, 'We sail out of the harbor, and the countries and cities recede.' For when a ship is sailing along quietly, everything which is outside of it will appear to those on board to have a motion corresponding to the movement of the ship; and the voyagers are of the erroneous opinion that they with all they have with them are at rest." Nietzsche's choppy discourse intends to make the reader's sailing less smooth and thus to let him become aware that our language and the conceptual frames we have raised on it are rather like a ship, that with our words and concepts we do not stand on firm land but are indeed at sea.

If Kant is enchanted by the name "land of truth," Zarathustra's sailors, "drunk with riddles, glad of the twilight," have experienced the very different enchantment of flutes that beckon them to every whirlpool. In *The Gay Science,* too, Nietzsche describes himself and those who are of his mind as "born guessers of riddles," who welcome the twilight of the setting of the sun of the old God. But this darkening of our world, with its ever deepening, ever more ominous shadows, does not fill him with dread but with a new cheerfulness. That cheerfulness lets him invert the traditional light metaphor: what to those still bound to the dead God must seem a sad and gloomy twilight will appear to those stretched out between present and future "like a new, scarcely describable kind of light, happiness, relief, exhilaration, encouragement, dawn":

> We philosophers and "free spirits" feel as if a new dawn were shining on us when we receive the tidings that "the old god is dead"; our heart overflows with gratitude, amazement, anticipation, expectation. At last the horizon appears free again to us, even granted that it is not bright; at last our ships may venture out again, venture out to face any danger; all the daring of the lover of knowledge is permitted again; the sea, *our* sea, lies open again; perhaps there has never yet been such an "open sea."

Zarathustra tells his vision and riddle to sailors, who, "be-cause they do not want to grope along a thread with cowardly hand" and would rather guess than deduce, are lured astray to every whirlpool. These sailors then are very different from the culture hero Theseus, who, having sailed to Crete and slain the Minotaur, finds his way out of the labyrinth with the help of Ariadne's thread. Theseus and those like him are here condemned as cowards. Zarathustra, of whom Nietzsche says that he is more courageous than all other thinkers taken together, demands a very different audience: "How much truth does a spirit *endure,* how much truth does it *dare?* More and more that became for me the real measure of value. Error (faith in the ideal) is not blindness, error is *cowardice.*" Nietzsche links this cowardice to the desire to deduce: deduction is a defense against truth, masking itself by claiming to serve truth.

"Deduce" is Kaufmann's translation of *erschliessen. Erschliessen,* however, means not so much "to deduce," which better translates *schliessen* ("to lock"), as it does "to unlock," "to open up," for example, land for cultivation by cutting roads into what was wilderness so that what was remote and mysterious is made accessible. *Erschliessen* is a first step toward taking possession. Thinking, too, may have that function. Think of Descartes's promise that his method would lead us to "know the force and action of fire, water, air, the stars, heavens and all bodies that environ us, as distinctly as we know the different crafts of the artisans" and thus render us "the masters and possessors of nature." Descartes presents himself to his readers as the Theseus of a culture founded on technology.

Zarathustra's sailors have come to question this culture. Inseparable from their questioning is a longing for the sea, for the labyrinth. Just as Zarathustra's sailors are lured by the whirlpool's abyss, so Nietzsche, in an earlier draft of *Ecce Homo,* speaks of the fascinated curiosity that draws him to the labyrinth, a curiosity, he suggests, that not only delights in the friendship of Ariadne but is also not afraid to make the acquaintance of the Minotaur, presumably not to slay it, as the culture hero Theseus did. Another passage makes the opposition to Theseus even clearer: "There are cases where what is needed is an Ariadne's thread leading into the labyrinth. He who has the task to bring on the great war, the war against the virtuous (—the good and virtuous Zarathustra calls them, also 'last men,' also 'beginning of the end'—) has to be willing to buy some experiences almost at any price; the price could even be the danger of losing oneself." What makes it so difficult for us to endure the truth about reality is the desire to hold on to ourselves. To hold on to ourselves, we also have to hold on to the world in which we exist, to comprehend it. Nietzsche grounds the desire for knowledge as this has been traditionally understood in the need for security. Security demands stability and order. This demand has to turn against all that is fleeting and confusing. So understood, the demand for knowledge has its telos in the defeat of chaos and time, of labyrinth and Minotaur.

The question is whether there is a reality beyond chaos and time that answers to what is here demanded or whether all such "realities" are only fictions born of cowardice, of an inability to affirm reality as it is.

Just as Nietzsche inverts the traditional valuation implied by the metaphors of land and sea, so he reverses the direction traditionally associated with Ariadne's thread, which he would have us follow back into the labyrinth. The significance of this reversal becomes clear when we compare Nietzsche's use of this figure with that of Descartes, who in the *Rules* offers the reader his newfound method as an Ariadne's thread that would lead him out of the labyrinth of fleeting appearance, where appearance is thought relative to the point in space and even more in time that the knowing subject is assigned by the perceiving body. To find our way out of this labyrinth we have to free ourselves from the rule of perspective. Reflection serves such liberation. To gain a more adequate grasp of nature, we must withdraw from the world that usually claims and moves us; to gain a more certain ground, we have to be willing to surrender the "ground" offered by common sense. Cartesian doubt is such a surrender which brackets our ordinary ways of knowing the world only in order to gain a more complete mastery over it.

If we are to master the world, we must discover in the world's heterogeneous multiplicity homogeneity and simplicity. To reflect is already to take a first step in this direction. By transforming the world of everyday experience into a collection of objects for a thinking subject, we establish that subject as the common measure of all these objects. As the subject comes to resemble a pure, disembodied, and dispassionate eye, the world comes to be like a picture. As long as this picture is seen or sensed, it remains relative to the sensing body and subject to the accident of its location in space and time: no more than a superficial appearance. To penetrate beneath that surface and to ensure access to reality, Descartes insists on a second reduction of experience. Now the thinking subject, not the "eye," is made the measure of what is. Reality is now equated with what presents itself to thought. So understood, reality is essentially without colors or sounds, tastes or smells. These belong only to its appearance, to the surface. Even subjected to this twofold reduction, reality might still prove too complex to be mastered by us. The demand for mastery leads thus inevitably to the transformation of what is to be mastered into a kind of mosaic: the world is to be analyzed into simple parts and then to be reconstructed out of these parts. Science may be understood as such reconstruction.

Descartes's statement of his method is an attempt to lay down the conditions that must be met if such reconstruction is to be possible. It has a counterpart in Wittgenstein's *Tractatus,* which brings out one consequence of such reconstruction; subjected to the requirements of such cognitive mastery, the world turns out to have no room for value: "In the world everything is as it is and happens as it does happen. *In* it there is no value—and if there were, it would be of no value." This loss of value has its foundation in the very first reduction I have sketched, in the transformation of the self engaged in the world by care and desire into a subject that stands before a world of now mute facts, as before a picture. We begin to understand what is at issue when Nietzsche challenges, both as thinker and as writer, the pursuit of truth and the commitment to objectivity that is inseparable from it, as is the "white-ness" of scientific discourse. At issue is the meaning of human existence. Nihilism and the pursuit of truth, understood as the correspondence of our thoughts or propositions to the objects themselves, that is, as they are thought to exist independent of the colors and values with which desire and love, distaste and hatred have endowed them, are inextricably intertwined. Both have their foundation in a will to power that, to secure itself, has to so master its world that it renders it mute and colorless.

It is easy to challenge Descartes's confidence in his method, his faith that human beings are capable of the truth and able to fashion themselves into the masters and possessors of nature. Descartes himself raised the question of whether even his simple natures or clear and distinct ideas might not prove deceptive, and he tried to defeat such doubts with his proofs of the existence of a God who is not a deceiver, proofs that were to establish once and for all that our understanding is indeed attuned to reality and thus were to secure the cognitive anthropocentrism presupposed by the new science. However, all such proofs are inescapably circular. Either we are already convinced of the understanding's ability to discipline itself so that there is no need for a God to shore up such conviction, or such conviction is lacking, and then no argument can be found that will make up for that lack. Nietzsche not only lacks such conviction and dismisses the truth Descartes would have us pursue as a fiction born of a cowardice that refuses to admit how profoundly we are at sea; more important, he also would not welcome such a truth, although, or perhaps precisely because, he knows about the very real power the Cartesian project has given us over nature, even our own nature. Descartes's promise of mastery was not an idle *Ver-sprechen,* an empty promise that sacrificed reality for a fantastic fiction. But just this forces us to share Nietzsche's concern about the price that has to be paid for the power gained: the very success of the attempt to secure human existence threatens to allow us to lose touch with the chaos we bear within ourselves, which is the source of our creativity and of our ability to love. Insisting on security, for lack of courage, we deny the labyrinth of Ariadne.

Who is Nietzsche's Ariadne? In keeping with Ariadne's labyrinthine character, different interpretations can be supported: Ariadne as Cosima Wagner; Ariadne as Arachne, the spider woman, the monster in the web of language; Ariadne as Jung's anima. The last interpretation can appeal to the fact that "On the Great Longing," Zarathustra's hymn to his soul, was originally called "Ariadne." Zarathustra there speaks of having freed his soul, of having nourished it, of having made it overfull, readying it for him who, still nameless, awaits the naming of future song, and of having bid his soul sing. Nietzsche's perfect reader should listen to this song beneath the surface of the words, just as the reader of Plato's dialogues should open himself to the unspoken words graven in his soul. Nietzsche, however, has a very different understanding of the soul. "Soul" is for him "only a word for something about the body." Thus, he speaks of the *Leitfaden des Leibes,* the guiding thread of the body. When Nietzsche calls on us to follow the thread of Ariadne back into the labyrinth, he is calling on us to return to our own corporeal soul, to its silent labyrinthine discourse, which finally supports all we care about and value. Nietzsche bids us descend into this labyrinth, even if such descent threatens destructions, bids us leave the terra firma of what has come to be expected and taken for granted for the open sea, even if such seafaring must end in shipwreck.

In the *Inferno,* Dante says of Ulysses that neither fondness for his son nor reverence for his father nor love of Penelope could keep him from sailing beyond the landlocked Mediterranean, through the warning markers Hercules had set up so that no man would pass beyond; longing to gain experience of the world, he sailed west with those few companions who had not deserted him, only to be shipwrecked before that dark, monstrous mountain which lies furthest from Jerusalem.

Nietzsche's description of the great health recalls this passage, although we are referred not to Dante's Ulysses but to the Argonauts. Nietzsche, too, describes himself and his companions as craving "to have experienced the whole range of values and desiderata to date," and, having "sailed around all the coasts of this ideal 'Mediterranean,'" still curious, still undeterred by shipwreck and suffering, eager to sail on, dreaming of "an as yet undiscovered country, whose boundaries nobody has surveyed yet, something beyond all the lands and the nooks of the ideal so far, a world overrich in what is beautiful, strange, questionable, terrible, and divine," daring, for the sake of that dream, a shipwreck from which there may be no return.

Nietzsche demands of those who would follow him courage in the face of the constant possibility and final inevitability of shipwreck. Those who evade that possibility, who think themselves secure on firm land of one sort or another and are unwilling to recognize that we are all at sea and that there is no ship not threatened by shipwreck, also have to refuse the abysmal depth of reality, that is to say, have to refuse life.

This has special significance for philosophy. If Nietzsche is right, almost always philosophy has been an evasion of life born of the spirit of revenge. The image of the dying Socrates presides over this evasion—as the image of "the human being whom knowledge and reason have liberated from the fear of death," it is "the emblem that, above the entrance gate of science, reminds all of its mission— namely, to make existence appear comprehensible and thus justified." The spirit of revenge bids us understand being against time, lets us oppose the illusory appearance of being to the sea of changing appearance as a terra firma. It teaches that the soul's true home lies beyond time, that we become most truly ourselves when we transcend ourselves as beings subject to time. This allows Socrates to interpret the true philosopher's death not as a shipwreck but as a homecoming of the self to itself.

Nietzsche, too, would have us come home to our soul, but he understands this homecoming not as an ascent to a timeless realm of pure forms but as a descent into the chaos each individual bears within himself, into his own labyrinth. As there is something inhuman about Socrates' ascent into the light of the forms, so there is something inhuman about Zarathustra's descent into himself: both

threaten the destruction of the individual in his being with others. Both Socrates and Zarathustra therefore insist on a compensatory movement that lets the thinker whose pursuit of wisdom leads him beyond all community rejoin those whom he has left behind. In the myth of the cave, Socrates thus has the prisoner who has escaped its darkness return, and similarly Zarathustra must leave the privacy of his cave high upon his mountain—the joining of cave and mountain hints at what joins, but also separates, Zarathustran and Socratic wisdom—and return to those he has left behind in order to become human again. Thus descending, Zarathustra must do violence to his private wisdom, just as his attempts to give voice to this wisdom must do violence to ordinary language. As Zarathustra's going is not only his own *Untergang,* or "going under," but also a leaping over those who hesitate and lag behind, which is to be their *Untergang,* so his speaking is not only the *Untergang* of his own wisdom but also a leaping over of common sense that threatens the shipwreck of all sense.

Consider Zarathustra's teaching of the eternal recurrence. This is not the place to review the many attempts to domesticate that doctrine so that it no longer can offend common sense. Here, I only want to call attention to the explosive power of this forcing together of time and eternity, which represents a refusal to keep reason confined within the limits marked out by Kant's antinomies, warning philosophers not to pass beyond. Hans Blumenberg speaks of a *Sprengmetapher,* a metaphor that like dynamite explodes inherited sense to open up our saying to an unsayable depth, and points to the role such metaphors have played in the mystical tradition with its *via negationis.* Particularly suggestive are remarks that invite a comparison of Nietzsche's doctrine of the eternal recurrence with Nicolaus Cusanus's rhetoric of the circle whose circumference becomes a straight line as its radius becomes infinite. Just as the fifteenth-century cardinal offers his readers the coincidence of opposites as a gate to God's infinity, so Nietzsche offers his readers the coincidence of time and eternity as a gate to a reality that is deeper than our reason. Intended in both cases is the shipwreck of common sense.

To be sure, Nietzsche links *Untergang* to *Ubergang,* "going under" to "going over," passing beyond the old to the new. The metaphor of the seafaring discoverer invites such a reading. But while the word "overman" gestures toward the new land that Nietzsche would have us discover, it names no more than an ill-defined hope that remains in the subjunctive. Nietzsche thus writes only *as if* he confronted that still undiscovered, overrich country that lures him. He knows that he is in no position to begin surveying its boundaries. He also knows that, like those of Dante's Ulysses, his curiosity and craving will not be sated by any discovery. In the end, what lures him is not so much the promise of a new land as the depth of the sea, the whirlpool that means shipwreck. Like his Zarathustra, Nietzsche wants to go *zu Grunde,* to perish.

To be sure, *zu Grunde gehen* in Zarathustra means not just to perish but to descend to the *Grund,* to the ground of human existence. Once again we are made to think of Plato's Socrates, especially of the *Phaedo,* whose *ars mo-*

riendi similarly links perishing and recovery of what is essential. In wanting to return to the *Grund,* Nietzsche joins all those philosophers who have looked for the ground that would give our existence its measure, even if he looks for this ground not to some Platonic or Christian heaven but to the earth, to nature. Recall Nietzsche's determination of *Homo natura* as the terrifying *ewige Grundtext,* the eternal basic text that we have to free from layers of misinterpretation so that it will once again provide our texts, our interpretations of who we are and should be, with a measure. But what right does Nietzsche have to posit such an eternal ground, a ground furthermore that is also said to be a text—a text that has authority precisely because we are not its author? All too readily, Nietzsche's appeal to this *Grundtext* recalls the traditional understanding of the book of nature written by God. What justifies the thought that, once we remove all the misrepresentations of past thinking, something like a *Grund-Text* will appear? Is the very word *Grundtext* not an oxymoron that on reflection plunges us into an abyss? *Grund* and *Text*—how do these belong together? Is not a text necessarily a human product, a conjecture that falsely claims the authority of a *Grund?* Where can we find a *Grund* to speak to us as a text would, presenting our existence with a measure? When we try to descend beneath the surface created by our discourse, strip reality of our fictions, what remains? Something that deserves to be called a *Grundtext?* Will we not stare rather into an *Abgrund,* into an abyss?

There is, to be sure, much in Nietzsche that celebrates superficiality. But Nietzsche is also profoundly impatient with superficiality, especially with the shallowness that has shaped modernity, including its common sense, including especially also the edifices philosophers have raised on that common sense. Against all these, Nietzsche raises his hammer. But such destruction leaves us no place to stand. No longer another Columbus eager to discover a better Europe, another America, Nietzsche now appears as a mad discoverer who, dreaming of a lost continent beneath the waves, begins to break apart the planks of his ship. At this point, one should expect those few sailors who have followed the music of his words to revolt, to stay his hand, to assess the damage that has been done, and, once the ship has been saved, to rethink the goal of the voyage. But perhaps they, too, have become captive to the enchantment of the flutes that lured their captain.

Karsten Harries, "The Philosopher at Sea," in Nietzsche's New Seas: Explorations in Philosophy, Aesthetics, and Politics, *edited by Michael Allen Gillespie and Tracy B. Strong, The University of Chicago Press, 1988, pp. 21-44.*

Terry Eagleton   (essay date 1990)

[*An English critic and educator, Eagleton is the author of numerous Marxist literary studies, including* Myths of Power: A Marxist Study of the Brontës *(1975) and* Criticism and Ideology: A Study in Marxist Literary Theory *(1976). In the following excerpt from his* The Ideology of the Aesthetic *(1990), Eagleton examines Nietzsche's critique of idealism.*]

It is not difficult to trace certain general parallels between historical materialism and the thought of Friedrich Nietzsche. For Nietzsche is in his own way a full-blooded materialist, whatever scant regard he may pay to the labour process and its social relations. One might say that the root of all culture for Nietzsche is the human body, were it not that the body itself is for him a mere ephemeral expression of the will to power. He asks himself in **The Gay Science** whether philosophy has 'not been merely an interpretation of the body and a *misunderstanding of the body*', and notes with mock solemnity in the **Twilight of the Idols** that no philosopher has yet spoken with reverence and gratitude of the human nose. Nietzsche has more than a smack of vulgar Schopenhauerian physiologism about him, as when he speculates that the spread of Buddhism may be attributed to a loss of vigour consequent on the Indian diet of rice. But he is right to identify the body as the enormous blindspot of all traditional philosophy: 'philosophy says away with the *body,* this wretched *idée fixe* of the senses, infected with all the faults of logic that exist, refuted, even impossible, although it be impudent enough to pose as if it were real!' He, by contrast, will return to the body and attempt to think everything through again in terms of it, grasping history, art and reason as the unstable products of its needs and drives. His work thus presses the original project of aesthetics to a revolutionary extreme, for the body in Nietzsche returns with a vengeance as the ruin of all disinterested speculation. The aesthetic, he writes in **Nietzsche Contra Wagner,** is 'applied physiology'.

It is the body, for Nietzsche, which produces whatever truth we can achieve. The world is the way it is only because of the peculiar structure of our senses, and a different biology would deliver us a different universe entirely. Truth is a function of the material evolution of the species: it is the passing effect of our sensuous interaction with our environment, the upshot of what we need to survive and flourish. The will to truth means constructing the kind of world within which one's powers can best thrive and one's drives most freely function. The urge to knowledge is an impulse to conquer, an apparatus for simplifying and falsifying the rich ambiguity of things so that we might take possession of them. Truth is just reality tamed and tabulated by our practical needs, and logic is a false equivalencing in the interests of survival. If Kant's transcendental unity of apperception has any meaning at all, it refers not to the ghostly forms of the mind but to the provisional unity of the body. We think as we do because of the sort of bodies we have, and the complex relations with reality which this entails. It is the body rather than the mind which interprets the world, chops it into manageable chunks and assigns it approximate meanings. What 'knows' is our multiple sensory powers, which are not only artefacts in themselves—the products of a tangled history—but the sources of artefacts, generating as they do those life-enhancing fictions by which we prosper. Thought, to be sure, is more than just a biological reflex: it is a specialized function of our drives which can refine and spiritualize them over time. But it remains the case that everything we think, feel and do moves within a frame of interests rooted in our 'species being', and can have no reality independently of this. Communication itself, which for Nietzsche as for Marx is effectively synonymous with consciousness, develops only under duress, as part of a material struggle for survival, however much we may later come to delight in it as an activity in itself. The body, a 'richer, clearer, more tangible phenomenon' than consciousness, figures in effect for Nietzsche as the unconscious—as the submerged sub-text of all our more finely reflective life. Thought is thus symptomatic of material force, and a 'psychology' is that sceptical hermeneutic which lays bare the lowly motives which impel it. One does not so much contest ideas as find inscribed within them the traces of humanity's hungering. Thinking is thus inherently 'ideological', the semiotic mark of a violence that now lies erased beneath it. What fascinates Nietzsche is the incessant hankering which lies at the core of reason, the malice, rancour or ecstasy which drives it on, the development of instinct in instinct's own repression; what he attends to in a discourse is the low murmur of the body speaking, in all of its greed or guilt. Like Marx, Nietzsche is out to bring down thought's credulous trust in its own autonomy, and above all that ascetic spirituality (whether its name is science, religion or philosophy) which turns its eyes in horror from the blood and toil in which ideas are actually born. That blood and toil is what he names 'genealogy', in contrast to the consoling evolutionism of 'history'. ('That gruesome dominion of nonsense and accident that has so far been called "history" ', he scoffs in ***Beyond Good and Evil.***) Genealogy unmasks the disreputable origins of noble notions, the chanciness of their functions, illuminating the dark workshop where all thought is fashioned. High-toned moral values are the bloodstained fruit of a barbarous history of debt, torture, obligation, revenge, the whole horrific process by which the human animal was systematically degutted and debilitated to be rendered fit for civilized society. History is just a morbid moralization through which humanity learns to be ashamed of its own instincts, and 'every smallest step on earth has been paid for by spiritual and physical torture . . . how much blood and cruelty lies at the bottom of all "good things"!' For Nietzsche as for Marx, 'morality' is not so much a matter of problems as a problem all in itself; philosophers may have queried this or that moral value, but they have not yet problematized the very concept of morality, which for Nietzsche is 'merely a sign language of the affects'.

Nietzsche has more than a smack of vulgar Schopenhauerian physiologism about him, as when he speculates that the spread of Buddhism may be attributed to a loss of vigour consequent on the Indian diet of rice. But he is right to identify the body as the enormous blindspot of all traditional philosophy.

—Terry Eagleton

Rather as for Marx the productive forces become shackled and constrained by a set of social relations, so for Nietzsche the productive life-instincts are enfeebled and corrupted into what we know as moral subjecthood, the gutless, abstract 'herd' morality of conventional society. This is essentially a movement from coercion to hegemony: 'Morality is preceded by *compulsion*; indeed, it itself remains compulsion for some time, to which one submits to avoid disagreeable consequences. Later it becomes custom, later still free obedience, and finally almost becomes instinct: then, like every thing long customary and natural, it is linked with gratification—and now is called *virtue*.' What we have seen in Rousseau and other middle-class moralists as the supremely positive 'aesthetic' transition from law to spontaneity, naked power to pleasurable habit, is for Nietzsche the last word in self-repression. The old barbaric law yields to the Judaeo-Christian invention of the 'free' subject, as a masochistic introjection of authority opens up that interior space of guilt, sickness and bad conscience which some like to call 'subjectivity'. Healthy vital instincts, unable to discharge themselves for fear of social disruption, turn inward to give birth to the 'soul', the police agent within each individual. The inward world thickens and expands, acquires depth and import, thus heralding the death of 'wild, free, prowling men' who injured and exploited without a care. The new moral creature is an 'aestheticized' subject, in so far as power has now become pleasure; but it signals at the same time the demise of the old style of aesthetic human animal, which lived out its beautiful barbaric instincts in splendid unconstraint.

Such, for Nietzsche, were the warriors who originally imposed their despotic powers on a population humbly waiting to be hammered into shape. 'Their work is an instinctive creation and imposition of forms; they are the most involuntary, unconscious artists there are . . . They do not know what guilt, responsibility, or consideration are, these born organisers; they exemplify that terrible artists' egoism that has the look of bronze and knows itself justified to all eternity in its "work", like a mother in her child.' It is this brutal ruling-class dominion which drives underground the free instincts of those it subjugates, creating the self-loathing life of science, religion, asceticism. But such sickly subjecthood is thus the product of a magnificent artistry, and reflects that formative discipline in its own festering masochism:

> This secret self-ravishment, this artists' cruelty, this delight in imposing a form on oneself as a hard, recalcitrant, suffering material and in burning a will, a critique, a contradiction, a contempt, a no into it, this uncanny, dreadfully joyous labour of a soul voluntarily at odds with itself that makes itself suffer out of joy in making suffer—eventually this entirely *active* 'bad conscience'—you will have guessed it—as the womb of all ideal and imaginative phenomena, also brought to light an abundance of strange new beauty and affirmation, and perhaps beauty itself . . .

There is no question of Nietzsche simply *regretting* the horrific birth of the humanist subject, unlike some of his less wary modern-day acolytes. In its alluring unity of discipline and spontaneity, sadistic form and malleable material, such a craven, self-punitive animal is an aesthetic artefact all of its own. If art is rape and violation, the humanist subject reaps the perverse aesthetic delights of a ceaseless self-violation, a sado-masochism Nietzsche much admires. And since art is that phenomenon which gives the law to itself, rather than receiving it passively from elsewhere, there is a sense in which the anguished moral self is a more exemplary aesthetic type than the old warrior class, who master an essentially alien material. The authentic art work is creature and creator in one, which is truer of the moral subject than of the imperious war-lord. There is something beautiful about the bad conscience: Nietzsche derives erotic stimulation from humanity's self-torture, and so, he implies, does humanity itself. Moreover, this compulsively self-ravishing creature is not only a work of art in itself, but the source of all sublimation, and so of all aesthetic phenomena. Culture has its roots in self-odium, and triumphantly vindicates that sorry condition.

All of this may seem gratifyingly remote from Marxism; but the parallel lies in a certain shared teleologism, however uncomfortably the word may ring in the ears of at least Nietzsche's present-day disciples. Teleology is a grossly unfashionable concept today even among Marxists, let alone Nietzscheans; but like many a demonized notion it is perhaps due for a little redemption. For Nietzsche, the breaking down of the old, reliable instinctual structure of the human animal is on the one hand a catastrophic loss, bringing forth the cringing, self-lacerating subject of moral ideology, and throwing humanity on the mercy of that most treacherous, deluded of all its faculties, consciousness. On the other hand, this declension marks a major advance: if the corruption of instinct makes human life more precarious, it also opens up at a stroke fresh possibilities of experiment and adventure. The repression of the drives is the basis of all great art and civilization, leaving as it does a void in human being which culture alone can fill. Moral man is thus an essential bridge or transition to the overman: only when the old savage inclinations have been sublimed by the imposition of 'herd' morality, by the craven love of the law, will the human animal of the future be able to take these propensities in hand and bend them to his autonomous will. The subject is born in sickness and subjection; but this is an essential workshop for the tempering and organizing of otherwise destructive powers, which in the shape of the overman will burst through moral formations as a new kind of productive force. The individual of the future will then buckle such powers to the task of forging himself into a free creature, releasing difference, heterogeneity and unique selfhood from the dull compulsion of a homogeneous ethics. The death of instinct and the birth of the subject is in this sense a fortunate Fall, in which our perilous reliance on calculative reason is at once an insidious softening of fibre and the advent of an enriched existence. The moral law was necessary in its day for the refining of human powers, but has now become a fetter which must be thrown off. 'Profoundest gratitude for that which morality has achieved hitherto', Nietzsche writes in *The Will to Power,* 'but now it is only a burden which may become a fatality!' 'Many chains have been placed upon man', he remarks in *The Wanderer and his Shadow,* 'that he might unlearn behaving as an animal: and in point of fact he has become

milder, more spiritual, more joyful, and more circumspect than any animal. But now he still suffers from having borne his chains too long . . .' There can be no sovereign individual without straitjacketing custom: having been disciplined to internalize a despotic law which flattens them to faceless monads, human beings are now ready for that higher aesthetic self-government in which they will bestow the law upon themselves, each in his or her own uniquely autonomous way. One kind of introjection, in short, will yield ground to another, in which the wealth of evolved consciousness will be incorporated as a fresh kind of instinctual structure, lived out with all the robust spontaneity of the old barbaric drives.

There is surely a remote analogy between this vision and historical materialism. For Marxism, too, the transition from traditional society to capitalism involves a falsely homogenizing law—of economic exchange, or bourgeois democracy—which erodes concrete particularity to a shadow. But this 'fall' is felicitous, one upwards rather than downwards, since within this dull carapace of abstract equality are fostered the very forces which might break beyond the kingdom of necessity to some future realm of freedom, difference and excess. In necessarily fashioning the organized collective worker, and in evolving a plurality of historical powers, capitalism for Marx plants the seeds of its own dissolution as surely as the epoch of the subject in Nietzsche's eyes prepares the ground for that which will overturn it. And Marx, like Nietzsche, would sometimes seem to view this overturning as an overcoming of morality as such. When Nietzsche speaks of the way in which consciousness abstracts and impoverishes the real, his language is cognate with Marx's discourse on exchange value:

> Owning to the nature of *animal consciousness,* the world of which we can become conscious is only a surface- and sign-world, a world that is made common and meaner; whatever becomes conscious *becomes* by the same token shallow, thin, relatively stupid, general, sign, herd signal; all becoming conscious involves a great and thorough corruption, falsification, reduction to superficialities, and generalization.

What is true of consciousness as such, in Nietzsche's extreme nominalist view, is for Marx an effect of commodification, whereby a complex wealth of use-value is stripped to a meagre index of exchange. For both philosophers, however, history moves by its bad side: if for Marx this commodifying process emancipates humanity from the privilege and parochialism of traditional society, laying down the conditions for free, equal, universal intercourse, for Nietzsche the dreary narrative of humanity's 'becoming calculable' is a necessity of its species-being, for without such calculability it would never survive. Logic is a fiction in Nietzsche's eyes, since no two things can be identical; but like the equivalencing of exchange value, it is at once repressive and potentially emancipatory.

The present age, then, is for both Nietzsche and Marx propaedeutic to a more desirable condition, at once impeding and enabling it, a protective matrix now definitively outgrown. If the two are alike in this respect, they are also strikingly similar in others. Both scorn all anodyne idealism and otherworldliness: 'The true world,' comments Nietzsche in notably Marxist idiom, 'has been erected on a contradiction of the real world.' Each lays claim to an energy—of production, 'life' or the will to power—which is the source and measure of all value but lies beyond such value. They are equally at one in their negative utopianism, which specifies the general forms of a future rather than pre-drafts its contents; and each imagines that future in terms of surplus, excess, overcoming, incommensurability, recovering a lost sensuousness and specificity through a transfigured concept of measure. Both thinkers deconstruct idealized unities into their concealed material conflictiveness, and are deeply wary of all altruistic rhetoric, beneath which they detect the fugitive motions of power and self-interest. If only those actions are moral which are done purely for the sake of others, Nietzsche remarks wryly in **Dawn,** then there are no moral actions at all. Neither theorist ascribes a high value to consciousness, which is berated for its idealist *hubris* and thrust back to its modest location within a broader field of historical determinations. For Nietzsche, consciousness as such is incurably idealist, stamping a deceptively stable 'being' on the material process of 'change, becoming, multiplicity, opposition, contradiction, war'. For Marx, this metaphysical or reificatory impulse of the mind would seem to inhere in the specific conditions of commodity fetishism, where change is similarly frozen and naturalized. Both are sceptical of the category of the subject, although Nietzsche a good deal more so than Marx. For the later Marx, the subject appears simply as a support for the social structure; in Nietzsche's view the subject is a mere trick of grammar, a convenient fiction to sustain the deed.

If Nietzsche's thought can be paralleled to Marxism, it can also be deciphered by it. The contempt which Nietzsche evinces for bourgeois morality is understandable enough in the conditions of the German empire of his time, where the middle class was for the most part content to seek influence within Bismarck's autocratic regime rather than offer it a decisive political challenge. Deferential and pragmatic, the German bourgeoisie disowned its historic revolutionary role for the benefits of a capitalism installed in large measure from 'above'—by the protectionist Bismarckian state itself—and for the protection which such an accommodation to ruling-class policies might furnish against what was rapidly to become the greatest socialist party in the world. Deprived of proper political representation by Bismarck's implacable opposition to parliamentary government, thwarted and overshadowed by an arrogant aristocratism, the middle class compromised and manoeuvred within the structures of state power, timorous in its political demands on its superiors and terrified by the swelling socialist clamour of its subordinates. In the face of this inert, conformist stratum Nietzsche swaggeringly affirms the virile, free-booting values of the old nobility or warrior caste. Yet it is equally possible to see this autarchic individualism as an idealized version of the bourgeoisie itself, with all the daring, dynamism and self-sufficiency it might attain in more propitious social circumstances. The active, adventurous *Übermensch* casts a nostalgic glance backwards to the old military nobility; but in his insolently explicit enterprise he also prefigures a reconstituted bourgeois subject. 'To have and to want to

have more—*growth,* in one word—that is life itself', comments Nietzsche in **The Will to Power,** in the course of an anti-socialist diatribe. If only manufacturers were noble, he reflects in **The Gay Science,** there might not be any socialism of the masses.

The project, however, is more complex and paradoxical than some Carlylean or Disraelian dream of grafting the heroic vigour of aristocracy onto a leaden bourgeoisie. It concerns, rather, an acute contradiction within the middle class itself. The problem is that the moral, religious and juridical 'superstructure' of that class is entering into conflict with its own productive energies. Conscience, duty, legality are essential foundations of the bourgeois social order; yet they also serve to impede the unbridled self-development of the bourgeois subject. That self-development is ironically at odds with the very 'metaphysical' values—absolute grounds, stable identities, unfissured continuities—upon which middle-class society trades for its political security. The dream of each entrepreneur is to be wholly unconstrained in his own activity, while receiving protection in the corporate forms of law, politics, religion and ethics from the potentially injurious activities of others of his kind. Such constraints, however, must then apply equally to himself, undermining the very autonomy they were meant to safeguard. Individual sovereignty and incommensurability are of the essence, yet would seem attainable only by a herd-like levelling and homogenizing. As sheer anarchic process or productive force, the bourgeois subject threatens in its sublimely inexhaustible becoming to undercut the very stabilizing social representations it requires. It is the bourgeois himself, if only he would acknowledge it, who is the true anarchist and nihilist, kicking away at every step the metaphysical foundation on which he depends. To realize itself fully, then, this strange, self-thwarting subject must somehow overthrow itself; and this is surely a central meaning of the self-overcoming *Übermensch*. The aesthetic as self-actualization is in conflict with the aesthetic as social harmony, and Nietzsche is recklessly prepared to sacrifice the latter to the former. Bourgeois man as moral, legal and political subject is 'more sick, uncertain, changeable, indeterminate than any other animal, there is no doubt of that—he is the *sick* animal'; yet he is also the bold adventurer who has 'dared more, done more new things, braved more and challenged fate more than all the other animals put together: he, the great experimenter with himself, discontented and insatiable, wrestling with animals, nature, and gods for ultimate dominion—he, still unvanquished, eternally directed toward the future, whose own restless energies never leave him in peace . . .'. This magnificent self-entrepreneurship tragically entails the morbid germ of consciousness; but Nietzsche will, so to speak, lift such productive dynamism from 'base' to 'superstructure', shattering the metaphysical forms of the latter with the furious creativity of the former.

Both subjects and objects are for Nietzsche mere fictions, the provisional effects of deeper forces. Such an eccentric view is perhaps no more than the daily truth of the capitalist order: the objects which are for Nietzsche sheer transient nodes of force are as commodities no more than ephemeral points of exchange. The 'objective' world for

Nietzsche, if one can speak in such terms, would seem at once turbulently vital and blankly meaningless—an accurate enough phenomenology, no doubt, of market society. The human subject, for all its ontological privilege, is likewise stripped in such conditions to the reflex of deeper, more determinant processes. It is this fact that Nietzsche will seize on and turn to advantage, hollowing out this already deconstructed figure to clear a path for the advent of the overman. As the ideal entrepreneur of the future, this bold creature has learnt to relinquish all the old consolations of soul, essence, identity, continuity, living provisionally and resourcefully, riding with the vital current of life itself. In him, the existing social order has come to sacrifice its security to its liberty, embracing the groundlessness of existence as the very source of its ceaseless self-experiment. If bourgeois society is caught in a cleft stick between energy and ontology, between prosecuting its ends and legitimating them, then the latter must yield to the former. To allow the old metaphysical subject to splinter apart is to tap directly into the will to power itself, appropriating this force to fashion a new, ungrounded, aesthetic being who carries his justification entirely in himself. In a reversal of Kierkegaard, ethics will then have given way to aesthetics, as the fiction of a stable order is swept aside for the more authentic fiction of eternal self-creation.

The most notable difference between Nietzsche and Marx is that Nietzsche is not a Marxist. Indeed he is not only not a Marxist, but a belligerent opponent of almost every enlightened liberal or democratic value. We must resist all sentimental weakness, he reminds himself: 'life itself is *essentially* appropriation, injury, overpowering of what is alien and weaker; suppression, hardness, imposition of one's own forms, incorporation, and at least, at its mildest, exploitation . . .'. Much of Nietzsche's writing reads like a brochure for a youth adventure scheme, or the dyspeptic grousings at liberal effeteness of some pensioned-off Pentagon general. He desires

> spirits strengthened by war and victory, for whom conquest, adventure, danger, and even pain have become needs; it would require habituation to the keen air of the heights, to winter journeys, to ice and mountains in every sense; it would require even a kind of sublime wickedness, an ultimate, supremely self-confident mischievousness in knowledge that goes with great health.

We must steel ourselves to the sufferings of others, and ride our chariots over the morbid and decadent. Sympathy and compassion as we have them are the diseased virtues of Judaeo-Christianity, symptoms of that self-odium and disgust for life which the lower orders, in their rancorous resentment, have by a stroke of genius persuaded their own masters to internalize. The poor have cunningly infected the strong with their own loathsome nihilism, so Nietzsche will speak up in turn for cruelty and delight in domination, for 'everything haughty, manly, conquering, domineering'. Like William Blake, he suspects that pity and altruism are the acceptable faces of aggression, pious masks of a predatory regime; and he can see nothing in socialism but a disastrous extension of abstract levelling. So-

cialism is insuffiently revolutionary, a mere collectivized version of the enfeebled bourgeois virtues which fails to challenge the whole fetish of morality and of the subject. It is simply an alternative brand of social ethics, bound in this sense to its political antagonist; the only worthwhile future must involve a transvaluation of all values.

One does not have to glimpse in Nietzsche a precursor of the Third Reich to be repelled by this grovelling self-abasement before the phallus, with all its brutal misogyny and militarist fantasizing. If Nietzsche means such talk as 'the annihilation of the decaying races' literally, then his ethics are appalling; if he intends it metaphorically, then he is recklessly irresponsible and cannot be entirely exculpated from the sinister uses to which such ugly rhetoric was later put. It is remarkable how blandly most of his present-day acolytes have edited out these more repugnant features of the Nietzschean creed, as a previous generation edited in a proto-fascist anti-Semitism. The *Übermensch*, to be sure, is not some latter-day Genghis Khan letting rip his murderous impulses but a tempered, refined individual of serenity and self-control, sensitive and magnanimous in his bearing. Indeed one proper objection to him is less that he will exterminate the poor than that he represents little advance, for all the flamboyant flourishing with which he is heralded, on the well-balanced, self-disciplined individual of a familiar cultural idealism. Even so, it is a crucial distinction between Nietzsche and Marx that the release of individual human powers from the fetters of social uniformity—a goal which both thinkers propose—is to be achieved for Marx in and through the free self-realization of all, and for Nietzsche in disdainful isolation. Nietzsche's contempt for human solidarity belongs with his fundamental values, not simply with his denunciation of a current conformism. The overman may display compassion and benevolence, but these are simply aspects of the pleasurable exercise of his powers, the noble decision of the strong to unbend magnanimously to the weak. If he decides that such compassionate unbending is inappropriate, then the weak are at his mercy. It is aesthetically gratifying from time to time for the overman to deploy his fullness of strength to succour others, always delightfully conscious that he could equally use it to crush them.

Given that the free individual cannot be the product of collective action, Nietzsche's answer to how he emerges at all must remain somewhat vacuous. It cannot be by voluntarist transformation, since Nietzsche has no time for such mental fictions as 'acts of will'. Indeed 'will power' and 'will to power' would seem effective opposites in his thought. But nor can it be by any vulgar historical evolutionism, for the overman strikes violently, unpredictably, into the complacent continuum of history. It would just seem the case that certain privileged subjects such as Friedrich Nietzsche are able mysteriously to transcend the nihilism of modern life and leap at a bound into another dimension. Such a leap can certainly not occur through the exercise of critical reason, which Nietzsche believes impossible. How could the intellect, that crude, fumbling instrument of the will to power, pick itself up by its own bootstraps and reflect critically on the interests of which it is the blind expression? 'A critique of the faculty of knowledge', Nietzsche writes, 'is senseless: how should a

Cover of Der Spiegel 35, no. 24 (8 June 1981), captioned "The Return of a Philosopher: Nietzsche the Thinker, Hitler the Perpetrator."

tool be able to criticise itself when it can only use itself for the critique?' Like several of his present-day followers, he would seem to assume that all such critique entails a serene disinterestedness; and then there is nothing between this impossible metalinguistic dream and a starkly Hobbesian conception of reason as the obedient slave of power. Cognition, as we have seen, is just a fictional simplification of the world for pragmatic ends: like the artefact itself, the concept edits, schematizes, disregards the inessential, in a reductive falsification essential for 'life'. There would seem no way, then, in which it could gain an analytic hold on its own operations, even if Nietzsche's own writings would appear paradoxically to do precisely this. As Jürgen Habermas has remarked [in *Knowledge and Human Interests*], Nietzsche 'denies the critical power of reflection with and only with *the means of reflection itself*'. Marx, for his part, would endorse Nietzsche's insistence on the practical nature of knowledge, its anchorage in material interests, but reject the pragmatist corollary that an overall emancipatory critique is thereby necessarily undercut. What concerns Marx are just those historically specific, 'perspectival' interests which, being what they are, can only realize themselves by passing over from their own particularity to a profoundly interested enquiry into the structure of a whole social formation. The link for Marx between local and general, pragmatic and totalizing thought, is secured in the first place by the contradictory nature of class society itself, which would require global transformation if certain highly specific demands were to find their fulfilment.

If Nietzsche is able to know that all reasoning is simply the product of the will to power, then this knowledge itself shares something of reason's classical range and authority, unlocking the very essence of the real. It is just that this essence turns out to be the truth that there are only ever sectoral interpretations, all of which are in fact false. The quarrel between Marx and Nietzsche turns not on whether there is something more fundamental than reasoning—both thinkers insist that there is—but on the consequent locus and status of reason within this more determining context. To dethrone reason from its vainglorious supremacy is not necessarily to reduce it to the function of a can-opener. Indeed just as Nietzsche at one point acknowledges that reason and passion are not simple opposites—it is mistaken, he argues in *The Will to Power,* to talk as if every passion did not possess its quantum of reason—so critical reason for Marxism is a potential within the growth of historical interests. The critical reason which might enable an overcoming of capitalism is for Marx immanent within that system rather as for Nietzsche reason is a quality immanent to desire. Marxist critique is neither parachuted into history from some metaphysical outer space, nor confined to a reflex of narrowly particular interests. Instead, it seizes insolently on the ideals of bourgeois society itself, and enquires why it is that in current conditions those ideals are curiously, persistently unrealizable.

Marxism is much preoccupied with power, but refers this issue to certain conflicts of interest bound up with material production. Nietzsche, by contrast, hypostasizes power as an end in itself, with no rationale beyond its own self-gratifying expansion. The aim of Nietzschean power is not material survival but richness, profusion, excess; it struggles for no other reason than to realize itself. Ironically, then, there is a sense in which for Nietzsche power is ultimately disinterested. On the one hand, it is wholly inseparable from the play of specific interests; on the other hand, it broods eternally upon its own being in sublime indifference to any of its localized expressions. In this as in other ways, Nietzschean power is fundamentally aesthetic: it bears its ends entirely within itself, positing them as mere points of resistance essential to its own self-actualizing. Through the contingent goals it throws up, power returns eternally to itself, and nothing can be extraneous to it. It is thus that Nietzsche can be branded by Heidegger as the last of the metaphysicians—not that the will to power is any sort of Hegelian essence behind the world (since for Nietzsche's full-blooded phenomenalism there is absolutely nothing behind 'appearances'), but that it is the sole, fundamental, universal form the world takes. Will to power means the dynamic self-enhancement of all things in their warring multiplicity, the shifting force-field by which they expand, collide, struggle and appropriate; and it is thus no kind of 'being' at all. But since it denotes that differential relation of quanta of forces which is the shape of everything, it inevitably continues to fulfil the conceptual function of such 'being'. So it is that a modern devotee of the master, Gilles Deleuze, can write with a certain rhetorical strain that 'The will to power is plastic, inseparable from each case in which it is determined; just as the eternal return is being, but being which is affirmed of becoming, the will to power is unitary, but unity which is affirmed of multiplicity.'

We have already encountered more than once the idea of a force which is 'inseparable from each case in which it is determined', and this is the law of the aesthetic. The will to power is and is not a unitary essence in just the way that the inner form of the artefact is and is not a universal law. The 'law' regulating the work of art is not of the kind that could be abstracted from it, even provisionally, to become the subject of argument and analysis; it evaporates without trace into the stuff of the artwork as a whole, and so must be intuited rather than debated. Just the same is true of the Nietzschean will, which is at once the inward shape of all there is, yet nothing but local, strategic variations of force. As such, it can provide an absolute principle of judgement or ontological foundation while being nothing of the sort, as fleeting and quicksilver as the Fichtean process of becoming. The Kantian 'law' of taste, similarly, is at once universal and particular to the object. Poised at this conveniently ambivalent point, the idea of the will to power can be used in one direction to lambaste those metaphysicians who would hunt out an essence behind appearances, and in another direction to denounce the myopic hedonists, empiricists and utilitarians who are unable to peer beyond their own (mainly English) noses to applaud the mighty cosmic drama unfolding around them. It permits Nietzsche to combine a full-blooded foundationalism, one which has searched out the secret of all existence, with a scandalous perspectivism which can upbraid as effeminate fantasy the abject will to truth. Will to power is just the universal truth that there is no universal truth, the interpretation that all is interpretation; and this paradox, not least in the hands of Nietzsche's modern inheritors, allows an iconoclastic radicalism to blend with a prudently pragmatist suspicion of all 'global' theorizing. As with Schellingian 'indifference' or Derridean 'difference', it is impossible to trump this quasi-transcendental principle because it is entirely empty.

It is worth enquiring whether the will to power is for Nietzsche a matter of 'fact' or 'value'. It would seem that it cannot be a good in itself, for if it is coterminous with everything, by what standard could this be assessed? One cannot in Nietzsche's view speak of the value or valuelessness of existence as a whole, since this would presuppose some normative criteria outside of existence itself. 'The value of life cannot be estimated', he writes in *The Twilight of the Idols;* and this is at least one sense in which he is not a nihilist. The will to power simply *is;* yet it is also at the source of all value. The sole objective measure of value, Nietzsche comments in *The Will to Power,* is enhanced and organized power; so that what is valuable is less the will to power 'in itself', whatever that might mean, than the ways it promotes and enriches itself in co-ordinated complexes of energy. Since human life is one such possible enrichment, Nietzsche can claim that 'life itself forces us to posit values; life itself values through us when we posit values'. But the will to power would seem to promote and complexify itself anyway, by virtue of its very 'essence'. Dandelions, for instance, are a triumph of the will to power, restlessly expanding their dominion by appropriating new areas of space. If it belongs to the 'nature' of the will to power to enhance itself, then as a 'principle' it hovers indeterminately between fact and value, its sheer existence a perpetual valuation.

If the world for Nietzsche is valueless, meaningless chaos, then the point would seem to be to create one's own values in defiance of its blank indifference. Nietzsche is accordingly stern with those sentimental moralists who hold that to live well is to live in accordance with Nature. Such thinkers merely project their own arbitrary values onto reality and then, in an act of ideological consolation, unite narcissistically with this self-image. In a subtle gesture of dominion, philosophy always fashions the world in its own likeness. Nietzsche is out to disrupt this imaginary closure, maliciously reminding us of Nature's sheer amorality:

> 'According to nature' you want to *live*? O you noble Stoics, what deceptive words these are! Imagine a being like nature, wasteful beyond measure, indifferent beyond measure, without purposes or consideration, without mercy and justice, fertile and desolate and uncertain at the same time; imagine indifference itself as a power—how *could* you live according to this indifference?

Humanity, in what Nietzsche terms a 'monstrous stupidity', regards itself as the measure of all things, and considers anything to be beautiful which reflects back its own visage. But the very indifference of the Nietzschean universe, in contrast to this anthropomorphism, sounds ironically close to some of his own most cherished values. He writes in *Beyond Good and Evil* of Nature's 'prodigal and indifferent magnificence which is outrageous but noble', implying that Nature's indifference to value is precisely its

value. The imaginary circle between humanity and world is thus ruptured with one hand only to be resealed with the other: it is the very haughty heedlessness of Nature which would seem to mirror Nietzsche's own ethics.

It is in this sense that Nietzsche, for all his mockery of the sentimentalists, is not exactly an existentialist. At one level, he would indeed appear to argue such a case: the world's lack of inherent value forbids you from taking a moral cue from it, leaving you free to generate your own gratuitous values by hammering this brutely meaningless material into aesthetic shape. The ethical here is purely decisionistic: 'Genuine philosophers . . . are commanders and legislators: they say: *thus* shall it be!' But to live in this style is precisely to imitate Nature as it truly is, an achievement beyond the purveyors of the pathetic fallacy. For the way the world is is no way in particular: reality is will to power, a variable complex of self-promoting powers, and to live a life of autonomous self-realization is therefore to live in accordance with it. It is precisely by becoming an end in oneself that one most accurately mirrors the universe. Nietzsche appears to equivocate between existentialist and naturalistic cases; but this opposition can be deconstructed, to give him the best of all possible ideological worlds. The splendid ungrounded autonomy of legislating one's own values in the teeth of an amoral reality can itself be metaphysically grounded, in the way the world essentially is. 'Life' is hard, savage indifference; but this is a value as much as a fact, a form of exuberant, indestructible energy to be ethically imitated. The will to power does not dictate any *particular* values, as the sentimentalists believe of Nature; it just demands that you do what it does, namely live in a changeful, experimental, self-improvisatory style through the shaping of a multiplicity of values. In this sense it is the 'form' of the will which the overman affirms rather than any moral content, since the will has in fact no moral content. 'Content henceforth becomes something merely formal—our life included', Nietzsche writes in *The Will to Power.* And this is one sense in which the will would seem at once the highest kind of value, and no value at all.

There is a problem, however, about *why* one should affirm the will to power. One cannot call it a value to *express* this force, since everything expresses it anyway. There is no point in legislating that things should do what they cannot help doing just by virtue of what they are. What is valuable is *enhancing* the will; but what is the basis of *this* value judgement, and whence do we derive the criteria which might determine what is to count as an enhancement? Do we just know this aesthetically or intuitively, as when Nietzsche speaks of the pleasurable *feeling* of power? 'What health is', remarks Heidegger ominously in his study of Nietzsche, 'only the healthy can say . . . What truth is, only one who is truthful can discern.' If the will to power is itself quite amoral, what is so morally positive about enriching it? Why should one cooperate with this force, any more than with a sentimentalized Nature? It is clear that one can choose, like Schopenhauer, to deny the will to power—even though all such denials must for Nietzsche be perverted expressions of it. But it is unclear on what grounds one judges that such negation is bad, and that affirming the will is good. Unless, of course, one has already projected certain supremely positive values into this force, such that promoting it becomes an indubitable virtue. Cannot the effects of the will to power be celebrated only if one is already in possession of some criteria of value by which to assess them?

The truth, of course, is that Nietzsche does indeed smuggle certain already assumed values into the concept of the will to power, in just the circular manner for which he scorns the dewy-eyed naturalists. In a mystificatory gesture quite as deluded as theirs, he naturalizes certain quite specific social values—domination, aggression, exploitation, appropriation—as the very essence of the universe. But since such relations of conflict are not a 'thing', their essentialism is mystified in its turn. When accused of subjectivism, Nietzsche can retreat to a kind of positivism: he is not so much promoting any particular values as describing the way life is. Life is callous, wasteful, merciless, dispassionate, inimical as such to human value; but these terms are of course thoroughly normative. True value is to acknowledge that the amorality of the competitive life-struggle is the finest thing there is. The market place would seem hostile to value of a traditional spiritual kind; but this plain-minded insistence on certain brute facts of life is itself, inevitably, a value-judgement. 'My idea', writes Nietzsche, 'is that each specific body strives to become master over the whole of space, and to spread out its power—its Will-to-Power—repelling whatever resists its expansion. But it strikes continually upon a like endeavour of other bodies, and ends by adjusting itself ("unifying") with them.' Few more explicit theorizations of capitalist competition could be imagined; but Nietzsche is out in his own way to spiritualize this predatory state. The will to power may be in one sense philosophical code for the market place, but it also delivers an 'aristocratic' rebuke to the sordid instrumentalism of such struggle, urging instead a vision of power as an aesthetic delight in itself. Such an irrationalism of power, scornful of all base purpose, dissociates itself from an ignoble utilitarianism in the very act of reflecting the irrationalism of capitalist production.

How does one come, unlike a Schopenhauer, to 'choose' the will to power? Either the act of choosing to affirm the will is an effect of the will itself, in which case it is hard to see how it can be a 'choice'; or it is not, in which case it would seem to fall, impossibly for Nietzsche, outside the will to power's cosmic scope. Nietzsche's own response to this dilemma is to deconstruct the entire opposition between free will and determinism. In the act of affirming the will, liberty and necessity blend undecidably together; and the primary Nietzschean image of this aporia is the activity of the artist. Artistic creation is no mere matter of 'volition'—a metaphysical delusion for Nietzsche if ever there was one; but it figures nonetheless as our finest instance of emancipation.

Indeed art is Nietzsche's theme from beginning to end, and the will to power is the supreme artefact. This is not to say that he places much credence in classical aesthetics: if the world is a work of art it is not as an organism but as 'in all eternity chaos—in the sense not of a lack of necessity but of a lack of order, arrangement, form, beauty, wis-

dom, and whatever other names there are for our aesthetic anthropomorphisms'. The aesthetic is not a question of harmonious representation but of the formless productive energies of life itself, which spins off sheerly provisional unities in its eternal sport with itself. What is aesthetic about the will to power is exactly this groundless, pointless self-generating, the way it determines itself differently at every moment out of its own sublimely unsearchable depths. The universe, Nietzsche comments in *The Will to Power,* is a work of art which gives birth to itself; and the artist or *Übermensch* is one who can tap this process in the name of his own free self-production. Such an aesthetics of production is the enemy of all contemplative Kantian taste—of that disinterested gaze on the reified aesthetic object which suppresses the turbulent, tendentious process of its making.

The critical eunuchs must thus be overthrown by the virile artistic practitioners. Art is ecstasy and rapture, demonic and delirious, a physiological rather than spiritual affair. It is a matter of supple muscles and sensitized nerves, an exquisite toning and refining of the body which blends sensual intoxication with effortless discipline. Nietzsche's ideal artist sounds more like a commando than a visionary. Art is sexualized to its root: 'Making music is just another way of making children.' The attempt to render it disinterested is merely another castrating feminine assault on the will to power, along with science, truth and asceticism. As Heidegger notes in a shabby little comment: 'True, Nietzsche speaks against feminine aesthetics. But in doing so he speaks for masculine aesthetics, hence for aesthetics.' The overman is artist and artefact, creature and creator in one, which is precisely not to suggest that he lets rip his spontaneous impulses. On the contrary, Nietzsche denounces the 'blind indulgence of an affect' as the cause of the greatest evils, and views greatness of character as a manly control of the instincts. The highest aesthetic condition is self-hegemony: after the long, degrading labour of submission to moral law, the *Übermensch* will finally attain sovereignty over his now sublimed appetites, realizing and reining them in with all the nonchalance of the superbly confident artist cuffing his materials into shape. The whole of existence is accordingly aestheticized: we must be 'poets of our lives', Nietzsche proclaims, in the minutest everyday matters. The overman improvises his being from moment to moment out of a superabundance of power and high spirits, stamping form on the flux of the world, forging chaos into fleeting order. 'To become master of the chaos one is; to compel one's chaos to become form' is the highest aesthetic achievement, which only the most dedicated sado-masochist can attain. The truly strong man is serene enough to submit to such lacerating self-discipline; those who resent this constraint are the weak who fear to become slaves.

The constraint in question, in fact, is of an enhancing rather than oppressive kind. What is at stake, as Heidegger puts it, is 'not the mere subjection of chaos to a form, but that mastery which enables the primal wilderness of chaos and the primordiality of law to advance under the same yoke, inevitably bound to one another with equal necessity'. The law of the future human animal is of a curiously antinomian kind, utterly unique to each individual. Nothing outrages Nietzsche more than the insulting suggestion that individuals might be in some way commensurable. The law which the *Übermensch* confers on himself, like the 'law' of the artefact, is in no sense heteronomous to him, but simply the inner necessity of his incomparable self-fashioning. The aesthetic as model or principle of social consensus is utterly routed by this radical insistence on autonomy; and it is here, perhaps, that Nietzsche's thought is at its most politically subversive. The *Übermensch* is the enemy of all established social *mores*, all proportionate political forms; his delight in danger, risk, perpetual self-reconstitution recalls the 'crisis' philosophy of a Kierkegaard, as equally disdainful of meekly habitual conduct. The aesthetic as autonomous self-realization is now at loggerheads with the aesthetic as custom, *habitus*, social unconscious; or, more precisely, the latter have now been audaciously appropriated from the public domain to the personal life. The overman lives from habitual instinct, absolved from the clumsy reckonings of consciousness; but what is admirable in him is inauthentic in society as a whole. Hegemony is wrested from the political arena and relocated within each incommensurable subject. Nietzsche's writings betray a profoundly masochistic love of the law, an erotic joy in the severity with which artists of their own humanity wrench the materials of their being into burnished form. But the idea of a law entirely peculiar to the individual simply allows him to reconcile his disgust for morbid self-indulgence with an extreme libertarianism.

We have seen that the moral law for Nietzsche, as with the Mosaic code for St Paul, is merely a ladder to be kicked away once mounted. It forms a protective shelter within which one grows to maturity; but it must then be abandoned, in a Kierkegaardian 'suspension of the ethical', for the adventure of free self-creation. What this enterprise involves is the transmuting into instinct of all that consciousness has painfully acquired in the epoch when it reigned supreme. In that period, the human organism learnt to absorb into its structure the 'untruth' essential for it to flourish; it remains to be seen whether it can now in turn incorporate the truth—which is to say, the recognition that there is no truth. The overman is he who can assimilate and naturalize even this terrible knowledge, convert it to finely instinctual habit, dance without certainties on the brink of the abyss. For him, the very groundlessness of the world had become a source of aesthetic delight and an opportunity for self-invention. In thus living out acquired cultural values as unconscious reflex, the overman reduplicates at a higher level the barbarian who simply unleashed his drives. In a reversal of the classic aesthetic project, instinct will now incorporate reason: consciousness, duly 'aestheticized' as bodily intuition, will take over the life-sustaining functions once fulfilled by the 'lower' drives; and the consequence will be that deconstruction of the opposition between intellect and instinct, volition and necessity, of which art is the supreme prototype. 'Artists seem to have more sensitive noses in these matters', Nietzsche writes, 'knowing only too well that precisely when they no longer do anything 'voluntarily' but do everything of necessity, their feeling of freedom, subtlety, full power, of creative placing, disposing, and forming reaches its peak—in short, that necessity and "freedom of the will" then become one in them.'

Nietzsche's narrative, then, begins with an original inerrancy of blind impulse, ambivalently admirable and terrible; shifts to a moral conscience which imperils but also enriches such impulses; and culminates in a higher synthesis in which body and mind are united under the aegis of the former. An originary brutal coercion gives birth to an era of moral hegemony, which in turn paves the way for the self-hegemony of the overman. This new dispensation combines, in transfigured form, the spontaneity of the first period with the legality of the second. A 'bad' introjection of the law in the ethical-subjective stage gives way to a 'good' such internalization in the coming aesthetic epoch, when freedom and governance will each find its root in the other. For such a remorselessly anti-Hegelian thinker as Nietzsche, this scenario has something of a familiar ring. Its perturbing originality is to press to a third stage the two-phase movement, familiar to aestheticizing thought, from coercion to hegemony. The concept of hegemony is retained; but the law to which one will finally yield consent is nothing but the law of one's unique being. In taking over the aesthetic model of a free appropriation of law, but in stripping that law of its uniformity and universalism, Nietzsche brings low any notion of social consensus. 'And how should there be a "common good"!', he scoffs in *Beyond Good and Evil*. 'The term contradicts itself: whatever can be common always has little value.' In *The Twilight of the Idols* he dismisses conventional virtue as little more than 'mimicry', thus scornfully overturning the whole Burkeian vision of aesthetic mimesis as the basis of social mutuality. Aesthetics and politics are now outright antagonists: all great periods of culture have been periods of political decline, and the whole concept of the 'culture-state', of the aesthetic as civilizing, educational, socially therapeutic, is just another dismal emasculation of art's sublimely amoral power.

Nietzsche's aristocratic disdain for a common measure is by no means wholly unacceptable to bourgeois individualism. But it strikes at the root of conventional order, and so catches the bourgeoisie on its sorest point of contradiction between its dream of autonomy and demand for legality. In the end, Nietzsche is claiming that the present regime of legal and moral subjecthood simply mediates between two states of anarchy, one 'barbaric' and the other 'artistic'. If this is hardly glad tidings for orthodox society, neither is his impudent severing of all connection between art and truth. If art is 'true' for Nietzsche, it is only because its illusoriness embodies the truth that there is no truth. 'Truth is ugly,' he writes in *The Will to Power*. 'We possess art lest we perish of the truth.' Art expresses the will to power; but the will to power is nothing but semblance, transient appearance, sensuous surface. Life itself is 'aesthetic' because it aims only at 'semblance, meaning, error, deception, simulation, delusion, self-delusion'; and art is true to this reality precisely in its falsity. It is also false to it, since it imprints an ephemeral stability of being on this meaningless warring of forces; there is no way in which the will to power can be represented without being in that moment distorted. Art expresses the brute senselessness of the will, but simultaneously conceals this lack of meaning by the fashioning of significant form. In doing so, it tricks us into a momentary belief that the world has some significant shape to it, and so fulfils something of the function of the Kantian imaginary.

The more false art is, then, the truer it is to the essential falsity of life; but since art is *determinate* illusion, it thereby conceals the truth of that falsity. At a single stroke, art symptomatizes and shields us from the terrible (un)truth of the universe, and thus is doubly false. On the one hand, its consolatory forms protect us from the dreadful insight that there is actually nothing at all, that the will to power is neither real, true nor self-identical; on the other hand, the very content of those forms is the will itself, which is no more than an eternal dissembling. Art as dynamic process is true to the untruth of the will to power; art as product or appearance is untrue to this (un)truth. In artistic creation, then, the will to power is harnessed and turned for an instant against its own cruel indifference. To produce forms and values from this tumultuous force is in once sense to work against it; but it is to do so with a touch of its own dispassionate serenity, in the knowledge that all such values are purely fictive.

One might put the same point differently by claiming that art for Nietzsche is at once masculine and feminine. If it is strenuous, muscular, productive, it is also fickle, mendacious, seductive. Indeed Nietzsche's entire philosophy turns on a curious amalgam of these sexual stereotypes. This most outrageously masculinist of creeds is devoted to hymning the 'feminine' values of form, surface, semblance, elusiveness, sensuality, against the patriarchal metaphysics of essence, truth and identity. In the concept of the will to power, these two sets of sexual characteristics are subtly interwoven. To live according to the will is to live robustly, imperiously, released from all female obeisance to law into splendid phallic autonomy. But to have mastered oneself in this style is to be set free to live mischievously, pleasurably, ironically, luxuriating in a teasing sport of masks and personae, gliding in and out of every passion and subject-position with all the serene self-composure of the sage. Nietzsche is thus able to speak up for the 'feminine' principle precisely as one of the most virulent sexists of his age, a title he shares with the obsessively misogynistic Schopenhauer. If truth is indeed a woman, then the claim is complimentary to neither.

In the aftermath of Fichte and Schelling, Nietzsche is the most flamboyant example we have of a full-blooded aestheticizer, reducing everything there is—truth, cognition, ethics, reality itself—to a species of artefact. 'It is only as an *aesthetic phenomenon*', he writes in celebrated phrase, 'that existence and the world are eternally *justified*', which means among other things that the blood-sport of history is at least a *sport*, which intends no harm because it intends nothing but itself. Thought itself must be aestheticized, shedding its leaden earnestness to become dance, laughter, high spirits. The key ethical terms are noble and base rather than good and bad, questions of style and taste rather than of moral judgement. Right living is a matter of artistic consistency, hammering one's existence into an austerely unified style. Art itself is blessing and deification: it must be wrested from the monkish idealists and restored to the body, to orgy and festive ritual. Aesthetic value-judgements must rediscover their true foundation in the libidinal drives. Art instructs us in the profound truth of how to live superficially, to halt at the sensuous surface rather than hunt the illusory essence beneath it. Perhaps superficiality is the true essence of life, and depth a mere veil thrown over the authentic banality of things.

To claim that there is nothing but surface is to argue, in effect, that society must relinquish its traditional metaphysical justifications for what it does. It is a feature of the rationalizing, secularizing activity of middle-class society, as we have seen already, that it tends to undermine some of the very metaphysical values on which that society depends in part for its legitimation. Nietzsche's thought points one bold way out of this embarrassing contradiction: society should renounce such metaphysical pieties and live daringly, groundlessly, in the eternal truth of its material activity. It is this activity which in the concept of the will to power has been raised to the aesthetic dignity of an end in itself. Bourgeois productive energies must furnish their own foundation; the values which ratify the social order must be conjured directly out of its own vital forces, out of the 'facts' of its incessant striving and struggling, not hypocritically superadded from some supernatural source. History must learn to be self-generative and self-legitimating, open its ears to the hard lesson of the aesthetic. This whole proliferating network of dominance, aggressiveness and appropriation must confront the death of God and have the courage to be its own rationale. The death of God is the death of the superstructure; society must make do instead with the 'base' of its own productive forces, the will to power.

Viewed in this light, Nietzsche's work signals a legitimation crisis in which the brute facts of bourgeois society are no longer easily ratifiable by an inherited notion of 'culture'. We must tear aside the 'mendacious finery of that alleged reality of the man of culture', acknowledging that none of the social legitimations on offer—Kantian duty, moral sense, Utilitarian hedonism and the rest—are any longer convincing. Rather than search anxiously for some alternative metaphysical guarantee, we should embrace the will to power—which is to say, the metaphysical guarantee that no ultimate ground is needed, that violence and domination are just expressions of the way the universe is and require no justification beyond this. It is this that Nietzsche means by living aesthetically, celebrating power as an end in itself. But this turns out to be simply one more justification, investing life with all the glamour of the cosmic ideologies we should supposedly surpass.

Nietzsche pits the productive vitality of social life against its drive for consensus, thus turning one current of the aesthetic against another. On the one hand, a rampant aestheticization sweeps boldly across the whole of conventional society, undoing its ethics and epistemology, shattering its supernatural consolations and scientific totems, and demolishing in its radical individualism all possibility of stable political order. On the other hand, this aestheticizing force can be seen as the very life-blood of that conventional society—as the urge to infinite productivity as an end in itself, with each producer locked in eternal combat with the others. It is as though Nietzsche finds in this organized social irrationalism something of art's own splendidly autotelic nature. In contempt for the timorous bourgeois, he unveils as his ideal that violently self-willing creature, conjuring himself up anew at every moment, who was for Kierkegaard the last word in 'aesthetic' futility. But this ferocious new creation, stamping his overbearing shape on the world with all the *hauteur* of the old transcendental ego, is hardly as new as he appears. If the furious dynamism of the *Übermensch* terrifies the stout metaphysical citizen, he may also figure as his fantastic *alter ego,* in the sphere of production if not in the sacred precincts of family, church and state. To live adventurously, experimentally, may jeopardize metaphysical certitudes; but such resourceful self-improvization is hardly an unfamiliar lifestyle in the market place. Nietzsche is an astonishingly radical thinker, who hacks his way through the superstructure to leave hardly a strut of it standing. As far as the base goes, his radicalism leaves everything exactly as it was, only a good deal more so.

Terry Eagleton, "True Illusions: Friedrich Nietzsche," in his The Ideology of the Aesthetic, *Basil Blackwell, 1990, pp. 234-61.*

Daniel W. Conway   (essay date 1990)

[*In the following essay Conway offers a deconstructionist analysis of* Thus Spake Zarathustra.]

Deconstruction presupposes the critic's insight into the contingency of the construction of authority. By exposing the empowering presuppositions of the author's discourse, deconstruction effectively discredits any claim to an epistemically privileged authority. But does deconstruction adequately provide for the author's *own* insight into the construction of textual authority? How does deconstruction (or any other self-conscious interpretative strategy) deal with a text whose textuality *presupposes* the kind of indeterminacy and self-referentiality upon which deconstruction operates? These questions are especially central to an engagement with Nietzsche's most forbidding book, **Thus Spoke Zarathustra.** Rather than deny or ignore the contingency of his own textual authority, Nietzsche *anticipates* the deconstruction of **Zarathustra,** thus forging a deconstructive relation between himself and his readers. By *accommodating* the deconstruction of his own authority, Nietzsche encourages/forces his readers similarly to acknowledge the contingent construction of their own claims to authority. A genuinely free and empowered agency, Nietzsche believes, involves the recognition that one's own claims to authority are just as partial, fragile, and contingent as those of anyone else. Underlying Nietzsche's self-compromising ideal is the conviction that partiality, fragility, and contingency do not in themselves constitute objections to one's specific claims to authority. In order to encourage his readers to reconstruct **Zarathustra** on their own (similarly contingent) authority, Nietzsche accommodates the deconstruction of his textual authority, thus providing his readers with an example of the ideal agency he recommends to them.

Zarathustra is notorious for its textual discontinuities, which philosophers have customarily attributed to Nietzsche's literary and/or emotional immaturity. In light of the deflationary readings of **Zarathustra** that this strategy has produced, a deconstructive reading of the text becomes quite attractive. In this essay, I focus primarily on the traditionally troublesome second part of the text, in which the reader encounters several glaring discontinuities. In what follows, I advance an interpretation of part 2 that accounts for these discontinuities within Nietzsche's general plan to accommodate a deconstruction of his own textual authority. My general strategy is to chart as related processes the devaluation of Zarathustra's model of self-understanding and the deconstruction of Nietzsche's textual authority, tracking the latter process to the former. By investigating the deconstructive relation between Nietzsche and his readers, I hope to suggest a reading of **Zarathustra** as Nietzsche's attempt to promote the freedom and empowerment of his readers.

At the close of part 1, Zarathustra takes leave of his disciples and bids them to enact in their own lives his teaching of the *Übermensch.* But before parting with his disciples, "He spoke thus and the tone of his voice had changed. 'Now I go alone, my disciples. You too go now, alone. Thus I want it. Verily, I counsel you go away and resist Zarathustra! And even better: be ashamed of him! Perhaps he deceived you.' " Zarathustra's unprecedented reversal is attributable to his suspicion that his pedagogy has failed to effect the desired change in his disciples. His evidence? As a farewell gift, they have presented him with a *staff.* Although at first "delighted with the staff," Zarathustra later "weighed the staff in his hand, doubtfully." By outfitting Zarathustra with a staff, his disciples have indicated that they view themselves as a flock and him as their shepherd, thus invoking a standard symbol of Christian redemption. Because Zarathustra's revolutionary teaching is supposed to liberate humankind from its perceived *need* for redemption, his disciples' perception of him as their potential redeemer constitutes *prima facie* evidence of his failure to convey his teaching. Yet despite this evidence, Zarathustra concludes part 1 by hopefully invoking the mysterious vision of "the great noon, when man stands in the middle of his way between beast and *Übermensch.*" Having ostensibly led his auditors to the brink of *Übermenschlichheit,* Zarathustra retreats triumphantly to his mountain solitude.

The beginning of part 2 marks an abrupt end to Zarathustra's respite in solitude. While interpreting a disconcerting dream, he suddenly realizes that his teaching is now "in danger": "Verily, all-too-well do I understand the Sign and admonition of the dream. . . . My enemies have grown powerful and have distorted my teaching till those dearest to me must be ashamed of the gifts I gave them." At first glance, the beginning of part 2 might therefore appear to herald a significant advance in Zarathustra's pedagogical project. Zarathustra vowed in part 1 to return only when all his auditors had denied him. He now ascertains that the anticipated apostasy is complete, and he prepares to resume his teaching: "I have lost my friends; the hour has come to seek my lost ones." But we must be wary of Zarathustra's enthusiasm. He is much more concerned to secure an outlet for his "impatient, overflowing love" than to promote the welfare of his disciples: "let all who suffer be my physicians." He seems largely unconcerned that his disciples have renounced him not from strength, as he had originally envisioned, but from weakness—a weakness he himself has fostered. He furthermore does not consider the possibility that his auditors may have denied him for good reason, as a charlatan whose teaching *ought* to be rejected. In light of Zarathustra's suspiciously selfish motives for resuming his pedagogy, his surprise upon waking from the dream appears largely disingenuous: did he not upon returning to solitude bid his disciples to "be ashamed of Zarathustra"? Why, then, is he *surprised* at his disciples' apparent apostasy? Was their presentation to him of a shepherd's staff not sufficient evidence of their rejection of his teaching? Furthermore, who are these heretofore unmentioned "enemies" on whom Zarathustra now blames the distortion of his teaching?

This discontinuity between the conclusion of part 1 and the beginning of part 2 is customarily attributed (when it is acknowledged at all) to the text's overall lack of a unified dramatic structure. But Zarathustra's curious behavior at the beginning of part 2 is perfectly consistent with his (repressed) suspicions at the close of part 1. In order to preserve the integrity of his current model of self-understanding in the face of his palpable failure, Zarathustra succumbs here to self-deception. The textual discontinuity thus reflects a fundamental conflict within Zarathustra's own understanding of himself as the herald of the *Übermensch*. He consequently resumes his pedagogy in part 2 not because his earlier efforts were somehow inadequate (a hypothesis that he cannot yet seriously entertain) but because some mysterious "enemies" have sabotaged his teaching. Throughout part 2, the distance separating Zarathustra from his "enemies" serves as a measure of his self-deception; only toward the end of part 2 does Zarathustra acknowledge that he is his own "enemy."

In order to account for the discontinuity between the close of part 1 and the beginning of part 2 we must therefore resist the temptation to identify Zarathustra strictly with Nietzsche. To be sure, Zarathustra eventually "grows into" the role reserved for him as Nietzsche's "official" proxy and spokesman. But in the first half of the book, Zarathustra serves as an example of an individual who finds it nearly impossible to treat his own authority as contingently constructed. This developmental account of the central character is warranted by the general dramatic structure of the book: Nietzsche envisions **Zarathustra** as a philosophical *Bildungsroman,* in which the central character gradually acquires self-knowledge as his experiences in the world collectively invalidate his original understanding of himself. The *Bildungsroman* genre enables Nietzsche to unite symbiotically the structure and content of **Zarathustra;** as I have suggested, the deconstruction of Nietzsche's textual authority corresponds to the gradual devaluation of Zarathustra's original understanding of himself as the teacher of the *Übermensch*. Nietzsche's reliance on the *Bildungsroman* genre thus links his own fate inextricably to that of Zarathustra, with whom he entrusts the promulgation of his teaching.

In order to appreciate Zarathustra's need for self-deception in part 2, let us briefly review the original model of self-understanding under which he operates in the pro-

logue. While ensconced in solitude, Zarathustra apparently witnessed an event of which he presumes humankind still ignorant: the death of God. Because God has served historically as the guarantor of all human value, we need no longer depend upon an external authority for our value. We are consequently free now to renounce the God-inspired view of ourselves as inherently sinful or deficient. Zarathustra thus ostensibly promotes Nietzsche's teaching of human *innocence:* although the death of God means that no redemption is forthcoming, *no redemption of the human condition is in order*. Mortality, contingency, and tragedy are *not* deficiencies of the human condition and therefore do not countenance an appeal to an external (or transcendent) guarantor of human value. Prompted by this insight into the death of God, Zarathustra departs his solitude in order to impart to mankind his vision of the *Übermensch,* an ideal of human freedom and power whose achievement represents the overcoming of the traditional Christian-Platonic appraisal of human nature as inherently deficient.

For about a decade now there has been a growing uneasiness with regard to Nietzsche: might he not be more inaccessible, more unapproachable, and more inevitably "betrayed" than any philosopher before or since? Might he not be more veiled and also more thoughtlessly read, and therefore more richly endowed with a future, than any other philosopher?

—Michel Haar, in his "Nietzsche and Metaphysical Language," in **The New Nietzsche,** *edited by David B. Allison, 1977.*

Having descended the mountain, Zarathustra confidently presents his revolutionary teaching to the crowd: "*I teach you the* Übermensch. Man is something that shall be overcome. What have you done to overcome him?" By addressing his auditors in this traditional, preacherly manner, Zarathustra assumes his auditors' need for such a teaching and his own ability to promulgate it. In going under, Zarathustra thus presupposes the causal efficacy of his discourse to effect a transformation of his auditors' lives. His mission is to supply his auditors with the knowledge that God is dead, which his auditors need simply parlay into *Übermenschlichkeit* by dint of an act of will. Zarathustra's preacherly manner furthermore indicates that he has adopted the traditional posture of the Platonic teacher of virtue, whose pedagogical authority rests on an allegedly privileged status *vis-à-vis* his auditors. Zarathustra's uncritical adoption of a pedagogical posture is crucial, for his understanding of himself as teacher of the *Übermensch* ideal proves to be incompatible with the teaching itself. As a teacher of virtue, he views the construction of his authority as neither contingent nor arbitrary. He consequently exempts himself from his own teaching on the grounds that he has already renounced his belief in the dead God; he is not a member of the community to which he speaks. His knowledge of the death of God apparently renders him sufficient unto himself, independent of his fellow human beings. He therefore imparts his teaching to humankind but requires nothing in return. Given Zarathustra's "privileged" status as a teacher of virtue, his auditors cannot help but appear deficient and obtuse to him. With respect to his auditors, then, Zarathustra commands the privilege of *autarky* and can only *give* to others.

In his opening speech of the prologue, Zarathustra anthropomorphically likened the sun to himself, declaring their common need for audience or community: "Behold, I am weary of my wisdom, like a bee that has gathered too much honey; I need hands outstretched to receive it. . . . For that I must descend to the depths, as you do in the evening when you go behind the sea and still bring light to the underworld, you overrich star. Like you, I must *go under*—go down as is said by man, to whom I want to descend." Having since adopted the posture of the Platonic teacher of virtue, Zarathustra now cosmomorphizes himself and assumes for himself the sun's privilege of autarky. In assuming that he has become his own "sun," independent of his "deficient" auditors, Zarathustra betrays a fundamental *mis*understanding of his own teaching: although the death of God frees us from our dependence on an external guarantor of value, we are still dependent for our well-being on some form of community, in which agents give and receive reciprocally. Zarathustra admitted as much when he acknowledged his need for "hands outstretched to receive [his wisdom]," but his initial confrontation with his "deficient" auditors led him to deny any dependence on them. Zarathustra's autarkic model of self-understanding is therefore incompatible with his vision of the *Übermensch*. Because he speaks from the privileged perspective he means to preclude, he rejects his teaching even as he utters it. This discordance manifests itself as an asymmetry between *what* he teaches and *how* he teaches it: Zarathustra *says* he comes to bury God, but his *manner* praises Him instead.

Zarathustra's fundamental methodological error, to which he is recidivistically prone, is to exempt himself from the categories in terms of which he understands his auditors. Fully prepared to expose the contingently Christian and ascetic construction of his auditors' authority, he refuses to view his own authority as similarly constructed. He therefore unwittingly reproduces at another level the very presuppositions of which he seeks to disabuse his auditors, thus presenting the *Übermensch* as the redeemer of his auditors' need for redemption. By treating his auditors' ignorance of their own sufficiency as *itself* a deficiency, Zarathustra unwittingly reinforces the Christian construction of "original sin" that he ostensibly seeks to subvert. Rather than liberate his auditors, Zarathustra transfers their relation of dependence from God to himself.

The failure of Zarathustra's pedagogy in part 1 attests to the incoherence of his enterprise. Handicapped by his traditional presentation of a revolutionary teaching, he was unable to attract any receptive auditors. Nietzsche therefore devotes part 2 of *Zarathustra* to a standard feature of the *Bildungsroman* genre: rather than abandon his original preconceptions about the world in the face of contrary experience, the novitiate dismisses his initial experiences as aberrant and sets out in search of the "real" world, in which his experiences are consonant with his preconceptions. Dissatisfied with his reception thus far, Zarathustra resolves in part 2 to discover an audience untainted by the receptive deficiencies that thwarted his pedagogy in part 1. Rather than return to his "lost ones," as he promised upon interpreting his dream, Zarathustra departs the town of the Motley Cow in search of an audience to which he can impart his vision of the *Übermensch*.

Zarathustra's "solution" to his pedagogical problems is crucial to an understanding of his self-deception: "Like a cry and a shout of joy I want to sweep over wide seas, till I find the Blessed Isles where my friends are dwelling. And my enemies among them! How I now love all to whom I may speak! My enemies too are part of my bliss." Most of the speeches of part 2 ostensibly take place on the Blessed Isles, a utopian community "discovered" by Zarathustra, where receptive auditors anxiously await the arrival of a liberating teacher. Here he need no longer concern himself with modifying his pedagogy to accommodate deficient auditors. Yet Zarathustra's effortless emigration to the Blessed Isles in part 2 may strike the reader as a surprisingly facile solution to his earlier pedagogical difficulties. Why has he never before mentioned these idyllic Blessed Isles if in fact his friends and enemies blissfully dwell there together? Nietzsche's deployment of an image of detachment and isolation (specifically, an island) only reinforces the suspicion that Zarathustra's "discovery" of a receptive audience represents a self-deceived retreat from the failures of his pedagogy; the allusion to the "Isles of the Blest" of Greek mythology further suggests that Zarathustra has engineered an afterworldly redemption of his pedagogical struggles. As we shall see, Zarathustra has in fact "invented" the conditions of his own pedagogical success.

In many respects, the text of part 2 resembles that of part 1: under the aegis of his sun-inspired autarky, Zarathustra continues to promote the *Übermensch* ideal to virtually anonymous auditors. The text thus reflects Zarathustra's own perspective on his enterprise and proceeds as if his pedagogy were highly successful. But in order to accommodate the internal tension occasioned by Zarathustra's self-deception, Nietzsche now begins to chronicle Zarathustra's misgivings about his career as the teacher of the *Übermensch*. By informing the text of part 2 with several radical discontinuities, Nietzsche inaugurates a subtext in which Zarathustra honestly surveys the evidence mounting against his current model of self-understanding. Within this subtext Zarathustra's *Bildungsgang* continues unimpaired by self-deception. The dominant text, which derives its authority solely from Zarathustra's own, remains stubbornly Apollonian; under the spell of the coming "great noon," Zarathustra continues to operate under his autarkic model of self-understanding. The subtext, however, comprises a Dionysian attack on Zarathustra's model of self-understanding. The interplay of Apollonian text and Dionysian subtext consequently parallels the tension inherent to Zarathustra's pedagogical project.

The eruptions of this subtext challenge Zarathustra's model of self-understanding by providing *internal* evidence against it: Zarathustra's subtextual forays gainsay his pretentions to autarky and thus expose the incoherence of his enterprise. As we have seen, the authority of Nietzsche's text derives entirely from Zarathustra's own authority as an autarkic agent. In challenging Zarathustra's autarkic model of self-understanding, the eruptions of the subtext thus also challenge the authority of the text itself. The emergence of this subtext consequently serves to catalyze a deconstruction of **Zarathustra**; the dramatic structure of the text mirrors the internal structure of Zarathustra's enterprise. By thus orchestrating the eruptions of the subtext, Nietzsche both anticipates and accommodates the deconstruction of his own textual authority. He is entirely reliant upon Zarathustra to promulgate his teaching, and Zarathustra's *Untergang* is destined inexorably for "demise."

To designate the occasional eruptions of this subtext, Nietzsche employs Dionysian images as signposts. Throughout part 2 we encounter intermittent chapters staged amid the imagery of dream, night, tomb, intoxication, song, dithyramb, underworld, and shadow. For example, Zarathustra's alarm at the beginning of part 2 is triggered by a *dream* in which his own reflection in a child's mirror reveals a devil's visage. Nietzsche's title for this inaugural chapter of part 2—"The Child with the Mirror"—suggests that this subtext is related to the text as a *mirror* that reflects the failures of Zarathustra's pedagogical career. Because Zarathustra enacts the reflections in this mirror, however, he does not enjoy the critical distance that informs our "privileged" standpoint; his own appraisal of the mirror's reflections is prejudiced by his autarkic model of self-understanding. We have already seen him interpret his initial dream as an endorsement of his pedagogy rather than as a challenge to it. Zarathustra's continued susceptibility to self-deception thus not only generates the subtext but also mitigates its potential utility for him as a mirror.

At the beginning of part 2, Zarathustra's interpretation of his dream persuades him to go under once again: "New ways I go, a new speech comes to me; weary I grow, like all creators, of the old tongues." This "new speech" largely comprises a series of fulminations against the obtuse auditors in the town of the Motley Cow, to whom he originally presented his teaching before emigrating to the Blessed Isles. Here Zarathustra gloats over his good fortune, for on the Blessed Isles he need no longer associate with the "rabble" to whom he initially tried to speak: "Oh, I found it here my brothers! Here, in the highest spheres, the fount of pleasure wells up for me! And here is a life of which the rabble does not drink." Zarathustra's "discovery" of the Blessed Isles furthermore vindicates his claim to an autarkic privilege. He is now certain that his pedagogical failures in part 1 are wholly attributable to the deficiencies of his original auditors. Zarathustra thus celebrates his arrival on the Blessed Isles by lampooning those whom he left behind: the pitying, the priests, the virtuous,

the rabble, the preachers of equality (that is, the tarantulas), and the famous wise men (chapters 3-8).

But Zarathustra's celebration comes to an abrupt end in chapter 9 of part 2, as the Dionysian subtext interrupts the course of the text. From the very outset of his pedagogical career, when he brazenly likened the sun to himself, Zarathustra has identified himself exclusively with light, with giving, with the redemptive "Great Noon." He has consequently denied his need for (and susceptibility to) any additional *Bildung*. The text has been illuminated thus far by Zarathustra's own solar radiance. But in *The Night Song*, which Nietzsche describes as Zarathustra's "immortal lament at being condemned by the overabundance of light and power, by his sun nature, not to love," the Dionysian subtext challenges Zarathustra's claim to an autarkic privilege by temporarily eclipsing the Apollonian daylight of the text. Submerged now in the darkness of the subtext, Zarathustra acknowledges that he longs also to receive: "Light am I; ah, that I were night! But this is my loneliness that I am girt with light. Ah, that I were dark and nocturnal! . . . But I live in my own light; I drink back into myself the flames that break out of me. I do not know the happiness of those who receive." Zarathustra's yearning in *The Night Song* "to receive light" implies that autarky is an unacceptable (and illusory) alternative to membership in a reciprocal community. Here he acknowledges that a coherent model of self-understanding must be predicated on the recognition of others as "suns" in their own right: "Many suns revolve in the void: to all that is dark they speak with their light—to me they are silent." Zarathustra consequently longs to renounce his autarkic "privilege" and take his place *within* the community to which he speaks: "And even you would I bless, you little sparkling stars and glowworms up there, and be overjoyed with your gifts of light." Zarathustra's *Night Song* finally questions whether his teaching can be imparted at all under the aegis of an autarkic model of self-understanding: "They take from me, but do I touch their souls? There is a cleft between giving and receiving; and the narrowest cleft is the last to be bridged." This "cleft between giving and receiving" corresponds to the original asymmetry between Zarathustra's untimely teaching and his traditional model of self-understanding. Zarathustra admits here that his autarkic posture has compromised his pedagogical project: "My happiness in giving died in giving; my virtue tired of itself in its overflow." *The Night Song* thus comprises Zarathustra's first consideration—albeit a subtextual one—of the possibility that *he* is responsible for the failure of his pedagogy.

The doubts expressed by Zarathustra in *The Night Song* are amplified in the final song of the subtextual eruption, *The Tomb Song*. Here Zarathustra leaves the Blessed Isles, crossing the sea to the Isle of Tombs; Nietzsche thus implies that Zarathustra's model of self-understanding has thrust him once again into the unwanted role of "gravedigger." Freed from the self-deception indigenous to the Blessed Isles, Zarathustra here reflects subtextually on his pedagogical failures—an exercise he cannot yet perform in the light of day, lest his enterprise come to an end. Fully expecting an immediate and universal reception of his teaching, Zarathustra has come to loathe his original auditors for their apparent recalcitrance and ingratitude. He consequently accuses his "enemies" of misleading him with an unrealistic exception of pedagogical success: "Thus spoke my purity once in a fair hour: 'All beings shall be divine to me.' Then you assaulted me with filthy ghosts; alas, where has this fair hour fled now? . . . All nausea I once vowed to renounce: then you changed those near and nearest me into putrid boils. Alas, where did my noblest vow flee then?" Zarathustra subsequently discloses that his experiences in the world have in fact sullied the innocence of his solitude: "You have taken from me the irretrievable: thus I speak to you my enemies. For you murdered the visions and dearest wonders of my youth. . . . you have cut short my eternal bliss, as a tone that breaks off in a cold night." Zarathustra's loss of innocence attests to the incoherence of his enterprise. He goes under to promote an ideal of human sufficiency, yet as an autarkic agent, he cannot help but deem his auditors deficient. On the subtextual level, then, Zarathustra's *Untergang* engenders an *absurdum practicum*: his claim to an autarkic privilege *guarantees* the failure of his pedagogy. *The Tomb Song* thus portends the eclipse of Zarathustra's sun-inspired autarky.

But the sentiments expressed in these songs do not yet mirror Zarathustra's "daylight" appraisal of his destiny as the teacher of the *Übermensch*. Despite the eruption of the Dionysian subtext, Zarathustra remains committed to his autarkic model of self-understanding. His strength of will enables him to "endure" and "overcome" these subtextual distractions. Immediately following *The Tomb Song*, Zarathustra ignores these "irrational" songs and takes solace in the potential receptivity of his current auditors, those individuals who allegedly overcome themselves.

Zarathustra turns hopefully to his new auditors, who he assumes have eagerly internalized his teaching of the *Übermensch*; evidence of pedagogical success on the Blessed Isles would presumably dispel the doubts raised by these songs. Nietzsche devotes chapters 13-17 of the text of part 2 to a narrative tour in which Zarathustra surveys the gamut of his auditors on the Blessed Isles. Zarathustra displays for the reader various individuals who are renowned on the Blessed Isles for their feats of self-overcoming: the ascetics of the spirit, the hypercritical men of today, foundationalists (that is, disinterested perceivers), scholars, and poets (chapters 13-17). But to his dismay, Zarathustra soon discovers that his emigration to the Blessed Isles has degenerated into a *via negativa*. Although each candidate is admittedly virtuous in some important regard, all nevertheless remain "fragmentary" in their common failure to renounce their God-inspired commitment to the deficiency of human nature. The virtue specialists who inhabit the Blessed Isles are nothing more than "inverse cripples" who compensate for their perceived deficiencies by cultivating one virtue to the exclusion of all others. Zarathustra is consequently forced to conclude this *via negativa* by admitting that his pedagogy has produced no *Übermensch*—even on the Blessed Isles. In fact, his disciples on the Blessed Isles are virtually indistinguishable from his previous auditors in the town of the Motley Cow, whom he thought he had left behind. The ridicule that he heaped upon his former disciples (chapters

3-8) thus reverberates mockingly, as a dismissal of his current auditors as well. Yet Zarathustra still fails to acknowledge that his *via negativa* is ultimately self-consuming in scope.

At this critical juncture, the Dionysian subtext once again interrupts the course of the text, in the chapters "On Great Events" and "The Soothsayer." In the former chapter, Zarathustra's "shadow" offers the following warning: "It is time! It is high time." But Zarathustra is as yet unable to decipher this parabolic message, requiring, it would seem, a more straightforward clue that "it is high time" to abandon his current model of self-understanding. Nor does Zarathustra recognize his shadow's "descent to hell" as a portent of his own imminent *Untergang* (that is, "demise"), for he does not yet view these subtextual eruptions as accurate reflections of his own inadequacies.

But in the latter chapter, the darkness prefigured in *The Night Song* and *The Tomb Song* finally descends: here the high nocturnal imagery of Zarathustra's nightmare embellishes the failure of his pedagogy. The soothsayer's prophecy that "the best grew weary of their works" echoes Zarathustra's confession in *The Night Song* that he no longer derives joy from his teaching. The ripe, sweet figs that earlier symbolized Zarathustra's teachings have now turned "rotten and brown." The soothsayer's prophecy moreover likens Zarathustra's teaching to an ambiguous Promethean gift: "and if fire should descend on us, we should turn to ashes; indeed, we have wearied the fire itself." Finally, Zarathustra's own fluid metaphor for his "new speech" in part 2 is here distorted into a portent of death: "All our wells have dried up; even the sea has withdrawn." The soothsayer finally concludes his prophecy by suggesting that Zarathustra's teaching has in fact precipitated the advent of nihilism: "Verily, we have become too weary even to die. We are still waking and living on—in tombs." As Zarathustra's subsequent nightmare confirms by casting him in the role of "night watchman and guardian of tombs," the "deadly doctrine" that the soothsayer describes is Zarathustra's own teaching. Despite his apparent efforts to liberate humankind from the shadow of the dead God, his teaching has nevertheless been internalized as the paralyzing doctrine that "All is empty, all is the same, all has been!" Zarathustra consequently dreams of himself as a servant "in the castle of Death."

Upon hearing Zarathustra's account of the nightmare, his favorite disciple eagerly volunteers an interpretation. Interestingly enough, the youth diagnoses the awful dream as yet another endorsement of the *success* of Zarathustra's pedagogy: "Are you not yourself the wind with the shrill whistling that tears open the gates of the castles of death? Are you not yourself the coffin full of colorful sarcasms and the angelic grimaces of life?" Zarathustra's *Bildungsgang* in part 2 thus comes full circle: for him to witness his favorite disciple's interpretation of the dream is like looking into a mirror—a child's mirror—for the second time. And once again, his "devilish" reflection has been interpreted charitably. This time around, however, owing perhaps to the therapeutic eruptions of the subtext, Zarathustra is able to distance himself from his own enterprise; his newly acquired *Bildung* renders him suspicious of his disciple's Zarathustresque interpretation of the nightmare. Nietzsche's imagery here suggests that the youth's interpretation of the nightmare has initiated the dissolution of Zarathustra's self-deception.

This spell of self-deception is finally shattered in the chapter "On Redemption," which begins as Zarathustra crosses over a great bridge. As he earlier did on the subtextual level, Nietzsche signals the end of Zarathustra's self-deception on the textual level by means of the latter's departure from the Blessed Isles. On the other side of the bridge, a hunchback informs Zarathustra that "one thing is still needed" before he and his fellow cripples can "believe in [Zarathustra's] doctrine"; Zarathustra must first "heal the blind and make the lame walk." Once again, Zarathustra's failure as the teacher of the *Übermensch* is manifest, for these auditors perceive him as a potential redeemer of human deficiencies, just as at the close of part 1.

Zarathustra consequently takes this opportunity to clarify his teaching one final time. As a Platonic teacher of virtue, he believes that he need only inform his auditors of the death of God; they in turn will transform themselves into *Übermenschen* by dint of an act of will. At the beginning of part 2, Zarathustra proclaimed that "willing liberates: that is the true teaching of will and liberty—thus Zarathustra teaches it." He later responded to the subtextual challenge of *The Tomb Song* by reaffirming his faith in human creativity: "Indeed, in me there is something invulnerable and unbearable, something that explodes rock: that is *my will*. . . . You are still the shatterer of all tombs. Hail to thee, my will!" But in the aftermath of his soothsayer-induced nightmare, Zarathustra is obliged to revise his teaching significantly: "Will—that is the name of the liberator and joy-bringer; thus I taught you, my friends. But now learn this too: the will itself is still a prisoner." Within the context of the nightmare, we recall, Zarathustra was able to open all gates save a single one; his "watchman's keys" symbolize the creative "Yea-savings" of the will and the open gates his successful self-overcomings. As Zarathustra discloses in his speech "On Redemption," the single unyielding gate symbolizes the *past:* "Powerless against all that has been done, he is an angry spectator of all that is past. The will cannot will backwards; and that he cannot break time and time's covetousness, that is the will's loneliest melancholy." As Zarathustra himself now realizes, his teaching is much more complicated than he initially thought when he straightforwardly presented it to the crowd. Although the will cannot objectively *change* the past, for example, alter the Christian-Platonic heritage of self-depreciation that defines us as historical agents, a form of redemption is nevertheless possible: "All 'it was' is a fragment, a riddle, a dreadful accident . . . until the creative will says to it 'But thus I will it; thus shall I will it.'" But the redemption of the will from its "revenge against the past," a feat that would require "something higher than any reconciliation," is among the darkest of Zarathustra's teachings. Zarathustra himself asks, "how shall this be brought about? Who could teach [the will] also to will backwards?"

The subsequent aposiopesis in Zarathustra's speech sig-

nals an epiphantic moment of realization: the will that could say to the past "But thus I willed it" is *not* the will that Zarathustra reveres. The redemption Zarathustra seeks involves a *liberation* from his past, and his own strategy for "willing backwards" calls for the advent of a redemptive *Übermensch*: "When my eyes flee from the now to the past, they always find the same: fragments and limbs and dreadful accidents—but no human beings. The now and the past on earth—alas, my friends, that is what I find most unendurable; and I should not know how to live if I were not also a seer of that which must come." Zarathustra thus realizes that he too envisions the *Übermensch* as a redeemer—albeit of our need for redemption. Although he ostensibly promotes the sufficiency of the human condition, he wants no part of a destiny that requires him to engage in a potentially interminable exchange with "fragments" and "cripples."

Zarathustra's predicament at the close of part 2 is succinctly represented in his final exchange with the hunchback, who apprises Zarathustra of the asymmetry between his words and manner: "But why does Zarathustra speak otherwise to his pupils than to himself?" That is, why does Zarathustra say one thing but teach another? Despite his pretensions to autarky, Zarathustra's primary goal all along has been to discern in his disciples a sign that they have internalized his teaching; he longs, as the *Night Song* confirmed, also to receive from them, and the failure of his pedagogy is attributable to his unacknowledged need for them *not* to internalize his teaching. Throughout part 2, Zarathustra has sought in vain to witness his teaching reflected in his auditors, discovering only "fragments" and "cripples." But we now see that Zarathustra has pursued the wrong evidence all along. Fully convinced of the efficacy of his discourse, he sought in his disciples only a reflection of his "official" teaching. In fact, whenever the subtext afforded him a contrary mirror image, he simply reassimilated his reflection. Now that his self-deception has been exposed, however, Zarathustra realizes that he has effectively advanced two separate, incompatible ideals of *Übermenschlichkeit*. The "official" Nietzschean teaching that Zarathustra failed to promulgate comprises two tenets: the death of God and the innocence of the human condition. The inadvertent teaching that Zarathustra successfully promulgated comprises only the former tenet and thus encourages his auditors to welcome a new redeemer of their human deficiencies. In this light, his pedagogy has been ironically successful after all: his disciples have in fact replicated his manner perfectly and have afforded him a reflection of his inadvertent teaching. Like him, they not only view the *Übermensch* as a potential redeemer of human deficiencies but also view themselves as needing external redemption. Zarathustra thus finally realizes that *he* is the enemy responsible for the distortion of his teaching. Because he refused to acknowledge his dependence on his auditors for their recognition of him as a teacher of virtue, Zarathustra unwittingly sabotaged his teaching; in order to secure their recognition, he was obliged to set himself up as the successor god, as the anti-*Übermensch*. After all, did *his* reflection in the child's mirror not reveal "a devil's grimace and scornful laughter"?

The climax of Zarathustra's crisis occurs, appropriately

enough, in the ambiguous midnight/noon midpoint of the text, "The Stillest Hour." At this juncture, the solar radiance of Zarathustra's autarky is rudely eclipsed, as the Dionysian subtext finally supplants the text of part 2. The deconstruction of the text is now complete. Zarathustra's mode of self-understanding, the source of authority for both Zarathustra and Nietzsche, has devalued itself. Here Zarathustra finally accepts the verdict originally pronounced in *The Tomb Song:* "As yet my words have not moved mountains, and what I said did not reach men. Indeed, I have gone to men, but as yet I have not arrived." Zarathustra therefore concludes that "it is beyond [his] strength" to impart a teaching he neither embodies nor esteems. The *Bildungsgang* of part 2 thus delivers a tragic conclusion: Zarathustra is unable to convince even *himself* of the merit of his own teaching. He knows that God is dead, but he is powerless to inform his own practices with this knowledge. Zarathustra's pronouncement of the death of God therefore signals only an interregnum period until a successor arrives; as we have seen, Zarathustra both assumes and denies the role of successor god. In the meantime, Zarathustra and his auditors, deprived of the guarantor of their value, now deem themselves irremediably deficient. As the soothsayer prophesied, Zarathustra's revolutionary teaching of liberation has degenerated into an enervating damnation: "All is empty, all is the same, all has been!"

We must bear in mind, however, that the deconstruction of *Zarathustra* marks the midpoint of the book and not its conclusion. To view the deconstruction of Nietzsche's textual authority as a purely negative result would therefore be mistaken or at any rate premature. I believe that Nietzsche anticipated the deconstruction of his textual authority and fashioned *Zarathustra* to accommodate the contingency and fragility of his authority. As we have seen, Nietzsche promotes an ideal of human sufficiency that is predicated on the innocence of the human condition; for Nietzsche, the mortality, contingency, and tragedy of the human condition do not detract from its value. But by promoting this ideal through a literary medium, Nietzsche risks exerting on his readers a dangerously formative influence such that they might come to regard *him* as the new guarantor of their value. In order to allay his greatest fear as a philosopher—that he might be involuntarily conscripted as the new redeemer—Nietzsche welcomes the deconstruction of his own textual authority, thus preemptively sabotaging his potential candidacy for the position of interim God. Zarathustra's unwitting complicity in the Christian-Platonic moral tradition is designed to obviate a similar fate for Nietzsche. Appropriating for his own purposes a familiar myth, Nietzsche sacrifices his own "son/sun"—not to redeem humankind but to free humankind from its perceived need for redemption. Of course, some readers will still revere Nietzsche's authority even in the wake of Zarathustra's dismal failure and "demise"; such readers lie ultimately beyond Nietzsche's authorial control.

Having accommodated the deconstruction of his textual authority, Nietzsche in parts 3-4 encourages his readers to reconstruct *Zarathustra* on the strength of their own authority, whose construction he has shown by implication

to be similarly contingent; only in this way can he promote the sufficiency of his readers without appealing to a privileged standpoint. Parts 3-4 of the text chronicle Zarathustra's gradual convalescence from his midbook crisis, a convalescence that corresponds to a reconstruction of the authority of the text independently of Nietzsche's authority.

Part 3 comprises a series of comic failures. Apprised of his own failure to embrace the *Übermensch* ideal, Zarathustra resolves to impart this teaching to *himself* before resuming his public pedagogy: "Thus I am in the middle of my work, going to my children and returning from them: for his children's sake Zarathustra must perfect himself." Zarathustra unwittingly reproduces in this autodidactic enterprise the same presuppositions that invalidated his original pedagogical project. Still convinced of the causal efficacy of his discourse, he comically seeks to provide himself with the knowledge whereby he might willfully transform himself. Because he unwittingly resumes an autarkic posture, the incipient reconstruction of the text of part 3 is interrupted on two occasions by the emergence of the subtext: the chapters "The Vision and the Riddle" and "On the Three Evils" both reflect the incoherence of Zarathustra's autodidactic enterprise. Only in "The Convalescent," following the final eruption of the Dionysian subtext, does Zarathustra finally renounce his claim to an autarkic privilege, thus setting the stage for part 4, in which he coherently, if not successfully, promotes the *Übermensch* ideal.

In part 4, the text proceeds without subtextual interruption, for Zarathustra has finally abandoned the autarkic posture that undermined his pedagogy and precipitated his self-deception. Yet how can Zarathustra continue his pedagogy if he does not assume his customary posture as Platonic teacher of virtue? This concern is only exacerbated as part 4 begins, for the supposedly transfigured Zarathustra exhibits no interest whatsoever in teaching. Perhaps his rejection of an autarkic privilege requires him to abandon his pedagogical project as well; after all, Zarathustra seems content in the opening scene of part 4 to spend his time *fishing*.

But as Zarathustra confides upon scaling a nearby mountain, his apparent indifference to his teaching is a "mere cunning" designed to appease his anxious animal companions. He now likens himself to a fisher of men, insofar as he now views his audience "as an abysmal, rich sea—a sea full of colorful fish and crabs, which even gods might covet, that for their sakes they would wish to become fishermen and net throwers: so rich is the world in queer things, great and small. Especially the human world, the human sea: *that* is where I now cast my golden fishing rod and say: Open up, you human abyss!" In parts 1-2, we recall, Zarathustra was primarily interested in becoming empty, with *giving* to humankind; here in part 4 however, he also longs to *receive* from his auditors, to draw them to himself. Zarathustra now consciously embraces the ideal of reciprocal community that was originally suggested in *The Night Song.* In exchanging his autarkic privilege for a "golden fishing rod," Zarathustra has not retired after all from the promotion of virtue but has instead corrected the error that thwarted his earlier attempts at pedagogy. Rather than risk inadvertently setting himself up as the new redeemer, Zarathustra no longer predicates his teaching on the priviledged authority of the teacher of virtue. In order to avoid another "demise," Zarathustra now refuses to go under: "Thus men may now come *up* to me; for I am still waiting for the sign that the time has come for my descent. I still do not myself go under, as I must under the eyes of men."

But if Zarathustra refuses to go under, then in what sense does he promote the virtue of others at all? Why would anyone voluntarily come to *him* in search of moral advice and edification—especially now that he has relinquished his claim to a privileged authority? Anticipating this objection, Zarathustra acknowledges that his fishing expedition *is* foolish, yet he defends it nonetheless, as an improvement upon his former "solemnity" (*Feierlichkeit*): "Has a man ever caught fish on high mountains? And even though what I want and do up here be folly, it is still better than if I became solemn down there from waiting . . . [like] an impatient one who shouts down into the valleys, 'Listen or I shall whip you with the scourge of God!' " In the absence of receptive auditors, Zarathustra originally viewed his promotion of *Übermenschlichkeit* as self-sacrificial; as he confessed in "On Redemption," he could endure "the now and the past" only by anticipating the advent of a redemptive *Übermensch*. His unconditional gift for humankind, which he had originally likened to a surfeit of honey, has consequently degenerated into a "honey sacrifice" (*Honig-Opfer*). Zarathustra therefore renounces his initial model of self-understanding; one cannot consistently maintain, as he did, that one's gift for mankind is both unconditional *and* sacrificial.

In contrast to the "honey sacrifice" that culminated in his "demise," Zarathustra now recommends a new metaphor for his teaching: "Why sacrifice? I *squander* [*verschwende*] what is given me, I—a squanderer with a thousand hands; how could I call that sacrificing?" Here Zarathustra overcomes the internal incoherence that compromised his initial efforts to promote the *Übermensch* ideal: like the bee, he too squanders his "honey." He consequently imposes no conditions whatsoever on his teaching—he does not even require anyone to *listen* to him: "That is why I wait here, cunning and mocking on high mountains, neither impatient nor patient . . . For my destiny . . . does not hurry and press me, and it leaves me time for jests and sarcasms, so that I could climb this mountain today to catch fish." As a squanderer, Zarathustra now embraces the folly endemic to his enterprise: he *is* foolish to fish on high mountains. Yet his conscious folly is "useful" to him as his unwitting folly was not. First of all, by acknowledging the folly of his enterprise, Zarathustra obviates the solemnity that earlier consumed him. Although he seriously pursues his promotion of virtue, he no longer justifies himself solely in terms of pedagogical success. Second, Zarathustra enjoys greater pedagogical freedom as a self-conscious fool: "Up here *I may speak more freely* than before hermits' caves and hermits' domestic animals." The self-conscious fool can actually exploit the folly of his enterprise to his own advantage. Since "no one" takes seriously the teaching of a fool, Zarathustra is free to articulate to "everyone" an alternative moral ideal. Zarathustra's advantage as a squanderer thus resembles Nietzsche's own: having accommodated the deconstruction of his own authority, Nietzsche is now free to promote the sufficiency of others without simultaneously exerting on them an unduly formative influence.

Yet even as a squanderer, Zarathustra must present his teaching as in some sense authoritative; the same holds for Nietzsche as well if he is to contribute at all to the well-being of his readers. Zarathustra must now confront the problem of audience that he has habitually ignored: why should anyone come up to him at all? Here Zarathustra reveals that he tempts his prospective auditors with some extraordinary "bait": "With my best bait I shall today lure the queerest human fish. My *happiness* I cast out far and wide . . . to see if many human fish might not learn to wriggle and wiggle from my happiness, until, biting at my sharp, hidden hooks, they must come up to *my* height." In part 4, Zarathustra has actually turned his initial problem of self-reference to his own advantage: he is now both fisherman *and* bait. Earlier in his pedagogical career, Zarathustra failed because he could do no more for his auditors than gesture darkly toward an uninstantiated ideal that he inconsistently described to them; as we recall, he too fell short of the prescribed ideal. At the midpoint of the text it became clear that if Zarathustra's auditors are to renounce their belief in God as the guarantor of human value, then simply to teach or to herald the *Übermensch*, as Zarathustra had done in parts 1-2, is inadequate. Rather than attempt to promote this ideal discursively, as he did in parts 1-2, Zarathustra now submits his own life as a concrete exemplification of it. In part 4, Zarathustra has in fact *become* the *Übermensch*, but *not* the *Übermensch* he originally heralded and inadvertently taught. The *Übermensch* is not he who transcends the human but he who embraces the human as it is: mortal, contingent, and tragic. As the *Übermensch*, Zarathustra no longer views the folly of his enterprise as an objection to it, for his teaching of virtue is now inseparable from his practical exemplification of virtue.

Zarathustra stakes his claim to authority by virtue of the freedom, power, and happiness evident in his own life. As an actual exemplar of *Übermenschlichkeit*, he claims for himself "only" the authority of his own limited perspective; as he reminds the "higher men" who seize his "bait," "I am a law only for my kind [*das Meinen*], I am no law for all." Yet in emphasizing his role as an *exemplar* of Nietzsche's ideal, Zarathustra does not necessarily forfeit his authority as a *teacher*, for his life now constitutes a kind of teaching that others can acquire through imitation and emulation. Zarathustra's newly won authority is secured not *internally*, by appeal to a priviledged standpoint, but *externally*, by appeal to the consensus of those "queer human fish" who voluntarily seek to cultivate the virtue he exemplifies as their own. Zarathustra's pedagogical authority now lies beyond his control and Nietzsche's as well.

Zarathustra's exemplification of *Übermenschlichkeit* thus transfers the onus of authority from his discourse to his practices in the world. Here Nietzsche's insight echoes that of Plato and Aristotle: to be a virtuous exemplar is to promote the virtue of others. By exemplifying the ideal that Nietzsche recommends, Zarathustra completes Nietzsche's teaching while minimizing the chances that Nietzsche might become yet another redeemer or god. To reinforce the dependence of "his" ideal on the authority of his readers, Nietzsche officially resigns his remaining narrative authority toward the end of the book and bequeaths to us Zarathustra, an admittedly fictional character whose own authority as a teacher extends no further than we voluntarily allow. By means of this "anonymous" reconstruction of the text, Nietzsche encourages/forces his readers to rely on their own limited, contingently constructed authority; "his" ideal must actually become their own, to the extent that his own authority is ultimately irrelevant. Nietzsche thus provides for the reconstruction of *Zarathustra* on the authority of his readers, as they progress toward *Übermenschlichkeit.*

Daniel W. Conway, "Nietzsche Contra Nietzsche: The Deconstruction of 'Zarathustra'," in Nietzsche as Postmodernist: Essays Pro and Contra, *edited by Clayton Koelb, The State University of New York Press, 1990, pp. 91-110.*

Clayton Koelb   (essay date 1990)

[*Koelb is an American critic and educator. His works include* Inventions of Reading: Rhetoric and the Literary Imagination *(1988) and* Kafka's Rhetoric: The Passion of Reading *(1989). In the following essay Koelb asserts that Nietzsche's insistence on the figurative origin of language reveals his basic philosophical method, whereby ideas are apprehended through a rhetorical manipulation of metaphors and double meanings rather than a purely conceptual logic "beyond" language.*]

There is a prima facie case to be made for Nietzsche's early and abiding interest in the rhetorical aspect of all discourse. Much of that case has already been made by Paul de Man in *Allegories of Reading* and has become widely known and frequently discussed. Because of de Man and others associated with the "new Nietzsche," who come mainly from France, many readers are now familiar with the formerly obscure little fragment **"On Truth and Lie in an Extra-moral Sense" ("Über Wahrheit und Lüge im aussermoralischen Sinn")** and its relation to Nietzsche's lecture notes on rhetoric made in the early 1870s. These documents give us a clear sense of Nietzsche's transition from philology to philosophy in the period from 1868 to 1876, when he was in effect working as both philosopher and professional philologist at the same time. Consideration of classical rhetoric as expounded by scholars such as Richard Volkmann and Gustav Gerber provided Nietzsche with important materials from which could be built a bridge between the study of language and the reexamination of some of philosophy's fundamental questions.

Section 3 of the lecture notes deals specifically with "The Relation of the Rhetorical to Language" and introduces the important notion that rhetoric cannot be identified with an artificial and unnatural supplement to "natural" language. What we call rhetoric, Nietzsche argues, is only a further development of a process already at work in all language:

> There is obviously no unrhetorical "naturalness" of language to which one could appeal; the language itself is the result of audible rhetorical arts. The power to discover and to make operative that which works and impresses, with respect to each thing, a power which Aristotle calls rhetoric, is, at the same time, the essence of language; the latter is based just as little as rhetoric is upon that which is true, upon the essence of things . . . The *tropes,* the non-literal significations, are considered to be the most artistic means of rhetoric. But, with respect to their meanings, all words are tropes in themselves, and from the beginning.

There is an obvious but important similarity between these notions and the position taken in **"On Truth and Lie"** about the nature of truth:

> What therefore is truth? A mobile army of metaphors, metonymies, anthropomorphisms: in short a sum of human relations which became poetically and rhetorically intensified, metamorphosed, adorned, and after long usage seems to a nation fixed, canonic, and binding; truths are illusions of which one has forgotten that they *are* illusions; worn-out metaphors which have become powerless to affect the senses; coins which have their obverse effaced and are no longer of account as coins but merely as metal.

These sentiments are well known and might seem to require little additional comment. It is worth noting, however, that Nietzsche makes sure that his own language here is itself highly rhetorical: the worn-out nature of the metaphors-become-truths is to be explained only metaphorically, by recourse to a figure which acts out the literal meaning of "worn-out." The text makes an effort to set forth the worn-out nature of the figurative expression "worn-out" by (paradoxically) revivifying it, by making its effaced literal import evident again. The illustrative image, in addition, pictures a process only rhetorically analogous to the one under discussion. From the standpoint of logic, the image of the coin depicts an action that tends in the opposite direction: instead of the tenor's effacing the vehicle, as in the metaphor "worn-out" and other worn-out metaphors, the vehicle of the coin is revealed by the effacement of its tenor. But rhetoric overwhelms logic by means of the play on the word *Bild,* which refers on the one hand to the "picture" stamped on the coin and on the other to the character of the trope as "image." Nietzsche tells us that these "coins" (worn-out metaphors) have "lost their quality as image," or in other words that they function no longer as representations but as things.

The rhetorical quality of this discourse about rhetoric is not merely witty and clever; it is a way of coming to terms with the consequences of the argument Nietzsche is making. Supposing that Nietzsche accepts his own conclusion that all discourse is metaphorical and that all truth is simply an unacknowledged catachresis, two principal reactions seem possible for the philosopher determined to pursue the truth. On the one hand, one might try to develop ways to circumvent language altogether and thus avoid its contaminating metaphoricity, or on the other hand, one might decide to join the forces one cannot beat and look to the resources of language itself for strategies by which one might subvert our tendency to accept as truth "the obligation to lie according to a fixed convention, to lie gregariously in a style binding for all." Nietzsche's reaction is never the former; often it is recognizably the latter; at other times, however, he appears to act as if he did not accept the conclusion of **"On Truth and Lie,"** to write as if language were a perfectly transparent medium, and to assume the pose of an authority untroubled by the rhetorical nature of his own discourse. Even the essay **"On Truth and Lie"** itself adopts this pose and even in the passage under discussion. It appears to be telling us the real truth about the truth (that it is a mobile army of metaphors) from a perspective that is somehow privileged. But that perspective undermines itself by relying so overtly on the process of figuration to make its point. Self-deconstructing propositions of this type are to be found relatively frequently in Nietzsche's writing and contribute importantly to his reputation as a literary writer.

The self-deconstructing Nietzsche is a figure that has already become familiar in one form or another over the past decade, and it is not my intention to paint that portrait again. While self-deconstruction is an important feature of Nietzsche's rhetorical style, it is not the aspect on which I want to focus attention now. I prefer to draw out a slightly different implication of the position taken in the lecture notes on rhetoric and in **"On Truth and Lie"** that focuses attention on its inventive rather than its subversive function in Nietzsche's philosophical project. That is what one might call, following Gregory Ulmer's extension of Derrida's term, the "grammatological" rather than the deconstructive turn in Nietzsche. If indeed all language (and thus all truth) is figurative and therefore subject to deconstruction, it offers the possibility of becoming an almost endlessly fertile source for philosophical thinking. If there is no distinction to be made between the figurative nature of even the most ordinary language and truth, then one way to think about "truth" in fresh ways would be to "let language do some thinking for us" by interrogating the figures themselves.

Interrogating them, however, would not mean attempting to discriminate between their "true" and "false" significations. Since all significations are the result of troping, according to **"On Truth and Lie,"** there is no way to carry out such a discrimination. It would have to mean accepting both the literal and figurative meanings as belonging to the same order—both, of course, figurative. While one point of view would see this leveling as destroying the value of both, Nietzsche often works on the assumption that all available meanings are equally useful. From this assumption comes a strategy for writing (in this case, writing a kind of philosophy) that derives from reading. The writer reads an already deconstructed language and from that reading forms a new discourse that actualizes both the literal and the figurative, both the assertion and its subversion. The discovery that all truth is nothing but figuration ceases to be an alarming or paralyzing problem for the philosopher; on the contrary, it opens up new space for investigation. Rhetoric, since Plato the thing that philoso-

phy has sought to purge from its midst, becomes the wellspring of philosophy.

Before pursuing this line any farther, I have to grant that Nietzsche seems to retain no small dose of ambivalence about a philosophy founded on rhetoric. This is evident enough in the direction taken by the argument in **"On Truth and Lie,"** where words like "dissimulation" (*Verstellung*) and "deception" (*Täuschung*) figure prominently. He even asks, rhetorically, whether language is "the adequate expression of all realities." The implication of such a vocabulary is that there exists some bedrock of reality which the metaphorical nature of speech hides from us. But does this bedrock of reality actually exist? There is no consistent answer to this question to be found in Nietzsche's writings. In the following sentence from **"On Truth and Lie,"** for example, it is impossible to determine the author's opinion on the subject under discussion: "The 'Thing-in-itself' (it is just this which would be the pure ineffective truth) is also quite incomprehensible to the creator of language and not worth making any great endeavor to obtain." We simply cannot tell whether the "creator of language" (*Sprachbildner*) has taken a proper or improper perspective in Nietzsche's eyes. Is the *Ding-an-sich* incomprehensible to the creator of language because of the shallowness of his own perception or because of the inconsequence of the notion of a Ding-an-sich, a truth which is "ineffective" (*folgenlos*)? There are explicit statements scattered through Nietzsche's works to support both views.

I do not propose to try to settle this perhaps unsettlable question. My interest in any case lies less with the issue of Nietzsche's "realism," if that is how one would want to put it, than with the way in which his assumptions about the pervasive and unavoidable metaphoricity of language, ambivalent though they were, became fruitful in his philosophical praxis. One thing we can say for certain is that the notions advanced in **"On Truth and Lie"** did not precipitate a paralyzing crisis in Nietzsche's own project of writing. He did not feel that his discourse was so contaminated by dissimulation and deception that there was no point in engaging in it. On the contrary, he wrote away with considerable zeal and with an apparent faith that writing was still very worthwhile, even at times "truthful." In aphorism 381 of **The Gay Science,** for example, Nietzsche excuses the brevity of his aphoristic style by claiming that "there are truths that are singularly shy and ticklish and cannot be caught except suddenly—that must be *surprised* or left alone." The implication is that Nietzsche has indeed surprised some of these shy "truths" (*Wahrheiten*) in the lightning flash of his writing.

It is fair enough, then, to say that Nietzsche's reaction to the conclusions reached through his study of rhetoric was not to shun rhetoric but to immerse himself in it. Nowhere is that decision more evident than in **The Gay Science** (1882), a work which in several ways announces itself as the marriage of philosophy and poetry. The epigraph to the first edition, slightly misquoted from Emerson, emphasizes the close relationship between the poet (*Dichter*) and the philosopher (*Weiser*). Emerson had included the saint in this brotherhood, but Nietzsche quietly deletes him. The confrontation of gaiety with science in the title not only suggests the importation of a lighter tone into philosophy but also refers quite directly to the "gaya scienza" of poetry itself. Nietzsche's book is to be both a work of *Wissenschaft,* [*science, knowledge*] as philosophy was supposed to be, and an example of the art of poetry. The book begins with a section in rhymes and, in the second edition, ends with another. It is an enterprise in which both joy and science are founded upon serious attention to language.

Nietzsche thought paying attention to language was worthwhile as part of the process of thinking. In the notes from the fall of 1881, for example, he writes down a number of wordplays or puns (*Wortspiele*) for possible use later. It is characteristic of Nietzsche that he would do so, but certainly not characteristic for the mainstream of philosophy in the nineteenth century (or—with the exception of those following in the Nietzschean tradition, such as Heidegger and Derrida—of the twentieth century either). Nietzsche has the kind of verbal imagination that sees, in the accidental, the interplay of signifiers, the impetus for thought. The shared syllable of *ridiculosus* and *cultura* suggests to him a shared quality, and he notes the possibility of the "*Ridicultur eines Menschen.*" He might have seen in this portmanteau word the occasion for satire directed against those whose notion of culture is so philistine as to be ridiculous, or he might have been thinking more positively of the potential for culture to emerge out of things that are laughable (such as the word *Ridicultur* itself). Whichever way Nietzsche might have thought to use the joke, it clearly belongs to the same project as the set of notes in which it is embedded.

The rhymes which open *The Gay Science* show Nietzsche attempting publicly to demonstrate the integration of a form of rhetorical or poetic invention into his philosophical discourse. He starts right off by using wordplay to explain the nature of his enterprise. The first piece of verse, **"Invitation"** (**"Einladung"**), plays on the two possible readings of *sieben,* one as the number "seven," the other as a deprecatory prefix:

> Wagt's mit meiner Kost, ihr Esser!
> Morgen schmeckt sie euch schon besser
> Und schon übermorgen gut!
> Wollt ihr dann noch mehr,—so machen
> Meine alten sieben Sachen
> Mir zu sieben neuen Muth.

> Take a chance and try my fare:
> It will grow on you, I swear;
> Soon it will taste good to you.
> If by then you should want more,
> All the things I've done before
> Will inspire things quite new.

Interestingly enough, this wordplay seems to repeat the sense of the Ridicultur joke in the notes. The locution *Siebensachen* refers to one's belongings in a belittling fashion: they are "odds and ends" or "trifles," as for example in Goethe's little poem comparing the "works of the masters" with his own poor Siebensachen. The *sieben* barely hangs onto its character as a number in this locution; the issue is not, after all, how many *Sachen* there are but rath-

er the perception that they are of no account. *Sieben* acts to put these things in their place by suggesting that they are few and paltry. The very same word, though, when used in the next line, works in just the opposite direction. It refers to an operation that adds rather than reduces value. By looking again at those Siebensachen, the reader (even when the reader is the author) can rediscover the augmentative power of the number seven embedded in the old text. Seven, after all, is a number of mystical power often associated with increase in the Bible and other canonical texts. The reader's stock of ideas increases in the very recognition of this possibility, and like Nietzsche, he or she is quickly in possession of fresh *Muth* (that is, "spirit" or "courage") for generating more and more ideas. One might even get "culture" out of this ridiculous stuff.

The notion of adding acts here as a metaphor for the results of reading (and rereading), as does eating or tasting earlier in the verse. The point of the poem is that what at first seems valueless can become valuable upon rereading. That is what the reader of *The Gay Science* is supposed to discover about this book, just as Nietzsche has discovered it about the word *sieben.* Nietzsche, though by no means a great poet, is an extremely skillful rhetorician. He not only preaches his point; he practices it in such a way as to drive home the doctrine being preached. We are not simply told that creative acts of interpretation can turn trifles into treasures; we are shown how the German language encourages just such a transformation of sieben. Even if the reader at first considers the book before him to be "indigestible" (one of Nietzsche's favorite metaphors), repeated reading will be able to make something of it. But the obligation and the responsibility rest, as they have since Plato, with the reader. The author cannot do the job for him.

This point is stressed in the twenty-third poem in the group, **"Interpretation"**:

> Leg ich mich aus, so leg ich mich hinein:
> Ich kann nicht selbst mein Interprete sein.
> Doch wer nun steigt auf seiner eignen Bahn,
> Trägt auch mein Bild zu hellerm Licht hinan.

> Interpreting myself, I always read
> Myself into my books. I clearly need
> Some help. But all who climb on their own way
> Carry my image, too, into the breaking day.

The equation between "sich auslegen" (interpret oneself) and "sich hineinlegen" (get oneself into trouble) is another paradoxical word-play. Since *ein* ("in") and *aus* ("out") are semantic opposites, the assertion that "sich hineinlegen" and "sich auslegen" are parts of the same process might come as a surprise, but since the locutions are so similar phonologically (the parallel structure "Leg ich mich . . . leg ich mich" emphasizes this point), the author's surprising conclusion seems justified. If self-interpretation on the part of the author can only get him into trouble, then, he must count on the reader to do the work of interpreting, even if that reader has no particular interest in advancing Nietzsche's project. It is interesting to compare this text with a slightly earlier version written in February 1882 and found in the *Nachlass.* The first line is the same, but the last three go in a somewhat different direction: "So mög ein Freund mein Interprete sein. / Und wenn er steigt auf seiner eignen Bahn, / Trägt er des Freundes Bild mit sich hinan." [So may a friend be my interpreter. / And should he climb on his own way, / He'll carry his friend's image onward with him.] In this version, written with a specific person in mind, Nietzsche presupposes that the interpreting other will be well disposed toward him. The relation between reader and author is that of friend and friend. This supposition is dropped from the published version. The context of the other poems of "Scherz, List, und Rache" makes clear that Nietzsche does not expect an audience necessarily friendly to him or to his project, especially since the material presented is not always easy to take. Poem 54, for example, admits that **The Gay Science** will need a reader with strong teeth and a strong stomach ("ein gut Gebiss und einen guten Magen") to consume what Nietzsche has to offer.

Even the unsympathetic reader, the one whom Nietzsche himself has put off with his "hardness" (*Härte*) and willingness to step on others to reach the heights, will be a better interpreter of Nietzsche than Nietzsche himself. There is a certain charming modesty about this, but we quickly realize that there is in fact not the slightest trace of self-deprecation in what Nietzsche is proposing. The protagonist of the poem may not be the author himself, but it does turn out to be his image (*Bild*). The goal of interpretation is to place the author's image (in both senses of "picture" and "trope") in a clearer light, and it is proposed that the reader is better equipped for that task than the author—even indeed when the reader is climbing along "his own way" and not necessarily Nietzsche's. Read my metaphors in whatever way you will, Nietzsche seems to be saying, as long as you keep reading them. That which is closest to me, my image, will emerge clearly in the process.

This notion that the reader can do the author's business while in fact attending strictly to his own is a particularly postmodern concept that goes somewhat, but not entirely, against the grain of the traditional imagery of reading invoked by Nietzsche himself in his **"Invitation."** The idea is traditional in that it still assumes that the reader's role is to take over from the author a burden the author is no longer in a position to assume, but it departs from the tradition in supposing that readerly independence, not subservience, will facilitate the transfer of the burden. In the Platonic formulation of the principal Western orthodoxy of reading, the author is understood as the parent of the text ("pater logou"), both progenitor of and absolute authority over his offspring; the reader is a kind of foster parent responsible to the wishes and intentions of the "father of the discourse," subservient to him in all matters pertaining to the welfare of the precious child. The goal of this fostering care could properly be described by Nietzsche's words, to carry the "image" of the author into the clear light of productive interpretation. This very traditional goal, however, is paradoxically alleged by Nietzsche to be most likely of attainment when the reader steadfastly pursues his own path without worrying about what path the author might have chosen.

This same idea is presented in the seventh poem, **"Vademecum—Vadetecum":**

> Es lockt dich meine Art und Sprach,
> Du folgest mir, du gehst mir nach?
> Geh nur dir selber treulich nach:—
> So folgst du mir—gemach! gemach!

> Lured by my style and tendency,
> you follow and come after me?
> Follow your self faithfully—
> take time—and thus you follow me.

The poem is concerned with *folgen* and *nachgehen* in their figurative senses of "comply with" and "inquire into" and thus once again with the issue of interpretation. Again the assertion is made that the proper method of inquiry into Nietzsche's writing is faithful investigation of the reader's self and that this act of self-examination will be the best way to imitate and obey (*folgen*) Nietzsche himself. This advice is at once both surprising and expected. It is very traditional in that it takes the Socratic position that the beginning of wisdom is self-knowledge, that to "follow" the philosopher is not so much to learn his doctrines as to obey the Delphic injunction to "know thyself." It is unexpected—and deliberately so—at the beginning of a volume so full of advice, warnings, precepts, and other forms of guidance. Nietzsche acknowledges that he is offering here a kind of guidebook, a vademecum for the philosophically inclined, but in the moment of acknowledging it he turns it against itself. The advice he gives here is that the best way of taking his advice is not to take anyone's advice but your own. Nietzsche evidently loved the logical involution implied by this game.

The gesture made by the text's rhetoric once again authorizes radical reinterpretation as the most valid mode of reading. We can read "vademecum" as "vadetecum" and vice versa, just as we could read "sich auslegen" as "sich hineinlegen" in poem 25. Nietzsche is showing us a method for rhetorical reading but at the same time is urging that we must ourselves take up this tool and not simply wait for Nietzsche to do it for us. It is Nietzsche's version of the traditional invitation "Tolle, lege" but with the notion of "reading" substantially revised.

Nietzsche is prepared to defend the value of incessant rereading even in the extreme case of rereading his own earlier readings. The thirty-sixth poem, **"Juvenalia"** (*"Jugendschriften"*) exemplifies the process:

> Meiner Weisheit A und O
> Klang mir hier: was hört' ich doch!
> Jetzo klingt mir's nicht mehr so,
> Nur das ew'ge Ah! und Oh!
> Meiner Jugend hör ich noch.

> My youthful wisdom's A and O
> I heard again. What did I hear?
> Words
> not of wisdom but of woe:
> Only the endless Ah and Oh
> Of youth lies heavy in
> my ear.

The commonplace German expression "das A und das O" ("the alpha and the omega") is regularly used to mean the sum total of something, even the "be-all and end-all." The clear implication of the poem is that the author did at one time think the sum total of his wisdom to be something grand, all-inclusive, and definitive. That interpretation comes under scrutiny when a now somewhat older Nietzsche looks back at his early writing and finds it "nicht mehr so," no longer what he once thought it was. The text is the same, but its meaning has radically changed. That change is cleverly exemplified in the rereading of the poem's own initial text, the phrase "A und O," now revealed as the semiarticulate cries of one whose feelings are more powerful than his means to express them. The transformation of "A und O" into "Ah! und Oh!" involves a dramatic change of signification with no change at all in the (oral) signifier. The change in the graphic signifier (the addition of *-h!*) is the mark of an alteration in perspective that both does and does not change the nature of the material interpreted. One could argue equally persuasively that there is no difference between the signifiers *A* and *Ah!*, *O* and *Oh!*, and that there is a huge difference; that is, one could take the point of view of a phonologically oriented linguist such as Saussure, or a graphically oriented grammatologist such as Derrida. The crucial thing here—which a Saussurian would be as quick to see as a Derridean—is the interplay of sameness and difference, in which the phonological samesness stands as a figure for a persisting, invariable text and graphic difference for the highly mutable act of reading.

The referential malleability of particular instances of discourse stands everywhere in these poems as a figure for the metaphoricity, and thus infinite interpretability, of all language, even of the whole world. Aphorism 374 in the body of the book (*Our new "infinite"*) makes explicit the presupposition inherent in the poems of "Scherz, List, und Rache":

> How far the perspective character of existence extends or indeed whether existence has any other character than this; whether existence without interpretation, without "sense," does not become "nonsense"; whether, on the other hand, all existence is not essentially actively engaged in *interpretation*—that cannot be decided even by the most industrious and most scrupulously conscientious analysis and self-examination of the intellect . . . Rather has the world become "infinite" for us all over again, inasmuch as we cannot reject the possibility that *it may include infinite interpretations.*

The world (Nietzsche uses *Welt* and *Dasein* interchangeably here) is analogized to a text of a certain sort. This is not the "book of the world" of the church fathers, a text whose form and meaning are ordained by God and whose legibility is guaranteed by God's perfection; this book is constantly reading itself and in that self-reading is making interpretive changes such as that from *A* to *Ah!*. The world, moreover, often reads itself in ways that testify to the absence of any guiding divine perfection: "Alas, too many *ungodly* possibilities of interpretation are included in the unknown, too much deviltry, stupidity, and foolishness of interpretation—even our own human, all too human folly, which we know."

But the poems of "Scherz, List, und Rache" demonstrate in their own way that even interpretation that is devilish or foolish has its uses. Nietzsche warns of his own deviltry

in poem 9, **"My Roses,"** in which he observes that, while his "happiness" (presumably the happiness of engaging in the gay science) wants to bring happiness to others ("es will beglücken"), it also has a special fondness for teasing (*Necken*) and malicious tricks (*Tücken*). Those who want to pick the roses of this philosopher will often prick their fingers on his thorns. Teasing and trickery are part of a method which retains the traditional aim of philosophy, to get to the bottom of things ("den Grund") but does not suppose that it can achieve that aim by means of research (*Forschung*):

> Ein Forscher ich? Oh spart diess Wort!—
> Ich bin nur *schwer*—so manche Pfund'!
> Ich Falle, falle immerfort
> Und endlich auf den Grund!
>
> A seeker, I? Oh, please be still!
> I'm merely *heavy*—weigh
> many a pound.
> I fall, and I keep falling till
> At last I reach the ground.

Walter Kaufmann makes a noble try at translating Nietzsche's wordplay by rendering the title **"Der Gründliche"** as **"The Thorough Who Get to the Bottom of Things,"** but even this laudable effort actually obscures the rhetoric of the original. The point of the poem is that one can be *gründlich* in the sense of getting to the bottom of things *without* being *gründlich* in the sense of thorough or rigorous—without, that is, being a *Forscher*. The title is revealed by the poem to be readable as both ironic and not ironic, since the denial of Gründlichkeit as a method is shown to in no way to prevent achievement of the *Grund,* the bottom of things.

The method proposed as Nietzsche's alternative to Forschung is cast in terms which will become very familiar to readers of **The Gay Science** and **Zarathustra** but is presented here with an almost dismissive comic casualness. The author proclaims that he is not thorough, he is merely *schwer* ("heavy" or "difficult" or "indigestible") and therefore keeps falling (or declining) until he reaches the ground. What makes him heavy and difficult is that he is full of *Pfunde*, but these "pounds" are things that add rhetorical weight, rhetorical Pfunde that are barely distinguishable from *Funde* ("discoveries"). The paronomasia Pfund'/Fund' is called for by the figurative context, since discoveries are far more likely than pounds to make a philosopher *schwer*. It is certainly this sort of intellectual "weightiness" that is at issue when the same vocabulary returns in a more sober guise much later in the book. Aphorism 341, the famous passage which Nietzsche considered the first announcement of the basic idea of **Zarathustra,** eternal recurrence, bears the title **"Das grösste Schwergewicht,"** again stressing the importance of being "weighty." And Aphorism 342, a passage almost identical to the opening section of **Zarathustra,** plays repeatedly on the term *untergehen,* a synonym of *fallen.* We can be sure that Nietzsche was very serious about *Schwergewicht* and *untergehen,* even if we harbor doubts about the seriousness of *schwer* and *fallen* in the poem **"Der Gründliche."** This is the devilish, foolish, unthorough method in operation, of course. That which is introduced as a teasing joke opens the way to something important: one falls, as it were, to the bottom of things by making jokes that are heavy and difficult. The process of falling to the philosophical ground is illustrated with particular consistency in the poems of "Scherz, List, und Rache" but is an important strategy in all of Nietzsche's writing. It is essentially a strategy of rhetorical reading, and it is plainly visible in a number of aphorisms in the main body of **The Gay Science.** Here the prose format makes no special pretension to literariness, but what we might regard as literary methods (because they are rhetorical) can be found as readily as in the rhymes. Nietzsche proceeds as if everyday language were a joyous *Wissenschaft* the power of which can be unlocked by an innovative act of reading. That is his method in **The Genealogy of Morals,** where he discovers *in language* the repressed relation between concepts of good and evil and facts of power, and this is his method in numerous aphorisms in **The Gay Science,** where wordplay and other forms of rhetorical reading play a significant role. His rumination on the role of deception in art, a passage that could have served as a program for Thomas Mann's entire literary career, concludes with a typically rhetorical, if somewhat misogynistic, discussion of the artistic nature of women. Women are actresses even in the act of love, he claims. One discovers "that they pretend even when they—give themselves" ("dass sie 'sich geben,' selbst noch, wenn sie—sich geben"). Nietzsche finds a way to actualize both the figurative and literal meanings of "sich geben" at once and to make that actualization the basis for an earnest discussion of a problem he considers to be philosophically important. The very same procedure is at work in no. 383, the last aphorism of the volume, in which he plays on the two senses of the word *Grillen* ("moping" and "crickets"): "Who will sing a song for us, a morning song, so sunny, so light, so fledged that it will *not* chase away the blues [*Grillen*] but invite them instead to join in the singing and dancing?" The blues are also a form of singing, as Kaufmann's translation cleverly reminds us.

This pun on *Grillen* appears in the context of a discussion of "the virtues of the right reader ['des rechten Lesens']—what forgotten and unknown virtues they are!" Right reading turns out to be exactly what our discussion of Nietzsche's rhetorical practice would lead us to think it is: a playful but radical rereading of the familiar. Nietzsche puts it as directly as could be at the end of number 382.:

> Another ideal runs ahead of us . . . : the ideal of a spirit who plays naively—that is, not deliberately but from overflowing power and abundance—with all that was hitherto called holy, good, untouchable, divine . . . ; the ideal of a human, superhuman well-being and benevolence that will often appear *inhuman*—for example, when it confronts all earthly seriousness so far, all solemnity in gesture, word, tone, eye, morality, and task so far, as if it were their most incarnate and involuntary parody—and in spite of all this, it is perhaps only with him that *great seriousness* really begins, that the real question mark is posed for the first time.

The fundamental Nietzschean project that he came to call the "transvaluation" or "revaluation of all values" ("Umwertung aller Werte") has as its other name "das rechte Lesen," right reading, and it is less a doctrine than a practice. While orthodox thinkers—or even some unorthodox ones such as Harold Bloom—might want to label this practice *mis*reading, Nietzsche is explicit in calling it right, correct, proper. It is a right and proper practice particularly because it refuses to exclude the naively playful as a necessary part of seriousness. The playful and the serious, the sad and the joyful, the blues and the crickets, all belong together. The kind of philosophy Nietzsche seeks is one which "die Grillen *nicht* verscheucht," that is, does not banish the blues, nor the crickets, nor caprices and whims (another figurative meaning of *Grillen*). These Grillen, one imagines, are most likely to be found among the roses mentioned in "Scherz, List, und Rache," those plants so full of tricks and teases, songs and caprices—the roses that stand as a figure for the aphorisms of **The Gay Science.**

Nietzsche's practice in **The Gay Science** has been very much in accord with the advice given in number 383 by the "spirits of my own book," as he calls them. He frequently calls upon the "Grillen" of the verbal imagination to stimulate his philosophical invention. He is not embarrassed to resort openly to some of the least revered forms of rhetorical whimsy, such as paronomasia. The pun on "Pfund'/Fund' " in **"Der Gründliche"** is a taste of things to come, as for example in number 310, which explicitly takes off from the phonological similarity of "Wille und Welle" ("will and wave"). Though not in verse, this aphorism is really in many ways more of a poem than any of the rhymes of "Scherz, List, und Rache." (One might recall also no. 22, "L'ordre du jour pour le roi," which is also essentially poetic in its mode of presentation.) It has a poetic quality because it presents and elaborates an image asking for interpretation rather than proposing a set of observations or opinions. But the image it presents—this elaborate personification of breakers on a beach—is given *as a reading* of the equation suggested by the paronomasia, the similarity of will and wave, and thus defines sharply the parameters of permissible interpretation. Everything that is said about the waves is to be understood as somehow applicable to the will: "Thus live waves—thus live we who will—more I shall not say."

Exactly this same paronomastic fancy shows itself elsewhere, as in number 371 ("We incomprehensible ones"), which depends on the interplay of *verwechseln, wechseln,* and *wachsen:* those who are incomprehensible are "misidentified" (*verwechselt*) precisely because "we ourselves keep growing [*wachsen*], keep changing [*wechseln*], we shed our old bark, we shed our skins every spring." The phonological relationship between the German words for "misidentify," and "change," and "grow" is not exploited here because of any supposedly genuine connection between language and something we might want to call reality; it is on the contrary an explicitly rhetorical device, a trick, a caprice. It is a way of acknowledging that Nietzsche's "truth" is no more exempt from contamination by metaphor than anyone else's. Furthermore, it announces that Nietzsche's method of philosophical discovery is a form of rhetorical *inventio* that is quite content to plunder the storehouse of available signifiers for all the ideas it will yield up.

The authorial persona reads the mother tongue as if he were a Cratylist and believed in some deep and essential connection between signifier and signified; as if, that is, the phonological similarity between *Wille* and *Welle* or *wachsen* and *wechseln* reflected a similarity existing at some "deeper" level. But the Cratylism of such passages must be understood as nothing more than a heuristic device, since we know from numerous declarations on the subject (**"On Truth and Lie"** among them) that Nietzsche was as skeptical as could be about language as a repository of truth. The truth that Nietzsche proposes to have found here is one of his own manufacture, reached by attending scrupulously to the *surface* of the linguistic sign. He embraces the relationships among signifiers, not because he believes they reflect the relationships obtaining among things-in-themselves, but because that is all he has to work with. Nietzsche is filled with what he calls the "consciousness of appearance":

> Appearance is for me that which lives and is effective and goes so far in its self-mocking that it makes me feel that this is appearance and will-o'-the-wisp and a dance of spirits and nothing more—that among all these dreamers, I, too, who "know," am dancing my dance; that the knower is a means for prolonging the earthly dance and thus belongs to the masters of ceremony of existence; and that the sublime consistence and interrelatedness of all knowledge perhaps is and will be the highest means to *preserve* the universality of dreaming and the mutual comprehension of all dreamers and thus also the *continuation of the dream.*

Fancies like the elaborate discourse on Wille/Welle can only be understood as belonging to the dance of a "knower" engaged in preserving the universality of dreaming. It is one of Nietzsche's ways to be, like the Greeks, "superficial—*out of profundity*" ("oberflächlich—*aus Tiefe*").

Nietzsche's inclination toward superficiality, his interest in exploiting the resources of language understood as surface, is matched by an equally strong urge toward depth. Being one of the "masters of ceremony of existence" requires something other than the kind of thoughtless assurance that goes with superficiality as we normally understand it. To be superficial out of profundity means to engage with the great sea of signifiers and to read it actively. You cannot be superficial in Nietzsche's sense by letting others read for you, by quietly accepting conventional interpretations as self-evidently correct. To let convention stand as truth—that is the surest way to be superficial out of superficiality. The great virtue of the artist/philosopher Nietzsche values so highly is that he is always active, always making his own readings, even rereading in a different way that which he had read before.

"Right reading" is thus an art whereby a particular human will engages the great, endlessly figurative body of language and makes his own sense of it. "The will to power *interprets*," and as Stanley Corngold observes, the Nietzschean self is nowhere more clearly in evidence than in its efforts at reading, including especially its attempts to read the self. The interaction between language, a system of tropes received essentially fully formed and belonging to the community, and the will, the individual human self that is for Nietzsche not only *a* "generative concept" but *the* generative concept par excellence. Everything of intellectual value arises out of this interaction, including that most fundamental of philosophical goods, knowledge. We see Nietzsche working on precisely this problem—in a typically rhetorical way—in aphorism number 355 of **The Gay Science,** where he seeks to explain "the origin of our concept of 'knowledge' ":

> I take this explanation from the street. I heard one of the common people say, "he knew me right away." Then I asked myself: What is it that the common people take for knowledge? What do they want when they want "knowledge"? Nothing more than this: Something strange is reduced to something familiar. And we philosophers—have we really meant *more* than this when we have spoken of knowledge?

How much this passage depends on the process of reading the German language is in part revealed by the text's lack of any point in the English translation. Kaufmann was forced to employ a series of footnotes to alert the reader to the play on various expressions formed out of the verb *kennen,* but to a reader with no German the crux of the matter would still remain mysterious. That crux is of course that what is known (*Erkenntnis*) is, for a German-speaker, only a variation on what is familiar ("das Bekannte"). In English, the relationship between knowledge and familiarity is entirely semantic, but in German it is phonological and morphological as well, suggesting a stronger and deeper affiliation. The verb *erkennen,* from which is formed the term German philosophers use for "knowledge" (*Erkenntnis*), has in its everyday usage the sense of "recognize." The sentence Kaufmann translates as "he knew me right away" can also be rendered as "he recognized me," with the attendant connotation of perceived familiarity (*recognize* is *re-cognize,* that is, *know again*). Nietzsche analyzes the sentence "er hat mich erkannt" as meaning the equivalent of something like "er hat das Bekannte an mir gesehen," an analysis that is perfectly reasonable for such a sentence spoken on the street. From there Nietzsche reasons that the people of the "Volk" understand knowledge to be the rediscovery of something already known rather than the discovery of "new" facts or relationships.

In his commentary on this passage, Kaufmann suggests that Nietzsche may have been thinking primarily of Hegel in suggesting that philosophers have often considered knowledge in this same way. It is just as likely, though, that he was thinking of Plato and the very ancient tradition that all knowledge is in fact nothing more than a recognition or remembering (as in the famous geometry lesson in the *Meno*). The truth (Greek *aletheia*) is that which is "un-forgotten." Nietzsche goes on to level a critique at such philosophers for thinking that the discovery of the familiar is the acquisition of knowledge ("was bekannt ist, ist erkannt"). The critique goes in a peculiarly Neitzschean direction, however, because Nietzsche is not entirely sure that "knowledge," in the sense of a fundamental grasping of something, really exists. The error of philosophers might not lie so much in taking up the common people's notion of knowledge-as-familiarity as in reformulating it in the high-sounding terms of epistemology.

Nietzsche understands "knowing" (*erkennen*) in a rather different way: for him it means "to see as a problem" ("als Problem zu sehen"), an approach that is hardest to take with something that is familiar. *Erkennen* would thus be most difficult in the case of "das Bekannte," the familiar. Nietzsche implies, though he does not explicitly say, that the philosopher's task must in part be to take what is familiar and to see it as a problem. How does one do that? How does one "defamiliarize" the familiar? I borrow the language of Russian Formalism here, not to imply any kinship between that movement and Nietzsche's work, but to suggest the fundamentally literary and rhetorical dimensions of the issue. The process of making the familiar problematic is precisely the process we have seen again and again in Nietzsche's practice of rhetorical rereading. What could be more familiar to us than the language of daily life, expressions like "er hat mich erkannt" or "Siebensachen" or "das A und das O"? It takes a special sort of imagination to see these commonplaces as problematic, an imagination that Nietzsche understands as belonging to both the poet and the philosopher. The mainstream of the Western intellectual tradition has tended to view this verbal mode of imagination as exclusively literary, however, and to regard as unorthodox those philosophers like Heidegger (particularly of the post-*Kehre* years), Derrida, and Nietzsche himself who embrace it openly. But philosophy, like literature, may not be in a position to free itself from the verbal imagination without suffering a crippling impoverishment. Nietzsche indicates exactly what form that impoverishment can take: the limitation of philosophical knowledge to a set of transformations of the unfamiliar into the familiar. Such a limitation, were it successful, would leave entirely to literature the most difficult and perhaps the most important intellectual task, that of seeing the familiar as a problem.

Clayton Koelb, "Reading as a Philosophical Strategy: Nietzsche's 'The Gay Science'," in Nietzsche as Postmodernist: Essays Pro and Contra, *edited by Clayton Koelb, The State University of New York Press, 1990, pp. 143-60.*

FURTHER READING

Biography

Gilman, Sander L., ed. *Conversations with Nietzsche: A Life in the Words of His Contemporaries.* Translated by David J. Parent. New York: Oxford University Press, 1987, 276 p.
> A compendium of reminiscences by personal acquaintances of Nietzsche.

Hayman, Ronald. *Nietzsche: A Critical Life.* 1980. Reprint. New York: Viking Penguin, 1982, 424 p.
> Authoritative critical biography.

Pletsch, Carl. *Young Nietzsche: Becoming a Genius.* New York: The Free Press, 1991, 261 p.

Biography of Nietzsche's formative years which views genius as a self-conscious, creative strategy for defining one's artistic or philosophical identity.

Criticism

Allen, Christine Garside. "Nietzsche's Ambivalence about Women." In *The Sexism of Social and Political Theory: Women and Reproduction from Plato to Nietzsche,* edited by Lorenne M.G. Clark and Lynda Lange, pp. 117-133. Toronto: University of Toronto Press, 1979.
> Critiques Nietzsche's misogynistic remarks. According to Allen, while Nietzsche admired the "Dionysian" qualities of women, his ambivalence towards them was stagnant and narrow-minded, rather than a means to deeper insight.

Allison, David B., ed. *The New Nietzsche: Contemporary Styles of Interpretation.* 1977. Reprint. Cambridge, Mass.: MIT Press, 1985, 274 p.
> Collection of essays which emphasizes poststructuralist, hermeneutic, and theological interpretations of Nietzsche. Contributors include Martin Heidegger, Jacques Derrida, and Gilles Deleuze.

Aschheim, Steven E. *The Nietzsche Legacy in Germany 1890-1990.* Berkeley: University of California Press, 1992, 337 p.
> Historical survey of Nietzsche's cultural and political legacy in Germany.

Asher, Kenneth. "Deconstruction's Use and Abuse of Nietzsche." *Telos* 62 (Winter 1984-85): 169-78.
> Contends that deconstruction's proponents have misappropriated and distorted Nietzsche's ideas about language and value.

Blondel, Eric. *Nietzsche: The Body and Culture.* Translated by Seán Hand. Stanford, Calif.: Stanford University Press, 1991, 353 p.
> Proposes an interpretation of Nietzsche which would strive to avoid metaphysical dualism and its denigration of the body as an object unworthy of philosophical consideration.

Bloom, Harold, ed. *Friedrich Nietzsche: Modern Critical Views.* New York: Chelsea House, 1987, 255 p.
> Collection of essays that examine Nietzsche's ideas about aesthetics, personal identity, and the entangled relations between philosophy and literature. Contributors include Maurice Blanchot, Paul de Man, and Richard Rorty.

Burgard, Peter, ed. *Nietzsche and the Feminine.* London: University Press of Virginia, 1994, 349 p.
> Collection of essays that debates the significance of Nietzsche's opinions about women and their relevance to contemporary feminist scholarship.

Camus, Albert. "Nietzsche and Nihilism." In his *The Rebel: An Essay on Man in Revolt,* pp. 65-80. New York: Alfred A. Knopf, 1957.
> Argues that Nietzsche's imperative to affirm existence in its totality ironically confines him to a nihilistic perspective, a stunted rebellion which merely inverts the errors of metaphysical thought.

Foucault, Michel. "Nietzsche, Genealogy, History." In his *Language, Counter-Memory, Practice,* pp. 139-164. Edited and translated by Donald F. Bouchard. Ithaca, N.Y.: Cornell University Press, 1977.

> Discusses Nietzsche's critique in *The Genealogy of Morals* of the traditional historian's search for original causes and the Nietzschean counter-project of "genealogical" inquiry.

Girard, René. "Dionysus versus the Crucified." *MLN* 99, No. 4 (September 1984): 816-35.

> Analyzes the sacrificial nature of the deaths of Dionysus and Christ and concludes that Nietzsche's famous dictum, "God is dead," far from symbolizing the modern decline of religious faith, actually signifies the birth of new deities from the collective murder of God.

Heidegger, Martin. *Nietzsche.* 4 vols. Translated by David Farrell Krell, Frank A. Capuzzi, and Joan Stambaugh. San Francisco: Harper & Row, 1979-87.

> A highly influential, much-cited study of the central themes of Nietzsche's philosophy, which Heidegger views as the culmination and end point of metaphysical thinking.

Hinman, Lawrence M. "Nietzsche, Metaphor, and Truth." *Philosophy and Phenomenology* XLIII, No. 2 (December 1982): 179-99.

> Assesses the validity of Nietzsche's claims that language and truth are derived exclusively from metaphor.

Jaspers, Karl. *Nietzsche: An Introduction to the Understanding of his Philosophical Activity.* 1965. Reprint. South Bend, Ind.: Regnery-Gateway, Inc., 1979, 496 p.

> Exhaustive interpretation of Nietzsche's philosophy as a precursor to existentialism.

Kaufmann, Walter. *Nietzsche: Philosopher, Psychologist, Antichrist.* Princeton, N.J.: Princeton University Press, 1950, 532 p.

> Thorough account of Nietzsche's philosophy by the principal translator of his works into English.

Koelb, Clayton, ed. *Nietzsche as Postmodernist: Essays Pro and Contra.* Albany, N.Y.: State University of New York Press, 1990, 350 p.

> Collection of essays which debate the question of whether Nietzsche's philosophy represents an incipient form of postmodernist discourse.

Lampert, Laurence. *Nietzsche's Teaching: An Interpretation of Thus Spoke Zarathustra.* London: Yale University Press, 1986, 378 p.

> Thorough analysis of *Thus Spoke Zarathustra* which cites the eternal return as the central theme of Nietzsche's book.

Marks, John. "Tracking Nietzsche." *The Georgia Review* XLVII, No. 2 (Summer 1993): 341-57.

> A colloquial account of the author's visit to Röcken, Germany, to look for Nietzsche's grave, mingled with reflections on the scope and meaning of Nietzsche's legacy in Germany.

Mencken, H. L. *Friedrich Nietzsche.* 1913. Reprint. London: Transaction Publishers, 1993, 304 p.

> Popular exposition of Nietzsche's philosophy by the famous American journalist and social critic, who regarded Nietzsche as a profound influence on his own ideas and a close intellectual kinsman.

Norris, Christopher. "Nietzsche, Philosophy and Deconstruction." In his *Deconstruction: Theory and Practice*, pp. 56-73. 1982. Reprint. London: Routledge, 1988.

> Explains how Nietzsche's philosophy represents a prototypical method of deconstruction, which Martin Heidegger and Jacques Derrida subsequently adopted in a more rigorous fashion.

Patton, Paul, ed. *Nietzsche, Feminism and Political Theory.* London: Routledge, 1993, 247 p.

> Collection of essays on the largely neglected question of Nietzsche's relevance to feminist and political theory.

Silk, M. S., and Stern, J. P. *Nietzsche on Tragedy.* London: Cambridge University Press, 1981, 441 p.

> Comprehensive study of *The Birth of Tragedy* which seeks to understand Nietzsche's first book in the contexts of classical philology in nineteenth-century Germany and Nietzsche's early interest in Arthur Schopenhauer and Richard Wagner.

Thiele, Leslie Paul. *Friedrich Nietzsche and the Politics of the Soul: A Study of Heroic Individualism.* Princeton, N. J.: Princeton University Press, 1990, 233 p.

> Cites such themes as the eternal return and the overman in support of his assertion that, for Nietzsche, the "primary task of life is held to be the heroic struggle of individuation."

Von der Luft, Eric. "Sources of Nietzsche's 'God Is Dead!' and Its Meaning for Heidegger." *Journal of the History of Ideas* 45, No. 2 (April- June 1984): 263-76.

> Examines the concept of the death of God in its traditional Christian sense of the two-day interim between Jesus' crucifixion and resurrection, as well as its more philosophical sense of the loss of transcendent value, as manifested in the works of Kant, Hegel, Kierkegaard, Nietzsche, and Heidegger.

Warren, Mark. *Nietzsche and Political Thought.* Cambridge, Mass.: MIT Press, 1988, 311 p.

> Assesses the significance of Nietzsche's philosophy for postmodern political theory, with particular emphasis on Nietzsche's conception of historical nihilism.

Zuckert, Catherine. "Nietzsche's Rereading of Plato." *Political Theory* 13, No. 2 (May 1985): 213-38.

> Considers the evolution of Nietzsche's varying opinions on Plato, whom Nietzsche viewed as a self-interested dissimulator whose conception of truth as the ideal is a highly politicized "mask" for his real philosophic activity.

Additional coverage of Nietzsche's life and career is contained in the following sources published by Gale Research: *Contemporary Authors,* **Vols. 107, 121;** *Dictionary of Literary Biography,* **Vol. 129; and** *Twentieth Century Literary Criticism,* **Vols. 10, 18.**

Mrs. Humphry Ward

1851-1920

(Born Mary Augusta Arnold) English novelist, nonfiction writer, and autobiographer.

INTRODUCTION

Ward was a popular and prolific novelist who is closely identified with the Victorian era in English life and literature. In her numerous novels she examined the social and moral issues that occupied Victorian readers, including women's role in society and the clash between science and evangelical theology. A dominant figure in late-Victorian public life who was known as much for her political activism and philanthropic activities as for her novels, Ward is chiefly remembered for providing a literary record of the intellectual life of England during a period when many long-held social values and public policies were being challenged.

Biographical Information

Ward was the granddaughter of Thomas Arnold, the influential headmaster of Rugby School, and the niece of the poet and essayist Matthew Arnold. Her father, also named Thomas Arnold, moved to New Zealand in 1847 and later accepted a position as a school inspector in Tasmania, where he married Julia Sorrell and where Ward was born in 1851. Ward's father resigned his post in 1856 after his religious conversion to Roman Catholicism and moved his family to England. Ward attended a series of boarding schools and joined her family in Oxford in 1865, when her father became a tutor there during a temporary return to Protestantism. In Oxford, Ward pursued independent studies, particularly in Spanish history, and later contributed sketches on that subject to a biographical reference work. Through her family Ward became acquainted with leading intellectuals and philosophers at Oxford University, among them Walter Pater, Mark Pattison, and T. H. Green. In 1872 she married Thomas Humphry Ward, an academic, and subsequently moved with him to London. During the 1870s Ward contributed articles on literature and history to such periodicals as *Macmillan's,* the *Saturday Review,* and the *Pall Mall Gazette* and began her prolific career as a novelist with the publication of *Miss Bretherton* in 1884. In addition to writing, Ward devoted much of her time to volunteer work and helped to found the Passmore Edwards Settlement, later renamed in her honor, a social aid facility that provided vocational training, child-care assistance, and social activities for the poor in London's Bloomsbury district. She headed the Women's Anti-Suffrage League in opposing the right of women to vote, believing that women's influence in political matters could be better achieved through alternate means. During the First World War, Ward championed

the British cause in journalistic writings and in 1918 published her autobiography. She died in 1920.

Major Works

Ward's works largely comprise moralistic considerations of various issues that engaged Victorian society. Her most famous novel, *Robert Elsmere*, details the theological crisis of an Anglican clergyman who renounces his faith and devotes himself to performing charitable works. In the story Elsmere is plagued by doubts regarding the miraculous underpinnings of Christian doctrine and finally settles on a simplified version of Christianity that rejects Christ's divinity. Elsmere resigns his country parish and moves to London, where he establishes a new church and begins offering assistance to the neighborhood poor. Often viewed as an attack on evangelical Christianity, *Robert Elsmere* typifies Ward's works in that it promotes spiritual independence and social improvement at the expense of traditional religious institutions and beliefs. Religious questions provided the basis for such later novels as *Helbeck of Bannisdale* (1898), in which a Roman Catholic faces a crisis of faith when he falls in love with a skeptic, and *The Case of Richard Meynell* (1911), a sequel to *Robert El-*

smere. Other novels combine romantic interest with questions of political or social reform, including women's suffrage and concepts of feminine duty. Ward also wrote a number of works based on historic characters, notably *The Marriage of William Ashe* (1905), which was inspired by the affair of Lord Byron with Lady Caroline Lamb. During the First World War, Ward undertook a series of articles at the request of Theodore Roosevelt that were later collected and published as *England's Effort* (1916), *Towards the Goal* (1917), and *Fields of Victory* (1919).

Critical Reception

Robert Elsmere created a sensation following a review by former prime minister William Gladstone in 1888, and Ward subsequently enjoyed great popular success. Victorian critics often challenged Ward's theoretical assumptions and arguments, but readers responded favorably to the combination of intellectual instruction, moral seriousness, and romantic appeal in her novels. As social attitudes and concerns changed in the Edwardian and Georgian eras of the early twentieth century, Ward's works were sharply criticized as didactic thesis novels displaying stereotypical characterizations and lacking humor. By the end of World War I, her works were generally considered anachronistic, their conservative moral code seeming remote from the preoccupations of postwar society. Her works remained little discussed and little read until the 1970s, when critics rediscovered in Ward's novels valuable documentary evidence of the intellectual life of Victorian England.

PRINCIPAL WORKS

Miss Bretherton (novel) 1884
Robert Elsmere (novel) 1888
The History of David Grieve (novel) 1892
Marcella (novel) 1894
The Story of Bessie Costrell (novel) 1895
Sir George Tressady (novel) 1896
Helbeck of Bannisdale (novel) 1898
Eleanor (novel) 1900
Lady Rose's Daughter (novel) 1903
The Marriage of William Ashe (novel) 1905
Fenwick's Career (novel) 1906
The Testing of Diana Mallory (novel) 1908
Daphne; or, Marriage à la Mode (novel) 1909
Canadian Born (novel) 1910
The Case of Richard Meynell (novel) 1911
The Coryston Family (novel) 1913
The Mating of Lydia (novel) 1913
Delia Blanchflower (novel) 1915
Eltham House (novel) 1915
England's Effort (nonfiction) 1916
A Great Success (novel) 1916
Lady Connie (novel) 1916
Missing (novel) 1917
Towards the Goal (nonfiction) 1917
The War and Elizabeth (novel) 1918
A Writer's Recollections (autobiography) 1918

Cousin Philip (novel) 1919
Fields of Victory (nonfiction) 1919
Harvest (novel) 1920

CRITICISM

W. E. Gladstone   (essay date 1888)

[*Gladstone was a prominent English statesman and author who served four times as Prime Minister and wrote numerous learned essays on such diverse subjects as politics, theology, classical history, and literature. In his literary criticism, Gladstone often uses criteria based on his deep commitments to Christian religious and moral beliefs to judge the plausibility of characters or actions. In the following excerpt from his influential, favorable review of* Robert Elsmere, *Gladstone challenges theological issues presented in the novel.*]

Human nature, when aggrieved, is apt and quick in devising compensations. The increasing seriousness and strain of our present life may have had the effect of bringing about the large preference, which I understand to be exhibited in local public libraries, for works of fiction. This is the first expedient of revenge. But it is only a link in a chain. The next step is, that the writers of what might be grave books, *in esse* or *in posse,* have endeavoured with some success to circumvent the multitude. Those who have systems or hypotheses to recommend in philosophy, conduct, or religion induct them into the costume of romance. Such was the second expedient of nature, the counterstroke of her revenge. When this was done in *Télémaque, Rasselas,* or *Coelebs,* it was not without literary effect. Even the last of these three appears to have been successful with its own generation. It would now be deemed intolerably dull. But a dull book is easily renounced. The more didactic fictions of the present day, so far as I know them, are not dull. We take them up, however, and we find that, when we meant to go to play, we have gone to school. The romance is a gospel of some philosophy, or of some religion; and requires sustained thought on many or some of the deepest subjects, as the only rational alternative to placing ourselves at the mercy of our author. We find that he has put upon us what is not indeed a treatise, but more formidable than if it were. For a treatise must nowhere beg the question it seeks to decide, but must carry its reader onwards by reasoning patiently from step to step. But the writer of the romance, under the convenient necessity which his form imposes, skips in thought, over undefined distances, from stage to stage, as a bee from flower to flower. A creed may (as here) be accepted in a sentence, and then abandoned in a page. But we the common herd of readers, if we are to deal with the consequences, to accept or repel the influence of the book, must, as in a problem of mathematics, supply the missing steps. Thus, in perusing as we ought a propagandist romance, we must terribly increase the pace; and it is the pace that kills.

Among the works to which the preceding remarks might apply, the most remarkable within my knowledge is **Robert Elsmere.** It is indeed remarkable in many respects. It is a novel of nearly twice the length, and much more than twice the matter, of ordinary novels. It dispenses almost entirely, in the construction of what must still be called its plot, with the aid of incident in the ordinary sense. We have indeed near the close a solitary individual crushed by a waggon, but this catastrophe has no relation to the plot, and its only purpose is to exhibit a good deathbed in illustration of the great missionary idea of the piece. The *nexus* of the structure is to be found wholly in the workings of character. The assumption and the surrender of a Rectory are the most salient events, and they are simple results of what the actor has thought right. And yet the great, nay, paramount function of character-drawing, the projection upon the canvas of human beings endowed with the true forces of nature and vitality, does not appear to be by any means the master-gift of the authoress. In the mass of matter which she has prodigally expended there might obviously be retrenchment; for there are certain laws of dimension which apply to a novel, and which separate it from an epic. In the extraordinary number of personages brought upon the stage in one portion or other of the book, there are some which are elaborated with greater pains and more detail, than their relative importance seems to warrant. **Robert Elsmere** is hard reading, and requires toil and effort. Yet, if it be difficult to persist, it is impossible to stop. The prisoner on the treadmill must work severely to perform his task: but if he stops he at once receives a blow which brings him to his senses. Here, as there, it is human infirmity which shrinks; but here, as not there, the propelling motive is within. Deliberate judgment and deep interest alike rebuke a fainting reader. The strength of the book, overbearing every obstacle, seems to lie in an extraordinary wealth of diction, never separated from thought; in a close and searching faculty of social observation; in generous appreciation of what is morally good, impartially exhibited in all directions: above all in the sense of mission with which the writer is evidently possessed, and in the earnestness and persistency of purpose with which through every page and line it is pursued. The book is eminently an offspring of the time, and will probably make a deep or at least a very sensible impression; not, however, among mere novel-readers, but among those who share, in whatever sense, the deeper thought of the period.

The action begins in a Westmoreland valley, where the three young daughters of a pious clergyman are grouped around a mother infirm in health and without force of mind. All responsibility devolves accordingly upon Catherine, the eldest of the three; a noble character, living only for duty and affection. When the ear heard her, then it blessed her; and when the eye saw her, it gave witness to her. Here comes upon the scene Robert Elsmere, the eponymist and hero of the book, and the ideal, almost the idol, of the authoress.

He had been brought up at Oxford, in years when the wholesale discomfiture of the great religious movement in the University, which followed upon the secession of Cardinal Newman, had been in its turn succeeded by a new religious reaction. The youth had been open to the personal influences of a tutor, who is in the highest degree beautiful, classical, and indifferentist; and of a noble-minded ra-

tionalising teacher, whose name, Mr. Grey, is the thin disguise of another name, and whose lofty character, together with his gifts, and with the tendencies of the time, had made him a power in Oxford. But, in its action on a nature of devout susceptibilities as well as active talents, the place is stronger than the man, and Robert casts in his lot with the ministry of the Church. Let us stop at this point to notice the terms used. At St. Mary's 'the sight and the experience touched his inmost feeling, and satisfied all the poetical and dramatic instincts of a passionate nature.' He 'carried his religious passion . . . into the service of the great positive tradition around him.' This great, and commonly life-governing decision, is taken under the influence of forces wholly emotional. It is first after the step taken that we have an inkling of any reason for it. This is not an isolated phenomenon. It is a key to the entire action. The work may be summed up in this way: it represents a battle between intellect and emotion. Of right, intellect wins; and, having won, enlists emotion in its service.

Elsmere breaks upon us in Westmoreland, prepared to make the great commission the business of his life, and to spend and be spent in it to the uttermost. He is at once attracted by Catherine; attention forthwith ripens into love; and love finds expression in a proposal. But, with a less educated intelligence, the girl has a purpose of life not less determined than the youth. She believes herself to have an outdoor vocation in the glen, and above all an indoor vocation in her family, of which she is the single prop. A long battle of love ensues, fought out with not less ability, and with even greater tenacity, than the remarkable conflict of intellects, carried on by correspondence, which ended in the marriage between Mr. and Mrs. Carlyle. The resolute tension of the two minds has many phases; and a double crisis, first of refusal, secondly of acceptance. This part of the narrative, wrought out in detail with singular skill, will probably be deemed the most successful, the most normal, of the whole. It is thoroughly noble on both sides. The final surrender of Catherine is in truth an opening of the eyes to a wider view of the evolution of the individual, and of the great vocation of life; and it involves no disparagement. The garrison evacuates the citadel, but its arms have not been laid down, and its colours are flying still.

So the pair settle themselves in a family living, full of the enthusiasm of humanity, which is developed with high energy in every practical detail, and based upon the following of the Incarnate Saviour. Equipped thus far with all that renders life desirable, their union is blessed by the birth of a daughter, and everything thrives around them for the formation of an ideal parish.

But the parish is adorned by a noble old English mansion, and the mansion inhabited by a wealthy Squire, who knows little of duty, but is devoted to incessant study. As an impersonated intellect, he is abreast of all modern inquiry, and, a 'Tractarian' in his youth, he has long abandoned all belief. At the outset, he resents profoundly the Rector's obtrusive concern for his neglected tenantry. But the courage of the clergyman is not to be damped by isolation, and in the case of a scandalously insanitary hamlet, after an adequate number of deaths, Mr. Wendover puts aside the screen called his agent, and rebuilds with an ample generosity. This sudden and complete surrender seems to be introduced to glorify the hero of the work, for it does not indicate any permanent change in the social ideas of Mr. Wendover, but only in his relations to his clergyman.

There is, however, made ready for him a superlative revenge. Robert has enjoyed the use of his rich library, and the two hold literary communications, but with a compact of silence on matters of belief. This treaty is honourably observed by the Squire. But the clergyman invites his fate. Mr. Wendover makes known to him a great design for a 'History of Testimony,' worked out through many centuries. The book speaks indeed of 'the long wrestle' of the two men, and the like. But of Elsmere's wrestling there is no other trace or sign. What weapons the Rector wielded for his faith, what strokes he struck, has not even in a single line been recorded. The discourse of the Squire points out that theologians are men who decline to examine evidence, that miracles are the invention of credulous ages, that the preconceptions sufficiently explain the results. He wins in a canter. There cannot surely be a more curious contrast than that between the real battle, fought in a hundred rounds, between Elsmere and Catherine on marriage, and the fictitious battle between Elsmere and the Squire on the subject of religion, where the one side is a paean, and the other a blank. A great creed, with the testimony of eighteen centuries at its back, cannot find an articulate word to say in its defence, and the downfall of the scheme of belief shatters also, and of right, the highly ordered scheme of life that had nestled in the Rectory of Murewell, as it still does in thousands of other English parsonages.

It is notable that Elsmere seeks, in this conflict with the Squire, no aid or counsel whatever. He encounters indeed by chance Mr. Newcome, a Ritualistic clergyman, whom the generous sympathies of the authoress place upon the roll of his friends. But the language of Mr. Newcome offers no help to his understanding. It is this: —

> Trample on yourself. Pray down the demon, fast, scourge, kill the body, that the soul may live. What are we miserable worms, that we should defy the Most High, that we should set our wretched faculties against His Omnipotence?

Mr. Newcome appears everywhere as not only a respectable but a remarkable character. But as to what he says here, how much does it amount to? Considered as a medicine for a mind diseased, for an unsettled, dislocated soul, is it less or more than pure nonsense? In the work of an insidious non-believer, it would be set down as part of his fraud. Mrs. Ward evidently gives it in absolute good faith. It is one in a series of indications, by which this gifted authoress conveys to us what appears to be her thoroughly genuine belief that historical Christianity has, indeed, broad grounds and deep roots in emotion, but in reason none whatever.

The revelation to the wife is terrible; but Catherine clings to her religion on a basis essentially akin to that of Newcome; and the faith of these eighteen centuries, and of the prime countries of the world,

> Bella, immortal, benefica
> Fede, ai trionfi avvezza,
> [Manzoni, *Cinque Maggio.*]

is dismissed without a hearing.

For my own part, I humbly retort on Robert Elsmere. Considered intellectually, his proceedings in regard to belief appear to me, from the beginning as well as in the downward process, to present dismal gaps. But the emotional part of his character is complete, nay redundant. There is no moral weakness or hesitation. There rises up before him the noble maxim, assigned to the so-called Mr. Grey (with whom he has a consultation of foregone conclusions), 'Conviction is the conscience of the mind.'

He renounces his parish and his orders. He still believes in God, and accepts the historical Christ as a wonderful man, good among the good, but a *primus inter pares.* Passing through a variety of stages, he devotes himself to the religion of humanity; reconciles to the new gospel, by shoals, skilled artisans of London who had been totally inaccessible to the old one; and nobly kills himself with overwork, passing away in a final flood of light. He founds and leaves behind him the 'New Christian Brotherhood' of Elgood Street; and we are at the close apprised, with enthusiastic sincerity, that this is the true effort of the race, and

> Others I doubt not, if not we,
> The issue of our toils shall see.

Who can grudge to this absolutely pure-minded and very distinguished writer the comfort of having at last found the true specific for the evils and miseries of the world? None surely who bear in mind that the Salvation Army has been known to proclaim itself the Church of the future, or who happen to know that Bunsen, when in 1841 he had procured the foundation of the bishopric of Jerusalem, suggested in private correspondence his hope that this might be the Church which would meet the glorified Redeemer at His coming.

It is necessary here to revert to the Squire. Himself the $\mu o \iota \rho \alpha \ \pi \epsilon \pi \rho \omega \mu \epsilon \nu \eta$, the supreme arbiter of destinies in the book, he is somewhat unkindly treated; his mind at length gives way, and a darkling veil is drawn over the close. Here seems to be a little literary intolerance, something even savouring of a religious test. Robert Elsmere stopped in the downward slide at theism, and it calms and glorifies his deathbed. But the Squire had not stopped there. He had said to Elsmere, 'You are playing into the hands of the Blacks. All this theistic philosophy of yours only means so much grist to their mill in the end.' But the great guide is dismissed from his guiding office as summarily as all other processes are conducted, which are required by the purpose of the writer. Art everywhere gives way to purpose. Elsmere no more shows cause for his theism than he had shown it against his Christianity. Why was not Mr. Wendover allowed at least the consolations which gave a satisfaction to David Hume?

Not yet, however, may I wholly part from this sketch of the work. It is so large that much must be omitted. But there is one limb of the plan which is peculiar. Of the two sisters not yet named, one, Agnes by name, appears only as quasi-chaperon or as 'dummie.' But Rose, the third, has beauty, the gift of a musical artist, and quick and plastic social faculties. Long and elaborate love relations are developed between her and the *poco-curante* tutor and friend, Mr. Langham. Twice she is fairly embarked in passion for him, and twice he jilts her. Still she is not discouraged, and she finally marries a certain Flaxman, an amiable but somewhat manufactured character. From the standing point of art, can this portion of the book fail to stir much misgiving? We know from Shakespeare how the loves of two sisters can be comprised within a single play. But while the drama requires only one connected action, the novel, and eminently this novel, aims rather at the exhibition of a life: and the reader of these volumes may be apt to say that in working two such lives, as those of Catherine and Rose, through so many stages, the authoress has departed from previous example, and has loaded her ship, though a gallant one, with more cargo than it will bear.

It may indeed be that Mrs. Ward has been led to charge her tale with such a weight of matter from a desire to give philosophical completeness to her representation of the main springs of action which mark the life of the period. For in Robert Elsmere we have the tempered but aggressive action of the sceptical intellect; in Catherine the strong reaction against it; in Rose the art-life; and in Langham the literary and cultivated indifference of the time. The comprehensiveness of such a picture may be admitted, without withdrawing the objection that, as a practical result, the cargo is too heavy for the vessel.

Apart from this question, is it possible to pass without a protest the double jilt? Was Rose, with her quick and self-centred life, a well-chosen *corpus vile* upon whom to pass this experiment? More broadly, though credible perhaps for a man, is such a process in any case possible by the laws of art for a woman? Does she not violate the first conditions of her nature in exposing herself to so piercing an insult? An enhancement of delicate self-respect is one among the compensations, which Providence has supplied in woman, to make up for a deficiency in some ruder kinds of strength.

Again, I appeal to the laws of art against the final disposal of Catherine. Having much less of ability than her husband, she is really drawn with greater force and truth; and possesses so firm a fibre that when, having been bred in a school of some intolerance, she begins to blunt the edge of her resistance, and to tolerate in divers ways, without adopting, the denuded system of her husband, we begin to feel that the key-note of her character is being tampered with. After his death, the discords become egregious. She remains, as she supposes, orthodox and tenaciously Evangelical. But every knee must be made to bow to Elsmere. So she does not return to the northern valley and her mother's declining age, but in London devotes her weekdays to carrying on the institutions of charity he had founded on behalf of his new religion. He had himself indignantly remonstrated with some supposed clergyman, who, in the guise of a Broad Churchman, at once held Elsmere's creed and discharged externally the office of an Anglican priest. He therefore certainly is not responsible for having taught her to believe the chasm between them was a narrow one. Yet she leaps or steps across it every

Sunday, attending her church in the forenoon, and looming as regularly every afternoon in the temple of the New Brotherhood. Here surely the claims of system have marred the work of art. Characters might have been devised whom this see-saw would have suited well enough; but for the Catherine of the first volume it is an unmitigated solecism; a dismal, if not even a degrading compromise.

It has been observed that the women of the book are generally drawn with more felicity than the men. As a work of art, Rose is in my view the most successful of the women, and among the men the Squire. With the Squire Mrs. Ward is not in sympathy, for he destroys too much, and he does nothing but destroy. She cannot be in sympathy with Rose; for Rose, who is selfishly and heartlessly used, is herself selfish and heartless; with this aggravation, that she has grown up in immediate contact with a noble elder sister, and yet has not caught a particle of nobleness, as well as in view of an infirm mother to whom she scarcely gives a care. On the other hand, in her Robert, who has all Mrs. Ward's affection and almost her worship, and who is clothed with a perfect panoply of high qualities, she appears to be less successful and more artificial. In the recently published correspondence of Sir Henry Taylor, who was by no means given to paradox, we are told that great earnestness of purpose and strong adhesive sympathies in an author are adverse to the freedom and independence of treatment, the disembarrassed movement of the creative hand, which are required in the supreme poetic office of projecting character on the canvas. If there be truth in this novel and interesting suggestion, we cannot wonder at finding the result exhibited in **Robert Elsmere,** for never was a book written with greater persistency and intensity of purpose. Every page of its principal narrative is adapted and addressed by Mrs. Ward to the final aim which is bone of her bone and flesh of her flesh. This aim is to expel the preternatural element from Christianity, to destroy its dogmatic structure, yet to keep intact the moral and spiritual results. The Brotherhood presented to us with such sanguine hopefulness is a 'Christian' brotherhood, but with a Christianity emptied of that which Christians believe to be the soul and springhead of its life. For Christianity, in the established Christian sense, is the presentation to us not of abstract dogmas for acceptance, but of a living and a Divine Person, to whom they are to be united by a vital incorporation. It is the reunion to God of a nature severed from God by sin, and the process is one, not of teaching lessons, but of imparting a new life, with its ordained equipment of gifts and powers.

It is I apprehend a complete mistake to suppose, as appears to be the supposition of this remarkable book, that all which has to be done with Scripture, in order to effect the desired transformation of religion, is to eliminate from it the miraculous element. Tremendous as is the sweeping process which extrudes the Resurrection, there is much else, which is in no sense miraculous, to extrude along with it. The Procession of Palms, for example, is indeed profoundly significant, but it is in no way miraculous. Yet, in any consistent history of a Robert Elsmere's Christ, there could be no Procession of Palms. Unless it be the healing of the ear of Malchus, there is not a miraculous event between the commencement of the Passion and the

Crucifixion itself. Yet the notes of a superhuman majesty overspread the whole. We talk of all religions as essentially one; but what religion presents to its votaries such a tale as this? Bishop Temple, in his sermons at Rugby, has been among the later teachers who have shown how the whole behaviour of our Lord, in this extremity of His abasement, seems more than ever to transcend all human limits, and to exhibit without arguing His Divinity. The parables, again, are not less refractory than the miracles, and must disappear along with them: for what parables are there which are not built upon the idea of His unique and transcendant office? The Gospel of Saint John has much less of miracle than the Synoptics; but it must of course descend from its pedestal, in all that is most its own. And what is gained by all this condemnation, until we get rid of the Baptismal formula? It is a question not of excision from the gospels, but of tearing them into shreds. Far be it from me to deny that the parts which remain, or which remain legible, are vital parts; but this is no more than to say that there may remain vital organs of a man, after the man himself has been cut in pieces.

I have neither space nor capacity at command for the adequate discussion of the questions, which shattered the faith of Robert Elsmere: whether miracles can happen, and whether 'an universal preconception' in their favour at the birth of Christianity 'governing the work of all men of all schools,' adequately accounts for the place which has been given to them in the New Testament, as available proofs of the Divine Mission of our Lord. But I demur on all the points to the authority of the Squire, and even of Mr. Grey.

The impossibility of miracle is a doctrine which appears to claim for its basis the results of physical inquiry. They point to unbroken sequences in material nature, and refer every phenomenon to its immediate antecedent as adequate to its orderly production. But the appeal to these great achievements of our time is itself disorderly, for it calls upon natural science to decide a question which lies beyond its precinct. There is an extraneous force of will which acts upon matter in derogation of laws purely physical, or alters the balance of those laws among themselves. It can be neither philosophical nor scientific to proclaim the impossibility of miracle, until philosophy or science shall have determined a limit, beyond which this extraneous force of will, so familiar to our experience, cannot act upon or deflect the natural order.

Next, as to that avidity for miracle, which is supposed by the omniscient Squire to account for the invention of it. Let it be granted, for argument's sake, that if the Gospel had been intended only for the Jews, they at least were open to the imputation of a biassing and blinding appetite for signs and wonders. But scarcely had the Christian scheme been established among the Jews, when it began to take root among the Gentiles. It will hardly be contended that these Gentiles, who detested and despised the Jewish race, had any predisposition to receive a religion at their hands or upon their authority. Were they then, during the century which succeeded our Lord's birth, so swayed by a devouring thirst for the supernatural as to account for the early reception, and the steady if not rapid growth, of the Christian creed among them? The statement of the Squire, which carries Robert Elsmere, is that the preconception in favour of miracles at the period 'governed the work of all men of all schools.' A most gross and palpable exaggeration. In philosophy the Epicurean school was atheistic, the Stoic school was ambiguously theistic, and doubt nestled in the Academy. Christianity had little direct contact with these schools, but they acted on the tone of thought, in a manner not favourable but adverse to the preconception.

Meantime the power of religion was in decay. The springs of it in the general mind and heart were weakened. A deluge of profligacy had gone far to destroy, at Rome, even the external habit of public worship; and Horace, himself an indifferentist, denounces the neglect and squalor of the temples; while further on we have the stern and emphatic testimony of Juvenal: —

> Esse aliquid Manes, et subterranea regna,
> Et contum, et Stygio ranas in gurgite nigras,
> Nec pueri credunt, nisi qui nondum aere lavantur.

The age was not an age of faith, among thinking and ruling classes, either in natural or in supernatural religion. There had been indeed a wonderful 'evangelical preparation' in the sway of the Greek language, in the unifying power of the Roman State and Empire, and in the utter moral failure of the grand and dominant civilisations; but not in any virgin soil, yearning for the sun, the rain, or the seed of truth.

But the Squire, treading in the footprints of Gibbon's fifteenth Chapter, leaves it to be understood that, in the appeal to the supernatural, the new religion enjoyed an exclusive as well as an overpowering advantage; that it had a patent for miracle, which none could infringe. Surely this is an error even more gross than the statement already cited about all men of all schools. The supernatural was interwoven with the entire fabric of the religion of the Roman State, which, if weak and effete as a religious discipline, was of extraordinary power as a social institution. It stood, if not on faith yet on nationality, on tradition, on rich endowments, on the deeply interested attachment of a powerful aristocracy, and on that policy of wide conciliation, which gave to so many creeds, less exclusive than the Christian, a cause common with its own.

Looking for a comprehensive description of miracles, we might say that they constitute a language of heaven embodied in material signs, by which communication is established between the Deity and man, outside the daily course of nature and experience. Distinctions may be taken between one kind of miracle and another. But none of these are distinctions in principle. Sometimes they are alleged to be the offspring of a divine power committed to the hands of particular men; sometimes they are simple manifestations unconnected with human agency, and carrying with them their own meaning, such as the healings in Bethesda; sometimes they are a system of events and of phenomena subject to authoritative and privileged interpretation. Miracle, portent, prodigy and sign are all various forms of one and the same thing, namely an invasion of the known and common natural order from the side of the supernatural. In the last-named case, there is an expression of the authorised human judgment upon it, while in the earlier ones there is only a special appeal to it. They rest upon one and the same basis. We may assign to miracle a body and a soul. It has for its body something accepted as being either in itself or in its incidents outside the known processes of ordinary nature, and for its soul the alleged message which in one shape or another it helps to convey from the Deity to man. This supernatural element, as such, was at least as familiar to the Roman heathenism, as to the Christian scheme. It was indeed more highly organised. It was embodied in the regular and normal practice of the ministers of religion, and especially, under the jurisdiction of the pontifical college, it was the regular and standing business of the augurs to observe, report, and interpret the supernatural signs, by which the gods gave reputed instructions to men outside the course of nature. Sometimes it was by strange atmospheric phenomena; sometimes by physical prodigies, as when a woman produced a snake, or a calf was born with its head in its thigh; whereupon, says Tacitus, *secuta haruspicum interpretatio.* Sometimes through events only preternatural from the want of assignable cause, as when the statue of Julius Caesar, on an island in the Tiber, turned itself round from west to east. Sometimes with an approximation to the Christian signs and wonders, as when Vespasian removed with spittle the *tabes oculorum,* and restored the impotent hand. It does not readily appear why in principle the Romans, who had the supernatural for their daily food in a shape sustained by the unbroken tradition of their country, should be violently attracted by the mere exhibition of it from a despised source, and in a manner less formal, less organised, and less known. In one important way we know the accepted supernatural of the Romans operated with direct and telling power against the Gospel. *Si coelum stetit, si terra movit, Christianos ad leones.* Or, in the unsuspected language of Tacitus, *dum latius metuitur, trepidatione vulgi, invalidus quisque obtriti.* When the portents were unfavourable, and there was fear of their extension, the weak had to suffer from the popular alarms.

The upshot of the matter then appears to be something like this.

The lowly and despised preachers of Christian portent were confronted everywhere by the highborn and accomplished caste sworn to the service of the gods, familiar from centuries of tradition with the supernatural, and supported at every point with the whole force and influence of civil authority. Nor has there ever probably been a case of a contest so unequal, as far as the powers of this world are concerned. Tainted in its origin by its connection with the detested Judaism, odious to the prevailing tone by its exclusiveness, it rested originally upon the testimony of men few, poor and ignorant, and for a length of time no human genius was enlisted in its service, with the single exception of Saint Paul. All that we of this nineteenth century know, and know so well, under the name of vested interests, is insignificant compared with the embattled fortress that these humble Christians had to storm. And the Squire, if he is to win the day with minds less ripe for conversion than Robert Elsmere, must produce some other suit of weapons from his armoury.

With him I now part company, as his thoroughgoing negation parts company with the hybrid scheme of Mrs. Ward. It is of that scheme that I now desire to take a view immediately practical.

In a concise but striking notice in the *Times* [7 April 1888] it is placed in the category of 'clever attacks upon revealed religion.' It certainly offers us a substitute for revealed religion; and possibly the thought of the book might be indicated in these words: 'The Christianity accepted in England is a good thing; but come with me, and I will show you a better.'

It may, I think, be fairly described as a devout attempt, made in good faith, to simplify the difficult mission of religion in the world by discarding the supposed lumber of the Christian theology, while retaining and applying, in their undiminished breadth of scope, the whole personal, social, and spiritual morality which has now, as matter of fact, entered into the patrimony of Christendom; and, since Christendom is the dominant power of the world, into the patrimony of the race. It is impossible indeed to conceive a more religious life than the later life of Robert Elsmere, in his sense of the word religion. And that sense is far above the sense in which religion is held, or practically applied, by great multitudes of Christians. It is, however, a new form of religion. The question is, can it be actually and beneficially substituted for the old one. It abolishes of course the whole authority of Scripture. It abolishes also Church, priesthood or ministry, sacraments, and the whole established machinery which trains the Christian as a member of a religious society. These have been regarded by fifty generations of men as wings of the soul. It is still required by Mrs. Ward to fly, and to fly as high as ever; but it is to fly without wings. For baptism, we have a badge of silver, and inscription in a book. For the Eucharist there is at an ordinary meal a recital of the fragment, 'This do in remembrance of Me.' The children respond, 'Jesus, we remember thee always.' It is hard to say that prayer is retained. In the Elgood Street service 'it is rather an act of adoration and faith, than a prayer properly so called,' and it appears that memory and trust are the instruments on which the individual is to depend, for maintaining his communion with God. It would be curious to know how the New Brotherhood is to deal with the great mystery of marriage, perhaps the truest touchstone of religious revolution.

It must be obvious to every reader that in the great duel between the old faith and the new, as it is fought in ***Robert Elsmere,*** there is a great inequality in the distribution of the arms. Reasoning is the weapon of the new scheme; emotion the sole resource of the old. Neither Catherine nor Newcome have a word to say beyond the expression of feeling; and it is when he has adopted the negative side that the hero himself is fully introduced to the faculty of argument. This is a singular arrangement, especially in the case of a writer who takes a generous view of the Christianity that she only desires to supplant by an improved device. The explanation may be simple. There are abundant signs in the book that the negative speculatists have been consulted if not ransacked; but there is nowhere a sign that the authoress has made herself acquainted with the Christian apologists, old or recent; or has weighed the evidences derivable from the Christian history; or has taken measure of the relation in which the doctrines of grace have historically stood to the production of the noblest, purest, and greatest characters of the Christian ages. If such be the case, she has skipped lightly (to put it no higher) over vast mental spaces of literature and learning relevant to the case, and has given sentence in the cause without hearing the evidence. . . .

W. E. Gladstone, " 'Robert Elsmere' and the Battle of Belief," in The Nineteenth Century, *No. 135, May, 1888, pp. 766-88.*

Walter Pater   (essay date 1888)

[*In the following excerpt, originally published in* The Guardian *in 1888, Pater praises characterization in* Robert Elsmere *but questions the validity of Elsmere's theological conversion in the novel.*]

Those who, in this bustling age, turn to fiction not merely for a little passing amusement, but for profit, for the higher sort of pleasure, will do well, we think (after a conscientious perusal on our own part) to bestow careful reading on **Robert Elsmere**. A *chef d'oeuvre* of that kind of quiet evolution of character through circumstance, introduced into English literature by Miss Austen, and carried to perfection in France by George Sand (who is more to the point, because, like Mrs. Ward, she was not afraid to challenge novel-readers to an interest in religious questions), it abounds in sympathy with people as we find them, in aspiration towards something better—towards a certain ideal—in a refreshing sense of second thoughts everywhere. The author clearly has developed a remarkable natural aptitude for literature by liberal reading and most patient care in composition—composition in that narrower sense which is concerned with the building of a good sentence; as also in that wider sense, which ensures, in a work like this, with so many joints, so many currents of interest, a final unity of impression on the part of the reader, and easy transition by him from one to the other. Well-used to works of fiction which tell all they have to tell in one thin volume, we have read Mrs. Ward's three volumes with unflagging readiness. For, in truth, that quiet method of evolution, which she pursues undismayed to the end, requires a certain lengthiness; and the reader's reward will be in a secure sense that he has been in intercourse with no mere flighty remnants, but with typical forms, of character, firmly and fully conceived. We are persuaded that the author might have written a novel which should have been all shrewd impressions of society, or all humorous impressions of country life, or all quiet fun and genial caricature. Actually she has chosen to combine something of each of these with a very sincerely felt religious interest; and who will deny that to trace the influence of religion upon human character is one of the legitimate functions of the novel? In truth, the modern "novel of character" needs some such interest, to lift it sufficiently above the humdrum of life; as men's horizons are enlarged by religion, of whatever type it may be—and we may say at once that the religious type which is dear to Mrs. Ward, though avowedly "broad," is not really the broadest. Having conceived her work thus, she has brought a rare instinct for probability and nature to the difficult task of combining this religious motive and all the learned thought it involves, with a very genuine interest in many varieties of average mundane life.

We should say that the author's special ethical gift lay in a delicately intuitive sympathy, not, perhaps, with all phases of character, but certainly with the very varied class of persons represented in these volumes. It may be congruous with this, perhaps, that her success should be more assured in dealing with the characters of women than with those of men. The men who pass before us in her pages, though real and tangible and effective enough, seem, nevertheless, from time to time to reveal their joinings. They are composite of many different men we seem to have known, and fancy we could detach again from the *ensemble* and from each other. And their goodness, when they are good, is—well! a little conventional; the kind of goodness that men themselves discount rather largely in their estimates of each other. Robert himself is certainly worth knowing—a really attractive union of manliness and saintliness, of shrewd sense and unworldly aims, and withal with that kindness and pity the absence of which so often abates the actual value of those other gifts. Mrs. Ward's literary power is sometimes seen at its best (it is a proof of her high cultivation of this power that so it should be) in the analysis of minor characters, both male and female. Richard Leyburn, deceased before the story begins, but warm in the memory of the few who had known him, above all of his great-souled daughter Catherine, strikes us, with his religious mysticism, as being in this way one of the best things in the book: —

> Poor Richard Leyburn! Yet where had the defeat lain?
>
> "Was he happy in his school life?" Robert asked gently. "Was teaching what he liked?"
>
> "Oh! yes, only——" Catherine paused and then added hurriedly, as though drawn on in spite of herself by the grave sympathy of his look, "I never knew anybody so good who thought himself of so little account. He always believed that he had missed everything, wasted everything, and that anybody else would have made infinitely more out of his life. He was always blaming, scourging himself. And all the time he was the noblest, purest, most devoted ——"
>
> She stopped. Her voice had passed beyond her control. Elsmere was startled by the feeling she showed. Evidently he had touched one of the few sore places in this pure heart. It was as though her memory of her father had in it elements of almost intolerable pathos, as though the child's brooding love and loyalty were in perpetual protest even now after this lapse of years against the verdict which an over-scrupulous, despondent soul had pronounced upon itself. Did she feel that he had gone uncomforted out of life—even by her—even by religion? Was that the sting?

A little later she gives the record of his last hours: —

> "Catherine! Life is harder, the narrower way

narrower than ever. I die"—and memory caught still the piteous long-drawn breath by which the voice was broken—"in much—much perplexity about many things. You have a clear soul, an iron will. Strengthen the others. Bring them safe to the day of account."

And then the smaller—some of them, ethically, very small—women; Lady Wynnstay, Mrs. Fleming, Mrs. Thornburgh; above all, Robert's delightful Irish mother, and Mrs. Darcy; how excellent they are! Mrs. Darcy we seem to have known, yet cannot have enough of, rejoiced to catch sight of her capital letter on the page, as we read on. In truth, if a high and ideal purpose, really learned in the school of Wordsworth and among the Westmorland hills which Mrs. Ward describes so sympathetically, with fitting dignity and truth of style, has accompanied the author throughout; no less plain, perhaps more pleasing to some readers, is the quiet humour which never fails her, and tests, while it relieves, the sincerity of her more serious thinking: —

> At last Mrs. Darcy fluttered off, only, however, to come hurrying back with little, short, scudding steps, to implore them all to come to tea with her as soon as possible in the garden that was her special hobby, and in her last new summer-house.
>
> "I build two or three every summer," she said; "now there are twenty-one! Roger laughs at me," and there was a momentary bitterness in the little eerie face; "but how can one live without hobbies? That's one—then I've two more. My album—oh, you *will* all write in my album, won't you? When I was young—when I was Maid of Honour"—and she drew herself up slightly—"everybody had albums. Even the dear Queen herself! I remember how she made M. Guizot write in it; something quite stupid, after all. *Those* hobbies—the garden and the album—are *quite* harmless, aren't they? They hurt nobody, do they?" Her voice dropped a little, with a pathetic expostulating intonation in it, as of one accustomed to be rebuked.

Mrs. Ward's women, as we have said, are more organic, sympathetic, and really creative, than her men, and make their vitality evident by becoming, quite naturally, the centres of very life-like and dramatic *groups* of people, family or social; while her men are the very *genii* of isolation and division. It is depressing to see so really noble a character as Catherine soured, as we feel, and lowered, as time goes on, from the happy resignation of the first volume (in which solemn, beautiful, and entire, and so very real, she is like a poem of Wordsworth) down to the mere passivity of the third volume, and the closing scene of Robert Elsmere's days, very exquisitely as this episode of unbelieving yet saintly biography has been conceived and executed. Catherine certainly, for one, has no profit in the development of Robert's improved gospel. The "stray sheep," we think, has by no means always the best of the argument, and her story is really a sadder, more testing one than his. Though both alike, we admit it cordially, have a genuine sense of the eternal moral charm of "renunciation," something even of the thirst for martyrdom,

for those wonderful, inaccessible, cold heights of the *Imitation,* eternal also in their aesthetic charm.

These characters and situations, pleasant or profoundly interesting, which it is good to have come across, are worked out, not in rapid sketches, nor by hazardous epigram, but more securely by patient analysis; and though we have said that Mrs. Ward is most successful in female portraiture, her own mind and culture have an unmistakable virility and grasp and scientific firmness. This indispensable intellectual process, which will be relished by admirers of George Eliot, is relieved constantly by the sense of a charming landscape background, for the most part English. Mrs. Ward has been a true disciple in the school of Wordsworth, and really undergone its influence. Her Westmorland scenery is more than a mere background; its spiritual and, as it were, *personal* hold on *persons,* as understood by the great poet of the Lakes, is seen actually at work, in the formation, in the refining, of character. It has been a stormy day: —

> Before him the great hollow of High Fell was just coming out from the white mists surging round it. A shaft of sunlight lay across its upper end, and he caught a marvellous apparition of a sunlit valley hung in air, a pale strip of blue above it, a white thread of stream wavering through it, and all around it and below it the rolling rain-clouds.

There is surely something of "natural magic" in that! The wilder capacity of the mountains is brought out especially in a weird story of a haunted girl, an episode well illustrating the writer's more imaginative psychological power; for, in spite of its quiet general tenour, the book has its adroitly managed elements of sensation—witness the ghost, in which the average human susceptibility to supernatural terrors takes revenge on the sceptical Mr. Wendover, and the love-scene with Madame de Netteville, which, like those other exciting passages, really furthers the development of the proper ethical interests of the book. The Oxford episodes strike us as being not the author's strongest work, as being comparatively conventional, coming, as they do, in a book whose predominant note is reality. Yet her sympathetic command over, her power of evoking, the genius of places, is clearly shown in the touches by which she brings out the so well-known grey and green of college and garden—touches which bring the real Oxford to the mind's eye better than any elaborate description—for the beauty of the place itself resides also in delicate touches. The book passes indeed, successively, through distinct, broadly conceived phases of scenery, which, becoming veritable parts of its texture, take hold on the reader, as if in an actual sojourn in the places described. Surrey—its genuine though almost suburban wildness, with the vicarage and the wonderful abode, above all, the ancient library of Mr. Wendover, all is admirably done, the landscape naturally counting for a good deal in the development of the profoundly meditative, country-loving souls of Mrs. Ward's favourite characters.

Well! Mrs. Ward has chosen to use all these varied gifts and accomplishments for a certain purpose. Briefly, Robert Elsmere, a priest of the Anglican Church, marries a very religious woman; there is the perfection of "mutual love"; at length he has doubts about "historic Christianity"; he gives up his orders; carries his learning, his fine intellect, his goodness, nay, his saintliness, into a kind of Unitarianism; the wife becomes more intolerant than ever; there is a long and faithful effort on both sides, eventually successful, on the part of these mentally divided people, to hold together; ending with the hero's death, the genuine piety and resignation of which is the crowning touch in the author's able, learned, and thoroughly sincere apology for Robert Elsmere's position.

For good or evil, the sort of doubts which troubled Robert Elsmere are no novelty in literature, and we think the main issue of the "religious question" is not precisely where Mrs. Ward supposes—that it has advanced, in more senses than one, beyond the point raised by Renan's *Vie de Jésus.* Of course, a man such as Robert Elsmere came to be ought not to be a clergyman of the Anglican Church. The priest is still, and will, we think, remain, one of the necessary types of humanity; and he is untrue to his type, unless, with whatever inevitable doubts in this doubting age, he feels, on the whole, the preponderance in it of those influences which make for faith. It is his triumph to achieve as much faith as possible in an age of negation. Doubtless, it is part of the ideal of the Anglican Church that, under certain safeguards, it should find room for latitudinarians even among its clergy. Still, with these, as with all other genuine priests, it is the positive not the negative result that justifies the position. We have little patience with those liberal clergy who dwell on nothing else than the difficulties of faith and the propriety of concession to the opposite force. Yes! Robert Elsmere was certainly right in ceasing to be a clergyman. But it strikes us as a blot on his philosophical pretensions that he should have been both so late in perceiving the difficulty, and then so sudden and trenchant in dealing with so great and complex a question. Had he possessed a perfectly philosophic or scientific temper he would have hesitated. This is not the place to discuss in detail the theological position very ably and seriously argued by Mrs. Ward. All we can say is that, one by one, Elsmere's objections may be met by considerations of the same *genus,* and not less equal weight, relatively to a world so obscure, in its origin and issues, as that in which we live.

Robert Elsmere was a type of a large class of minds which cannot be sure that the sacred story is true. It is philosophical, doubtless, and a duty to the intellect to recognize our doubts, to locate them, perhaps to give them practical effect. It may be also a moral duty to do this. But then there is also a large class of minds which cannot be sure it is false—minds of very various degrees of conscientiousness and intellectual power, up to the highest. They will think those who are quite sure it is false unphilosophical through lack of doubt. For their part, they make allowance in their scheme of life for a great possibility, and with some of them that bare concession of possibility (the subject of it being what it is) becomes the most important fact in the world. The recognition of it straightway opens wide the door to hope and love; and such persons are, as we fancy they always will be, the nucleus of a Church. Their particular phase of doubt, of philosophic uncertainty, has been the secret of millions of good Christians, multitudes

of worthy priests. They knit themselves to believers, in various degrees, of all ages. As against the purely negative action of the scientific spirit, the high-pitched Grey, the theistic Elsmere, the "ritualistic priest," the quaint Methodist Fleming, both so admirably sketched, present perhaps no unconquerable differences. The question of the day is not between one and another of these, but in another sort of opposition, well defined by Mrs. Ward herself, between—

> Two estimates of life—the estimate which is the offspring of the scientific spirit, and which is for ever making the visible world fairer and more desirable in mortal eyes; and the estimate of Saint Augustine.

To us, the belief in God, in goodness at all, in the story of Bethlehem, does not rest on evidence so diverse in character and force as Mrs. Ward supposes. At his death Elsmere has started what to us would be a most unattractive place of worship, where he preaches an admirable sermon on the purely human aspect of the life of Christ. But we think there would be very few such sermons in the new church or chapel, for the interest of that life could hardly be very varied, when all such sayings as that "though He was rich, for our sakes He became poor" have ceased to be applicable to it. It is the infinite nature of Christ which has led to such diversities of genius in preaching as St. Francis, and Taylor, and Wesley.

And after all we fear we have been unjust to Mrs. Ward's work. If so, we should read once more, and advise our readers to read, the profoundly thought and delicately felt chapter—chapter forty-three in her third volume—in which she describes the final spiritual reunion, on a basis of honestly diverse opinion, of the husband and wife. Her view, we think, could hardly have been presented more attractively. For ourselves we can only thank her for pleasure and profit in the reading of her book, which has refreshed actually the first and deepest springs of feeling, while it has charmed the literary sense.

Walter Pater, "Robert Elsmere," in his Essays from "The Guardian," *Macmillan and Co., Limited, 1901, pp. 53-70.*

Oscar Wilde on *Robert Elsmere*:

Robert Elsmere is of course a masterpiece—a masterpiece of the 'genre ennuyeux,' the one form of literature that the English people seem to thoroughly enjoy. A thoughtful young friend of ours once told us that it reminded him of the sort of conversation that goes on at a meat tea in the house of a serious Nonconformist family, and we can quite believe it. Indeed it is only in England that such a book could be produced. England is the home of lost ideas.

Oscar Wilde, "The Decay of Lying," in his Intentions, *1891.*

The Bookman (London) (essay date 1892)

[*The following excerpt assesses Ward's works from her early essays to the publication of* The History of David Grieve.]

[Mrs. Ward's] popularity is a significant fact to the student of the English life of to-day. Not that any single page of hers is stamped with that seal of faithfulness and art that would make of it a historic document for time to come. But round all she has written there clings an aroma which distinctively belongs to the thought and ideals of a very large part of the national life. It lurks in her phrases, in her modes of thinking, and literary historians might well wish Mrs. Ward all the power with which her admirers credit her, that the durability of the material which secretes this flavour of our time might be ensured. Rightly understood, it reveals the mental condition of a far larger portion of the nation than the one in whose name the critics speak.

Her literary evolution has been far from simple. The connection between her earlier critical work and her recent fiction is hardly obvious at first sight. Her essays in *Macmillan's Magazine,* some ten years ago, were not cast in a popular form. They were not the food on which her later admirers have fed for the most part. All things considered, it is not so much to be regretted as to be wondered at that she ever left this field for fiction. From a purely literary point of view these essays are the best work she has ever done, if we except, perhaps, the translation of Amiel's Journal. They are good examples of honest, second-best criticism. In their solidity, their thoroughness, they belong rather to a past age. They have none of the slightness, the too often flimsy impressionism we are content with to-day. Commonplace they are at times, but never affected; cultivated, temperate, sane, and with never a spark of genius in them from beginning to end. Had she rested here she might have been our most faithful guide through the byeways of Continental literature. Perhaps only a few readers of *Robert Elsmere* would be interested in the subject of these essays—in Gustavo Becquer, Garnier, in the literature of French souvenirs, etc. But read in the light of her later fiction, they are curiously significant. The cast of mind, the ideals that have more space for betrayal and development in the novels, are lurking in these earlier works. *Robert Elsmere* is foreshadowed in her deep interest in Renan's *Memories,* inasmuch as "they touch the note which vibrates deepest in the modern world—the note of religious difference." "The greatest of the controversies of humanity," by which is meant the struggle between creeds and reason, is a constantly recurring phrase. In the essays and the novels there is the same uneasy consciousness of the changes passing over the world, the timid sympathy, the halting approval, the same talk of the modern spirit with the same curiously inadequate comprehension of what it means, the same combination of healthy instincts with morbid thinking, the same dislike of strong contrasts, of brutal certainties, the same air of tolerance and the lack of catholicity, the same gentle and fair mindedness, the same note of intellectual Pharisaism, the same repetition of the catchwords of a sect.

To her first attempt at fiction Mrs. Ward brought a well-stored mind, a fluent and vigorous pen, an amount of cultivation somewhat unusual, and perhaps unnecessary, for a novelist. Her familiarity with London literary society and her own mental experiences furnished the rest of her capital. Heavy baggage certainly; and she dropped none by the way. In *Miss Bretherton* there was no second-hand reporting, for Mrs. Ward knew London drawing-rooms and private views; she knew Oxford and Surrey. Only they are seen through such a highly rarefied medium, that they are no longer the London or the Oxford or the Surrey of ordinary folks. "Phrases of Joubert and Stendhal" and "subtleties of artistic and critical speculation float about" in the thick air as its inhabitants fly through the fog in hansoms to join kindred spirits in intellectual West End circles. The jargon and cant of art are heard on every side. We are not even spared the 'Paradoxe sur le Comédien.' The love of nature expressed is probably genuine enough, but the description of Surrey commons is a wild mixture of Hugo and heather, Balzac and bracken, gorse and Chateaubriand. The one strong human passion in the book— the devotion of Kendal to his sister, is made subordinate to intellectual interests, and becomes only another manifestation of priggishness. Kendal's keenest regret for the woman he is said to love seems to be "that her youth had been spoilt by her entire want of that inheritance from the past which is the foundation of all good work in the present." When the girl owns to her ignorance of French, instead of rejoicing in her fine honesty, he makes haste to give her an educational lecture on the benefits to be derived from the study of French prose. The reader's grievance is that Mrs. Ward does not herself attach the fitting label to Kendal's coat-tails, or endow her heroine with devilry enough to flout him. And the end of it is that we leave *Miss Bretherton* with a wild craving for the wilderness, the uttermost parts of the sea, the fastnesses of Philistia, where neither art nor letters do penetrate, and where the cultivated person is altogether unknown.

Since then Mrs. Ward has learnt much, and her aptness in learning has been rewarded by a great popularity. *Robert Elsmere,* at least, was a long step on. It touched on commoner human interests; it was more readable. Well-bred mediocrity no longer spoke as it had been told to speak of art and literature; it took to solving religious and social problems instead. Now Mrs. Ward in her late protest against her critics has defended the Novel with a Purpose. She is quite right. A vast deal of cant has been talked on this subject. "Art for Art's sake"—that, too, is vanity like every canon and formula of criticism that is exclusive and intolerant. Genius is its own justification, and the methods of Flaubert and Dickens have both forced acceptance. Divest your novel of all moral atmosphere, if you will; weave into it even fanatical irrelevancies, if you will. If the creative power be there; if the tale be quick with human life, the verdict will be for you in spite of your theories or your lack of them. Those who condemned *Robert Elsmere* intelligently, did so, not because it had a purpose, but because they felt it to be a dramatic failure, or because of the provincial tone of its thought. Indeed, to the fulfilment of its "purpose" must be set down much of the praise it deserves. There is a distinct continuity about it. It develops its ideas in a sane and wholesome fashion. That those whose beliefs were fast grounded were not convinced by

Robert's logic; or that others considered the book made a great fuss about small difficulties, has nothing to do with the case. Mrs. Ward, it is true, may have had propagandist intentions, but surely her purpose as a missionary and as a writer of fiction was fulfilled in presenting a sympathetic type of the compromising modern mind in face of religious difficulties. In *David Grieve* she was more ambitious and much less successful. The sated minds of readers demanded more variety in his experiences, and after giving him this, there is no moral or mental unity left about him at all. He is painted over with successive veneers of revivalism, atheism, socialism, sensualism. And the sum of all the coatings is the impossible one of Elsmerism. He reaps none of the harvest he has sown; he does not pay in hard coin the penalties he has merited. They were but shadowy picture fires he passed through. Surely here Mrs. Ward lost her way. Many a less instructive writer, with a firmer mental grasp, would have shaped the facts of David's case in harmony with the stern inevitable morality of real life.

Yet her people are not mere puppets. Elsmere is almost a success, so is Langham; Rose is charming; Robert's mother, with her strange garments and her Irish wit, is a sympathetic figure. Aunt Hannah is made of flesh and blood, and Lomax the wanderer is a reality. Unfortunately Mrs. Ward has an unfortunate habit of arresting our interest in her people's actions while she is looking after her hero's soul or her heroine's education, or drawing out the spiritual experiences of the supernumeraries. "I am so made," says Mrs. Ward, "that I cannot picture a human being's development without wanting to know the whole, his religion as well as his business, his thoughts as well as his actions." This sounds like a threat for the future; let us pray, therefore, that the *dramatis personae* be rigorously few. She has too little trust in the power of the untrained, untrimmed bits of human life for stirring human feeling. Her lack of artistic simplicity is instanced in the example she gives of "one of those experiences which remain with us as a sort of perpetual witness to the poetry which life holds in it, and yields up to one at any moment," for the "experience" was a spectacular rendering of *Romeo and Juliet* in a garden at Venice, with a moon and the canal in sight, a balcony, a sundial catching the moonbeams, a beautiful actress in white brocade, and other highly decorative accessories. She says she has a liking for "serious endings." No one will quarrel with the seriousness, but only with her manifestations of it. She wishes to wring from her readers the tears due to human suffering. Internal chill is her means of doing so in Miss Bretherton; tubercular disease of the larynx in Robert Elsmere; in *David Grieve* it is sarcoma and diphtheria. Yet there is no reason in the world why Madame Chàteauvieux, or Elsmere, or Lucy should have died, except to satisfy that ghoulish tradition of the Sunday-school literature of the last generation. This triumph of the lachrymose over the pathetic betrays Mrs. Ward's inherent weakness and reveals her kindred.

Critics do her wrong by turning and rending her because she is lacking in what is not hers to give. Stripped of their outer garb of culture, her works belong to an order of writing to which critics as a rule pay but little attention. There is in England a very large class of persons who are serious, given to speculation, yet timid and unadventurous in mind. A generation ago they were less highly educated. In those days they read Miss Yonge. Now they are attracted by mild philosophical inquiries. They are influential, and they are worth influencing. On them depends whether ideals and impulses born within a narrow circle become popular forces bearing the life of the nation along. To widen their minds by ever so little, to point to further horizons, to teach forbearance to the new and unknown, is a work the best might be proud to take part in. That work is not for the inaccessible idealist, the austere logician, the fastidious artist. Subtle refinement, strong sensation, naked truth are alien to the mass of timid souls—the great middle class of the intellect. They may indeed be impressed and commanded by the greatest genius which is never very far away from the level of any human mind, high or low. But they are docile, and prefer to be instructed by one whose kinship they can feel. To this class Mrs. Ward appeals as a great moral force. Not that she is on their level; but she is at least within sight of it. She is concerned with their problems, owns, perhaps with a difference, their social ideals, interprets what lies just outside their borders. Within certain bounds, her admirers are fastidious. Academically, they are learned enough, cultured enough. The purely literary side of their demands it is not easy to satisfy. The cultivation, therefore, the full mind, which Mrs. Ward brings to bear on the questions towards the solution of which they would be discreetly guided, is not only flattering, it is indispensable. In thought and ideals the guide must not soar too far away from their levels: the form in which these are wrapped cannot be too fine. In the character of the public for whom these books were consciously or unconsciously written, lie the interest and the explanation of their success, and instead of pedantically pointing to artistic or dramatic flaws in their workmanship, we should be better employed in contentedly recognising that Mrs. Ward is a strong influence that reaches, and is effectual, where artists extolled by the critics would be powerless and unowned.

G. Y., "The Work of Mrs. Humphry Ward," in The Bookman, *London, Vol. II, No. 9, June, 1892, pp. 76-8.*

Lionel Johnson   (essay date 1894)

[*In the following excerpt, originally published in* The Academy *in 1894, Johnson reviews* Marcella.]

That *Marcella* is a good novel, and a very much better novel than *Robert Elsmere* or *David Grieve,* would seem to be the unanimous verdict of its readers. It may be not amiss to consider the reasons of this clear superiority to its predecessors.

Mrs Humphry Ward, in a quaint preface to *David Grieve,* defended with great energy her choice of theme and treatment in that book, and in *Robert Elsmere.* Undoubtedly fiction in prose has been successfully written with so infinite a variety of aims and ideals, written so lightly and loosely, so sternly and strictly, so waywardly and airily, so straightforwardly and precisely, that it is impossible to say what is or is not a novel: what a novel may or may not contain. But one thing is certain. If a novel be fantastic, capricious, a curious combination of humour and philosophy, and wisdom and wit, constantly digressing and divagating, a thing of whims and fancies: why, if the writer be a writer of genius, he may discuss the differential calculus or Home Rule, death duties or the North Pole, at any point in his narrative. But if a writer sets out with certain strong convictions concerning matters in which the truth, whatever it be, is a question of spiritual life and death to the majority of civilised men—matters, too, intimately connected with scholarship and learning of many kinds— then a fair treatment of those matters in a novel is impossible. A man's loss of faith in traditional Christianity is a possible theme for a novelist, if minute detail, points of critical scholarship, be avoided, and the tragedy, or tragicomedy, be presented with the strong and human features of its spiritual drama. But some readers of **Robert Elsmere** were perpetually leaving their chairs to consult their books: "Yes! but So-and-so has answered that in his first chapter." "That view is shaken by the discovery of such-and-such a document." "They are beginning to question it in Germany." "Perhaps so, but even the Vatican Decrees do not demand that." "Where did I put the last number of the Something-or-other?" Now, few readers care to read novels under those conditions. Imagine a novel turning upon a scholar's change of view about the Homeric problem, written by an ardent advocate of the "advanced" view: imagine the scholarly reader exclaiming, "Very likely, but Wilamowitz-Moellendorff is not infallible," and "Wolf would not maintain that now." It would have been possible to let the reader understand that critical studies in history had destroyed Elsmere's old faith, without any unfair or inartistic treatment of the matter; but Mrs Ward was not content with that. She introduced definite examples of the historical difficulties, in a way necessarily superficial, and therefore unfair. It would have been at once fairer and more artistic, more reverent and more scholarly, to have prefaced the story by a reasoned and elaborate essay upon the question. As it is, the treatment hurts the feelings of orthodox Christians, and must irritate those of scholars, orthodox or not. A second blemish was the description of the orthodox Christians. Consumptive, emaciated, hectic, wasted, unearthly, gaunt, worn, thin, starving, ascetic, mystical, passionate, vehement, agonised, ardent and uncritical—these were the adjectives. Their eyes were dreamy and bright, their hands long and thin, their voices had a vibrating intensity. They were often most lovable, and had a magnetic charm of personality. The intellect was a snare to them, and they fled from the learning of Germany with a *Vade Satana!* Newcome, the High Church vicar, "had the saint's wasted unearthly look, the ascetic's brow high and narrow"; when he appealed to Elsmere, it was with "a hurricane of words hot from his inmost being." Wishart, the young Liberal Catholic convert, was "a pale, small, hectic creature, possessed of that restless energy of mind which often goes with the heightened temperature of consumption." He poured forth "a stream of argument and denunciation which had probably lain lava-hot at the heart of the young convert for years." Ancrum was a valetudinarian, sinking out of sheer exhaustion into the arms of Rome. Catherine Elsmere and Dora Lomax were womanly and devout and strong, but with something of a mulish obstinacy in their religion. It was always a religion of passionate dreams passionately be-

lieved. Mrs Ward's orthodox Christians were amusing to her orthodox readers; but as representatives of orthodoxy, they seemed somewhat inadequate caricatures.

Marcella has none of these defects, or of defects like them; no political economist, no social reformer, will impatiently put the book down to confute its reasonings out of Mill or Marx. No class of politicians, or of social theorists, is represented by obviously unfair examples: no one is intolerably and divinely right, no one pathetically and stubbornly wrong. No reader can say that whole chapters should have been cast into an independent essay or pamphlet. Yet the story is no less ardent and earnest than its predecessors: like them, it deals with matters of immense importance, matters keenly debatable and extremely difficult; like them, it is full of human passion and spiritual trial, full of conflict and love and death. Unlike them, it is a good novel: they were but novels with good things plentiful in them: this novel is a satisfying whole. It is largely planned, some readers may think too largely and elaborately. Even so, the workmanship may be held atonement enough for the elaboration. Mrs Ward is not of those fashionable writers whose agitation over their psychology makes them ignore their grammar. There is an occasional excess of phrase, overwrought expressions and an encumbering weight of words; but never any clumsy carelessness, no huddled jumble of sentences, unrhythmical and disproportioned. Of all the general impressions made upon the reader by Mrs Ward's book, the strongest impression is that here is very careful work. Perhaps no impression is less commonly left by modern writers. Mrs Ward's novels are written with a very vigilant eye to demonstrating the necessity of "conduct," of a resolute morality, of a care for the things of the spirit; but what human, what delightful worldliness, what a sense of living forces, the writer brings to her task! The background, environment, atmosphere, whatever be the right word, are admirable in their reality and truth. "Society," the "masses," the "landed class," the "political world," the "old families," the "new generation," the "labour movement," Mrs Ward may depict them rightly or wrongly, but her portraiture is enchantingly alive.

Mrs Ward's books are masterly work, seriously to be considered, comfortably to be enjoyed; the abominable amateur of cleverness has had no hand in them. One can fancy Dr Johnson rolling out sonorous condemnation of certain monstrously fashionable novels of to-day, somewhat in this manner: "Madam, you have not atoned for the tedium of your narration by the novelty of your morals, nor for the disorder of your style by the indecorum of your sentiments." But though we may dislike Mrs Ward's stories, we cannot be disrespectful nor contemptuous towards them. Even the vitriolic and vivacious exquisites of criticism, who flout the "earnest" novel as only fit for "Brixton parlours," cannot flout away the honourable excellence of *Marcella.*

As in its predecessors, so in *Marcella,* the burden of the story is the progress of some strenuous soul towards reason, patience, self-discipline: a regulated and well-grounded ardour, as Mrs Ward comprehends and realises them. Difficulty! that is the characteristic word: the recognition of complexities in life: an ordeal never ended, always to be endured: a testing and a purifying of fine gold in the fire. There is a moral collision of two fine natures, with a shock rending the hearts of both: on one side, clear-eyed and wise patience, strong to stand firm, in spite of passion persuading, not ignobly, the contrary course; on the other side, a vehement spirit of protest, revolt, impatient conviction, born of a not ignoble intolerance of a sad wisdom, just, and proof against the folly of an emotion, unjust in its very generosity. On one side Aldous Raeburn, on the other Marcella Boyce; common to both, a sense of social disorder, sorrow, trouble. Aldous has the "strength to sit still," the power to serve, if need be, while he "stands and waits": a depth of moral purpose, a depth of mental courage, a depth of emotional sincerity. Marcella has the storm and stress of youth, inexperience, personal ambition and headlong sympathy. Both have family pride: Aldous in its finer form of real "nobility," implying responsibility; Marcella in the more sentimental form, picturesque and vivid, less assured and unassertive. Her father's conduct in earlier life had outcast him from his equals: she had been brought up apart from her parents, a prey to her childish cravings for sympathy, full of nervous passion, impressionable and restless and expectant. She falls in with "Venturist" socialism in her London youth, with an exciting Bohemianism of thought and feeling: her beauty, ardour, pride, give her visions of becoming a Saint Teresa, a Joan of Arc, to "the social movement," the cause of the poor and the oppressed. Her father's succession to the old place in the country brings her front to front with village life, as a field for her half-unconscious patronage and whole genuine commiseration. Aldous Raeburn, heir to a great estate and title, living hard by with his grandfather, falls in love with her, discerning her better than she knows herself. And at this point begins the active drama of the book, which we will not attempt to tell. It is enough to say that Aldous and Marcella are parted by the means that joined them, their common concentration upon social difficulties. As she was passionately prejudiced by her personal feelings of compassion in the matter that separated them, so also her love for him was at heart a yielding to personal ambition. At the end, great suffering, a quickening of her conscience and deepening of her mind, a purgation in manifold and multiform trials of life, bring her back to him. She had passed through the fires.

A number of admirable characters assist in the drama. The most memorable is Harry Wharton, "gentleman labour leader," young and able, and all that the part seems to demand. His character is one of the most masterly and natural in recent fiction. Honestly a champion of the poor; intellectually and emotionally a social reformer of "advanced and progressive" views; winning and buoyant, a notable personality, he sells his labour journal to a syndicate of capitalists at the crisis of a great strike which he has fostered. He sells it to relieve his personal necessities, largely due to gambling debts incurred at a very aristocratic and retiring haunt. He is a familiar figure at great gatherings of "society," a favourite with great Tory dames and magnates of all kinds. He wins Marcella to his side by maintaining with equal fervour and far greater knowledge

her policy of "thorough." The discovery of his conduct, no surprise to Aldous and others, acquaintances of his early youth, was among her severest wounds: she had almost loved him. Seldom has a novelist portrayed with finer truth the divorce between intellect and conscience, between sentimental public sympathies and cynical private selfishness. A divorce; yet the elements and various strains so subtly intermix and overlap that the character is always easy, unforced, persuasive. The expositor of "Hohenstiel-Schwangau" would have enjoyed the exposure of Harry Wharton. Edward Hallin is less masterly, because he is the whitest of white souls: the scholar-priest of social reform, neither scholar nor priest by profession, but very much of both in his life. He is the idealist with a grasp of facts: the sternest of believers in the strength of justice, truth, complete and absolute honesty. The Cambridge friend of Aldous, he inspired Aldous with his spirit, the spirit that never compromises with half lies and expedient immoralities, and the "necessary" insincerities of public life. A little more insistence upon his virtues, and he would have been a tedious saint, an Aristides: as it is, he is pleasant and human and pathetic. He stands over against Wharton, as an influence upon Marcella; and he is throughout, by his influence, the better and guardian angel of her and Aldous in their love. Mrs Boyce, Marcella's mother, is an impressive figure; whether she be an acceptable figure or not is less obvious. Her husband's disgrace killed her pride in him, and her joy in existence: she lived apart, unapproachable, but not repellent. She lived in her past, she loved Dante, she was no cynic; but she was a quietly embittered spectator of the life about her, a little ironical and very lovable, whilst neither wanting nor accepting any love but that of her irritable and no longer brilliant husband. Aldous's grandfather, Lord Maxwell, is as stately an old noble of a type familiar both in literature and in life, as his sister is a narrow and dignified lady unable to comprehend "modern notions." The labour leaders, the "Venturist" theorists, all the examples of rugged force, or democratic culture, or self-educated enthusiasm, or business-like energy, devoted in various ways to the solution of "the social problem," are happily drawn; they are neither idealised, nor caricatured, nor yet presented with indifference. They help to illustrate the complexity of our tangled life, the characters and natures of the powers at work in it: the necessity of the work, the partiality and imperfection of all methods, apart from honesty and knowledge and faith. The book seems to suggest that the co-operation of the highest qualities of all classes can alone do any good: to suggest, for the book, though intensely moral, is not didactic. In the play of life upon life, the personal struggles of men and women, with their humour and gravity, hope and fear, sorrow and joy, all very human and alive, *Marcella* succeeds and satisfies. It has an abundant brilliance of scenes, either passionate or amusing. Here is a rendering of modern life, crowded and moving, in which high tragedy and excellent comedy take their parts, each with a bearing upon the other that is true to life and true to art.

Lionel Johnson, "Mrs. Humphry Ward: 'Marcella'," in Reviews & Critical Papers, *edited by Robert Shafer, Elkin Mathews, 1921, pp. 58-65.*

A. St. John Adcock   (essay date 1903)

[*An English author whose works often concern the city of London, Adcock served as editor of the London* Bookman *from 1923 until his death in 1930. In the following excerpt, he presents an appreciative survey of Ward's career to 1903.*]

To think over the successful problem or purposeful novels of the last fifteen years is to indulge in what is very much of a meditation among the tombs. Books of their week, of their season, of their year, selling in tens of thousands, read and discussed by everyone, extravagantly praised and extravagantly condemned, so long as they lived they were intensely and aggressively alive; but "whom the gods love die early," and they are, most of them, already little more than half-forgotten names. They ran through their popularity as swiftly and as splendidly as a spendthrift runs through his inheritance, and died bankrupt and neglected after a career that was as brief as it was astonishing.

For though no other type of fiction is qualified, by the very nature of it, to achieve such a dazzling and uproarious notoriety easily and instantly, none loses its hold on the public sooner or is, as a rule, more inherently mortal. "It is not difficult to obtain readers," as Dr. Johnson puts it, "when we discuss a question which everyone is desirous to understand, which is debated in every assembly and has divided the nation into parties. . . . To the quick circulation of such productions all the motives of interest and vanity concur; the disputant enlarges his knowledge, the zealot animates his passion, and every man is desirous to inform himself concerning affairs so vehemently agitated and variously represented." But, with rare exceptions, it is the fate of controversial novelists, "even when they contend for philosophical or theological truth, to be soon laid aside and slighted. Either the question is decided and there is no more place for doubt and opposition, or mankind despair of understanding it and, grown weary of disturbance, content themselves with quiet ignorance."

It is by no ordinary talent, then, but by some rare creative power for which one can find no other name than genius, that out of this perishable material Mrs. Humphry Ward has fashioned novels of high and permanent value, and given them a vital and compelling interest, so that they have outlived, and continue to outlive, the once-current phases of thought and the stirring political or religious movements that are embodied in them.

Mrs. Humphry Ward is akin to Matthew Arnold mentally and spiritually, no less than by ties of blood: she has the same intellectual scepticism, the same passion for religious truth; she has been largely influenced, too, by the great French and German thinkers who influenced him, and in Robert Elsmere, in David Grieve, in certain lesser persons of her other books, she has given these teachings a practical application, and shown and analysed, with a fine insight, their workings upon high-minded and emotional men who take themselves and all things earnestly. It is done with a tense human appeal that is irresistible and unfailing, for though every religious movement passes, the hopes and doubts and world-old questionings in which it has its rise are never finally put by, but are such as come

and will come, more or less prevailingly, to most men of average intelligence until the end of time; and, in the main, it is this and their vivid actuality of incident and character that give the greatest of these novels their root in life and their continuing charm.

Beginning her career as an author, in 1881, with *Milly and Olly,* an unambitious, small book for younger readers, in 1884 Mrs. Ward published *Miss Bretherton,* a clever little sketch of theatrical life, whose beautiful heroine reflects the fascinating personality of a famous actress who, after a brief and brilliant triumph, retired from the stage while she was still young and her fame at its zenith; and in Miss Bretherton's lofty ideal of her art, in her insistence on reconciling that art with morality, as well as in the general trend and masterful characterisation of the book, one has glimpses and foreshadowings of the psychological instinct and profound knowledge of humanity, the large sympathy and altruistic purpose that reached their fullest expression in *Robert Elsmere* and *David Grieve,* and had their share in the making of each one of the notable series of novels that have succeeded them.

But *Robert Elsmere* did not appear until 1888. In the meantime, Mrs. Ward had translated Amiel's Journal, and in that intimate record of a spiritual pilgrimage one traces, perhaps, the beginnings and shadowy suggestion of Elsmere's own less stoical and more complex personality. Such sayings of Amiel's as "There is but one thing needful—to possess God"; or "It is the historical task of Christianity to assume with every succeeding age a fresh metamorphosis and to be for ever spiritualising more and more her understanding of the Christ and of salvation"; or "Our century wants a new theology—that is to say, a more profound explanation of the nature of Christ and of the light which it flashes upon heaven and upon humanity"—these, in a manner, anticipate the mind of Elsmere himself, the convictions in which, after much travail of soul, he found something of peace at last.

The success of *Robert Elsmere* was instant and startling. In the press, the critics cried it up or down with equal vehemence; the pulpits fulminated against it, or gave it qualified approval; courses of lectures were delivered about it; pamphlets were published to prove that its doctrines were noble and elevating or utterly pernicious; and while its prosperity was still on the increase, a critical article by Mr. Gladstone, in the *Nineteenth Century,* lent a fresh impetus to its popularity and sealed it for admission into those vast serious circles where the ordinary novel is not, or was not in those days, taken into account.

The absorbing interest of the book was granted even by those who held its teachings in abhorrence; yet it is quite unusually long and its plot is of the very simplest. It relies chiefly, indeed, as all enduring work in fiction does and must, upon the verisimilitude of its characters and the hold they take upon the reader's sympathies. You may be irritated by the narrow creed of Catherine, by her blind, unquestioning faith, her conventional habit of thought and the dull obstinacy with which she cramps her own life, and the lives of those she loves, in a rigid and unintelligent fulfilment of the dying wishes of her father; but your very irritation is a testimony to her actuality—if she were less true to life, less real to the imagination, you could not be sufficiently interested in her to resent the innocent ignorance and saintly littlenesses in her that count for so much in the shaping of Elsmere's destiny and her own. Moreover, if she had not been so uncompromising and her religious beliefs so shrined above the reach of reason, Elsmere's love romance would have been too insipid to have been worth telling, and, after their marriage, there could not have been that fierce and agonising spiritual conflict betwixt them, and all the intensity must have been absent from that painfully dramatic scene in which, after long heart-searching and pitying hesitancy, Elsmere brings himself to confess to her that he can no longer believe in the divinity of Christ, that he is an outcast from the sanctities of her religion and must resign his living and sever himself from communion with the Church outside whose pale she inexorably believed there was no hope of salvation.

The unanswerable arguments in that heretical book of the Squire's (a sinister personage, drawn with consummate fidelity and effectiveness, as are all, even the least important, men and women in the novel) are rightly not revealed, for if they failed to persuade us, as they and converse with the Squire are said to have persuaded Elsmere, then his conversion from Christianity to a sort of theism must of necessity have been unconvincing and unreal, and to that extent the story would have been crudely inartistic. Yet one general outcry against the book was that these potent reasonings were not duly set forth in it; that while the other side had such powerful advocates as the broadly philosophical Oxford tutor, Henry Grey, and the brilliant, selfishly cynical Langham, Christianity was allowed no champion other than the simple, ascetic, ritualistic priest, Newcome, who could oppose little to Elsmere's doubts but Scriptural commonplaces and exhortations to fast and pray and crucify the flesh.

The aim of **Robert Elsmere** was, as Mr. Gladstone said, "to expel the preternatural element from Christianity, to destroy its dogmatic structure, yet to keep intact the moral and spiritual results," and he protested that at the hands of Mrs. Humphry Ward "a great creed with the testimony of eighteen centuries at its back cannot find an articulate word to say in its defence." But this was, of course, to regard what was primarily a novel concerned with life and character and the play of human passions and errors, as nothing but a cut and dried essay in theological polemics. Assuming that the defence of Christianity could have been and had been presented with the triumphant results that certain critics considered inevitable, then Elsmere's doubts must have been laid, and he had remained firm in the faith instead of deserting the Church and suffering that bitter estrangement from his wife—obviously, in a word, there would have been no story to tell, or a story that would substitute a dramatised compendium of Christian evidences and philosophic doubts for the engrossing soul's tragedy that took the world by storm.

For the vogue and influence of **Robert Elsmere** were by no means limited to England. The book was translated into various languages; it carried its torch of controversy flaming all across the Continent and through America and the colonies, giving an impetus to religious thought everywhere by the very opposition and resentment it aroused. Nowhere was its success more marked than in Germany, where it was the subject of earnest and elaborate criticism and discussion, and inspired one author to write what appears to have been a sequel to it under the title of *Catherine Elsmere's Widowhood.*

"Why do people read a book like **Robert Elsmere,** and why do they take any interest in it?" a newspaper interviewer inquired of Colonel Ingersoll. "Simply because they are not satisfied with the religion of our day," replied the American apostle of free-thought. He considered that the book was conservative. "It is an effort to save something," he said—"a few shreds and patches and ravellings from the wreck"; and he was not far wrong in describing Elsmere's new religion as "after all, only a system of outdoor relief." But what then? Having studied and got to know a lot of things he is really none the wiser for knowing, Elsmere breaks away from the orthodox Christian tenets, forlornly assured that "the miraculous Christ story rests on a tissue of mistakes," that "Christ was only a wise man, and miracles do not happen," and proceeds to construct out of the salvage of his shattered theology a simple humanitarian gospel that is something nearer to his heart's desire:

> Ruled by the Scripture and his own advice,
> Each has a blind by-path to Paradise;

and though in the last resort his reformed gospel is no more demonstrable than was the one he has discarded, that is no flaw in the novel. On the contrary, it harmonises entirely with the broad, insistently human note of the whole book, for it is an essentially human futility that Elsmere's new religion, like every new religion that men have formulated, should be as elusive and as dark with potential uncertainties as the old.

David Grieve, which followed Elsmere after a lapse of four years, is in many respects the greater novel of the two. The narrative moves with an easier, larger sweep, and is managed with an assured mastery of construction and matured literary style. Here again there is conflict between the revelations of ancient theology and the revelations of modern science, but only as strong undercurrents and not as the all-absorbing main stream of the lives that are troubled and subtly influenced by them. David himself is more of a faulty, inconsistent, full-blooded natural man than Elsmere; he tries a wider range of emotions, his experiences are more varied and have more of colour in them. Between the early years when he and his elfish, wilful, hapless sister Louie tended their uncle's sheep in the Derbyshire hills, and the quiet end, where he is a widower with one son, a prosperous, middle-aged publisher and bookseller in Manchester, running his business on co-operative principles and taking a keen, practical interest in the current questions of labour and poverty, he had burnt through lawless ecstasies of love and joy and grief, and an intoxication of black despair against which Elsmere's narrower scope of feeling and straiter moral temperament and training had ramparted him inviolably.

In **Marcella,** and in **Sir George Tressady,** which is by way of being a sequel to it, Mrs. Ward handles contemporary politics and the tangled social problems of the hour with consummate art and effectiveness. Through a stormy atmosphere of political rivalries and parliamentary intrigues, an impulsive, fascinatingly tantalising individuality, constantly led astray in her judgment by her acute sympathy with the poor and the unhappy, and as constantly brought back to a sane comprehension of things by her innate common-sense and great-heartedness, Marcella emerges, at last, statuesquely magnificent, but sensitively feminine, one of the most capricious, truthful, and charmingly womanly women that fiction has given us. She is willing at first to marry Raeburn because she foresees that his wealth and position will assist her incalculably in her endeavours after social reformation; she indignantly breaks off their engagement on the eve of marriage because Raeburn feels that he cannot conscientiously support her petition for the reprieve of Hurd, the wretched hunchback poacher who shot one of his keepers in a midnight affray, and she is racked with grief for the condemned man's heart-broken wife and sickly children; then, having spent some months as a nurse, toiling among the London slum-dwellers, and having come to a larger knowledge of the world and of him and of herself, she marries him for love only, when he had lost all hope of ever winning her. The scene of her final self-surrender, and the tact and characteristic nobility with which Raeburn acquiesces in her remorseful self-humiliation without allowing her to feel humiliated is very finely done.

The poacher Hurd, his wife and family, his squalid home life and warped morality, are drawn with a knowledge and biting realism that make them live in the memory with the detail and vividness of personal observation. Mrs. Ward knows the rural mind and the drab life of the countryside intimately, and the peasants and village folk transcribed in her pages, with all their cramped sympathies, their wry humour and pathetic patience, their sluggish subtleties and simplicities of thought and emotion, are as racy of the soil and as distinctly individualised as any even in that wonderful miscellany of rustics Mr. Thomas Hardy has created. There is Uncle Reuben, in *David Grieve,* with his grim, uncomfortable religion, and his inarticulate kindnesses; there is his hard, unscrupulous wife Hannah, who terrorises over him and holds him in fierce subjection, till his struggling, half-suffocated conscience nerves him to scrape and save and make secret restitution to his brother's children of the money Hannah is filching from them, and then to confess to her, fearfully, what he has done, with such nearly fatal results that her frenzy of rage culminates in a stroke of paralysis. There is the crazy old schoolmaster, 'Lias Dawson, and his gentle, long-enduring wife, Margaret. There are, to say nothing of many another, old Patton, the wistful Mrs. Brunt, and the rest of that memorable group of villagers in *Marcella,* with the vivacious, quaintly malicious and independent Mrs. Jellison, and her somewhat morose daughter, the gamekeeper's wife. Mrs. Ward understands these humble thoroughly, and is keenly sensitive to the hardness and monotony and the hopeless limitations of their existences, and recognises and feelingly denounces the petty injustice they are often compelled to put up with at the hands of the squires, landlords, and masters on whom they are pitifully dependent. She inveighs against the crying iniquity of the game laws, and

against the insanitary and tumble-down state of the labourers' cottages with a fiery earnestness that Charles Kingsley himself, in all his savage tilting at those same old grievances, scarcely surpassed.

Nowhere is this minute knowledge of village life and character used more tellingly than in *The Story of Bessie Costrell,* a little masterpiece of sustained narrative power and realistic romance, the poignant pathos of whose closing scene touches one by its simple directness as no other passage of Mrs. Ward's writing does, except, perhaps, that amazingly vivid picture of the foundry accident in *Helbeck of Bannisdale,* when the wondering, frightened little girl is brought in among the rugged workmen as the burial service is about to be read before the furnace in which her father has perished.

But Mrs. Ward appears to approach the lower classes in London in a curiously different spirit; she does not evince the same intimacy with them, or move among them on the same friendly, equal footing. She uses them more in masses and as material necessary to the foundation of social propaganda, as a race to be taken in hand by rescue associations or the Charity Organisation Society, as unfortunates to be elevated in the bulk by means of lectures and serviceable institutions. She does not, with any effectiveness, show these town-bred men and women as separate entities and as they live in their own homes. Elsmere goes to preach to them and regenerate them by means of his new "Brotherhood"; or, accompanied by aristocratic friends, faces a crowd of them in debate at a public hall; Marcella and her husband establish an extra residence at Mile End and receive tired seamstresses and pallid artisans at informal "At Homes" where they would be awkward and unlike their normal selves, and to which those who were best worth knowing would be too proud to come; whilst earlier in her history Marcella had been to work among the poor as a member of a Nursing Home, and seeing, in that capacity, much of the worse side of lower London, was cured of some of her humanitarian illusions and impelled towards reconciliation with her aristocratic lover, whose apparent lack of humanity had stung her into revolt.

Speaking of this lover reminds one that though Mrs. Ward never hampers herself with anything intricate in the way of a plot, the love romances that grow up amid the strain and stress of the social, political, or religious problems that are handled in her novels, have an infinite freshness and variety. Once or twice the ending is unhappy, but only once does it fall a little short of being convincing, and that is in the case of *Helbeck of Bannisdale.* Laura Fountain, inoculated with the advanced Radicalism and materialistic philosophy of her dead father, goes with her stepmother to live in the ruined mansion of Bannisdale, and there comes into contact with the strict, bigoted Roman Catholicism of the Jesuitical Helbeck. After scorning and ridiculing his fastings and prayings and his conventional superstitions, she comes to respect and, after flagrant outbreaks of rebellion, even to love the serious, sincere gentleman, who in return loves her with a passion that is only less than his love of heaven. Finally, in her utter devotion to him she is desirous of learning something of his religion in the hope of being converted to it. But his creeds are, she fears, irreconcilably alien to her very nature, and on the night of his sister's death, it is borne in upon her that she can never share his faith and her disbelief must always be a barrier between them, and in a dark access of despair she puts an end to her life. It is so powerfully and plausibly accomplished, this solution of the difficulty, that one is carried away in the reading and takes the probability of it for granted, but on after reflection it affects one as strained and unlikely, and lacks the sequential fitness that gives the suicide of Bessie Costrell its tragic touch of inevitability. This element of Roman Catholicism, in contrast with an opposing system of religion or morality, is introduced again in *Eleanor* and in *Lady Rose's Daughter,* but amid vastly different surroundings and to subserve widely different purposes.

It is impossible to do more here than touch very superficially on certain aspects and general tendencies of Mrs. Humphry Ward's work; and if it were not impossible, it would be unnecessary. A more practical and reliable testimony to the force of her genius is to be found in the far-reaching success that has attended the publication of each new novel of hers since *Robert Elsmere. David Grieve* was almost as extensively translated and has since been written and lectured about in half the languages of Europe; an able and appreciative address by a German Professor who treated the book as a typical presentation of certain phases of English religious opinion, having been recently reprinted in the *Anglia.* Of her later books, *Marcella* has been done into French, and *Helbeck of Bannisdale* is very shortly to appear in a well-known French journal.

Among living women novelists in England, Mrs. Humphry Ward occupies a unique eminence. Probably none has achieved a greater or sounder European reputation; and certainly none of them has done more to revivify and humanise the Christian ideal, or to stimulate thought and the enthusiasm for social reform; no other has exercised a more fruitful influence on the intellects and emotions of the religious, the sceptical, the serious-minded publics of her day and generation.

A. St. John Adcock, "Mrs. Humphry Ward," in The Bookman, *London, Vol. XXIV, No. 144, September, 1903, pp. 199-204.*

Mrs. Ward's lack of humour betrayed her, as the years went on, to a sort of pontifical self-assurance, or, it may be more simply said, to a lack of sympathy with forms of thought and fancy which had not yet secured academic authority. It is a pity that circumstances forced her to adopt the facile art of fiction, towards which she had no real bent.

—Edmund Gosse, in his Silhouettes, 1925.

William Lyon Phelps   (essay date 1910)

[*In the following excerpt, Phelps challenges Ward's high literary reputation.*]

It is high time that somebody spoke out his mind about Mrs. Humphry Ward. Her prodigious vogue is one of the most extraordinary literary phenomena of our day. A roar of approval greets the publication of every new novel from her active pen, and it is almost pathetic to contemplate the reverent awe of her army of worshippers when they behold the solemn announcement that she is "collecting material" for another masterpiece. Even professional reviewers lose all sense of proportion when they discuss her books, and their so-called criticisms sound like publishers' advertisements. Sceptics are warned to remain silent, lest they become unpleasantly conspicuous. When *Lady Rose's Daughter* appeared, the critic of a great metropolitan daily remarked that whoever did not immediately recognise the work as a masterpiece thereby proclaimed himself as a person incapable of judgment, taste, and appreciation. This is a fair example of the attitude taken by thousands of her readers, and it is this attitude, rather than the value of her work, that we must, first of all, consider.

In the year 1905 an entirely respectable journal said of Mrs. Ward, "There is no more interesting and important figure in the literary world to-day." In comparing this superlative with the actual state of affairs, we find that we were asked to believe that Mrs. Ward was a literary personage not second in importance to Tolstoi, Ibsen, Björnson, Heyse, Sudermann, Hauptmann, Anatole France, Jules Lemaître, Rostand, Swinburne, Thomas Hardy, Meredith, Kipling, and Mark Twain. At about the same time a work appeared intended as a textbook for the young, which declared Mrs. Ward to be "the greatest living writer of fiction in English literature," and misspelled her name—an excellent illustration of carelessness in adjectives with in-accuracy in facts. Over and over again we have heard the statement that the "mantle" of George Eliot has fallen on Mrs. Ward. Is it really true that her stories are equal in value to *Adam Bede, The Mill on the Floss,* and *Middlemarch*?

The object of this essay is not primarily to attack a dignified and successful author; it is rather to enquire, in a proper spirit of humility, and with a full realisation of the danger incurred, whether or not the actual output justifies so enormous a reputation. For in some respects I believe the vogue of Mrs. Ward to be more unfortunate than the vogue of the late lamented Duchess, of Laura Jean Libbey, of Mrs. E. D. E. N. Southworth, of Marie Corelli, and of Hall Caine. When we are asked to note that 300,000 copies of the latest novel by any of these have been sold before the book is published, there is no cause for alarm. We know perfectly well what that means. It is what is called a "business proposition"; it has nothing to do with literature. It simply proves that it is possible to make as splendid a fortune out of the trade of book-making, and by equally respectable methods, as is made in other legitimate avenues of business. But the case is quite different with Mrs. Ward. Whatever she is, she is not vulgar, sensational, or cheap; she has never made the least compromise with her moral ideals, nor has she ever attempted to play to the gallery. Her constituency is made up largely of serious-minded, highly respectable people, who live in good homes, who are fairly well read, and who ought to know the difference between ordinary and extraordinary literature. Her books have had a bad effect in blurring this distinction in the popular mind; for while she has never written a positively bad book, —with the possible exception of *Bessie Costrell,* —I feel confident that she has never written supremely well; that, compared with the great masters of fiction, she becomes immediately insignificant. If there ever was a successful writer whose work shows industry and talent rather than genius, that writer is Mrs. Ward. If there ever was a successful writer whose work is ordinary rather than extraordinary, it is Mrs. Ward.

To those of us who delight in getting some enjoyment even out of the most depressing facts, the growth of Mrs. Ward's reputation has its humorous aspect. The same individuals (mostly feminine) who in 1888 read *Robert Elsmere* with dismay, who thought the sale of the work should be prohibited, and the copies already purchased removed from circulating libraries, are the very same ones who now worship what they once denounced. She was then regarded as a destroyer of Christian faith. Well, if she was Satan then, she is Satan still (one Western clergyman, in advocating at that time the suppression of the work, said he believed in hitting the devil right between the eyes). She has given no sign of recantation, or even of penitence. I remember one fond mother, who, fearful of the effect of the book on her daughter's growing mind, marked all the worst passages, and then told Alice she might read it, provided she skipped all the blazed places! That indicated not only a fine literary sense, but a remarkable knowledge of human nature. I wonder what the poor girl did when she came to the danger signals! And, as a matter of fact, how valuable or vital would a Christian faith be that could be destroyed by the perusal of *Robert Elsmere*? It is almost difficult now to bring to distinct recollection the tremendous excitement caused by Mrs. Ward's first successful novel, for it is a long time since I heard its name mentioned. The last public notice of it that I can recall was a large sign which appeared some fifteen years ago in a New Haven apothecary's window to the effect that one copy of *Robert Elsmere* would be presented free to each purchaser of a cake of soap!

Although *Robert Elsmere* was an immediate and prodigious success, and made it certain that whatever its author chose to write next would be eagerly bought, it is wholly untrue to say that her subsequent novels have depended in any way on *Elsmere* for their reputation. There are many instances in professional literary careers where one immensely successful book—*Lorna Doone,* for example—has floated a long succession of works that could not of themselves stay above water; many an author has succeeded in attaching a life-preserver to literary children who cannot swim. Far otherwise is the case with Mrs. Ward. It is probable that over half the readers of *Diana Mallory* have never seen a copy of *Robert Elsmere,* for which, incidentally, they are to be congratulated. But many of us can easily recollect with what intense eagerness the novel that followed that sensation was awaited. Every one wondered if it would be equally good; and many

confidently predicted that she had shot her bolt. As a matter of fact, not only was *David Grieve* a better novel than *Robert Elsmere,* but, in my judgement, it is the best book its author has ever written. Oscar Wilde said that *Robert Elsmere* was *Literature and Dogma* with the literature left out. Now, *David Grieve* has no dogma at all, but in a certain sense it does belong to literature. It has some actual dynamic quality. The character of David, and its development in a strange environment, are well analysed; and altogether the best thing in the work, taken as a whole, is the perspective. It is a difficult thing to follow a character from childhood up, within the pages of one volume, and have anything like the proper perspective. It requires for one thing, hard, painstaking industry; but Mrs. Ward has never been afraid of work. She cannot be accused of laziness or carelessness. The ending of this book is, of course, weak, like the conclusion of all her books, for she has never learned the fine art of saying farewell, either to her characters or to the reader.

It was in the year 1894—a year made memorable by the appearance of *Trilby,* the *Prisoner of Zenda, The Jungle Book, Lord Ormont and his Aminta, Esther Waters,* and other notable novels—that Mrs. Ward greatly increased her reputation and widened her circle of readers by the publication of *Marcella.* Here she gave us a political-didactic-realistic novel, which she has continued to publish steadily ever since under different titles. It was gravely announced that this new book would deal with socialism and the labour question. Many readers, who felt that she had said the last word on agnosticism in *Elsmere,* now looked forward with reverent anticipation not only to the final solution of socialistic problems, but to some coherent arrangement of their own vague and confused ideas. Naturally, they got just what they deserved—a voluminous statement of various aspects of the problem, with no solution at all. It is curious how many persons suppose that their favourite author or orator has done something toward settling questions, when, as a matter of fact, all he has done is to *state* them, and then state them again. This is especially true of philosophical and metaphysical difficulties. Think how eagerly readers took up Professor James's exceedingly clever book on Pragmatism, hoping at last to find rest in some definite principle. And if there ever was a blind alley in philosophy, it is Pragmatism—the very essence of agnosticism.

Now, *Marcella,* as a document, is both radical and reactionary. There is an immense amount of radical talk; but the heroine's schemes fail, the Labour party is torn by dissension, Wharton proves to be a scoundrel, and the rebel Marcella marries a respectable nobleman. There is not a single page in the book, with all its wilderness of words, that can be said to be in any sense a serious contribution to the greatest of all purely political problems. And, as a work of art, it is painfully limited; but since it has the same virtues and defects of all her subsequent literary output, we may consider what these virtues and defects are.

In the first place, Mrs. Ward is totally lacking in one almost fundamental quality of the great novelist—a keen sense of humour. Who are the English novelists of the first class? They are Defoe, Richardson, Fielding, Scott, Jane

Austen, Dickens, Thackeray, George Eliot, Stevenson, and perhaps Hardy. Every one of these shows humour enough and to spare, with the single exception of Richardson, and he atoned for the deficiency by a terrible intensity that has seldom, if ever, been equalled in English fiction. Now, the absence of humour in a book is not only a positive loss to the reader, in that it robs him of the fun which is an essential part of the true history of any human life, and thereby makes the history to that extent inaccurate and unreal, but the writer who has no humour seldom gets the right point of view. There is infinitely more in the temperament of the humorist than mere laughter. Just as the poet sees life through the medium of a splendid imagination, so the humorist has the almost infallible guide of sympathy. The humorist sees life in a large, tolerant, kindly way; he knows that life is a tragi-comedy, and he makes the reader feel it in that fashion.

Again, the lack of humour in a writer destroys the sense of proportion. The humorist sees the salient points—the merely serious writer gives us a mass of details. In looking back over the thousands of pages of fiction that Mrs. Ward has published, how few great scenes stand out bright in the memory! The principle of selection—so important a part of all true art—is conspicuous only by its absence. This is one reason for the sameness of her books. All that we can remember is an immense number of social functions and an immense amount of political gossip—a long, sad level of mediocrity. This perhaps helps to explain why German fiction is so markedly inferior to the French. The German, in his scientific endeavour to get in the whole of life, gives us a mass of unrelated detail. A French writer by a few phrases makes us see a character more clearly than a German presents him after many painful pages of wearisome description.

Mrs. Ward is not too much in earnest in following her ideals of art; no one can be. But she is too sadly serious. There is a mental tension in her books, like the tension of overwork and mental exhaustion, like the tension of overwrought nerves; her books are, in fact, filled with tired and over-worked men and women, jaded and gone stale. How many of her characters seem to need a change—what they want is rest and sleep! Many of them ought to be in a sanatorium.

Her books are devoid of charm. One does not have to compare her with the great masters to feel this deficiency; it would not be fair to compare her with Thackeray. But if we select among all the novelists of real distinction the one whom, perhaps, she most closely approaches, —Anthony Trollope, —the enormous distance between *Diana Mallory* and *Framley Parsonage* is instantly manifest. We think of Trollope with a glow of reminiscent delight; but although Trollope and Mrs. Ward talk endlessly on much the same range of subject-matter, how far apart they really are! Mrs. Ward's books are crammed with politicians and clergymen, who keep the patient reader informed on modern aspects of political and religious thought; but the difficulty is that they substitute phrases for ideas. Mrs. Ward knows all the political and religious cant of the day; she is familiar with the catch-words that divide men into hostile camps; but in all these dreary pages of serious conver-

sation there is no real illumination. She completely lacks the art that Trollope possessed, of making ordinary people attractive. But to find out the real distance that separates her productions from literature, one should read, let us say, *The Marriage of William Ashe* and then take up *Pride and Prejudice*. The novels of Mrs. Ward bear about the same relation to first-class fiction that maps and atlases bear to great paintings.

This lack of charm that I always feel in reading Mrs. Ward's books (and I have read them all) is owing not merely to the lack of humour. It is partly due to what seems to be an almost total absence of freshness, spontaneity, and originality. Mrs. Ward works like a well-trained and high-class graduate student, who is engaged in the preparation of a doctor's thesis. Her discussions of socialism, her scenes in the House of Commons and on the Terrace, her excursions to Italy, her references to political history, her remarks on the army, her disquisitions on theology, her pictures of campaign riots, her studies of defective drainage, her representations of the labouring classes, —all these are "worked up" in a scholarly and scientific manner; there is the modern passion for accuracy, there is the German completeness of detail, —there is, in fact, everything except the breath of life. She works in the descriptive manner, from the outside in—not in the inspired manner which goes with imagination, sympathy, and genius. She is not only a student, she is a journalist; she is a special correspondent on politics and theology; but she is not a creative writer. For she has the critical, not the creative, temperament.

The monotonous sameness of her books, which has been mentioned above, is largely owing to the sameness of her characters. She changes the frames, but not the portraits. First of all, in almost any of her books we are sure to meet the studious, intellectual young man. He always has a special library on some particular subject, with the books all annotated. One wearies of this perpetual character's perpetual library, crowded, as it always is, with the latest French and German monographs. Her heroes smell of books and dusty dissertations, and the conversations of these heroes are plentifully lacking in native wit and originality—they are the mere echoes of their reading. Let us pass in review a few of these serious students—Robert Elsmere, Langham, Aldous Reyburn (who changes into Lord Maxwell, but who remains a prig), the melancholy Helbeck, the insufferable Manisty, Jacob Delafield, William Ashe, Oliver Marsham—all, all essentially the same, tiresome, dull, heavy men—what a pity they were not intended as satires! Second, as a foil to this man, we have the Byronic, clever, romantic, sentimental, insincere man—who always degenerates or dies in a manner that exalts the dull and superior virtues of his antagonist. Such a man is Wharton, or Sir George Tressady, or Captain Warkworth, or Cliffe—they have different names in different novels, but they are the same character. Curiously enough, the only convincing men that appear in her pages are *old* men—men like Lord Maxwell or Sir James Chide. In portraying this type she achieves success.

What shall we say of her heroines? They have the same suspicious resemblance so characteristic of her heroes;

they are represented as physically beautiful, intensely eager for morality and justice, with an extraordinary fund of information, and an almost insane desire to impart it. Her heroine is likely to be or to become a power in politics; even at a tender age she rules society by the brilliancy of her conversation; in a crowded drawing-room the Prime Minister hangs upon her words; diplomats are amazed at her intimate knowledge of foreign relations, and of the resources of the British Empire; and she can entertain a whole ring of statesmen and publicists by giving to each exactly the right word at the right moment. Men who are making history come to her not only for inspiration but for guidance, for she can discourse fluently on all phases of the troublesome labour question. And yet, if we may judge of this marvellous creature not by the attitude of the other characters in the book, but by the actual words that fall from her lips, we are reminded of the woman whom Herbert Spencer's friends selected as his potential spouse. They shut him up with her, and awaited the result with eagerness, for they told him she had a great mind; but on emerging from the trial interview Spencer remarked that she would not do at all: "The young lady is, in my opinion, too highly intellectual; or, I should rather say—morbidly intellectual. A small brain in a state of intense activity." Was there ever a better formula for Mrs. Ward's constantly recurring heroine? Now, as a foil to Marcella, Diana Mallory, and the others, Mrs. Ward gives us the frivolous, mischief-making, would-be brilliant, and actually vulgar woman, who makes much trouble for the heroine and ultimately more for herself—the wife of Sir George Tressady, the young upstart in *Diana Mallory,* and all the rest of them. By the introduction of these characters there is an attempt to lend colour to the dull pages of the novels. These women are at heart adventuresses, but they are apt to lack the courage of their convictions; instead of being brilliant and terrible, —like the great adventuresses of fiction, —they are as dull in sin as their antagonists are dull in virtue. Mrs. Ward cannot make them real; compare any one of them with Thackeray's Beatrix or with Becky Sharp—to say nothing of the long list of sinister women in French and Russian fiction.

There are no "supreme moments" in Mrs. Ward's books; no great dramatic situations; she has tried hard to manage this, for she has had repeatedly one eye on the stage. When *The Marriage of William Ashe* and *Lady Rose's Daughter* appeared, one could almost feel the strain for dramatic effect. It was as though she had realised that her previous books were treatises rather than novels, and had gathered all her energies together to make a severe effort for real drama. But, unfortunately, the scholarly and critical temperament is not primarily adapted for dramatic masterpieces. In the endeavour to recall thrilling scenes in her novels, scenes that brand themselves for ever on the memory, one has only to compare her works with such stories as *Far From the Madding Crowd* or *The Return of the Native,* and her painful deficiency is immediately apparent.

In view of what I believe to be the standard mediocrity of her novels, how shall we account for their enormous vogue? The fact is, whether we like it or not, that she is one of the most widely read of all living novelists. Well, in the first place, she is absolutely respectable and safe. It is assuredly to her credit that she has never stooped for popularity. She has never descended to melodrama, claptrap, or indecency. She is never spectacular and declamatory like Marie Corelli, and she is never morally offensive like some popular writers who might be mentioned. She writes for a certain class of readers whom she thoroughly understands: they are the readers who abhor both vulgarity and pruriency, and who like to enter vicariously, as they certainly do in her novels, into the best English society. In her social functions her readers can have the pleasure of meeting prime ministers, lords, and all the dwellers in Mayfair, and they know that nothing will be said that is shocking or improper. Her books can safely be recommended to young people, and they reflect the current movement of English thought as well as could be done by a standard English review. She has a well-furnished and highly developed intellect; she is deeply read; she makes her readers think that they are thinking. She tries to make up for artistic deficiencies by an immense amount of information. Fifty years ago it is probable that she would not have written novels at all, but rather thoughtful and intellectual critical essays, for which her mind is admirably fitted. She unconsciously chose the novel simply because the novel has been, during the last thirty years, the chief channel of literary expression. But in spite of her popularity, it should never be forgotten that the novel is an art-form, not a medium for doctrinaires.

Then, with her sure hand on the pulse of the public, she is always intensely modern, intensely contemporary; again like a well-trained journalist. She knows exactly what Society is talking about, for she emphatically belongs to it. This is once more a reason why so many people believe that she holds the key to great problems of social life, and that her next book will give the solution. Many hoped that her novel on America, carefully worked up during her visit here, would give the final word on American social life. Both England and the United States were to find out what the word "American" really means.

Mrs. Ward is an exceedingly talented, scholarly, and thoughtful woman, of lofty aims and actuated only by noble motives; she is hungry for intellectual food, reading both old texts and the daily papers with avidity. She has a highly trained, sensitive, critical mind, —but she is destitute of the divine spark of genius. Her books are the books of to-day, not of to-morrow; for while the political and religious questions of to-day are of temporary interest, the themes of the world's great novels are what Richardson called "love and nonsense, men and women"—and these are eternal.

William Lyon Phelps, "Mrs. Humphry Ward," in his Essays on Modern Novelists, *The Macmillan Company, 1910, pp. 191-207.*

Arnold Bennett   (essay date 1908)

[*Bennett was an Edwardian novelist who is credited with bringing techniques of European Naturalism to the English novel. He is best known as the author of* The Old Wives' Tale *(1908) and the Clayhanger trilogy (1910-1916), realistic novels depicting life in an English manufacturing town.*

In the following excerpt, originally published in New Age *in 1908, he offers a negative appraisal of Ward's works, particularly criticizing the heroines of her novels.*]

That a considerable social importance . . . attaches to the publication of a novel by Mrs. Humphry Ward may be judged from the fact that the *Manchester Guardian* specially reviewed the book on its leader page. This strange phenomenon deserves to be studied, because the *Manchester Guardian*'s reviewing easily surpasses that of any other daily paper, except, possibly, the *Times* in its Literary Supplement. The *Guardian* relies on mere, sheer intellectual power, and as a rule it does not respect persons. Its theatrical critics, for example, take joy in speaking the exact truth—never whispered in London—concerning the mandarins of the stage. Now it is remarkable that the only strictly first-class morning daily in these isles should have printed the *Guardian*'s review of **Diana Mallory** (signed "B. S."); for the article respected persons. I do not object to Mrs. Humphry Ward being reviewed with splendid prominence. I am quite willing to concede that a new book from her constitutes the matter of a piece of news, since it undoubtedly interests a large number of respectable and correct persons. A novel by Miss Marie Corelli, however, constitutes the matter of a greater piece of news; yet I have seen no review of *Holy Orders,* even in a corner, in the *Guardian.* Surely the *Guardian* was not prevented from dealing faithfully with *Holy Orders* by the fact that it received no review copy, or by the fact that Miss Corelli desired no review. Its news department in general is conducted without reference to the desires of Miss Marie Corelli, and it does not usually boggle at an expenditure of four-and-sixpence. Why, then, Mrs. Humphry Ward being reviewed specially, is not Miss Marie Corelli reviewed specially? If the answer be that Mrs. Humphry Ward's novels are better, as literature, than Miss Corelli's, I submit that the answer is insufficient, and lacking in Manchester sincerity.

Let me duly respect Mrs. Humphry Ward. She knows her business. She is an expert in narrative. She can dress up even the silliest incidents of sentimental fiction—such as that in which the virgin heroine, in company with a young man, misses the last train home (see **Helbeck of Bannisdale**)—in a costume of plausibility. She is a conscientious worker. She does not make a spectacle of herself in illustrated interviews. Even in agitating against votes for women she can maintain her dignity. (She would be an ideal President of the Authors' Society.) But, then, similar remarks apply, say, to Mr. W. E. Norris. Mr. W. E. Norris is as accomplished an expert as Mrs. Humphry Ward. He is in possession of a much better style. He has humour. He is much more true to life. He has never compromised the dignity of his vocation. Nevertheless, the prospect of the *Guardian* reviewing Mr. W. E. Norris on its leader-page is remote, for the reason that though he pleases respectable and correct persons, he does not please nearly so many respectable and correct persons as does Mrs. Humphry Ward. If anybody has a right to the leader-page of our unique daily, Mrs. Humphry Ward is that body. My objection to the phenomenon is that the *Guardian* falsified its item of news. It deliberately gave the impression that a serious work of art had appeared in **Diana Mallory**. It

ought to have known better. It did know better. If our unique daily is to yield to the snobbishness which ranks Mrs. Humphry Ward among genuine artists, where among dailies are we to look for the shadow of a great rock?

Mrs. Humphry Ward's novels are praiseworthy as being sincerely and skilfully done, but they are not works of art. They are possibly the best stuff now being swallowed by the uneducated public; and they deal with the governing classes; and when you have said that you have said all. Nothing truly serious can happen in them. It is all make-believe. No real danger of the truth about life! . . . I should think not, indeed! The fearful quandary in which the editor of *Harper's* found himself with *Jude the Obscure* was a lesson to all Anglo-Saxon editors for ever more! Mrs. Humphry Ward has never got nearer to life than, for instance, *Rita* has got—nor so near! Gladstone, a thoroughly bad judge of literature, made her reputation, and not on a postcard, either! Gladstone had no sense of humour—at any rate when he ventured into literature. Nor has Mrs. Humphry Ward. If she had she would not concoct those excruciating heroines of hers. She probably does not know that her heroines are capable of rousing temperaments such as my own to ecstasies of homicidal fury. Moreover, in literature all girls named Diana are insupportable. Look at Diana Vernon, beloved of Mr. Andrew Lang, I believe! What a creature! Imagine living with her! You can't! Look at Diana of the Crossways. Why did Diana of the Crossways marry? Nobody can say—unless the answer is that she was a ridiculous ninny. Would Anne Elliot have made such an inexplicable fool of herself? Why does Diana Mallory "go to" her preposterous Radical ex-M.P.? Simply because she is tiresomely absurd. Oh, those men with strong chins and irreproachable wristbands! Oh, those cultured conversations! Oh, those pure English maids! That skittishness! That impulsiveness! That noxious winsomeness!

I have invented a destiny for Mrs. Humphry Ward's heroines. It is terrible, and just. They ought to be caught, with their lawful male protectors, in the siege of a great city by a foreign army. Their lawful male protectors ought, before sallying forth on a forlorn hope, to provide them with a revolver as a last refuge from a brutal and licentious soldiery. And when things come to a crisis, in order to be concluded in our next, the revolvers ought to prove to be unloaded. I admit that this invention of mine is odious, and quite un-English, and such as would never occur to a right-minded subscriber to Mudie's. But it illustrates the mood caused in me by witnessing the antics of those harrowing dolls.

Arnold Bennett, "Mrs. Humphry Ward's Heroines," in his Books and Persons: Being Comments on a Past Epoch, 1908-1911, *George H. Doran Company, 1917, pp. 47-52.*

Herbert L. Stewart (essay date 1920)

[*In the following excerpt, Stewart examines Ward's theological novels.*]

There are few of [Mrs Ward's] books from which the religious interest is wholly absent, and there are at least five in which it may be said to predominate. *Robert Elsmere* is the best known, but in any such general survey we must not omit *The History of David Grieve, Helbeck of Bannisdale, Eleanor,* and *The Case of Richard Meynell.* The first point which calls for notice is one that all of these novels exhibit alike, and that constitutes a notable merit in the authoress when compared with many others who have imported speculations about faith into a work of fiction. We all know with tolerable exactness what Mrs Ward herself believed, or at least some things that she emphatically disbelieved. But her first concern was neither to proclaim what she thought true nor to repudiate what she thought false. The Evangelical school, the Broad school, the Romanising school—all pass before us in order, and if the writer's sole or even her chief object had been to take sides among them she would have deserved all the artistic censure that some quarterlies have bestowed upon her work. Her first desire was to enter with what St Paul called "charity" into the attitude of all candid souls who have set out, in however blundering a fashion, upon the great quest, to give all the credit that seemed to be their due, and to wean the angry disputants of each school not from the zeal that springs from conviction but from the bitterness that has its roots in misunderstanding. It would be too much to expect of anyone that this purpose should be achieved with perfect impartiality, and one can recall places where far less than equal justice has been done. For instance, George Eliot was at least as remote intellectually from Methodism as Mrs Ward can be, but the fervid Wesleyan must feel that sympathy is further from her perfect work in the hand which drew Mrs Fleming in *Robert Elsmere,* or the smithy prayer-meeting in *David Grieve,* than in the hand which gave us Dinah Morris in *Adam Bede.* The prejudices of temperament are hard to overcome, but we should be thankful to those who manage to overcome them as consistently as Mrs Ward has done, and thus set a pattern to that great number who do not even attempt to overcome them at all. On the whole she deserves the high eulogium passed upon her own Henry Grey, for she was sympathetic to "every genuine utterance of the spiritual life of man."

Again, while many others have introduced religious and anti-religious debate into a novel, she is one of a very few who have given us studies of *cultured* unbelief as it exists at the present time. We know how Dickens and Thackeray, for example, used to poke fun at the narrow evangelicals. Sam Weller in *Pickwick,* making his unseemly jests about Regeneration; Miss Murdstone in *David Copperfield,* rolling her dark eyes with delight over the congregation around her as often as the prayer-book mentioned "miserable sinners"; Miss Miggs in *Barnaby Rudge,* who hoped that she knew her own unworthiness and hated and despised herself as every good Christian should; Lady Emily in *Vanity Fair,* tying up her parcels of tracts, with mild exhortation for real ladies and warmer stuff about "The Frying Pan and the Fire" for the servants' hall— such matter as this has become quite familiar, and can be produced, now that the pattern has been set, in almost any quantity by very indifferent artists. It is often very successful wit, but its fault lies in the absence of humour, that lack of a background in charity which our own sobered age increasingly demands, Charlotte Brontë used to keep up the

fun at the expense of the High Church. Mr Wells never lets us rest from laughing at the formulae of "vindictive theologians." And Mr Winston Churchill—the American of that name—provides us in such books as *The Inside of the Cup* with most effective satire upon those who are zealots for dogma, but not zealots for the housing of the poor or the living wage. Mrs Ward's interest in religion was different. She was concerned with the state of mind of persons of culture, and although "culture" is an object of scorn just now to those who think it just the English word for Kultur, and keep themselves in readiness to explode the moment it is named, yet this is a misunderstanding which must soon pass away.

Mrs Ward spent her life in the atmosphere of the intellectuals; the university was her spiritual home; it is of the leaders of thought that she loved to write. She had the great advantage of personal acquaintance with literary and scientific men of wide celebrity, and it is their varying moods and attitudes towards religion which she has drawn with the most unerring hand. Taine, Edmond Scherer, Mark Pattison, Jowett, Walter Pater, and many others are made to pass before us in *A Writer's Recollections* by a critic who knew them well, and she has made us very much her debtors by helping us to know them too. Everyone must have been struck by her frequent allusions to two men, Ernest Renan and Matthew Arnold. The brilliant gifts of the former were enough to impress any keen receptive mind during the seventies, and we may well pardon the partiality of an admiring niece if Arnold's *bons mots* are treated by her as if they now formed part of the linguistic inheritance for all educated Englishmen. One may, perhaps, object that such phrases as "Barbarians, Philistines, Populace," "Hellenist and Hebraist," "Stream of tendency not ourselves that makes for righteousness" are not quite such universal counters of human thought as Mrs Ward seemed to assume, and not a few may be puzzled to find them used as if they came from *Hamlet* or *Faust.* So too we may smile at a writer who is still harking back for illustration to something that was done or said or felt by Renan, for the men of our own time have had many other teachers, and recognise many other landmarks as at least equally significant with the *Vie de Jésus.*

Stocks, the Wards' country home in the village of Aldbury, Hertfordshire.

But very few of those who grumble so were under the immediate influence of these magicians. Arnold and Renan were perhaps the two most original minds with which Mrs Ward in her youth was brought into close contact, and it is to her credit that she so appreciated each of them as to be unable afterwards to escape from the power of his personality.

The historic impulse which produced the first, and still the most famous, of her theological novels is quite apparent. In the five years from 1869 to 1873 Matthew Arnold made his well-known contribution to the great debate. The four books, *Culture and Anarchy, St Paul and Protestantism, Literature and Dogma, God and the Bible,* form together a manifesto of humanitarian Christianity. No one who reads **Robert Elsmere** can mistake the source from which some of its most arresting features were drawn. The strange re-interpreting of St Paul on the Resurrection, the spiritualising of the words "risen with Christ," the breaking away from the "envelope of miracle," the dissolving of supernatural occurrences into mere clothing for moral ideas—for all these, if a chief inspiration was found in the *Lay Sermons* of Thomas Hill Green, it is no less the thought and often the very words of Arnold which persistently recur.

But at this stage Mrs Ward was also in somewhat sharp revolt against some of her distinguished uncle's positions. The hero of her book could find no satisfaction in the Broad Church. She quotes Renan's judgment that if the prophecies of Daniel have to be placed by criticism in the period of the Maccabees, there is no option for critics but a resolute schism. And she adds, curiously enough, that the Protestant "is in truth more bound to the book of Daniel than M. Renan." In those days Mrs Ward could see no place for religious compromise, depicted Elsmere as confronted with a situation which left no room for choice to an honest man, set before us in the proposals of the cynical squire on the one hand and the idealistic Oxford tutor on the other the great contrast between temporising disguise and resolute veracity. "It can't be said," declares Henry Grey, "that the Broad Church movement has helped us much. How greatly it promised! How little it has performed!"

In the sequel to **Robert Elsmere,** published more than twenty years afterwards under the name **The Case of Richard Meynell,** this attitude of bold secession is very suggestively modified. Meynell is a Modernist, but by no means willing to be in consequence a schismatic. He believes that the time is ripe for a new Reformation, and, though he thinks that this should be a Reformation from within, he is determined that it shall adopt no half-measures of timidity or concealment. Like Erasmus, he would move slowly, but he would not be so slow as to make no perceptible movement at all. If his movement fails he is prepared to be its victim, taking no refuge in the comfortable thought that Providence has bestowed upon him "no gift for martyrdom." But he is determined that, so far as lies in the power of himself and his friends, it is the orthodox resistance that shall be made to fail, and that the old historic Church of England, once more reformed,

shall rise as she did three centuries ago to meet the new dawn.

Thus Meynell's case is that the so-called "orthodox" have no more right to expel Modernists than Modernists to expel the orthodox. If we defend the retention of the Roman cathedrals, though the English people had cast off Roman supremacy, why cannot we assert a similar ownership in the same fabrics if the supremacy of the Thirty-nine Articles has now to be repudiated. In the end this must no doubt be a trial of strength between parties, and the voice of the nation as a whole must decide. Hence arises Meynell's curious emphasising of the significant increase in the *number* of Modernists as compared with the days of Elsmere. Speaking to the daughter of that vigorous secessionist, he says: "All *within* the gates seemed lost. Your father went out into the wilderness, and there, amid everything that was poor and mean and new, he laid down his life. But we! —we are no longer alone, or helpless. The tide has come up to the stranded ship—the launching of it depends now only on the faithfulness of those within it."

Almost exactly equidistant in time of composition between **Robert Elsmere** and **Richard Meynell** came that fascinating pair of romances in which Mrs Ward gave us her study of the Church of Rome. **Helbeck of Bannisdale** appeared in 1898, **Eleanor** in 1900. If we trace our authoress's interest in the broader Anglicans to the stimulus imparted by her uncle, it may equally well have been filial piety which made her touch so delicate when she drew those in willing and glad subjection under the Roman obedience. Charles Hargrove, whose frequent changes of creed the editor of this Journal has lately been setting before us, is among the very few parallels one may quote to the chameleon-like religious career of the younger Thomas Arnold. That a son of the famous headmaster of Rugby should have begun as a disciple of his father, seceded in early manhood to the Church of Rome, swung over after a few years to Rationalism, and having remained there for a period should have made a fresh submission—not again to be recanted—to the Holy See, was by itself a sufficiently curious phenomenon to set any thoughtful mind upon the task of its unravelling.

In **Helbeck of Bannisdale** Mrs Ward has given us a psychological picture of an old Catholic household, whose representative is a man of the finest feeling, torn between the promptings of human nature and what he takes to be the inexorable obligations of his religion, preserving in a hostile neighbourhood the loyalty of his mistaken creed, and struggling in vain to reconcile his duties towards the true faith with an attachment he has formed, in spite of himself, to a girl who is, alas! among the "sinners of the Gentiles." **Eleanor** has its scene laid in Italy, the Italy that had just passed through the period of hot contention between the papal power and the national movement, and makes us realise with great vividness the two sides—the party of Pius IX. and the party of Victor Emmanuel; but to many of us the most important interest of the book centres round the case of Father Benecke, who has published a book about the Church and her history which is condemned by Propaganda. Shall he recant and escape deprivation? Or stand firm, and be a martyr? Father Benecke's dilemma, like that of Elsmere and Helbeck, brings home to us the everlasting issue between the spirit of the past and the spirit of the future.

Mr. G. W. E. Russell declared that, so far as he knew, the Rev. Robert Elsmere was the only human being whose religious faith had been shattered by the discovery that "miracles do not happen." "That long-legged weakling," wrote Mr Russell, "with his auburn hair and 'boyish innocence of mood' and sweet ignorance of the wicked world went down, it will be remembered, like a ninepin before the assaults of a sceptical squire who had studied in Germany."

Probably this is, on the whole, the most inept comment that was made by any critic upon the hero of Mrs Ward's great novel. Whether religious faith is, or is not, bound up with acceptance of the miraculous, is a matter upon which there is fair ground for difference of opinion, and the present writer at least is in thorough agreement with what he takes to be Mr Russell's view upon it. It may be conceded, too, that Elsmere after his ordination was curiously unacquainted, for a man of his training and powers, with the trend of modern unbelief. But it is absurd to suggest that he is an unintelligible or even a very unusual type, and that he is not—as the dramatic critics say—"psychologically convincing." He presents no greater problem than, for example, the Rev. James Anthony Froude at the time when he wrote *The Nemesis of Faith.* There is not the least doubt that many men, brought up to Holy Orders in the Oxford of forty years ago, were similarly immune from the infection of the Zeitgeist. No one who is in the least familiar with the moods of the theological student of our own time has the least difficulty in recognising Elsmere's distress, and most of us could quote parallels from men whom we have personally known.

The reason is obvious. To many—perhaps to the greater number of Christians—the whole fabric of faith stands as a solid system of which no part can be invalidated without invalidating the rest. That which, so far as Mr Russell was aware, had never occurred in the experience of any human being except "a character in a popular work of fiction" has, as others are well aware, occurred historically again and again, when religious faith has been shattered by discoveries about the antiquity of the earth, the dimensions of stellar space, the evolution of species, and the higher criticism of scripture. In all these cases the rule *falsus in uno falsus in omnibus* was applied, to the immense dislocation of fixed beliefs, and it was the principle of a supernatural—or a miraculous—revelation which was on each occasion held to have been overthrown. The inference may have been exaggerated, or it may have been wholly wrong; but there is no doubt of its occurrence as a fact of religious psychology. It is no failure of insight into the moods of the human mind which we can justly charge against Mrs Ward, for the verisimilitude of her characters—Roman, High Anglican, Broad Anglican, and Agnostic—is well-nigh perfect.

It may be argued with far greater force against her, as Gladstone and many others argued, that the prestige of learning and intellect are by no means so exclusively on the side of her own school as she has tried to suggest. And

it may be maintained that she has undertaken far more than she can effect in trying to find the essence of Christianity in Thomas Hill Green. But these discussions would carry us much too far. What I wish to consider is her proposed practical solution of the issue about Modernism as she has set it forth in *The Case of Richard Meynell.* Here she touched the newest and most urgent problem of our own time, and revealed, I think, the most vulnerable side in her whole programme for the future of the Church.

Some historian will yet be much interested in that singular alliance between Freethought and Erastianism of which Mrs Ward in her latest phase was so striking a representative. It is significant that in matters of Church Reform she again and again appealed to "England" as the ultimate authority, and one cannot help feeling that she had often in mind Reformers not so much like John Knox as like Henry VIII. The national Church, she kept reminding us, is a national possession, with its cathedrals, its ecclesiastical fabrics of every kind, its endowments—its "plant," as she occasionally, breaking into the vernacular of commerce, rather startles us by summing the matter up. Her idea seemed to be that just as state machinery, provided from the public purse, must not be monopolised by the interests of a single class, so the spiritual organisation is in essence a public affair, and must be wide enough to allow a home to men of every Christian faith. Why it should thus be limited to those whose attitude is *Christian,* or whether she would set any limits at all, Mrs Ward did not make quite clear. She did not meet such embarrassing proposals as that of Mr Ronald Knox in *Reunion All Round,* or such dilemmas as are set in *A Spiritual Æneid.* "For the life of me," says Mr Knox, "I could never see why we had to regret being out of communion with a good man like Dr Horton, more than being out of communion with a good man like Professor Gilbert Murray, who repudiates Theism."

Perhaps the most extraordinary position taken up by Richard Meynell is that the High Churchman ought to be as willing to tolerate the Broad as the Broad is to tolerate the High. For what this really means is that, while the Broad keeps his own view, the High ought either to become Broad or at least to act as if he had become so. The demand for tolerance is by no means identical as applied to each of these two parties. Rather, one is forced to say, must the orthodox be driven to exclusiveness by the very same logic which drives the liberal to charity. Those to whom dogma is comparatively indifferent may, and indeed must, adopt a generous attitude towards those whose honest beliefs they cannot themselves share. But men to whom dogma is essential cannot without absurdity be other than unbending towards men who preach that creeds are a matter of ceaseless change. The Modernist can remain in the Church undisturbed by the fact that his brother in the next parish imposes penances, pronounces absolution, and reserves the sacrament; for, although he does not himself approve such doings, he does not think of them as endangering souls in another world, or of the communion of saints as fundamentally vitiated by these divergences of practice. But the sacerdotalist cannot in the same way look on without fierce protest while his neighbour in Holy Orders is teaching that belief in the miraculous is superstition, that there was no Virgin Birth, and that the Tomb at Jerusalem did not on the third day yield up the body of the Lord; for he does not simply dissent from all this as a lamentable error of judgment: he regards it as a blasphemy, and a mood of complaisant indulgence for peace's sake towards those who commit it is, for him, denying his Lord before men.

I speak of this with all the more vigour because I do not share in any degree most of the objections which the orthodox level against Modernism. Perhaps, however, I understand them all the better just because of some very real objections with which I wholly sympathise against the presence of certain so-called Modernists, and because the principle involved appears to be the same. From time to time we have to hear or read sermons in which, for example, the notion of "subjective immortality" is insinuated, elegant Emersonian scorn is poured upon those— generally psychic researchers—who dare to take the survival of man as a genuine and perhaps even a verifiable fact, and the idea of evil as a mere negation of good or a necessary form of finitude is played with under some such nonsensical phrase as "supra-moral sphere." Are we to pretend that the Christian Church should make room for incoherences like these? And, if not, is our revolt different in kind from that which inspires the Anglo-Catholic to cut himself loose from association with Modernists in general! Are not the yearly secessions to Rome, however deeply we may deplore the fact that men feel driven to make them, thus the tokens of both clear-sighted and resolute candour? Aptly indeed from his own point of view may the High Churchman find a parallel to this theological issue in that old affiliation case tried before Solomon, and see men like Meynell typified by the latitudinarian mother who cried out, "Let it be neither mine nor thine, but let us divide it." And, though we may think that his point of view is wrong, we cannot fairly reproach him for acting upon the situation as he sees it, or set him in discreditable contrast with those who act differently because they see differently. The present writer, Modernist as he is in his own sympathies to an extent by which many evangelicals would be appalled, cannot acquiesce in this programme of easy-going complaisance for those to whom it would mean a denial of truth. Not thus shall the new Reformation be achieved. The coming change must involve no disguises, for the thing at stake is too momentous. Perhaps the Church should be divided in two, but where the differences are radical the division must be radical. Those within her pale who believe, however erroneously, that saving truth lies in rigid dogma, should not be browbeaten in the name of toleration into taking liberties with that which— as they hold—is not theirs to compromise. The stigma of narrowness is not to be expunged by the mop of prevarication.

One might point out, as further illustrating this tendency in Mrs Ward, how the spirit of revolt which has been so conspicuous in her theological novels is moderated into an enthusiasm for what Lord Eldon called the "wisdom of our ancestors" when she deals with problems of government. No one will be surprised, or at any loss to guess the reason, when he finds in *A Writer's Recollections* such grateful adoration of Mr Kipling and such nasty resent-

ment towards Mr Wells. Some of us feel that old church tradition deserves at least as respectful a treatment as old political usages, that ecclesiastical authority is not more open to reproach than the prestige of an hereditary ruling class, and that there are dogmas about imperialism not less obsolete in the living thought of our new world than any dogmas of old theology. But Mrs Ward's mind was curiously blended—half conservative and half liberal, —and to those who, like England herself, "love not coalitions," this sort of compromise is far from satisfactory. It is not, indeed, uncommon in cultivated circles. Like many others, this novelist was a very orthodox aristocrat, though a quite unorthodox theologian. Robust rationalism in dealing with religious tenets can easily make its peace with a tenacious traditionalism in one's theory of the State, so that the abuse of radical politicians in *Marcella* and of the suffragettes in *Delia Blanchflower* gives willing place to a quite different tone when the radicals are causing upheaval of the Church in *Richard Meynell* or an Italian countess is plunging into political discussion against Pio Nono in *Eleanor.* The Germans, as Dr Sarolea has aptly remarked, used to combine great freedom of thought about the divinity of Christ with a docile subservience to the divine right of their Kaiser. Imperialistic politics almost everywhere can be cherished by some side by side with the most vigorous spirit of theological anarchy. And although I mean nothing so offensive or so absurd as a likening of Mrs Ward to German exponents both of religious agnosticism and of earthly Realpolitik, I cannot refrain from noticing that the liberal trend of her thought was restrained by some astonishing limits. Inconsistency, however, is a poor charge in these days when our world has been shaken to its base, and we have much ground for thankfulness to this writer of fiction for at least some healthy ethical conventionalism. As we think, for instance, of the abyss of immoral nonsense into which the sex novel so often degenerates, even those pious folk who have been most shocked by *Robert Elsmere* must not forget what they owe to the authoress of *Daphne* and *The Marriage of William Ashe.*

There are many others too who in these times of religious disturbance are "wandering between two worlds—one dead, the other powerless to be born." Few have been able to present this state of mind with even a tithe of the vividness and strength with which this novelist has set it before us. . . .

[Mrs Ward] was in error, I think, in supposing that the path of progress now lies in any other direction than that in which it has always lain, that fundamental discords can with advantage be superficially disguised, or that truth will be furthered by minimising rather than by intensifying the "clash of Yes and No."

Herbert L. Stewart, "Mrs. Humphry Ward and the Theological Novel," in The Hibbert Journal, *Vol. XVIII, No. 4, July, 1920, pp. 675-86.*

Edward Wagenknecht   (essay date 1943)

[*In the following excerpt, Wagenknecht characterizes*

Ward's works as typifying conservative Victorian tastes in literature.]

Life is always much less systematic than histories of literature; and there are currents and counter-currents in every period. During the latter end of Victoria's reign in England some writers were already giving their allegiance to the ideals of the age that was to come, while others, not necessarily inferior to them, were still finding their creative inspiration in the old patterns. . . .

Mrs. Humphry Ward is the first [among the literary conservatives of the late Victorian era]. It is the fashion nowadays to see her in a light very similar to that in which Lytton Strachey placed her grandfather, Thomas Arnold. She is the perfect symbol of everything that was "stuffy" in Victorianism. She has been caricatured by H. G. Wells and Arnold Bennett [in *The Sea Lady* and *The Book of Carlotta* respectively]; and even her friend, Henry James, who spent many hours trying to pump some of his wisdom into her, is said to have declared that the dear lady never understood a word he said.

In all save time Mrs. Ward is as remote as the polar star, as remote, as indifferent, and as cold. We do not understand her. Whether the fault is hers or ours, who can say?

—*John Middleton Murry, in his* The Evolution of an Intellectual, *1927.*

The most remarkable thing about Mrs. Ward is that having first achieved such prestige as surely no other novelist with so little creative power had ever enjoyed before her, she should have been so quickly forgotten. She died as recently as March 24, 1920; though no doubt it would be possible to argue that as an artist she died with Catherine Elsmere in 1911, on the last page of *The Case of Richard Meynell*. Among her later books, *The Coryston Family* (1913), *Eltham House* (1915), and *Lady Connie* (1916) are perhaps the best; from these she descended to the four war novels which stand gathering dust in old bookshops to remind us that she was an important cog in the British propaganda machine to get America into the First World War.

Yet for many years Mrs. Ward was regarded as George Eliot's successor, and her books were approached with comparable reverence. None other than Tolstoy called her the greatest living English novelist. The general public was equally enthusiastic; in America the competition between rival pirate publishers of *Robert Elsmere* waxed so keen that one actually brought out an edition at four cents a copy, only to be outdone at last by the Maine Balsam Fir Company, which gave away a book with every cake of soap! "No book since *Uncle Tom's Cabin*," wrote William Roscoe Thayer, "has had so sudden and wide a diffusion among all classes of readers; and I believe no other book of equal seriousness ever had so quick a hearing."

Robert Elsmere (1888), *The History of David Grieve* (1892), *Helbeck of Bannisdale* (1898), and *The Case of Richard Meynell* (1911) are Mrs. Ward's distinctively religious novels; here she does what George Eliot always refused to do—she makes religious doubt the subject of fiction. Robert Elsmere, like George Eliot herself, is driven to relinquish orthodoxy through the critical study of Christian evidences; he leaves the Church of England to found a religious-humanitarian center in London, which is motivated by ideals similar to those that inspired Mrs. Ward's own Passmore Edwards Settlement, and at last finds his spiritual equilibrium in a passionate loyalty to a purely human Christ. The most moving part of the book concerns the struggle between the hero and his rigidly orthodox wife, so impervious to his opinions, so unshaken in her love and loyalty. *David Grieve* presents the ideal of a "natural religion" developing spontaneously through conscience and social sensitiveness. *Helbeck of Bannisdale* reverses the *Elsmere* problem on its personal side; this time the man is a passionate Catholic, the girl an unbeliever. And *Richard Meynell* reworks *Elsmere* toward another conclusion. Richard, who marries Elsmere's daughter and inherits his battle, refuses to leave the church; instead he attempts to build a place for Modernists within its fold.

Life had prepared Mrs. Ward very thoroughly for the understanding of such problems. She was born, Mary Augusta Arnold, in Tasmania, June 11, 1851. Her father was the younger Thomas Arnold, whose conversion to Catholicism brought him home from that country, while his daughter was yet a child, to become a professor in the Catholic University of Dublin. Later he left the Catholic Church; still later, he returned to it, this time permanently.

Mary did not go to Dublin; her childhood was spent instead in Wordsworth's Lake Country. When she was sixteen she moved to Oxford, where she was influenced by Mark Pattison and others, and where she specialized in the early Christian history of Spain. Whatever may be said of her as a novelist there can be no question about her scholarship; when she came to deal with the problems that wrecked Elsmere's orthodoxy she knew whereof she spake, for she had been over the ground independently before him. She continued to reside in Oxford until 1881, when her husband, T. Humphry Ward, whom she had married in 1872, went to London as art critic of the *Times*.

This removal brought Mrs. Ward closer to the main stream of English life. In her own austere way she ceased to be a cloistered scholar and became a woman of the world. As a critic she turned from ancient Spaniards to modern Frenchmen. She became interested in politics and enjoyed the friendship of many learned men. In her later years—passionate anti-suffragist though she was—she engineered her son's career in Parliament; the wags called him "the member for Mrs. Humphry Ward." *Marcella* (1894), *Sir George Tressady* (1896), *The Marriage of William Ashe* (1905), and *The Coryston Family* (1913) all involve Parliamentary considerations; as a group they are second in importance only to the religious group.

But whether she writes of politics or of religion, there is

still a bookish quality about Mrs. Ward; we know the libraries of her heroes better than we know their hearts. It is not that she fails to understand them. She understands them completely, and she sets them forth so admirably, so justly, and with such admirable detachment, that we sometimes get a touch of smugness or snobbery. But, as Henry James puts it of the people in *Robert Elsmere,* they are "not simply enough seen and planted on their feet."

Five times Mrs. Ward chose to make a novel out of a historic scandal [Chateaubriand and Madame de Beaumont in *Eleanor* (1900); Madame du Deffand and Julie de Lespinasse in *Lady Rose's Daughter* (1903); Byron and the Lambs in *The Marriage of William Ashe;* Romncy and Lady Hamilton in *Fenwick's Career* (1906); Lord Holland and Lady Webster in *Eltham House.* Elise Delaunay in *The History of David Grieve* is an almost heartless caricature of Marie Bashkirtseff]. In no one of these instances does she trust her imagination and dare to present her characters in their native setting. She is too good a scholar for that; she might get something wrong. Instead, she takes them all over into her own time, changes their names, and decks them out in modern dress. She never hesitates to refer openly to history or to literature; the characters she has created always seem more real to her when she can remember that they are like something she has read about. In *The Marriage of William Ashe,* where Cliffe is already Byron, she very nearly breaks the spell altogether by referring several times to his historical prototype.

Much of this Mrs. Ward herself knew as well as any critic. She was, to be sure, rather a pontifical person.

> What is important [writes Katherine Mansfield] is the messages that her characters have to deliver; she sees herself, we fancy, as the person of the great house, receiving these messages and translating them to the eager, inquiring crowd about the gates, and then—returning to the library. [*Novels and Novelists,* 1930]

Yet she realized her limitations, and her own analysis of them in the Prefaces to the Westmoreland Edition is fundamentally just. "Had I dragged my heroine through ways of a more commonplace difficulty and miriness," she says of the Marcella of *Sir George Tressady,* "she would have been more appealing, and the scene with Letty stronger." And she repudiates the latter half of *Lady Rose's Daughter* because she knows she herself lacked the spiritual robustness necessary to achieve the tragic ending the logic of the story demanded.

In general, Mrs. Ward's story-telling impulse was "set in motion by an event, a tale, a character, which causes a stir in the mind like that of a seed germinating, till the leaf and flower of the story are thrown up, one hardly knows how, but with a certain heat and violence, and a happy sense of *discovery*"; but among all her books only *The Story of Bessie Costrell* (1895) was, she tells us, written, in anything like its entirety, in what might be called a state of inspiration. For the most part she knew just what she was doing; she wrote "intellectually, following out a logical sequence"; she achieved no effects that she could not explain.

For her immediate popularity, Mrs. Ward's limitations were no doubt quite as valuable as her gifts. A great and original artist in fiction—a Meredith, a Conrad—must create the taste by which he is enjoyed. Mrs. Ward essayed no technical experiments; her technique was as old-fashioned as her morality. She wrote about the subjects which intelligent people in her time wished to consider, and she handled them intelligently, with assured competence and impeccable taste.

It is not quite fair to her to say that "the subjects she treats with complete assurance are those proper to the platform and the lecture-room." Such a statement omits the important fact that she still stands as one of the few writers who have been able to put passion into the novel of ideas. This was what James liked about *Elsmere,* that with all its faults it was still "a history of our moral life and not simply of our physical accidents."

The frightfully insular French portions of *David Grieve* are mere synthetic stuff, but the English scenes here and there suggest *The Old Wives' Tale. Helbeck* has power despite the Gordian knot-cutting of Laura's suicide. And "the tears of things" are in Lady Kitty Ashe's death scene (despite its sentimentality) and in the common tragedy of Bessie Costrell (which is not sentimental at all). In such things we get Mrs. Ward at her best.

Edward Wagenknecht, "Victorian Sunset," in his Cavalcade of the English Novel: From Elizabeth to George VI, *Holt, Rinehart and Winston, 1943, pp. 386-405.*

Vineta Colby   (essay date 1970)

[*Colby is an American educator and critic who has written several studies of Victorian literature. In the following excerpt, she examines the appeal of Ward's works to Victorian readers.*]

It is a telling comment on Victorianism that one of its leading family dynasties was not Marlborough, Medici, Borgia, Fugger, or Rothschild, but Arnold. The founder of this line was not a warrior, a statesman, a banker, or a patron of the arts, but a clergyman and schoolmaster. Though some of his descendants practiced the arts of criticism, poetry, and fiction, not one of them deviated from the family mission of public service and education. . . .

The Arnolds were not a royal dynasty, but early and permanently associated with them was a cachet of *noblesse oblige.* In a bourgeois, secular society they represented an ideal—the cultivated mind and conscience, the aristocracy of learning, dedicated public service and ethical conduct, the religion not so much of the Book as of the book. What is curious to us today about their careers is their enormous popular success and influence in their own times. Every modern society has produced its share of educators, critics and social reformers, but in Victorian England they enjoyed a unique prestige. Measured in practical terms, their power was probably negligible. Rather than influencing social action, they registered or reflected certain significant trends in public opinion, most especially the zeal for self-improvement and, in the old Calvinist-Utilitarian spirit, the recognition that since self and society were mutually dependent, social reform was morally as well as practically imperative upon the individual.

The Arnolds reflected more. Not only did their collective effort epitomize the positive, energetic, progressive thrust of Victorian society. Simultaneously it reflected the doubt, confusion, and frequently the despair of their age. The complacency of the Establishment, the sublime dogmatism of the Evangelicals, the healthy but often mindless vigor of Kingsley's "muscular Christianity," were notably absent with them. Instead there was a sensibility of conscience that in some members of the family led to painful religious conflict, in others to morbid melancholy, and in still others to outright protest and action. Oddly enough, it was a female Arnold, Mary Augusta, later Mrs. Humphry Ward, who proved the most effectually active of the crusading Arnolds. No rebel, certainly no iconoclast, indeed as staid and genteel a figure as Victorian society ever produced, she wielded a more powerful influence on the religious thinking of her day and achieved more concrete social reform than did her grandfather Thomas Arnold of Rugby fame or her uncle Matthew. No creative thinker or artist in her own right, she was endowed only with high intelligence, fervent moral conviction, and a warm feminine sympathy for the sufferings—intellectual, spiritual and practical—of others. The Victorians often confused such talents as these for genius, but in no era are they to be underestimated.

Her medium was the novel. Through it she reached a wider audience than Matthew Arnold reached through poetry and criticism. He was the artist, she merely the polemicist. He has endured, she is today unread—and no one can question the justice of that verdict. What one does question today is the reason for her popularity as a novelist in her own time. The publishing phenomenon of *Robert Elsmere,* that record-smashing best-seller of the late 1880's in both England and America, is mystifying to the modern reader of the novel. One can account for most best-sellers, of the period—Marie Corelli, Hall Caine, M. E. Braddon—on grounds of their vulgarity and sensationalism. But *Robert Elsmere* and the dozen or so novels that Mrs. Ward produced after it, almost all of them financial successes if not best-sellers, are neither vulgar nor sensational. To explain their popularity one must look not at the novels themselves so much as at the public who bought and presumably read them.

Mrs. Ward's understanding of the psychology of her readers was based to some extent on a shrewd, businesslike insight into public taste. But it was also the result of her wholehearted identification with that public. Her attitude, to be sure, was condescending. The strain of Arnold in her kept her always figuratively on the lecture platform, a level above the mass of her readers. But even if slightly *de haut en bas,* she was one with her readers and their middle-class aspirations. Readers recognized in her high-mindedness and didacticism not a patronizing contempt for their ignorance, but an earnest respect for their desire for enlightenment and self-improvement. She complimented them by considering them capable of absorbing profound issues of theology and philosophy, learned dis-

quisitions on history and literature, long debates on politics and social reform. . . .

Perhaps the highest tribute one could pay Mrs. Ward was made by a critic who disliked her work intensely, William Lyon Phelps: "She has a well-furnished and highly developed intellect; she is deeply read; she makes her readers think that they are thinking." And thinking they were. We have come to recognize more clearly today the profound ethical-moral-intellectual revolutions that were stirring up the later years of Victorianism. Our faulty conception of the age as one of stuffy, rigid, smug conservatism is being sharply revised. We know now that thinking Englishmen in the last century were keenly aware of the crumbling away of the foundations of their religious faith and of the challenges to the established social order rising everywhere. Their zeal for education reflected their desire to understand the swiftly changing world around them.

It was Mrs. Ward's genius to have seized precisely the issues of most burning public interest—religion, politics, social reform—and to have framed these in the relatively attractive form of fiction. She added the piquancy of story to the statistics of parliamentary Blue Books, the rhetoric of the pulpit, and the recondite speculations of the learned journals. The Master of Balliol, Benjamin Jowett, admired *Robert Elsmere* but wrote off its success as "really due to what everybody else is thinking." The grand old man Gladstone, though alarmed at the religious skepticism of the novel, praised its earnestness and sincerity and recognized that it was "eminently an offspring of the time . . . [which] will probably make a deep, or at least a very sensible impression, not however among mere novel readers, but among those who share, in whatever sense, the deeper thought of the period." Even its most disapproving critics, who found absolutely no literary or artistic merit in the book, grudgingly conceded, as did Rowland Prothero in the *Edinburgh Review* (April, 1892), that "she gave utterance—however hesitating and uncertain the voice—to some indeterminate, inarticulate, but widespread feeling that needed expression."

Such a comment as this last, indeed, epitomizes critical reaction to all of Mrs. Ward's novels. Her books said what her readers wanted to hear—not so much smugly confirming their prejudices and preconceptions as airing their questions, marshaling pertinent evidence and information, and finally guiding but not pushing them to a more rational, enlightened position. Mrs. Ward's readers knew that, although more learned than most of them, she was "one of us." And she in turn knew that she could count on their sympathetic response and cooperation. More than twenty years after the first great success of *Robert Elsmere,* in a preface to the Westmoreland edition of the novel, she wrote:

> At a moment when the particular ideas put forward have a high degree of life and significance for a great many people, the public in a sense cooperates in the book. Such a novel as *Robert Elsmere* is entirely related to a particular time and milieu; and those who are drawn to read it, unconsciously lend it their own thoughts, the passion of their own assents and denials. Some happy chance bestows on a novel this suggestive,

symbolic character; and the reader's eager sympathy, or antagonism, completes the effort of the writer.

Furthermore, Mrs. Ward's novels appealed to the essential idealism of her nineteenth-century readers. Her settings were always roughly contemporary, even when she drew on historical materials for her plots (the Lady Caroline Lamb-Byron relationship in *The Marriage of William Ashe,* the life of the painter George Romney in *Fenwick's Career,* the rivalry between Julie de l'Espinasse and Mme du Deffand in *Lady Rose's Daughter,* the marriage of Lord and Lady Holland in *Eltham House*). The English society that they portrayed was sufficiently realistic in detail—precise geographical setting and minute description of clothes, furniture, and customs—but its image was highly idealized and reflects a widespread ambivalence—the desire to see England as simultaneously the guardian of a proud old aristocratic tradition and the leader of vigorous progressive reform. Her most sympathetic characters are crusaders but not rebels. They fight valiantly to correct, improve, ameliorate, but they cherish their old country houses, they marry within their social class, and they have no intentions of upsetting tradition. Even her most ambitious middle-class readers relished Mrs. Ward's romantic nostalgia for the past. They delighted in passages like this one from *The Marriage of William Ashe* describing a costume ball where all the guests are dressed as figures from English history:

> It is said that as a nation the English have no gift for pageants. Yet every now and then—as no doubt in the Elizabethan mask—they show a strange felicity in the art. Certainly the dance that followed would have been difficult to surpass even in the ripe days and motherlands of pageantry. To the left, a long line, consisting mainly of young girls in their first bloom, dressed as Gainsborough and his great contemporaries delighted to paint those flowers of England—the folds of plain white muslin crossed over the young breast, a black velvet at the throat, a rose in the hair, the simple skirt showing the small pointed feet, and sometimes a broad sash defining the slender waist. Here were Stanleys, Howards, Percys, Villierses, Butlers, Osbornes—soft slips of girls bearing the names of England's rough and turbulent youth, bearing themselves tonight with a shy or laughing dignity, as though the touch of history and romance were on them. And facing them, the youths of the same families, no less handsome than their sisters and brides—in Romney's blue coats, or the splendid red of Reynolds and Gainsborough.

At the same time, however, her readers were moving with the currents of change and progress. Inside the drawing rooms of stately old country houses her aristocratic characters debate politics; then they go forth to Parliament, to settlement houses in the slums, to the cottages of the workers in the fields or the miners—legislating reform, nursing, teaching. Some of her most romantic heroes, like Aldous Raeburn in *Marcella* and Sir George Tressady, are descendants of those young aristocrats in Disraeli's novels who were impelled almost religiously by a sense of their duty to society. Her heroine Marcella may have sounded

girlishly naive to some contemporary readers, but she spoke for a good many of them: "The time has come for a wider basis. Paternal government and charity were very well in their way—democratic self-government will manage to do without them!"

Time and experience mellow but do not substantially alter these views. Enlightened social reform, Mrs. Ward tells her readers—with their warm approval—is not only a practical necessity but a religious obligation. Man ultimately serves God best by serving his fellowmen. Thus Raeburn, now Lord Maxwell and leader of his political party reasons:

> The vast extension of the individual will and power which science has brought to humanity during the last hundred years was always present to him as food for a natural exultation—a kind of pledge of the boundless prospects of the race. On the other hand, the struggle of society brought face to face with this huge increment of the individual power, forced to deal with it for its own higher and mysterious ends, to moralise and socialise it lest it should destroy itself and the State altogether; the slow steps by which the modern community has succeeded in asserting itself against the individual, in protecting the weak from his weakness, the poor from his poverty, in defending the woman and child from the fierce claims of capital, in forcing upon trade after trade the axiom that no man may lawfully build his wealth upon the exhaustion and degradation of his fellow—these things stirred in him the far deeper enthusiasms of the moral nature. Nay more! Together with all the other main facts which mark the long travail of man's ethical and social nature, they were among the only "evidences" of religion a critical mind allowed itself—the most striking signs of something "greater than we know" working among the dust and ugliness of our common day. Attack wealth as wealth, possession as possession, and civilisation is undone. But bring the force of the social conscience to bear as keenly and ardently as you may, upon the separate activities of factory and household, farm and office; and from the results you will only get a richer individual freedom, one more illustration of the divinest law man serves—that he must "die to live," must surrender to obtain (*Sir George Tressady*).

Granted the hunger of Mrs. Ward's public for knowledge and enlightenment, it is still difficult to reconcile such passages as these with the facts of best-sellerdom. This was, to be sure, a public that devoured other equally weighty novels. J. H. Shorthouse's formidably erudite *John Inglesant,* that fictitious adult education course in seventeenth-century English theology, was another best-seller contemporary with *Robert Elsmere.* But Mrs. Ward's high rank among popular novelists over the next three decades was not won by scholarship alone. It was the result of her instinctive grasp of her public's tastes and desires—for knowledge, for comforting reassurance of their social and political convictions, but, equally, for entertainment. She entertained her readers fundamentally in the same ways as did her less highly respected literary colleagues: only with the difference that she shunned their overt vulgarity and shrillness, their flamboyance and exaggeration. Her education, her good taste, her Arnoldian sense of mission saved her from their excesses, but not from their subject matter. After *Elsmere* her novels show a steadily increasing attention to elements of popular best-sellerdom—licit and illicit love, intrigue, family secrets, "fast" upper-class society, adultery, illegitimacy, sordid slum poverty, graphic details of physical suffering, deathbeds, morbid states of mind.

This is not to suggest that Mrs. Ward was succumbing to the contagions of Zolaism, which she honestly deplored. She continued, without a trace of hypocrisy, to affirm the values of her bourgeois Victorian society; the wicked are punished; the innocent who sin through error or accident must suffer; marriage vows are sacred. Perhaps unconsciously, out of sheer innocence, Mrs. Ward made the best of both worlds. On the other hand, observing her keen intelligence and her lively interest in society, it is difficult to believe that she was not perfectly conscious of what she was doing. She was marketing her product. But she was also faithfully and diligently guiding that public *up* to her standards. She was the observer and recorder of the present, but also the guardian of tradition. By reading her novels in chronological order, one can trace the development of English moral sensibilities from Victorianism through World War I.

In *Robert Elsmere* she sprinkled just enough delicate touches of romance to refresh the reader in intermissions from the heady theological passages that form the bulk of her novel. Once she had tasted fame with *Elsmere,* however, Mrs. Ward courted her public more openly. Her next novel, *The History of David Grieve,* introduced a rebellious young girl who goes off to live in the wild bohemia of Paris and is sufficiently corrupted to tease the thrill-seeking public and sufficiently punished to satisfy the proper Victorian. From there on Mrs. Ward proceeded cautiously but steadily, growing more daring as her society grew more "modern." In 1903, in *Lady Rose's Daughter,* she introduced a heroine who is illegitimate, determined to run away with a man who will not marry her, yet who ends not in tragedy but as the wife of a duke. Mrs. Ward acknowledged that her heroine's rescue from disgrace was a defect in the book, but significantly she calls it an artistic rather than a moral mistake—"a certain treachery to the artistic conscience." As for the "sin" of the heroine's mother, Lady Rose, who leaves a cold, strait-laced husband for another man, Mrs. Ward seeks moral support in the best literary precedents: "Colonel Delaney [the husband] made the penalties of it as heavy as he could. Like Karennine in Tolstoy's great novel he refused to sue for a divorce, and for something of the same reasons. Divorce was in itself impious, and sin should not be made easy."

Not all her heroines are so lucky, but their fates are often more interesting for their melodrama than for their morality. The intrigue-filled story of another illegitimate young girl is introduced into the theological novel *The Case of Richard Meynell* (1911), obviously to leaven and spice the solemn material of the book. After being tricked into a false marriage by a scoundrel, this unfortunate girl wan-

ders off in a snowstorm, falls over a precipice, and dies in agony. The heroine of *The Testing of Diana Mallory* (1906), spotlessly virtuous herself, suffers bitterly for the sins of her mother, a gambler and a murderess. Certainly Mrs. Ward's most appealing heroines from the point of view of the literary marketplace, are her impetuous, headstrong beauties who destroy themselves but win the author's, and presumably the reader's, pity and forgiveness. Typical of these is the charming but neurotic Kitty Ashe in *The Marriage of William Ashe* (1905). Kitty is an Edwardian "golden girl," a kind of ancestor to those beautiful, reckless heroines in F. Scott Fitzgerald a generation later. We deplore her destructiveness, but the author loves her and wants her readers to share that love. Kitty travels in a "fast" set, the Archangels (obviously modeled on the glittering and exclusive "Souls," that informal club of which Lord Curzon, Arthur James Balfour, and Margot Tennant were members). She smokes cigarettes and flirts outrageously. All this her handsome, rich, adoring, politically ambitious husband accepts tolerantly. But when she writes a novel exposing his political secrets, he finally leaves her. Her "sin" however, is nothing so innocuous as novel-writing. Distraught and betrayed by a jealous rival, she runs away with another man—a satanic, Byronic figure—and she pays amply. The lover treats her brutally, and she dies, painfully and penitently, of tuberculosis.

The pattern in its broadest outlines is too clear-cut to be merely accidental and unconscious. Mrs. Ward knew well enough that she was writing on the level of women's magaziner. Her heroines' clothes are from Worth, described down to the last ribbon and bit of expensive lace. Their jewels, their furs, their coiffures—all conform to a conventionally romantic scheme. The doors of smart Mayfair townhouses and fine old country houses are opened wide for her readers: the furnishings, the pictures on the walls, the menus, the smallest details of social behavior—nothing that would intrigue and delight the "common" reader escapes her camera eye. She courted that reader persistently, even attempting to enlarge her public by dramatizing some of her novels and by writing one original play. Characteristically, she plunged into the theater with vigor and worked as conscientiously at her plays as at her novels. But for the most part her efforts were disastrous.

In . . . these attempts to woo the public Mrs. Ward displayed a curious mixture of vanity, shrewdness, and naïveté. There is something almost disarming in her sublime faith in her work, a trust and self-confidence that made it possible for her to stand, on the one hand, as the guardian and mentor of an idealistic, earnest public and, on the other, as a purveyor of sex and sensationalism. Mrs. Ward's heroes and heroines are full of "rushing passions" and "trembling yearnings." But all is described in respectable literary language, with none of the shrillness and grammatical solecisms of Marie Corelli or M. E. Braddon. The young and innocent reader could not be corrupted by Mrs. Ward; the more worldly reader could make of her what he would: "Falloden's sense approved her wholly: the white dress; the hat that framed her brow; the slender gold chains that rose and fell on her gently rounded breast;

her height and grace. Passion beat within him" (*Lady Connie*).

Such a passage indicates the limits of Mrs. Ward's pre-Freudian innocence; her novels abound with similar ones. Human passion was exalted to romantic stereotype. Relations between the sexes, though at times represented as unhappy, were more often idealized and seen through a haze of romantic convention. Even more romantically idealized were relations between women. A good deal of the passion felt by Mrs. Ward's female characters is sublimated in relationships that modern readers would immediately designate as lesbian. To Mrs. Ward, however, these served as decorous outlets for her characters' passions while, at the same time, they were not only proper but even poetic and elevating. Such relationships flourished both in fiction and in real life in the nineteenth century. George Eliot, Mrs. Browning, Dinah Mulock Craik, and Jane Carlyle had circles of adoring female friends and disciples. Mrs. Ward herself, apparently fulfilled in her marriage and in motherhood, had ardent female admirers. What her novels reflect, therefore, is far more romantic convention than sexual perversion or repression.

Nevertheless, one must acknowledge that the total effect of such implied, latent, or merely accidental sexuality helped to sell her books. One of her greatest popular successes, for example, was *Eleanor* (1900), a vastly ambitious novel. Its purpose was nothing less than to portray the whole "revolution" of modern Italy, a country that Mrs. Ward had adopted in her prosperity as a second home and loved deeply. To an extent, she succeeds in her purpose. She surveys with exhausting thoroughness the total condition of Italy at the end of the nineteenth century (with a guidebook tour of the campagna thrown in to emphasize the contrasts between the ancient and the modern world)—the war in Abyssinia, the civil struggles, the battle within the Roman Church between modernism and conservatism. To heighten and render palatable her quite profound exposition, she weaves it into a love triangle involving an aging and sickly widow Eleanor, her intellectual cousin Edward Manisty, who is writing a book on Italy, and an innocent young American visitor, Lucy. Eleanor is brilliant, sensitive, grieving over a tragic past but clinging to life because she loves her cousin and is helping him with his book. She recognizes Lucy as a rival long before the younger girl or Manisty is aware of their mutual attraction. Desperately, Eleanor takes Lucy away to a remote village in the mountains. For a while the women live alone, Lucy nursing and worshiping the older woman: "The two fell into each other's embrace. Lucy, with the maternal tenderness that should have been Eleanor's, pressed her lips on the hot brow that lay upon her breast, murmuring words of promise, of consolation, of self-reproach, feeling her whole being passing out to Eleanor's in a great tide of passionate will and pity." Ultimately, Eleanor realizes the wrong she is doing, brings the lovers together, and dies in tearful but happy self-sacrifice.

What is most striking about *Eleanor* to the modern reader—and what begins to emerge as a recurring motif in Mrs. Ward's novels—is an emotional debauch innocent in intention, no doubt, but profoundly disturbing in its impli-

cations. At the root of her most serious and elevated fiction there is a sickly morbidity that undeniably appealed to a proper middle-class reading public. The simple pathos of the popular Victorian deathbed scenes is missing, but in its place there is an obsession with disease (many of her characters die gratuitously of painful, lingering illnesses) and suffering. "How ill she is," a character observes of Eleanor, "and how distinguished!" At the climax of the novel, in a passionate plea to Lucy to marry the man they both love, Eleanor lets her dressing gown fall from her shoulders:

> She showed the dark hollows under the wasted collar-bones, the knife-like shoulders, the absolute disappearance of all that had once made the difference between grace and emaciation. She held up her hands before the girl's terrified eyes. The skin was still white and delicate, otherwise they were the hands of a skeleton.
>
> "You can look at *that*," she said fiercely, under her breath—"and then insult me by refusing to marry the man you love, because you choose to remember that I was once in love with him."

Mrs. Ward produced her own version of Gothic horror. Her learning, her serious intentions and keen intelligence gave her novels their critical distinction in their time, but there were other attractions about them. In accounting for her popularity, therefore, one must measure not only the particular qualities of the Victorian public—their earnestness and eagerness for knowledge—but the general nature of readers seeking thrills and forbidden delights. Consciously or unconsciously, Mrs. Ward exploited both sources to the fullest and reaped rich rewards.

Vineta Colby, "Light on a Darkling Plain: Mrs. Humphry Ward," in her The Singular Anomaly: Women Novelists of the Nineteenth Century, *New York University Press, 1970, pp. 111-74.*

William S. Peterson   (essay date 1976)

[*Peterson is an American educator and critic who has written extensively about the poet Robert Browning. In the following excerpt, Peterson offers a detailed, volume-by-volume analysis of Ward's* Robert Elsmere.]

Archibald Tait once observed, 'The great evil is—that the liberals are deficient in religion and the religious are deficient in liberality.' This was the profound religious dilemma of the Victorian age to which Mrs Ward addressed herself in *Robert Elsmere.* How could a young man like Elsmere be both religious and liberal (i. e., intellectually enlightened)? The solution which she offered to her contemporaries was based upon the familiar Arnoldian dialectic: the destruction of orthodoxy by modern rationalism must be followed by a new synthesis which would offer a reasonable religion for nineteenth-century men and women. The three stages of the dialectic are suggested in several ways. First, Robert himself undergoes a change as the story progresses. He begins as a conventional Christian, falls unsuspectingly into a morass of unbelief, and at last regains his footing by discovering what Matthew Arnold called the 'joy whose grounds are true'. Second, the

Arnoldian dialectic is reflected in the characters who dominate each of the three volumes of the novel. The first volume belongs to Catherine, the representative of orthodoxy; the second belongs to Wendover, an embittered sceptic; and the third to Robert, the founder of the purified new faith.

Even the settings of *Robert Elsmere* evoke a similar dialectical pattern. The moral centre of volume i is Long Whindale (i. e., Longsleddale), a Westmorland valley of Wordsworthian beauty and freshness which symbolizes the simplicity of the earlier faith. In volume ii the really decisive actions take place in Squire Wendover's library, which is filled with poisonous books that nearly ensnare Robert's soul. They do in fact capture his mind, but his deepest spiritual life is untouched, so that in the third volume he is able to create in the East End of London (outwardly the City of Destruction) a City of God—though in an Arnoldian rather than an Augustinian sense. Like Dr Arnold in the closing lines of 'Rugby Chapel', Elsmere becomes an inspiring Carlylean hero, a modern Moses, leading the confused ranks of humanity through the wilderness of this world 'On, to the bound of the waste, / On, to the City of God'.

Yet such a schematic view of the novel overlooks the hints of change that are evident in Long Whindale, in Catherine, and in the old faith. The opening chapter of *Robert Elsmere,* which has often been admired for its beautiful portrayal of the arrival of spring in a Westmorland valley, is more than a clever exercise in Ruskinian landscape description. From the first paragraph onward, we learn that the impression of changelessness in Long Whindale is an illusion. It is not only the season which is robbing the valley of its natural austerity; there are signs everywhere of a more advanced civilization encroaching upon the ancient fells. Burwood Farm, Catherine Leyburn's home, has a bow window, neat flower-beds, and close-shaven lawn, all of which were unknown in Long Whindale a generation or two before:

> The windows in [the sheds] were new, the doors fresh-painted and closely shut; curtains of some soft outlandish make showed themselves in what had once been a stable, and the turf stretched smoothly up to a narrow gravelled path in front of them, unbroken by a single footmark. No, evidently the old farm, for such it undoubtedly was, had been but lately, or comparatively lately, transformed to new and softer uses; that rough patriarchal life of which it had once been a symbol and centre no longer bustled and clattered through it. It had become the shelter of new ideals, the home of another and a milder race than had once possessed it.

There is a new church in the valley, and the vicar is a typically middle-class Victorian clergyman incapable of achieving the intimate relationships with the peasants that his predecessors had enjoyed. Even the description in Chapter 1 of Rose playing her violin at Burwood, with the music floating and eddying about the valley, which may appear to be an echo of Wordsworth's 'The Solitary Reaper', is in fact something quite different: the song is not of 'old, unhappy, far-off things' but a modern Andante by Spohr.

All of this is important because it points forward to the later, almost imperceptible changes in Catherine and her religious faith. After Robert has abandoned Christianity, Mrs Ward supplies this analysis of the corresponding but more subtle transformation of his wife:

> She would live and die steadfast to the old faiths. But her present mind and its outlook was no more the mind of her early married life than the Christian philosophy of to-day is the Christian philosophy of the Middle Ages. She was not conscious of change, but change there was. She had, in fact, undergone that dissociation of the moral judgement from a special series of religious formulae which is the crucial, the epoch-making fact of our time.

Many reviewers, including Gladstone, were bewildered by Mrs Ward's assertion in the penultimate paragraph of the novel that Catherine quietly attended the services of the New Brotherhood of Christ after the death of Robert, because they felt it was out of character for her. Yet from the very beginning of *Robert Elsmere* Mrs Ward had been warning her readers that Catherine and her faith were no more exempt from the universal law of ceaseless, inexorable change than was Long Whindale.

Given this close symbolic relationship between the heroine and landscape of Book One, it is not surprising that Mrs Ward was able to create Catherine only after her visit in 1885 to Longsleddale. (Mrs Ward nearly always had to find settings for her novels before she could people them with characters.) Catherine towers over the other characters in Book One, because she is in her natural element, while her sisters and Robert have deeper affinities to the modern world outside the valley:

> [Her] complexion had caught the freshness and purity of Westmoreland air and Westmoreland streams. About face and figure there was a delicate austere charm, something which harmonised with the bare stretches and lonely crags of the fells, something which seemed to make her a true daughter of the mountains, partaker at once of their gentleness and their severity. She was in her place here, beside the homely Westmoreland house and under the shelter of the fells.

Catherine moves with 'a beautiful dignity and freedom, as of mountain winds and mountain streams'; in her more tender moments she reminds Robert of March flowers breaking through the Westmorland soil; and when Robert compares her to the 'mountains, to the exquisite river, to that great purple peak', even the unsentimental Rose acknowledges the justice of the analogy with her cynical response that 'she is not unlike that high cold peak!'.

If Mrs Gaskell had not already appropriated the title, Mrs Ward might well have called her novel *North and South,* for the important conflicts of the story all hinge—as they often do also in Scott's fiction that she read so assiduously in childhood—upon psychological and social contrasts resulting from geography. The North is the past, a preindustrial world characterized by unspoilt natural beauty and simple faith. The South is the present, the familiar Victorian world of modern knowledge and doubt. When Robert finds himself a guest at the vicarage of Long Whindale, he realizes with delight that he has moved backward in time to a less complicated era. Though his decision to marry Catherine, whom he meets in this tranquil valley, suggests Robert's desire to wed himself to the moral simplicities of her world, ultimately he is an intruder in Long Whindale, a citizen of the intellectually sophisticated South, who cannot live comfortably with Catherine's naive religion. He belongs to the present, and she belongs to the past. This, rather than any specific theological differences that develop between them, is the source of trouble in their marriage.

The movement of the characters about the valley and its environs is keyed to the same geographical symbolism. Significantly, Long Whindale, which lies on a north-west-south-east axis, is tame and featureless throughout its lower half but is bordered by steep, rugged crags at the northern head of the valley. Shanmoor (the real name of which is Kentmere), the neighbouring valley to the south-west, is more heavily populated and 'civilized'; it is while on a picnic there that Catherine's resistance to Robert's charms begins to weaken. But Marrisdale (i. e., Bannisdale), the valley to the north-east, is completely uninhabited; and it is there that Catherine goes alone to wrestle with her desires and temporarily persuade herself that she cannot marry Robert. In order to stiffen her will, she instinctively turns to the north.

Long Whindale itself is a series of time-layers, as if it were an archaeologist's *tell* in which the deepest strata are uncovered as one moves north. The earliest form of human civilization is represented at the craggy northern end by High Ghyll (which recalls Wuthering Heights), the farmhouse of the Backhouses, with its atmosphere of superstition, brutality, and ignorance. At approximately the centre of the valley are the church, the vicarage, and Burwood Farm. At the southern tip of Long Whindale is the road that leads to the nearest city, Whinborough (Kendal). The church, in other words, occupies an intermediate position between primitive superstition and modern civilization. 'There are no fairies and no ghosts . . . any more', wrote Froude in *The Nemesis of Faith;* 'only the church bells and the church music have anything of the old tones, and they are silent, too, except at rare, mournful, gusty intervals'. Robert, in his pursuit of Catherine, penetrates ever deeper into this mysterious past, even beyond the Long Whindale church, until he proposes to her at last on a ghostly path above High Ghyll at midnight on Midsummer's Eve.

The frequent allusions to Wordsworth in Book One (Catherine, for example, is compared with his 'Louisa', and Richard Leyburn's portrait resembles that of the poet) function in the same way as do the Wordsworthian references in Matthew Arnold's poetry—that is to say, they evoke memories of an earlier age of innocence and simple religious trust. The Wordsworthian 'forest-glade' and Christianity alike belong to the uncomplicated past, which can be viewed only from a distance with longing and nostalgia by modern personalities like Elsmere.

Mrs Ward's Westmorland valley, like Hardy's Wessex or Emily Brontë's Yorkshire moors, is a powerful spiritual force which shapes the lives of its inhabitants. In an unpublished lecture (1909) on Hardy, Mrs Ward argued that the greatest literary figures, such as Shakespeare and Goethe, transcend any tie with a local scene; but she admired and emulated nevertheless 'that Antaean band of writers'—most notably Hardy and Emily Brontë—'which draws its life from a particular soil, and must constantly renew it there'. Mrs Ward's roots were in Westmorland, and she was always at her best when writing about it. For her the Cumbrian fells were richly alive, speaking to harried nineteenth-century men and women of the serene (but, alas, discredited) faith of their ancestors.

Catherine, far from being a 'repellent, evangelical monster' [as Clara Lederer has described her in *Nineteenth Century Fiction,* December 1951], is the *genius loci* of this pastoral setting, a beautiful spirit who hovers over the valley's poor peasants like 'Sister Dora', Mark Pattison's sister, among the miners of Walsall, and who, like George Eliot's Dorothea Brooke (in *Middlemarch*), is a saint that has had the misfortune of being born in the wrong century. Of course Catherine's religious ardour has its less attractive side, which is **amply** documented in the novel. Langham calls her 'the **Thirty**-nine Articles in the flesh', and Rose, when Agnes suggests that Catherine may marry, exclaims: 'Marry! . . . You might as well talk of marrying Westminster Abbey'. Mrs Ward makes no attempt to conceal the substratum of fanaticism in her heroine. In the **Elsmere** notebook and twice in the novel itself she is identified with Madame Guyon, the ascetic, self-tormenting mystic of the Quietist school. Mrs Ward also notes the resemblance between Catherine and her bigoted Methodist aunt and sees her as secretly sympathizing with Newcome, another religious fanatic. Mrs Ward obviously regards Catherine with strongly ambivalent feelings: she responds to her heroine's intense spiritual fervour yet insists that such a childish faith in the modern age is, intellectually speaking, an anachronism. When Catherine is swept unwillingly into the nineteenth century by her marriage to Robert, some kind of catastrophe is inevitable. 'Half the tragedy of our time', writes Mrs Ward, 'lies in this perpetual clashing of two estimates of life—the estimate which is the offspring of the scientific spirit, and which is for ever making the visible world fairer and more desirable in mortal eyes; and the estimate of Saint Augustine'.

But in the Westmorland section of **Robert Elsmere** such portents are merely hinted at in muted tones. Book One is, as Mrs Ward said, 'very tame & domestic', possessing the flavour of a provincial comedy of manners done by Jane Austen. Mrs Thornburgh, bustling self-importantly about in her match-making efforts, is Mrs Bennett of *Pride and Prejudice* transplanted in Westmorland; Mr Thornburgh, the vicar of Long Whindale, who emerges from his study occasionally to offer ironic comments on his wife's activities, plays the part of Mr Bennett. 'One does not see these types, [Robert] said to himself, in the cultivated monotony of Oxford or London. [Mrs Thornburgh] was like a bit of a bygone world—Miss Austen's or Miss Ferrier's—unearthed for his amusement'. 'How Miss Austenish it sounded' to Robert at Mrs Thornburgh's party: 'the managing rector's wife, her still more managing old maid of a sister, the neighbouring clergyman who played the flute, the local doctor, and a pretty daughter just out'.

The 'Miss Austenish' tone is executed surprisingly well by Mrs Ward, particularly in a marvellously comic scene describing a musical duet by the vicar of Shanmoor and the inimitable Miss Barks, but for Mrs Ward such drawing-room satire is not the essence of her novel, as it was for Jane Austen, but only a light-spirited prelude to the ensuing crisis in the history of Robert's mind.

Though much of the second volume of *Robert Elsmere* is ostensibly devoted to a description of the hero as a happily married and energetic young country parson in Surrey, fishing and preaching with equal enthusiasm, Mrs Ward had little first-hand knowledge of rural life. She was, as she said, 'a townswoman, living in Oxford or London', and the photographic realism of the passages about Murewell Rectory (which was in reality Peperharrow Vicarage, where the Wards had lived in the summer of 1882) cannot conceal her apparent ignorance of the lives led by Robert's parishioners. Robert, we are told, had known the people of Murewell since early childhood, yet despite this assertion, none of them really emerges as a distinct individual in these chapters. What really matters in the Surrey section of the novel is the clash of ideas that takes place within Robert's mind. If Catherine, the spokesman of orthodoxy (as Mrs Ward understands orthodoxy), is the dominant figure of the first volume, then here the strongest personality is the local squire, an embodiment of atheistic rationalism; and, caught between these two powerful forces, Robert is nearly crushed.

Roger Wendover (whose name, ironically, is that of a medieval chronicler of ecclesiastical miracles) is in both physical appearance and cast of mind, though not in the external circumstances of his life, a fictionalized version of Mark Pattison. Pattison and Wendover both devote their lives to a literary *magnum opus* which is never completed; each has an insane father; each has associated with Newman but later turns to scepticism; each exalts the life of the mind above a life of action; each dies a bitter, frustrated, painful death. In the manuscript drafts of the novel the resemblance between the two men is even more pronounced. A cancelled passage in Chapter 18 portrays a long-standing quarrel between Wendover and the Provost of St Anselm's (i. e., Jowett) over the true nature of a university. Pattison, as Rector of Lincoln, attempted to foster research and scholarship in the German fashion, whereas Jowett, as Master of Balliol, subscribed to the rival theory that his college should offer a liberal education to prepare young men for public service. Wendover—in almost the exact language which Pattison had used in *Suggestions on Academical Organisation* (1868) to denounce Jowett's ideals—complains that the Provost has 'ruined a University' by turning it into a 'boarding-house university'.

In the *Robert Elsmere* manuscripts there are several cancelled references to an unhappy love-affair of Wendover's which immediately calls to mind Pattison's marital difficulties. Wendover proposes clumsily to the beautiful young daughter of Lord Windermere, who accepts him but then throws him over at the last moment for a cousin her own age. This episode (as in Pattison's case) deepens the Squire's melancholia and compels him to find solace in study and travel.

Why, then, did Mrs Ward claim (in 1888) that 'the Squire is in no sense a portrait of Pattison', and (in 1909) that ' "the Rector" suggested the Squire only so far as outward aspect, a few personal traits, and the two main facts of great learning and a general impatience of fools are concerned'? The answer, of course, is that the picture of Wendover, a spiritually sick man, is hardly flattering, and there can be no doubt that Mrs Ward genuinely loved Pattison. Yet, as she wrote in *A Writer's Recollections,* 'When his *Memoirs* appeared [in February 1885, just as she was proposing *Robert Elsmere* to Macmillan], after his death, a book of which Mr. Gladstone once said to me that he reckoned it as among the most tragic and the most memorable books of the nineteenth century, I understood him more clearly, and more tenderly, than I could have done as a girl'. Squire Wendover was Mrs Ward's affectionate tribute to Pattison's role in shaping her own mind, tempered by an awareness that his complete rationalism had led in the end to a cul-de-sac of despair.

Mrs Ward did not accept the view that 'unbelief' was an expression of secret 'sin' (at one point in the novel she directly quotes John Wordsworth's lecture in order to refute it), but she was convinced that an exclusively intellectual life could damage a man's moral instincts. To dwell continually in the realm of thought was to behold Medusa directly and thus take the chance of being turned into stone. On the mantelpiece of the Squire's library Robert observes

> a head of Medusa, and the frightful stony calm of it struck on Elsmere's ruffled nerves with extraordinary force. It flashed across him that here was an apt symbol of that absorbing and overgrown life of the intellect which blights the heart and chills the senses. And to that spiritual Medusa, the man before him was not the first victim he had known.

Wendover—like Pattison and those furtive inhabitants of the Bodleian that Mrs Ward had watched years before, and like Edith Lansdale of 'Lansdale Manor'—has incurred a 'fearful risk' by his pathological craving for knowledge. In his 'God-like isolation' from the poor at his gates, he plays out the part of the soul in 'The Palace of Art' and Wendover Hall, 'as beautiful as a dream', becomes inevitably a nightmare filled with Tennysonian 'white-eyed phantasms' which haunt him as death nears.

In depicting the moral catastrophe which overtakes the Squire, Mrs Ward may also have had in mind Matthew Arnold's Empedocles, who tells himself, as he toils up the 'charred, blacked, melancholy waste' of Etna, that 'something has impaired thy spirit's strength, / And dried its self-sufficing fount of joy'. Now a slave to thought and 'dead to every natural joy', Empedocles looks back upon the serene spiritual harmony of the past (both his own past and that of the human race) as an illusion whose unreality must be affirmed by every enlightened thinker. Wendover is attracted to Robert for the same reason that Empedocles listens with gratitude (but also sorrow) to the simple nature-myths sung by his companion, Callicles: the youth poignantly reminds the older man of what he himself once was. However, Wendover's attempt to make a disciple and surrogate son of Robert has sinister implications, for he is feeding parasitically upon the emotional vitality of another to compensate for his own state of dessication. 'Nothing but a devouring flame of thought— / But a naked, eternally restless mind!' (as Empedocles says of himself), Squire Wendover is for Mrs Ward an object lesson in the terrors of modern rational thought divorced from ethical considerations.

Mrs Ward offers us a lengthy analysis of the contents of the Squire's library not only because she is fond of describing books (similar passages appear in several of her novels) but also because she is providing what amounts to an annotated bibliography of nineteenth-century intellectual history. As Langham detects the gradual shifts in the Squire's interests as reflected in his library—'from the Fathers to the Philosophers, from Hooker to Hume'—he comments, 'How history repeats itself in the individual!'. In the manuscript of **Robert Elsmere** (Chapter 20) Mrs Ward emphasizes that Robert's intellectual transformation is also a paradigm of 'that tumult and agony of the modern mind, which spreads itself year by year in ever wider circles of disturbance, troubling profundities of feeling & breaking up calm surfaces of life':

> What was taking place in Robert during this period of his young intellectual development was the reproduction in miniature of what takes place on a large scale in any of the critical moments of human history. *It was the slow & gradual substitution of one set of preconceptions for another;* the steady imperceptible advance from the presuppositions of English orthodoxy, involving a double order of things, spiritual & material, continually interrupting & intersecting each other, to the presuppositions of science, in which the mind assumes the "rationality of the world" & the unity of all experience. Just as the world moves from the generalisation of St. Thomas Aquinas to that of Bacon & Locke, from the generalisation of Hegel to that of Comte, or from that of Rousseau to that of the modern student of anthropology and primitive culture, and for the common understanding of man the great kaleidescope of experience changes, & passes into ever fresh combinations & leading patterns, with every alteration of the point of view; so, in the history of the individual the same moments of crisis occur, preceded by the same periods of half-conscious preparation. All that vast confusion of circumstance which had been to a greater or less degree enslaved and brought to order by one master set of conceptions resumes as it were its inherent right of sway, and dictates another system of the mind, as a nation changes the form of its government. . . .

> And with this fundamental change everything changes. Opinion in all directions throws itself into fresh lines; and action seeks for itself new outlets.

Mrs Ward saw the nineteenth century as one of these epochs of far-reaching intellectual change, and she regarded her own hours of quiet struggle in the Bodleian (which she attributed to Robert in the Squire's library) as a symbol of the contemporary upheaval in systems of ideas.

Though the Squire and his library operate as a catalyst, they are not the underlying cause of Robert's loss of faith. 'I recognise that his influence immensely accelerated a process already begun', explains Elsmere. Mrs Ward also remarks that 'now at every step the ideas, impressions, arguments bred in him by his months of historical work and ordinary converse with the squire rushed in.. . to cripple resistance, to check an emerging answer, to justify Mr. Wendover'. In a letter to Meredith Townsend written in 1888, Mrs Ward argued this thesis even more vigorously: 'The Squire's influence is described as only the match which ultimately lights the mine. I have tried to show that everything really depended not on the Squire but on the nature of the historical training which had gone before.'

The **Elsmere** notebook indicates that Mrs Ward at first intended to describe the 'converging pressure of science & history', and Darwin's name is listed under 'Books wanted' in the notebook (a character in **The Testing of Diana Mallory** [1908] declares that 'Darwin has transformed the main conceptions of the human mind'); but, as Mrs Ward wrote in the subsequent Introduction to **Robert Elsmere**:

> As far as my personal recollection goes, the men of science entered but little into the struggle of ideas that was going on [in the 1870s]. The main Darwinian battle had been won long before 1870; science was quietly verifying and exploring along the new lines; it was in literature, history, and theology that evolutionary conceptions were most visibly and dramatically at work.

What shakes Robert's belief in Christianity is neither the Squire nor Darwinism but his own patient study of the documents and records of the late Roman Empire. In a half-hearted effort to conceal the confessional element in the novel, Mrs Ward has her hero absorbed in French rather than Spanish history, but nevertheless his conclusion is identical to the position she had adopted after preparing the Spanish articles for the *Dictionary of Christian Biography:* that the 'kings, bishops, judges, poets, priests, men of letters' of the early Christian era lived in such an atmosphere of credulity and superstition that the entire historical basis of Christianity must be called into question.

The climactic moment arrives when Robert realizes (in the words of Matthew Arnold) that 'miracles do not happen'—meaning particularly the miraculous resurrection of Jesus. Mrs Ward repeatedly asserted that this crucial statement was a result of inductive historical reasoning, yet she failed to acknowledge the obvious fact that a disbelief in miracles rests upon certain *a priori* assumptions about the operation of 'natural' laws. By embracing a dogmatic monism that was completely uncritical in its acceptance of 'reason', Elsmere, it might be argued, merely leaped from one system of authority to another. Instinctively a true believer, Mrs Ward was evidently incapable of genuine agnosticism; orthodox Christianity had to be discarded, but she (and Robert Elsmere) turned at once to constructing a new faith from the wreckage of the old. As Dr Arnold remarked in one of his sermons, 'For indeed to be for ever wavering in doubt is an extreme misery.'

What is disappointing about the culmination of Robert's mental struggles is that his cry of agony, though intense and heart-felt, seems to be expressed in the most banal terms: *'O God! My wife—my work!'*. To modern readers accustomed to acknowledging the redemptive value of total despair, this response may sound very tame, and we are not surprised to learn that 'at his worst there was never a moment when Elsmere felt himself utterly forsaken'. Yet if Elsmere's angst strikes us as almost cosily domestic, it should be said, in fairness to Mrs Ward, that she was not unaware of the potential depths of spiritual anguish. Robert weathers the storm with relative ease because he (like Mrs Ward) discovers almost instantly a middle ground between unreasonable orthodoxy and destructive rationalism. Laura Fountain in **Helbeck of Bannisdale**, who is unable to find such a convenient synthesis, commits suicide; Robert, however, is never really forced to peer into the abyss (though he is conscious at times that it is there beneath his feet), since Mrs Ward has already prepared an escape route for him.

Robert accordingly turns to a celebration of the human Christ and to a Theism which cannot be discredited by historical research. Mr Grey says to him:

> Spiritually you have gone through the last wrench, I promise it you! You being what you are, nothing can cut this ground from under your feet. Whatever may have been the forms of belief, *faith*, the faith which saves, has always been rooted here! All things change, —creeds and philosophies and outward systems, —but God remains!

But it is a faith based on intuition rather than historical evidence or revealed Scriptures. Robert argues that the chief distinction between Christianity and Theism is that the latter *'can never be disproved'*, for 'at the worst it must always remain in the position of an alternative hypothesis'.

The dramatic interest of the novel turns primarily upon the struggle of will between Robert and Catherine after he has made his decision to leave the Church and his clerical vocation. The preservation of Catherine's love is supremely important to Robert, because it is for him the primary evidence of divine love and a reassuring link with the old faith. Robert, in fact, regards his wife as a symbol of the deep spirituality of Christianity: she has a 'Madonna-like face', and Robert addresses her as 'Madonna mine'. A cancelled passage in the **Elsmere** manuscript (Chapter 25) reveals even more explicitly the significance of Catherine in Robert's religious life:

> A sort of allegory of himself ran vaguely through his mind. He felt as though he had been forcing his way for weeks through some dense & baffling forest, tangled by the creeper[s], bewildered by the closeness of the trees, stifled for lack of air, crushed by the sense of the impenetratable [sic] distance & discoverable issues. And suddenly the trees thin around him, the air grows lighter,

the wood falls back, and under the blessed sky & wind of an uncovered heaven, there rises in a clearing made by pious hands a white & tender image, —a vision of the Mother & Child. And forgetting all the passion & the desperation of that long struggle through the blinding hindering branches, he falls on his knees, the heart crying out with joy, the black oppression lifted.

This dream-fantasy, filled with phrases from the opening canto of the *Divine Comedy*, discloses the symbolic weight of the recurrent scenes in which Robert stumbles through the dark Surrey woods. On the very night that he renounces Christianity, he moves mechanically along a darkened lane until 'the trees before him thinned' and he hears the voice of Catherine calling for him. After returning from Oxford, he must pass through a 'frowning mass of wood' before he can dimly see Catherine's figure behind the muslin curtains of the rectory window. When his wife temporarily flees the rectory, he searches for her among 'a thick interwoven mass of young trees' until he at last finds her in a clearing. Much later, in a delirium produced by fatigue and illness, Robert again catches a glimpse of his Madonna, whose faith he has formally rejected but whose spiritual beauty is nevertheless a solace to his troubled soul: 'The strangest whirlwind of thoughts fled through him in the darkness, suggested very often by the figures on the seventeenth-century tapestry which lined the walls. Were those the trees in the wood-path? Surely that was Catherine's figure . . . ?'.

The Surrey portion of **Robert Elsmere** is also richer in colourful incident and characterization than the foregoing analysis might suggest. The brooding figure of the Squire casts an appalling shadow over the pastoral landscape. His sister, Mrs Darcy (who, incidentally, is a portrait of the wife of E. H. Craddock, Principal of Brasenose), lends an appropriately demented quality to the atmosphere of Wendover Hall. Newcome (whose name and mannerisms may have been suggested by Newman), the High Church clergyman, is a grotesque figure out of a child's nightmare. Above all, there is the strange, remote personality of Edward Langham, spiritual kin to the Squire, in whom unbelief has produced the moral paralysis of an Obermann or an Amiel. Mrs Ward claimed, in fact, that Langham was modelled exclusively upon these two introspective personalities, but he is also reminiscent of both Pater and Clough, particularly in his unsuccessful resolve to leave Oxford. His courtship of Rose—which is one the most fascinating episodes of the novel though admittedly too long for a mere subplot—owes much to Clough's 'Amours de Voyage' and Matthew Arnold's 'Marguerite' poems. Thematically the courtship is related to the main story, for we are meant to see that Langham's passivity, even when in love, contrasts unfavourably with Robert's earlier vigour as a suitor.

Rose herself is a refreshing character in a novel peopled so largely with intensely religious personalities. She is beautiful, vivacious, 'aesthetic' (indeed, in many respects very much like Emilia Pattison), yet Mrs Ward must punish her at least lightly because she is too self-assertive. As her juvenile tales demonstrate, Mrs Ward was preoccupied with the idea that a frivolous girl is morally strengthened only through an unhappy love affair. Hence we are informed that after Langham breaks off their engagement, 'deep undeveloped forces of character [begin to] stir within her'. Henry James, however, recognized the real implications of Rose's eventual 'third volume-y' marriage to Flaxman, the wealthy, handsome, but very colourless aristocrat. James sensed that Mrs Ward had provided such a conventional husband for Rose precisely because (perhaps at a subconscious level) the author's Puritan instincts disapproved of Rose's artistic ambitions. 'I can't help wishing that you had made her serious, deeply so, in her own line, as Catherine, for instance, is serious in hers', James wrote. But Mrs Ward, like Robert Elsmere, still worshipped the traditional religious and cultural values represented by the shrine in the forest clearing, and art and scholarship, though valuable in themselves, were lower in her scale of values than a strict standard of morality.

Mrs Ward believed that the final third of **Robert Elsmere,** which is set largely in the East End of London, was the finest part of her novel, but most readers would probably be inclined to apply to it T. S. Eliot's famous observation on Tennyson's *In Memoriam* that the author's doubt is a more intense and vivid reality than his faith. Elsmere, never a strong personality, is flattened into an instrument of propaganda once he is no longer afflicted by scepticism. 'One fears a little sometimes', James remarked wryly to Mrs Ward, 'that he may suffer a sunstroke, damaging if not fatal, from the high, oblique light of your admiration for him.' Elsmere's sufferings in Surrey compel our sympathy; his apotheosis in London as the saint of a new cult becomes a dull spectacle.

Mrs Ward also again laboured under the handicap of placing her hero in a milieu about which she knew little. When Robert is writing articles in his house in Bedford Square (which corresponds to descriptions of the Wards' house in Russell Square) or moves in the glittering social world of Madame de Netteville, Mrs Ward is obviously on familiar ground, but her descriptions of slum life are based on only a few visits to the East End in the company of her sister-in-law, who was a nurse, and conscientious research in printed sources. Though Mrs Ward was of course a perceptive observer, such a superficial acquaintance with working-class existence was hardly sufficient for one who professed to offer a new religion to the poor. When she made similar brief ventures into the world of the lower classes while writing **David Grieve**, Alice Green (the widow of J. R. Green) remarked sarcastically that Mrs Ward was going to Manchester 'for a three day study of the working class'.

From the **Elsmere** notebook and her letters written between 1885 and 1887, we know some of the books which Mrs Ward read to inform herself about the alien world of the East End. In the notebook one of the titles listed is Gissing's *Demos: A Story of English Socialism* (1886). She also studied the published letters of Edward Denison (1872), who spent much time among the London poor trying to teach them the elements of Christianity. James Knowles thought that Walter Besant's novel *All Sorts and Conditions of Men* (1884) had influenced Mrs Ward's treatment of 'Elgood Street', but there is no solid evidence to support this view. She was, however, intrigued by the problems of instructing the poor, and she turned to the lectures of Joseph Payne and Huxley's *Lay Sermons* (1870) for suggestions as to how scientific concepts could be communicated in simple fashion. She read widely in the autobiographies and memoirs of working men such as William Lovett and Thomas Cooper.

Having abandoned the Church and living now in the shadow of the British Museum, Elsmere would seem to be destined for a scholarly career, but his eyes turn quickly to the brutalized masses, devoid of any religious sentiments, that crowd the eastern and southern edges of London. Though he briefly engages in charitable work under the direction of a Broad Church vicar, Robert concludes that the Revd Mr Vernon is involved 'in endless contradictions and practical falsities of speech and action' because the essence of the Broad Church strategy is the concealment of one's opinions. The vein of Pattisonian radicalism in Mrs Ward's thinking made her impatient with such apparent duplicity, just as she had strongly disapproved of Jowett's willingness to subscribe to the Thirty-nine Articles. In a letter written in 1895, Mrs Ward remarked, 'I deeply regret—& wrote **Robert Elsmere** to shew it—the whole action and attitude of the Broad churchmen of those days.' Elsmere declares (in language reminiscent of John Morley's) that there is no room for compromise:

> Miracle is to our time what the law was to the early Christians. We must make up our minds about it one way or the other. And if we decide to throw it over as Paul threw over the law, then we must *fight* as he did. There is no help in subterfuge, no help in anything but a perfect sincerity. . . . The ground must be cleared; then may come the rebuilding.

Robert also has encounters with High Churchmen, Comtists (whose 'potent spirit of social help' he admires), Unitarians (with whom he identifies intellectually but not emotionally), and every variety of Secularist and Socialist, all of them moving helplessly about under the cloud of spiritual darkness that covers the East End. Eventually he decides that he must establish his own centre of activities, free of all sectarian ties, in an empty warehouse on Elgood Street. Undoubtedly with the example of Toynbee Hall in mind, Robert creates the New Brotherhood of Christ, described by one sceptical witness as 'a new church', which offers a multitude of social, educational, and religious activities for the working people of the neighbourhood.

Superficially, the New Brotherhood appears to be a 'purified' or attenuated version of Christianity. The faith has only two articles ('In Thee, O Eternal, have I put my trust' and 'This do in remembrance of me'), and its simple liturgy recalls that of James Martineau's Unitarian prayer book, which first appeared in 1862. The walls of the Elgood Street hall are lined with recesses which will hold the names of present and deceased members of the New Brotherhood, reminding us that Mrs Ward had once thus envisioned the cathedral of the new faith. In short, the New Brotherhood gives the impression of offering a modest, unpolemical alternative to orthodox Christianity that is nonetheless deeply Christian in spirit and ethics.

That is evidently how Mrs Ward wished the third volume

of her novel to be read. However, the Arnoldian theme of reconciliation and the Pattisonian theme of intransigence are always straining against each other in Mrs Ward's religious fiction, and there are frequent indications that the ultimate goal of the New Brotherhood is not to modify but to supplant traditional Christianity. The one sermon we hear Robert preach at Murewell is on the Messianic text 'This day is the scripture fulfilled in your ears!', for he is destined to become the Christ of Mrs Ward's neo-Christianity. As he declares in a lecture to a crowd of working men on Easter Eve:

> No—an idea cannot be killed from without—it can only be supplanted, transformed, by another idea, and that one of equal virtue and magic. Strange paradox! In the moral world you cannot pull down except by gentleness—you cannot revolutionise except by sympathy. Jesus only superseded Judaism by absorbing and recreating all that was best in it.

Clearly the implication is that the New Brotherhood today stands in the same relationship to Christianity as Christianity did in the first century to Judaism. Like Jesus, Robert gathers round himself a small circle of disciples who will carry on the work of Elgood Street after his martyrdom; but even before his death, pious legends and myths are beginning to be associated with Robert's name, thus suggesting how the earliest oral accounts of Jesus' ministry eventually developed into the versions found in the Synoptic Gospels.

Some readers and reviewers of **Robert Elsmere,** recognizing its revolutionary implications, have wondered why Mrs Ward chose to disguise this fundamentally new religion as a reformed Christianity. Was it merely timidity on her part? In **The Future of University Hall,** a lecture delivered and published in 1892, she explained that Christianity had so interwoven itself with European history and culture that the modern Englishman cannot escape it 'without wasteful and paralysing revolt'. Theoretically Buddhist mysticism might be of equal spiritual value to Christian mysticism, but in fact—as she told Felicia Skene in 1889—Christianity was superior to other religions because it had been associated with the greatest of all human cultures. The Christian colouration of the New Brotherhood, then, is a result of convenience and historical accident rather than of any intrinsic merit which the faith of Jesus might possess that would distinguish it from other religions.

One of the temptations in the urban wilderness which Robert as the new Christ must face and overcome is the siren call of an alluring Frenchwoman, Madame de Netteville. In several of her novels Mrs Ward created a similar feminine type, intellectually gifted but morally depraved (and nearly always of French birth or descent), who presides over a brilliant salon. Madame de Netteville's attempted seduction of Robert has class as well as sexual overtones. Her drawing room represents the most beautifully decorated room in the Palace of Art, and she wishes to lure Robert into it so that he will stop his ears to the cries of the poor without. But Robert, his mind filled with painful images of the suffering he has witnessed in Elgood Street, declines to separate himself from the moral realities of that world beyond the gates of the Palace of Art:

> When, every now and then, in the pauses of their own conversation, Elsmere caught something of the chatter going on at the other end of the table, or when the party became fused into one for a while under the genial influence of a good story or the exhilaration of a personal skirmish, the whole scene—the dainty oval room, the lights, the servants, the exquisite fruit and flowers, the gleaming silver, the tapestried walls—would seem to him for an instant like a mirage, a dream, yet with something glittering and arid about it which a dream never has.

The grim paradox—which Mrs Ward was to explore often in her later novels—was that this drawing room, both in its furnishings and guests, symbolized the finest aspects of modern civilization, yet it was threatened with extinction by the moral indifference of those who frequented Madame de Netteville's salon. Like Squire Wendover's library, the fashionable drawing room, admirable in many ways, becomes crowded with daemonic shapes when it attempts to ignore its obligations to the peasants in the valley below.

On the same night that Robert spurns the advances of Madame de Netteville, Catherine for the first time learns from Hugh Flaxman the full story of her husband's self-sacrificial labours among the London poor. Having experienced these simultaneous moral crises, 'Elsmere and his wife', we are told, 'were lovers as of old'. The reconciliation which John Morley had predicted was finally achieved. The last chapter begins: 'There is little more to tell. The man who lived so fast was no long time dying'. Fatally ill with throat cancer in Algiers (where the Wards had visited in 1881), Robert remains faithful to the new creed until the end, never wavering in his trust of God, though he professes ignorance of what form of existence may await him in the afterlife.

The gospel according to Robert Elsmere may seem in some respects a hasty and premature theological synthesis, but it is impossible not to admire the eloquence and fervour with which Mrs Ward proclaimed it both in this novel and throughout the rest of her life. Though her religious ideas were tainted by the facile optimism of her century, she never lost touch—despite, as it were, her official ideology—with the tragic element of life which she had learned from orthodox Christianity. It is not enough to say that Robert Elsmere dies because Mrs Ward has the usual Victorian weakness for sentimental death-bed scenes. He dies because (in words that echo the closing paragraph of *Middlemarch*) 'his effort was but a fraction of the effort of the race', and only through the martyrdom of humanity's most precious spirits can the rest of us climb upward on the shadowy ladder of faith that leads to God.

William S. Peterson, in his Victorian Heretic: Mrs. Humphry Ward's "Robert Elsmere," *Leicester University Press, 1976, 259 p.*

Mildred L. Culp (essay date 1982)

[*In the following excerpt, Culp considers the relationship between the artistic and the ideological in* Robert Elsmere.]

Two recent studies of the Victorian religious upheaval have drawn considerable attention to **Robert Elsmere**—published in 1888 by Mary Augusta Ward, the niece of Matthew Arnold and granddaughter of Rugby's Thomas Arnold. Neither of them, however, fully treats the issue of closure and ideological crisis in the novel. In *Gains and Losses: Novels of Faith and Doubt in Victorian England* Robert Lee Wolff rightly recognizes that Mrs. Ward's book, with its emphasis on philanthropy as a cure for the unbelief caused by biblical criticism and skepticism toward Christian evidences, was, far more than frequently discussed texts like George Eliot's *Middlemarch* or Thomas Hardy's *Jude the Obscure*, "the great classic novel of Victorian doubt." And in *Victorian Heretic: Mrs. Humphry Ward's "Robert Elsmere,"* William S. Peterson has definitively established the chronology of the book as May, 1882, to May, 1886.

What remains to be analyzed is the problem of the relationship between the ideological tension and the lack of closure in the novel, for there is a very definite correlation between ideology and form which becomes more evident when we explore the way in which Mrs. Ward illustrates the relationship between biblical criticism, religion, and science, and the way in which the novel comes to a close. On the one hand, Peterson suggests that **Robert Elsmere** was intended to attain a certain literary stature. However, Wolff dismisses the whole issue by stating that "the novel . . . has high literary merit . . . [but in] the end, literary merit is and will remain a matter of taste."

As useful as these additions to Victorian scholarship have proved to be, they do not exhaust the interacting of the artistic and ideological factors in the production of Mrs. Ward's novel. Reiterating what U. C. Knoepflmacher said [in *Religious Humanism and the Victorian Novel*, 1965], both Peterson and Wolff maintain that **Robert Elsmere** is best analyzed as a work of historical fiction. Consequently, the relationship between the ideological and aesthetic strata of **Robert Elsmere** has been both misjudged and misrepresented. A reconsideration of the book will reveal that the ideological endorsement of science has rich artistic consequences.

Robert Elsmere is a *roman à thèse* confronting head-on a mid- to late-nineteenth century development seen most frequently among the intellectual elite of England and discussed in literature from Matthew Arnold's "Dover Beach" to Edmund Gosse's *Father and Son*. Mary Ward's hero is a minister whose very being finds expression in faith, for the concern for religious truth remains after formal ties with the Church are broken. The intellect transforms Elsmere's belief, yet as the author states, "after the crash, *faith* emerged as strong as ever, only craving and eager to make a fresh peace, a fresh compact with the reason." And it is this very statement which must be analyzed in its relation to the book's ending.

As a cultural document, this weighty text may be perceived as a highly successful rendering of Mrs. Humphry

Ward's conclusion that it is impossible to embrace the insights and method of biblical criticism while engaging in the act of unquestioning religious faith. The formal choice of the open ending mirrors an ideological *aporia* in Victorian society, while suggesting that one's loyalty should favor inquiry over a religious leader. And the technique of the novel, as Mark Schorer has said [in "Technique as Discovery," *The Hudson Review*, Spring, 1948], must be seen as the author's "means . . . of discovering, exploring, developing . . . [her] subject, conveying its meaning, and, finally, of evaluating it." **Robert Elsmere** should then be viewed as an unusually subtle work of fiction whose form reflects its author's commitment not so much to create *homo religiosus*, as to join faith and reason and thereby foster critical inquiry.

Before discussing the impact of science upon form, it is well to be clear about what Mrs. Ward understood by science. Previous analyses have failed to focus squarely upon the tension in the novel, which is caused by the interplay of rationalism and anti-intellectualism. That is, Mrs. Ward suggests that critical inquiry or the spirit of science is causing cultural upheaval. Interestingly, this interpretation had been articulated in a letter by T. H. Huxley to Charles Kingsley, which suggested that religion could be saved "from the rise of science by combining it with the spirit of science" [Knoepflmacher].

In its fullest sense, Victorian science, from Mrs. Ward's perspective, is understood as an attitude of mind or critical methodology applied specifically to historical or biblical criticism and, ultimately, to faith. What the author imposes upon her hero is an Arnoldian solution, a stance halfway between orthodoxy, which she finds unreasonable, and rationalism, which appears potentially destructive to her. In particular, Elsmere, a projection of Mrs. Ward, comes to think more deeply than he did in his days at Oxford, when he first endorses science for its rational method rather than its addition to knowledge. Consequently, the impact of the critical spirit in the novel is seen in the traditional Victorian conflict between head and heart. And Mary Ward reveals her bias toward the progressive scientific mind as opposed to a prescientific spirit.

By considering the method of science rather than scientific advance as both a constructive and destructive force in matters of religion, one comes to understand that the ideas are reflected in the form, and that **Robert Elsmere** makes a cultural statement. After all, Mrs. Ward herself observed in her introduction to the Westmoreland Edition that in terms of "the main Darwinian battle . . . it was in literature, history, and theology that evolutionary conceptions were most visibly and dramatically at work." The rise of science, Mrs. Ward thus recognized, was accompanied by a critical spirit which some reflective Victorians, like herself, welcome in their attempt to find answers to their questions about faith.

In this regard, **Robert Elsmere** is best understood as an instance of the way in which the scientific spirit (not science) in the guise of biblical criticism was shaking the foundations of the intellectual elite in nineteenth-century England. And it exemplifies in its very form the author's continued concern over the impact of this development.

Moreover, perceiving this overall feature of the novel enables the reader to grasp the significance of the ending. In *The Genesis of Secrecy* Frank Kermode has said just this, for "without some foreunderstanding of the whole we can make no sense of the part. . . ."

But the great church historian Owen Chadwick neglects the aesthetic factor, then asserts [in *The Victorian Church*] that the author's crisis of faith—and by implication Elsmere's—is unrelated to science: "Notice that science had nothing to do with it." Likewise, Robert Lee Wolff says that science is unimportant in Elsmere's life. Emphasizing the confessional element of the novel, William S. Peterson appears to be more concerned with content than method. And U. C. Knoepflmacher refers to Mrs. Ward's support of the "scientific" spirit but his argument, too, does not unfold and demonstrate this idea. The following analysis discloses the formal and ideational dimensions of the open ending as a single aesthetic unity.

An examination of the relationship of poetic texture to the problem of the invasion of the spirit of science reveals the rich implications of the problem of closure in ***Robert Elsmere.*** For here an aesthetic phenomenon directly reflects a cultural issue. In other words, open form was brought about by a nagging cultural question that could not be answered. This open form is evident in the way in which Mrs. Ward's novel, in a spirit of ideological compromise, has Robert's "quiet evolution of character through circumstance" culminate in the determination to reconceptualize the Christ. The ending is rendered highly problematic by virtue of its openness on both aesthetic and ideological grounds, in that shortly after the climax, the hero dies. Kermode might well be thinking of an ending such as this when he asks readers to observe "the absence of some usual satisfactions, the disappointment of conventional expectations . . . [which] connote the existence of other satisfactions, inaccessible to those who see without perceiving and hear without understanding." He also suggests that by coming to terms with a specific dimension of a work, we may then grasp the significance of the whole of the text. Precisely for this reason the end of ***Robert Elsmere*** merits analysis in terms of an openness that is embodied both ideologically and formally.

The ending is indeed problematic, because Elsmere has found a comfortable religious stance, but Mrs. Ward has him die just after his religious views are translated into action. Is the author suggesting that his spiritual quest has ended and he therefore must die? If this is the case, why does she use [what Enid Huws Jones describes in *Mrs. Humphry Ward* as] "the well-tried and still popular mid-Victorian recipe, rich and varied in its scenes and characters, streaked with judicious laughter and . . . tears" and then jolt the reader by presenting a short, innovative (for 1888) open ending? In other words, what is the rationale behind the decision to use a conventional fictional mode to express one's views on Anglican church history and the choice of what might appear to be an inappropriate conclusion?

From a different perspective, it may be argued that the ending of ***Robert Elsmere*** is unsuited to the book as reflecting the author's inability to maintain a balance between the intellectual and the poetic. Then Mrs. Ward could be faulted for a failure of imagination in resorting to the death of her hero. Moreover, she could be criticized for attracting those interested in the Victorian ferment without presenting an analysis of its significance. In this regard, Mrs. Ward could then be accused of lacking the imaginative resources to portray the intellectual and emotional opportunities available to her character.

But the answer to these possible charges Mary Ward herself provided in a remark about her *roman à clef* showing "a certain representative and pioneering force." This seemingly casual statement actually is the key to her narrative technique. For when one asks what ***Robert Elsmere*** represents, and in what way is it pioneering, an analysis that is both aesthetic and ideational becomes necessary. From this standpoint, the book is on the frontier of the Victorian religious and scientific debate. Thus, a superficial analysis might suggest that the inability to solve the problem is an artistic failure. The analysis here suggests, on the contrary, that the absence of closure is both ideologically necessary and aesthetically inevitable.

Although in most novels the death of the hero is ordinarily a sign of closure, in ***Robert Elsmere*** Mrs. Ward uses this narrative device for precisely the opposite purpose. Its function is to reveal the fact that the focus is upon critical inquiry (the scientific spirit), not the specific character who manifests it and who represents a particular religious position. Preparing us for this development, the author remarks in an early Westmoreland scene that the hero's hair has been cut short because of a fever. From the outset, then, Robert is a Samson sapped of his physical strength. The author thus communicates less interest in *him*, than in what he finally discloses aesthetically and ideologically. From this perspective, the religious crisis may be perceived at once as a beginning and an ending. It, too, is a form of fever, a *delirium tremens* among the intellectual elite marking the transition from one ideological stance to another. Such illness is evident in other semi-autobiographical novels, including Samuel Butler's *Ernest Pontifex, or The Way of All Flesh,* begun about 1872, and William Hale White's *The Autobiography of Mark Rutherford,* completed just seven years before the publication of ***Robert Elsmere.***

Like a sacred text, then, Mrs. Ward's novel comes to be seen as having secrets, in Kermode's sense, lending themselves to interpretation by "those who seek spiritual senses behind the carnal." That is, one has at the end of the book an acute lack of a sense of closure on both the aesthetic and ideological level. For the attention has been upon the minister whose life is influenced by a number of characters, but then he is abandoned. And this idea of closure which is not a closure has been beautifully suggested by J. Hillis Miller in his perceptive theoretical discussion of novelistic ending ["The Problematic of Ending in Narrative," *Nineteenth-Century Fiction,* June, 1978]: "This ending must . . . simultaneously be thought of as a tying up, a neat knotting leaving no loose threads hanging out, no characters unaccounted for, and at the same time as an untying, as the combing out of the tangled narrative threads so that they may be clearly seen, shining side by side, all mystery or complexity revealed." Applying this method to *Robert Elsmere,* one may interpret the formal embodiment of Mrs. Ward's view of the impossibility of unifying the older and newer religious position with which Elsmere comes into contact. Moreover, the novelist's indication that the focus is less upon human life than the life of ideas viewed scientifically is disclosed.

The key here is Mary Ward's evident indifference to Elsmere's death. The author wants the reader to turn away from the character and become immersed in the scientific spirit. As Kermode has indicated in *The Sense of an Ending,* "Men, like poets . . . die *in mediis rebus.*" And Hugh Flaxman's question about the longevity of the sect bears this out, as does Catherine's attendance at two kinds of church services. Through Elsmere's openness to religious inquiry fostered by the critical spirit, Mrs. Ward seeks to advance religion beyond the death of any religious hero. The scientific spirit therefore necessitates openendedness in an aesthetic sense. The narrative is seen here as operating on levels of proclamation and silence. Thus, the lack of closure suggests the openness brought about in response to the spirit of science itself, and the importance of critical thinking over physical existence. This orientation releases Mrs. Ward herself, along with the reader who stands on the inside, from the burden of reflecting upon Elsmere as a representative human being when the main concern is how he utilizes scientific inquiry. In addition, it spares the author's characterization from the possibility of becoming rigid in terms of its perspective of scientific thinking. Thus, Elsmere is left standing in direct contrast with the other characters whose positions are absolutely fixed. And the reader is asked to look beyond him to what the novel has really been communicating.

The validity of arguing that the spirit of science has transformed what would normally be closure into non-closure is reinforced by the lines on the last page of the novel. After three long volumes, Mary Ward uses just a few lines plus a slightly modified stanza from Arthur Clough to state that the New Brotherhood of Christ, Robert's religious sect of working class laborers who endorse faith over creed, is flourishing and will continue to flourish. These closing statements are not truly a closure, but only a perfunctory gesture. Indeed, with them the author dispenses with the whole apparatus of closure. And there is a good reason for this. If the reader's focus were more on character than idea, this would most certainly be a flaw. But Mrs. Ward does this to suggest that her spotlight is primarily upon idea, not character. That is, she is more interested in the continuation of the idea than her hero. In short, as fiction mirrors history, the lack of closure in *Robert Elsmere* reflects what Miller is referring to in another context when he says that "the whole drama is ending and beginning at once, a beginning/ending which . . . [presupposes] something outside of itself, something anterior or ulterior."

The ending, then, comes as a double surprise. For in a seemingly simple narrative structure, it may be seen as operating on two levels. First, it is harmonious with the text which has prepared the reader for the death of the hero. This closure which is no closure is as distressing and perplexing as the issue under discussion and thereby engages the reader's sympathy for the author's intellectual stance and compassion toward the culture's upheaval. The technique also affirms Mary Ward's advocacy of openness, so that the ideological stance becomes manifest in the ending.

Then, more subtly, the ending evolves into a masterly critique of culture. This second, less expected development relates to Mrs. Ward's understanding of the evolutionary quality of novel writing and novel reading. Believing and showing, as a contemporary critic remarked, "that the present grows out of the past," the author is demonstrating that the scientific spirit must be nurtured, but that it must not be allowed to overtake narrative responses to culture, or culture itself. That is, a novel, particularly when it examines religion, must not be reduced to analysis: it needs to retain its aesthetic qualities and not become obsessed with scientific inquiry or the scientific spirit. Fiction, in the words of Leslie Fiedler, existing in a culturally ambiguous situation, "serves as the scriptures of an underground religion." In this regard, Elsmere's death, which occurs when the hero seems to be at his zenith, becomes a celebration of the essential mystery of human culture and the manifestation of it through the imagination.

Mildred L. Culp, "Literary Dimensions of 'Robert Elsmere': Idea, Character, and Form," in The International Fiction Review, *Vol. 9, No. 1, Winter, 1982, pp. 35-40.*

J. E. Sait   (essay date 1988)

[In the following excerpt, Sait discusses Ward's works of the First World War era.]

Undoubtedly the Great War was recognised as the Great Subject by commercially minded writers of fiction and non-fiction. However, few writers achieved any major work in the battlefield and much of the non-combatant literature which did appear has suffered from critical neglect. Neither of the two major critical studies of literature in the Great War, Bernard Bergonzi's *Heroes' Twilight: A Study of the Literature of the Great War* and Paul Fussell's *The Great War and Modern Memory* refers to Mrs. Humphry Ward. This neglect is justified to a certain extent in that both male writers are concerned only with male writers. However, their concern with the literature which emanated from the battlefields reaches some generalisations which reflect on Mrs. Ward's own work. Bergonzi asserts: 'The dominant movement in the literature of the Great War was . . . from a myth-dominated to a demythologized world.' The myth-dominated world to a certain extent depended on the classical university education of many of the middle class combatant writers. Although Mary Augusta Ward had not had a formal university education, as a member of the Arnold family and long term intellectual resident of Oxford, she was no mean classical scholar. Paul Fussell concludes that literature, in time, made the experience of the war coherent: 'Ex post facto, literary narrative has supplied . . . coherence and irony, educing the pattern: innocence savaged and destroyed.' These two critical assertions, both dealing with the role of literature in the Great War rather than the effect of the Great War on literature, do, however, suggest the general trend of Mrs. Ward's literary development during this period: the loss of the innocent certainty of traditionally assured Victorian middle class values which had been enshrined in the mythology of married love. As the war progressed Mrs. Ward's fiction becomes both more nostalgically aware of the Victorian world being left behind, and more bewilderingly intrigued through 'a strange new consciousness' with the social shape of the world to come, and most particularly with the place of women in it.

During the war Mrs. Ward published six . . . novels, her autobiography, and three non-fiction books solely devoted to the propagandising of Britain's war activities. Four of the novels made no overt reference to the Great War: *Delia Blanchflower* (January 1915), *Eltham House* (October 1915), *A Great Success* (March 1916), and *Lady Connie* (November 1916). However, all four novels deal with widening social disaffection and outright social conflict. The war fiction comprises *Missing* (October 1917) and *The War and Elizabeth* (November 1918) and concentrates on those left behind. Two post-war novels pursue war issues in civilian settings: *Cousin Philip* (November 1919) and her last work *Harvest* (April 1920). The non-fiction war works, *England's Effort* (June 1916), *Towards the Goal* (June 1917) and *Fields of Victory* (July 1919) went through vast editions but made little money for the author.

Delia Blanchflower, begun in the Spring of 1914 and finished before the war began, contains no overt mention of the European conflict and can therefore be used as an artistic yardstick to measure Mrs. Ward's concerns in the last days before the war. The major themes of money, property, marriage, propriety, and the place and function of women, dominate this essentially anti-suffrage novel. In fact, the only struggle to be mentioned is the Suffrage campaign. The dramatisation of the enfranchisement question depicts with some complexity and subtlety a range of women from the headstrong heroine whose purity, as her name implies, can never really be stained, to the fanatically driven Gertrude Marvell, with, in between, Susy Amberley, the Rector's put-upon daughter, Marion Andrews, unhappily kept in domestic servitude to her indolent mother, and Lady Tonbridge, an admirable woman and social benefactress who also desired the vote but does not wish it achieved through militancy. Delia becomes the ward of Mark Winnington, an older man heroic in the management of his estates and in his career as a cricketer. The situation recalls *Marcella,* and *The Marriage of William Ashe.* Despite her emotional attachment to Winnington, and her obvious sexual attraction to him, Delia persists in her militancy until a growing sense of alienation coincides with a spectacular outrage in which both Gertrude Marvell and a small crippled child perish. The whole tone of the work recalls Tennyson's mid-Victorian, mock-epic, *The Princess* (1847) with the same arguments reaching fundamentally the same domestic solution:

> either sex alone
> Is half itself, and in true marriage lies
> Nor equal, nor unequal: each fulfils
> Defect in each, and always thought in thought,
> Purpose in purpose, will in will, they grow,

> The single pure and perfect animal,
> The two-celled heart beating, with one full stroke,
> Life.

Or, as Mary Ward puts it, after Delia's consoling marriage to Mark:

> Delia must still wrestle all her life with the meaning of that imperious call to women which this century has sounded; and of those further stages, upwards and onwards, to which the human spirit, in Man or Woman, is perennially urged by the revealing forces that breathe through human destiny.

The novel's dedication, 'To The Younger Generation', indicates more of optimism than condescension, for if the novel contains any wisdom, it is the 'no solution as yet' variety. The novel's conclusion, in an ironic parody of its obvious model, *Middlemarch,* reduces the universal to the individual, the social to the private, as the young heroine marries the older guardian. This is the last such blessed Victorian alliance to occur in Mrs. Ward's work and presents the strongest contrast with the novels which follow, particularly the non-sexual alliance in *The War and Elizabeth* and the failed alliance in *Cousin Philip.*

The same reductive quality reappears in *Eltham House,* but the much more pessimistic tone begins a process of deepening tragic vision. Before the action of the novel begins, Caroline Marsworth has left her husband, Sir John Marsworth, to marry Alec Wing. Her young son, Dickie, dies of pneumonia, and her other child, Carina, is taken from her. The novel itself concerns Wing's attempt to win himself a prominent political position in the new government and in London Society. But his wife cannot be accepted by polite (female) society and Elizabeth Washington, the Prime Minister's wife, whips up the religious sections of the party and brings about Wing's political failure. The novel closes with Carrie's death from cancer and the cynical knowledge that Wing, spoiled, arrogant, and unworthy of her, will be socially rehabilitated. While the novel contains echoes of other pieces, notably Helbeck in the character of Sir John, it begins a much more complex perception of social and sexual mores. Below the surface of many earlier novels, Mrs. Ward has more than intimated the sharp sexual attraction which motivates the love themes. In *Eltham House,* the obvious obsessive sexual attraction between Alec and Carrie ennobles the heroine and degrades the hero, at least in the readers' eyes. However, in society the reverse is the case. Wing may not achieve through his marriage his political desires, but he may still be invited alone to dine with fashionable society. After Carrie's death, the Prime Minister, whose sound character and moral sensitivity have sympathetically provided the best index to the novelist's own ideas, ponders the situation:

> Yes, she had loved much—and how wastefully! What was left of all that love and charm? Alec Wing would forget her before long, and would return, absolved, to political life, and make in time—probably soon—a second marriage which would complete his rehabilitation. Her child would remember her a little. Her cousin and

friend would mourn her sincerely. And a bright memory and legend of her as something rare—something perhaps unique—would linger no doubt for years in the society through which she passed, over which she had so briefly reigned. But when all was said, how little! —compared with the enchanting beauty, the passionate joys and sufferings, the magic, the kindness, and the grace of the living woman.

Washington was glad to have known her; he wished he had known her better.

The novel contains only one vague reference to the war:

> The talk fell on Germany, and that possible Armageddon of the future, of which the world in general thought then so little, and the men closely in touch with European affairs so much.

However, it is not possible to read Mrs. Ward's examination of British political and social institutions, particularly the ruling classes, without the sense that the War was causing a reassessment. Her treatment of divorce, and the subsequent social ostracism, indicates a reappraisal of Victorian middle class morality. The reader wonders at the value of the former social institutions which shape and sustain society. The author freely admitted using the Holland story of 1797 as the framework, setting the novel in the deceptively stable Edwardian period. This suggests that in the historical subject cast in the times when doom impended Mrs. Ward reassesses the ideas and values of her own time:

> So it was that the figure of Caroline Wing rose out of the mists that encircle one's first thoughts of a new subject; and in the dark days of last winter [1914-1915], those hours that could be spent in writing were entirely occupied in weaving the story of her discomfiture at the hands of circumstance—a story that for months was like 'a wind-warm space' amid the horrors and griefs and tasks of the war, into which one could retreat for a little while every day and forget the newspapers.

Carrie's struggle for social acceptance differs markedly from Delia's struggle for the vote (although the depiction of both defeats resembles all too closely Mrs. Ward's response to Britain's initial experiences in the Great War). The Anti-Suffrage campaign seems artificial compared to the sympathy aroused by Carrie's desire for social acceptance, for the values of love, and the natural affection of woman and child. The correlation between Mrs. Ward's daily newspaper reading and the failure of Carrie's campaign may have contributed considerably to the emotional intensity of the novel, an intensity devoid of sentimentality as the social values rather than the character ultimately assume primary importance.

The importance of social values reappears in Mrs. Ward's next, and sparest, novel, *A Great Success* (1916). At first it seems a rather slight, short-waisted romance about a married couple. The writer-husband, Arthur Meadows, achieves a success which takes him into the lionizing upper levels of society while his artist wife, Doris, is snubbed. The novel contrasts simple artistic and human (social) success and centres on the selfishness of the indi-

vidual devoted only to society's public virtues. The men, portrayed in the novel's foreground as weak, lazy, vain, or selfish, indicate a new shift in values. As the novel progresses, the men move aside and the reader concentrates on four important women. The two positive, or virtuous women, Doris Meadows and Miss Wigram, an accountant, have still some feudal loyalties; the Italian hoyden, Miss Flink (a possible parody of Marie Corelli) contrasts neatly with the selfish and ill-mannered Lady Dunstable who seeks to lead a masculine salon of intellects, thus neglecting her role as mother. In some ways the values being lauded are the conservative ones of home, hearth and family, but the absence of any powerful, or even interesting, male figure resonates with the state of England at war, an England being depopulated of men, an England being rescued by women. The wisdom of Miss Fields (a sort of social secretary to Lady Dunstable), Mrs. Meadows and Miss Wigram, stemming as it does from a more than eponymous association with the natural and ordinary worlds, triumphs over the blind affection of the men. Frequent references to the Olympians and to Circe, suggest the mythology of classical gods and heroes, victimised by their sexual desires and innate vanity, while Doris Meadows and the chaste Miss Wigram seem much more like goddesses of wisdom, good sense and fair play. The loss of innocence here involves a feet-of-clay awakening whereby the reader, even more than the female characters, recognises the inadequacy of the male way of life, and the perverting power of corrupt women who play masculine games with sexuality or social vulnerability. Alienation and isolation, both expressed here, find no completely satisfactory resolution in either the rescue of Lord Dunstable's son or the intimations of new life for the Meadows couple. Something is definitely wrong with the state of England.

The sense of dissatisfaction with England persists in the last piece of non-war fiction, *Lady Connie,* set in the more remote past of the 1880s, and decidedly analogous to the opening skirmishes of the war. The decadence of the social world out of touch with its natural bases in *A Great Success* has been translated to the academic world of Oxford, the seat of 'wisdom', where folly creates a tragedy. The basic plot line of the 'girl meets boy' romance novel takes some unusual turns here. As might be expected, the two principal characters, Lady Connie Bledlow and Douglas Falloden, are from the upper classes, but the boy's father loses all their money. The wealthy orphaned girl has been sent to Oxford to be cared for by her studious uncle, Ewen Hooper, and his 'languid incompetent' wife. The Oxford setting of much of the novel mingles the nostalgia of spring and summer days with the bitchiness, favouritism, and outright cruelty consistent with any institution of learning dissociated from significant political power. Doubtless it reflects Mrs. Ward's earlier life there, with pen portraits of eminent persons, particularly Edward Wenlock, who substitutes for Mark Pattison. None of the characters appears absolutely innocent, though several are inexperienced, ignorant, and just a trifle stupid. Lady Connie's sexual interest in Douglas leads her to taunt him with a rival, Otto Radowitz, a young Polish student studying Music. Falloden and some fellow college bloods who have already made open war on the boy because of his wit and rather effeminate French ways, decide to douse him in 'Neptune . . . the Graeco-Roman fountain in the inner quad.' Radowitz's hand is mutilated by a broken pipe in the 'lark' where he is outnumbered ten to one. Through numerous such resonances Mrs. Ward makes what first appear to be generalized condemnatory comparisons to the war. A more overt reference appears later when, to rescue some remains of fortune, Falloden's family are forced to sell their pictures to a German ship owner, Herr Schwarz, who looks at the boy's arrogance with no knowledge of the Radowitz affair:

> 'Some day—we will teach them a lesson!' he said, under his breath, his eyes wandering over the rose-garden, and the deer-park beyond. The rapidly growing docks of Bremen and Hamburg, their crowded shipping, the mounting tide of their business, came flashing into his mind—ran through it in a series of images. This England, with her stored wealth, and her command of the seas—must she always stand between Germany and her desires? . . . What a country to conquer and to loot!

The similarities between the materialist grasping of Herr Schwarz and the calculating arrogance of Douglas Falloden with his streak of cruelty would resonate with any contemporary reader for whom dissatisfaction with the ruling classes and their part in instigating the war was general during the opening years of combat. Doubtless the use of Radowitz and Poland as an analogue for Belgium, mutilated by the Germans, would also have struck the contemporary reader. However, Mrs. Ward is not all negative. Falloden redeems himself through nursing Radowitz and Radowitz forgives Falloden by finding himself, by chance, at the death scene of Falloden's father, where he substitutes for the son. The last redemptive section of the novel re-establishes the true English values, and reverberates with references to the war. The two Oxford men, Alexander Sorell and Douglas Falloden, become the two types of Englishmen, both capable of good acts but both flawed:

> The antagonism between men of Sorell's type—disinterested, pure-minded, poetic, and liable, often, in action to the scrupulosity which destroys action; and the men of Falloden's type—strong, claimant, self-centred, arrogant, determined—is perennial. Nor can the man of the one type ever understand the attraction for women of the other.

The notion of war as a mission which would redeem the powerless and the flawed finds explicit expression in the first chapter of the final part:

> 'Nora!' —she looked around the Oxford street with a sudden ardour, her eyes running over the groups of undergraduates hurrying back to hall—'do you think these English boys could ever—well, *fight*—and *die*—for what you call ideas—for their country—as Otto Radowitz could die for Poland?'
>
> 'Try them!' The reply rung out defiantly. Connie laughed.
>
> 'They'll never have the chance. Who'll ever attack England? If we only had something—something splendid, and not too far away! —to look back upon, as the Italians look back on Garibaldi—or to long and to suffer for as the Poles long and suffer for Poland!'
>
> 'We shall some day!' said Nora hopefully. 'Mr. Sorell says every nation gets its turn to fight for its life.'

Falloden's care for Radowitz in his frailty becomes a measure of his individual fight for life and love, and an ironic comparison of the fight for the civilised values of Europe as Mrs. Ward saw them. Falloden's success, in achieving a betrothal with Lady Connie, leaves in the closing pages a more subtle bittersweet taste for the reader and for Sorell, the most honourable character:

> Sorell's mind was full of mingled emotion—as torn and jagged as the clouds rushing overhead. The talk and laughter in the cottage came back to him. How hollow and vain it sounded in the spiritual ear! What could ever make up to that poor boy, who could have no more, at the most, than a year or two to live, for the spilt wine of his life? —the rifled treasure of his genius? And was it not true to say that his loss had made the profit of the lovers—of whom one had been the author of it? When Falloden and Constance believed themselves to be absorbed in Otto, were they not really playing the great game of sex like any ordinary pair?
>
> It was the question that Otto himself had asked—that any cynic must have asked. But Sorell's tender humanity passed beyond it. For the mysterious impulse which had brought Falloden to the help of Otto was as real in its sphere as the anguish and the pain: aye, for the philosophic spirit, more real than they, and fraught with a healing and disciplining power that none could measure.

Her interest in the female mythologies of the hearth and domestic functions which prevailed in her early fiction has given way to an examination of a pointedly masculine and decrepit mythology of greco-romanism. However, this mythology has no emotional force, operating, not as a thorough texture within the novel, but rather as a thin thread. The recognition of a world of mixed morality or relativistic values, devoid of the old powerful mythologies which used to clothe virtues in classical metaphors but which now had become dilapidated like the college fountain, thrusts the reader and the writer out of the nineteenth century world of religious ideas and into the twentieth century world of rapid, careless action. The act of damaging, and ultimately destroying, Radowitz, is not gratuitously designed to resolve the plot as one finds in other sensational actions in the earlier novels of love and ideas. Rather here that action becomes the core, or middle climax, around which characters must move and find new values.

The interpretation of action, not the expression of ideas in conflict, becomes the principal aim of Mrs. Ward's three non-fiction war books. This must appear somewhat surprising as propaganda was the basis for these three works. But the ideas of 'honour', 'virtue', 'loyalty', 'justice', 'truth' and so on, the topical abstractions of war-time, have now less significance in Mrs. Ward's non-fiction than one might expect. Instead 'work', not so much a concept, as an action, and compatible as such with her own profession of writing, becomes the most significant feature. Theodore Roosevelt, the former American President, spurred Mrs. Ward into that action with a letter which mentioned how England was being depicted in America, shirking. She replied:

> We are thought to be not taking the war seriously, even now. Drunkenness, strikes, difficulties in recruiting the new armies, the losses of the Dardanelles expedition, the failure to save Serbia and Montenegro, tales of the luxurious expenditure in the private life of rich and poor, and of waste or incompetence in military administration—these are made much of . . . You who know something of the vastness of the English effort—you urge upon me that English writers whose work and name are familiar to the American public are bound to speak for their country, bound to try and make Americans feel what we here feel through every nerve—that cumulative force of a great nation, which has been slow to rouse, and is now immoveably, irrevocably, set upon its purpose.

England's Effort, the result of this motivation, becomes a series of hymns in praise of England's actions.

Although Mrs. Ward espouses a journalistic style, the novelist's sense of shape and balance manifest themselves in the handling of her main theme. The six letters of ***EE*** fall tidily into two groups, with the first and final letters acting both as brackets and as part of the groups. After the preamble of the first letter, the matter settles into a description of a winter visit to the Fleet, the source of England's legendary reputation:

> My heart goes out to you, great ships, and you, gallant unwearied men, who keep your watch upon them! That watch has been kept for generations . . . While the Navy lives, England lives, and Germany's vision of a world governed by the ruthless will of the scientific soldier is doomed.

After this symbol of timeless energy, Ward turns in the next two letters to examine action unleashed in the munition and engineering workshops. Here women have gained prominence by taking the place of men in the shops and promote, through work, a sense of innovation:

> There will be a new wind blowing through England when this war is done. Not only will the scientific intelligence, the general education, and the industrial plant of the nation have gained enormously from this huge impetus of war; but men and women, employers and employed, shaken perforce out of their old grooves, will look at each other, surely, with new eyes, in a world which has not been steeped for nothing in effort and sacrifice, in common griefs and a common passion of will.

However, despite a sense of curiosity: 'One's thoughts begin to follow out some of the possible social results of

this national movement', she retreats from an exploration of it: 'As to the problem of what is to be done with women after the war, one may safely leave it to the future.' The next two letters, dealing with effort behind the lines and at the front, have the basic desire 'to show something—however inadequately—of the work of men who have done a magnificent piece of organisation.' She observes and transcribes the 'work' in supply, hospitals, and finally military action:

> 'How many years have we been at war?' one tends to ask oneself in bewilderment, as the spectacle unrolls itself. 'Is it possible that all this is the work of eighteen months?'

It would be quite easy to see in her bewilderment a mid-nineteenth century admiration of work as 'proof of moral rectitude', and that the war was merely causing her to reassert conservative attitudes. While she does occasionally adopt a reactionary posture, as in incidents when her snobbery becomes overt, she more often sees 'work' as a vast and comprehensive effort for change which will alter the perception of both the world of 'before the war' and 'now'. The last letter, observing the home front, looks at the sacrifice and work of all classes. Of the sons of aristocrats she says:

> Whatever may be said henceforth of these 'golden lads' of ours, 'shirker' and 'loafer' they can never be called again. They have died too lavishly, their men have loved and trusted them too well for that; and some of the working-class leaders, with the natural generosity of English hearts, have confessed it abundantly.

Indeed, she dwells on the courage and sacrifice of the sons of the rich to an inordinate degree because they are her closer acquaintances. But the Tommies also come in for commendation, as the whole of this last letter turns work into effort and finally into heroism of a new kind. The shape of the entire book is thus confirmed subtextually as the transformation of slothful dross, through work, into the gold of heroism.

The subtlety and novelistic control of ***England's Effort*** does not appear as strong in ***Towards the Goal*** (June 1917). There, having revealed her correspondent to be Theodore Roosevelt, Mrs. Ward's style becomes more casual as she becomes more assured of the Allies' coming Victory. America enters the war during the course of the third letter (Easter Eve 1917) and her sense of the American audience also governs the way she reports the French War Zones. Only in the latter sections of the book where reported and eye-witness accounts of German atrocities at Senlis, Vareddes, and Gerbéviller portray action, does she lose sight of the propaganda intent on the more interesting field of human drama. I think that unconsciously she created a subtext which at first manifests a fascination with the machinery of war, particularly the aeroplane, while still maintaining the idea that 'war is work.' This gives way to a perception of the garden of France ruined by machinery. This too, is ultimately overlain with an extraordinary series of classical references first to the Iliad and then finally, and most tellingly, to the *Odyssey*. The Trojan war naturally enough would have some literary parallels to the experiences and activities which she observes, but the curiosity becomes the way France and the Classical world of Uncle Matthew's Hellenism have combined. The Germans are philistines or, more frequently, barbarians, who run amok under the influence of drink. Again, she witnesses and accepts a new perception of reality: 'The fact is that old axioms are being everywhere revised in the light of this war.' However, these letters do not carry that thought far, no doubt because her work has been divided between journalism and novel-writing where in *England's Effort* she substituted her non-fiction for a novel.

With *Missing* (October 1917), Mrs. Ward combined the old concerns of the pre-war novels (money, position, the role of women, sexual attraction and so on) with the foreground of the war and used a plotting style reminiscent of both Mrs. Henry Wood and Wilkie Collins, all to the creating of a strange new consciousness. Significantly religion does not appear as an important factor, a sure sign that she is leaving more of the nineteenth century behind her. The main plot depicts the grieving young wife, Nelly Serrat, being cared for by Sir William Farrell, while her husband is away first fighting, then missing in action. The complication comes with Nelly's sister, Bridget Cookson, who plots to throw Nelly and Farrell together and finally suppresses the knowledge of George's identity in an army hospital because she is socially and financially ambitious, hoping eventually for Nelly and Sir William to marry. Nelly finds George on his death-bed, shares a few days with him, and ultimately recovers from his death, perhaps to marry Farrell. Within this melodramatic plot-line Ward plays with variations on the theme of consciousness. The Westmoreland setting provides instant and obvious references to Wordsworth, including a moonlight boat ride and descriptions of the scenes between Nelly and George which are pure 'spots of Time'. Nelly eventually emerges from passive dependence to a new consciousness of her own strength, and a rejection of Bridget's mean-spirited nature. The Farrell family who even in war-time live in 'ease and lavishness' also must wake to a new consciousness of the war effort and the economies to be undertaken. Most important of all, the new consciousness of Mrs. Ward brings with it a new style of Realism, despite the appearance of melodrama.

Mrs. Ward's new Realism comes in part from the war material with its stories of bravery, wounded soldiers, and war-time hospitals behind the lines, and in part from relation of that material to perennial social conflicts. The old-fashioned and the new-fangled, the battle of the sexes and the struggle within the individual to know what is right, and knowing it, to act upon that knowledge: all these become part of the novelist's thematic material, observed realistically and rendered dramatically. The opposition of character is nothing new in Mrs. Ward's fiction: mother against daughter (*Marcella*), husband against wife (*The Marriage of William Ashe*), lover against lover (*Delia Blanchflower, Helbeck* and so on). But *Missing* concentrates on sibling and lover conflicts, and the divided self. Sir William and his sister, Cicely, are mildly at odds, while Nelly and her sister, Bridget, are certainly in unacknowledged conflict. Marsworth and Cicely function as a Benedict and Beatrice match requiring the help and tricks of the other 'lovers', if one can call Sir William that.

The conflict between old and new appears in the various acceptable roles of women: Cecily and Bridget both represent kinds of the 'new' woman, the former the 'fast' woman in make-up and outrageous, rather French dress, the latter a pseudo-intellectual who has not the will to stick at anything. Naturally these two do not care for each other. Mrs. Ward delineates carefully the principal conflict within Nelly between her feelings for George and her gratitude and growing affection for Sir William. Nelly grieves when George is reported missing, but it is only the writer's intrusion into her consciousness which informs the reader that Nelly thinks him dead, and then that knowledge transforms her from passivity to awareness and self-control:

> It often seemed to her that during the year since George's death, her mind had been wrenched and hammered into another shape. It had grown so much older she scarcely knew it herself.

At the novel's end various characters speculate as to whether she will ever marry Farrell. Nelly's own thoughts on the matter are more pragmatic than the romanticising of her friends:

> Her heart was full of intensest love and yearning; but the love was no longer a torment. She knew now that if she had been able to tell George everything, he would never have condemned her; he would only have opened his arms and comforted her . . . It seemed to her that even while George stood spiritually beside her, in this scene of their love, he was bidding her think kindly and gratefully of the man whom he had blessed in dying—the man who, in loving her, had meant him no harm.

The contrast between the characters who romanticise the 'little widow' and turn her into a kind of saint, and Nelly's own thoughts which have a basis in acknowledged sexual attraction, serves to heighten the sense of realism. The further rationalising and spiritualising within Nelly's consciousness also adds a realistic sense of unresolved self-questioning. The war itself, as an omnipresent unresolved conflict, likewise heightens the realism. The slice of life presented here has not been organically idealised into a whole. This novel then makes a considerable advance in Mrs. Ward's development away from the idealising, and the ideation, of the 'high' society political novels.

The new Realism which allows Mrs. Ward to depict both the confused subjective deliberations of her heroine, and the fragmented society suffering from the conflicting pressures of materialism, idealism and self-preservation, could be seen as a product of the writer's own war-time experiences. Her visits to the Fleet and the battlefields of France, and the alteration this gave to her social perception, can hardly have failed to impinge on her fictional work, once she committed herself to writing about the war in tract and novel. In fact, as her daughter notes, the war occupied her time in many ways:

> the lighter side of her War labours was the intense and meticulous interest she took in the

> 'War economies' . . . Her daughter Dorothy was at this time deep in the organization of 'Women on the Land'—a movement of considerable importance in Hertfordshire— . . . All this gave her many ideas for her four War novels . . . *Missing* had a considerable popular success [Janet Penrose Trevelyan, *The Life of Mrs. Humphry Ward*].

She took more than ideas and themes from the war and her work in it. Images and motifs from the war non-fiction permeate *Missing.* The machine-like nature of the war noted in *Towards the Goal* reappears in Nelly's visit to France: 'Here, the war came home to her, as a vast machine by which George, like millions of others, had been caught and crushed.' The garden of France from that work has been translated into the ideal landscape of Wordsworth and the Arnolds' Lake District, bringing with it the sense that that world is imperilled both from without and within. The importance of work observed constantly in *England's Effort* also reappears where work transforms the idle upper classes. Nelly's final transformation also occurs because of her involvement in hospital work. Likewise, the new perception of women and women's work in *England's Effort* reappears in *Missing,* though without any further extension of its implications. The new Realism which penetrates the fiction from the non-fiction results in more affective works which display neither cliché nor sentimentality.

While *Missing* presented Mrs. Ward with the challenge of generating a new Realism as a response to the new consciousness achieved through examining 'work' both as a war theme in fiction where private grief and public duty come to an understanding, and as an analogue for the writer's occupation, its use of the Westmoreland setting must have contributed to another important effort: *A Writer's Recollections* (October 1918). While much of this autobiography may have existed before the war began, and it is evident from the fact that this terminates at 1900 that a longer work was planned, undoubtedly the war caused Mrs. Ward to re-examine her past. The past of her childhood in the Lake District, her intellectual life at Oxford, and the society of London, take on a special, ideal nature, and a strong sense of *ave atque vale*. Only in the 'Epilogue' does the war make itself felt, as she observes the beginning of a new era:

> if religious ideals have got greatly profited by the war, it is plain that in the field of social change we are on the eve of transformations—throughout Europe—which may well rank in history with the establishment of the Pax Romana, or the incursion of the northern races upon the Empire; with the Renaissance or the French Revolution. In our case, the vast struggle, in the course of which millions of British men and women have been forcibly shaken out of all their former ways of life, and submitted to a sterner discipline than anything they have yet known, while at the same time, they have been roused by mere change of circumstances and scene to a strange new consciousness of themselves and the world, cannot pass away without permanently affecting the life of the State, and the relation of all citizens to each other . . . a

> new heat of intelligence, a new passion of sympathy and justice has been roused in our midst by this vast and terrible effort, which, when the war is over, will burn out of itself the rotten things in our social structure, and make reforms easy, which, but for the war, might have rent us in sunder.

The new beginning which she hints at appears more forcefully in her next novel.

The War and Elizabeth (November 1918) must have been written at much the same time as *Recollections,* and just as that work had a remarkable young woman as its central character, the novel concentrates on a nearly flawless heroine who has a reformer's zeal. The romantic plot between Mannering and Elizabeth recalls George Eliot's Casaubon in *Middlemarch* and the Pitt-Crawley episodes with Becky in *Vanity Fair.* However, the romance is just as decidedly without the earlier novels' satire or pessimism as it is without sexual attraction between the two characters. (Two subsidiary plots of young lovers create as much sexual interest as the novel needs.) Miss Bremerton's abilities match many of Mrs. Ward's own: her knowledge of languages, her interest in the Classics, and her fascination with husbandry, forestry, estate management, and poor crippled children. She also apparently shares Mrs. Ward's disability: a tendency not to notice when she tramples on the feelings of younger women by dominating male conversation. But Elizabeth is also the New Woman, 'who wants to *do* things, and isn't always thinking about getting married'. Again, as in *Towards the Goal, England's Effort, Recollections,* and *Missing,* the young woman's enormous capacity for work forms the core around which character development occurs.

While *Missing* introduced a greater realism in Ward's fiction, *The War and Elizabeth* lays more stress on the creation of a denser text with a strong symbolic level. This symbolic level related particularly to the Greek and Roman culture, perhaps because certain issues such as the state of the nation and civilization in Europe, exemplified in the ancient world, as well as the role of women in society (and indeed the link between the two aspects), could not easily be resolved on the surface level of the narrative. However, Mrs. Ward's handling of the symbolism does not suggest allegory. Rather she intends to create a suggestive penumbra-like effect halfway between the bright surface of the narrative and a fully developed shadowing allegory, thus allowing the reader to associate more fully. The most persistent symbolism, classical analogies, involves a momentary identification of a character from the surface narrative with another character in classical mythology. Thus Elizabeth's stubborn determination that the Squire must not impede the use of his land for food compares with Penelope's rejection of her suitors. However, the author gives a nice twist to the allusion, allowing the Squire obliquely to compare himself to Penelope when he is forced to dismantle his barricade: 'and yet she was only undoing her own work! —she was not forcing a grown man to undo his!' Here the author can play at sexual role reversal, one of the important elements of the surface narrative where Elizabeth is the truest soldier, and the men, rather weaker, except for Desmond who is compared to 'the young Odysseus . . . when he left his mother on his first journey to hunt the boar'. The reader cannot totally ascribe Penelope's character to Elizabeth because her suitor/lover has married a Greek girl in Alexandria, and she herself finally settles for the Squire, his family, and the control of his estate. However, the reader retains an impression of that distant Trojan war without ascribing Germans to one side or the other in it. Instead the reader senses the values of that classical civilization in jeopardy. Towards the end of the novel, Ward marries classical and Christian allusions as Desmond, dying from war wounds, lies in the Squire's library:

> By the light of one lamp, which was screened from the bed, one saw dimly the fantastic shapes in the glass cases which lined the walls—the little Tanagra figures with their sun-hats and flowing dress—bronzes of Apollo or Hermes—a bronze bull—an ibex—a cup wreathed with acanthus. And in the shadow at the far end rose the great Nikê. She seemed to be asking what the white bed and the shrouded figure upon it might mean—protesting that these were not her symbols, or a language that she knew.
>
> Yet at times, as the light varied she seemed to take another aspect. To Aubrey, sitting beside his brother, the Nikê more than once suggested the recollection of a broken Virgin hanging from the fragment of a ruined church which he remembered on a bit of road near Mametz, at which he had seen passing soldiers look stealthily and long. Her piteous arms, empty of the babe, suggested motherhood to boys fresh from home; and there were moments when this hovering Nikê seemed to breathe a mysterious tenderness like hers—became a proud and splendid angel of consolation—only, indeed to resume, with some fresh change in its shadows, its pagan indifference, its exultant loneliness.

Here again, the allusions are suggestive. The Nikê as goddess of Victory signals Desmond's heroic apotheosis, the eventual victory of the Allies, and the mediation between men and the gods, particularly Pallas Athena and Zeus (wisdom and might). Her classical role then forecasts a Victory through the triumph of right which will make men like the gods. The Virgin's empty arms suggest the Pieta as much as the mother and infant; thus Desmond's death becomes a sanctified sacrifice contributing to a general salvation and the specific conversion of his father to the war cause. Mrs. Ward's sub-textual manipulations import a cultural tradition rather than a specific allegory, a tradition which implies order and love amidst a world of chaos. This novel in the surface and sub-text comes closest to both Fussell's and Bergonzi's conception of the role of literature in the Great War.

Order opposed to chaos has considerable meaning on the surface level of the narrative. Elizabeth rescues the Squire's collection of antiquities from disorder. Doing the same for the estate, she creates order in the external world. In the process she civilises the Squire and his surroundings. The emotional lives of all the characters seem chaotic to say the least. However, the novel ends with ordering, pairing and marriages. Part of the chaos comes from the old order trying to ignore a new situation which has arisen. Unfortunately both the admirable design of the novel and the subtlety of its imagery and symbols does not always sustain the reader through the boredom of the romantic sub-plots.

The treatment of the war echoes that in *Missing* in its examination of those left behind. Their war activities take on more importance because Desmond serves at the front as a less significant emotional interest than George Serat. Again Ward explores the role of women and their changing social importance, and finds a more positive attitude in the scope of Elizabeth's work, but a rather negative attitude, at least to this reader, in her marriage to the squire at the end.

After the war ended, Mrs. Ward wrote and published *Fields of Victory* (July 1919) which explained how Britain really won the war:

> there is yet no doubt in any British military mind that it was the British Army which brought the war to its victorious end.

She needs to explain to Americans and to others who had stayed at home just how this was done. The book contains a wealth of detailed explanation, maps, photographs, and the curious sense that Mrs. Ward is in the vanguard of the millions-to-be Great War Tourists. She reports more than one battle in the present tense, which provides an extraordinary sense of immediacy, and she again reiterates the 'unusual' work of women. But here her tone becomes a trifle patronising, and once again she backs away from the social implications:

> Of the noble army of women, who, since 1917, have formed part of the great force behind the fighting lines I have been rapidly sketching— what shall one say but good and grateful things? . . . It is clear that, during the concluding year of the war, they rendered services of which British women may reasonably be proud; and in the retreat of last March, by universal testimony, they bore themselves with special coolness and pluck. . . . It was yet another page in that history of a new womanhood we are all collaborating in to-day.

In spite of the claim for collaboration, the patronising tone suggests that women can now be returned to their appropriate place on the shelf. The work concludes with a plea for civilization, and Christian ideals. This sense of conservatism, despite her own first-hand perception of the horrors of the war, and the alteration to her own perceptions, perhaps results from her uncertainty about the place of women in society post-war, a situation she explores in her next piece of fiction.

Cousin Philip (November 1919) *almost* confronts the changing role of women as a result of the war. Helena Pitstone has been made the ward of her cousin Philip, Lord Buntingford. However, having worked in a war canteen, and as a chauffeur, she feels that she has earned the right to self-determination, stating her manifesto: 'we—the women of the present day—are not going to accept our principles—moral—or political—or economic—on anybody's authority.' Mrs. Ward contrasts Helena with her chaperone, Lucy Friend, a war widow, who emerges from her five-year absence from the world as if she had come from a nunnery into a New England. Lucy wonders, in a somewhat Wordsworthian frame of mind, about life for women after the war:

> Mrs. Friend was left to reflect on the New Woman. Was it in truth the war that had produced her? and if so, how and why?

Helena's friendship for Lucy makes her less antipathetic to the reader, as does her bravery during the soldiers' riot, and her competent driving (something her cousin and most of his men friends, though soldiers, have not learned how to do). Overall, the New Woman does not leave an entirely satisfactory impression, but then neither does the Old Man. Although Lord Buntingford knows best, most of the time, the novel's somewhat sensational, Lady Audley-like plot, reveals his earlier impetuous marriage to an artist. At the novel's conclusion he is left with an idiot son to bring up and married off to a less than satisfactory woman, Lady Cynthia Welwyn, who has been chasing him for some time and would appear to be past bearing any further children herself. The plots of Mrs. Ward's earlier novels would have demanded the marriage of the headstrong but reformed young woman to the older, wiser, man who would be her 'stay and support'. However, if the war has altered characters, it has also altered the plot. Unfortunately, it has not altered it enough. Helena does fall in love with Philip, but in an almost *Enoch Arden* fashion she goes to the woods, gets over it, and finally marries Geoffrey French. Even Lucy may marry the Vicar. Thus, all the ends are tidied up. However, the tidying up suggests a novelist's desires rather than a reflection of reality, and the reader feels that Mrs. Ward has made an attempt to confront the problem of the New Woman after the war, but really has no idea what to do with her. This is not quite the case with her last novel.

Harvest (April 1920) might in many ways be said to marry nineteenth century traditions of the Brontës and George Eliot to a twentieth century sense of women's sexuality. Motifs from *The Tenant of Wildfell Hall, Wuthering Heights* and *Jane Eyre* jostle with situations and sensibilities from *Felix Holt, Adam Bede,* and *The Mill on the Floss.* Both Tennyson's *The Promise of May* and Hardy's *Tess of the D'Urbervilles* also receive quietly bucolic nods, particularly in the conjunction of female sexuality and the ripening countryside. But unlike Eliot and Hardy, Mrs. Ward chooses a much more sensational core for this last novel set on the land. Rachel Henderson rents a farm where, with the aid of her friend Janet Leighton, two land girls, and a couple of elderly hired men, she harvests the crop of 1918. However, she also harvests the crop sown in her previous years when, married to an English wastrel in Canada, she sought and obtained a divorce after the death of their child. This in itself would not debar her in Mrs. Ward's mind from a further happy (or preferably as in *Eltham House,* unhappy) marriage. Unfortunately, she has also committed adultery before her divorce when she was desperately in need of comfort and sympathy. This moral lapse, and the threatened disclosure of it, contribute a sense of guilt and terror to her developing relationship with Captain Ellesborough. Finally, just at the moment of

reconciliation and forgiveness, her former husband, maddened by drink and dying of tuberculosis, shoots her. At the moment of highest sexual and emotional awareness, the human life is harvested.

Despite the apparent negative depiction of female sexuality, Ward maintains a strong sympathy for her heroine, both through a lavish sense of her inner consciousness (always the novelist's best technique for eliciting sympathy) and through the depiction of wretched men. Rachel struggles with life and love, and Mrs. Ward unfolds that struggle omnisciently. Thus, Rachel appears warm, human and flawed. The men, on the other hand, seem either twisted, as in the case of Roger Delane, or narrowly stereotyped and stereotyping as in the case of Captain Ellesborough. The puritan education of the latter manifests itself in conservative pronouncements:

> He believed the world was coming back to the old things. The war had done it—made people think. . . . 'Men are better cooks than women when they give their minds to it!'

However, love transforms Ellesborough too, as he reads Rachel's diary, sitting beside her body:

> They were as her still living voice in his ears, and as the words sank into memory they pierced though all the rigidities of a noble nature, rending and kneading as they went.

The greater knowledge of the inner workings of the minds of men and women contributes to a new perception of the capacity to change.

The new perception and sympathetic understanding of character emerges as a direct result of the war. Mrs. Ferguson, the commandant of the timber girls, remarks on this to Janet:

> You see, we women who are doing all this new work with men, we know a jolly deal more about them than we ever did before. I can tell you, it searches us out, this joint life—both women and men. In this camp you can't hide what you are— the sort of man—or the sort of woman.

Because women have taken occupations formerly held by men, they become aware of the way men think and act. Not only that, but it has become harder for either sex to dissemble in the presence of the other. Had Rachel had a better opportunity to know Roger Delane before she married him, she would have seen through his lies. This, then is to be the real harvest of the war: a view into the world of the opposite sex which will enlighten women and men. The 'strange new consciousness' which came through the change of scene and circumstance brought on by the war, has turned Mrs. Ward inside out. The social reformer of the early novels had depicted characters as victims of social conditions (albeit in a liberal rather than Marxist sense) but the characters remained only half-realised automatons for the novelist because of her fundamental belief in Victorian social institutions. After the war social reform collapses into individual private struggle for renewal. This limits the social enquiry: the novel proposes no new Eden.

If one reads *Harvest* as the summation of Mrs. Ward's career as a writer of fiction, a number of interesting implications arise which ultimately reflect the significance of the war. A marked tendency in the later novels to dispense with the omniscient benevolent male figure reappears here bringing a general sense of fallibility to the characters without suggesting either cynicism or disillusionment to the reader. However, a notion persists that the past will somehow blight the present as evil seeds have their inevitable fruition. More worrying is the idea that benevolent characters may never be fulfilled. On the final page Janet is condemned to friendship rather than love. The wasting of human life contrasts neatly with the prodigality of nature in the long harvest. But the contrast of the effects of war and peace on the landscape focus most strongly Mrs. Ward's new consciousness, as in this passage regarding the logging of the forests:

> Two years before it had been known only to the gamekeeper and the shooting guests of the neighbouring landowner. Now a great timber camp filled it. The gully ran far and deep into the heart of the forest country, with the light railway winding along the bottom, towards an unseen road. The steep sides of the valley—Rachel and Janet stood on the edge of one of them—were covered with felled trees, cut the preceding winter and left as they fell. The dead branch and leaf of the trees had turned a rich purple, and dyed all the inside of the long deep cup. But along its edges stretched the forest, still untouched, and everywhere, in the bar spaces left here and there by the felling among the 'rubble and wood wreck', green and gold mosses and delicate grasses had sprung up, a brilliant enamel, inlaid with a multitude of wild flowers.. ..
>
> 'German prisoners!' said Janet, and strained her eyes to see thinking all the time of a letter she had received that morning from her soldier brother fighting with the English troops to the west of Rheims:
>
> 'The beggars are on the run! . . . But, oh, Lord, the sight they've made of all this beautiful country! Trampled, and ruined, and smashed! all of it. Deliberate loot and malice everywhere, and tales of things done in the villages that make one see red. We captured a letter to his wife on a dead German this morning: "Well, the offensive is a failure, but we've done one thing—we've smashed up another bit of France!" How are we going to live with these people in the same world after the war?'

The simplicity of the passage, and the almost simple-minded propaganda here written after the war, gives a sense of the problem which Mrs. Ward sees in Europe. But the simplicity of style combined with the sensation in the novel's plot and characterizations points to a failure of realism. The war has been too much. However, Mrs. Ward does not revert to the old sensational artifices of the earlier novels, rather the sensationalism here is on a grand scale uninvolved with ideas but caught up with universal earthbound feelings. The struggle between good and evil of which the war had made so much at last penetrates and pervades the neutral liberalism of the earlier works making the characters naturalistic. This naturalism results in closer ties between the surface narrative and the subtextual allegory of universal war at the same time that it reduces the characters to cyphers in some vast design of Nature's which even the novelist cannot quite discern. The War has triumphed and the old ways of the 19th century writer lie pretty much in ruins.

The obvious difficulties facing the critic who attempts to calculate the effect of the war on the writers of established literary reputation and professional commitment, particularly those born in the middle of the previous century, rests in the diversity of the writers and the state of literature itself. The changes in Mrs. Ward's career, and in her version of the novel of ideas, can be taken only as one example, not necessarily isolated, or unique, but perhaps indicative. She saw her transformation both as common to many writers and a response to market pressures, but she also felt the increasing literary response to the war was entered into very reluctantly:

> In the first two years of the war, the cry both of writers and public—so far as the literature of imagination was concerned—tended to be— 'anything but the war!' There was an eager wish in both, for a time, in the first onrush of the great catastrophe, to escape from it and the newspapers, into the world behind it. That world looks to us now as the Elysian fields looked to Aeneas as he approached them from the heights—full not only of souls in a blessed calm, but of those who had yet to make their way into existense as it terribly is, had still to taste reality and pain. We were thankful for a time to go back to that kind, conscious, unforeseeing world. But that is no longer possible. The war has become our life, and will be so for years after the signing of peace.

She reiterates this in a less consciously literary way at the beginning of *England's Effort:*

> My literary profession, indeed, has been to me as to others, since August 4th, 1914, something to be interposed for a short time, day by day, between a mind tormented and obsessed by the spectacle of war, and the terrible reality it could not otherwise forget. To take up one's pen and lose oneself for a while in memories of life as it was long, long before the war—there was refreshment and renewal in that! Once, —last spring—I tried to base a novel on a striking war incident which had come my way. Impossible! The zest and pleasure which for any story-teller goes with the first shaping of a story, died away, at the very beginning. For the day's respite had gone. The little 'wind-warm space' had disappeared. Life and thought were all given up, without mercy or relief, to the fever and nightmare of the war. I fell back upon my early recollections of Oxford thirty or forty years ago—and it was like rain in the desert [*Lady Connie*]. So that, in the course of months it had become a habit with me never to write about the war; and outside the hours of writing to think and talk of nothing else. . . .

Like many artists Mrs. Ward sought initially to escape the reality of the war, conceiving literature as a space where disbelief might be temporarily suspended in romance. As the Great War progressed and Mrs. Ward became involved with it as a writer of non-fiction material, her ability to escape its grim reality even in fiction diminished. The shifts from romance in *Lady Connie* to realism in *Missing* to symbolism in *The War and Elizabeth* to the failure of Victorianism in *Cousin Philip* and finally to naturalism in *Harvest* show a remarkable series of adjustments which the war forced upon her. Her attitude to women too shifted from the notion of domestic female to a certainty that women need not restrict themselves to the traditional roles of homemaker and nurse, but she was uncertain about what precisely would be their next functions in the less than brave new world. More telling is her depiction of weak men, beset by past indiscretions, and present inadequacies. The great optimism of the Victorian age which would lavish time in arguments about religion and the finer issues of social welfare gives way to a more compulsive sense of human nature as raw, coarse, and unstructured by refining ideals like material Nature itself. Ultimately when the old plot devices are used, they seem inadequate shorings-up against a flooding realisation of the inchoate powers of Nature and the puniness of Man.

Undoubtedly the Great War influenced many writers who held liberal ideas and ideals to further enlightened social projects, but for Mrs. Ward it forced a retreat into the puritanism evident in *Harvest*. The frailty of old age did not cause the retreat so much as the confrontation with the catastrophe of the War. Coming from the more leisured life of the Victorian intellectual, albeit involved with social issues, she had seen improvement as possible within the system. Her 'strange new consciousness' after the War acknowledged that the system she knew was not only in its death throes, but that the very basic element in that system, the conception of the individual, was flawed. In this perception of the individual's relation to the social fabric, she is not alone. Like Ford Madox Ford in *Parade's End* (1924-1928) or Virginia Woolf in *Jacob's Room* (1922), Mrs. Ward acknowledges not only the breakdown of the Old Order of Victorian patriarchal benevolent government, but also the shattering of its reflection in society and the family. But unlike these, and many other writers of a younger generation (i. e. Conrad, Kipling, Wells, Lawrence, Strachey, Forster and her nephew, Aldous Huxley), she could not entirely free herself from the strong belief in many of the positive values of that older world. She has neither the energy, nor the vision, nor the cynicism, nor perhaps the courage, to become a social satirist, or a psycho-sexual analyser of the human condition. Had she lived to produce another novel after *Harvest,* she might, like other writers, have been able to marry her early espousal of the principles of social improvement with the later liberal socialism of the Webbs, or George Bernard Shaw. But she did not, so *Harvest* remains a retreat to the essential building block of society, the relations between men and women, on the land, with very few of the old social institutions as a background for their support.

J. E. Sait, " 'A Strange New Consciousness': Mrs. Humphry Ward and the Great War," in AUMLA, No. 69, May, 1988, pp. 98-132.

FURTHER READING

Biography

Jones, Enid Huws. *Mrs. Humphry Ward.* New York: St. Martin's Press, 1973, 180 p.
> Appreciative biography. According to Jones, "Ward's life is not so much a story of literary development, success and decline as the story of seventy years of history lived through by a privileged, talented, zestful woman who told nearly all she saw."

Trevelyan, Janet Penrose. *The Life of Mrs. Humphry Ward.* New York: Dodd, Mead, and Co., 1923, 317 p.
> Account of Ward's life by her daughter.

Criticism

Bellringer, Alan W. "Mrs. Humphry Ward's Autobiographical Tactics: *A Writer's Recollections.*" *Prose Studies* 8, No. 3 (December 1985): 40-50.
> Examines Ward's autobiography, which Bellringer credits with keeping "her reputation afloat" during the decades that her works were seldom discussed.

Birch, Dinah. "The Great Mary." *London Review of Books* 12, No. 17 (13 September 1990): 13-14.
> Review of John Sutherland's *Mrs. Humphry Ward: Eminent Victorian, Pre-Eminent Edwardian*. Commenting on *Robert Elsmere*, Birch states: "What makes it compelling is its sense of unremitting struggle—intellectual, spiritual, and emotional. *Robert Elsmere* presents a world in which every kind of progress, every moment of happiness, must be fought for and paid for."

Collister, Peter. "A Postlude to Gladstone on *Robert Elsmere*: Four Unpublished Letters." *Modern Philology* 79, No. 3 (February 1982): 284-96.
> Reprints three letters by William Gladstone and one by Ward written between March 1889 and September 1895, following Gladstone's landmark review of *Robert Elsmere*.

Eliot, Sarah Barnwell. "Some Recent Fiction: II." *The Sewanee Review* III, No. 1 (November 1894): 90-104.
> Includes a favorable review of *Marcella*.

Gosse, Edmund. "Mrs. Humphry Ward." In his *Silhouettes,* pp. 203-10. New York: Charles Scribner's Sons, 1925.
> Portrait occasioned by the publication of *The Life of Mrs. Humphry Ward* by Janet Penrose Trevelyan.

Gwynn, Stephen. *Mrs. Humphry Ward.* New York: Henry Holt and Co., 1917, 127 p.
> Appreciative assessment of Ward's works, concluding that "future criticism will not overlook the fact that [Ward] almost alone of her contemporaries avoided dealing in the crudities of passion and won her popularity by a singularly austere appeal; addressing herself not to the senses or the simpler feelings, but to those emotions which connect themselves with high and often abstract intellectual interests."

Harris, Frank. "Mrs. Humphry Ward." In his *Latest Con-*

temporary Portraits, pp. 95-102. New York: The Macaulay Co., 1927.

> Unflattering reminiscence describing Ward as "a prim little governess body without a spark even of talent, lifted up by impertinent praise to be a teacher and seer, taking her limitations for excellences and her shortcomings for virtues, . . . an intolerable pedagogue in petticoats writing interminable prosy tales of nobodies."

More, Paul Elmer. "Oxford, Women, and God." In his *A New England Group and Others,* Shelburne Essays, Eleventh Series, pp. 257-87. Boston: Houghton Mifflin Co., 1921.

> Discusses Ward's portrait of Oxford life in the 1860s and 1870s in her autobiography, *A Writer's Recollections.*

Murry, John Middleton. "The Gulf Between." In his *The Evolution of an Intellectual,* pp. 115-25. London: Jonathan Cape, 1927.

> Assesses Ward's relevance in an essay originally published at the conclusion of World War I. According to Murry, Ward is "the embodiment of [a] remoter age. The novels by which she attained her reputation are merely elaborate chronicles for those spiritual struggles which now appear to us to be storms in a teacup. . . . The sense of proportion is so utterly different from our own, the values have so changed, that we find ourselves a million times more remote from the thoughts of Mrs. Humphry Ward than we are from those of any one of a dozen ancient Chinese poets."

Norton-Smith, J. "An Introduction to Mrs. Humphry Ward, Novelist." *Essays in Criticism* 18, No. 4 (October 1968): 420-28.

> Discusses the style, structure, and appeal of Ward's works.

Otte, George. "Mrs. Humphry Ward, the Great War, and the Historical Loom." *CLIO* 19, No. 3 (Spring 1990): 271-84.

> Examines the impact of World War I on Ward's conception of history and human progress.

Peterson, William S. "Mrs. Humphry Ward on *Robert Elsmere*: Six New Letters." *Bulletin of the New York Public Library* 74, No. 9 (November 1970): 587-97.

> Reprints six previously unpublished letters by Ward containing rebuttals of criticisms of *Robert Elsmere* and clarifying her intentions in the novel.

———. "Gladstone's Review of *Robert Elsmere*: Some Unpublished Correspondence." *The Review of English Studies* XXI, No. 84 (1970): 442-61.

> Reprints correspondence between Ward and William Gladstone written in the weeks following Gladstone's review of *Robert Elsmere.*

Rives, Françoise. "The Marcellas, Lauras, Dianas . . . of Mrs. Humphry Ward." *Caliban* XVII, No. 1 (1980): 69-79.

> Discusses Ward's portraits of women.

Ryals, Clyde de L. "Editor's Introduction." In *Robert Elsmere,* by Mrs. Humphry Ward, edited by Clyde de L. Ryals, pp. vii-xl. Lincoln: University of Nebraska Press, 1967.

> Discusses the biographical and cultural contexts of *Robert Elsmere,* as well as the religious thesis it comprises.

Smith, Esther Marian Greenwell. *Mrs. Humphry Ward.* Boston: Twayne, 1980, 163 p.

> Includes chapters on Ward's religious works, social reform novels, romances, and First World War writings.

Steele, J. S. "Mrs. Humphry Ward." *The Critic* XXI, No. 635 (21 April 1894): 265-66.

> Appreciative sketch identifying Ward as "a latter-day George Eliot."

Sutton-Ramspeck, Beth. "The Slayer and the Slain: Women and Sacrifice in Mary Ward's *Eleanor.*" *South Atlantic Review* 52, No. 4 (November 1987): 39-60.

> Describes the conflict between the female protagonists of *Eleanor* in terms of the "slayer and slain" motif—the successor must destroy the predecessor—suggesting that this pattern "reveals a profound tension: ostensibly a book celebrating the ethic of female sacrifice, *Eleanor* subtly attacks the destructive consequences of that ideal."

Trevelyan, Janet. "Mrs. Humphry Ward and *Robert Elsmere.*" In *Spectator Harvest,* edited by Wilson Harris, pp. 65-9. 1952. Reprint. Freeport, N.Y.: Books for Libraries Press, 1970.

> Centenary reminiscence by Ward's daughter.

Walters, J. Stuart. *Mrs. Humphry Ward: Her Work and Influence.* London: Kegan Paul, Trench, Trübner & Co., 1912, 208 p.

> Divides Ward's literary works into four categories: stories of religious controversy, stories of social reform, studies of character, and studies of such aspects of society as politics and the arts.

Willey, Basil. "How *Robert Elsmere* Struck Some Contemporaries." In *Essays and Studies, 1957,* edited by Margaret Willy, pp. 53-68. London: John Murray, 1957.

> Proposes that "if we can somewhat recapture the moods in which [*Robert Elsmere*] was written, read, praised and condemned, we shall at least have reminded ourselves of an important moment in the history of ideas."

Additional coverage of Ward's life and career is contained in the following source published by Gale Research: *Dictionary of Literary Biography,* Vol. 18.

Twentieth-Century Literary Criticism

Cumulative Indexes
Volumes 1-55

How to Use This Index

The main references

Calvino, Italo
    1923-1985.....CLC **5, 8, 11, 22, 33, 39,**
                                        73; SSC 3

list all author entries in the following Gale Literary Criticism series:

BLC = *Black Literature Criticism*
CLC = *Contemporary Literary Criticism*
CLR = *Children's Literature Review*
CMLC = *Classical and Medieval Literature Criticism*
DA = *DISCovering Authors*
DC = *Drama Criticism*
HLC = *Hispanic Literature Criticism*
LC = *Literature Criticism from 1400 to 1800*
NCLC = *Nineteenth-Century Literature Criticism*
PC = *Poetry Criticism*
SSC = *Short Story Criticism*
TCLC = *Twentieth-Century Literary Criticism*
WLC = *World Literature Criticism, 1500 to the Present*

The cross-references

See also CANR 23; CA 85-88;
    obituary CA 116

list all author entries in the following Gale biographical and literary sources:

AAYA = *Authors & Artists for Young Adults*
AITN = *Authors in the News*
BEST = *Bestsellers*
BW = *Black Writers*
CA = *Contemporary Authors*
CAAS = *Contemporary Authors Autobiography Series*
CABS = *Contemporary Authors Bibliographical Series*
CANR = *Contemporary Authors New Revision Series*
CAP = *Contemporary Authors Permanent Series*
CDALB = *Concise Dictionary of American Literary Biography*
CDBLB = *Concise Dictionary of British Literary Biography*
DLB = *Dictionary of Literary Biography*
DLBD = *Dictionary of Literary Biography Documentary Series*
DLBY = *Dictionary of Literary Biography Yearbook*
HW = *Hispanic Writers*
JRDA = *Junior DISCovering Authors*
MAICYA = *Major Authors and Illustrators for Children and Young Adults*
MTCW = *Major 20th-Century Writers*
SAAS = *Something about the Author Autobiography Series*
SATA = *Something about the Author*
YABC = *Yesterday's Authors of Books for Children*

Literary Criticism Series
Cumulative Author Index

A.
See Arnold, Matthew

A. E. .... TCLC 3, 10
See also Russell, George William
See also DLB 19

A. M.
See Megged, Aharon

A. R. P-C
See Galsworthy, John

Abasiyanik, Sait Faik 1906-1954
See Sait Faik
See also CA 123

Abbey, Edward 1927-1989 ...... CLC 36, 59
See also CA 45-48; 128; CANR 2, 41

Abbott, Lee K(ittredge) 1947- ...... CLC 48
See also CA 124; DLB 130

Abe, Kobo 1924-1993 ..... CLC 8, 22, 53, 81
See also CA 65-68; 140; CANR 24; MTCW

Abelard, Peter c. 1079-c. 1142 ... CMLC 11
See also DLB 115

Abell, Kjeld 1901-1961 .... CLC 15
See also CA 111

Abish, Walter 1931- .... CLC 22
See also CA 101; CANR 37; DLB 130

Abrahams, Peter (Henry) 1919- ..... CLC 4
See also BW 1; CA 57-60; CANR 26;
DLB 117; MTCW

Abrams, M(eyer) H(oward) 1912-... CLC 24
See also CA 57-60; CANR 13, 33; DLB 67

Abse, Dannie 1923-............. CLC 7, 29
See also CA 53-56; CAAS 1; CANR 4;
DLB 27

Achebe, (Albert) Chinua(lumogu)
1930- ..... CLC 1, 3, 5, 7, 11, 26, 51, 75;
BLC; DA; WLC
See also BW 2; CA 1-4R; CANR 6, 26;
CLR 20; DLB 117; MAICYA; MTCW;
SATA 38, 40

Acker, Kathy 1948- .... CLC 45
See also CA 117; 122

Ackroyd, Peter 1949-.......... CLC 34, 52
See also CA 123; 127

Acorn, Milton 1923-.............. CLC 15
See also CA 103; DLB 53

Adamov, Arthur 1908-1970 ...... CLC 4, 25
See also CA 17-18; 25-28R; CAP 2; MTCW

Adams, Alice (Boyd) 1926- ... CLC 6, 13, 46
See also CA 81-84; CANR 26; DLBY 86;
MTCW

Adams, Andy 1859-1935.......... TCLC 56
See also YABC 1

Adams, Douglas (Noel) 1952- ... CLC 27, 60
See also AAYA 4; BEST 89:3; CA 106;
CANR 34; DLBY 83; JRDA

Adams, Francis 1862-1893....... NCLC 33

Adams, Henry (Brooks)
1838-1918 .... TCLC 4, 52; DA
See also CA 104; 133; DLB 12, 47

Adams, Richard (George)
1920- .... CLC 4, 5, 18
See also AITN 1, 2; CA 49-52; CANR 3,
35; CLR 20; JRDA; MAICYA; MTCW;
SATA 7, 69

Adamson, Joy(-Friederike Victoria)
1910-1980 .... CLC 17
See also CA 69-72; 93-96; CANR 22;
MTCW; SATA 11, 22

Adcock, Fleur 1934-.............. CLC 41
See also CA 25-28R; CANR 11, 34;
DLB 40

Addams, Charles (Samuel)
1912-1988 .... CLC 30
See also CA 61-64; 126; CANR 12

Addison, Joseph 1672-1719 .... LC 18
See also CDBLB 1660-1789; DLB 101

Adler, C(arole) S(chwerdtfeger)
1932- .... CLC 35
See also AAYA 4; CA 89-92; CANR 19,
40; JRDA; MAICYA; SAAS 15;
SATA 26, 63

Adler, Renata 1938-............. CLC 8, 31
See also CA 49-52; CANR 5, 22; MTCW

Ady, Endre 1877-1919 .... TCLC 11
See also CA 107

Aeschylus
525B.C.-456B.C......... CMLC 11; DA

Afton, Effie
See Harper, Frances Ellen Watkins

Agapida, Fray Antonio
See Irving, Washington

Agee, James (Rufus)
1909-1955 .... TCLC 1, 19
See also AITN 1; CA 108;
CDALB 1941-1968; DLB 2, 26

Aghill, Gordon
See Silverberg, Robert

Agnon, S(hmuel) Y(osef Halevi)
1888-1970 .... CLC 4, 8, 14
See also CA 17-18; 25-28R; CAP 2; MTCW

Aherne, Owen
See Cassill, R(onald) V(erlin)

Ai 1947-.................... CLC 4, 14, 69
See also CA 85-88; CAAS 13; DLB 120

Aickman, Robert (Fordyce)
1914-1981 .... CLC 57
See also CA 5-8R; CANR 3

Aiken, Conrad (Potter)
1889-1973 ... CLC 1, 3, 5, 10, 52; SSC 9
See also CA 5-8R; 45-48; CANR 4;
CDALB 1929-1941; DLB 9, 45, 102;
MTCW; SATA 3, 30

Aiken, Joan (Delano) 1924-........ CLC 35
See also AAYA 1; CA 9-12R; CANR 4, 23,
34; CLR 1, 19; JRDA; MAICYA;
MTCW; SAAS 1; SATA 2, 30, 73

Ainsworth, William Harrison
1805-1882 .... NCLC 13
See also DLB 21; SATA 24

Aitmatov, Chingiz (Torekulovich)
1928-...................... CLC 71
See also CA 103; CANR 38; MTCW;
SATA 56

Akers, Floyd
See Baum, L(yman) Frank

Akhmadulina, Bella Akhatovna
1937-...................... CLC 53
See also CA 65-68

Akhmatova, Anna
1888-1966 .... CLC 11, 25, 64; PC 2
See also CA 19-20; 25-28R; CANR 35;
CAP 1; MTCW

Aksakov, Sergei Timofeyvich
1791-1859 .... NCLC 2

Aksenov, Vassily................. CLC 22
See also Aksyonov, Vassily (Pavlovich)

Aksyonov, Vassily (Pavlovich)
1932-...................... CLC 37
See also Aksenov, Vassily
See also CA 53-56; CANR 12

Akutagawa Ryunosuke
1892-1927 .... TCLC 16
See also CA 117

Alain 1868-1951 .... TCLC 41

Alain-Fournier.................... TCLC 6
See also Fournier, Henri Alban
See also DLB 65

Alarcon, Pedro Antonio de
1833-1891 .... NCLC 1

Alas (y Urena), Leopoldo (Enrique Garcia)
1852-1901 .... TCLC 29
See also CA 113; 131; HW

Albee, Edward (Franklin III)
1928- ...... CLC 1, 2, 3, 5, 9, 11, 13, 25,
53; DA; WLC
See also AITN 1; CA 5-8R; CABS 3;
CANR 8; CDALB 1941-1968; DLB 7;
MTCW

Alberti, Rafael 1902- .... CLC 7
See also CA 85-88; DLB 108

Alcala-Galiano, Juan Valera y
See Valera y Alcala-Galiano, Juan

Alcott, Amos Bronson 1799-1888 .. NCLC 1
See also DLB 1

Alcott, Louisa May
1832-1888 .... NCLC 6; DA; WLC
See also CDALB 1865-1917; CLR 1;
DLB 1, 42, 79; JRDA; MAICYA;
YABC 1

Aldanov, M. A.
See Aldanov, Mark (Alexandrovich)

Aldanov, Mark (Alexandrovich)
1886(?)-1957 . . . . TCLC 23
See also CA 118

Aldington, Richard 1892-1962 . . . . . . CLC 49
See also CA 85-88; CANR 45; DLB 20, 36,
100

Aldiss, Brian W(ilson)
1925- . . . . CLC 5, 14, 40
See also CA 5-8R; CAAS 2; CANR 5, 28;
DLB 14; MTCW; SATA 34

Alegria, Claribel 1924- . . . . CLC 75
See also CA 131, CAAS 15; HW

Alegria, Fernando 1918- . . . . CLC 57
See also CA 9-12R; CANR 5, 32; HW

Aleichem, Sholom . . . . TCLC 1, 35
See also Rabinovitch, Sholem

Aleixandre, Vicente 1898-1984 . . . CLC 9, 36
See also CA 85-88; 114; CANR 26;
DLB 108; HW; MTCW

Alepoudelis, Odysseus
See Elytis, Odysseus

Aleshkovsky, Joseph 1929-
See Aleshkovsky, Yuz
See also CA 121; 128

Aleshkovsky, Yuz . . . . CLC 44
See also Aleshkovsky, Joseph

Alexander, Lloyd (Chudley) 1924- . . CLC 35
See also AAYA 1; CA 1-4R; CANR 1, 24,
38; CLR 1, 5; DLB 52; JRDA; MAICYA;
MTCW; SATA 3, 49

Alfau, Felipe 1902- . . . . CLC 66
See also CA 137

Alger, Horatio, Jr. 1832-1899 . . . . . NCLC 8
See also DLB 42; SATA 16

Algren, Nelson 1909-1981 . . . . CLC 4, 10, 33
See also CA 13-16R; 103; CANR 20;
CDALB 1941-1968; DLB 9; DLBY 81,
82; MTCW

Ali, Ahmed 1910- . . . . CLC 69
See also CA 25-28R; CANR 15, 34

Alighieri, Dante 1265-1321 . . . . CMLC 3

Allan, John B.
See Westlake, Donald E(dwin)

Allen, Edward 1948- . . . . CLC 59

Allen, Paula Gunn 1939- . . . . CLC 84
See also CA 112; 143; NNAL

Allen, Roland
See Ayckbourn, Alan

Allen, Sarah A.
See Hopkins, Pauline Elizabeth

Allen, Woody 1935- . . . . CLC 16, 52
See also AAYA 10; CA 33-36R; CANR 27,
38; DLB 44; MTCW

Allende, Isabel 1942- . . . . CLC 39, 57; HLC
See also CA 125; 130; HW; MTCW

Alleyn, Ellen
See Rossetti, Christina (Georgina)

Allingham, Margery (Louise)
1904-1966 . . . . CLC 19
See also CA 5-8R; 25-28R; CANR 4;
DLB 77; MTCW

Allingham, William 1824-1889 . . . NCLC 25
See also DLB 35

Allison, Dorothy E. 1949- . . . . CLC 78
See also CA 140

Allston, Washington 1779-1843 . . . . NCLC 2
See also DLB 1

Almedingen, E. M. . . . . CLC 12
See also Almedingen, Martha Edith von
See also SATA 3

Almedingen, Martha Edith von 1898-1971
See Almedingen, E. M.
See also CA 1-4R; CANR 1

Almqvist, Carl Jonas Love
1793-1866 . . . . NCLC 42

Alonso, Damaso 1898-1990 . . . . CLC 14
See also CA 110; 131; 130; DLB 108; HW

Alov
See Gogol, Nikolai (Vasilyevich)

Alta 1942- . . . . CLC 19
See also CA 57-60

Alter, Robert B(ernard) 1935- . . . . . CLC 34
See also CA 49-52; CANR 1

Alther, Lisa 1944- . . . . CLC 7, 41
See also CA 65-68; CANR 12, 30; MTCW

Altman, Robert 1925- . . . . CLC 16
See also CA 73-76; CANR 43

Alvarez, A(lfred) 1929- . . . . CLC 5, 13
See also CA 1-4R; CANR 3, 33; DLB 14,
40

Alvarez, Alejandro Rodriguez 1903-1965
See Casona, Alejandro
See also CA 131; 93-96; HW

Amado, Jorge 1912- . . . . . CLC 13, 40; HLC
See also CA 77-80; CANR 35; DLB 113;
MTCW

Ambler, Eric 1909- . . . . CLC 4, 6, 9
See also CA 9-12R; CANR 7, 38; DLB 77;
MTCW

Amichai, Yehuda 1924- . . . . . . CLC 9, 22, 57
See also CA 85-88; MTCW

Amiel, Henri Frederic 1821-1881 . . NCLC 4

Amis, Kingsley (William)
1922- . . CLC 1, 2, 3, 5, 8, 13, 40, 44; DA
See also AITN 2; CA 9-12R; CANR 8, 28;
CDBLB 1945-1960; DLB 15, 27, 100, 139;
MTCW

Amis, Martin (Louis)
1949- . . . . CLC 4, 9, 38, 62
See also BEST 90:3; CA 65-68; CANR 8,
27; DLB 14

Ammons, A(rchie) R(andolph)
1926- . . . . . . CLC 2, 3, 5, 8, 9, 25, 57
See also AITN 1; CA 9-12R; CANR 6, 36;
DLB 5; MTCW

Amo, Tauraatua i
See Adams, Henry (Brooks)

Anand, Mulk Raj 1905- . . . . CLC 23
See also CA 65-68; CANR 32; MTCW

Anatol
See Schnitzler, Arthur

Anaya, Rudolfo A(lfonso)
1937- . . . . CLC 23; HLC
See also CA 45-48; CAAS 4; CANR 1, 32;
DLB 82; HW 1; MTCW

Andersen, Hans Christian
1805-1875 . . NCLC 7; DA; SSC 6; WLC
See also CLR 6; MAICYA; YABC 1

Anderson, C. Farley
See Mencken, H(enry) L(ouis); Nathan,
George Jean

Anderson, Jessica (Margaret) Queale
. . . . CLC 37
See also CA 9-12R; CANR 4

Anderson, Jon (Victor) 1940- . . . . . . CLC 9
See also CA 25-28R; CANR 20

Anderson, Lindsay (Gordon)
1923- . . . . CLC 20
See also CA 125; 128

Anderson, Maxwell 1888-1959 . . . . . TCLC 2
See also CA 105; DLB 7

Anderson, Poul (William) 1926- . . . . CLC 15
See also AAYA 5; CA 1-4R; CAAS 2;
CANR 2, 15, 34; DLB 8; MTCW;
SATA 39

Anderson, Robert (Woodruff)
1917- . . . . CLC 23
See also AITN 1; CA 21-24R; CANR 32;
DLB 7

Anderson, Sherwood
1876-1941 . . . . TCLC 1, 10, 24; DA;
SSC 1; WLC
See also CA 104; 121; CDALB 1917-1929;
DLB 4, 9, 86; DLBD 1; MTCW

Andouard
See Giraudoux, (Hippolyte) Jean

Andrade, Carlos Drummond de . . . . . . CLC 18
See also Drummond de Andrade, Carlos

Andrade, Mario de 1893-1945 . . . . . TCLC 43

Andreas-Salome, Lou 1861-1937 . . . TCLC 56
See also DLB 66

Andrewes, Lancelot 1555-1626 . . . . LC 5

Andrews, Cicily Fairfield
See West, Rebecca

Andrews, Elton V.
See Pohl, Frederik

Andreyev, Leonid (Nikolaevich)
1871-1919 . . . . TCLC 3
See also CA 104

Andric, Ivo 1892-1975 . . . . CLC 8
See also CA 81-84; 57-60; CANR 43;
MTCW

Angelique, Pierre
See Bataille, Georges

Angell, Roger 1920- . . . . CLC 26
See also CA 57-60; CANR 13, 44

Angelou, Maya
1928- . . . . CLC 12, 35, 64, 77; BLC; DA
See also AAYA 7; BW 2; CA 65-68;
CANR 19, 42; DLB 38; MTCW;
SATA 49

Annensky, Innokenty Fyodorovich
1856-1909 . . . . TCLC 14
See also CA 110

Anon, Charles Robert
See Pessoa, Fernando (Antonio Nogueira)

Anouilh, Jean (Marie Lucien Pierre)
1910-1987 . . . . . . CLC 1, 3, 8, 13, 40, 50
See also CA 17-20R; 123; CANR 32;
MTCW

Author Index

Auel, Jean M(arie) 1936-......... **CLC 31**
See also AAYA 7; BEST 90:4; CA 103;
CANR 21

Auerbach, Erich 1892-1957 ...... **TCLC 43**
See also CA 118

Augier, Emile 1820-1889 .... **NCLC 31**

August, John
See De Voto, Bernard (Augustine)

Augustine, St. 354-430 .... **CMLC 6**

Aurelius
See Bourne, Randolph S(illiman)

Austen, Jane
1775-1817 ... **NCLC 1, 13, 19, 33; DA;
WLC**
See also CDBLB 1789-1832; DLB 116

Auster, Paul 1947- .... **CLC 47**
See also CA 69-72; CANR 23

Austin, Frank
See Faust, Frederick (Schiller)

Austin, Mary (Hunter)
1868-1934 .... **TCLC 25**
See also CA 109; DLB 9, 78

Autran Dourado, Waldomiro
See Dourado, (Waldomiro Freitas) Autran

Averroes 1126-1198 .... **CMLC 7**
See also DLB 115

Avison, Margaret 1918-......... **CLC 2, 4**
See also CA 17-20R; DLB 53; MTCW

Axton, David
See Koontz, Dean R(ay)

Ayckbourn, Alan
1939- .... **CLC 5, 8, 18, 33, 74**
See also CA 21-24R; CANR 31; DLB 13;
MTCW

Aydy, Catherine
See Tennant, Emma (Christina)

Ayme, Marcel (Andre) 1902-1967... **CLC 11**
See also CA 89-92; CLR 25; DLB 72

Ayrton, Michael 1921-1975 .... **CLC 7**
See also CA 5-8R; 61-64; CANR 9, 21

Azorin........................ **CLC 11**
See also Martinez Ruiz, Jose

Azuela, Mariano
1873-1952 .... **TCLC 3; HLC**
See also CA 104; 131; HW; MTCW

Baastad, Babbis Friis
See Friis-Baastad, Babbis Ellinor

Bab
See Gilbert, W(illiam) S(chwenck)

Babbis, Eleanor
See Friis-Baastad, Babbis Ellinor

Babel, Isaak (Emmanuilovich)
1894-1941(?) ..... **TCLC 2, 13; SSC 16**
See also CA 104

Babits, Mihaly 1883-1941 .... **TCLC 14**
See also CA 114

Babur 1483-1530................. **LC 18**

Bacchelli, Riccardo 1891-1985 ..... **CLC 19**
See also CA 29-32R; 117

Bach, Richard (David) 1936-....... **CLC 14**
See also AITN 1; BEST 89:2; CA 9-12R;
CANR 18; MTCW; SATA 13

Bachman, Richard
See King, Stephen (Edwin)

Bachmann, Ingeborg 1926-1973..... **CLC 69**
See also CA 93-96; 45-48; DLB 85

Bacon, Francis 1561-1626 .... **LC 18**
See also CDBLB Before 1660

Bacovia, George.................. **TCLC 24**
See also Vasiliu, Gheorghe

Badanes, Jerome 1937-............ **CLC 59**

Bagehot, Walter 1826-1877 ...... **NCLC 10**
See also DLB 55

Bagnold, Enid 1889-1981.......... **CLC 25**
See also CA 5-8R; 103; CANR 5, 40;
DLB 13; MAICYA; SATA 1, 25

Bagrjana, Elisaveta
See Belcheva, Elisaveta

Bagryana, Elisaveta
See Belcheva, Elisaveta

Bailey, Paul 1937- .... **CLC 45**
See also CA 21-24R; CANR 16; DLB 14

Baillie, Joanna 1762-1851 .... **NCLC 2**
See also DLB 93

Bainbridge, Beryl (Margaret)
1933- .... **CLC 4, 5, 8, 10, 14, 18, 22, 62**
See also CA 21-24R; CANR 24; DLB 14;
MTCW

Baker, Elliott 1922-............... **CLC 8**
See also CA 45-48; CANR 2

Baker, Nicholson 1957-........... **CLC 61**
See also CA 135

Baker, Ray Stannard 1870-1946 ... **TCLC 47**
See also CA 118

Baker, Russell (Wayne) 1925-...... **CLC 31**
See also BEST 89:4; CA 57-60; CANR 11,
41; MTCW

Bakhtin, M.
See Bakhtin, Mikhail Mikhailovich

Bakhtin, M. M.
See Bakhtin, Mikhail Mikhailovich

Bakhtin, Mikhail
See Bakhtin, Mikhail Mikhailovich

Bakhtin, Mikhail Mikhailovich
1895-1975 .... **CLC 83**
See also CA 128; 113

Bakshi, Ralph 1938(?)-............ **CLC 26**
See also CA 112; 138

Bakunin, Mikhail (Alexandrovich)
1814-1876 .... **NCLC 25**

Baldwin, James (Arthur)
1924-1987 ...... **CLC 1, 2, 3, 4, 5, 8, 13,
15, 17, 42, 50, 67; BLC; DA; DC 1;
SSC 10; WLC**
See also AAYA 4; BW 1; CA 1-4R; 124;
CABS 1; CANR 3, 24;
CDALB 1941-1968; DLB 2, 7, 33;
DLBY 87; MTCW; SATA 9, 54

Ballard, J(ames) G(raham)
1930- .... **CLC 3, 6, 14, 36; SSC 1**
See also AAYA 3; CA 5-8R; CANR 15, 39;
DLB 14; MTCW

Balmont, Konstantin (Dmitriyevich)
1867-1943 .... **TCLC 11**
See also CA 109

Balzac, Honore de
1799-1850 .... **NCLC 5, 35; DA; SSC 5;
WLC**
See also DLB 119

Bambara, Toni Cade
1939- .... **CLC 19; BLC; DA**
See also AAYA 5; BW 2; CA 29-32R;
CANR 24; DLB 38; MTCW

Bamdad, A.
See Shamlu, Ahmad

Banat, D. R.
See Bradbury, Ray (Douglas)

Bancroft, Laura
See Baum, L(yman) Frank

Banim, John 1798-1842 .... **NCLC 13**
See also DLB 116

Banim, Michael 1796-1874 ...... **NCLC 13**

Banks, Iain
See Banks, Iain M(enzies)

Banks, Iain M(enzies) 1954- .... **CLC 34**
See also CA 123; 128

Banks, Lynne Reid .... **CLC 23**
See also Reid Banks, Lynne
See also AAYA 6

Banks, Russell 1940- .... **CLC 37, 72**
See also CA 65-68; CAAS 15; CANR 19;
DLB 130

Banville, John 1945-.............. **CLC 46**
See also CA 117; 128; DLB 14

Banville, Theodore (Faullain) de
1832-1891 .... **NCLC 9**

Baraka, Amiri
1934- .... **CLC 1, 2, 3, 5, 10, 14, 33;
BLC; DA; PC 4**
See also Jones, LeRoi
See also BW 2; CA 21-24R; CABS 3;
CANR 27, 38; CDALB 1941-1968;
DLB 5, 7, 16, 38; DLBD 8; MTCW

Barbellion, W. N. P............... **TCLC 24**
See also Cummings, Bruce F(rederick)

Barbera, Jack (Vincent) 1945-...... **CLC 44**
See also CA 110; CANR 45

Barbey d'Aurevilly, Jules Amedee
1808-1889 .... **NCLC 1**
See also DLB 119

Barbusse, Henri 1873-1935 .... **TCLC 5**
See also CA 105; DLB 65

Barclay, Bill
See Moorcock, Michael (John)

Barclay, William Ewert
See Moorcock, Michael (John)

Barea, Arturo 1897-1957 .... **TCLC 14**
See also CA 111

Barfoot, Joan 1946- .... **CLC 18**
See also CA 105

Baring, Maurice 1874-1945 .... **TCLC 8**
See also CA 105; DLB 34

Barker, Clive 1952- .... **CLC 52**
See also AAYA 10; BEST 90:3; CA 121;
129; MTCW

Barker, George Granville
1913-1991 .... **CLC 8, 48**
See also CA 9-12R; 135; CANR 7, 38;
DLB 20; MTCW

Barker, Harley Granville
See Granville-Barker, Harley
See also DLB 10

Barker, Howard 1946- .... **CLC 37**
See also CA 102; DLB 13

Barker, Pat 1943- .... **CLC 32**
See also CA 117; 122

Barlow, Joel 1754-1812 .... **NCLC 23**
See also DLB 37

Barnard, Mary (Ethel) 1909- ...... **CLC 48**
See also CA 21-22; CAP 2

Barnes, Djuna
1892-1982 ... **CLC 3, 4, 8, 11, 29; SSC 3**
See also CA 9-12R; 107; CANR 16; DLB 4,
9, 45; MTCW

Barnes, Julian 1946- .... **CLC 42**
See also CA 102; CANR 19; DLBY 93

Barnes, Peter 1931- .... **CLC 5, 56**
See also CA 65-68; CAAS 12; CANR 33,
34; DLB 13; MTCW

Baroja (y Nessi), Pio
1872-1956 .... **TCLC 8; HLC**
See also CA 104

Baron, David
See Pinter, Harold

Baron Corvo
See Rolfe, Frederick (William Serafino
Austin Lewis Mary)

Barondess, Sue K(aufman)
1926-1977 .... **CLC 8**
See also Kaufman, Sue
See also CA 1-4R; 69-72; CANR 1

Baron de Teive
See Pessoa, Fernando (Antonio Nogueira)

Barres, Maurice 1862-1923 ...... **TCLC 47**
See also DLB 123

Barreto, Afonso Henrique de Lima
See Lima Barreto, Afonso Henrique de

Barrett, (Roger) Syd 1946- .... **CLC 35**
See also Pink Floyd

Barrett, William (Christopher)
1913-1992 .... **CLC 27**
See also CA 13-16R; 139; CANR 11

Barrie, J(ames) M(atthew)
1860-1937 .... **TCLC 2**
See also CA 104; 136; CDBLB 1890-1914;
CLR 16; DLB 10, 141; MAICYA;
YABC 1

Barrington, Michael
See Moorcock, Michael (John)

Barrol, Grady
See Bograd, Larry

Barry, Mike
See Malzberg, Barry N(athaniel)

Barry, Philip 1896-1949 .... **TCLC 11**
See also CA 109; DLB 7

Bart, Andre Schwarz
See Schwarz-Bart, Andre

Barth, John (Simmons)
1930- ...... **CLC 1, 2, 3, 5, 7, 9, 10, 14,
27, 51; SSC 10**
See also AITN 1, 2; CA 1-4R; CABS 1;
CANR 5, 23; DLB 2; MTCW

Barthelme, Donald
1931-1989 ...... **CLC 1, 2, 3, 5, 6, 8, 13,
23, 46, 59; SSC 2**
See also CA 21-24R; 129; CANR 20;
DLB 2; DLBY 80, 89; MTCW; SATA 7,
62

Barthelme, Frederick 1943- .... **CLC 36**
See also CA 114; 122; DLBY 85

Barthes, Roland (Gerard)
1915-1980 .... **CLC 24, 83**
See also CA 130; 97-100; MTCW

Barzun, Jacques (Martin) 1907- .... **CLC 51**
See also CA 61-64; CANR 22

Bashevis, Isaac
See Singer, Isaac Bashevis

Bashkirtseff, Marie 1859-1884 ... **NCLC 27**

Basho
See Matsuo Basho

Bass, Kingsley B., Jr.
See Bullins, Ed

Bass, Rick 1958- .... **CLC 79**
See also CA 126

Bassani, Giorgio 1916- .... **CLC 9**
See also CA 65-68; CANR 33; DLB 128;
MTCW

Bastos, Augusto (Antonio) Roa
See Roa Bastos, Augusto (Antonio)

Bataille, Georges 1897-1962 .... **CLC 29**
See also CA 101; 89-92

Bates, H(erbert) E(rnest)
1905-1974 .... **CLC 46; SSC 10**
See also CA 93-96; 45-48; CANR 34;
MTCW

Bauchart
See Camus, Albert

Baudelaire, Charles
1821-1867 ..... **NCLC 6, 29; DA; PC 1;
WLC**

Baudrillard, Jean 1929- .... **CLC 60**

Baum, L(yman) Frank 1856-1919 ... **TCLC 7**
See also CA 108; 133; CLR 15; DLB 22;
JRDA; MAICYA; MTCW; SATA 18

Baum, Louis F.
See Baum, L(yman) Frank

Baumbach, Jonathan 1933- ...... **CLC 6, 23**
See also CA 13-16R; CAAS 5; CANR 12;
DLBY 80; MTCW

Bausch, Richard (Carl) 1945- ...... **CLC 51**
See also CA 101; CAAS 14; CANR 43;
DLB 130

Baxter, Charles 1947- .... **CLC 45, 78**
See also CA 57-60; CANR 40; DLB 130

Baxter, George Owen
See Faust, Frederick (Schiller)

Baxter, James K(eir) 1926-1972 .... **CLC 14**
See also CA 77-80

Baxter, John
See Hunt, E(verette) Howard, Jr.

Bayer, Sylvia
See Glassco, John

Beagle, Peter S(oyer) 1939- .... **CLC 7**
See also CA 9-12R; CANR 4; DLBY 80;
SATA 60

Bean, Normal
See Burroughs, Edgar Rice

Beard, Charles A(ustin)
1874-1948 .... **TCLC 15**
See also CA 115; DLB 17; SATA 18

Beardsley, Aubrey 1872-1898 ..... **NCLC 6**

Beattie, Ann
1947- .... **CLC 8, 13, 18, 40, 63; SSC 11**
See also BEST 90:2; CA 81-84; DLBY 82;
MTCW

Beattie, James 1735-1803 .... **NCLC 25**
See also DLB 109

Beauchamp, Kathleen Mansfield 1888-1923
See Mansfield, Katherine
See also CA 104; 134; DA

Beaumarchais, Pierre-Augustin Caron de
1732-1799 .... **DC 4**

**Beauvoir, Simone (Lucie Ernestine Marie
Bertrand) de**
1908-1986 .... **CLC 1, 2, 4, 8, 14, 31, 44,
50, 71; DA; WLC**
See also CA 9-12R; 118; CANR 28;
DLB 72; DLBY 86; MTCW

Becker, Jurek 1937- .... **CLC 7, 19**
See also CA 85-88; DLB 75

Becker, Walter 1950- .... **CLC 26**

Beckett, Samuel (Barclay)
1906-1989 ...... **CLC 1, 2, 3, 4, 6, 9, 10,
11, 14, 18, 29, 57, 59, 83; DA; SSC 16;
WLC**
See also CA 5-8R; 130; CANR 33;
CDBLB 1945-1960; DLB 13, 15;
DLBY 90; MTCW

Beckford, William 1760-1844 .... **NCLC 16**
See also DLB 39

Beckman, Gunnel 1910- .... **CLC 26**
See also CA 33-36R; CANR 15; CLR 25;
MAICYA; SAAS 9; SATA 6

Becque, Henri 1837-1899 .... **NCLC 3**

Beddoes, Thomas Lovell
1803-1849 .... **NCLC 3**
See also DLB 96

Bedford, Donald F.
See Fearing, Kenneth (Flexner)

Beecher, Catharine Esther
1800-1878 .... **NCLC 30**
See also DLB 1

Beecher, John 1904-1980 .... **CLC 6**
See also AITN 1; CA 5-8R; 105; CANR 8

Beer, Johann 1655-1700 .... **LC 5**

Beer, Patricia 1924- .... **CLC 58**
See also CA 61-64; CANR 13; DLB 40

Beerbohm, Henry Maximilian
1872-1956 .... **TCLC 1, 24**
See also CA 104; DLB 34, 100

Begiebing, Robert J(ohn) 1946- ..... **CLC 70**
See also CA 122; CANR 40

Behan, Brendan
1923-1964 .... **CLC 1, 8, 11, 15, 79**
See also CA 73-76; CANR 33;
CDBLB 1945-1960; DLB 13; MTCW

Behn, Aphra
1640(?)-1689 .... **LC 1; DA; DC 4; WLC**
See also DLB 39, 80, 131

Behrman, S(amuel) N(athaniel)
1893-1973 . . . . **CLC 40**
See also CA 13-16; 45-48; CAP 1; DLB 7,
44

Belasco, David 1853-1931 . . . . **TCLC 3**
See also CA 104; DLB 7

Belcheva, Elisaveta 1893- . . . . **CLC 10**

Beldone, Phil "Cheech"
See Ellison, Harlan

Beleno
See Azuela, Mariano

Belinski, Vissarion Grigoryevich
1811-1848 . . . . **NCLC 5**

Belitt, Ben 1911- . . . . **CLC 22**
See also CA 13-16R; CAAS 4; CANR 7;
DLB 5

Bell, James Madison
1826-1902 . . . . **TCLC 43; BLC**
See also BW 1; CA 122; 124; DLB 50

Bell, Madison (Smartt) 1957- . . . . . . **CLC 41**
See also CA 111; CANR 28

Bell, Marvin (Hartley) 1937- . . . . . **CLC 8, 31**
See also CA 21-24R; CAAS 14; DLB 5;
MTCW

Bell, W. L. D.
See Mencken, H(enry) L(ouis)

Bellamy, Atwood C.
See Mencken, H(enry) L(ouis)

Bellamy, Edward 1850-1898 . . . . . . **NCLC 4**
See also DLB 12

Bellin, Edward J.
See Kuttner, Henry

Belloc, (Joseph) Hilaire (Pierre)
1870-1953 . . . . **TCLC 7, 18**
See also CA 106; DLB 19, 100, 141;
YABC 1

Belloc, Joseph Peter Rene Hilaire
See Belloc, (Joseph) Hilaire (Pierre)

Belloc, Joseph Pierre Hilaire
See Belloc, (Joseph) Hilaire (Pierre)

Belloc, M. A.
See Lowndes, Marie Adelaide (Belloc)

Bellow, Saul
1915- . . . . . . **CLC 1, 2, 3, 6, 8, 10, 13, 15,
25, 33, 34, 63, 79; DA; SSC 14; WLC**
See also AITN 2; BEST 89:3; CA 5-8R;
CABS 1; CANR 29; CDALB 1941-1968;
DLB 2, 28; DLBD 3; DLBY 82; MTCW

Belser, Reimond Karel Maria de
1929- . . . . **CLC 14**

Bely, Andrey . . . . **TCLC 7**
See also Bugayev, Boris Nikolayevich

Benary, Margot
See Benary-Isbert, Margot

Benary-Isbert, Margot 1889-1979 . . . **CLC 12**
See also CA 5-8R; 89-92; CANR 4;
CLR 12; MAICYA; SATA 2, 21

Benavente (y Martinez), Jacinto
1866-1954 . . . . **TCLC 3**
See also CA 106; 131; HW; MTCW

Benchley, Peter (Bradford)
1940- . . . . **CLC 4, 8**
See also AITN 2; CA 17-20R; CANR 12,
35; MTCW; SATA 3

Benchley, Robert (Charles)
1889-1945 . . . . **TCLC 1, 55**
See also CA 105; DLB 11

Benedikt, Michael 1935- . . . . **CLC 4, 14**
See also CA 13-16R; CANR 7; DLB 5

Benet, Juan 1927- . . . . **CLC 28**
See also CA 143

Benet, Stephen Vincent
1898-1943 . . . . **TCLC 7; SSC 10**
See also CA 104; DLB 4, 48, 102; YABC 1

Benet, William Rose 1886-1950 . . . **TCLC 28**
See also CA 118; DLB 45

Benford, Gregory (Albert) 1941- . . . . **CLC 52**
See also CA 69-72; CANR 12, 24;
DLBY 82

Bengtsson, Frans (Gunnar)
1894-1954 . . . . **TCLC 48**

Benjamin, David
See Slavitt, David R(ytman)

Benjamin, Lois
See Gould, Lois

Benjamin, Walter 1892-1940 . . . . . . **TCLC 39**

Benn, Gottfried 1886-1956 . . . . **TCLC 3**
See also CA 106; DLB 56

Bennett, Alan 1934- . . . . **CLC 45, 77**
See also CA 103; CANR 35; MTCW

Bennett, (Enoch) Arnold
1867-1931 . . . . **TCLC 5, 20**
See also CA 106; CDBLB 1890-1914;
DLB 10, 34, 98

Bennett, Elizabeth
See Mitchell, Margaret (Munnerlyn)

Bennett, George Harold 1930-
See Bennett, Hal
See also BW 1; CA 97-100

Bennett, Hal . . . . **CLC 5**
See also Bennett, George Harold
See also DLB 33

Bennett, Jay 1912- . . . . **CLC 35**
See also AAYA 10; CA 69-72; CANR 11,
42; JRDA; SAAS 4; SATA 27, 41

Bennett, Louise (Simone)
1919- . . . . **CLC 28; BLC**
See also BW 2; DLB 117

Benson, E(dward) F(rederic)
1867-1940 . . . . **TCLC 27**
See also CA 114; DLB 135

Benson, Jackson J. 1930- . . . . **CLC 34**
See also CA 25-28R; DLB 111

Benson, Sally 1900-1972 . . . . **CLC 17**
See also CA 19-20; 37-40R; CAP 1;
SATA 1, 27, 35

Benson, Stella 1892-1933 . . . . **TCLC 17**
See also CA 117; DLB 36

Bentham, Jeremy 1748-1832 . . . . . **NCLC 38**
See also DLB 107

Bentley, E(dmund) C(lerihew)
1875-1956 . . . . **TCLC 12**
See also CA 108; DLB 70

Bentley, Eric (Russell) 1916- . . . . . . **CLC 24**
See also CA 5-8R; CANR 6

Beranger, Pierre Jean de
1780-1857 . . . . **NCLC 34**

Berger, Colonel
See Malraux, (Georges-)Andre

Berger, John (Peter) 1926- . . . . . . **CLC 2, 19**
See also CA 81-84; DLB 14

Berger, Melvin H. 1927- . . . . **CLC 12**
See also CA 5-8R; CANR 4; CLR 32;
SAAS 2; SATA 5

Berger, Thomas (Louis)
1924- . . . . **CLC 3, 5, 8, 11, 18, 38**
See also CA 1-4R; CANR 5, 28; DLB 2;
DLBY 80; MTCW

Bergman, (Ernst) Ingmar
1918- . . . . **CLC 16, 72**
See also CA 81-84; CANR 33

Bergson, Henri 1859-1941 . . . . **TCLC 32**

Bergstein, Eleanor 1938- . . . . **CLC 4**
See also CA 53-56; CANR 5

Berkoff, Steven 1937- . . . . **CLC 56**
See also CA 104

Bermant, Chaim (Icyk) 1929- . . . . . . **CLC 40**
See also CA 57-60; CANR 6, 31

Bern, Victoria
See Fisher, M(ary) F(rances) K(ennedy)

Bernanos, (Paul Louis) Georges
1888-1948 . . . . **TCLC 3**
See also CA 104; 130; DLB 72

Bernard, April 1956- . . . . **CLC 59**
See also CA 131

Berne, Victoria
See Fisher, M(ary) F(rances) K(ennedy)

Bernhard, Thomas
1931-1989 . . . . **CLC 3, 32, 61**
See also CA 85-88; 127; CANR 32;
DLB 85, 124; MTCW

Berrigan, Daniel 1921- . . . . **CLC 4**
See also CA 33-36R; CAAS 1; CANR 11,
43; DLB 5

Berrigan, Edmund Joseph Michael, Jr.
1934-1983
See Berrigan, Ted
See also CA 61-64; 110; CANR 14

Berrigan, Ted . . . . **CLC 37**
See also Berrigan, Edmund Joseph Michael,
Jr.
See also DLB 5

Berry, Charles Edward Anderson 1931-
See Berry, Chuck
See also CA 115

Berry, Chuck . . . . **CLC 17**
See also Berry, Charles Edward Anderson

Berry, Jonas
See Ashbery, John (Lawrence)

Berry, Wendell (Erdman)
1934- . . . . **CLC 4, 6, 8, 27, 46**
See also AITN 1; CA 73-76; DLB 5, 6

Berryman, John
1914-1972 . . . . . . **CLC 1, 2, 3, 4, 6, 8, 10,
13, 25, 62**
See also CA 13-16; 33-36R; CABS 2;
CANR 35; CAP 1; CDALB 1941-1968;
DLB 48; MTCW

Bertolucci, Bernardo 1940- . . . . **CLC 16**
See also CA 106

Bertrand, Aloysius 1807-1841 . . . . **NCLC 31**

Bertran de Born c. 1140-1215 . . . . . **CMLC 5**

Besant, Annie (Wood) 1847-1933 . . . **TCLC 9**
See also CA 105

Bessie, Alvah 1904-1985. . . . . **CLC 23**
See also CA 5-8R; 116; CANR 2; **DLB 26**

Bethlen, T. D.
See Silverberg, Robert

Beti, Mongo. . . . . **CLC 27; BLC**
See also Biyidi, Alexandre

Betjeman, John
1906-1984 . . . . **CLC 2, 6, 10, 34, 43**
See also CA 9-12R; 112; CANR 33;
CDBLB 1945-1960; DLB 20; DLBY 84;
MTCW

Bettelheim, Bruno 1903-1990 . . . . . . **CLC 79**
See also CA 81-84; 131; CANR 23; MTCW

Betti, Ugo 1892-1953 . . . . **TCLC 5**
See also CA 104

Betts, Doris (Waugh) 1932- . . . . **CLC 3, 6, 28**
See also CA 13-16R; CANR 9; DLBY 82

Bevan, Alistair
See Roberts, Keith (John Kingston)

Beynon, John
See Harris, John (Wyndham Parkes Lucas)
Beynon

Bialik, Chaim Nachman
1873-1934 . . . . **TCLC 25**

Bickerstaff, Isaac
See Swift, Jonathan

Bidart, Frank 1939- . . . . **CLC 33**
See also CA 140

Bienek, Horst 1930- . . . . **CLC 7, 11**
See also CA 73-76; DLB 75

Bierce, Ambrose (Gwinett)
1842-1914(?) . . . . **TCLC 1, 7, 44; DA;**
SSC 9; WLC
See also CA 104; 139; CDALB 1865-1917;
DLB 11, 12, 23, 71, 74

Billings, Josh
See Shaw, Henry Wheeler

Billington, (Lady) Rachel (Mary)
1942- . . . . **CLC 43**
See also AITN 2; CA 33-36R; CANR 44

Binyon, T(imothy) J(ohn) 1936- . . . . **CLC 34**
See also CA 111; CANR 28

Bioy Casares, Adolfo
1914- . . . . **CLC 4, 8, 13; HLC**
See also CA 29-32R; CANR 19, 43;
DLB 113; HW; MTCW

Bird, C.
See Ellison, Harlan

Bird, Cordwainer
See Ellison, Harlan

Bird, Robert Montgomery
1806-1854 . . . . **NCLC 1**

Birney, (Alfred) Earle
1904- . . . . **CLC 1, 4, 6, 11**
See also CA 1-4R; CANR 5, 20; DLB 88;
MTCW

Bishop, Elizabeth
1911-1979 . . . . . . **CLC 1, 4, 9, 13, 15, 32;**
DA; PC 3
See also CA 5-8R; 89-92; CABS 2;
CANR 26; CDALB 1968-1988; DLB 5;
MTCW; SATA 24

Bishop, John 1935- . . . . **CLC 10**
See also CA 105

Bissett, Bill 1939- . . . . **CLC 18**
See also CA 69-72; CAAS 19; CANR 15;
DLB 53; MTCW

Bitov, Andrei (Georgievich) 1937- . . . **CLC 57**
See also CA 142

Biyidi, Alexandre 1932-
See Beti, Mongo
See also BW 1; CA 114; 124; MTCW

Bjarme, Brynjolf
See Ibsen, Henrik (Johan)

Bjornson, Bjornstjerne (Martinius)
1832-1910 . . . . **TCLC 7, 37**
See also CA 104

Black, Robert
See Holdstock, Robert P.

Blackburn, Paul 1926-1971 . . . . . . **CLC 9, 43**
See also CA 81-84; 33-36R; CANR 34;
DLB 16; DLBY 81

Black Elk 1863-1950 . . . . **TCLC 33**
See also CA 144

Black Hobart
See Sanders, (James) Ed(ward)

Blacklin, Malcolm
See Chambers, Aidan

Blackmore, R(ichard) D(oddridge)
1825-1900 . . . . **TCLC 27**
See also CA 120; DLB 18

Blackmur, R(ichard) P(almer)
1904-1965 . . . . **CLC 2, 24**
See also CA 11-12; 25-28R; CAP 1; DLB 63

Black Tarantula, The
See Acker, Kathy

Blackwood, Algernon (Henry)
1869-1951 . . . . **TCLC 5**
See also CA 105

Blackwood, Caroline 1931- . . . . **CLC 6, 9**
See also CA 85-88; CANR 32; DLB 14;
MTCW

Blade, Alexander
See Hamilton, Edmond; Silverberg, Robert

Blaga, Lucian 1895-1961 . . . . **CLC 75**

Blair, Eric (Arthur) 1903-1950
See Orwell, George
See also CA 104; 132; DA; MTCW;
SATA 29

Blais, Marie-Claire
1939- . . . . **CLC 2, 4, 6, 13, 22**
See also CA 21-24R; CAAS 4; CANR 38;
DLB 53; MTCW

Blaise, Clark 1940- . . . . **CLC 29**
See also AITN 2; CA 53-56; CAAS 3;
CANR 5; DLB 53

Blake, Nicholas
See Day Lewis, C(ecil)
See also DLB 77

Blake, William
1757-1827 . . . . . **NCLC 13, 37; DA; WLC**
See also CDBLB 1789-1832; DLB 93;
MAICYA; SATA 30

Blasco Ibanez, Vicente
1867-1928 . . . . **TCLC 12**
See also CA 110; 131; HW; MTCW

Blatty, William Peter 1928- . . . . **CLC 2**
See also CA 5-8R; CANR 9

Bleeck, Oliver
See Thomas, Ross (Elmore)

Blessing, Lee 1949- . . . . **CLC 54**

Blish, James (Benjamin)
1921-1975 . . . . **CLC 14**
See also CA 1-4R; 57-60; CANR 3; DLB 8;
MTCW; SATA 66

Bliss, Reginald
See Wells, H(erbert) G(eorge)

Blixen, Karen (Christentze Dinesen)
1885-1962
See Dinesen, Isak
See also CA 25-28; CANR 22; CAP 2;
MTCW; SATA 44

Bloch, Robert (Albert) 1917- . . . . **CLC 33**
See also CA 5-8R; CANR 5; DLB 44;
SATA 12

Blok, Alexander (Alexandrovich)
1880-1921 . . . . **TCLC 5**
See also CA 104

Blom, Jan
See Breytenbach, Breyten

Bloom, Harold 1930- . . . . **CLC 24**
See also CA 13-16R; CANR 39; DLB 67

Bloomfield, Aurelius
See Bourne, Randolph S(illiman)

Blount, Roy (Alton), Jr. 1941- . . . . . **CLC 38**
See also CA 53-56; CANR 10, 28; MTCW

Bloy, Leon 1846-1917. . . . . **TCLC 22**
See also CA 121; DLB 123

Blume, Judy (Sussman) 1938- . . . **CLC 12, 30**
See also AAYA 3; CA 29-32R; CANR 13,
37; CLR 2, 15; DLB 52; JRDA;
MAICYA; MTCW; SATA 2, 31

Blunden, Edmund (Charles)
1896-1974 . . . . **CLC 2, 56**
See also CA 17-18; 45-48; CAP 2; DLB 20,
100; MTCW

Bly, Robert (Elwood)
1926- . . . . **CLC 1, 2, 5, 10, 15, 38**
See also CA 5-8R; CANR 41; DLB 5;
MTCW

Boas, Franz 1858-1942. . . . . **TCLC 56**
See also CA 115

Bobette
See Simenon, Georges (Jacques Christian)

Boccaccio, Giovanni
1313-1375 . . . . **CMLC 13; SSC 10**

Bochco, Steven 1943- . . . . **CLC 35**
See also AAYA 11; CA 124; 138

Bodenheim, Maxwell 1892-1954 . . . **TCLC 44**
See also CA 110; DLB 9, 45

Bodker, Cecil 1927- . . . . **CLC 21**
See also CA 73-76; CANR 13, 44; CLR 23;
MAICYA; SATA 14

Boell, Heinrich (Theodor) 1917-1985
See Boll, Heinrich (Theodor)
See also CA 21-24R; 116; CANR 24; DA;
DLB 69; DLBY 85; MTCW

Boerne, Alfred
See Doeblin, Alfred

Bogan, Louise 1897-1970..... CLC 4, 39, 46
See also CA 73-76; 25-28R; CANR 33;
DLB 45; MTCW

Bogarde, Dirk .... CLC 19
See also Van Den Bogarde, Derek Jules
Gaspard Ulric Niven
See also DLB 14

Bogosian, Eric 1953- .... CLC 45
See also CA 138

Bograd, Larry 1953-.............. CLC 35
See also CA 93-96; SATA 33

Boiardo, Matteo Maria 1441-1494 .... LC 6

Boileau-Despreaux, Nicolas
1636-1711 .... LC 3

Boland, Eavan (Aisling) 1944-... CLC 40, 67
See also CA 143; DLB 40

Boll, Heinrich (Theodor)
1917-1985 .... CLC 2, 3, 6, 9, 11, 15, 27,
39, 72; WLC
See also Boell, Heinrich (Theodor)
See also DLB 69; DLBY 85

Bolt, Lee
See Faust, Frederick (Schiller)

Bolt, Robert (Oxton) 1924-........ CLC 14
See also CA 17-20R; CANR 35; DLB 13;
MTCW

Bomkauf
See Kaufman, Bob (Garnell)

Bonaventura.................... NCLC 35
See also DLB 90

Bond, Edward 1934-...... CLC 4, 6, 13, 23
See also CA 25-28R; CANR 38; DLB 13;
MTCW

Bonham, Frank 1914-1989......... CLC 12
See also AAYA 1; CA 9-12R; CANR 4, 36;
JRDA; MAICYA; SAAS 3; SATA 1, 49,
62

Bonnefoy, Yves 1923-........ CLC 9, 15, 58
See also CA 85-88; CANR 33; MTCW

Bontemps, Arna(ud Wendell)
1902-1973 .... CLC 1, 18; BLC
See also BW 1; CA 1-4R; 41-44R; CANR 4,
35; CLR 6; DLB 48, 51; JRDA;
MAICYA; MTCW; SATA 2, 24, 44

Booth, Martin 1944-............. CLC 13
See also CA 93-96; CAAS 2

Booth, Philip 1925-.............. CLC 23
See also CA 5-8R; CANR 5; DLBY 82

Booth, Wayne C(layson) 1921- ..... CLC 24
See also CA 1-4R; CAAS 5; CANR 3, 43;
DLB 67

Borchert, Wolfgang 1921-1947 ..... TCLC 5
See also CA 104; DLB 69, 124

Borel, Petrus 1809-1859........ NCLC 41

Borges, Jorge Luis
1899-1986 ... CLC 1, 2, 3, 4, 6, 8, 9, 10,
13, 19, 44, 48, 83; DA; HLC; SSC 4;
WLC
See also CA 21-24R; CANR 19, 33;
DLB 113; DLBY 86; HW; MTCW

Borowski, Tadeusz 1922-1951...... TCLC 9
See also CA 106

Borrow, George (Henry)
1803-1881 .... NCLC 9
See also DLB 21, 55

Bosman, Herman Charles
1905-1951 .... TCLC 49

Bosschere, Jean de 1878(?)-1953... TCLC 19
See also CA 115

Boswell, James
1740-1795 .... LC 4; DA; WLC
See also CDBLB 1660-1789; DLB 104, 142

Bottoms, David 1949-............. CLC 53
See also CA 105; CANR 22; DLB 120;
DLBY 83

Boucicault, Dion 1820-1890...... NCLC 41

Boucolon, Maryse 1937-
See Conde, Maryse
See also CA 110; CANR 30

Bourget, Paul (Charles Joseph)
1852-1935 .... TCLC 12
See also CA 107; DLB 123

Bourjaily, Vance (Nye) 1922- .... CLC 8, 62
See also CA 1-4R; CAAS 1; CANR 2;
DLB 2, 143

Bourne, Randolph S(illiman)
1886-1918 .... TCLC 16
See also CA 117; DLB 63

Bova, Ben(jamin William) 1932-.... CLC 45
See also CA 5-8R; CAAS 18; CANR 11;
CLR 3; DLBY 81; MAICYA; MTCW;
SATA 6, 68

Bowen, Elizabeth (Dorothea Cole)
1899-1973 ...... CLC 1, 3, 6, 11, 15, 22;
SSC 3
See also CA 17-18; 41-44R; CANR 35;
CAP 2; CDBLB 1945-1960; DLB 15;
MTCW

Bowering, George 1935-........ CLC 15, 47
See also CA 21-24R; CAAS 16; CANR 10;
DLB 53

Bowering, Marilyn R(uthe) 1949-... CLC 32
See also CA 101

Bowers, Edgar 1924- .... CLC 9
See also CA 5-8R; CANR 24; DLB 5

Bowie, David.................... CLC 17
See also Jones, David Robert

Bowles, Jane (Sydney)
1917-1973 .... CLC 3, 68
See also CA 19-20; 41-44R; CAP 2

Bowles, Paul (Frederick)
1910- .... CLC 1, 2, 19, 53; SSC 3
See also CA 1-4R; CAAS 1; CANR 1, 19;
DLB 5, 6; MTCW

Box, Edgar
See Vidal, Gore

Boyd, Nancy
See Millay, Edna St. Vincent

Boyd, William 1952-........ CLC 28, 53, 70
See also CA 114; 120

Boyle, Kay
1902-1992 ..... CLC 1, 5, 19, 58; SSC 5
See also CA 13-16R; 140; CAAS 1;
CANR 29; DLB 4, 9, 48, 86; DLBY 93;
MTCW

Boyle, Mark
See Kienzle, William X(avier)

Boyle, Patrick 1905-1982......... CLC 19
See also CA 127

Boyle, T. C.
See Boyle, T(homas) Coraghessan

Boyle, T(homas) Coraghessan
1948- .... CLC 36, 55; SSC 16
See also BEST 90:4; CA 120; CANR 44;
DLBY 86

Boz
See Dickens, Charles (John Huffam)

Brackenridge, Hugh Henry
1748-1816 .... NCLC 7
See also DLB 11, 37

Bradbury, Edward P.
See Moorcock, Michael (John)

Bradbury, Malcolm (Stanley)
1932- .... CLC 32, 61
See also CA 1-4R; CANR 1, 33; DLB 14;
MTCW

Bradbury, Ray (Douglas)
1920- ... CLC 1, 3, 10, 15, 42; DA; WLC
See also AITN 1, 2; CA 1-4R; CANR 2, 30;
CDALB 1968-1988; DLB 2, 8; MTCW;
SATA 11, 64

Bradford, Gamaliel 1863-1932..... TCLC 36
See also DLB 17

Bradley, David (Henry, Jr.)
1950- .... CLC 23; BLC
See also BW 1; CA 104; CANR 26; DLB 33

Bradley, John Ed(mund, Jr.)
1958- .... CLC 55
See also CA 139

Bradley, Marion Zimmer 1930-..... CLC 30
See also AAYA 9; CA 57-60; CAAS 10;
CANR 7, 31; DLB 8; MTCW

Bradstreet, Anne
1612(?)-1672 .... LC 4; DA; PC 10
See also CDALB 1640-1865; DLB 24

Bragg, Melvyn 1939- .... CLC 10
See also BEST 89:3; CA 57-60; CANR 10;
DLB 14

Braine, John (Gerard)
1922-1986 .... CLC 1, 3, 41
See also CA 1-4R; 120; CANR 1, 33;
CDBLB 1945-1960; DLB 15; DLBY 86;
MTCW

Brammer, William 1930(?)-1978 .... CLC 31
See also CA 77-80

Brancati, Vitaliano 1907-1954..... TCLC 12
See also CA 109

Brancato, Robin F(idler) 1936-..... CLC 35
See also AAYA 9; CA 69-72; CANR 11,
45; CLR 32; JRDA; SAAS 9; SATA 23

Brand, Max
See Faust, Frederick (Schiller)

Brand, Millen 1906-1980 . . . . **CLC 7**
See also CA 21-24R; 97-100

Branden, Barbara . . . . **CLC 44**

Brandes, Georg (Morris Cohen)
1842-1927 . . . . **TCLC 10**
See also CA 105

Brandys, Kazimierz 1916- . . . . **CLC 62**

Branley, Franklyn M(ansfield)
1915- . . . . **CLC 21**
See also CA 33-36R; CANR 14, 39;
CLR 13; MAICYA; SAAS 16; SATA 4,
68

Brathwaite, Edward (Kamau)
1930- . . . . **CLC 11**
See also BW 2; CA 25-28R; CANR 11, 26;
DLB 125

Brautigan, Richard (Gary)
1935-1984 . . . . **CLC 1, 3, 5, 9, 12, 34, 42**
See also CA 53-56; 113; CANR 34; DLB 2,
5; DLBY 80, 84; MTCW; SATA 56

Braverman, Kate 1950- . . . . **CLC 67**
See also CA 89-92

Brecht, Bertolt
1898-1956 . . . . . . **TCLC 1, 6, 13, 35; DA;
DC 3; WLC**
See also CA 104; 133; DLB 56, 124; MTCW

Brecht, Eugen Berthold Friedrich
See Brecht, Bertolt

Bremer, Fredrika 1801-1865 . . . . . **NCLC 11**

Brennan, Christopher John
1870-1932 . . . . **TCLC 17**
See also CA 117

Brennan, Maeve 1917- . . . . **CLC 5**
See also CA 81-84

Brentano, Clemens (Maria)
1778-1842 . . . . **NCLC 1**

Brent of Bin Bin
See Franklin, (Stella Maraia Sarah) Miles

Brenton, Howard 1942- . . . . **CLC 31**
See also CA 69-72; CANR 33; DLB 13;
MTCW

Breslin, James 1930-
See Breslin, Jimmy
See also CA 73-76; CANR 31; MTCW

Breslin, Jimmy . . . . **CLC 4, 43**
See also Breslin, James
See also AITN 1

Bresson, Robert 1907- . . . . **CLC 16**
See also CA 110

Breton, Andre 1896-1966 . . . **CLC 2, 9, 15, 54**
See also CA 19-20; 25-28R; CANR 40;
CAP 2; DLB 65; MTCW

Breytenbach, Breyten 1939(?)- . . **CLC 23, 37**
See also CA 113; 129

Bridgers, Sue Ellen 1942- . . . . **CLC 26**
See also AAYA 8; CA 65-68; CANR 11,
36; CLR 18; DLB 52; JRDA; MAICYA;
SAAS 22

Bridges, Robert (Seymour)
1844-1930 . . . . **TCLC 1**
See also CA 104; CDBLB 1890-1914;
DLB 19, 98

Bridie, James . . . . **TCLC 3**
See also Mavor, Osborne Henry
See also DLB 10

Brin, David 1950- . . . . **CLC 34**
See also CA 102; CANR 24; SATA 65

Brink, Andre (Philippus)
1935- . . . . **CLC 18, 36**
See also CA 104; CANR 39; MTCW

Brinsmead, H(esba) F(ay) 1922- . . . . **CLC 21**
See also CA 21-24R; CANR 10; MAICYA;
SAAS 5; SATA 18, 78

Brittain, Vera (Mary)
1893(?)-1970 . . . . **CLC 23**
See also CA 13-16; 25-28R; CAP 1; MTCW

Broch, Hermann 1886-1951 . . . . . . **TCLC 20**
See also CA 117; DLB 85, 124

Brock, Rose
See Hansen, Joseph

Brodkey, Harold 1930- . . . . **CLC 56**
See also CA 111; DLB 130

Brodsky, Iosif Alexandrovich 1940-
See Brodsky, Joseph
See also AITN 1; CA 41-44R; CANR 37;
MTCW

Brodsky, Joseph . . **CLC 4, 6, 13, 36, 50; PC 9**
See also Brodsky, Iosif Alexandrovich

Brodsky, Michael Mark 1948- . . . . . **CLC 19**
See also CA 102; CANR 18, 41

Bromell, Henry 1947- . . . . **CLC 5**
See also CA 53-56; CANR 9

Bromfield, Louis (Brucker)
1896-1956 . . . . **TCLC 11**
See also CA 107; DLB 4, 9, 86

Broner, E(sther) M(asserman)
1930- . . . . **CLC 19**
See also CA 17-20R; CANR 8, 25; DLB 28

Bronk, William 1918- . . . . **CLC 10**
See also CA 89-92; CANR 23

Bronstein, Lev Davidovich
See Trotsky, Leon

Bronte, Anne 1820-1849 . . . . **NCLC 4**
See also DLB 21

Bronte, Charlotte
1816-1855 . . . **NCLC 3, 8, 33; DA; WLC**
See also CDBLB 1832-1890; DLB 21

Bronte, (Jane) Emily
1818-1848 . . . . **NCLC 16, 35; DA; PC 8;
WLC**
See also CDBLB 1832-1890; DLB 21, 32

Brooke, Frances 1724-1789 . . . . **LC 6**
See also DLB 39, 99

Brooke, Henry 1703(?)-1783 . . . . **LC 1**
See also DLB 39

Brooke, Rupert (Chawner)
1887-1915 . . . . **TCLC 2, 7; DA; WLC**
See also CA 104; 132; CDBLB 1914-1945;
DLB 19; MTCW

Brooke-Haven, P.
See Wodehouse, P(elham) G(renville)

Brooke-Rose, Christine 1926- . . . . . . **CLC 40**
See also CA 13-16R; DLB 14

Brookner, Anita 1928- . . . . . . **CLC 32, 34, 51**
See also CA 114; 120; CANR 37; DLBY 87;
MTCW

Brooks, Cleanth 1906- . . . . **CLC 24**
See also CA 17-20R; CANR 33, 35;
DLB 63; MTCW

Brooks, George
See Baum, L(yman) Frank

Brooks, Gwendolyn
1917- . . . . . . **CLC 1, 2, 4, 5, 15, 49; BLC;
DA; PC 7; WLC**
See also AITN 1; BW 2; CA 1-4R;
CANR 1, 27; CDALB 1941-1968;
CLR 27; DLB 5, 76; MTCW; SATA 6

Brooks, Mel . . . . **CLC 12**
See also Kaminsky, Melvin
See also DLB 26

Brooks, Peter 1938- . . . . **CLC 34**
See also CA 45-48; CANR 1

Brooks, Van Wyck 1886-1963 . . . . . . **CLC 29**
See also CA 1-4R; CANR 6; DLB 45, 63,
103

Brophy, Brigid (Antonia)
1929- . . . . **CLC 6, 11, 29**
See also CA 5-8R; CAAS 4; CANR 25;
DLB 14; MTCW

Brosman, Catharine Savage 1934- . . . . **CLC 9**
See also CA 61-64; CANR 21

Brother Antoninus
See Everson, William (Oliver)

Broughton, T(homas) Alan 1936- . . . **CLC 19**
See also CA 45-48; CANR 2, 23

Broumas, Olga 1949- . . . . **CLC 10, 73**
See also CA 85-88; CANR 20

Brown, Charles Brockden
1771-1810 . . . . **NCLC 22**
See also CDALB 1640-1865; DLB 37, 59,
73

Brown, Christy 1932-1981 . . . . **CLC 63**
See also CA 105; 104; DLB 14

Brown, Claude 1937- . . . . **CLC 30; BLC**
See also AAYA 7; BW 1; CA 73-76

Brown, Dee (Alexander) 1908- . . **CLC 18, 47**
See also CA 13-16R; CAAS 6; CANR 11,
45; DLBY 80; MTCW; SATA 5

Brown, George
See Wertmueller, Lina

Brown, George Douglas
1869-1902 . . . . **TCLC 28**

Brown, George Mackay 1921- . . . . **CLC 5, 48**
See also CA 21-24R; CAAS 6; CANR 12,
37; DLB 14, 27, 139; MTCW; SATA 35

Brown, (William) Larry 1951- . . . . . . **CLC 73**
See also CA 130; 134

Brown, Moses
See Barrett, William (Christopher)

Brown, Rita Mae 1944- . . . . . **CLC 18, 43, 79**
See also CA 45-48; CANR 2, 11, 35;
MTCW

Brown, Roderick (Langmere) Haig-
See Haig-Brown, Roderick (Langmere)

Brown, Rosellen 1939- . . . . **CLC 32**
See also CA 77-80; CAAS 10; CANR 14, 44

Brown, Sterling Allen
1901-1989 . . . . **CLC 1, 23, 59; BLC**
See also BW 1; CA 85-88; 127; CANR 26;
DLB 48, 51, 63; MTCW

Brown, Will
See Ainsworth, William Harrison

Brown, William Wells
1813-1884 . . . . NCLC 2; BLC; DC 1
See also DLB 3, 50

Browne, (Clyde) Jackson 1948(?)-. . . CLC 21
See also CA 120

Browning, Elizabeth Barrett
1806-1861 . . . . . NCLC 1, 16; DA; PC 6;
WLC
See also CDBLB 1832-1890; DLB 32

Browning, Robert
1812-1889 . . . . NCLC 19; DA; PC 2
See also CDBLB 1832-1890; DLB 32;
YABC 1

Browning, Tod 1882-1962 . . . . CLC 16
See also CA 141; 117

Bruccoli, Matthew J(oseph) 1931- . . CLC 34
See also CA 9-12R; CANR 7; DLB 103

Bruce, Lenny . . . . CLC 21
See also Schneider, Leonard Alfred

Bruin, John
See Brutus, Dennis

Brulls, Christian
See Simenon, Georges (Jacques Christian)

Brunner, John (Kilian Houston)
1934- . . . . CLC 8, 10
See also CA 1-4R; CAAS 8; CANR 2, 37;
MTCW

Brutus, Dennis 1924- . . . . CLC 43; BLC
See also BW 2; CA 49-52; CAAS 14;
CANR 2, 27, 42; DLB 117

Bryan, C(ourtlandt) D(ixon) B(arnes)
1936- . . . . CLC 29
See also CA 73-76; CANR 13

Bryan, Michael
See Moore, Brian

Bryant, William Cullen
1794-1878 . . . . NCLC 6, 46; DA
See also CDALB 1640-1865; DLB 3, 43, 59

Bryusov, Valery Yakovlevich
1873-1924 . . . . TCLC 10
See also CA 107

Buchan, John 1875-1940 . . . . TCLC 41
See also CA 108; DLB 34, 70; YABC 2

Buchanan, George 1506-1582 . . . . LC 4

Buchheim, Lothar-Guenther 1918- . . . CLC 6
See also CA 85-88

Buchner, (Karl) Georg
1813-1837 . . . . NCLC 26

Buchwald, Art(hur) 1925-. . . . . CLC 33
See also AITN 1; CA 5-8R; CANR 21;
MTCW; SATA 10

Buck, Pearl S(ydenstricker)
1892-1973 . . . . CLC 7, 11, 18; DA
See also AITN 1; CA 1-4R; 41-44R;
CANR 1, 34; DLB 9, 102; MTCW;
SATA 1, 25

Buckler, Ernest 1908-1984. . . . . CLC 13
See also CA 11-12; 114; CAP 1; DLB 68;
SATA 47

Buckley, Vincent (Thomas)
1925-1988 . . . . CLC 57
See also CA 101

Buckley, William F(rank), Jr.
1925- . . . . CLC 7, 18, 37
See also AITN 1; CA 1-4R; CANR 1, 24;
DLB 137; DLBY 80; MTCW

Buechner, (Carl) Frederick
1926- . . . . CLC 2, 4, 6, 9
See also CA 13-16R; CANR 11, 39;
DLBY 80; MTCW

Buell, John (Edward) 1927-. . . . . . . CLC 10
See also CA 1-4R; DLB 53

Buero Vallejo, Antonio 1916- . . . CLC 15, 46
See also CA 106; CANR 24; HW; MTCW

Bufalino, Gesualdo 1920(?)-. . . . . . . CLC 74

Dugayev, Boris Nikolayevich 1880-1934
See Bely, Andrey
See also CA 104

Bukowski, Charles
1920-1994 . . . . CLC 2, 5, 9, 41, 82
See also CA 17-20R; 144; CANR 40;
DLB 5, 130; MTCW

Bulgakov, Mikhail (Afanas'evich)
1891-1940 . . . . TCLC 2, 16
See also CA 105

Bulgya, Alexander Alexandrovich
1901-1956 . . . . TCLC 53
See also Fadeyev, Alexander
See also CA 117

Bullins, Ed 1935- . . . . CLC 1, 5, 7; BLC
See also BW 2; CA 49-52; CAAS 16;
CANR 24; DLB 7, 38; MTCW

Bulwer-Lytton, Edward (George Earle Lytton)
1803-1873 . . . . NCLC 1, 45
See also DLB 21

Bunin, Ivan Alexeyevich
1870-1953 . . . . TCLC 6; SSC 5
See also CA 104

Bunting, Basil 1900-1985. . . . CLC 10, 39, 47
See also CA 53-56; 115; CANR 7; DLB 20

Bunuel, Luis 1900-1983 . . CLC 16, 80; HLC
See also CA 101; 110; CANR 32; HW

Bunyan, John 1628-1688 . . LC 4; DA; WLC
See also CDBLB 1660-1789; DLB 39

Burford, Eleanor
See Hibbert, Eleanor Alice Burford

Burgess, Anthony
CLC 1, 2, 4, 5, 8, 10, 13, 15, 22, 40, 62,
81
See also Wilson, John (Anthony) Burgess
See also AITN 1; CDBLB 1960 to Present;
DLB 14

Burke, Edmund
1729(?)-1797 . . . . LC 7; DA; WLC
See also DLB 104

Burke, Kenneth (Duva)
1897-1993 . . . . CLC 2, 24
See also CA 5-8R; 143; CANR 39; DLB 45,
63; MTCW

Burke, Leda
See Garnett, David

Burke, Ralph
See Silverberg, Robert

Burney, Fanny 1752-1840 . . . . NCLC 12
See also DLB 39

Burns, Robert
1759-1796 . . . . . LC 3; DA; PC 6; WLC
See also CDBLB 1789-1832; DLB 109

Burns, Tex
See L'Amour, Louis (Dearborn)

Burnshaw, Stanley 1906-. . . . . CLC 3, 13, 44
See also CA 9-12R; DLB 48

Burr, Anne 1937- . . . . CLC 6
See also CA 25-28R

Burroughs, Edgar Rice
1875-1950 . . . . TCLC 2, 32
See also AAYA 11; CA 104; 132; DLB 8;
MTCW; SATA 41

Burroughs, William S(eward)
1914- . . . . CLC 1, 2, 5, 15, 22, 42, 75;
DA; WLC
See also AITN 2; CA 9-12R; CANR 20;
DLB 2, 8, 16; DLBY 81; MTCW

Burton, Richard F. 1821-1890. . . . NCLC 42
See also DLB 55

Busch, Frederick 1941- . . . CLC 7, 10, 18, 47
See also CA 33-36R; CAAS 1; CANR 45;
DLB 6

Bush, Ronald 1946- . . . . CLC 34
See also CA 136

Bustos, F(rancisco)
See Borges, Jorge Luis

Bustos Domecq, H(onorio)
See Bioy Casares, Adolfo; Borges, Jorge
Luis

Butler, Octavia E(stelle) 1947- . . . . . CLC 38
See also BW 2; CA 73-76; CANR 12, 24,
38; DLB 33; MTCW

Butler, Robert Olen (Jr.) 1945-. . . . . CLC 81
See also CA 112

Butler, Samuel 1612-1680 . . . . LC 16
See also DLB 101, 126

Butler, Samuel
1835-1902 . . . . . . TCLC 1, 33; DA; WLC
See also CA 104; CDBLB 1890-1914;
DLB 18, 57

Butler, Walter C.
See Faust, Frederick (Schiller)

Butor, Michel (Marie Francois)
1926- . . . . CLC 1, 3, 8, 11, 15
See also CA 9-12R; CANR 33; DLB 83;
MTCW

Buzo, Alexander (John) 1944-. . . . . . CLC 61
See also CA 97-100; CANR 17, 39

Buzzati, Dino 1906-1972 . . . . CLC 36
See also CA 33-36R

Byars, Betsy (Cromer) 1928-. . . . . . . CLC 35
See also CA 33-36R; CANR 18, 36; CLR 1,
16; DLB 52; JRDA; MAICYA; MTCW;
SAAS 1; SATA 4, 46

Byatt, A(ntonia) S(usan Drabble)
1936- . . . . CLC 19, 65
See also CA 13-16R; CANR 13, 33;
DLB 14; MTCW

Byrne, David 1952-. . . . . CLC 26
See also CA 127

Byrne, John Keyes 1926-. . . . . CLC 19
See also Leonard, Hugh
See also CA 102

Byron, George Gordon (Noel)
1788-1824 . . . . . . **NCLC 2, 12; DA; WLC**
See also CDBLB 1789-1832; DLB 96, 110

C.3.3.
See Wilde, Oscar (Fingal O'Flahertie Wills)

Caballero, Fernan 1796-1877 . . . . . **NCLC 10**

Cabell, James Branch 1879-1958 . . . **TCLC 6**
See also CA 105; DLB 9, 78

Cable, George Washington
1844-1925 . . . . **TCLC 4; SSC 4**
See also CA 104; DLB 12, 74

Cabral de Melo Neto, Joao 1920- . . . **CLC 76**

Cabrera Infante, G(uillermo)
1929- . . . . **CLC 5, 25, 45; HLC**
See also CA 85-88; CANR 29; DLB 113;
HW; MTCW

Cade, Toni
See Bambara, Toni Cade

Cadmus
See Buchan, John

Caedmon fl. 658-680 . . . . **CMLC 7**

Caeiro, Alberto
See Pessoa, Fernando (Antonio Nogueira)

Cage, John (Milton, Jr.) 1912- . . . . . **CLC 41**
See also CA 13-16R; CANR 9

Cain, G.
See Cabrera Infante, G(uillermo)

Cain, Guillermo
See Cabrera Infante, G(uillermo)

Cain, James M(allahan)
1892-1977 . . . . **CLC 3, 11, 28**
See also AITN 1; CA 17-20R; 73-76;
CANR 8, 34; MTCW

Caine, Mark
See Raphael, Frederic (Michael)

Calasso, Roberto 1941- . . . . **CLC 81**
See also CA 143

Calderon de la Barca, Pedro
1600-1681 . . . . **LC 23; DC 3**

Caldwell, Erskine (Preston)
1903-1987 . . . . **CLC 1, 8, 14, 50, 60**
See also AITN 1; CA 1-4R; 121; CAAS 1;
CANR 2, 33; DLB 9, 86; MTCW

Caldwell, (Janet Miriam) Taylor (Holland)
1900-1985 . . . . **CLC 2, 28, 39**
See also CA 5-8R; 116; CANR 5

Calhoun, John Caldwell
1782-1850 . . . . **NCLC 15**
See also DLB 3

Calisher, Hortense
1911- . . . . **CLC 2, 4, 8, 38; SSC 15**
See also CA 1-4R; CANR 1, 22; DLB 2;
MTCW

Callaghan, Morley Edward
1903-1990 . . . . **CLC 3, 14, 41, 65**
See also CA 9-12R; 132; CANR 33;
DLB 68; MTCW

Calvino, Italo
1923-1985 . . . . . **CLC 5, 8, 11, 22, 33, 39,**
73; SSC 3
See also CA 85-88; 116; CANR 23; MTCW

Cameron, Carey 1952- . . . . **CLC 59**
See also CA 135

Cameron, Peter 1959- . . . . **CLC 44**
See also CA 125

Campana, Dino 1885-1932 . . . . **TCLC 20**
See also CA 117; DLB 114

Campbell, John W(ood, Jr.)
1910-1971 . . . . **CLC 32**
See also CA 21-22; 29-32R; CANR 34;
CAP 2; DLB 8; MTCW

Campbell, Joseph 1904-1987 . . . . **CLC 69**
See also AAYA 3; BEST 89:2; CA 1-4R;
124; CANR 3, 28; MTCW

Campbell, (John) Ramsey 1946- . . . . **CLC 42**
See also CA 57-60; CANR 7

Campbell, (Ignatius) Roy (Dunnachie)
1901-1957 . . . . **TCLC 5**
See also CA 104; DLB 20

Campbell, Thomas 1777-1844 . . . . **NCLC 19**
See also DLB 93; 144

Campbell, Wilfred . . . . **TCLC 9**
See also Campbell, William

Campbell, William 1858(?)-1918
See Campbell, Wilfred
See also CA 106; DLB 92

Campos, Alvaro de
See Pessoa, Fernando (Antonio Nogueira)

Camus, Albert
1913-1960 . . . . **CLC 1, 2, 4, 9, 11, 14, 32,**
63, 69; DA; DC 2; SSC 9; WLC
See also CA 89-92; DLB 72; MTCW

Canby, Vincent 1924- . . . . **CLC 13**
See also CA 81-84

Cancale
See Desnos, Robert

Canetti, Elias 1905- . . . . . . **CLC 3, 14, 25, 75**
See also CA 21-24R; CANR 23; DLB 85,
124; MTCW

Canin, Ethan 1960- . . . . **CLC 55**
See also CA 131; 135

Cannon, Curt
See Hunter, Evan

Cape, Judith
See Page, P(atricia) K(athleen)

Capek, Karel
1890-1938 . . . . . **TCLC 6, 37; DA; DC 1;**
WLC
See also CA 104; 140

Capote, Truman
1924-1984 . . . . . . **CLC 1, 3, 8, 13, 19, 34,**
38, 58; DA; SSC 2; WLC
See also CA 5-8R; 113; CANR 18;
CDALB 1941-1968; DLB 2; DLBY 80,
84; MTCW

Capra, Frank 1897-1991 . . . . **CLC 16**
See also CA 61-64; 135

Caputo, Philip 1941- . . . . **CLC 32**
See also CA 73-76; CANR 40

Card, Orson Scott 1951- . . . . **CLC 44, 47, 50**
See also AAYA 11; CA 102; CANR 27;
MTCW

Cardenal (Martinez), Ernesto
1925- . . . . **CLC 31; HLC**
See also CA 49-52; CANR 2, 32; HW;
MTCW

Carducci, Giosue 1835-1907 . . . . **TCLC 32**

Carew, Thomas 1595(?)-1640 . . . . **LC 13**
See also DLB 126

Carey, Ernestine Gilbreth 1908- . . . . **CLC 17**
See also CA 5-8R; SATA 2

Carey, Peter 1943- . . . . **CLC 40, 55**
See also CA 123; 127; MTCW

Carleton, William 1794-1869 . . . . . . **NCLC 3**

Carlisle, Henry (Coffin) 1926- . . . . . . **CLC 33**
See also CA 13-16R; CANR 15

Carlsen, Chris
See Holdstock, Robert P.

Carlson, Ron(ald F.) 1947- . . . . **CLC 54**
See also CA 105; CANR 27

Carlyle, Thomas 1795-1881 . . **NCLC 22; DA**
See also CDBLB 1789-1832; DLB 55; 144

Carman, (William) Bliss
1861-1929 . . . . **TCLC 7**
See also CA 104; DLB 92

Carnegie, Dale 1888-1955 . . . . **TCLC 53**

Carossa, Hans 1878-1956 . . . . **TCLC 48**
See also DLB 66

Carpenter, Don(ald Richard)
1931- . . . . **CLC 41**
See also CA 45-48; CANR 1

Carpentier (y Valmont), Alejo
1904-1980 . . . . **CLC 8, 11, 38; HLC**
See also CA 65-68; 97-100; CANR 11;
DLB 113; HW

Carr, Emily 1871-1945 . . . . **TCLC 32**
See also DLB 68

Carr, John Dickson 1906-1977 . . . . . . **CLC 3**
See also CA 49-52; 69-72; CANR 3, 33;
MTCW

Carr, Philippa
See Hibbert, Eleanor Alice Burford

Carr, Virginia Spencer 1929- . . . . **CLC 34**
See also CA 61-64; DLB 111

Carrier, Roch 1937- . . . . **CLC 13, 78**
See also CA 130; DLB 53

Carroll, James P. 1943(?)- . . . . **CLC 38**
See also CA 81-84

Carroll, Jim 1951- . . . . **CLC 35**
See also CA 45-48; CANR 42

Carroll, Lewis . . . . **NCLC 2; WLC**
See also Dodgson, Charles Lutwidge
See also CDBLB 1832-1890; CLR 2, 18;
DLB 18; JRDA

Carroll, Paul Vincent 1900-1968 . . . . **CLC 10**
See also CA 9-12R; 25-28R; DLB 10

Carruth, Hayden
1921- . . . . . . **CLC 4, 7, 10, 18, 84; PC 10**
See also CA 9-12R; CANR 4, 38; DLB 5;
MTCW; SATA 47

Carson, Rachel Louise 1907-1964 . . . **CLC 71**
See also CA 77-80; CANR 35; MTCW;
SATA 23

Carter, Angela (Olive)
1940-1992 . . . . . . **CLC 5, 41, 76; SSC 13**
See also CA 53-56; 136; CANR 12, 36;
DLB 14; MTCW; SATA 66;
SATA-Obit 70

Carter, Nick
See Smith, Martin Cruz

Carver, Raymond
1938-1988 . . . **CLC 22, 36, 53, 55; SSC 8**
See also CA 33-36R; 126; CANR 17, 34;
DLB 130; DLBY 84, 88; MTCW

Cary, (Arthur) Joyce (Lunel)
1888-1957 . . . . **TCLC 1, 29**
See also CA 104; CDBLB 1914-1945;
DLB 15, 100

Casanova de Seingalt, Giovanni Jacopo
1725-1798 . . . . **LC 13**

Casares, Adolfo Bioy
See Bioy Casares, Adolfo

Casely-Hayford, J(oseph) E(phraim)
1866-1930 . . . . **TCLC 24; BLC**
See also BW 2; CA 123

Casey, John (Dudley)   1939- . . . . **CLC 59**
See also BEST 90:2; CA 69-72; CANR 23

Casey, Michael   1947- . . . . **CLC 2**
See also CA 65-68; DLB 5

Casey, Patrick
See Thurman, Wallace (Henry)

Casey, Warren (Peter)   1935-1988 . . . **CLC 12**
See also CA 101; 127

Casona, Alejandro . . . . **CLC 49**
See also Alvarez, Alejandro Rodriguez

Cassavetes, John   1929-1989 . . . . **CLC 20**
See also CA 85-88; 127

Cassill, R(onald) V(erlin)   1919- . . . **CLC 4, 23**
See also CA 9-12R; CAAS 1; CANR 7, 45;
DLB 6

Cassity, (Allen) Turner   1929- . . . . **CLC 6, 42**
See also CA 17-20R; CAAS 8; CANR 11;
DLB 105

Castaneda, Carlos   1931(?)- . . . . **CLC 12**
See also CA 25-28R; CANR 32; HW;
MTCW

Castedo, Elena   1937- . . . . **CLC 65**
See also CA 132

Castedo-Ellerman, Elena
See Castedo, Elena

Castellanos, Rosario
1925-1974 . . . . **CLC 66; HLC**
See also CA 131; 53-56; DLB 113; HW

Castelvetro, Lodovico   1505-1571 . . . . . **LC 12**

Castiglione, Baldassare   1478-1529 . . . **LC 12**

Castle, Robert
See Hamilton, Edmond

Castro, Guillen de   1569-1631 . . . . **LC 19**

Castro, Rosalia de   1837-1885 . . . . . **NCLC 3**

Cather, Willa
See Cather, Willa Sibert

Cather, Willa Sibert
1873-1947 . . . . **TCLC 1, 11, 31; DA;
SSC 2; WLC**
See also CA 104; 128; CDALB 1865-1917;
DLB 9, 54, 78; DLBD 1; MTCW;
SATA 30

Catton, (Charles) Bruce
1899-1978 . . . . **CLC 35**
See also AITN 1; CA 5-8R; 81-84;
CANR 7; DLB 17; SATA 2, 24

Cauldwell, Frank
See King, Francis (Henry)

Caunitz, William J.   1933- . . . . **CLC 34**
See also BEST 89:3; CA 125; 130

Causley, Charles (Stanley)   1917- . . . . . **CLC 7**
See also CA 9-12R; CANR 5, 35; CLR 30;
DLB 27; MTCW; SATA 3, 66

Caute, David   1936- . . . . **CLC 29**
See also CA 1-4R; CAAS 4; CANR 1, 33;
DLB 14

Cavafy, C(onstantine) P(eter) . . . . . . **TCLC 2, 7**
See also Kavafis, Konstantinos Petrou

Cavallo, Evelyn
See Spark, Muriel (Sarah)

Cavanna, Betty . . . . **CLC 12**
See also Harrison, Elizabeth Cavanna
See also JRDA; MAICYA; SAAS 4;
SATA 1, 30

Caxton, William   1421(?)-1491(?) . . . . . **LC 17**

Cayrol, Jean   1911- . . . . **CLC 11**
See also CA 89-92; DLB 83

Cela, Camilo Jose
1916- . . . . **CLC 4, 13, 59; HLC**
See also BEST 90:2; CA 21-24R; CAAS 10;
CANR 21, 32; DLBY 89; HW; MTCW

Celan, Paul . . . . **CLC 53, 82; PC 10**
See also Antschel, Paul
See also DLB 69

Celine, Louis-Ferdinand
. . . . **CLC 1, 3, 4, 7, 9, 15, 47**
See also Destouches, Louis-Ferdinand
See also DLB 72

Cellini, Benvenuto   1500-1571 . . . . **LC 7**

Cendrars, Blaise
See Sauser-Hall, Frederic

Cernuda (y Bidon), Luis
1902-1963 . . . . **CLC 54**
See also CA 131; 89-92; DLB 134; HW

Cervantes (Saavedra), Miguel de
1547-1616 . . . . . . **LC 6, 23; DA; SSC 12;
WLC**

Cesaire, Aime (Fernand)
1913- . . . . **CLC 19, 32; BLC**
See also BW 2; CA 65-68; CANR 24, 43;
MTCW

Chabon, Michael   1965(?)- . . . . **CLC 55**
See also CA 139

Chabrol, Claude   1930- . . . . **CLC 16**
See also CA 110

Challans, Mary   1905-1983
See Renault, Mary
See also CA 81-84; 111; SATA 23, 36

Challis, George
See Faust, Frederick (Schiller)

Chambers, Aidan   1934- . . . . **CLC 35**
See also CA 25-28R; CANR 12, 31; JRDA;
MAICYA; SAAS 12; SATA 1, 69

Chambers, James   1948-
See Cliff, Jimmy
See also CA 124

Chambers, Jessie
See Lawrence, D(avid) H(erbert Richards)

Chambers, Robert W.   1865-1933 . . . **TCLC 41**

Chandler, Raymond (Thornton)
1888-1959 . . . . **TCLC 1, 7**
See also CA 104; 129; CDALB 1929-1941;
DLBD 6; MTCW

Chang, Jung   1952- . . . . **CLC 71**
See also CA 142

Channing, William Ellery
1780-1842 . . . . **NCLC 17**
See also DLB 1, 59

Chaplin, Charles Spencer
1889-1977 . . . . **CLC 16**
See also Chaplin, Charlie
See also CA 81-84; 73-76

Chaplin, Charlie
See Chaplin, Charles Spencer
See also DLB 44

Chapman, George   1559(?)-1634 . . . . . . **LC 22**
See also DLB 62, 121

Chapman, Graham   1941-1989 . . . . . . **CLC 21**
See also Monty Python
See also CA 116; 129; CANR 35

Chapman, John Jay   1862-1933 . . . . . **TCLC 7**
See also CA 104

Chapman, Walker
See Silverberg, Robert

Chappell, Fred (Davis)   1936- . . . . **CLC 40, 78**
See also CA 5-8R; CAAS 4; CANR 8, 33;
DLB 6, 105

Char, Rene(-Emile)
1907-1988 . . . . **CLC 9, 11, 14, 55**
See also CA 13-16R; 124; CANR 32;
MTCW

Charby, Jay
See Ellison, Harlan

Chardin, Pierre Teilhard de
See Teilhard de Chardin, (Marie Joseph)
Pierre

Charles I   1600-1649 . . . . **LC 13**

Charyn, Jerome   1937- . . . . **CLC 5, 8, 18**
See also CA 5-8R; CAAS 1; CANR 7;
DLBY 83; MTCW

Chase, Mary (Coyle)   1907-1981 . . . . . . **DC 1**
See also CA 77-80; 105; SATA 17, 29

Chase, Mary Ellen   1887-1973 . . . . **CLC 2**
See also CA 13-16; 41-44R; CAP 1;
SATA 10

Chase, Nicholas
See Hyde, Anthony

Chateaubriand, Francois Rene de
1768-1848 . . . . **NCLC 3**
See also DLB 119

Chatterje, Sarat Chandra   1876-1936(?)
See Chatterji, Saratchandra
See also CA 109

Chatterji, Bankim Chandra
1838-1894 . . . . **NCLC 19**

Chatterji, Saratchandra . . . . **TCLC 13**
See also Chatterje, Sarat Chandra

Chatterton, Thomas   1752-1770 . . . . **LC 3**
See also DLB 109

Chatwin, (Charles) Bruce
1940-1989 . . . . **CLC 28, 57, 59**
See also AAYA 4; BEST 90:1; CA 85-88;
127

Chaucer, Daniel
See Ford, Ford Madox

Chaucer, Geoffrey
1340(?)-1400 . . . . **LC 17; DA**
See also CDBLB Before 1660

Chaviaras, Strates 1935-
See Haviaras, Stratis
See also CA 105

Chayefsky, Paddy . . . . **CLC 23**
See also Chayefsky, Sidney
See also DLB 7, 44; DLBY 81

Chayefsky, Sidney 1923-1981
See Chayefsky, Paddy
See also CA 9-12R; 104; CANR 18

Chedid, Andree 1920- . . . . **CLC 47**

Cheever, John
1912-1982 . . . . . . **CLC 3, 7, 8, 11, 15, 25,**
64; DA; SSC 1; WLC
See also CA 5-8R; 106; CABS 1; CANR 5,
27; CDALB 1941-1968; DLB 2, 102;
DLBY 80, 82; MTCW

Cheever, Susan 1943- . . . . **CLC 18, 48**
See also CA 103; CANR 27; DLBY 82

Chekhonte, Antosha
See Chekhov, Anton (Pavlovich)

Chekhov, Anton (Pavlovich)
1860-1904 . . . . . **TCLC 3, 10, 31, 55; DA;**
SSC 2; WLC
See also CA 104; 124

Chernyshevsky, Nikolay Gavrilovich
1828-1889 . . . . **NCLC 1**

Cherry, Carolyn Janice 1942-
See Cherryh, C. J.
See also CA 65-68; CANR 10

Cherryh, C. J. . . . . **CLC 35**
See also Cherry, Carolyn Janice
See also DLBY 80

Chesnutt, Charles W(addell)
1858-1932 . . . . **TCLC 5, 39; BLC; SSC 7**
See also BW 1; CA 106; 125; DLB 12, 50,
78; MTCW

Chester, Alfred 1929(?)-1971 . . . . **CLC 49**
See also CA 33-36R; DLB 130

Chesterton, G(ilbert) K(eith)
1874-1936 . . . . **TCLC 1, 6; SSC 1**
See also CA 104; 132; CDBLB 1914-1945;
DLB 10, 19, 34, 70, 98; MTCW;
SATA 27

Chiang Pin-chin 1904-1986
See Ding Ling
See also CA 118

Ch'ien Chung-shu 1910- . . . . **CLC 22**
See also CA 130; MTCW

Child, L. Maria
See Child, Lydia Maria

Child, Lydia Maria 1802-1880 . . . . **NCLC 6**
See also DLB 1, 74; SATA 67

Child, Mrs.
See Child, Lydia Maria

Child, Philip 1898-1978 . . . . **CLC 19, 68**
See also CA 13-14; CAP 1; SATA 47

Childress, Alice
1920- . . . . **CLC 12, 15; BLC; DC 4**
See also AAYA 8; BW 2; CA 45-48;
CANR 3, 27; CLR 14; DLB 7, 38; JRDA;
MAICYA; MTCW; SATA 7, 48

Chislett, (Margaret) Anne 1943- . . . . **CLC 34**

Chitty, Thomas Willes 1926- . . . . **CLC 11**
See also Hinde, Thomas
See also CA 5-8R

Chomette, Rene Lucien 1898-1981 . . **CLC 20**
See also Clair, Rene
See also CA 103

Chopin, Kate . . . . **TCLC 5, 14; DA; SSC 8**
See also Chopin, Katherine
See also CDALB 1865-1917; DLB 12, 78

Chopin, Katherine 1851-1904
See Chopin, Kate
See also CA 104; 122

Chretien de Troyes
c. 12th cent. - . . . . **CMLC 10**

Christie
See Ichikawa, Kon

Christie, Agatha (Mary Clarissa)
1890-1976 . . . . . . **CLC 1, 6, 8, 12, 39, 48**
See also AAYA 9; AITN 1, 2; CA 17-20R;
61-64; CANR 10, 37; CDBLB 1914-1945;
DLB 13, 77; MTCW; SATA 36

Christie, (Ann) Philippa
See Pearce, Philippa
See also CA 5-8R; CANR 4

Christine de Pizan 1365(?)-1431(?) . . . . **LC 9**

Chubb, Elmer
See Masters, Edgar Lee

Chulkov, Mikhail Dmitrievich
1743-1792 . . . . **LC 2**

Churchill, Caryl 1938- . . . . **CLC 31, 55**
See also CA 102; CANR 22; DLB 13;
MTCW

Churchill, Charles 1731-1764 . . . . **LC 3**
See also DLB 109

Chute, Carolyn 1947- . . . . **CLC 39**
See also CA 123

Ciardi, John (Anthony)
1916-1986 . . . . **CLC 10, 40, 44**
See also CA 5-8R; 118; CAAS 2; CANR 5,
33; CLR 19; DLB 5; DLBY 86;
MAICYA; MTCW; SATA 1, 46, 65

Cicero, Marcus Tullius
106B.C.-43B.C. . . . . **CMLC 3**

Cimino, Michael 1943- . . . . **CLC 16**
See also CA 105

Cioran, E(mil) M. 1911- . . . . **CLC 64**
See also CA 25-28R

Cisneros, Sandra 1954- . . . . . . **CLC 69; HLC**
See also AAYA 9; CA 131; DLB 122; HW

Clair, Rene . . . . **CLC 20**
See also Chomette, Rene Lucien

Clampitt, Amy 1920- . . . . **CLC 32**
See also CA 110; CANR 29; DLB 105

Clancy, Thomas L., Jr. 1947-
See Clancy, Tom
See also CA 125; 131; MTCW

Clancy, Tom . . . . **CLC 45**
See also Clancy, Thomas L., Jr.
See also AAYA 9; BEST 89:1, 90:1

Clare, John 1793-1864 . . . . **NCLC 9**
See also DLB 55, 96

Clarin
See Alas (y Urena), Leopoldo (Enrique
Garcia)

Clark, Al C.
See Goines, Donald

Clark, (Robert) Brian 1932- . . . . **CLC 29**
See also CA 41-44R

Clark, Curt
See Westlake, Donald E(dwin)

Clark, Eleanor 1913- . . . . **CLC 5, 19**
See also CA 9-12R; CANR 41; DLB 6

Clark, J. P.
See Clark, John Pepper
See also DLB 117

Clark, John Pepper 1935- . . . . **CLC 38; BLC**
See also Clark, J. P.
See also BW 1; CA 65-68; CANR 16

Clark, M. R.
See Clark, Mavis Thorpe

Clark, Mavis Thorpe 1909- . . . . **CLC 12**
See also CA 57-60; CANR 8, 37; CLR 30;
MAICYA; SAAS 5; SATA 8, 74

Clark, Walter Van Tilburg
1909-1971 . . . . **CLC 28**
See also CA 9-12R; 33-36R; DLB 9;
SATA 8

Clarke, Arthur C(harles)
1917- . . . . . . **CLC 1, 4, 13, 18, 35; SSC 3**
See also AAYA 4; CA 1-4R; CANR 2, 28;
JRDA; MAICYA; MTCW; SATA 13, 70

Clarke, Austin 1896-1974 . . . . **CLC 6, 9**
See also CA 29-32; 49-52; CAP 2; DLB 10,
20

Clarke, Austin C(hesterfield)
1934- . . . . **CLC 8, 53; BLC**
See also BW 1; CA 25-28R; CAAS 16;
CANR 14, 32; DLB 53, 125

Clarke, Gillian 1937- . . . . **CLC 61**
See also CA 106; DLB 40

Clarke, Marcus (Andrew Hislop)
1846-1881 . . . . **NCLC 19**

Clarke, Shirley 1925- . . . . **CLC 16**

Clash, The . . . . **CLC 30**
See also Headon, (Nicky) Topper; Jones,
Mick; Simonon, Paul; Strummer, Joe

Claudel, Paul (Louis Charles Marie)
1868-1955 . . . . **TCLC 2, 10**
See also CA 104

Clavell, James (duMaresq)
1925- . . . . **CLC 6, 25**
See also CA 25-28R; CANR 26; MTCW

Cleaver, (Leroy) Eldridge
1935- . . . . **CLC 30; BLC**
See also BW 1; CA 21-24R; CANR 16

Cleese, John (Marwood) 1939- . . . . . **CLC 21**
See also Monty Python
See also CA 112; 116; CANR 35; MTCW

Cleishbotham, Jebediah
See Scott, Walter

Copeland, Stewart (Armstrong)
1952- .... CLC 26
See also Police, The

Coppard, A(lfred) E(dgar)
1878-1957 .... TCLC 5
See also CA 114; YABC 1

Coppee, Francois 1842-1908 ...... TCLC 25

Coppola, Francis Ford 1939-....... CLC 16
See also CA 77-80; CANR 40; DLB 44

Corbiere, Tristan 1845-1875 ..... NCLC 43

Corcoran, Barbara 1911- .... CLC 17
See also CA 21-24R; CAAS 2; CANR 11,
28; DLB 52; JRDA; SATA 3, 77

Cordelier, Maurice
See Giraudoux, (Hippolyte) Jean

Corelli, Marie 1855-1924........ TCLC 51
See also Mackay, Mary
See also DLB 34

Corman, Cid...................... CLC 9
See also Corman, Sidney
See also CAAS 2; DLB 5

Corman, Sidney 1924-
See Corman, Cid
See also CA 85-88; CANR 44

Cormier, Robert (Edmund)
1925- .... CLC 12, 30; DA
See also AAYA 3; CA 1-4R; CANR 5, 23;
CDALB 1968-1988; CLR 12; DLB 52;
JRDA; MAICYA; MTCW; SATA 10, 45

Corn, Alfred (DeWitt III) 1943-.... CLC 33
See also CA 104; CANR 44; DLB 120;
DLBY 80

Cornwell, David (John Moore)
1931- .... CLC 9, 15
See also le Carre, John
See also CA 5-8R; CANR 13, 33; MTCW

Corrigan, Kevin................... CLC 55

Corso, (Nunzio) Gregory 1930-... CLC 1, 11
See also CA 5-8R; CANR 41; DLB 5, 16;
MTCW

Cortazar, Julio
1914-1984 ...... CLC 2, 3, 5, 10, 13, 15,
33, 34; HLC; SSC 7
See also CA 21-24R; CANR 12, 32;
DLB 113; HW; MTCW

Corwin, Cecil
See Kornbluth, C(yril) M.

Cosic, Dobrica 1921- .... CLC 14
See also CA 122; 138

Costain, Thomas B(ertram)
1885-1965 .... CLC 30
See also CA 5-8R; 25-28R; DLB 9

Costantini, Humberto
1924(?)-1987 .... CLC 49
See also CA 131; 122; HW

Costello, Elvis 1955-.............. CLC 21

Cotter, Joseph Seamon Sr.
1861-1949 .... TCLC 28; BLC
See also BW 1; CA 124; DLB 50

Couch, Arthur Thomas Quiller
See Quiller-Couch, Arthur Thomas

Coulton, James
See Hansen, Joseph

Couperus, Louis (Marie Anne)
1863-1923 .... TCLC 15
See also CA 115

Court, Wesli
See Turco, Lewis (Putnam)

Courtenay, Bryce 1933-........... CLC 59
See also CA 138

Courtney, Robert
See Ellison, Harlan

Cousteau, Jacques-Yves 1910-...... CLC 30
See also CA 65-68; CANR 15; MTCW;
SATA 38

Coward, Noel (Peirce)
1899-1973 .... CLC 1, 9, 29, 51
See also AITN 1; CA 17-18; 41-44R;
CANR 35; CAP 2; CDBLB 1914-1945;
DLB 10; MTCW

Cowley, Malcolm 1898-1989 .... CLC 39
See also CA 5-8R; 128; CANR 3; DLB 4,
48; DLBY 81, 89; MTCW

Cowper, William 1731-1800....... NCLC 8
See also DLB 104, 109

Cox, William Trevor 1928- ... CLC 9, 14, 71
See also Trevor, William
See also CA 9-12R; CANR 4, 37; DLB 14;
MTCW

Cozzens, James Gould
1903-1978 .... CLC 1, 4, 11
See also CA 9-12R; 81-84; CANR 19;
CDALB 1941-1968; DLB 9; DLBD 2;
DLBY 84; MTCW

Crabbe, George 1754-1832....... NCLC 26
See also DLB 93

Craig, A. A.
See Anderson, Poul (William)

Craik, Dinah Maria (Mulock)
1826-1887 .... NCLC 38
See also DLB 35; MAICYA; SATA 34

Cram, Ralph Adams 1863-1942.... TCLC 45

Crane, (Harold) Hart
1899-1932 .... TCLC 2, 5; DA; PC 3;
WLC
See also CA 104; 127; CDALB 1917-1929;
DLB 4, 48; MTCW

Crane, R(onald) S(almon)
1886-1967 .... CLC 27
See also CA 85-88; DLB 63

Crane, Stephen (Townley)
1871-1900 .... TCLC 11, 17, 32; DA;
SSC 7; WLC
See also CA 109; 140; CDALB 1865-1917;
DLB 12, 54, 78; YABC 2

Crase, Douglas 1944-............. CLC 58
See also CA 106

Crashaw, Richard 1612(?)-1649...... LC 24
See also DLB 126

Craven, Margaret 1901-1980....... CLC 17
See also CA 103

Crawford, F(rancis) Marion
1854-1909 .... TCLC 10
See also CA 107; DLB 71

Crawford, Isabella Valancy
1850-1887 .... NCLC 12
See also DLB 92

Crayon, Geoffrey
See Irving, Washington

Creasey, John 1908-1973.......... CLC 11
See also CA 5-8R; 41-44R; CANR 8;
DLB 77; MTCW

Crebillon, Claude Prosper Jolyot de (fils)
1707-1777 .... LC 1

Credo
See Creasey, John

Creeley, Robert (White)
1926- ..... CLC 1, 2, 4, 8, 11, 15, 36, 78
See also CA 1-4R; CAAS 10; CANR 23, 43;
DLB 5, 16; MTCW

Crews, Harry (Eugene)
1935- .... CLC 6, 23, 49
See also AITN 1; CA 25-28R; CANR 20;
DLB 6, 143; MTCW

Crichton, (John) Michael
1942-...................... CLC 2, 6, 54
See also AAYA 10; AITN 2; CA 25-28R;
CANR 13, 40; DLBY 81; JRDA;
MTCW; SATA 9

Crispin, Edmund .... CLC 22
See also Montgomery, (Robert) Bruce
See also DLB 87

Cristofer, Michael 1945(?)- .... CLC 28
See also CA 110; DLB 7

Croce, Benedetto 1866-1952 ...... TCLC 37
See also CA 120

Crockett, David 1786-1836 .... NCLC 8
See also DLB 3, 11

Crockett, Davy
See Crockett, David

Crofts, Freeman Wills
1879-1957 .... TCLC 55
See also CA 115; DLB 77

Croker, John Wilson 1780-1857 .. NCLC 10
See also DLB 110

Crommelynck, Fernand 1885-1970 .. CLC 75
See also CA 89-92

Cronin, A(rchibald) J(oseph)
1896-1981 .... CLC 32
See also CA 1-4R; 102; CANR 5; SATA 25,
47

Cross, Amanda
See Heilbrun, Carolyn G(old)

Crothers, Rachel 1878(?)-1958..... TCLC 19
See also CA 113; DLB 7

Croves, Hal
See Traven, B.

Crowfield, Christopher
See Stowe, Harriet (Elizabeth) Beecher

Crowley, Aleister.................. TCLC 7
See also Crowley, Edward Alexander

Crowley, Edward Alexander 1875-1947
See Crowley, Aleister
See also CA 104

Crowley, John 1942-.............. CLC 57
See also CA 61-64; CANR 43; DLBY 82;
SATA 65

Crud
See Crumb, R(obert)

Crumarums
See Crumb, R(obert)

Crumb, R(obert) 1943- .... **CLC 17**
See also CA 106

Crumbum
See Crumb, R(obert)

Crumski
See Crumb, R(obert)

Crum the Bum
See Crumb, R(obert)

Crunk
See Crumb, R(obert)

Crustt
See Crumb, R(obert)

Cryer, Gretchen (Kiger) 1935- ...... **CLC 21**
See also CA 114; 123

Csath, Geza 1887-1919 .... **TCLC 13**
See also CA 111

Cudlip, David 1933- .... **CLC 34**

Cullen, Countee
1903-1946 ...... **TCLC 4, 37; BLC; DA**
See also BW 1; CA 108; 124;
CDALB 1917-1929; DLB 4, 48, 51;
MTCW; SATA 18

Cum, R.
See Crumb, R(obert)

Cummings, Bruce F(rederick) 1889-1919
See Barbellion, W. N. P.
See also CA 123

Cummings, E(dward) E(stlin)
1894-1962 ...... **CLC 1, 3, 8, 12, 15, 68;**
DA; PC 5; WLC 2
See also CA 73-76; CANR 31;
CDALB 1929-1941; DLB 4, 48; MTCW

Cunha, Euclides (Rodrigues Pimenta) da
1866-1909 .... **TCLC 24**
See also CA 123

Cunningham, E. V.
See Fast, Howard (Melvin)

Cunningham, J(ames) V(incent)
1911-1985 .... **CLC 3, 31**
See also CA 1-4R; 115; CANR 1; DLB 5

Cunningham, Julia (Woolfolk)
1916- .... **CLC 12**
See also CA 9-12R; CANR 4, 19, 36;
JRDA; MAICYA; SAAS 2; SATA 1, 26

Cunningham, Michael 1952- .... **CLC 34**
See also CA 136

Cunninghame Graham, R(obert) B(ontine)
1852-1936 .... **TCLC 19**
See also Graham, R(obert) B(ontine)
Cunninghame
See also CA 119; DLB 98

Currie, Ellen 19(?)- .... **CLC 44**

Curtin, Philip
See Lowndes, Marie Adelaide (Belloc)

Curtis, Price
See Ellison, Harlan

Cutrate, Joe
See Spiegelman, Art

Czaczkes, Shmuel Yosef
See Agnon, S(hmuel) Y(osef Halevi)

D. P.
See Wells, H(erbert) G(eorge)

Dabrowska, Maria (Szumska)
1889-1965 .... **CLC 15**
See also CA 106

Dabydeen, David 1955- .... **CLC 34**
See also BW 1; CA 125

Dacey, Philip 1939- .... **CLC 51**
See also CA 37-40R; CAAS 17; CANR 14,
32; DLB 105

Dagerman, Stig (Halvard)
1923-1954 .... **TCLC 17**
See also CA 117

Dahl, Roald 1916-1990 ..... **CLC 1, 6, 18, 79**
See also CA 1-4R; 133; CANR 6, 32, 37;
CLR 1, 7; DLB 139; JRDA; MAICYA;
MTCW; SATA 1, 26, 73; SATA-Obit 65

Dahlberg, Edward 1900-1977 ... **CLC 1, 7, 14**
See also CA 9-12R; 69-72; CANR 31;
DLB 48; MTCW

Dale, Colin .... **TCLC 18**
See also Lawrence, T(homas) E(dward)

Dale, George E.
See Asimov, Isaac

Daly, Elizabeth 1878-1967 .... **CLC 52**
See also CA 23-24; 25-28R; CAP 2

Daly, Maureen 1921- .... **CLC 17**
See also AAYA 5; CANR 37; JRDA;
MAICYA; SAAS 1; SATA 2

Damas, Leon-Gontran 1912-1978 ... **CLC 84**
See also BW 1; CA 125; 73-76

Daniel, Samuel 1562(?)-1619 .... **LC 24**
See also DLB 62

Daniels, Brett
See Adler, Renata

Dannay, Frederic 1905-1982 .... **CLC 11**
See also Queen, Ellery
See also CA 1-4R; 107; CANR 1, 39;
DLB 137; MTCW

D'Annunzio, Gabriele
1863-1938 .... **TCLC 6, 40**
See also CA 104

d'Antibes, Germain
See Simenon, Georges (Jacques Christian)

Danvers, Dennis 1947- .... **CLC 70**

Danziger, Paula 1944- .... **CLC 21**
See also AAYA 4; CA 112; 115; CANR 37;
CLR 20; JRDA; MAICYA; SATA 30,
36, 63

Dario, Ruben 1867-1916 .... **TCLC 4; HLC**
See also CA 131; HW; MTCW

Darley, George 1795-1846 .... **NCLC 2**
See also DLB 96

Daryush, Elizabeth 1887-1977 .... **CLC 6, 19**
See also CA 49-52; CANR 3; DLB 20

Daudet, (Louis Marie) Alphonse
1840-1897 .... **NCLC 1**
See also DLB 123

Daumal, Rene 1908-1944 .... **TCLC 14**
See also CA 114

Davenport, Guy (Mattison, Jr.)
1927- .... **CLC 6, 14, 38; SSC 16**
See also CA 33-36R; CANR 23; DLB 130

Davidson, Avram 1923-
See Queen, Ellery
See also CA 101; CANR 26; DLB 8

Davidson, Donald (Grady)
1893-1968 .... **CLC 2, 13, 19**
See also CA 5-8R; 25-28R; CANR 4;
DLB 45

Davidson, Hugh
See Hamilton, Edmond

Davidson, John 1857-1909 .... **TCLC 24**
See also CA 118; DLB 19

Davidson, Sara 1943- .... **CLC 9**
See also CA 81-84; CANR 44

Davie, Donald (Alfred)
1922- .... **CLC 5, 8, 10, 31**
See also CA 1-4R; CAAS 3; CANR 1, 44;
DLB 27; MTCW

Davies, Ray(mond Douglas) 1944- .. **CLC 21**
See also CA 116

Davies, Rhys 1903-1978 .... **CLC 23**
See also CA 9-12R; 81-84; CANR 4;
DLB 139

Davies, (William) Robertson
1913- ..... **CLC 2, 7, 13, 25, 42, 75; DA;**
WLC
See also BEST 89:2; CA 33-36R; CANR 17,
42; DLB 68; MTCW

Davies, W(illiam) H(enry)
1871-1940 .... **TCLC 5**
See also CA 104; DLB 19

Davies, Walter C.
See Kornbluth, C(yril) M.

Davis, Angela (Yvonne) 1944- ...... **CLC 77**
See also BW 2; CA 57-60; CANR 10

Davis, B. Lynch
See Bioy Casares, Adolfo; Borges, Jorge
Luis

Davis, Gordon
See Hunt, E(verette) Howard, Jr.

Davis, Harold Lenoir 1896-1960 .... **CLC 49**
See also CA 89-92; DLB 9

Davis, Rebecca (Blaine) Harding
1831-1910 .... **TCLC 6**
See also CA 104; DLB 74

Davis, Richard Harding
1864-1916 .... **TCLC 24**
See also CA 114; DLB 12, 23, 78, 79

Davison, Frank Dalby 1893-1970 ... **CLC 15**
See also CA 116

Davison, Lawrence H.
See Lawrence, D(avid) H(erbert Richards)

Davison, Peter (Hubert) 1928- ..... **CLC 28**
See also CA 9-12R; CAAS 4; CANR 3, 43;
DLB 5

Davys, Mary 1674-1732 .... **LC 1**
See also DLB 39

Dawson, Fielding 1930- .... **CLC 6**
See also CA 85-88; DLB 130

Dawson, Peter
See Faust, Frederick (Schiller)

Day, Clarence (Shepard, Jr.)
1874-1935 .... **TCLC 25**
See also CA 108; DLB 11

Day, Thomas 1748-1789 .... **LC 1**
See also DLB 39; YABC 1

Day Lewis, C(ecil)
1904-1972 .... CLC **1, 6, 10**
See also Blake, Nicholas
See also CA 13-16; 33-36R; CANR 34;
CAP 1; DLB 15, 20; MTCW

Dazai, Osamu .... TCLC **11**
See also Tsushima, Shuji

de Andrade, Carlos Drummond
See Drummond de Andrade, Carlos

Deane, Norman
See Creasey, John

de Beauvoir, Simone (Lucie Ernestine Marie
Bertrand)
See Beauvoir, Simone (Lucie Ernestine
Marie Bertrand) de

de Brissac, Malcolm
See Dickinson, Peter (Malcolm)

de Chardin, Pierre Teilhard
See Teilhard de Chardin, (Marie Joseph)
Pierre

Dee, John 1527-1608 .... LC **20**

Deer, Sandra 1940-............... CLC **45**

De Ferrari, Gabriella .... CLC **65**

Defoe, Daniel
1660(?)-1731 .... LC **1; DA; WLC**
See also CDBLB 1660-1789; DLB 39, 95,
101; JRDA; MAICYA; SATA 22

de Gourmont, Remy
See Gourmont, Remy de

de Hartog, Jan 1914-............. CLC **19**
See also CA 1-4R; CANR 1

de Hostos, E. M.
See Hostos (y Bonilla), Eugenio Maria de

de Hostos, Eugenio M.
See Hostos (y Bonilla), Eugenio Maria de

Deighton, Len .... CLC **4, 7, 22, 46**
See also Deighton, Leonard Cyril
See also AAYA 6; BEST 89:2;
CDBLB 1960 to Present; DLB 87

Deighton, Leonard Cyril 1929-
See Deighton, Len
See also CA 9-12R; CANR 19, 33; MTCW

Dekker, Thomas 1572(?)-1632....... LC **22**
See also CDBLB Before 1660; DLB 62

de la Mare, Walter (John)
1873-1956 .. TCLC **4, 53; SSC 14; WLC**
See also CDBLB 1914-1945; CLR 23;
DLB 19; SATA 16

Delaney, Franey
See O'Hara, John (Henry)

Delaney, Shelagh 1939- .... CLC **29**
See also CA 17-20R; CANR 30;
CDBLB 1960 to Present; DLB 13;
MTCW

Delany, Mary (Granville Pendarves)
1700-1788 .... LC **12**

Delany, Samuel R(ay, Jr.)
1942- .... CLC **8, 14, 38; BLC**
See also BW 2; CA 81-84; CANR 27, 43;
DLB 8, 33; MTCW

De La Ramee, (Marie) Louise 1839-1908
See Ouida
See also SATA 20

de la Roche, Mazo 1879-1961 ...... CLC **14**
See also CA 85-88; CANR 30; DLB 68;
SATA 64

Delbanco, Nicholas (Franklin)
1942- .... CLC **6, 13**
See also CA 17-20R; CAAS 2; CANR 29;
DLB 6

del Castillo, Michel 1933- .... CLC **38**
See also CA 109

Deledda, Grazia (Cosima)
1875(?)-1936 .... TCLC **23**
See also CA 123

Delibes, Miguel .... CLC **8, 18**
See also Delibes Setien, Miguel

Delibes Setien, Miguel 1920-
See Delibes, Miguel
See also CA 45-48; CANR 1, 32; HW;
MTCW

DeLillo, Don
1936- ..... CLC **8, 10, 13, 27, 39, 54, 76**
See also BEST 89:1; CA 81-84; CANR 21;
DLB 6; MTCW

de Lisser, H. G.
See De Lisser, Herbert George
See also DLB 117

De Lisser, Herbert George
1878-1944 .... TCLC **12**
See also de Lisser, H. G.
See also BW 2; CA 109

Deloria, Vine (Victor), Jr. 1933-.... CLC **21**
See also CA 53-56; CANR 5, 20; MTCW;
SATA 21

Del Vecchio, John M(ichael)
1947- .... CLC **29**
See also CA 110; DLBD 9

de Man, Paul (Adolph Michel)
1919-1983 .... CLC **55**
See also CA 128; 111; DLB 67; MTCW

De Marinis, Rick 1934-........... CLC **54**
See also CA 57-60; CANR 9, 25

Demby, William 1922-....... CLC **53; BLC**
See also BW 1; CA 81-84; DLB 33

Demijohn, Thom
See Disch, Thomas M(ichael)

de Montherlant, Henry (Milon)
See Montherlant, Henry (Milon) de

Demosthenes 384B.C.-322B.C. .... CMLC **13**

de Natale, Francine
See Malzberg, Barry N(athaniel)

Denby, Edwin (Orr) 1903-1983..... CLC **48**
See also CA 138; 110

Denis, Julio
See Cortazar, Julio

Denmark, Harrison
See Zelazny, Roger (Joseph)

Dennis, John 1658-1734........... LC **11**
See also DLB 101

Dennis, Nigel (Forbes) 1912-1989.... CLC **8**
See also CA 25-28R; 129; DLB 13, 15;
MTCW

De Palma, Brian (Russell) 1940-.... CLC **20**
See also CA 109

De Quincey, Thomas 1785-1859 ... NCLC **4**
See also CDBLB 1789-1832; DLB 110; 144

Deren, Eleanora 1908(?)-1961
See Deren, Maya
See also CA 111

Deren, Maya .... CLC **16**
See also Deren, Eleanora

Derleth, August (William)
1909-1971 .... CLC **31**
See also CA 1-4R; 29-32R; CANR 4;
DLB 9; SATA 5

de Routisie, Albert
See Aragon, Louis

Derrida, Jacques 1930-............ CLC **24**
See also CA 124; 127

Derry Down Derry
See Lear, Edward

Dersonnes, Jacques
See Simenon, Georges (Jacques Christian)

Desai, Anita 1937-............ CLC **19, 37**
See also CA 81-84; CANR 33; MTCW;
SATA 63

de Saint-Luc, Jean
See Glassco, John

de Saint Roman, Arnaud
See Aragon, Louis

Descartes, Rene 1596-1650 .... LC **20**

De Sica, Vittorio 1901(?)-1974 ..... CLC **20**
See also CA 117

Desnos, Robert 1900-1945........ TCLC **22**
See also CA 121

Destouches, Louis-Ferdinand
1894-1961 .... CLC **9, 15**
See also Celine, Louis-Ferdinand
See also CA 85-88; CANR 28; MTCW

Deutsch, Babette 1895-1982 .... CLC **18**
See also CA 1-4R; 108; CANR 4; DLB 45;
SATA 1, 33

Devenant, William 1606-1649 ...... LC **13**

Devkota, Laxmiprasad
1909-1959 .... TCLC **23**
See also CA 123

De Voto, Bernard (Augustine)
1897-1955 .... TCLC **29**
See also CA 113; DLB 9

De Vries, Peter
1910-1993 .... CLC **1, 2, 3, 7, 10, 28, 46**
See also CA 17-20R; 142; CANR 41;
DLB 6; DLBY 82; MTCW

Dexter, Martin
See Faust, Frederick (Schiller)

Dexter, Pete 1943-............ CLC **34, 55**
See also BEST 89:2; CA 127; 131; MTCW

Diamano, Silmang
See Senghor, Leopold Sedar

Diamond, Neil 1941- .... CLC **30**
See also CA 108

di Bassetto, Corno
See Shaw, George Bernard

Dick, Philip K(indred)
1928-1982 .... CLC **10, 30, 72**
See also CA 49-52; 106; CANR 2, 16;
DLB 8; MTCW

Dickens, Charles (John Huffam)
1812-1870 . . . . . **NCLC 3, 8, 18, 26; DA;**
WLC
See also CDBLB 1832-1890; DLB 21, 55,
70; JRDA; MAICYA; SATA 15

Dickey, James (Lafayette)
1923- . . . . **CLC 1, 2, 4, 7, 10, 15, 47**
See also AITN 1, 2; CA 9-12R; CABS 2;
CANR 10; CDALB 1968-1988; DLB 5;
DLBD 7; DLBY 82, 93; MTCW

Dickey, William 1928- . . . . **CLC 3, 28**
See also CA 9-12R; CANR 24; DLB 5

Dickinson, Charles 1951- . . . . **CLC 49**
See also CA 128

Dickinson, Emily (Elizabeth)
1830-1886 . . **NCLC 21; DA; PC 1; WLC**
See also CDALB 1865-1917; DLB 1;
SATA 29

Dickinson, Peter (Malcolm)
1927- . . . . **CLC 12, 35**
See also AAYA 9; CA 41-44R; CANR 31;
CLR 29; DLB 87; JRDA; MAICYA;
SATA 5, 62

Dickson, Carr
See Carr, John Dickson

Dickson, Carter
See Carr, John Dickson

Didion, Joan 1934- . . . . . **CLC 1, 3, 8, 14, 32**
See also AITN 1; CA 5-8R; CANR 14;
CDALB 1968-1988; DLB 2; DLBY 81,
86; MTCW

Dietrich, Robert
See Hunt, E(verette) Howard, Jr.

Dillard, Annie 1945- . . . . **CLC 9, 60**
See also AAYA 6; CA 49-52; CANR 3, 43;
DLBY 80; MTCW; SATA 10

Dillard, R(ichard) H(enry) W(ilde)
1937- . . . . **CLC 5**
See also CA 21-24R; CAAS 7; CANR 10;
DLB 5

Dillon, Eilis 1920- . . . . **CLC 17**
See also CA 9-12R; CAAS 3; CANR 4, 38;
CLR 26; MAICYA; SATA 2, 74

Dimont, Penelope
See Mortimer, Penelope (Ruth)

Dinesen, Isak . . . . **CLC 10, 29; SSC 7**
See also Blixen, Karen (Christentze
Dinesen)

Ding Ling . . . . **CLC 68**
See also Chiang Pin-chin

Disch, Thomas M(ichael) 1940- . . . **CLC 7, 36**
See also CA 21-24R; CAAS 4; CANR 17,
36; CLR 18; DLB 8; MAICYA; MTCW;
SAAS 15; SATA 54

Disch, Tom
See Disch, Thomas M(ichael)

d'Isly, Georges
See Simenon, Georges (Jacques Christian)

Disraeli, Benjamin 1804-1881 . . **NCLC 2, 39**
See also DLB 21, 55

Ditcum, Steve
See Crumb, R(obert)

Dixon, Paige
See Corcoran, Barbara

Dixon, Stephen 1936- . . . . . **CLC 52; SSC 16**
See also CA 89-92; CANR 17, 40; DLB 130

Dobell, Sydney Thompson
1824-1874 . . . . **NCLC 43**
See also DLB 32

Doblin, Alfred . . . . **TCLC 13**
See also Doeblin, Alfred

Dobrolyubov, Nikolai Alexandrovich
1836-1861 . . . . **NCLC 5**

Dobyns, Stephen 1941- . . . . **CLC 37**
See also CA 45-48; CANR 2, 18

Doctorow, E(dgar) L(aurence)
1931- . . . . . **CLC 6, 11, 15, 18, 37, 44, 65**
See also AITN 2; BEST 89·3; CA 45-48;
CANR 2, 33; CDALB 1968-1988; DLB 2,
28; DLBY 80; MTCW

Dodgson, Charles Lutwidge 1832-1898
See Carroll, Lewis
See also CLR 2; DA; MAICYA; YABC 2

Dodson, Owen (Vincent)
1914-1983 . . . . **CLC 79; BLC**
See also BW 1; CA 65-68; 110; CANR 24;
DLB 76

Doeblin, Alfred 1878-1957 . . . . **TCLC 13**
See also Doblin, Alfred
See also CA 110; 141; DLB 66

Doerr, Harriet 1910- . . . . **CLC 34**
See also CA 117; 122

Domecq, H(onorio) Bustos
See Bioy Casares, Adolfo; Borges, Jorge
Luis

Domini, Rey
See Lorde, Audre (Geraldine)

Dominique
See Proust, (Valentin-Louis-George-Eugene-)
Marcel

Don, A
See Stephen, Leslie

Donaldson, Stephen R. 1947- . . . . **CLC 46**
See also CA 89-92; CANR 13

Donleavy, J(ames) P(atrick)
1926- . . . . **CLC 1, 4, 6, 10, 45**
See also AITN 2; CA 9-12R; CANR 24;
DLB 6; MTCW

Donne, John
1572-1631 . . . . **LC 10, 24; DA; PC 1**
See also CDBLB Before 1660; DLB 121

Donnell, David 1939(?)- . . . . **CLC 34**

Donoso (Yanez), Jose
1924- . . . . **CLC 4, 8, 11, 32; HLC**
See also CA 81-84; CANR 32; DLB 113;
HW; MTCW

Donovan, John 1928-1992 . . . . **CLC 35**
See also CA 97-100; 137; CLR 3;
MAICYA; SATA 29

Don Roberto
See Cunninghame Graham, R(obert)
B(ontine)

Doolittle, Hilda
1886-1961 . . . . . **CLC 3, 8, 14, 31, 34, 73;**
DA; PC 5; WLC
See also H. D.
See also CA 97-100; CANR 35; DLB 4, 45;
MTCW

Dorfman, Ariel 1942- . . . . **CLC 48, 77; HLC**
See also CA 124; 130; HW

Dorn, Edward (Merton) 1929- . . . **CLC 10, 18**
See also CA 93-96; CANR 42; DLB 5

Dorsan, Luc
See Simenon, Georges (Jacques Christian)

Dorsange, Jean
See Simenon, Georges (Jacques Christian)

Dos Passos, John (Roderigo)
1896-1970 . . . . . . **CLC 1, 4, 8, 11, 15, 25,**
34, 82; DA; WLC
See also CA 1-4R; 29-32R; CANR 3;
CDALB 1929-1941; DLB 4, 9; DLBD 1;
MTCW

Dossage, Jean
See Simenon, Georges (Jacques Christian)

Dostoevsky, Fedor Mikhailovich
1821-1881 . . . . . . **NCLC 2, 7, 21, 33, 43;**
DA; SSC 2; WLC

Doughty, Charles M(ontagu)
1843-1926 . . . . **TCLC 27**
See also CA 115; DLB 19, 57

Douglas, Ellen
See Haxton, Josephine Ayres

Douglas, Gavin 1475(?)-1522 . . . . **LC 20**

Douglas, Keith 1920-1944 . . . . **TCLC 40**
See also DLB 27

Douglas, Leonard
See Bradbury, Ray (Douglas)

Douglas, Michael
See Crichton, (John) Michael

Douglass, Frederick
1817(?)-1895 . . . . **NCLC 7; BLC; DA;**
WLC
See also CDALB 1640-1865; DLB 1, 43, 50,
79; SATA 29

Dourado, (Waldomiro Freitas) Autran
1926- . . . . **CLC 23, 60**
See also CA 25-28R; CANR 34

Dourado, Waldomiro Autran
See Dourado, (Waldomiro Freitas) Autran

Dove, Rita (Frances)
1952- . . . . **CLC 50, 81; PC 6**
See also BW 2; CA 109; CAAS 19;
CANR 27, 42; DLB 120

Dowell, Coleman 1925-1985 . . . . **CLC 60**
See also CA 25-28R; 117; CANR 10;
DLB 130

Dowson, Ernest Christopher
1867-1900 . . . . **TCLC 4**
See also CA 105; DLB 19, 135

Doyle, A. Conan
See Doyle, Arthur Conan

Doyle, Arthur Conan
1859-1930 . . . . **TCLC 7; DA; SSC 12;**
WLC
See also CA 104; 122; CDBLB 1890-1914;
DLB 18, 70; MTCW; SATA 24

Doyle, Conan 1859-1930
See Doyle, Arthur Conan

Doyle, John
See Graves, Robert (von Ranke)

Doyle, Roddy 1958(?)- . . . . **CLC 81**
See also CA 143

Doyle, Sir A. Conan
See Doyle, Arthur Conan

Doyle, Sir Arthur Conan
See Doyle, Arthur Conan

Dr. A
See Asimov, Isaac; Silverstein, Alvin

Drabble, Margaret
1939- . . . . **CLC 2, 3, 5, 8, 10, 22, 53**
See also CA 13-16R; CANR 18, 35;
CDBLB 1960 to Present; DLB 14;
MTCW; SATA 48

Drapier, M. B.
See Swift, Jonathan

Drayham, James
See Mencken, H(enry) L(ouis)

Drayton, Michael 1563-1631 . . . . **LC 8**

Dreadstone, Carl
See Campbell, (John) Ramsey

Dreiser, Theodore (Herman Albert)
1871-1945 . . . . **TCLC 10, 18, 35; DA;**
WLC
See also CA 106; 132; CDALB 1865-1917;
DLB 9, 12, 102, 137; DLBD 1; MTCW

Drexler, Rosalyn 1926- . . . . **CLC 2, 6**
See also CA 81-84

Dreyer, Carl Theodor 1889-1968 . . . . **CLC 16**
See also CA 116

Drieu la Rochelle, Pierre(-Eugene)
1893-1945 . . . . **TCLC 21**
See also CA 117; DLB 72

Drop Shot
See Cable, George Washington

Droste-Hulshoff, Annette Freiin von
1797-1848 . . . . **NCLC 3**
See also DLB 133

Drummond, Walter
See Silverberg, Robert

Drummond, William Henry
1854-1907 . . . . **TCLC 25**
See also DLB 92

Drummond de Andrade, Carlos
1902-1987 . . . . **CLC 18**
See also Andrade, Carlos Drummond de
See also CA 132; 123

Drury, Allen (Stuart) 1918- . . . . **CLC 37**
See also CA 57-60; CANR 18

Dryden, John
1631-1700 . . . **LC 3, 21; DA; DC 3; WLC**
See also CDBLB 1660-1789; DLB 80, 101,
131

Duberman, Martin 1930- . . . . **CLC 8**
See also CA 1-4R; CANR 2

Dubie, Norman (Evans) 1945- . . . . . . **CLC 36**
See also CA 69-72; CANR 12; DLB 120

Du Bois, W(illiam) E(dward) B(urghardt)
1868-1963 . . . . . . **CLC 1, 2, 13, 64; BLC;**
DA; WLC
See also BW 1; CA 85-88; CANR 34;
CDALB 1865-1917; DLB 47, 50, 91;
MTCW; SATA 42

Dubus, Andre 1936- . . . **CLC 13, 36; SSC 15**
See also CA 21-24R; CANR 17; DLB 130

Duca Minimo
See D'Annunzio, Gabriele

Ducharme, Rejean 1941- . . . . **CLC 74**
See also DLB 60

Duclos, Charles Pinot 1704-1772 . . . . . **LC 1**

Dudek, Louis 1918- . . . . **CLC 11, 19**
See also CA 45-48; CAAS 14; CANR 1;
DLB 88

Duerrenmatt, Friedrich
. . . . **CLC 1, 4, 8, 11, 15, 43**
See also Duerrenmatt, Friedrich
See also DLB 69, 124

Duerrenmatt, Friedrich
1921-1990 . . . . . . **CLC 1, 4, 8, 11, 15, 43**
See also Duerrenmatt, Friedrich
See also CA 17-20R; CANR 33; DLB 69,
124; MTCW

Duffy, Bruce (?)- . . . . **CLC 50**

Duffy, Maureen 1933- . . . . **CLC 37**
See also CA 25-28R; CANR 33; DLB 14;
MTCW

Dugan, Alan 1923- . . . . **CLC 2, 6**
See also CA 81-84; DLB 5

du Gard, Roger Martin
See Martin du Gard, Roger

Duhamel, Georges 1884-1966 . . . . **CLC 8**
See also CA 81-84; 25-28R; CANR 35;
DLB 65; MTCW

Dujardin, Edouard (Emile Louis)
1861-1949 . . . . **TCLC 13**
See also CA 109; DLB 123

Dumas, Alexandre (Davy de la Pailleterie)
1802-1870 . . . . **NCLC 11; DA; WLC**
See also DLB 119; SATA 18

Dumas, Alexandre
1824-1895 . . . . **NCLC 9; DC 1**

Dumas, Claudine
See Malzberg, Barry N(athaniel)

Dumas, Henry L. 1934-1968 . . . . . **CLC 6, 62**
See also BW 1; CA 85-88; DLB 41

du Maurier, Daphne
1907-1989 . . . . **CLC 6, 11, 59**
See also CA 5-8R; 128; CANR 6; MTCW;
SATA 27, 60

Dunbar, Paul Laurence
1872-1906 . . . . . . **TCLC 2, 12; BLC; DA;**
PC 5; SSC 8; WLC
See also BW 1; CA 104; 124;
CDALB 1865-1917; DLB 50, 54, 78;
SATA 34

Dunbar, William 1460(?)-1530(?) . . . . **LC 20**

Duncan, Lois 1934- . . . . **CLC 26**
See also AAYA 4; CA 1-4R; CANR 2, 23,
36; CLR 29; JRDA; MAICYA; SAAS 2;
SATA 1, 36, 75

Duncan, Robert (Edward)
1919-1988 . . . . **CLC 1, 2, 4, 7, 15, 41, 55;**
PC 2
See also CA 9-12R; 124; CANR 28; DLB 5,
16; MTCW

Dunlap, William 1766-1839 . . . . **NCLC 2**
See also DLB 30, 37, 59

Dunn, Douglas (Eaglesham)
1942- . . . . **CLC 6, 40**
See also CA 45-48; CANR 2, 33; DLB 40;
MTCW

Dunn, Katherine (Karen) 1945- . . . . . **CLC 71**
See also CA 33-36R

Dunn, Stephen 1939- . . . . **CLC 36**
See also CA 33-36R; CANR 12; DLB 105

Dunne, Finley Peter 1867-1936 . . . . **TCLC 28**
See also CA 108; DLB 11, 23

Dunne, John Gregory 1932- . . . . **CLC 28**
See also CA 25-28R; CANR 14; DLBY 80

Dunsany, Edward John Moreton Drax
Plunkett 1878-1957
See Dunsany, Lord
See also CA 104; DLB 10

Dunsany, Lord . . . . **TCLC 2**
See also Dunsany, Edward John Moreton
Drax Plunkett
See also DLB 77

du Perry, Jean
See Simenon, Georges (Jacques Christian)

Durang, Christopher (Ferdinand)
1949- . . . . **CLC 27, 38**
See also CA 105

Duras, Marguerite
1914- . . . . . . **CLC 3, 6, 11, 20, 34, 40, 68**
See also CA 25-28R; DLB 83; MTCW

Durban, (Rosa) Pam 1947- . . . . **CLC 39**
See also CA 123

Durcan, Paul 1944- . . . . **CLC 43, 70**
See also CA 134

Durkheim, Emile 1858-1917 . . . . . . **TCLC 55**

Durrell, Lawrence (George)
1912-1990 . . . . **CLC 1, 4, 6, 8, 13, 27, 41**
See also CA 9-12R; 132; CANR 40;
CDBLB 1945-1960; DLB 15, 27;
DLBY 90; MTCW

Dutt, Toru 1856-1877 . . . . **NCLC 29**

Dwight, Timothy 1752-1817 . . . . . . **NCLC 13**
See also DLB 37

Dworkin, Andrea 1946- . . . . **CLC 43**
See also CA 77-80; CANR 16, 39; MTCW

Dwyer, Deanna
See Koontz, Dean R(ay)

Dwyer, K. R.
See Koontz, Dean R(ay)

Dylan, Bob 1941- . . . . . . **CLC 3, 4, 6, 12, 77**
See also CA 41-44R; DLB 16

Eagleton, Terence (Francis) 1943-
See Eagleton, Terry
See also CA 57-60; CANR 7, 23; MTCW

Eagleton, Terry . . . . **CLC 63**
See also Eagleton, Terence (Francis)

Early, Jack
See Scoppettone, Sandra

East, Michael
See West, Morris L(anglo)

Eastaway, Edward
See Thomas, (Philip) Edward

Eastlake, William (Derry) 1917- . . . . . **CLC 8**
See also CA 5-8R; CAAS 1; CANR 5;
DLB 6

Eastman, Charles A(lexander)
1858-1939 . . . . **TCLC 55**
See also YABC 1

Eberhart, Richard (Ghormley)
    1904- . . . . CLC 3, 11, 19, 56
  See also CA 1-4R; CANR 2;
    CDALB 1941-1968; DLB 48; MTCW

Eberstadt, Fernanda   1960- . . . . CLC 39
  See also CA 136

Echegaray (y Eizaguirre), Jose (Maria Waldo)
    1832-1916 . . . . TCLC 4
  See also CA 104; CANR 32; HW; MTCW

Echeverria, (Jose) Esteban (Antonino)
    1805-1851 . . . . NCLC 18

Echo
  See Proust, (Valentin-Louis-George-Eugene-)
    Marcel

Eckert, Allan W.   1931- . . . . CLC 17
  See also CA 13-16R; CANR 14, 45;
    SATA 27, 29

Eckhart, Meister   1260(?)-1328(?) . . CMLC 9
  See also DLB 115

Eckmar, F. R.
  See de Hartog, Jan

Eco, Umberto   1932- . . . . CLC 28, 60
  See also BEST 90:1; CA 77-80; CANR 12,
    33; MTCW

Eddison, E(ric) R(ucker)
    1882-1945 . . . . TCLC 15
  See also CA 109

Edel, (Joseph) Leon   1907- . . . . . . CLC 29, 34
  See also CA 1-4R; CANR 1, 22; DLB 103

Eden, Emily   1797-1869 . . . . NCLC 10

Edgar, David   1948- . . . . CLC 42
  See also CA 57-60; CANR 12; DLB 13;
    MTCW

Edgerton, Clyde (Carlyle)   1944- . . . . CLC 39
  See also CA 118; 134

Edgeworth, Maria   1767-1849 . . . . . . NCLC 1
  See also DLB 116; SATA 21

Edmonds, Paul
  See Kuttner, Henry

Edmonds, Walter D(umaux)   1903- . . CLC 35
  See also CA 5-8R; CANR 2; DLB 9;
    MAICYA; SAAS 4; SATA 1, 27

Edmondson, Wallace
  See Ellison, Harlan

Edson, Russell . . . . CLC 13
  See also CA 33-36R

Edwards, G(erald) B(asil)
    1899-1976 . . . . CLC 25
  See also CA 110

Edwards, Gus   1939- . . . . CLC 43
  See also CA 108

Edwards, Jonathan   1703-1758 . . . . LC 7; DA
  See also DLB 24

Efron, Marina Ivanovna Tsvetaeva
  See Tsvetaeva (Efron), Marina (Ivanovna)

Ehle, John (Marsden, Jr.)   1925- . . . . CLC 27
  See also CA 9-12R

Ehrenbourg, Ilya (Grigoryevich)
  See Ehrenburg, Ilya (Grigoryevich)

Ehrenburg, Ilya (Grigoryevich)
    1891-1967 . . . . CLC 18, 34, 62
  See also CA 102; 25-28R

Ehrenburg, Ilyo (Grigoryevich)
  See Ehrenburg, Ilya (Grigoryevich)

Eich, Guenter   1907-1972 . . . . CLC 15
  See also CA 111; 93-96; DLB 69, 124

Eichendorff, Joseph Freiherr von
    1788-1857 . . . . NCLC 8
  See also DLB 90

Eigner, Larry . . . . CLC 9
  See also Eigner, Laurence (Joel)
  See also DLB 5

Eigner, Laurence (Joel)   1927-
  See Eigner, Larry
  See also CA 9-12R; CANR 6

Eiseley, Loren Corey   1907-1977 . . . . . CLC 7
  See also AAYA 5; CA 1-4R; 73-76;
    CANR 6

Eisenstadt, Jill   1963- . . . . CLC 50
  See also CA 140

Eisner, Simon
  See Kornbluth, C(yril) M.

Ekeloef, (Bengt) Gunnar
    1907-1968 . . . . CLC 27
  See also Ekelof, (Bengt) Gunnar
  See also CA 123; 25-28R

Ekelof, (Bengt) Gunnar . . . . CLC 27
  See also Ekeloef, (Bengt) Gunnar

Ekwensi, C. O. D.
  See Ekwensi, Cyprian (Odiatu Duaka)

Ekwensi, Cyprian (Odiatu Duaka)
    1921- . . . . CLC 4; BLC
  See also BW 2; CA 29-32R; CANR 18, 42;
    DLB 117; MTCW; SATA 66

Elaine . . . . TCLC 18
  See also Leverson, Ada

El Crummo
  See Crumb, R(obert)

Elia
  See Lamb, Charles

Eliade, Mircea   1907-1986 . . . . CLC 19
  See also CA 65-68; 119; CANR 30; MTCW

Eliot, A. D.
  See Jewett, (Theodora) Sarah Orne

Eliot, Alice
  See Jewett, (Theodora) Sarah Orne

Eliot, Dan
  See Silverberg, Robert

Eliot, George
    1819-1880 . . . . NCLC 4, 13, 23, 41; DA;
                                          WLC
  See also CDBLB 1832-1890; DLB 21, 35, 55

Eliot, John   1604-1690 . . . . LC 5
  See also DLB 24

Eliot, T(homas) S(tearns)
    1888-1965 . . . . . CLC 1, 2, 3, 6, 9, 10, 13,
      15, 24, 34, 41, 55, 57; DA; PC 5; WLC 2
  See also CA 5-8R; 25-28R; CANR 41;
    CDALB 1929-1941; DLB 7, 10, 45, 63;
    DLBY 88; MTCW

Elizabeth   1866-1941 . . . . TCLC 41

Elkin, Stanley L(awrence)
    1930- . . . CLC 4, 6, 9, 14, 27, 51; SSC 12
  See also CA 9-12R; CANR 8; DLB 2, 28;
    DLBY 80; MTCW

Elledge, Scott . . . . CLC 34

Elliott, Don
  See Silverberg, Robert

Elliott, George P(aul)   1918-1980 . . . . . CLC 2
  See also CA 1-4R; 97-100; CANR 2

Elliott, Janice   1931- . . . . CLC 47
  See also CA 13-16R; CANR 8, 29; DLB 14

Elliott, Sumner Locke   1917-1991 . . . CLC 38
  See also CA 5-8R; 134; CANR 2, 21

Elliott, William
  See Bradbury, Ray (Douglas)

Ellis, A. E. . . . . CLC 7

Ellis, Alice Thomas . . . . CLC 40
  See also Haycraft, Anna

Ellis, Bret Easton   1964- . . . . CLC 39, 71
  See also AAYA 2; CA 118; 123

Ellis, (Henry) Havelock
    1859-1939 . . . . TCLC 14
  See also CA 109

Ellis, Landon
  See Ellison, Harlan

Ellis, Trey   1962- . . . . CLC 55

Ellison, Harlan
    1934- . . . . CLC 1, 13, 42; SSC 14
  See also CA 5-8R; CANR 5; DLB 8;
    MTCW

Ellison, Ralph (Waldo)
    1914- . . . . . . CLC 1, 3, 11, 54; BLC; DA;
                                          WLC
  See also BW 1; CA 9-12R; CANR 24;
    CDALB 1941-1968; DLB 2, 76; MTCW

Ellmann, Lucy (Elizabeth)   1956- . . . . CLC 61
  See also CA 128

Ellmann, Richard (David)
    1918-1987 . . . . CLC 50
  See also BEST 89:2; CA 1-4R; 122;
    CANR 2, 28; DLB 103; DLBY 87;
    MTCW

Elman, Richard   1934- . . . . CLC 19
  See also CA 17-20R; CAAS 3

Elron
  See Hubbard, L(afayette) Ron(ald)

Eluard, Paul . . . . TCLC 7, 41
  See also Grindel, Eugene

Elyot, Sir Thomas   1490(?)-1546 . . . . . LC 11

Elytis, Odysseus   1911- . . . . CLC 15, 49
  See also CA 102; MTCW

Emecheta, (Florence Onye) Buchi
    1944- . . . . CLC 14, 48; BLC
  See also BW 2; CA 81-84; CANR 27;
    DLB 117; MTCW; SATA 66

Emerson, Ralph Waldo
    1803-1882 . . . . . . NCLC 1, 38; DA; WLC
  See also CDALB 1640-1865; DLB 1, 59, 73

Eminescu, Mihail   1850-1889 . . . . . NCLC 33

Empson, William
    1906-1984 . . . . CLC 3, 8, 19, 33, 34
  See also CA 17-20R; 112; CANR 31;
    DLB 20; MTCW

Enchi Fumiko (Ueda)   1905-1986 . . . . CLC 31
  See also CA 129; 121

Ende, Michael (Andreas Helmuth)
    1929- . . . . CLC 31
  See also CA 118; 124; CANR 36; CLR 14;
    DLB 75; MAICYA; SATA 42, 61

Endo, Shusaku   1923- . . . . . CLC 7, 14, 19, 54
  See also CA 29-32R; CANR 21; MTCW

Faust, Irvin 1924-................. **CLC 8**
See also CA 33-36R; CANR 28; DLB 2, 28;
DLBY 80

Fawkes, Guy
See Benchley, Robert (Charles)

Fearing, Kenneth (Flexner)
1902-1961 .... **CLC 51**
See also CA 93-96; DLB 9

Fecamps, Elise
See Creasey, John

Federman, Raymond 1928- ...... **CLC 6, 47**
See also CA 17-20R; CAAS 8; CANR 10,
43; DLBY 80

Federspiel, J(uerg) F. 1931-........ **CLC 42**

Feiffer, Jules (Ralph) 1929-.... **CLC 2, 8, 64**
See also AAYA 3; CA 17-20R; CANR 30;
DLB 7, 44; MTCW; SATA 8, 61

Feige, Hermann Albert Otto Maximilian
See Traven, B.

Fei-Kan, Li
See Li Fei-kan

Feinberg, David B. 1956-.......... **CLC 59**
See also CA 135

Feinstein, Elaine 1930-............ **CLC 36**
See also CA 69-72; CAAS 1; CANR 31;
DLB 14, 40; MTCW

Feldman, Irving (Mordecai) 1928-.... **CLC 7**
See also CA 1-4R; CANR 1

Fellini, Federico 1920-1993........ **CLC 16**
See also CA 65-68; 143; CANR 33

Felsen, Henry Gregor 1916- .... **CLC 17**
See also CA 1-4R; CANR 1; SAAS 2;
SATA 1

Fenton, James Martin 1949- .... **CLC 32**
See also CA 102; DLB 40

Ferber, Edna 1887-1968........... **CLC 18**
See also AITN 1; CA 5-8R; 25-28R; DLB 9,
28, 86; MTCW; SATA 7

Ferguson, Helen
See Kavan, Anna

Ferguson, Samuel 1810-1886..... **NCLC 33**
See also DLB 32

Ferling, Lawrence
See Ferlinghetti, Lawrence (Monsanto)

Ferlinghetti, Lawrence (Monsanto)
1919(?)- .... **CLC 2, 6, 10, 27; PC 1**
See also CA 5-8R; CANR 3, 41;
CDALB 1941-1968; DLB 5, 16; MTCW

Fernandez, Vicente Garcia Huidobro
See Huidobro Fernandez, Vicente Garcia

Ferrer, Gabriel (Francisco Victor) Miro
See Miro (Ferrer), Gabriel (Francisco
Victor)

Ferrier, Susan (Edmonstone)
1782-1854 .... **NCLC 8**
See also DLB 116

Ferrigno, Robert 1948(?)-.......... **CLC 65**
See also CA 140

Feuchtwanger, Lion 1884-1958 ..... **TCLC 3**
See also CA 104; DLB 66

Feuillet, Octave 1821-1890 ...... **NCLC 45**

Feydeau, Georges (Leon Jules Marie)
1862-1921 .... **TCLC 22**
See also CA 113

Ficino, Marsilio 1433-1499 .... **LC 12**

Fiedeler, Hans
See Doeblin, Alfred

Fiedler, Leslie A(aron)
1917- .... **CLC 4, 13, 24**
See also CA 9-12R; CANR 7; DLB 28, 67;
MTCW

Field, Andrew 1938-.............. **CLC 44**
See also CA 97-100; CANR 25

Field, Eugene 1850-1895 .... **NCLC 3**
See also DLB 23, 42, 140; MAICYA;
SATA 16

Field, Gans T.
See Wellman, Manly Wade

Field, Michael .... **TCLC 43**

Field, Peter
See Hobson, Laura Z(ametkin)

Fielding, Henry
1707-1754 .... **LC 1; DA; WLC**
See also CDBLB 1660-1789; DLB 39, 84,
101

Fielding, Sarah 1710-1768 .... **LC 1**
See also DLB 39

Fierstein, Harvey (Forbes) 1954- ... **CLC 33**
See also CA 123; 129

Figes, Eva 1932-................. **CLC 31**
See also CA 53-56; CANR 4, 44; DLB 14

Finch, Robert (Duer Claydon)
1900- .... **CLC 18**
See also CA 57-60; CANR 9, 24; DLB 88

Findley, Timothy 1930- .... **CLC 27**
See also CA 25-28R; CANR 12, 42;
DLB 53

Fink, William
See Mencken, H(enry) L(ouis)

Firbank, Louis 1942-
See Reed, Lou
See also CA 117

Firbank, (Arthur Annesley) Ronald
1886-1926 .... **TCLC 1**
See also CA 104; DLB 36

Fisher, M(ary) F(rances) K(ennedy)
1908-1992 .... **CLC 76**
See also CA 77-80; 138; CANR 44

Fisher, Roy 1930-................ **CLC 25**
See also CA 81-84; CAAS 10; CANR 16;
DLB 40

Fisher, Rudolph
1897-1934 .... **TCLC 11; BLC**
See also BW 1; CA 107; 124; DLB 51, 102

Fisher, Vardis (Alvero) 1895-1968.... **CLC 7**
See also CA 5-8R; 25-28R; DLB 9

Fiske, Tarleton
See Bloch, Robert (Albert)

Fitch, Clarke
See Sinclair, Upton (Beall)

Fitch, John IV
See Cormier, Robert (Edmund)

Fitgerald, Penelope 1916- .... **CLC 61**

Fitzgerald, Captain Hugh
See Baum, L(yman) Frank

FitzGerald, Edward 1809-1883 .... **NCLC 9**
See also DLB 32

Fitzgerald, F(rancis) Scott (Key)
1896-1940 .... **TCLC 1, 6, 14, 28, 55;
DA; SSC 6; WLC**
See also AITN 1; CA 110; 123;
CDALB 1917-1929; DLB 4, 9, 86;
DLBD 1; DLBY 81; MTCW

Fitzgerald, Penelope 1916-...... **CLC 19, 51**
See also CA 85-88; CAAS 10; DLB 14

Fitzgerald, Robert (Stuart)
1910-1985 .... **CLC 39**
See also CA 1-4R; 114; CANR 1; DLBY 80

FitzGerald, Robert D(avid)
1902-1987 .... **CLC 19**
See also CA 17-20R

Fitzgerald, Zelda (Sayre)
1900-1948 .... **TCLC 52**
See also CA 117; 126; DLBY 84

Flanagan, Thomas (James Bonner)
1923- .... **CLC 25, 52**
See also CA 108; DLBY 80; MTCW

Flaubert, Gustave
1821-1880 .... **NCLC 2, 10, 19; DA;
SSC 11; WLC**
See also DLB 119

Flecker, (Herman) James Elroy
1884-1915 .... **TCLC 43**
See also CA 109; DLB 10, 19

Fleming, Ian (Lancaster)
1908-1964 .... **CLC 3, 30**
See also CA 5-8R; CDBLB 1945-1960;
DLB 87; MTCW; SATA 9

Fleming, Thomas (James) 1927-.... **CLC 37**
See also CA 5-8R; CANR 10; SATA 8

Fletcher, John Gould 1886-1950... **TCLC 35**
See also CA 107; DLB 4, 45

Fleur, Paul
See Pohl, Frederik

Flooglebuckle, Al
See Spiegelman, Art

Flying Officer X
See Bates, H(erbert) E(rnest)

Fo, Dario 1926-.................. **CLC 32**
See also CA 116; 128; MTCW

Fogarty, Jonathan Titulescu Esq.
See Farrell, James T(homas)

Folke, Will
See Bloch, Robert (Albert)

Follett, Ken(neth Martin) 1949- .... **CLC 18**
See also AAYA 6; BEST 89:4; CA 81-84;
CANR 13, 33; DLB 87; DLBY 81;
MTCW

Fontane, Theodor 1819-1898 ..... **NCLC 26**
See also DLB 129

Foote, Horton 1916-.............. **CLC 51**
See also CA 73-76; CANR 34; DLB 26

Foote, Shelby 1916- .... **CLC 75**
See also CA 5-8R; CANR 3, 45; DLB 2, 17

Forbes, Esther 1891-1967.......... **CLC 12**
See also CA 13-14; 25-28R; CAP 1;
CLR 27; DLB 22; JRDA; MAICYA;
SATA 2

Forche, Carolyn (Louise)
1950- .... **CLC 25, 83; PC 10**
See also CA 109; 117; DLB 5

Frye, (Herman) Northrop
1912-1991 . . . . **CLC 24, 70**
See also CA 5-8R; 133; CANR 8, 37;
DLB 67, 68; MTCW

Fuchs, Daniel 1909-1993 . . . . **CLC 8, 22**
See also CA 81-84; 142; CAAS 5;
CANR 40; DLB 9, 26, 28; DLBY 93

Fuchs, Daniel 1934- . . . . **CLC 34**
See also CA 37-40R; CANR 14

Fuentes, Carlos
1928- . . . . . . **CLC 3, 8, 10, 13, 22, 41, 60;**
DA; HLC; WLC
See also AAYA 4; AITN 2; CA 69-72;
CANR 10, 32; DLB 113; HW; MTCW

Fuentes, Gregorio Lopez y
See Lopez y Fuentes, Gregorio

Fugard, (Harold) Athol
1932- . . . . **CLC 5, 9, 14, 25, 40, 80; DC 3**
See also CA 85-88; CANR 32; MTCW

Fugard, Sheila 1932- . . . . **CLC 48**
See also CA 125

Fuller, Charles (H., Jr.)
1939- . . . . **CLC 25; BLC; DC 1**
See also BW 2; CA 108; 112; DLB 38;
MTCW

Fuller, John (Leopold) 1937- . . . . **CLC 62**
See also CA 21-24R; CANR 9, 44; DLB 40

Fuller, Margaret . . . . **NCLC 5**
See also Ossoli, Sarah Margaret (Fuller
marchesa d')

Fuller, Roy (Broadbent)
1912-1991 . . . . **CLC 4, 28**
See also CA 5-8R; 135; CAAS 10; DLB 15,
20

Fulton, Alice 1952- . . . . **CLC 52**
See also CA 116

Furphy, Joseph 1843-1912 . . . . **TCLC 25**

Fussell, Paul 1924- . . . . **CLC 74**
See also BEST 90:1; CA 17-20R; CANR 8,
21, 35; MTCW

Futabatei, Shimei 1864-1909 . . . . . . **TCLC 44**

Futrelle, Jacques 1875-1912 . . . . . . **TCLC 19**
See also CA 113

G. B. S.
See Shaw, George Bernard

Gaboriau, Emile 1835-1873 . . . . . . **NCLC 14**

Gadda, Carlo Emilio 1893-1973 . . . . **CLC 11**
See also CA 89-92

Gaddis, William
1922- . . . . **CLC 1, 3, 6, 8, 10, 19, 43**
See also CA 17-20R; CANR 21; DLB 2;
MTCW

Gaines, Ernest J(ames)
1933- . . . . **CLC 3, 11, 18; BLC**
See also AITN 1; BW 2; CA 9-12R;
CANR 6, 24, 42; CDALB 1968-1988;
DLB 2, 33; DLBY 80; MTCW

Gaitskill, Mary 1954- . . . . **CLC 69**
See also CA 128

Galdos, Benito Perez
See Perez Galdos, Benito

Gale, Zona 1874-1938 . . . . **TCLC 7**
See also CA 105; DLB 9, 78

Galeano, Eduardo (Hughes) 1940- . . . **CLC 72**
See also CA 29-32R; CANR 13, 32; HW

Galiano, Juan Valera y Alcala
See Valera y Alcala-Galiano, Juan

Gallagher, Tess 1943- . . . . **CLC 18, 63; PC 9**
See also CA 106; DLB 120

Gallant, Mavis
1922- . . . . **CLC 7, 18, 38; SSC 5**
See also CA 69-72; CANR 29; DLB 53;
MTCW

Gallant, Roy A(rthur) 1924- . . . . **CLC 17**
See also CA 5-8R; CANR 4, 29; CLR 30;
MAICYA; SATA 4, 68

Gallico, Paul (William) 1897-1976 . . . **CLC 2**
See also AITN 1; CA 5-8R; 69-72;
CANR 23; DLB 9; MAICYA; SATA 13

Gallup, Ralph
See Whitemore, Hugh (John)

Galsworthy, John
1867-1933 . . . . **TCLC 1, 45; DA; WLC 2**
See also CA 104; 141; CDBLB 1890-1914;
DLB 10, 34, 98

Galt, John 1779-1839 . . . . **NCLC 1**
See also DLB 99, 116

Galvin, James 1951- . . . . **CLC 38**
See also CA 108; CANR 26

Gamboa, Federico 1864-1939 . . . . . . **TCLC 36**

Gann, Ernest Kellogg 1910-1991 . . . . **CLC 23**
See also AITN 1; CA 1-4R; 136; CANR 1

Garcia, Cristina 1958- . . . . **CLC 76**
See also CA 141

Garcia Lorca, Federico
1898-1936 . . . . **TCLC 1, 7, 49; DA;**
DC 2; HLC; PC 3; WLC
See also CA 104; 131; DLB 108; HW;
MTCW

Garcia Marquez, Gabriel (Jose)
1928- . . . . **CLC 2, 3, 8, 10, 15, 27, 47, 55;**
DA; HLC; SSC 8; WLC
See also Marquez, Gabriel (Jose) Garcia
See also AAYA 3; BEST 89:1, 90:4;
CA 33-36R; CANR 10, 28; DLB 113;
HW; MTCW

Gard, Janice
See Latham, Jean Lee

Gard, Roger Martin du
See Martin du Gard, Roger

Gardam, Jane 1928- . . . . **CLC 43**
See also CA 49-52; CANR 2, 18, 33;
CLR 12; DLB 14; MAICYA; MTCW;
SAAS 9; SATA 28, 39, 76

Gardner, Herb . . . . **CLC 44**

Gardner, John (Champlin), Jr.
1933-1982 . . . . . **CLC 2, 3, 5, 7, 8, 10, 18,**
28, 34; SSC 7
See also AITN 1; CA 65-68; 107;
CANR 33; DLB 2; DLBY 82; MTCW;
SATA 31, 40

Gardner, John (Edmund) 1926- . . . . . **CLC 30**
See also CA 103; CANR 15; MTCW

Gardner, Noel
See Kuttner, Henry

Gardons, S. S.
See Snodgrass, W(illiam) D(e Witt)

Garfield, Leon 1921- . . . . **CLC 12**
See also AAYA 8; CA 17-20R; CANR 38,
41; CLR 21; JRDA; MAICYA; SATA 1,
32, 76

Garland, (Hannibal) Hamlin
1860-1940 . . . . **TCLC 3**
See also CA 104; DLB 12, 71, 78

Garneau, (Hector de) Saint-Denys
1912-1943 . . . . **TCLC 13**
See also CA 111; DLB 88

Garner, Alan 1934- . . . . **CLC 17**
See also CA 73-76; CANR 15; CLR 20;
MAICYA; MTCW; SATA 18, 69

Garner, Hugh 1913-1979 . . . . **CLC 13**
See also CA 69-72; CANR 31; DLB 68

Garnett, David 1892-1981 . . . . **CLC 3**
See also CA 5-8R; 103; CANR 17; DLB 34

Garos, Stephanie
See Katz, Steve

Garrett, George (Palmer)
1929- . . . . **CLC 3, 11, 51**
See also CA 1-4R; CAAS 5; CANR 1, 42;
DLB 2, 5, 130; DLBY 83

Garrick, David 1717-1779 . . . . **LC 15**
See also DLB 84

Garrigue, Jean 1914-1972 . . . . **CLC 2, 8**
See also CA 5-8R; 37-40R; CANR 20

Garrison, Frederick
See Sinclair, Upton (Beall)

Garth, Will
See Hamilton, Edmond; Kuttner, Henry

Garvey, Marcus (Moziah, Jr.)
1887-1940 . . . . **TCLC 41; BLC**
See also BW 1; CA 120; 124

Gary, Romain . . . . **CLC 25**
See also Kacew, Romain
See also DLB 83

Gascar, Pierre . . . . **CLC 11**
See also Fournier, Pierre

Gascoyne, David (Emery) 1916- . . . . . **CLC 45**
See also CA 65-68; CANR 10, 28; DLB 20;
MTCW

Gaskell, Elizabeth Cleghorn
1810-1865 . . . . **NCLC 5**
See also CDBLB 1832-1890; DLB 21, 144

Gass, William H(oward)
1924- . . . **CLC 1, 2, 8, 11, 15, 39; SSC 12**
See also CA 17-20R; CANR 30; DLB 2;
MTCW

Gasset, Jose Ortega y
See Ortega y Gasset, Jose

Gautier, Theophile 1811-1872 . . . . . **NCLC 1**
See also DLB 119

Gawsworth, John
See Bates, H(erbert) E(rnest)

Gaye, Marvin (Penze) 1939-1984 . . . **CLC 26**
See also CA 112

Gebler, Carlo (Ernest) 1954- . . . . . . **CLC 39**
See also CA 119; 133

Gee, Maggie (Mary) 1948- . . . . **CLC 57**
See also CA 130

Gee, Maurice (Gough) 1931- . . . . **CLC 29**
See also CA 97-100; SATA 46

Goines, Donald
1937(?)-1974 . . . . **CLC 80; BLC**
See also AITN 1; BW 1; CA 124; 114;
DLB 33

Gold, Herbert 1924- . . . . **CLC 4, 7, 14, 42**
See also CA 9-12R; CANR 17, 45; DLB 2;
DLBY 81

Goldbarth, Albert 1948- . . . . **CLC 5, 38**
See also CA 53-56; CANR 6, 40; DLB 120

Goldberg, Anatol 1910-1982 . . . . **CLC 34**
See also CA 131; 117

Goldemberg, Isaac 1945- . . . . **CLC 52**
See also CA 69-72; CAAS 12; CANR 11,
32; HW

Golding, William (Gerald)
1911-1993 . . . . **CLC 1, 2, 3, 8, 10, 17, 27,
58, 81; DA; WLC**
See also AAYA 5; CA 5-8R; 141;
CANR 13, 33; CDBLB 1945-1960;
DLB 15, 100; MTCW

Goldman, Emma 1869-1940 . . . . . . **TCLC 13**
See also CA 110

Goldman, Francisco 1955- . . . . **CLC 76**

Goldman, William (W.) 1931- . . . . **CLC 1, 48**
See also CA 9-12R; CANR 29; DLB 44

Goldmann, Lucien 1913-1970 . . . . . . **CLC 24**
See also CA 25-28; CAP 2

Goldoni, Carlo 1707-1793 . . . . **LC 4**

Goldsberry, Steven 1949- . . . . **CLC 34**
See also CA 131

Goldsmith, Oliver
1728-1774 . . . . **LC 2; DA; WLC**
See also CDBLB 1660-1789; DLB 39, 89,
104, 109, 142; SATA 26

Goldsmith, Peter
See Priestley, J(ohn) B(oynton)

Gombrowicz, Witold
1904-1969 . . . . **CLC 4, 7, 11, 49**
See also CA 19-20; 25-28R; CAP 2

Gomez de la Serna, Ramon
1888-1963 . . . . **CLC 9**
See also CA 116; HW

Goncharov, Ivan Alexandrovich
1812-1891 . . . . **NCLC 1**

Goncourt, Edmond (Louis Antoine Huot) de
1822-1896 . . . . **NCLC 7**
See also DLB 123

Goncourt, Jules (Alfred Huot) de
1830-1870 . . . . **NCLC 7**
See also DLB 123

Gontier, Fernande 19(?)- . . . . **CLC 50**

Goodman, Paul 1911-1972 . . . . **CLC 1, 2, 4, 7**
See also CA 19-20; 37-40R; CANR 34;
CAP 2; DLB 130; MTCW

Gordimer, Nadine
1923- . . . . **CLC 3, 5, 7, 10, 18, 33, 51, 70;
DA**
See also CA 5-8R; CANR 3, 28; MTCW

Gordon, Adam Lindsay
1833-1870 . . . . **NCLC 21**

Gordon, Caroline
1895-1981 . . . **CLC 6, 13, 29, 83; SSC 15**
See also CA 11-12; 103; CANR 36; CAP 1;
DLB 4, 9, 102; DLBY 81; MTCW

Gordon, Charles William 1860-1937
See Connor, Ralph
See also CA 109

Gordon, Mary (Catherine)
1949- . . . . **CLC 13, 22**
See also CA 102; CANR 44; DLB 6;
DLBY 81; MTCW

Gordon, Sol 1923- . . . . **CLC 26**
See also CA 53-56; CANR 4; SATA 11

Gordone, Charles 1925- . . . . **CLC 1, 4**
See also BW 1; CA 93-96; DLB 7; MTCW

Gorenko, Anna Andreevna
See Akhmatova, Anna

Gorky, Maxim . . . . **TCLC 8; WLC**
See also Peshkov, Alexei Maximovich

Goryan, Sirak
See Saroyan, William

Gosse, Edmund (William)
1849-1928 . . . . **TCLC 28**
See also CA 117; DLB 57, 144

Gotlieb, Phyllis Fay (Bloom)
1926- . . . . **CLC 18**
See also CA 13-16R; CANR 7; DLB 88

Gottesman, S. D.
See Kornbluth, C(yril) M.; Pohl, Frederik

Gottfried von Strassburg
fl. c. 1210- . . . . **CMLC 10**
See also DLB 138

Gould, Lois . . . . **CLC 4, 10**
See also CA 77-80; CANR 29; MTCW

Gourmont, Remy de 1858-1915 . . . . **TCLC 17**
See also CA 109

Govier, Katherine 1948- . . . . **CLC 51**
See also CA 101; CANR 18, 40

Goyen, (Charles) William
1915-1983 . . . . **CLC 5, 8, 14, 40**
See also AITN 2; CA 5-8R; 110; CANR 6;
DLB 2; DLBY 83

Goytisolo, Juan
1931- . . . . **CLC 5, 10, 23; HLC**
See also CA 85-88; CANR 32; HW; MTCW

Gozzano, Guido 1883-1916 . . . . **PC 10**
See also DLB 114

Gozzi, (Conte) Carlo 1720-1806 . . **NCLC 23**

Grabbe, Christian Dietrich
1801-1836 . . . . **NCLC 2**
See also DLB 133

Grace, Patricia 1937- . . . . **CLC 56**

Gracian y Morales, Baltasar
1601-1658 . . . . **LC 15**

Gracq, Julien . . . . **CLC 11, 48**
See also Poirier, Louis
See also DLB 83

Grade, Chaim 1910-1982 . . . . **CLC 10**
See also CA 93-96; 107

Graduate of Oxford, A
See Ruskin, John

Graham, John
See Phillips, David Graham

Graham, Jorie 1951- . . . . **CLC 48**
See also CA 111; DLB 120

Graham, R(obert) B(ontine) Cunninghame
See Cunninghame Graham, R(obert)
B(ontine)
See also DLB 98, 135

Graham, Robert
See Haldeman, Joe (William)

Graham, Tom
See Lewis, (Harry) Sinclair

Graham, W(illiam) S(ydney)
1918-1986 . . . . **CLC 29**
See also CA 73-76; 118; DLB 20

Graham, Winston (Mawdsley)
1910- . . . . **CLC 23**
See also CA 49-52; CANR 2, 22, 45;
DLB 77

Grant, Skeeter
See Spiegelman, Art

Granville-Barker, Harley
1877-1946 . . . . **TCLC 2**
See also Barker, Harley Granville
See also CA 104

Grass, Guenter (Wilhelm)
1927- . . . . . **CLC 1, 2, 4, 6, 11, 15, 22, 32,
49; DA; WLC**
See also CA 13-16R; CANR 20; DLB 75,
124; MTCW

Gratton, Thomas
See Hulme, T(homas) E(rnest)

Grau, Shirley Ann
1929- . . . . **CLC 4, 9; SSC 15**
See also CA 89-92; CANR 22; DLB 2;
MTCW

Gravel, Fern
See Hall, James Norman

Graver, Elizabeth 1964- . . . . **CLC 70**
See also CA 135

Graves, Richard Perceval 1945- . . . . **CLC 44**
See also CA 65-68; CANR 9, 26

Graves, Robert (von Ranke)
1895-1985 . . . . . . **CLC 1, 2, 6, 11, 39, 44,
45; PC 6**
See also CA 5-8R; 117; CANR 5, 36;
CDBLB 1914-1945; DLB 20, 100;
DLBY 85; MTCW; SATA 45

Gray, Alasdair 1934- . . . . **CLC 41**
See also CA 126; MTCW

Gray, Amlin 1946- . . . . **CLC 29**
See also CA 138

Gray, Francine du Plessix 1930- . . . . **CLC 22**
See also BEST 90:3; CA 61-64; CAAS 2;
CANR 11, 33; MTCW

Gray, John (Henry) 1866-1934 . . . . **TCLC 19**
See also CA 119

Gray, Simon (James Holliday)
1936- . . . . **CLC 9, 14, 36**
See also AITN 1; CA 21-24R; CAAS 3;
CANR 32; DLB 13; MTCW

Gray, Spalding 1941- . . . . **CLC 49**
See also CA 128

Gray, Thomas
1716-1771 . . . . . . **LC 4; DA; PC 2; WLC**
See also CDBLB 1660-1789; DLB 109

Grayson, David
See Baker, Ray Stannard

Grayson, Richard (A.) 1951- . . . . **CLC 38**
See also CA 85-88; CANR 14, 31

Greeley, Andrew M(oran) 1928- . . . . **CLC 28**
See also CA 5-8R; CAAS 7; CANR 7, 43;
MTCW

Green, Brian
See Card, Orson Scott

Green, Hannah
See Greenberg, Joanne (Goldenberg)

Green, Hannah . . . . **CLC 3**
See also CA 73-76

Green, Henry . . . . **CLC 2, 13**
See also Yorke, Henry Vincent
See also DLB 15

Green, Julian (Hartridge) 1900-
See Green, Julien
See also CA 21-24R; CANR 33; DLB 4, 72;
MTCW

Green, Julien . . . . **CLC 3, 11, 77**
See also Green, Julian (Hartridge)

Green, Paul (Eliot) 1894-1981 . . . . . . **CLC 25**
See also AITN 1; CA 5-8R; 103; CANR 3;
DLB 7, 9; DLBY 81

Greenberg, Ivan 1908-1973
See Rahv, Philip
See also CA 85-88

Greenberg, Joanne (Goldenberg)
1932- . . . . **CLC 7, 30**
See also AAYA 12; CA 5-8R; CANR 14,
32; SATA 25

Greenberg, Richard 1959(?)- . . . . **CLC 57**
See also CA 138

Greene, Bette 1934- . . . . **CLC 30**
See also AAYA 7; CA 53-56; CANR 4;
CLR 2; JRDA; MAICYA; SAAS 16;
SATA 8

Greene, Gael . . . . **CLC 8**
See also CA 13-16R; CANR 10

Greene, Graham
1904-1991 . . . . **CLC 1, 3, 6, 9, 14, 18, 27,
37, 70, 72; DA; WLC**
See also AITN 2; CA 13-16R; 133;
CANR 35; CDBLB 1945-1960; DLB 13,
15, 77, 100; DLBY 91; MTCW; SATA 20

Greer, Richard
See Silverberg, Robert

Greer, Richard
See Silverberg, Robert

Gregor, Arthur 1923- . . . . **CLC 9**
See also CA 25-28R; CAAS 10; CANR 11;
SATA 36

Gregor, Lee
See Pohl, Frederik

Gregory, Isabella Augusta (Persse)
1852-1932 . . . . **TCLC 1**
See also CA 104; DLB 10

Gregory, J. Dennis
See Williams, John A(lfred)

Grendon, Stephen
See Derleth, August (William)

Grenville, Kate 1950- . . . . **CLC 61**
See also CA 118

Grenville, Pelham
See Wodehouse, P(elham) G(renville)

Greve, Felix Paul (Berthold Friedrich)
1879-1948
See Grove, Frederick Philip
See also CA 104; 141

Grey, Zane 1872-1939 . . . . **TCLC 6**
See also CA 104; 132; DLB 9; MTCW

Grieg, (Johan) Nordahl (Brun)
1902-1943 . . . . **TCLC 10**
See also CA 107

Grieve, C(hristopher) M(urray)
1892-1978 . . . . **CLC 11, 19**
See also MacDiarmid, Hugh
See also CA 5-8R; 85-88; CANR 33;
MTCW

Griffin, Gerald 1803-1840 . . . . **NCLC 7**

Griffin, John Howard 1920-1980 . . . . **CLC 68**
See also AITN 1; CA 1-4R; 101; CANR 2

Griffin, Peter . . . . **CLC 39**

Griffiths, Trevor 1935- . . . . **CLC 13, 52**
See also CA 97-100; CANR 45; DLB 13

Grigson, Geoffrey (Edward Harvey)
1905-1985 . . . . **CLC 7, 39**
See also CA 25-28R; 118; CANR 20, 33;
DLB 27; MTCW

Grillparzer, Franz 1791-1872 . . . . . **NCLC 1**
See also DLB 133

Grimble, Reverend Charles James
See Eliot, T(homas) S(tearns)

Grimke, Charlotte L(ottie) Forten
1837(?)-1914
See Forten, Charlotte L.
See also BW 1; CA 117; 124

Grimm, Jacob Ludwig Karl
1785-1863 . . . . **NCLC 3**
See also DLB 90; MAICYA; SATA 22

Grimm, Wilhelm Karl 1786-1859 . . **NCLC 3**
See also DLB 90; MAICYA; SATA 22

**Grimmelshausen, Johann Jakob Christoffel
von** 1621-1676 . . . . **LC 6**

Grindel, Eugene 1895-1952
See Eluard, Paul
See also CA 104

Grisham, John 1955(?)- . . . . **CLC 84**
See also CA 138

Grossman, David 1954- . . . . **CLC 67**
See also CA 138

Grossman, Vasily (Semenovich)
1905-1964 . . . . **CLC 41**
See also CA 124; 130; MTCW

Grove, Frederick Philip . . . . **TCLC 4**
See also Greve, Felix Paul (Berthold
Friedrich)
See also DLB 92

Grubb
See Crumb, R(obert)

Grumbach, Doris (Isaac)
1918- . . . . **CLC 13, 22, 64**
See also CA 5-8R; CAAS 2; CANR 9, 42

Grundtvig, Nicolai Frederik Severin
1783-1872 . . . . **NCLC 1**

Grunge
See Crumb, R(obert)

Grunwald, Lisa 1959- . . . . **CLC 44**
See also CA 120

Guare, John 1938- . . . . **CLC 8, 14, 29, 67**
See also CA 73-76; CANR 21; DLB 7;
MTCW

Gudjonsson, Halldor Kiljan 1902-
See Laxness, Halldor
See also CA 103

Guenter, Erich
See Eich, Guenter

Guest, Barbara 1920- . . . . **CLC 34**
See also CA 25-28R; CANR 11, 44; DLB 5

Guest, Judith (Ann) 1936- . . . . **CLC 8, 30**
See also AAYA 7; CA 77-80; CANR 15;
MTCW

Guild, Nicholas M. 1944- . . . . **CLC 33**
See also CA 93-96

Guillemin, Jacques
See Sartre, Jean-Paul

Guillen, Jorge 1893-1984 . . . . **CLC 11**
See also CA 89-92; 112; DLB 108; HW

Guillen (y Batista), Nicolas (Cristobal)
1902-1989 . . . . . **CLC 48, 79; BLC; HLC**
See also BW 2; CA 116; 125; 129; HW

Guillevic, (Eugene) 1907- . . . . **CLC 33**
See also CA 93-96

Guillois
See Desnos, Robert

Guiney, Louise Imogen
1861-1920 . . . . **TCLC 41**
See also DLB 54

Guiraldes, Ricardo (Guillermo)
1886-1927 . . . . **TCLC 39**
See also CA 131; HW; MTCW

Gunn, Bill . . . . **CLC 5**
See also Gunn, William Harrison
See also DLB 38

Gunn, Thom(son William)
1929- . . . . **CLC 3, 6, 18, 32, 81**
See also CA 17-20R; CANR 9, 33;
CDBLB 1960 to Present; DLB 27;
MTCW

Gunn, William Harrison 1934(?)-1989
See Gunn, Bill
See also AITN 1; BW 1; CA 13-16R; 128;
CANR 12, 25

Gunnars, Kristjana 1948- . . . . **CLC 69**
See also CA 113; DLB 60

Gurganus, Allan 1947- . . . . **CLC 70**
See also BEST 90:1; CA 135

Gurney, A(lbert) R(amsdell), Jr.
1930- . . . . **CLC 32, 50, 54**
See also CA 77-80; CANR 32

Gurney, Ivor (Bertie) 1890-1937 . . . **TCLC 33**

Gurney, Peter
See Gurney, A(lbert) R(amsdell), Jr.

Gustafson, Ralph (Barker) 1909- . . . . **CLC 36**
See also CA 21-24R; CANR 8, 45; DLB 88

Gut, Gom
See Simenon, Georges (Jacques Christian)

Guthrie, A(lfred) B(ertram), Jr.
1901-1991 . . . . **CLC 23**
See also CA 57-60; 134; CANR 24; DLB 6;
SATA 62; SATA-Obit 67

Guthrie, Isobel
See Grieve, C(hristopher) M(urray)

Guthrie, Woodrow Wilson 1912-1967
  See Guthrie, Woody
  See also CA 113; 93-96

Guthrie, Woody.................. **CLC 35**
  See also Guthrie, Woodrow Wilson

Guy, Rosa (Cuthbert) 1928-........ **CLC 26**
  See also AAYA 4; BW 2; CA 17-20R;
  CANR 14, 34; CLR 13; DLB 33; JRDA;
  MAICYA; SATA 14, 62

Gwendolyn
  See Bennett, (Enoch) Arnold

H. D. .... **CLC 3, 8, 14, 31, 34, 73; PC 5**
  See also Doolittle, Hilda

Haavikko, Paavo Juhani
  1931-................... **CLC 18, 34**
  See also CA 106

Habbema, Koos
  See Heijermans, Herman

Hacker, Marilyn 1942- .... **CLC 5, 9, 23, 72**
  See also CA 77-80; DLB 120

Haggard, H(enry) Rider
  1856-1925 .... **TCLC 11**
  See also CA 108; DLB 70; SATA 16

Haig, Fenil
  See Ford, Ford Madox

Haig-Brown, Roderick (Langmere)
  1908-1976 .... **CLC 21**
  See also CA 5-8R; 69-72; CANR 4, 38;
  CLR 31; DLB 88; MAICYA; SATA 12

Hailey, Arthur 1920- .... **CLC 5**
  See also AITN 2; BEST 90:3; CA 1-4R;
  CANR 2, 36; DLB 88; DLBY 82; MTCW

Hailey, Elizabeth Forsythe 1938-... **CLC 40**
  See also CA 93-96; CAAS 1; CANR 15

Haines, John (Meade) 1924-....... **CLC 58**
  See also CA 17-20R; CANR 13, 34; DLB 5

Haldeman, Joe (William) 1943-..... **CLC 61**
  See also CA 53-56; CANR 6; DLB 8

Haley, Alex(ander Murray Palmer)
  1921-1992 .... **CLC 8, 12, 76; BLC; DA**
  See also BW 2; CA 77-80; 136; DLB 38;
  MTCW

Haliburton, Thomas Chandler
  1796-1865 .... **NCLC 15**
  See also DLB 11, 99

Hall, Donald (Andrew, Jr.)
  1928- .... **CLC 1, 13, 37, 59**
  See also CA 5-8R; CAAS 7; CANR 2, 44;
  DLB 5; SATA 23

Hall, Frederic Sauser
  See Sauser-Hall, Frederic

Hall, James
  See Kuttner, Henry

Hall, James Norman 1887-1951 ... **TCLC 23**
  See also CA 123; SATA 21

Hall, (Marguerite) Radclyffe
  1886(?)-1943 .... **TCLC 12**
  See also CA 110

Hall, Rodney 1935- .... **CLC 51**
  See also CA 109

Halliday, Michael
  See Creasey, John

Halpern, Daniel 1945- .... **CLC 14**
  See also CA 33-36R

Hamburger, Michael (Peter Leopold)
  1924- .... **CLC 5, 14**
  See also CA 5-8R; CAAS 4; CANR 2;
  DLB 27

Hamill, Pete 1935-.............. **CLC 10**
  See also CA 25-28R; CANR 18

Hamilton, Clive
  See Lewis, C(live) S(taples)

Hamilton, Edmond 1904-1977....... **CLC 1**
  See also CA 1-4R; CANR 3; DLB 8

Hamilton, Eugene (Jacob) Lee
  See Lee-Hamilton, Eugene (Jacob)

Hamilton, Franklin
  See Silverberg, Robert

Hamilton, Gail
  See Corcoran, Barbara

Hamilton, Mollie
  See Kaye, M(ary) M(argaret)

Hamilton, (Anthony Walter) Patrick
  1904-1962 .... **CLC 51**
  See also CA 113; DLB 10

Hamilton, Virginia 1936-.......... **CLC 26**
  See also AAYA 2; BW 2; CA 25-28R;
  CANR 20, 37; CLR 1, 11; DLB 33, 52;
  JRDA; MAICYA; MTCW; SATA 4, 56

Hammett, (Samuel) Dashiell
  1894-1961 .... **CLC 3, 5, 10, 19, 47**
  See also AITN 1; CA 81-84; CANR 42;
  CDALB 1929-1941; DLBD 6; MTCW

Hammon, Jupiter
  1711(?)-1800(?) .... **NCLC 5; BLC**
  See also DLB 31, 50

Hammond, Keith
  See Kuttner, Henry

Hamner, Earl (Henry), Jr. 1923- ... **CLC 12**
  See also AITN 2; CA 73-76; DLB 6

Hampton, Christopher (James)
  1946- .... **CLC 4**
  See also CA 25-28R; DLB 13; MTCW

Hamsun, Knut............. **TCLC 2, 14, 49**
  See also Pedersen, Knut

Handke, Peter 1942- .. **CLC 5, 8, 10, 15, 38**
  See also CA 77-80; CANR 33; DLB 85,
  124; MTCW

Hanley, James 1901-1985 ... **CLC 3, 5, 8, 13**
  See also CA 73-76; 117; CANR 36; MTCW

Hannah, Barry 1942-.......... **CLC 23, 38**
  See also CA 108; 110; CANR 43; DLB 6;
  MTCW

Hannon, Ezra
  See Hunter, Evan

Hansberry, Lorraine (Vivian)
  1930-1965 ...... **CLC 17, 62; BLC; DA;
  DC 2**
  See also BW 1; CA 109; 25-28R; CABS 3;
  CDALB 1941-1968; DLB 7, 38; MTCW

Hansen, Joseph 1923-............. **CLC 38**
  See also CA 29-32R; CAAS 17; CANR 16,
  44

Hansen, Martin A. 1909-1955..... **TCLC 32**

Hanson, Kenneth O(stlin) 1922- .... **CLC 13**
  See also CA 53-56; CANR 7

Hardwick, Elizabeth 1916- .... **CLC 13**
  See also CA 5-8R; CANR 3, 32; DLB 6;
  MTCW

Hardy, Thomas
  1840-1928 ...... **TCLC 4, 10, 18, 32, 48,
  53; DA; PC 8; SSC 2; WLC**
  See also CA 104; 123; CDBLB 1890-1914;
  DLB 18, 19, 135; MTCW

Hare, David 1947- .... **CLC 29, 58**
  See also CA 97-100; CANR 39; DLB 13;
  MTCW

Harford, Henry
  See Hudson, W(illiam) H(enry)

Hargrave, Leonie
  See Disch, Thomas M(ichael)

Harjo, Joy 1951- .... **CLC 83**
  See also CA 114; CANR 35; DLB 120

Harlan, Louis R(udolph) 1922-..... **CLC 34**
  See also CA 21-24R; CANR 25

Harling, Robert 1951(?)- .... **CLC 53**

Harmon, William (Ruth) 1938-..... **CLC 38**
  See also CA 33-36R; CANR 14, 32, 35;
  SATA 65

Harper, F. E. W.
  See Harper, Frances Ellen Watkins

Harper, Frances E. W.
  See Harper, Frances Ellen Watkins

Harper, Frances E. Watkins
  See Harper, Frances Ellen Watkins

Harper, Frances Ellen
  See Harper, Frances Ellen Watkins

Harper, Frances Ellen Watkins
  1825-1911 .... **TCLC 14; BLC**
  See also BW 1; CA 111; 125; DLB 50

Harper, Michael S(teven) 1938- ... **CLC 7, 22**
  See also BW 1; CA 33-36R; CANR 24;
  DLB 41

Harper, Mrs. F. E. W.
  See Harper, Frances Ellen Watkins

Harris, Christie (Lucy) Irwin
  1907- .... **CLC 12**
  See also CA 5-8R; CANR 6; DLB 88;
  JRDA; MAICYA; SAAS 10; SATA 6, 74

Harris, Frank 1856(?)-1931....... **TCLC 24**
  See also CA 109

Harris, George Washington
  1814-1869 .... **NCLC 23**
  See also DLB 3, 11

Harris, Joel Chandler 1848-1908 ... **TCLC 2**
  See also CA 104; 137; DLB 11, 23, 42, 78,
  91; MAICYA; YABC 1

Harris, John (Wyndham Parkes Lucas)
  Beynon 1903-1969 .... **CLC 19**
  See also CA 102; 89-92

Harris, MacDonald
  See Heiney, Donald (William)

Harris, Mark 1922- .... **CLC 19**
  See also CA 5-8R; CAAS 3; CANR 2;
  DLB 2; DLBY 80

Harris, (Theodore) Wilson 1921-.... **CLC 25**
  See also BW 2; CA 65-68; CAAS 16;
  CANR 11, 27; DLB 117; MTCW

Henderson, Sylvia
See Ashton-Warner, Sylvia (Constance)

Henley, Beth .... CLC 23
See also Henley, Elizabeth Becker
See also CABS 3; DLBY 86

Henley, Elizabeth Becker 1952-
See Henley, Beth
See also CA 107; CANR 32; MTCW

Henley, William Ernest
1849-1903 .... TCLC 8
See also CA 105; DLB 19

Hennissart, Martha
See Lathen, Emma
See also CA 85-88

Henry, O. .... TCLC 1, 19; SSC 5; WLC
See also Porter, William Sydney

Henry, Patrick 1736-1799 .... LC 25

Henryson, Robert 1430(?)-1506(?). ... LC 20

Henry VIII 1491-1547 .... LC 10

Henschke, Alfred
See Klabund

Hentoff, Nat(han Irving) 1925- ..... CLC 26
See also AAYA 4; CA 1-4R; CAAS 6;
CANR 5, 25; CLR 1; JRDA; MAICYA;
SATA 27, 42, 69

Heppenstall, (John) Rayner
1911-1981 .... CLC 10
See also CA 1-4R; 103; CANR 29

Herbert, Frank (Patrick)
1920-1986 .... CLC 12, 23, 35, 44
See also CA 53-56; 118; CANR 5, 43;
DLB 8; MTCW; SATA 9, 37, 47

Herbert, George 1593-1633 .... LC 24; PC 4
See also CDBLB Before 1660; DLB 126

Herbert, Zbigniew 1924- .... CLC 9, 43
See also CA 89-92; CANR 36; MTCW

Herbst, Josephine (Frey)
1897-1969 .... CLC 34
See also CA 5-8R; 25-28R; DLB 9

Hergesheimer, Joseph
1880-1954 .... TCLC 11
See also CA 109; DLB 102, 9

Herlihy, James Leo 1927-1993 ...... CLC 6
See also CA 1-4R; 143; CANR 2

Hermogenes fl. c. 175- .... CMLC 6

Hernandez, Jose 1834-1886 ...... NCLC 17

Herrick, Robert
1591-1674 .... LC 13; DA; PC 9
See also DLB 126

Herring, Guilles
See Somerville, Edith

Herriot, James 1916- .... CLC 12
See also Wight, James Alfred
See also AAYA 1; CANR 40

Herrmann, Dorothy 1941- .... CLC 44
See also CA 107

Herrmann, Taffy
See Herrmann, Dorothy

Hersey, John (Richard)
1914-1993 ...... CLC 1, 2, 7, 9, 40, 81
See also CA 17-20R; 140; CANR 33;
DLB 6; MTCW; SATA 25;
SATA-Obit 76

Herzen, Aleksandr Ivanovich
1812-1870 .... NCLC 10

Herzl, Theodor 1860-1904 .... TCLC 36

Herzog, Werner 1942- .... CLC 16
See also CA 89-92

Hesiod c. 8th cent. B.C.- .... CMLC 5

Hesse, Hermann
1877-1962 .... CLC 1, 2, 3, 6, 11, 17, 25,
69; DA; SSC 9; WLC
See also CA 17-18; CAP 2; DLB 66;
MTCW; SATA 50

Hewes, Cady
See De Voto, Bernard (Augustine)

Heyen, William 1940- .... CLC 13, 18
See also CA 33-36R; CAAS 9; DLB 5

Heyerdahl, Thor 1914- .... CLC 26
See also CA 5-8R; CANR 5, 22; MTCW;
SATA 2, 52

Heym, Georg (Theodor Franz Arthur)
1887-1912 .... TCLC 9
See also CA 106

Heym, Stefan 1913- .... CLC 41
See also CA 9-12R; CANR 4; DLB 69

Heyse, Paul (Johann Ludwig von)
1830-1914 .... TCLC 8
See also CA 104; DLB 129

Hibbert, Eleanor Alice Burford
1906-1993 .... CLC 7
See also BEST 90:4; CA 17-20R; 140;
CANR 9, 28; SATA 2; SATA-Obit 74

Higgins, George V(incent)
1939- .... CLC 4, 7, 10, 18
See also CA 77-80; CAAS 5; CANR 17;
DLB 2; DLBY 81; MTCW

Higginson, Thomas Wentworth
1823-1911 .... TCLC 36
See also DLB 1, 64

Highet, Helen
See MacInnes, Helen (Clark)

Highsmith, (Mary) Patricia
1921- .... CLC 2, 4, 14, 42
See also CA 1-4R; CANR 1, 20; MTCW

Highwater, Jamake (Mamake)
1942(?)- .... CLC 12
See also AAYA 7; CA 65-68; CAAS 7;
CANR 10, 34; CLR 17; DLB 52;
DLBY 85; JRDA; MAICYA; SATA 30,
32, 69

Hijuelos, Oscar 1951- ...... CLC 65; HLC
See also BEST 90:1; CA 123; HW

Hikmet, Nazim 1902(?)-1963 ...... CLC 40
See also CA 141; 93-96

Hildesheimer, Wolfgang
1916-1991 .... CLC 49
See also CA 101; 135; DLB 69, 124

Hill, Geoffrey (William)
1932- .... CLC 5, 8, 18, 45
See also CA 81-84; CANR 21;
CDBLB 1960 to Present; DLB 40;
MTCW

Hill, George Roy 1921- .... CLC 26
See also CA 110; 122

Hill, John
See Koontz, Dean R(ay)

Hill, Susan (Elizabeth) 1942- .... CLC 4
See also CA 33-36R; CANR 29; DLB 14,
139; MTCW

Hillerman, Tony 1925- .... CLC 62
See also AAYA 6; BEST 89:1; CA 29-32R;
CANR 21, 42; SATA 6

Hillesum, Etty 1914-1943 .... TCLC 49
See also CA 137

Hilliard, Noel (Harvey) 1929- ...... CLC 15
See also CA 9-12R; CANR 7

Hillis, Rick 1956- .... CLC 66
See also CA 134

Hilton, James 1900-1954 .... TCLC 21
See also CA 108; DLB 34, 77; SATA 34

Himes, Chester (Bomar)
1909-1984 .... CLC 2, 4, 7, 18, 58; BLC
See also BW 2; CA 25-28R; 114; CANR 22;
DLB 2, 76, 143; MTCW

Hinde, Thomas .... CLC 6, 11
See also Chitty, Thomas Willes

Hindin, Nathan
See Bloch, Robert (Albert)

Hine, (William) Daryl 1936- .... CLC 15
See also CA 1-4R; CAAS 15; CANR 1, 20;
DLB 60

Hinkson, Katharine Tynan
See Tynan, Katharine

Hinton, S(usan) E(loise)
1950- .... CLC 30; DA
See also AAYA 2; CA 81-84; CANR 32;
CLR 3, 23; JRDA; MAICYA; MTCW;
SATA 19, 58

Hippius, Zinaida .... TCLC 9
See also Gippius, Zinaida (Nikolayevna)

Hiraoka, Kimitake 1925-1970
See Mishima, Yukio
See also CA 97-100; 29-32R; MTCW

Hirsch, E(ric) D(onald), Jr. 1928- ... CLC 79
See also CA 25-28R; CANR 27; DLB 67;
MTCW

Hirsch, Edward 1950- .... CLC 31, 50
See also CA 104; CANR 20, 42; DLB 120

Hitchcock, Alfred (Joseph)
1899-1980 .... CLC 16
See also CA 97-100; SATA 24, 27

Hitler, Adolf 1889-1945 .... TCLC 53
See also CA 117

Hoagland, Edward 1932- .... CLC 28
See also CA 1-4R; CANR 2, 31; DLB 6;
SATA 51

Hoban, Russell (Conwell) 1925- .. CLC 7, 25
See also CA 5-8R; CANR 23, 37; CLR 3;
DLB 52; MAICYA; MTCW; SATA 1,
40, 78

Hobbs, Perry
See Blackmur, R(ichard) P(almer)

Hobson, Laura Z(ametkin)
1900-1986 .... CLC 7, 25
See also CA 17-20R; 118; DLB 28;
SATA 52

Hochhuth, Rolf 1931- .... CLC 4, 11, 18
See also CA 5-8R; CANR 33; DLB 124;
MTCW

Hochman, Sandra 1936- .... CLC 3, 8
See also CA 5-8R; DLB 5

Hochwaelder, Fritz 1911-1986...... **CLC 36**
See also CA 29-32R; 120; CANR 42;
MTCW

Hochwalder, Fritz
See Hochwaelder, Fritz

Hocking, Mary (Eunice) 1921-..... **CLC 13**
See also CA 101; CANR 18, 40

Hodgins, Jack 1938-............. **CLC 23**
See also CA 93-96; DLB 60

Hodgson, William Hope
1877(?)-1918............... **TCLC 13**
See also CA 111; DLB 70

Hoffman, Alice 1952-............. **CLC 51**
See also CA 77-80; CANR 34; MTCW

Hoffman, Daniel (Gerard)
1923-.................... **CLC 6, 13, 23**
See also CA 1-4R; CANR 4; DLB 5

Hoffman, Stanley 1944-............ **CLC 5**
See also CA 77-80

Hoffman, William M(oses) 1939-... **CLC 40**
See also CA 57-60; CANR 11

Hoffmann, E(rnst) T(heodor) A(madeus)
1776-1822........... **NCLC 2; SSC 13**
See also DLB 90; SATA 27

Hofmann, Gert 1931-............. **CLC 54**
See also CA 128

Hofmannsthal, Hugo von
1874-1929........... **TCLC 11; DC 4**
See also CA 106; DLB 81, 118

Hogan, Linda 1947-............. **CLC 73**
See also CA 120; CANR 45

Hogarth, Charles
See Creasey, John

Hogg, James 1770-1835.......... **NCLC 4**
See also DLB 93, 116

Holbach, Paul Henri Thiry Baron
1723-1789.................... **LC 14**

Holberg, Ludvig 1684-1754......... **LC 6**

Holden, Ursula 1921-............. **CLC 18**
See also CA 101; CAAS 8; CANR 22

Holderlin, (Johann Christian) Friedrich
1770-1843........... **NCLC 16; PC 4**

Holdstock, Robert
See Holdstock, Robert P.

Holdstock, Robert P. 1948-........ **CLC 39**
See also CA 131

Holland, Isabelle 1920-.......... **CLC 21**
See also AAYA 11; CA 21-24R; CANR 10,
25; JRDA; MAICYA; SATA 8, 70

Holland, Marcus
See Caldwell, (Janet Miriam) Taylor
(Holland)

Hollander, John 1929-...... **CLC 2, 5, 8, 14**
See also CA 1-4R; CANR 1; DLB 5;
SATA 13

Hollander, Paul
See Silverberg, Robert

Holleran, Andrew 1943(?)-........ **CLC 38**
See also CA 144

Hollinghurst, Alan 1954-.......... **CLC 55**
See also CA 114

Hollis, Jim
See Summers, Hollis (Spurgeon, Jr.)

Holmes, John
See Souster, (Holmes) Raymond

Holmes, John Clellon 1926-1988.... **CLC 56**
See also CA 9-12R; 125; CANR 4; DLB 16

Holmes, Oliver Wendell
1809-1894................ **NCLC 14**
See also CDALB 1640-1865; DLB 1;
SATA 34

Holmes, Raymond
See Souster, (Holmes) Raymond

Holt, Victoria
See Hibbert, Eleanor Alice Burford

Holub, Miroslav 1923-............. **CLC 4**
See also CA 21-24R; CANR 10

Homer c. 8th cent. B.C.-..... **CMLC 1; DA**

Honig, Edwin 1919-............... **CLC 33**
See also CA 5-8R; CAAS 8; CANR 4, 45;
DLB 5

Hood, Hugh (John Blagdon)
1928-.................... **CLC 15, 28**
See also CA 49-52; CAAS 17; CANR 1, 33;
DLB 53

Hood, Thomas 1799-1845....... **NCLC 16**
See also DLB 96

Hooker, (Peter) Jeremy 1941-...... **CLC 43**
See also CA 77-80; CANR 22; DLB 40

Hope, A(lec) D(erwent) 1907-.... **CLC 3, 51**
See also CA 21-24R; CANR 33; MTCW

Hope, Brian
See Creasey, John

Hope, Christopher (David Tully)
1944-...................... **CLC 52**
See also CA 106; SATA 62

Hopkins, Gerard Manley
1844-1889........ **NCLC 17; DA; WLC**
See also CDBLB 1890-1914; DLB 35, 57

Hopkins, John (Richard) 1931-...... **CLC 4**
See also CA 85-88

Hopkins, Pauline Elizabeth
1859-1930............. **TCLC 28; BLC**
See also BW 2; CA 141; DLB 50

Hopkinson, Francis 1737-1791...... **LC 25**
See also DLB 31

Hopley-Woolrich, Cornell George 1903-1968
See Woolrich, Cornell
See also CA 13-14; CAP 1

Horatio
See Proust, (Valentin-Louis-George-Eugene-)
Marcel

Horgan, Paul 1903-............. **CLC 9, 53**
See also CA 13-16R; CANR 9, 35;
DLB 102; DLBY 85; MTCW; SATA 13

Horn, Peter
See Kuttner, Henry

Hornem, Horace Esq.
See Byron, George Gordon (Noel)

Horovitz, Israel 1939-............ **CLC 56**
See also CA 33-36R; DLB 7

Horvath, Odon von
See Horvath, Oedoen von
See also DLB 85, 124

Horvath, Oedoen von 1901-1938... **TCLC 45**
See also Horvath, Odon von
See also CA 118

Horwitz, Julius 1920-1986......... **CLC 14**
See also CA 9-12R; 119; CANR 12

Hospital, Janette Turner 1942-..... **CLC 42**
See also CA 108

Hostos, E. M. de
See Hostos (y Bonilla), Eugenio Maria de

Hostos, Eugenio M. de
See Hostos (y Bonilla), Eugenio Maria de

Hostos, Eugenio Maria
See Hostos (y Bonilla), Eugenio Maria de

Hostos (y Bonilla), Eugenio Maria de
1839-1903.................. **TCLC 24**
See also CA 123; 131; HW

Houdini
See Lovecraft, H(oward) P(hillips)

Hougan, Carolyn 1943-........... **CLC 34**
See also CA 139

Household, Geoffrey (Edward West)
1900-1988................... **CLC 11**
See also CA 77-80; 126; DLB 87; SATA 14,
59

Housman, A(lfred) E(dward)
1859-1936...... **TCLC 1, 10; DA; PC 2**
See also CA 104; 125; DLB 19; MTCW

Housman, Laurence 1865-1959..... **TCLC 7**
See also CA 106; DLB 10; SATA 25

Howard, Elizabeth Jane 1923-... **CLC 7, 29**
See also CA 5-8R; CANR 8

Howard, Maureen 1930-..... **CLC 5, 14, 46**
See also CA 53-56; CANR 31; DLBY 83;
MTCW

Howard, Richard 1929-...... **CLC 7, 10, 47**
See also AITN 1; CA 85-88; CANR 25;
DLB 5

Howard, Robert Ervin 1906-1936... **TCLC 8**
See also CA 105

Howard, Warren F.
See Pohl, Frederik

Howe, Fanny 1940-.............. **CLC 47**
See also CA 117; SATA 52

Howe, Julia Ward 1819-1910..... **TCLC 21**
See also CA 117; DLB 1

Howe, Susan 1937-............... **CLC 72**
See also DLB 120

Howe, Tina 1937-............... **CLC 48**
See also CA 109

Howell, James 1594(?)-1666........ **LC 13**

Howells, W. D.
See Howells, William Dean

Howells, William D.
See Howells, William Dean

Howells, William Dean
1837-1920............ **TCLC 7, 17, 41**
See also CA 104; 134; CDALB 1865-1917;
DLB 12, 64, 74, 79

Howes, Barbara 1914-............ **CLC 15**
See also CA 9-12R; CAAS 3; SATA 5

Hrabal, Bohumil 1914-........ **CLC 13, 67**
See also CA 106; CAAS 12

Hsun, Lu....................... **TCLC 3**
See also Shu-Jen, Chou

Hubbard, L(afayette) Ron(ald)
1911-1986 .... CLC **43**
See also CA 77-80; 118; CANR 22

Huch, Ricarda (Octavia)
1864-1947 .... TCLC **13**
See also CA 111; DLB 66

Huddle, David 1942- .... CLC **49**
See also CA 57-60; DLB 130

Hudson, Jeffrey
See Crichton, (John) Michael

Hudson, W(illiam) H(enry)
1841-1922 .... TCLC **29**
See also CA 115; DLB 98; SATA 35

Huetter, Ford Madox
See Ford, Ford Madox

Hughart, Barry 1934-............. CLC **39**
See also CA 137

Hughes, Colin
See Creasey, John

Hughes, David (John) 1930- .... CLC **48**
See also CA 116; 129; DLB 14

Hughes, (James) Langston
1902-1967 ..... CLC **1, 5, 10, 15, 35, 44;**
BLC; DA; DC 3; PC 1; SSC 6; WLC
See also AAYA 12; BW 1; CA 1-4R;
25-28R; CANR 1, 34; CDALB 1929-1941;
CLR 17; DLB 4, 7, 48, 51, 86; JRDA;
MAICYA; MTCW; SATA 4, 33

Hughes, Richard (Arthur Warren)
1900-1976 .... CLC **1, 11**
See also CA 5-8R; 65-68; CANR 4;
DLB 15; MTCW; SATA 8, 25

Hughes, Ted
1930- .... CLC **2, 4, 9, 14, 37; PC 7**
See also CA 1-4R; CANR 1, 33; CLR 3;
DLB 40; MAICYA; MTCW; SATA 27,
49

Hugo, Richard F(ranklin)
1923-1982 .... CLC **6, 18, 32**
See also CA 49-52; 108; CANR 3; DLB 5

Hugo, Victor (Marie)
1802-1885 .. NCLC **3, 10, 21; DA; WLC**
See also DLB 119; SATA 47

Huidobro, Vicente
See Huidobro Fernandez, Vicente Garcia

Huidobro Fernandez, Vicente Garcia
1893-1948 .... TCLC **31**
See also CA 131; HW

Hulme, Keri 1947- .... CLC **39**
See also CA 125

Hulme, T(homas) E(rnest)
1883-1917 .... TCLC **21**
See also CA 117; DLB 19

Hume, David 1711-1776............. LC **7**
See also DLB 104

Humphrey, William 1924-......... CLC **45**
See also CA 77-80; DLB 6

Humphreys, Emyr Owen 1919-..... CLC **47**
See also CA 5-8R; CANR 3, 24; DLB 15

Humphreys, Josephine 1945-.... CLC **34, 57**
See also CA 121; 127

Hungerford, Pixie
See Brinsmead, H(esba) F(ay)

Hunt, E(verette) Howard, Jr.
1918- .... CLC **3**
See also AITN 1; CA 45-48; CANR 2

Hunt, Kyle
See Creasey, John

Hunt, (James Henry) Leigh
1784-1859 .... NCLC **1**

Hunt, Marsha 1946-............. CLC **70**
See also BW 2; CA 143

Hunt, Violet 1866-1942 .... TCLC **53**

Hunter, E. Waldo
See Sturgeon, Theodore (Hamilton)

Hunter, Evan 1926- .... CLC **11, 31**
See also CA 5-8R; CANR 5, 38; DLBY 82;
MTCW; SATA 25

Hunter, Kristin (Eggleston) 1931-... CLC **35**
See also AITN 1; BW 1; CA 13-16R;
CANR 13; CLR 3; DLB 33; MAICYA;
SAAS 10; SATA 12

Hunter, Mollie 1922-............. CLC **21**
See also McIlwraith, Maureen Mollie
Hunter
See also CANR 37; CLR 25; JRDA;
MAICYA; SAAS 7; SATA 54

Hunter, Robert (?)-1734............. LC **7**

Hurston, Zora Neale
1903-1960 .... CLC **7, 30, 61; BLC; DA;**
SSC 4
See also BW 1; CA 85-88; DLB 51, 86;
MTCW

Huston, John (Marcellus)
1906-1987 .... CLC **20**
See also CA 73-76; 123; CANR 34; DLB 26

Hustvedt, Siri 1955-............... CLC **76**
See also CA 137

Hutten, Ulrich von 1488-1523....... LC **16**

Huxley, Aldous (Leonard)
1894-1963 ..... CLC **1, 3, 4, 5, 8, 11, 18,**
35, 79; DA; WLC
See also AAYA 11; CA 85-88; CANR 44;
CDBLB 1914-1945; DLB 36, 100;
MTCW; SATA 63

Huysmans, Charles Marie Georges
1848-1907
See Huysmans, Joris-Karl
See also CA 104

Huysmans, Joris-Karl............. TCLC 7
See also Huysmans, Charles Marie Georges
See also DLB 123

Hwang, David Henry
1957-................. CLC **55; DC 4**
See also CA 127; 132

Hyde, Anthony 1946-............. CLC **42**
See also CA 136

Hyde, Margaret O(ldroyd) 1917- ... CLC **21**
See also CA 1-4R; CANR 1, 36; CLR 23;
JRDA; MAICYA; SAAS 8; SATA 1, 42,
76

Hynes, James 1956(?)-............ CLC **65**

Ian, Janis 1951- .... CLC **21**
See also CA 105

Ibanez, Vicente Blasco
See Blasco Ibanez, Vicente

Ibarguengoitia, Jorge 1928-1983.... CLC **37**
See also CA 124; 113; HW

Ibsen, Henrik (Johan)
1828-1906 ...... TCLC **2, 8, 16, 37, 52;**
DA; DC 2; WLC
See also CA 104; 141

Ibuse Masuji 1898-1993.......... CLC **22**
See also CA 127; 141

Ichikawa, Kon 1915-............. CLC **20**
See also CA 121

Idle, Eric 1943-................. CLC **21**
See also Monty Python
See also CA 116; CANR 35

Ignatow, David 1914-...... CLC **4, 7, 14, 40**
See also CA 9-12R; CAAS 3; CANR 31;
DLB 5

Ihimaera, Witi 1944- .... CLC **46**
See also CA 77-80

Ilf, Ilya........................ TCLC 21
See also Fainzilberg, Ilya Arnoldovich

Immermann, Karl (Lebrecht)
1796-1840 .... NCLC **4**
See also DLB 133

Inclan, Ramon (Maria) del Valle
See Valle-Inclan, Ramon (Maria) del

Infante, G(uillermo) Cabrera
See Cabrera Infante, G(uillermo)

Ingalls, Rachel (Holmes) 1940-..... CLC **42**
See also CA 123; 127

Ingamells, Rex 1913-1955 .... TCLC **35**

Inge, William Motter
1913-1973 .... CLC **1, 8, 19**
See also CA 9-12R; CDALB 1941-1968;
DLB 7; MTCW

Ingelow, Jean 1820-1897 .... NCLC **39**
See also DLB 35; SATA 33

Ingram, Willis J.
See Harris, Mark

Innaurato, Albert (F.) 1948(?)- .. CLC **21, 60**
See also CA 115; 122

Innes, Michael
See Stewart, J(ohn) I(nnes) M(ackintosh)

Ionesco, Eugene
1912-1994 .... CLC **1, 4, 6, 9, 11, 15, 41;**
DA; WLC
See also CA 9-12R; 144; MTCW; SATA 7

Iqbal, Muhammad 1873-1938 ..... TCLC **28**

Ireland, Patrick
See O'Doherty, Brian

Iron, Ralph
See Schreiner, Olive (Emilie Albertina)

Irving, John (Winslow)
1942-................. CLC **13, 23, 38**
See also AAYA 8; BEST 89:3; CA 25-28R;
CANR 28; DLB 6; DLBY 82; MTCW

Irving, Washington
1783-1859 .... NCLC **2, 19; DA; SSC 2;**
WLC
See also CDALB 1640-1865; DLB 3, 11, 30,
59, 73, 74; YABC 2

Irwin, P. K.
See Page, P(atricia) K(athleen)

Isaacs, Susan 1943- .... CLC **32**
See also BEST 89:1; CA 89-92; CANR 20,
41; MTCW

Isherwood, Christopher (William Bradshaw)
1904-1986 . . . . **CLC 1, 9, 11, 14, 44**
See also CA 13-16R; 117; CANR 35;
DLB 15; DLBY 86; MTCW

Ishiguro, Kazuo 1954- . . . . . . **CLC 27, 56, 59**
See also BEST 90:2; CA 120; MTCW

Ishikawa Takuboku
1886(?)-1912 . . . . **TCLC 15; PC 10**
See also CA 113

Iskander, Fazil 1929- . . . . **CLC 47**
See also CA 102

Ivan IV 1530-1584 . . . . **LC 17**

Ivanov, Vyacheslav Ivanovich
1866-1949 . . . . **TCLC 33**
See also CA 122

Ivask, Ivar Vidrik 1927-1992. . . . . . . **CLC 14**
See also CA 37-40R; 139; CANR 24

Jackson, Daniel
See Wingrove, David (John)

Jackson, Jesse 1908-1983 . . . . **CLC 12**
See also BW 1; CA 25-28R; 109; CANR 27;
CLR 28; MAICYA; SATA 2, 29, 48

Jackson, Laura (Riding) 1901-1991
See Riding, Laura
See also CA 65-68; 135; CANR 28; DLB 48

Jackson, Sam
See Trumbo, Dalton

Jackson, Sara
See Wingrove, David (John)

Jackson, Shirley
1919-1965 . . . . . **CLC 11, 60; DA; SSC 9;
WLC**
See also AAYA 9; CA 1-4R; 25-28R;
CANR 4; CDALB 1941-1968; DLB 6;
SATA 2

Jacob, (Cyprien-)Max 1876-1944 . . . **TCLC 6**
See also CA 104

Jacobs, Jim 1942-. . . . . **CLC 12**
See also CA 97-100

Jacobs, W(illiam) W(ymark)
1863-1943 . . . . **TCLC 22**
See also CA 121; DLB 135

Jacobsen, Jens Peter 1847-1885 . . **NCLC 34**

Jacobsen, Josephine 1908- . . . . **CLC 48**
See also CA 33-36R; CAAS 18; CANR 23

Jacobson, Dan 1929- . . . . **CLC 4, 14**
See also CA 1-4R; CANR 2, 25; DLB 14;
MTCW

Jacqueline
See Carpentier (y Valmont), Alejo

Jagger, Mick 1944-. . . . . **CLC 17**

Jakes, John (William) 1932- . . . . **CLC 29**
See also BEST 89:4; CA 57-60; CANR 10,
43; DLBY 83; MTCW; SATA 62

James, Andrew
See Kirkup, James

James, C(yril) L(ionel) R(obert)
1901-1989 . . . . **CLC 33**
See also BW 2; CA 117; 125; 128; DLB 125;
MTCW

James, Daniel (Lewis) 1911-1988
See Santiago, Danny
See also CA 125

James, Dynely
See Mayne, William (James Carter)

James, Henry
1843-1916 . . . . . . **TCLC 2, 11, 24, 40, 47;
DA; SSC 8; WLC**
See also CA 104; 132; CDALB 1865-1917;
DLB 12, 71, 74; MTCW

James, M. R.
See James, Montague (Rhodes)
See also SSC 16

James, Montague (Rhodes)
1862-1936 . . . . **TCLC 6**
See also CA 104

James, P. D. . . . . **CLC 18, 46**
See also White, Phyllis Dorothy James
See also BEST 90:2; CDBLB 1960 to
Present; DLB 87

James, Philip
See Moorcock, Michael (John)

James, William 1842-1910. . . . . **TCLC 15, 32**
See also CA 109

James I 1394-1437 . . . . **LC 20**

Jameson, Anna 1794-1860 . . . . **NCLC 43**
See also DLB 99

Jami, Nur al-Din 'Abd al-Rahman
1414-1492 . . . . **LC 9**

Jandl, Ernst 1925- . . . . **CLC 34**

Janowitz, Tama 1957- . . . . **CLC 43**
See also CA 106

Jarrell, Randall
1914-1965 . . . . **CLC 1, 2, 6, 9, 13, 49**
See also CA 5-8R; 25-28R; CABS 2;
CANR 6, 34; CDALB 1941-1968; CLR 6;
DLB 48, 52; MAICYA; MTCW; SATA 7

Jarry, Alfred 1873-1907. . . . . . . **TCLC 2, 14**
See also CA 104

Jarvis, E. K.
See Bloch, Robert (Albert); Ellison, Harlan;
Silverberg, Robert

Jeake, Samuel, Jr.
See Aiken, Conrad (Potter)

Jean Paul 1763-1825 . . . . **NCLC 7**

Jeffers, (John) Robinson
1887-1962 . . . . **CLC 2, 3, 11, 15, 54; DA;
WLC**
See also CA 85-88; CANR 35;
CDALB 1917-1929; DLB 45; MTCW

Jefferson, Janet
See Mencken, H(enry) L(ouis)

Jefferson, Thomas 1743-1826 . . . . **NCLC 11**
See also CDALB 1640-1865; DLB 31

Jeffrey, Francis 1773-1850. . . . . . . **NCLC 33**
See also DLB 107

Jelakowitch, Ivan
See Heijermans, Herman

Jellicoe, (Patricia) Ann 1927- . . . . . . **CLC 27**
See also CA 85-88; DLB 13

Jen, Gish . . . . **CLC 70**
See also Jen, Lillian

Jen, Lillian 1956(?)-
See Jen, Gish
See also CA 135

Jenkins, (John) Robin 1912- . . . . **CLC 52**
See also CA 1-4R; CANR 1; DLB 14

Jennings, Elizabeth (Joan)
1926- . . . . **CLC 5, 14**
See also CA 61-64; CAAS 5; CANR 8, 39;
DLB 27; MTCW; SATA 66

Jennings, Waylon 1937-. . . . . **CLC 21**

Jensen, Johannes V. 1873-1950. . . . **TCLC 41**

Jensen, Laura (Linnea) 1948- . . . . . . **CLC 37**
See also CA 103

Jerome, Jerome K(lapka)
1859-1927 . . . . **TCLC 23**
See also CA 119; DLB 10, 34, 135

Jerrold, Douglas William
1803-1857 . . . . **NCLC 2**

Jewett, (Theodora) Sarah Orne
1849-1909 . . . . **TCLC 1, 22; SSC 6**
See also CA 108; 127; DLB 12, 74;
SATA 15

Jewsbury, Geraldine (Endsor)
1812-1880 . . . . **NCLC 22**
See also DLB 21

Jhabvala, Ruth Prawer
1927- . . . . **CLC 4, 8, 29**
See also CA 1-4R; CANR 2, 29; DLB 139;
MTCW

Jiles, Paulette 1943-. . . . . **CLC 13, 58**
See also CA 101

Jimenez (Mantecon), Juan Ramon
1881-1958 . . . . **TCLC 4; HLC; PC 7**
See also CA 104; 131; DLB 134; HW;
MTCW

Jimenez, Juan Ramon 1881-1958
See Jimenez (Mantecon), Juan Ramon

Jimenez, Ramon
See Jimenez (Mantecon), Juan Ramon

Jimenez Mantecon, Juan
See Jimenez (Mantecon), Juan Ramon

Joel, Billy . . . . **CLC 26**
See also Joel, William Martin

Joel, William Martin 1949-
See Joel, Billy
See also CA 108

John of the Cross, St. 1542-1591 . . . . **LC 18**

Johnson, B(ryan) S(tanley William)
1933-1973 . . . . **CLC 6, 9**
See also CA 9-12R; 53-56; CANR 9;
DLB 14, 40

Johnson, Benj. F. of Boo
See Riley, James Whitcomb

Johnson, Benjamin F. of Boo
See Riley, James Whitcomb

Johnson, Charles (Richard)
1948- . . . . **CLC 7, 51, 65; BLC**
See also BW 2; CA 116; CAAS 18;
CANR 42; DLB 33

Johnson, Denis 1949-. . . . . **CLC 52**
See also CA 117; 121; DLB 120

Johnson, Diane 1934-. . . . . **CLC 5, 13, 48**
See also CA 41-44R; CANR 17, 40;
DLBY 80; MTCW

Johnson, Eyvind (Olof Verner)
1900-1976 . . . . **CLC 14**
See also CA 73-76; 69-72; CANR 34

Johnson, J. R.
See James, C(yril) L(ionel) R(obert)

Kaufman, Bob (Garnell)
1925-1986 .... **CLC 49**
See also BW 1; CA 41-44R; 118; CANR 22;
DLB 16, 41

Kaufman, George S. 1889-1961 ..... **CLC 38**
See also CA 108; 93-96; DLB 7

Kaufman, Sue .... **CLC 3, 8**
See also Barondess, Sue K(aufman)

Kavafis, Konstantinos Petrou 1863-1933
See Cavafy, C(onstantine) P(eter)
See also CA 104

Kavan, Anna 1901-1968 ...... **CLC 5, 13, 82**
See also CA 5-8R; CANR 6; MTCW

Kavanagh, Dan
See Barnes, Julian

Kavanagh, Patrick (Joseph)
1904-1967 .... **CLC 22**
See also CA 123; 25-28R; DLB 15, 20;
MTCW

Kawabata, Yasunari
1899-1972 .... **CLC 2, 5, 9, 18**
See also CA 93-96; 33-36R

Kaye, M(ary) M(argaret) 1909- ..... **CLC 28**
See also CA 89-92; CANR 24; MTCW;
SATA 62

Kaye, Mollie
See Kaye, M(ary) M(argaret)

Kaye-Smith, Sheila 1887-1956 ..... **TCLC 20**
See also CA 118; DLB 36

Kaymor, Patrice Maguilene
See Senghor, Leopold Sedar

Kazan, Elia 1909- .... **CLC 6, 16, 63**
See also CA 21-24R; CANR 32

Kazantzakis, Nikos
1883(?)-1957 .... **TCLC 2, 5, 33**
See also CA 105; 132; MTCW

Kazin, Alfred 1915- .... **CLC 34, 38**
See also CA 1-4R; CAAS 7; CANR 1, 45;
DLB 67

Keane, Mary Nesta (Skrine) 1904-
See Keane, Molly
See also CA 108; 114

Keane, Molly .... **CLC 31**
See also Keane, Mary Nesta (Skrine)

Keates, Jonathan 19(?)- .... **CLC 34**

Keaton, Buster 1895-1966 .... **CLC 20**

Keats, John
1795-1821 ... **NCLC 8; DA; PC 1; WLC**
See also CDBLB 1789-1832; DLB 96, 110

Keene, Donald 1922- .... **CLC 34**
See also CA 1-4R; CANR 5

Keillor, Garrison .... **CLC 40**
See also Keillor, Gary (Edward)
See also AAYA 2; BEST 89:3; DLBY 87;
SATA 58

Keillor, Gary (Edward) 1942-
See Keillor, Garrison
See also CA 111; 117; CANR 36; MTCW

Keith, Michael
See Hubbard, L(afayette) Ron(ald)

Keller, Gottfried 1819-1890 ...... **NCLC 2**
See also DLB 129

Kellerman, Jonathan 1949- .... **CLC 44**
See also BEST 90:1; CA 106; CANR 29

Kelley, William Melvin 1937- ...... **CLC 22**
See also BW 1; CA 77-80; CANR 27;
DLB 33

Kellogg, Marjorie 1922- .... **CLC 2**
See also CA 81-84

Kellow, Kathleen
See Hibbert, Eleanor Alice Burford

Kelly, M(ilton) T(erry) 1947- .... **CLC 55**
See also CA 97-100; CANR 19, 43

Kelman, James 1946- .... **CLC 58**

Kemal, Yashar 1923- .... **CLC 14, 29**
See also CA 89-92; CANR 44

Kemble, Fanny 1809-1893 .... **NCLC 18**
See also DLB 32

Kemelman, Harry 1908- .... **CLC 2**
See also AITN 1; CA 9-12R; CANR 6;
DLB 28

Kempe, Margery 1373(?)-1440(?) ..... **LC 6**

Kempis, Thomas a 1380-1471 .... **LC 11**

Kendall, Henry 1839-1882 .... **NCLC 12**

Keneally, Thomas (Michael)
1935- ...... **CLC 5, 8, 10, 14, 19, 27, 43**
See also CA 85-88; CANR 10; MTCW

Kennedy, Adrienne (Lita)
1931- .... **CLC 66; BLC**
See also BW 2; CA 103; CABS 3;
CANR 26; DLB 38

Kennedy, John Pendleton
1795-1870 .... **NCLC 2**
See also DLB 3

Kennedy, Joseph Charles 1929- ...... **CLC 8**
See also Kennedy, X. J.
See also CA 1-4R; CANR 4, 30, 40;
SATA 14

Kennedy, William 1928- ... **CLC 6, 28, 34, 53**
See also AAYA 1; CA 85-88; CANR 14,
31; DLB 143; DLBY 85; MTCW;
SATA 57

Kennedy, X. J. .... **CLC 42**
See also Kennedy, Joseph Charles
See also CAAS 9; CLR 27; DLB 5

Kent, Kelvin
See Kuttner, Henry

Kenton, Maxwell
See Southern, Terry

Kenyon, Robert O.
See Kuttner, Henry

Kerouac, Jack ..... **CLC 1, 2, 3, 5, 14, 29, 61**
See also Kerouac, Jean-Louis Lebris de
See also CDALB 1941-1968; DLB 2, 16;
DLBD 3

Kerouac, Jean-Louis Lebris de 1922-1969
See Kerouac, Jack
See also AITN 1; CA 5-8R; 25-28R;
CANR 26; DA; MTCW; WLC

Kerr, Jean 1923- .... **CLC 22**
See also CA 5-8R; CANR 7

Kerr, M. E. .... **CLC 12, 35**
See also Meaker, Marijane (Agnes)
See also AAYA 2; CLR 29; SAAS 1

Kerr, Robert .... **CLC 55**

Kerrigan, (Thomas) Anthony
1918- .... **CLC 4, 6**
See also CA 49-52; CAAS 11; CANR 4

Kerry, Lois
See Duncan, Lois

Kesey, Ken (Elton)
1935- ...... **CLC 1, 3, 6, 11, 46, 64; DA;
WLC**
See also CA 1-4R; CANR 22, 38;
CDALB 1968-1988; DLB 2, 16; MTCW;
SATA 66

Kesselring, Joseph (Otto)
1902-1967 .... **CLC 45**

Kessler, Jascha (Frederick) 1929- .... **CLC 4**
See also CA 17-20R; CANR 8

Kettelkamp, Larry (Dale) 1933- .... **CLC 12**
See also CA 29-32R; CANR 16; SAAS 3;
SATA 2

Keyber, Conny
See Fielding, Henry

Keyes, Daniel 1927- .... **CLC 80; DA**
See also CA 17-20R; CANR 10, 26;
SATA 37

Khayyam, Omar
1048-1131 .... **CMLC 11; PC 8**

Kherdian, David 1931- .... **CLC 6, 9**
See also CA 21-24R; CAAS 2; CANR 39;
CLR 24; JRDA; MAICYA; SATA 16, 74

Khlebnikov, Velimir .... **TCLC 20**
See also Khlebnikov, Viktor Vladimirovich

Khlebnikov, Viktor Vladimirovich 1885-1922
See Khlebnikov, Velimir
See also CA 117

Khodasevich, Vladislav (Felitsianovich)
1886-1939 .... **TCLC 15**
See also CA 115

Kielland, Alexander Lange
1849-1906 .... **TCLC 5**
See also CA 104

Kiely, Benedict 1919- .... **CLC 23, 43**
See also CA 1-4R; CANR 2; DLB 15

Kienzle, William X(avier) 1928- .... **CLC 25**
See also CA 93-96; CAAS 1; CANR 9, 31;
MTCW

Kierkegaard, Soren 1813-1855 .... **NCLC 34**

Killens, John Oliver 1916-1987 ..... **CLC 10**
See also BW 2; CA 77-80; 123; CAAS 2;
CANR 26; DLB 33

Killigrew, Anne 1660-1685 .... **LC 4**
See also DLB 131

Kim
See Simenon, Georges (Jacques Christian)

Kincaid, Jamaica 1949- ... **CLC 43, 68; BLC**
See also BW 2; CA 125

King, Francis (Henry) 1923- ..... **CLC 8, 53**
See also CA 1-4R; CANR 1, 33; DLB 15,
139; MTCW

King, Martin Luther, Jr.
1929-1968 .... **CLC 83; BLC; DA**
See also BW 2; CA 25-28; CANR 27, 44;
CAP 2; MTCW; SATA 14

King, Stephen (Edwin)
1947- .... **CLC 12, 26, 37, 61**
See also AAYA 1; BEST 90:1; CA 61-64;
CANR 1, 30; DLB 143; DLBY 80;
JRDA; MTCW; SATA 9, 55

King, Steve
See King, Stephen (Edwin)

Kingman, Lee. CLC 17
See also Natti, (Mary) Lee
See also SAAS 3; SATA 1, 67

Kingsley, Charles 1819-1875 . . . . . NCLC 35
See also DLB 21, 32; YABC 2

Kingsley, Sidney 1906- . . . . CLC 44
See also CA 85-88; DLB 7

Kingsolver, Barbara 1955- . . . . . . CLC 55, 81
See also CA 129; 134

Kingston, Maxine (Ting Ting) Hong
1940- . . . . CLC 12, 19, 58
See also AAYA 8; CA 69-72; CANR 13,
38; DLBY 80; MTCW; SATA 53

Kinnell, Galway
1927- . . . . CLC 1, 2, 3, 5, 13, 29
See also CA 9-12R; CANR 10, 34; DLB 5;
DLBY 87; MTCW

Kinsella, Thomas 1928- . . . . CLC 4, 19
See also CA 17-20R; CANR 15; DLB 27;
MTCW

Kinsella, W(illiam) P(atrick)
1935- . . . . CLC 27, 43
See also AAYA 7; CA 97-100; CAAS 7;
CANR 21, 35; MTCW

Kipling, (Joseph) Rudyard
1865-1936 . . . . . . TCLC 8, 17; DA; PC 3;
SSC 5; WLC
See also CA 105; 120; CANR 33;
CDBLB 1890-1914; DLB 19, 34, 141;
MAICYA; MTCW; YABC 2

Kirkup, James 1918- . . . . CLC 1
See also CA 1-4R; CAAS 4; CANR 2;
DLB 27; SATA 12

Kirkwood, James 1930(?)-1989 . . . . . . CLC 9
See also AITN 2; CA 1-4R; 128; CANR 6,
40

Kis, Danilo 1935-1989 . . . . CLC 57
See also CA 109; 118; 129; MTCW

Kivi, Aleksis 1834-1872 . . . . NCLC 30

Kizer, Carolyn (Ashley)
1925- . . . . CLC 15, 39, 80
See also CA 65-68; CAAS 5; CANR 24;
DLB 5

Klabund 1890-1928 . . . . TCLC 44
See also DLB 66

Klappert, Peter 1942- . . . . CLC 57
See also CA 33-36R; DLB 5

Klein, A(braham) M(oses)
1909-1972 . . . . CLC 19
See also CA 101; 37-40R; DLB 68

Klein, Norma 1938-1989 . . . . CLC 30
See also AAYA 2; CA 41-44R; 128;
CANR 15, 37; CLR 2, 19; JRDA;
MAICYA; SAAS 1; SATA 7, 57

Klein, T(heodore) E(ibon) D(onald)
1947- . . . . CLC 34
See also CA 119; CANR 44

Kleist, Heinrich von
1777-1811 . . . . NCLC 2, 37
See also DLB 90

Klima, Ivan 1931- . . . . CLC 56
See also CA 25-28R; CANR 17

Klimentov, Andrei Platonovich 1899-1951
See Platonov, Andrei
See also CA 108

Klinger, Friedrich Maximilian von
1752-1831 . . . . NCLC 1
See also DLB 94

Klopstock, Friedrich Gottlieb
1724-1803 . . . . NCLC 11
See also DLB 97

Knebel, Fletcher 1911-1993 . . . . CLC 14
See also AITN 1; CA 1-4R; 140; CAAS 3;
CANR 1, 36; SATA 36; SATA-Obit 75

Knickerbocker, Diedrich
See Irving, Washington

Knight, Etheridge
1931-1991 . . . . CLC 40; BLC
See also BW 1; CA 21-24R; 133; CANR 23;
DLB 41

Knight, Sarah Kemble 1666-1727 . . . . . LC 7
See also DLB 24

Knister, Raymond 1899-1932 . . . . . . TCLC 56
See also DLB 68

Knowles, John
1926- . . . . CLC 1, 4, 10, 26; DA
See also AAYA 10; CA 17-20R; CANR 40;
CDALB 1968-1988; DLB 6; MTCW;
SATA 8

Knox, Calvin M.
See Silverberg, Robert

Knye, Cassandra
See Disch, Thomas M(ichael)

Koch, C(hristopher) J(ohn) 1932- . . . CLC 42
See also CA 127

Koch, Christopher
See Koch, C(hristopher) J(ohn)

Koch, Kenneth 1925- . . . . CLC 5, 8, 44
See also CA 1-4R; CANR 6, 36; DLB 5;
SATA 65

Kochanowski, Jan 1530-1584 . . . . LC 10

Kock, Charles Paul de
1794-1871 . . . . NCLC 16

Koda Shigeyuki 1867-1947
See Rohan, Koda
See also CA 121

Koestler, Arthur
1905-1983 . . . . CLC 1, 3, 6, 8, 15, 33
See also CA 1-4R; 109; CANR 1, 33;
CDBLB 1945-1960; DLBY 83; MTCW

Kogawa, Joy Nozomi 1935- . . . . CLC 78
See also CA 101; CANR 19

Kohout, Pavel 1928- . . . . CLC 13
See also CA 45-48; CANR 3

Koizumi, Yakumo
See Hearn, (Patricio) Lafcadio (Tessima
Carlos)

Kolmar, Gertrud 1894-1943 . . . . . . TCLC 40

Konrad, George
See Konrad, Gyoergy

Konrad, Gyoergy 1933- . . . . . . CLC 4, 10, 73
See also CA 85-88

Konwicki, Tadeusz 1926- . . . . CLC 8, 28, 54
See also CA 101; CAAS 9; CANR 39;
MTCW

Koontz, Dean R(ay) 1945- . . . . CLC 78
See also AAYA 9; BEST 89:3, 90:2;
CA 108; CANR 19, 36; MTCW

Kopit, Arthur (Lee) 1937- . . . . CLC 1, 18, 33
See also AITN 1; CA 81-84; CABS 3;
DLB 7; MTCW

Kops, Bernard 1926- . . . . CLC 4
See also CA 5-8R; DLB 13

Kornbluth, C(yril) M. 1923-1958 . . . . TCLC 8
See also CA 105; DLB 8

Korolenko, V. G.
See Korolenko, Vladimir Galaktionovich

Korolenko, Vladimir
See Korolenko, Vladimir Galaktionovich

Korolenko, Vladimir G.
See Korolenko, Vladimir Galaktionovich

Korolenko, Vladimir Galaktionovich
1853-1921 . . . . TCLC 22
See also CA 121

Kosinski, Jerzy (Nikodem)
1933-1991 . . . . CLC 1, 2, 3, 6, 10, 15, 53,
70
See also CA 17-20R; 134; CANR 9; DLB 2;
DLBY 82; MTCW

Kostelanetz, Richard (Cory) 1940- . . CLC 28
See also CA 13-16R; CAAS 8; CANR 38

Kostrowitzki, Wilhelm Apollinaris de
1880-1918
See Apollinaire, Guillaume
See also CA 104

Kotlowitz, Robert 1924- . . . . CLC 4
See also CA 33-36R; CANR 36

Kotzebue, August (Friedrich Ferdinand) von
1761-1819 . . . . NCLC 25
See also DLB 94

Kotzwinkle, William 1938- . . . CLC 5, 14, 35
See also CA 45-48; CANR 3, 44; CLR 6;
MAICYA; SATA 24, 70

Kozol, Jonathan 1936- . . . . CLC 17
See also CA 61-64; CANR 16, 45

Kozoll, Michael 1940(?)- . . . . CLC 35

Kramer, Kathryn 19(?)- . . . . CLC 34

Kramer, Larry 1935- . . . . CLC 42
See also CA 124; 126

Krasicki, Ignacy 1735-1801 . . . . NCLC 8

Krasinski, Zygmunt 1812-1859 . . . . NCLC 4

Kraus, Karl 1874-1936 . . . . TCLC 5
See also CA 104; DLB 118

Kreve (Mickevicius), Vincas
1882-1954 . . . . TCLC 27

Kristeva, Julia 1941- . . . . CLC 77

Kristofferson, Kris 1936- . . . . CLC 26
See also CA 104

Krizanc, John 1956- . . . . CLC 57

Krleza, Miroslav 1893-1981 . . . . CLC 8
See also CA 97-100; 105

Kroetsch, Robert 1927- . . . . . . CLC 5, 23, 57
See also CA 17-20R; CANR 8, 38; DLB 53;
MTCW

Kroetz, Franz
See Kroetz, Franz Xaver

Kroetz, Franz Xaver 1946- . . . . CLC 41
See also CA 130

Kroker, Arthur 1945- . . . . CLC 77

Kropotkin, Peter (Aleksieevich)
1842-1921 . . . . **TCLC 36**
See also CA 119

Krotkov, Yuri 1917- . . . . **CLC 19**
See also CA 102

Krumb
See Crumb, R(obert)

Krumgold, Joseph (Quincy)
1908-1980 . . . . **CLC 12**
See also CA 9-12R; 101; CANR 7;
MAICYA; SATA 1, 23, 48

Krumwitz
See Crumb, R(obert)

Krutch, Joseph Wood 1893-1970 . . . . **CLC 24**
See also CA 1-4R; 25-28R; CANR 4;
DLB 63

Krutzch, Gus
See Eliot, T(homas) S(tearns)

Krylov, Ivan Andreevich
1768(?)-1844 . . . . **NCLC 1**

Kubin, Alfred 1877-1959 . . . . **TCLC 23**
See also CA 112; DLB 81

Kubrick, Stanley 1928- . . . . **CLC 16**
See also CA 81-84; CANR 33; DLB 26

Kumin, Maxine (Winokur)
1925- . . . . **CLC 5, 13, 28**
See also AITN 2; CA 1-4R; CAAS 8;
CANR 1, 21; DLB 5; MTCW; SATA 12

Kundera, Milan
1929- . . . . **CLC 4, 9, 19, 32, 68**
See also AAYA 2; CA 85-88; CANR 19;
MTCW

Kunitz, Stanley (Jasspon)
1905- . . . . **CLC 6, 11, 14**
See also CA 41-44R; CANR 26; DLB 48;
MTCW

Kunze, Reiner 1933- . . . . **CLC 10**
See also CA 93-96; DLB 75

Kuprin, Aleksandr Ivanovich
1870-1938 . . . . **TCLC 5**
See also CA 104

Kureishi, Hanif 1954(?)- . . . . **CLC 64**
See also CA 139

Kurosawa, Akira 1910- . . . . **CLC 16**
See also AAYA 11; CA 101

Kushner, Tony 1957(?)- . . . . **CLC 81**
See also CA 144

Kuttner, Henry 1915-1958 . . . . **TCLC 10**
See also CA 107; DLB 8

Kuzma, Greg 1944- . . . . **CLC 7**
See also CA 33-36R

Kuzmin, Mikhail 1872(?)-1936 . . . . **TCLC 40**

Kyd, Thomas 1558-1594 . . . . . . **LC 22; DC 3**
See also DLB 62

Kyprianos, Iossif
See Samarakis, Antonis

La Bruyere, Jean de 1645-1696 . . . . . . **LC 17**

Lacan, Jacques (Marie Emile)
1901-1981 . . . . **CLC 75**
See also CA 121; 104

**Laclos, Pierre Ambroise Francois Choderlos
de** 1741-1803 . . . . **NCLC 4**

La Colere, Francois
See Aragon, Louis

Lacolere, Francois
See Aragon, Louis

La Deshabilleuse
See Simenon, Georges (Jacques Christian)

Lady Gregory
See Gregory, Isabella Augusta (Persse)

Lady of Quality, A
See Bagnold, Enid

**La Fayette, Marie (Madelaine Pioche de la
Vergne Comtes** 1634-1693 . . . . . . **LC 2**

Lafayette, Rene
See Hubbard, L(afayette) Ron(ald)

Laforgue, Jules 1860-1887 . . . . **NCLC 5**

Lagerkvist, Paer (Fabian)
1891-1974 . . . . **CLC 7, 10, 13, 54**
See also Lagerkvist, Par
See also CA 85-88; 49-52; MTCW

Lagerkvist, Par
See Lagerkvist, Paer (Fabian)
See also SSC 12

Lagerloef, Selma (Ottiliana Lovisa)
1858-1940 . . . . **TCLC 4, 36**
See also Lagerlof, Selma (Ottiliana Lovisa)
See also CA 108; CLR 7; SATA 15

Lagerlof, Selma (Ottiliana Lovisa)
See Lagerloef, Selma (Ottiliana Lovisa)
See also CLR 7; SATA 15

La Guma, (Justin) Alex(ander)
1925-1985 . . . . **CLC 19**
See also BW 1; CA 49-52; 118; CANR 25;
DLB 117; MTCW

Laidlaw, A. K.
See Grieve, C(hristopher) M(urray)

Lainez, Manuel Mujica
See Mujica Lainez, Manuel
See also HW

Lamartine, Alphonse (Marie Louis Prat) de
1790-1869 . . . . **NCLC 11**

Lamb, Charles
1775-1834 . . . . **NCLC 10; DA; WLC**
See also CDBLB 1789-1832; DLB 93, 107;
SATA 17

Lamb, Lady Caroline 1785-1828 . . **NCLC 38**
See also DLB 116

Lamming, George (William)
1927- . . . . **CLC 2, 4, 66; BLC**
See also BW 2; CA 85-88; CANR 26;
DLB 125; MTCW

L'Amour, Louis (Dearborn)
1908-1988 . . . . **CLC 25, 55**
See also AITN 2; BEST 89:2; CA 1-4R;
125; CANR 3, 25, 40; DLBY 80; MTCW

Lampedusa, Giuseppe (Tomasi) di . . . **TCLC 13**
See also Tomasi di Lampedusa, Giuseppe

Lampman, Archibald 1861-1899 . . **NCLC 25**
See also DLB 92

Lancaster, Bruce 1896-1963 . . . . **CLC 36**
See also CA 9-10; CAP 1; SATA 9

Landau, Mark Alexandrovich
See Aldanov, Mark (Alexandrovich)

Landau-Aldanov, Mark Alexandrovich
See Aldanov, Mark (Alexandrovich)

Landis, John 1950- . . . . **CLC 26**
See also CA 112; 122

Landolfi, Tommaso 1908-1979 . . . **CLC 11, 49**
See also CA 127; 117

Landon, Letitia Elizabeth
1802-1838 . . . . **NCLC 15**
See also DLB 96

Landor, Walter Savage
1775-1864 . . . . **NCLC 14**
See also DLB 93, 107

Landwirth, Heinz 1927-
See Lind, Jakov
See also CA 9-12R; CANR 7

Lane, Patrick 1939- . . . . **CLC 25**
See also CA 97-100; DLB 53

Lang, Andrew 1844-1912 . . . . **TCLC 16**
See also CA 114; 137; DLB 98, 141;
MAICYA; SATA 16

Lang, Fritz 1890-1976 . . . . **CLC 20**
See also CA 77-80; 69-72; CANR 30

Lange, John
See Crichton, (John) Michael

Langer, Elinor 1939- . . . . **CLC 34**
See also CA 121

Langland, William
1330(?)-1400(?) . . . . **LC 19; DA**

Langstaff, Launcelot
See Irving, Washington

Lanier, Sidney 1842-1881 . . . . **NCLC 6**
See also DLB 64; MAICYA; SATA 18

Lanyer, Aemilia 1569-1645 . . . . **LC 10**

Lao Tzu . . . . **CMLC 7**

Lapine, James (Elliot) 1949- . . . . **CLC 39**
See also CA 123; 130

Larbaud, Valery (Nicolas)
1881-1957 . . . . **TCLC 9**
See also CA 106

Lardner, Ring
See Lardner, Ring(gold) W(ilmer)

Lardner, Ring W., Jr.
See Lardner, Ring(gold) W(ilmer)

Lardner, Ring(gold) W(ilmer)
1885-1933 . . . . **TCLC 2, 14**
See also CA 104; 131; CDALB 1917-1929;
DLB 11, 25, 86; MTCW

Laredo, Betty
See Codrescu, Andrei

Larkin, Maia
See Wojciechowska, Maia (Teresa)

Larkin, Philip (Arthur)
1922-1985 . . . . **CLC 3, 5, 8, 9, 13, 18, 33,
39, 64**
See also CA 5-8R; 117; CANR 24;
CDBLB 1960 to Present; DLB 27;
MTCW

Larra (y Sanchez de Castro), Mariano Jose de
1809-1837 . . . . **NCLC 17**

Larsen, Eric 1941- . . . . **CLC 55**
See also CA 132

Larsen, Nella 1891-1964 . . . . . **CLC 37; BLC**
See also BW 1; CA 125; DLB 51

Larson, Charles R(aymond) 1938- . . . **CLC 31**
See also CA 53-56; CANR 4

Latham, Jean Lee 1902- . . . . **CLC 12**
See also AITN 1; CA 5-8R; CANR 7;
MAICYA; SATA 2, 68

Lustig, Arnost 1926-.............. **CLC 56**
See also AAYA 3; CA 69-72; SATA 56

Luther, Martin 1483-1546.......... **LC 9**

Luzi, Mario 1914-................ **CLC 13**
See also CA 61-64; CANR 9; DLB 128

Lynch, B. Suarez
See Bioy Casares, Adolfo; Borges, Jorge
Luis

Lynch, David (K.) 1946-........... **CLC 66**
See also CA 124; 129

Lynch, James
See Andreyev, Leonid (Nikolaevich)

Lynch Davis, B.
See Bioy Casares, Adolfo; Borges, Jorge
Luis

Lyndsay, Sir David 1490-1555 ...... **LC 20**

Lynn, Kenneth S(chuyler) 1923-.... **CLC 50**
See also CA 1-4R; CANR 3, 27

Lynx
See West, Rebecca

Lyons, Marcus
See Blish, James (Benjamin)

Lyre, Pinchbeck
See Sassoon, Siegfried (Lorraine)

Lytle, Andrew (Nelson) 1902-...... **CLC 22**
See also CA 9-12R; DLB 6

Lyttelton, George 1709-1773........ **LC 10**

Maas, Peter 1929- .... **CLC 29**
See also CA 93-96

Macaulay, Rose 1881-1958 ..... **TCLC 7, 44**
See also CA 104; DLB 36

Macaulay, Thomas Babington
1800-1859 .... **NCLC 42**
See also CDBLB 1832-1890; DLB 32, 55

MacBeth, George (Mann)
1932-1992 .... **CLC 2, 5, 9**
See also CA 25-28R; 136; DLB 40; MTCW;
SATA 4; SATA-Obit 70

MacCaig, Norman (Alexander)
1910- .... **CLC 36**
See also CA 9-12R; CANR 3, 34; DLB 27

MacCarthy, (Sir Charles Otto) Desmond
1877-1952 .... **TCLC 36**

MacDiarmid, Hugh
.... **CLC 2, 4, 11, 19, 63; PC 9**
See also Grieve, C(hristopher) M(urray)
See also CDBLB 1945-1960; DLB 20

MacDonald, Anson
See Heinlein, Robert A(nson)

Macdonald, Cynthia 1928-...... **CLC 13, 19**
See also CA 49-52; CANR 4, 44; DLB 105

MacDonald, George 1824-1905..... **TCLC 9**
See also CA 106; 137; DLB 18; MAICYA;
SATA 33

Macdonald, John
See Millar, Kenneth

MacDonald, John D(ann)
1916-1986 .... **CLC 3, 27, 44**
See also CA 1-4R; 121; CANR 1, 19;
DLB 8; DLBY 86; MTCW

Macdonald, John Ross
See Millar, Kenneth

Macdonald, Ross..... **CLC 1, 2, 3, 14, 34, 41**
See also Millar, Kenneth
See also DLBD 6

MacDougal, John
See Blish, James (Benjamin)

MacEwen, Gwendolyn (Margaret)
1941-1987 .... **CLC 13, 55**
See also CA 9-12R; 124; CANR 7, 22;
DLB 53; SATA 50, 55

Machado (y Ruiz), Antonio
1875-1939 .... **TCLC 3**
See also CA 104; DLB 108

Machado de Assis, Joaquim Maria
1839-1908 .... **TCLC 10; BLC**
See also CA 107

Machen, Arthur................... **TCLC 4**
See also Jones, Arthur Llewellyn
See also DLB 36

Machiavelli, Niccolo 1469-1527 .. **LC 8; DA**

MacInnes, Colin 1914-1976...... **CLC 4, 23**
See also CA 69-72; 65-68; CANR 21;
DLB 14; MTCW

MacInnes, Helen (Clark)
1907-1985 .... **CLC 27, 39**
See also CA 1-4R; 117; CANR 1, 28;
DLB 87; MTCW; SATA 22, 44

Mackay, Mary 1855-1924
See Corelli, Marie
See also CA 118

Mackenzie, Compton (Edward Montague)
1883-1972 .... **CLC 18**
See also CA 21-22; 37-40R; CAP 2;
DLB 34, 100

Mackenzie, Henry 1745-1831 .... **NCLC 41**
See also DLB 39

Mackintosh, Elizabeth 1896(?)-1952
See Tey, Josephine
See also CA 110

MacLaren, James
See Grieve, C(hristopher) M(urray)

Mac Laverty, Bernard 1942-....... **CLC 31**
See also CA 116; 118; CANR 43

MacLean, Alistair (Stuart)
1922-1987 .... **CLC 3, 13, 50, 63**
See also CA 57-60; 121; CANR 28; MTCW;
SATA 23, 50

Maclean, Norman (Fitzroy)
1902-1990 .... **CLC 78; SSC 13**
See also CA 102; 132

MacLeish, Archibald
1892-1982 .... **CLC 3, 8, 14, 68**
See also CA 9-12R; 106; CANR 33; DLB 4,
7, 45; DLBY 82; MTCW

MacLennan, (John) Hugh
1907-1990 .... **CLC 2, 14**
See also CA 5-8R; 142; CANR 33; DLB 68;
MTCW

MacLeod, Alistair 1936- .... **CLC 56**
See also CA 123; DLB 60

MacNeice, (Frederick) Louis
1907-1963 .... **CLC 1, 4, 10, 53**
See also CA 85-88; DLB 10, 20; MTCW

MacNeill, Dand
See Fraser, George MacDonald

Macpherson, (Jean) Jay 1931-...... **CLC 14**
See also CA 5-8R; DLB 53

MacShane, Frank 1927-.......... **CLC 39**
See also CA 9-12R; CANR 3, 33; DLB 111

Macumber, Mari
See Sandoz, Mari(e Susette)

Madach, Imre 1823-1864........ **NCLC 19**

Madden, (Jerry) David 1933- .... **CLC 5, 15**
See also CA 1-4R; CAAS 3; CANR 4, 45;
DLB 6; MTCW

Maddern, Al(an)
See Ellison, Harlan

Madhubuti, Haki R.
1942- .... **CLC 6, 73; BLC; PC 5**
See also Lee, Don L.
See also BW 2; CA 73-76; CANR 24;
DLB 5, 41; DLBD 8

Madow, Pauline (Reichberg) .... **CLC 1**
See also CA 9-12R

Maepenn, Hugh
See Kuttner, Henry

Maepenn, K. H.
See Kuttner, Henry

Maeterlinck, Maurice 1862-1949 ... **TCLC 3**
See also CA 104; 136; SATA 66

Maginn, William 1794-1842....... **NCLC 8**
See also DLB 110

Mahapatra, Jayanta 1928-......... **CLC 33**
See also CA 73-76; CAAS 9; CANR 15, 33

Mahfouz, Naguib (Abdel Aziz Al-Sabilgi)
1911(?)-
See Mahfuz, Najib
See also BEST 89:2; CA 128; MTCW

Mahfuz, Najib................. **CLC 52, 55**
See also Mahfouz, Naguib (Abdel Aziz
Al-Sabilgi)
See also DLBY 88

Mahon, Derek 1941-.............. **CLC 27**
See also CA 113; 128; DLB 40

Mailer, Norman
1923- ...... **CLC 1, 2, 3, 4, 5, 8, 11, 14,
28, 39, 74; DA**
See also AITN 2; CA 9-12R; CABS 1;
CANR 28; CDALB 1968-1988; DLB 2,
16, 28; DLBD 3; DLBY 80, 83; MTCW

Maillet, Antonine 1929-........... **CLC 54**
See also CA 115; 120; DLB 60

Mais, Roger 1905-1955 .... **TCLC 8**
See also BW 1; CA 105; 124; DLB 125;
MTCW

Maistre, Joseph de 1753-1821.... **NCLC 37**

Maitland, Sara (Louise) 1950-...... **CLC 49**
See also CA 69-72; CANR 13

Major, Clarence
1936- .... **CLC 3, 19, 48; BLC**
See also BW 2; CA 21-24R; CAAS 6;
CANR 13, 25; DLB 33

Major, Kevin (Gerald) 1949-....... **CLC 26**
See also CA 97-100; CANR 21, 38;
CLR 11; DLB 60; JRDA; MAICYA;
SATA 32

Maki, James
See Ozu, Yasujiro

Martines, Julia
See O'Faolain, Julia

Martinez, Jacinto Benavente y
See Benavente (y Martinez), Jacinto

Martinez Ruiz, Jose 1873-1967
See Azorin; Ruiz, Jose Martinez
See also CA 93-96; HW

Martinez Sierra, Gregorio
1881-1947 . . . . **TCLC 6**
See also CA 115

Martinez Sierra, Maria (de la O'LeJarraga)
1874-1974 . . . . **TCLC 6**
See also CA 115

Martinsen, Martin
See Follett, Ken(neth Martin)

Martinson, Harry (Edmund)
1904-1978 . . . . **CLC 14**
See also CA 77-80; CANR 34

Marut, Ret
See Traven, B.

Marut, Robert
See Traven, B.

Marvell, Andrew
1621-1678 . . . . . **LC 4; DA; PC 10; WLC**
See also CDBLB 1660-1789; DLB 131

Marx, Karl (Heinrich)
1818-1883 . . . . **NCLC 17**
See also DLB 129

Masaoka Shiki . . . . **TCLC 18**
See also Masaoka Tsunenori

Masaoka Tsunenori 1867-1902
See Masaoka Shiki
See also CA 117

Masefield, John (Edward)
1878-1967 . . . . **CLC 11, 47**
See also CA 19-20; 25-28R; CANR 33;
CAP 2; CDBLB 1890-1914; DLB 10;
MTCW; SATA 19

Maso, Carole 19(?)- . . . . **CLC 44**

Mason, Bobbie Ann
1940- . . . . **CLC 28, 43, 82; SSC 4**
See also AAYA 5; CA 53-56; CANR 11,
31; DLBY 87; MTCW

Mason, Ernst
See Pohl, Frederik

Mason, Lee W.
See Malzberg, Barry N(athaniel)

Mason, Nick 1945- . . . . **CLC 35**
See also Pink Floyd

Mason, Tally
See Derleth, August (William)

Mass, William
See Gibson, William

Masters, Edgar Lee
1868-1950 . . . . . . **TCLC 2, 25; DA; PC 1**
See also CA 104; 133; CDALB 1865-1917;
DLB 54; MTCW

Masters, Hilary 1928- . . . . **CLC 48**
See also CA 25-28R; CANR 13

Mastrosimone, William 19(?)- . . . . . . **CLC 36**

Mathe, Albert
See Camus, Albert

Matheson, Richard Burton 1926- . . . **CLC 37**
See also CA 97-100; DLB 8, 44

Mathews, Harry 1930- . . . . **CLC 6, 52**
See also CA 21-24R; CAAS 6; CANR 18,
40

Mathews, John Joseph 1894-1979 . . . **CLC 84**
See also CA 19-20; 142; CANR 45; CAP 2

Mathias, Roland (Glyn) 1915- . . . . . . **CLC 45**
See also CA 97-100; CANR 19, 41; DLB 27

Matsuo Basho 1644-1694 . . . . **PC 3**

Mattheson, Rodney
See Creasey, John

Matthews, Greg 1949- . . . . **CLC 45**
See also CA 135

Matthews, William 1942- . . . . **CLC 40**
See also CA 29-32R; CAAS 18; CANR 12;
DLB 5

Matthias, John (Edward) 1941- . . . . . . **CLC 9**
See also CA 33-36R

Matthiessen, Peter
1927- . . . . **CLC 5, 7, 11, 32, 64**
See also AAYA 6; BEST 90:4; CA 9-12R;
CANR 21; DLB 6; MTCW; SATA 27

Maturin, Charles Robert
1780(?)-1824 . . . . **NCLC 6**

Matute (Ausejo), Ana Maria
1925- . . . . **CLC 11**
See also CA 89-92; MTCW

Maugham, W. S.
See Maugham, W(illiam) Somerset

Maugham, W(illiam) Somerset
1874-1965 . . . . . . **CLC 1, 11, 15, 67; DA;
SSC 8; WLC**
See also CA 5-8R; 25-28R; CANR 40;
CDBLB 1914-1945; DLB 10, 36, 77, 100;
MTCW; SATA 54

Maugham, William Somerset
See Maugham, W(illiam) Somerset

Maupassant, (Henri Rene Albert) Guy de
1850-1893 . . . . **NCLC 1, 42; DA; SSC 1;
WLC**
See also DLB 123

Maurhut, Richard
See Traven, B.

Mauriac, Claude 1914- . . . . **CLC 9**
See also CA 89-92; DLB 83

Mauriac, Francois (Charles)
1885-1970 . . . . **CLC 4, 9, 56**
See also CA 25-28; CAP 2; DLB 65;
MTCW

Mavor, Osborne Henry 1888-1951
See Bridie, James
See also CA 104

Maxwell, William (Keepers, Jr.)
1908- . . . . **CLC 19**
See also CA 93-96; DLBY 80

May, Elaine 1932- . . . . **CLC 16**
See also CA 124; 142; DLB 44

Mayakovski, Vladimir (Vladimirovich)
1893-1930 . . . . **TCLC 4, 18**
See also CA 104

Mayhew, Henry 1812-1887 . . . . . . **NCLC 31**
See also DLB 18, 55

Maynard, Joyce 1953- . . . . **CLC 23**
See also CA 111; 129

Mayne, William (James Carter)
1928- . . . . **CLC 12**
See also CA 9-12R; CANR 37; CLR 25;
JRDA; MAICYA; SAAS 11; SATA 6, 68

Mayo, Jim
See L'Amour, Louis (Dearborn)

Maysles, Albert 1926- . . . . **CLC 16**
See also CA 29-32R

Maysles, David 1932- . . . . **CLC 16**

Mazer, Norma Fox 1931- . . . . **CLC 26**
See also AAYA 5; CA 69-72; CANR 12,
32; CLR 23; JRDA; MAICYA; SAAS 1;
SATA 24, 67

Mazzini, Guiseppe 1805-1872 . . . . **NCLC 34**

McAuley, James Phillip
1917-1976 . . . . **CLC 45**
See also CA 97-100

McBain, Ed
See Hunter, Evan

McBrien, William Augustine
1930- . . . . **CLC 44**
See also CA 107

McCaffrey, Anne (Inez) 1926- . . . . . . **CLC 17**
See also AAYA 6; AITN 2; BEST 89:2;
CA 25-28R; CANR 15, 35; DLB 8;
JRDA; MAICYA; MTCW; SAAS 11;
SATA 8, 70

McCann, Arthur
See Campbell, John W(ood, Jr.)

McCann, Edson
See Pohl, Frederik

McCarthy, Charles, Jr. 1933-
See McCarthy, Cormac
See also CANR 42

McCarthy, Cormac 1933- . . . . **CLC 4, 57**
See also McCarthy, Charles, Jr.
See also DLB 6, 143

McCarthy, Mary (Therese)
1912-1989 . . . **CLC 1, 3, 5, 14, 24, 39, 59**
See also CA 5-8R; 129; CANR 16; DLB 2;
DLBY 81; MTCW

McCartney, (James) Paul
1942- . . . . **CLC 12, 35**

McCauley, Stephen (D.) 1955- . . . . . **CLC 50**
See also CA 141

McClure, Michael (Thomas)
1932- . . . . **CLC 6, 10**
See also CA 21-24R; CANR 17; DLB 16

McCorkle, Jill (Collins) 1958- . . . . . . **CLC 51**
See also CA 121; DLBY 87

McCourt, James 1941- . . . . **CLC 5**
See also CA 57-60

McCoy, Horace (Stanley)
1897-1955 . . . . **TCLC 28**
See also CA 108; DLB 9

McCrae, John 1872-1918 . . . . **TCLC 12**
See also CA 109; DLB 92

McCreigh, James
See Pohl, Frederik

McCullers, (Lula) Carson (Smith)
1917-1967 . . . . **CLC 1, 4, 10, 12, 48; DA;
SSC 9; WLC**
See also CA 5-8R; 25-28R; CABS 1, 3;
CANR 18; CDALB 1941-1968; DLB 2, 7;
MTCW; SATA 27

McCulloch, John Tyler
See Burroughs, Edgar Rice

McCullough, Colleen 1938(?)- ...... CLC 27
See also CA 81-84; CANR 17; MTCW

McElroy, Joseph 1930- .... CLC 5, 47
See also CA 17-20R

McEwan, Ian (Russell) 1948- ... CLC 13, 66
See also BEST 90:4; CA 61-64; CANR 14,
41; DLB 14; MTCW

McFadden, David 1940- .... CLC 48
See also CA 104; DLB 60

McFarland, Dennis 1950- .... CLC 65

McGahern, John 1934- .... CLC 5, 9, 48
See also CA 17-20R; CANR 29; DLB 14;
MTCW

McGinley, Patrick (Anthony)
1937- .... CLC 41
See also CA 120; 127

McGinley, Phyllis 1905-1978 ...... CLC 14
See also CA 9-12R; 77-80; CANR 19;
DLB 11, 48; SATA 2, 24, 44

McGinniss, Joe 1942- .... CLC 32
See also AITN 2; BEST 89:2; CA 25-28R;
CANR 26

McGivern, Maureen Daly
See Daly, Maureen

McGrath, Patrick 1950- .... CLC 55
See also CA 136

McGrath, Thomas (Matthew)
1916-1990 .... CLC 28, 59
See also CA 9-12R; 132; CANR 6, 33;
MTCW; SATA 41; SATA-Obit 66

McGuane, Thomas (Francis III)
1939- .... CLC 3, 7, 18, 45
See also AITN 2; CA 49-52; CANR 5, 24;
DLB 2; DLBY 80; MTCW

McGuckian, Medbh 1950- .... CLC 48
See also CA 143; DLB 40

McHale, Tom 1942(?)-1982 .... CLC 3, 5
See also AITN 1; CA 77-80; 106

McIlvanney, William 1936- .... CLC 42
See also CA 25-28R; DLB 14

McIlwraith, Maureen Mollie Hunter
See Hunter, Mollie
See also SATA 2

McInerney, Jay 1955- .... CLC 34
See also CA 116; 123

McIntyre, Vonda N(eel) 1948- ..... CLC 18
See also CA 81-84; CANR 17, 34; MTCW

McKay, Claude ..... TCLC 7, 41; BLC; PC 2
See also McKay, Festus Claudius
See also DLB 4, 45, 51, 117

McKay, Festus Claudius 1889-1948
See McKay, Claude
See also BW 1; CA 104; 124; DA; MTCW;
WLC

McKuen, Rod 1933- .... CLC 1, 3
See also AITN 1; CA 41-44R; CANR 40

McLoughlin, R. B.
See Mencken, H(enry) L(ouis)

McLuhan, (Herbert) Marshall
1911-1980 .... CLC 37, 83
See also CA 9-12R; 102; CANR 12, 34;
DLB 88; MTCW

McMillan, Terry (L.) 1951- ..... CLC 50, 61
See also BW 2; CA 140

McMurtry, Larry (Jeff)
1936- .... CLC 2, 3, 7, 11, 27, 44
See also AITN 2; BEST 89:2; CA 5-8R;
CANR 19, 43; CDALB 1968-1988;
DLB 2, 143; DLBY 80, 87; MTCW

McNally, T. M. 1961- .... CLC 82

McNally, Terrence 1939- ...... CLC 4, 7, 41
See also CA 45-48; CANR 2; DLB 7

McNamer, Deirdre 1950- .... CLC 70

McNeile, Herman Cyril 1888-1937
See Sapper
See also DLB 77

McPhee, John (Angus) 1931- ...... CLC 36
See also BEST 90:1; CA 65-68; CANR 20;
MTCW

McPherson, James Alan
1943- .... CLC 19, 77
See also BW 1; CA 25-28R; CAAS 17;
CANR 24; DLB 38; MTCW

McPherson, William (Alexander)
1933- .... CLC 34
See also CA 69-72; CANR 28

McSweeney, Kerry .... CLC 34

Mead, Margaret 1901-1978 .... CLC 37
See also AITN 1; CA 1-4R; 81-84;
CANR 4; MTCW; SATA 20

Meaker, Marijane (Agnes) 1927-
See Kerr, M. E.
See also CA 107; CANR 37; JRDA;
MAICYA; MTCW; SATA 20, 61

Medoff, Mark (Howard) 1940- ... CLC 6, 23
See also AITN 1; CA 53-56; CANR 5;
DLB 7

Medvedev, P. N.
See Bakhtin, Mikhail Mikhailovich

Meged, Aharon
See Megged, Aharon

Meged, Aron
See Megged, Aharon

Megged, Aharon 1920- .... CLC 9
See also CA 49-52; CAAS 13; CANR 1

Mehta, Ved (Parkash) 1934- .... CLC 37
See also CA 1-4R; CANR 2, 23; MTCW

Melanter
See Blackmore, R(ichard) D(oddridge)

Melikow, Loris
See Hofmannsthal, Hugo von

Melmoth, Sebastian
See Wilde, Oscar (Fingal O'Flahertie Wills)

Meltzer, Milton 1915- .... CLC 26
See also AAYA 8; CA 13-16R; CANR 38;
CLR 13; DLB 61; JRDA; MAICYA;
SAAS 1; SATA 1, 50

Melville, Herman
1819-1891 .... NCLC 3, 12, 29, 45; DA;
SSC 1; WLC
See also CDALB 1640-1865; DLB 3, 74;
SATA 59

Menander
c. 342B.C.-c. 292B.C. .... CMLC 9; DC 3

Mencken, H(enry) L(ouis)
1880-1956 .... TCLC 13
See also CA 105; 125; CDALB 1917-1929;
DLB 11, 29, 63, 137; MTCW

Mercer, David 1928-1980 .... CLC 5
See also CA 9-12R; 102; CANR 23;
DLB 13; MTCW

Merchant, Paul
See Ellison, Harlan

Meredith, George 1828-1909 ... TCLC 17, 43
See also CA 117; CDBLB 1832-1890;
DLB 18, 35, 57

Meredith, William (Morris)
1919- .... CLC 4, 13, 22, 55
See also CA 9-12R; CAAS 14; CANR 6, 40;
DLB 5

Merezhkovsky, Dmitry Sergeyevich
1865-1941 .... TCLC 29

Merimee, Prosper
1803-1870 .... NCLC 6; SSC 7
See also DLB 119

Merkin, Daphne 1954- .... CLC 44
See also CA 123

Merlin, Arthur
See Blish, James (Benjamin)

Merrill, James (Ingram)
1926- .... CLC 2, 3, 6, 8, 13, 18, 34
See also CA 13-16R; CANR 10; DLB 5;
DLBY 85; MTCW

Merriman, Alex
See Silverberg, Robert

Merritt, E. B.
See Waddington, Miriam

Merton, Thomas
1915-1968 .. CLC 1, 3, 11, 34, 83; PC 10
See also CA 5-8R; 25-28R; CANR 22;
DLB 48; DLBY 81; MTCW

Merwin, W(illiam) S(tanley)
1927- ...... CLC 1, 2, 3, 5, 8, 13, 18, 45
See also CA 13-16R; CANR 15; DLB 5;
MTCW

Metcalf, John 1938- .... CLC 37
See also CA 113; DLB 60

Metcalf, Suzanne
See Baum, L(yman) Frank

Mew, Charlotte (Mary)
1870-1928 .... TCLC 8
See also CA 105; DLB 19, 135

Mewshaw, Michael 1943- .... CLC 9
See also CA 53-56; CANR 7; DLBY 80

Meyer, June
See Jordan, June

Meyer, Lynn
See Slavitt, David R(ytman)

Meyer-Meyrink, Gustav 1868-1932
See Meyrink, Gustav
See also CA 117

Meyers, Jeffrey 1939- .... CLC 39
See also CA 73-76; DLB 111

Meynell, Alice (Christina Gertrude Thompson)
1847-1922 .... TCLC 6
See also CA 104; DLB 19, 98

Meyrink, Gustav .... TCLC 21
See also Meyer-Meyrink, Gustav
See also DLB 81

Michaels, Leonard
1933- . . . . **CLC 6, 25; SSC 16**
See also CA 61-64; CANR 21; DLB 130;
MTCW

Michaux, Henri 1899-1984 . . . . . . **CLC 8, 19**
See also CA 85-88; 114

Michelangelo 1475-1564. . . . . **LC 12**

Michelet, Jules 1798-1874 . . . . . . **NCLC 31**

Michener, James A(lbert)
1907(?)- . . . . **CLC 1, 5, 11, 29, 60**
See also AITN 1; BEST 90:1; CA 5-8R;
CANR 21, 45; DLB 6; MTCW

Mickiewicz, Adam 1798-1855 . . . . . **NCLC 3**

Middleton, Christopher 1926- . . . . . . **CLC 13**
See also CA 13-16R; CANR 29; DLB 40

Middleton, Stanley 1919- . . . . **CLC 7, 38**
See also CA 25-28R; CANR 21; DLB 14

Migueis, Jose Rodrigues 1901- . . . . . **CLC 10**

Mikszath, Kalman 1847-1910 . . . . . **TCLC 31**

Miles, Josephine
1911-1985 . . . . **CLC 1, 2, 14, 34, 39**
See also CA 1-4R; 116; CANR 2; DLB 48

Militant
See Sandburg, Carl (August)

Mill, John Stuart 1806-1873 . . . . . **NCLC 11**
See also CDBLB 1832-1890; DLB 55

Millar, Kenneth 1915-1983 . . . . **CLC 14**
See also Macdonald, Ross
See also CA 9-12R; 110; CANR 16; DLB 2;
DLBD 6; DLBY 83; MTCW

Millay, E. Vincent
See Millay, Edna St. Vincent

Millay, Edna St. Vincent
1892-1950 . . . . . . **TCLC 4, 49; DA; PC 6**
See also CA 104; 130; CDALB 1917-1929;
DLB 45; MTCW

Miller, Arthur
1915- . . . . **CLC 1, 2, 6, 10, 15, 26, 47, 78;
DA; DC 1; WLC**
See also AITN 1; CA 1-4R; CABS 3;
CANR 2, 30; CDALB 1941-1968; DLB 7;
MTCW

Miller, Henry (Valentine)
1891-1980 . . . . **CLC 1, 2, 4, 9, 14, 43, 84;
DA; WLC**
See also CA 9-12R; 97-100; CANR 33;
CDALB 1929-1941; DLB 4, 9; DLBY 80;
MTCW

Miller, Jason 1939(?)- . . . . **CLC 2**
See also AITN 1; CA 73-76; DLB 7

Miller, Sue 1943- . . . . **CLC 44**
See also BEST 90:3; CA 139; DLB 143

Miller, Walter M(ichael, Jr.)
1923- . . . . **CLC 4, 30**
See also CA 85-88; DLB 8

Millett, Kate 1934- . . . . **CLC 67**
See also AITN 1; CA 73-76; CANR 32;
MTCW

Millhauser, Steven 1943- . . . . **CLC 21, 54**
See also CA 110; 111; DLB 2

Millin, Sarah Gertrude 1889-1968 . . **CLC 49**
See also CA 102; 93-96

Milne, A(lan) A(lexander)
1882-1956 . . . . **TCLC 6**
See also CA 104; 133; CLR 1, 26; DLB 10,
77, 100; MAICYA; MTCW; YABC 1

Milner, Ron(ald) 1938- . . . . **CLC 56; BLC**
See also AITN 1; BW 1; CA 73-76;
CANR 24; DLB 38; MTCW

Milosz, Czeslaw
1911- . . . **CLC 5, 11, 22, 31, 56, 82; PC 8**
See also CA 81-84; CANR 23; MTCW

Milton, John 1608-1674 . . . **LC 9; DA; WLC**
See also CDBLB 1660-1789; DLB 131

Minehaha, Cornelius
See Wedekind, (Benjamin) Frank(lin)

Miner, Valerie 1947- . . . . **CLC 40**
See also CA 97-100

Minimo, Duca
See D'Annunzio, Gabriele

Minot, Susan 1956- . . . . **CLC 44**
See also CA 134

Minus, Ed 1938- . . . . **CLC 39**

Miranda, Javier
See Bioy Casares, Adolfo

Mirbeau, Octave 1848-1917 . . . . . . **TCLC 55**
See also DLB 123

Miro (Ferrer), Gabriel (Francisco Victor)
1879-1930 . . . . **TCLC 5**
See also CA 104

Mishima, Yukio
. . . . **CLC 2, 4, 6, 9, 27; DC 1; SSC 4**
See also Hiraoka, Kimitake

Mistral, Frederic 1830-1914 . . . . . **TCLC 51**
See also CA 122

Mistral, Gabriela. . . . . **TCLC 2; HLC**
See also Godoy Alcayaga, Lucila

Mistry, Rohinton 1952- . . . . **CLC 71**
See also CA 141

Mitchell, Clyde
See Ellison, Harlan; Silverberg, Robert

Mitchell, James Leslie 1901-1935
See Gibbon, Lewis Grassic
See also CA 104; DLB 15

Mitchell, Joni 1943- . . . . **CLC 12**
See also CA 112

Mitchell, Margaret (Munnerlyn)
1900-1949 . . . . **TCLC 11**
See also CA 109; 125; DLB 9; MTCW

Mitchell, Peggy
See Mitchell, Margaret (Munnerlyn)

Mitchell, S(ilas) Weir 1829-1914 . . **TCLC 36**

Mitchell, W(illiam) O(rmond)
1914- . . . . **CLC 25**
See also CA 77-80; CANR 15, 43; DLB 88

Mitford, Mary Russell 1787-1855. . **NCLC 4**
See also DLB 110, 116

Mitford, Nancy 1904-1973 . . . . **CLC 44**
See also CA 9-12R

Miyamoto, Yuriko 1899-1951 . . . . . **TCLC 37**

Mo, Timothy (Peter) 1950(?)- . . . . . . **CLC 46**
See also CA 117; MTCW

Modarressi, Taghi (M.) 1931- . . . . . . **CLC 44**
See also CA 121; 134

Modiano, Patrick (Jean) 1945- . . . . . **CLC 18**
See also CA 85-88; CANR 17, 40; DLB 83

Moerck, Paal
See Roelvaag, O(le) E(dvart)

Mofolo, Thomas (Mokopu)
1875(?)-1948 . . . . **TCLC 22; BLC**
See also CA 121

Mohr, Nicholasa 1935- . . . . . . **CLC 12; HLC**
See also AAYA 8; CA 49-52; CANR 1, 32;
CLR 22; HW; JRDA; SAAS 8; SATA 8

Mojtabai, A(nn) G(race)
1938- . . . . **CLC 5, 9, 15, 29**
See also CA 85-88

Moliere 1622-1673 . . . . **LC 10; DA; WLC**

Molin, Charles
See Mayne, William (James Carter)

Molnar, Ferenc 1878-1952. . . . . . . **TCLC 20**
See also CA 109

Momaday, N(avarre) Scott
1934- . . . . **CLC 2, 19; DA**
See also AAYA 11; CA 25-28R; CANR 14,
34; DLB 143; MTCW; NNAL; SATA 30,
48

Monette, Paul 1945- . . . . **CLC 82**
See also CA 139

Monroe, Harriet 1860-1936 . . . . . . **TCLC 12**
See also CA 109; DLB 54, 91

Monroe, Lyle
See Heinlein, Robert A(nson)

Montagu, Elizabeth 1917- . . . . **NCLC 7**
See also CA 9-12R

Montagu, Mary (Pierrepont) Wortley
1689-1762 . . . . **LC 9**
See also DLB 95, 101

Montagu, W. H.
See Coleridge, Samuel Taylor

Montague, John (Patrick)
1929- . . . . **CLC 13, 46**
See also CA 9-12R; CANR 9; DLB 40;
MTCW

Montaigne, Michel (Eyquem) de
1533-1592 . . . . **LC 8; DA; WLC**

Montale, Eugenio 1896-1981 . . . **CLC 7, 9, 18**
See also CA 17-20R; 104; CANR 30;
DLB 114; MTCW

Montesquieu, Charles-Louis de Secondat
1689-1755 . . . . **LC 7**

Montgomery, (Robert) Bruce 1921-1978
See Crispin, Edmund
See also CA 104

Montgomery, L(ucy) M(aud)
1874-1942 . . . . **TCLC 51**
See also AAYA 12; CA 108; 137; CLR 8;
DLB 92; JRDA; MAICYA; YABC 1

Montgomery, Marion H., Jr. 1925- . . **CLC 7**
See also AITN 1; CA 1-4R; CANR 3;
DLB 6

Montgomery, Max
See Davenport, Guy (Mattison, Jr.)

Montherlant, Henry (Milon) de
1896-1972 . . . . **CLC 8, 19**
See also CA 85-88; 37-40R; DLB 72;
MTCW

Munford, Robert   1737(?)-1783 . . . . **LC 5**
See also DLB 31

Mungo, Raymond   1946- . . . . **CLC 72**
See also CA 49-52; CANR 2

Munro, Alice
1931- . . . . **CLC 6, 10, 19, 50; SSC 3**
See also AITN 2; CA 33-36R; CANR 33;
DLB 53; MTCW; SATA 29

Munro, H(ector) H(ugh)   1870-1916
See Saki
See also CA 104; 130; CDBLB 1890-1914;
DA; DLB 34; MTCW; WLC

Murasaki, Lady . . . . **CMLC 1**

Murdoch, (Jean) Iris
1919- . . . . . . **CLC 1, 2, 3, 4, 6, 8, 11, 15,**
22, 31, 51
See also CA 13-16R; CANR 8, 43;
CDBLB 1960 to Present; DLB 14;
MTCW

Murnau, Friedrich Wilhelm
See Plumpe, Friedrich Wilhelm

Murphy, Richard   1927- . . . . **CLC 41**
See also CA 29-32R; DLB 40

Murphy, Sylvia   1937- . . . . **CLC 34**
See also CA 121

Murphy, Thomas (Bernard)   1935- . . . **CLC 51**
See also CA 101

Murray, Albert L.   1916- . . . . **CLC 73**
See also BW 2; CA 49-52; CANR 26;
DLB 38

Murray, Les(lie) A(llan)   1938- . . . . . **CLC 40**
See also CA 21-24R; CANR 11, 27

Murry, J. Middleton
See Murry, John Middleton

Murry, John Middleton
1889-1957 . . . . **TCLC 16**
See also CA 118

Musgrave, Susan   1951- . . . . **CLC 13, 54**
See also CA 69-72; CANR 45

Musil, Robert (Edler von)
1880-1942 . . . . **TCLC 12**
See also CA 109; DLB 81, 124

Musset, (Louis Charles) Alfred de
1810-1857 . . . . **NCLC 7**

My Brother's Brother
See Chekhov, Anton (Pavlovich)

Myers, Walter Dean   1937- . . . **CLC 35; BLC**
See also AAYA 4; BW 2; CA 33-36R;
CANR 20, 42; CLR 4, 16; DLB 33;
JRDA; MAICYA; SAAS 2; SATA 27, 41,
71

Myers, Walter M.
See Myers, Walter Dean

Myles, Symon
See Follett, Ken(neth Martin)

Nabokov, Vladimir (Vladimirovich)
1899-1977 . . . . . **CLC 1, 2, 3, 6, 8, 11, 15,**
23, 44, 46, 64; DA; SSC 11; WLC
See also CA 5-8R; 69-72; CANR 20;
CDALB 1941-1968; DLB 2; DLBD 3;
DLBY 80, 91; MTCW

Nagai Kafu . . . . **TCLC 51**
See also Nagai Sokichi

Nagai Sokichi   1879-1959
See Nagai Kafu
See also CA 117

Nagy, Laszlo   1925-1978 . . . . **CLC 7**
See also CA 129; 112

Naipaul, Shiva(dhar Srinivasa)
1945-1985 . . . . **CLC 32, 39**
See also CA 110; 112; 116; CANR 33;
DLBY 85; MTCW

Naipaul, V(idiadhar) S(urajprasad)
1932- . . . . **CLC 4, 7, 9, 13, 18, 37**
See also CA 1-4R; CANR 1, 33;
CDBLB 1960 to Present; DLB 125;
DLBY 85; MTCW

Nakos, Lilika   1899(?)- . . . . **CLC 29**

Narayan, R(asipuram) K(rishnaswami)
1906- . . . . **CLC 7, 28, 47**
See also CA 81-84; CANR 33; MTCW;
SATA 62

Nash, (Frediric) Ogden   1902-1971 . . **CLC 23**
See also CA 13-14; 29-32R; CANR 34;
CAP 1; DLB 11; MAICYA; MTCW;
SATA 2, 46

Nathan, Daniel
See Dannay, Frederic

Nathan, George Jean   1882-1958 . . . **TCLC 18**
See also Hatteras, Owen
See also CA 114; DLB 137

Natsume, Kinnosuke   1867-1916
See Natsume, Soseki
See also CA 104

Natsume, Soseki . . . . **TCLC 2, 10**
See also Natsume, Kinnosuke

Natti, (Mary) Lee   1919-
See Kingman, Lee
See also CA 5-8R; CANR 2

Naylor, Gloria
1950- . . . . **CLC 28, 52; BLC; DA**
See also AAYA 6; BW 2; CA 107;
CANR 27; MTCW

Neihardt, John Gneisenau
1881-1973 . . . . **CLC 32**
See also CA 13-14; CAP 1; DLB 9, 54

Nekrasov, Nikolai Alekseevich
1821-1878 . . . . **NCLC 11**

Nelligan, Emile   1879-1941 . . . . **TCLC 14**
See also CA 114; DLB 92

Nelson, Willie   1933- . . . . **CLC 17**
See also CA 107

Nemerov, Howard (Stanley)
1920-1991 . . . . **CLC 2, 6, 9, 36**
See also CA 1-4R; 134; CABS 2; CANR 1,
27; DLB 6; DLBY 83; MTCW

Neruda, Pablo
1904-1973 . . . . . **CLC 1, 2, 5, 7, 9, 28, 62;**
DA; HLC; PC 4; WLC
See also CA 19-20; 45-48; CAP 2; HW;
MTCW

Nerval, Gerard de   1808-1855 . . . . . . **NCLC 1**

Nervo, (Jose) Amado (Ruiz de)
1870-1919 . . . . **TCLC 11**
See also CA 109; 131; HW

Nessi, Pio Baroja y
See Baroja (y Nessi), Pio

Nestroy, Johann   1801-1862 . . . . . . **NCLC 42**
See also DLB 133

Neufeld, John (Arthur)   1938- . . . . . . **CLC 17**
See also AAYA 11; CA 25-28R; CANR 11,
37; MAICYA; SAAS 3; SATA 6

Neville, Emily Cheney   1919- . . . . **CLC 12**
See also CA 5-8R; CANR 3, 37; JRDA;
MAICYA; SAAS 2; SATA 1

Newbound, Bernard Slade   1930-
See Slade, Bernard
See also CA 81-84

Newby, P(ercy) H(oward)
1918- . . . . **CLC 2, 13**
See also CA 5-8R; CANR 32; DLB 15;
MTCW

Newlove, Donald   1928- . . . . **CLC 6**
See also CA 29-32R; CANR 25

Newlove, John (Herbert)   1938- . . . . . **CLC 14**
See also CA 21-24R; CANR 9, 25

Newman, Charles   1938- . . . . **CLC 2, 8**
See also CA 21-24R

Newman, Edwin (Harold)   1919- . . . . **CLC 14**
See also AITN 1; CA 69-72; CANR 5

Newman, John Henry
1801-1890 . . . . **NCLC 38**
See also DLB 18, 32, 55

Newton, Suzanne   1936- . . . . **CLC 35**
See also CA 41-44R; CANR 14; JRDA;
SATA 5, 77

Nexo, Martin Andersen
1869-1954 . . . . **TCLC 43**

Nezval, Vitezslav   1900-1958 . . . . . . **TCLC 44**
See also CA 123

Ng, Fae Myenne   1957(?)- . . . . **CLC 81**

Ngema, Mbongeni   1955- . . . . **CLC 57**
See also BW 2; CA 143

Ngugi, James T(hiong'o) . . . . **CLC 3, 7, 13**
See also Ngugi wa Thiong'o

Ngugi wa Thiong'o   1938- . . . . . **CLC 36; BLC**
See also Ngugi, James T(hiong'o)
See also BW 2; CA 81-84; CANR 27;
DLB 125; MTCW

Nichol, B(arrie) P(hillip)
1944-1988 . . . . **CLC 18**
See also CA 53-56; DLB 53; SATA 66

Nichols, John (Treadwell)   1940- . . . . **CLC 38**
See also CA 9-12R; CAAS 2; CANR 6;
DLBY 82

Nichols, Leigh
See Koontz, Dean R(ay)

Nichols, Peter (Richard)
1927- . . . . **CLC 5, 36, 65**
See also CA 104; CANR 33; DLB 13;
MTCW

Nicolas, F. R. E.
See Freeling, Nicolas

Niedecker, Lorine   1903-1970 . . . . **CLC 10, 42**
See also CA 25-28; CAP 2; DLB 48

Nietzsche, Friedrich (Wilhelm)
1844-1900 . . . . **TCLC 10, 18, 55**
See also CA 107; 121; DLB 129

Nievo, Ippolito   1831-1861 . . . . **NCLC 22**

Nightingale, Anne Redmon 1943-
See Redmon, Anne
See also CA 103

Nik.T.O.
See Annensky, Innokenty Fyodorovich

Nin, Anais
1903-1977 . . . . . . **CLC 1, 4, 8, 11, 14, 60;**
SSC 10
See also AITN 2; CA 13-16R; 69-72;
CANR 22; DLB 2, 4; MTCW

Nissenson, Hugh 1933- . . . . **CLC 4, 9**
See also CA 17-20R; CANR 27; DLB 28

Niven, Larry . . . . **CLC 8**
See also Niven, Laurence Van Cott
See also DLB 8

Niven, Laurence Van Cott 1938-
See Niven, Larry
See also CA 21-24R; CAAS 12; CANR 14,
44; MTCW

Nixon, Agnes Eckhardt 1927- . . . . . . **CLC 21**
See also CA 110

Nizan, Paul 1905-1940 . . . . **TCLC 40**
See also DLB 72

Nkosi, Lewis 1936- . . . . **CLC 45; BLC**
See also BW 1; CA 65-68; CANR 27

Nodier, (Jean) Charles (Emmanuel)
1780-1844 . . . . **NCLC 19**
See also DLB 119

Nolan, Christopher 1965- . . . . **CLC 58**
See also CA 111

Norden, Charles
See Durrell, Lawrence (George)

Nordhoff, Charles (Bernard)
1887-1947 . . . . **TCLC 23**
See also CA 108; DLB 9; SATA 23

Norfolk, Lawrence 1963- . . . . **CLC 76**
See also CA 144

Norman, Marsha 1947- . . . . **CLC 28**
See also CA 105; CABS 3; CANR 41;
DLBY 84

Norris, Benjamin Franklin, Jr.
1870-1902 . . . . **TCLC 24**
See also Norris, Frank
See also CA 110

Norris, Frank
See Norris, Benjamin Franklin, Jr.
See also CDALB 1865-1917; DLB 12, 71

Norris, Leslie 1921- . . . . **CLC 14**
See also CA 11-12; CANR 14; CAP 1;
DLB 27

North, Andrew
See Norton, Andre

North, Anthony
See Koontz, Dean R(ay)

North, Captain George
See Stevenson, Robert Louis (Balfour)

North, Milou
See Erdrich, Louise

Northrup, B. A.
See Hubbard, L(afayette) Ron(ald)

North Staffs
See Hulme, T(homas) E(rnest)

Norton, Alice Mary
See Norton, Andre
See also MAICYA; SATA 1, 43

Norton, Andre 1912- . . . . **CLC 12**
See also Norton, Alice Mary
See also CA 1-4R; CANR 2, 31; DLB 8, 52;
JRDA; MTCW

Norway, Nevil Shute 1899-1960
See Shute, Nevil
See also CA 102; 93-96

Norwid, Cyprian Kamil
1821-1883 . . . . **NCLC 17**

Nosille, Nabrah
See Ellison, Harlan

Nossack, Hans Erich 1901-1978 . . . . . **CLC 6**
See also CA 93-96; 85-88; DLB 69

Nosu, Chuji
See Ozu, Yasujiro

Nova, Craig 1945- . . . . **CLC 7, 31**
See also CA 45-48; CANR 2

Novak, Joseph
See Kosinski, Jerzy (Nikodem)

Novalis 1772-1801 . . . . **NCLC 13**
See also DLB 90

Nowlan, Alden (Albert) 1933-1983 . . **CLC 15**
See also CA 9-12R; CANR 5; DLB 53

Noyes, Alfred 1880-1958 . . . . **TCLC 7**
See also CA 104; DLB 20

Nunn, Kem 19(?)- . . . . **CLC 34**

Nye, Robert 1939- . . . . **CLC 13, 42**
See also CA 33-36R; CANR 29; DLB 14;
MTCW; SATA 6

Nyro, Laura 1947- . . . . **CLC 17**

Oates, Joyce Carol
1938- . . . . . . **CLC 1, 2, 3, 6, 9, 11, 15, 19,**
33, 52; DA; SSC 6; WLC
See also AITN 1; BEST 89:2; CA 5-8R;
CANR 25, 45; CDALB 1968-1988;
DLB 2, 5, 130; DLBY 81; MTCW

O'Brien, E. G.
See Clarke, Arthur C(harles)

O'Brien, Edna
1936- . . . **CLC 3, 5, 8, 13, 36, 65; SSC 10**
See also CA 1-4R; CANR 6, 41;
CDBLB 1960 to Present; DLB 14;
MTCW

O'Brien, Fitz-James 1828-1862 . . . **NCLC 21**
See also DLB 74

O'Brien, Flann . . . . **CLC 1, 4, 5, 7, 10, 47**
See also O Nuallain, Brian

O'Brien, Richard 1942- . . . . **CLC 17**
See also CA 124

O'Brien, Tim 1946- . . . . **CLC 7, 19, 40**
See also CA 85-88; CANR 40; DLBD 9;
DLBY 80

Obstfelder, Sigbjoern 1866-1900 . . . **TCLC 23**
See also CA 123

O'Casey, Sean
1880-1964 . . . . **CLC 1, 5, 9, 11, 15**
See also CA 89-92; CDBLB 1914-1945;
DLB 10; MTCW

O'Cathasaigh, Sean
See O'Casey, Sean

Ochs, Phil 1940-1976 . . . . **CLC 17**
See also CA 65-68

O'Connor, Edwin (Greene)
1918-1968 . . . . **CLC 14**
See also CA 93-96; 25-28R

O'Connor, (Mary) Flannery
1925-1964 . . . . **CLC 1, 2, 3, 6, 10, 13, 15,**
21, 66; DA; SSC 1; WLC
See also AAYA 7; CA 1-4R; CANR 3, 41;
CDALB 1941-1968; DLB 2; DLBY 80;
MTCW

O'Connor, Frank . . . . **CLC 23; SSC 5**
See also O'Donovan, Michael John

O'Dell, Scott 1898-1989 . . . . **CLC 30**
See also AAYA 3; CA 61-64; 129;
CANR 12, 30; CLR 1, 16; DLB 52;
JRDA; MAICYA; SATA 12, 60

Odets, Clifford 1906-1963 . . . . **CLC 2, 28**
See also CA 85-88; DLB 7, 26; MTCW

O'Doherty, Brian 1934- . . . . **CLC 76**
See also CA 105

O'Donnell, K. M.
See Malzberg, Barry N(athaniel)

O'Donnell, Lawrence
See Kuttner, Henry

O'Donovan, Michael John
1903-1966 . . . . **CLC 14**
See also O'Connor, Frank
See also CA 93-96

Oe, Kenzaburo 1935- . . . . **CLC 10, 36**
See also CA 97-100; CANR 36; MTCW

O'Faolain, Julia 1932- . . . . **CLC 6, 19, 47**
See also CA 81-84; CAAS 2; CANR 12;
DLB 14; MTCW

O'Faolain, Sean
1900-1991 . . . . **CLC 1, 7, 14, 32, 70;**
SSC 13
See also CA 61-64; 134; CANR 12;
DLB 15; MTCW

O'Flaherty, Liam
1896-1984 . . . . **CLC 5, 34; SSC 6**
See also CA 101; 113; CANR 35; DLB 36;
DLBY 84; MTCW

Ogilvy, Gavin
See Barrie, J(ames) M(atthew)

O'Grady, Standish James
1846-1928 . . . . **TCLC 5**
See also CA 104

O'Grady, Timothy 1951- . . . . **CLC 59**
See also CA 138

O'Hara, Frank
1926-1966 . . . . **CLC 2, 5, 13, 78**
See also CA 9-12R; 25-28R; CANR 33;
DLB 5, 16; MTCW

O'Hara, John (Henry)
1905-1970 . . . . **CLC 1, 2, 3, 6, 11, 42;**
SSC 15
See also CA 5-8R; 25-28R; CANR 31;
CDALB 1929-1941; DLB 9, 86; DLBD 2;
MTCW

O Hehir, Diana 1922- . . . . **CLC 41**
See also CA 93-96

Okigbo, Christopher (Ifenayichukwu)
1932-1967 . . . . . **CLC 25, 84; BLC; PC 7**
See also BW 1; CA 77-80; DLB 125;
MTCW

Olds, Sharon 1942-. . . . . **CLC 32, 39**
See also CA 101; CANR 18, 41; DLB 120

Oldstyle, Jonathan
See Irving, Washington

Olesha, Yuri (Karlovich)
1899-1960 . . . . **CLC 8**
See also CA 85-88

Oliphant, Margaret (Oliphant Wilson)
1828-1897 . . . . **NCLC 11**
See also DLB 18

Oliver, Mary 1935-. . . . . **CLC 19, 34**
See also CA 21-24R; CANR 9, 43; DLB 5

Olivier, Laurence (Kerr)
1907-1989 . . . . **CLC 20**
See also CA 111; 129

Olsen, Tillie
1913- . . . . **CLC 4, 13; DA; SSC 11**
See also CA 1-4R; CANR 1, 43; DLB 28;
DLBY 80; MTCW

Olson, Charles (John)
1910-1970 . . . . . **CLC 1, 2, 5, 6, 9, 11, 29**
See also CA 13-16; 25-28R; CABS 2;
CANR 35; CAP 1; DLB 5, 16; MTCW

Olson, Toby 1937- . . . . **CLC 28**
See also CA 65-68; CANR 9, 31

Olyesha, Yuri
See Olesha, Yuri (Karlovich)

Ondaatje, (Philip) Michael
1943- . . . . **CLC 14, 29, 51, 76**
See also CA 77-80; CANR 42; DLB 60

Oneal, Elizabeth 1934-
See Oneal, Zibby
See also CA 106; CANR 28; MAICYA;
SATA 30

Oneal, Zibby . . . . **CLC 30**
See also Oneal, Elizabeth
See also AAYA 5; CLR 13; JRDA

O'Neill, Eugene (Gladstone)
1888-1953 . . . . . . **TCLC 1, 6, 27, 49; DA;**
WLC
See also AITN 1; CA 110; 132;
CDALB 1929-1941; DLB 7; MTCW

Onetti, Juan Carlos 1909- . . . . **CLC 7, 10**
See also CA 85-88; CANR 32; DLB 113;
HW; MTCW

O Nuallain, Brian 1911-1966
See O'Brien, Flann
See also CA 21-22; 25-28R; CAP 2

Oppen, George 1908-1984 . . . . **CLC 7, 13, 34**
See also CA 13-16R; 113; CANR 8; DLB 5

Oppenheim, E(dward) Phillips
1866-1946 . . . . **TCLC 45**
See also CA 111; DLB 70

Orlovitz, Gil 1918-1973 . . . . **CLC 22**
See also CA 77-80; 45-48; DLB 2, 5

Orris
See Ingelow, Jean

Ortega y Gasset, Jose
1883-1955 . . . . **TCLC 9; HLC**
See also CA 106; 130; HW; MTCW

Ortiz, Simon J(oseph) 1941- . . . . **CLC 45**
See also CA 134; DLB 120

Orton, Joe . . . . **CLC 4, 13, 43; DC 3**
See also Orton, John Kingsley
See also CDBLB 1960 to Present; DLB 13

Orton, John Kingsley 1933-1967
See Orton, Joe
See also CA 85-88; CANR 35; MTCW

Orwell, George
. . . . **TCLC 2, 6, 15, 31, 51; WLC**
See also Blair, Eric (Arthur)
See also CDBLB 1945-1960; DLB 15, 98

Osborne, David
See Silverberg, Robert

Osborne, George
See Silverberg, Robert

Osborne, John (James)
1929- . . . . **CLC 1, 2, 5, 11, 45; DA; WLC**
See also CA 13-16R; CANR 21;
CDBLB 1945-1960; DLB 13; MTCW

Osborne, Lawrence 1958- . . . . **CLC 50**

Oshima, Nagisa 1932- . . . . **CLC 20**
See also CA 116; 121

Oskison, John Milton
1874-1947 . . . . **TCLC 35**
See also CA 144

Ossoli, Sarah Margaret (Fuller marchesa d')
1810-1850
See Fuller, Margaret
See also SATA 25

Ostrovsky, Alexander
1823-1886 . . . . **NCLC 30**

Otero, Blas de 1916-1979. . . . . **CLC 11**
See also CA 89-92; DLB 134

Otto, Whitney 1955-. . . . . **CLC 70**
See also CA 140

Ouida . . . . **TCLC 43**
See also De La Ramee, (Marie) Louise
See also DLB 18

Ousmane, Sembene 1923- . . . . **CLC 66; BLC**
See also BW 1; CA 117; 125; MTCW

Ovid 43B.C.-18th cent. (?) . . . **CMLC 7; PC 2**

Owen, Hugh
See Faust, Frederick (Schiller)

Owen, Wilfred (Edward Salter)
1893-1918 . . . . . . **TCLC 5, 27; DA; WLC**
See also CA 104; 141; CDBLB 1914-1945;
DLB 20

Owens, Rochelle 1936-. . . . . **CLC 8**
See also CA 17-20R; CAAS 2; CANR 39

Oz, Amos 1939- . . . **CLC 5, 8, 11, 27, 33, 54**
See also CA 53-56; CANR 27; MTCW

Ozick, Cynthia
1928- . . . . **CLC 3, 7, 28, 62; SSC 15**
See also BEST 90:1; CA 17-20R; CANR 23;
DLB 28; DLBY 82; MTCW

Ozu, Yasujiro 1903-1963 . . . . **CLC 16**
See also CA 112

Pacheco, C.
See Pessoa, Fernando (Antonio Nogueira)

Pa Chin
See Li Fei-kan

Pack, Robert 1929-. . . . . **CLC 13**
See also CA 1-4R; CANR 3, 44; DLB 5

Padgett, Lewis
See Kuttner, Henry

Padilla (Lorenzo), Heberto 1932-. . . **CLC 38**
See also AITN 1; CA 123; 131; HW

Page, Jimmy 1944-. . . . . **CLC 12**

Page, Louise 1955-. . . . . **CLC 40**
See also CA 140

Page, P(atricia) K(athleen)
1916- . . . . **CLC 7, 18**
See also CA 53-56; CANR 4, 22; DLB 68;
MTCW

Paget, Violet 1856-1935
See Lee, Vernon
See also CA 104

Paget-Lowe, Henry
See Lovecraft, H(oward) P(hillips)

Paglia, Camille (Anna) 1947-. . . . . . **CLC 68**
See also CA 140

Paige, Richard
See Koontz, Dean R(ay)

Pakenham, Antonia
See Fraser, (Lady) Antonia (Pakenham)

Palamas, Kostes 1859-1943 . . . . **TCLC 5**
See also CA 105

Palazzeschi, Aldo 1885-1974. . . . . . . **CLC 11**
See also CA 89-92; 53-56; DLB 114

Paley, Grace 1922-. . . . **CLC 4, 6, 37; SSC 8**
See also CA 25-28R; CANR 13; DLB 28;
MTCW

Palin, Michael (Edward) 1943-. . . . . **CLC 21**
See also Monty Python
See also CA 107; CANR 35; SATA 67

Palliser, Charles 1947-. . . . . **CLC 65**
See also CA 136

Palma, Ricardo 1833-1919. . . . . . . **TCLC 29**

Pancake, Breece Dexter 1952-1979
See Pancake, Breece D'J
See also CA 123; 109

Pancake, Breece D'J. . . . . **CLC 29**
See also Pancake, Breece Dexter
See also DLB 130

Panko, Rudy
See Gogol, Nikolai (Vasilyevich)

Papadiamantis, Alexandros
1851-1911 . . . . **TCLC 29**

Papadiamantopoulos, Johannes 1856-1910
See Moreas, Jean
See also CA 117

Papini, Giovanni 1881-1956. . . . . . . **TCLC 22**
See also CA 121

Paracelsus 1493-1541. . . . . **LC 14**

Parasol, Peter
See Stevens, Wallace

Parfenie, Maria
See Codrescu, Andrei

Parini, Jay (Lee) 1948-. . . . . **CLC 54**
See also CA 97-100; CAAS 16; CANR 32

Park, Jordan
See Kornbluth, C(yril) M.; Pohl, Frederik

Parker, Bert
See Ellison, Harlan

Parker, Dorothy (Rothschild)
1893-1967 . . . . **CLC 15, 68; SSC 2**
See also CA 19-20; 25-28R; CAP 2;
DLB 11, 45, 86; MTCW

Parker, Robert B(rown) 1932-. . . . . . **CLC 27**
See also BEST 89:4; CA 49-52; CANR 1,
26; MTCW

Parkes, Lucas
See Harris, John (Wyndham Parkes Lucas) Beynon

Parkin, Frank 1940- . . . . **CLC 43**

Parkman, Francis, Jr.
1823-1893 . . . . **NCLC 12**
See also DLB 1, 30

Parks, Gordon (Alexander Buchanan)
1912- . . . . **CLC 1, 16; BLC**
See also AITN 2; BW 2; CA 41-44R;
CANR 26; DLB 33; SATA 8

Parnell, Thomas 1679-1718 . . . . **LC 3**
See also DLB 94

Parra, Nicanor 1914- . . . . **CLC 2; HLC**
See also CA 85-88; CANR 32; HW; MTCW

Parrish, Mary Frances
See Fisher, M(ary) F(rances) K(ennedy)

Parson
See Coleridge, Samuel Taylor

Parson Lot
See Kingsley, Charles

Partridge, Anthony
See Oppenheim, E(dward) Phillips

Pascoli, Giovanni 1855-1912 . . . . . . **TCLC 45**

Pasolini, Pier Paolo
1922-1975 . . . . **CLC 20, 37**
See also CA 93-96; 61-64; DLB 128;
MTCW

Pasquini
See Silone, Ignazio

Pastan, Linda (Olenik) 1932- . . . . . . **CLC 27**
See also CA 61-64; CANR 18, 40; DLB 5

Pasternak, Boris (Leonidovich)
1890-1960 . . . . . . **CLC 7, 10, 18, 63; DA;**
PC 6; WLC
See also CA 127; 116; MTCW

Patchen, Kenneth 1911-1972 . . . **CLC 1, 2, 18**
See also CA 1-4R; 33-36R; CANR 3, 35;
DLB 16, 48; MTCW

Pater, Walter (Horatio)
1839-1894 . . . . **NCLC 7**
See also CDBLB 1832-1890; DLB 57

Paterson, A(ndrew) B(arton)
1864-1941 . . . . **TCLC 32**

Paterson, Katherine (Womeldorf)
1932- . . . . **CLC 12, 30**
See also AAYA 1; CA 21-24R; CANR 28;
CLR 7; DLB 52; JRDA; MAICYA;
MTCW; SATA 13, 53

Patmore, Coventry Kersey Dighton
1823-1896 . . . . **NCLC 9**
See also DLB 35, 98

Paton, Alan (Stewart)
1903-1988 . . . . . . **CLC 4, 10, 25, 55; DA;**
WLC
See also CA 13-16; 125; CANR 22; CAP 1;
MTCW; SATA 11, 56

Paton Walsh, Gillian 1937-
See Walsh, Jill Paton
See also CANR 38; JRDA; MAICYA;
SAAS 3; SATA 4, 72

Paulding, James Kirke 1778-1860 . . **NCLC 2**
See also DLB 3, 59, 74

Paulin, Thomas Neilson 1949-
See Paulin, Tom
See also CA 123; 128

Paulin, Tom . . . . **CLC 37**
See also Paulin, Thomas Neilson
See also DLB 40

Paustovsky, Konstantin (Georgievich)
1892-1968 . . . . **CLC 40**
See also CA 93-96; 25-28R

Pavese, Cesare 1908-1950 . . . . **TCLC 3**
See also CA 104; DLB 128

Pavic, Milorad 1929- . . . . **CLC 60**
See also CA 136

Payne, Alan
See Jakes, John (William)

Paz, Gil
See Lugones, Leopoldo

Paz, Octavio
1914- . . . . **CLC 3, 4, 6, 10, 19, 51, 65;**
DA; HLC; PC 1; WLC
See also CA 73-76; CANR 32; DLBY 90;
HW; MTCW

Peacock, Molly 1947- . . . . **CLC 60**
See also CA 103; DLB 120

Peacock, Thomas Love
1785-1866 . . . . **NCLC 22**
See also DLB 96, 116

Peake, Mervyn 1911-1968 . . . . . . **CLC 7, 54**
See also CA 5-8R; 25-28R; CANR 3;
DLB 15; MTCW; SATA 23

Pearce, Philippa . . . . **CLC 21**
See also Christie, (Ann) Philippa
See also CLR 9; MAICYA; SATA 1, 67

Pearl, Eric
See Elman, Richard

Pearson, T(homas) R(eid) 1956- . . . . **CLC 39**
See also CA 120; 130

Peck, Dale 1968(?)- . . . . **CLC 81**

Peck, John 1941- . . . . **CLC 3**
See also CA 49-52; CANR 3

Peck, Richard (Wayne) 1934- . . . . . . **CLC 21**
See also AAYA 1; CA 85-88; CANR 19,
38; JRDA; MAICYA; SAAS 2; SATA 18,
55

Peck, Robert Newton 1928- . . . . **CLC 17; DA**
See also AAYA 3; CA 81-84; CANR 31;
JRDA; MAICYA; SAAS 1; SATA 21, 62

Peckinpah, (David) Sam(uel)
1925-1984 . . . . **CLC 20**
See also CA 109; 114

Pedersen, Knut 1859-1952
See Hamsun, Knut
See also CA 104; 119; MTCW

Peeslake, Gaffer
See Durrell, Lawrence (George)

Peguy, Charles Pierre
1873-1914 . . . . **TCLC 10**
See also CA 107

Pena, Ramon del Valle y
See Valle-Inclan, Ramon (Maria) del

Pendennis, Arthur Esquir
See Thackeray, William Makepeace

Penn, William 1644-1718 . . . . **LC 25**
See also DLB 24

Pepys, Samuel
1633-1703 . . . . **LC 11; DA; WLC**
See also CDBLB 1660-1789; DLB 101

Percy, Walker
1916-1990 . . . . **CLC 2, 3, 6, 8, 14, 18, 47,**
65
See also CA 1-4R; 131; CANR 1, 23;
DLB 2; DLBY 80, 90; MTCW

Perec, Georges 1936-1982 . . . . **CLC 56**
See also CA 141; DLB 83

Pereda (y Sanchez de Porrua), Jose Maria de
1833-1906 . . . . **TCLC 16**
See also CA 117

Pereda y Porrua, Jose Maria de
See Pereda (y Sanchez de Porrua), Jose
Maria de

Peregoy, George Weems
See Mencken, H(enry) L(ouis)

Perelman, S(idney) J(oseph)
1904-1979 . . . **CLC 3, 5, 9, 15, 23, 44, 49**
See also AITN 1, 2; CA 73-76; 89-92;
CANR 18; DLB 11, 44; MTCW

Peret, Benjamin 1899-1959 . . . . **TCLC 20**
See also CA 117

Peretz, Isaac Loeb 1851(?)-1915 . . . **TCLC 16**
See also CA 109

Peretz, Yitzkhok Leibush
See Peretz, Isaac Loeb

Perez Galdos, Benito 1843-1920 . . . **TCLC 27**
See also CA 125; HW

Perrault, Charles 1628-1703 . . . . **LC 2**
See also MAICYA; SATA 25

Perry, Brighton
See Sherwood, Robert E(mmet)

Perse, St.-John . . . . **CLC 4, 11, 46**
See also Leger, (Marie-Rene Auguste) Alexis
Saint-Leger

Peseenz, Tulio F.
See Lopez y Fuentes, Gregorio

Pesetsky, Bette 1932- . . . . **CLC 28**
See also CA 133; DLB 130

Peshkov, Alexei Maximovich 1868-1936
See Gorky, Maxim
See also CA 105; 141; DA

Pessoa, Fernando (Antonio Nogueira)
1888-1935 . . . . **TCLC 27; HLC**
See also CA 125

Peterkin, Julia Mood 1880-1961 . . . . **CLC 31**
See also CA 102; DLB 9

Peters, Joan K. 1945- . . . . **CLC 39**

Peters, Robert L(ouis) 1924- . . . . **CLC 7**
See also CA 13-16R; CAAS 8; DLB 105

Petofi, Sandor 1823-1849 . . . . **NCLC 21**

Petrakis, Harry Mark 1923- . . . . **CLC 3**
See also CA 9-12R; CANR 4, 30

Petrarch 1304-1374 . . . . **PC 8**

Petrov, Evgeny . . . . **TCLC 21**
See also Kataev, Evgeny Petrovich

Petry, Ann (Lane) 1908- . . . . . . **CLC 1, 7, 18**
See also BW 1; CA 5-8R; CAAS 6;
CANR 4; CLR 12; DLB 76; JRDA;
MAICYA; MTCW; SATA 5

Petursson, Halligrimur 1614-1674 . . . . **LC 8**

Philipson, Morris H. 1926- .... **CLC 53**
See also CA 1-4R; CANR 4

Phillips, David Graham
1867-1911 .... **TCLC 44**
See also CA 108; DLB 9, 12

Phillips, Jack
See Sandburg, Carl (August)

Phillips, Jayne Anne
1952- .... **CLC 15, 33; SSC 16**
See also CA 101; CANR 24; DLBY 80;
MTCW

Phillips, Richard
See Dick, Philip K(indred)

Phillips, Robert (Schaeffer) 1938-... **CLC 28**
See also CA 17-20R; CAAS 13; CANR 8;
DLB 105

Phillips, Ward
See Lovecraft, H(oward) P(hillips)

Piccolo, Lucio 1901-1969.......... **CLC 13**
See also CA 97-100; DLB 114

Pickthall, Marjorie L(owry) C(hristie)
1883-1922 .... **TCLC 21**
See also CA 107; DLB 92

Pico della Mirandola, Giovanni
1463-1494 .... **LC 15**

Piercy, Marge
1936- .... **CLC 3, 6, 14, 18, 27, 62**
See also CA 21-24R; CAAS 1; CANR 13,
43; DLB 120; MTCW

Piers, Robert
See Anthony, Piers

Pieyre de Mandiargues, Andre 1909-1991
See Mandiargues, Andre Pieyre de
See also CA 103; 136; CANR 22

Pilnyak, Boris .... **TCLC 23**
See also Vogau, Boris Andreyevich

Pincherle, Alberto 1907-1990 ... **CLC 11, 18**
See also Moravia, Alberto
See also CA 25-28R; 132; CANR 33;
MTCW

Pinckney, Darryl 1953- .... **CLC 76**
See also BW 2; CA 143

Pindar 518B.C.-446B.C. .... **CMLC 12**

Pineda, Cecile 1942- .... **CLC 39**
See also CA 118

Pinero, Arthur Wing 1855-1934 ... **TCLC 32**
See also CA 110; DLB 10

Pinero, Miguel (Antonio Gomez)
1946-1988 .... **CLC 4, 55**
See also CA 61-64; 125; CANR 29; HW

Pinget, Robert 1919- .... **CLC 7, 13, 37**
See also CA 85-88; DLB 83

Pink Floyd .... **CLC 35**
See also Barrett, (Roger) Syd; Gilmour,
David; Mason, Nick; Waters, Roger;
Wright, Rick

Pinkney, Edward 1802-1828 ..... **NCLC 31**

Pinkwater, Daniel Manus 1941-.... **CLC 35**
See also Pinkwater, Manus
See also AAYA 1; CA 29-32R; CANR 12,
38; CLR 4; JRDA; MAICYA; SAAS 3;
SATA 46, 76

Pinkwater, Manus
See Pinkwater, Daniel Manus
See also SATA 8

Pinsky, Robert 1940- .... **CLC 9, 19, 38**
See also CA 29-32R; CAAS 4; DLBY 82

Pinta, Harold
See Pinter, Harold

Pinter, Harold
1930- ..... **CLC 1, 3, 6, 9, 11, 15, 27, 58,
73; DA; WLC**
See also CA 5-8R; CANR 33; CDBLB 1960
to Present; DLB 13; MTCW

Pirandello, Luigi
1867-1936 ...... **TCLC 4, 29; DA; WLC**
See also CA 104

Pirsig, Robert M(aynard)
1928- .... **CLC 4, 6, 73**
See also CA 53-56; CANR 42; MTCW;
SATA 39

Pisarev, Dmitry Ivanovich
1840-1868 .... **NCLC 25**

Pix, Mary (Griffith) 1666-1709 ...... **LC 8**
See also DLB 80

Pixerecourt, Guilbert de
1773-1844 .... **NCLC 39**

Plaidy, Jean
See Hibbert, Eleanor Alice Burford

Planche, James Robinson
1796-1880 .... **NCLC 42**

Plant, Robert 1948- .... **CLC 12**

Plante, David (Robert)
1940- .... **CLC 7, 23, 38**
See also CA 37-40R; CANR 12, 36;
DLBY 83; MTCW

Plath, Sylvia
1932-1963 ..... **CLC 1, 2, 3, 5, 9, 11, 14,
17, 50, 51, 62; DA; PC 1; WLC**
See also CA 19-20; CANR 34; CAP 2;
CDALB 1941-1968; DLB 5, 6; MTCW

Plato 428(?)B.C.-348(?)B.C.... **CMLC 8; DA**

Platonov, Andrei .... **TCLC 14**
See also Klimentov, Andrei Platonovich

Platt, Kin 1911- .... **CLC 26**
See also AAYA 11; CA 17-20R; CANR 11;
JRDA; SAAS 17; SATA 21

Plick et Plock
See Simenon, Georges (Jacques Christian)

Plimpton, George (Ames) 1927-..... **CLC 36**
See also AITN 1; CA 21-24R; CANR 32;
MTCW; SATA 10

Plomer, William Charles Franklin
1903-1973 .... **CLC 4, 8**
See also CA 21-22; CANR 34; CAP 2;
DLB 20; MTCW; SATA 24

Plowman, Piers
See Kavanagh, Patrick (Joseph)

Plum, J.
See Wodehouse, P(elham) G(renville)

Plumly, Stanley (Ross) 1939- ...... **CLC 33**
See also CA 108; 110; DLB 5

Plumpe, Friedrich Wilhelm
1888-1931 .... **TCLC 53**
See also CA 112

Poe, Edgar Allan
1809-1849 ..... **NCLC 1, 16; DA; PC 1;
SSC 1; WLC**
See also CDALB 1640-1865; DLB 3, 59, 73,
74; SATA 23

Poet of Titchfield Street, The
See Pound, Ezra (Weston Loomis)

Pohl, Frederik 1919- .... **CLC 18**
See also CA 61-64; CAAS 1; CANR 11, 37;
DLB 8; MTCW; SATA 24

Poirier, Louis 1910-
See Gracq, Julien
See also CA 122; 126

Poitier, Sidney 1927- .... **CLC 26**
See also BW 1; CA 117

Polanski, Roman 1933- .... **CLC 16**
See also CA 77-80

Poliakoff, Stephen 1952- .... **CLC 38**
See also CA 106; DLB 13

Police, The.................... **CLC 26**
See also Copeland, Stewart (Armstrong);
Summers, Andrew James; Sumner,
Gordon Matthew

Pollitt, Katha 1949- .... **CLC 28**
See also CA 120; 122; MTCW

Pollock, (Mary) Sharon 1936-...... **CLC 50**
See also CA 141; DLB 60

Pomerance, Bernard 1940-........ **CLC 13**
See also CA 101

Ponge, Francis (Jean Gaston Alfred)
1899-1988 .... **CLC 6, 18**
See also CA 85-88; 126; CANR 40

Pontoppidan, Henrik 1857-1943 ... **TCLC 29**

Poole, Josephine .... **CLC 17**
See also Helyar, Jane Penelope Josephine
See also SAAS 2; SATA 5

Popa, Vasko 1922- .... **CLC 19**
See also CA 112

Pope, Alexander
1688-1744 .... **LC 3; DA; WLC**
See also CDBLB 1660-1789; DLB 95, 101

Porter, Connie (Rose) 1959(?)- ..... **CLC 70**
See also BW 2; CA 142

Porter, Gene(va Grace) Stratton
1863(?)-1924 .... **TCLC 21**
See also CA 112

Porter, Katherine Anne
1890-1980 ...... **CLC 1, 3, 7, 10, 13, 15,
27; DA; SSC 4**
See also AITN 2; CA 1-4R; 101; CANR 1;
DLB 4, 9, 102; DLBY 80; MTCW;
SATA 23, 39

Porter, Peter (Neville Frederick)
1929- .... **CLC 5, 13, 33**
See also CA 85-88; DLB 40

Porter, William Sydney 1862-1910
See Henry, O.
See also CA 104; 131; CDALB 1865-1917;
DA; DLB 12, 78, 79; MTCW; YABC 2

Portillo (y Pacheco), Jose Lopez
See Lopez Portillo (y Pacheco), Jose

Post, Melville Davisson
1869-1930 .... **TCLC 39**
See also CA 110

Potok, Chaim 1929- . . . . CLC 2, 7, 14, 26
See also AITN 1, 2; CA 17-20R; CANR 19,
35; DLB 28; MTCW; SATA 33

Potter, Beatrice
See Webb, (Martha) Beatrice (Potter)
See also MAICYA

Potter, Dennis (Christopher George)
1935- . . . . CLC 58
See also CA 107; CANR 33; MTCW

Pound, Ezra (Weston Loomis)
1885-1972 . . . . . . CLC 1, 2, 3, 4, 5, 7, 10,
13, 18, 34, 48, 50; DA; PC 4; WLC
See also CA 5-8R; 37-40R; CANR 40;
CDALB 1917-1929; DLB 4, 45, 63;
MTCW

Povod, Reinaldo 1959- . . . . CLC 44
See also CA 136

Powell, Anthony (Dymoke)
1905- . . . . CLC 1, 3, 7, 9, 10, 31
See also CA 1-4R; CANR 1, 32;
CDBLB 1945-1960; DLB 15; MTCW

Powell, Dawn 1897-1965 . . . . CLC 66
See also CA 5-8R

Powell, Padgett 1952- . . . . CLC 34
See also CA 126

Powers, J(ames) F(arl)
1917- . . . . CLC 1, 4, 8, 57; SSC 4
See also CA 1-4R; CANR 2; DLB 130;
MTCW

Powers, John J(ames) 1945-
See Powers, John R.
See also CA 69-72

Powers, John R. . . . . CLC 66
See also Powers, John J(ames)

Pownall, David 1938- . . . . CLC 10
See also CA 89-92; CAAS 18; DLB 14

Powys, John Cowper
1872-1963 . . . . CLC 7, 9, 15, 46
See also CA 85-88; DLB 15; MTCW

Powys, T(heodore) F(rancis)
1875-1953 . . . . TCLC 9
See also CA 106; DLB 36

Prager, Emily 1952- . . . . CLC 56

Pratt, E(dwin) J(ohn)
1883(?)-1964 . . . . CLC 19
See also CA 141; 93-96; DLB 92

Premchand . . . . TCLC 21
See also Srivastava, Dhanpat Rai

Preussler, Otfried 1923- . . . . CLC 17
See also CA 77-80; SATA 24

Prevert, Jacques (Henri Marie)
1900-1977 . . . . CLC 15
See also CA 77-80; 69-72; CANR 29;
MTCW; SATA 30

Prevost, Abbe (Antoine Francois)
1697-1763 . . . . LC 1

Price, (Edward) Reynolds
1933- . . . . CLC 3, 6, 13, 43, 50, 63
See also CA 1-4R; CANR 1, 37; DLB 2

Price, Richard 1949- . . . . CLC 6, 12
See also CA 49-52; CANR 3; DLBY 81

Prichard, Katharine Susannah
1883-1969 . . . . CLC 46
See also CA 11-12; CANR 33; CAP 1;
MTCW; SATA 66

Priestley, J(ohn) B(oynton)
1894-1984 . . . . CLC 2, 5, 9, 34
See also CA 9-12R; 113; CANR 33;
CDBLB 1914-1945; DLB 10, 34, 77, 100,
139; DLBY 84; MTCW

Prince 1958(?)- . . . . CLC 35

Prince, F(rank) T(empleton) 1912- . . CLC 22
See also CA 101; CANR 43; DLB 20

Prince Kropotkin
See Kropotkin, Peter (Aleksieevich)

Prior, Matthew 1664-1721 . . . . LC 4
See also DLB 95

Pritchard, William H(arrison)
1932- . . . . CLC 34
See also CA 65-68; CANR 23; DLB 111

Pritchett, V(ictor) S(awdon)
1900- . . . . CLC 5, 13, 15, 41; SSC 14
See also CA 61-64; CANR 31; DLB 15,
139; MTCW

Private 19022
See Manning, Frederic

Probst, Mark 1925- . . . . CLC 59
See also CA 130

Prokosch, Frederic 1908-1989 . . . . CLC 4, 48
See also CA 73-76; 128; DLB 48

Prophet, The
See Dreiser, Theodore (Herman Albert)

Prose, Francine 1947- . . . . CLC 45
See also CA 109; 112

Proudhon
See Cunha, Euclides (Rodrigues Pimenta) da

Proulx, E. Annie 1935- . . . . CLC 81

Proust, (Valentin-Louis-George-Eugene-)
Marcel
1871-1922 . . . TCLC 7, 13, 33; DA; WLC
See also CA 104; 120; DLB 65; MTCW

Prowler, Harley
See Masters, Edgar Lee

Prus, Boleslaw . . . . TCLC 48
See also Glowacki, Aleksander

Pryor, Richard (Franklin Lenox Thomas)
1940- . . . . CLC 26
See also CA 122

Przybyszewski, Stanislaw
1868-1927 . . . . TCLC 36
See also DLB 66

Pteleon
See Grieve, C(hristopher) M(urray)

Puckett, Lute
See Masters, Edgar Lee

Puig, Manuel
1932-1990 . . . CLC 3, 5, 10, 28, 65; HLC
See also CA 45-48; CANR 2, 32; DLB 113;
HW; MTCW

Purdy, Al(fred Wellington)
1918- . . . . CLC 3, 6, 14, 50
See also CA 81-84; CAAS 17; CANR 42;
DLB 88

Purdy, James (Amos)
1923- . . . . CLC 2, 4, 10, 28, 52
See also CA 33-36R; CAAS 1; CANR 19;
DLB 2; MTCW

Pure, Simon
See Swinnerton, Frank Arthur

Pushkin, Alexander (Sergeyevich)
1799-1837 . . . . NCLC 3, 27; DA; PC 10;
WLC
See also SATA 61

P'u Sung-ling 1640-1715 . . . . LC 3

Putnam, Arthur Lee
See Alger, Horatio, Jr.

Puzo, Mario 1920- . . . . CLC 1, 2, 6, 36
See also CA 65-68; CANR 4, 42; DLB 6;
MTCW

Pym, Barbara (Mary Crampton)
1913-1980 . . . . CLC 13, 19, 37
See also CA 13-14; 97-100; CANR 13, 34;
CAP 1; DLB 14; DLBY 87; MTCW

Pynchon, Thomas (Ruggles, Jr.)
1937- . . . . . CLC 2, 3, 6, 9, 11, 18, 33, 62,
72; DA; SSC 14; WLC
See also BEST 90:2; CA 17-20R; CANR 22;
DLB 2; MTCW

Q
See Quiller-Couch, Arthur Thomas

Qian Zhongshu
See Ch'ien Chung-shu

Qroll
See Dagerman, Stig (Halvard)

Quarrington, Paul (Lewis) 1953- . . . . CLC 65
See also CA 129

Quasimodo, Salvatore 1901-1968 . . . CLC 10
See also CA 13-16; 25-28R; CAP 1;
DLB 114; MTCW

Queen, Ellery . . . . CLC 3, 11
See also Dannay, Frederic; Davidson,
Avram; Lee, Manfred B(ennington);
Sturgeon, Theodore (Hamilton); Vance,
John Holbrook

Queen, Ellery, Jr.
See Dannay, Frederic; Lee, Manfred
B(ennington)

Queneau, Raymond
1903-1976 . . . . CLC 2, 5, 10, 42
See also CA 77-80; 69-72; CANR 32;
DLB 72; MTCW

Quevedo, Francisco de 1580-1645 . . . . LC 23

Quiller-Couch, Arthur Thomas
1863-1944 . . . . TCLC 53
See also CA 118; DLB 135

Quin, Ann (Marie) 1936-1973 . . . . CLC 6
See also CA 9-12R; 45-48; DLB 14

Quinn, Martin
See Smith, Martin Cruz

Quinn, Simon
See Smith, Martin Cruz

Quiroga, Horacio (Sylvestre)
1878-1937 . . . . TCLC 20; HLC
See also CA 117; 131; HW; MTCW

Quoirez, Francoise 1935- . . . . CLC 9
See also Sagan, Francoise
See also CA 49-52; CANR 6, 39; MTCW

Raabe, Wilhelm 1831-1910 . . . . TCLC 45
See also DLB 129

Rabe, David (William) 1940- . . . CLC 4, 8, 33
See also CA 85-88; CABS 3; DLB 7

Rabelais, Francois
1483-1553 . . . . LC 5; DA; WLC

Rabinovitch, Sholem 1859-1916
See Aleichem, Sholom
See also CA 104

Radcliffe, Ann (Ward) 1764-1823 . . **NCLC 6**
See also DLB 39

Radiguet, Raymond 1903-1923 . . . . **TCLC 29**
See also DLB 65

Radnoti, Miklos 1909-1944 . . . . . . **TCLC 16**
See also CA 118

Rado, James 1939- . . . . **CLC 17**
See also CA 105

Radvanyi, Netty 1900-1983
See Seghers, Anna
See also CA 85-88; 110

Rae, Ben
See Griffiths, Trevor

Raeburn, John (Hay) 1941- . . . . **CLC 34**
See also CA 57-60

Ragni, Gerome 1942-1991 . . . . **CLC 17**
See also CA 105; 134

Rahv, Philip 1908-1973 . . . . **CLC 24**
See also Greenberg, Ivan
See also DLB 137

Raine, Craig 1944- . . . . **CLC 32**
See also CA 108; CANR 29; DLB 40

Raine, Kathleen (Jessie) 1908- . . **CLC 7, 45**
See also CA 85-88; DLB 20; MTCW

Rainis, Janis 1865-1929 . . . . **TCLC 29**

Rakosi, Carl . . . . **CLC 47**
See also Rawley, Callman
See also CAAS 5

Raleigh, Richard
See Lovecraft, H(oward) P(hillips)

Rallentando, H. P.
See Sayers, Dorothy L(eigh)

Ramal, Walter
See de la Mare, Walter (John)

Ramon, Juan
See Jimenez (Mantecon), Juan Ramon

Ramos, Graciliano 1892-1953 . . . . . **TCLC 32**

Rampersad, Arnold 1941- . . . . **CLC 44**
See also BW 2; CA 127; 133; DLB 111

Rampling, Anne
See Rice, Anne

Ramuz, Charles-Ferdinand
1878-1947 . . . . **TCLC 33**

Rand, Ayn
1905-1982 . . . . . . **CLC 3, 30, 44, 79; DA;
WLC**
See also AAYA 10; CA 13-16R; 105;
CANR 27; MTCW

Randall, Dudley (Felker)
1914- . . . . **CLC 1; BLC**
See also BW 1; CA 25-28R; CANR 23;
DLB 41

Randall, Robert
See Silverberg, Robert

Ranger, Ken
See Creasey, John

Ransom, John Crowe
1888-1974 . . . . **CLC 2, 4, 5, 11, 24**
See also CA 5-8R; 49-52; CANR 6, 34;
DLB 45, 63; MTCW

Rao, Raja 1909- . . . . **CLC 25, 56**
See also CA 73-76; MTCW

Raphael, Frederic (Michael)
1931- . . . . **CLC 2, 14**
See also CA 1-4R; CANR 1; DLB 14

Ratcliffe, James P.
See Mencken, H(enry) L(ouis)

Rathbone, Julian 1935- . . . . **CLC 41**
See also CA 101; CANR 34

Rattigan, Terence (Mervyn)
1911-1977 . . . . **CLC 7**
See also CA 85-88; 73-76;
CDBLB 1945-1960; DLB 13; MTCW

Ratushinskaya, Irina 1954- . . . . **CLC 54**
See also CA 129

Raven, Simon (Arthur Noel)
1927- . . . . **CLC 14**
See also CA 81-84

Rawley, Callman 1903-
See Rakosi, Carl
See also CA 21-24R; CANR 12, 32

Rawlings, Marjorie Kinnan
1896-1953 . . . . **TCLC 4**
See also CA 104; 137; DLB 9, 22, 102;
JRDA; MAICYA; YABC 1

Ray, Satyajit 1921-1992 . . . . **CLC 16, 76**
See also CA 114; 137

Read, Herbert Edward 1893-1968 . . . . **CLC 4**
See also CA 85-88; 25-28R; DLB 20

Read, Piers Paul 1941- . . . . . . **CLC 4, 10, 25**
See also CA 21-24R; CANR 38; DLB 14;
SATA 21

Reade, Charles 1814-1884 . . . . **NCLC 2**
See also DLB 21

Reade, Hamish
See Gray, Simon (James Holliday)

Reading, Peter 1946- . . . . **CLC 47**
See also CA 103; DLB 40

Reaney, James 1926- . . . . **CLC 13**
See also CA 41-44R; CAAS 15; CANR 42;
DLB 68; SATA 43

Rebreanu, Liviu 1885-1944 . . . . **TCLC 28**

Rechy, John (Francisco)
1934- . . . . **CLC 1, 7, 14, 18; HLC**
See also CA 5-8R; CAAS 4; CANR 6, 32;
DLB 122; DLBY 82; HW

Redcam, Tom 1870-1933 . . . . **TCLC 25**

Reddin, Keith . . . . **CLC 67**

Redgrove, Peter (William)
1932- . . . . **CLC 6, 41**
See also CA 1-4R; CANR 3, 39; DLB 40

Redmon, Anne . . . . **CLC 22**
See also Nightingale, Anne Redmon
See also DLBY 86

Reed, Eliot
See Ambler, Eric

Reed, Ishmael
1938- . . . **CLC 2, 3, 5, 6, 13, 32, 60; BLC**
See also BW 2; CA 21-24R; CANR 25;
DLB 2, 5, 33; DLBD 8; MTCW

Reed, John (Silas) 1887-1920 . . . . . . **TCLC 9**
See also CA 106

Reed, Lou . . . . **CLC 21**
See also Firbank, Louis

Reeve, Clara 1729-1807 . . . . **NCLC 19**
See also DLB 39

Reid, Christopher (John) 1949- . . . . . **CLC 33**
See also CA 140; DLB 40

Reid, Desmond
See Moorcock, Michael (John)

Reid Banks, Lynne 1929-
See Banks, Lynne Reid
See also CA 1-4R; CANR 6, 22, 38;
CLR 24; JRDA; MAICYA; SATA 22, 75

Reilly, William K.
See Creasey, John

Reiner, Max
See Caldwell, (Janet Miriam) Taylor
(Holland)

Reis, Ricardo
See Pessoa, Fernando (Antonio Nogueira)

Remarque, Erich Maria
1898-1970 . . . . **CLC 21; DA**
See also CA 77-80; 29-32R; DLB 56;
MTCW

Remizov, A.
See Remizov, Aleksei (Mikhailovich)

Remizov, A. M.
See Remizov, Aleksei (Mikhailovich)

Remizov, Aleksei (Mikhailovich)
1877-1957 . . . . **TCLC 27**
See also CA 125; 133

Renan, Joseph Ernest
1823-1892 . . . . **NCLC 26**

Renard, Jules 1864-1910 . . . . **TCLC 17**
See also CA 117

Renault, Mary . . . . **CLC 3, 11, 17**
See also Challans, Mary
See also DLBY 83

Rendell, Ruth (Barbara) 1930- . . **CLC 28, 48**
See also Vine, Barbara
See also CA 109; CANR 32; DLB 87;
MTCW

Renoir, Jean 1894-1979 . . . . **CLC 20**
See also CA 129; 85-88

Resnais, Alain 1922- . . . . **CLC 16**

Reverdy, Pierre 1889-1960 . . . . **CLC 53**
See also CA 97-100; 89-92

Rexroth, Kenneth
1905-1982 . . . . . . **CLC 1, 2, 6, 11, 22, 49**
See also CA 5-8R; 107; CANR 14, 34;
CDALB 1941-1968; DLB 16, 48;
DLBY 82; MTCW

Reyes, Alfonso 1889-1959 . . . . **TCLC 33**
See also CA 131; HW

Reyes y Basoalto, Ricardo Eliecer Neftali
See Neruda, Pablo

Reymont, Wladyslaw (Stanislaw)
1868(?)-1925 . . . . **TCLC 5**
See also CA 104

Reynolds, Jonathan 1942- . . . . **CLC 6, 38**
See also CA 65-68; CANR 28

Reynolds, Joshua 1723-1792 . . . . **LC 15**
See also DLB 104

Reynolds, Michael Shane 1937- . . . . **CLC 44**
See also CA 65-68; CANR 9

Reznikoff, Charles 1894-1976 ...,... **CLC 9**
See also CA 33-36; 61-64; CAP 2; DLB 28, 45

Rezzori (d'Arezzo), Gregor von
1914- .... **CLC 25**
See also CA 122; 136

Rhine, Richard
See Silverstein, Alvin

Rhodes, Eugene Manlove
1869-1934 .... **TCLC 53**

R'hoone
See Balzac, Honore de

Rhys, Jean
1890(?)-1979 .... **CLC 2, 4, 6, 14, 19, 51**
See also CA 25-28R; 85-88; CANR 35;
CDBLB 1945-1960; DLB 36, 117; MTCW

Ribeiro, Darcy 1922- .... **CLC 34**
See also CA 33-36R

Ribeiro, Joao Ubaldo (Osorio Pimentel)
1941- .... **CLC 10, 67**
See also CA 81-84

Ribman, Ronald (Burt) 1932- .... **CLC 7**
See also CA 21-24R

Ricci, Nino 1959- .... **CLC 70**
See also CA 137

Rice, Anne 1941- .... **CLC 41**
See also AAYA 9; BEST 89:2; CA 65-68;
CANR 12, 36

Rice, Elmer (Leopold)
1892-1967 .... **CLC 7, 49**
See also CA 21-22; 25-28R; CAP 2; DLB 4,
7; MTCW

Rice, Tim 1944- .... **CLC 21**
See also CA 103

Rich, Adrienne (Cecile)
1929- .... **CLC 3, 6, 7, 11, 18, 36, 73, 76;**
PC 5
See also CA 9-12R; CANR 20; DLB 5, 67;
MTCW

Rich, Barbara
See Graves, Robert (von Ranke)

Rich, Robert
See Trumbo, Dalton

Richards, David Adams 1950- ...... **CLC 59**
See also CA 93-96; DLB 53

Richards, I(vor) A(rmstrong)
1893-1979 .... **CLC 14, 24**
See also CA 41-44R; 89-92; CANR 34;
DLB 27

Richardson, Anne
See Roiphe, Anne (Richardson)

Richardson, Dorothy Miller
1873-1957 .... **TCLC 3**
See also CA 104; DLB 36

Richardson, Ethel Florence (Lindesay)
1870-1946
See Richardson, Henry Handel
See also CA 105

Richardson, Henry Handel .... **TCLC 4**
See also Richardson, Ethel Florence
(Lindesay)

Richardson, Samuel
1689-1761 .... **LC 1; DA; WLC**
See also CDBLB 1660-1789; DLB 39

Richler, Mordecai
1931- .... **CLC 3, 5, 9, 13, 18, 46, 70**
See also AITN 1; CA 65-68; CANR 31;
CLR 17; DLB 53; MAICYA; MTCW;
SATA 27, 44

Richter, Conrad (Michael)
1890-1968 .... **CLC 30**
See also CA 5-8R; 25-28R; CANR 23;
DLB 9; MTCW; SATA 3

Riddell, J. H. 1832-1906 .... **TCLC 40**

Riding, Laura .... **CLC 3, 7**
See also Jackson, Laura (Riding)

Riefenstahl, Berta Helene Amalia 1902-
See Riefenstahl, Leni
See also CA 108

Riefenstahl, Leni .... **CLC 16**
See also Riefenstahl, Berta Helene Amalia

Riffe, Ernest
See Bergman, (Ernst) Ingmar

Riggs, (Rolla) Lynn 1899-1954 .... **TCLC 56**
See also CA 144

Riley, James Whitcomb
1849-1916 .... **TCLC 51**
See also CA 118; 137; MAICYA; SATA 17

Riley, Tex
See Creasey, John

Rilke, Rainer Maria
1875-1926 .... **TCLC 1, 6, 19; PC 2**
See also CA 104; 132; DLB 81; MTCW

Rimbaud, (Jean Nicolas) Arthur
1854-1891 ..... **NCLC 4, 35; DA; PC 3;**
WLC

Rinehart, Mary Roberts
1876-1958 .... **TCLC 52**
See also CA 108

Ringmaster, The
See Mencken, H(enry) L(ouis)

Ringwood, Gwen(dolyn Margaret) Pharis
1910-1984 .... **CLC 48**
See also CA 112; DLB 88

Rio, Michel 19(?)- .... **CLC 43**

Ritsos, Giannes
See Ritsos, Yannis

Ritsos, Yannis 1909-1990 ..... **CLC 6, 13, 31**
See also CA 77-80; 133; CANR 39; MTCW

Ritter, Erika 1948(?)- .... **CLC 52**

Rivera, Jose Eustasio 1889-1928 ... **TCLC 35**
See also HW

Rivers, Conrad Kent 1933-1968 ...... **CLC 1**
See also BW 1; CA 85-88; DLB 41

Rivers, Elfrida
See Bradley, Marion Zimmer

Riverside, John
See Heinlein, Robert A(nson)

Rizal, Jose 1861-1896 .... **NCLC 27**

Roa Bastos, Augusto (Antonio)
1917- .... **CLC 45; HLC**
See also CA 131; DLB 113; HW

Robbe-Grillet, Alain
1922- ...... **CLC 1, 2, 4, 6, 8, 10, 14, 43**
See also CA 9-12R; CANR 33; DLB 83;
MTCW

Robbins, Harold 1916- .... **CLC 5**
See also CA 73-76; CANR 26; MTCW

Robbins, Thomas Eugene 1936-
See Robbins, Tom
See also CA 81-84; CANR 29; MTCW

Robbins, Tom .... **CLC 9, 32, 64**
See also Robbins, Thomas Eugene
See also BEST 90:3; DLBY 80

Robbins, Trina 1938- .... **CLC 21**
See also CA 128

Roberts, Charles G(eorge) D(ouglas)
1860-1943 .... **TCLC 8**
See also CA 105; CLR 33; DLB 92;
SATA 29

Roberts, Kate 1891-1985 .... **CLC 15**
See also CA 107; 116

Roberts, Keith (John Kingston)
1935- .... **CLC 14**
See also CA 25-28R

Roberts, Kenneth (Lewis)
1885-1957 .... **TCLC 23**
See also CA 109; DLB 9

Roberts, Michele (B.) 1949- .... **CLC 48**
See also CA 115

Robertson, Ellis
See Ellison, Harlan; Silverberg, Robert

Robertson, Thomas William
1829-1871 .... **NCLC 35**

Robinson, Edwin Arlington
1869-1935 .... **TCLC 5; DA; PC 1**
See also CA 104; 133; CDALB 1865-1917;
DLB 54; MTCW

Robinson, Henry Crabb
1775-1867 .... **NCLC 15**
See also DLB 107

Robinson, Jill 1936- .... **CLC 10**
See also CA 102

Robinson, Kim Stanley 1952- ...... **CLC 34**
See also CA 126

Robinson, Lloyd
See Silverberg, Robert

Robinson, Marilynne 1944- .... **CLC 25**
See also CA 116

Robinson, Smokey .... **CLC 21**
See also Robinson, William, Jr.

Robinson, William, Jr. 1940-
See Robinson, Smokey
See also CA 116

Robison, Mary 1949- .... **CLC 42**
See also CA 113; 116; DLB 130

Rod, Edouard 1857-1910 .... **TCLC 52**

Roddenberry, Eugene Wesley 1921-1991
See Roddenberry, Gene
See also CA 110; 135; CANR 37; SATA 45

Roddenberry, Gene .... **CLC 17**
See also Roddenberry, Eugene Wesley
See also AAYA 5; SATA-Obit 69

Rodgers, Mary 1931- .... **CLC 12**
See also CA 49-52; CANR 8; CLR 20;
JRDA; MAICYA; SATA 8

Rodgers, W(illiam) R(obert)
1909-1969 .... **CLC 7**
See also CA 85-88; DLB 20

Rodman, Eric
See Silverberg, Robert

Rodman, Howard   1920(?)-1985 . . . . . **CLC 65**
See also CA 118

Rodman, Maia
See Wojciechowska, Maia (Teresa)

Rodriguez, Claudio   1934- . . . . **CLC 10**
See also DLB 134

Roelvaag, O(le) E(dvart)
1876-1931 . . . . **TCLC 17**
See also CA 117; DLB 9

Roethke, Theodore (Huebner)
1908-1963 . . . . . . **CLC 1, 3, 8, 11, 19, 46**
See also CA 81-84; CABS 2;
CDALB 1941-1968; DLB 5; MTCW

Rogers, Thomas Hunton   1927- . . . . . **CLC 57**
See also CA 89-92

Rogers, Will(iam Penn Adair)
1879-1935 . . . . **TCLC 8**
See also CA 105; 144; DLB 11

Rogin, Gilbert   1929- . . . . **CLC 18**
See also CA 65-68; CANR 15

Rohan, Koda . . . . **TCLC 22**
See also Koda Shigeyuki

Rohmer, Eric . . . . **CLC 16**
See also Scherer, Jean-Marie Maurice

Rohmer, Sax . . . . **TCLC 28**
See also Ward, Arthur Henry Sarsfield
See also DLB 70

Roiphe, Anne (Richardson)
1935- . . . . **CLC 3, 9**
See also CA 89-92; CANR 45; DLBY 80

Rojas, Fernando de   1465-1541 . . . . . . **LC 23**

**Rolfe, Frederick (William Serafino Austin
Lewis Mary)**   1860-1913 . . . . . . **TCLC 12**
See also CA 107; DLB 34

Rolland, Romain   1866-1944 . . . . **TCLC 23**
See also CA 118; DLB 65

Rolvaag, O(le) E(dvart)
See Roelvaag, O(le) E(dvart)

Romain Arnaud, Saint
See Aragon, Louis

Romains, Jules   1885-1972 . . . . **CLC 7**
See also CA 85-88; CANR 34; DLB 65;
MTCW

Romero, Jose Ruben   1890-1952 . . . **TCLC 14**
See also CA 114; 131; HW

Ronsard, Pierre de   1524-1585 . . . . **LC 6**

Rooke, Leon   1934- . . . . **CLC 25, 34**
See also CA 25-28R; CANR 23

Roper, William   1498-1578 . . . . **LC 10**

Roquelaure, A. N.
See Rice, Anne

Rosa, Joao Guimaraes   1908-1967 . . . **CLC 23**
See also CA 89-92; DLB 113

Rosen, Richard (Dean)   1949- . . . . . . **CLC 39**
See also CA 77-80

Rosenberg, Isaac   1890-1918 . . . . **TCLC 12**
See also CA 107; DLB 20

Rosenblatt, Joe . . . . **CLC 15**
See also Rosenblatt, Joseph

Rosenblatt, Joseph   1933-
See Rosenblatt, Joe
See also CA 89-92

Rosenfeld, Samuel   1896-1963
See Tzara, Tristan
See also CA 89-92

Rosenthal, M(acha) L(ouis)   1917- . . . **CLC 28**
See also CA 1-4R; CAAS 6; CANR 4;
DLB 5; SATA 59

Ross, Barnaby
See Dannay, Frederic

Ross, Bernard L.
See Follett, Ken(neth Martin)

Ross, J. H.
See Lawrence, T(homas) E(dward)

Ross, Martin
See Martin, Violet Florence
See also DLB 135

Ross, (James) Sinclair   1908- . . . . **CLC 13**
See also CA 73-76; DLB 88

Rossetti, Christina (Georgina)
1830-1894 . . . **NCLC 2; DA; PC 7; WLC**
See also DLB 35; MAICYA; SATA 20

Rossetti, Dante Gabriel
1828-1882 . . . . **NCLC 4; DA; WLC**
See also CDBLB 1832-1890; DLB 35

Rossner, Judith (Perelman)
1935- . . . . **CLC 6, 9, 29**
See also AITN 2; BEST 90:3; CA 17-20R;
CANR 18; DLB 6; MTCW

Rostand, Edmond (Eugene Alexis)
1868-1918 . . . . **TCLC 6, 37; DA**
See also CA 104; 126; MTCW

Roth, Henry   1906- . . . . **CLC 2, 6, 11**
See also CA 11-12; CANR 38; CAP 1;
DLB 28; MTCW

Roth, Joseph   1894-1939 . . . . **TCLC 33**
See also DLB 85

Roth, Philip (Milton)
1933- . . . . . . **CLC 1, 2, 3, 4, 6, 9, 15, 22,
31, 47, 66; DA; WLC**
See also BEST 90:3; CA 1-4R; CANR 1, 22,
36; CDALB 1968-1988; DLB 2, 28;
DLBY 82; MTCW

Rothenberg, Jerome   1931- . . . . **CLC 6, 57**
See also CA 45-48; CANR 1; DLB 5

Roumain, Jacques (Jean Baptiste)
1907-1944 . . . . **TCLC 19; BLC**
See also BW 1; CA 117; 125

Rourke, Constance (Mayfield)
1885-1941 . . . . **TCLC 12**
See also CA 107; YABC 1

Rousseau, Jean-Baptiste   1671-1741 . . . **LC 9**

Rousseau, Jean-Jacques
1712-1778 . . . . **LC 14; DA; WLC**

Roussel, Raymond   1877-1933 . . . . . **TCLC 20**
See also CA 117

Rovit, Earl (Herbert)   1927- . . . . **CLC 7**
See also CA 5-8R; CANR 12

Rowe, Nicholas   1674-1718 . . . . **LC 8**
See also DLB 84

Rowley, Ames Dorrance
See Lovecraft, H(oward) P(hillips)

Rowson, Susanna Haswell
1762(?)-1824 . . . . **NCLC 5**
See also DLB 37

Roy, Gabrielle   1909-1983 . . . . **CLC 10, 14**
See also CA 53-56; 110; CANR 5; DLB 68;
MTCW

Rozewicz, Tadeusz   1921- . . . . **CLC 9, 23**
See also CA 108; CANR 36; MTCW

Ruark, Gibbons   1941- . . . . **CLC 3**
See also CA 33-36R; CANR 14, 31;
DLB 120

Rubens, Bernice (Ruth)   1923- . . . **CLC 19, 31**
See also CA 25-28R; CANR 33; DLB 14;
MTCW

Rudkin, (James) David   1936- . . . . . . **CLC 14**
See also CA 89-92; DLB 13

Rudnik, Raphael   1933- . . . . **CLC 7**
See also CA 29-32R

Ruffian, M.
See Hasek, Jaroslav (Matej Frantisek)

Ruiz, Jose Martinez . . . . **CLC 11**
See also Martinez Ruiz, Jose

Rukeyser, Muriel
1913-1980 . . . . **CLC 6, 10, 15, 27**
See also CA 5-8R; 93-96; CANR 26;
DLB 48; MTCW; SATA 22

Rule, Jane (Vance)   1931- . . . . **CLC 27**
See also CA 25-28R; CAAS 18; CANR 12;
DLB 60

Rulfo, Juan   1918-1986 . . . . **CLC 8, 80; HLC**
See also CA 85-88; 118; CANR 26;
DLB 113; HW; MTCW

Runeberg, Johan   1804-1877 . . . . . . **NCLC 41**

Runyon, (Alfred) Damon
1884(?)-1946 . . . . **TCLC 10**
See also CA 107; DLB 11, 86

Rush, Norman   1933- . . . . **CLC 44**
See also CA 121; 126

Rushdie, (Ahmed) Salman
1947- . . . . **CLC 23, 31, 55**
See also BEST 89:3; CA 108; 111;
CANR 33; MTCW

Rushforth, Peter (Scott)   1945- . . . . . **CLC 19**
See also CA 101

Ruskin, John   1819-1900 . . . . **TCLC 20**
See also CA 114; 129; CDBLB 1832-1890;
DLB 55; SATA 24

Russ, Joanna   1937- . . . . **CLC 15**
See also CA 25-28R; CANR 11, 31; DLB 8;
MTCW

Russell, George William   1867-1935
See A. E.
See also CA 104; CDBLB 1890-1914

Russell, (Henry) Ken(neth Alfred)
1927- . . . . **CLC 16**
See also CA 105

Russell, Willy   1947- . . . . **CLC 60**

Rutherford, Mark . . . . **TCLC 25**
See also White, William Hale
See also DLB 18

Ruyslinck, Ward
See Belser, Reimond Karel Maria de

Ryan, Cornelius (John)   1920-1974 . . . **CLC 7**
See also CA 69-72; 53-56; CANR 38

Ryan, Michael   1946- . . . . **CLC 65**
See also CA 49-52; DLBY 82

Rybakov, Anatoli (Naumovich)
1911- .... **CLC 23, 53**
See also CA 126; 135

Ryder, Jonathan
See Ludlum, Robert

Ryga, George 1932-1987 .... **CLC 14**
See also CA 101; 124; CANR 43; DLB 60

S. S.
See Sassoon, Siegfried (Lorraine)

Saba, Umberto 1883-1957 .... **TCLC 33**
See also CA 144; DLB 114

Sabatini, Rafael 1875-1950 .... **TCLC 47**

Sabato, Ernesto (R.)
1911- .... **CLC 10, 23; HLC**
See also CA 97-100; CANR 32; HW;
MTCW

Sacastru, Martin
See Bioy Casares, Adolfo

Sacher-Masoch, Leopold von
1836(?)-1895 .... **NCLC 31**

Sachs, Marilyn (Stickle) 1927- ..... **CLC 35**
See also AAYA 2; CA 17-20R; CANR 13;
CLR 2; JRDA; MAICYA; SAAS 2;
SATA 3, 68

Sachs, Nelly 1891-1970 .... **CLC 14**
See also CA 17-18; 25-28R; CAP 2

Sackler, Howard (Oliver)
1929-1982 .... **CLC 14**
See also CA 61-64; 108; CANR 30; DLB 7

Sacks, Oliver (Wolf) 1933- .... **CLC 67**
See also CA 53-56; CANR 28; MTCW

Sade, Donatien Alphonse Francois Comte
1740-1814 .... **NCLC 3**

Sadoff, Ira 1945-................. **CLC 9**
See also CA 53-56; CANR 5, 21; DLB 120

Saetone
See Camus, Albert

Safire, William 1929-............. **CLC 10**
See also CA 17-20R; CANR 31

Sagan, Carl (Edward) 1934-........ **CLC 30**
See also AAYA 2; CA 25-28R; CANR 11,
36; MTCW; SATA 58

Sagan, Francoise .... **CLC 3, 6, 9, 17, 36**
See also Quoirez, Francoise
See also DLB 83

Sahgal, Nayantara (Pandit) 1927-... **CLC 41**
See also CA 9-12R; CANR 11

Saint, H(arry) F. 1941- .... **CLC 50**
See also CA 127

St. Aubin de Teran, Lisa 1953-
See Teran, Lisa St. Aubin de
See also CA 118; 126

Sainte-Beuve, Charles Augustin
1804-1869 .... **NCLC 5**

Saint-Exupery, Antoine (Jean Baptiste Marie Roger) de
1900-1944 .... **TCLC 2, 56; WLC**
See also CA 108; 132; CLR 10; DLB 72;
MAICYA; MTCW; SATA 20

St. John, David
See Hunt, E(verette) Howard, Jr.

Saint-John Perse
See Leger, (Marie-Rene Auguste) Alexis
Saint-Leger

Saintsbury, George (Edward Bateman)
1845-1933 .... **TCLC 31**
See also DLB 57

Sait Faik .... **TCLC 23**
See also Abasiyanik, Sait Faik

Saki .... **TCLC 3; SSC 12**
See also Munro, H(ector) H(ugh)

Salama, Hannu 1936-.............. **CLC 18**

Salamanca, J(ack) R(ichard)
1922- .... **CLC 4, 15**
See also CA 25-28R

Sale, J. Kirkpatrick
See Sale, Kirkpatrick

Sale, Kirkpatrick 1937-........... **CLC 68**
See also CA 13-16R; CANR 10

Salinas (y Serrano), Pedro
1891(?)-1951 .... **TCLC 17**
See also CA 117; DLB 134

Salinger, J(erome) D(avid)
1919- ...... **CLC 1, 3, 8, 12, 55, 56; DA;**
SSC 2; WLC
See also AAYA 2; CA 5-8R; CANR 39;
CDALB 1941-1968; CLR 18; DLB 2, 102;
MAICYA; MTCW; SATA 67

Salisbury, John
See Caute, David

Salter, James 1925- .... **CLC 7, 52, 59**
See also CA 73-76; DLB 130

Saltus, Edgar (Everton)
1855-1921 .... **TCLC 8**
See also CA 105

Saltykov, Mikhail Evgrafovich
1826-1889 .... **NCLC 16**

Samarakis, Antonis 1919- .... **CLC 5**
See also CA 25-28R; CAAS 16; CANR 36

Sanchez, Florencio 1875-1910 ..... **TCLC 37**
See also HW

Sanchez, Luis Rafael 1936-........ **CLC 23**
See also CA 128; HW

Sanchez, Sonia 1934-... **CLC 5; BLC; PC 9**
See also BW 2; CA 33-36R; CANR 24;
CLR 18; DLB 41; DLBD 8; MAICYA;
MTCW; SATA 22

Sand, George
1804-1876 ...... **NCLC 2, 42; DA; WLC**
See also DLB 119

Sandburg, Carl (August)
1878-1967 .... **CLC 1, 4, 10, 15, 35; DA;**
PC 2; WLC
See also CA 5-8R; 25-28R; CANR 35;
CDALB 1865-1917; DLB 17, 54;
MAICYA; MTCW; SATA 8

Sandburg, Charles
See Sandburg, Carl (August)

Sandburg, Charles A.
See Sandburg, Carl (August)

Sanders, (James) Ed(ward) 1939- ... **CLC 53**
See also CA 13-16R; CANR 13, 44;
DLB 16

Sanders, Lawrence 1920-.......... **CLC 41**
See also BEST 89:4; CA 81-84; CANR 33;
MTCW

Sanders, Noah
See Blount, Roy (Alton), Jr.

Sanders, Winston P.
See Anderson, Poul (William)

Sandoz, Mari(e Susette)
1896-1966 .... **CLC 28**
See also CA 1-4R; 25-28R; CANR 17;
DLB 9; MTCW; SATA 5

Saner, Reg(inald Anthony) 1931- .... **CLC 9**
See also CA 65-68

Sannazaro, Jacopo 1456(?)-1530 ...... **LC 8**

Sansom, William 1912-1976....... **CLC 2, 6**
See also CA 5-8R; 65-68; CANR 42;
DLB 139; MTCW

Santayana, George 1863-1952 ...... **TCLC 40**
See also CA 115; DLB 54, 71

Santiago, Danny .... **CLC 33**
See also James, Daniel (Lewis); James,
Daniel (Lewis)
See also DLB 122

Santmyer, Helen Hoover
1895-1986 .... **CLC 33**
See also CA 1-4R; 118; CANR 15, 33;
DLBY 84; MTCW

Santos, Bienvenido N(uqui) 1911-... **CLC 22**
See also CA 101; CANR 19

Sapper .... **TCLC 44**
See also McNeile, Herman Cyril

Sappho fl. 6th cent. B.C.-.... **CMLC 3; PC 5**

Sarduy, Severo 1937-1993 .... **CLC 6**
See also CA 89-92; 142; DLB 113; HW

Sargeson, Frank 1903-1982 .... **CLC 31**
See also CA 25-28R; 106; CANR 38

Sarmiento, Felix Ruben Garcia
See Dario, Ruben

Saroyan, William
1908-1981 ..... **CLC 1, 8, 10, 29, 34, 56;**
DA; WLC
See also CA 5-8R; 103; CANR 30; DLB 7,
9, 86; DLBY 81; MTCW; SATA 23, 24

Sarraute, Nathalie
1900- .... **CLC 1, 2, 4, 8, 10, 31, 80**
See also CA 9-12R; CANR 23; DLB 83;
MTCW

Sarton, (Eleanor) May
1912- .... **CLC 4, 14, 49**
See also CA 1-4R; CANR 1, 34; DLB 48;
DLBY 81; MTCW; SATA 36

Sartre, Jean-Paul
1905-1980 .... **CLC 1, 4, 7, 9, 13, 18, 24,**
44, 50, 52; DA; DC 3; WLC
See also CA 9-12R; 97-100; CANR 21;
DLB 72; MTCW

Sassoon, Siegfried (Lorraine)
1886-1967 .... **CLC 36**
See also CA 104; 25-28R; CANR 36;
DLB 20; MTCW

Satterfield, Charles
See Pohl, Frederik

Saul, John (W. III) 1942- .... **CLC 46**
See also AAYA 10; BEST 90:4; CA 81-84;
CANR 16, 40

Saunders, Caleb
See Heinlein, Robert A(nson)

Saura (Atares), Carlos 1932-....... **CLC 20**
See also CA 114; 131; HW

Sauser-Hall, Frederic 1887-1961.... **CLC 18**
See also CA 102; 93-96; CANR 36; MTCW

Saussure, Ferdinand de
1857-1913 .... **TCLC 49**

Savage, Catharine
See Brosman, Catharine Savage

Savage, Thomas 1915- .... **CLC 40**
See also CA 126; 132; CAAS 15

Savan, Glenn .... **CLC 50**

Saven, Glenn 19(?)- .... **CLC 50**

Sayers, Dorothy L(eigh)
1893-1957 .... **TCLC 2, 15**
See also CA 104; 119; CDBLB 1914-1945;
DLB 10, 36, 77, 100; MTCW

Sayers, Valerie 1952- .... **CLC 50**
See also CA 134

Sayles, John (Thomas)
1950- .... **CLC 7, 10, 14**
See also CA 57-60; CANR 41; DLB 44

Scammell, Michael .... **CLC 34**

Scannell, Vernon 1922- .... **CLC 49**
See also CA 5-8R; CANR 8, 24; DLB 27;
SATA 59

Scarlett, Susan
See Streatfeild, (Mary) Noel

Schaeffer, Susan Fromberg
1941- .... **CLC 6, 11, 22**
See also CA 49-52; CANR 18; DLB 28;
MTCW; SATA 22

Schary, Jill
See Robinson, Jill

Schell, Jonathan 1943- .... **CLC 35**
See also CA 73-76; CANR 12

Schelling, Friedrich Wilhelm Joseph von
1775-1854 .... **NCLC 30**
See also DLB 90

Scherer, Jean-Marie Maurice 1920-
See Rohmer, Eric
See also CA 110

Schevill, James (Erwin) 1920- ...... **CLC 7**
See also CA 5-8R; CAAS 12

Schiller, Friedrich 1759-1805 .... **NCLC 39**
See also DLB 94

Schisgal, Murray (Joseph) 1926- ..... **CLC 6**
See also CA 21-24R

Schlee, Ann 1934- .... **CLC 35**
See also CA 101; CANR 29; SATA 36, 44

Schlegel, August Wilhelm von
1767-1845 .... **NCLC 15**
See also DLB 94

Schlegel, Friedrich 1772-1829 .... **NCLC 45**
See also DLB 90

Schlegel, Johann Elias (von)
1719(?)-1749 .... **LC 5**

Schlesinger, Arthur M(eier), Jr.
1917- .... **CLC 84**
See also AITN 1; CA 1-4R; CANR 1, 28;
DLB 17; MTCW; SATA 61

Schmidt, Arno (Otto) 1914-1979 .... **CLC 56**
See also CA 128; 109; DLB 69

Schmitz, Aron Hector 1861-1928
See Svevo, Italo
See also CA 104; 122; MTCW

Schnackenberg, Gjertrud 1953- ..... **CLC 40**
See also CA 116; DLB 120

Schneider, Leonard Alfred 1925-1966
See Bruce, Lenny
See also CA 89-92

Schnitzler, Arthur
1862-1931 .... **TCLC 4; SSC 15**
See also CA 104; DLB 81, 118

Schor, Sandra (M.) 1932(?)-1990 ... **CLC 65**
See also CA 132

Schorer, Mark 1908-1977 .... **CLC 9**
See also CA 5-8R; 73-76; CANR 7;
DLB 103

Schrader, Paul (Joseph) 1946- ...... **CLC 26**
See also CA 37-40R; CANR 41; DLB 44

Schreiner, Olive (Emilie Albertina)
1855-1920 .... **TCLC 9**
See also CA 105; DLB 18

Schulberg, Budd (Wilson)
1914- .... **CLC 7, 48**
See also CA 25-28R; CANR 19; DLB 6, 26,
28; DLBY 81

Schulz, Bruno
1892-1942 .... **TCLC 5, 51; SSC 13**
See also CA 115; 123

Schulz, Charles M(onroe) 1922- .... **CLC 12**
See also CA 9-12R; CANR 6; SATA 10

Schumacher, E(rnst) F(riedrich)
1911-1977 .... **CLC 80**
See also CA 81-84; 73-76; CANR 34

Schuyler, James Marcus
1923-1991 .... **CLC 5, 23**
See also CA 101; 134; DLB 5

Schwartz, Delmore (David)
1913-1966 ...... **CLC 2, 4, 10, 45; PC 8**
See also CA 17-18; 25-28R; CANR 35;
CAP 2; DLB 28, 48; MTCW

Schwartz, Ernst
See Ozu, Yasujiro

Schwartz, John Burnham 1965- .... **CLC 59**
See also CA 132

Schwartz, Lynne Sharon 1939- ..... **CLC 31**
See also CA 103; CANR 44

Schwartz, Muriel A.
See Eliot, T(homas) S(tearns)

Schwarz-Bart, Andre 1928- .... **CLC 2, 4**
See also CA 89-92

Schwarz-Bart, Simone 1938- .... **CLC 7**
See also BW 2; CA 97-100

Schwob, (Mayer Andre) Marcel
1867-1905 .... **TCLC 20**
See also CA 117; DLB 123

Sciascia, Leonardo
1921-1989 .... **CLC 8, 9, 41**
See also CA 85-88; 130; CANR 35; MTCW

Scoppettone, Sandra 1936- .... **CLC 26**
See also AAYA 11; CA 5-8R; CANR 41;
SATA 9

Scorsese, Martin 1942- .... **CLC 20**
See also CA 110; 114

Scotland, Jay
See Jakes, John (William)

Scott, Duncan Campbell
1862-1947 .... **TCLC 6**
See also CA 104; DLB 92

Scott, Evelyn 1893-1963.......... **CLC 43**
See also CA 104; 112; DLB 9, 48

Scott, F(rancis) R(eginald)
1899-1985 .... **CLC 22**
See also CA 101; 114; DLB 88

Scott, Frank
See Scott, F(rancis) R(eginald)

Scott, Joanna 1960- .... **CLC 50**
See also CA 126

Scott, Paul (Mark) 1920-1978.... **CLC 9, 60**
See also CA 81-84; 77-80; CANR 33;
DLB 14; MTCW

Scott, Walter
1771-1832 .... **NCLC 15; DA; WLC**
See also CDBLB 1789-1832; DLB 93, 107,
116, 144; YABC 2

Scribe, (Augustin) Eugene
1791-1861 .... **NCLC 16**

Scrum, R.
See Crumb, R(obert)

Scudery, Madeleine de 1607-1701..... **LC 2**

Scum
See Crumb, R(obert)

Scumbag, Little Bobby
See Crumb, R(obert)

Seabrook, John
See Hubbard, L(afayette) Ron(ald)

Sealy, I. Allan 1951- .... **CLC 55**

Search, Alexander
See Pessoa, Fernando (Antonio Nogueira)

Sebastian, Lee
See Silverberg, Robert

Sebastian Owl
See Thompson, Hunter S(tockton)

Sebestyen, Ouida 1924- .... **CLC 30**
See also AAYA 8; CA 107; CANR 40;
CLR 17; JRDA; MAICYA; SAAS 10;
SATA 39

Secundus, H. Scriblerus
See Fielding, Henry

Sedges, John
See Buck, Pearl S(ydenstricker)

Sedgwick, Catharine Maria
1789-1867 .... **NCLC 19**
See also DLB 1, 74

Seelye, John 1931- .... **CLC 7**

Seferiades, Giorgos Stylianou 1900-1971
See Seferis, George
See also CA 5-8R; 33-36R; CANR 5, 36;
MTCW

Seferis, George .... **CLC 5, 11**
See also Seferiades, Giorgos Stylianou

Segal, Erich (Wolf) 1937- .... **CLC 3, 10**
See also BEST 89:1; CA 25-28R; CANR 20,
36; DLBY 86; MTCW

Seger, Bob 1945-................. **CLC 35**

Seghers, Anna .... **CLC 7**
See also Radvanyi, Netty
See also DLB 69

Shu-Jen, Chou 1881-1936
See Hsun, Lu
See also CA 104

Shulman, Alix Kates 1932- . . . . . . **CLC 2, 10**
See also CA 29-32R; CANR 43; SATA 7

Shuster, Joe 1914- . . . . **CLC 21**

Shute, Nevil . . . . **CLC 30**
See also Norway, Nevil Shute

Shuttle, Penelope (Diane) 1947- . . . . . **CLC 7**
See also CA 93-96; CANR 39; DLB 14, 40

Sidney, Mary 1561-1621 . . . . **LC 19**

Sidney, Sir Philip 1554-1586 . . . . **LC 19; DA**
See also CDBLB Before 1660

Siegel, Jerome 1914- . . . . **CLC 21**
See also CA 116

Siegel, Jerry
See Siegel, Jerome

Sienkiewicz, Henryk (Adam Alexander Pius)
1846-1916 . . . . **TCLC 3**
See also CA 104; 134

Sierra, Gregorio Martinez
See Martinez Sierra, Gregorio

Sierra, Maria (de la O'LeJarraga) Martinez
See Martinez Sierra, Maria (de la
O'LeJarraga)

Sigal, Clancy 1926- . . . . **CLC 7**
See also CA 1-4R

Sigourney, Lydia Howard (Huntley)
1791-1865 . . . . **NCLC 21**
See also DLB 1, 42, 73

Siguenza y Gongora, Carlos de
1645-1700 . . . . **LC 8**

Sigurjonsson, Johann 1880-1919 . . . **TCLC 27**

Sikelianos, Angelos 1884-1951 . . . . **TCLC 39**

Silkin, Jon 1930- . . . . **CLC 2, 6, 43**
See also CA 5-8R; CAAS 5; DLB 27

Silko, Leslie (Marmon)
1948- . . . . **CLC 23, 74; DA**
See also CA 115; 122; CANR 45; DLB 143

Sillanpaa, Frans Eemil 1888-1964 . . . **CLC 19**
See also CA 129; 93-96; MTCW

Sillitoe, Alan
1928- . . . . **CLC 1, 3, 6, 10, 19, 57**
See also AITN 1; CA 9-12R; CAAS 2;
CANR 8, 26; CDBLB 1960 to Present;
DLB 14, 139; MTCW; SATA 61

Silone, Ignazio 1900-1978 . . . . **CLC 4**
See also CA 25-28; 81-84; CANR 34;
CAP 2; MTCW

Silver, Joan Micklin 1935- . . . . **CLC 20**
See also CA 114; 121

Silver, Nicholas
See Faust, Frederick (Schiller)

Silverberg, Robert 1935- . . . . **CLC 7**
See also CA 1-4R; CAAS 3; CANR 1, 20,
36; DLB 8; MAICYA; MTCW; SATA 13

Silverstein, Alvin 1933- . . . . **CLC 17**
See also CA 49-52; CANR 2; CLR 25;
JRDA; MAICYA; SATA 8, 69

Silverstein, Virginia B(arbara Opshelor)
1937- . . . . **CLC 17**
See also CA 49-52; CANR 2; CLR 25;
JRDA; MAICYA; SATA 8, 69

Sim, Georges
See Simenon, Georges (Jacques Christian)

Simak, Clifford D(onald)
1904-1988 . . . . **CLC 1, 55**
See also CA 1-4R; 125; CANR 1, 35;
DLB 8; MTCW; SATA 56

Simenon, Georges (Jacques Christian)
1903-1989 . . . . **CLC 1, 2, 3, 8, 18, 47**
See also CA 85-88; 129; CANR 35;
DLB 72; DLBY 89; MTCW

Simic, Charles 1938- . . . **CLC 6, 9, 22, 49, 68**
See also CA 29-32R; CAAS 4; CANR 12,
33; DLB 105

Simmons, Charles (Paul) 1924- . . . . . **CLC 57**
See also CA 89-92

Simmons, Dan 1948- . . . . **CLC 44**
See also CA 138

Simmons, James (Stewart Alexander)
1933- . . . . **CLC 43**
See also CA 105; DLB 40

Simms, William Gilmore
1806-1870 . . . . **NCLC 3**
See also DLB 3, 30, 59, 73

Simon, Carly 1945- . . . . **CLC 26**
See also CA 105

Simon, Claude 1913- . . . . . . **CLC 4, 9, 15, 39**
See also CA 89-92; CANR 33; DLB 83;
MTCW

Simon, (Marvin) Neil
1927- . . . . **CLC 6, 11, 31, 39, 70**
See also AITN 1; CA 21-24R; CANR 26;
DLB 7; MTCW

Simon, Paul 1942(?)- . . . . **CLC 17**
See also CA 116

Simonon, Paul 1956(?)- . . . . **CLC 30**
See also Clash, The

Simpson, Harriette
See Arnow, Harriette (Louisa) Simpson

Simpson, Louis (Aston Marantz)
1923- . . . . **CLC 4, 7, 9, 32**
See also CA 1-4R; CAAS 4; CANR 1;
DLB 5; MTCW

Simpson, Mona (Elizabeth) 1957- . . . **CLC 44**
See also CA 122; 135

Simpson, N(orman) F(rederick)
1919- . . . . **CLC 29**
See also CA 13-16R; DLB 13

Sinclair, Andrew (Annandale)
1935- . . . . **CLC 2, 14**
See also CA 9-12R; CAAS 5; CANR 14, 38;
DLB 14; MTCW

Sinclair, Emil
See Hesse, Hermann

Sinclair, Iain 1943- . . . . **CLC 76**
See also CA 132

Sinclair, Iain MacGregor
See Sinclair, Iain

Sinclair, Mary Amelia St. Clair 1865(?)-1946
See Sinclair, May
See also CA 104

Sinclair, May . . . . **TCLC 3, 11**
See also Sinclair, Mary Amelia St. Clair
See also DLB 36, 135

Sinclair, Upton (Beall)
1878-1968 . . . . . . **CLC 1, 11, 15, 63; DA;**
WLC
See also CA 5-8R; 25-28R; CANR 7;
CDALB 1929-1941; DLB 9; MTCW;
SATA 9

Singer, Isaac
See Singer, Isaac Bashevis

Singer, Isaac Bashevis
1904-1991 . . . . **CLC 1, 3, 6, 9, 11, 15, 23,**
38, 69; DA; SSC 3; WLC
See also AITN 1, 2; CA 1-4R; 134;
CANR 1, 39; CDALB 1941-1968; CLR 1;
DLB 6, 28, 52; DLBY 91; JRDA;
MAICYA; MTCW; SATA 3, 27;
SATA-Obit 68

Singer, Israel Joshua 1893-1944 . . . **TCLC 33**

Singh, Khushwant 1915- . . . . **CLC 11**
See also CA 9-12R; CAAS 9; CANR 6

Sinjohn, John
See Galsworthy, John

Sinyavsky, Andrei (Donatevich)
1925- . . . . **CLC 8**
See also CA 85-88

Sirin, V.
See Nabokov, Vladimir (Vladimirovich)

Sissman, L(ouis) E(dward)
1928-1976 . . . . **CLC 9, 18**
See also CA 21-24R; 65-68; CANR 13;
DLB 5

Sisson, C(harles) H(ubert) 1914- . . . . . **CLC 8**
See also CA 1-4R; CAAS 3; CANR 3;
DLB 27

Sitwell, Dame Edith
1887-1964 . . . . **CLC 2, 9, 67; PC 3**
See also CA 9-12R; CANR 35;
CDBLB 1945-1960; DLB 20; MTCW

Sjoewall, Maj 1935- . . . . **CLC 7**
See also CA 65-68

Sjowall, Maj
See Sjoewall, Maj

Skelton, Robin 1925- . . . . **CLC 13**
See also AITN 2; CA 5-8R; CAAS 5;
CANR 28; DLB 27, 53

Skolimowski, Jerzy 1938- . . . . **CLC 20**
See also CA 128

Skram, Amalie (Bertha)
1847-1905 . . . . **TCLC 25**

Skvorecky, Josef (Vaclav)
1924- . . . . **CLC 15, 39, 69**
See also CA 61-64; CAAS 1; CANR 10, 34;
MTCW

Slade, Bernard . . . . **CLC 11, 46**
See also Newbound, Bernard Slade
See also CAAS 9; DLB 53

Slaughter, Carolyn 1946- . . . . **CLC 56**
See also CA 85-88

Slaughter, Frank G(ill) 1908- . . . . . . **CLC 29**
See also AITN 2; CA 5-8R; CANR 5

Slavitt, David R(ytman) 1935- . . . . **CLC 5, 14**
See also CA 21-24R; CAAS 3; CANR 41;
DLB 5, 6

Slesinger, Tess 1905-1945 . . . . **TCLC 10**
See also CA 107; DLB 102

Slessor, Kenneth 1901-1971 . . . . **CLC 14**
See also CA 102; 89-92

Slowacki, Juliusz 1809-1849 . . . . . **NCLC 15**

Smart, Christopher 1722-1771 . . . . **LC 3**
See also DLB 109

Smart, Elizabeth 1913-1986 . . . . **CLC 54**
See also CA 81-84; 118; DLB 88

Smiley, Jane (Graves) 1949- . . . **CLC 53, 76**
See also CA 104; CANR 30

Smith, A(rthur) J(ames) M(arshall)
1902-1980 . . . . **CLC 15**
See also CA 1-4R; 102; CANR 4; DLB 88

Smith, Betty (Wehner) 1896-1972 . . . **CLC 19**
See also CA 5-8R; 33-36R; DLBY 82;
SATA 6

Smith, Charlotte (Turner)
1749-1806 . . . . **NCLC 23**
See also DLB 39, 109

Smith, Clark Ashton 1893-1961 . . . . **CLC 43**
See also CA 143

Smith, Dave . . . . **CLC 22, 42**
See also Smith, David (Jeddie)
See also CAAS 7; DLB 5

Smith, David (Jeddie) 1942-
See Smith, Dave
See also CA 49-52; CANR 1

Smith, Florence Margaret
1902-1971 . . . . **CLC 8**
See also Smith, Stevie
See also CA 17-18; 29-32R; CANR 35;
CAP 2; MTCW

Smith, Iain Crichton 1928- . . . . **CLC 64**
See also CA 21-24R; DLB 40, 139

Smith, John 1580(?)-1631 . . . . **LC 9**

Smith, Johnston
See Crane, Stephen (Townley)

Smith, Lee 1944- . . . . **CLC 25, 73**
See also CA 114; 119; DLB 143; DLBY 83

Smith, Martin
See Smith, Martin Cruz

Smith, Martin Cruz 1942- . . . . **CLC 25**
See also BEST 89:4; CA 85-88; CANR 6,
23, 43

Smith, Mary-Ann Tirone 1944- . . . . . **CLC 39**
See also CA 118; 136

Smith, Patti 1946- . . . . **CLC 12**
See also CA 93-96

Smith, Pauline (Urmson)
1882-1959 . . . . **TCLC 25**

Smith, Rosamond
See Oates, Joyce Carol

Smith, Sheila Kaye
See Kaye-Smith, Sheila

Smith, Stevie . . . . **CLC 3, 8, 25, 44**
See also Smith, Florence Margaret
See also DLB 20

Smith, Wilbur A(ddison) 1933- . . . . . **CLC 33**
See also CA 13-16R; CANR 7; MTCW

Smith, William Jay 1918- . . . . **CLC 6**
See also CA 5-8R; CANR 44; DLB 5;
MAICYA; SATA 2, 68

Smith, Woodrow Wilson
See Kuttner, Henry

Smolenskin, Peretz 1842-1885 . . . . **NCLC 30**

Smollett, Tobias (George) 1721-1771 . . **LC 2**
See also CDBLB 1660-1789; DLB 39, 104

Snodgrass, W(illiam) D(e Witt)
1926- . . . . **CLC 2, 6, 10, 18, 68**
See also CA 1-4R; CANR 6, 36; DLB 5;
MTCW

Snow, C(harles) P(ercy)
1905-1980 . . . . **CLC 1, 4, 6, 9, 13, 19**
See also CA 5-8R; 101; CANR 28;
CDBLB 1945-1960; DLB 15, 77; MTCW

Snow, Frances Compton
See Adams, Henry (Brooks)

Snyder, Gary (Sherman)
1930- . . . . **CLC 1, 2, 5, 9, 32**
See also CA 17-20R; CANR 30; DLB 5, 16

Snyder, Zilpha Keatley 1927- . . . . . . **CLC 17**
See also CA 9-12R; CANR 38; CLR 31;
JRDA; MAICYA; SAAS 2; SATA 1, 28,
75

Soares, Bernardo
See Pessoa, Fernando (Antonio Nogueira)

Sobh, A.
See Shamlu, Ahmad

Sobol, Joshua . . . . **CLC 60**

Soderberg, Hjalmar 1869-1941 . . . . **TCLC 39**

Sodergran, Edith (Irene)
See Soedergran, Edith (Irene)

Soedergran, Edith (Irene)
1892-1923 . . . . **TCLC 31**

Softly, Edgar
See Lovecraft, H(oward) P(hillips)

Softly, Edward
See Lovecraft, H(oward) P(hillips)

Sokolov, Raymond 1941- . . . . **CLC 7**
See also CA 85-88

Solo, Jay
See Ellison, Harlan

Sologub, Fyodor . . . . **TCLC 9**
See also Teternikov, Fyodor Kuzmich

Solomons, Ikey Esquir
See Thackeray, William Makepeace

Solomos, Dionysios 1798-1857 . . . **NCLC 15**

Solwoska, Mara
See French, Marilyn

Solzhenitsyn, Aleksandr I(sayevich)
1918- . . . . . . **CLC 1, 2, 4, 7, 9, 10, 18, 26,
34, 78; DA; WLC**
See also AITN 1; CA 69-72; CANR 40;
MTCW

Somers, Jane
See Lessing, Doris (May)

Somerville, Edith 1858-1949 . . . . . . **TCLC 51**
See also DLB 135

Somerville & Ross
See Martin, Violet Florence; Somerville,
Edith

Sommer, Scott 1951- . . . . **CLC 25**
See also CA 106

Sondheim, Stephen (Joshua)
1930- . . . . **CLC 30, 39**
See also AAYA 11; CA 103

Sontag, Susan 1933- . . . **CLC 1, 2, 10, 13, 31**
See also CA 17-20R; CANR 25; DLB 2, 67;
MTCW

Sophocles
496(?)B.C.-406(?)B.C . . . . . **CMLC 2; DA;
DC 1**

Sorel, Julia
See Drexler, Rosalyn

Sorrentino, Gilbert
1929- . . . . **CLC 3, 7, 14, 22, 40**
See also CA 77-80; CANR 14, 33; DLB 5;
DLBY 80

Soto, Gary 1952- . . . . **CLC 32, 80; HLC**
See also AAYA 10; CA 119; 125; DLB 82;
HW; JRDA

Soupault, Philippe 1897-1990 . . . . . . **CLC 68**
See also CA 116; 131

Souster, (Holmes) Raymond
1921- . . . . **CLC 5, 14**
See also CA 13-16R; CAAS 14; CANR 13,
29; DLB 88; SATA 63

Southern, Terry 1926- . . . . **CLC 7**
See also CA 1-4R; CANR 1; DLB 2

Southey, Robert 1774-1843 . . . . **NCLC 8**
See also DLB 93, 107, 142; SATA 54

Southworth, Emma Dorothy Eliza Nevitte
1819-1899 . . . . **NCLC 26**

Souza, Ernest
See Scott, Evelyn

Soyinka, Wole
1934- . . . . **CLC 3, 5, 14, 36, 44; BLC;
DA; DC 2; WLC**
See also BW 2; CA 13-16R; CANR 27, 39;
DLB 125; MTCW

Spackman, W(illiam) M(ode)
1905-1990 . . . . **CLC 46**
See also CA 81-84; 132

Spacks, Barry 1931- . . . . **CLC 14**
See also CA 29-32R; CANR 33; DLB 105

Spanidou, Irini 1946- . . . . **CLC 44**

Spark, Muriel (Sarah)
1918- . . . . **CLC 2, 3, 5, 8, 13, 18, 40;
SSC 10**
See also CA 5-8R; CANR 12, 36;
CDBLB 1945-1960; DLB 15, 139; MTCW

Spaulding, Douglas
See Bradbury, Ray (Douglas)

Spaulding, Leonard
See Bradbury, Ray (Douglas)

Spence, J. A. D.
See Eliot, T(homas) S(tearns)

Spencer, Elizabeth 1921- . . . . **CLC 22**
See also CA 13-16R; CANR 32; DLB 6;
MTCW; SATA 14

Spencer, Leonard G.
See Silverberg, Robert

Spencer, Scott 1945- . . . . **CLC 30**
See also CA 113; DLBY 86

Spender, Stephen (Harold)
1909- . . . . **CLC 1, 2, 5, 10, 41**
See also CA 9-12R; CANR 31;
CDBLB 1945-1960; DLB 20; MTCW

Spengler, Oswald (Arnold Gottfried)
1880-1936 . . . . **TCLC 25**
See also CA 118

Spenser, Edmund
1552(?)-1599 .... **LC 5; DA; PC 8; WLC**
See also CDBLB Before 1660

Spicer, Jack 1925-1965 ..... **CLC 8, 18, 72**
See also CA 85-88; DLB 5, 16

Spiegelman, Art 1948- .... **CLC 76**
See also AAYA 10; CA 125; CANR 41

Spielberg, Peter 1929- .... **CLC 6**
See also CA 5-8R; CANR 4; DLBY 81

Spielberg, Steven 1947- .... **CLC 20**
See also AAYA 8; CA 77-80; CANR 32;
SATA 32

Spillane, Frank Morrison 1918-
See Spillane, Mickey
See also CA 25-28R; CANR 28; MTCW;
SATA 66

Spillane, Mickey .... **CLC 3, 13**
See also Spillane, Frank Morrison

Spinoza, Benedictus de 1632-1677 .... **LC 9**

Spinrad, Norman (Richard) 1940-... **CLC 46**
See also CA 37-40R; CAAS 19; CANR 20;
DLB 8

Spitteler, Carl (Friedrich Georg)
1845-1924 .... **TCLC 12**
See also CA 109; DLB 129

Spivack, Kathleen (Romola Drucker)
1938- .... **CLC 6**
See also CA 49-52

Spoto, Donald 1941-.............. **CLC 39**
See also CA 65-68; CANR 11

Springsteen, Bruce (F.) 1949- ...... **CLC 17**
See also CA 111

Spurling, Hilary 1940-............ **CLC 34**
See also CA 104; CANR 25

Squires, (James) Radcliffe
1917-1993 .... **CLC 51**
See also CA 1-4R; 140; CANR 6, 21

Srivastava, Dhanpat Rai 1880(?)-1936
See Premchand
See also CA 118

Stacy, Donald
See Pohl, Frederik

Stael, Germaine de
See Stael-Holstein, Anne Louise Germaine
Necker Baronn
See also DLB 119

Stael-Holstein, Anne Louise Germaine Necker
Baronn 1766-1817 .... **NCLC 3**
See also Stael, Germaine de

Stafford, Jean 1915-1979... **CLC 4, 7, 19, 68**
See also CA 1-4R; 85-88; CANR 3; DLB 2;
MTCW; SATA 22

Stafford, William (Edgar)
1914-1993 .... **CLC 4, 7, 29**
See also CA 5-8R; 142; CAAS 3; CANR 5,
22; DLB 5

Staines, Trevor
See Brunner, John (Kilian Houston)

Stairs, Gordon
See Austin, Mary (Hunter)

Stannard, Martin 1947-........... **CLC 44**
See also CA 142

Stanton, Maura 1946- .... **CLC 9**
See also CA 89-92; CANR 15; DLB 120

Stanton, Schuyler
See Baum, L(yman) Frank

Stapledon, (William) Olaf
1886-1950 .... **TCLC 22**
See also CA 111; DLB 15

Starbuck, George (Edwin) 1931-.... **CLC 53**
See also CA 21-24R; CANR 23

Stark, Richard
See Westlake, Donald E(dwin)

Staunton, Schuyler
See Baum, L(yman) Frank

Stead, Christina (Ellen)
1902-1983 .... **CLC 2, 5, 8, 32, 80**
See also CA 13-16R; 109; CANR 33, 40;
MTCW

Stead, William Thomas
1849-1912 .... **TCLC 48**

Steele, Richard 1672-1729 .... **LC 18**
See also CDBLB 1660-1789; DLB 84, 101

Steele, Timothy (Reid) 1948-....... **CLC 45**
See also CA 93-96; CANR 16; DLB 120

Steffens, (Joseph) Lincoln
1866-1936 .... **TCLC 20**
See also CA 117

Stegner, Wallace (Earle)
1909-1993 .... **CLC 9, 49, 81**
See also AITN 1; BEST 90:3; CA 1-4R;
141; CAAS 9; CANR 1, 21; DLB 9;
DLBY 93; MTCW

Stein, Gertrude
1874-1946 ...... **TCLC 1, 6, 28, 48; DA;**
WLC
See also CA 104; 132; CDALB 1917-1929;
DLB 4, 54, 86; MTCW

Steinbeck, John (Ernst)
1902-1968 ...... **CLC 1, 5, 9, 13, 21, 34,**
45, 75; DA; SSC 11; WLC
See also AAYA 12; CA 1-4R; 25-28R;
CANR 1, 35; CDALB 1929-1941; DLB 7,
9; DLBD 2; MTCW; SATA 9

Steinem, Gloria 1934-............. **CLC 63**
See also CA 53-56; CANR 28; MTCW

Steiner, George 1929-............. **CLC 24**
See also CA 73-76; CANR 31; DLB 67;
MTCW; SATA 62

Steiner, K. Leslie
See Delany, Samuel R(ay, Jr.)

Steiner, Rudolf 1861-1925 .... **TCLC 13**
See also CA 107

Stendhal
1783-1842 ..... **NCLC 23, 46; DA; WLC**
See also DLB 119

Stephen, Leslie 1832-1904 .... **TCLC 23**
See also CA 123; DLB 57, 144

Stephen, Sir Leslie
See Stephen, Leslie

Stephen, Virginia
See Woolf, (Adeline) Virginia

Stephens, James 1882(?)-1950 ...... **TCLC 4**
See also CA 104; DLB 19

Stephens, Reed
See Donaldson, Stephen R.

Steptoe, Lydia
See Barnes, Djuna

Sterchi, Beat 1949-.............. **CLC 65**

Sterling, Brett
See Bradbury, Ray (Douglas); Hamilton,
Edmond

Sterling, Bruce 1954-............. **CLC 72**
See also CA 119; CANR 44

Sterling, George 1869-1926 .... **TCLC 20**
See also CA 117; DLB 54

Stern, Gerald 1925- .... **CLC 40**
See also CA 81-84; CANR 28; DLB 105

Stern, Richard (Gustave) 1928-... **CLC 4, 39**
See also CA 1-4R; CANR 1, 25; DLBY 87

Sternberg, Josef von 1894-1969..... **CLC 20**
See also CA 81-84

Sterne, Laurence
1713-1768 .... **LC 2; DA; WLC**
See also CDBLB 1660-1789; DLB 39

Sternheim, (William Adolf) Carl
1878-1942 .... **TCLC 8**
See also CA 105; DLB 56, 118

Stevens, Mark 1951- .... **CLC 34**
See also CA 122

Stevens, Wallace
1879-1955 .... **TCLC 3, 12, 45; DA;**
PC 6; WLC
See also CA 104; 124; CDALB 1929-1941;
DLB 54; MTCW

Stevenson, Anne (Katharine)
1933- .... **CLC 7, 33**
See also CA 17-20R; CAAS 9; CANR 9, 33;
DLB 40; MTCW

Stevenson, Robert Louis (Balfour)
1850-1894 .... **NCLC 5, 14; DA;**
SSC 11; WLC
See also CDBLB 1890-1914; CLR 10, 11;
DLB 18, 57, 141; JRDA; MAICYA;
YABC 2

Stewart, J(ohn) I(nnes) M(ackintosh)
1906- .... **CLC 7, 14, 32**
See also CA 85-88; CAAS 3; MTCW

Stewart, Mary (Florence Elinor)
1916- .... **CLC 7, 35**
See also CA 1-4R; CANR 1; SATA 12

Stewart, Mary Rainbow
See Stewart, Mary (Florence Elinor)

Stifter, Adalbert 1805-1868...... **NCLC 41**
See also DLB 133

Still, James 1906-................ **CLC 49**
See also CA 65-68; CAAS 17; CANR 10,
26; DLB 9; SATA 29

Sting
See Sumner, Gordon Matthew

Stirling, Arthur
See Sinclair, Upton (Beall)

Stitt, Milan 1941-................ **CLC 29**
See also CA 69-72

Stockton, Francis Richard 1834-1902
See Stockton, Frank R.
See also CA 108; 137; MAICYA; SATA 44

Stockton, Frank R............... **TCLC 47**
See also Stockton, Francis Richard
See also DLB 42, 74; SATA 32

Stoddard, Charles
See Kuttner, Henry

Stoker, Abraham 1847-1912
See Stoker, Bram
See also CA 105; DA; SATA 29

Stoker, Bram . . . . TCLC 8; WLC
See also Stoker, Abraham
See also CDBLB 1890-1914; DLB 36, 70

Stolz, Mary (Slattery) 1920- . . . . CLC 12
See also AAYA 8; AITN 1; CA 5-8R;
CANR 13, 41; JRDA; MAICYA;
SAAS 3; SATA 10, 71

Stone, Irving 1903-1989 . . . . CLC 7
See also AITN 1; CA 1-4R; 129; CAAS 3;
CANR 1, 23; MTCW; SATA 3;
SATA-Obit 64

Stone, Oliver 1946- . . . . CLC 73
See also CA 110

Stone, Robert (Anthony)
1937- . . . . CLC 5, 23, 42
See also CA 85-88; CANR 23; MTCW

Stone, Zachary
See Follett, Ken(neth Martin)

Stoppard, Tom
1937- . . . . . . CLC 1, 3, 4, 5, 8, 15, 29, 34,
63; DA; WLC
See also CA 81-84; CANR 39;
CDBLB 1960 to Present; DLB 13;
DLBY 85; MTCW

Storey, David (Malcolm)
1933- . . . . CLC 2, 4, 5, 8
See also CA 81-84; CANR 36; DLB 13, 14;
MTCW

Storm, Hyemeyohsts 1935- . . . . CLC 3
See also CA 81-84; CANR 45

Storm, (Hans) Theodor (Woldsen)
1817-1888 . . . . NCLC 1

Storni, Alfonsina
1892-1938 . . . . TCLC 5; HLC
See also CA 104; 131; HW

Stout, Rex (Todhunter) 1886-1975 . . . CLC 3
See also AITN 2; CA 61-64

Stow, (Julian) Randolph 1935- . . CLC 23, 48
See also CA 13-16R; CANR 33; MTCW

Stowe, Harriet (Elizabeth) Beecher
1811-1896 . . . . NCLC 3; DA; WLC
See also CDALB 1865-1917; DLB 1, 12, 42,
74; JRDA; MAICYA; YABC 1

Strachey, (Giles) Lytton
1880-1932 . . . . TCLC 12
See also CA 110; DLBD 10

Strand, Mark 1934- . . . . . . CLC 6, 18, 41, 71
See also CA 21-24R; CANR 40; DLB 5;
SATA 41

Straub, Peter (Francis) 1943- . . . . . . CLC 28
See also BEST 89:1; CA 85-88; CANR 28;
DLBY 84; MTCW

Strauss, Botho 1944- . . . . CLC 22
See also DLB 124

Streatfeild, (Mary) Noel
1895(?)-1986 . . . . CLC 21
See also CA 81-84; 120; CANR 31;
CLR 17; MAICYA; SATA 20, 48

Stribling, T(homas) S(igismund)
1881-1965 . . . . CLC 23
See also CA 107; DLB 9

Strindberg, (Johan) August
1849-1912 . . . . . TCLC 1, 8, 21, 47; DA;
WLC
See also CA 104; 135

Stringer, Arthur 1874-1950 . . . . . . TCLC 37
See also DLB 92

Stringer, David
See Roberts, Keith (John Kingston)

Strugatskii, Arkadii (Natanovich)
1925-1991 . . . . CLC 27
See also CA 106; 135

Strugatskii, Boris (Natanovich)
1933- . . . . CLC 27
See also CA 106

Strummer, Joe 1953(?)- . . . . CLC 30
See also Clash, The

Stuart, Don A.
See Campbell, John W(ood, Jr.)

Stuart, Ian
See MacLean, Alistair (Stuart)

Stuart, Jesse (Hilton)
1906-1984 . . . . CLC 1, 8, 11, 14, 34
See also CA 5-8R; 112; CANR 31; DLB 9,
48, 102; DLBY 84; SATA 2, 36

Sturgeon, Theodore (Hamilton)
1918-1985 . . . . CLC 22, 39
See also Queen, Ellery
See also CA 81-84; 116; CANR 32; DLB 8;
DLBY 85; MTCW

Sturges, Preston 1898-1959 . . . . . . TCLC 48
See also CA 114; DLB 26

Styron, William
1925- . . . . CLC 1, 3, 5, 11, 15, 60
See also BEST 90:4; CA 5-8R; CANR 6, 33;
CDALB 1968-1988; DLB 2, 143;
DLBY 80; MTCW

Suarez Lynch, B.
See Bioy Casares, Adolfo; Borges, Jorge
Luis

Su Chien 1884-1918
See Su Man-shu
See also CA 123

Sudermann, Hermann 1857-1928 . . TCLC 15
See also CA 107; DLB 118

Sue, Eugene 1804-1857 . . . . NCLC 1
See also DLB 119

Sueskind, Patrick 1949- . . . . CLC 44

Sukenick, Ronald 1932- . . . . . CLC 3, 4, 6, 48
See also CA 25-28R; CAAS 8; CANR 32;
DLBY 81

Suknaski, Andrew 1942- . . . . CLC 19
See also CA 101; DLB 53

Sullivan, Vernon
See Vian, Boris

Sully Prudhomme 1839-1907 . . . . . . TCLC 31

Su Man-shu . . . . TCLC 24
See also Su Chien

Summerforest, Ivy B.
See Kirkup, James

Summers, Andrew James 1942- . . . . . CLC 26
See also Police, The

Summers, Andy
See Summers, Andrew James

Summers, Hollis (Spurgeon, Jr.)
1916- . . . . CLC 10
See also CA 5-8R; CANR 3; DLB 6

Summers, (Alphonsus Joseph-Mary Augustus)
Montague 1880-1948 . . . . TCLC 16
See also CA 118

Sumner, Gordon Matthew 1951- . . . . CLC 26
See also Police, The

Surtees, Robert Smith
1803-1864 . . . . NCLC 14
See also DLB 21

Susann, Jacqueline 1921-1974 . . . . . . CLC 3
See also AITN 1; CA 65-68; 53-56; MTCW

Suskind, Patrick
See Sueskind, Patrick

Sutcliff, Rosemary 1920-1992 . . . . . . CLC 26
See also AAYA 10; CA 5-8R; 139;
CANR 37; CLR 1; JRDA; MAICYA;
SATA 6, 44, 78; SATA-Obit 73

Sutro, Alfred 1863-1933 . . . . TCLC 6
See also CA 105; DLB 10

Sutton, Henry
See Slavitt, David R(ytman)

Svevo, Italo . . . . TCLC 2, 35
See also Schmitz, Aron Hector

Swados, Elizabeth 1951- . . . . CLC 12
See also CA 97-100

Swados, Harvey 1920-1972 . . . . CLC 5
See also CA 5-8R; 37-40R; CANR 6;
DLB 2

Swan, Gladys 1934- . . . . CLC 69
See also CA 101; CANR 17, 39

Swarthout, Glendon (Fred)
1918-1992 . . . . CLC 35
See also CA 1-4R; 139; CANR 1; SATA 26

Sweet, Sarah C.
See Jewett, (Theodora) Sarah Orne

Swenson, May
1919-1989 . . . . CLC 4, 14, 61; DA
See also CA 5-8R; 130; CANR 36; DLB 5;
MTCW; SATA 15

Swift, Augustus
See Lovecraft, H(oward) P(hillips)

Swift, Graham 1949- . . . . CLC 41
See also CA 117; 122

Swift, Jonathan
1667-1745 . . . . . . LC 1; DA; PC 9; WLC
See also CDBLB 1660-1789; DLB 39, 95,
101; SATA 19

Swinburne, Algernon Charles
1837-1909 . . . . . . TCLC 8, 36; DA; WLC
See also CA 105; 140; CDBLB 1832-1890;
DLB 35, 57

Swinfen, Ann . . . . CLC 34

Swinnerton, Frank Arthur
1884-1982 . . . . CLC 31
See also CA 108; DLB 34

Swithen, John
See King, Stephen (Edwin)

Sylvia
See Ashton-Warner, Sylvia (Constance)

Symmes, Robert Edward
See Duncan, Robert (Edward)

Symonds, John Addington
1840-1893 .... **NCLC 34**
See also DLB 57, 144

Symons, Arthur 1865-1945 .... **TCLC 11**
See also CA 107; DLB 19, 57

Symons, Julian (Gustave)
1912- .... **CLC 2, 14, 32**
See also CA 49-52; CAAS 3; CANR 3, 33;
DLB 87; DLBY 92; MTCW

Synge, (Edmund) J(ohn) M(illington)
1871-1909 .... **TCLC 6, 37; DC 2**
See also CA 104; 141; CDBLB 1890-1914;
DLB 10, 19

Syruc, J.
See Milosz, Czeslaw

Szirtes, George 1948- .... **CLC 46**
See also CA 109; CANR 27

Tabori, George 1914- .... **CLC 19**
See also CA 49-52; CANR 4

Tagore, Rabindranath
1861-1941 .... **TCLC 3, 53; PC 8**
See also CA 104; 120; MTCW

Taine, Hippolyte Adolphe
1828-1893 .... **NCLC 15**

Talese, Gay 1932- .... **CLC 37**
See also AITN 1; CA 1-4R; CANR 9;
MTCW

Tallent, Elizabeth (Ann) 1954- ..... **CLC 45**
See also CA 117; DLB 130

Tally, Ted 1952- .... **CLC 42**
See also CA 120; 124

Tamayo y Baus, Manuel
1829-1898 .... **NCLC 1**

Tammsaare, A(nton) H(ansen)
1878-1940 .... **TCLC 27**

Tan, Amy 1952- .... **CLC 59**
See also AAYA 9; BEST 89:3; CA 136;
SATA 75

Tandem, Felix
See Spitteler, Carl (Friedrich Georg)

Tanizaki, Jun'ichiro
1886-1965 .... **CLC 8, 14, 28**
See also CA 93-96; 25-28R

Tanner, William
See Amis, Kingsley (William)

Tao Lao
See Storni, Alfonsina

Tarassoff, Lev
See Troyat, Henri

Tarbell, Ida M(inerva)
1857-1944 .... **TCLC 40**
See also CA 122; DLB 47

Tarkington, (Newton) Booth
1869-1946 .... **TCLC 9**
See also CA 110; 143; DLB 9, 102;
SATA 17

Tarkovsky, Andrei (Arsenyevich)
1932-1986 .... **CLC 75**
See also CA 127

Tartt, Donna 1964(?)- .... **CLC 76**
See also CA 142

Tasso, Torquato 1544-1595 .... **LC 5**

Tate, (John Orley) Allen
1899-1979 .... **CLC 2, 4, 6, 9, 11, 14, 24**
See also CA 5-8R; 85-88; CANR 32;
DLB 4, 45, 63; MTCW

Tate, Ellalice
See Hibbert, Eleanor Alice Burford

Tate, James (Vincent) 1943- ... **CLC 2, 6, 25**
See also CA 21-24R; CANR 29; DLB 5

Tavel, Ronald 1940- .... **CLC 6**
See also CA 21-24R; CANR 33

Taylor, Cecil Philip 1929-1981 ..... **CLC 27**
See also CA 25-28R; 105

Taylor, Edward 1642(?)-1729.... **LC 11; DA**
See also DLB 24

Taylor, Eleanor Ross 1920- .... **CLC 5**
See also CA 81-84

Taylor, Elizabeth 1912-1975 ... **CLC 2, 4, 29**
See also CA 13-16R; CANR 9; DLB 139;
MTCW; SATA 13

Taylor, Henry (Splawn) 1942- ...... **CLC 44**
See also CA 33-36R; CAAS 7; CANR 31;
DLB 5

Taylor, Kamala (Purnaiya) 1924-
See Markandaya, Kamala
See also CA 77-80

Taylor, Mildred D. .... **CLC 21**
See also AAYA 10; BW 1; CA 85-88;
CANR 25; CLR 9; DLB 52; JRDA;
MAICYA; SAAS 5; SATA 15, 70

Taylor, Peter (Hillsman)
1917- ...... **CLC 1, 4, 18, 37, 44, 50, 71;**
SSC 10
See also CA 13-16R; CANR 9; DLBY 81;
MTCW

Taylor, Robert Lewis 1912- .... **CLC 14**
See also CA 1-4R; CANR 3; SATA 10

Tchekhov, Anton
See Chekhov, Anton (Pavlovich)

Teasdale, Sara 1884-1933.......... **TCLC 4**
See also CA 104; DLB 45; SATA 32

Tegner, Esaias 1782-1846........ **NCLC 2**

Teilhard de Chardin, (Marie Joseph) Pierre
1881-1955 .... **TCLC 9**
See also CA 105

Temple, Ann
See Mortimer, Penelope (Ruth)

Tennant, Emma (Christina)
1937- .... **CLC 13, 52**
See also CA 65-68; CAAS 9; CANR 10, 38;
DLB 14

Tenneshaw, S. M.
See Silverberg, Robert

Tennyson, Alfred
1809-1892 .. **NCLC 30; DA; PC 6; WLC**
See also CDBLB 1832-1890; DLB 32

Teran, Lisa St. Aubin de .... **CLC 36**
See also St. Aubin de Teran, Lisa

Teresa de Jesus, St. 1515-1582 ...... **LC 18**

Terkel, Louis 1912-
See Terkel, Studs
See also CA 57-60; CANR 18, 45; MTCW

Terkel, Studs .... **CLC 38**
See also Terkel, Louis
See also AITN 1

Terry, C. V.
See Slaughter, Frank G(ill)

Terry, Megan 1932- .... **CLC 19**
See also CA 77-80; CABS 3; CANR 43;
DLB 7

Tertz, Abram
See Sinyavsky, Andrei (Donatevich)

Tesich, Steve 1943(?)-.......... **CLC 40, 69**
See also CA 105; DLBY 83

Teternikov, Fyodor Kuzmich 1863-1927
See Sologub, Fyodor
See also CA 104

Tevis, Walter 1928-1984 .... **CLC 42**
See also CA 113

Tey, Josephine................... **TCLC 14**
See also Mackintosh, Elizabeth
See also DLB 77

Thackeray, William Makepeace
1811-1863 .... **NCLC 5, 14, 22, 43; DA;**
WLC
See also CDBLB 1832-1890; DLB 21, 55;
SATA 23

Thakura, Ravindranatha
See Tagore, Rabindranath

Tharoor, Shashi 1956- .... **CLC 70**
See also CA 141

Thelwell, Michael Miles 1939- ..... **CLC 22**
See also BW 2; CA 101

Theobald, Lewis, Jr.
See Lovecraft, H(oward) P(hillips)

Theodorescu, Ion N. 1880-1967
See Arghezi, Tudor
See also CA 116

Theriault, Yves 1915-1983........ **CLC 79**
See also CA 102; DLB 88

Theroux, Alexander (Louis)
1939- .... **CLC 2, 25**
See also CA 85-88; CANR 20

Theroux, Paul (Edward)
1941- .... **CLC 5, 8, 11, 15, 28, 46**
See also BEST 89:4; CA 33-36R; CANR 20,
45; DLB 2; MTCW; SATA 44

Thesen, Sharon 1946-............. **CLC 56**

Thevenin, Denis
See Duhamel, Georges

Thibault, Jacques Anatole Francois
1844-1924
See France, Anatole
See also CA 106; 127; MTCW

Thiele, Colin (Milton) 1920- .... **CLC 17**
See also CA 29-32R; CANR 12, 28;
CLR 27; MAICYA; SAAS 2; SATA 14,
72

Thomas, Audrey (Callahan)
1935- ....**CLC 7, 13, 37**
See also AITN 2; CA 21-24R; CAAS 19;
CANR 36; DLB 60; MTCW

Thomas, D(onald) M(ichael)
1935- .... **CLC 13, 22, 31**
See also CA 61-64; CAAS 11; CANR 17,
45; CDBLB 1960 to Present; DLB 40;
MTCW

Thomas, Dylan (Marlais)
1914-1953 ... **TCLC 1, 8, 45; DA; PC 2;**
SSC 3; WLC
See also CA 104; 120; CDBLB 1945-1960;
DLB 13, 20, 139; MTCW; SATA 60

Thomas, (Philip) Edward
1878-1917 .... **TCLC 10**
See also CA 106; DLB 19

Thomas, Joyce Carol 1938- .... **CLC 35**
See also AAYA 12; BW 2; CA 113; 116;
CLR 19; DLB 33; JRDA; MAICYA;
MTCW; SAAS 7; SATA 40, 78

Thomas, Lewis 1913-1993 .... **CLC 35**
See also CA 85-88; 143; CANR 38; MTCW

Thomas, Paul
See Mann, (Paul) Thomas

Thomas, Piri 1928- .... **CLC 17**
See also CA 73-76; HW

Thomas, R(onald) S(tuart)
1913- .... **CLC 6, 13, 48**
See also CA 89-92; CAAS 4; CANR 30;
CDBLB 1960 to Present; DLB 27;
MTCW

Thomas, Ross (Elmore) 1926- ...... **CLC 39**
See also CA 33-36R; CANR 22

Thompson, Francis Clegg
See Mencken, H(enry) L(ouis)

Thompson, Francis Joseph
1859-1907 .... **TCLC 4**
See also CA 104; CDBLB 1890-1914;
DLB 19

Thompson, Hunter S(tockton)
1939- .... **CLC 9, 17, 40**
See also BEST 89:1; CA 17-20R; CANR 23;
MTCW

Thompson, James Myers
See Thompson, Jim (Myers)

Thompson, Jim (Myers)
1906-1977(?) .... **CLC 69**
See also CA 140

Thompson, Judith .... **CLC 39**

Thomson, James 1700-1748 .... **LC 16**

Thomson, James 1834-1882 ...... **NCLC 18**

Thoreau, Henry David
1817-1862 ...... **NCLC 7, 21; DA; WLC**
See also CDALB 1640-1865; DLB 1

Thornton, Hall
See Silverberg, Robert

Thurber, James (Grover)
1894-1961 ... **CLC 5, 11, 25; DA; SSC 1**
See also CA 73-76; CANR 17, 39;
CDALB 1929-1941; DLB 4, 11, 22, 102;
MAICYA; MTCW; SATA 13

Thurman, Wallace (Henry)
1902-1934 .... **TCLC 6; BLC**
See also BW 1; CA 104; 124; DLB 51

Ticheburn, Cheviot
See Ainsworth, William Harrison

Tieck, (Johann) Ludwig
1773-1853 .... **NCLC 5, 46**
See also DLB 90

Tiger, Derry
See Ellison, Harlan

Tilghman, Christopher 1948(?)- ..... **CLC 65**

Tillinghast, Richard (Williford)
1940- .... **CLC 29**
See also CA 29-32R; CANR 26

Timrod, Henry 1828-1867 .... **NCLC 25**
See also DLB 3

Tindall, Gillian 1938- .... **CLC 7**
See also CA 21-24R; CANR 11

Tiptree, James, Jr. .... **CLC 48, 50**
See also Sheldon, Alice Hastings Bradley
See also DLB 8

Titmarsh, Michael Angelo
See Thackeray, William Makepeace

Tocqueville, Alexis (Charles Henri Maurice
Clerel Comte) 1805-1859..... **NCLC 7**

Tolkien, J(ohn) R(onald) R(euel)
1892-1973 .... **CLC 1, 2, 3, 8, 12, 38;**
DA; WLC
See also AAYA 10; AITN 1; CA 17-18;
45-48; CANR 36; CAP 2;
CDBLB 1914-1945; DLB 15; JRDA;
MAICYA; MTCW; SATA 2, 24, 32

Toller, Ernst 1893-1939.......... **TCLC 10**
See also CA 107; DLB 124

Tolson, M. B.
See Tolson, Melvin B(eaunorus)

Tolson, Melvin B(eaunorus)
1898(?)-1966 .... **CLC 36; BLC**
See also BW 1; CA 124; 89-92; DLB 48, 76

Tolstoi, Aleksei Nikolaevich
See Tolstoy, Alexey Nikolaevich

Tolstoy, Alexey Nikolaevich
1882-1945 .... **TCLC 18**
See also CA 107

Tolstoy, Count Leo
See Tolstoy, Leo (Nikolaevich)

Tolstoy, Leo (Nikolaevich)
1828-1910 ...... **TCLC 4, 11, 17, 28, 44;**
DA; SSC 9; WLC
See also CA 104; 123; SATA 26

Tomasi di Lampedusa, Giuseppe 1896-1957
See Lampedusa, Giuseppe (Tomasi) di
See also CA 111

Tomlin, Lily .... **CLC 17**
See also Tomlin, Mary Jean

Tomlin, Mary Jean 1939(?)-
See Tomlin, Lily
See also CA 117

Tomlinson, (Alfred) Charles
1927- .... **CLC 2, 4, 6, 13, 45**
See also CA 5-8R; CANR 33; DLB 40

Tonson, Jacob
See Bennett, (Enoch) Arnold

Toole, John Kennedy
1937-1969 .... **CLC 19, 64**
See also CA 104; DLBY 81

Toomer, Jean
1894-1967 ...... **CLC 1, 4, 13, 22; BLC;**
PC 7; SSC 1
See also BW 1; CA 85-88;
CDALB 1917-1929; DLB 45, 51; MTCW

Torley, Luke
See Blish, James (Benjamin)

Tornimparte, Alessandra
See Ginzburg, Natalia

Torre, Raoul della
See Mencken, H(enry) L(ouis)

Torrey, E(dwin) Fuller 1937-....... **CLC 34**
See also CA 119

Torsvan, Ben Traven
See Traven, B.

Torsvan, Benno Traven
See Traven, B.

Torsvan, Berick Traven
See Traven, B.

Torsvan, Berwick Traven
See Traven, B.

Torsvan, Bruno Traven
See Traven, B.

Torsvan, Traven
See Traven, B.

Tournier, Michel (Edouard)
1924- .... **CLC 6, 23, 36**
See also CA 49-52; CANR 3, 36; DLB 83;
MTCW; SATA 23

Tournimparte, Alessandra
See Ginzburg, Natalia

Towers, Ivar
See Kornbluth, C(yril) M.

Townsend, Sue 1946- .... **CLC 61**
See also CA 119; 127; MTCW; SATA 48,
55

Townshend, Peter (Dennis Blandford)
1945- .... **CLC 17, 42**
See also CA 107

Tozzi, Federigo 1883-1920........ **TCLC 31**

Traill, Catharine Parr
1802-1899 .... **NCLC 31**
See also DLB 99

Trakl, Georg 1887-1914........... **TCLC 5**
See also CA 104

Transtroemer, Tomas (Goesta)
1931- .... **CLC 52, 65**
See also CA 117; 129; CAAS 17

Transtromer, Tomas Gosta
See Transtroemer, Tomas (Goesta)

Traven, B. (?)-1969............. **CLC 8, 11**
See also CA 19-20; 25-28R; CAP 2; DLB 9,
56; MTCW

Treitel, Jonathan 1959- .... **CLC 70**

Tremain, Rose 1943-............. **CLC 42**
See also CA 97-100; CANR 44; DLB 14

Tremblay, Michel 1942-.......... **CLC 29**
See also CA 116; 128; DLB 60; MTCW

Trevor, Glen
See Hilton, James

Trevor, William
1928- .... **CLC 7, 9, 14, 25, 71**
See also Cox, William Trevor
See also DLB 14, 139

Trifonov, Yuri (Valentinovich)
1925-1981 .... **CLC 45**
See also CA 126; 103; MTCW

Trilling, Lionel 1905-1975 .... **CLC 9, 11, 24**
See also CA 9-12R; 61-64; CANR 10;
DLB 28, 63; MTCW

Trimball, W. H.
See Mencken, H(enry) L(ouis)

Waddington, Miriam 1917- .... **CLC 28**
See also CA 21-24R; CANR 12, 30;
DLB 68

Wagman, Fredrica 1937- .... **CLC 7**
See also CA 97-100

Wagner, Richard 1813-1883....... **NCLC 9**
See also DLB 129

Wagner-Martin, Linda 1936-....... **CLC 50**

Wagoner, David (Russell)
1926-.................... **CLC 3, 5, 15**
See also CA 1-4R; CAAS 3; CANR 2;
DLB 5; SATA 14

Wah, Fred(erick James) 1939-...... **CLC 44**
See also CA 107; 141; DLB 60

Wahloo, Per 1926-1975 .... **CLC 7**
See also CA 61-64

Wahloo, Peter
See Wahloo, Per

Wain, John (Barrington)
1925-............... **CLC 2, 11, 15, 46**
See also CA 5-8R; CAAS 4; CANR 23;
CDBLB 1960 to Present; DLB 15, 27,
139; MTCW

Wajda, Andrzej 1926-............. **CLC 16**
See also CA 102

Wakefield, Dan 1932-............. **CLC 7**
See also CA 21-24R; CAAS 7

Wakoski, Diane
1937-.......... **CLC 2, 4, 7, 9, 11, 40**
See also CA 13-16R; CAAS 1; CANR 9;
DLB 5

Wakoski-Sherbell, Diane
See Wakoski, Diane

Walcott, Derek (Alton)
1930-.... **CLC 2, 4, 9, 14, 25, 42, 67, 76;
BLC**
See also BW 2; CA 89-92; CANR 26;
DLB 117; DLBY 81; MTCW

Waldman, Anne 1945- .... **CLC 7**
See also CA 37-40R; CAAS 17; CANR 34;
DLB 16

Waldo, E. Hunter
See Sturgeon, Theodore (Hamilton)

Waldo, Edward Hamilton
See Sturgeon, Theodore (Hamilton)

Walker, Alice (Malsenior)
1944- .... **CLC 5, 6, 9, 19, 27, 46, 58;
BLC; DA; SSC 5**
See also AAYA 3; BEST 89:4; BW 2;
CA 37-40R; CANR 9, 27;
CDALB 1968-1988; DLB 6, 33, 143;
MTCW; SATA 31

Walker, David Harry 1911-1992.... **CLC 14**
See also CA 1-4R; 137; CANR 1; SATA 8;
SATA-Obit 71

Walker, Edward Joseph 1934-
See Walker, Ted
See also CA 21-24R; CANR 12, 28

Walker, George F. 1947-....... **CLC 44, 61**
See also CA 103; CANR 21, 43; DLB 60

Walker, Joseph A. 1935-.......... **CLC 19**
See also BW 1; CA 89-92; CANR 26;
DLB 38

Walker, Margaret (Abigail)
1915- .... **CLC 1, 6; BLC**
See also BW 2; CA 73-76; CANR 26;
DLB 76; MTCW

Walker, Ted..................... **CLC 13**
See also Walker, Edward Joseph
See also DLB 40

Wallace, David Foster 1962-....... **CLC 50**
See also CA 132

Wallace, Dexter
See Masters, Edgar Lee

Wallace, Irving 1916-1990...... **CLC 7, 13**
See also AITN 1; CA 1-4R; 132; CAAS 1;
CANR 1, 27; MTCW

Wallant, Edward Lewis
1926-1962 .... **CLC 5, 10**
See also CA 1-4R; CANR 22; DLB 2, 28,
143; MTCW

Walpole, Horace 1717-1797......... **LC 2**
See also DLB 39, 104

Walpole, Hugh (Seymour)
1884-1941 .... **TCLC 5**
See also CA 104; DLB 34

Walser, Martin 1927-............. **CLC 27**
See also CA 57-60; CANR 8; DLB 75, 124

Walser, Robert 1878-1956....... **TCLC 18**
See also CA 118; DLB 66

Walsh, Jill Paton................ **CLC 35**
See also Paton Walsh, Gillian
See also AAYA 11; CLR 2; SAAS 3

Walter, Villiam Christian
See Andersen, Hans Christian

Wambaugh, Joseph (Aloysius, Jr.)
1937-.................... **CLC 3, 18**
See also AITN 1; BEST 89:3; CA 33-36R;
CANR 42; DLB 6; DLBY 83; MTCW

Ward, Arthur Henry Sarsfield 1883-1959
See Rohmer, Sax
See also CA 108

Ward, Douglas Turner 1930-....... **CLC 19**
See also BW 1; CA 81-84; CANR 27;
DLB 7, 38

Ward, Mary Augusta
See Ward, Mrs. Humphry

Ward, Mrs. Humphry
1851-1920 .... **TCLC 55**
See also DLB 18

Ward, Peter
See Faust, Frederick (Schiller)

Warhol, Andy 1928(?)-1987........ **CLC 20**
See also AAYA 12; BEST 89:4; CA 89-92;
121; CANR 34

Warner, Francis (Robert le Plastrier)
1937-...................... **CLC 14**
See also CA 53-56; CANR 11

Warner, Marina 1946-............ **CLC 59**
See also CA 65-68; CANR 21

Warner, Rex (Ernest) 1905-1986.... **CLC 45**
See also CA 89-92; 119; DLB 15

Warner, Susan (Bogert)
1819-1885 .... **NCLC 31**
See also DLB 3, 42

Warner, Sylvia (Constance) Ashton
See Ashton-Warner, Sylvia (Constance)

Warner, Sylvia Townsend
1893-1978 .... **CLC 7, 19**
See also CA 61-64; 77-80; CANR 16;
DLB 34, 139; MTCW

Warren, Mercy Otis 1728-1814... **NCLC 13**
See also DLB 31

Warren, Robert Penn
1905-1989 .... **CLC 1, 4, 6, 8, 10, 13, 18,
39, 53, 59; DA; SSC 4; WLC**
See also AITN 1; CA 13-16R; 129;
CANR 10; CDALB 1968-1988; DLB 2,
48; DLBY 80, 89; MTCW; SATA 46, 63

Warshofsky, Isaac
See Singer, Isaac Bashevis

Warton, Thomas 1728-1790......... **LC 15**
See also DLB 104, 109

Waruk, Kona
See Harris, (Theodore) Wilson

Warung, Price 1855-1911......... **TCLC 45**

Warwick, Jarvis
See Garner, Hugh

Washington, Alex
See Harris, Mark

Washington, Booker T(aliaferro)
1856-1915 .... **TCLC 10; BLC**
See also BW 1; CA 114; 125; SATA 28

Washington, George 1732-1799...... **LC 25**
See also DLB 31

Wassermann, (Karl) Jakob
1873-1934 .... **TCLC 6**
See also CA 104; DLB 66

Wasserstein, Wendy
1950-............... **CLC 32, 59; DC 4**
See also CA 121; 129; CABS 3

Waterhouse, Keith (Spencer)
1929-..................... **CLC 47**
See also CA 5-8R; CANR 38; DLB 13, 15;
MTCW

Waters, Roger 1944-............. **CLC 35**
See also Pink Floyd

Watkins, Frances Ellen
See Harper, Frances Ellen Watkins

Watkins, Gerrold
See Malzberg, Barry N(athaniel)

Watkins, Paul 1964-............. **CLC 55**
See also CA 132

Watkins, Vernon Phillips
1906-1967 .... **CLC 43**
See also CA 9-10; 25-28R; CAP 1; DLB 20

Watson, Irving S.
See Mencken, H(enry) L(ouis)

Watson, John H.
See Farmer, Philip Jose

Watson, Richard F.
See Silverberg, Robert

Waugh, Auberon (Alexander) 1939-... **CLC 7**
See also CA 45-48; CANR 6, 22; DLB 14

Waugh, Evelyn (Arthur St. John)
1903-1966 ...... **CLC 1, 3, 8, 13, 19, 27,
44; DA; WLC**
See also CA 85-88; 25-28R; CANR 22;
CDBLB 1914-1945; DLB 15; MTCW

Waugh, Harriet 1944- .... **CLC 6**
See also CA 85-88; CANR 22

Ways, C. R.
See Blount, Roy (Alton), Jr.

Waystaff, Simon
See Swift, Jonathan

Webb, (Martha) Beatrice (Potter)
1858-1943 .... TCLC 22
See also Potter, Beatrice
See also CA 117

Webb, Charles (Richard) 1939- ...... CLC 7
See also CA 25-28R

Webb, James H(enry), Jr. 1946- .... CLC 22
See also CA 81-84

Webb, Mary (Gladys Meredith)
1881-1927 .... TCLC 24
See also CA 123; DLB 34

Webb, Mrs. Sidney
See Webb, (Martha) Beatrice (Potter)

Webb, Phyllis 1927- .... CLC 18
See also CA 104; CANR 23; DLB 53

Webb, Sidney (James)
1859-1947 .... TCLC 22
See also CA 117

Webber, Andrew Lloyd............. CLC 21
See also Lloyd Webber, Andrew

Weber, Lenora Mattingly
1895-1971 .... CLC 12
See also CA 19-20; 29-32R; CAP 1;
SATA 2, 26

Webster, John 1579(?)-1634(?) .... DC 2
See also CDBLB Before 1660; DA; DLB 58;
WLC

Webster, Noah 1758-1843 .... NCLC 30

Wedekind, (Benjamin) Frank(lin)
1864-1918 .... TCLC 7
See also CA 104; DLB 118

Weidman, Jerome 1913- .... CLC 7
See also AITN 2; CA 1-4R; CANR 1;
DLB 28

Weil, Simone (Adolphine)
1909-1943 .... TCLC 23
See also CA 117

Weinstein, Nathan
See West, Nathanael

Weinstein, Nathan von Wallenstein
See West, Nathanael

Weir, Peter (Lindsay) 1944- .... CLC 20
See also CA 113; 123

Weiss, Peter (Ulrich)
1916-1982 .... CLC 3, 15, 51
See also CA 45-48; 106; CANR 3; DLB 69,
124

Weiss, Theodore (Russell)
1916- .... CLC 3, 8, 14
See also CA 9-12R; CAAS 2; DLB 5

Welch, (Maurice) Denton
1915-1948 .... TCLC 22
See also CA 121

Welch, James 1940- .... CLC 6, 14, 52
See also CA 85-88; CANR 42

Weldon, Fay
1933(?)- .... CLC 6, 9, 11, 19, 36, 59
See also CA 21-24R; CANR 16;
CDBLB 1960 to Present; DLB 14;
MTCW

Wellek, Rene 1903- .... CLC 28
See also CA 5-8R; CAAS 7; CANR 8;
DLB 63

Weller, Michael 1942- .... CLC 10, 53
See also CA 85-88

Weller, Paul 1958- .... CLC 26

Wellershoff, Dieter 1925-......... CLC 46
See also CA 89-92; CANR 16, 37

Welles, (George) Orson
1915-1985 .... CLC 20, 80
See also CA 93-96; 117

Wellman, Mac 1945- .... CLC 65

Wellman, Manly Wade 1903-1986 .. CLC 49
See also CA 1-4R; 118; CANR 6, 16, 44;
SATA 6, 47

Wells, Carolyn 1869(?)-1942 ...... TCLC 35
See also CA 113; DLB 11

Wells, H(erbert) G(eorge)
1866-1946 .... TCLC 6, 12, 19; DA;
SSC 6; WLC
See also CA 110; 121; CDBLB 1914-1945;
DLB 34, 70; MTCW; SATA 20

Wells, Rosemary 1943-........... CLC 12
See also CA 85-88; CLR 16; MAICYA;
SAAS 1; SATA 18, 69

Welty, Eudora
1909- ...... CLC 1, 2, 5, 14, 22, 33; DA;
SSC 1; WLC
See also CA 9-12R; CABS 1; CANR 32;
CDALB 1941-1968; DLB 2, 102, 143;
DLBY 87; MTCW

Wen I-to 1899-1946 .... TCLC 28

Wentworth, Robert
See Hamilton, Edmond

Werfel, Franz (V.) 1890-1945 ...... TCLC 8
See also CA 104; DLB 81, 124

Wergeland, Henrik Arnold
1808-1845 .... NCLC 5

Wersba, Barbara 1932-........... CLC 30
See also AAYA 2; CA 29-32R; CANR 16,
38; CLR 3; DLB 52; JRDA; MAICYA;
SAAS 2; SATA 1, 58

Wertmueller, Lina 1928- .... CLC 16
See also CA 97-100; CANR 39

Wescott, Glenway 1901-1987....... CLC 13
See also CA 13-16R; 121; CANR 23;
DLB 4, 9, 102

Wesker, Arnold 1932- .... CLC 3, 5, 42
See also CA 1-4R; CAAS 7; CANR 1, 33;
CDBLB 1960 to Present; DLB 13;
MTCW

Wesley, Richard (Errol) 1945-....... CLC 7
See also BW 1; CA 57-60; CANR 27;
DLB 38

Wessel, Johan Herman 1742-1785 .... LC 7

West, Anthony (Panther)
1914-1987 .... CLC 50
See also CA 45-48; 124; CANR 3, 19;
DLB 15

West, C. P.
See Wodehouse, P(elham) G(renville)

West, (Mary) Jessamyn
1902-1984 .... CLC 7, 17
See also CA 9-12R; 112; CANR 27; DLB 6;
DLBY 84; MTCW; SATA 37

West, Morris L(anglo) 1916-..... CLC 6, 33
See also CA 5-8R; CANR 24; MTCW

West, Nathanael
1903-1940 ..... TCLC 1, 14, 44; SSC 16
See also CA 104; 125; CDALB 1929-1941;
DLB 4, 9, 28; MTCW

West, Owen
See Koontz, Dean R(ay)

West, Paul 1930- .... CLC 7, 14
See also CA 13-16R; CAAS 7; CANR 22;
DLB 14

West, Rebecca 1892-1983 .. CLC 7, 9, 31, 50
See also CA 5-8R; 109; CANR 19; DLB 36;
DLBY 83; MTCW

Westall, Robert (Atkinson)
1929-1993 .... CLC 17
See also AAYA 12; CA 69-72; 141;
CANR 18; CLR 13; JRDA; MAICYA;
SAAS 2; SATA 23, 69; SATA-Obit 75

Westlake, Donald E(dwin)
1933- .... CLC 7, 33
See also CA 17-20R; CAAS 13; CANR 16,
44

Westmacott, Mary
See Christie, Agatha (Mary Clarissa)

Weston, Allen
See Norton, Andre

Wetcheek, J. L.
See Feuchtwanger, Lion

Wetering, Janwillem van de
See van de Wetering, Janwillem

Wetherell, Elizabeth
See Warner, Susan (Bogert)

Whalen, Philip 1923- .... CLC 6, 29
See also CA 9-12R; CANR 5, 39; DLB 16

Wharton, Edith (Newbold Jones)
1862-1937 ...... TCLC 3, 9, 27, 53; DA;
SSC 6; WLC
See also CA 104; 132; CDALB 1865-1917;
DLB 4, 9, 12, 78; MTCW

Wharton, James
See Mencken, H(enry) L(ouis)

Wharton, William (a pseudonym)
.... CLC 18, 37
See also CA 93-96; DLBY 80

Wheatley (Peters), Phillis
1754(?)-1784 .... LC 3; BLC; DA; PC 3;
WLC
See also CDALB 1640-1865; DLB 31, 50

Wheelock, John Hall 1886-1978 .... CLC 14
See also CA 13-16R; 77-80; CANR 14;
DLB 45

White, E(lwyn) B(rooks)
1899-1985 .... CLC 10, 34, 39
See also AITN 2; CA 13-16R; 116;
CANR 16, 37; CLR 1, 21; DLB 11, 22;
MAICYA; MTCW; SATA 2, 29, 44

White, Edmund (Valentine III)
1940- .... CLC 27
See also AAYA 7; CA 45-48; CANR 3, 19,
36; MTCW

White, Patrick (Victor Martindale)
1912-1990 .. CLC 3, 4, 5, 7, 9, 18, 65, 69
See also CA 81-84; 132; CANR 43; MTCW

White, Phyllis Dorothy James 1920-
  See James, P. D.
  See also CA 21-24R; CANR 17, 43; MTCW

White, T(erence) H(anbury)
  1906-1964 . . . . **CLC 30**
  See also CA 73-76; CANR 37; JRDA;
  MAICYA; SATA 12

White, Terence de Vere 1912- . . . . . . **CLC 49**
  See also CA 49-52; CANR 3

White, Walter F(rancis)
  1893-1955 . . . . **TCLC 15**
  See also White, Walter
  See also BW 1; CA 115; 124; DLB 51

White, William Hale 1831-1913
  See Rutherford, Mark
  See also CA 121

Whitehead, E(dward) A(nthony)
  1933- . . . . **CLC 5**
  See also CA 65-68

Whitemore, Hugh (John) 1936- . . . . . **CLC 37**
  See also CA 132

Whitman, Sarah Helen (Power)
  1803-1878 . . . . **NCLC 19**
  See also DLB 1

Whitman, Walt(er)
  1819-1892 . . . . . **NCLC 4, 31; DA; PC 3;**
                              WLC
  See also CDALB 1640-1865; DLB 3, 64;
  SATA 20

Whitney, Phyllis A(yame) 1903- . . . . **CLC 42**
  See also AITN 2; BEST 90:3; CA 1-4R;
  CANR 3, 25, 38; JRDA; MAICYA;
  SATA 1, 30

Whittemore, (Edward) Reed (Jr.)
  1919- . . . . **CLC 4**
  See also CA 9-12R; CAAS 8; CANR 4;
  DLB 5

Whittier, John Greenleaf
  1807-1892 . . . . **NCLC 8**
  See also CDALB 1640-1865; DLB 1

Whittlebot, Hernia
  See Coward, Noel (Peirce)

Wicker, Thomas Grey 1926-
  See Wicker, Tom
  See also CA 65-68; CANR 21

Wicker, Tom . . . . **CLC 7**
  See also Wicker, Thomas Grey

Wideman, John Edgar
  1941- . . . . **CLC 5, 34, 36, 67; BLC**
  See also BW 2; CA 85-88; CANR 14, 42;
  DLB 33, 143

Wiebe, Rudy (Henry) 1934- . . . **CLC 6, 11, 14**
  See also CA 37-40R; CANR 42; DLB 60

Wieland, Christoph Martin
  1733-1813 . . . . **NCLC 17**
  See also DLB 97

Wieners, John 1934- . . . . **CLC 7**
  See also CA 13-16R; DLB 16

Wiesel, Elie(zer)
  1928- . . . . **CLC 3, 5, 11, 37; DA**
  See also AAYA 7; AITN 1; CA 5-8R;
  CAAS 4; CANR 8, 40; DLB 83;
  DLBY 87; MTCW; SATA 56

Wiggins, Marianne 1947- . . . . **CLC 57**
  See also BEST 89:3; CA 130

Wight, James Alfred 1916-
  See Herriot, James
  See also CA 77-80; SATA 44, 55

Wilbur, Richard (Purdy)
  1921- . . . . **CLC 3, 6, 9, 14, 53; DA**
  See also CA 1-4R; CABS 2; CANR 2, 29;
  DLB 5; MTCW; SATA 9

Wild, Peter 1940- . . . . **CLC 14**
  See also CA 37-40R; DLB 5

Wilde, Oscar (Fingal O'Flahertie Wills)
  1854(?)-1900 . . . . **TCLC 1, 8, 23, 41; DA;**
                   SSC 11; WLC
  See also CA 104; 119; CDBLB 1890-1914;
  DLB 10, 19, 34, 57, 141; SATA 24

Wilder, Billy . . . . **CLC 20**
  See also Wilder, Samuel
  See also DLB 26

Wilder, Samuel 1906-
  See Wilder, Billy
  See also CA 89-92

Wilder, Thornton (Niven)
  1897-1975 . . . . . . **CLC 1, 5, 6, 10, 15, 35,**
                82; DA; DC 1; WLC
  See also AITN 2; CA 13-16R; 61-64;
  CANR 40; DLB 4, 7, 9; MTCW

Wilding, Michael 1942- . . . . **CLC 73**
  See also CA 104; CANR 24

Wiley, Richard 1944- . . . . **CLC 44**
  See also CA 121; 129

Wilhelm, Kate . . . . **CLC 7**
  See also Wilhelm, Katie Gertrude
  See also CAAS 5; DLB 8

Wilhelm, Katie Gertrude 1928-
  See Wilhelm, Kate
  See also CA 37-40R; CANR 17, 36; MTCW

Wilkins, Mary
  See Freeman, Mary Eleanor Wilkins

Willard, Nancy 1936- . . . . **CLC 7, 37**
  See also CA 89-92; CANR 10, 39; CLR 5;
  DLB 5, 52; MAICYA; MTCW;
  SATA 30, 37, 71

Williams, C(harles) K(enneth)
  1936- . . . . **CLC 33, 56**
  See also CA 37-40R; DLB 5

Williams, Charles
  See Collier, James L(incoln)

Williams, Charles (Walter Stansby)
  1886-1945 . . . . **TCLC 1, 11**
  See also CA 104; DLB 100

Williams, (George) Emlyn
  1905-1987 . . . . **CLC 15**
  See also CA 104; 123; CANR 36; DLB 10,
  77; MTCW

Williams, Hugo 1942- . . . . **CLC 42**
  See also CA 17-20R; CANR 45; DLB 40

Williams, J. Walker
  See Wodehouse, P(elham) G(renville)

Williams, John A(lfred)
  1925- . . . . **CLC 5, 13; BLC**
  See also BW 2; CA 53-56; CAAS 3;
  CANR 6, 26; DLB 2, 33

Williams, Jonathan (Chamberlain)
  1929- . . . . **CLC 13**
  See also CA 9-12R; CAAS 12; CANR 8;
  DLB 5

Williams, Joy 1944- . . . . **CLC 31**
  See also CA 41-44R; CANR 22

Williams, Norman 1952- . . . . **CLC 39**
  See also CA 118

Williams, Tennessee
  1911-1983 . . . . . **CLC 1, 2, 5, 7, 8, 11, 15,**
        19, 30, 39, 45, 71; DA; DC 4; WLC
  See also AITN 1, 2; CA 5-8R; 108;
  CABS 3; CANR 31; CDALB 1941-1968;
  DLB 7; DLBD 4; DLBY 83; MTCW

Williams, Thomas (Alonzo)
  1926-1990 . . . . **CLC 14**
  See also CA 1-4R; 132; CANR 2

Williams, William C.
  See Williams, William Carlos

Williams, William Carlos
  1883-1963 . . . . **CLC 1, 2, 5, 9, 13, 22, 42,**
                     67; DA; PC 7
  See also CA 89-92; CANR 34;
  CDALB 1917-1929; DLB 4, 16, 54, 86;
  MTCW

Williamson, David (Keith) 1942- . . . . **CLC 56**
  See also CA 103; CANR 41

Williamson, Jack . . . . **CLC 29**
  See also Williamson, John Stewart
  See also CAAS 8; DLB 8

Williamson, John Stewart 1908-
  See Williamson, Jack
  See also CA 17-20R; CANR 23

Willie, Frederick
  See Lovecraft, H(oward) P(hillips)

Willingham, Calder (Baynard, Jr.)
  1922- . . . . **CLC 5, 51**
  See also CA 5-8R; CANR 3; DLB 2, 44;
  MTCW

Willis, Charles
  See Clarke, Arthur C(harles)

Willy
  See Colette, (Sidonie-Gabrielle)

Willy, Colette
  See Colette, (Sidonie-Gabrielle)

Wilson, A(ndrew) N(orman) 1950- . . **CLC 33**
  See also CA 112; 122; DLB 14

Wilson, Angus (Frank Johnstone)
  1913-1991 . . . . **CLC 2, 3, 5, 25, 34**
  See also CA 5-8R; 134; CANR 21; DLB 15,
  139; MTCW

Wilson, August
  1945- . . **CLC 39, 50, 63; BLC; DA; DC 2**
  See also BW 2; CA 115; 122; CANR 42;
  MTCW

Wilson, Brian 1942- . . . . **CLC 12**

Wilson, Colin 1931- . . . . **CLC 3, 14**
  See also CA 1-4R; CAAS 5; CANR 1, 22,
  33; DLB 14; MTCW

Wilson, Dirk
  See Pohl, Frederik

Wilson, Edmund
  1895-1972 . . . . **CLC 1, 2, 3, 8, 24**
  See also CA 1-4R; 37-40R; CANR 1;
  DLB 63; MTCW

Wilson, Ethel Davis (Bryant)
  1888(?)-1980 . . . . **CLC 13**
  See also CA 102; DLB 68; MTCW

Wilson, John 1785-1854 . . . . **NCLC 5**

Yeats, William Butler
1865-1939 ..... **TCLC 1, 11, 18, 31; DA;
WLC**
See also CA 104; 127; CANR 45;
CDBLB 1890-1914; DLB 10, 19, 98;
MTCW

Yehoshua, A(braham) B.
1936- .... **CLC 13, 31**
See also CA 33-36R; CANR 43

Yep, Laurence Michael 1948- ...... **CLC 35**
See also AAYA 5; CA 49-52; CANR 1;
CLR 3, 17; DLB 52; JRDA; MAICYA;
SATA 7, 69

Yerby, Frank G(arvin)
1916-1991 .... **CLC 1, 7, 22; BLC**
See also BW 1; CA 9-12R; 136; CANR 16;
DLB 76; MTCW

Yesenin, Sergei Alexandrovich
See Esenin, Sergei (Alexandrovich)

Yevtushenko, Yevgeny (Alexandrovich)
1933- .... **CLC 1, 3, 13, 26, 51**
See also CA 81-84; CANR 33; MTCW

Yezierska, Anzia 1885(?)-1970 ..... **CLC 46**
See also CA 126; 89-92; DLB 28; MTCW

Yglesias, Helen 1915- .... **CLC 7, 22**
See also CA 37-40R; CANR 15; MTCW

Yokomitsu Riichi 1898-1947 ...... **TCLC 47**

Yonge, Charlotte (Mary)
1823-1901 .... **TCLC 48**
See also CA 109; DLB 18; SATA 17

York, Jeremy
See Creasey, John

York, Simon
See Heinlein, Robert A(nson)

Yorke, Henry Vincent 1905-1974 ... **CLC 13**
See also Green, Henry
See also CA 85-88; 49-52

Yoshimoto, Banana .... **CLC 84**
See also Yoshimoto, Mahoko

Yoshimoto, Mahoko 1964-
See Yoshimoto, Banana
See also CA 144

Young, Al(bert James)
1939- .... **CLC 19; BLC**
See also BW 2; CA 29-32R; CANR 26;
DLB 33

Young, Andrew (John) 1885-1971 .... **CLC 5**
See also CA 5-8R; CANR 7, 29

Young, Collier
See Bloch, Robert (Albert)

Young, Edward 1683-1765 .... **LC 3**
See also DLB 95

Young, Marguerite 1909- .... **CLC 82**
See also CA 13-16; CAP 1

Young, Neil 1945- .... **CLC 17**
See also CA 110

Yourcenar, Marguerite
1903-1987 .... **CLC 19, 38, 50**
See also CA 69-72; CANR 23; DLB 72;
DLBY 88; MTCW

Yurick, Sol 1925- .... **CLC 6**
See also CA 13-16R; CANR 25

Zabolotskii, Nikolai Alekseevich
1903-1958 .... **TCLC 52**
See also CA 116

Zamiatin, Yevgenii
See Zamyatin, Evgeny Ivanovich

Zamyatin, Evgeny Ivanovich
1884-1937 .... **TCLC 8, 37**
See also CA 105

Zangwill, Israel 1864-1926. .... **TCLC 16**
See also CA 109; DLB 10, 135

Zappa, Francis Vincent, Jr. 1940-1993
See Zappa, Frank
See also CA 108; 143

Zappa, Frank .... **CLC 17**
See also Zappa, Francis Vincent, Jr.

Zaturenska, Marya 1902-1982. ... **CLC 6, 11**
See also CA 13-16R; 105; CANR 22

Zelazny, Roger (Joseph) 1937- ..... **CLC 21**
See also AAYA 7; CA 21-24R; CANR 26;
DLB 8; MTCW; SATA 39, 57

Zhdanov, Andrei A(lexandrovich)
1896-1948 .... **TCLC 18**
See also CA 117

Zhukovsky, Vasily 1783-1852 .... **NCLC 35**

Ziegenhagen, Eric .... **CLC 55**

Zimmer, Jill Schary
See Robinson, Jill

Zimmerman, Robert
See Dylan, Bob

Zindel, Paul 1936- .... **CLC 6, 26; DA**
See also AAYA 2; CA 73-76; CANR 31;
CLR 3; DLB 7, 52; JRDA; MAICYA;
MTCW; SATA 16, 58

Zinov'Ev, A. A.
See Zinoviev, Alexander (Aleksandrovich)

Zinoviev, Alexander (Aleksandrovich)
1922- .... **CLC 19**
See also CA 116; 133; CAAS 10

Zoilus
See Lovecraft, H(oward) P(hillips)

Zola, Emile (Edouard Charles Antoine)
1840-1902 ...... **TCLC 1, 6, 21, 41; DA;
WLC**
See also CA 104; 138; DLB 123

Zoline, Pamela 1941- .... **CLC 62**

Zorrilla y Moral, Jose 1817-1893.. **NCLC 6**

Zoshchenko, Mikhail (Mikhailovich)
1895-1958 .... **TCLC 15; SSC 15**
See also CA 115

Zuckmayer, Carl 1896-1977. .... **CLC 18**
See also CA 69-72; DLB 56, 124

Zuk, Georges
See Skelton, Robin

Zukofsky, Louis
1904-1978 .... **CLC 1, 2, 4, 7, 11, 18**
See also CA 9-12R; 77-80; CANR 39;
DLB 5; MTCW

Zweig, Paul 1935-1984. .... **CLC 34, 42**
See also CA 85-88; 113

Zweig, Stefan 1881-1942 .... **TCLC 17**
See also CA 112; DLB 81, 118

Literary Criticism Series
Cumulative Topic Index

This index lists all topic entries in the Gale Literary Criticism Series *Classical and Medieval Literature Criticism, Contemporary Literary Criticism, Literature Criticism from 1400 to 1800, Nineteenth-Century Literature Criticism,* and *Twentieth-Century Literary Criticism.*

Topic Index

Topic Index

TCLC Cumulative Nationality Index